THE OFFICIAL® PRICE GUIDE TO

FLEA MARKET TREASURES

Fifth Edition

HARRY L. RINKER

HOUSE OF COLLECTIBLES

THE BALLANTINE PUBLISHING GROUP • NEW YORK

Important Notice. All of the information, including valuations, in this book has been compiled from the most reliable sources, and every effort has been made to eliminate errors and questionable data. Nevertheless, the possibility of error, in a work of such immense scope, always exists. The publisher will not be held responsible for losses that may occur in the purchase, sale, or other transaction of items because of information contained herein. Readers who feel they have discovered errors are invited to *write* and inform us, so they may be corrected in subsequent editions. Those seeking further information on the topics covered in this book are advised to refer to the complete line of *Official Price Guides* published by the House of Collectibles.

House of Collectibles and the HC colophon are trademarks of Random House, Inc.

Published by: House of Collectibles
The Ballantine Publishing Group
201 East 50th Street
New York, NY 10022

Distributed by The Ballantine Publishing Group, a division of Random House, Inc., New York, and simultaneously in Canada by Random House of Canada Limited, Toronto.

www.randomhouse.com/BB/

Manufactured in the United States of America

ISBN: 0–676–60180–4

Cover design by Cathy Colbert

Fifth Edition: May 1999

10 9 8 7 6 5 4 3 2 1

CONTENTS

Chapter 6: The Flea Market Scene Today

Part Two: FLEA MARKET TREASURES – Categories A to Z

Part Three: REFERENCE SOURCES

PREFACE

Welcome to a somewhat unconventional price guide. It is designed to serve the non-traditionalist independent buyer and collector as well as the person collecting in "established" categories. The approach is informal. When you read the category introductions and carefully scan the listings, you will find a fair amount of humor. Do not be afraid to laugh. This book is about the pure fun and joy of collecting.

The flea market and garage sale markets are huge—far larger than the collector, dealer, and decorator markets to which over ninety percent of the books about antiques and collectibles cater. The more flea markets and garage sales I visit, the more I realize that seventy to eighty percent of the material found at flea markets cannot be researched in a general antiques and collectibles price guide. This title seeks to remedy that situation.

The Official Price Guide to Flea Market Treasures contains dozens of unconventional categories. It offers the opportunity to test the waters by introducing new collecting categories and having a little fun at the same time. Some categories eventually work their way into my ***Harry L. Rinker The Official Price Guide to Collectibles*** while others fall by the wayside. Alas, some collecting categories only enjoy a brief moment in the sun. This is why there are dozens of new categories included in this book for the first time and why some categories found in previous editions are missing.

CRITERIA

Availability and affordability are the primary factors determining what collecting categories do and do not appear in this book. Objects do not have to be 25, 50, or 100 years old to be included. If it is collected and offered for sale in quantity at flea markets, I have tried to include it.

Because many objects appeal to multiple buyers, I urge you to become familiar with the index. The object may be in this book. You simply are not looking in the right collecting category.

Discounted contemporary merchandise, manufacturer and store overstock, and holiday remnants are not included. Tube socks, cheap Asian knockoffs, clothing odds and ends, cassette tapes, and handcrafted products, all too common at some flea markets, are not collectible. This book is not a price guide to junk.

This is the second edition of this title to use category advisors. The increasing number of business card and seeker classified advertisements in trade periodicals convinced me that there was a wealth of fun categories and collectors of the somewhat unusual that should be included in this guide. Over fifty individuals responded positively to my request for assistance, many for the second time. The name and address of the advisor appears at the end of the introduction of the category to which they contributed.

The information in this book is solid, thorough and fresh. If objects are repeated, it is because they are extremely common and provide a means for those individuals with an interest in tracking the market.

IDEAL COMPANIONS

I recommend using ***The Official Price Guide to Flea Market Treasures*** in conjunction with two other titles. Information and values for objects in the more traditional collectibles categories seen at flea markets is found in ***Harry L. Rinker The Official Price Guide to Collectibles,*** also published by House of Collectibles. Its focus is on objects made after 1920.

Use Dana Morykan's and my **Garage Sale Manual and Price Guide,** published by Antique Trade Books, for information about recycled or reusable goods, items that appear regularly at flea markets. A sampling of reusable goods is found in this book's "Secondhand Rose" category.

GOOD-BYE, KRAUSE PUBLISHING

In the preface to the last edition, I said good-bye to my son, Harry Jr., the author of the first three editions of this work. He returned safely from doing his duty in the Army Reserves in Hungary and Bosnia. Harry Jr. chose to chart his own course rather than return to Rinker Enterprises when his tour of duty ended. He still is an avid collector and occasionally does some photography for his dad's business. Hopefully, he will find the satisfaction he is seeking in his new endeavors.

The fourth edition of this title was published by Krause Publishing shortly after it purchased Chilton Books with its Warman and Wallace-Homestead imprints. My staff and I very much enjoyed working on the fourth edition with Krause staff members Deborah Faupel, Jon Brecka, and William Gulbrandsen. As a strong fan of most of Krause's periodicals and books, I looked forward to Krause publishing this fifth edition. Although offered the opportunity, they decided in the negative.

HELLO, HOUSE OF COLLECTIBLES

Is there life after Warman's? You bet there is. Is it a good life? It is not only good. It is terrific.

The Official Price Guide to Flea Market Treasures is the eighth Rinker Enterprises title published by Ballantine Publishing Group's House of Collectibles. The other seven are: ***Harry L. Rinker The Official Price Guide to Collectibles; Dinnerware of the 20th Century: The Top 500 Patterns; Silverware of the 20th Century: The Top 250 Patterns; Stemware of the 20th Century: The Top 200 Patterns; The Official Price Guide to Antiques and Collectibles, Seventeenth Edition; The Official Price Guide to Collector Plates, Seventh Edition;*** and, ***The Official Price Guide to Country Antiques & Collectibles*** (authored by Dana Morykan). Do not be surprised if one or two additional titles are added to this list following the publication of the sixth edition of my flea market title.

Tim Kochuba, Randy Ladenheim-Gil, and Simon Vukelj at House of Collectibles initially welcomed me to House of Collectibles. Susan Randol, Executive Editor, now directs the House of Collectibles line. Laura Paczosa provides editorial expertise. Alex Klapwald continues to oversee production. Autumn Daughette assists Susan and Laura. These individuals are consummate publishing professionals; Rinker Enterprises and I are delighted with our partnership with Ballantine Publishing Group's House of Collectibles. Hopefully, it will continue long into the future.

CREDIT WHERE CREDIT IS DUE

Kathy Williamson's first project upon joining the staff of Rinker Enterprises was preparing the listings for the fourth edition of ***Price Guide to Flea Market Treasures.*** With Dana Morykan working on the manuscript for ***The Official Price Guide to Antiques & Collectibles*** and Dena George finishing ***The Official Price Guide to Collector Plates,*** Kathy assumed the principal responsibility for preparing this manuscript. She did a great job.

Everyone on the Rinker Enterprises team loves working on this book because it is so much fun to do. It is the one book in which we can let our hair down a little. It also allows us to show off some of the things we have around the house. Several illustrations are objects from the Rinker Enterprises' staff's personal collections. I will not identify which ones they are; in some cases the staff may not wish to admit to ownership.

Kathy and I worked together in identifying and contacting individuals who served as advisors. I also am responsible for the front matter, heads, and back matter.

Dana Morykan assisted with photograph selection and did much of the proofing. Dena George scanned the images and filled-in elsewhere when needed. Nancy Butt ensured the accuracy of the references to auction houses, collectors' clubs, newsletters, trade periodicals, and flea market locations listings. Virginia Reinbold and Richard Schmeltzle also contributed.

I very much appreciate the quality of the material submitted by those individuals who agreed to serve on the Board of Advisors. Their principal reward is seeing accurate information about their favorite collecting category appear in print. I hope they had as much fun preparing their listings as we had working with them.

Finally, a huge thanks to YOU—the reader and user of this book. We have worked hard to earn your trust. Hopefully, we succeeded.

LET ME KNOW WHAT YOU THINK

As much as I would like this book to be perfect, it is not. We all make mistakes. If you spot information that you believe is incorrect or have a suggestion to make that you think will improve the next edition, I encourage you to send your comments and/or criticisms to: Harry L. Rinker, Rinker Enterprises, Inc., 5093 Vera Cruz Road, Emmaus, PA 18049.

Harry L. Rinker
Vera Cruz, PA
March 1999

INTRODUCTION

GOOOOD MORNNNNINGGGG, Flea Marketeers. Welcome to *The Official Price Guide to Flea Market Treasures*. Today's specials are the very best goodies, tidbits, and knickknacks found in every flea market throughout the good old U.S. of A. It's all here—neatly printed and organized for your use and reading pleasure.

Sound a bit like a carnival barker? It should. Going to a good flea market will produce as much fun, enjoyment, treasures, and memories as a visit to any carnival. Flea marketeering is a grand adventure. You have an idea of what to expect, but you know there will be a number of surprises. If you are lucky, you will grab a brass ring.

This fifth edition continues the fine-tuning process found in the fourth edition. A major effort was made to change the majority of objects listed in each collecting category. Almost all the illustrations are new.

Why duplicate some object listings from edition to edition? There are two principal reasons. First, some objects are so common that anyone using this book as a reference expects to find them in it, and they should. Second, some categories have a limited number of listings. If they are not repeated, the category needs to be dropped. Finally, prices can stagnate. This is information worth knowing.

FIND IT HERE FIRST

Like its predecessors, *The Official Price Guide to Flea Market Treasures, Fifth Edition,* also provides a first look at many potential collecting categories. Collectibility is tested at the flea market level. Dealers are continually offering material not seen previously. The successful sale of new groups of items immediately attracts the attention of other dealers. Their enthusiasm spreads. Before long, a new collecting category enters the established market. Many collecting categories first presented in this book are now regular entries in general antiques and collectibles price guides and my *Harry L. Rinker The Official Price Guide to Collectibles*.

Not all efforts to establish a new collecting category succeed. This is why some categories that appeared in previous editions of *Price Guide to Flea Market Treasures* have been dropped from this edition.

Category advisors were used sparingly in the first three editions of this work. In an effort to add breadth and diversity to the categories appearing in this book, over 75 specialized collectors were approached and asked to contribute information about their collecting specialty. More than 50 responded positively. When an advisor is responsible for the information in a category, his or her full name and address is listed at the end of the category introduction.

This book follows the same approach as previous editions, which is to combine basic information about flea marketeering with price listings by category. Those familiar with previous editions will renew their acquaintance with an old friend. Those discovering this book for the first time have an opportunity to make a friend for life.

THREE PARTS

The Official Price Guide to Flea Market Treasures is divided into three principal parts.

Part One

The first part is a guide for flea marketeers. It helps you identify a "true" flea market, tells you how to find and evaluate flea markets, provides a list of the top thirty flea markets nationwide, gives tips for surviving the flea market experience and honing your shopping skills, and provides in-depth analysis of the current flea market scene.

Much of the information is duplicated from previous editions. You will find minor changes in the sections dealing with general guides to flea market locations, trade papers, and top thirty flea markets. Chapter 6, "The Flea Market Scene Today," has been totally rewritten to reflect changes within the flea market scene over the past two years.

In talking with individuals who purchased earlier editions of this book, I was surprised to learn how many "experienced" flea marketeers had skipped this first part. They made a mistake. Even the most experienced flea marketeer will find something of value. One of the worst mistakes you can make in the antiques and collectibles field is to assume that you know all you need to know.

Part Two

The second part of the book is devoted to price listings by category. Previous users are advised to thumb through the categories and not rely on the assumption that they know what the book contains. This fifth edition of *The Official Price Guide to Flea Market Treasures* contains over 50 new categories.

You deceive yourself if you assume this book is just another antiques and collectibles price guide. Not true. This book was prepared using the premise that everything imaginable turns up at a flea market—from the finest antiques to good reusable secondhand items. *The Official Price Guide to Flea Market Treasures* contains dozens of categories that are not found in any other antiques and/or collectibles price guide.

In a few categories you will not find specific priced items. Instead you are provided with general information that allows a broad understanding of the category. Occasionally, you are referred to specialized books on the subject.

One of the great joys about working on the categories in this book is that so many are supported with collectors' clubs, newsletters, and periodicals. You will find full addresses for these listed in the appropriate category before the price listing.

The Official Price Guide to Flea Market Treasures provides the Rinker Enterprises, Inc., staff and me an opportunity to let our hair down. If you are comfortable with a formal traditionalist price guide approach this price guide is not for you. Category introductions range from serious to humorous to sublime. If the key to a great flea market is that it evokes these emotions and more within you, why should this book do any less?

Part Three

Although I am not certain why, the third part of this book, which contains reference material for flea marketeers, including the "Flea Marketeer's Annotated Reference Library" and a list of "Antiques and Collectibles Trade Papers," is often completely overlooked by purchasers of this book. I strongly recommend that you become familiar with this section. The information not only helps you become highly proficient as a flea marketeer but also serves as your introduction to many other wonderful areas within the antiques and collectibles field.

LET'S GO!

It is time to honor the cry of the Circus ringmaster: "On with the show." Take a moment and read the program (the first section) before you watch the acts in the center ring (the second section) and then relive the memories (the third section). Most of all, don't forget—the entire purpose of the performance is for you to have fun.

Part One

A FLEA MARKET EDUCATION

Chapter 1
WHAT IS A FLEA MARKET?

It is difficult to explain the sense of excitement and anticipation felt by collectors and dealers as they get ready to shop a flea market. They are about to undertake a grand adventure, a journey into the unknown. Flea markets turn the average individual into an explorer in search of buried treasure. The search is not without adversity. Conditions ranging from a hostile climate to intense competition may be encountered. Victory is measured in "steals" and stories that can be shared at the end of the day.

Flea markets provide the opportunity for prospective collectors to get their feet wet in the exciting world of antiques and collectibles and for novice dealers to test their merchandise and selling skills at minimal expense. Many first contacts, some of which last a lifetime, are made between collectors and dealers there. More than any other environment in the antiques and collectibles trade, the flea market is the one forum where everyone is on equal footing.

Before you learn how to find, evaluate, and survive flea markets, it is important that you understand exactly what a flea market is, how it fits into the antiques and collectibles marketplace, and the many variations that exist. This is the first step to identifying the flea markets that are most likely to provide the greatest opportunities for you.

DEFINING A FLEA MARKET

Few terms in the antiques and collectibles field are as difficult to define as "flea market." If you visit the Rose Bowl Flea Market in Pasadena, California, you will find discontinued and knock-off merchandise, crafts, clothing (from tube socks to dresses), home-care items, plants of all types, and specialty foods as much in evidence as antiques and collectibles. On the other hand, if you visit the Ann Arbor Antiques Market in Michigan, you will find primarily middle and upper-level antiques and collectibles. Both are flea markets, yet they are light-years apart from one another.

The flea market concept is generations old. As it spread around the world, each country changed and adapted the form to meet its own particular needs. Regional differences developed. In New England, the Mid-Atlantic states, and the Midwest, the term generally is used to describe a place where antiques and collectibles are sold. In the South and Southwest, the term is more loosely interpreted to include craft, secondhand, and discounted goods.

It is not hard to see why this confusion exists. *Webster's Ninth New Collegiate Dictionary* (Springfield, MA: Merriam-Webster, Inc., 1984) defines a flea market as "a usually open-air market for secondhand articles and antiques." Individuals involved with antiques and collectibles do not equate secondhand (recycled or reusable) goods with antiques and collectibles. Although the dictionary may lump them together, collectors and dealers clearly differentiate one from the other.

The flea markets described in this book fit a much more narrow definition than the dictionary definition.

Flea market means a regularly scheduled market, held either indoors or outdoors, in which the primary goods offered for sale are those defined by the trade as antiques or collectibles. Occasionally, some handcrafted products and secondhand goods may be found among the offerings, especially in the seasonal and roadside flea markets where professional flea market dealers mix with individuals selling on a one-shot basis.

The problem with defining "flea market" with an antiques and collectibles perspective is that a multiplicity of flea market types exist. There are the seasonal flea markets such as Renninger's Extravaganza (Kutztown, Pennsylvania) and Brimfield's (Brimfield, Massachusetts), the monthlies such as the Metrolina Expo (Charlotte, North Carolina), and numerous weeklies scattered across the country.

One of the best ways to understand what an antiques and collectibles flea market encompasses is to discuss how it differs from three other closely related institutions in the antiques and collectibles trade: the antiques mall, the garage sale, and the antiques show. While the differences may appear subtle, they are significant to collectors and dealers.

Prior to the arrival of the antiques mall, there was a clearly defined ladder of quality within the antiques and collectibles community that progressed from garage sale to flea market to small show to major show or shop. This is how most goods moved through the market, and the route many dealers used to establish themselves in the trade. Two things changed the equation: collectors recognized the role flea markets played as the initial source of goods and actively participated as a means of eliminating the "middleman" and the antiques mall came into existence.

Antiques malls arrived on the scene in the early 1980s. As the decade of the 1990s ends, the trend is toward the Super

Mall, a mall with 300 plus dealers that offers a full range of services from direct sales to auctions. Malls developed because flea market sellers wanted a method to do business on a daily basis without the overhead of owning a shop. They also sought an indoor environment free from the vagaries of weather. Additionally, the buying public was delighted to find as many sellers as possible in one location.

Malls differ from flea markets in that they are open for business on a daily basis (a minimum of five and often seven days a week), the display and sales process is often handled by a manager or other mall representative, a more formal business procedure is used, and the quality of material is somewhat higher than that found at flea markets. The main drawbacks are that the buyer generally has no contact with the owner of the merchandise and price negotiation is difficult.

Garage sales are usually one-time events, often conducted by people with no pretensions of being antiques or collectibles dealers. They are merely attempting to get rid of items they no longer find useful. While it is true that some antiques and collectibles enter the market through this source, most individuals conducting garage sales have enough good sense to realize that this is the worst way to sell these items. Emphasis in a garage sale is on secondhand merchandise.

A recent development in the garage sale area is the annual or semiannual community garage sale. A promoter rents a large hall or auditorium and sells space to any individual wishing to set up. Usually there is a rule that no established antiques and collectibles dealers are allowed to take part. However, many dealers sneak in with friends or simply use a different name to rent a space in order to "pick" the merchandise during setup. Although community garage sales fit the dictionary definition of a flea market, the large volume of secondhand merchandise distinguishes them from the flea markets discussed in this book.

An antiques show consists of a number of professional dealers (weekend, full-time, or a combination of both) who meet in a fixed location on a regular basis, usually two to three times each year, to offer quality antiques and collectibles to collectors, interior decorators, and others. Once an antique or collectible reaches the show circuit, it is usually priced close to book value. Flea markets thrive on the concept that merchandise priced for sale is significantly below book value. While this is more myth than reality, it prevails.

Confusion arises because a number of monthly flea markets have dropped the term "flea market" from their titles. They call themselves "shows" or "markets." They do not use "flea" because of a growing list of problems, ranging from unscrupulous dealers to an abundance of unmarked reproductions, that plagued flea markets in the 1990s. Calling yourself something else does not change what you really are. Most monthly markets and shows are nothing more than flea markets in disguise.

SEASONAL FLEA MARKETS

Seasonal flea markets are those held a maximum of three times a year. Theoretically, they are held outdoors. However, many sites now provide either indoor or pavilion shelters for participants. Most have clearly established dates. For example, Renninger's Extravaganza is held the last weekend in April, June, and September.

If there is a Mecca in the flea market world, it is Brimfield. The name is magic. You are not an accomplished flea marketeer until you have been there. Actually, Brimfield is not a flea market, it is an event. In early May, July, and September over fifteen separate flea markets open and close. On Fridays the dealer count exceeds 1,500. Area motel rooms are booked over a year in advance. Traffic jams last hours.

For the past several years Renninger's has been promoting seasonal markets during the winter months at its Mount Dora, Florida, location. They are an important stop on the Southern winter circuit. Although there are a few seasonal markets in the Midwest, none are on a par with the Renninger's Extravaganzas and the Brimfield weeks.

MONTHLY FLEA MARKETS

The monthly flea market's strength rests on a steady dealer clientele supplemented by other dealers passing through the area, a frequency that allows dealers enough time to find new merchandise, and a setting that is usually superior to the seasonal and weekly flea markets. The monthlies range from the upscale Ann Arbor Antiques Market to the mid-range antiques and collectibles show copycat (for example, the Fairgrounds Antiques Market in Phoenix, Arizona) to the something-for-everybody flea market (like the Kane County Flea Market in St. Charles, Illinois).

Courtesy Antiques by the Bay – Alameda Point Antiques and Collectibles Faire

Most of the monthly flea markets have some outdoor spaces. The Kentucky Flea Market in Louisville, Kentucky, and the Fairgrounds Antiques Market in Phoenix, Arizona, are two exceptions. Flea markets with outdoor space operate only during warm weather months, generally April through November. A few of the larger operations (e.g., the Springfield Antiques Show & Flea Market in Springfield, Ohio) operate year-round. Double-check the schedule for any flea market you plan to visit between November and April, even those located in the South and Southwest.

Another strength of the monthly flea markets rests in the fact that they attract a large number of dealers who appear regularly. Collectors and dealers have time to cultivate good working relationships. A level of buying trust is created because the collector knows that he or she will be able to find the seller again if questions develop.

WEEKLY FLEA MARKETS

The weekly flea markets break down into two types: those held on a weekday and those held on a weekend. The weekday markets are primarily for dealers in the trade. Monday flea markets at Perkiomenville, Pennsylvania, and Wednesday flea markets at Shipshewana, Indiana, are legends. These markets begin in the predawn hours. The best buys are found by flashlight as participants check merchandise as it is being unpacked. Most selling ends by 9:00 a.m. These markets appeal primarily to individuals actively involved in the resale of antiques and collectibles. Most collectors prefer something a bit more civilized.

Courtesy Renninger's Extravaganza

Renninger's in Adamstown, Pennsylvania, shows the staying power of the weekend flea market. Within driving distance of several major population centers, yet far enough in the country to make the day an outing, Renninger's combines an ever-changing outdoor section with an indoor facility featuring primarily permanent dealers. Renninger's is open only on Sundays, except for Extravaganza weekends. Because buyers like to shop on Saturdays as well, Renninger's Promotions created Renninger's in Kutztown, Pennsylvania.

Weekend flea markets are now a fixture across the country and constitute the largest segment of the flea market community. It is common to find several in one location as each tries to capitalize on the success of the other. However, their quality varies tremendously.

The biggest problem with weekend flea markets is merchandise staleness. Many dealers add only a few new items each week. Collectors shop them on a four- to eight-week cycle. The way to avoid missing a shot at a major new piece is to maintain a close working relationship with several dealers. Most weekend flea market dealers shop the market. They can be your eyes when you are not there.

As with the monthly flea markets, you can buy from indoor dealers knowing that you are likely to find them if a problem develops later. Be much more careful when purchasing from the transient outside dealers. Get a valid name, address, and phone number from anyone from whom you make a purchase.

One of the things I like best about large weekend flea markets is that they feature one or more book dealers who specialize in antiques and collectibles books. I always stop at these booths to check on the latest titles. In some cases, I find a book I never saw advertised in the trade papers. Some of the dealers offer search services for out-of-print titles. Spending time getting to know these book dealers is something you will never regret.

ROADSIDE FLEA MARKETS

I have ignored roadside flea markets up to this point because the merchandise they offer is usually of garage sale quality. This is not to say that I have not found some great buys at roadside markets. However, when I consider the amount of time that I spend finding these few precious gems, I realize I can do much better at a traditional flea markets.

Chances are that you collect one or two specific categories. If so, not every type of flea market is right for you. How do you find the best markets? What type of evaluation can you do in advance to avoid the frustration of coming home empty-handed? These questions and more are answered in the next chapter.

Chapter 2

FINDING AND EVALUATING FLEA MARKETS

In order to attend a flea market, you have to locate one. It is not as easy as it sounds. In order to thoroughly research the available markets in any given area, you will have to consult a variety of sources. Even when you have finished, you are still likely to spot a flea market that you missed in your research along the way. I told you there was a strong sense of adventure in flea marketeering.

FLEA MARKET GUIDES

There are four national guides to United States flea markets. Buy them all.

The Flea Market Shopper's Companion: A Complete Guide for Buyers and Sellers Coast to Coast by James Goodridge (Citadel Press, Carol Publishing Group, 120 Enterprise Avenue, Secaucus, NJ 07094).

Prior to the publication of *The Flea Market Shopper,* James Goodridge edited four regional flea market guides published by Adams Publishing. Goodridge's new title combines the information into a single volume, a concession to the fact that today's flea marketeer is as much a national shopper as a regional shopper. The book lists flea markets alphabetically and provides information about size, trading days, parking, and types of traders. *The Flea Market Shopper* also contains buying and selling tips. This paperback retails for $14.95.

The Original Clark's Flea Market U.S.A.: A National Directory of Flea Markets and Swap Meets (Clark Publications, 5469 Inland Cove Ct., Milton, FL 32583 / (850) 623-0794).

Clark's, issued quarterly, lists over 2,000 flea markets and swap meets. The guide is organized alphabetically by state. The secondary organization is city or town closest to the flea market within the state. You will find information on name, address, days and occasionally hours of operation and telephone number. Information provided about each market varies greatly. Completely missing are directions for hard-to-find markets. I buy an issue every year or two as a safety check against my regular sources. A one-year subscription is $30.00. Single copies are available from the publisher at $8.00, a price that includes postage and handling.

The Official Directory to U.S. Flea Markets, Sixth Edition, edited by Kitty Werner (House of Collectibles, Division of Random House, 201 East 50th Street, New York, NY 10022).

The Official Directory under Kitty Werner's direction gets better with each edition. The book covers over 800 flea markets in the United States, Canada, and Europe. Yes, Canada and Europe—it's time someone paid attention to our northern neighbor and our cousins abroad. Each listing contains information about a flea market's dates, hours, admission, location, a very detailed description of the type of merchandise found, dealer rates, and a telephone number and full address for the chief contact person. I especially like the list of "Other Flea Markets" found at the end of most state listings. These are markets that did not respond to the questionnaire. Werner advises users to "please call first" to make certain they are open. You can purchase a copy of this guide in most larger bookstores. It is a bargain at $9.95.

U.S. Flea Market Directory, Second Edition, edited by Albert LaFarge (Avon Books, Confident Collector series, 1350 Avenue of the Americas, New York, NY 10019).

The second edition of *U.S. Flea Market* is welcome. Designed to compete with *The Official Directory,* it provides detailed information that includes maps and travel directions, days and times, number of dealers, description of goods sold, dealer information, and other useful tidbits for approximately 1,000 flea markets nationwide. As one might expect, LaFarge covers many of the same flea markets that are found in *The Official Directory.* However, there are enough differences to make both books a must buy. *U.S. Flea Market* retails for $6.99 and is available at most bookstores.

Antiques and collectibles flea markets are not unique to the United States. In fact, the modern flea market originated in Paris. Flea markets play a vital role throughout Europe, especially in France, Great Britain, and Germany.

Travel Keys (PO Box 160691, Sacramento, CA 95816) has published a separate flea market guide for France, Great Britain, and Germany, each edited by Peter B. Manston. Although badly in need of revision, the books still have value if you are traveling abroad. First, many of the flea markets are decades old—same time, same place. If possible, double-check before setting out. Once at a market, do not hesitate to ask dealers to recommend other flea market venues. Second, the introductory material is a must read, especially the section on export laws and regulations. This is information you will not find anywhere else. New editions are in the works. The first is due out in fall 1999.

NATIONAL AND REGIONAL SHOP GUIDES

National Guides

In the late 1990s a day "antiquing" means visiting a variety of selling markets. A flea market stop is combined with a visit to nearby antiques and collectibles malls. For this reason, I recommend Judy Lloyd's *No-Nonsense Antique Mall Directory.* It covers 5,000 malls throughout the United States. It is available only by mail order. Send a check for $20.50, the price includes fourth class postage, to FDS Antiques, PO Box 188, Higginsport, OH 45131.

I have mixed emotions about Kim and David Leggett's *Leggett's Antiques Atlas: The Guide to Antiquing in America* (Three Rivers Press, a division of Crown Publishers, Inc., 201 East 50th Street, New York, NY 10022). I find its size awkward and the information shallow, despite the ringing trade endorsements that appear prior to the title page. The vast majority of the listings consist only of the name, street address (often incomplete and no zip codes), and telephone number of an auction, shop, mall, or show. Those with more detailed listings obviously paid for the privilege as did the full page advertisers whose displays clutter the presentation. You make up your own mind about its value. At a cover price of $26, I have already made up mine.

Regional Guides

A number of specialized regional guides for locating antiques and collectibles flea markets, malls, and shops exist. Most are published by trade papers. A few are done privately. None focus solely on the flea market scene.

The *AntiqueWeek Central Antique Shop Guide* and *AntiqueWeek Eastern Antique Shop Guide* (AntiqueWeek, PO Box 90, Knightstown, IN 46148) are typical. Organization is by state, region, and by city and town within a region. Brief listings for each business are supplemented by display advertising. Each edition covers flea markets, malls, shops, shows, and more. The coverage gets better with each edition. The principal problem with these and similar guides is that you have to pay a fee to be listed. As a result, coverage is limited to those willing to pay. However, they are a great starting point and a bargain at $3.50 each.

When planning to visit a new area, contact some of the trade papers that serve the region and ask if they publish a regional guide or know of such a guide. Regional guides are inexpensive, ranging from $5 to $15. Many of the businesses listed in the guide sell it across the counter. I always pick up a copy. The storage pouch located behind the front driver's seat of my car is littered with road maps and regional guides, most of which show signs of heavy use.

RESOURCE DIRECTORY

David Maloney Jr.'s *Maloney's Antiques and Collectibles Resource Directory, 4th Edition* (Antique Trader Books, PO Box 1050 Dubuque, IA 52004) contains category listings for antiques shops and flea markets. The listings include addresses and telephone numbers. Hopefully, you own a copy of Maloney's book. If you do not, you should. Make a resolution—right now—to buy a copy the next time you visit a bookstore or the stand of an antiques and collectibles book seller at a flea market. The book retails for $28.95. It is the best investment anyone in the trade can make. If you do not think so, I will give you your money back.

TRADE NEWSPAPERS

The best source of flea market information is advertisements in trade newspapers. Some papers put all the flea market advertisements in one location, while others place them in their appropriate regional section. Most trade papers' events calendars include flea markets with the show listings. Once again, the problem rests with the fact that all advertising is paid advertising.

Not all flea markets advertise in every issue of a trade paper. Some advertise in papers outside their home area because the locals know where and when to find them. Flea markets that operate between April and September usually do not advertise in December and January. The only way to conduct a complete search is to obtain a four- to six-month run of a regional paper and carefully scan each issue. When doing this, keep your eyes open for reports and features about flea markets. As advertisers, flea markets expect to get written up at least once a year.

The following is a list of national and regional trade papers that I recommend you consult for flea market information. You will find their full addresses and phone numbers (when known) in the listing of trade newspapers at the back of this book.

National Trade Papers

The Antique Trader Weekly, Dubuque, IA
AntiqueWeek, Knightstown, IN
Antiques & the Arts Weekly, Newtown, CT
Collectors News, Grundy Center, IA
Maine Antique Digest, Waldoboro, ME
Warman's Today's Collector, Iola, WI

Regional Trade Papers

New England

MassBay Antiques / North Shore Weekly, Danvers, MA
New England Antiques Journal, Ware, MA
New Hampshire Antiques Monthly, Farmington, NH
The Fine Arts Trader, Randolph, MA
Treasure Chest, North Scituate, RI
Unravel the Gavel, Ctr. Belmont, NH

Middle Atlantic States

Antiques & Auction News, Mount Joy, PA
Antiques Tattler, Adamstown, PA
New York City's Antique News, New York, NY
New York-Pennsylvania Collector, Fishers, NY
Northeast Journal of Antiques & Art, Hudson, NY
Renninger's Antique Guide, Lafayette Hill, PA

South

Antique Finder Magazine, Panama City, FL
Antique Gazette, Nashville, TN
The Antique Shoppe, Keystone Heights, FL
Carolina Antique News, Charlotte, NC
Cotton & Quail Antique Trail, Monticello, FL
MidAtlantic Antiques Magazine, Henderson, NC
The Antique Shoppe of the Carolinas, Lancaster, NC
The Old News Is Good News Antiques Gazette, Hammond, LA
Second Hand Dealer News, Spring Hill, FL
Southern Antiques, Decatur, GA
Southern Antiquing and Collecting Magazine, Acworth, GA
The Vintage Times, Macon, GA
20th Century Folk Art News, Buford, GA

Midwest

The American Antiquities Journal, Springfield, OH
The Antique Collector and Auction Guide, Salem, OH
Antique Review, Worthington, OH
Auction Action News, Shawano, WI
Auction World, Benson, MN
The Collector, Heyworth, IL
Collectors Journal, Vinton, IA
Discover Mid-America, Kansas City, MO
Great Lakes Trader, Williamstown, MI
Indiana Antique Buyer's News, Silver Lake, IN
Ohio Collectors' Magazine, Diqua, OH
The Old Times, Maple Lake, MN
Yesteryear, Princeton, WI

Southwest

The Antique Traveler, Mineola, TX
Antiques & Collectibles Travelers' Guide, Apache Junction, AZ
Arizona Antique News, Phoenix, AZ
Auction Weekly, Phoenix, AZ
The Country Register, Inc, Phoenix, AZ

West Coast

Antique & Collectables, El Cajon, CA
Antique Journal, Alameda, CA
Antiques Plus, Salem, OR
Antiques Today, Carson City, NV
Collector, Pomona, CA
Old Stuff, McMinnville, OR
The Oregon Vintage Times, Eugene, OR
West Coast Peddler, Whittier, CA

This list is by no means complete. I am certain that I have missed a few regional papers. However, these papers provide a starting point. Do not be foolish and go flea marketeering without consulting them.

NATIONAL FLEA MARKET ASSOCIATION OF OWNERS & MANAGERS (NFMA)

In 1997 Jerry Stokes founded the National Flea Market Association of Owners & Managers (PO Box 18646, Charlotte, NC 28218). Its Mission Statement reads: "The National Flea Market Association is dedicated to creating and presenting the cleanest, most convenient shopping facilities for you and your family."

The Association issues a newsletter, offers educational programs, and holds conventions. Its Internet web site's (www.fleamarkets.org) intent is to exchange ideas, co-advertise, promote, and better the flea market shopping venues for people concerned.

The vast majority of the flea markets that comprise the membership of the NFMA are swap meets, places where you are more likely to find discounted new merchandise, farm produce, crafts, contemporary collectibles (many speculative), and blatant reproductions than antiques and collectibles. There will be an occasional jewel, but discovering it requires a great deal of hunting.

Courtesy Renninger's Extravaganza

WHICH FLEA MARKET IS RIGHT FOR YOU?

The best flea market is the one at which you find plenty to buy at good to great prices. This means that most flea markets are not right for you. Is it necessary to attend each one to make your determination? I do not think so.

I am a great believer in using the telephone. If long distance rates jump dramatically as a result of the publication of this book, I plan to approach AT&T and ask for a piece of the action. It is a lot cheaper to call than to pay for transportation, lodging, and meals, not to mention the value of your time. Do not hesitate to call promoters and ask them about their flea markets.

What type of information should you request? First, check the number of dealers. If the number falls below one hundred, think twice. Ask for a ratio of local dealers to transient dealers. A good mix is 75% local and 25% transient for monthly and weekly markets. Second, inquire about the type of merchandise being offered for sale. Make a point not to tell the promoter what you collect. If you do, you can be certain that the flea market has a number of dealers who offer the material. Do not forget to ask about the quality of the merchandise. Third, ask about the facilities. The more indoor space available, the higher the level of merchandise is likely to be. What happens if it rains?

Finally, ask yourself this question: Do you trust what the promoter has told you?

When you are done talking to the promoter, call the editor of one of the regional trade papers and ask his or her opinion about the market. If they have published an article or review of the market recently, request that a copy be sent to you. If you know someone who has attended, talk to that person. If you still have not made up your mind, try the local daily newspaper or chamber of commerce.

Do not be swayed by the size of a flea market's advertisement in a trade paper. The Kane County advertisement is often less that a sixteenth of a page. A recent full-page advertisement for Brimfield flea markets failed to include J & J Promotions or May's Antique Market, two of the major players on the scene. This points out the strong regional competition between flea markets. Be suspicious of what one promoter tells you about another promoter's market.

EVALUATING A FLEA MARKET

After you have attended a flea market, it is time to decide if you will attend it again, and if so, how frequently. Answer the following nineteen questions "yes" or "no." In this test, "no" is the right answer. If more than half the questions are "yes," forget about going back. There are plenty of flea markets from which to choose. If twelve or more are answered "no," give it another chance in a few months. If seventeen or more answers are "no," plan another visit soon.

Flea Market Quick Quiz

1. Was the flea market hard to find? ____ Yes ____ No
2. Did you have a difficult time moving between the flea market and your car in the parking area? ____ Yes ____ No
3. Did you have to pay a parking fee in addition to an admission fee? ____ Yes ____ No
4. Did the manager fail to provide a map of the market? ____ Yes ____ No
5. Was a majority of the market in an open, outdoor environment? ____ Yes ____ No
6. Were indoor facilities poorly lighted and ventilated? ____ Yes ____ No
7. Was there a problem with the number of toilet facilities or with the facilities' cleanliness? ____ Yes ____ No
8. Was your overall impression of the market one of chaos? ____ Yes ____ No
9. Did collectibles outnumber antiques? ____ Yes ____ No
10. Did secondhand goods and new merchandise outnumber collectibles? ____ Yes ____ No
11. Were reproductions, copycats, fantasy items, and fakes in abundance? (See Chapter 5.) ____ Yes ____ No
12. Was there a large representation of home crafts and/or discontinued merchandise? ____ Yes ____ No
13. Were the vast majority of antiques and collectibles that you saw in fair condition or worse? ____ Yes ____ No
14. Were individuals that you expected to encounter at the market absent? ____ Yes ____ No
15. Did you pass out fewer than five lists of your "wants"? ____ Yes ____ No
16. Did you buy fewer than five new items for your collection? ____ Yes ____ No
17. Were more than half the items that you bought priced near or at book value? ____ Yes ____ No
18. Was there a lack of good restaurants and/or lodging within easy access of the flea market? ____ Yes ____ No
19. Would you tell a friend never to attend the market? ____ Yes ____ No

There are some flea markets that scored well with me, and I would like to share them with you. They are listed in the next chapter.

Chapter 3
TOP 30 U.S. FLEA MARKETS

The list stops here. The first two editions of *Price Guide to Flea Market Treasures* contained a list of the top twenty flea markets. The list was expanded to twenty-five in the third and fourth editions. Now it stands at thirty; and, here it will remain in this and subsequent editions.

The Atlanta Antiques Center and Flea Market, Chamblee, Georgia, that appeared in previous editions is no longer in business. It is always sad to see an old friend pass away. However, I am delighted to report a significant increase in the number of antiques and collectibles available at the Rose Bowl Flea Market. It is a pleasure to put an old friend back on the list.

Deciding which markets will and will not appear on the list is not an easy task. There are thousands of flea markets throughout the United States. In each edition there are several markets that I excluded simply because of the arbitrary number I selected.

Everyone has regional favorites that failed to make the cut. There simply is not room to list them all. In making my choices, I used the following criteria. I wanted to provide a representative sample from the major flea market groups—seasonal, monthly, and weekly. Since this guide is designed for the national market, I made certain that the selection covered the entire United States. Finally, I selected flea markets that I feel will "turn on" a prospective or novice collector. Nothing is more fun than getting off to a great start.

This list is only a starting point. Almost every flea market has a table containing promotional literature for other flea markets in the area. Follow up on the ones of interest. Continue to check trade paper listings. There are always new flea markets being started.

Finally, not every flea market is able to maintain its past glories. Are there flea markets that you think should be on this list? Have you visited some of the listed flea markets and found them to be unsatisfactory? As each edition of this guide is prepared, this list will be evaluated. Send any thoughts and comments that you may have to: Harry L. Rinker, Rinker Enterprises, Inc., 5093 Vera Cruz Road, Emmaus, PA 18049.

The "Top 30" list contains the following information: name of flea market, location, frequency and general admission times, type of goods sold and general comments, number of dealers, indoor or outdoor, special features, 1999 admission fee, and address and phone number (if known) of manager or promoter.

SEASONAL FLEA MARKETS

1. "America's Largest" Antique and Collectible Sale

Portland Expo Center, Portland, OR. Multnomah County Expo Center, Exit 306B off I-5; Saturday and Sunday, early March, mid July, and late October; antiques and collectibles; 1,250+ dealers in March and October, indoors; 1,500+ dealers in July, indoor/outdoor; admission—$5 per person; parking—$4; Palmer/Wirfs & Associates, 4001 N.E. Halsey, Portland, OR 97232, (503) 282-0877, Fax: (503) 282-2953.

Also check out Palmer/Wirfs & Associates' Cow Palace Shows, San Francisco, CA. exit off Highway 101; Saturday and Sunday, February, May, August, and November, usually mid-month, Saturday 8 a.m. to 7 p.m.; Sunday 9 a.m. to 5 p.m; antiques and collectibles; over 400 dealers; indoor; admission—$5.

2. Brimfield

Route 20, Brimfield, MA 01010; six consecutive days in May, July, and September; antiques, collectibles, and secondhand goods; 3,000+ dealers. Indoor/outdoor; includes more than 20 individual antiques shows with staggered opening and closing dates, most shows with different promoters; admission—varies according to field, ranging from free admission to $3; average parking fee—$3.

Brimfield Acres North, 120 Richards Ave., Paxton, MA 01612, (508) 754-4185 or (413) 245-9471.

Central Park Antiques Shows, P.O. Box 224, Brimfield, MA 01010, (413) 596-9257, Fax: (413) 599-0298.

The Dealers' Choice and Faxon's Treasure Chest Midway Shows, P.O. Box 28, Fiskdale, MA 01518, (508) 347-3929.

Heart-O-The-Mart, P.O. Box 26, Brimfield, MA 01010, (413) 245-9556, Fax: (413) 245-3542.

J & J Promotions, P.O. Box 385, Brimfield, MA 01010, (413) 245-3436 or (978) 597-8155.

Jeanne Hertan Antiques Shows, P.O. Box 628, Somers, CT 06071, (860) 763-3760.

Mahogany Ridge, P.O. Box 129, Brimfield, MA 01010, (413) 245-9615.

May's Antique Show, P.O. Box 416, Brimfield, MA 01010, (413) 245-9271, Fax: (413) 245-9509.
The Meadows Antique Shows, Inc., P.O. Box 374, Brimfield, MA 01010, (413) 245-9427 or (413) 245-3215.
New England Motel Antiques Market, Inc., P.O. Box 186, Sturbridge, MA 01566, (508) 347-2179.
Shelton Antiques Shows, P.O. Box 124, Brimfield, MA 01010, (413) 245-3591.
Sturtevant, P.O. Box 468, Brimfield, MA 01010, (413) 245-7458.

You can subscribe to the *Brimfield Antique Guide* from Brimfield Publications, P.O. Box 442, Brimfield, MA 01010; (413) 245-9329. Three issues for $13.95, first class mail.

3. Renninger's Extravaganza

Noble Street, Kutztown, PA 19530; Thursday, Friday, and Saturday of last full weekend of April, June, and September, Thursday opens 10:00 a.m. for pre-admission only ($40 per car carrying one to four people), Friday, 7 a.m. to 6 p.m., and Saturday, 7 a.m. to 5 p.m; antiques and collectibles; 1,200+ dealers; indoor/outdoor; admission—$5 on Friday, $3 on Saturday; Renninger's Promotions, 27 Bensinger Drive, Schuylkill Haven, PA 17972; call Monday through Friday (717) 385-0104, Saturday (610) 683-6848, www.renningers.com.

MONTHLY FLEA MARKETS

4. Alameda Point Antiques and Collectibles Faire

Located at the former Naval Air Station, Alameda, exit off Hwy 880; first Sunday of every month, January through December, 9 a.m. to 3 p.m.; 400+ booths; antiques, collectibles and vintage furnishings—all items must be at least 20 years old; admission—$3; early bird admission 7 a.m. to 9 a.m.—$10; parking—free; Antiques By The Bay, Inc., 3200 Grand Ave., Oakland, CA 94610, (510) 869-5428.

Courtesy Renninger's Extravaganza

5. Allegan Antiques Market

Allegan Fairgrounds, Allegan, MI 49010; last Sunday of the month, April through September, 7:30 a.m. to 4:30 p.m; antiques and collectibles; 170+ dealers indoors/200 dealers outdoor—admission—$3; Larry L. Wood and Morrie Fulkerson, 2030 Blueberry Drive N.W., Grand Rapids, MI 49504, (616) 453-8780 for show information or (616) 887-7677.

6. Ann Arbor Antiques Market

5055 Ann Arbor-Saline Rd., Ann Arbor, MI 48103; May through August and October (third Sunday of the month), April and September (Saturday and Sunday, weekend of third Sunday of month); November market usually occurs second Sunday of month; 6 a.m. to 4 p.m; antiques and select collectibles; 350+ dealers; all under cover; locator service for specialties and dealers; admission— $5; M. Brusher, Manager, P.O. Box 1512, Ann Arbor, MI 48106, (734) 662-9453.

7. Birmingham Fairgrounds Flea Market

Birmingham Fairgrounds, Birmingham, AL 35208; exit 120 off I-20/59, follow signs for Alabama State Fair Complex; first weekend of every month, year-round, plus second and third weekends in December, Friday, 3 p.m. to 9 p.m., Saturday and Sunday, 9 a.m. to 6 p.m; antiques, collectibles, and new merchandise (somewhat swapmeet-like); 600+ antique market dealer spaces; mostly indoor; admission—free; parking—free; Birmingham Flea Market, 621 Lorna Square, Birmingham, AL 35216, 800-362-7538.

8. Burlington Antiques Show

Boone County Fairgrounds, Burlington, KY 41005; third Sunday of the month, April through October, 8 a.m. to 3 p.m.; antiques and collectibles; outdoor; admission— $2; early buyers 5 a.m. to 8 a.m.—$5; Paul Kohls, Manager, P.O. Box 58367, Cincinnati, OH 45258, (513) 922-5265.

9. Centreville Antiques Market

The St. Joseph County Grange Fairgrounds, M-86, Centreville, MI 49032; one Sunday per month, May through October, excluding September, 7 a.m. to 4 p.m.; antiques and collectibles (all merchandise guaranteed); 500+ dealers; admission—$4; Robert C. Lawler Management, 1510 N. Hoyne, Chicago, IL 60622, (773) 227-4464.

10. Fairgrounds Antiques Market

Arizona State Fairgrounds, 19th Avenue & McDowell, Phoenix, AZ 85009; third weekend of the month, year-round, except December (second weekend); no show in October, Saturday 9 a.m. to 5 p.m. and Sunday 10 a.m. to 4 p.m.; antiques, collectibles, and crafts. Antique glass and clock repairs; 200+ dealers; indoor; admission—$1; Jack Black Enterprises, P.O. Box 61172, Phoenix, AZ 85082-1172, (800) 678-9987 or (602) 943-1766.

11. Flea Market at the Nashville Fairgrounds

Tennessee State Fairgrounds, Wedgewood and Nolensville Rd., Nashville, TN 37204; fourth Saturday and Sunday of every month except December, Saturday 6 a.m. to 6 p.m., Sunday 7 a.m. to 5 p.m.; antiques and collectibles, crafts and some new merchandise, indoor/outdoor; about 2,000 booths; admission—free; parking—free; Nashville Fairgrounds Flea Market, PO Box 40208, Nashville, TN 37204, (615) 862-5016.

12. Gordyville USA Flea Market & Auction

Gifford, IL 61847: Route 136, 7.5 miles east of I-57; second weekend (Friday, Saturday, Sunday) of each month; first weekend in December, Friday 4 p.m. to 9 p.m., Saturday 9 a.m. to 6 p.m., and Sunday 9 a.m. to 4 p.m.; antiques, collectibles, vintage items, arts, crafts, indoor/outdoor; auctions start Saturday, 10 a.m., and Sunday, 11 a.m.; admission—free; Gordon Hannagan Auction Company, P.O. Box 490, Gifford, IL 61847, (217) 568-7117.

13. Kane County Antiques Flea Markets

Kane County Fairgrounds, Rte. 64 & Randall Road, St. Charles, IL 60174; first Sunday of every month and preceding Saturday, except New Year's and Easter, year-round; Saturday 12 p.m. to 5 p.m.and Sunday 7 a.m. to 4 p.m.; antiques, collectibles, and some crafts; (a favorite in the Midwest, especially with the Chicago crowd); combination indoor and outdoor; country breakfast served; admission—$5 (children under 12 free); Helen Robinson, Manager, P.O. Box 549, St. Charles, IL 60174, (630) 377-2252; www2.pair.com/kaneflea/

Courtesy Kane County Antiques Flea Markets

14. Kentucky Flea Market

Kentucky Fair and Exposition Center at junction of I-264 and I-65, Louisville, KY.; three-or four-day show, dates vary, check trade papers; antiques, collectibles, arts and crafts, and new merchandise; about 1,000 booths; indoor, (climate-controlled); admission—free; parking—$2 at facility; Stewart Promotions, 2950 Breckinridge Lane, Ste. 4A, Louisville, KY 40220, (502) 456-2244.

15. Lakewood Antiques Market

Lakewood Fairgrounds, I 75-85 to Exit 88 East, Atlanta, GA; second weekend of every month, Friday through Sunday, January through December, Friday and Saturday 9 a.m. to 6 p.m., Sunday 10 a.m. to 5 p.m.; antiques and collectibles, 800+ dealers, indoor/outdoor; admission—$3; parking—free; Diane Kent, lakewood Antiques Market, PO Box 6826, Atlanta, GA 30315, (404) 622-4488, Fax (404) 627-2999.

16. Long Beach Outdoor Antiques & Collectible Market

Veterans Stadium, Lakewood Boulevard and Conant Street, Long Beach, CA; third Sunday of each month, 8 a.m. to 3 p.m.; first Sunday in November, antiques and collectibles (including vintage clothing, pottery, quilts, primitives, advertising); 800+ dealers; admission—early admission (5:30 a.m. to 6:30 a.m.) $10, general admission $4.50; Americana Enterprises, Inc., P.O. Box 69219, Los Angeles, CA 90069, (323) 655-5703.

17. Metrolina Expo

7100 North Statesville Road, Charlotte, NC; I-77 to Exit 16A; first and third Friday, Saturday, and Sunday of every month, year-round; 8 a.m. to 5 p.m. Friday and Saturday, 9 a.m. to 5 p.m. Sunday; antiques and collectibles; indoor/outdoor; first weekend about 1,500 dealers; third weekend between 800 and 1,000 dealers. Metrolina hosts three Spectaculars yearly—April, June and November—that feature more than 5,000 dealers; admission: first weekend $3 per day, third weekend $2 per day, and spectaculars $5 per day; early buyer's fee and sneak preview fee are available; Metrolina Expo Center, P.O. Box 26652, Charlotte, NC 28221, (704) 596-4643 or 1-800-824-3770; www.metrolinaexpo.com.

18. Rose Bowl Flea Market

Rose Bowl in Pasadena, CA at Rosemont Ave. and Arroyo Blvd.; second Sunday of every month; antiques, collectibles, primitives, vintage clothing, jewelry, arts and crafts and new merchandise; about 2,200 vendors; regular admission (9 a.m. to 3 p.m.)—$5, early bird admission (7:30 a.m. to 9 a.m.)—$10; VIP admission (6 a.m. to 7:30 a.m.)—$15; Canning Attractions, PO Box 400, Maywood, CA 90270, (323) 560-SHOW (7469); www.rgcshows.com.

19. Rummage-O-Rama

Wisconsin State Fair Park, Milwaukee, WI, I-94 to 84th St. exit; held 13 times a year, January through May and September through December, first weekend of the month and sometimes an additional weekend (call for dates), 10 a.m. to 5 p.m.; indoor; antiques, collectibles, arts and crafts, new merchandise; varies between 300 to 600 vendors; admission—$1.75; parking—free; Rummage-O-Rama, Inc., PO Box 510619, New Berlin, WI 53151, (414) 521-2111.

20. Sandwich Antiques Market

The Fairgrounds, State Route 34, Sandwich, IL 60548; one Sunday per month, May through October, 8 a.m. to 4 p.m.; antiques and collectibles; 600+ dealers; admission—$4; Robert C. Lawler, Sandwich Antiques Market, 1510 N. Hoyne, Chicago, IL 60622, (773) 227-4464.

21. Scott Antiques Market

Ohio Expo Center, Columbus, OH; Saturday 9 a.m. to 6 p.m. and Sunday 10 a.m. to 5 p.m., November through June (weekend dates vary, check Scott advertisements in the trade papers); antiques and collectibles; 1,200+ booths; indoor; admission—free; parking—$3; Scott Antiques Market, P.O. Box 60, Bremen, OH 43107, (740) 569-4112, Fax: (740) 569-7595. (Scott conducts a second monthly flea market—The Scott Antique Market, Atlanta Exposition Centers, adjacent north and south facilities, I-285 to Exit 40 at Jonesboro Road, three miles east of Atlanta airport—second weekend of every month, about 2,400 dealers.)

22. Springfield Antiques Show & Flea Market

Clark County Fairgrounds, Springfield, OH, exit 59 on I-70; third weekend of the month, year-round, excluding July, Saturday 8 a.m. to 5 p.m. and Sunday 9 a.m. to 4 p.m.; Extravaganzas are held in May and September; more than half the market is antiques and collectibles; 400 dealers indoor/900 dealers outdoor in warm weather; admission—$2; Extravaganza admission—$3; early admission for Extravaganza (Friday morning)—$5; Steven and Barbara Jenkins, P.O. Box 2429, Springfield, OH 45501, (937) 325-0053.

Courtesy Super Flea

23. Super Flea

Greensboro Coliseum Complex, Greensboro, NC 27416; monthly but weekend of the month may vary (call for dates), Saturday 8 a.m. to 5 p.m., Sunday 10 a.m. to 5 p.m.; antiques, collectibles, arts and crafts, some new merchandise; about 300 dealers; indoor; admission—$2; parking—$3; Tim Smith, Super Flea, PO Box 16122, Greensboro, NC 27416, (336) 373-8515, www.superflea.com.

WEEKLY FLEA MARKETS

24. Adamstown

Route 272, Adamstown, PA 17517; Sundays; antiques, collectibles, and secondhand material; admission—free; three major markets:

Renninger's; year-round, 7:30 a.m. to 4 p.m. on Sundays, year-round, indoor/outdoor; Renninger's Promotions, 27 Bensinger Drive, Schuylkill Haven, PA 17972; phone on Sunday (717) 336-2177.

Shupp's Grove; April through October, 7 a.m. to 5 p.m., outdoor; Shupp's Grove, P.O. Box 892, Adamstown, PA 19501, (717) 484-4115.

Stoudtburg Antiques Mall, year-round, 7:30 a.m. to 5 p.m.; indoor/outdoor; Carl Barto, 2717 Long Farm Ln., Lancaster, PA 17601, (717) 569-3536 or (717) 484-4385.

25. Annex Antiques Fair and Flea Market

Avenue of the Americas, between 24th and 27th Street, New York City, 10116; year-round, Saturday and Sunday, 9 a.m. to 5 p.m.; mostly outdoor with a new indoor area; variety of merchandise including antiques and collectibles; 600+ dealers; admission—$1 for antique market, flea market is free; Annex Antique Fair, PO Box 7010, New York, NY 10116, (212) 243-5343.

26. Antique World and Marketplace

10995 Main Street, Clarence, NY 14031. (Main Street is Route 5); every Sunday, 8 a.m. to 4 p.m.; three buildings; (one devoted to antiques and collectibles, one to flea market material, and one as exhibition building); 350 dealers in winter/650 dealers in summer; indoor/outdoor; admission—free; Antique World, 10995 Main Street, Clarence, NY 14031; (716) 759-8483, Fax (716) 759-6167.

27. First Monday Trade Days

Canton, TX 75103 (two blocks from downtown square); Friday through Sunday (Friday before the first Monday of each month) 7 a.m. to dusk; antiques, collectibles, new merchandise, crafts (Note: This belongs in the book—not because it is a great source for antiques and collectibles, but because it is the best known swap meet–flea market in the world); 4,000+ booths; antiques and collectibles located on three-acre plot north of Courthouse; admission—free; parking—$3; City of Canton, P.O. Box 245, Canton, TX 75103. (903) 567-6556.

Courtesy Metrolina Expo

28. Lambertville Antiques Flea Market

Route 29, 1.5 miles south of Lambertville, NJ 08530; Wednesday, Saturday, and Sunday, 6 a.m. to 4 p.m.; antiques and collectibles; 150 dealers; indoor /outdoor; admission—free; Heidi and Tom Cekoric, 1864 River Road, Lambertville, NJ 08530, (609) 397-0456.

29. Renninger's Antique Center

Highway 441, Mount Dora, FL 32757; Saturdays and Sundays, 8 a.m. to 4 p.m. (indoor 9 a.m. to 5 p.m.); Extravaganzas on third weekend of November, January, and February. Friday 10 a.m. to 5 p.m., Saturday 8 a.m. to 5:30 p.m., and Sunday 8 a.m. to 5 p.m.; antiques and collectibles; 500+ dealers; indoor/outdoor; admission—free; Extravaganza admission—three-day pass $15, Friday $10, Saturday $5, and Sunday $3; Florida Twin Markets, Inc., P.O. Box 1699, Mount Dora, FL 32756, (352) 383-8393.

30. Shipshewana Auction and Flea Market

On State Route 5 near the southern edge of Shipshewana, IN 46565; Tuesdays 7 a.m. to 5 p.m., Wednesdays, 7 a.m. to 3 p.m. from May through October, antiques, collectibles, new merchandise, and produce (you name it, they sell it); can accommodate up to 800 dealers; indoor/outdoor; admission—free; Shipshewana Auction, Inc., P.O. Box 185, Shipshewana, IN 46565, (219) 768-4129, Fax (219) 768-7041.

Thus far you have learned to identify the various types of flea markets, how to locate them, the keys to evaluating whether or not they are right for you, and my recommendations for getting started. Next you need to develop the skills necessary for flea market survival.

Chapter 4
FLEA MARKET SURVIVAL GUIDE

Your state of exhaustion at the end of the day is the best gauge that I know to judge the value of a flea market—the greater your exhaustion, the better the flea market. A great flea market keeps you on the go from early morning, in some cases 5:00 a.m., to early evening, often 6:00 p.m. The key to survival is to do advance homework, have proper equipment, develop and follow a carefully thought-out shopping strategy, and do your follow-up chores as soon as you return home.

If you are a Type-A personality, your survival plan is essentially a battle plan. Your goal is to cover the flea market as thoroughly as possible and secure the objectives (bargains and hard-to-find objects) ahead of your rivals. You do not stop until total victory is achieved. If you do not have a Type-A personality it does not matter. You still need a survival plan if you want to maximize fun and enjoyment.

ADVANCE HOMEWORK

Consult a flea market's advertisement or brochure. Make certain you understand its dates and time. You never know when special circumstances may cause a change in dates and even location. Check the admission policy. It may be possible to buy a ticket in advance to avoid the wait in line at the ticket booth.

Determine if there is an early admission fee and what times are involved. Admitting collectors and others to the flea market through the use of an early admission fee is a growing practice at flea markets. In most cases the fee is the cost of renting a space. The management simply does not insist that you set up. Actually, this practice had been going on for some time before management formalized it. Friends of individuals renting space often tagged along as helpers or assistants. Once inside, the urge to shop superseded their desire to help their friend.

Review the directions. Are they detailed enough to allow you to find the flea market easily? Remember, it still may be dark when you arrive. If you are not certain, call the manager and ask for specific directions.

Make certain of parking provisions, especially when a flea market takes place within a city or town. Local residents who are not enamored with a flea market in their neighborhood take great pleasure in informing police of illegally parked cars and watching the cars get towed away. In some cases, parking may be more of a problem than locating the flea market. Avoid frustration and plan ahead.

Decide if you are going to stay overnight either the evening before the flea market opens or during the days of operation. In many cases local motel accommodations are minimal. It is common for dealers as well as collectors to commute fifty miles each way to attend Brimfield. The general attitude of most flea market managers is that accommodations are your problem, not theirs. If you are lucky, you can get a list of accommodations from a local Chamber of Commerce. The American Automobile Association regional guidebooks provide some help. However, if you attend a flea market expecting to find nearby overnight accommodations without a reservation, you are the world's biggest optimist.

If possible, obtain a map of the flea market grounds. Become familiar with the layout of the spaces. If you know some of your favorite dealers are going to set up, call and ask them for their space numbers. Mark the location of all toilet facilities and refreshment stands. You may not have time for the latter, but sooner or later you are going to need the former.

Finally, try to convince one or more friends, ideally someone whose area of collecting is totally different from yours, to attend the flea market with you. Each becomes a second set of eyes for the other. Meeting at predesignated spots makes exchanging information easy. It never hurts to share the driving and expenses. Best of all, war stories can be told and savored immediately.

Courtesy Super Flea

FLEA MARKET CHECKLIST

To have an enjoyable and productive day at the flea market, you need the right equipment. What you do not wear can be stored in your car trunk. Make certain that everything is in order the day before your flea market adventure.

Clothing Checklist

____ Hat
____ Sunglasses
____ Light jacket or sweatshirt
____ Poncho or raincoat
____ Waterproof work boots or galoshes

Field Gear Checklist

____ Canvas bag(s)
____ Cash, checkbook, and credit cards
____ Wants lists
____ Business (Collector) cards
____ Magnifying glass
____ Swiss Army pocket knife
____ Toilet paper
____ Sales receipts
____ Mechanical pencil or ballpoint pen
____ This price guide

Car Trunk Checklist

____ Three to six cardboard boxes
____ Newspaper, bubble wrap, diapers, and other appropriate material
____ Sun block
____ First-aid kit
____ Cooler with cold beverages

Clothing

Most flea markets you attend will either be outdoors or have an outdoor section. If you are lucky, the sun will be shining. Beware of sunburn. Select a hat with a wide brim. I prefer a hat with an outside hat band as well. First, it provides a place to stick notes, business cards, and other small pieces of paper I would most likely lose otherwise. Second, it provides a place to stick a feather or some other distinguishing item that allows my friends to spot me in the crowd. Some flea marketeers use the band as a holder for a card expounding their collecting wants. Make certain that your hat fits snugly. Some flea market sites are quite windy. An experienced flea market attendee's hat looks as though it has been through the wars. It has.

I carry sunglasses, but I confess that I rarely use them. I find that taking them on and off is more trouble than they are worth. Further, they distort colors. However, I have found them valuable at windswept and outdoor markets located in large fields. Since I usually misplace a pair a year, I generally buy inexpensive glasses.

The key to dressing for flea markets is a layered, comfortable approach. The early morning and late evening hours are often cool. A light jacket or sweatshirt is suggested. I found a great light jacket that is loaded with pockets. Properly outfitted, it holds all the material I would normally put in my carrying bag.

You must assume that it is going to rain. I have never been to Brimfield when it was not raining. Rain, especially at an outdoor flea market, is a disaster. What is astonishing is how much activity continues in spite of the rain. I prefer a poncho over a raincoat because it covers my purchases as well as my clothing. Most flea markets offer ponchos for sale when rain starts. They are lightweight and come with a storage bag. Of course, you have to be a genius to fold them small enough to get them back into their original storage bag. One I purchased at Kane County lasted years. Mrs. Robinson, being a shrewd promoter, just happened to have them imprinted with information about her flea market. I had a great time there so I have never objected to being a walking bulletin board on her behalf.

The ideal footwear for a flea market is a well broken-in pair of running or walking shoes. However, in the early morning when the ground is wet with dew, a pair of waterproof work boots is a much better choice. I keep my running shoes in the car trunk and usually change into them by 9:00 a.m. at most flea markets.

Rain at outdoor flea markets equals mud. The only defense is a good pair of galoshes. I have been at Brimfield when the rain was coming down so fiercely that dealers set up in tents were using tools to dig water diversion ditches. Cars, which were packed in the nearby fields, sank into the ground. In several cases, local farmers with tractors handsomely supplemented their income by pulling out the stuck autos.

Field Gear

I always go to a flea market planning to buy something. Since most flea market sellers provide the minimum packaging possible, I carry my own. My preference is a double-handled canvas bag with a flat bottom. It is not as easy an item to find as it sounds. I use one to carry my field gear along with two extra bags that start out folded. I find that I can carry three filled bags comfortably. This avoids the necessity of running back to the car each time a bag is filled.

If you are going to buy something, you have to pay for it. Cash is always preferred by the sellers. I carry my cash in a small white envelope with the amount with which I started marked at the top. I note and deduct each purchase as I go along. If you carry cash, be careful how you display it. Pickpockets and sticky-fingered individuals who cannot resist temptation do attend flea markets.

Since I want a record of my purchases, I pay by check whenever I can. I have tried to control my spending by only taking a few checks. Forget it. I can always borrow money on Monday to cover my weekend purchases. I carry a minimum of ten checks.

Most flea market sellers will accept checks with proper identification. For this reason, I put my driver's license and a major credit card in the front of my checkbook before entering the flea market. This saves me the trouble of taking out my wallet each time I make a purchase.

A surprising number of flea market sellers take credit cards. I am amazed at this practice since the only means they have of checking a card's validity is the canceled card booklet they receive each week. They wait until later to get telephone authorization, a potentially dangerous practice.

I buy as much material through the mail as I do at flea markets. One of the principal reasons I attend flea markets is to make contact with dealers. Since flea markets attract dealers from across the country, I expand my supplier sources at each flea market I attend.

The key is to have a wants list ready to give to any flea market seller that admits to doing business by mail. My wants list fills an 8½ inch by 11 inch sheet of writing paper. In addition to my wants, it includes my name, post office box address, UPS (i.e., street) address, and office and home telephone numbers. I also make it a point to get the full name and address of any dealer to whom I give my list. I believe in follow-up.

Not every dealer is willing to take a full-page wants list. For this reason, I hand out my business card. However, I am smart. The back of my business card contains an abbreviated list of my wants and a blank line for me to add additional information. Do not pass up this opportunity for free advertising by using only one-sided business cards. I have received quotes on a few great items as a result of my efforts.

I carry a simple variety-store ten-power magnifying glass. It is helpful to see marks clearly and to spot cracks in china and glass. Ninety-nine percent of the time I use it merely to confirm something that I saw with the naked eye. Jewelers loupes are overkill unless you are buying jewelry.

Years ago I purchased a good Swiss Army pocket knife, one which contains scissors as part of the blade package. It was one of the smartest investments that I made. No flea market goes by that I do not use the knife for one reason or another. If you do not want to carry a pocket knife, invest in a pair of operating room surgical scissors. They will cut through almost anything.

I am a buyer. Why do I carry a book of sales receipts? Alas, many flea market sellers operate in a nontraditional business manner. They are not interested in paper trails, especially when you pay cash. You need a receipt to protect yourself. More on this subject later.

I keep a roll of toilet paper in the car and enough for two sittings in my carrying bag. Do not laugh; I am serious. Most outdoor flea markets have portable toilets. After a few days, the toilet paper supply is exhausted. Even some indoor facilities run out. If I had five dollars from all the people to whom I supplied toilet paper at flea markets, I would be writing this book in Hawaii instead of Pennsylvania.

I carry a mechanical pencil (a ball-point pen works just as well). When I pick up someone's business card, I note why on the back of the card. Use the pencil to mark dealer locations on the flea market map. I do not always buy something when I first spot it. The map helps me relocate items when I wish to go back for a second look. I have wasted hours at flea markets backtracking to find an item that was not located where I thought it was.

Anyone who tells you they know everything about antiques and collectibles and their prices is a liar. I know the areas in which I collect quite well. But there are many categories where a quick source-check never hurts. Every general price guide is different. Find the one that best serves your needs and use it consistently. You know you have a good command of your price guide when you do not have to use the index to locate the value for the item you are seeking. I scored some major points with dealers and others when I offered to share information with them.

From the Car Trunk

My car trunk contains a number of cardboard boxes, several of which are archival file boxes with hand inserts on the side. I have them because I want to see that my purchases make it home safe and sound. One of the boxes is filled with newspaper, diapers, and some bubble wrap. It supplements the field wrapping so that I can stack objects on top of one another. I check the trunk seals on a regular basis. A leaking car trunk once ruined several key purchases I made on an antiquing adventure.

A wide-brim hat may protect the face and neck from the sun, but it leaves the arms exposed. I admire those individuals who can wear a long-sleeved shirt year-round. I am not one of them. In the summer, I wear short-sleeved shirts. For this reason, I keep a bottle of sun block in the trunk.

I also have a first-aid kit that includes aspirin. The most used object is a Band-Aid for unexpected cuts and scratches. The aspirin comes in handy when I have spent eight or more hours in the sun. My first-aid kit also contains packaged cleaning towelettes. I always use one before heading home.

It does not take much for me to get a flea market high. When I do, I can go the entire day without eating. The same does not hold true for liquid intake. Just as toilet paper is a precious commodity at flea markets, so is ice. I carry a small cooler in my trunk with six to a dozen cans of my favorite beverage of the moment. The fastest way to seal a friendship with a flea market dealer is to offer him or her a cold drink at the end of a hot day.

HOW TO SHOP A FLEA MARKET

After having attended flea markets for a number of years, I would like to share some suggestions for bagging the treasures found in the flea market jungle. Much of what I am about to tell you is simply common sense, but we all know that this is probably the most ignored of all the senses.

Most likely you will drive to the flea market. Parking is often a problem. It does not have to be. Most people park as close to the main gate as possible. However, since most flea markets have a number of gates, I usually try to park near a secondary gate. First, this allows me to get closer than I could by trying for the main gate. Second, I have long since learned that whatever gate I use is "my" main gate, and it serves well as home base for my buying operations.

As soon as I arrive at the flea market, I check three things before allowing my buying adrenaline to kick into high gear;—the location of the toilets, the location of the refreshment stands, and the relationship between outdoor and indoor facilities. The latter is very important. Dealers who regularly do the flea market are most likely to be indoors. If I miss them this time around, I can catch them the next. Dealers who are just passing through are most likely set up outdoors. If I miss them, I may never see them again.

I spend the first half hour at any flea market doing a quick tour in order to understand how the flea market is organized, spot those dealers that I would like to visit later, and develop a general sense of what is happening. I prefer to start at the point farthest from my car and work my way back, just the opposite of most flea market shoppers. This method makes trips back to the car shorter each time and reduces the amount of purchases that I am carrying over an extended period of time.

Whenever I go to a flea market to buy, I try to have one to four specific categories in mind. If one tries to look at everything, one develops "antiques and collectibles" shock. Collectors' minds short-circuit if they try to absorb too much. They never get past the first aisle. With specific goals, a quick look at a booth will tell me whether or not it is likely to feature merchandise of interest. If not, I pass it by.

Since time is always at a premium, I make it a practice to ask every dealer, "Do you have any...?" If they say "no," I usually go to the next booth. However, I have learned that dealers do not always remember what they have. When I am in a booth that should have the type of merchandise that I am seeking, I take a minute or two to do a quick scan to see if the dealer is right. In about 25% of the cases, I have found at least one example of the type of material for which I am looking.

I eat on the run, if I eat at all. A good breakfast before the market opens carries me until the evening hours when dusk shuts down the market. I am at the flea market to stuff my bag and car trunk, not my face.

When I find a flea market that I like, I try to visit it at least once in the spring and once in the late summer or early fall. In many flea markets the same dealers are located in the same spot each time. This is extremely helpful to a buyer. I note their location on my map of the market.

When I return the next time, I ask these dealers if they have brought anything that fills my needs. If they say "yes," I take a quick look and decide immediately what I do and do not want to buy. I ask them if they mind holding the items I agreed to buy so that I can move on quickly. I make a commitment to stop back and pay in a few hours. Some agree and some do not. Those who have done business with me previously and know my buying pattern are more willing to accede to my wishes than those who do not. I do not abuse the privilege, but I do not hesitate to take advantage of it either.

Guarantees

There is an adage among antiques and collectibles collectors that "if you bought something at a flea market, you own it." I do not support this approach. I feel every seller should unconditionally guarantee his merchandise. If I find a piece is misrepresented, I take it back.

I try to get a receipt for every purchase that I make. Since many individuals who sell at outdoor flea markets are part-time dealers, they often are unprepared to give a receipt. No problem. I carry a pad of blank receipts and ask them to fill one out.

In every case, I ask the dealers to include their name, shop name (if any), mailing address, and phone number on the receipt. If I do not think a dealer is telling me the truth, I ask for identification. If they give me any flack, I go to their vehicle (usually located in their booth or just outside their indoor stand) and make note of the license plate number. Flea market dealers, especially the outdoor group, are highly mobile. If a problem is discovered with the merchandise I bought, I want to reach the dealer in order to solve the problem.

Whenever possible, the receipt should contain a full description of the merchandise along with a completeness and condition statement. I also ask the dealer to write "money back guaranteed, no questions asked" on the receipt. This is the only valid guarantee that I know. Phrases such as "guaranteed as represented" and "money back" are open to interpretation and become relatively meaningless if a dispute develops. Many flea market dealers are reluctant to provide this guarantee, afraid that the buyer will switch a damaged item for a good one or swipe a part and return the item as incomplete.

Shopping Around

I always shop around. At a good flea market, I expect to see the same merchandise in several booths. Prices will vary, often by several hundred if not several thousand percent. I make a purchase immediately only when the price is a bargain, i.e., priced way below current market value. If a piece is near current market value, I inspect it, note its location on my map, and move on. If I do not find another in better good condition, at a cheaper price, or both, I go back and negotiate with the dealer.

I take the time to inspect carefully, in natural sunlight, any piece that I buy. First, I check for defects such as cracks, nicks, scratches, and signs of normal wear. Second, if the object involves parts, I make certain that it is complete. I have been known to take the time to carefully count parts. The last two times that I did not do this, the objects that I bought turned out to be incomplete when I got them home.

I frequently find myself asking a dealer to clean an object for my inspection. Outdoor flea markets are often quite dusty, especially in July and August. The insides of most indoor markets are generally not much better. Dirt can easily hide flaws. It also can discolor objects. Make certain you know exactly what you are buying.

I force myself to slow down and get to know those dealers from whom I hope to make future purchases. Though it may mean that I do not visit the entire flea market, I have found that the long-term benefits from this type of contact far outweigh the short-term gain of seeing every booth.

FLEA MARKET FOOD

Flea market food is best described as overcooked, greasy, and heartburn-inducing. I think I forgot to mention that my first-aid kit contains a roll of antacid pills. Gourmet eating facilities are usually nonexistent. Is it any wonder that I often go without eating?

Several flea markets take place on sites that also house a farmer's market. When this is the case, I take time to shop the market and purchase my food at one of its counters.

I do make it a point to inquire among the dealers where they go to have their evening meals. They generally opt for good food, plenty of it, and at inexpensive prices. At the end of the day I am hungry. I do not feel like driving home, cleaning up, and then eating. I want to eat where the clientele can stand the appearance and smell of a flea marketeer. I have rarely been disappointed when I followed a flea market dealer's recommendation.

The best survival tactic is probably to bring your own food. I simply find this too much trouble. I get heartburn just thinking about a lunch sitting for several hours inside a car on a hot summer day. No thanks; I buy what I need.

MAILING LIST/NEWSLETTER

Many flea markets actively recruit names for promotional mailings. Several send monthly, bi-monthly, or quarterly newsletters to their customers. I always take a minute or two to fill out their request card. It is not my nickel paying for the mailing.

FOLLOW-UP

Immediately upon returning home, or at worst the next day, unpack and record your purchases. If you wait, you are likely to forget important details. This is not the fun part of collecting. It is easy to ignore. Discipline yourself. Get in the habit. You know it is the right thing to do, so do it.

Review the business cards that you picked up and notes that you made. If letters are required, write them. If telephone calls are necessary, make them. Never lose sight of the fact that one of your principal reasons for going to the flea market is to establish long-term dealer contacts.

Finally, if your experiences at the flea market were positive or if you saw ways to improve the market, write a letter to the manager. He or she will be delighted in both instances. Competition among flea markets for dealers and customers is increasing. Good managers want to make their markets better than their competitors. Your comments and suggestions will be welcomed.

Courtesy Metrolina Expo

Chapter 5
HONING YOUR SHOPPING SKILLS

Earlier I mentioned that most buyers view flea markets as places where bargains and "steals" can be found. I have found plenty. However, the truth is that you have to hunt long and hard to find them, and in some cases, they evolve only after intense bargaining. Shopping a flea market properly requires skills. This chapter will help shape and hone your shopping skills and alert you to some of the pitfalls involved with buying at a flea market.

WITH WHAT TYPE OF DEALER ARE YOU DEALING?

There are essentially three types of dealers found at flea markets: the professional dealer, the weekend dealer, and the once-and-done dealer. Each brings a different level of expertise and merchandise to the flea market. Each offers pluses and minuses. Knowing which type you are dealing with is advantageous.

Professional Dealer

So many flea markets developed in the 1980s and 1990s that there are now professional flea market dealers who practice their craft full-time. Within any given week, you may find them at three or four different flea markets. They are the modern American gypsies. Their living accommodations and merchandise are usually found within the truck, van, or station wagon in which they are traveling. These individuals survive on shrewdness and hustle. They want to turn over their merchandise as quickly as possible for the best gain possible and are willing to do whatever is necessary to achieve this end.

Buy from professional flea market dealers with a questioning mind; i.e., question everything they tell you about an object from what it is to what they want for it. Their knowledge of the market comes from hands-on experience. It is often not as great as they think. They are so busy setting up, buying, selling, and breaking down that they have little time to do research or read trade literature. More than any other group of dealers in the trade, they are weavers of tales and sellers of dreams.

The professional flea market dealer's circuit can stretch from New England to California, from Michigan to Florida. These "professionals" are constantly on the move. If you have a problem with something one of these dealers sold you, finding him or her can prove difficult. Do not buy anything from a professional dealer unless you are absolutely certain about it.

Judge the credibility and integrity of the professional flea market dealer by the quality of the merchandise he or she displays. You should see middle- and high-quality material in better condition than you normally expect to find. If the offerings are heavily damaged and appear poorly maintained, walk away.

Do not interpret what I have said to imply that all professional flea market dealers are dishonest. The vast majority are fine, upstanding individuals. However, as a whole, this group has the largest share of rotten apples in its barrel—more than any other group of dealers in the flea market field. Since there is no professional organization to police the trade and promoters do not care as long as their space rent is paid, it is up to you to protect yourself.

The antiques and collectibles field works on the principle of *caveat emptor*, "let the buyer beware." It is important to remember that the key is to beware of the seller as well as his merchandise. It pays to know with whom you are doing business.

Weekend Dealers

Weekend flea market dealers are individuals who have a full-time job elsewhere and are dealing on the weekends to supplement their income. In most cases, their weekday job is outside the antiques and collectibles field. However, with the growth of the antiques mall, some of these weekend dealers are really full-time antiques and collectibles dealers. They spend their weekdays shopping and maintaining their mall locations, while selling on the weekend at their traditional flea market location.

In many cases, these dealers specialize, especially if they are in a large flea market environment. As a result, they are usually familiar with the literature relating to their areas of expertise. They also tend to live within a few hours' drive of the flea market in which they set up. This means that they can be found if the need arises.

Courtesy Antiques by the Bay – Alameda Point Antiques and Collectibles Faire

Once-and-Done Dealers

Once and done dealers range from an individual who is using the flea market to dispose of some inherited family heirlooms or portions of an estate to collectors who have culled their collection and are offering their duplicates and discards for sale. Bargains can often be found in both cases. In the first instance, bargains result from lack of pricing knowledge. However, unless you are an early arrival, chances are that the table will be picked clean by the regular dealers and pickers long before you show up. Bargains originate from the collectors because they know the price levels in their field. They realize that in order to sell their discards and duplicates, they will have to offer their merchandise at prices that are tempting to dealer and collector alike.

The once-and-done dealers are the least prepared to conduct sales on a business basis. Most likely they will not have a receipt book or a business card featuring their address and phone number. They almost never attempt to collect applicable sales tax. There is little long-term gain in spending time getting to know the individual who is selling off a few family treasures. However, do not leave without asking, "Is there anything else you have at home that you are planning to sell?"

Spend some time with the collector. Strike up a conversation. If you have mutual collecting interests, invite him or her to visit and view your collection. What you are really fishing for is an invitation to view his or her holdings. You will be surprised how often you will receive one when you show genuine interest.

WHAT IS IT?

You need to be concerned with two questions when looking at an object: What is it? and How much is it worth? In order to answer the second question, you need a correct answer to the first. Information provided about objects for sale at flea markets is minimal and often incorrect. The only state of mind that protects you is a defensive one.

There are several reasons for the amount of misidentification of objects at flea markets. The foremost is dealer ignorance. Many dealers simply do not take the time to do proper research. I also suspect that they are quite comfortable with the adage that "ignorance is bliss." As long as an object bears a resemblance to something good, it will be touted with the most prestigious label available.

When questioning dealers about an object, beware of phrases such as "I think it is...," "As best as I can tell," "It looks exactly like," and "I trust your judgment." Push the dealers until you pin them down. The more they vacillate, the more suspicious you should become. Insist that the sales receipt carry a full claim about the object.

In many cases misidentification is passed from person to person because the dealer who bought the object trusted what was said by the dealer who sold it to him. I am always amazed how convinced dealers are that they are right. There is little point in arguing with them. The only way to preserve both individuals' sanity is to walk away.

If you do not know what something is, do not buy it. The general price guide and any specific price guides that you have in your bag can point you in the right direction, but they are not the final word. If you simply must find out right that minute and do not have the reference book you need, check with the antiques and collectibles book dealer at the market to see if he has the title you need in stock.

STORIES, STORIES AND MORE STORIES

A flea market is a place where one's creative imagination and ability to believe what is heard are constantly tested. The number of cleverly crafted stories to explain the origin of pieces and why the condition is not exactly what one expects is endless. The problem is that they all sound plausible. Once again, I come back to the concept upon which flea market survival is founded: a questioning mind.

I often ask dealers to explain the circumstances through which they acquired a piece and what they know about the piece. Note what I said, I am not asking the seller to reveal his or her source. No one should be expected to do that. I am testing the openness and believability of the dealer. If the dealer claims there is something special about an object (e.g., it belonged to a famous person or was illustrated in a book), I ask to see proof. Word-of-mouth stories have little credibility in the long run.

Again, there are certain phrases that serve as tip-offs that something may be amiss. "It is the first one I have ever seen," "You will never find another one like it," "I saw one a few aisles over for more money," "One sold at auction a few weeks ago for double what I am asking," and "I am selling it to you for exactly what I paid for it" are just a few examples. If what you are hearing sounds too good to be true, it probably is.

Your best defense is to study and research the area in which you want to collect before going to flea markets. Emphasis should be placed equally on object identification and an understanding of the pricing structure within that collecting category. You will not be a happy person if you find that although an object you bought is what the seller claimed it was, you paid far more for it than it is worth.

PERIOD, REPRODUCTION, COPYCAT, FANTASY OR FAKE

The number of reproductions, copycats, and fantasy and fake items at flea markets is larger than in any other segment of the field. Antiques malls run a close second. In fact, it is common to find several dealers at a flea market selling reproductions, copycats, and fantasy items openly. When you recognize them, take time to study their merchandise. Commit the material to memory. In ten years, when the material has begun to age, you will be glad that you did.

Although the above terms are familiar to those who are active in the antiques and collectibles field, they may not be understood by some. A period piece is an example made during the initial period of production or an object licensed during a person's, group's, or show's period of fame or stardom. The commonly used term is "real." However, if you think about it, all objects are real, whether period or not. "Real" is one of those terms that should set your mind to questioning.

A reproduction is an exact copy of a period piece. There may be subtle changes in areas not visible to the naked eye, but essentially it is identical to its period counterpart. A copycat is an object that is similar, but not exactly like the period piece it is emulating. It may vary in size, form, or design elements. In some cases, it is very close to the original. In auction terms, copycats are known as "in the style of." A fantasy item is a form that was not issued during the initial period of production. An object licensed after Elvis's death would be an Elvis fantasy item. A Chippendale-style coffee table, a form which did not exist during the first Chippendale period, is another example.

The thing to remember is that reproductions, copycats, and fantasy items are generally mass-produced and start out life honestly. The wholesalers who sell them to dealers in the trade make it clear exactly what they are. Alas, some of the dealers do not do so when they resell them.

Because reproductions, copycats, and fantasy items are mass-produced, they appear in the market in quantity. When you spot a piece in your collecting area that you have never seen before, quickly check through the rest of the market. If the piece is mint, double-check. Handle the piece. Is it the right weight? Does it have the right color? Is it the quality that you expect? If you answer "no" to any of these questions, put it back.

The vast majority of items sold at any flea market are mass-produced, twentieth-century items. Encountering a new influx of never-seen-before items does not necessarily mean they are reproductions, copycats, or fantasy items. Someone may have uncovered a hoard. The trade term is "warehouse find." A hoard can seriously affect the value of any antique or collectible. All of a sudden the number of available examples rises dramatically. So usually does the condition level. Unless the owner of a hoard is careful, this sudden release of material can drive prices downward.

Courtesy Super Flea

A fake is an item deliberately meant to deceive. They are usually one-of-a-kind items, with many originating in shops of revivalist craftspersons. The folk art and furniture market is flooded with them. Do not assume that because an object is inexpensive, it is all right. You would be surprised how cheaply goods can be made in Third World countries.

It is a common assumption that reproductions, copycats, fantasy items, and fakes are of poor quality and can be easily spotted. If you subscribe to this theory, you are a fool. There are some excellent reproductions, copycats, fantasy items, and fakes. You probably have read on more than one occasion how a museum was fooled by an object in its collection. If museum curators can be fooled, so can you.

This is not the place for a lengthy dissertation on how to identify and differentiate period objects from reproductions, copycats, fantasies, or fakes. Read the books suggested in the "Flea Marketeer's Annotated Reference Library" that appears on page 334.

What follows are a few quick tips to put you on the alert:

1. If it looks new, assume it is new.
2. Examine each object carefully, looking for signs of age and repair that should be there.
3. Use all appropriate senses—sight, touch, smell, and hearing—to check an object.
4. Be doubly alert when something appears to be a "steal."
5. Make copies of articles from trade papers or other sources that you find about period, reproduction, copycat, fantasy, and fake items and keep them on file.
6. Finally, handle as many authentic objects as possible. The more genuine items you handle, the easier it will be to identify impostors.

WHAT'S A FAIR PRICE?

The best selling scenario at a flea market is a buyer and seller who are both extremely happy with the price paid and a seller who has made sufficient profit to allow him or her to stay in business and return to sell another day. Reality is not quite like this. Abundance of merchandise, competition among dealers, and negotiated prices often result in the seller being less than happy with the final price received. Yet the dealers sell because some money is better than no money.

Price haggling is part of the flea market game. In fact, the next section discusses this very subject in detail. The only real value an object has is what someone is willing to pay for it, not what someone asks for it. There is no fixed price for any antique, collectible, or secondhand object. All value is relative.

These considerations aside, there are a few points relating to price and value that the flea marketeer should be aware of. Try to understand these points. Remember, in the antiques and collectibles field there are frequently two or more sides to every issue and rarely any clear-cut right or wrong answer.

First, dealers have a right to an honest profit. If dealers are attempting to make a full-time living in the trade, they must triple their money in order to cover their inventory costs, pay their overhead expenses, which are not inconsequential, and pay themselves. Buy at thirty cents and sell at one dollar.

The problem is that many flea market dealers set up at flea markets not to make money but simply to have a good time. As a result, they willingly sell at much lower profit margins than those who are trying to make a living. It is not really that hard to tell which group is which. Keep the seller's circumstances in mind when haggling.

Second, selling is labor and capital-intensive. Check a dealer's booth when a flea market opens and again when it closes. Can you spot the missing objects? When a dealer has a "good" flea market, he or she usually sells between fifteen and thirty objects. In most cases, the inventory from which these objects sold consists of hundreds of pieces. Do not think about what the dealer sold, think about what was not sold. What did it cost? How much work is involved in packing, hauling, setting up, and repacking these items until the objects finally sell. Flea market sellers need a high profit margin to stay in business.

Third, learn to use price guide information correctly. Remember the prices are guides, not price absolutes. For their part, sellers must resist the temptation to become greedy and trap themselves in the assumption that they deserve book price or better for every item they sell. Sellers would do better to focus on what they paid for an object (which, in effect, does determine the final price) rather than on what they think they can get for it (it never sells as quickly as they think). They will make more on volume sales than they will trying to get top dollar for all their items.

Price guide prices represent what a "serious" collector in that category will pay provided he or she does not already own the object. An Elvis Presley guitar in its original box may book for over $500, but it has that value only to an Elvis Presley collector who does not already own one. Price guide prices tend to be on the high side.

Fourth, the IRS defines fair-market value as a situation where there is a willing buyer and seller, neither compelled to buy or sell, and both parties equally knowledgeable. While the first and second part of this equation usually applies, the third usually does not. There is no question that knowledge is power in the flea market game and sharing it can cost money. If money were the only issue, I could accept the idea of keeping quiet. However, I like to think that a sale involves transfer of information about the object as well as the object itself. If there were a fuller understanding of the selling situation by both sides, there would be a lot less grousing about prices after the deal is done.

Finally, forget about book value. The only value an object has is what it is worth to you. This is the price that you should pay. The only person who can make this judgment is you. It is a decision of the moment. Never forget that. Do not buy if you think the price is unfair. Do not look back if you find later that you overpaid. At the moment of purchase you thought the price was fair. In buying at a flea market, the buck stops in your heart and wallet.

FLEA MARKET HAGGLING

Few prices at a flea market are firm prices. No matter what anyone tells you, it is standard practice to haggle. You may not be comfortable doing it, but you might as well learn how. The money you save will be your own.

In my mind there are only three prices: a bargain price, a negotiable price, and a ridiculous price. If the price on an object is already a bargain, I pay it. I do this because I like to see the shocked look on a seller's face when I do not haggle. I also do it because I want that dealer to find similar material for me. Nothing encourages this more than paying the price asked.

If the price is ridiculous, marked several times above what it is worth, I simply walk away. No amount of haggling will ever get the price to where I think it belongs. All that will happen is that the dealer and I will become frustrated. Who needs it? Let the dealers sit with their pieces. Sooner or later, the message will become clear.

Courtesy Antiques by the Bay – Alameda Point Antiques and Collectibles Faire

I firmly believe it is the responsibility of the seller to set the asking price. When an object is not marked with a price, I become suspicious that the dealer is going to set the asking price based on what he or she thinks I can pay. I have tested this theory on more than one occasion by sending several individuals to inquire about the value of an unmarked item. In every case, a variety of prices were reported back to me. Since most of the material that I collect is mass-produced, I walk away from all unpriced merchandise. I will find another example somewhere else. This type of dealer does not deserve my business.

I have too much to do at a flea market to waste time haggling. If I find a piece that is close to what I am willing to pay, I make a counter-offer. I am very clear in what I tell the seller. "I am willing to pay "x" amount. This is my best offer. Will you take it?" Most dealers are accustomed to responding with "Let's halve the difference." Hard though it is at times, I never agree. I tell the dealer that I made my best offer to save time haggling, and I intend to stick by it.

If the flea market that I am attending is a monthly or weekly, I may follow the object for several months. If it has gone unsold at the end of four to five months, I speak with the dealer and call attention to the fact that he has been unsuccessful in selling the object for the amount asked. I make my counter-offer, which sometimes can be as low as half the value marked on the piece. While the dealer may not be totally happy selling the object at that price, the prospect of any sale is often better than keeping the object in inventory for several more months. If the object has been sold before I return, I do not get upset. In fact, I am glad the dealer received his price. He just did not get it from me.

IN SUMMARY

If you are gullible, flea markets may not be for you. While not a Darwinian jungle, the flea market has pitfalls and traps which must be avoided in order for you to be successful. The key is to know that these pitfalls and traps exist.

Successful flea marketeering comes from practice. There is no school where you can learn the skills you need. You fly by the seat of your pants, learn as you go. The tuition that you pay are the mistakes you make along the way.

You can lessen your mistakes by doing homework. Research and study what you want to collect before you start buying. Even the most experienced buyers get careless or are fooled. Buying from the heart is much easier than buying from the head.

Never get discouraged. Everyone else you see at the flea market has experienced or is experiencing exactly what is happening to you. When you become a seasoned veteran, you will look back upon the learning period and laugh. In the interim, at least try to smile.

Chapter 6
THE FLEA MARKET SCENE TODAY

"The Flea Market Scene Today" that appeared in the fourth edition of this book began: "While the flea market scene continually evolves, changes occur so gradually that they almost escape notice." Not true today. Change is occurring; and, it is very noticeable.

MORE THAN JUST A FLEA MARKET

Today flea markets are more than just a place to sell antiques and collectibles. A growing number of promoters are turning them into weekend happenings, some aspects of which are designed to make attending the flea market as much fun as possible.

The popularity of PBS' *Antiques Roadshow* and HGTV's *Appraise-It* led several promoters to add verbal appraisal clinics to their regular flea market activities. Several also offer mini-educational seminars covering everything from collecting tips, how to buy at auction, and keys to spotting reproductions, copycats, fantasy items, and fakes.

Extravaganzas, heavily promoted events occurring one to three times per year, continue to expand. Buyers like them because they attract a greater variety of dealers. More is better is the philosophy of the day.

While antiques and collectibles flea market promoters continue to prevent discount and discontinued merchandise sellers from setting up at their shows, they have expanded the number of craft sellers. They recognize that many antiques and collectibles buyers also buy craft products.

Those flea markets not fortunate to have a farmers' market nearby are providing space to individuals selling a wide range of food stuffs from farm produce to seafood. These individuals do well.

Flea market promoters also have learned to cooperate with each other and with other antiques and collectibles selling venues and tourist attractions in their area. They have realized there is strength in numbers. Rather than competing, rivals complement. Progressive promoters are creating packages that entice buyers to spend several days "antiquing" their community.

Finally, flea market promoters have cleaned up their act. Today's flea markets are better organized and cleaner than they were a decade ago. Many feature attractive new indoor facilities.

THE INTERNET

The Internet is having a very positive effect on flea markets. Gate admissions have risen significantly. Why? The answer is simple. Flea markets and auctions are the two principal buying sources for people selling and auctioning material on the Internet.

At the moment, Internet prices are among the strongest in the business. No matter what one pays at the flea market, there is usually someone buying on the Internet who will pay more. This is the philosophy that dominated the antiques and collectibles market during the boom times of the early 1980s. There are those who remember what happened when the bubble burst in the mid-1980s. Unfortunately, they are in the minority. Any individual who has been a flea market dealer for less than ten years has no memory of the late 1980s recession and its impact on the market. History does have a way of repeating itself.

Some promoters note a decrease in the number of dealers doing their shows. They blame the Internet; and, they are probably correct. As noted earlier, the good promoters are introducing a variety of reforms to strengthen the flea market scene. These should counter this Internet negative. Further, look for many of these deserters to return to the flea market scene when the glamour of selling on the Internet wears off. The smart seller realizes that the Internet offers a new selling approach that complements, not replaces his existing selling opportunities.

FLEA MARKET DECORATING STYLE

Professional decorators returned to the flea market scene in the mid-1990s. They primarily sought decorative accent pieces and objects that complemented existing decorating styles such as Country and Retro. They bought Look, not collectibility.

The possibility of an independent flea market decorating style never occurred to most individuals, not even in their wildest imagination. Yet, it has happened. Emelie Tolley and Chris Mead's *Flea Market Style* (Clarkson Potter, 1997, $30.00) is the movement's bible.

One is tempted to call flea market style the "junk is funk" style. Making fun of it is a mistake. Decorators and their customers take it very seriously. It will have a positive cash flow impact on flea markets for the next five years.

Will the flea market style be only a passing fad or become an established, traditional decorating style? Counting the number, length, and duration of articles appearing in architectural, decorator, living, and women's magazines is a key measure of a decorating craze's success. The flea market decorating style is in its infancy. If the article count is high and persists for a decade or longer, the look will be considered established. At the moment, fad appears more likely. The old adage of "take the money and run" applies. Fulfilling the demands of flea market style devotees is a major contributor to flea markets' current boom times.

"Anything decorators can do, I can do cheaper" is a deeply entrenched philosophy. There already are indications of a new wave of do-it-yourself decorators invading the flea market scene. They are not afraid to spend money.

Because flea market style is highly eclectic, predetermining what will and will not appeal to them is difficult. Two key types of material stand out: (1) big, showy, pizzazz oriented pieces and (2) pieces that are easily identified with a specific decade, e.g., the fifties or sixties.

The flea market style emphasizes the used look. Appearance, not condition, is everything. Signs of aging and use are acceptable as long as the piece still "looks good."

Finally, individuals purchasing flea market material for decorating purposes place far less emphasis on the investment aspect of their purchases than do collectors. Most collectors still are unable to get past the "what it is worth today and what it will potentially be worth tomorrow" philosophy. Kudos to those who downplay the commodity aspect of antiques and collectibles.

SECONDHAND ROSE

The number of individuals shopping flea markets for objects they can use on a daily basis continues to increase. Once again, especially regarding household items such as dinnerware, flatware, and stemware, buying at a flea market is cheaper than buying new. As a result, individuals are not concerned if the items break. They assume they will be able to return to the flea market and replace them or find something similar that is equally as good or better.

Flea market dealers realize their customer basis is shifting. Collectors were the principal buyers at antiques and collectibles flea markets fifteen years ago. Today three out of four buyers are reusers. Collector buyers are a distinct minority.

Booth merchandise is changing. Objects are in ready-to-use condition. Utilitarian, functional, and practical objects dominate. While most antiques and collectibles objects are twenty-five years old or older, they still fit the bill.

The reuse buyer is now so strong that it is questionable if collectors will ever regain their buying dominance. A few see this as a negative. Most think of it as a very positive development.

TWO NEGATIVES: REPRODUCTIONS AND DESIRABLES

The problem of reproductions (exact copies), copycats (stylistic copies), fantasy items (forms, shapes, and patterns that appear earlier but are not), and fakes (objects made to deceive) being sold as period pieces continues. It is buyer beware, caveat emptor. Refuse to buy from individuals selling this type of merchandise improperly marked, spread the word about them, and complain to the management about their presence. Nothing is likely to happen except perhaps you will feel better.

Parasitic toy scalpers, greedy individuals who capitalize on artificial toy shortages, have been replaced by the desirables dealers. A desirable is an object of recent origin with an artificial and highly speculative secondary market. Sports/racing collectibles and Beanie Babies are the two most common examples in today's flea market scene. Barbie is still around, but a shadow of her former self. Beanie Babies are on the way out, thank God. What will replace them remains to be determined. Have no doubt that something will.

A FINAL NOTE

As in previous editions of this title, this state of the market report concludes with the final paragraphs from the first edition's report. The words are as applicable today as they were in 1991.

"Permit me one final thought. The key to having an enjoyable experience at a flea market does not rest with the manager, the dealers, the physical setting or the merchandise. The key is you. Attend with reasonable expectations in mind. Go to have fun, to make a pleasant day of it. Even if you come home with nothing, savor the contacts that you made and the fact that you spent a few hours or longer among the goodies.

"As a smart flea marketeer, you know the value of customers to keep flea markets alive and functioning. When you find a good flea market, do not keep the information to yourself. Write or call the regional trade papers and ask them to do more stories about the market. Share your news with friends and others. Encourage them to attend. There is plenty for everyone."

Happy Hunting from all of us at Rinker Enterprises, Inc.

Part Two

FLEA MARKET TREASURES

Categories A to Z

PRICE NOTES

Flea market prices for antiques and collectibles are not as firmly established as those at malls, shops, and shows. As a result, it is imperative that you treat the prices found in this book as "guides," not "absolutes."

Prices given are based on the national retail price for an object that is complete and in fine condition. These are retail prices. They are what you would expect to pay to purchase the objects. They do not reflect what you might realize if you were selling objects. A "fair" selling price to a dealer or private collector ranges from 20% to 40% of the book price, depending on how commonly found the object is.

Prices quoted are for objects that show a minimum of wear and no major blemishes to the display surface. The vast majority of flea market objects are mass-produced. As such, they survive in quantity. Do not buy damaged or incomplete objects. It also pays to avoid objects that show signs of heavy use.

Regional pricing is a factor within the flea market area, especially when objects are being sold close to their place of manufacture. When faced with higher prices due to strong regional pricing, I offer the price an object would bring in a neighboring state or geographic area. In truth, regional pricing has all but disappeared due to the large number of nationally oriented antiques and collectibles price guides, magazines, newspapers, and collectors' clubs.

Finally, "you" determine price; it is what "you" are willing to pay. Flea market treasures have no fixed prices. What has value to one person may be totally worthless to another. Is it possible to make sense out of this chaos? Yes, but in order to do so, you have to jump in feet first: attend flea markets and buy.

Happy Hunting! May all your purchases turn out to be treasures.

ABBREVIATIONS

3D = three-dimensional
adv = advertising
C = century
c = circa
circ = circular
cov = cover or covered
d = diameter or depth
dec = decorated or decoration
dj = dust jacket
ed = edition
emb = embossed
expo = exposition
ext = exterior
FH = flat handle
ftd = footed
gal = gallon
ground = background
h = height, high
HH = hollow handle
hp = hand painted
illus = illustrated, illustration, or illustrations
imp = impressed
int = interior
j = jewels
K = karat
l = length, long
lb = pound
litho = lithograph or lithographed
MBP = mint in bubble pack
mfg = manufactured
MIB = mint in box
MIP = mint in package
MISB = mint in sealed box
mkd = marked
MOC = mint on card
MOP = mother of pearl
orig = original
oz = ounce or ounces
pc = piece
pp = page
pps = pages
pkg = package
pr = pair
pt = pint
qt = quart
rect = rectangular
sgd = signed
SP = silver plated
SS = sterling silver
ST = stainless steel
sq = square
unmkd = unmarked
Vol = volume
w = width, wide
yg = yellow gold
yr = year
# = number

ABINGDON POTTERY

Over the years, Roseville and Weller pottery—favorites of old-time traditional collectors of mass-produced pottery wares—have become more and more expensive. In the 1970s and 1980s, collectors with limited budgets began concentrating on firms such as Gonder, Hall, Hull, McCoy, Stangl and Vernon Kilns. Now this material is going up in value. Stretch your dollar by concentrating on some of the firms that still have limited collector appeal. Abingdon Potteries, Inc., Haeger Potteries and Pfaltzgraff Pottery Co., are a few suggestions. I'll bet you can think of many more.

The Abingdon Sanitary Manufacturing Co., began manufacturing bathroom fixtures in 1908 in Abingdon, Ill. In 1938, they began production of art pottery made with a vitreous body. This line continued until 1970 and included more than 1,000 shapes and pieces. Almost 150 colors were used to decorate these wares. Given these numbers, forget about collecting an example of every form in every color ever made. Find a few forms that you like and concentrate on them. There are some great ones.

Club: Abingdon Pottery Club, 210 Knox Hwy. 5, Abingdon, IL 61410.

Ashtray, Duo, #356 . . . . **$35.00**
Bookends, pr, Scotty, #650, 7½" h **200.00**
Bookends, pr, sea gull, 6" h **40.00**
Bowl, Crescent, #684 . . . . **15.00**
Candleholders, pr, Rope, #323 . . . . **40.00**
Candleholders, pr, Daisy **40.00**
Candleholders, pr, Sunburst **50.00**
Candleholders, pr, Wreath **65.00**
Console Bowl, oval, white, 19" l **18.00**
Cookie Jar, Granny, green **135.00**
Cookie Jar, Hippo, #549, 8" h **250.00**
Cookie Jar, Jack-In-The-Box, 10½" h **295.00**
Cookie Jar, Little Girl, #693D, 9½" h **125.00**
Cookie Jar, Little Ol'Lady, #471, 9" h **275.00**
Cookie Jar, Pineapple, #3664, 10½" h **75.00**
Cookie Jar, Three Bears, #696D, 8¾" h **250.00**
Cornucopia, low, #569 . . . . **15.00**
Cornucopia, Shell, #449, 4½" h **45.00**
Figure, kangaroo, #605D, 7" h **200.00**
Figure, peacock, #416, 7" h **55.00**
Figure, pouter pigeon, #388, 4¼" h **45.00**
Figure, swordfish, #657, 4½" h **55.00**
Flower Pot, La Fleur, #151, 5" h **15.00**
Jardiniere, La Fleur **15.00**
Pitcher, ice lip, #200, 2 qt **35.00**
Planter, Scroll and Leaf, yellow, 9 x 3½" **6.50**
Plate, Apple Blossom, #415, 11½" d **50.00**
Plate, Wild Rose, #344, 10 x 12" **125.00**
Vase, Echo, #352, 4" h **25.00**
Vase, large asters, #455, 11½" h **50.00**
Vase, Chinese Terrace, #698, 6" h **45.00**
Vase, Classic, blue, emb leaf band, orig label, 9⅞" h **25.00**
Vase, Fern Leaf, #420, 7¼" h **65.00**
Vase, Hollyhock, #496, 7½" h **30.00**
Vase, Sang, #304, white matte glaze, 10" h **40.00**
Vase, Sea Horse **18.00**
Wall Pocket, Daisy, #379 . . . . **70.00**
Wall Pocket, Ivy, #590D, 7" h **65.00**
Wall Pocket, Leaf, #724 . . . . **40.00**
Wall Pocket, Morning Glory, #377, 7½" h **35.00**

ACTION FIGURES

Action, action, action! Action is the key to action figures. Action figures show action. You can recognize them because they can be manipulated into an action pose or are molded into an action pose. There is a wealth or supporting accessories for most action figures, ranging from clothing to vehicles, that is as collectible as the figures themselves. A good rule is the more pizzazz, the better the piece.

This is a relatively new collecting field. Emphasis is placed on pieces in mint or near-mint condition. The best way to find them is with their original packaging. Better yet, buy some new and stick them away. Unless noted, prices quoted are for action figures out of their packaging.

Club: Classic Action Figure Collector's Club, P.O. Box 2095, Halesite, NY 11743.

Periodicals: *Action Figure News & Toy Review,* 556 Monroe Turnpike, Monroe, CT 06468; *Tomart's Action Figure Digest,* Tomart Publications, 3300 Encrete Ln., Dayton, OH 45439.

FIGURES

Addams Family, Playmates, Gomez, MIP **$15.00**
Addams Family, Playmates, Lurch, MIP **15.00**
Addams Family, Playmates, Morticia, MIP **35.00**
Advanced Dungeons and Dragons, LJN, Drex, 2nd series, 4" h **75.00**
Advanced Dungeons and Dragons, LJN, Kelek, 1st series, 4" h **20.00**
Advanced Dungeons and Dragons, LJN, Ringlerun, 1st series, 4" h **25.00**
Advanced Dungeons and Dragons, LJN, Strongheart, 1st series, 4" h **25.00**
A-Team, Galoob, 1984, 3¾" h, price for set of 4 . . . . **30.00**
Bart Simpson, Mattel, 1990 . . . . **5.00**
Battlestar Galactica, Mattel, Starbuck, 1978 . . . . **20.00**
Best of the West, Marx, Johnny West, quick draw, 1965 . . . . **75.00**
Big Jim, Mattel, baseball outfit with accessories **40.00**
Big Jim, Mattel, hockey outfit with helmet and skates **40.00**
Bionic Six, LJN, Bungi, MIP **15.00**
Bionic Six, LJN, Dr Scarab, MIP **10.00**
Bionic Six, LJN, Glove, MIP **15.00**
Bionic Woman, Kenner **45.00**
Bonanza, American Character, Hoss Cartwright, 1966 . . . . **100.00**
Captain Power, Mattel **8.00**
Captain Power, Mattel, Sgt Scout Baker **12.00**
Clash of the Titans, Mattel, Charon, 3¾" h **15.00**
C O P S, Hasbro, Officer Bowzer and Blitz, #7687, 1988 . . . . **15.00**
Defenders of the Earth, Galoob, Flash Gordon, MOC **30.00**
Defenders of the Earth, Galoob, Garax, MOC **40.00**
Defenders of the Earth, Galoob, Ming the Merciless, MOC **30.00**
Dukes of Hazzard, Mego, Bo, 3¾" h **10.00**
Grizzly Adams, Mattel, 1978 . . . . **25.00**
Indiana Jones, Kenner, Cairo Swordsman **15.00**
Indiana Jones, Kenner, German mechanic **25.00**
Karate Kommandos, Kenner, Chuck Norris, battle gear **12.00**
Lone Ranger, Gabriel, 9" h, MIB **125.00**
Magnum P I, LJN, Tom Selleck, 1983 . . . . **12.00**
Man From U N C L E, Gilbert, Illya Kuryakin **200.00**
M A S K, Kenner, Hurricane with Hondo Maclean, MOC **20.00**

M A S K, Kenner, Outlaw, 12" h, MOC 30.00
M A S K, Kenner, Pitstop Catapult with Syrax, MOC 35.00
M A S K, Kenner, Stinger with Bruno Sheppard, MOC 20.00
Masters of the Universe, Mattel, Beastman 15.00
Masters of the Universe, Mattel, Buzz Off 12.00
Masters of the Universe, Mattel, Clamp Champ 15.00
Masters of the Universe, Mattel, Faker 20.00
Masters of the Universe, Jitsu 15.00
Masters of the Universe, Man-E-Faces 15.00
Masters of the Universe, Rio Boast 10.00
Police Academy, Kenner, Carey Mahoney 6.00
Predator, Kenner, Cracked Tusk 15.00
Predator, Kenner, Clan Leader 15.00
Predator, Kenner, Lava Planet 10.00
Predator, Kenner, Scavage 10.00
Predator, Kenner, Spiked Tail 10.00
Predator, Kenner, Ultimate Predator, 12" h 25.00
Princess of Power, Mattel, Angela, MOC 25.00
Princess of Power, Mattel, Bow, MOC 35.00
Princess of Power, Mattel, She-RA, MOC 35.00
Princess of Power, Mattel, Sweetbee, MOC 30.00
Robin Hood Prince of Thieves, Kenner, Sheriff of Nottingham, with sword, #05850, 1991 . . . . 6.00
Robocop, Kenner, Anne Lewis, MOC 25.00
Robocop, Kenner, Gatalin' Blaster Robocop, MOC 35.00
Robocop, Kenner, Sgt Reed, MOC 20.00
Robocop, Kenner, Toxic Waster, MOC 20.00
Six Million Dollar Man, Kenner, Oscar Goldman 40.00
S P A W N, Chapel, Todd McFarland Toys, 2nd series, MOC 20.00
S P A W N, Cy-Gor, Todd McFarland Toys, 4th series, MOC 45.00
S P A W N, Pilot Spawn, Todd McFarland Toys, 2nd series, MOC 30.00
S P A W N, Todd McFarlane Toys, Violator, 1st series, MOC 20.00
Starsky and Hutch, Mego, Capt Dolly, MOC 70.00
Starsky and Hutch, Mego, Huggy Bear, 8" h, MOC 70.00
Starsky and Hutch, Mego, Starsky, 8" h, MOC 65.00
Steve Scout, Kenner, 8" h 35.00
Swamp Thing, Kenner, Anton Arcane, MOC 20.00
Swamp Thing, Kenner, Bio-Glow, MOC 15.00
Swamp Thing, Kenner, Tomahawk, MOC 25.00
The Tick, Bandai, Bounding Tick, 1st series, 5" h, MOC 15.00
The Tick, Bandai, Chairface Chippendale, 3" h, MOC 5.00
The Tick, Bandai, Dyna-Mole, 3" h, MOC 5.00
The Tick, Bandai, Human Bullet, 1st series, 5" h, MOC 12.00
Thundercats, LJN, Berbil Bert 35.00
Thundercats, LJN, Capt Shiner 30.00
Thundercats, LJN, Rataro 22.00
Thundercats, LJN, Tuska Warrior 18.00
Transformers, Hasbro, Air Raid 12.00
Transformers, Hasbro, Battletrap 15.00
Transformers, Hasbro, Beachcomber 8.00
Transformers, Hasbro, Bumblebee, yellow 15.00
Transformers, Hasbro, Chase 8.00
Transformers, Hasbro, Divebomb 35.00
Transformers, Hasbro, Fire Fight 12.00
Transformers, Hasbro, Firstaid 10.00
Transformers, Hasbro, Fizzle 6.00
Transformers, Hasbro, Freeway 8.00
Transformers, Hasbro, Gears 10.00
Transformers, Hasbro, Groove 10.00
Transformers, Hasbro, Huffer 8.00
Transformers, Hasbro, Ironhide 20.00
VR Troopers, Kenner, Dark Heart 4.00
VR Troopers, Kenner, Kaitlin Star 4.00
VR Troopers, Kenner, Skug 10.00
WWF, Hasbro, Big Boss Man, with glasses, 1st series 10.00
WWF, Hasbro, Rick Rude, 1st series 20.00
WWF, Hasbro, Rowdy Roddy Piper, 2nd series 15.00
WWF, Hasbro, Ultimate Warrior, 2nd series 15.00
WWF, LJN, Andre the Giant, short hair 20.00
WWF, LJN, Bobby Heenan 15.00
WWF, LJN, Hillbilly Jim 15.00
WWF, LJN, Junk Yard Dog 20.00
WWF, LJN, S D Jones 15.00
WWF, LJN, Hulk Hogan 50.00
WWF, LJN, Rowdy Roddy Piper 75.00
X-Men, Toy Biz, Juggernaut, #4909, power punch action, 5" h 10.00

VEHICLES, PLAYSETS & ACCESSORIES

Alien, Kenner, Evac Fighter $40.00
Alien, Kenner, Hovertread 20.00
Alien, Queen Hive Playset 75.00
Captain Action, Ideal, carrying case, headquarters, vinyl 400.00
Captain Action, Ideal, catalog, comic book style, Captain Action and Action Boy on cover 45.00
C.O.P.S., Hasbro, Cops Cycle, open 15.00
C.O.P.S., Highway Interceptor, with road 60.00
Knight Rider, Kenner, Knight 2000 Whip Shift car, 7" 40.00
Knight Rider, Kenner, Turbo Booster Knight 2000 car, diecast, launcher 40.00
Marvel Secret Wars, Mattel, Tower of Doom 40.00
Marvel Secret Wars, Mattel, Turbo Cycle 35.00
Masters of the Universe, Mattel, Castle Grayskull 125.00
Masters of the Universe, Mattel, Snake Mountain 125.00
Planet of the Apes, Mego, Action Stallion, motorized 100.00
Planet of the Apes, Mego, Forbidden Zone Trap 140.00
Princess of Power, Mattel, Sea Harp 25.00
Princess of Power, Mattel, Swift Wind 30.00
Robocop, Kenner, Robocycle 20.00
Six Million Dollar Man & Bionic Woman, Kenner, Bionic Man fashions, Mission to Mars 30.00
Six Million Dollar Man & Bionic Woman, Kenner, O.S.I. Headquarters 85.00
Spawn, Todd McFarlane Toys, Spawn Alley Playset 45.00
Spawn, Todd McFarlane Toys, Spawn Aircycle 50.00
Thundercats, LJN, Astral Moat Monster 55.00
Thundercats, LJN, Mutant Fist Pounder 30.00
Waltons, Mego, Walton's Farm House 160.00

Action Jackson, outfit, Mego, MIP, $10.00.

ADVENTURE GAMES

Adventure games have been played for hundreds of years. In an adventure game, each player is asked to assume the role of a character. The character's fate is determined by choices that he and other players make. The rules are often very complex; games can last for days, even months.

There are many different game scenarios ranging from sports and entertainment or war and conflict, to finance and fortune. The principal marketing source for current games is the comic book shop. Some comic book shops also handle discontinued games.

Collectors fall into two groups—those who buy discontinued games to play them and those who buy them solely for the purpose of collecting them. Both groups place strong emphasis on completeness. Many of the games contain more than 100 different playing pieces. Few take the time to count all the parts. This is why adventure games tend to be relatively inexpensive when found at garage sale and flea markets.

A small group of individuals have begun to collect playing pieces, many of which are hand painted. However, rarely does the price paid exceed the initial cost.

Club: American Game Collectors Assoc., P.O. Box 44, Dresler, PA 19025.

Against The Reich, West End Games, 1986 . . . . **$20.00**
Clash Of Empires, World Wide Wargames, 1986 . . . . **32.00**
Confrontation, Ariel, 1974 . . . . **47.00**
DAK, Simulation Canada, 1982 . . . . **4.00**
Decline and Fall, Ariel, 1977 . . . . **62.00**
Diplomacy, Calhamer, 1959 . . . . **75.00**
Drive on Damascus, World Wide Wargames, 1981 . . . . **32.00**
Dungeon, TSR, 1980 . . . . **17.00**
English Civil War, Ariel, 1978 . . . . **30.00**
Insurgency, Heritage Models, 1979 . . . . **25.00**
Magic: The Gathering, Wizards of the Coast, 363 cards **125.00**
Never Call Retreat, World Wide Wargames, 1983 . . . . **30.00**
Panderblitz, Avalon Hill, 1970 . . . . **14.00**
Ploy, 3M, 1970 . . . . **22.00**
Starship Troopers, Robert Heinlein, Avalon Hill, 1976, MIB **20.00**
Strategic Command, Transogram, 1950 . . . . **45.00**
Strategy, Ariel, 1973 . . . . **32.00**
Squad Leader, Avalon Hill, 1977 . . . . **15.00**
Tournament, Bear Hug **5.00**
Trenchfoot, Game Designer's Workshop, 1981 . . . . **20.00**
Twilight War, TSR, 1884 . . . . **35.00**

High-Bid, The Auction Game, 3M, 1965, $10.00.

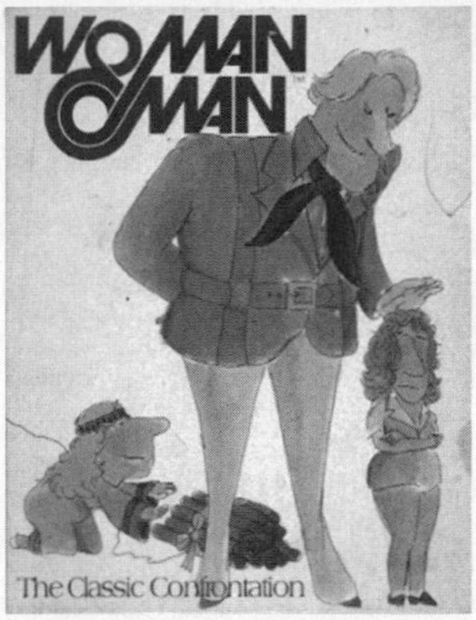

Woman & Man, Psychology Today, 1971, $10.00.

ADVERTISING CHARACTERS

Many companies created advertising characters as a means of guaranteeing product recognition by the buying public. Consumers are more apt to purchase an item with which they are familiar and advertising characters were a surefire method of developing familiarity.

The early development of advertising characters also enabled immigrants who could not read to identify products by the colorful figures found on the packaging.

Trademarks and advertising characters are found on product labels, in magazines, as premiums, and on other types of advertising. Character subjects may be based on a real person such as Nancy Green, the original "Aunt Jemima." However, more ofen than not, they are comical figures, often derived from popular contemporary cartoons. Other advertising characters were designed especially to promote a specific product, like Mr. Peanut and the Campbell Kids.

Clubs: Camel Joe & Friends, 2205 Hess Dr., Cresthill, IL 60435; Campbell Soup Collectors Club, 414 Country Ln. Ct., Wauconda, IL 60084; Sorry Charlie...No Fan Club For You, 7812 N. W. Hampton Rd., Kansas City, MO 64152.

Note: For additional listings see Aunt Jemima.

Campbell's Kids, display, Campbell Kid figure, diecut cardboard standup **$15.00**
Campbell's Kids, doll, vinyl head, 1 pc Magic Skin body, molded and painted hair, painted side glancing eyes, smiling watermelon type mouth, orig red and white cotton dress, apron, chef's hat, nylon socks and plastic shoes, mkd "Campbell's Kid, Made by Ideal Toy Corp," 10" h **50.00**
Campbell's Kids, pennant, felt, burnt orange, white inscription, c1930, 17½" l **30.00**
Campbell's Kids, salt and pepper shakers, pr, plastic, girl and boy, 1950s, 4½" h **35.00**
Charlie Tuna, pinback button, litho tin, "Charlie for President," red, white, and blue, 1960s, 1½" d **25.00**
Charlie Tuna, scale, oval, vinyl over metal, Charlie image, 1972, 10½ x 13" **75.00**
Chiquita Banana, doll pattern, Kellogg's Corn Flakes premium, uncut cotton fabric sheet, orig envelope, 1940s . . . **100.00**
Col Sanders, Kentucky Fried Chicken, hard plastic, figural Colonel Sanders, "Col Harland Sanders/Kentucky Fried Chicken" inscribed on base front, 12½" h, 1960s **50.00**

The Campbell Kids, jigsaw puzzle, Schooltime, Jaymar Kiddie puzzle, #319, 28 pcs, 13 x 10", $12.00.

Dino the Dinosaur, Sinclair Oil, tumbler, green illus, "Drive with Care and Buy Sinclair," c1930, 5" h **15.00**
Dutch Boy, keychain, plastic, dayglow, holding brushes behind back, c1940s, 2¼" h **30.00**
Gerber Baby, bank, Gerber Strained Peas with ABC blocks on blue and white paper label with Gerber Baby picture with "Gerber 1928–1978—Fifty Years of Caring," 1978 . . . . **10.00**
Gerber Baby, doll, Atlanta Novelty Co, 50th anniversary commemorative, soft stuffed body, molded vinyl head, arms, and legs, floating type eyes, rose bud mouth with molded tongue, unremovable blue cloth outfit, 1979 . . . . **35.00**
Gerber Baby, Swiss Bells, Arrow Molded Plastics, multi-colored musical plastic bells with Gerber baby face dec, vinyl band, 1969 . . . . **30.00**
Hush Puppy, frisbee, plastic, white dayglow, blue dog, red lettering, 1960–70s, 9¼" d **12.00**
Keebler Elf, doll, soft vinyl, movable head, stamped "1974 copyright by Keebler Co," 6½" h **20.00**
Nipper, RCA Victor, figure, chalkware, base mkd "Victor Windsor-Poling Co, Akron, OH," 4 h **95.00**
Pillsbury Doughboy, cookie jar **33.00**
Poll Parrot Shoes, spinner top, metal, diecut, yellow, red, and green, c1940s. **25.00**
Reddy Kilowatt, coaster, set of 20, paper, black, white, and red, each with image, wax paper backing, unused, 3½" d. **15.00**
Reddy Kilowatt, pin, brass, diecut, figural, red enamel accents, 1950s, 1" h **20.00**
Smokey Bear, figure, Aim Toothpaste premium, 1960s **18.00**
Snap, Crackle, and Pop, Kellogg's Rice Krispies, song book, 1937 . . . . **5.00**
Speedy, Alka Seltzer, bank, vinyl, 1950s, 5½" h **350.00**
Spuds Mackenzie, wristwatch **20.00**

ADVERTISING ITEMS

Divide advertising items into two groups: items used to merchandise a product and items used to promote a product. Merchandising advertising is a favorite with interior decorators and others who want it for its mood-setting ability. It is often big, splashy and showy. Promotional advertising (giveaways) are primarily collector-driven.

Almost every piece of advertising appeals to more than one collector. As a result, prices for the same piece will often differ significantly, depending on who the seller views as the final purchaser. Most advertising is bought for the purpose of display. As a result, emphasize theme and condition. The vast majority of advertising collectibles are two-dimensional. Place a premium on large three-dimensional objects.

Clubs: Advertising Cup and Mug Collectors of America, P.O. Box 680, Solon, IA 52333; Antique Advertising Assoc. of America, P.O. Box 1121, Morton Grove, IL 60053; Inner Seal Club (Nabisco), 6609 Billtown Rd., Louisville, KY 40299; Porcelain Advertising Collectors Club, P.O. Box 381, Marshfield Hills, MA 02051; The Ephemera Society of America, P.O. Box 95, Cazenovia, NY 13035; The Trade Card Collector's Assoc., P.O. Box 284, Marlton, NJ 08053; Tin Container Collectors Assoc., P.O. Box 44010, Aurora, CO 80044.

Periodicals: *Paper Collectors' Marketplace (PCM),* P.O. Box 128, Scandinavia, WI 54977.

Advertising Trade Card, Empire Wringer Co, printed color illus **$5.00**
Advertising Trade Card, Gold Coin Stoves & Ranges, children by pond. **25.00**
Advertising Trade Card, Richmond Stove Co, sepia **8.00**
Ashtray, Luchow's Restaurant Since 1882, blue and white, stein in center **20.00**
Astray, Old Judge Coffee, tin **90.00**
Ashtray, Seiberling Tire, Market St, Williamsport, PA **18.00**
Ashtray, Smith's General Store, Birdseye, IN, tin **4.00**
Bank, Arctic Circle Drive-In Restaurant, Acey the Cowboy Chicken, composition, 6½" h **100.00**
Bank, Blue Bonnet Sue **25.00**
Bank, Crunch Bird, vinyl **45.00**
Bank, Curad, Taped Crusader, vinyl, 1970s. **95.00**
Bank, Florida Oranges, Florida Orange Girl, vinyl. **35.00**
Bank, Grandma's Cookies, vinyl. **55.00**
Bank, Green Giant, Little Sprout, musical. **35.00**
Bank, Miller's Outpost, General Jeans, vinyl **125.00**
Bank, Norge Refrigerator, metal, painted, white, black base, 1930s, 4" h. **40.00**
Bank, Pillsbury Doughboy, MIB **40.00**
Bank, Rival Dog Food, tin, can shape. **15.00**
Beach Bag, Maxwell House Coffee, figural, coffee can **25.00**
Bill Hook, Ceresota Flour **45.00**
Blotter, Blue Coal, The Shadow illus. **18.00**
Blotter, Blue Valley Butter **6.00**
Blotter, Morton's Salt. **10.00**
Booklet, *Franco-American Soup,* color, 1908 . . . . **22.00**
Booklet, Adirondak Rest Camp, c1930. . . . . **10.00**

Box, National Biscuit Co, Uneeda Bakers, Royal Lunch, prototype before distribution, 8 x 6 x 6", $35.00.

Display, Sunshine Biscuits, tin, copper front face, glass window, 11½" h, $210.00. Photo courtesy Collectors Auction Services.

Bookmark, Buckwalter Stoves, celluloid, diecut, figural, teddy bear and stove illus on back, Whitehead and Hoag, 1907 . . . . 45.00
Bookmark, Ice Cream/Soda Water, diecut aluminum, inscribed "Brown Bros. Fine Confections," emb stylized floral pattern with top center string hole, early 1900s 25.00
Bowl, Use Jaxon Soap, cast iron, bail handle, 6" d 75.00
Box, cov, Dr Baker's Condition Powders, wood, dovetailed 45.00
Box, Castoria, Purepac Corp, NY, colorful baby head, 2 oz bottle, 5¼ x 1 x 2" 6.00
Box, Dr Hobson's Ox Marrow Pomade, picture of lady on label and box, includes jar dated 1921,1923, 3½ x 2 x 2" 15.00
Box, Imperial Peanut Butter, wood, dovetailed 35.00
Broadside, Pure Milk, "New System" illus, c1885 . . . . 32.00
Brochure, Cottolene, The Evolution of an Apple Pie, 1898 . . . . 28.00
Brochure, Wallpapers for Home Decor, c1930 . . . . 8.00
Cabinet, Putnam Dye 95.00
Change Tray, C Worz Saloon, 1907 . . . . 55.00
Change Tray, Franklin Life 30.00
Change Tray, Old Reliable Coffee, beautiful woman, 1907 . . . . 148.00
Change Tray, Velvet Ice Cream, oval, young woman eating ice cream 275.00
Greeting Card, Christmas, Breyer Ice Cream Company, c1920 . . . . 20.00
Cigarette Lighter, TraveLodge Motels, enameled sleepy bear on billboard illus 35.00
Clock, Premier Vacuum Cleaner, 1930s 160.00
Clock, Winston Cigarette, clock and counter display, lighted 60.00
Counter Card, National Oats, diecut, girl carrying basket, c1900 . . . . 35.00
Crock, Germ Proof Water Filter, Pasteur Chamberland, Dayton, OH 175.00
Dispenser, T-Lax, tin, black and yellow, "10¢," 19½ x 1⅝ x 1¼" 40.00
Display, B-1 Lemon Lime, automated, turquoise, white, and red, flashing colored "star" lights bheind translucent screen, "More zip in every sip!," 1960, 16 x 13 x 4" 100.00
Display, Campbell's Soup, rack, metal, 1930-40, 18 x 22 x 5" 75.00
Display, Columbia Ring, automated, centered diamond over twilight starry sky and suspended angel, when activated sign lights up, diamond sparkles, and angel is raised and lowered, mkd "Guardian angel protects Columbia 'Tru-Fit' diamond rings," c1950, 12" h 195.00
Display, Mohawk Carpet, automated, Indian boy standing on tree stump beating drum, "Carpet Craftmanship from the Looms of Mohawk," c1948, 23" h 285.00
Display, Shelby Razor Blade, card, 20 pkgs, 1940s, 9 x 12½" 18.00
Display, West Hairnets, countertop, litho tin, 1918, 6" sq 150.00
Display Rack, Beech-Nut/Beechies, metal, 2 shelf 20.00
Display Rack, Esquire Shoe Polish, metal, revolving 50.00
Display Rack, Uncle Josh Pork Rind 30.00
Doll, Uneeda Biscuit, boy, Ideal, 1914 . . . . 350.00
Door Push, Colonial Is Good Bread, adjustable, double sided, blue and black paint, 3 x 22" 75.00
Door Push, Duke's Mixture, porcelain 115.00
Door Push, Salada Tea, porcelain enamel 110.00
Figure, Insulite, Bill Drite, leprechaun, cast bronze, 4" h 125.00
Figure, RCA Victor Nipper, chalk, logo 45.00
Figure, Regan's Holsum Bread, cardboard, pudgy little girl, 9½" h 25.00
Hat, Ehler's Grade 'A' Ceylon Tea, red, white, and blue 20.00
Hatchet, Art Stove Co, 4" l 50.00
Ledger, pocket type, Chicago Stove Works, heaters and ranges illus, c1900 . . . . 10.00
Match Holder, Allyn & Blanchard Co, litho tin, spice can shape, 7" h 350.00
Match Holder, Bennett's Brilliantshine Metal Polish, litho tin, 5" h 355.00
Menu, R H Macy's, large, 1937 . . . . 25.00
Mirror, Buckwalter Stoves, pocket, oval, celluloid, detailed stove illus 75.00
Mirror, Dr Walter's Bitters, pocket, brass 48.00
Mirror, Stacy's Chocolates, pocket, image of yellow rising sun against pale blue sky 50.00
Mirror, The Boston Herald, pocket, multicolored image of running newsboy holding paper inscribed "The Boston Herald/New England's Greatest Newspaper," 1¾" 100.00
Mirror, Victor Talking Machine, pocket, black, white, and red, image of early 1900s phonograph record centered by label image, tradigional Nipper trademark art and "Aida-Celeste-Aida" 75.00
Mug, Buckeye Root Beer, pottery 45.00
Pamphlet, Shredded Wheat, 1918 . . . . 6.00
Paper Doll, McLaughlin's Coffee, ealry 1900s 6.50

Jar, Lance, metal and glass, painted advertising, 8" h, 6½" w, $154.00. Photo courtesy Collectors Auction Services.

Tin, Old Faithful Lighter Fluid, double sided, red, black, and white, 4 x 2 x 1", $55.00. Photo courtesy Past Tyme Pleasures.

Paperweight, Diamond Tool & Horseshoe Co, horseshoe shape **30.00**
Paperweight, Star Biscuits, metal, figural mouse and biscuit **85.00**
Pinback Button, ABC Soda Crackers, parrot illus, 1896 . . . . . . **35.00**
Pinback Button, Dandee Bread, tan, black, and white, early 1900s **20.00**
Pinback Button, International Apple Assn, red apple, black and white rim, 1930s **15.00**
Pin Cushion, Bunny Bread, felt **12.00**
Playing Cards, Hearn's Dept Store, sailboat back **22.00**
Pot Scraper, C D Kenny Teas, Coffees, Sugars, cast iron, S-shape handle, raised lettering **50.00**
Puppet, Dutch Boy Paint **30.00**
Reamer, C D Kenny Co, Teas, Coffees, Sugars, side handle, emb bottom, 3" d **50.00**
Record Cleaner, RCA Victor, round, celluloid **20.00**
Ring, chief Wahoo, Goudey Gum, Indian head **65.00**
Scissors, "Star Brand Shoes Are Better", 7" l **25.00**
Serving Tray, Cunningham's Ice Cream, oval, picture of factory, c1910-15, 18 x 15" **350.00**
Serving Tray, Fairfield Butter Co, round, 2 children at table with lace cloth, 13½" d **850.00**
Serving Tray, Hoefler Ice Cream, oval, young woman eating ice cream, c1915 . . . . . . **425.00**
Serving Tray, Red Raven, round, woman hugging oversized red raven, 12" d **95.00**
Shoe Horn, A S Beck Shoes, metal, 1940s **5.00**
Shot Glass, Adlerika Bowel Cleaner **15.00**
Sign, Aetna Auto Ass'n of the USA, porcelain diecut, double sided, shield shaped, dark blue ground, white stars above US map silhouette, red and white lettering, c1920s, 20 x 14" **500.00**
Sign, Bell System Public Telephone, round, porcelain **80.00**
Sign, Breidbach & Sons, Mfgs of Dyes, brass, c1900 . . . . . . **65.00**
Sign, Cranford Dairy, cardboard, Charles Twelvetrees illus, 4 x 9" **12.00**
Sign, Dauntless Coffee, young Roman soldier illus **55.00**
Sign, Donnell's De Luxe Ice Cream, porcelain, double sided, white ground, dark blue and red lettering, 1920s boy and girl sharing large sundae, "The Aristocrat of Ice Creams," c1920s, 24 x 16" **400.00**
Sign, Dutchess Trousers, tin, 20 x 25" **65.00**

AIRLINE AND AVIATION COLLECTIBLES

The airline mergers and bankruptcies have produced a wealth of obsolete material. There were enormous crowds at Eastern's liquidation sale in spring 1991. I have a bunch of stuff from Piedmont and Peoples, two airlines that flew into the sunset in the 1980s.

The wonderful thing about airline collectibles is that most of them initially were free. I try to make it a point to pick up several items, from bathroom soap to playing cards, each time I fly. Save the things most likely to be thrown out.

Club: Aeronautica & Air Label Collectors Club, P.O. Box 1239, Elgin, IL, 60121; C.A.L./N-Y-211 Collectors Society, 913 Wylde Oak Dr., Oshkosh, WI 54904; International Miniature Aircraft Collectors Society, P.O. Box 845, Greenwich, CT 06836; World Airline Historical Society, 13739 Picarsa Dr., Jacksonville, FL 32225.

Periodical: *Airliner,* P.O. Box 521238, Miami, FL 33125.

Ashtray, commemorative, ceramic, United Airlines Caravelle jet design in center, pilot's name on rim, c1982, 7 x 7" **$20.00**
Book, *Airplane of the USA,* Walker, John B, color photos, 1944, 60 pp **18.00**
Book, *Bird Boy, The,* Langworthy, 1st ed, 3 vol, 1912 . . . . . . **50.00**
Book, *Story of Lindbergh, The Lone Eagle, The,* Beamish, Richard J, 1st ed, 1927 . . . . . . **40.00**
Booklet, *Man Has Learned To Fly,* Monarch Food Products, ©1929, 24 pp, 4 x 6" **25.00**
Calendar, "Fly TWA," spiral bound, full color photo for each month, 16 x 24" **25.00**
Crew Bag Tag, Mid-Continent Airlines, metal, c1950 . . . . . . **10.00**
Flatware, United Airlines, fork, knife, and spoon, 1950–60 . . . . . . **25.00**
Game, The Airplane Game, Hasbro, 1966 . . . . . . **15.00**

Tin, Devotion Brand Coffee, 1 lb, press fit lid, Canco, 5¼ x 4", $132.00. Photo courtesy Past Tyme Pleasures.

Ashtray, Air France, ceramic, white, gold logo and cigarette rests, 3¼" d, $12.00.

Pin, Civil Air Patrol, diecut metal, gold colored, 3¹/₄" h, 3¹/₄" w, detailed, $38.50. Photo courtesy Collectors Auction Services.

Hat Badge, pilot, Delta-C&S, gold metal with red enamel, 1954 . . . . 95.00
Hot Plate, Century of Progress zeppelin, *Spirit of St Louis* 35.00
Jacket Wing, flight attendant, Western Airlines, gold wings, "W," 1980 . . . . 15.00
Jacket Wing, pilot, Eastern Airlines, black felt with metal enamel center disc, 1955 . . . . 95.00
Jacket Wing, pilot, Lake Central Airlines, sterling with red and black lettering, 1960 . . . . 95.00
Log Book, pilot, Piedmont Airlines, 1948–65 . . . . 20.00
Manual, Northeast Airlines, 3 ring binder, 2947 . . . . 25.00
Paperweight, United Airlines, bronze, "WA Patterson" 40.00
Pin, half wing, Northwest Airlines, US Airmail Official Carrier, 1950s 75.00
Pin, Stewardess, Eastern Airlines 25.00
Pinback Button, American Air Races, Mechanic, red on cream, 1933, 2¹/₂" d 50.00
Playing Cards, Cessna, double deck, full color photo of Cessna 120 on 1 deck, other with Cessna 140, orig box, 1940s 25.00
Postcard, Dirigible & Lakehurst, Lakehurst Naval Air Station in NJ and USS *Los Angeles Shenandoah* dirigibles scenes, numbered, unused, 1930s, set of 12 . . . . 200.00
Puzzle, frame tray, American Airlines, Milton Bradley, 707 jet in flight, 1960 . . . . 15.00

AKRO AGATE GLASS

When the Akro Agate Co., was founded in 1911, its principal product was marbles. The company was forced to diversify during the 1930s, developing floral-ware lines and children's dishes. Some collectors specialize in containers made by Akro Agate for the cosmetic industry.

Akro Agate merchandised many of its products as sets. Full sets that retain their original packaging command a premium price. Learn what pieces and colors constitute a set. Some dealers will mix and match pieces into a false set, hoping to get a better price.

Most Akro Agate pieces are marked "Made in USA" and have a mold number. Some, but not all, have a small crow flying through an "A" as a mark.

Club: Akro Agate Collectors Club, 10 Bailey St., Clarksburg, WV 26301.

Ashtray, advertising, "Edison Hotel," 3" d1 . . . . $40.00
Ashtray, Leaf, marbleized 4.50
Basket, marbleized orange and white, 2 handles 28.50
Bell, white 50.00
Bowl, cream and red, tab handle, 7¹/₂" d 28.00
Bowl, ftd, pumpkin, 8" d 150.00
Bowl, marbleized orange and white, emb leaves, 5" d 35.00
Bowl, pumpkin, tab handles, 7¹/₄" 32.50
Children's Dishes, cereal bowl, Interior Panel, transparent amber 15.00
Children's Dishes, creamer, Chiquita, cobalt blue 8.00
Children's Dishes, creamer, Raised Daisy, yellow 45.00
Children's Dishes, cup, Chiquita, green 4.00
Children's Dishes, cup, pumpkin, octagonal, closed handle 25.00
Children's Dishes, cup, Stippled Band, light amber 9.00
Children's Dishes, cup and saucer, Concentric Rib, transparent cobalt blue 50.00
Children's Dishes, cup and saucer, Raised Daisy, yellow 50.00
Children's Dishes, dinner plate, Stippled Band, light amber 2.50
Children's Dishes, pitcher, Stacked Disc, blue 15.00
Children's Dishes, plate, Chiquita, green 2.00
Children's Dishes, plate, octagonal, white 4.00
Children's Dishes, set, Interior Panel, 8 pcs, pink, orig box 100.00
Children's Dishes, set, Stacked Disc, 5 pcs, pitcher and 4 tumblers, bright blue and white 25.00
Children's Dishes, sugar, octagonal, green, white lid, closed handles 12.00
Children's Dishes, tumbler, Raised Daisy, yellow 25.00
Creamer, 3" h 225.00
Demitasse Cup and Saucer, blue and white 17.50
Finger Bowl, marbleized 10.00
Flowerpot, Graduated Dart, orange and white, 2" h 15.00
Flowerpot, ribbed top, marbleized, 4" h 8.00
Flowerpot, Ribs and Flutes, scalloped, yellow 3.75
Flowerpot, scalloped top, cobalt, 3¹/₄" h 8.00
Flowerpot, Stacked Disc, blue and white, 3" h 10.00
Flowerpot, Stacked Disc, marbleized, 3" h 6.00
Flowerpot, Stacked Disc, marbleized, 5¹/₂" h 15.00
Flowerpot, Westite, brown and white, 5¹/₄" h 15.00
Flowerpot, Westite, green marble, 4" h 6.00
Game, Tiddley Winks, J Pressman, boxed set 25.00
Ivy Bowl, orange and white 18.00
Ivy Bowl, Westite, brown and white 25.00
Jardiniere, bell shaped, rect top, cobalt, 4³/₄" 25.00
Jardiniere, Graduated Dart, scalloped, cobalt, 5" 25.00
Jardiniere, Graduated Dart, smooth top, pumpkin, 5" 25.00
Match Holder, red and white, 3" h 7.00
Mortar and Pestle, black 35.00
Pen Holder, Goodrich Tire, black, orange and white center, 3¹/₄" d 40.00
Planter, oval, marbleized, 6" 5.00
Planter, rect,#653, blue and white, 8" l 35.00
Powder Box, cov, Colonial Lady, blue and white 68.00
Powder Box, cov, Colonial Lady, pink and white 60.00
Powder Box, ribbed, yellow 25.00
Powder Jar, Concentric Ring, 3 ftd 20.00
Powder Jar, cov, Scottie, white 85.00
Shaving Mug, cov, black 15.00
Smoker Set, red and white, orig box 90.00
Table Lamp, blue pineapple body 95.00
Teapot, cov, octagonal, open handle, bright blue, white lid 24.00
Urn, ftd, sq, brown and white 7.50
Vase, Graduated Dart, #312, ftd, Westite, tab, green and white, 6¹/₄" h 28.00

ALADDIN

The Mantle Lamp Co., of America, founded in 1908 in Chicago, is best known for its lamps. However, in the late 1950s through the 1970s, it also was one of the leading producers of character lunch boxes.

Aladdin deserves a separate category because of the large number of lamp collectors who concentrate almost exclusively on this one company. There is almost as big a market for parts and accessories as for the lamps themselves. Collectors are constantly looking for parts to restore lamps in their possession.

Club: The Aladdin Knights of the Mystic Light, 3935 Kelley Rd., Kevil, KY 42053.

LAMPS

Bracket, Model C, aluminum font **$50.00**
Caboose, Model B, style B-400, galvanized steel font **100.00**
Caboose, Model 23, style B23000, aluminum **45.00**
Floor, Model B, style B-289, oxidized bronze, 1937–38 . . . . . **90.00**
Floor, Model B, style B-197, satin gold, 1939–40 . . . . **150.00**
Floor, Model 12, style 1253, Verde Antique **125.00**
Hanging, Model 9, style 516 shade **225.00**
Hanging, Model 12, 4 post, with parchment shade **250.00**
Parlor, Model 4 . . . . **450.00**
Shelf, Model 23, clear, drape font, 1975–82 . . . . **65.00**
Shelf, Model 23, Lincoln Drape, clear, no oil fill, 1975–82 . . . . **70.00**
Table, Model 12, brass, slanted sides **65.00**
Table, Model 23, aluminum font **35.00**
Table, Model B-53, Washington Drape, clear crystal, 1940–41 . . . . **65.00**
Table, Model B, style B-80, Beehive, clear crystal **80.00**
Table, Model B-137, Treasure, bronze, 1937–53 . . . . **75.00**
Vase, Model 12, style 1241, crystal, variegated tan, 1930–35, 12" h **200.00**

PARTS AND ACCESSORIES

Burner, Model 6 . . . . **$40.00**
Burner, Practicus, Sunbeam or Lumineer, with gallery, without flame spreader **75.00**
Chimney, orig ball style with 1908 crest logo **75.00**
Chimney Brush **15.00**
Flame Spreader, Model 11 . . . . **10.00**
Gallery, Model C **10.00**
Insect Screen **60.00**
Shade, glass, style 21C, English cased, red, 10" d **65.00**
Shade, paper, Aladdinite Parchment, table and hanging lamp, 15" d **200.00**
Shade, paper, Alpha, table and hanging lamp, dec **50.00**

Ivory alacite mounted on cast metal antiqued gold base, fluted whip-o-lite shades topped by alacite scrolled finials in bouquet, 1938, 23" h, $287.50. Price for pr. Photo courtesy Jackson's Auctioneers & Appraisers.

ALBUMS

The Victorian craze has drawn attention to the Victorian photograph album that enjoyed an honored place in the parlor. The more common examples had velvet or leather covers. However, the ones most eagerly sought by collectors are those featuring a celluloid cover with motifs ranging from floral to Spanish American War battleships.

Most albums housed "family" photographs, the vast majority of which are unidentified. If the photographs are head and shoulders or baby shots, chances they have little value, unless the individuals are famous. Photographs of military figures, actors and actresses and other oddities are worth checking out further.

Cardboard albums still have not found favor with collectors. However, check the interior contents. In many cases, they contain post cards, clippings, match covers or photographs that are worth far more than the album.

Cabinet Card, Victorian, celluloid front and back cov, Spanish-American War battleship motif on front **$200.00**
Cabinet Card, Victorian, celluloid front cov with young maiden dec, red velvet back cov **85.00**
Cabinet Card, Victorian, emb "Album" on celluloid front cov with floral design, green and orange floral pattern on velvet back cov **65.00**
Cabinet Card, Victorian, leather cov. **30.00**
Cabinet Card, Victorian, red velvet front and back cov with raised floral design and gold highlights **45.00**
Cartes de Visite, leather, gilt border, 41 cartes de visite, 1860s, 1 clasp missing, 8 x 10" **625.00**
Daguerrotype, gutta percha, baroque motif cov **45.00**
Greeting Card, celluloid cov, multicolored medallion of Gibson girl portrait center, 1910–20 . . . . **25.00**
Photo, plain, red velvet front and back cov, 8½ x 10½" **30.00**
Photo, emb leather, presented to Gracie by Mrs. Roger, 1882, 44 tintypes of Gracie with her family, friends, dolls, and pet chicken, ages 4 to 11 . . . . **750.00**
Photo, red velvet front and back cov, emb scroll design trim on front cov, emb brass clasp, gold edged heavy cardboard pages, 10½ x 14½" **55.00**
Souvenir, European photos, menus, billheads, booklets, and steamships, 50 pp, 1930–31 . . . . **20.00**

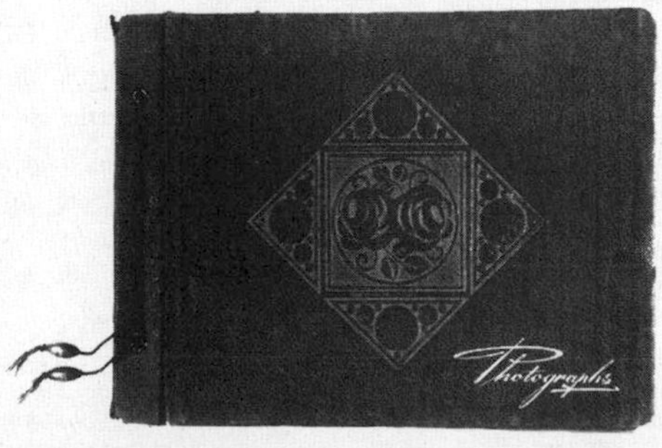

Photo Album, emb cardboard cov, dark blue, gold script "Photographs," 24 pp, c1935, 11 x 8½", $18.00.

ALIENS, SPACE-RELATED

IEEEEKK!! As the scream goes up for extraterrestrials, so does their collectibility. From *War of the Worlds* to *My Favorite Martian*, aliens have been landing in our collections. Aliens have gained in popularity with the influence of television and advances made in movie special effects. The *Mork and Mindy* show, starring comedian Robin Williams as a fun-loving extraterrestrial, and the *Star Wars* trilogy, with its strange alien creatures, are just two prime examples of alien familiarity.

So what is an alien? The alien is any creature, character, or being that is not of this planet. Aliens appear in many shapes and sizes, so be careful—you never know where an alien will turn up.

Alien, comic book, *Aliens*, #4, Dark Horse, Second Series, 1989 . . . . **$4.00**
Alien, game, Alien Game, Kenner, 1979 . . . . **20.00**
Alien, game, This Time It's War, Leading Edge, 1990 . . . . **35.00**
Alien, puzzle, jigsaw, H G Toys, Alien illus, 1979 . . . . **20.00**
Alien, model kit, MPC, Alien with teeth, unassembled, orig box **80.00**
Alien, mug, plastic, logo **5.00**
Alien, poster, Alien Warrier, G S, multicolored, 1988, 72" h **18.00**
Battlestar Galactica, Cylon Radio, Vanity Fair, ©1978 Universal City Studios Inc, figural hard plastic radio depicting head of Cylon warrior, MIB **65.00**
Battlestar Galactica, stuffed toy, Daggit, plush **15.00**
Battlestar Galactica, wallet, Larami Corp, ©1978 Universal City Studios, black vinyl, I D card and silver plastic badge, orig blister card **15.00**
Close Encounters of the Third Kind, lunch box, King Seeley, metal, color illus, 1977-78, 7 x 9 x 4" **25.00**
Close Encounters of the Third Kind, pinback button, "CONTACT," alien illus **1.50**
Dune, pinback button, Sandworm illus **1.50**
Dune, vehicle, Sandworm, LJN, battery operated, 1984 . . . . **18.00**
E T, address book, E T and "Addresses" on cov **1.00**
E T, figure, LJN, ©1982 Universal City Studios Inc, hard plastic, orig blister card, 3½" h **25.00**
E T, finger light, Knickerbocker, ©1982 Universal City Studios Inc, flesh colored molded vinyl finger, battery operated, glows when pressed, orig blister card with fan club adv, 2½ x 9" **45.00**
E T, glass, Pizza Hut promotional, "Phone Home" **2.50**
E T, stickers, puffy, set of 9, orig pkg . . . . **.75**
E T, wristwatch, Melody Glow Alarm Watch, Nelsonic **12.00**

Planet of the Apes, Prison Wagon, AHI/APJAC, 7 x 8", $115.00. MOC. Photo courtesy New England Auction Gallery.

Battlestar Galactica, game, Parker Brothers, 1978, $15.00.

Gremlins, sleeping bag, Ero Leisure, ©1984 Warner Bros Inc, padded, red, multicolored image, 30 x 56" **18.00**
Planet of the Apes, dart game, Transogram, ©1967 Apjac Productions Inc, 11" sq target, 2 soft plastic suction darts, orig box **75.00**
Planet of the Apes, magazine, Vol 1, #4, Jan 1965, 1974 Magazine Management, 8¼ x 11" **15.00**

ALUMINUM COOKWARE

Hand-wrought aluminum has been a popular collectible for several years, with prices rising steadily. It only stands to reason that aluminum cookware, hand-wrought aluminum's poorer relation, should spark collector interest, as well.

Prices are currently very reasonable and examples are plentiful. Look for pieces with unusual decorative elements, preferable made by the same companies which produced the giftware items found in the next section.

Butter Dish, cov, anodized **$5.00**
Cake Decorator, tube, 6 tips **10.00**
Cake Pan, 8" d **1.00**
Coaster, set of 4 . . . . **2.00**
Cocktail Shaker, wooden finial on lid **10.00**
Coffeepot, percolator, 5 pcs **5.00**
Dutch Oven, cov, 3 wood handles, 5 qt **10.00**
Fondue, wood handles, 1½ qt **10.00**
Ice Bucket, plastic handles **12.00**
Jelly Jar, cranberry glass bowl and spoon **25.00**
Pitcher, Norben Ware, anodized, 7¾" h **25.00**
Pressure Cooker, cov, 6 qt **12.00**
Spoon Rest, anodized, 8 x 5" **4.00**
Stock Pot, cov, 8 qt **10.00**
Tea Kettle, whistling, Bakelite handle **7.50**

ALUMINUM, HAND-WROUGHT

With increasing emphasis on post World War II collectibles, especially those from the 1950s, hand-wrought aluminum is enjoying a collecting revival. The bulk of the pieces were sold on the giftware market as decorative accessories.

Do not be confused by the term "hand-wrought." The vast majority of the pieces were mass-produced. The two collecting keys appear to be manufacturer and unusualness of form.

There is an enormous difference between flea market prices and prices at a major show within driving distance of New York City. Hand-wrought aluminum is quite trendy at the moment.

Club: Hammered Aluminum Collectors Assoc., P.O. Box 1346, Weatherford, TX 76086.

Newsletter: *The Continental Report,* 5128 Schultz Bridge Rd, Zionsville, PA 18092.

Basket, Hand Wrought by Federal S Co, fluted edge, double handle with square knot, sailing ship, 11" **$10.00**
Beverage Set, 5 pcs, World Hand Forged, hammered, pitcher with square knot handle, 4 tumblers with flared lip **60.00**
Bowl, cov, Shup Laird/Argental, wooden knob, applied leaves, 7¼" **12.00**
Buffet Server, Keystone Ware, #606, rect caddy with wrapped handle, 6 square ribbed glass inserts with fruit design on lids **25.00**
Cake Basket, Canterbury Arts, multicolored floral spray design, twisted handle, helmet mark faces left, 12" d. **28.00**
Candle Holders, pr, Everlast, Bamboo 3 leg stand, 2 candle cups each, tall rod **225.00**
Casserole, cov, Arthur Armour **180.00**
Casserole, cov, Cromwell, hammered, glass liner, ftd **12.00**
Cigarette Box, Wendell August, pine **157.00**
Coaster, Wendell August Forge, turtle, 5" **3.00**
Cocktail Shaker, Continental, #530, cork lined top, 12" h **40.00**
Condiment Set, oil and vinegar with salt and pepper, Everlast **10.00**
Crumb Tray, Wrought Farberware, stamped leaf pattern, 12" with well **12.00**
Ice Bucket, Canterbury Arts, hammered, double walled, rubber seal, 8" h **45.00**
Match Box Holder, Wendell August Forge **8.00**
Napkin Holder, Rodney Kent, hammered, floral dec bands and feet **10.00**
Pitcher, World Hand Forged, applied flower, 6 plain tumblers **95.00**
Platter, Everlast, rect, oval center well with tree, grape leaf dec in corners, 2 handles **42.00**
Salad Utensils, wooden, teardrop shape aluminum dec, dogwood pattern **10.00**
Tidbit Tray, Hammercraft Hand Hammered, grape cluster design, looped finger hold, 7½" d **5.00**
Tray, Farber & Shlevin, zinnia panel, spiral handle, 7½ x 14½" **18.00**
Tray, Rodney Kent, #425, tulip, handles, 14 x 20" **25.00**
Wine Cooler, Everlast, with stand **295.00**

AMERICAN BISQUE

The American Bisque Company, founded in Williamstown, West Virginia, in 1919, was originally established for the manufacture of china head dolls. Early on the company expanded its product line to include novelties such as cookie jar and ashtrays, serving dishes, and ceramic giftware.

B. E. Allen, founder of the Sterling China Company, invested heavily in the company and eventually purchased the remaining stock. In 1982 the company changed hands, operating briefly under the name American China Company. The plant ceased operations in 1983.

American Bisque items have various markings. The trademark "Sequoia Ware" is often found on items sold in gift shops. The Berkeley trademark was used on pieces sold through chain stores. The most common mark found consists of three stacked baby blocks with the letters A, B, and C.

Bank, Little Audrey **$550.00**
Cereal Bowl, Ballerina Mist, painted **4.00**
Cookie Jar, After School Cookies **45.00**
Cookie Jar, Albert Apple, mkd "ABC" **90.00**
Cookie Jar, bear with cookie **50.00**
Cookie Jar, cat in basket **35.00**
Cookie Jar, cat on beehive **35.00**
Cookie Jar, churn boy **200.00**
Cookie Jar, coffeepot **40.00**
Cookie Jar, Dutch girl **45.00**
Cookie Jar, lady pig **110.00**
Cookie Jar, rabbit with hat **100.00**
Cookie Jar, sailor elephant **95.00**
Cookie Jar, space ship, mkd "ABC" **325.00**
Cookie Jar, squirrel with top hat **150.00**
Dinner Plate, Ballerina Mist, painted **5.00**
Lamp, Billy the Kid **175.00**
Lunch Plate, Ballerina Mist, painted **3.00**
Planter, duck, wearing flower hat, 24K gold **24.00**
Planter, kitten, wailing **20.00**
Planter, puppy, 24K gold **35.00**

AMUSEMENT PARKS

From the park at the end of the trolley line to today's gigantic theme parks such as Six Flags Great Adventure, amusement parks have served many generations. No trip to an amusement park was complete without a souvenir, many of which are now collectible.

Prices are still modest in this new collecting field. When an item is returned to the area where the park was located, it often brings a 20% to 50% premium.

Club: National Amusement Park Historical Assoc., P.O. Box 83, Mount Prospect, IL 60056.

Advertising Trade Card, Atlantic City, multicolored boardwalk scene, adv for Maizena National Starch, printed in Germany **$75.00**
Ashtray, Disneyland, china, blue, bottom center with raised "Disneyland" crest design and "D" in shield with castle and pr of griffins, c1950s, 6½" d **50.00**

Poster, Greater Bucks County Fair, cardboard, black lettering, yellow ground, multicolored image, The Fair Publishing House, Norwalk, OH, 13 x 21". $12.00.

Booklet, Cedar Point Amusement Park, Breakers Hotel, 25th Annual Outing Convention—Midland Grocery Co, OH, June 1922, aerial view, 128 pp 15.00
Box, Goff's Atlantic City Salt Water Taffy, blue, woman wearing orange swimsuit, 8$^{7}/_{8}$" l 6.00
Folder, Disneyland, "Welcome to Disneyland," inside illus map of Disneyland with text and information, c1950s, 3 x 8$^{1}/_{2}$" 25.00
Game, Excursion to Coney Island, Milton Bradley, card game, c1885 . . . . 30.00
Hat, Disneyland, Mouseketeers, stiff black felt, large black plastic ears, white, blue, and orange "Disneyland/Mickey Mouse" patch, c1960 . . . . 25.00
Medal, Coney Island, steeplechase face, orig ribbon, 1924 . . . . 90.00
Pennant, Hershey Park, felt, white lettering on brown ground, c1950 . . . . 25.00
Photograph, Coney Island, set of 6, 1941 . . . . 17.00
Pinback Button, Asbury Park, black and white, bathing beach scene, c1900, 1$^{1}/_{4}$" d 10.00
Pinback Button, Dreamland Park, NY, white lettering on red ground, 1900s 5.00
Pinback Button, Hershey Park, multicolored, child emerging from cocoa bean, c1905 . . . . 35.00
Playing Cards, Dorney Park, Allentown, PA, Alfundo the Clown 5.00
Post Card, Coney Island, Aerial Swing, Luna Park, black and white, Jul 10, 1906 postmark, 3$^{1}/_{2}$ x 5$^{1}/_{2}$" 25.00
Post Card, Shooting the Chutes, Sylvan Beach, NY, water slide, 1928 postmark 5.00
Poster, panoramic view, multicolored, various rides including The Whip, Ferris Wheel, and Carousel, Riverside Print Co, c1910, 28 x 41" 175.00
Post Card, "Bathing Scene and Heinz's Pier, Atlantic City, NJ," illumination effect in tiny windows of distant building, center foreground water ripples, sun in sky center, German publisher marking "2202L J. Koehler" on back, message in pencil, 1908 postmark 50.00
Ride Tag, Coney Island, Steeplechase Park, cardboard string tag featuring grinning figure, dated 1948 on front in pencil, back text includes offer for any 6 rides for 50¢, hole-punched 6 times 50.00
Sheet Music, *Just Take Me Down To Wonderland,* ride illus on cov, 1907 . . . . 20.00
Souvenir Book, Disneyland, 32 pp, ©1965, 10$^{1}/_{2}$ x 10$^{1}/_{2}$" 25.00
Stereograph, Asbury Park, NJ, buildings, G W Pach, 1870s 10.00
Stereograph, Coney Island, hot air balloon, 1870s 70.00

Poster, paper, multicolor, midway scene, c1930s, 27 x 41", $132.00. Photo courtesy Wm. Morford.

Guardian Angel and Children, resin, 6$^{3}/_{4}$" h, $45.00. Photo courtesy Roman, Inc.

ANGELS

Angels were flying high in the mid-1990s. Angels and angel collectibles made the cover of *Time* and were the subject of a prime-time network television series. Some saw it as divine provenance. Others argued it was nothing more than a decorating craze.

There will always be a heavenly chorus of angel collectors, albeit somewhat reduced in size at the moment. Christmas-theme angel collectibles sell well.

Club: Angel Collector's Club of America, 12225 S. Potomac St., Phoenix, AZ 85044.

Enesco, ornament, angel with holder, Memories of Yesterday Series, M Atwell, 1997 . . . . $18.00
Lefton, Angel of the Month, #1987J, 3" h 32.00
Lefton, Birthday Girl, with stone, #6224, 5" h 18.00
Lefton, bisque, #2323, 4$^{3}/_{4}$" h 30.00
Lefton, Boy of the Month, #1952, 4$^{1}/_{2}$" h 20.00
Lefton, Boy of the Month, #2300, 5" h 30.00
Lladro, ornament, Angel of the Stars, 1995 . . . . 195.00
Margaret Furlong Designs, Holly Angel, Annual Ornament Series, M Furlong, 1983, 3" h 15.00
Ornament, angel holding bouquet, crepe paper, scrap, and tinsel, 12" h 25.00
Ornament, scrap and tinsel dec, 4" h 12.00
Ornament, wax, spun glass wings, leather hinges, 4" 60.00
Sarah's Attic, figurine, Angel Adora with Bunny, #3990, Angels in the Attic Series, 1991 . . . . 65.00
Tree Topper, hard plastic, white and gold robe, clear wings, 1950s, 10" l 20.00
Tree Topper, spun glass and scrap, Western Germany, 1940s, 6" h 12.00
United Design Corp, figurine, Autumn Angel, AA-035, D Newburn, 1993 . . . . 70.00

ANIMAL DISHES, COVERED

Covered animal dishes were a favorite of housewives during the first half of the 20th century. Grandmother Rinker and her sisters had numerous hens on nest scattered throughout their homes. They liked the form. It did not make any difference how old or new they were. Reproductions and copycats abound. You have to be alert for these late examples.

Look for unusual animals and forms. Many early examples were enhanced through hand-painted decorations. Pieces with painting in excellent condition command a premium.

Open-neck swan, milk glass, split rib base, 5½" l, $99.00. Photo courtesy Gene Harris Antique Auction Center, Inc.

Centenary Swan with Stand, Swarovski Crystal, 2" h swan, 2" h stand, $150.00.

Chick and Eggs, emerging chick, white milk glass, Atterbury, 11" h **$185.00**
Cow, milk glass, Vasserystahl, 4¾" h, 5½" l **500.00**
Dog on Carpet, milk glass, Vasserystahl **130.00**
Dog, white milk glass, patterned quilt top, sgd Vallerystahl **175.00**
Eagle on Nest, white milk glass, "The American Hen" inscribed on banner **85.00**
Elephant, amber glass **150.00**
Frog, sitting, green glass, Co-Operative Flint Glass Co, 1920-30s **85.00**
Hen on Nest, blue frosted glass, quilted base, 6½" l **75.00**
Hen on Nest, chocolate milk glass, Westmoreland, 7½" l . . . **300.00**
Hen on Nest, marbleized glass, white and dark blue, lacy base, Atterbury, 7½" l **165.00**
Jumbo the Elephant, crystal, Indiana Glass Co, reissue, 1981, 4 x 7" **20.00**
Swan, raised wing #2, milk glass, orig paint and eyes, 9¾" l **225.00**
Turkey, milk glass, 7" h **180.00**
Turtle, snail on back, blue milk glass, 7½" l **600.00**

ANIMAL FIGURES

Animal collectors are a breed apart. Collecting is a love affair. As long as their favorite animal is pictured or modeled, they are more than willing to buy the item. In many cases, they own real life counterparts to go with their objects. My son's menagerie includes a cat, dog, tarantula, lovebird, two rabbits, a Golden Ball python, and three tanks of tropical fish.

Clubs: Canine Collectors Club, 736 N. Western Ave., Ste. 314, Lake Forest, IL 60045; Cat Collectors, 33161 Wendy Dr., Sterling Heights, MI 48130; The Frog Pond, P.O. Box 193, Beech Grove, IN 46107; The National Elephant Collectors Society, 380 Medford St., Somerville, MA 02145.

Newsletter: *Jumbo Jargon,* 1002 W. 25th St., Erie PA 16502; *The Model Horse Trader,* 143 Mercer Way, Upland, CA 91786.

Periodical: *Hobby Horse News,* 5053 Dryehaven Dr., Tallahassee, FL 32311; *T R R Pony Express,* 71 Aloha Circle, North Little Rock, AR 72120.

Alley Cat, glass, dusty rose iridized, Fenton **$65.00**
Alligator, Ceramic Arts Studio **50.00**
Bird, glass, purple, gold leaf base, Barbini, 5½" h **75.00**
Boxer Dog, sitting, ceramic Morten **75.00**
Calf, ceramic, brown, Brayton Laguna **85.00**
Cat, glass, clear, green eyes **45.00**
Cat, stylized, black matte, Royal Dux Bohemia triangle mark, 7½" h **21.00**
Chicks, glass, New Martinsville **45.00**
Cockatoo, ceramic, Brad Keeler **55.00**
Dachshund, china, Beswick, 9" l **53.00**
Donkey and Pheasant, glass, clear, Duncan & Miller **425.00**
Dove, glass, clear, Duncan & Miller **165.00**
Eagle, bisque, mkd "Bald Eagle by Andrea, Japan," 15" h **85.00**
Elephant, china, white, numbered, 3" h, price for pair **17.00**
Goose, fat, crystal, Duncan **225.00**
Hen, glass, New Martinsville **75.00**
Lamb, ceramic, plain, Ceramic Arts Studio **60.00**
Lamb, china, pink roses and bows, Cordelia, 4½" h **18.00**
Owl, carved wood, old brown finish, round base, 3¾" h **45.00**
Owl, ceramic, Roselane **20.00**
Owl, white milk glass, Imperial **48.00**
Penguin, ceramic, maroon, Homer Laughlin, Harlequin **285.00**
Percheron Horse, china, unmkd, 10½" h **14.00**
Pony, standing, clear, Heisey **95.00**
Robin, glass, ruby, twig nest, ftd, Westmoreland **95.00**
Squirrel, on base, New Martinsville **45.00**
Swan, glass, opalescent blue, Duncan & Miller, 6½" leaf **95.00**

ANTI-AXIS COLLECTIBLES

The Golden Rule may tell us to turn the other cheek, but during World War II we learned to hate our enemies. Anti-Axis material, items which were derogatory of the leaders of Germany, Japan, and Italy, was plentiful and many American families showed their patriotism through the display of these humorous novelties.

Advisor: Ken Fleck, 496 Second St., Highspire, PA 17034, (717) 939-8441.

Ashtray, Hitler face, flat, open mouth, Redware **$150.00**
Ashtray, Tojo face, flat, open mouth, Redware **150.00**
Ashtray, Hitler head, standup, open mouth, Redware **175.00**
Dartboard, "Bom Jap," flakeboard, yellow, black, and red, different war scenes with Jap soldier in center **150.00**
Display, cardboard, standup, Hitler, Mussolini, and Stalin with "Nuts" below 3 boxes of Double Kay Nuts, dated 1940 . . . . . . **275.00**
Figure, carved wood, skunk with Hitler's head, painted swastika on butt, small **150.00**
Hankie, silk, Brussels boy urinating on German flag, made in Belgium **35.00**

Poster, "More Toolie You Crackie—More Happy Jappie," $175.00.

Milkshake Mixer, Hamilton Beach, green porcelain, metal, c1940s, $121.00. Photo courtesy Gary Metz's Muddy River Trading Co.

Pinback Button, "Ax the Axis," plastic, $1\frac{1}{2}$" **45.00**
Pinback Button, "Beat the Axis," wood, $2\frac{3}{4}$" h **50.00**
Pinback Button, "Eat to Beat the Devil," litho tin, multicolored, Hitler's face being punched, 1" **45.00**
Pinback Button, "To Hell with Mussie," celluloid, $1\frac{1}{4}$" **35.00**
Pinback Button, "Wanted for Murder," celluloid, Hitler's face, $1\frac{1}{4}$" **35.00**
Postcard, "I'm Bringing Home the Bacon!," WAC leading Hitler by rope, multicolored linen **6.00**
Postcard, "Keep 'Em Flying!," Uncle Sam kicking 3 Jap soldiers, multicolored linen **6.00**
Postcard, "Remember Pearl Harbor!," Uncle Sam spanking Jap on his lap, multicolored linen **6.00**
Postcard, "Slam the Axis," set of 6, with mailer envelope **50.00**
Postcard, "Swat that Fly," English, fly with Hitler's head, multicolored **25.00**
Poster, "Tighten Your Grip," swastika being crushed by blacksmith pliers **150.00**
Poster, "We've Made A Monkey Out Of You," Uncle Sam as organ grinder, Hitler as monkey, red, white, and blue **125.00**
Scarf, silk, multicolored scene of rooster on top of German flag, made in France **75.00**
Sheet Music, *Let's Put the Axe to the Axis* **40.00**
Sheet Music, *Put Another Nail in Hitler's Coffin* **40.00**
Sheet Music, *Scrap the Axis & the Japs* **35.00**

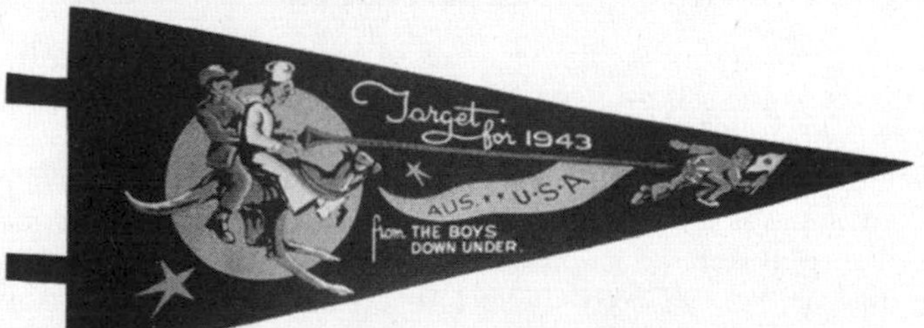

Pennant, made in Australia, "Target for the 1943 from the Boys Down Under," $100.00.

APPLIANCES, ELECTRICAL

Nothing illustrates our ability to take a relatively simple task—e.g. toast a piece of bread—and create a wealth of different methods for achieving it quite like a toaster. Electrical appliances are viewed as one of the best documents of stylistic design in utilitarian form.

Collectors tend to concentrate on one form. Toasters are the most commonly collected, largely because several books have been written about them. Electric fans have a strong following. Waffle irons are pressing toasters for popularity. Modernistic collectors seek bar drink blenders from the 1930s through the 1950s.

Clubs: Electrical Breakfast Club, P.O. Box 306, White Mills, PA 18473; Old Appliance Club, P.O. Box 65, Ventura, CA 93002; Porcelier Collectors Club, 21 Tamarac Swamp Rd., Wallingford, CT 06492; Upper Crust: The Toaster Collectors Assoc., P.O. Box 529, Temecula, CA 92593.

Blender, Dorby Whipper, Model E, chrome motor, black Bakelite handle, off/on toggle, clear, measured Vidrio glass, 1940s **$25.00**
Blender, Kenmore, Sears, white enameled body **20.00**
Blender, Kwik Way, St Louis, MO, white metal motor top over angular, clear glass base, no switch, decal label, $7\frac{1}{2}$" h **20.00**
Broiler, Royal Master Appliance Co, Miriam, OH, 1930s. **25.00**
Butter Churn, Mixmaster, stainless steel, wood paddles, clear glass jar, 4 qt. **35.00**
Chafing Dish, American Beauty, American Electrical Heater Co, Detroit, MI, 3 part, nickel on copper, sealed element in base, hot water container, separate plugs, mkd "fast" and "slow," black painted wood handles and knob, 1910s. **50.00**
Chafing Dish, Universal, Landers, Frary & Clark, nickel on copper faceted body, 3 parts, sealed element in base hot water pan, 3 prong heat adjustment in base, large black wooden handle and knob, 1910s **50.00**
Clock Timer, Montgomery Ward & Co, cream body, flat swivel base, silver and red, 1940s **15.00**
Coffee Grinder, Kitchen Aid. **65.00**
Coffee Maker, Farberware, S W Farber, Brooklyn, NY, Coffee Robot, chrome body, glass bowl, thermostat, 1937. . . . . **35.00**
Coffee Maker, Percolator, Porcelier, Black-Eyed Susan **65.00**
Coffee Maker, Percolator, Porcelier, Golden Wheat **60.00**
Coffee Maker, Percolator, Porcelier, Starflower **60.00**
Coffee Maker, Percolator, Royal Rochester, #366 B-29, nickel plated copper, black wooden handles, 1920s, 10" h **15.00**
Coffee Mill, Kitchen Aid, Hobart Model A9, Art Deco style, white motor base, clear glass top threads onto base, threaded black metal lid, 1936, $13\frac{3}{4}$" h **60.00**

Toaster, Universal, Landers, Frary & Clark, New Britain, CT, $35.00.

Drink Mixer, Made-Rite, Weining Co, Cleveland, OH, 1930s 20.00
Egg Cooker, Rochester Stamping Co, Rochester, NY, egg shaped, 4 part, chrome, small base, int fitted with skillet with turned black wooden handle, 6 egg holder with lift out handle, enclosed heating element, 1910s 40.00
Food Cooker, Quality Brand, Model #950, Great Northern Mfg Co, Chicago, IL, cylindrical body, insulated sides and lid, fitted int, aluminum pan lids, brown with red stripe on body, lift out rods, 1920s, 14" h 40.00
Fry Pan, Electric Skillet, GE, cast aluminum turquoise base with glass top 50.00
Iron, Royal, Brock Snyder Mfg Co, wood handle 15.00
Malt Mixer, Machine Craft, Los Angeles, CA, Model B, 18$^{3}/_{4}$" h 60.00
Mixer, Handymix, Mary Dunbar, Chicago Elect Mfg Co, #D-121125, stand, 2 beaters, push button, 11$^{1}/_{2}$" h 16.00
Popcorn Popper, White Cross, National Stamping & Electrical Co, Chicago, tin can base with heater and cord, wire basket fits into can, metal top with stirrer mounted through handle, side wooden handle, late 1910s 30.00
Roaster, Dominion, chrome, attached cord 25.00
Tea Kettle, Universal, Model #973, Landers, Frary & Clark, bright nickel squatty body and base in 1 pc, long spout, high curved black painted wood handle, vertically curved mounts, 1910s 45.00
Toaster, Sears Kenmore, Model #307-6323-1, chrome, rounded body, 2 slice pop-up, Bakelite handles and knob, early 1940s 15.00
Toaster, Toastmaster, Waters Center Co, Model 1-A-3, Art Deco, sq, chrome, vertical fluted sides, 1929 . . . . . 35.00
Waffle Iron, Westinghouse, chrome, black Bakelite handles with incised leaf design, 1950s 30.00
Water Pot, Dormeyer, Hurri-Hot Electri-Cup, automatic, chrome body, 1950s 10.00

ASHTRAYS

Most price guides include ashtrays under advertising. The problem is that there are a number of terrific ashtrays in shapes that have absolutely nothing to do with advertising. Ashtrays get a separate category from me.

With the nonsmoking movement gaining strength, the ashtray is an endangered species. The time to collect them is now.

Advertising, Cliff House, San Francisco, shell, litho $15.00
Advertising, Crane Plumbing, cast iron 20.00
Advertising, General Electric Motor 15.00
Advertising, General Motors, brass, "Who Serves Progress Serves America," and "Designed And Produced By Terstedt Div./General Motors Corp" inscription, 4" d 40.00
Advertising, General Streamline Jumbo, figural tire, emb glass insert 25.00
Advertising, Hanley Brewing Co, Providence, RI 35.00
Advertising, Mountain States Telephone & Telegraph, granite 85.00
Advertising, Old Judge Coffee, tin 90.00
Advertising, Old Shay-Fort Pitt Beer, aluminum 14.00
Advertising, Pyrene Fire Extinguisher, figural, Bakelite 40.00
Advertising, Twin Beers Store, chalkware, dated 1931, 4$^{1}/_{2}$" d 40.00
Advertising, William Marvy Co Sign Makers, glass, red, white, and blue rim, "Porcelain Enameled Signs and Barber Poles," 1950s, 5" d 18.00
Art Deco, chrome 7.50
Bird, figural, chrome, Art Deco 18.00
Clown, playing banjo, multicolored shiny glaze, Japan, 3$^{1}/_{4}$" h 30.00
Commemorative, Civil War Centennial, china, white, color center illus and symbols, 6$^{1}/_{2}$" d 30.00
Fiesta Ware, green 25.00
Fish, Frankoma 15.00
Frog, sitting, porcelain, Japan, 4$^{1}/_{2}$" h 20.00
Guitar, figural, wood, 8$^{1}/_{4}$" l 5.00
Hat, figural, blue 7.50
House, figural, multicolored luster, semi-matte glaze, Japan, 3$^{3}/_{4}$" h 15.00
Pinup Girl, tin, Vargas, 1950s 10.00
Scottish Terrier, figural, glass insert, 4$^{1}/_{2}$" h, 5$^{3}/_{4}$" w 25.00
Space, dark blue, white cupids dec, mkd "Wedgwood," 4$^{1}/_{2}$" d 30.00
Squirrel, cigarette holder and snuffer center, Art Deco, Hamilton, 2$^{3}/_{4}$ x 5$^{3}/_{4}$" 25.00
Triangle Shape, apple blossom dec, mkd "Town/Hand Made Aluminum," 3$^{1}/_{2}$" d 4.00

AUNT JEMIMA COLLECTIBLES

Aunt Jemima's Pancake flour has been a breakfast tradition for over 100 years. The self-rising pancake mix was invented in St. Joseph, Missouri, in 1889. The product has been marketed by several companies in the century since its introduction. The R. T. Davis Milling Company was the first to introduce Aunt Jemima to a worldwide audience. This introduction was at the 1893 Chicago World's Fair. At this fair Nancy Green, the first Aunt Jemima, served more than one million pancakes. Aunt Jemima Mills Company became the producer of Aunt Jemima in a modernized version and is still being used by Quaker Oats.

Over the years Aunt Jemima has also been used on many different food products. These products include corn meal, flour, cake mixes, soup mix, syrup and frozen breakfast foods. In the marketing of these products many types of related premiums have been used. The most widely known of these were the red plastic kitchen items produced by F & F Mold and Die of Dayton Ohio. These premiums were first introduced in 1948 and offered through the 1950s.

Due to the popularity of Aunt Jemima items with collectors reproductions have become a major problem. The most recent items to appear in quantity are kitchen and alarm clocks. These are old clocks that have had Aunt Jemima images added to the face. This is done using a color copy of the face with artwork added. Some of these use a current logo cut from a product box and not a logo of the same vintage as the clock. These clocks can be found in any style. There is no consistency to the clocks used. No information has surfaced that indicates any of these clocks are original. Most other premium items appear as offers on product boxes. Asking prices on these fantasy clocks have ranged from $50.00 to $1,000.00. Some even have fake boxes. Some have a small offer for the Aunt Jemima Cookie Jar on back.

Advisor: Lynn and Kevin Burkett, P.O. Box 671, Hillsdale, MI 49242-0671, (517) 437-2149, e-mail: slburkett@dmci.net.

Apron, yellow oilcloth **$100.00**
Cake Decorations, Mother Goose characters, 12 different, several colors, price for each **5.00**
Cigarette Lighter, different styles **150.00**
Clock, clear plastic, encased waffle, 1980s **175.00**
Coloring Book, "Hurray It's Aunt Jemima Day," 1964 . . . . . . **125.00**
Cookie Jar, F & F Mold and Die **600.00**
Cookie Jar, soft plastic, mkd "Aunt Jemima's Cookie Jar" **325.00**
Creamer and Sugar, cov, F & F Mold and Die **150.00**
Mask, paper, different styles **500.00**
Matchbook, Aunt Jemima's Kitchen, Disneyland **45.00**
Measuring Cup, clear glass, Aunt Jemima's face, 2 cups **175.00**
Muffin Pan, cast iron, mkd "Aunt Jemima Meal" **175.00**
Needle Book, different styles **200.00**
Pancake Mold, aluminum, wooden handle, 4 animal shapes **100.00**
Pancake Shaker, plastic, blue **65.00**
Pancake Shaker, plastic, yellow, Aunt Jemima's face on top **65.00**
Pancake Turner, metal, "Hurray It's Aunt Jemima" on handle **45.00**
Puzzle, 2 pcs with string **150.00**
Recipe Book, *Magical Recipes* **35.00**
Recipe Book, *New Temptilatin Recipes* **65.00**
Recipe Book, *Pancakes Unlimited* **65.00**
Recipe Cards, set of 16, with mailing envelope **150.00**
Salt and Pepper Shakers, pr, F & F Mold and Die, 3½" h, mint **50.00**
Salt and Pepper Shakers, pr, F & F Mold and Die, 5½" h, mint **85.00**

Sign, tin over cardboard with easel back, c1920s, 9 x 13", $1,500.00.

Shipping Box, cardboard, unusual shape, $350.00.

Shipping Crate, wood construction, various sizes and styles **500.00**
Spice Jar, cinnamon, paprika, and nutmeg, F & F Mold and Die, near mint, price for each **75.00**
Sporks, Mother Goose characters, 12 different, several colors, price for each **15.00**
Syrup Pitcher, F & F Mold and Die **75.00**
Tin, cooking oil, red ground, 5 gallons **1,000.00**

AUTOGRAPHS

Collecting autographs is a centuries' old hobby. A good rule to follow is the more recognizable the person, the more likely the autograph is to have value. Content is a big factor in valuing autograph material. A clipped signature is worth far less than a lengthy handwritten document by the same person.

Before spending big money for an autograph, have it authenticated. Many movie and sports stars have secretaries and other individuals sign their material, especially photographs. An "autopen" is a machine that can sign up to a dozen documents at one time. The best proof that a signature is authentic is to get it from the person who stood there and watched the celebrity sign it.

Clubs: The Manuscript Society, 350 N. Niagara St., Burbank, CA 95105; Universal Autograph Collectors Club, P.O. Box 6181, Washington, DC 20044.

Newsletter: *Autographs & Memorabilia,* P.O. Box 224, Coffeyville, KS 67337; *The Autograph Review,* 305 Carlton Rd, Syracuse, NY 13207.

Periodicals: *Autograph Collector,* 510-A S. Corona Mall, Corona, CA 91720; *Autograph Times,* 1125 W. Baseline Rd. #2-153-M, Mesa, AZ 85210; *The Collector,* P.O. Box 255, Hunter, NY 12442.

Allen, Brooke, First Day Cover **$20.00**
Anka, Paul, photo, black and white, 8 x 10" **10.00**
Austin, Tracy, card, 5 x 3" **10.00**
Baker, Josephine, card, "J. Baker," 3 x 5" **200.00**
Barton, Clara, letter, 4 pp, Jul 29, 1905, 5 x 7" **350.00**
Capote, Truman, news article, photo at top, black ink signature across photo, 3 x 7" **75.00**
Carter, Jimmy, speech, 5 pp, Jul 12, 1972, blue ink signature **185.00**
Chamberlain, Wilt, photo, black and white, 8 x 10" **30.00**
Close, Glen, magazine cov, *American Film,* May 1884 . . . . . . **15.00**
Cole, Nat King, postcard, Jan 2, 1949 . . . . . . **150.00**
Coward, Noel, card, 5½ x 3¼" **125.00**

Cummings, Constance, photo, black and white, 3 1/2 x 5 1/2" 10.00
Dangerfield, Rodney, photo, black and white glossy, portrait pose, white borders trimmed, 7 x 9" 10.00
DeLuise, Dom, photo, black and white glossy, inscribed, white borders trimmed, 7 x 9" 10.00
Diller, Phyllis, photo, black and white glossy, 5 x 7" 5.00
Garland, Beverly, photo, black and white, 5 x 7" 15.00
Haley, Alex, card, 5 x 3" 15.00
Hayes, Rutherford B, Executive Mansion card, "Spiegel Grove-Fremont Ohio" 475.00
Herbert, Victor, typed letter, New York, Apr 13, 1916 . . . . 175.00
Hoover, Herbert, typed letter, thank you to Mr Wilson Mills, 7 x 10 1/2" 145.00
Jabbar, Kareem Abdul, and Julius Irving, First Day cover 45.00
Joel, Billy, color photo, 8 x 10" 40.00
Porter, Cole, sgd and inscribed photo, black and white studio portrait of Cole in middle age, inscribed "To Harold Krevolin, Sincerely Cole Porter" in black ink, 2 3/5 x 3 3/5" 600.00
Rhetton, Mary Lou, card, 5 x 3" 5.00
Rehnquist, William, Supreme Court Card 45.00
Roosevelt, Eleanor, White House card 75.00
Sherman, John, Secretary of State, letter, personal stationary, OH, 1886, 5 x 8" 45.00
Staubach, Roger, card, 5 x 3" 10.00
Thurston, Howard, membership card for Society of American Magicians, 1929 . . . . 95.00
The Moody Blues, sgd Yamaha acoustic guitar, "Justin Hayward; Ray Thomas; Graeme Edge; John Lodge, Tuesday Afternoon" 632.00
Turner, Ted, business stationary 15.00
Muhammad, Elijah, check, Jul 31, 1971 . . . . 375.00

AUTOMOBILE COLLECTIBLES

An automobile swap meet is 25% cars and 75% car parts. Restoration and rebuilding of virtually all car models is a never-ending process. The key is to find the exact part needed. Too often, auto parts at flea markets are not priced. The seller is going to judge how badly he thinks you want the part before setting the price. You have to keep your cool.

Two areas that are attracting outside collector interest are promotional toy models and hood ornaments. The former have been caught up in the craze for 1950s and 1960s Japanese tin. The latter have been discovered by the art community, who view them as wonderful examples of modern streamlined design.

Clubs: Hubcap Collectors Club, P.O. Box 54, Buckley, MI 49620; Spark Park Collectors of America, 4262 County Rd. 121, Fulton, MO 65251.

Periodicals: *Car Toys,* 7950 Deering Ave., Canoga Park, CA 91304; *Hemmings Motor News,* P.O. Box 100, Rt. 9 W. Bennington, VT 05201; *Mobilia,* P.O. Box 575, Middlebury, VT 05753; *PL8S: The License Plate Collector's Hobby Magazine,* P.O. Box 222, East Texas, PA 18046.

Badge, Chrysler Plymouth, Main Plant, Ord mech, Edward Bachman, Executive, rect, plated steel frame, employee photo and signature, 1 5/8 x 2 5/16" $30.00
Carbuerator, Buick, 1924–25 . . . . 25.00
Catalog, Avanti, Studebaker, shop and parts manual, 1964 . . . . 50.00
Engine, Maxwell, 1914 . . . . 200.00
Folder, Dodge, color, 30 x 21" open size, 1952 . . . . 35.00
Game, Assembly Line, The Game of, Selchow & Righter, action game, 1960s 30.00
Gearshift Knob, plastic, red, tapered sides, red jewel center 25.00
Headlamp, bull's-eye, Marchal, 12" d. 700.00
Hood Ornament, lion, dated 1924 . . . . 30.00
Hood Ornament, steer horns 50.00
Hubcaps, set of 4, Plymouth, 1939–40 . . . . 250.00
License Plate, Massachusetts, 4 digits, 1911 . . . . 70.00
License Plate, Pennsylvania, black on white, "329" in center, "City of Allentown" over "License No." across top, "Expires Oct. 1, 1928" across bottom 15.00
Owner's Kit, Plymouth, includes 36 pp illus manual, Plymouth service certificate, Chrysler parts leaflet, Mopar radio booklet, and monthly bank payment folder, orig 6 x 9" brown paper folder, 1951 . . . . 20.00
Owner's Manual, Chandler Big Six, 1927 . . . . 55.00
Owner's Manual, Ford Model T, 1914 . . . . 15.00
Owner's Manual, Rambler, 1927 . . . . 35.00
Owner's Manual, Volkswagen, Operation and Maintenance, 1971–72 models, vinyl cov, 130 pp 10.00
Parking Meter, Duncan, 2-hour limit 100.00
Postcard, DeSoto adv, color, 4 door sedan, 1939 . . . . 4.00
Poster, Buick, "Kansas City," blck and white, 1921–22, 25 x 38" 85.00
Radiator Ornament, Pontiac, feather headdress, 1958 . . . . 15.00
Radiator Ornament, Willys Knight 250.00
Sheet Music, *In My Merry Oldsmobile,* 1905, 10 1/2 x 14" 60.00
Sheet Music, *The Motor March,* tour car illus on cov, 1906 . . . . 30.00
Spark Plug, Beacon Lite, glass insulator, 7/8" 25.00
Spark Plug, Cross Country, 7/8" 18.00

Display, Magic Rust Eraser, countertop, cardboard, 1957, 16 1/2" w, $55.00. Photo courtesy Collectors Auction Services.

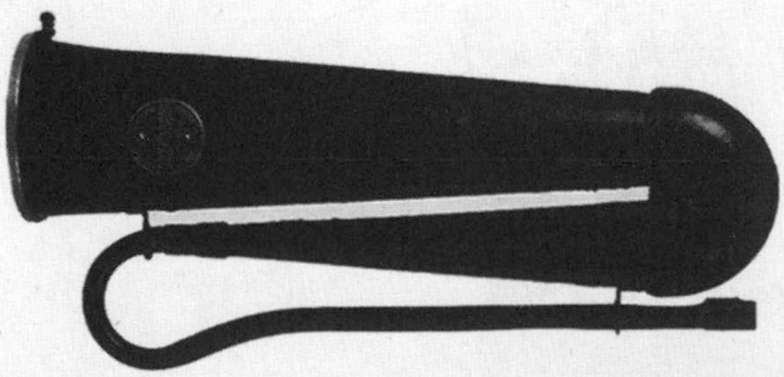

Car Horn, metal, 14 1/2" l, $27.50. Photo courtesy Collectors Auction Services.

AUTO RACING

Man's quest for speed is as old as time. Automobile racing dates before the turn of the century. Many of the earliest races took place in Europe. By the first decade of the 20th century, automobile racing was part of the American scene.

The Indianapolis 500 began in 1911 and was interrupted only by World War II. In addition to Formula 1 racing, the NASCAR circuit has achieved tremendous popularity with American racing fans. Cult heroes such as Richard Petty have become household names. This is a field of heroes and also-rans. Collectors love the winners. A household name counts. Losers are important only when major races are involved. Pre-1945 material is especially desirable since few individuals were collecting these items prior to that time.

The field has problems with reproductions and copycats. Check every item carefully. Beware of paying premium prices for items made within the last 20 years. Although interest in Indy 500 collectibles remains strong, the current market is dominated by NASCAR collectibles. In fact, the market is so strong that racing collectibles have their own separate show circuit and supporting literature. Because racing collecting is in its infancy, price speculation is rampant. Market manipulators abound. In addition, copycat, fantasy and contemporary limited edition items are being introduced into the market as quickly as they can be absorbed. A shake-out appears to be years in the future. In the interim, check your engine and gear up for fast action.

Clubs: Auto Racing Memories, P.O. Box 12226, St. Petersburg, FL 33733; National Indy 500 Collectors Club, 10505 N. Delaware St, Indianapolis, IN 46280; The National Racing Club, 615 Hwy. A1A North, Ste. 105, Ponte Vedra Beach, FL 32082.

Newsletter: *Quarter Milestones,* 53 Milligan Ln., Johnson City, TN 37601.

Periodicals: *Collector's World,* P.O. Box 562029, Charlotte, NC 28256; *Racing Collectibles Price Guide,* Po Box 608114, Orlando, FL 32860; *TRACE Magazine,* P.O. Box 716, Kannapolis, NC 28082; *Tuff Stuff's RPM,* P.O. Box 1637, Glen Allen, VA 23060.

Autograph, Kyle Petty, photo **$25.00**
Book, *Salute to the 75th Anniversary of the Indianapolis 500,* Marlboro, 1986 . . . . **15.00**
Bottle, Fan Fuelers sports drink, Kyle Petty, 32 oz **6.00**
Decal, Valvoline Racing Oil, 1973 NHRA Spring Nationals, 4 x 5½" **5.00**

Lamp, Winston 500, paper and wood with plastic car, souvenir, wall-mounted, some soiling, $187.00. Photo courtesty Collectors Auction Services.

Demitasse Cup and Saucer, white, china, 1¾" h cup shows speedway emblem on 1 side without inscription, 3¾" d saucer shows "Lard Roadster/Milwaukee" racing car posed against vacated spectator standing under "Indy 500," both with full color art and blue accent trim line **25.00**
Game, Spedem Auto Race, Alderman-Fairchild, board game, patented Apr 20, 1922 . . . . **95.00**
Game, Speed Circuit, 3M, board game, 1971 . . . . . . **15.00**
Game, Wide World of Sports—Auto Racing, Milton Bradley, board game, 1974 . . . . **15.00**
Magazine, *TACH,* American Hot Rod Assoc. **6.00**
Pass, Indianapolis Motor Speedway, 1939 . . . . **75.00**
Pennant, William Grove Park and Speedway, green felt, 1950s, 16" l **25.00**
Pinback Button, Cobe Cup Race, Jun 18–19, 1909, Crown Point, IN, red, early race car with 2 men **35.00**
Pinback Button, Merrimack Valley Automobile Race, Sep 6–10, 1909, Lowell, MA, red and white, early race car **20.00**
Program, Monterey Historic Auto Races, CA, 1979 . . . . . **15.00**
Program, Pocono 500, PA, 1971 . . . . **10.00**

AUTUMN LEAF

The Hall China Co. developed Autumn Leaf china as a dinnerware premium for the Jewel Tea Co. in 1933. The giveaway was extremely successful. The "Autumn Leaf" name did not originate until 1960. Previously, the pattern was simply known as "Jewel" or "Autumn." Autumn Leaf remained in production until 1978.

Pieces were added and dropped from the line over the years. Limited production pieces are most desirable. Look for matching accessories in glass, metal and plastic made by other companies. Jewel Tea toy trucks were also made.

Club: National Autumn Leaf Collector's Club, 62200 E236 Rd. Wyandotte, OK 74370.

Baker, open, 6½" d **$35.00**
Ball Jug, #3 . . . . **22.00**
Bean Pot, cov, 2 handles **192.50**
Bowl, Radiance, 6" d **8.00**
Bowl, Radiance, 9" d **25.00**
Bread and Butter Plate **3.00**
Cereal Bowl **6.50**
Coaster, price for 10 . . . . **38.50**
Coffeepot, Rayed, no drip, 8 cup **22.00**
Coffeepot, Rayed, with drip, 8 cup **55.00**
Coffeepot Lid **10.00**

Salt and Pepper Shakers, range size, handled, $32.00

Cookie Jar, cov, Zeisel 110.00
Gravy Boat, no underplate 20.00
Hotpad, round, tin back, 7¼" d 10.00
Jug, Rayed, 2½ pt 22.00
Luncheon Plate, 8" d 5.50
Norris Jug, cov, 1991 . . . . . 71.50
Pie Baker, spotted, 9" d 50.00
Platter, oval, 11½" l 27.50
Salad Bowl, 2 qt 11.00
Salad Plate 3.00
Soup Bowl 14.00
Sugar, cov, ruffled 11.00
Tablecloth, sailcloth, 54 x 62" 82.50
Tea Towel, 2 sewn together, 16 x 33" 71.50
Tidbit, 2 tier 71.50
Tumbler, frosted, 5½" h 10.00

AVON COLLECTIBLES

Avon products, with the exception of California Perfume Co., material, are not found often at flea markets any longer. The 1970s were the golden age of Avon collectibles. There are still a large number of dedicated collectors, but the legion that fueled the pricing fires of the 1970s has been hard hit by desertions. Avon material today is more likely to be found at garage sales than at flea markets.

Club: National Assoc. of Avon Collectors, Inc., P.O. Box 7006, Kansas City, MO 64113.

Periodical: *Avon Times*, P.O. Box 9868, Kansas City, MO 64134.

Candy Cane Twins Set, 2 cameo lipsticks with candy cane box, 1966 . . . . . $20.00
Cape Cod, candlestick cologne, 1975–80, 5 oz 8.00
Cape Cod, candy dish, 3½" h 112.00
Cape Cod, dinner plate, 1982–83 . . . . . 14.00
Cape Cod, heart box, 1989, 4" w 13.00
Cape Cod, napkin rings, set of 4, 1989, 1½" d 20.00
Cape Cod, sauce boat, ftd, 8" l 25.00
Cape Cod, wine goblet, issued to Reps with Presidents Celebration 1976, emb bottom 8.00
Cotillion, Little Girl Blue, 1972–73 . . . . . 7.00
Eight Ball, black and white 2.50
Handkerchief Savings Bank, metal, Ben Franklin on $100 bill, white handkerchief inside, 4½" h 9.00
Little Wiggly Game & Bubble Bath, 1973, 8 oz 3.50
Old Faithful, brown glass, brown plastic head and gold keg, 1972–73, 5 oz 10.00
Randy Pandy Soap Dish, rubber, 1972-74 . . . . . 2.00
Roll-A-Fluff Set, red Charisma puff, green Regence puff, white Brocade puff, 1967–70 . . . . . 15.00
Sonnet, yule tree, green, 1974–79 . . . . . 3.00
Stop 'N Go, green glass and cap, 4 oz 5.00
Tai Winds After Shave, President Lincoln, 1973 . . . . . 6.50
Ted E Bear Baby Lotion Dispenser, plastic, 1981–82, 10 oz 2.00
Wild Country After Shave, western boot, 1973–75 . . . . . 2.50

Hand Lotion, Country style, (graniteware) coffeepot, 10 oz, $1.75.

BADGES

Have you ever tried to save a name tag or badge that attaches directly to your clothing or fits into a plastic holder? We are victims of a throwaway society. This is one case in which progress has not been a boon for collectors.

Fortunately, our grandparents and great-grandparents loved to save the membership, convention, parade and other badges that they acquired. The badges' colorful silk and cotton fabric often contained elaborate calligraphic lettering and lithographed scenes in combination with celluloid and/or metal pinbacks and pins. They were badges of honor. They had an almost military quality about them.

Look for badges with attached three-dimensional miniatures. Regional value is a factor. I found a great Emmaus, PA, badge priced at $2 at a flea market in Florida: back home, its value is more than $20.

Chauffeur, New York, 1928 . . . . . $10.00
Convention, Grain Dealers, brass, Minneapolis name and skyline on hanger bar, red, white, and blue ribbon, pendant inscribed "24th Annual Convention, 1920," 3½" h 10.00
Deputy Constable, silvered brass, emb design, spring clip metal fastener, 1930s, 2½" h 20.00
Employee, Bethlehem Steel Co, Industrial Police, shield, plated brass, raised letters, brass number, 2⅜ x 2½" 45.00
Employee, Conmar Products Corp, Newark, NJ, round, plated brass frame, black enamel letters, employee photo and number, black woman, 1¾" d 30.00
Employee, Franklin Sugar Refining Co, round, plated steel frame, employee photo, 2" d 20.00
Employee, Ingersoll-Rand, Phillipsburg, NJ, oval, plated brass, red enamel plant strip, black enamel employee number, employee photo, 1⅜ x 1¾" 20.00

Shell–Mex and B P Ltd, metal cloisonné, 2" h, 2¼" w, $60.50. Photo courtesy Collectors Auction Services.

Sheriff, Spec Dept Sheriff, Rennselaer, NY 35.00
Souvenir, 1920 Pennsylvania GAR Encampment, brown bronze luster metal link badge depicting official symbol at center of hanger bar holding dark red unmkd fabric ribbon joining "Representative" link bar, profile portrait of "Commander George W. Rhoads," reverse with "54th Annual Encampment/Dept. of Penna. G.A.R./Indiana Pa. June 1920" 15.00
Souvenir, Fire Parade, brass, 2 bars, upper bar with "Hackettstown Fire Dept," lower bar with "Elizabeth Oct 11, 1906," hanging celluloid pendant with fireman portrait illus, 4" h 20.00
Souvenir, State Firemans Tournament, Decatur, IL, Jul 1895, brass hanger bar with fine china suspending 1¾" two-sided celluloid pendant with brass rim, 1 side with color scene of fireman rescuing infant from burning building, reverse has blue inscription on white ground. 20.00
Special Police, silvered brass, star shaped, black lettering, 1930s, 2½" h 22.00
Taxi Driver, silvered brass, engraved "City Of Mt. Vernon," and "131," c1930s 65.00
War Daughters, dark brown luster metal hanger bar and pendant joined by red, white, and blue striped fabric ribbon, hanger bar has initials "FCL," pendant has rim inscription "Daughters of Union Veterans Of The Civil War 1861-1865," entwined "DUV" at center 15.00
Womans Corps, dark brown luster metal hanger bar and pendant joined by red, white, and blue striped fabric ribbon, bar has "F.C.L.," pendant has official emblem and inscription "Woman's Relief Corps 1883". 10.00

BAKELITE

This is a great example of a collecting category gone price-mad. Bakelite is a trademark used for a variety of synthetic resins and plastics used to manufacture colorful, inexpensive, ulitarian objects. The key word is inexpensive. That can also be interpreted as cheap. There is nothing cheap about Bakelite collectibles in today's market. Collectors, especially those from large metropolitan areas who consider themselves design-conscious, want Bakelite in whatever form they can find.

Buy a Bakelite piece because you love it. The market has already started to collapse for commonly found material. Can the high-end pieces be far behind?

Cake Server, green handle $5.00
Cigarette Holder, Art Deco, 12" l 35.00
Clock, Telechron, black, octagonal. 38.00
Flatware, child's, knife, fork, and spoon, butterscotch handles, price for set 20.00
Flatware, service for 6, red handles, price for 26 pcs. 85.00
Jewelry, bangle bracelet, bright yellow, red, black, and green enamel dec 25.00
Jewelry, brooch, yellow carved fawn, painted spots and features, c1930 . . . . 70.00
Jewelry, earrings, pr, black, gold dec 25.00
Jewelry, pendant, cameo, sterling chain 28.00
Jewelry, pin, pink, figural cherries, cluster of 3 . . . . 20.00
Jewelry, ring, marbled blue-green tapered dome, laminated black dot center, c1940 . . . . 60.00
Mending Kit, red, thimble cap 16.00
Napkin Ring, figural dog 25.00

Dresser Set, 3 pcs, amber, imitation mother-of-pearl, black and green Art Nouveau design, 14½" l mirror, 9" l brush, $16.50.

Napkin Ring, hexagonal, red, yellow, and green, orig box, price for set of 6 . . . . 30.00
Pencil Sharpener, Charlie McCarthy 45.00
Pencil Sharpener, G-Man Gun, red 45.00
Poker Chip Caddy, brown, round 15.00
Salt and Pepper Shakers, pr, half moon, green and yellow, matching tray 18.00
Salt and Pepper Shakers, pr, shotgun bullets, green 15.00
Shaving Brush, Klenzo, 2 part handle. 8.50
Table Lighter, standing nude, Dunhill, 3 x 5" h 125.00
Telephone, Kelloggs Series 1000, brown, Art Deco, chrome dial. 90.00
Television, Admiral, #19A11, table top style, dark brown, 7" screen, 1948 . . . . 125.00
Tip Tray, red 8.00

BANDANNAS

Women associate bandannas with keeping their hair in place. Men visualize stage coach holdups or rags used to wipe the sweat from their brows. Neither approach recognizes the colorful and decorative role played by the bandanna.

Some of the earliest bandannas are political. By the turn of the century, bandannas joined pillow cases as the leading souvenir textile found at sites, ranging from beaches to museums. Hillary Weiss's *The American Bandanna: Culture on Cloth from George Washington to Elvis* (Chronicle Books, 1990), provides a visual feast for this highly neglected collecting area.

The bandanna played an important role in the Scouting movement, serving as a neckerchief for both Boy Scouts and Girl Scouts. Many special neckerchiefs were issued. There is also a close correlation between scarves and bandannas. Bandanna collectors tend to collect both.

Autry, Gene, silk, purple, green, dark blue, and white images and design, 1940s, 18 x 21" $75.00
Boy Scout, National Jamboree, 1953 . . . . 30.00
Carter, James E, "Carter-Mondale," white and green, 1980, 28" sq 25.00
Cleveland, Grover, black and white center portrait, red, white, and blue striped border, 16½" sq 60.00
Crockett, Davy, Davy as bronc rider center image, blue, yellow, red, and white Indian blankets, ranch symbols, spurs, botts, and cowboy hat design, 13½ x 14" 40.00
Eisenhower, Dwight D, "Win With Ike For President," blue and white image, bright red ground, 26" sq. 60.00
Garfield, James A, Garfield/Arthur portraits, black and white, 1880, 20 x 21" 275.00

Hoover, Herbert, red, white, and blue, 1932, 17 x 18" **50.00**
Lone Ranger, printed white and blue design, bright red ground, portrait, rail fence, crossed guns, coiled lasso, and horseshoe design, Cheerios premium, 1949–50, 21 x 23" **65.00**
Mickey Mouse, cotton, black, white, and red Mickey, Goofy, Minnie, and Donald figures, green border, c1960, 22" sq **35.00**
Radio Orphan Annie Flying W Bandanna, red and white fabric with brown accents on border horseshoe motifs and circular background portraits of Radio Orphan Annie, Sandy, Joe Corntassel, and Ginger, 1934 Ovaltine premium, 17 x 18½" **70.00**
Remember Pearl Harbor, linen weave, white fabric, red and blue ink with slogan repeated at each corner, warships and fighter planes centered by "Island of Oahu" map, 13 x 14" **65.00**
Roosevelt, Theodore, center portrait, red, white, and brown, 21 x 24" **150.00**

BANKS, STILL

Banks are classified into two types—mechanical (action) and still (non-action). Chances are that any mechanical bank you find at a flea market today is a reproduction. If you find one that you think is real, check it out in one of the mechanical bank books before buying it.

The still or non-action bank dominates the flea market scene. There is no limit to the methods for collecting still banks. Some favor type (advertising), others composition (cast iron, tin, plastic, etc.), figural (shaped like something) or theme (Western).

Beware of still-bank reproductions, just as you are with mechanical banks, especially in the cast-iron sector. Most banks were used, so look for wear in places you would expect to find it. Save your money and do not buy if you are uncertain of a bank's authenticity.

Club: Still Bank Collectors Club of America, 4175 Millersville Rd, Indianapolis, IN 46205.

Newsletter: Glass Bank Collector, P.O. Box 155, Poland, NY 13431.

Advertising, Admiral Appliances, vinyl, figural Admiral **$25.00**
Advertising, Arctic Circle Drive-In Restaurant, composition, figural Adcey the Cowboy Chicken, 6½" h **100.00**
Advertising, Big Boy, holding suspenders, vinyl, ©1977, 9½" h **16.50**
Advertising, Bokar Coffee, tin **12.00**
Advertising, Campbell's, figural Garden Vegetable soup can, metal, paper label, contains seed packets, 4½" h **12.00**
Advertising, Citco, Model T Delivery truck, painted metal, orig box, 6" h **33.00**
Advertising, Curad, Taped Crusader, vinyl, 1970s **95.00**
Advertising, Elephant Castle Restaurant, figural elephant, ceramic **45.00**
Advertising, Esso, tiger, vinyl, 1970s **45.00**
Advertising, Florida Oranges, Florida Orange Girl, vinyl **35.00**
Advertising, KFC, figural Colonel Sanders holding cane, vinyl **35.00**
Advertising, King Royal, 1960s **195.00**
Advertising, Kraft Macaroni & Cheese, Cheesasaurus Rex, vinyl **35.00**

Advertising, "Put a Tiger in Your Tank," hard rubber, 8" h, $35.00. Photo courtesy Collectors Auction Services.

Advertising, Magic Chef Ovens, figural Magic Chef, vinyl **25.00**
Advertising, Pepto Bismol, figural, 24 Hour Bug, vinyl, 1970s **95.00**
Advertising, Poppin' Fresh, ceramic, white, figural, plastic trap, Pillsbury Co copyright 1985 . . . . . . **15.00**
Advertising, Sinclair, figural Dino Dinosaur, metal, 8½" l. . . . **242.00**
Advertising, Snoboy Produce, figural Snoboy, vinyl, 8" h **190.00**
Advertising, Wonder Bread, figural wrapped bread loaf, vinyl, red, yellow, and blue spotted design with blue smiling cartoon face at each end, plastic disk trap, c1970s, 3 x 3 x 5" **90.00**
Advertising, Zeller's Department Store, figural Zeddy Bear, vinyl **55.00**
Cast Iron, globe, worn polychrome paint, 4⅝" h **135.00**
Cast Iron, mailbox, red and blue with raised white "Letters" on front, 1930s, 1¾ x 2½ x 4" **20.00**
Cast Iron, McKinley/Teddy, gold painted 3D elephant with raised jugate images of McKinley and Teddy Roosevelt, raised inscription "Prosperity" above their heads, 2½ x 3½" **400.00**
Cast Iron, safe, bronze finish, applied medallions of ladies' heads, 6½" h **50.00**
Ceramic, camera, Rolleicord, painted and glazed, opalescent luster, gold name and knobs, mkd "PAC/Japan," 1950s **55.00**
Character, Casper the Friendly Ghost, Renzi Co **20.00**
Character, Chewbacca, ceramic, painted and glazed, orig trap and "Sigma" sticker, Lucasfilm Ltd copyright 1983, 9½" h **25.00**
Figaro, Hagen-Renaker, ceramic, painted and glazed, Figaro with 1 paw raised, open area at mouth where coins are placed, 1950s, 3½ x 5 x 5¼" **200.00**

American Eagle Coin Bank, Emigrant Industrial Savings Bank, made by Contemporary Ceramics, Chatham, NJ, ceramic eagle, approx 8" h, orig box, $15.00.

Composition, painted, Story Town USA, storybook shoe house shape, yellow shoe with red roof, brown, blue, and black accents, raised name on front, c1960s, missing trap, 2½ x 5½ x 4¼" 25.00
Glass, Atlas-Mason Jar, clear glass jar with raised name and logo on front, complete with 2 pc metal lid, 1930s, 3¾" h 40.00
Glass, figural pig 10.00
Metal, Jackpot Dime, 6 x 3½" 20.00
Papier-mâché, Beatles, rubber plug, Pride Creations, 8" h 100.00

BARBED WIRE

Barbed wire is a farm, Western or military collectible. It is usually collected in 18-inch lengths and mounted on boards for display. While there are a few rare examples that sell in the hundreds of dollars for a piece, the majority of strands are common types that sell between $2 and $5 per sample.

Club: American Barbed Wire Collectors Society, 1023 Baldwin Rd., Bakersfield, CA 93304.

BARBERSHOP AND BEAUTY PARLOR COLLECTIBLES

Let's not discriminate. This is the age of the unisex hair salon. This category has been male-oriented for far too long. Haven't you wondered where a woman had her hair done in the 19th century? Don't forget drug store products. Not everyone had the funds or luxury to spend time each day at the barbershop or beauty salon.

Club: National Shaving Mug Collectors Assoc., 320 S. Glenwood St., Allentown, PA 18104.

Barber Bottle, Bonheur Eau De Quinine, reverse painted label, "The BonHeaur Co. Inc., Syracuse, N.Y.," smooth base, rolled lip, 6½" h $85.00
Barber Bottle, Fore After Shaving Bottle, glass and paper, A R Winarick Inc, New York, NY, 9½" h 60.00
Barber Bottle, Kings Barber Barbicide 20.00
Barber Bottle, Mrs S Allen's World's Hair Balsam, aqua, open pontil, tooled lip, "335 Broome St. New York," 6½" h 50.00
Barber Bottle, Opaline, 6¾" h 30.00
Barber Bottle, West Point Hair Tonic, screw lid, paper label, "Copyright 1935 by West Point Laboratories New York" at bottom of label, 8¼" h 25.00
Barber Bottle, Witch Hazel, milk glass, globular body, straight neck, floral deck, 7" h 60.00
Barber Chair, child's, wood with metal and porcelain base, glass eyes, detailed carving to horse, 48" h 3,000.00
Barber Pole, glass pole with red and white stripes, porcelain hexagonal end caps, metal wall mount, light-up style, 23" h, 5½" w 165.00
Barber Pole, top half of floor model, Padar, orig hand crank and glass tube, refinished, 1920 . . . . . 300.00
Barber Pole, white milk glass globe above black painted metal base with cylindrical white milk glass globe below, lower globe painted with gold-outlinedred and blue stripes, wall mounted, light-up style, replaced globe on top, 30" h 550.00

Bottle, Wild Root Hair Tonic, The Wildroot Co, Inc, Buffalo, NY, clear glass, paper labels on front and back, some orig contents, 4½" h, $55.00. Photo courtesy Collectors Auction Services.

Barber Pole, white milk glass globe atop white porcelain end caps on clear glass cylinder enclosing metal pole with red, white, and blue stripes, wall mount, 6" crack in glass cylinder, replaced center pole, 36" h 390.00
Barber Pole, William Marvy Co, serial #5492, metal frame and end caps, light-up milk glass cylinder with painted red and blue stripes, wall mounted, 24" h. 154.00
Barber Pole, wooden pole top with turned finial, hp red, white, and blue stripes, 42" g, 2½" d 110.00
Blade Bank, Yankee, tin, c1900 . . . . . 55.00
Box, Fairies Bath Perfume, unopened, 1920s 6.00
Can, Lucky Tiger Dandruff Remover, reverse with building of Lucky Tiger Remedy Co, 1 gal, 10½" h 90.00
Catalog, Human Hair Goods, color lithos, 1896, 24 pp 65.00
Decal, Rayette Dandruff Lotion, unused, 18½" h 60.00
Display, Pal Razor, cardboard, with 10 cartons of unopened Pal Gold Thin Razors, 17" h 130.00
Hair Net, Doloris 4.75
Hair Net, Jal-Net 5.50
Hair Tonic, Lan-Tox 12.00
Hair Treatment, Marchand's Hair Rinse 4.25
Hair Wax, Lucky Tiger, large jar 10.00
Jar, Antiseptic, frosted glass, metal lid, 10" h 55.00
Manual, The Barber's Hairdressers & Manicure's Manual, red cloth cov with black lettering, 82 pp, AB Moler, ©1900, 5¾x 4½" 45.00
Razor, bone handle, carved western scene, HC Wentworth & Co, Germany, #2266, 6" l 40.00
Razor, rubber handle with dec detail, 6" l. 35.00
Shaving Brush, aluminum handle, emb design, c1910 . . . . . 8.50
Shaving Mug, occupational, "A.J. Harris," detailed dec of man driving horse drawn buggy, 3½" h. 357.50

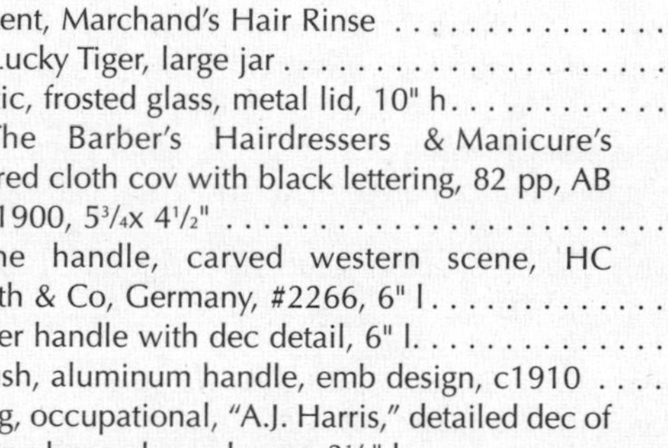

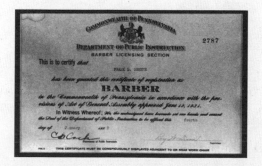

License, Commonwealth of Pennsylvania, Department of Public Instructions, 12½ x 9½" matted size, 1921, $18.00.

Shaving Mug, occupational, Telegraph, "C G Albright," laurel surround, gold leaf trim, 3¾" h 250.00
Shaving Mug, patriotic, "Frank Barbera," eagle with crossed American and Italian flags, full pink wrap, base stamped "Elite L. France," 3⅞" h. 253.00
Sign, Barber Bhop, reverse painting on glass, lights, 7" h. . . . 130.00
Sign, Beauty Shoppe, porcelain, 1-sided, 12" h. 375.00
Sign, Klondike Head Rub, cardboard, emb lettering and bottle, 8½ x 11" 155.00
Sign, Zepp's Dandruff Card, celluloid over metal, car board back, NJ Aluminum Co, Newark, NJ, 6 x 6" 250.00
Sign, Zepp's Hair Dressing, porcelain, flange, 2-sided, reverse with "Noonan's Hair Petrole For Falling Hair," Nelke-Veribrite Signs, NY, 12" h, 16½" w 300.00
Sterilizer, Antiseptic, wooden frame with metal edging and glass front and sides, 3 glass shelves, Emil J Paidar Co, Chicago & NY, 20" h. 235.00
Strop, razor blade stropping kit, Ingersoll, MIB 12.00
Tin, Bermarine Hair Dressing, sample, litho, round, 1⅝" d 20.00
Tin, Colgate's Rapid-Shave Powder, litho, round, 4" h 15.00
Tin, Griffen Safety Razor, litho, rect, 2¼" h. 60.00
Tin, Stein's Face Powder, litho, round, 4⅝ d 10.00
Toiletry Kit, Walgreen's, red box, includes talc, styptic powder and shaving cream, 1938. . . . . 125.00
Vending Machine, Gillette Razor Blade, metal, paper label, Modern Merchandising Corp, St Louis, MO, no key, 19" h 85.00

BARBIE DOLL COLLECTIBLES

As a doll, Barbie is unique. She burst upon the scene in the late 1950s and has remained a major factor in the doll market for more than 40 years. No other doll has enjoyed this longevity. Every aspect of Barbie is collectible, from the doll to her clothing to her play accessories. Although collectors place the greatest emphasis on Barbie material from the 1950s and 1960s, there is some great stuff from the 1970s and 1980s that should definately not be overlooked. Whenever possible, try to get original packaging. This is especially important for Barbie material from the 1980s forward.

Club: Barbie Doll Collectors Club International, P.O. Box 586, White Plains, NY 10603.

Periodicals: *Barbie Bazaar,* 5617 6th Ave., Kenosha, WI 53140; *Miller's Barbie Collector,* P.O. Box 8722, Spokane, WA 99203.

McDonald's Happy Meal Box, Beachfront Fun, 1992, $1.50.

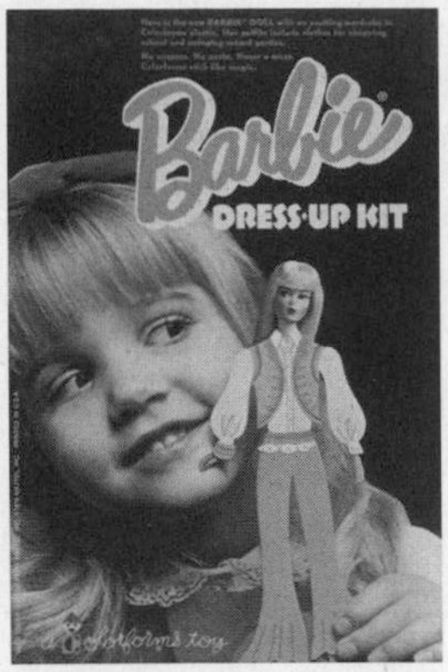

Barbie Dress-Up Kit, Colorforms, 1970, $40.00.

CLOTHING AND ACCESSORIES, MIB

Altogether Elegant, #1242, jacket, dress, gloves, bag, and shoes, 1970–71 . . . . $65.00
Baby-Dolls, #1957, 1968 . . . . 50.00
Barbie-Q Outfit, #962, 1959 . . . . 45.00
Bride's Dream, #947, 1963-65. . . . . 85.00
Dr Ken, #793, 1963–65. . . . . 95.00
Graduation, #795, cap, gown, and diploma, 1963–64 . . . . . . 95.00
Hooray For Leather, #1477, leather type skirt, knit top, and shoes, 1969–70 . . . . 55.00
Lawn Swing and Planter, # 0411, 1964 . . . . 90.00
Let's Dance, #978 . . . . 50.00
Long On Looks, #1227, 1969 . . . . 85.00
Malibu Barbie Beach Party Case, vinyl, white, hot pink, and orange designs, plastic window reveals Barbie wearing swimsuit, includes accessories, orig wrist bracelet, 1979 . . . . 175.00
Musical Rocking Chair, #31191, 1973 . . . . 20.00
Peachy Fleece Coat, #915 . . . . 50.00
Picnic Set, #967, blue jeans, red and white checkered blouse, straw hat, woven picnic basket, cork wedge shoes, green and grey fish on nylon line, sinker, and bamboo pole, 1959–61 . . . . 90.00
Plantation Belle, #966, 1959–60 . . . . 75.00
Red Sweater Fashion Pak, 1962 . . . . 40.00
Senior Prom, #951, green satin evening gown, light blue band, layered green tulle overskirt, green open-toed heels with pearl dec, 1963–64 . . . . 85.00
Skin Diver, #1406, 1964 . . . . 40.00
Time For Tennis, #790 . . . . 50.00
Wild 'N Wonderful, multicolored top and skirt, hot pants, plastic cut-out boots, 1969. 65.00

DOLLS

Allan, #1000, straight legs, red hair, 1964 . . . . $95.00
Barbie, Fashion Play Barbie, 1986 . . . . 15.00
Barbie, Fashion Queen Barbie, #870, 1963, MIB 350.00
Barbie, Swirl Ponytail Barbie, 1964, MIB 250.00
Barbie, Twist 'n Turn Barbie,1967, MIB. 350.00
Francie, Quick Curl Francie, #4222, 1973 . . . . 70.00
Ken, Mod Hair Ken, #4234, 1974 . . . . 40.0
Ken, Sparkle Eyes Ken, #3149, 1961 . . . . 20.00
Ken, Talking, #1111, 1969. . . . . 95.00
Midge, #860, straight legs, brunette, 1963 . . . . 120.00
P J, Gymnast P J, #7263, 1974. . . . . 70.00
P J, Live Action P J, #1156, 1971 . . . . 90.00
Skipper, Deluxe Quick Curl Skipper, #9428, 1975 . . . . 60.00

OTHER

Barbie Mattel-a-Phone, pink **$50.00**
Cookbook, Random House **45.00**
Game, Barbie Game—Queen of the Prom, Mattel, 1961 . . . . **40.00**
Play Set, DreamStore—FashionDepartment, 1982–84 . . . . **45.00**
Game, Barbie Keys To Fame, Mattel **30.00**
Manicure Set, Barbie Good Grooming Manicure Set, orig box **35.00**
Play Set, Barbie Fashion Stage, 1981 . . . . **65.00**
Play Set, Mountain Ski Cabin, #4283, 1972 . . . . **30.00**
Play Set, Olympic Ski Village, 1975 . . . . **45.00**
Play Set, The World of Barbie House, #1048, 1968 . . . . **45.00**
Playing Cards, Barbie Plastic Coasted Playing Cards, Nasta, Inc, 1979 . . . . **10.00**
Vehicle, Beach Bus, 1974–77 . . . . **50.00**
Vehicle, Corvette, Irwin Corp, ©Mattel, coral open-topped car, aqua, 2-seat interior, chrome trim, movable wheels, 1962–63 . . . . **85.00**
Vehicle, Country Camper, #4994, 1971 . . . . **25.00**
Vehicle, Starcycle, #2149, 1978 . . . . **20.00**
Vehicle, 10 Speed Bicycle, turning wheels, movable kickstand, 1974–77 . . . . **25.00**
Vehicle, Travelin' Trailer, #5489, 1982 . . . . **20.00**

BARWARE

During the late 1960s and early 1970s it became fashionable for homeowners to convert basements into family rec rooms, often equipped with bars. Most were well stocked with both utilitarian items (shot glasses and ice crushers) and decorative accessories. Objects with advertising are usually more valuable than their generic counterparts.

Cocktail Set, Art Deco, glass shaker, 6 tall glasses, 5 shorter glasses, frosted stippled surface, gold and colored mid bands, 1950s **$60.00**
Cocktail Shaker, aluminum, Buenilum, hand-wrought, straight sides, grooved Modernistic top, clear plastic knob lid **20.00**
Cocktail Shaker, The Konga, aluminum, plastic knobs, 1930s, 11¼" h. **150.00**
Decanter, Cambridge, Cleo pattern, pink, orig stopper **225.00**
Decanter, Waterford, Irish, cut crystal, Belfray pattern **150.00**
Ice Bucket, aluminum, hand-wrought, Lehman, double twisted handles, plastic knob **15.00**
Martini Set, glass, pheasants on pitcher and lgases, brass stirrer **18.00**

Cocktail Set, West Virginia Specialty Glass Co., ribbed standing cobalt glass dumbbell shaker, cocktail cups with sterling silver trim, 13" h x 4" d shaker, c1935, $200.00. Photo courtesy Norton Auctioneers.

Matchbook, Carstairs White Seal Blended Whiskey, oversized, blue, gold, and red, seal balancing ball on cov and matches, 1940s, unused, 3½ x 4½" **10.00**
Mixer, Yo-Yo Cocktail Mixer, Alabe Crafts, Cincinnati, OH, plastic and metal, 7¼" l **35.00**
Playing Cards, Johnnie Walker Black Label Scotch, yellow logo, black ground, "12 Years Old" **15.00**
Recipe Book, *Bottoms Up,* cocktail shaker shape, with attached bottle opener and cork screw, Bizza Co, NY, 1928, 6½ x 9" **100.00**
Recipe Book, *Tipple Tips on How to Fix 'em,* West Bend Aluminum Co, 1934, 24 pp **5.00**
Shot Glass, clear **1.00**
Stemware, cocktail, Tiffin, Cadena pattern, yellow, 5¼" h **25.00**

BASEBALL CARDS

Collecting baseball cards is no longer just for kids. It is an adult game. Recent trends include buying and stashing away complete boxed sets of cards, placing special emphasis on rookie and other types of cards, and speculation on a few "rare" cards that have a funny habit of turning up on the market far more frequently than one would expect from such rarities.

Baseball cards date from the late 19th century. The earliest series are tobacco company issues dating between 1909 and 1915. During the 1920s American Caramel, National Caramel, and York Caramel issued cards.

Goudey Gum Co. (1933 to 1941) and Gum, Inc. (1939), caried on the tradition in the 1930s. When World War II ended, Bowman Gum of Philadelphia, the successor to Gum, Inc., became the baseball giant. Topps, Inc., of Brooklyn, NY, followed. Topps purchased Bowman in 1956 and enjoyed almost a monopoly in card production until 1981 when Fleer of Philadelphia and Donruss of Memphis challenged its leadership.

In addition to sets produced by these major companies, there are hundreds of other sets issued by a variety of sources, ranging from product manufacturers, such as Sunbeam Bread, to Minor League teams. There are so many secondary sets now issued annually that it is virtually impossible for a collector to keep up with them at all. The field is plagued with reissued sets and cards, as well as outright forgeries. The color photocopier has been used to great advantage by unscrupulous dealers. Never buy cards from someone whom you can't find six months later.

The listing below is simply designed to give you an idea of baseball card prices in good to very good condition and to show you how they change, depending on the age of the cards that you wish to collect. For detailed information about card prices, consult the following price guides: James Beckett, *Beckett Baseball Card Price Guide No. 19,* Beckett Publications, 1997; Bob Lemke, ed., *Standard Catalog of Baseball Cards, 8th Edition,* Krause Publications, 1998; and *Sports Collectors Digest Baseball Card Price Guide, 12th Edition,* Krause Publications, 1998. Although Beckett is the name most often mentioned in connection with price guides, I have found the Krause guides to be more helpful.

Periodicals: *Beckett Baseball Card Monthly,* 15850 Dallas Parkway, Dallas, TX 75248; *Sports Cards,* 700 E. State St., Iola, WI 54990.

Bowman, 1948, complete set (48) **$450.00**
Bowman, 1948, #7 Pete Reiser **10.00**
Bowman, 1948, #9, Walker Cooper **2.50**

Bowman, 1950, complete set (252) **1,100.00**
Bowman, 1950, #78, Mickey Owen **2.50**
Bowman, 1950, #227, Bob Miller **2.00**
Bowman, 1955, complete set (320) **600.00**
Bowman, 1955, #81, Bobby Morgan **1.00**
Bowman, 1955, #168, Yogi Berra **11.00**
Donruss, 1981, complete set (605) **5.00**
Donruss, 1981, #179, Dusty Baker **.05**
Donruss, 1981, #251, Pete Rose **.25**
Donruss, 1988, complete set (660) **1.25**
Donruss, 1988, #277, Rickey Henderson **.02**
Fleer, 1961, complete set (154) **150.00**
Fleer, 1961, #153, Cy Young **5.00**
Fleer, 1981, complete set (660) **5.00**
Fleer, 1981, #5, Mike Schmidt **.25**
Fleer, 1981, #13, Keith Moreland **.03**
Hostess, 1975, complete set (150) **28.00**
Hostess, 1975, #59, Reggie Smith **.09**
Kellogg's, 1970, complete set (75) **25.00**
Kellogg's, 1970, #36, Jim Fregosi **.19**
Leaf, 1960, complete set (145) **220.00**
Leaf, 1960, 144, Jim Bunning **6.00**
Leaf Gold All-Stars, 1993, complete set (20) **5.00**
Score, 1990, complete set (704) **1.50**
Score, 1990, #140, George Brett **.05**
Topps, 1952, #33, Warren Spahn, regular back **200.00**
Topps, 1952, #36, Gil Hodges, black back **172.50**
Topps, 1952, #65, Enos Slaughter, black back **172.50**
Topps, 1956, complete set (340) **900.00**
Topps, 1956, #10, Yogi Berra **15.50**
Topps, 1958, complete set (494) **600.00**
Topps, 1958, #55, Chico Carrasquel **1.50**
Topps, 1961, complete set (587) **600.00**
Topps, 1961, #2, Roger Maris **20.00**
Topps, 1968, complete set (598) **375.00**
Topps, 1968, #86, Willie Stargell **1.00**
Topps, 1971, complete set (752) **250.00**
Topps, 1971, #525, Ernie Banks **5.25**
Topps, 1978, complete set (726) **38.00**
Topps, 1978, #112, Houston Astros team card **.12**
Topps, 1980, complete set (726) **60.00**
Topps, 1980, #160, Eddie Murray **1.75**
Topps, 1980, #482, Rickey Henderson **22.00**
Topps, 1981, complete set (726) **60.00**
Topps, 1981, #643, Lloyd Moseby **.50**
Topps, 1982, complete set (792) **15.50**
Topps, 1982, #80, Jim Palmer **.09**
Upper Deck, 1990, complete set (800) **3.00**
Upper Deck, 1990, #37, Tino Martinez **.05**
Upper Deck, 1990, #174, Mitch Williams **.01**
Upper Deck, 1993, complete set (840) **5.00**
Upper Deck, 1993, #38, Ryne Sandberg **.02**

BASEBALL MEMORABILIA

What a feast for the collector! Flea markets often contain caps, bats, gloves, autographed balls and photos of your favorite all-stars, baseball statues, regular and world series game programs and team manuals or rosters. Do not overlook secondary material such as magazine covers with a baseball theme. Condition and personal preference should always guide the eye.

Be careful of autograph forgeries. The general feeling among collectors is that more than 50 percent of the autographed baseballs being offered for sale have faked signatures. But do not let this spoil your fun. There is plenty of good stuff out there.

Clubs: Sociey for American Baseball Research, P.O. Box 93183, Cleveland, OH 44101; The Glove Collector Club, 14057 Rolling Hills Ln., Dallas, TX 75240.

Newsletter: *Diamond Duds,* P.O. Box 19153, Silver Springs, MD 20904.

Periodicals: *Baseball Hobby News,* 4540 Kearney Villa Rd., San Diego, CA 92123; *Sports Collectors Digest,* 700 E. State St, Iola, WI 54990; *Tuff Stuff,* P.O. Box 569, Dubuque, IA 52004.

Bank , Cleveland Indians, ceramic, 1950s **$185.00**
Baseball, autographed, Carl Hubbel, bold black marker signature **30.00**
Baseball, autographed, Cubs Team, 1986 **45.00**
Baseball, autographed, Ted Williams, blue ink signature "Best Wishes Ted Williams 1952" **125.00**
Beer Tray, Gil Hodges, round, 4 coasters, color picture **45.00**
Doll, Los Angeles Dodgers, 1960 **65.00**
Doll, New York Yankees, black and white uniform outfit, printed blue and white cap, 1960–70 **15.00**
Game, All-Pro Baseball, Ideal, 1967 **40.00**
Game, Base-Ball, Game of, McLaughlin Brothers, ©1886 **3,000.00**
Pass, Rochester Trolley, colorful baseball scene, 1935 **22.00**
Pencil, mechanical, Detroit Tigers/1940 champions, bat shape, brown inscription **30.00**
Pennant, Philadelphia Athletics, felt, navy blue, white inscription, 28" l **50.00**

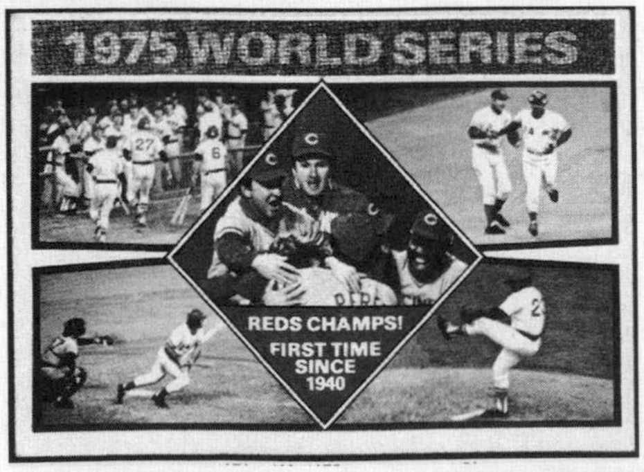

Topps, #462, 1975 World Series, front, 50¢.

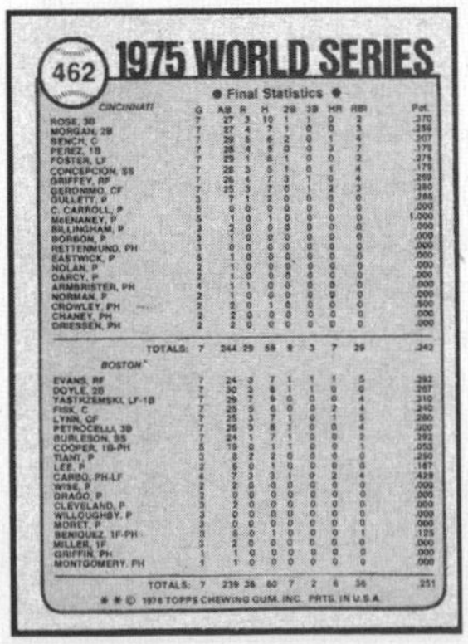

Topps, #462, 1975 World Series, back, 50¢.

Bank, figural baseball, glass, Pegasus horse one side, Indian head other side, metal screw cap on bottom with coin slot, 3" h, 3" d, $77.00. Photo courtesy Collectors Auction Services.

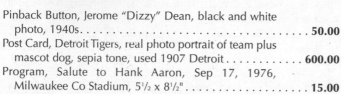

Storage basket, willow, 2 handles, 25½" h, 22" d, $150.00.

Pinback Button, Jerome "Dizzy" Dean, black and white photo, 1940s 50.00
Post Card, Detroit Tigers, real photo portrait of team plus mascot dog, sepia tone, used 1907 Detroit 600.00
Program, Salute to Hank Aaron, Sep 17, 1976, Milwaukee Co Stadium, 5½ x 8½" 15.00

BASKETBALL

As the price of baseball cards and baseball memorabilia continue to rise, collectors are turning to other sports categories based on the affordability of their material. Basketball and football are "hot" sport collecting fields.

Collecting generally centers around one team, as it does in most other sport collecting categories. Items have greater value in their "hometown" than they do "on the road." You know a category is gaining strength when its secondary material starts to bring consistently strong prices.

Periodicals: *Beckett Basketball Card Magazine,* 15850 Dallas Parkway, Dallas, TX 75248; *Sports Cards* and *Sports Collectors Digest,* 700 E. State St, Iola, WI 54990; *Tuff Stuff,* P.O. Box 569, Dubuque, IA 52004.

Autograph, Chris Mullin, card, 3 x 5" $7.00
Autograph, Nate Thurmond, basketball 25.00
Cereal Box, Karl Malone, Kellogg's Frosted Mini Wheats, Team USA, 1992 . . . . 20.00
Cereal Box, Michael Jordan, Wheaties, 1½ oz 3.00
Cereal Box, Larry Bird, Kellogg's Corn Flakes, Team USA, 1992 . . . . 15.00
Game, Basket Ball, Russell Mfg Co, #217, 1929 . . . . 85.00
Game, Harlem Globetrotters Game, Milton Bradley, 1971 . . . . 15.00
Magazine, *Basketball's Best,* Wilt Chamberlain, 1964–65 . . . . 20.00
Magazine, *Hoop,* Larry Bird, Jul 1986 . . . . 8.00
Pennant, Larry Johnson, Win Craft, 1992 . . . . 5.00
Punchboard, Play Basket Ball, 5¢, Havana Blend Cigar adv, red, blue, and white, 7¼ x 10" 17.50
Starting Lineup Figure, Kenner, Charles Barkley 20.00
Starting Lineup Figure, Kenner, Larry Bird 15.00
Trading Card, Fleer, 1993–94, complete set (400) 2.50
Trading Card, Skybox, 1990–91, complete set (423) 2.50
Trading Card, Topps, 1971–72, complete set (223) 95.00
Trading Card, Topps, 1972–73, #1, Wilt Chamberlain 4.00
Trading Card, Topps, 1973–74, #1, Kareem Abdul-Jabbar 3.50

BASKETS

A tisket, a tasket, who's got the basket? Baskets, ranging from old timers to contemporary craft types, are readily found at flea markets.

American Indian, Southeast, oblong, woven, polychrome plaiting of glossy natural and dark brown river cane, 4" h, 9¼" l $115.00
Bicycle, woven plastic cane, white, red and blue stripes, orig leather straps, c1960 . . . . 50.00
Bushel, stave construction, wrapped with wire bands, wooden rim, bentwood rim handles, old varnish finish, partial paper label 165.00
Cheese, woven splint, dark brown stained ext 55.00
Clothespin, willow, early 20th century, 14¼ x 12½" 85.00
Easter, round, colorful, high handle, Mexico, c1955 . . . . 5.00
Egg, woven splint, bentwood handle, weathered gray scrubbed finish, 15 x 17" 55.00
Gathering, woven splint, bentwood handle, rim repair, 15 x 19½", 6" H 45.00
Laundry, oval, woven splint, bentwood rim handles 50.00
Loom, hanging, cane, faded curlicued ribbon and string dec, 6¾" h, 7½" w 35.00
Pea Picking, oval, wide overlapping split wood, attached feet, full circular bentwood handle, 6" h, 16" l, 11" w 75.00
Pet, small round wooden feet, worn cushion 25.00
Picnic, woven splint, swivel handles, wooden lid, worn finish 65.00
Sewing, cov, round, tightly woven, stained brown, mkd "China" 10.00
Utility, boat shaped, woven handle, 7¼" h 55.00
Wedding, Navajo, polychrome, coiled, woven in typical material and design, 3" h, 12½" d 80.50
Wine, willow, divided int holds 12 bottles, factory made, early 20th century, 21¾" l 65.00

BATMAN

"Galloping globs of bat guano, Caped Crusader!" and similar cries may be heard as the Dark Knight and his sidekick are summoned to restore peace to Gotham City.

The saga of the search for Batman and Robin-related items began with Batman's appearance in 1939 in issue #27 of Detective Comics. Today, Boy Wonder and Caped Crusader collectibles are found in almost every medium imaginable. Local flea markets

Batmobile, Husky, #1403, diecast with painted Batman and Robin figures, 3" l, on orig bubble card, $160.00. Photo courtesy New England Auction Gallery.

offer a large variety of batgoodies capable of making any bat collector go batty!

Club: Batman TV Series Fan Club, P.O. Box 107, Venice, CA 90294.

Action Figure, Batman, animated series, Kenner, Anti-Freeze Batman **$15.00**
Action Figure, Batman, animated series, Kenner, Joker **30.00**
Action Figure, Batman, animated series, Kenner, Mr. Freeze . . **25.00**
Action Figure, Batman, animated series, Kenner, Robin **30.00**
Action Figure, Batman Returns, Kenner, Arctic Batman **20.00**
Action Figure, Batman Returns, Kenner, Catwoman **25.00**
Action Figure, Batman-The Dark Knight, Kenner, Bruce Wayne **20.00**
Action Figure, Batman-The Dark Knight, Kenner, Sky Escape Joker **45.00**
Batcave, Mego, 1980 . . . . **35.00**
Bat-Chute, CDC, unused, 1966 . . . . **40.00**
Batmobile, Simms, Inc, Aurora, IL, plastic, Batman and Robin figures inside clear plastic shell, on card with Batman punching Joker illus, 1966, 8" l **150.00**
Batmobile and Batboat Set, Corgi Jr, 1979, MOC **70.00**
Bat-Scope, Kellogg's premium, 1966 . . . . **40.00**
Cape, B&K, 1966, MIP **25.00**
Coloring Book, Whitman, Batman Meets Blockbuster, 40 pp, 1966, 8 x 11", neatly colored **8.00**
Doll, Robin, Mego, 1974, 7½" h **10.00**
Drinking Glass, Batgirl, Pepsi Super Series, 1976 . . . . **10.00**
Frame Tray Puzzle, Watkins-Strathmore, 1966 . . . . **10.00**
Game, Batman Card Game, Ideal, 1966 . . . . **50.00**
Game, Batman Forever, Battle at the Big Top, Parker Brothers, 1995 . . . . **15.00**

Bubble Gum Card, Flying Foes, #3 of 6 Penguin Puzzle Cards, ©1966, National Periodical Publications, $2.00.

Game, Batman Game, Milton Bradley, board game, 1966 . . . . **75.00**
Game, Batman Pin Ball Game, Marx, plastic and litho tin, ©National Periodical Publications, 1966 . . . . **100.00**
Mask, rubber, full head, ©DC Comics, 1989 . . . . **45.00**
Night Light, Sanpit, 1966, MOC **25.00**
Pinback Button, Button World, dynamic duo image, "Charter Member, Batman & Robin Society," 1966, 3" d **8.00**
Record, Picture Disc, RCA, 1988, unused **25.00**

BAUER POTTERY

J. A. Bauer established the Bauer Pottery in Los Angeles in 1909. Flowerpots were among the first items manufactured, followed by utilitarian items. Dinnerware was introduced in 1930. Artware came a decade later. The firm closed in 1962.

Newsletters: *Bauer Quarterly*, P.O. Box 2524, Berkeley, CA 94702.

Brusche Contempo, gravy boat, pink speck **$20.00**
Brusche Contempo, vegetable bowl, indigo brown, 7½" d **20.00**
La Linda, carafe, chartreuse, wood handle **20.00**
La Linda, chop plate, 13" d **25.00**
La Linda, creamer, turquoise **20.00**
La Linda, dinner plate, chartreuse, 9" d **15.00**
La Linda, shaker, turquoise **15.00**
La Linda, teapot, 8 cup, olive green **35.00**
La Linda, tumbler, 8 oz **13.00**
Monterey Moderne, butter dish **65.00**
Monterey Moderne, creamer and sugar, orange **55.00**
Monterey Moderne, cup, turquoise **20.00**
Monterey Moderne, pitcher, 2 qt, green **45.00**
Monterey Moderne, platter, yellow, 17" l **45.00**
Monterey Moderne, vegetable bowl, divided, blue **45.00**
Ring, casserole, red-brown, 6½" d **50.00**
Ring, cereal bowl, ivory **115.00**
Ring, coffee server, wood handle, 6 cup **28.00**
Ring, creamer and sugar, yellow **55.00**
Ring, dinner plate, white, 10" d **20.00**
Ring, pickle dish **20.00**
Ring, ramekin, orange-red **15.00**
Ring, saucer **45.00**
Ring, souffle dish **25.00**
Ring, soup bowl, burgundy, 7½" d **25.00**
Ring, tumbler, delph blue, metal handle, 6 oz **30.00**
Ring, vase, cylindrical, 6" h **45.00**

BEANIE BABIES

While there is an extremely active secondary resale market for Ty's Beanie Babies, it is highly manipulated and speculative. Prices fluctuate wildly. The Beanie Babies' bubble will burst, as did other contemporary collectibles such as Holiday Barbie, Precious Moments, and Tickle Me Elmo. The only question is when.

Many factors can contribute to the collapse of a speculative secondary market for a contemporary item. Several already are impacting on the Beanie Babies market. Dozens of companies have launched competitive products, e.g., the Idea Factory's Meanies and Walt Disney's cartoon character plush toys. Even Avon has gotten into the act. A general feeling has developed that prices have reached the ridiculous level. Many Beanie Babies advertised in the hundreds of dollars are going unsold. Finally, counterfeits are flooding the secondary market. United States Customs agents in Chicago have seized hundreds of couterfeit examples of high-end Beanie Babies, including 456 examples of Grunt, the red razorback boar. One collector reportedly paid $1,500 for a counterfeit Peanut the Elephant sold on the Internet.

The market is flooded with Beanie Baby price guides. Consider carefully how accurately they reflect the secondary retail market. A few years from now, their only value will be the ability to look nostalgically back on the craze and think "if I only sold then." The values listed below are highly conservativbe and far more realistic than those found in many Beanie Baby price guides. They reflect the market, they **DO NOT** prop the market. With a few exceptions, e.g., the very first Beanie Babies, most are selling at one-half to one-third of book—the more recent the example, the greater the discount. The Beanie Baby market collapse is at hand. A year from now, sellers will thank their lucky stars if they can get these prices.

The items are priced each. Beanie Babies without tags have little or no value. New Tag = hang tag with star; Old Tag = hang tag without star; R = retired; D = discontinued.

Periodicals: *Beans! Magazine,* P.O. Box 569, Dubuque, IA 52004; *Mary Beth's Beanie World Montly,* P.O. Box 500, Missouri City, TX 77459.

Ants the Anteater, new tag . . . **$15.00**
Bernie the St Bernard, new tag . . . **5.00**
Bones the Dog, R 5/1/98, old tag . . . **25.00**
Chip the Calico Cat, new tag . . . **5.00**
Coral the Fish, R 1/1/97, old tag . . . **60.00**
Cubbie the Bear, R 12/31/97, new tag . . . **10.00**
Cubbie the Bear, R 12/31/77, old tag . . . **35.00**
Digger the Crab, orange, R 7/1/95, old tag . . . **325.00**
Flash the Dolphin, R 5/11/97, new tag . . . **20.00**
Flash the Dolphin, R 5/11/97, old tag . . . **50.00**
Garcia the Bear, tie-dyed, R 10/1/97, new tag . . . **75.00**
Garcia the Bear, tie-dyed, R 10/1/97, old tag . . . **120.00**
Hoppity the Bunny, pink, R 5/1/98, new tag . . . **8.00**
Humphrey the Camel, R 12/31/95, old tag . . . **800.00**
Inky the Octopus, tan, with mouth, D 7/1/95, old tag . . . **300.00**
Inky the Octopus, tan, without mouth, D 7/1/94, old tag . . . **400.00**
Lucky the Ladybug, 11 printed spots, R 5/1/98, new tag . . . **8.00**
McDonald's Teenie Beanie Babies, 1997, R 4/97, new tag . . . **5.00**
McDonald's Teenie Beanie Babies, 1998, R 6/97, new tag . . . **3.00**
Pounce the Cat, new tag . . . **5.00**
Seamore the Seal, R 101/97, new tag . . . **60.00**
Seamore the Seal, R 10/1/97, old tag . . . **120.00**

Crunch the Shark, new tag, 1996, $9.00.

Sparky the Dalmatian, R 5/11/97, new tag . . . **30.00**
Squealer the Pig, R 5/1/98, new tag . . . **8.00**
Squealer the Pig, R 5/1/98, old tag . . . **35.00**
Stripes the Tiger, orange, D 7/1/96, old tag . . . **150.00**
Tank the Armadillo, 7 ridges, R 7/1/96, new tag . . . **80.00**
Tank the Armadillo, 7 ridges, R 7/1/96, old tag . . . **95.00**
Teddy the Teal Bear, new or old face, R 7/1/95, old tag . . . **550.00**
Twigs the Giraffe, R 5/1/98, new tag . . . **8.00**
Twigs the Gireaffe, R 5/1/98, old tag . . . **25.00**
Velvet the Panther, R 10/1/97, new tag . . . **40.00**
Velvet the Panther, R 10/1/97, old tag . . . **15.00**
Wise the Owl, new tag . . . **5.00**
Zip the Cat, all black, D 7/1/95, old tag . . . **750.00**

BEATLES

Ahhh! look, it's the Fab Four! The collector will never need Help to find Beatle memorabilia at a flea market—place mats, dishes, records, posters and much more. The list is a Magical Mystery Tour. John, Paul, George and Ringo can be found in a multitude of shapes and sizes. Examine them carefully. They are likely to be heavily played with, so conditions will vary from poor to good.

Clubs: Beatles Connection, P.O. Box 1066, Pinellas Park, FL 34665; Working Class Hero Beatles Club, 3311 Niagara St., Pittsburgh, PA 15123.

Periodicals: *Beatlefan,* P.O. Box 33515, Decatur, GA 30033; *Good Day Sunshine,* P.O. Box 1008, Los Angeles, CA 90066; *Instant Karma,* P.O. Box 256, Sault Ste. Marie, MI 49783; *Strawberry Fields Forever,* P.O. Box 880981, San Diego, CA 92168.

Animation Cel, from cartoon *Yellow Submarine,* gouache on celluloid, George with arms outstretched, almost full-length, three-quarters seen from behind, scene references along bottom edge, 7½" h . . . **$450.00**
Banner, rayon, metal shaft, photos, "Die Beatles," German . . . **8.00**
Binder, 3-ring, vinyl cov cardboard, Standard Plastic Products, ©NEMS Enterprises Ltd, photo image on front surrounded by facsimile signatures, 1964, 10¼ x 11¾" . . . **90.00**
Coin Purse, fabric, gold colored metal top rim and closure, each side features John Lennon illus with facsimile signature on guitar, 1960s, 3½ x 4" . . . **85.00**
Comb, plastic, Beatles and signature label, Lido Toys, 1964, 3¼ x 15" . . . **90.00**

Puzzle, The Beatles Yellow Submarine, "Sgt. Pepper Band," copyright 1968 King Features Syndicate, unopened box, 650 pcs, 19 x 19", $5.00.

Game, Beatles Flip Your Wig Game, Milton Bradley, 1964 . . . . **125.00**

Lobby Card, Mexican, text in English and Spanish, inset black-and-white photo with image of Beatles sitting in directors chairs having their hair combed, c1970s re-release, 12 x 16¼" **100.00**

Magazine, *Post,* Aug 8–15, 1964, 8 pp article, color photos **15.00**

Pin Set, set of 8, hard plastic pin with metal clasps, hp, figural pin including 1 for each Beatle, Blue Meanie and 3 other characters from *Yellow Submarine,* c1968 . . . . . **75.00**

Poster, *Help,* Americn three-sheet, 1965, 41 x 81" **632.00**

Record, *She Loves You/I'll Get You,* 45 rpm, Swan, paper sleeve with black and white group photo on front and back, 1964 . . . . **65.00**

Sheet Music, *Help!,* cov photo, ©1965 Northern Songs Ltd, 8½ x 11" **25.00**

Sweatshirt, red cotton, design on chest in black with Beatles portraits and "Yea Yea/Beatles" worn and washed, c1964 . . . . **90.00**

Thermos, metal, color illus, blue plastic cup, 6½" h **75.00**

Ticket, *The Beatles/Hard Day's Night,* cardboard, black and yellow, photo image, Washington Theater, Royal Oak, MI **20.00**

BEATNIK MEMORABILIA

After World War II, a variety of disaffected people—returning G.I.'s, jazz musicians, liberal writers, and other nonconformists—began to coalesce in Greenwich Village in New York City and the North beach area of San Francisco. They were dissatisfied with the conventional values of society. They were interested in seeing the world in terms of creativity rather than commerce. They were provocative in appearance and attitude.

In the 1950s, a number of authors, including Allen Ginsberg, Jack Kerouac, and William Burroughs received mainstream exposure. They, and those who believed as they did in an alternative view of society, became known as "Beats" or "Beatniks." Books, records, posters, pamphlets, leaflets, and other items associated with the era are highly collectible. Although widely ridiculed in their day, the contributions they made to art, literature, and music are recognized for their importance and significance in American culture. The "Beats" continued the tradition of Bohemian nonconformity and produced thousands of very desirable items for collectors from 1947–1962.

Advisor: Richard M. Synchef, 22 Jefferson Ave., San Rafael, CA 94903, (415) 507-9933.

Note: Prices listed for items in excellent to near mint condition. All books are first editions with dust jackets in near fine or better condition.

Beatnik Kit, contains beret, cigarette holder, and beard, plastic package, c1950s, 12 x 11" **$50.00**

Book, *Beat Generation and the Angry Young Men, The,* Feldman, Gene, and Gartenberg, Max (eds.), Dell, NY, 1959 . . . . **125.00**

Book, *H Is For Heroin,* Hulburd, David, Doubleday & Co, NY, "A Teen-age narcotic tells her story," 1952 . . . . **90.00**

Booklet, *Beat Talk,* Studio Press, Tulsa, OK, 1960, 30 pp **100.00**

Booklet, *Berlin,* Ferlinghetti, Lawrence, Golden Mountain Press, 1961, 8 pp of poetry **100.00**

Folder, The Beat Generation, MGM promotional film tie-in, 1959, 8 pp, 8½ x 11", $250.00.

Booklet, *Nova Convention, The,* Nov 30–Dec 2, 1978, New York City, Burroughs, 12 pp **150.00**

Booklet, *Prospectus for a Naked Lunch,* Burroughs, William, Grove Press, NY, 1962, 16 pp **175.00**

Handbill, poetry reading, Kenneth Rexroth, Ginsberg, Ferlinghetti, Kandel, University of California at Santa Barbara gym, April 18, 1970 . . . . **450.00**

Magazine, *Fruitcup,* Beach Books Texts and Documents, San Francisco, 1969 . . . . **90.00**

Magazine, *Journal for the Protection of All Beings,* #1, City Lights Books, San Francisco, 1961 . . . . **175.00**

Magazine, *Life,* "Squaresville vs Beatsville," Sept 21 1959 . . . . **50.00**

Magazine, *Playboy,* The Beat Issue, Jul 1959 . . . . **80.00**

Magazine, *Startling Detective,* "My Life as a Beatnik," Mar 1961 . . . . **75.00**

Magazine, *The Second Coming,* William Borrough's chapter from *Nova Express,* Mar 1962 . . . . **150.00**

Paperback Book, *Beatville,* USA, Mandel, George, Avon, New York, 1961 . . . . **50.00**

Paperback Book, *Naked Lunch,* Burroughs, William, Grove Press, New York, 1962 . . . . **400.00**

Paperback Book, *Planet News,* Ginsberg, Allen, City Lights Books, San Francisco, Pocket Poet Series #23, 1968 . . . . **200.00**

Paperback Book, *Wholly Communion,* Lorrimar Films, London, 1965 . . . . **85.00**

Poster, *The Beard,* Michael McClure's award-winning play, premiere, Mar 31, 1965, San Francisco **550.00**

Poster, poetry reading, Ginsberg, Felinghetti, McClure, di Prima, University of California, Berkeley, Aug 19, 1971 . . . . **250.00**

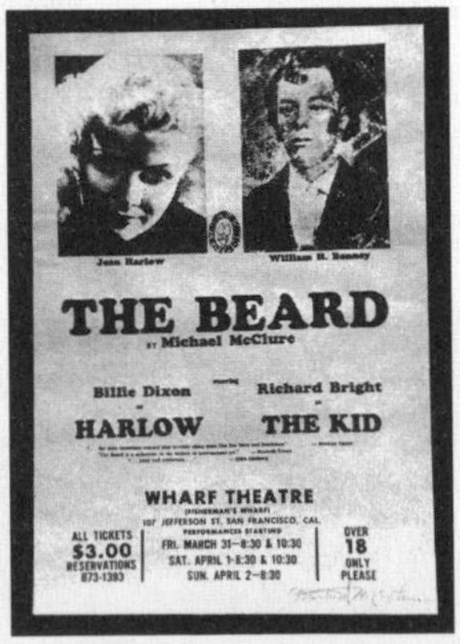

Handbill, The Beard, **Michael McClure's controversial award-winning play, premiere performance, 11 x 7", $350.00.**

Record, *Lenny Bruce—American,* monaural LP, Fantasy Records, #7011, red vinyl, 1961 . . . . **120.00**
Record, *Poetry for the Beat Generation,* Kerouac, Jack, monaural LP, Hanover Records, Kerouac reading poetry accompanied by Steve Allen on piano **450.00**
Record, The Beatniks, 45 rpm, movie promotional tie-in, 1960 . . . . **125.00**

BEER CANS

Beer can collecting was very popular in the 1970s. Times have changed. The field is now dominated by the serious collector and most trading and selling goes on at specialized beer can-ventions.

The list below contains a number of highly sought-after cans. Do not assume these prices are typical. Most cans fall in the 25-cent to 50-cent range. Do not pay more unless you are certain of the resale market.

There is no extra value to be gained by having a full beer can. In fact, selling a full can of beer without a license, even if only to a collector, violates the liquor laws in a large number of states. Most collectors punch a hole in the bottom of the can and drain out the beer.

Finally, before you ask, Billy Beer, either in individual cans, six packs or cases, is not worth hundreds or thousands of dollars. The going price for a can among collectors is between 5 cents and $1. Billy Beer has lost its fizz.

Club: Beer Can Collectors of America, 747 Mercus Ct., Fenton, MO 63026.

Black Label, Carling Brewing Co, red can, black label, map of US or world, pull top, 12 oz **$10.00**
Buffalo Brew, Cold Spring Brewing Co, orange can, block house illus, flat top, 12 oz **2.00**
Bull Dog Lager, Acme Breweries, Inc, maroon can, white label, flat top, 12 oz **60.00**
Busch Bavarian, Anheuser-Busch, circles on face, blue outer circle, pull top, 12 oz **3.00**
Coors Banquet Beer, Adolph Coors Co, Golden, CO, yellow can, bright gold trim, flat top, 12 oz **25.00**
Falstaff Draft, Falstaff Brewing Corp, white can, Falstaff shield, "Draft" on blue ribbon, tab top, 16 oz **10.00**
Fisher Premium Light, General Brewing Corp, Azusa, CA, metallic gold and red label, gold scrolling, "Premium Light" on blue band, flat top, 12 oz **20.00**
Hamm's Draft Beer Genuine Draft, Theodore Hamm Brewing Co, barrel shaped can, blue label, pull top, 12 oz **3.00**
Heritage House, Pittsburgh, PA, pull top, 12 oz **3.50**
Manheim, Reading, PA, flat top, 10 oz **8.00**
Old Milwaukee Genuine Draft, Pabst Brewing Co, red and white can, flat top, 16 oz **5.00**
Pabst Blue Ribbon Bock, Pabst Brewing Co, Pabst shield, goat on red ribbon, tab top, 12 oz **5.00**
Progress, Oklahoma City, OK, flat top, 11 oz **75.00**
Regal Premium, Florida Brewing Co, white can, blue label, flat top, 12 oz **2.00**
Rheingold Extra Dry Lager, Rheingold Brewing Co, white can, red label, flat top, 12 oz **20.00**
Schmidt's, E&B Brewing Co, silver can, black shield, white label, flat top, 12 oz **40.00**
Zobelein's East Side, Los Angeles Brewing Co, blue can, red label, large eagle, cone top, 12 oz **90.00**

BELLS

Bell collectors are fanatics. They tend to want every bell they can find. Admittedly, most confine themselves to bells that will fit on a shelf, but there are those who derive great pleasure from an old school bell sitting on their front lawn.

Be alert for wine glasses that have been converted into bells. They are worth much less than bells that began life as bells. Also, collect Limited Edition bells because you like them, rather than with the hope they will rise in value. Many Limited Edition bells do not ring true on the resale market.

Clubs: American Bell Assoc. International, Inc, P.O. Box 19443, Indianapolis, IN 46219.

Brass, owl, emb feathers and features, 4" h **$45.00**
China, figural, chef, holding wine bottle and glass, Occupied Japan, 3" h **24.00**
China, figural cow, light blue, pink roses, gilded handle, Limoges, 4" h **40.00**
Cow, brass, iron clapper, 3½" h **30.00**
Cow, sheet iron, handmade, orig leather strap, unmkd, 5" h **25.00**
Desk, bronze, white marble base, side tap, c1875 . . . . **45.00**
Glass, cranberry, gold edge, acid leaves **30.00**
Glass, Degenhart, Bicentennial, canary **15.00**
Glass, Imperial, Carnival, figural, Southern Belle, white **38.00**
Hand, brass, figural, turtle, bell bracket and striker on shell **30.00**
Horse, metal strap, 4 graduated cast bells, painted black, probably nailed to wagon shaft, 8" l **125.00**
Lawn Ornament, metal, cast iron dolphin frame on wooden base, engraved "Dunrovin 1940," 26" h **385.00**

BELT BUCKLES

This is a category loaded with reproductions and fakes. Beware of any cast buckle signed Tiffany. Suprisingly, many collectors do not mind the fakes. They like the designs and collect them for what they are.

A great specialized collection can be built around military buckles. These can be quite expensive. Once again, beware of recasts and fakes, especially Nazi buckles.

Club: Buckle Buddies International, 3208 Jackson Dr., Holiday, FL 34691.

Advertising, Bull's Head, lady's **$35.00**
Advertising, Hire's Root Beer, "Drink Hires" **5.00**

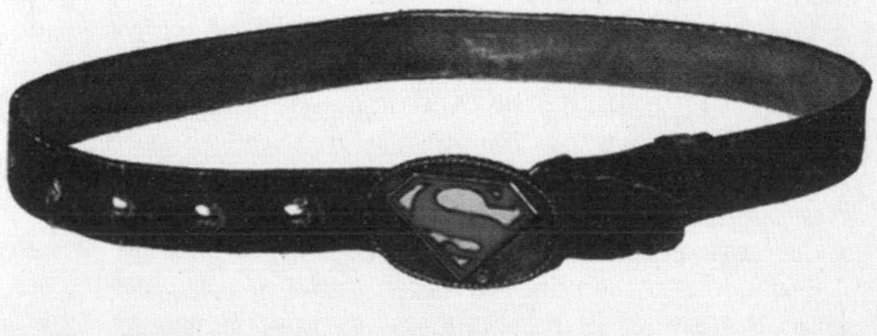

Child's, cloisonné Superman buckle with belt, $71.50. Photo courtesy Collectors Auction Services.

Advertising, Planters Peanuts, figural Mr Peanut, metal, gold tone **10.00**
Advertising, Stroh's Beer **5.00**
Brass, New York City Police **75.00**
Character, Davy Crockett, silvered metal, raised border, inscription, Old Betsy rifle, $1\frac{1}{2} \times 3"$ **25.00**
Character, Mickey Mouse, Sun Rubber Co, 1937 . . . . **45.00**
Character, Red Ryder, silvered brass, cowboy on bronco, name spelled twice in rope script, 1940s, 2" sq. **35.00**
Military, Austrian, steel, gray painted finish **55.00**
Mother-of-Pearl, chrome hasp, c1930. . . . . **10.00**
Sterling Silver, baroque, c1900 . . . . **65.00**

BIBLES

The general rule to follow is that any Bible less than 200 years old has little or no value in the collectibles market. For a number of reasons, individuals are reluctant to buy religious items. Bibles are proof positive that nothing is worth anything without a buyer.

Many have trouble accepting this argument. They see a large late 19th century family Bible filled with engravings of religious scenes and several pages containing information about the family. It is old and impressive. It has to be worth money. Alas, it as mass produced and survived in large quantities. The most valuable thing about it is the family data and this can be saved simply by copying the few pages involved on a photocopier.

An average price for a large family Bible from the turn of the century is between $25 and $50. Of course, there are Bibles that sell for a lot more than this. Never speculate when buying a Bible; God would not like it.

Dutch, 1657, Amsterdam, *Biblia Sacra, dat is de Geheele Heylighe Schhrifture,* Christoffel Van Sichem, 2 vol, engraved title, woodcuts, old suede and calf, 12 x 5" . . . **$500.00**
English, 1668, *Holy Bible,* Cambridge, John Field, engraved title with fine architectural border by John Chantry, Van Hove copperplates, 19th century mottled calf, neatly rebacked, gilt edges, 8 x 10" **350.00**
English, 1798, *Bible,* Nuremberg, J L Bugel, 2 engraved titles, over 250 plates, contemporaty calf gilt over wooden boards, loose binding, lacking clasps, 8 x 10" . . . **350.00**
English, 1810, London, *The Christian's New and Complete British Family Bible,* A Hogg, morocco gilt, 12 x 5" **195.00**
German, *Biblia, Das 1st: Die Ganze Gottliche Heilige Schrift...Erst Auflage,* Reading, PA, Gottlob Jungmann, contemporary polished calf binding, 1,235 pp, 8 x 10" . . . **125.00**

BICENTENNIAL

America's 200th birthday in 1976 was PARTY TIME for the nation. Everyone and everything in the country had something stamped, painted, printed, molded, cast and pressed with the commemorative dates 1776–1976. The American spirit of "overdo" and "outdo" always puts our nation in a great mood. We certainly overdid it during the Bicentennial.

The average flea market will have a wide variety of Bicentennial goodies. Prices have come down in recent years as the patriotic spirit waned and the only buyers left in the market were the collectors. Remember the Bicentennial was only 23 years ago. This is one category where you only want to buy in fine or better condition.

"Bicentennial Observance of Signing the Declaration of Independence," red and blue with "1776–1976," Liberty Bell, eagle, and flag, banner with $3\frac{1}{4}"$ h, $2.00.

Drinking Glass, A&P Ann Page Peanut Butter Bicentennial Celebration, Liberty Bell, 1976 . . . . **$2.00**
Drinking Glass, Coca-Cola Heritage Collector Series, Patrick Henry, "Give Me Liberty or Give Me Death," 1976. . . . . **3.00**
Drinking Glass, National Flag Foundation, Anchor Hocking, Early Flags of Our Nation, series 1974-96 . . . . **3.00**
Drinking Glass, Pittsburgh Press Bicentennial Collection, Confederate Battle Flag, 1974 . . . . **7.00**
Drinking Glass, Wendy's *New York Times* Headlines Limited Edition Series, "Nation and Millions in City Joyously Hail Bicentennial," 1981 . . . . **3.00**
Jar, clear glass, emb "Liberty Cherries Jar 1776-1976," metal lid with flag and black letters, $6 \times 6\frac{1}{2}"$ **8.00**
Pinback Button, oval, white Statue of Liberty, brown accents, yellow ground, red and white dates "1776" and "1976," white lettered "Bicentennial," $2\frac{3}{8}"$ l. **10.00**

BICYCLES

Bicycles are divided into two groups—antique and classic. Chances of finding an antique bicycle, such as a high wheeler, at a flea market are slim. Chances of spotting a great balloon tire classic are much greater.

Do no pay much for a bicycle that is incomplete, rusted, or repaired with non-original parts. Replacement of parts that deteriorate, e.g., leather seats, is acceptable. It is not uncommon to heavily restore a bicycle, i.e., to make it look like new. If the amount of original parts is less than half, question an extremely high price.

There is a great market in secondary material from accessories to paper ephemera in bicycle collectibles. Since most bicycle fanatics haunt the automobile flea markets, you might just get lucky and find a great bicycle item at a low cost at an antiques and collectibles flea market.

Clubs: Classic Bicycle & Whizzer Club of America, 35769 Simon Dr., Clinton Township, MI 48035; International Veteran Cycle Assoc., 248 Highland Dr., Findlay, OH 45840; The Wheelmen, 55 Bucknell Ave., Trenton, NJ 08619.

Newsletter: *Bicycle Trader,* P.O. Box 3324, Ashland, OR 97520; *Classic & Antique Bicycle Exchange,* 325 W. Hornbeam Dr., Longwood, FL 32779.*Classic Bike News,* 5046 E. Wilson Rd., Clio, MI 48420.

Periodicals: *Antique/Classic Bicycle News,* P.O. Box 1049, Ann Arbor, MI 48106; *National Antique & Classic Bicycle,* P.O. Box 5600, Pittsburgh, PA 15207.

BICYCLES

Columbia, boy's, Five Star Superb, 3-speed, 2-tone cream and maroon, orig paint, 1952 . . . . **$875.00**
Elgin, girl's, orig pod stop-tail light, Stewart warner floating hub, c1940s **375.00**
Firestone, Deluxe Speed Cruiser, 1959 . . . . **450.00**
Firestone Pilot, boy's, orig red and white paint, basket, and chrome carrier, orig condition, 26" **165.00**
Rover Tandem, repainted, c1900 . . . . **300.00**
Schwinn, boy's, Collegiate Sport, 5-speed, bright yellow, c1970 . . . . **75.00**
Schwinn, boy's, Scrambler, red paint, c1975, 20" **50.00**
Schwinn, Jaguar Mark 2, 3-speed, with horn tank, phantom rack and tail light, book rack, crash rail seat, and Westwind white wall tires, 1955 . . . . **450.00**
Schwinn, girl's, Fair Lady, yellow, 1960s **65.00**
Schwinn, girl's, Lil Chik, blue and white, orig condition, c1969, 20" **110.00**
Schwinn, Whizzer Pacemaker, orig paint, 24" cantilever frame **700.00**
Sting Ray Toronado, orig condition, 1970s **75.00**
Swiss, Alenax, boy's, light blue, lever action, 27" **325.00**
Westfield 50th Anniversary, girl's, with headlight, full coverage chain guard and drop stand, orig condition, c1937 . . . . **165.00**

BICYCLE RELATED

Book, *Cycle Guide*, Bicycling and Trade Review, Philadelphia, PA, Mar, Apr, May, and Jun, 1897 . . . . **$25.00**
Cabinet Card, photo of White Cycling Academy, c1890–1910, 6 x 8" **65.00**
Catalog, Keating Bicycles, 1897–1898 . . . . **45.00**
Light Schwinn Phantom, chrome, battery operated **60.00**
Pedals, girl's, glass reflectors, Schwinn **50.00**
Pinback Button, "A.C.C. Meet/Linton vs. Elkes/Charles River Park Cambridge/May 30, 1898," with 6-man pacer, 1¼" d **35.00**
Pinback Button, "Kenilworth-Wheelmen/1897/Phila. Aug. 4,5,6,7," with K-W and LAW logos, 1¾" d **35.00**
Plate, transfer dec, "Les Sports No. 11 Bicyclette," women and men riding safeties, sgd "Terre De Fer France, 19th century **40.00**
Sheet Music, *New York and Coney Island Cycle March Two-Step*, E T Paull Music Co, NY, c1896 . . . . **60.00**
Sign, electric, "Columbia Since 1877, America's First Bicycle," plastic, ribbed metal frame, c1950–60 . . . . **105.00**

Western Flyer, Westfield, MA, reflector on front, luggage rack, chrome light, streamers in handle bars, 38" h, 72" l, $665.50. Photo courtesy Collectors Auction Services.

Radio Patrol, Trailing The Safeblowers, #1173, $20.00.

BIG LITTLE BOOKS

The first Big Little Book was published by Whitman Publishing Co., in 1933. As with any successful endeavor, copycats soon appeared. Saalfield Publishing Co., was first with the introduction of its line of Little Big Books. Lesser known and less successful imitators include Engel-Van Wiseman, Lynn Publishing Co., Goldsmith Publishing Co., and Dell Publishing Co.

Condition and story content are the keys to determining value. Prices listed are for books in fine condition.

Air Fighters of America, #1448 . . . . **$18.00**
Alley Oop and Dinny, #763 . . . . **20.00**
Apple Mary and Dennie Foil the Swindlers, #1130 . . . . **18.00**
Big Chief Wahoo, #1443 . . . . **20.00**
Blaze Brandon with the Foreign Legion, #1447 . . . . **10.00**
Blondie, Who's The Boss?, #1423 . . . . **20.00**
Captain Easy Behind Enemy Lines, #1474 . . . . **15.00**
Coach Bernie Bierman's Brick Barton and the Winning Eleven, #1480 . . . . **10.00**
Convoy Patrol, #1446 . . . . **10.00**
Flame Boy and the Indians' Secret, #1464 . . . . **10.00**
Gangbusters Step In, #1433 . . . . **10.00**
Houdini's Magic, #715 . . . . **40.00**
International Spy, Dr Doom Faces Death at Dawn, #1148 . . . . **15.00**
Jim Starr of the Border Patrol, #1428 . . . . **15.00**
Lieutenant Commander Don Winslow U S N, #1107 . . . . **25.00**
Little Women, #757 . . . . **20.00**
Our Gang Adventures, #1456 . . . . **35.00**
Texas Kid, #1429 . . . . **15.00**

BISQUE

Every time I look at a bisque figure, I think of grandmothers. I keep wondering why I never see a flea market table labeled "Only things a grandmother would love."

Bisque is pottery ware that has been fired once and not glazed. It is a technique that is centuries' old and is still being practiced today. Unfortunately, some of today's figures are exact copies of those made hundreds of years ago. Be especially aware of bisque piano babies.

Collectors differentiate between Continental (mostly German) and Japanese bisque with premiums generally paid for Continental pieces. However, the Japanese made some great bisque. Do not confuse the chape five-and-dime "Occupied Japan" bisque with the better pieces.

Cigar Holder, tree stump, bird chasing insect, Germany, 19th C, $4\frac{1}{4}$" h . . . **$35.00**
Fairy Lamp, cat's head, white, amber eyes, $3\frac{1}{4}$" h . . . **250.00**
Figure, baby, crawling, brown human hair, blue gown, pink sash and slippers, $3\frac{1}{2}$" h . . . **195.00**
Figure, girl, dancing, cream and green pleated dress, white lace collar, blond hair, mkd "Heubach," $8\frac{1}{4}$" h . . . **165.00**
Figure, Mickey Mouse, riding Pluto, repainted, c1930, $2\frac{1}{8}$" h . . . **75.00**
Figure, Russian man, playing concertina, sq base, mkd "Gardner," $7\frac{1}{2}$" h . . . **425.00**
Match Holder, Dutch girl, copper and gold trim . . . **35.00**
Nodder, Indian Princess, light blue robe, gold trim $3\frac{3}{4}$" h . . . **125.00**
Nodder, jester, seated holding pipe, pastel peach and white, gold trim $2\frac{1}{2}$ x $3\frac{1}{2}$" . . . **75.00**
Planter, girl with water jug, sitting by well, coral and green . . . **50.00**
Salt, figural walnut, cream, branch base, matching spoon, 3" d . . . **70.00**
Shoe, man's, real shoelaces, brown and white, 5 x $1\frac{3}{4}$ x 2" . . . **75.00**

BIZARRE ART

There is some really great stuff made by senior citizen groups and community organizations that can be found at local bazaars, church rummage sales and so on. Of course, after a few years, these items often turn up at flea markets.

Some bazaar craftspeople also create unique decorative accessories that may hold some resale value. Other stuff is just "stuff" and can be had for pennies on the dollar. Perhaps some day this tacky stuff will catch a decorator's eye and skyrocket in value!

Boo Boo Bear, made from washcloth . . . **$.50**
Coasters, set of 4, with holder, needlepoint on plastic mesh, colorful . . . **2.50**
Cat Toy, felt, catnip stuffing . . . **2.00**
Dog Pull Toy, braided cloth . . . **1.50**
Door Decoration, straw hat, fabric flowers dec, cloth band . . . **5.00**
Footstool, fabric cov over large juice cans . . . **2.00**
Ornament, candy airplane, handmade . . . **1.00**
Ornament, cinnamon sticks, dec, handmade . . . **1.00**
Ornament, reindeer, made from clothespin and felt . . . **1.00**
Ornament, sled, made from popsicle sticks, glitter dec . . . **1.50**
Telephone Book Cover, needlepoint on plastic mesh . . . **4.00**
Toilet Paper Holder, crocheted, round, plain . . . **1.00**
Toilet Paper Holder, crocheted, poodle style . . . **5.00**
Wreath, made from pinecones, well made and dec . . . **5.00**

BLACK MEMORABILIA

Black memorabilia is enjoying its second renaissance. It is one of the "hot" areas in the present market. The category is viewed quite broadly, ranging from slavery-era items to objects showing ethnic stereotypes. Prices range all over the place. It pays to shop around.

Because Black memorabilia embodies a wide variety of forms, the Black memorabilia collector is constantly competing with collectors from other areas, e.g., cookie jar, kitchen and salt and pepper collectors. Surprisingly enough, it is the collectors of Black memorabilia who realize the extent of the material available and tend to resist high prices.

Reproductions, from advertising signs (Bull Durham Tobacco) to mechanical banks (Jolly Nigger), are an increasing problem. Remember—if it looks new, chances are that it is new.

Club: Black Memorabilia Collector's Assoc., 2482 Devoe Ter., Bronx, NY 10468.

Newsletter: *Lookin Back At Black,* 6087 Glen Harbor Dr., San Jose, CA 95123.

Advertising Trade Card, Singer Sewing Machine, black women smoking, 1 using machine, c1890, 3 x 5" . . . **$7.50**
Bobbing Head, black boy holding banana and apple, painted composition, charcoal black with white eyes with thin blue accents, brown eyebrown markings, pink lips, gold earring suspended through each ear, reverse image of red diaper, coin slot across shoulders, "Kenmar Japan" foil sticker on underside, c1960s, 7" h, $3\frac{1}{2}$" d . . . **75.00**
Book, *Color,* 1925 . . . **130.00**
Book, *Little Brown Koko,* Hunt, Blanche, American Colortype Co, 96 pp, 1952 . . . **20.00**
Broadside, Carncross Minstrels, Blacks playing banjo and leaning against title, black babies playing instruments, blue and white, Ledger Job Printing, Philadelphia, PA, c1885, $10\frac{1}{2}$ x 31" . . . **195.00**
Clock, ceramic mammy with white turban and dress with blue trim, holding round clock face, back mkd "Model W, The Sessions Clock Co, Forestville, Conn, U.S.A." and patent numbers . . . **25.00**
Cookie Jar, promotional, molded plastic and painted, Aunt Jemima in red dress with white shawl and apron carrying tray, base stamped "Aunt Jemima" above "F & F Mold & Die Works, Dayton Ohio" in shield above "Made in U.S.A.," c1950 . . . **100.00**
Doll, pr, stuffed stockinette children,little boy with pink floral print shirt and blue coveralls, black yarn hair, girl with pink floral print dress, black yarn pigtails with yellow and red bows, both with white cotton stitched and embroidered eyes and mouth, each $5\frac{1}{2}$" h . . . **100.00**
Doll, mammy, red cotton stuffed body with white polka dots, white skirt with red polka dots and white apron, red cotton turban, molded canvas head with painted black, white, and red facial features, black yarn hair, 16" h . . . **50.00**
Magazine Cover, *Life,* Slave Auction, 1956 . . . **15.00**
Magazine Cover, *Saturday Evening Post,* black picking cotton, Aug 28, 1903 . . . **20.00**

Milk glass, egg-shaped dome with Black face coming through and "More Chicken," $4\frac{3}{8}$" h, $412.50. Photo courtesy Gene Harris Antique Auction Center, Inc.

Fruit Crate Label, Dixie Boy Brand, color photograph, 9 x 8½", 1930s, $18.00.

Cast Iron, owls, pr, detailed casting, 6 x 5½", $88.00. Photo courtesy Bill Bertoia Auctions.

Match Holder, adv, Coon Chicken Inn, metal **250.00**
Memo Holder, molded plastic, painted green mammy with green turban and scarf with red dots, green, brown, and white dress, stamped "Mammy Memo Holder, No. 123" **25.00**
Mug, ceramic, caricature of black man, glossy brown face and arms with fuchsia accent on eyelids and lids, white outfit with blue trim, upraised hand holds tan rolling pin inserted into side of head, stamped "Japan" on underside, 4" h **50.00**
Wall Plaque, painted chalk, mammy with red turban and bow, c1950 . . . . **15.00**
Whisk Broom, wood handle, caricature of black woman's face with white eyes and red lips, dark blue cap and blouse with white collar and chest buttons, unmkd, 1940s, 4½" h **25.00**

BLUE RIDGE

Southern Potteries of Erwin, Tenn., produced Blue Ridge dinnerware from the late 1930s until 1956. Four hundred patterns graced eight basic shapes.

Club: Blue Ridge Collectors Club, 208 Harris St., Erwin, TN 37650.

Newsletter: *National Blue Ridge Newsletter,* 144 Highland Dr., Blountville, TN 37617.

Periodical: *Blue Ridge Beacon Magazine,* P.O. Box 629, Mountain City, GA 30562.

Apple and Pear, tidbit tray, 3 tiers **$40.00**
Brittany, demitasse saucer **10.00**
Buttercup, fruit bowl, 6" d **10.00**
Chanticleer, bowl, 6½" d **18.00**
Cherries, soup bowl **5.00**
Crab Apple, cereal bowl, 6" d **5.00**
Daffodil, sugar **12.00**
Dogtooth Violet, vase, 7¾" h **75.00**
Fantasia, teapot, Skyline shape **65.00**
French Peasant, cake plate, Maple Leaf shape **90.00**
Forest Fruit, plate **7.00**
Greenbriar, gravy boat **10.00**
Jigsaw, child's feeding dish **90.00**
Mardi Gras, pie baker **25.00**
Mardi Gras, plate, 9½" d **3.00**
Nocturne, creamer, Colonial shape **15.00**

BOOKENDS

Prices listed below are for pairs. Woe to the dealer who splits pairs apart!

Club: Bookend Collector Club, 4510 NW 17th Pl., Gainesville, FL 32605.

Arts and Crafts, metal, verse **$135.00**
Brass, Cheshire cat, c1930 . . . . **135.00**
Brass, key, c1935, 8" h **75.00**
Brass, leaping rabbit inside moon, c1935, 5" h **110.00**
Bronze, Maiden's Fountain, c1928, 5" h **175.00**
Cast Iron, children kissing, Hubley **155.00**
Cast Iron, country cottage, Hubley, c1924, 5½" h **70.00**
Cast Iron, The Thinker, c1928, 5" h **35.00**
Ceramic, Peony, Roseville, yellow **130.00**
Chalkware, Donald Duck, carrying schoolbooks, 7" h **20.00**
Chalkware, Pink Lady, polished stone base, c1943, 5½" h **125.00**
Glass, Daddy Bear, New Martinsville, 4½" h **100.00**
Ivory, elephants, teakwood base **165.00**
Metal, Nouveau Girls, c1920, 5" h **110.00**
Pewter, Bear and Beehive, c1940, 8" h **100.00**
Plaster, Lincoln Memorial, bronze finish, detailed **25.00**
Pressed Wood, swordfish **15.00**
Wood, oaken door, metal ring door knocker, c1975 . . . . **15.00**

BOOKMARKS

Don't you just hate it when you lose your place in that book you've been reading? Bookmarks can help keep your sanity and they're easy to find, easy to display and fun to own.

Bookmark collecting dates back to the early 19th century. A bookmark is any object used to mark a reader's place in a book. Bookmarks have been made from a wide variety of materials, including celluloid, cloth, cross-stitched needlepoint in punched paper, paper, sterling silver, wood and woven silk. Heavily embossed leather markers were popular between 1800 and 1860. Advertising markers appeared after 1860.

Woven silk markers are a favorite among collectors. T. Stevens of Coventry, England, manufacturer of Stevensgraphs, is among the most famous makers. Paterson, N. J. was the silk weaving center in the United states, John Best & Co., Phoenix Silk Manufacturing Co., produced bookmarks. Other important U. S. companies that made woven silk bookmarks were J. J. Mannion of Chicago and Tilt & Son of Providence, R. I.

The best place to search for bookmarks is specialized paper shows. Be sure to check all related categories. Most dealers file them under subject headings, e.g., Insurance, Ocean Liners, World's Fair and so on.

Club: Antique Bookmark Collector's Assoc., 2224 Cherokee, St., Louis, MO 63118.

Newsletter: *Bookmark Collector,* 1002 W 25th St, Erie, PA 16502.

Advertising, Brown Bros Fine Confections, diecut aluminum, emb stylized floral pattern on upper rim, early 1900s **$20.00**
Advertising, Climax Cattarah Cure, woman with fur coat. **10.00**
Advertising, Cracker Jack, litho tin, brown terrier, c1930 . . . . . **18.00**
Advertising, Crown Flour, diecut celluloid, young baker holding large toasty brown bread loaf under each arm, brown and red inscriptions, reverse with black and white monthly calendar for 1904, 4" h. **75.00**
Advertising, Hood's Sarsaparilla, children holding books, colorful, 1900 . . . . . **10.00**
Advertising, Meadow Gold Butter, Fox River Butter Co, diecut celluloid, multicolored art with yellow flowers on green leaves with product, locations on reverse, early 1900s. 3¼" h **40.00**
Cloisonne, butterfly, metal bookmark hook **2.00**
Cross-stitched, punched paper, sometimes found attached to silk ribbon, large, 3⅝ x 7¾". **4.50**
Handmade, needlepoint on plastic mesh, yarn dec. **2.00**

BOOKS

There are millions of books out there. Some are worth a fortune. Most are hardly worth the paper they were printed on. Listing specific titles serves little purpose in a price guide such as this. By following these 10 guidelines, you can quickly determine if the books that you have uncovered have value potential.

1. Check your book titles in *American Book Prices Current,* which is published annually by Bancroft-Parkman, Inc., and is available at most libraries, as well as Huxford's *Old Book Value Guide,* published by Collector Books. When listing your books in preparation for doing research, include the full name of the author, expanded title, name of publisher, copyright date and edition and/or printing number.

2. Examine the bindings. Decorators buy handsomely bound books by the foot at prices ranging from $40 to $75 per foot.

3. Carefully research any children's book. Illustration quality is an important value key. Little Golden Books are one of the hottest book areas in the market today. In the late 1970s and early 1980s, Big Little Books were hot.

4. Buy all hardcover books about antiques and collectibles that you find that are less than $5. There is a growing demand for out-of-print antiques and collectibles books.

5. Check the edition number. Value, in most cases, rests with the first edition. However, not every first edition is valuable. Consult *Blank's Bibliography of Americn First Editions* or Tannen's *How to Identify and Collect American First Editions.*

6. Look at the multi-faceted aspects of the book and the subject that it covers. Books tend to be collected by type, e.g., mysteries, westerns, etc. Many collectors buy books as supplements to their main collection. A Hopalong Cassidy collector, although focusing

Hopalong Cassidy Returns, **Clarence E. Mulford author, Triangle Books, NY, 1940s, 310 pp, $15.00.**

primarily on the objects licensed by Bill Boyd, will want to own the Mulford novels in which Hopalong Cassidy originated.

7. Local histories and atlases always have a good market, particularly those printed between 1880 and 1930. Add to this centennial and other celebration volumes.

8. Check to see if the book was signed by the author. Generally an author's signature increases the value of the book. However, it was a common practice to put engraved signatures of authors in front of books during the last part of the 19th century. The Grant signature in the first volume of his two-volume memoir set is not original, but printed.

9. Book-club editions have little or no value with the exception of books done by George and Helen Macy's Limited Editions Club.

10. Accept the fact that the value of most books falls in the 50 cent to $2 range and, that after all your research is done, this is probably what you'll get.

Club: *Antiquarian Booksellers Assoc. of America,* 20 W. 44th St., 4th Flr., New York, NY, 10036.

Newsletter: *Rare Book Bulletin,* P.O. Box 201, Peoria, IL 61650.

Periodicals: *AB Bookman's Weekly,* P.O. Box AB, Clifton, NJ 07015; *Biblio Magazine,* 845 Wilamette St., P.O. Box 10603, Eugene, OR 97401; *Book Source Monthly,* 2007 Syosett Dr., P.O. Box 567, Cazenovia, NY 13035; *Firsts: The Book Collector's Magazine,* P.O. Box 65166, Tucson, AZ 85728.

BOOTJACKS

Unless you are into horseback riding, a bootjack is one of the most useless devices that you can have around the house. why do so many individuals own one? The answer in our area is "just for nice." Actually, they are seen as a major accessory in trying to capture the country look. Cast iron reproductions are a major problem, especially for "Naughty Nellie" and "Beetle" designs.

Brass, beetle, 10" l **$90.00**
Cast Iron, Downs & Co, adv **85.00**
Cast Iron, closed loop, painted **70.00**
Cast Iron, cricket, emb lacy design, 11¾" l. **25.00**
Cast Iron, lyre shape, 10¼" l **48.00**
Cast Iron, scissor action, mkd "Pat 1877" **85.00**
Wood, fish, relief carving, red stain, 19" l. **30.00**
Wood, folk art, monkey, painted suit, c1900, 15" l **30.00**
Wood, maple, hand hewn **15.00**

BOTTLE OPENERS, FIGURAL

Although this listing focuses on cast iron figural bottle openers, the most sought after type of bottle openers, do not forget the tin advertising openers. Also known to some as church keys, the bulk still sell between $2 and $10, a very affordable price range.

Clubs: Figural Bottle Opener Collectors Club, 9697 Gwynn Park Dr., Ellicott City, MD 21042; Just For Openers, P.O. Box 64, Chapel Hill, NC 27514.

Note: Listings are for cast iron bottle openers unless noted.

Advertising, Dr Brown's Celery Tonic **$20.00**
Advertising, Effinger Beer, Baraboo, WI, hand shape, pointing finger. **15.00**
Amish Boy, barefoot, black pants, hat, and suspenders, red shirt, Wilton Products. **235.00**
Clown, brass, wall mount, white bow tie with red polka dots, bald head, sgd "495" on back, John Wright Co, 4⅛" h, 4" w. **85.00**
Cowboy, with guitar, yellow, brown, and gray guitar, green cactus, black shoes, red bandanna, John Wright Co, 4⅞" h **100.00**
Dachshund, brass **50.00**
DoDo Bird, cream, black highlights, red beak, 2¾" h **150.00**
Elephant, sitting on hind legs, trunk up, mouth open, flat, pink, black base **80.00**
Fish, tail raised, yellow and green body, John Wright Co, 4¾" l **135.00**
Horseshoe **25.00**
Mademoiselle, streetwalker by lamp post, black, flesh face, hands, and legs, yellow light, John Wright Co, 2½" h **135.00**
Monkey, dark brown body and face, tan mask, orange-brown tree, John Wright Co, 2½" h **135.00**
Mr Dry, wall mount, man wearing black top hat, red hair, blue bags under eyes, red lips, flesh-tone face, Wilton Products, 5½" h, 3½" w **125.00**
Pelican, red and black, yellow beak, orange feet, green base, John Wright Co, 3¾" h **55.00**
Seagull, on stump, polychrome paint, 3¼" h. **175.00**

BOTTLES

Bottle collecting is such a broad topic that the only way one can hope to survive is by specialization. It is for this reason that there are several bottle topics are found elsewhere in this book. Bottles have a bad habit of multiplying. Do not start collecting them until you have plenty of room. I know one person whose entire basement is filled with Coca-Cola bottles bearing the imprint of different cities.

There are many bottle categories that are still relatively inexpensive to collect. In many cases, you can find a free source of supply in old dumps. Before getting too deeply involved, it pays to talk with other bottle collectors and to visit one or more specialized bottle collector shows.

Club: Federation of Historical Bottle Collectors, 88 Sweetbriar Branch, Longwood, FL 32750.

Periodical: *Antique Bottle and Glass Collector,* P.O. Box 180, East Greenville, PA 18041.

Note: Consult *Maloney's Antiques & Collectibles Resource Directory,* by David J. Maloney, Jr., at your local library for additional information on regional bottle clubs.

BEVERAGES

Adirondack Spring Mineral Water, emerald green, qt. **$88.00**
Booths High & Dry Gin, light blue, 10¼" h **5.00**
Clarke & Co Mineral Water, yellow olive **88.00**
D A Knowlton Mineral Water, olive green **55.00**
Double Line Soda, Kokomo, IN **6.00**
Excelsior Spring Mineral Water, yellow green **55.00**
Mountain Valley Mineral Water **13.00**
Sharon Sulphur Water, light blue green, 1 pt. **22.00**
W A Gilbey Silver Stream Schnapps, clear, 8" h **6.00**
W P Knicker-Bocker Soda Water, medium sapphire blue **135.00**

FOOD

Burnetts Standard Flavoring Extract, aqua, 5½" h **$4.00**
Cloverleaf Dairy, Quincy, MA, emb, qt. **35.00**
Cross & Blackwell Mint Sauce **3.00**
Hebeerlings, banana flavoring, paper label, 8" h. **8.00**
Highland Maple Sap Syrup **9.00**
Louis & Co, lemon extract. **10.00**
Marvel Sweet Pickles. **12.00**
Mrs Chapins Mayonnaise, clear, pt. **5.00**
Sauers Extracts, clear, 6" h. **4.00**
Valentines Meat Juice, amber, 3" h. **4.00**

HEALTH AND BEAUTY

Arnold's Vegetable Hair Balsam, 6⅛" h. **$18.00**
Curity Nursing Bottle, turtle, circle with crown, 1885, 8 oz **30.00**
Drake's Plantation Bitters, log cabin shape, strawberry puce, 9¾" h **135.00**
Dr Campbells Scotch Bitters, strapside flash shape, yellow amber, smooth base, tooled mouth, 1880–90, ½ pt **425.00**
Dr C Grattans Diptheria Remedy, aqua, 7" h. **25.00**
Dr Gillmore's Laxative Kidney & Liver Bitters, oval, orange-amber, 10⅛" h **99.00**
Fish Bitters, reddish amber, 11¾" h **165.00**
Fletchers Castoria, aqua, 6" h **5.00**
Fulton M McRae Yazoo Valley Bitters, yellow-amber, 8⅝" h **154.00**

Pepper Sauce Bottles, American, smooth base, tooled mouth, orig labels, approx 8¼" h; left: "Pepper Sauce Derby Brand Glaser, Crandell Co. Chicago Ill," clear; right: "Challenge Mills Brand Pepper Saucer, 534 Washington St. New York," aqua: $75.00 each. Photo courtesy Glass-Works Auctions.

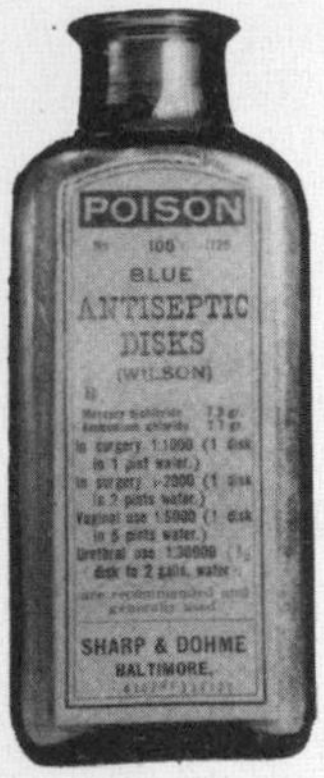

Poison Bottle, yellow amber, smooth base, tooled mouth, 99% orig label, American, 1890–1910, $4\frac{7}{8}$" h, $187.00. Photo courtesy Glass-Works Auctions.

Great English Sweeny Specific, aqua, 6" h **5.00**
Lufkin Eczema Remedy, clear, label, 7" h **8.00**
Thompsons Herbal Compound, aqua, label, $6\frac{3}{4}$" h. **8.00**

HOUSEHOLD

Black Cat Stove Enamel, clear, 6" h **$3.00**
Dutchers Dead Shot For Bed Bugs, aqua, label, $4\frac{7}{8}$" h **60.00**
Hercules Disinfectant, amber, 6" h. **4.00**
Lazell's Sacher Powder, label, ground stopper. **20.00**
Shulife—For Shoes, olive green, $3\frac{3}{4}$" h. **5.00**

POISON

Cobalt Blue, lattice and diamond pattern, smooth base, tooled lip, orig emb "POISON" stopper, 1890–1910, $5\frac{1}{2}$" h **$90.00**
Mercury Bichloride, rect, amber, $2\frac{11}{16}$" h **15.00**
Tinct Iodine, amber, skull and crossbones, 3" h. **40.00**

BOXES

We have reached the point with some 20th century collectibles where the original box may be more valuable than the object that came in it. If the box is colorful and contains a picture of the product, it has value.

Boxes have always been a favorite among advertising collectors. They are three-dimensional and often fairly large in size. The artwork reflects changing period tastes. Decorators like the pizzazz that boxes offer. The wood box with a lithographed label is a fixture in the country household.

Arm & Hammer Baking soda, cardboard, unused, 1930s **$5.00**
Armour's Sliced Bacon, cardboard **12.00**
Baker's Chocolate, wood, shipping, 12 lbs **15.00**
Beech-Nut Chewing Gum, cardboard, 6" l **40.00**
Blanar Banana **55.00**
Bossie's Best Brand Butter, 1 lb **2.00**
Diamond Spring & Cold Spring Brewery, wood **40.00**
Dr Charles Flesh Food, cardboard, 3 x $1\frac{1}{2}$" **7.50**
Excelsior Bird Food, cardboard, 1 lb **5.00**
Fairy Soap, individual **22.00**
Game, Tiddledy Winks, Milton Bradley, 1939, empty **20.00**
Gay Times Soft Drink, children illus **20.00**
Goff's Atlantic City Salt Water Taffy, $8\frac{7}{8}$ x $4\frac{7}{8}$ x $2\frac{1}{2}$" **7.50**
Jackson Fly Killer, display, wood **25.00**
Mr Delish Popcorn, bellhop illus, 1950s, 2 x 5 x 9" **3.50**
Payday, Salted Nut Roll, Hollywood Brands, Inc, 8 x 10 x 2" **15.00**
Pencil, Faber Castell **12.00**
Reese Cigars, wood. **20.00**
Squirrel Brandy Peanut Taffy, wood **30.00**
Toy, Structo, #402, machinery truck and steam shovel. **65.00**
Wrigley's Spearmint Gum, 1929 . . . . **35.00**

Mason's Blacking Box, wood, paper litho label mkd "Crump Label Co, N.Y.," scuffs, scratches to label, 1 wire lid hinge broken, 5" h, $11\frac{1}{2}$" w, $159.50. Photo courtesy Collectors Auction Services.

BOYD'S BEARS AND FRIENDS

Gary and Tina Lowenthal of McSherrytown, Pennsylvania, began the Boyd plush toy line in 1979. The Boyd name came from Boyd, Maryland, the location of the Lowenthal's antiques business in a previous life.

An active secondary market, especially on the Internet, has developed for discontinued Boyd plush toys and cast resin collectibles. Prices should be viewed as highly speculative. Like many collectibles of this type, their primary appeal is to the buyer's heart, not their head. Boyd does not realize production numbers. Scarcity is more related to speculative hoarding than actual lack of product.

Bearstone, Amelia's Enterprise, Carrot Juice, 1995. . . . . **$33.00**
Bearstone, Boyds Bailey with Suitcase, 1996 . . . . **55.00**
Bearstone, Charlotte & Bebe, The Gardeners, 1994. . . . . **71.00**
Bearstone, Daphne Hare & Maisey Ewe, 1993 . . . . **78.00**
Bearstone, Emma, The Witchy Bear, 1995. . . . . **43.00**
Bearstone, Greenville & Neville, The Sign, white bottom, 1993. . . . . **16.00**
Bearstone, Homer on the Plate, 1994. . . . . **48.00**
Bearstone, Manaheim The Eco-Moose, 1994 . . . . **38.00**
Toy, Structo, #402, machinery truck and steam shovel. **65.00**
Dollstone, Anne, The Masterpiece, 1996 . . . . **35.00**
Dollstone, Kristi with Nicole, Skater's Waltz, 1996 . . . . **54.00**

Folkstone Collection, votive, Yukon and Kodiak, Nome Sweet Home, 4" h, $38.00. Photo courtesy the Boyds Collection Ltd.

Dollstone, Rebecca with Elliot, Birthday, 1996 . . . . **38.00**
Folkstone, Athena The Wedding Angel, 1996 . . . . **42.00**
Folkstone, Buster Goes a 'Courtin', 1996 . . . . **33.00**
Folkstone, Florence, the Kitchen Angel, 1995 . . . . **40.00**
Folkstone, Jingle Moose, 1994 . . . . **46.00**
Folkstone, Rufus, Hoe Down, 1995 . . . . **23.00**
Shoe Box Bears, Gertrude "Gertie" Grizberg, 1996. . . . . **15.00**

BOYD CRYSTAL ART GLASS

The Boyds, Bernard and his son, purchased the Degenhart Glass Factory in 1978. Since that time, they have reissued a number of the Degenhart forms. Their productions can be distinguished by the color of the glass and the "D" in a diamond mark. The Boyd family continues to make contemporary collectible glass at its factory in Cambridge, Ohio.

Club: Boyd Art Glass Collectors Guild, P.O. Box 52, Hatboro, PA 19040.

Newsletters: *Boyd's Crystal Art Glass,* 1203 Morton Ave, P.O. Box 127, Cambridge, OH 43725; *Jody & Darrell's Glass Collectibles Newsletter,* P.O. Box 180833, Arlington, TX 76094.

Animal, Bingo Deer, custard **$8.00**
Animal, Debbie Duck, English Yew **5.00**
Animal, Joey Pony, chocolate. **30.00**
Animal, Joey Pony, nile green **15.00**
Animal, kitten on pillow **15.00**
Animal, owl, light rose **9.00**
Animal, rooster, orange calico **10.00**
Animal, Sammy the Squirrel, autumn beige **5.00**
Animal, Sueee Pig, autumn beige **7.50**
Basket, milk white, hp dec, 4½" d **20.00**
Card Holder, grape, cardinal red **7.00**
Figurine, Chuckles the Clown, confetti **7.00**
Figurine, Chuckles the Clown, vaseline **8.00**
Figurine, Hobo Clown, Freddie, cobalt, 3" h. **8.50**
Figurine, Jeremy, vaseline, 1¼" h **6.00**
Salt, chick, butterscotch, #5, 1979 . . . . **25.00**
Salt, chick, English yew, #43, 1983 . . . . **6.00**

BOY SCOUTS

Collecting Boy Scout memorabilia has become a mature field with well-established subcategories. In fact, separate books have been published to detail at least seventeen of these subs. The field also shows maturity in that several subcategories have waxed and waned while overall strength of Boy Scout collecting has continued to grow.

It is said that 90% of Boy Scout collectors collect nothing but cloth patches. At least, that is their main focus. But there are many kinds of cloth patches and each kind has devotees. Some collect merit badges, Cub Scout insignia, High Adventure patches, Jamboree patches, Council patches, and many collect Order of the Arrow patches. (They call it OA). This is an Honor Camper organization within Boy Scouting. Only a limited number of boys get to join it, but they are the ones most heavily involved in Scouting. It is likely they will be involved again as adults and they will want to collect OA patches.

Books published by collectors give elaborate lists of all the thousands of OA patches. In fact, there are references showing almost all the official Boy Scout items ever made. However, a novice has a lot to learn before he can understand the specialized notation used to condense the listings.

Because OA patches were issued locally in small quantity and collectors all over the country are seeking them, prices on scarce issues have been driven up to thousands of dollars. Another group that has run up high prices are old Insignia and Uniforms from early days of Scouting (before 1940). Also, values of good old Handbooks have boomed. Recently the premium value for mint Insignia and Handbooks has shown particular growth as collectors seek to upgrade their collections.

Boy Scout collectors buy, sell and trade at Trade-O-Rees in almost every part of the Country. Most of them are held annually on Friday and Saturday under the management of local collectors. They usually attract from 50 to 200 collectors. These events are great learning opportunities as experienced collectors willingly help out those with less knowledge.

Advisor: Cal Holden, Box 264, Doylestown, OH 44230, (330) 658-2793.

Clubs: American Scouting Historical Society, 2580 Silver Cloud Ct., Park City, UT 84060; American Scouting Traders Assoc., P.O. Box 21013, San Francisco, CA 94121; International Badgers Club, 2903 W. Woodbine Dr., Maryville, TN 37801; National Scouting Collectors Society, 806 E. Scott St., Tuscola, IL 61953.

Periodicals: *Fleur de Lis,* 5 Dawes Ct., Novato, CA 94947; *Scout Memorabilia,* P.O. Box 1121, Manchester, NH 03105.

Book, *Winter Camping,* proof copy in wraps, slight wear, 1927. . . . . **$25.00**
Diary, Boy Scout, cov scuffed, 1941. . . . . **20.00**
Equipment Catalog, 1917 . . . . **25.00**
Handbook, *Boy Scout Handbook,* soft cov, 1910 . . . . **700.00**
Handbook, *Boy Scout Handbook,* 1st ed, 10th printing, spine stripped, edge worn **100.00**
Handbook, *Boy Scout Handbook,* 3rd ed, 1st printing, slight wear **40.00**
Handbook, *Scout Master Handbook,* 3rd ed, 2 vol, 1937 . . . . **30.00**
Hat Pin, Den Mother's, "Cub Scouts BSA," painted. **4.00**
Medal, Eagle, Robbins 3, ribbon slightly faded, 1940 . . . . . . **80.00**
Merit Badge, First Aid, square, 1920s. **3.00**
Merit Badge, Music, narrow, tan, 1936–46. . . . . **5.00**
Merit Badge, Plumbing, square, 1920s **25.00**
Neckerchief, square, red, NJ, 1937. **110.00**
Patch, Order of the Arrow, Lodge 62, Sioux, first jacket patch, fully embroidered. **1,050.00**

Left: Rover Scouts Patch, cut edge, squatty crown, $150.00.
Right: Explorer Scout Universal Patch, light green, $15.00.

Left: Eagle Medal, no BSA, Robbins 3, (93354), $80.00
Right: Silver Award Medal, type 1, boxed, (1949–54), $900.00.

Patch, Order of the Arrow, Lodge 151, first fully embroidered flap 8.00
Patch, Order of the Arrow, Lodge 542, Kiminschi, first and only flap, not fully embroidered 2,100.00
Patch, Region 1, type R2, felt, 77 mm d 90.00
Patch, Region 10, type 3B 20.00
Patch, Sea Scout Skipper, gauze back 5.00
Patch, Star, type 3, fat star, no knot, early 1920s 200.00
Patch, Tenderfoot, type 7, embroidered cut edge, gauze back 3.00
Pennant, felt, blue, white inscription, c1940, 30" l 20.00
Pin, Tenderfoot, silver plated, horizontal slogan, safety pin clasp 110.00
Pin, Wolf, Cubs BSA, first type, square 50.00
Pinback Button, "Do A Good Turn Daily," multicolored portrait, dark blue ground, 1920s 15.00

Lodge 1 First Flap, cut edge, verticle embroidered turtle, horizontal red embroidery, $50.00.

BRASS

Brass is a durable, malleable and ductile metal alloy, consisting mainly of copper and zinc. It appears in this guide because of the wide variety of objects made from it.

Andirons, pr, fire dogs, back rods damaged, 20$^1/_2$" h $80.00
Bed Warmer, oversized lid with tooled designs and heart, turned wood handle, 44$^1/_2$" l 75.00
Blotter, rocker shape, knob handle 10.00
Call Bell, red granite base, 6$^1/_4$" h 25.00
Clothes Tree, 4 top hooks, 4 legs, sq tubular trim on base 45.00
Dipper, dovetailed brass bowl, wrought iron handle, 6$^1/_2$" d 55.00
Inkwell, Victorian, pierced scrolled back plate, 2 ink pots, pen tray 110.00
Knife, Golden Wedding Whiskey adv 20.00
Lamp, skater's, clear globe, mkd "Pat'd Dec 24, 1867" 110.00
Matchsafe, Internal Tailoring adv, nickel plated, emb Indians and lion 55.00
Pail, Brown & Bros, Waterbury, 1856, 3 gal 65.00
Plant Stand, gilded, white onyx shelf and top 50.00
Salt, cov, paw feet, 4$^3/_4$" h, 3" d 75.00
Trivet, reticulated top, worn tooling, 7$^1/_2$" d. 100.00
Wafer Iron, geometric floral design, wrought iron handles, 17" l 65.00

BREAD BOXES

Bread boxes are too much fun to be hidden in the Kitchen Collectibles category. There are plenty of great examples, both in form and decoration. They have disappeared from the modern kitchen. I miss them.

Graniteware, green and white, hinged lid, 1920s, 19" l. $95.00
Graniteware, round, white, black letters and trim, fully vented top. 125.00
Metal, fruit decal, painte yellow. 15.00
Metal, Red Poppy pattern 17.00
Metal, white enamel paint, stenciled "Bread," c1900 . . . . 32.00
Wood, carved "Give Us This Daily," 12$^1/_2$" h. 80.00

BREWERIANA

Beer is a liquid bread, or so I was told growing up in Pennsylvania German country. It is hard to deny German linkage with the brewing industry when your home community contained the Horlacher, Neuweiler and Uhl breweries.

Brewery signs and trays, especially from the late 19th and early 20th century, contain some of the finest advertising lithography of the period. The three-dimensional advertising figures from the 1930s through the 1970s are no slouches either. Brewery advertising has become expensive. Never fear. You can build a great breweriana collection concentrating on barroom accessories such as foam scrappers, coasters and tab knobs.

Menu, Schlitz Brewing Company, Milwaukee, WI, 1950s, 7$^1/_2$ x 10$^1/_4$", $6.00.

Clubs: American Breweriana Assoc., Inc., P.O. Box 11157, Pueblo, CO 81001; National Assoc. of Breweriana Advertising, 2343 Met-To-Wee Ln, Wauwatosa, WI 53226.

Ashtray, Budweiser, glass, round, 1950s, 5" d **$8.00**
Blotter, Bergdoll Brewing Co, black and white portrait of Louis Bergdoll, holly dec, 60th anniversary, 1909, unused, 7½ x 3" **50.00**
Booklet, Budweiser, 20 pp, 1965, 5 x 7" **7.00**
Bottle, Blatz, figural, fishing lure, MIB **35.00**
Bottle, Enterprise Brewing Co, qt **8.00**
Bottle, Schwarzenbach Brewing Co, clear, 7¼" h **3.00**
Butter Pat, Magnolia Brewing, Houston, ornate. **32.00**
Can, Bartels Beer, Edwardsville, PA **52.00**
Can, Gunther Beer, Baltimore, MD **17.00**
Can, Koch's Beer, Dunkirk, NY **10.00**
Can, Regency Beer, Eagle Brewery, Catasauqua, PA **67.00**
Can, Sunshine Beer, Reno, NV. **70.00**
Change Tray, Billings Brewing Co, Billings, MT. **100.00**
Change Tray, Budweiser. **8.00**
Change Tray, Miller Beer, duck illus **20.00**
Clicker, Gunther's Beer **20.00**
Clock, Lowenbrau. **18.00**
Coaster, metal, Simon Pure Beer **5.00**
Container, Corbys Stir, plstic, 1950s, 6" h **20.00**
Corkscrew, Pabst, wood handle **22.00**
Display, Beefeater Gin, figural, composition, 1960s **80.00**
Display, Bert and Harry Piel, vinyl, 1965, 11⅕" h. **40.00**
Foam Scraper, Birk's Beer **18.00**
Lapel Pin, Pabst Breweries, enameled 14K gold **25.00**
Matchsafe, Genesee **65.00**
Matchsafe, Schlitz. **55.00**
Mug, Stroh's At The Fair, May 1–Oct 31, 1982, Knoxville, TN, mkd on bottom "King World 44413" **45.00**
Pin, Miller Brewing Co, employee's **12.00**
Pinback Button, Poth's Beer, white lettering, khaki ground, c1900, 1" d **12.00**
Pinback Button, Schlitz Beer, red lettering, white ground, crossed key center, early 1900s, 1¼" d. **20.00**
Playing Cards, Budweiser, label **8.00**
Pocket Protector, Falstaff Beer, 1960s **4.00**
Sign, Budweiser, plastic with light-up bottle, 1960s, 5 x 12". **45.00**
Sign, Old Milwaukee, glass and metal, 13". **25.00**
Statue, Bert and Harry Piel, metal, 1955, 9" h. **50.00**
Statue, Hamm's, bear, changeable calendar **75.00**
Stein, Blatz, barrel shape, glaze flakes **30.00**
Stein, Budweiser, ceramic, 1989, 8½" h **20.00**

Light, reverse glass, Daeufer's, Allentown, PA, 1930s, 15" d, $75.00. Photo courtesy Fink's Off The Wall Auctions.

Coaster, Sunshine Brewing Company, full color printing, "Get a Sunny Thing Going," 1940s, 3½" d, $4.00.

Stein, Hamm's Beer, Octoberfest, McCoy, 1973 . . . . **25.00**
Stein, Schlitz. **18.00**
Tap Handle, Bass Ale, Bass Brewery, London, England, 2 handles, lucite, red and white logos **10.00**
Tap Handle, Whitbread, Whitbred Ltd, London, England, wooden handle, 2-sided **4.00**
Tip Tray, Miller High Life, 1940s, 4" l **30.00**
Tray, Beck's Brewing, buffalo, 1950s, 13" d. **50.00**
Tray, Ehret Beer, oval. **55.00**
Wall Lamp, Budweiser, price for pair **22.00**

BREYER HORSES

The Breyer line of plastic model horses has been on the market since the 1950s. During the past five decades the company has not only produced a line of horses but also dogs, wildlife and farm animals. In 1984 Breyer Molding Company was sold to Reeves International and moved from Chicago to New Jersey. The Breyer company is still in business today.

Breyer consists of four lines that are separated by height. *Traditional* (horses and animals in separate categories) which average around nine inches; *Classic,* which averages six inches; *Little Bit,* which stand around four inches; and *Stablemates,* which average three inches.

Advisor: Antina Richards-Pennock, PO Box 8924, Rockford, IL 61125, (815) 398-6175.

Club: Breyer Collectors Club, (company-sponsored), 14 Industrial Rd., Pequannock, NJ 07440.

Newsletter: *The Model Horse Trader,* 143 Mercer Way, Upland, CA 91786.

Periodicals: *Hobby Horse News,* 2053 Dyrehaven Dr., Tallahassee, FL 32311, *TRR Pony Express,* 71 Aloha Cir., North Little Rock, AR 72120.

TRADITIONAL SERIES

American Buckskin Stock Mare, #222, buckskin. **$37.00**
American Buckskin Stock Stallion, #221, buckskin **38.00**
American Buckskin Stock Foal, #224, buckskin **26.00**
Brahma Bull Glossy, #70, gray/white **45.00**
Family Arabian Foal, #6, palomino. **18.00**
Family Arabian Mare, #5, palomino **25.00**
Five Gaiter, #52, sorrel **45.00**
Five Gaiter "Project Universe," #117, pinto **50.00**

Western Horse, #59, alabaster, $50.00.

Foundation Stallion, #64, black, MIB **45.00**
Gem Twist, #495, white. **35.00**
Misty's Twilight, #470, pinto **31.00**
Morganglanz, #59, chestnut **42.00**
Old Timer, with hat, #206, bay **40.00**
Polled Hereford Bull, #74, brown/white **25.00**
Proud Arabian Mare, #217, white **36.00**
Running Foal, #849, pinto, MIB **25.00**
Sea Star, #16, chestnut **15.00**
Spanish Barb-Porcelain, #79194, grulla **165.00**
Western Pony, with saddle, #41, pinto **30.00**

OTHER SERIES, CLASSIC

Black Beauty (4 horses), #3040, mixed, MIB. **55.00**
Little Bit Quarter Horse, #9015, bay. **11.00**
Stablemate Draft Horse, #5055, chestnut **10.00**

Elephant, #91, gray, $25.00.

BRITISH ROYALTY COLLECTIBLES

This is one of those categories where you can get in on the ground floor. Every king and queen, potential king and queen and their spouses is collectible. Buy commemorative items when they are new. I have a few Prince Harry items. We may not have royal blood in common, but...

Most individuals collect by monarch, prince, or princess. Take a different approach—collect by form, e.g., mugs, playing cards, etc. British royalty commemoratives were made at all quality levels. Stick to high-quality examples.

It is fun to find recent issues at flea markets for much less than their original selling price. Picking is competitive. There are a lot of British royalty commemorative collectors.

Club: Commemorative Collector's Society, Lumless House, Gainsborough Rd., Winthrope, New Newark, Nottingham NG24 2NR, U.K.

Newsletter: *British Royalty Commemorative Collectors Newsletter,* P.O. Box 294, Lititz, PA 17543.

Bank, Edward VII, Oxo Cubes, tin **$60.00**
Beaker, King George V and Queen Mary, black and white portraits with small portrait of Edward, Prince of Wales, color dec and rim gilding, bone china, 3$\frac{3}{4}$" h **70.00**
Bell, Queen Elizabeth II Silver Jubilee, applied roses, silver trim, Crown Staffordshire, 1977, 5$\frac{1}{2}$" h **30.00**
Biscuit Tin, George V Silver Jubilee, Mc Vitie & Price Biscuit Manufacturers, mkd "Free Sample" on bottom, 1935, 5$\frac{1}{2}$ x 4$\frac{1}{2}$" **30.00**
Bowl, Birth of Prince William of Wales, color portraits and nursery scenes, Jun 21, 1982 . . . . . **35.00**
Cigarette Case, George VI Coronation, book type, emb medallions design on front cov, clasp, May 12, 1937 . . . . . **38.00**
Coaster, Charles and Diana, black and white portrait, multicolor dec, cork back **7.00**
Coca-Cola Bottle, Prince Charles Wedding to Lady Diana Spencer, Jul 29, 1981 . . . . . **40.00**
Figurine, Queen Elizabeth and Duke of Edinburgh, plastic, white and black, 4" h **35.00**
Glass, Edward VII Coronation, clear, etched portrait and inscriptions, May 12, 1937 . . . . . **35.00**
Jigsaw Puzzle, Princess Anne, cardboard, multicolor, 400 pcs. **60.00**
Magazine, *The Illustrated London News,* Queen Elizabeth II Coronation **20.00**
Mug, Queen Elizabeth, 80th Anniversary, portrait in floral wreath, inscirbed "To Celebrate the 80th Birthday of her Majesty Queen Elizabeth the Queen Mother, August 4, 1980," Spode **75.00**
Pendant, Queen Victoria Diamond Jubilee, diecut brass, center profile Portrait "Victoria Regina," formed in Maltese Cross style, front includes dates of her birth, crowning, marriage, and 1837–1897 "Longest Reign," reverse inscription "To Commemorate The Longest And Most Illustrious Reign In England's History/Diamond Jubilee" **50.00**
Pinback Button, King Edward VII Coronation, multicolored portrait, gold ground, 1901 . . . . . **20.00**
Pinback Button, King George V, multicolored portrait in naval uniform, gold ground, c1902 . . . . . **20.00**
Plate, George V and Queen Mary, Silver Jubilee, 1910-1935, Almaware, 6" d **27.00**

Cup, Edward VII Coronation, multicolor design by Dame Laura Knight, lion handle, mkd "Myott Son, Made in England, 3$\frac{1}{4}$" h, $60.00.

Pocket Watch, Queen Elizabeth II Coronation, silvered metal, back engraved with royal family crest, 2" d. **250.00**
Program George V Coronation, issued by City of London, Jun 22, 1911 . . . . **25.00**
Stamp Set, King George VI and Queen Elizabeth Coronation, orig 4 x 6" envelope with $9\frac{1}{2}$ x 12" stamp block sheet of 60 perforated commemorative stamps, c1937. . . . . **20.00**
Teapot, cov, Edward VIII Coronation, portrait and shield, gold trim, May 12, 1937 . . . . **95.00**
Thimble, set of 4, Birth of Prince William of Wales, Queen Mother, Queen Elizabeth, Princess Diana, and crown illus, Caverswall, Jun 21, 1982. . . . . **60.00**

BUBBLEGUM TRADING CARDS

Based on the publicity received by baseball cards, you would think that they were the only bubble gum cards sold. Wrong, wrong, wrong! There is a wealth of non-sport bubble gum cards.

Prices for many of these card sets are rather modest. Individual cards often sell for less than $1.00. Classic cards were issued in the 1950s, but many more recently released sets are sure to become collectible.

Club: United States Cartophilic Society, P.O. Box 4020, St. Augustine, FL 32085.

Periodicals: *Non Sport Update,* 4019 Green St., P.O. Box 5858, Harrisburg, PA 17110; *Non Sports Illustrated,* P.O. Box 126, Lincoln, MA 01773; *The Wrapper,* 1811 More Ct., St. Charles, IL 60174.

Addams Family, Donruss, 66 cards, 1964 . . . . **$250.00**
Alien, Topps, 84 cards, 22 stickers, 1979 . . . . **30.00**
All Pro Skateboard, Donruss, 44 cards, 1978 . . . . **55.00**
Animal Cards, Frostick, 44 cards, 1930s. **185.00**
A-Team, Topps, 66 cards, 12 stickers, 1983 . . . . **8.00**
Baby, Topps, 66 cards, 11 stickers **10.00**
Batman, Topps, 55 cards, 1966 . . . . **100.00**
Bay City Rollers, Topps, 66 cards, 1975 . . . . **140.00**
Beverly Hillbillies, Topps, 66 cards, 1963. . . . . **375.00**
Bionic Woman, Donruss, 44 cards, 1976. . . . . **33.00**
Black Hole, Topps, 88 cards, 22 stickers, 1979. . . . . **18.00**
Casey & Kildare, Topps, 110 cards, 1962 . . . . **200.00**
Civil War News, Topps, 88 cards, 1962 . . . . **550.00**
Crazy Magazine Covers, Fleer, 9 cards, 40 stickers, 1974 . . . . **20.00**
Daktari, Philly, 66 cards **95.00**
Dark Shadows, Philly, 66 cards, series #1, 1968 . . . . **375.00**
DC/Warner Bros Cartoon Cards, 30 cards, 1974. . . . . **200.00**
Desert Storm, Topps, 88 cards, 22 stickers, 1991 . . . . **42.00**
Disneyland, Donruss, 66 cards, puzzle back, 1965. . . . . **90.00**
Dukes of Hazzard, Donruss, 66 cards, 1980. . . . . **30.00**
Empire Strikes Back, Topps, 132 cards, 33 stickers, series #1, 1980. . . . . **90.00**
Evel Knievel, Topps, 60 cards, 1974 . . . . **180.00**
Excalibar, Comic Images, 45 cards, 1989 . . . . **16.00**
Famous Airplanes, Heinz, 25 cards, 1940. . . . . **310.00**
Fighting Marines, Topps, 96 cards, 1953. . . . . **700.00**
Flying Nun, Donruss, 66 cards, 1968. . . . . **215.00**
Freddie & The Dreamers, Donruss, 66 cards, 1965 . . . . **60.00**
Frontier Days, Bowman, 128 cards, 1953 . . . . **750.00**
Get Smart, Topps, 66 cards, 1966. **380.00**
Ghostbusters II, Topps, 88 cards, 11 stickers, 1989 . . . . **12.00**

Davy Crockett, King of the Wild Frontier Series, Topps, set of 80, $2\frac{1}{8}$ x $3\frac{3}{4}$", $75.00 per set.

G I Joe, Hasbro, 192 cards, 1986. . . . . **50.00**
Gilligan's Island, Topps, 55 cards, 1965 . . . . **825.00**
Gong Show, Fleer, 66 cards, 10 stickers, 1979 . . . . **25.00**
Grease, Topps, 66 cards, 11 stickers, series #1, 1978 . . . . **20.00**
Green Hornet, Donruss, 44 cards, 1966. . . . . **270.00**
Happy Days, Topps, 44 cards, 11 stickers, 1976 . . . . **35.00**
Honeymooners, Comic Images, 51 cards, 1988 . . . . **110.00**
Hysterical History, Topps, 66 cards, 1976. . . . . **90.00**
Independence Day, Topps, 72 cards, 1996 . . . . **10.00**
Isolation Booth, Topps, 88 cards, 1957. . . . . **190.00**
Jaws 2, Topps, 59 cards, 11 stickers, 1978 . . . . **14.00**
Kennedy, John F, Topps, 77 cards, 1964 . . . . **150.00**
Kiss, Donruss, 66 cards, series #1, 1978. . . . . **45.00**
Kustom Cars, Fleer, 9 cards, 30 stickers, 1974 . . . . **85.00**
Leave It to Beaver, Pacific, 60 cards, 1985 . . . . **45.00**
Lost In Space, Topps, 55 cards, 1966 . . . . **575.00**
MAD Magazine, Lime Rock, 55 cards, series #1, 1992 . . . . **7.00**
Magnum P I, Donruss, 66 cards, 1983 . . . . **16.00**
Man From U N C L E, Topps, 55 cards, 1966 . . . . **120.00**
Mod Squad, Topps, 55 cards, 1969 . . . . **175.00**
Monkees, Donruss, 44 cards, 1966 . . . . **125.00**
Munsters, Leaf, 72 cards, 1966 . . . . **475.00**
Nancy Kerrigan, Topps, 88 cards, 1994 . . . . **15.00**
National Lampoon, 21st Century Archives, 100 cards, 1993. . . . . **15.00**
Night of the Living Dead, Imagine, 60 cards, 1st printing, green border, 1987 . . . . **25.00**
Nintendo, Topps, 60 cards, 33 stickers, 1989 . . . . **20.00**
Odd Rods, Donruss, 44 sticker cards, 1970 . . . . **110.00**
Outer Limits, Bubbles-Topps, 50 cards, 1964 . . . . **425.00**
Planet of the Apes, Topps, 66 cards, 1975 . . . . **75.00**
Precious Moments, Enesco, 16 cards, 1993 . . . . **15.00**
Rat Patrol, Topps, 66 cards, 1966. . . . . **85.00**

U S Presidents, Bowman, #34, Franklin D Roosevelt, 1952, $2\frac{1}{2}$ x $3\frac{3}{4}$", $2.50

Rocky II, Topps, 99 cards, 22 stickers, 1979 . . . . **16.00**
Saturday Night Fever, Donruss, 66 cards, 1978 . . . . **20.00**
Simpsons, Topps, 88 cards, 22 stickers, 1990 . . . . **15.00**
Soupy Sales, Topps, 66 cards, 1967 . . . . **225.00**
Space 1999, Donruss, 66 cards, 1976 . . . . **23.00**
Sports Cars, Topps, 66 cards, 1961 . . . . **130.00**
Star Trek, Topps, 88 cards, 22 stickers, 1979 . . . . **45.00**
Star Trek: Deep Space 9, SkyBox, 100 cards, 1994 . . . . **15.00**
Star Trek: The Next Generation, Impel, 120 cards, 1992 . . . . . **15.00**
Star Wars, Kenner, Action Masters set, 15 cards, 1994–95 . . . . **75.00**
Star Wars, Wonder Bread, 16 cards, 1977 . . . . **15.00**
Street Fighter, Upper Deck, 90 cards, 1995 . . . . **15.00**
Superman II, Topps, 99 cards, 22 stickers, 1983 . . . . **15.00**
Teenage Mutant Ninja Turtles Movie, Topps, 132 cards, 11 stickers, 1990 . . . . **20.00**
Terror Tales, Topps, 88 cards, 1967 . . . . **440.00**
Three's Company, Topps, 16 cards, 44 stickers, 1978 . . . . **20.00**
Total Recall, Pacific, 110 cards, 1990 . . . . **20.00**
Toy Story, SkyBox, 90 cards, 1995 . . . . **15.00**
Transformers, Hasbro, 192 cards, 1985 . . . . **55.00**
Trivia Battle, Topps, 132 cards, 11 stickers, 2 game cards, 1984 . . . . **20.00**
Trolls (Russ), Topps, 66 cards, 11 stickers, 1992 . . . . **10.00**
Wacky Packages, Topps, 44 stickers, 1985 . . . . **9.00**

BURMA SHAVE

The famous Burma Shave jingle ad campaign was the brainstorm of Allan Odell, son of Burma-Vita's founder, Clinton M. Odell. The first sets, six signs placed 100 feet apart, appeared in 1926 on a stretch of road from Minneapolis to Albert Lea. Success was instantaneous and the Burma Shave name was fixed in the minds of drivers across the country. If You...Don't Know...Whose Signs These Are...You Haven't Driven...Very Far...Burma Shave.

Advisor: Steve Soelberg, 29126 Laro Dr., Agoura Hills, CA, 91301, (818) 889-9909.

Aerosol Can **$100.00**
After Shave **50.00**
Blades **10.00**
Gift Set **100.00**
Jar, cov, empty **15.00**
Jar, open, empty **10.00**
Letterhead **25.00**
Lotion Bottle, empty **15.00**
Lotion Bottle, full **50.00**
Printer's Blocks **50.00**
Shaving Cream Tube **25.00**
Sign, roadside, individual **175.00**
Sign, roadside, set of six **1,000.00**
Talc **50.00**
Toy Truck, metal **50.00**
Trolley Ad **150.00**

BUSTER BROWN

R. F. Outcault could have rested on his Yellow Kid laurels. Fortunately, he did not and created a second great cartoon character—Buster Brown. The strip first appeared in the Sunday, May 4, 1902, *New York Herald*. Buster's fame was closely linked to Tige, his toothily grinning evil-looking bulldog.

Clock, electric, light up, tin body with glass face, 15" d, $522.50. Photo courtesy Collectors Auction Services.

Most of us remember Buster Brown and Tige because of Buster Brown Shoes. The shoe advertisements were popular on radio and television shows of the 1950s. "Look for me in there too."

Club: R. F. Outcault Society, 103 Doubloon Dr., Slidell, LA 70461.

Bandanna, Buster Tige, Smilen Ed, and Froggy, 1940s, unused **$95.00**
Bill Hook, Buster Brown Shoes adv **65.00**
Book, *Buster Disturbs The Family,* Stokes Co, ©1917, $5\frac{1}{2}$ x $6\frac{1}{2}$" **125.00**
Booklet, Ringen Stove adv, Buster Brown illus, c1905 . . . . **30.00**
Candy Container, Buster & Tige, composition, c1910, 5" h **250.00**
Card Game, Buster Brown at the Circus, Selchow & Righter, early 1900s, 4 x 5" box **175.00**
Clicker, Buster Brown Hosiery, red, white, and blue, 1930–40 . . . . **22.00**
Compact, brass, emb logo "Buster Brown Shoes, First Because of The Last," Buster holding shoe beside Tige, reverse with hinged door and small mirror, c1930, 2" d. . . . **65.00**
Dictionary, premium, *Buster Brown Webster Selected Dictionary* **32.00**
Figure, bisque, c1930s, 4" h. **200.00**
Frame, good graphic decal, 1950s, 5 x 7" **30.00**
Lapel Stud, white metal, silver finish, Buster with hand on Tige's head, c1900. $1\frac{1}{4}$" w **40.00**
Paint Book, Buster's and Mary Jane's Painting Book, Stokes Co, 1907, 10 x 14" **100.00**
Pin, brass, Buster and Tige head **5.00**
Pinback Button, Buster Brown Blue Ribbon Shoes, sepia, photo-like portrait of Buster and Tige, paper text on back, 1902-10, 1" d. **18.00**

Buster Brown Cloth Party Game, full color lithograph on canvas type, published by Selchow & Righter Company, NY, 22" h, 12" w, $385.00. Photo courtesy Collectors Auction Services.

Valentine, diecut, mechanical, Buster standing behind large walnut shell, "All in a Nutshell, Valentine Greeting," eyes roll when nutshell is raised, c1900 . . . . 20.00

CALCULATORS

The Texas Instruments TI-2500 Datamath entered the market in the early 1970s. This electronic calculator, the marvel of its era, performed four functions—addition, subtraction, multiplication, and division. This is all it did. It retailed for over $100.00. Within less than a decade, calculators selling for less than $20.00 were capable of doing five times as many functions.

Early electronic calculators are dinosaurs. They deserve to be preserved. When collecting them, make certain to buy examples that retain their power transformer, instruction booklet, and original box. Make certain any calculator that you buy works. There are few around who know how to repair one.

It is a little too early for a category on home computers. But a few smart collectors are starting to stash away the early Texas Instrument and Commodore models.

Club: International Assoc. of Calculator Collectors, 14561 Livingston St., Tustin, CA 92780.

Brother 408AX, c1972 . . . . **$45.00**
Figural, cash register, 6 x 7" **35.00**
Figural, tape measure **25.00**
Hewlett Packard 80 . . . . **60.00**
Radio Shack EC-231, Statesman Thin **30.00**
Sharp EL-8016 . . . . **15.00**
Texas Instruments SR-51 . . . . **40.00**
Toy, Hello Kitty, fold-open style **15.00**
Toy, Math To Go **25.00**

CALENDAR PLATES

Calendar plates are one of the traditional, affordable collecting categories. A few years ago, they sold in the $10 to $20 range; now that figure has jumped to $35 to $50.

Value rests with the decorative motif and the place for which it was issued. A fun collection would be to collect the same plate and see how many different merchants and other advertisers utilized it.

Newsletter: *The Calendar,* 710 N. Lake Shore Dr., Barrington, IL 60010.

1906, Indian with calendar in head dress center, mkd "Imperial China" **$60.00**
1907, Christmas scenes, holly center **75.00**
1907, Order of Elks **50.00**
1908, dog portrait center **55.00**
1908, mountain scene **35.00**
1908, Victorian lady in flowered hat and dress center, brown calendar around border, souvenir of Snyder, OK. . . . **30.00**
1908, Merry Christmas, 4 large cat faces **45.00**
1908, crossed American flags, Oyster Bay, NY **35.00**
1909, Queen Louise portrait center **26.00**
1909, Santa in zeppelin dropping presents to children **50.00**
1909, horsehead center **22.00**
1909, dog's head, "John S. Stewart" adv **40.00**
1909, flowers center, souvenir of Mt Sterling, IA **20.00**
1909, Gibson-type girl portrait head center **24.00**
1909, water lilies center, "Mercersburg, PA" adv **45.00**
1910, boxer dog portrait center **45.00**

CALENDARS

The primary reason calendars are collected is for the calendar art. Prices hinge on quality of printing and the pizazz of the subject. A strong advertising aspect adds to the value.

A highly overlooked calendar collecting area is the modern art and photographic calendar. For whatever reason, there is little interest in calendars dating after 1940. Collectors are making a major mistake. There are some great calendars from this later time period selling for less than $2.00.

"Gentlemen's" calendars did not grace the kitchen wall, but they are very collectible. Illustrations range from the pinup beauties of Elvgren and Moran and the *Esquire* Vargas ladies in the 1930s to the Playboy Playmates of the 1960s. Early Playboy calendars sell in the $50.00 plus range.

But, what's the fun of having something you cannot display openly? The following list will clear corporate censors with no problems.

Club: Calendar Collector Society, 18222 Flower Hill Way #299, Gaithersburg, MD 20879.

1881, Brooks & Co Vanishes, black comic scenes **$350.00**
1890, Walter A Wood Mowing & Reaping Machine Co. **75.00**
1895, Royal Fire Insurance **45.00**
1901, Lipton Tea, little girl in pink dress, 10 x 12" **110.00**
1903, A & P Tea, shopkeeper and products **180.00**
1905, Giant Powder Co. **175.00**
1906, Deering Harvester, young woman illus **65.00**
1906, Frank Coe's Fertilizer **70.00**
1908, Lister Animal Fertilizer **45.00**
1908, Swift's Premium **150.00**
1910, Hanley & Kinsetta Coffee, lithographed, 10 x 15" **30.00**
1913, Ceresota Flour, girl and flour bag illus **85.00**
1914, Ashland Brewery **65.00**
1916, Metropolitan Insurance **15.00**
1919, Hood's Sarsaparilla, orig envelope **45.00**
1920, Globe Feeds, children and chickens **110.00**
1921, Milton Bradley, full color illus and songs **15.00**
1927, Commercial State Bank **75.00**
1939, Sunshine Cookies **18.00**
1940, Keen Kutter **60.00**
1951, Four Seasons, Norman Rockwell illus **35.00**

Tarzan, 1978, Ballantine Books, color litho, orig cardboard mailer, 13 x 24½", $65.00.

1963, Pasadena Tournament of Roses 15.00
1978, Elvis Presley 12.00

CALIFORNIA POTTERIES

California pottery collectors divide into three distinct groups—art pottery, dinnerware, and figurine collectors. California art pottery is trendy and expensive. Dinnerware prices are stable. Figurine prices are cooling following a major price run in the mid- and late 1990s.

California pottery collectors focus on firm, pattern, or period within their adopted specialty. Over a dozen checklist books dealing with a specific manufacturer have been published in the last ten years. Each was followed by a short speculative period in the company's product.

Periodical: *The Pottery Collectors Express,* P.O. Box 221, Mayview, MO 64071.

Batchelder, tile, peacock illus, unglazed, "Batchelder Los Angeles" imp mark, 6" sq. **$95.00**
Brastoff, Sascha, dinner plate, Winrock pattern, 11" d 20.00
Brayton Laguna, figure, Mexican Man, 9" h 60.00
Brayton Laguna, figure, Mexican peasant couple hugging, textured bisque, high glaze, in-mold mark, 12½" h 60.00
Cleminsons, plate, crowing rooster, 9½" d 8.00
Cleminsons, wall pocket, chef, stamped mark, 7¼" h 25.00
Freeman-McFarlin, figure, mermaid holding shell dish, pink tinted bisque, high glaze, c1957 . . . . 35.00
Hagan-Renaker, standing goose, white, orange bill and feet, 6½" h 35.00
Keeler, Brad, figure, blue jay, mkd "Brad Keeler #735," 7¼" h 25.00
La Mirada Pottery, wall pocket, fish shape, chartreuse crackle glaze 15.00
Manker, William, condiment tray, fish shape, stamped, 11¾ x 16¾" 100.00
Pierce, Howard, figure, hippo, 6" l, stamped 25.00
Schoop, Hedi, figure, clown, playing cello, mkd, c1943, 12½" h 80.00
Schoop, Hedi, tray, King of Diamonds 45.00
Twin Winton, ice bucket, Hillbilly line, in-mold mark 25.00
Twin Winton, salt and pepper shakers, pr, Hillbilly line 10.00
Wallace China, ashtray, "Season's Greetings Wallace China Co, Los Angeles, California," c1950 . . . . 25.00
Will-George/The Claysmiths, figure, small bird on branch, paper label, 2 x 5" 22.50

Brastoff, Sascha, mug, Alaska line, totem motif, sgd "Sascha B.," 5" h, $55.00. Photo courtesy Jackson's Auctioneers & Appraisers.

Figure, Justin X Grape, mkd "The California Raisins ©1987 Calrab, Applause, China," 5½" h, $15.00.

CALIFORNIA RAISINS

California Raisins are those adorable claymation raisins seen on television commercials sponsored by the California Raisin Advisory Board. The American viewing public fell in love with the Raisins' conga line performance of Marvin Gaye's hit single "I Heard It Through the Grapevine." The exploitation of these wrinkled raisins soon followed, much to the delight of the Advisory Board. California Raisins were soon found dancing their way across a myriad of merchandise from address books to welcome mats.

Bookmark, paper, punched hole for tassel **$4.00**
Bubble Bath, Rockin Raisin, purple, 24 oz 10.00
Candy Container, glass, plastic lid, dancing raisins on sides, 8" h 25.00
Coloring Book, Sports Crazy, Marvel Books, Canada, ©Calrab, Applause, 1988, 8 x 11" 20.00
Doll, stuffed, plush, Acme, ©Calrab, 30" h 25.00
Figure, F F Strings, Hardee's premium 5.00
Figure, Raisin playing guitar, turquoise sneakers, made in China, 1988, 2½" h 10.00
Figure, Santa Raisin Man, green sneakers, Santa hat, made in China, 1988, 3" h 10.00
Game, The California Raisins Board Game, 18¾ x 9½" box 15.00
Lunch Box, Thermos, plastic, with thermos 30.00
Pinback Button, "California Raisins For President," 1¾" d 3.00
Radio, AM, posable arms and legs, orig box, 1988 . . . .
Tote Bag, pink canvas, 3 Conga Dancers illus 15.00
Umbrella, 1988 . . . .
Wall Clock, figural wrist watch, white plasticc 50.00

CAMARK POTTERY

Camark pottery derives its name from its location in Camden, Arkansas. The company was organized in 1926 and produced decorative and utilitarian items in hundreds of shapes, colors, and forms. The pottery closed in 1986.

Club: Arkansas Pottery Collectors Society, P.O. Box 7617, Little Rock, AR 72217.

Ashtray, sunburst **$15.00**
Basket, USA 028, 4½" h 24.00
Casserole, chicken lid 40.00
Creamer, USA 898, 2" h 18.00
Figure, cat, USA N62, 10" h 60.00
Figure, lion 35.00
Figure, pointer 35.00

Pitcher, bulbous, cat handle, 8½" h 50.00
Planter, elephant , 11 x 8" 60.00
Planter, rolling pin, N1 51 . . . . 8.00
Vase, boot, USA 565 . . . . 20.00
Vase, fluted, 7" h. 30.00
Wall Pocket, torch, USA N22, 6" h. 20.00

CAMBRIDGE GLASS

The Cambridge Glass Company of Cambridge, Ohio, began operation in 1901. Its first products were clear tablewares. Later color, etched, and engraved pieces were added to the line. Production continued until 1954. The Imperial Glass Company of Bellaire, Ohio, bought some of the Cambridge molds and continued production of these pieces.

Club: National Cambridge Collectors, Inc., P.O. 416, Cambridge, OH 43725.

Periodical: *The Daze,* P.O. Box 57, Otisville, MI 48463.

Apple Blossom, basket, pink $18.00
Apple Blossom, salt and pepper shakers, pr 30.00
Caprice, bonbon, blue, low, ftd, 6" sq 50.00
Caprice, bowl, alpine blue, oval, handle, #65, 11" l 95.00
Caprice, bowl, blue, bell shaped, 10½" d 155.00
Caprice, bowl, crystal, crimped, 4 ftd, 13" d. 40.00
Caprice, candy dish, cov, crystal, 3 ftd 45.00
Caprice, cigarette box, cov, crystal, 3½ x 2½" 20.00
Caprice, comport, blue, low, ftd, #130, 7" d. 50.00
Caprice, console set, pink, 13" d ftd bowl, pr of #70 candlesticks with prisms 250.00
Caprice, creamer and sugar, blue, individual 52.00
Caprice, creamer and sugar, crystal, table size 22.00
Caprice, cup and saucer, crystal. 16.50
Caprice, lemon dish, blue, 2 handles 25.00
Caprice, luncheon plate, blue, 8½" d. 35.00
Caprice, plate, blue, ftd, 11" d. 75.00
Caprice, plate, crystal, ftd, 11" d 50.00
Caprice, rose bowl, alpine blue, 6" d 150.00
Caprice, sherbet, crystal, tall 12.00
Caprice, torte plate, blue, 4 toes, 13" d 90.00
Caprice, tray, blue, oval, 6" l 50.00
Caprice, tumbler, ftd, crystal, 5 oz 18.00
Chantilly, cocktail shaker, metal top 95.00
Chantilly, creamer and sugar, sterling base 58.00
Chantilly, water goblet. 20.00
Diane, bowl, 11" d 35.00
Diane, cocktail, tall. 18.00
Diane, cup and saucer, scroll handle 30.00
Diane, oil bottle, orig stopper, 6 oz 10.00
Diane, torte plate, 14⅝" d 45.00
Elaine, compote, Gadroon etching 58.00
Everglades, relish, 3 parts 45.00
Gloria, ice bucket, pink, chrome handle 65.00
Rosepoint, basket, 6" sq. 65.00
Rosepoint, candlesticks, pr, 5" h. 115.00
Rosepoint, champagne 25.00
Rosepoint, cheese and cracker set 115.00
Rosepoint, cocktail, 3 oz. 35.00
Rosepoint, compote, 6" d 55.00
Rosepoint, cup and saucer. 35.00
Rosepoint, goblet, 10 oz 65.00
Rosepoint, plate, 2 handles, 6½" d. 55.00
Rosepoint, relish, 3 part, 4 toed, 10" d 95.00
Rosepoint, sherbet, 6 oz 22.00
Rosepoint, tumbler, ftd, 5 oz 42.00
Rosepoint, wine, 3½ oz. 55.00
Wild Flower, champagne. 30.00
Wild Flower, cup and saucer 20.00

CAMEOS

Cameos are a form of jewelry that has never lost its popularity. Cameos have been made basically the same way for centuries. Most are dated by their settings, although this is risky, since historic settings can be duplicated very easily.

Normally, one thinks of a cameo as carved from a piece of conch shell. However, the term cameo means a gem that is carved in relief. You can find cameos carved from gemstones and lava. Lava cameos are especially desirable.

Beware of plastic and other forms of copycat and fake cameos. Look carefully at the side. If you spot layers, shy away. A real cameo is carved from a single piece. Your best defense when buying a cameo is to buy from a dealer that you can find later and then have the authenticity of the cameo checked by a local retail jeweler.

Bracelet, designed with 7 hardstone, shell, and lava cameos depicting classical females, 14k yg mount $920.00
Brooch, antique ivory cameo, depicting female in profile in high relief, engraved 18k yellow gold frame with applied wiretwist. 757.50
Brooch, hardstone cameo, Roman soldier in profile, 18k yg frame 1,495.00
Brooch, hardstone cameo, Mercury in profile, seed pearl and 18k yg wiretwist frame 920.00
Brooch, shell cameo, female in profile adorned with grapes and grape leaves, in goldtone metal frame 287.50
Brooch, Victorian agate, depicting classical male in pr file, some veining, 14k yg mount. 1,092.00
Button, pearl, carved cameo and lily of the valley dec 10.00
Earpendants, antique malachite cameos, depicting bust of male withing a ropetwist frame in 18k yg. 1,150.00
Earrings, hobe shell, rhinestones, smoked crystals. 45.00
Hair Ribbon Holder, dated 1913 . . . . 12.50
Necklace, hard stone, silver filigree chain with jet beads, mkd "Czech" 65.00
Pendant, plastic, molded, plastic link chain, c1920. . . . . 85.00
Ring, lady's, 14k yg. 30.00

Victorian Shell Cameo Brooch, classical male with olive leaf crown in profile, swivel mount, heavy link 14k yellow gold frame, $805.00. Photo courtesy Skinner, Inc., Boston, MA.

Sign, Kodak Cameras Film, with hanger, metal, 2-sided, new old stock, in orig box, 18" h, 24" h with hanger, $55.00. Photo courtesy Collectors Auction Services.

CAMERAS

Just because a camera is old does not mean that it is valuable. Rather, assume that the more examples of a camera that were made the less likely it is to be of some value. Collectors are after unusual cameras or examples from companies that failed quickly.

A portion of a camera's value rests on how it works. Check all bellows cameras by shining a strong light over the outside surface while looking at the inside. Also, check the seating on removable lenses.

It is only recently that collectors have begun to focus in on the 35mm camera. You can still build a collection of early models at a modest cost per camera.

There is a growing market in camera accessories and ephemera. A camera has minimum value if you do not know how it works. Whenever possible, insist on the original instruction booklet as part of the purchase.

Clubs: American Photographic Historical Society, Inc., 1150 Avenue of the Americas, New York, NY 10036; American Society of Camera Collectors, 7415 Reseda Blvd., Reseda, CA 91335; National Stereoscopic Assoc., P.O. Box 14801, Columbus, OH 43214; Photographic Historical Society, Inc., P.O. Box 39563, Rochester, NY 14604.

Periodical: *Classic Camera,* P.O. Box 1270, New York, NY 10156.

CAMERA

Ansco, Kiddie Camera, red covering and strap, c1926–29 . . . . . **15.00**
Ansco, studio, fixed tailboard, double extension bellows, sliding back, c1947, 8 x 10" **100.00**
Asahi, Pentax Auto 110 Super, electronic self-timer, single stroke advance, slow speed warning in finder, 24mm f2.8 lens, c1982 . . . . . **65.00**
Blair Camera Co, Hawk-Eye Junior, box, 1895–1900 . . . . . **75.00**
Brownie Jr, 6-20 . . . . . **38.00**
Canon, Dial 35, 35 mm, 1963–67 . . . . . **50.00**
Conley Camera Co, Kewpie #2A, box **15.00**
Eastman Kodak Co, Auto Colorsnap 35, black and gray plastic, 35 mm, 1962–64 . . . . . **12.00**
Eastman Kodak Co, Buckeye Camera, folding, leather cov, c1899 . . . . . **125.00**
Eastman Kodak Co, Duex Camera, helical telescoping front, double lens, 620 film, 1940–42 . . . . . **15.00**
Eastman Kodak Co, Pocket Instamatic, Model 60, 110 film, 1972 . . . . . **20.00**
Lure Camera Ltd, plastic, 110 film, c1973 . . . . . **3.00**
Minolta, 24 rapid 24 x 24mm, 35mm range finder, built-in meter **80.00**
Olympus, Pen S 2.8, Zuiko 30mm f2.8 lens, Copal X shutter, 1960–64 . . . . . **45.00**
Pho-Tak Corp, Eagle Eye, box, metal, eye-level optical finder, 110mm lens, c1950–54 . . . . . **5.00**
Polaroid, Pathfinder 110A, 1957–60 . . . . . **50.00**
Supersport Dolly, folding, 12 exp, 120 film, with rangefinder, c1935–41 . . . . . **125.00**
Universal, Uniflash, plastic, Vitar f16/60mm lens, orig flash and box, c1940 . . . . . **20.00**
Yashica, Atoron Electro, 8 x 11mm, black finish, case, flash, filters, and presentation box, c1970 . . . . . **50.00**

CAMERA RELATED

Bag, plastic, camera shape, transparent plastic tinted magenta lens and back, c1985 . . . . . **10.00**
Bank, Kodak Disc bank, black plastic, camera shape, aluminum colored cov, c1983 . . . . . **2.50**
Book, *Lecia Guide,* W D Emanuel, Focal Press, 112 pp, 1945–53 . . . . . **8.00**
Box, Eastman's Kodak Developing Powders, "For Use in Brownie Tank Developer," c1900 . . . . . **8.00**
Magazine, *Studio Light,* 107 issues, 1917–29 . . . . . **200.00**
Puzzle, Kolorcube, Eastman Kodak Co, Kodak logo on each square **8.00**
Radio, transistor, shaped like Kodak Instant Color Film PR10 pack, wrist strap, made in Hong Kong **10.00**
Windup, figural film box, Eastman Kodak Co **3.00**

CAMERAS, NOVELTY

Over the years, collectors of cameras have been a serious bunch with a hierarchy interested in sophisticated, top-end equipment or beautiful antique pieces. Recently, more interest has been drawn to cameras exhibiting vibrant multicolor designs with a flair for grabbing one's attention.

Plastic cameras depicting cartoon characters Mickey Mouse, Bugs Bunny, Punky Brewster, Holly Hobbie, Teenage Mutant Ninja Turtles, etc., are a fun collecting area that can really brighten up a shelf. The most striking are the "face" cameras resembling some of these characters, clowns, bears, or Santa Claus, and even a full figure Charlie Tuna.

Early 1930s Kodak box and folding cameras can be found in red, blue, brown, green, pink, and some even more exotic colors. The challenge exists in finding an example of each model in each color. What an admirable display!

Character, Roy Rogers, plastic case, metal front plate with Roy and Trigger and facsimile signature, with orig box and Camera Club Membership Card, mfg by George, $115.00. Photo courtesy New England Auction Gallery.

The Art Deco crowd will want both sizes of the Beau Brownies and the diamond, lightning bolt, and step patterns of the folding Petites.

Collecting the cardboard covered disposable cameras is the new craze that is just beginning to catch on. Here the rewrapped and reloaded models advertising products such as Winchester bullets, Playboy, Budweiser, college sports teams, cereals, etc., are the most desirable. Their graphic art designs are colorful—making them stand out is any collection.

Note: Prices listed are for cameras in excellent condition.

Advertising, Budweiser, disposable **$15.00**
Advertising, Cinnamon Toast Crunch, disposable **8.00**
Advertising, J C Whitney, "Everything Automotive" **12.00**
Advertising, Marlboro, plastic, 110 film **45.00**
Box, Kodak, Beau Brownie, Art Deco front, pink, sizes 2 and 2A **175.00**
Box, Kodak, Brownie, various colors, sizes 2 and 2A **40.00**
Box, Macy, Flash 120, metal, black crinkle enamel finish, Art Deco faceplate **10.00**
Character, cat, Micro 110, oversized hinged lens cov shaped like cat holding fish, c1988 . . . . **10.00**
Character, Dick Tracy, plastic, black, Seymore Products. **45.00**
Character, Donald Duck, olive drab, 127 film. **45.00**
Character, Holly Hobbie, white plastic, decals, 126 film **30.00**
Character, Mickey Mouse, plastic, black, red plastic straps, 127 film, early 1960s, 3 x 3 x 5" **50.00**
Character, Roy Rogers and Trigger, plastic, black, metal flash attachment, vinyl carrying strap, Herbert George Co, Chicago, 1940–50, 3 x 3¼ x 3¼". **100.00**
Character, Smurf, Illco Toy Co, blue plastic, musical, plays *Rock-a-bye-Baby,* 1982 . . . . **5.00**
Character, Spider Man, plastic, 126 film. **30.00**
Disposable, Encore De Luxe, cardboard, c1940s **25.00**
Disposable, Fling 35, yellow box with multicolored K logo on front. **9.00**
Disposable, Mal-It Camera Mfg Co, Inc, cardboard. **35.00**
Disposable, Time Magazine **10.00**
Disposable, University of Nebraska, Herbie Husker, "Huskers" on front. **12.00**
Figural, can, Gent Coffee, EIKO **35.00**
Folding, Petite, Kodak, with replacement black bellows. **75.00**
Folding, Kodak, Rainbow Hawk-Eye, sizes 2 and 2A. **80.00**
Folding, Kodak, Vest Pocket Rainbow Hawk-Eye **40.00**
Toy, Fisher-Price, pocket, 110 film, c1984 . . . . **20.00**
Toy, Squirt Camera, L S, made in Hong Kong, molded black plastic features **5.00**

Disposable Camera, Harley–Davidson, Let The Good Times Roll, $20.00.

CANDLEWICK

Imperial Glass Corporation issued its No. 400 pattern, Candlewick, in 1936 and continued to produce it until 1982. In 1985 the Candlewick molds were dispersed to a number of sources, e.g., Boyd Crystal Art Glass, through sale.

Over 650 items and sets are known. Shapes include round, oval, oblong, heart, and square. The largest assortment of pieces and sets were made during the late 1940s and early 1950s. Watch for reproductions!

Club: The National Candlewick Collector's Club, 275 Milledge Ter., Athens, GA 30606.

Ashtray Set, 400/550, colored **$22.00**
Bowl, 400/183, 3 toed **60.00**
Bowl, 400/233, square **140.00**
Bud Vase, 400/25 . . . . **53.00**
Butter Dish, 400/144. . . . . **30.00**
Cake Plate, 400/67D, low **50.00**
Candle Holder, 400/100 . . . . **12.00**
Candy Box, 400/59 . . . . **48.00**
Celery, 400/105 . . . . **35.00**
Centre Bowl, 400/138 . . . . **125.00**
Cocktail, 400/18 . . . . **60.00**
Compote, 400/45 . . . . **22.00**
Dinner Plate, 400/10D, 10½" d **35.00**
Heart, 400/73H, handled. **175.00**
Hostess Helper, 400/37 . . . . **125.00**
Hurricane, 400/152R. **295.00**
Lazy Susan, 400/1503 . . . . **195.00**
Lemon Tray, 400/221 . . . . **42.00**
Marmalade, 400/19. . . . . **55.00**
Match Holder, 400/118 . . . . **45.00**
Plate, 400/42E **11.00**
Punch Cup, 400/211 . . . . **35.00**
Relish, 400/1112, with dressing set, 3 part **115.00**
Seafood Icer, 400/18 . . . . **65.00**
Sugar Dip, 400/64. . . . . **8.00**

CANDY COLLECTIBLES

Who doesn't love some form of candy? Forget the chocoholics. I'm a Juicy Fruit man. Once you start looking for candy related material, you are quickly overwhelmed by how much is available. Do not forget the boxes. They are usually discarded. Ask your local drugstore or candy shop to save the more decorative ones for you. What is free today may be worth money tomorrow.

Club: Candy Container Collectors Club of America, P.O. Box 352, Chelmsford, MA 01824.

Advertising Trade Card, John Colgan Taffy Tolu Chewing Gum, sepia, cherubs and product. **$45.00**
Advertising Trade Card, Newton Brothers Pepsin Chewing Gum, diecut, emb, 1887 . . . . **85.00**
Calendar, 1901, George Smith & Son Bakers & Confectioners, Colonial couple, full pad. **25.00**
Calendar, 1912, Fern Brand Chocolates, emb, multicolored **6.00**
Candy Box, Whitman Candy, Pickaninny Peppermints, black children **12.00**

Candy Container, tin, football, brown, ribbon trim, 2" l, $

Candy Container, cardboard, barrel shape, paper oak stave finish, "Old Doc Brox, Horehound Drops, Double Strength," E R Brach & Sons **475.00**
Candy Container, composition, rabbit holding flowers, made in Germany, 7¾" h **120.00**
Candy Container, glass, clown, sitting on rocking horse, blue **225.00**
Candy Container, glass, rabbit, holding basket on arm, mkd "USA," 4½" h **50.00**
Candy Container, tin, church, white, 8 cutout windows, brown door and window, 3½" h **125.00**
Candy Dish, cov, Diana, clear **15.00**
Candy Dish, cov, Queen Mary, clear **20.00**
Candy Dish, cov, Heisey, Greek Key, ftd **55.00**
Catalog, Eppelsheimer & Co, New York, chocolate molds, 34 pp, c1928 . . . . **48.00**
Display, Clark's Teaberry Gum, countertop, Vaseline Glass, emb, pedestal **40.00**
Poster, Wrigley's Gum, "Pioneer Women Helped Build Our Great Country," woman wearing bonnet, Otis Shepard illus, c1943, 28 x 11" **100.00**
Sign, Wrigley's Chewing Gum, woman selling gum to girl **375.00**
Toy Train, Baby Ruth, car, Lionel **36.00**

CAP PISTOLS

Classic collectors collect the one-shot, cast iron pistols manufactured during the first third of the 20th century. Kids of the 1950s collect roll-cap pistols. Children of the 1990s do not know what they are missing. Prices for roll-cap pistols are skyrocketing. Buy them only if they are in working order. Ideally, acquire them with their appropriate accessories, e.g., holsters, fake bullets, etc.

Club: Toy Gun Collectors of America, 3009 Oleander Ave., San Marcos, CA 92069.

Daisy Cap Pistol, 9½" l, dark bronze luster finish white metal, dark brown marbled wood grain plastic grips, each with Daisy bull's-eye emblem, Daisy logo on left side under cylinder, left side of barrel mkd "Daisy Mfg Co," top loading, 1960s **$100.00**
Dent, Villa, cast iron, 1934, 4¾" l **60.00**
Hamilton, Cheyenne, 9½" l, die cast nickel finish, smooth white grips with "CS," logo in gold on right grip, 1955–60 . . . . **82.00**
Hubley, Colt .45, die cast with revolving cylinder, bullets, engraved, nickel, gold cylinder, ivory grips **121.00**
Hubley, Cowboy Cap Pistol, 11½" l, nickel finish metal, white plastic steer head grips, side opens for loading, 1½ x 5 x 11½" box **386.00**
Hubley, Wyatt Earp, "Buntline Special," long barrel, die cast nickel finish, canyon brown steerhead grips with star medallion, 1955–61 . . . . **160.00**
Kilgore, Roy Rogers, 8½" l, silvered white metal, marbled ivory gray plastic grips, each with "RR" brand initials plus raised horse head designs, Roy's name on left side under cylinder area, barrel with various ranch brand symbols plus logo of maker, top loading, 1950s . . . **225.00**
Leslie-Henry, Davy Crocket, full size horsehead grips **395.00**
Leslie-Henry, Gene Autry 44 Cap Pistol with holster set, 10½" l, nickel finish white metal, ivory white plastic raised horse head grips, cylinder rotates when trigger is pulled, left side opens for loading, holster belt with bright silver luster metal buckle, holster decorative disk, rivet caps, bullet clip holds 3 red wooden toy bullets, 1950s **325.00**
Lone Star, Gambler, 3½" l, black die cast metal, grained white plastic grips, designed to fire single cap plus potato pellet to be formed by pressing int bullet cartridge into common potato, c1960s, ¾ x 3¾ x 3¾" box **35.00**
Lone Star, James Bond, 100 Shot Repeater, 1965 . . . . **200.00**
Marshal, 11½" l, silvered metal, ivory plastic grips, white plastic belt with 6 bullets, 1960s **75.00**
Marx, Davy Crockett Flintlock Pistol, 10¾" l, brown marbelized hard plastic body, gold accents including name on 1 side of barrel, cast metal hammer and firing plate for single caps, late 1950s **126.00**
Mattel, Fanner Shootin' Shell, 9" l, die cast, revolving cylinder accepts bullets, chrome plated, stag grips, 1958–65 . . . . **41.00**
Roy Rogers, 2½" l, gold finish metal, "RR" symbol on each grip, black leather holster, 1950s **50.00**
Schmidt, Hopalong Cassidy, nickel body, normal black grips and white busts, 1 grip cracked, 1950–55 . . . . **195.00**
Schmidt, Roy Rogers, die cast nickel, long ribbed barrel, fully engraved frame, checkered copper grips with Roy Rogers and Trigger, red jewels, 1950–60 . . . . **285.00**
Stevens, Spitfire, 4½" l, silvered cast iron, ivory white plastic grips, each depicting 3 fighter planes, left grip plate opens for loading **75.00**
Stevens, The Sheriff, 8½" l, nickel finish cast iron, ivory white plastic insert grips, right grip with raised image of crossed 6-shooters and cowboy head, left grip with raised image of horse head, both with inset red cut glass stone, top loading, 1¼ x 4½ x 8½" box **156.00**

Schmidt, Roy Rogers, 10" l pistol, imitation leather studded holster and belt, 3 x 3" metal belt buckle with emb Roy inside horseshoe, $420.00. Photo courtesy New England Auction Gallery.

CARNIVAL CHALKWARE

Carnival chalkware is my candidate for the kitsch collectible of the 1980s. No one uses *quality* to describe these inexpensive prizes given out by games of chance at carnivals, amusement parks, and ocean boardwalks.

The best pieces are those depicting a specific individual or character. Since most were bootlegged (made without permission), they often appear with a fictious name, e.g., "Smile Doll" is really supposed to be Shirley Temple. The other strong collecting subcategory is the animal figure. As long as the object comes close to capturing the appearance of a pet, animal collectors will buy it.

Casper the Friendly Ghost, wooden pull toy, colorful paper labels, 10" h. Photo courtesy New England Auction Gallery.

Ashtray, Amos & Andy, mkd "I'se Regusted," c1930–40, 7½" h **$195.00**
Bank, Army Sgt Bilko, at ease, c1945–50, 12" h **75.00**
Bank, cat, sitting, large bow tie, c1945–50, 12" h **35.00**
Bank, clown, standing behind small drum, c1940–50, 12" h **65.00**
Bank, cow, sitting, c1945–50, 9½" h **45.00**
Figure, Barney Google, c1930–40, 6½" h **95.00**
Figure, Bell Hop, ©J Y Jenkins Studio, Venice, CA, 13" h **85.00**
Figure, Betty Boop, c1930–40, 14½" h **295.00**
Figure, bird, with nest, c1940–50, 9½" h **40.00**
Figure, boy, with newspapers, c1935–45, 7" h **30.00**
Figure, Charlie McCarthy, sitting in chair, c1935–50, 9½" h **60.00**
Figure, chipmunk, sitting, holding nut, c1945–50, 5½" h **20.00**
Figure, cowboy, wearing 10 gal hat, hand behind head, c1935–45, 12" h **55.00**
Figure, Indian, on horse back, c1930–40, 11" h **55.00**
Figure, Lovebirds, kissing, mkd "Eagle Love," c1940–50, 6¼" h **30.00**
Figure, majorette, mkd "El Segundo Novelty Company," 1949, 12" h **55.00**
Lamp, buffalo, American Bison, charging, orig back glass, c1930–40, 8½ x 10" **145.00**

CARTOON COLLECTIBLES

This is a category with something for each generation. The characters represented here enjoyed a life in comic books and newspaper pages or had a career on movie screens and television.

Every collector has a favorite. Buy examples that bring back pleasant memories. "That's All Folks."

Note: For information on collector clubs/fan clubs for individual cartoon characters, refer to *Maloney's Antiques & Collectibles Resource Directory* by David J. Maloney, Jr., published by Antique Trader Books.

Barney Google, figure, Schoenhut, wood, jointed, cloth jacket, shirt, and pants, mid 1920s, 7¼" h **$400.00**
Beanie and Cecil, toy guitar, molded black plastic, colorful paper label of Beanie and friends in Leakin' Lena and smiling Cecil image in background, red wooden handle on right side, Cecils eyes and mouth move as music plays, Mattel, ©1961 Bob Clampett, complete with 4 orig vinyl strings and pick **50.00**
Beetle Bailey, Fold-A-Way Camp Swampy Playset, MPC, fold-open cardboard box, plastic soldiers, jeeps, trucks, and exploding bridge, five 3" detailed character figures, 1964 .... **175.00**
Betty Boop, mug **22.00**
Blondie and Dagwood, Blondie and Dagwood Interchangeable Blocks, Gaston Mfg, painted wooden blocks, 7 x 9" box, 1951 .... **35.00**
Bugs Bunny, coloring book, front cov shows Bugs taking photo of Elmer who is balancing carrot on his nose, Whitman, #1147, ©Warner Bros, 8 x 10¾", unused **25.00**
Bugs Bunny, necktie, clip-on, c1940, 10½" l **50.00**
Bullwinkle, badge, plastic, "Bullwinkle's Deputy Mountie," Stoffel Seals, Tuckahoe, NY, c1980s, 2¾" h **45.00**
Casper the Friendly Ghost, bank, glow-in-the-dark, 1967 .... **75.00**
Dagwood, sandwich bag, waxed paper, large Bumstead image, 1952 .... **25.00**
Deputy Dawg, record, 78 rpm, Peter Pan Records, full color glossy envelops, ©1962 Terrytoons **20.00**
Felix the Cat, candy container, composition, figural, "Germany" printed in purple on underside, mid 1920s, 6" h **700.00**
Huckleberry Hound, figure, ceramic **55.00**
Jiggs, pin, enamel, diecut full figure Jiggs in brass, holding cigar and cane, red and black enamel accents, c1920, 1¼" h **100.00**
Joe Palooka, lunch box, litho tin, 1948 .... **45.00**
Krazy Kat, clip, enamel and brass, brass bar with black enamel figure of Krazy Kat playing mandolin, "So's Your Old Man," c1920s, 1¼" l **100.00**
Little Lulu, centerpiece, Hallmark, diecut peg hole at top with photo of Lulu shooting marbles as gang looks on, clubhouse and tree in background, ©Western Publishing Co, Inc, c1970s, 9¼ x 14" envelope **25.00**
Maggie and Jiggs, salt and pepper shakers, pr, figural, mkd "Made In Japan," 1930s, 2½" h **65.00**

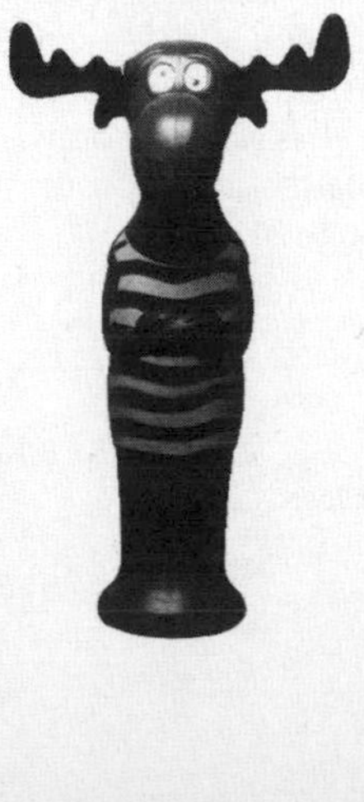

Soaky, Bullwinkle, Colgate-Palmolive, 1960s, $50.00.

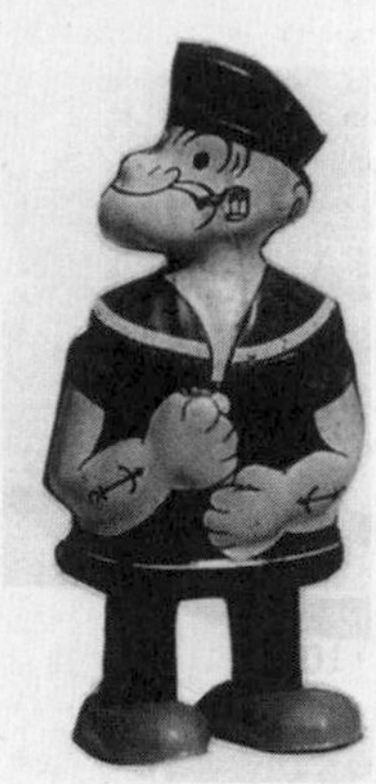

Popeye, tin windup, Chein, mkd "Chein Made in USA" on shirt back, with key, 6" h, $275.00. Photo courtesy Collectors Auction Services.

National, Model 130, serial #622,909, marble shelf on front, older restoration, c1908, 19" h, $935.00. Photo courtesy Collectors Auction Services.

Moon Mullins, nodder, bisque, Germany, 3⅞" h **60.00**
Pink Panther, dish, plastic, 3 sections **30.00**
Popeye, ball, juggler, litho tin, 1929 . . . . **55.00**
Popeye, chalk, white and colored pcs, 1953, MIB **24.00**
Porky Pig, bookends, pr, metal, figural, smiling full figure Porky wearing red vest, blue bow tie atop green base, name in orange on front next to brown accent tree, c1947, 3 x 3¾ x 4½" h **100.00**
Porky Pig, comic book, Porky's Book of Tricks, premium, cov shows Porky dressed as Santa as Bugs tries on his beard and Sniffles polishes his boots, 48 black and white pp of stories, puzzles, and games, colorful image of smiling Porky in Christmas wreath with imprint of PA department store, ©1942 Leon Schlesinger Prod, Inc, 5½ x 8½" **25.00**
Schmoo, figural planter, white ceramic, smiling Schmoo image, his back serving as planter, late 1940s, 4¾" h, 3¼" d **45.00**
Slow Poke Rodriguez, glass, Pepsi Collector series, both sides show Slow Poke walking along with hand to mouth, ©Warner Bros, 1973, 6¼" h **25.00**
Speedy Gonzales, bank **25.00**
Woody Woodpecker, breakfast set, mug and log shape cereal bowl, F & F Mold Co **50.00**
Woody Woodpecker, clock, animated, 1960s **145.00**
Yellow Kid, ice cream mold, full figure, hinged, 4¾" h **185.00**

CASH REGISTERS

If you want to buy a cash register, you had better be prepared to put plenty of money in the till. Most are bought for decorative purposes. Serious collectors would go broke in a big hurry if they had to pay the prices listed below for every machine they buy.

Beware of modern reproductions. Cash registers were meant to be used. Signs of use should be present. There is also a tendency to restore a machine to its original appearance through replating and rebuilding. Well and good. But when all is said and done, how do you tell the refurbished machine from a modern reproduction? When you cannot, it is hard to sustain long-term value.

Club: Cash Register Collectors Club of America, P.O. Box 20534, Dayton, OH 45420.

American, copper plated, 50 key **$1,000.00**
McCaskey, oak, orig decal, metal account files, 2 drawers, refinished, 23 x 23 x 27" **150.00**
Michigan, #1, 22 keys **200.00**
National, #52, brass, emb, ornate ledge on 3 sides, 17" h, restored **862.50**
National, #317, marble change shelf, printer, 5¢ to $1.00, 16" h **1,200.00**
National, #342, brass, crank operated, drawer, 24" h **600.00**
National, #349, 2 drawers, 1910 . . . . **800.00**
National, #552-5, brass, oak base **450.00**
National, #542, brass, keys up to $99.99, receipt machine at side, running totals at other side, crank operated, brass cash drawer, 24" h **600.00**
Peninsula, Muren, nickel plated, c1912 . . . . **250.00**
Toy, Tom Thumb, Western Stamping Co, steel, complete with play money and "thank you" card, 1950–60 . . . . **15.00**
Toy, Uncle Sam's Cash Store Register, Durable Toy & Novelty Corp, #150, steel, black enamel finish, c1940, 5" h **30.00**

CASSETTE TAPES

Flea markets thrive on two types of goods—those that are collectible and those that serve a secondhand function. Cassette tapes fall into the latter group. Buy them for the purpose of playing them.

The one exception is when the promotional pamphlet covering the tape shows a famous singer or group. In this case, you may be paying for the piece of paper ephemera rather than the tape, but you might as well have the whole shooting match.

Several times within recent years there have been a number of articles in the trade papers about collecting eight-tracks. When was the last time you saw an eight-track machine? They are going to be as popular in thirty years as the wire tape recorder is today. Interesting idea—too bad it bombed.

Average price 50¢ to $2.

CAST IRON

This is a category where you should be suspicious that virtually everything you see is a reproduction or copycat. More often than not, the object will not be original. Even cast iron frying pans are being reproduced.

One of the keys to spotting the newer material is the rust. If it is orange in color and consists of small pinpoint flakes, forget it. Also check paint patina. It should have a mellow tone from years of exposure to air. Bright paint should be suspect.

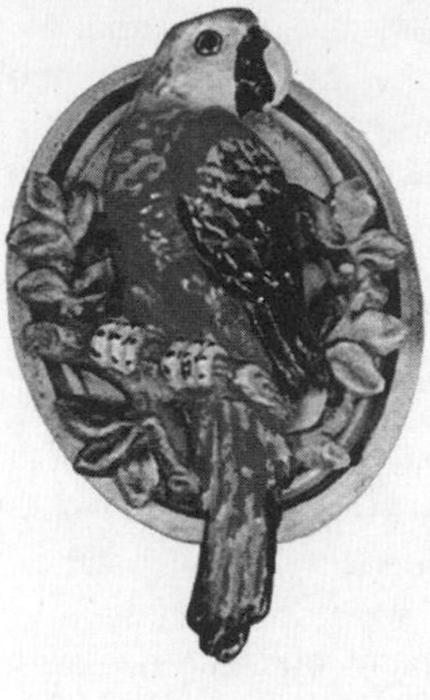

Door Knocker, Hubley, multicolored parrot on branch, 4¼ x 2¾", $110.00. Photo courtesy Bill Bertoia Auctions.

Cast iron is a favorite of the country collector. It evokes memories of the great open kitchen fireplaces and wood/coal burning stoves of our ancestors. Unfortunately, few discover what a great cooking utensil cast iron can really be.

Club: Griswold & Cast Iron Cookware Assoc., P.O. Box 243, Perrysburg, NY 14129.

Newsletter: *Cast Iron Cookware News,* 28 Angela Ave., San Anselmo, CA 94960; *Kettles 'n Cookware,* P.O. Box 247, Perrysburg, NY 14129.

Andirons, pr, birds, copper wash, owl perched on branch, yellow glass eyes, c1920, 14" h **$165.00**
Baking Pan, Wagner, #1508 . . . . **250.00**
Bank, Cocker Spaniel, Hubley **120.00**
Bookends, pr, elephants, red polychrome, 4" h **85.00**
Bottle Opener, Cocker Spaniel, black **65.00**
Bottle Opener, sailor **65.00**
Bottle Opener, trout **75.00**
Bread Stick Pan, Griswold, #21 . . . . **150.00**
Cigarette Dispenser, elephant, bronze repaint, 8½" l **30.00**
Griddle, round, Wagner, #7 . . . . **35.00**
Door Knocker, basket of flowers, orig polychrome paint, 3¾" l **30.00**
Door Stop, basket of tulips, Hubley, tall slender basket, 13" h **550.00**
Door Stop, crying baby, kneeling on pillow, fists clenched at shoulders, 8¾" h **83.00**
Door Stop, penguin, standing upright, wearing bowtie, 10½" h **165.00**
Door Stop, sea dragon, head resting at base, upraised scaly body and tail, 14" h **83.00**
Garden Urn, removable ears, white repaint, 28½" h **290.00**
Pencil Holder, penguin **70.00**
Spittoon, white porcelain int, c1850, 5½" h, 8½" d **435.00**
Toy, coupe, Arcade, blue and nickel with decal, 5" l **165.00**
Toy, motorcycle cop, Champion, blue and white, 4⅞" l **132.00**
Toy, fire truck, Arcade, red with blue and silver, Arcade balloon wheels, decal label, repaired, 9¾" l **165.00**
Toy, steam shovel, Kenton, red with nickel plate, 4⅞" l **192.50**
Toy, train, Overland Limited, 9" l engine and 2 passenger cars mkd "Doric" and "Ionic," nickel finish with copper japanned tin on car tops **110.00**
Toy, train, Pennsylvania, 9¾" l engine with tender and 3 passenger cars mkd "Pennsylvania R.R. Co. Eloise," worn dark finish with bronze detail, 1 set wheels missing **220.00**

Toy O Rama, multicolor, 40 pp, 1955–56, 7 x 10¼", $40.00.

CATALOGS

Catalogs are used as excellent research sources. The complete manufacturing line of a given item is often described, along with prices, styles, colors, etc. Old catalogs provide a good way to date objects.

Many old catalogs are reprinted for use by collectors as an aid to identification of their specialities, such as Imperial and The Cambridge Glass Co.

Collecting Hint: The price of an old catalog is affected by the condition, data, type of material advertised, and location of advertiser.

Armstrong Cork Co, Lancaster, PA, 52 pp, 1940, 8 x 10¾" **$36.00**
Borg-Warner Corp, appliances, 8 pp, c1940 . . . . **8.00**
Butler Bros, Chicago, IL, kitchenware, hardware, housewares and electrical goods, 102 pp, 1949, 8¼ x 10¾" **28.00**
Dennison Mfg Co, Framingham, MA, holiday decorations, 36 pp, 1926, 5½ x 8¼" **42.00**
Eastman Kodak Co, Rochester, NY, 28 pp, 1920s, 4¾ x 6¾" **11.00**
Montgomery Ward, Chicago, IL, Fall and Winter, 1,412 pp, 1972, 8 x 11" **24.00**
Montgomery Ward, Chicago, IL, Spring and Summer, 1,256 pp, 1970, 8 x 11" **22.00**
Porter Paint Co, St Louis, MO, "The Painters' Friend," 206 pp, 1939, 6¾ x 9¾" **28.00**
Royal Tailor, The, Chicago, IL, 12 pp, 1913, 10 x 13" **13.00**
S & H Green Stamp Premiums, 1928 . . . . **25.00**
Scott's Standard Postage Stamp Catalog, 1,300 pp, 1938 . . . . . **12.00**
Sears, Roebuck & Co, Chicago, IL, auto accessories, 34 pp, c1920, 8 x 11" **22.00**
Sears, Roebuck & Co, Chicago, IL, Spring and Summer, 1,008 pp, 1943, 8 x 11" **38.00**
Spiegel, May, Stern Co, Chicago, IL, 48 pp, c1929, 9½ x 13½" **19.00**
Standard Mail Order Co, New York, NY, clothing and shoes, 64 pp, 1914, 6 x 8½" **9.00**

CAT COLLECTIBLES

It is hard to think of a collecting category that does not have one or more cat-related items in it. Chessie the Cat is railroad oriented; Felix is a cartoon, comic, and toy collectible. There rests the problem. The poor cat collector is always competing with an outside collector for a favorite cat item.

Sign, tin, Cherry Blossom Shoe Polish, 27⅞" h, 17¾" w, $88.00. Photo courtesy Collectors Auction Services.

Cat collectors are apparently as stubborn as their pets because I have never seen a small cat collectibles collection. The one additional thing that I have noticed is that, unlike most dog collectibles collectors, cat collectors are more willing to collect objects portraying other breeds of cats than the one that they own.

Club: Cat Collectors, 33161 Wendy Dr., Sterling Heights, MI 48310.

Advertising Trade Card, Choose Black Cat Reinforced Hosiery, multicolored diecut **$15.00**
Ashtray, ceramic, brown crouching cat, front paws extended, mkd "Made in China," 5" l **20.00**
Book, *Felix The Cat,* Big Little Book, Whitman, #1129, 1936 . . . . . . **50.00**
Box, cat shape, Oriental blue design with pink flowers, mkd "Made in China," 7½" l, 4½" h **65.00**
Calendar, wall, 3 parts, "Little Mischief," Tuck, several peeking cat faces, 1903 . . . . . . **25.00**
Cuff Links, pr, black arched back cat, silver color details **25.00**
Door Knocker, brass, Cheshire Cat, engraved, England, c1920 . . . . . . **55.00**
Figure, bisque, dark gray stripe tabby, seated and looking down, wiping 1 eye with paw, "Price Products Taiwan" paper label, 3¾" h **15.00**
Figure, brass cat on 7" sq marble base, 10" h **150.00**
Figure, ceramic, waving cat, green, pink, and purple floral and bamboo pattern, "Made in China" paper label, 10" h **50.00**
Figure, chalkware, long haired white cat lying on beige loveseat with red florals, lace doily top of loveseat, "Lauren Rarems" paper label, 4" h **40.00**
Pinback Button, Morris For President, Nine Lives Cat Food, multicolored photo portrait, bright red, white, and blue border, 1988, 2¼" d **10.00**
Plate, milk glass, three kittens **30.00**
Pocket Mirror, White Cat Union Suits, celluloid, black and white, cartoon illus, early 1900s, 2¾" l **65.00**

CAVES & CAVERNS

An amazing variety of antique items are available on American (and foreign) caves and caverns. Collectibles on caves and caverns can be broken down into two categories, i. e., paper items and non-paper items.

Paper collectibles include books, pamphlets, brochures, postcards, photos, stereo views, posters, sheet music, postage stamps, and even stock certificates from cave corporations. The items can be from caves located in this country or from caves throughout the world. Books and pamphlets on United States caves date from the early 1800s with tourist brochures and postcards dating from the turn of the century. Photos and stereo views of caves started with the Waldack views of Mammoth Cave in the 1860s. Early cave posters (mainly of French and Belgium caves) date to the late 1800s with more recent posters from caves throughout the world. Cave postage stamps have never been produced in the United States, but are available from many other countries.

Non-paper collectibles include souvenir items such as china plates, silver spoons, felt pennants, paperweights, and miscellaneous items such as glasses, hats, nodders, ashtrays, patches, matchbooks, etc.

China cave souvenirs made in Germany and Austria were imported by Wheelock, JonRoth, and others from the early 1900s through about 1934. Many caves imported these souvenirs in the shape of plates, vases, ashtrays, pitchers, and an amazing variety of other shapes including fish, boats, and musical instruments. After 1934 Staffordshire English china was imported by Mammoth Cave, Howe Caverns, Luray Caverns, and Carlsbad Caverns. In recent years most souvenirs are made in Japan and China.

Items pertaining to Floyd Collins, the famous cave explorer who died in Sand Cave in 1925, are also considered cave collectibles. Floyd Collins' items include books, postcards, sheet music, newspaper clippings, and even souvenir china showing his casket in Crystal Cave.

It should be noted that items removed from caves such as stalagtites and other formations, as well as archaeological pieces (arrowheads, etc) are never considered cave collectibles. In most states removing anything from a cave is illegal and can result in a fine or jail time, as happened in a recent Kentucky case.

Advisors: Bill and Judy Smith, P.O. Box 217, Marengo, IN 47140, (812) 945-5721, e-mail: Glstis@aol.com.

Book, *Life of the Cave, The,* Mohr & Poulson, dj **$8.00**
Book, *Mammoth Cave and the Cave Region of Kentucky,* Randolph, hardcover, 1924 . . . . . . **30.00**
Book, *Tragedy of Sand Cave,* Hartley, second ed, hardcover,, 1925 . . . . . . **45.00**
Book, *Underground Empire,* dj, 1948 . . . . . . **25.00**
Brochure, Cobb Caverns Texas **5.00**
Brochure, Mammoth Cave, 1930–1998 . . . . . . **1.00**
Dutch Shoe, china, shows Floyd Collins' casket in Crystal Cave, imported by JonRoth, c1932 . . . . . . **50.00**

Manual, The Mammoth Cave of Kentucky, **Horace Carter Hovey and Richard Ellsworht Call, 1st ed, gilt hard cover, 1897, $45.00.**

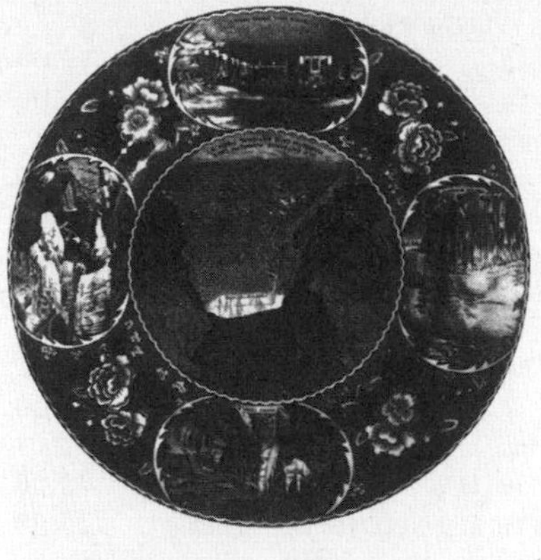

Souvenir Plate, Mammoth Cave Entrance, Staffordshird, c1950, $20.00.

Letter Opener, wood, Cave of the Winds, Niagara Falls, New York **40.00**
Matchbook Cover, Skyline Caverns **1.00**
Nodder, Mammoth Cave **35.00**
Pamphlet, Beautiful Caverns of Luray, The, 1920–1950 . . . . . . **20.00**
Pamphlet, Exploring Endless Caves, Reeds, 1926 . . . . **4.00**
Pamphlet, Jim White's Own Story, Carlsbad Caverns, sgd by Jim White **3.00**
Pamphlet, National Park Service Cave Booklets **3.00**
Paperweight, glass, Cave of the Winds, Colorado, c1950 . . . . . . **3.00**
Patch, Carlsbad Caverns **2.00**
Pennant, felt, Mammoth Cave, c1950 . . . . **5.00**
Postcard, chrome card of Mammoth Cave, c1950 . . . . **.10**
Postcard, linen card of Howe Caverns, c1920 . . . . **.10**
Postcard, real photo of guide at entrance of Mammoth Cave **10.00**
Postcard, strickler card of Luray Caverns, c1906 . . . . **.25**
Sheet Music, *Death of Floyd Collins, The,* 1925 . . . . **5.00**
Sheet Music, *I Want A Cave Man,* c1920 . . . . **8.00**
Sheet Music, *Mammoth Cave Waltz, The,* 1850 . . . . **25.00**
Souvenir Plate, Howe Caverns, made in Japan, c1950 . . . . **3.00**
Souvenir Plate, Luray Caverns Titania's Veil, Staffordshire, c1948 . . . . **20.00**
Souvenir Plate, Mammoth Cave Bridal Altar, imported by Wheelock, c1908 . . . . **25.00**
Souvenir Spoon, SS, Luray Caverns, c1900 . . . . **25.00**
Stereo View, Big Room, Carlsbad Caverns, c1930 . . . . **5.00**
Stereo View, James view of Luray Caverns, 1882 . . . . **10.00**
Stereo View, Waldack magnesium view of Mammoth Cave, 1866 . . . . **12.00**

CELLULOID

Celluloid is the trade name for a thin, tough, flammable material made of cellulose nitrate and camphor. Originally used for toilet articles, it quickly found a use as inexpensive jewelry, figurines, vases, and other household items. In the 1920s and 1930s, it was used heavily by the toy industry.

Be on the lookout for dealers who break apart dresser sets and sell the pieces individually as a way of getting more money. Also check any ivory or tortoise shell piece that is offered to you. Both were well imitated by quality celluloid.

Club: Victorian Era Celluloid Collectors Assoc., P.O. Box 470, Alpharetta, GA 30239.

Candlestick, pr, 8½" h **$35.00**
Canister Set, 3 pc, floral dec **12.00**
Card Holder, black base, 2 Mickey Mouse figures, "Walt Disney Enterprises Ltd/Japan" paper stick, 1930s **90.00**
Clothespin Set, miniature **15.00**
Compact, Rex Fifth Avenue, round, floral transfer on lid, 1939-40 . . . . **65.00**
Doll, cowboy, Japan, 1940-50, 7½" h **24.00**
Dresser Tray, jeweled dec **20.00**
Fan, painted flowers, dated 1914, replaced flowers **25.00**
Figure, baseball player, jointed, holds ball and glove, "#1" on back, Occupied Japan **125.00**
Manicure Set, leather roll-up case, 8 pcs **9.00**
Memo Book, Spirit of St Louis **18.00**
Mirror, Buckwalter Stove Co, Royersford, PA **65.00**
Pencil Clip, Diamond Edge, black, white, and red, silvered tin clip, early 1900s, ⅞" d **10.00**
Pin, Uncle Sam, diecut, movable arms and legs **35.00**
Purse, beaded, celluloid frame, sunburst style, butterfly motif **35.00**
Rattle, five faces **12.00**
Rattle, teething ring, silhouette pictures, dated 1916 . . . . **85.00**
Ruler, diecut, Western Union, silver and blue logo, tel graph and cable rates on back, 1905 patent, 7½" l **25.00**
Serving Tray, tortoise shell, 1960s **5.00**
Sharpening Stone, Circle Service Station, Hanover, PA **40.00**
Stamp Case, Tom Moore Cigar adv **35.00**
Toy, airship, hollow, red and blue, wood wheels, pull string, US Star Co logo on tail fin, 1930s, 1½ x 2¼ x 5½" **100.00**
Toy, boy, riding tricycle, Occupied Japan, MIB **95.00**

CEREAL BOXES

There is no better example of a collectible category gone mad than cereal boxes. Cereal boxes from the first half of the twentieth century sell in the $15.00 to $50.00 range. Cereal boxes from the 1950s through the 1970s can sell for $50.00 and up. Where's the sense?

The answer rests in the fact that the post–World War II cereal box market is being manipulated by a shrewd speculator who is drawing upon his past experience with the lunch box market. Eventually, the bubble will burst. Don't get involved unless you have money to burn.

Club: Sugar-Charged Cereal Collectors, 5400 Cheshire Meadows Way, Fairfax, VA 22032.

Periodical: *Flake: The Breakfast Nostalgia Magazine,* P.O. Box 481, Cambridge, MA 02140.

Alpha Bits, Post, premium offer, 1960s **$20.00**
Batman, Ralston, shrink wrapped plastic bank on front, 1989 . . . . **10.00**
Cheerios, General Mills, American Airlines Game Kit, 1956 . . . . **20.00**
Cocoa Puffs, General Mills, conductor's hat on back, 1959 . . . . **45.00**
Cocoa Pebbles, Post, Bedrock Bike Race poster, 1987 . . . . **3.00**
Corn Chex, Party Mix recipe on back, 1950s **65.00**
Corn Flakes, Kellogg's, Dingle-Dandies on back, 1955 . . . . . **100.00**
Corn Flakes, Kellogg's, Norman Rockwell illus, Atomic Sub offer, 1955 . . . . **50.00**
Ghostbusters, Ralston, frisbee offer, 1985 . . . . **10.00**
Grape-Nuts Flakes, Post, Hopalong Cassidy **200.00**

Hopalong Cassidy, Post, ©Wm Boyd, Wheat Meal Sample, 4 x 3", $210.00. Photo courtesy New England Auction Gallery.

Pep, Kellogg's, Mango Ford car and instruction sheet, 1950 . . . . **15.00**
Puffed Rice, Quaker, Gabby Hayes cannon ring offer, 1951 . . . . **350.00**
Quisp, Quaker, space trivia game on back, 1985 . . . . **25.00**
Rainbow Brite, Ralston, Crazy Chain offer, 1985 . . . . **30.00**
Raisin Bran, Post, Hopalong Cassidy western badge premium, 1950–51 . . . . **400.00**
Ranger Joe Rice Honnies and Wheat Honnies, Honeyville airport on back, 1950s **100.00**
Rice Krispies, Kellogg's, Howdy Doody and Clarabell masks, 1954 . . . . **300.00**
Sugar Crisp, Post, Dick Tracy Decoder offer, 1958 . . . . **100.00**
Sugar Frosted Flakes, Kellogg's, Mary Hartline magic doll offer, 1955 . . . . **225.00**
Sugar Pops, Kellogg's, Fun Niks offer, 1970 . . . . **50.00**
Sugar Smacks, Kellogg's, action cutouts on back, 1959 . . . . **100.00**
Trix, General Mills, sample box, 1954, $4^{1}/_{4}$" h **45.00**
Trix, General Mills, Trix Plush rabbit offer, 1985 . . . . **10.00**
Wheaties, General Mills, baseball's Johnny Bench Commemorative, 1989 . . . . **10.00**

CEREAL PREMIUMS

Forget cereal boxes. The fun rests with the goodies inside the box that you got for buying the cereal in the first place. Cereal premiums have changed a great deal over the past decade. No self-respecting manufacturer in the 1950s would have included a tube of toothpaste as their premium. Yuck!

Collectors make a distinction between premiums that came with the box and those for which you had to send away. The latter group is valued more highly because the items are often more elaborate and better made.

Club: Sugar-Charged Cereal Collectors, 5400 Cheshire Meadows Way, Fairfax, VA 22032.

Periodicals: *Flake: The Breakfast Nostalgia Magazine,* P.O. Box 481, Cambridge, MA 02140; *Toy Ring Journal,* P.O. Box 544, Birmingham, MI 48012.

Booklet, *The Frolie Grasshopper Circus,* multicolored, grasshoppers and clowns, whimsical scenes, American Cereal Co, Quaker Oats, 1895 . . . . **$65.00**
Breakfast Buddies, Winnie the Pooh characters, Nabisco, 1965 . . . . **10.00**
Card, pop-out, Dale Evans, Post Cereals, unused, M **15.00**
Cards, Sherman and Peabody Wiggle Pictures, Wheat Hearts, General Mills, 1960 . . . . **10.00**
Cereal Set, Marky Maypo figure and bowl, Maltex, 1961 . . . . **75.00**
Comic Book, Sugar Bear In The Race For Outer Space, 12 pp, Post Cereal, 1960s **15.00**
Comic Book, Yogi Bear Birthday Party, Kellogg's, 1962 . . . . **25.00**
Doll, stuffed, Huckleberry Hound, Kellogg's, 1960, 18" h **25.00**
Doll, stuffed, Toucan Sam, Kellogg's, 1964, 8" h **30.00**
Door Knocker, Woody Woodpecker, Kellogg's, 1964 . . . . **65.00**
Handbook, *Kellogg's Cadet Aviation Corps,* 28 pp, Kellogg's, ©1938, 6 x 9" **25.00**
Hand Puppet, Lamb Chop and Hush Puppy, Life, Quaker Oats, 1962, $7^{1}/_{2}$" h, price for each **25.00**
Huckleberry Hound Stampets Printing Set, Kellogg's, 1961 . . . . **25.00**
Medal, Frontier hero and Indian war medals, Rice Honeys, Nabisco, 1954 . . . . **8.00**
Model, punch-out, C-54 Skymaster war plane, Kellogg's pep, WWII **24.00**
Mug and Bowl Set, Yogi Bear mug, Huckleberry Hound bowl, Kellogg's, 1960 . . . . **25.00**
Musical Cornyphone, with instructions, Kellogg's, 1963, 9" l **20.00**
Racing Robot, Wheat Honey's, Nabisco, 1961, 2" h **15.00**
Record, *Hey There, It's Yogi Bear,* Kellogg's, 1964 . . . . **35.00**
Record, The Banana Splits, Kellogg's, 1968 . . . . **45.00**
Shari Lewis Finger Puppets, Life, Quaker Oats, 1962 . . . . **15.00**
Sponge, Twinkles the elephant, General Mills, 1960–61 . . . . **25.00**
Spoon, Yogi Bear, Kellogg's, 1960, 6" l **10.00**
Treasure Chest, Cap'n Crunch, Quaker Oats, 1966, 4 x 6 x 5" **50.00**

CHARACTER BANKS

These lovable creatures just beg for your money. Although pre-1940 bisque, cast iron, and tin character banks exist, this form reached its zenith in the age of injection molded vinyl plastic. Post-war examples are bright, colorful, and usually large in size. They make a great display collection.

Watch out for contemporary banks, especially ceramic models. Anything bank less than ten years old should be considered garage sale fodder—$1 to $2 at most.

Andy Gump Thrift Bank, tin, General Thrift Products Co, Chicago, IL, black ink stamp on bottom for First National Bank, East Chicago, IN, 1930s **$200.00**
Bullwinkle, hard vinyl, glossy painted body, plastic trap, ©Ward, 1977, 10" h **75.00**
Casper the Friendly Ghost, Renzi Co **20.00**

Dino and Pebbles, Hanna Barbera's Flintstones, molded vinyl, Homecraft Products, Vinyl Prod Corp, 1971, 13" h, $7^{3}/_{4}$" w, $45.00.

Donald Duck, ceramic, still, paint loss and crazing, 6" h, $22.00. Photo courtesy Collectors Auction Services.

Davy Crockett, metal **35.00**
Ernie Pig, figural, painted composition, pig dressed in football outfit, "GTA Feeds" decal, "Lit-O-Bit" decal, Ernie name in raised letters beneath coin slot, rubber trap, 1970s **175.00**
Fred and Wilma Flintstone, figural, Fred and Wilma holding hands against cave wall background, names incised in heart on bank reverse, 8¼" h **200.00**
Little Orphan Annie, dime register, litho tin, 1936 . . . . **200.00**
Scooby Doo, figural, gumball, plastic, clear smiling face holding white bone against dark brown back of head, yellow base with coin slot, Hasbro, 1968, 9" h **15.00**
Smokey Bear, figural, composition, smiling Smokey sitting on log, 1960s **85.00**
Snoopy, ceramic, 40th Anniversary **25.00**
Stan Laurel, hard vinyl, plastic trap, Larry Harmon Pictures Corp, ©Play Pal Plastics, 1972 . . . . **45.00**

CHASE CHROME AND BRASS COMPANY

The Chase Chrome and Brass Company was founded in the late 1870s by Augustus S. Chase and some partners. Through numerous mergers and acquisitions, the company grew and grew. The mergers helped to expand the product line into chrome, copper, brass, and other metals. Several name changes occurred until the company was sold as a subsidiary of Kennecott Corp in its merger with Standard Oil in 1981.

One of the most popular products this company made was the chrome Art Deco line, which really appealed to housewives in the 1930–1942 period.

Chase items can be found with some really neat styling and are usually marked. Just like the aluminum wares, it does not need polishing and is becoming just as hot with today's collectors.

Club: Chase Collectors Society, 2149 West Jibsail Loop, Mesa, AZ 85202.

Ashtray, chrome, Art Deco **$20.00**
Bank, barrel shape, brass chromium finish, double bolt lock, key **9.00**
Bud Vase, chromium, central tube with 3 applied tubes, stepped circular base **45.00**
Cake Server, chrome, yellow Bakelite handle, 12 x 8" **100.00**
Candy Dish, 2 part, round, upside down whale in middle, circular handle **45.00**
Champagne Bucket, Bacchus, Rockwell Kent, 9¼" h **500.00**
Cocktail Set, chrome, cylindrical shaker and ice bucket with black enameled lines, 11½ x 3¾" **100.00**
Smoking Stand, chrome, maroon Bakelite top inset with hooded ashtray, 21½ x 11" **165.00**
Snack Set, plate and matching cup, rainbow colors, set of 8 . . . . **185.00**
Sorbet and Cordial Set, with tray, chrome, cobalt glass, 15½ x 5" tray **100.00**
Tea Set, with tray, chrome, spherical, ftd, ivory Bakelite handles, 8½ x 8" teapot **150.00**
Tumbler, rainbow colors, set of 7 . . . . **20.00**

CHILDREN'S BOOK SERIES

Most of these children's book series, often referred to as young adult books, are collected by series. Not surprisingly, books whose main character is male are generally collected by men; those with a heroine are collected by women. Obtaining a complete run of a particular series is possible and would make for an interesting collection. Happy hunting!

Club: The Society of Phantom Friends, P.O. Box 1437, North Highlands, CA 95660.

Periodicals: *Mystery & Adventure Series Review,* P.O. Box 3488, Tucscon, AZ 85722; *Yellowback Library,* P.O. Box 36172, Des Moines, IA 50315.

BOBBSEY TWINS by Laura Lee Hope

Bobbsey Twins at the Seashore, #3 . . . . **$19.00**
Bobbsey Twins in Echo Valley, #36, 1943 . . . . **22.50**
Bobbsey Twins on a Ranch, #26, 1935 . . . . **10.00**
Bobbsey Twins on an Airplane Trip, #26, 1933 . . . . **35.00**
Bobbsey Twins, or Merry Days Indoors & Out **22.50**

FREDDY'S ADVENTURES by Walter R. Brooks

Freddy and the Baseball Team, 1955 . . . . **$150.00**
Freddy and the Flying Saucer Plans, 1957 . . . . **135.00**
Freddy Goes to the North Pole, 1951 . . . . **100.00**
Freddy Plays Football, 1949 . . . . **200.00**
Freddy the Cowboy, 1950 . . . . **325.00**
Freddy the Detective, 1944 . . . . **40.00**

HARDY BOYS by Franklin W. Dixon

Clue of the Broken Blade, #21, 1942 . . . . **$25.00**
Ghost at Skeleton Rock, #37, 1957 . . . . **25.00**
House on the Cliff, #2, 1927 . . . . **50.00**
Hunting for Hidden Gold, #5, 1928 . . . . **135.00**

Freddy and the Perilous Adventure, Walter R. Brooks, Kurt Wises illus., Knopf, 1942, $48.00.

Tom Swift and His Flying Lab, **Victor Appleton II author, 208 pp, Grosset & Dunlap, 1954, $20.00.**

JERRY TODD SERIES by Leo Edwards

Jerry Todd, Editor-in-Grief, #10, 1930 . . . . **$60.00**
Jerry Todd & the Buffalo Bill Bathtub, #13, 1936 . . . . **75.00**
Jerry Todd's Poodle Parlor, #15, 1938 . . . . **60.00**

JUDY BOLTON MYSTERIES SERIES by Margaret Sutton

Haunted Attic, #2, 1932 . . . . **$50.00**
Phantom Friend, #30, 1959 . . . . **90.00**
Unfinished House, #11, 1938 . . . . **30.00**

MOTOR BOYS by Clarence Young

Motor Boys Afloat, #5, 1908 . . . . **$50.00**
Motor Boys on the Pacific, #8, 1909 . . . . **17.50**
Motor Boys Overland, #2, 1906 . . . . **50.00**
Motor Boys: Ned, Bob & Jerry on the Firing Line, 1919 . . . . . . **25.00**

NANCY DREW by Carolyn Keene

Clue in the Ancient Disguise, #60, 1982 . . . . **$25.00**
Clue of the Black Keys, #28, 1954 . . . . **25.00**
Haunted Showboat, #35, 1957 . . . . **55.00**
Mystery at the Ski Jump, #29, 1952 . . . . **60.00**
Secret of the Golden Pavilion, #36, 1959 . . . . **50.00**
Secret of the Red Gate Farm, #6, 1931 . . . . **50.00**

TOM SWIFT by Victor Appleton II

Tom Swift and His Electric Rifle, 1911 . . . . **$20.00**
Tom Swift and His Electric Retroscope, #14, 1959 . . . . **25.00**
Tom Swift and the Great Oil Gusher, 1924 . . . . **20.00**
Tom Swift and His Sky Train, #34, 1931 . . . . **150.00**

CHILDREN'S COLLECTIBLES

Mothers of the world unite. This category is for you. The children who used it hardly remember it. It's the kind of stuff that keeps your children forever young in your mind.

There is virtually nothing written about this collecting category so what to collect is wide open. One collector I know has hundreds of baby planters. To each their own.

Clubs: Children's Things Collectors Society, P.O. Box 983, Durant, IA 52747; Toy Dish Collectors Club, P.O. Box 159, Bethlehem, CT 06751.

Advertising Trade Card, A N & T Coy Linen Netting, diecut standup, little girl wearing net dress, "Fishermen are filled with joy At the sight of Netty Coy" **$25.00**
Baby Scale, pink, 1940s **38.00**
Bonnet, baby's, cotton, tatted, ribbon rosettes **15.00**
Book, *Mother Goose Rhymes,* Saalfield, illus by Fern Bisel Peat, linen, 1929, 7¼ x 8½" **15.00**
Book, *The Tale of Cuffy Bear,* Arthur Scott Bailey, Grossett & Dunlap, 1915, 112 pp **10.00**
Booklet, *Our Baby's First & Second Years,* Carnick's Soluble Food, baby on front cov, advice and product information, 64 pp **20.00**
Catalog, Best & Co Lilliputian Bazaar, children and infants specialty shop, 1935, 48 pp **20.00**
Chair, oak, pressed back, acorn finials, turned spindles back and sides, rolled arms attached to seat, rect foot rest, turned legs and front stretcher, 42" h **175.00**
Cookbook, Kitchen Fun: A Cookbook for Children **7.00**
Cradle, pine, primitive, simple scalloped bracket on curved hood, old black repaint, New England, 36" l **275.00**
Dish Set, Farm Breakfast Set, service for 3, tin and plastic, 1972 . . . . **35.00**
Game, Children's Hour, Parker Brothers, board game, "A Laugh A Minute," contains 3 games including "Porky the Pig," 1950–60s **30.00**
Lamp, ceramic, figural bear base, 3 bears motif on shade, 14½" h **65.00**
Pedal Car, hook and ladder pumper, sheet metal, worn metallic red paint, 45" l **85.00**
Plate, chicks dec, Roseville **110.00**
Puzzle, Criss Cross Spelling Strips, McLoughlin Brothers, New York, NY, c1880, 10 x 9" **100.00**
Puzzle, Farm Friends Puzzle Box, Milton Bradley, Springfield, MA, 3 puzzle set, 1913–35, 13 x 17" box **75.00**
Record, *Mind Your Mommy/London Bridge,* Voco Inc, cardboard picture record, 1948 . . . . **8.00**
Record, *The Ugly Duckling,* Mercury Childcraft Records, 1940s **2.50**
Sled, pansies and geometric designs, yellow on red painted panel, "R H White/Boston/Kitchen D P" stenciled signature on bottom, orig finish, 36" l **150.00**
Tea Set, Blue Willow Tea Set, Ideal, plastic, teapot, creamer, sugar bowl, 4 cups and saucers, serving platter . . . **45.00**
Tea Set, Holly Hobby Tea Set, Chein, metal teapot, 4 blue plastic cups, 4 metal plates and saucers, set of 4 plastic knives, forks, and spoons, 1970s **35.00**

Toy, Bar-Bee-Q, GW, Japan, battery operated, metal, combination grill and rotisserie, black grill, silver hood, box mkd "A GW Quality Toy," orig box and instructions, 9" h, 4¾" d, $165.00.

Toy, Four Leaf Clover Bubble Pipe, Chemical Sundries Co, Chicago, 1962 . . . . **5.00**
Toy, Dial Pla-Phone, Gong Bell, blue steel, numbers and letters cardboard insert, clear plastic dial, 1950s **50.00**
Toy, Junior Typewriter, Marx, metal litho base and carriage, dial face, plastic knobs, type dial, c1957 . . . . **10.00**
Tricycle, Thunderbolt, pulley type, wooden seat, 34" l. **200.00**

CHINTZ CHINA

Chinta China—or "All-Over-Floral" as it is known in England—can be best described as wallpaper applied to ceramics. One of the hottest collectibles of 1996, chintz cooled slightly in 1997 and has become even hotter in 1998, attracting a whole new group of collectors. Chintz was first made in the early 1800s and continued in various forms until well into the 1960s. Some new collectors are buying the German, Czechoslovakian, Japanese and Dutch chintz ceramics because the prices are much lower than the English earthenware chintz made in Staffordshire. English bone china chintz—especially Shelley—and Victorian chintz are becoming more popular here in North America but it is the 1930–1960 chintz which still commands the highest prices. Factories such as James Kent, Crown Ducal, Lord Nelson, and Midwinter produced a number of chintz patterns, but Grimwade's Royal Winton was the leading manufacturer and is considered the "Cadillac" of chintz.

Chintz ware was exported to North America, particularly Canada in huge quantities from the 1920s until the 1960s. Since it was cheap and cheerful when it was sold, it can turn up anywhere. Although breakfast sets have been selling for $1,000–$4,000, the English Chintz Club reported two Julia breakfast sets bought in charity shops and flea markets for under $5 within the past few months!

Grimwade's alone produced over seventy chintz patterns although some are considered much more collectible than others. Prices can vary widely on the same teapot or cake plate depending on which pattern was used. Most of the Royal Winton, James Kent and Lord Nelson pieces have the pattern name incorporated into the backstamp, making identification simple. Read the *Charlton Standard Catalogue of Chintz, Second Edition* in order to familiarize yourself with the different patterns and shapes and then head to the nearest garage sale or flea market.

Christie's South Kensington in London have an annual chintz auction in August. The first all-chintz auction in North America was held in Copake, NY, in 1998. Prices have gone so high that Royal Winton, James Kent, and Lord Nelson now have begun to reproduce chintz. Although most pieces are marked, Royal Winton produced some general giftwares in Summertime and Florence early in 1998 that have caused confusion for new collectors. Check the web site chintznet.com for examples of new and old backstamps. Remember that the new Royal Winton chintz has a circle around the backstamp; this did not appear on the original pieces.

Advisor: Susan Scott, 882 Queen St. West, Toronto, Ontario M6J 1G3, fax (416) 658-4675, e-mail: scottca@ibm.net.

Clubs: Royal Winton International Collector's Club, Dancer's End, Northall, LU6 2EU, England, Tel: 011441525220272, Fax: 011441525222442, e-mail: The Chintz Collector, P.O. Box 50888, Pasadena, CA 91115 (626) 441-4708, Fax: (626) 441-4122.

A G RICHARDSON & CO LTD, CROWN DUCAL

Butter Dish, Spring Blossom, square **$325.00**
Compote, Purple Chintz, yellow border, octagonal **495.00**
Jug, Blue Chintz, 6 1/2" h **650.00**
Jug, Primula, 3 3/4" h **250.00**

ELIJAH COTTON, LORD NELSON

Bud Vase, Marina **$165.00**
Cup and Saucer, Briar Rose **135.00**
Saucer Boat and Stand, Rosetime **185.00**

GRIMWADE'S, ROYAL WINTON

Candy Box, cov, ftd, Shrewsbury **$425.00**
Creamer and Sugar, Nantwich, Ascot shape **175.00**
Coffeepot, Fireglow, Perth shape **1,150.00**
Cruet Set, salt, pepper, and cov mustard with tray, Kew **750.00**
Cup and Saucer, Crocus **155.00**
Cup and Saucer, Spring Glory **60.00**
Jug, Sweet Pea, globe shape, 5" **650.00**
Plate, Julia, Ascot shape, 8" sq **285.00**
Salt and Pepper Shakers, pr, with tray, Summertime, Fife shape **25.00**
Sandwich Tray, Majestic, Ascot shape, 10 1/4 x 6" **265.00**

JAMES KENT, LTD

Breakfast Set, Apple Blossom **$1,200.00**
Bud Vase, Rosalynde, 2 1/2" **175.00**
Jug, Silverdale, Dutch shape, 3 3/4" **200.00**

Royal Winton Breakfast Set, Florence, Countess shape, $3,500.00.

Lord Nelson stacking teapot, Royal Brocade, $895.00.

Nut Dish, individual, Apple Blossom 55.00
Plate, Marigold, 7¾" 145.00
Sugar Bowl, Hydrangea, octagonal 85.00
Teapot, Du Barry, 3 cup. 575.00
Toast Rack, 4-slice, Du Barry, large 595.00

W R MIDWINTER, LTD

Biscuit Barrel, Brama/Springtime, chrome lid $495.00
Demitasse, Brama 130.00
Jam Pot, Lorna Doone/Bird Chintz, chrome lid, round. 95.00
Sugar Shaker, Brama, metal top 375.00

SHELLEY POTTERIES, LTD

Cup, Saucer, and 5½" Plate, Primrose Chintz $225.00
Cup and Saucer, Rock Garden, Henley shape. 155.00
Hot Water Pot, Melody, 7¾" 700.00
Plate, Maytime, 8½" sq 175.00

CHRISTMAS

Of all the holiday collectibles, Christmas is the most popular. It has grown so large as a category that many collectors specialize in only one area, e.g., Santa Claus figures or tree ornaments.

Anything Victorian is "hot." The Victorians popularized Christmas. Many collectors love to recapture that spirit. However, prices for Victorian items, from feather trees to ornaments, are quickly moving out of sight.

This is a field where knowledgeable individuals can find bargains. Learn to tell a late nineteenth/early twentieth century ornament from a modern example. A surprising number of dealers cannot. If a dealer thinks a historic ornament is modern and prices it accordingly, he is actually playing Santa Claus by giving you a present. Ho, Ho, Ho!

Club: Golden Glow of Christmas Past, 6401 Winsdale St., Minneapolis, MN 55427.

Bank, Santa, painted hollow plaster, coin clot in back, Duquesne Statuary Co, Pittsburgh, c1950s, 12" h $65.00
Bobbing Head, Santa, painted composition, spring mounted head, c1960s, 6" h 50.00
Book, *Night Before Christmas or A Visit from St Nicholas,* McLaughlin Bros, 1896 . . . . 20.00
Candy Container, elf, cylinder type, wire neck, 8" h 25.00
Candy Container, Santa, cardboard, spring head, West Germany, 13" h. 60.00

Santa Bank, Noel Decorations, Inc, orig box, $242.00. Photo courtesy Bill Bertoia Auctions.

Christmas Tree Ornaments, box of 6 pine cones, Shiny Brite, Japan, 2⅝" h, $2.00.

Catalog, Montgomery Ward Christmas Book, 240 pp, 1950, 8 x 11" 20.00
Catalog, Treasure Island of Toys, "Santa Claus Takes Pete Panda To The Treasure Island Of Toys," 28 pp, 1940, 7½ x 10¼" 20.00
Figure, choir boy, hard plastic, 3½" h. 4.50
Figure, Santa, full beard and hair, chime hat, 6¼" h 70.00
Greeting Card, "Merry Christmas From Our House," American, 1930s. 2.50
Light Bulb, bird, milk glass, painted, Japan 15.00
Light Bulb, house, milk glass, pink and white, Japan 10.00
Memo Pad, celluloid cov, brunette woman within holly and berry wreath accented by red bow at bottom above 1909 copyright, Whitehead & Hoag Co, unused, 2 x 3". 20.00
Nativity Scene, plastic, Hong Kong, 3¾ x 4¾" 12.00
Ornament, cat in shoe, glass 38.00
Ornament, flamingo, blue mercury glass 40.00
Pinback Button, Santa holding writing quill feather while conversing on candlestick telephone, "First Trust & Savings Bank, Kankakee, Illinois/Christmas Club," 1¼" d 40.00
Pinback Button, Santa reaching into pack as children await at doorway, 1¼" d 8.00
Planter, sleeping Santa sitting in chair, 5 x 6½ x 4¾". 18.00
Stocking, red flannel, stenciled Santa and sleigh. 5.00
Tree, brush, green, glass bead dec, red base, 9" h. 15.00
Tree, cellophane, 15" h 15.00
Tree Stand, revolving. 20.00

CHRISTMAS AND EASTER SEALS

Collecting Christmas and Easter Seals is one of the most inexpensive "stamp" hobbies. Sheets usually sell for between 50¢ and $1.00. Most collectors do not buy single stamps, except for the very earliest Christmas seals.

Club: Christmas Seal and Charity Stamp Society, P.O. Box 39696, Minneapolis, MN 55439.

CIGARETTE AND CIGAR

Cigarette products contain a warning that they might be hazardous to your health. Cigarette and cigar memorabilia should also contain a warning that they may be hazardous to your pocketbook. With each passing year, the price for cigarette and cigar-related material goes higher and higher. If it ever stabilizes and then drops, a number of collectors are going to see their collections go up in smoke.

The vast majority of cigarette and cigar material is two-dimensional, from advertising trade cards to posters. Seek out three-dimensional pieces. There are some great cigarette and cigar tins.

Clubs: Cigar label Collectors International, P.O. Box 66, Sharon Center, OH 44274; Cigarette Pack Collectors Assoc., 61 Searle St., Georgetown, MA 01833; International Seal, Label & Cigar Band Society, 8915 E. Bellevue St, Tucson, AZ 85715.

Ashtray, Fatima Turkish Cigarettes, ceramic, 3¼" d **$100.00**
Cigar Band, German Iron Cross **16.00**
Cigar Band, Priscilla **35.00**
Cigar Box, Yellow Cab, rect, front color illus of Yellow Cab with lettering, int Yellow Cab litho, 7 x 5½" **130.00**
Cigar Box Label, Challenge Cup **45.00**
Cigar Box Label, Idle Hours **55.00**
Cigar Box Label, Scarlet Crown Cigars **25.00**
Cigar Cutter, cast iron, emb fancy filigree on front and base, 3½" h **200.00**
Cigarette Dispenser, music box shape, lift lid **185.00**
Cigarette Maker, E-Z Maker, 1933 . . . . **35.00**
Cigarette Pack, Aide De Camp, Westminster Tobacco Co, London, c1938 . . . . **6.00**
Cigarette Pack, Black Death Filter Cigarettes, c1985 . . . . **3.00**
Cigarette Pack, Charleston, Denmark, c1955 . . . . **3.00**
Cigarette Pack, Lady Hamilton, J & B Soter Tobacco Corp, NY, c1935 . . . . **8.00**
Cigarette Pack, Lucky Strike, American Tobacco Co, NY, c1935 . . . . **25.00**
Cigarette Pack, Viceroy, B & W, Louisville, KY, c1955 . . . . **6.00**
Cigarette Pack, Winston, R J Reynolds Tobacco Co, Richmond, VA, 4 per pack, c1965 . . . . **6.00**
Flip Book, Fatima Cigarettes **15.00**
Match Holder, Kool Cigarettes, tin **25.00**
Pinback Button, Union Made Cigars, red, white, blue, and black, light green cigar label, c1890, 1¼" d **20.00**
Pocket Mirror, Philip Morris **20.00**
Poster, Kool Cigarettes, smoking penguin pointing to pack, c1933, 12 x 18 . . . . **35.00**
Sign, Charles the Great Cigars, tin, c1910, 11⅔ x 17½" **275.00**
Sign, El Wadora Cigars, tin, c1930, 24 x 36" **45.00**
Sign, Nickel King Cigars, cardboard, 16 x 18" **35.00**
Sign, Viceroy Cigarettes, neon, red and yellow **180.00**

Cigar Box, Charmer Perfecto Extra, 10¢ size, tax stam, series 115, Class C, $15.00. Photo courtesy Frank's Antiques.

Advertising, AAA, chrome plated, Regens, 2⅛" h, $30.00.

CIGARETTE LIGHTERS

Cigarette lighters come in all shapes and sizes. Collections could be assembled focusing on several different categories, i.e., flat advertising lighters, figural lighters, or even figural advertising lighters. The possibilities are endless. Buy lighters in good condition only. Scratches and/or missing parts greatly detract from a lighter's value. Remember, cigarette lighters were mass produced and therefore plentiful.

Clubs: International Lighter Collectors, P.O. Box 536, Quitman, TX 75783; Pocket Lighter Preservation Guild & Historical Society, Inc., 380 Brooks Dr., Ste. 209A, Hazelwood, MO 63042.

Advertising, Alpine, pocket, Japan, c1960s, 2" h **$10.00**
Advertising, Camel, gift box, Zippo, c1993, 2¼" h **15.00**
Advertising, Salem, chromium, Zippo, c1991, 2¼" h **15.00**
Art Deco, Electro-Match, black plastic, gold trim, table, Korex Co, c1950s, 5¾" h **15.00**
Art Deco, Octette, chromium and black enamel, table, Ronson, 3½" h **50.00**
Electric, figural gremlin, Aircraft Novelty Co, 1930s, 4¼" h **50.00**
Electric, figural telephone, metal and painted enamel, table, built-in clock and ashtrays on each side, late 1930s, 3½" h **50.00**
Figural, hound dog, chromium, table, Ronson, c1934, 4½" h **30.00**
Figural, penguin, gold and SP, c1960, 2" h **40.00**
Figural, rose, chromium, table, mid 1960s, 2½" h **20.00**
Figural, slot machine, Bently Gifts, Inc, N Bellmore, NY, Japan patent **35.00**
Flaminaire, Swiss, lighter and watch, case **50.00**
Table Model, Zippo, Pat #251791 . . . . **60.00**

CIRCUS

Traveling tent circuses were an exciting event in rural towns across the country—evidence the large amount of memorabilia left behind.

I keep threatening to take my son to see the great annual circus parade in Milwaukee featuring the equipment from the Circus World Museum in Baraboo, Wisconsin. I need him to be my traveling companion because my wife, Connie, wants nothing to do with my circus fantasies. She insists that living with me is all the circus she needs.

Clubs: Circus Fans Assoc. of America, 1544 Piedmont Ave., ME, Ste. 41, Atlanta, GA, 30324; Circus Historical Society, 3477 Vienna Ct., Westerville, OH 43081.

Book, punch-out, Whitman, 6 pp, unpunched, 1954, 10 x 14½ **$40.00**
Cabinet Photo, fat lady, inscribed "Miss Gertie Plathm 510 lbs, 5 ft, 11 in," late 1890s **25.00**
Game, Game of Day at the Circus, McLoughlin Bros, 1898 . . . . **1,000.00**
Game, Merry Circus Game, Milton Bradley, 1960 . . . . **12.00**
Menu, Greatest Show on Earth, Nov 12, 1898, full color **100.00**
Newspaper, *St Paul Dispatch,* MN, Jun 30, 1876, The Great Circus, back page ad **12.00**
Pennant, felt, Ringling Bros and Barnum & Bailey Circus, brown, white lettering and circus scenes, yellow trim and streamers, 1940s **25.00**
Pinback Button, "Arabian Circus/Barton Show Grounds/By Akdar Temple/May 1st to 6th Tulsa, Okla/Trade You Smiles," red fez on cream ground, tin back, 1¼" d **10.00**
Pinback Button, "Clyde Beatty/Cole Bros Circus," black and gray photo of man holding young lion or leopard in his arms, 1 gloved hand under animal's mouth, 1930s, 1¾" d **20.00**
Pinback Button, "The Barnum Festival," copper colored plastic disk with detailed raised bust of Barnum facing right, accented by 7 flags and inscribed below "Bridgeport Connecticut," reverse with needlepost and brass clutch, 1" d **10.00**
Postcard, Barnum & Bailey, complete set of 12, "Souvenir from the Barnum & Bailey, Greatest Show on Earth," published by L Fränzl, Germany, c1902 . . . . **500.00**
Poster, Bill Lynch-Shows, World's Largest Midway, Art Deco style, 29 x 42" **110.00**
Poster, Carson and Barnes Wild Animal Circus, 1961 . . . . **50.00**
Poster, Cole Brothers Circus, Big Railroad Show, Kay Hanneford, Greatest Bareback Rider of All Time, full color litho, Erie Litho & Ptg, Erie, PA, 18 x 26" **126.50**
Poster, Dailey Brothers Big Railroad Circus Presents/Pina Medel/World's Most Beautiful and Graceful Circus Star, color photo portrait, 42 x 14" **165.00**
Poster, King Brothers Combined 3 Ring Circus, crouching tiger, woodcut style, 1950s, 28 x 40" **49.50**
Poster, Ringling Brothers and Barnum & Bailey Circus, The Greatest Show on Earth, laughing white-faced clown, 20 x 28" **82.50**
Poster, Tiger Bills Wild West, Big Free Street Parade, clown images, wrinkled, 1930s, 28 x 41" **110.00**
Program, Martin Bros Circus Magazine, souvenir, 64 pp, 1936 . . . . **20.00**
Stereograph, Windsor & Whipple, Olean, NY, people with elephant **35.00**
Ticket, Adam Forepaugh Sells Bros, complimentary, ornate, numbered, 1910, price for set of 4 . . . . **20.00**
Ticket, Hunt's Three Ring Circus, annual pass, engraved, hand sgd by Charles A Hunt to "G. A. Hunt and Party," 1933 . . . . **20.00**

Poster, Carson and Barnes Circus, paper, red, yellow, and blue, 42 x 28", $66.00. Photo courtesy Poster Mail Auction.

CLICKERS

If you need a clicker, you would probably spend hours trying to locate a modern one. I am certain that they exist. You can find a clicker at a flea market in a matter of minutes. As an experiment, I tried looking up the word in a dictionary. It was not there. Times change.

Clickers made noise, a slight sharp sound. I believe their principal purpose was to drive parents crazy. I understand they played a major role at parochial school, but cannot attest to the fact since I attended public school.

Advertising, Bonnie Laddie Shoes, purple, emb boy **$24.00**
Advertising, Castles Ice Cream, blue and white, bird and "I'm Chirping For Castles Ice Cream" **33.00**
Advertising, Forbes Coffee, red, white, and blue, trademark logo and "Forbes Quality Brand Coffee" **44.00**
Advertising, Gunther's Beer, red and white, "Just Click For Gunther's Beer, The Beer That Clicks" **22.00**
Advertising, Jack & Jill Gelatin Dessert **40.00**
Advertising, Maxwell House, blue and gray, "Drink Maxwell House Coffee" **52.00**
Advertising, Purity Salt, multicolor, product image **38.50**
Advertising, Saltines Crackers **10.00**
Advertising, Smile, "Drink Smile" **35.00**
Advertising, Steelco Stainless Steel, blue and white, "4450 Ravenswood Chicago, The Greatest Name In Fine Cookware" **24.00**
Advertising, Stroehmann Bread, red, white, and yellow, 2 clowns holding "Stroehmann Bread" banner, 4½" l **43.00**
Advertising, Tastykake, 1940–50 . . . . **12.00**
Character, Mickey Mouse, playing banjo, 1930s **40.00**
Christmas, Santa and fireplace scene **25.00**
Figural, banjo, 1930s **15.00**
Halloween, orange, black, and white, witch and pumpkin **15.00**

Left: Sun Dial Shoes, $25.00.
Right: Weather Bird Shoes, red and black, 4¼" h, $26.00.
Photos courtesy Frank's Antiques.

CLOCKS

Look for clocks that are fun (have motion actions) or that are terrific in a decorating scheme (a school house clock in a country setting). Clocks are bought to be seen and used.

Avoid buying any clock that does not work. You do not know whether it is going to cost $5, $50, or $500 to repair. Are you prepared to risk the higher numbers? Likewise, avoid clocks with extensively damaged cases. There are plenty of clocks in fine condition awaiting purchase.

Club: National Assoc. of Watch and Clock Collectors, Inc., 514 Poplar St., Columbia, PA 17512.

Advertising, Dr Pepper, light-up, metal body, glass front, plastic face, 15" h **$143.00**
Advertising, Frostie Root Beer, cuckoo, Frostie on pendulum. **125.00**
Advertising, Jacob Lucks Clothier, Watkins, NY, figural dog, black man holding sign above **160.00**
Advertising, St Joseph Aspirin, light-up, metal with glass face and front, "Buy St. Joseph Aspirin," Pam Clock Co, Inc, NY, body stamped "Sep. 1954," metal rim painted black, 14½" d **275.00**
Alarm, brass, double bell, Bradley, Germany **35.00**
Alarm, ebonized cast iron case, paper on zinc dial, 30 hr time and alarm movement, fixed pendulum, paper label, Terry Clock Co, 6" h **30.00**
Alarm, metal, Seth Thomas, 1910–20, 10¼" h **50.00**
Banjo, mahogany, New England, white painted metal dial surmounted by brass ball finial, solid throat panel flanked by scrolled side arms, molded edge paneled box door centering an oval glass window, restoration, 35½" h, 10" w **1,035.00**
Character, Charlie Tuna, alarm, windup, 1969 . . . . **125.00**
Character, Cinderella, Westclox, alarm, windup, white metal case, orig box, 2½ x 4½ x 4" **50.00**
Character, Raggedy Ann & Andy, Janex, talking. **40.00**
Commemorative, Admiral Dewey, gilded iron case, 30 hr lever movement, 10" h. **165.00**
Cuckoo, carved case, bird with glass eyes on top, 30 hr three-train movement, single cuckoo bird and 2 doors open to dancing figures, Germany, 1940, 19" h. **110.00**
Figural, refrigerator, white metal, GE label, Warren Telechron Co, Ashland, MA, 8½" h. **185.00**
Figural, fry pan, Erie Hollow Ware, Griswold, 11 x 14" . . . **1,000.00**

Advertising, Dodge Brothers, metal face, wood frame, early 20th C, 15¼" sq, $357.50. Photo courtesy Collectors Auction Services.

Alarm Clock, electric, General Electric, Bakelite, butterscotch, 5" h, $57.50. Photo courtesy Jackson's Auctioneers & Appraisers.

Figural, tape measure, black, Lux. **30.00**
Mantel, fruitwood, Chelsea, c1910 . . . . **80.00**
Schoolhouse, Sessions Clock Co, Forestville, CT, oak case, paper on tin dial, 8 day time movement with pendulum, c1900, 19¼" h. **500.00**
Schoolhouse, Seth Thomas, oak case, 8 day **150.00**
Wall, regulator, Brewster & Ingraham, Bristol, CT, rosewood veneered case, applied rippled molding, enameled zinc dial, 8 day time and strike movement with pendulum, 1860, 22" h **275.00**

CLOTHES SPRINKLERS

Before steam irons, clothes requiring ironing had to be manually dampened with water. Some housewives used soda pop bottles or other common bottles, with sprinkler caps attached, while others owned more decorative figural bottles made especially for this purpose. These are the bottles that are now sought after by collectors willing to pay $20.00 and up for the more common examples and as much as several hundred dollars for the extremely rare bottles. It is estimated that close to 100 different sprinkle bottles were manufactured.

The sprinkle bottle had a cap with several holes (on rarer bottles, the head was the cap) to allow controlled dampening. In addition to the sprinkle bottle, the well-equipped laundry room had a wetter-downer, which had a single hole for moistening large pieces of laundry. The Dutch Boy sprinkler and Dutch Girl wetter-downer were sold as a set.

Most sprinkler bottles are ceramic or glass, but a few are plastic, such as the ladies known as "Merry Maids." There are many variations of sprinkle bottles, the most common being the green and yellow "Sprinkle Plenty" Chinaman, the gray elephant and sadirons. Others are much harder to find, such as the Kitchen Prayer Lady, the Dachshund and the Fireman.

Advisor: Loretta Anderson, 1208 Lakeshore Dr., Rockwall, TX 75087, (214) 771-9638.

Bottle, plastic, adv. **$40.00**
Bottle, plastic, plain, various styles. **20.00**
Cat, black, 7½". **150.00**
Cat, Siamese, various shades of cream and tan, Cardinal Co **200.00**
Cat, stray **100.00**
Cat, various colors, marble eyes, Cardinal Co. **300.00**
Chinaman, Emperor **100.00**
Chinaman, Sprinkle Plenty, common, yellow and green **45.00**

Chinaman, holding iron, ceramic, "Sprinkle Plenty," brown pants, $125.00.

Chaps, leather, Mobiloil, white and red with metal buttons and hooks, $258.50. Photo courtesy Collectors Auction Services.

Chinaman, Sprinkle Plenty, head is sprinkler **125.00**
Chinaman, white, blue trim, Cleminson Co **55.00**
Clothespin, various colors **225.00**
Dachshund, green coat, red bow tie, very rare **500.00**
Dearie is Weary, yellow dress, holding iron, head is sprinkler, rare **350.00**
Dutch Boy **250.00**
Dutch Girl, plastic. **75.00**
Dutch Girl, wetter-downer. **250.00**
Elephant, happy face, fat and squatty, trunk curled up for handle, rare. **275.00**
Elephant, trunk up, gray and pink, common **95.00**
Elephant, trunk up, shamrock on tummy, white and pink . . . **150.00**
Fireman, holding hose with sprinkler, cap in front, rare **600.00**
Kitchen Prayer Lady, Enesco, rare. **500.00**
Mammy, white dress with red trim **300.00**
Mary Poppins, clear glass, holding umbrella and purse **90.00**
Mary Poppins, wearing hat and dress with striped skirt, Cleminson. **300.00**
Merry Maid, glass, various colors, new. **100.00**
Myrtle, white dress with polka-dot top, sprinkler in back of head, Pfaltzgraff. **300.00**
Poodle, standing on hind legs, pink or gray **300.00**
Rooster, long neck, plastic cap, 10" h. **175.00**
Sadiron, ceramic, blue flowers. **95.00**
Sadiron, ceramic, ivy. **85.00**
Sadiron, ceramic, souvenir, theme park adv **95.00**
Sadiron, ceramic, woman ironing **95.00**
Sadiron, plastic, green. **30.00**

CLOTHING AND ACCESSORIES

Decide from the outset whether you are buying clothing and accessories for use or display. If you are buying for use, apply very strict standards with respect to condition and long term survival prospects. If you only want the items for display, you can be a little less fussy about condition.

Vintage clothing was a hot collectible craze in the 1980s. Things have cooled off a bit. Emphasis in the 1990s seems to be on accessories, with plastic purses from the 1950s leading the parade.

Club: The Costume Society of America, P.O. Box 73, Earleville, MD 21919.

Newsletter: *Lill's Vintage Clothing Newsletter,* 19 Jamestown Dr., Cincinnati, OH 45241; *The Vintage Connection,* 904 N. 65th St., Springfield, OH, 97478.

Apron, cotton, hand sewn, patchwork design, waist length, ties **$25.00**
Baby Pants, Playtex Waterpfoof Dress-Eez, snap, orig box. **6.00**
Bloomers, crepe satin, peach, silk embroidery, lace **20.00**
Blouse, white cotton, Victorian cutwork **20.00**
Change Purse, mesh, Art Nouveau head. **45.00**
Change Purse, tin, small face, mouth opens for change. **35.00**
Coat, brown velvet, brown floral ribbon striped silk lining, labeled "A. Guerin & I. Ferrier 12 East 32nd St. New York," sleeves and front trim removed, 1890s **143.00**
Collar, linen, sq cutwork corners **25.00**
Dress, cotton, strapless, floral pring, 1950s. **30.00**
Dress, evening, brown, matching velvet capelet, feather trim, c1930. . . . . **45.00**
Dress, polyester, red, sleeveless, gold coin drop trim, back bow and zipper, 1950s **20.00**
Dress, psychedelic, Mollie Parnis, 1960s **85.00**
Dress, Victorian, teenager's, white, French lace insertions, tucks of embroidery **135.00**
Evening Jacket, wool brocade, beaded front and sleeves, 1940s **100.00**
Gloves, pr, lady's, leather, France. **15.00**
Handbag, beaded, celluloid compact top and chain **225.00**
Handbag, gold mesh, German silver frame, pink coral stones, silk lining. **68.00**
Hat, wool, curved brim with net, 1950s. **35.00**
Necktie, Oleg Cassini, 1960s. **6.00**
Necktie, polyester, c1960 . . . . **8.00**
Pajamas, men's, flannel, Harwick, size medium **6.50**
Shawl, wool, green, beige, and olive green plaid, fringed **25.00**

Stockings, lady's, black, $16.00.

Shoes, pr, lady's, leather beige, pearl and rhinestone shoe clips, 1960s **10.00**
Slip, crinoline, various colors, 1950s **20.00**
Slip, satin, full length, lace trim, 1940s. **20.00**
Stockings, pr, baby's, hand knitted, 19th C **7.50**
Sweater, wool, appliqued flowers, 1950s **15.00**
Top Hat, Victorian, beaver **65.00**

CLOTHING, PAPER

Paper clothing was an innovation of the 1960s that never quite caught on. What could be more convenient than disposable clothing? Perhaps the drawbacks were only evident after the article was worn. A paper bikini hardly seems practical.

Bikini, yellow, with matching hat and carrying pouch **$10.00**
Dress, adv, Campbell's Soup, sleeveless, repeated design, dark trim **200.00**
Dress, Flower Fantasy, Hallmark, A-line, Capri, floral design, yellow yarn **40.00**
Dress, Flower Fantasy, Hallmark, A-line, Sierra, ties at back of neck, floral print, yellow yarn. **40.00**
Dress, Island Paradise, Hallmark, muumuu, sleeveless **20.00**
Dress, Paperdelic, style B, ruffled hem, sleeveless, plain **10.00**
Dress, Paperdelic, style B, ruffled hem, sleeveless, tie-dyed **10.00**

COCA-COLA COLLECTIBLES

John Pemberton, a pharmacist from Atlanta, Georgia, is credited with creating the formula for Coca-Cola. Less than two years later, he sold out to Asa G. Candler. Candler improved the formula and began advertising. By the 1890s America was Coca-Cola conscious.

Coke, a term first used in 1941, is now recognized worldwide. American collectors still focus primarily on Coca-Cola material designed for the American market. Although it would take a little effort to obtain, a collection of foreign Coke advertising would make a terrific display. What a perfect excuse to fly to the Orient.

Club: Coca-Cola Collectors Club, 400 Monemar Ave., Baltimore, MD 21228; The Coca-Cola Collectors Club, P.O. Box 49166, Atlanta, GA 30359; The Cola Club, P.O. Box 158715, Nashville, TN 37215.

Airline Cooler, stainless steel liner, 1950s, $350.00. Photo courtesy Gary Metz's Muddy River Trading Co.

Left: Sign, tin, diecut, emb, 1933, 12 x 39", $82.50. Photo courtesy Gary Metz's Muddy River Trading Co.
Right: Thermometer, tin, diecut, emb, 29½" h, 8½" w, $82.50. Photo courtesy Collectors Auction Services.

Bank, figural vending machine, plastic, 1960s **$100.00**
Binder, sales, small **300.00**
Booklet, *The Truth About Coca-Cola,* 1912. . . . . **30.00**
Bookmark, celluloid, heart shape, c1898, 2 x 2¼" **600.00**
Bottle, amber, "Coca-Cola" in double diamond, "Toledo, Ohio" at bottom. **175.00**
Bottle Opener, hand **10.00**
Calendar, 1945, Boy Scout Law with Boy Scout, Norman Rockwell illus **550.00**
Calendar, 1952, "Coke adds Zest" **185.00**
Calendar, 1970, reference, Santa with bottle of Coke and "Season's Greetings" **5.00**
Carrier, cardboard. **12.00**
Change Tray, oval, woman in wide brimmed hat holding glass, 1913 . . . . **625.00**
Clock, countertop, light-up, "Drink Coca-Cola" with sq clock, 1950s **750.00**
Clock, figural can, 1970–80s **35.00**
Clock, metal frame, light-up, "Drink Coca-Cola" in center octagon with bottle, c1942, 16" sq **800.00**
Clock, plastic, light-up, rect, "Time To Enjoy Coca-Cola, Be Really Refreshed," 1960s. **250.00**
Cooler, 6-pack size, metal and stainless steel, aluminum handle with orig zinc lining, Acton Mfg, 1950s. **375.00**
Dish, souvenir, 1964 New York World's Fair **65.00**
Display, canvas awning, "Drink Coca-Cola" in center, vertical stripes on sides, "Refreshment Center" on front scalloped trim, c1948 . . . . **600.00**
Display, cardboard, "Santa Glasses Are Here!," 1970s. **30.00**
Doll, stuffed, Frozen Coca-Cola, blue and white striped suit, red and white striped Santa hat, 1969, 14" h **100.00**
Door Handle, figural Coke bottle, plastic and metal, 1950s **225.00**
Drinking Glass, flare shape, with syrup line, c1904, 3¾" h **575.00**
Earrings, clip-on, bottle caps, 1970s. **30.00**
Eyeglasses, 3-dimensional, "Relax with the pause that refreshes, drink Coca-Cola in bottles," 1950s **55.00**
Fan, cardboard, 1940s. **22.00**
Game, Bingo board, "Coca-Cola" in center," 1950s **3.00**
Game, Cribbage, MIB **55.00**
Key Chain, miniature bottle, c1950 . . . . **6.00**
Matchbook, c1930 . . . . **5.00**
Notepad, celluloid, Hilda Clark, 1903, 2½ x 5" **600.00**
Pin, "Safe Driver," 1950–60 . . . . **30.00**
Pinback Button, "Drink Coca-Cola," red and white, c1950, 1⅛" d **10.00**

Sign, round, porcelain, mounted on orig base, base emb "Drink Coca-Cola," 62" h, 30½" d, $247.50. Photo courtesy Collectors Auction Services.

Pinback Button, "Member of Coca-Cola Bottle Club," 1930s **65.00**
Score Pad, unused **18.00**
Serving Tray, ice skater, 1940 . . . . . **200.00**
Serving Tray, Thanksgiving, TV, 1961 . . . . . **20.00**
Serving Tray, woman wearing bathing suit, towel draped over shoulder, holding glass, 1929 . . . . . **325.00**
Sheet Music, *Rum and Coca-Cola,* Andrews Sisters, 1940s **18.00**
Sign, cardboard, trolley, bathing girl in white 2 pc bathing suit, being offered a bottle of Coke, red "Coca-Cola" at right, white ground, 1946, 11 x 28" **325.00**
Sign, cardboard, diecut, Old Man North holding 6 pack of bottles and large bottle, "Serve Ice Cold," 1953, 16 x 21" **275.00**
Sign, plywood, diecut, 2-sided, inverted triangle, mint green ground, light blue down-pointing arrow with "Ice Cold" at top and bottle at bottom, red banner with white "Drink Coca-Cola," Kay Displays, 1930s **750.00**
Sign, porcelain, fountain service, yellow ground, red parellelogram with white script "Coca-Cola," white banner with red "Drink" and blue "Fountain Service," 1950s, 12 x 18" **687.50**
Sign, tin, bottle, raised gray border, 1953, 18 x 33" **450.00**
Sign, tin, diecut, fishtail, turned edges, red ground, white script "Coca-Cola," 1962, 12 x 16" **500.00**
Sign, tin, emb, green ground, rect red sign with "Ice Cold Coca-Cola Sold Here" beside bottle, 1932, 19 x 27" **375.00**
Statue, Salesman of the Month, 1930s, 6½" h **600.00**
Toy, dispenser, plastic, Chilton, with box, 1970s **40.00**
Truck, Buddy-L, orange, 1959 . . . . . **725.00**

COINS, AMERICAN

Just because a coin is old does not mean that it is valuable. Value often depends more on condition than on age. This being the case, the first step in deciding if any of your coins are valuable is to grade them. Coins are graded on a scale of 70 with 70 being the best and 4 being good.

Start your research by acquiring Marc Hudgeons's *The Official 1996 Blackbook Price Guide to United States Coins, 34th Edition* (House of Collectibles: 1995). Resist the temptation to look up your coins immediately. Read the hundred-page introduction, over half of which deals with the question of grading.

Do not overlook the melt (weight) value of silver content coins. In many cases, weight value will be far greater than collectible value. If only we had have sold when the industry was paying twenty times face value in the midst of the 1980s silver craze!

Club: American Numismatic Assoc., 818 N. Cascade Ave., Colorado Springs, CO 80903.

Periodical: Krause Publications has several coin-related magazines. Contact the company at 700 E. State St., Iola, WI 54990.

COINS, FOREIGN

The foreign coins that you are most likely to find at a flea market are the leftover change that someone brought back with them from their travels. Since the coins were in circulation, they are common and of a low grade. In some countries, they have been withdrawn from circulation and cannot even be redeemed for face value.

If you are a dreamer and think you have uncovered hidden wealth, use Chester L. Krause and Clifford Mishler's *Standard Catalog of World Coins* (Krause Publications). This book covers world coinage from 1701 to the present.

Avoid any ancient coinage. There are excellent fakes on the market. You need to be an expert to tell the good from the bad. Coins are one of those categories where it pays to walk away when the deal is too good. Honest coin dealers work on very small margins. They cannot afford to give away anything of value.

COLLEGE COLLECTIBLES

Rah, rah, rah, sis-boom-bah! The Yuppies made a college education respectable again. They tout their old alma mater, and usually have a souvenir of their college days in their office at home or work.

You will not find a Harvard graduate with a room full of Yale memorabilia and vice versa. These items have value only to someone who attended the school. The exception is sport-related college memorabilia. This has a much broader appeal, either to a conference collector or a general sports collector.

Periodical: *Sports Collectors Digest,* 700 E. State St., Iola, WI 54990.

Broadside, Roanoke College, Eighth Annual Contest, gold lettering, 1861, 10 x 5" **$25.00**
Calendar, University of Wisconsin, Madison, Bascom Hall photo, 1916 . . . . . **100.00**
Freshman Admittance, Polytechnic College, PA, black lettering, orange ground, 1868 . . . . . **20.00**
Matriculation Card, University of Pennsylvania, 1820–21 . . . . . **60.00**
Nodder, basketball player, composition, rounded gold base, sticker inscribed "Millersville," 1960s, 7" h **22.00**
Pinback Button, Alabama, Sugar Bowl, New Orleans, LA, red on white, c1950s **15.00**
Pinback Button, Michigan College Stadium, dark copper luster medalet with "Dwight B. Waldo" under "It's The Extra Drive That Wins," reverse with aerial view of "Western Stadium/Kalamazoo, Michigan," dated 1939 . . . . . **10.00**
Pinback Button, Folder, Yale Athletic Association Fall Meeting, 3 panels, violet, black lettering, 1874 . . . . . **40.00**
Pinback Button, Fordham, Sugar Bowl, New Orleans, LA, purple, 1942 . . . . . **5.00**

Commencement Program, University of Iowa, steel engraving, 3 pp, 5 x 5¹/₄", 1891, $10.00.

Program, Amherst College Class Day of 1863 . . . . **8.00**
Program, Missouri vs Georgia Tech, Bluebonnet Bowl, 1962 . . . . **15.00**
Program, Notre Dame vs West Virginia, Fiesta Bowl, 1989 . . . . **6.00**
Program, Texas A & M vs Iowa State, All-American Bowl, 1978 . . . . **10.00**
Program, U C L A vs Florida, Aloha Bowl, 1987 . . . . **5.00**
Score Card, Yale, baseball, Yale vs Trinity, Harvard, and Princeton, bi-fold, 1878, price for set of 3 . . . . **40.00**
Spoon, souvenir, Cornell University, Art Nouveau woman **50.00**
Spoon, souvenir, Notre Dame **100.00**
Spoon, souvenir, Wellesley College, woman in cap and gown handle **50.00**
Ticket Stub, Clemson vs Missouri, Gator Bowl, 1949 . . . . . . **10.00**
Ticket Stub, Texas vs Missouri, Cotton Bowl, 1946 . . . . **15.00**
Yearbook, Princeton University, 1952 . . . . **28.00**
Yearbook, University of Texas at Austin, 1918, 480 pp **12.00**

COLLEGE PLATES

Did you party hearty or did you grind? Pull "all nighters" or live for keg parties? Do the words *streaking, panty raids, tail gate, Woodstock, Ivy League, Hook 'em Horns, Rush Week, Flirtation Walk, tie dye, protest, ROTC, Big Bands, Rock & Roll or Hula Hoop* cause you to stop and smile as a flood of nostalgia hits you?

College plates evoke all these thoughts and more. A golden time in our lives when we were almost, but not quite, on our own. These plates come in all colors and designs and were made by Wedgwood, Spode, Lenox, Lamberton, Syracuse, Staffordshire, and Rowland Marcellus. Their heyday was in the 1930s, but many were made in the 20s, 40s, and some as late as the 80s for certain schools. They can still be found in flea markets, garage sales, and church bazaars if you are lucky. They range in price from as low as a few dollars per plate to as high as $30.00. In the East the prices are 30 to 50% higher. Although they are called college plates, there were plates made for prep schools and military academies.

They make wonderful gifts for the new graduate as well as the old as they are a unique reminder of their particular school.

Advisor: Pat Klein, P.O. Box 262, East Berlin, CT 06023, (860) 828-3973.

Alabama College, AL, Wedgwood, pink, Reynolds Hall **$10.00**
Alfred University, NY, white, The Chapel **5.00**
Bates College, ME, Wedgwood, pink, The Chapel 1939 . . . . . . **9.00**
Bentley College, MA, Solomon R Baker Library **10.00**
Boston University, MA, Wedgwood, pink, School of Theology and the Chapel **13.75**
Brown University, RI, Wedgwood, brown, John Nichols Brown Gate **20.00**
Citadel, SC, Wedgwood, blue, The Color Guard **18.00**
City College of NY, Wedgwood, pink, School of Business, 1947 . . . . **25.00**
Columbia Medical Center, Jackson China Co, blue **7.00**
Connecticut College, Wedgwood, black, Harkness Chapel **20.00**
Culver Military Academy, IN, Royal Winton, Dining Hall **8.00**
Dartmouth College, NH, Royal Cauldon, green, Observatory Hill **20.00**
Ethel Walker School, CT, Wedgwood, Phelps House **18.00**
Emma Willard, NY, Wedgwood, pink, Slocum Doorway **32.00**
Georgetown University, DC, Wedgwood, blue, Old North, 1954 . . . . **30.00**
Harvard University, MA, Wedgwood, blue, Freshman Halls, 1927 . . . . **25.00**
Indiana University, IN, Wedgwood, pink, Memorial Hall **20.00**
Kent State, OH, Wedgwood, blue, Administration Building, 1960 . . . . **10.00**
Lafayette College, NY, Lamberton, Dormitory Row **16.00**
Medical College of Virginia, Wedgwood, pink, Egyptian Building, 1938 . . . . **15.00**
Miss Porters School, Wedgwood, black, Headmasters House **20.00**
New York University, Wedgwood, pink, Hall of Fame, 1932 . . . . **8.00**
Northeastern University, MA, University center with insets, 1960 . . . . **8.00**
Peekskill Military Academy, NY, Wedgwood, James B Ford Upper House **16.00**
Princeton University, NJ, Wedgwood, blue, Holder Court and Tower **37.00**
Radcliffe College, MA, Wedgwood, pink, Longfellow Hall, 1934 . . . . **15.00**
St Mark's School, Syracuse China, blue, seal in center **3.00**
St Paul's School, Wedgwood, pink, The Rectory, 1956 . . . . **23.00**
Stanford University, CA, Wedgwood, green, Arcade and Library **15.00**
Tufts University, MA, Wedgwood, pink, Ballou Hall, 1950 . . . . **15.00**
Tulane University, LA, Wedgwood, green, Newcomb Gymnasium **20.00**
University of Connecticut, Balfour, State Seal with buildings **5.00**
Vassar College, NY, Wedgwood, pink, Taylor Hall, 1929 . . . . . **23.00**

Yale University, New Haven, CT, Timothy Dwight College, Wedgwood, 1949, $25.00.

Washington & Jefferson, PA, Lamberton, Main Hall **22.50**
Yale University, CT, Syracuse China college seal **15.00**

COLORING BOOKS

The key is to find these gems uncolored. Some collectors will accept a few pages colored, but the coloring had better be neat. If it is scribbled, forget it.

Most of the value rests on the outside cover. The closer the image is to the actual character or personality featured, the higher the value. The inside pages of most coloring books consist of cheap newsprint. It yellows and becomes brittle over time. However, resist buying only the cover. Collectors prefer to have the entire book.

Addams Family, Saalfield, #4331, 1965 . . . . **$25.00**
A-Team Coloring and Activity Book, Modern Promotions, © 1983 Steven J Cannell Productions **3.50**
Barnie Google, 1968 . . . . **10.00**
Ben Casey, Saalfield, #9532, ©Bing Crosby Productions, 1963 . . . . **15.00**
Boo Boo Bear, Watkins-Strathmore, ©1963, 96 pp, 8 x 11" **25.00**
Boots and Her Buddies, Saalfield, #331, ©Stephen Slesinger, Inc, 1941 . . . . **30.00**
Captain Kangaroo Trace and Color, Samuel Lowe, #4967, 1977 . . . . **12.00**
Charlie Chaplin, Donohue & Co, ©1917, 10 x 17" **80.00**
Cheerful Tearful, Western Publishing, 1966 . . . .
Dick Tracy, Saalfield, #2536, ©1946, $8\frac{1}{4}$ x 11" **25.00**
Donald Duck, Whitman, 1946, $7\frac{1}{2}$ x $8\frac{1}{2}$", unused **20.00**
Doris Day, Whitman, ©1955 Doris Day, "A Warner Brothers Star" **25.00**
Fantastic Osmonds, Saalfield, #4622, ©1973 Osbro Productions **30.00**
Fonzie, Treasure Books, ©1976 Paramount Pictures Corp, $8\frac{1}{4}$ x $10\frac{3}{4}$" **15.00**
Fritzi Ritz, Abbott Publishing, #3335, 1940s **25.00**
Goodbye, Mr Chips, Saalfield, #9569, ©Metro Goldwyn-Mayer, 1969 . . . . **20.00**
Hong Kong Phooey, Saalfield, ©1975, 32 pp, $8\frac{1}{2}$ x 11", unused **15.00**
Indian Scout Kit Carson, Abbott Publishing Co, ©1957, 8 x 11" **25.00**
Leave It To Beaver, Saalfield, ©1958, ©1958, 8 x $10\frac{3}{4}$" **75.00**
Lennon Sisters, Whitman, #158, ©1958 Teleklew Productions, Inc **25.00**

Wagon Train, Whitman Publishing, #1122, 1959, $8\frac{1}{2}$ x 11", unused, $25.00.

Merry Christmas Story and Coloring Book from Newberrys, ©1960, Promotional Publishing Co., NY, $10\frac{1}{4}$" h, $7\frac{1}{4}$" w, $15.00.

Little Scouts, Whitman, #680, ©1953 Roland Coe **12.00**
My Three Sons, Whitman, #1113, ©1967 Columbia Broadcast System, Inc **12.00**
Partridge Family, Saalfield, ©1971 Columbia Pictures Industries, Inc, $8\frac{1}{2}$ x 11" **25.00**
Peanuts Pictures to Color, Saalfield, #5331, 1960 . . . . **25.00**
Rainbow Brite "I'm A Fit Kid," ©Hallmark Cards, 1983 . . . . **3.00**
Rocky and Bullwinkle, "Bullwinkle's How To Have Fun Outdoors Without Getting Clobbered," unused **20.00**
Shazam, Whitman, pinup poster on back cov, National Periodical Publications, ©1975 . . . . **12.00**
Straight Arrow, Stephens Publishing Co, National Biscuit Co, ©1949, 20 pp, $10\frac{3}{4}$ x $14\frac{1}{4}$" **25.00**
Thunderbirds, Whitman, #1115, 1968 . . . . **15.00**
Tom & Jerry, Watkins-Strathmore, ©1957, 192 pp, 8 x 11", unused **45.00**
Walt Disney, Haley Mills In Search of the Castaways, Whitman, #1139, ©1962 Walt Disney Productions **15.00**
Walt Disney, Mickey Mouse Club, Whitman, ©1955, 164 pp, 11 x 13" **50.00**

COMBS

The form is pretty basic. Value rests in how and in what material the comb is presented. Some hair combs are fairly elaborate and actually should be considered as jewelry accessories.

Beware of combs being sold separately that were originally part of larger dresser sets. Their value is less than combs that were meant to stand alone.

You can build an interesting collection inexpensively by collecting giveaway combs. You will be amazed to see how many individuals and businesses used this advertising media, from politicians to funeral parlors.

Club: Antique Comb Collectors Club International, 3748 Sunray Dr., Holiday, FL 34691.

Brass, purse, folding, emb cracker barrel design **$35.00**
Celluloid, creamy ivory **18.00**
Celluloid, side comb, butterscotch, rhinestone band, c1900 . . . . **10.00**
Celluloid, stamped gold plated brass filigree butterfly motif, set with circular and marquise shaped multicolored rhinestones, mounted on 2-pronged celluloid comb, rev imp with E A Bliss Co maker's mark, $3\frac{3}{4}$" w, $4\frac{3}{4}$" h **275.00**
Celluloid, tuck comb, faux tortoise shell, amethyst colored rhinestones **75.00**

Celluloid, tuck comb, faux tortoise shell, peacock motif, rhinestone accents, early 1900s 40.00
Lucite, purse, folding, gold speckled case, Curry Arts 25.00
Plastic, blue, "Vote Muskie, Comb Nixon Out of Your Hair," inscriptions both sides, 7" l. 15.00
Plastic, side comb, crown design, brilliant rhinestones, faux tortoise shell, 1940s 35.00
Plastic, side comb, rhinestone band with pearl end. 25.00
Plastic, side comb, tiara design, silver colored metal, brilliant rhinestones, hinged, clear 30.00
Plastic, faux mother-of-pearl, purse, folding, Marhill, 1960s 25.00

COMEDIAN COLLECTIBLES

Laughter is said to be the best medicine. If this is true, why does it hurt so much when Abbot & Costello meet the Mummy?

Comedians of all eras have bestowed upon the public the gift of laughter. In return the public has made them stars.

Comedian collectibles range throughout the known mediums of radio, vaudeville, television, standup, and cinema. The plight of Charlie Chaplin echoes in the antics of Whoopie Goldberg. Comedian collectibles also reflect the diversity of those mediums. So feel free to laugh out loud the next time you find a Groucho Marx eyeglass and mustache mask—I do.

Clubs: Abbott & Costello Fan Club, P.O. Box 2081, North Hollywood, CA 91610; International Jack Benny Fan Club, 4759 Wilkie St., Oakland, CA 94619; Marx Brotherhood, 335 Fieldstone Dr., New Hope, PA 18938; Three Stooges Fan Club, P.O. Box 747, Gwynedd Valley, PA 19437.

Abbott & Costello, game, Who's On First, Selchow Righter, ©1978 ZIV International $20.00
Ball, Lucille, coloring book, I Love Lucy, Whitman, ©1954 Lucille Ball and Desi Arnaz, 11¼ x 13¾" 450.00
Ball, Lucille, doll, cloth, stuffed, molded plastic face, yellow yarn hair, red and white fabric outfit, 1950s, 27" h 150.00
Ball, Lucille, paper dolls, Luci, Desi, and Little Ricky, Whitman, ©1953 . . . . 75.00
Berle, Milton, book, *Milton Berle's Jumbo Fun Book,* illus, jokes, games, and recipes, 48 pp, ©1940 The Quaker Oats Co 15.00
Burns, George, picture, color, with name plaque, framed, from the Friars Club, 25 x 21" 632.00

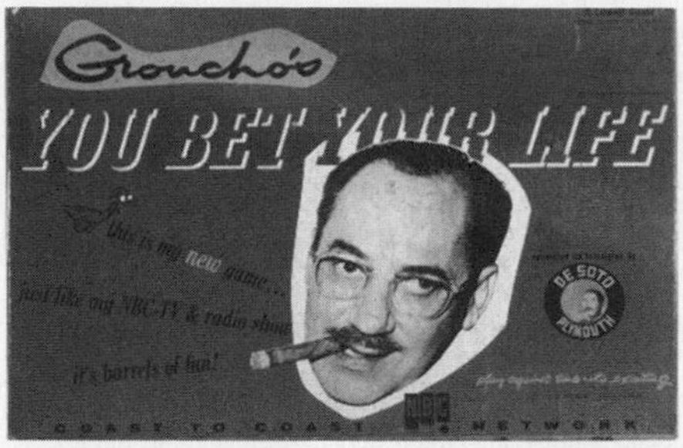

Groucho Marx, game, Groucho's You Bet Your Life, Lowell, 1955, $55.00.

Burns, George, stand-up figure, cardboard, life-size, George Burns with cigar 747.00
Gillis, Dobie, nodder, composition, 1960s, 7" h 100.00
Gleason, Jackie, climbing toy, Poor Soul, c1955 . . . . 120.00
Gleason, Jackie, cocktail napkins, Honeymooners, set of 50, orig box, 1955. . . . . 40.00
Gleason, Jackie, uniform, bus driver, includes cap, coin changer, coins, bus tickets, and ticket puncher, VIP, orig box, 1956 . . . . 395.00
Hope, Bob, pinback button, black and white, *Beau James* promo, 1957, 2½" d 40.00
Laurel & Hardy, bank, hard vinyl, figural Hardy, multi-colored, Play Pal Plastics, 1974, 7½" h 30.00
Laurel & Hardy, Feelable Movables Kit, includes 12" diecut cardboard figures, pre-cut velour outfits, puppet string holders, Edu-Craft, ©Larry Harmon, 1970s, MIB 40.00
Laurel & Hardy, hand puppets, pr, fabric body, painted soft vinyl head, molded black derby hat, orig stitched Knickerbocker Toy Co tag, ©1966 Larry Harmon, 11" h 200.00
Laurel & Hardy, mask, pr, Laurel & Hardy faces, molded plastics, 1960s, 6½ x 10" 35.00
Laurel & Hardy, puzzle, frame tray, Whitman, Laurel, Hardy, and gorilla cartoon illus, 1967. . . . . 14.00
Laurel & Hardy, salt and pepper shakers, pr, china, 4" h Laurel shaker and 3" h Hardy shaker, each with bow tie, mkd "Bewwick Ward, Made in England," cork stopper in bottom, c1930s 200.00
Lewis, Jerry, bubble bath container, tapered cardboard accented by light blue artificial wig cap, applied blue flannel felt fabric center torso, plastic eye disks with smaller jiggle disks, attached black and white cardboard string tag picturing Jerry Lewis with reference to movie *The Family Jewels,* House of Tre-Jur, ©Maradel Products, Inc, 1964, 10½" h. 50.00
Martin & Lewis, charm, green plastic frame, inset glossy black and white photos, 1" h, 1950s. 45.00
Marx Brothers, figurines, set of 3, painted hollow bisque, "Royal Crown" symbol mkd on bottom, 1970s, 6½" h. 65.00
Marx Brothers, Groucho Marx goggles and cigar, plastic, carded, 1955. . . . . 40.00
Marx Brothers, *TV Guide,* Jul 18, 1952, cov photo 20.00
Newhart, Bob, script, TV series, sgd "Bob" 25.00
Pinky Lee, tray, tin, full color litho, 10½ x 14½" 20.00
Rowan & Martin, drawing set, Laugh-In, Lakeside, orig box, unused, 1968 . . . . 60.00
Rowan & Martin, magazine, *Laugh-In,* Vol 1, #2, Nov 1968. . . . . 15.00

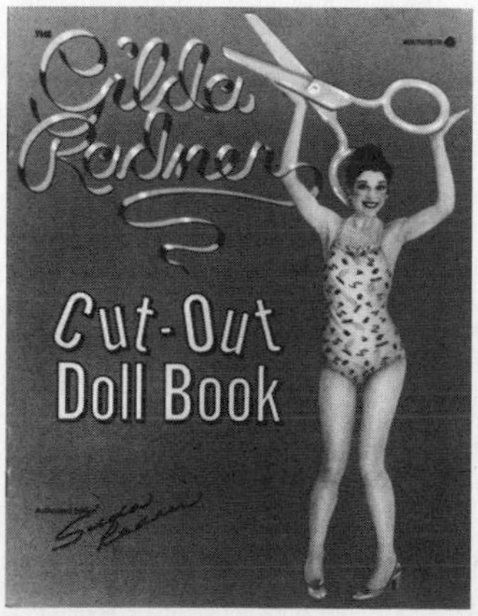

Gilda Radner Cut-Out Doll Book, Avon Books, 1975, 14 pp, 8½ x 11", uncut, $17.50.

Soupy Sales, autograph, postcard, black and white glossy photo, "Sincerely Soupy Sales" 20.00
Soupy Sales, pinback button, "Charter Member/Soupy Sales Society," 1960, 3 1/2" d 15.00
Three Stooges, record, 45 rpm, *Yuletide Songs,* cardboard sleeve, ©1959 Norman Maurer Productions 25.00
W C Fields, record, 78 rpm, 3 record set, *Temperance Lecture* and *The Day I Drank A Glass Of Water,* biography and black and white photo inside front cov, United Artists, 1946 . . . . 45.00
Williams, Robin, doll, Mork, plastic, poseable, red plastic backpack talking unit, Mattel, ©1979 Paramount Pictures Corp 25.00
Williams, Robin, lunch box, King-Seeley Thermos, steel box, plastic thermos, 1979 . . . . 30.00

COMIC BOOKS

Comic books come in all shapes and sizes. The number that have survived is almost endless. Although there were reprint books of cartoon strips in the 1910s, 1920s, and 1930s, the modern comic book originated in June 1938 when DC issued Action Comics No. 1, marking the first appearance of Superman.

Comics are divided into Golden Age, Silver Age, and Contemporary titles. Before you begin buying, read John Hegenberger's *Collector's Guide to Comic Books* (Wallace-Homestead, 1990) and D. W. Howard's *Investing in Comics* (The World of Yesterday, 1988).

The dominant price guide for comics is Robert Overstreet's *The Overstreet Comic Book Price Guide.* However, more and more you see obsolete comics being offered in shops and at conventions for ten to twenty-five percent less than Overstreet's prices. The comic book market may be facing a reevaluation crisis similar to what happened in the stamp market several years ago when the editors of the Scott catalog lowered the value significantly for many stamps.

Note that most comics, due to condition, are not worth more than 50¢ to a couple of dollars. Very strict grading standards are applied to comics less than 10 years old. The following list shows the potential in the market. You need to check each comic book separately.

Periodicals: *Comic Buyer's Guide,* 700 E. State St, Iola, WI 54990; *Overstreet's Comic Book Marketplace,* Gemstone Publishing (West), P.O. Box 180700, Coronado, CA 92178.

Dennis the Menace and Ruff, Dennis the Menace and His Friends Series, Fawcett Publications, #7, 1971, $1.50.

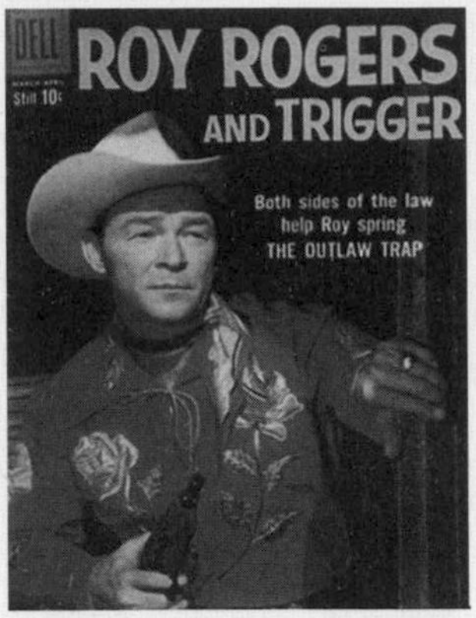

Roy Rogers & Trigger, March/April 1944, Vol. #1, 10 1/4" h, 7 1/4" w, $75.00. Photo courtesy Collectors Auction Services.

Archie, Adventures of the Fly, #6 . . . . $45.00
Barbarians, The, Atlas Comics/Seaboard Periodicals, Jun 1975 . . . . 1.20
Batman, #110 . . . . 40.00
Bewitched, Dell, #7, Dec 1966, 7 x 10" 10.00
Brenda Lee Story, The, Dell, Sep 1962 . . . . 22.00
Captain America, Marvel Comic, Vol 1, #100, Apr 1968 . . . . . 10.00
Casper & Friends, Harvey, #4 . . . . 1.00
Chuck Norris, Marvel, #4, 1987 . . . . 2.00
Conan The Barbarian, Shadow in the Tomb, Marvel, #31 . . . . . 4.00
Danny Thomas Show, The, #1249, Nov–Jan 1962, 7 1/2 x 10" 12.00
Dr Jekyll and Mr Hyde, Classics Illustrated, #8 . . . . 3.75
Fantastic Voyages of Sinbad, The, Gold Key, #5, Sep 1952 . . . . 11.00
Gabby Hayes Adventure Comics, Toby Press, Dec 1953 . . . . . 36.00
GI Joe, Vol 2, #18, winter 1952, 7 x 10" 20.00
Hong Kong Phooey, Charlton Comics, #1, Jun 1975 . . . . 9.00
Hopalong Cassidy, Fawcett, Vol 5, #29, Mar 1949 . . . . 55.00
Johnny Quest, Comico, #6 . . . . 2.00
Kissyfur, DC Comics, Sep 1989 80
Lawman, Dell, #970, Feb 1959 . . . . 36.00
Life Story, Fawcett, Vol 1, Apr 1949 . . . . 30.00
Little Jack Frost, Avon Products, #1, 1951 . . . . 20.00
Little Stooges, The, Gold Key, #1, Sep 1972 . . . . 5.50
Love Memories, Fawcett, #4, Jul 1950 . . . . 17.00
Marines In Battle, Atlas Comics, #7, 1950s 21.00
Real Ghostbusters, The, Now Comics, #32, Aug 1988 80
Fantastic Voyages of Sinbad, The, Gold Key, #5, Sep 1952 . . . . 11.00

COMMEMORATIVE GLASSES

Before there were modern promotional drinking glasses (the kind you get from a fast food restaurant, gas station, or by eating the contents of a glass food container) people bought glasses as souvenirs. The earliest examples have acid-etched decorations. Although these are tough to find, they are not all that expensive. One collector I know specializes in advertising spirit glasses. Her collection numbers in the hundreds.

Bicentennial Heritage Collector Series, Spirit 1776, Coca-Cola, Declaration of Independence/Paul Revere $7.00
Bicentennial Presidents and Patriots Collector's Series, image and biographical sketch on front, 1975 Burger Chef Systems, Inc, 5 1/4" h 8.00
Civil War Centennial Series, clear, red, white, and blue illus, 5 3/4" h 3.00

Colorado Rush to the Rockies Centennial 1859–1959, Discovery of gold at Little Dry Creek—Summer of 1858 . . . . **8.00**
End of Prohibition, clear, GOP elephant and DEM donkey on beer keg illus, "At Last! 1933," 3 5/8" h **30.00**
Green Mill Whiskey, adv, spirit glass, S M Denison, Wholesale Liquor Dealer, Chillicothe, OH, c1910, 2 1/4" h **15.00**
Historical Mission Series, mission illus, Coca-Cola Co, 5 5/8" h **7.00**
Indy 500, spirit glass, Johnny Rutherford 1976 Winner, 2 1/2" h **6.00**
Laurel Race Course, Washington, DC, 25th Year, winners from '52–'75 on back, 1976 . . . . **9.00**
Michigan 150th Anniversary, red numerals encircled by white lettering, red and blue Pepsi logo onback, 5 9/16" h **4.00**
National Sports Festival, Indianapolis, Jul 23–31, flared, red, white, and blue, 1982, 5 1/2" h **6.00**
Le Tour De France, Le Havre, Jul 1995 . . . . **7.00**
Pittsburg Press Bicentennial Collection Seeries, 1974–76 . . . . **10.00**
Presidents and Patriots Series, Burger Chef, 1975 . . . . **5.00**
Remember Pearl Harbor, clear, red slogan, white date, red, white, and blue airplanes, warships, Hawaiian island, and Pearl Harbor Bay, 4 3/4" h **75.00**
Seattle Liquor Co, adv, spirit glass, 1123 First Avenue, Seattle, WA, gold rim, c1908, 2 5/16" h **20.00**
Texas Centennial Exposition, clear, dark blue seal and cowboy on rearing horse illus, 3 1/2" h **22.00**
The Wonderful World of Ohio Series, iced tea, Fort Recovery State Memorial, Greenville **5.00**
World Series, clear, weighted bottom, white lettering, list of World Series winners from 1924 through 1951, gold batter illus, 5 3/4" h **20.00**
World's Fair, Knoxville, TN, 1982, red and black design, 5 5/8" h **5.00**
World's Fair, New York, clear, Theme Building and Court of Communications illus, 1939, 4 1/2" h **25.00**
World's Fair, Seattle, iced tea, frosted, World of Art **6.00**

COMMEMORATIVE MEDALS

From the late nineteenth century through the 1930s, commemorative medals were highly prized possessions. The U.S. Mint and other mints still carry on the tradition today, but to a far lesser degree.

Distinguish between medals issued in mass and those struck for a limited purpose, in some cases in issues of one for presentation. An old medal should have a surface patina that has developed over the years causing it to have a very mellow appearance. Never, never clean a medal. Collectors like the patina.

In most medals, the metal content has little value. However, medals were struck in both silver and gold. If you are not certain, have the metal tested.

Club: Token and Medal Society, Inc., 9230 S.W. 59th St., Miami, FL 33173.

Apollo XII, "Return To The Moon," gold colored metal, raised portraits, Nov 19–20, 1969 . . . . **$12.50**
Cincinnati Industrial Exposition, Brewery Award, brass, 6-sided, "Complimentary Grand Medal" and George Washington profile on front, reverse with date, expo title, and "The Christian Moerlein Brewing Co, Cincinnati O," 1883, 1 1/4" d **60.00**
Civil War, copper, Major General George McClellan, USA, eagle, shield, and flag design, slogan on back "I Am Born To Defend My Country," 1 1/4" d **35.00**
Civil War Centennial, bronze, McDowell & Beauregard busts, "Battle of Manaassas" above, "Bull Run" below, reverse with cannons and flags, 1961 . . . . **12.00**
Columbian Exposition, aluminum, raised detailed image of Manufacturers and Liberal Arts Building, Berry Brothers Varnishes adv, 3/8" d **10.00**
Constitution Anniversary, busts of Washington and Reagan, reverse with Preamble and Seal, 1987 . . . . **77.50**
Constitution Centennial, reverse with "Centennial Anniversary of the Adoption of the Constititution of the United States" **7.00**
John Fitzgerald Kennedy Memorial, brass, orig box and 4 pp insert, 1 1/2" d **15.00**
Lindberg Flight, brass, portrait and rim inscription **12.00**
Paris Exposition, "Exposition Coloniale Internationale Paris 1931" **6.00**
Surrender at Yorktown, bronze, Washington & Lafayette busts, reverse with surrender scene **55.00**
United States Census, eagle on shield, loop on back, 1900, 1 3/4" d **37.00**
World's Fair, Chicago, brass, emb, Travel and Transport building on front, reverse with Century of Progress symbol, 1934, 1 1/4" d **10.00**

COMPACTS

Old compacts are the "new" hot collectibles. Compacts are small portable cosmetic makeup boxes that contain powder, mirror, and puff. The vanity case is the more elaborate compact. It contains multiple compartments for powder, rouge, and/or lipstick. Compacts that were used up until the 1960s, when women opted for the "au natural" look, are considered vintage. There are compacts and vanities to suit every palate and purse.

Vintage compacts were made in a variety of shapes, sizes, combinations, and materials. There were square, round, oval, oblong, and triangle shape. They were made in almost every conceivable natural or man-made material.

The most desirable compacts are the figural, enameled, Art Deco, commemorative, souvenir, and patriotic. Compacts were often a reflection of the times. During the war years the military hat

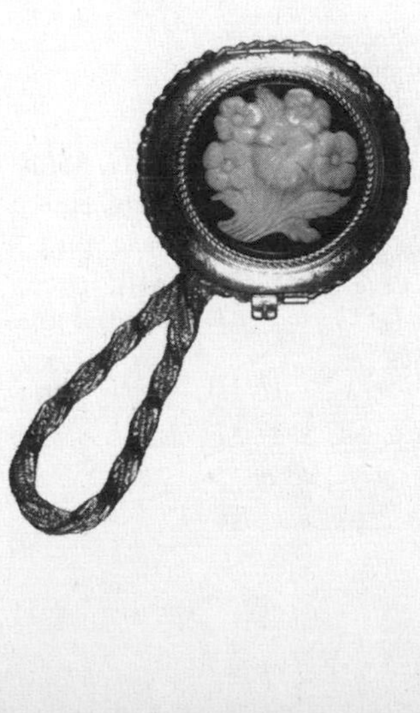

Revlon, #9508, goldtone, demitasse hand mirror compact, plastic floral dec, designed by Van Cleef & Arpels, $50.00.

was very popular. The World's Fair and Niagara Falls are two of the most popular examples of the souvenir compact. To keep their name in the public eye, manufacturers jumped on the bandwagon and had their logos printed on compacts which were given away as premiums. Figural compacts took the form of hearts, suitcases, balls, baskets, musical instruments, hands, praying hands, and animals.

There are also many vintage compacts that are multipurpose—combined with other accessories. The compact/watch, compact/music box, compact/fan, compact/purse, compact/perfume, compact/lighter, compact/cane, compact/hatpin are but a few of the combination compacts that not only appeal to the compact collector, but also to collectors of the secondary accessory.

Compacts have come into their own as a collectible. They are listed as a separate category in price guides, they are being sold at prestigious auction houses and displayed in museums and several books and many articles on the collectible compact have been written.

The beauty and intricate workmanship of these compacts are works of fantasy and art in miniature.

Advisor: Roselyn Gerson, P.O. Box 100, Malverne, NY 11565.

Club: Compact Collectors, P.O. Box 40, Lynbrook, NY 11563 (516) 593-8746, fax: (516) 593-0610.

Note: Roselyn Gerson is the author of *Ladies' Compacts of the Nineteenth & Twentieth Centuries,* Wallace-Homestead, PA, out-of-print; *Vintage Ladies' Compacts,* Collector Books, KY; *Vintage Vanity Bags & Purses,* Collector Books, KY; *Vintage and Contemporary Purse Accessories,* Collector Books, KY. She is also the founder and editor of *Powder Puff,* the Compact Collectors' Chronicle, P.O. Box 40, Lynbrook, NY 11563.

Agme, "Dial-A-Scene," gold and silvertone compact, silvertone lid framed by goldtone border, 2 centered openings on lid reveal scenes of Paris, moveable dials on sides, Switzerland, 2 x 3¼" $150.00

Astor-Pak, round compact, bone colored plastic, silvertone Scottie dog centered on top of ivorene lid, reverse side black, 3½" d 110.00

Cara Noma Langlois, goldtone vanity, flower basket centered on incised web lid dec, int reveals mirror, powder and rouge compartments, 3¼ x 2¼" 70.00

Ciner, mini compact, square, goldtone, with matching lipstick, compact lid and lipstick tube cov in brown alligator leather, int mirror and powder well, goldtone alligator applied to top of lipstick tube and centered on compact lid, brown corduroy fitted case, powder lid sgd, 2" sq 175.00

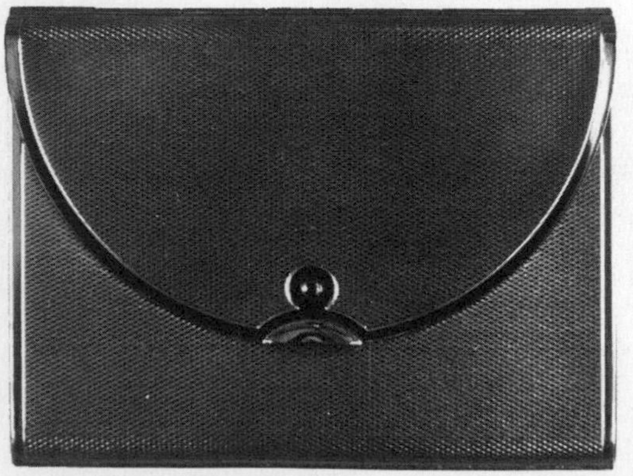

Coty, goldtone, sgd case, puff with logo, framed mirror, 3½ x 2⅝ x ½", $70.00.

Henriette, brass, bell shaped, c1930, $70.00.

Coty, goldtone vanity, wishbone and star set with rhinestone lid dec, int reveals rouge and powder compartments, 3¾ x 2¼" 80.00

Coty, "Memo," goldtone compact, with matching lipstick/perfume combination, book shape, emb basketweave design on lid, cartouche on polished goldtone spine, lipstick/perfume combination designed to resemble pencil, 1 side of tube contains creamy lipstick, other side contains small bottle of Chypre perfume, 3½ x 2¼" lipstick, 3½" 175.00

Dunhill, "Clearview," blue leather compact, int reveals mirror windshield wiper, attached sleeve for lipstick, 2½ x 3½" 150.00

E A M, black enamel and silvertone tango chain vanity, silvertone cartouche centered on lid, int reveals mirror, powder and rouge compartments, lipstick attached by enamel link chain, 2½ x 3½" 150.00

E A M, blue cloisonne enamel silvertone vanity, floral lid dec, int reveals metal mirror, powder and rouge compartments, metal link wrist chain, 2½ x 1½" 135.00

Elgin, square compact, hammered goldtone, American, rhinestone Christmas bell center lid dec, red crystal moveable clapper, 2¾" sq 80.00

Elizabeth Arden, polished goldtone, harlequin shape compact, 3 x 1⅝" 150.00

Karess, round compact, woman's profile, rose, and star on goldtone top lid dec, on dark blue and black background framed with goldtone bars, silvertone bottom lid, 1¾" d 125.00

Kigu, round compact, worldglobe shape, continents in goldtone, oceans in silvertone, plastic int, England, 2⅞" d 225.00

Le Rage, compact/bracelet, goldtone, wrist watch shape, hours on lid of compact set with green and clear stones, moveable hands, bubble link chain, int reveals mirror and puff, England, 1½" d 350.00

Marhill, 2¾ x 2½" compact with matching 1¼" sq pill box, mother-of-pearl enhanced with goldtone bands and raised painted flowers set with sparkle lid dec 55.00

Raquel, gold emb green leather vanity, book shape, int reveals metal framed mirror, powder and rouge compartments, 2 x 3" 95.00

R & G Co, compact/perfume combination, gold and silvertone, screw top perfume closure on top complete

Langlois, sgd "Cara Nome," white metal, cutout flower basket logo on blue celluloid ground, engine turned vertical lines, $60.00.

with perfume wand, engine turned lid with blue bag and letter "M" dec, front lid opens to revel powder well and mirror, 1¾ x 2" **110.00**

Rex, round brushed silver tango chain compact, polished goldtone floral lid dec, lipstick attached by chain to compact, 3⅓" d **185.00**

S G D G, powder grinder vanity, silvertone, int reveals metal mirror which separated powder and rouge compartments, int powder well lifts up to reveal solid powder grinder, France, 2 x 2" **80.00**

Stratton, Wedgwood, Jasperware, convertible goldtone compact, lid inset with cameo of "Three Graces" Aglair, Euprosyne and Thalia, blue label on int beveled mirror reads "The cameo on this STRATTON PRODUCT is made by "Josiah Wedgwood & Sons, Ltd," 3¼" d **75.00**

Tiffany & Co, oval compact, sterling, int mirror and powder well, case sgd, 2¼ x 1¼" **125.00**

Unknown Manufacturer, mini compact, goldtone, fan shape, yellow, pink, silvertone, and goldtone floral dec lid, pearl twist lock closure, int mirror and powder well, 2½ x 1½" **60.00**

Unknown Manufacturer, mini compact, round, green enamel, goldtone star design lid dec, 1½" d **85.00**

Unknown Manufacturer, oblong vanity, Bakelite, clear and green colored rhinestone ext dec, int reveals mirror, removable cov powder and rouge containers and lipstick compartment, carrying cord, tassel, 2¼ x 4" **375.00**

Unknown Manufacturer, photo compact, green leather, beveled mirror, open slot on lid to insert photo protected by clear plastic around goldtone frame, 3" sq **110.00**

Unknown Manufacturer, red faux leather compact, hat box shape, snaps open and shut, faux zipper, int reveals mirror and puff, carrying handle, 3 x 2¼" **100.00**

Unknown Manufacturer, round compact/coin holder combination, copper, raised elephant front lid dec, slots for int reveal metal powder sifter and puff, 2⅛" d . . . **150.00**

Unknown Manufacturer, round compact, dark green marbleized Bakelite, pink carved Bakelite roses and painted green leaves lid dec, int reveals beveled mirror and powder compartment, plastic link carrying chain with finger ring, 2½" d **175.00**

Unknown Manufacturer, round compact, white enamel, baseball shape, "Giants" centered on front lid with blue and white painted stitching, int reveals mirror and powder compartments, 3" d **90.00**

Unknown Manufacturer, round silvertone compact, plastic discs on sides depicting musician in relief playing instruments, 2¼" d. **65.00**

Unknown Manufacturer, silvertone compact, souvenir of Washington DC, heart shape, polished goldtone DC attractions lid dec, 2¾ x 3" **50.00**

Unknown Manufacturer, U.S. Navy hat, plastic **80.00**

Volupte, brushed goldtone compact, artist's palette shape, paint tube, brushes, and colors lid dec, int mirror and powder compartment, 3 x 2¾" **175.00**

Volupte, *Gone With the Wind,* square silvertone compact, black enamel lids, "Scarlett O'Hara" and painted enamel Southern scene front lid dec, int reveals mirror and powder well, insert reads "*Gone With the Wind* Selznick Int. Pictures M.G.M. Release," 2⅞" sq **125.00**

Volupte, square compact, goldtone, lid resembles gift package, raised gift card and bow lid dec, 3" sq **50.00**

Volupte, round compact, white enamel, red anchor and blue rope lid dec, 2½" d **60.00**

CONDOM TINS

Condom tins have finally come "out of the closet"! Referred to by *Playboy* as "Sin Tins," there was a time when people were too embarassed to collect them or admit they owned one. Now it's agreed these tins are little works of art! They were manufactured by several different companies, from the early 1920s until the late 1950s. The earliest were round and made of aluminum, all embossed with no color. They were all 1⅝" diameter, friction fit, the most common being 3 Merry Widows. However, even though the aluminum containers are earlier, the later tins with colorful lithography are definately more collectible, most of which came from the 1940s. They came in 1⅝" round, 1⅝" square, and the most popular (and most numerous) the hinged rectangulars, most of which are 2⅛ x 1⅝", the size of (and sometimes mistaken for) aspirin tins! All of these containers (whether aluminum or tin) and/or say "For Medical Purpose Only!" One of the fun things about condom tins are many of their amusing names, Examples: Blue Goose, Duble-Tip, Silk Skin, Seal-Tite, and Nunbetter. Incidentally, condoms were also marketed in paper and cardboard containers, from the early 1920s to the present. These are also collectible, but not nearly as desirable as the tins.

Collectors should look for condom tins that are the most colorful and graphic. As is the case with most antique advertising pieces, the ones with pictures are more sought after than the ones having only lettering. And of course, Condition! Condition! Condition!

Along with the aluminum 3 Merry Widows, there are four condom tins one should not spend much money on, as they are very plentiful. Ultrex Platinum, Ramses, Sheik, and Dean's Peacocks. In fact the Dean's Peacocks (pretty as it is) has been named "The 'Prince Albert' of condom tins!" (And the Ultrex Platinum, is the 'Edgeworth.'

Advisors: Dennis & George, (from Nov to May): 323 Sandpiper Ln., Delray Beach, FL 33483, (561) 243-3072, (from Jun to Oct): 3407 Lake Montebello Dr., Baltimore MD 21218, (410) 889-3964.

Dennis and George are the authors of the book *Remember Your Rubbers!*, Schiffer Publishing, 1988, the first book in history on collectible condom containers, beautiful hardback with a dust jacket, over 300 color pictures with prices.

Note: The following tins are all rectangular unless noted. Prices are for tins in pristine condition only.

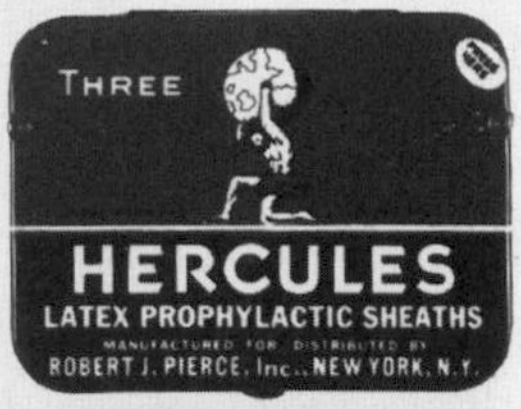

Top: Hercules, Robert J. Pierce, Inc, New York, NY, $500.00

Bottom: Oriental, unknown mfg, $450.00.

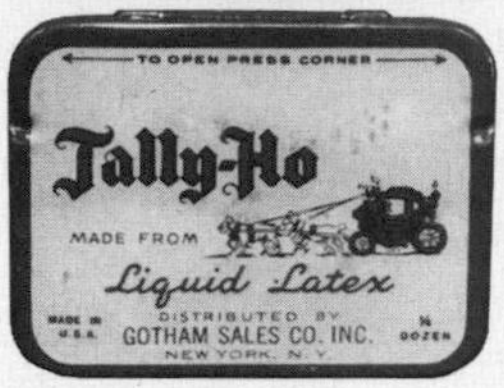

Top: Three Graces, (Faith, Hope, and Charity), unknown mfg, $300.00.

Bottom, Tally-Ho, Gotham Sales Co, Inc, New York, NY, $450.00.

Akron Tourist Tubes, Akron Rubber Supply Co, Akron, OH, dirigible circling over trees **$500.00**
Apris, Killian Mfg Co, Akron, OH, leaping gazelle **150.00**
Cadets, Julius Schmid, Inc, New york, NY, 3 saluting soldiers **125.00**
Caravan, Tiger Skin Rubber Co, New York, NY, desert scene **150.00**
Carmen, round, unknown manufacturer, beautiful semi-nude girl with fan, Rolf Armstrong artist **300.00**
Chariots, Goodwear Rubber Co, New York, NY, horse race **200.00**
Dean's Peacocks, Dean Rubber Mfg, Co, Kansas City, MO, colorful peacock in garden. **10.00**
Derbies, Jay Dee Drug Co, Chicago, IL, jockey's cap and 2 riding crops **100.00**
De-Luxe Blue Ribbon, American Hygienic Co, Baltimore, MD, German Shepherd dog **350.00**
Double-Tip, Department Sales Co, New York, NY, girl and her reflection in river. **300.00**
Esquire, Crown Rubber Co, Los Angeles, CA, man in top hat **400.00**
Gold Dollar, Allied Latex Sales Co, New York, NY, gold coins. **250.00**
Golden Pheasant, W H Reed & Co, Inc, bird on branch **100.00**
Le Transparent Trojan, Youngs Rubber Corp, Inc, New York, NY, Eiffel Tower. **175.00**
Nutex Lifeguards, round, Nutex Sales Co, Philadelphia, PA, 3 lifeguards arm in arm. **1,000.00**
Patrol, Wilson-Robinson Co, Inc, Boston, MA, war planes. **700.00**
Polly, round, unknown manufacturer, parrot **300.00**
Rainbow, Dean Rubber Mfg Co, beautiful rainbow **550.00**
Seal-Tite, Allied Latex Sales Division, E Newark, NJ, mortar & pestle **75.00**
Shadows, Young Rubber Corp, New York, NY, "As Thin as a Shadow—Strong as an Ox!" **125.00**
Sheik, Julius Schmid, Inc, New York, NY, arab on horseback **25.00**
Silver-Tex, Killian Mfg Co, Akron, OH, Deco design **75.00**
Silver Knight, L J McFaddin Co, Cedar Rapids, IA, knighthead **250.00**
Sphinx, Julius Schmid, Inc, New York, NY, Sphinx and pyramids. **300.00**
Texide, L E Shunk Latex Products, Inc, Akron, OH, rubber plantation native workers **50.00**
Three Knights, Goodwill Rubber Co, New York, NY, knights on horseback. **150.00**
Three Pirates, Akron Rubber Supply Co, Akron, OH, girls on ship dressed in pirate costumes **400.00**
Trey-Pak, C I Lee Co, Inc, New York, NY, "3 of Hearts" **250.00**
Trianon, Gotham Rubber Co, Chicago, IL, Disney-like castle **350.00**
Ultrex Platinum, Dean Rubber Mfg Co, Kansas City, MO, plain. . . . . **.50**

CONSTRUCTION SETS

Children love to build things. Building block sets originated in the nineteenth century. They exist in modern form as Legos and Lego imitators.

Construction toys also are popular, especially with young boys who aspire to be engineers. The best known is the Erector Set, but it also had plenty of imitators. Alfred Carlton Gilbert, Jr., began his business by producing magic sets as the Mysto Manufacturing Company. With the help of his father, he bought out his partner and created the A. C. Gilbert Company located on Erector Square in New Haven, Connecticut.

Clubs: A. C. Gilbert Heritage Society, 16 Palmer St., Medford, MA 02155; Anchor Block Foundation, 1670 Hawkwood Ct., Charlottesville, VA 22901; Girder and Panel Collectors Club, Box 494, Bolton, MA 01470.

A C Gilbert, Erector Set, #1, complete with box **$150.00**
A C Gilbert, Erector Set, Engineers Set, #7½, early 1950s **55.00**
A C Gilbert, Erector Set, Lunar Vehicle Set, #10127, 1963. . . . . **50.00**
A C Gilbert, Erector Set, Trumodel Set, #77, Sears, 1929 . . . . **125.00**
A C Gilbert, Erector Set, Radar Scope Set, #10042 . . . . **35.00**
A C Gilbert, Erector Set, Master Builder Set, #10093. . . . . . . **300.00**
Auburn, Flexible Building Blocks, 1960s **10.00**
Halsam, Frontierland Logs, #915, 1950s. **35.00**
Kenner, Girder & Panel Hydro-Dynamic Building Set, with motorized pump, #2195, 1961 . . . . **75.00**
Lincoln Logs, #1A, 1920 . . . . **22.00**
Lincoln Logs, #29 . . . . **130.00**
Marx, Riverside Construction Set, 1960s. **125.00**
Meccano, Engineering Erector Set **20.00**
Remco, Jumbo Construction Set, 1968 . . . . **125.00**
Scott Manufacturing, Bilt-E-Z Skyscraper Building Blocks, c1925 . . . . **175.00**
Tinkertoy, Electric, with motor **55.00**
Tinkertoy, Senior, complete with instructions **35.00**

COOKBOOKS

There are eighteenth and nineteenth century cookbooks. But, they are expensive, very expensive. It pays to look through old piles of books in hopes that a dealer has overlooked one of these gems. But, in truth, you are going to go unrewarded ninety-nine percent or more of the time.

The cookbooks that you are most likely to find date from the twentieth century. Most were promotional giveaways. A fair number came with appliances. Some were associated with famous authors.

A few years ago, you could buy them in the 50¢ to $1.00 range and had a large selection from which to choose. No longer. These later cookbooks have been discovered. Now you are going to pay between $5.00 and $20.00 for most of them.

Cover art does affect price. Most are bought onlyfor display purposes. Seek out the ones that feature a recognizable personality on the cover.

Club: Cookbook Collectors Club of America, Inc, P.O. Box 56, St James, MO 65559.

Periodical: *Cookbook Collectors' Exchange*, P.O. Box 32369, San Jose, CA 95152.

Alphabet for Gourmets, M Fisher, 1949 . . . . **$8.50**
American Home Cookbook by Ladies of Detroit, 1878 . . . . . . **45.00**
Art of Cooking and Serving, Crisco, 252 pp, 1937 . . . . **6.50**
Busy Woman's Cookbook, Williams-Heller, 342 pp, 1951 . . . . . **6.00**
Campbell's Main Dishes **8.00**
Chinese Cookery Made Easy, I Chang, 256 pp, 1959 . . . . **6.00**
Come Into The Kitchen, 32 pp, 1930 . . . . **40.00**
Desserts of the World, Jell-O **5.00**
Electric Cooking With Your Kenmore, 1941 . . . . **2.00**
Gifts from Our Kitchen, C Laklan, 256 pp, 1955 . . . . **2.50**
Joys of Jell-O **5.00**
McNess Cookbook, 63 pp, c1910 . . . . **5.00**
My Grandmother's Cookery Book, S Wooley, 112 pp, 1976 . . . . **5.00**
Pillsbury Family Cookbook, 1963 . . . . **10.00**
Potato Cook Book—State of Maine, 63 pp, 1950 . . . . **3.00**
Quaker Cereal Products and How To Use Them, 56 pp, 5 x 7" **35.00**
Souvenir from Kraft, NY World's Fair, 3 leaflets, 1939 . . . . **8.50**

COOKIE CUTTERS

When most individuals think of cookie cutters, they envision the metal cutters, often mass produced, that were popular during the nineteenth century and first third of the twentieth century. This is too narrow a view. Do not overlook the plastic cutters of recent years. Not only are they detailed and colorful, they also come in a variety of shapes quite different from their metal counterparts.

If you want to build a great specialized collection, look for cutters that were giveaway premiums by flour and baking related business. Most of these cutters are priced in the $10.00 to $40.00 range.

Club: Cookie Cutter Collectors Club, 1167 Teal Rd. SW, Dellroy, OH 44620.

Newsletter: *Cookies,* 9610 Greenview Ln., Manassas, VA 20109.

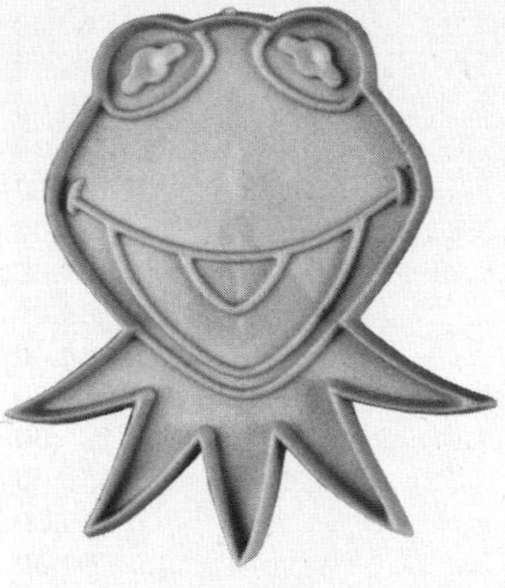

Character, Kermit the Frog, plastic, green, 25¢.

Advertising, Egg Baking Powder, Co, 1902, 1½" d. **$40.00**
Advertising, Fanchon Flour, round, fold down handle **10.00**
Advertising, Robin Hood Flour, set of 6 . . . . **25.00**
Character, Blondie, 1948, MIB. **125.00**
Character, Strawberry Shortcake, Hallmark **10.00**
Character, Tom & Jerry, dated 1956 . . . . **10.00**
Figural, flame, Garland Stoves and Ranges **22.00**
Figural, prancing horse, bobtail, flat back, 6½ x 7½". **100.00**
Metal, pretzel, handle **3.00**
Metal, sprinkling can, Wilton. **2.50**
Plastic, gingerbread boy, blue, Betty Crocker **2.00**
Plastic, Jack O'Lantern, white, inner design, Regal **1.00**
Plastic, Pioneer Seed Company, white **1.00**
Plastic, Quaker Oats, standing bear, yellow **3.00**
Plastic, tree, green, Southwest Indian Foundation, orig card **5.00**
Tin, bird, spread wings, 4½" l **15.00**
Tin, Dutchman, 5¼" h **115.00**
Tin, scissors, 5¼" l. **100.00**

COOKIE JARS

Talk about categories that have gone nuts over the past years. Thanks to the Andy Warhol sale, cookie jars became the talk of the town. Unfortunately, the prices reported for the Warhol cookie jars were so far removed from reality that many individuals were deceived into believing their cookie jars are far more valuable than they really are.

The market seems to be having trouble finding the right pricing structure. A recent cookie jar price guide lowballed a large number of jar prices. Big city dealers are trying to sell cookie jars as art objects at high prices instead of the kitsch they really are. You have to be the judge. Remember, all you are buying is a place to store your cookies.

Club: Cookie Jar Club, P.O. Box 451005, Miami, FL 33245.

Newsletter: *Cookie Jarrin',* 1501 Maple Ridge Rd., Walterboro, SC 29488; *Crazed Over Cookie Jars,* P.O. Box 254, Savanna, IL 61074.

Asparagus Bunch, McCoy **$38.00**
Bananas, Red Wing, turquoise **170.00**
Bear and Beehive, McCoy **55.00**
Brown Bear, Brush **65.00**

Bulldog Cafe, Treasure Craft 60.00
Caboose, McCoy 75.00
Child in Shoe, Twin Winton 40.00
Cinderella, Napco 300.00
Cookie Cabin, McCoy 60.00
Cookie Kettle, American Bisque 45.00
Donald Duck, sitting, Walt Disney Productions 375.00
Dutch Girl, Pottery Guild 65.00
Elephant, Twin Winton 40.00
Mammy, Shirley Corl 125.00
Meat and Vegetable Truck, Henry Cavanaugh 275.00
Raggedy Ann, Twin Winton 250.00
Simba, Treasure Craft 75.00
Snowy Woods Santa, Fitz & Floyd 90.00

COPPER PAINTINGS

Copper paintings, actually pictures stamped out of copper or copper foil, deserve a prize as one of the finest "ticky-tacky" collectibles ever created. I remember getting a four-picture set from a bank as a premium in the late 1950s or early 1960s. It is one of the few things that I have no regrets about throwing out.

However, to each his own—somewhere out there are individuals who like this unique form of mass-produced art. Their treasures generally cost them in the $15 to $50 range depending on subject.

COSTUMES

Remember how much fun it was to play dress-up as a kid? Seems silly to only do it once a year at Halloween. Down South and in Europe, Mardis Gras provides an excuse; but, in my area, we eat doughnuts instead.

Collectors are beginning to discover children's Halloween costumes. While you may be staggered by some of the prices listed below, I see costumes traded at these prices all the time.

There doesn't seem to be much market in adult costumes, those used in the theater and for theme parties. Costume rental shops are used to picking them up for a few dollars each.

Annie Oakley, Herman Iskin & Co, Telford, PA, red, white, and blue, Annie illus on pockets $175.00
Astronaut, plastic mask, boxed, Halco, 1962 . . . . 55.00
Bambi, Ben Cooper, 1950s 40.00
Bat Masterson, boxed 45.00
Beetle Bailey, Spook Town Halloween Costume, orig box, 1960s 50.00
California Raisin 25.00
Dress, homemade, black and orange jack-o'-lanterns, c1940 . . . . 70.00
Dr Zaius, Planet of the Apes, Ben Cooper 65.00
Farmer Alfalfa, 1950s 45.00
Grandpa Munster, Ben Cooper, 1964 . . . . 225.00
Hee Haw, 1976 . . . . 20.00
Herman Munster, Ben Cooper, 1964 . . . . 225.00
Huckleberry Hound, Ben Cooper, 1960 . . . . 50.00
Jet Man, Ben Cooper, 1950s 45.00
Kiss, mask only 35.00
Klinger, M*A*S*H, Ben Cooper, 1981 . . . . 75.00
Klingon, Ben Cooper, 1975 . . . . 15.00
Land of the Giants, Professor 325.00
Lone Ranger, Herman Iskin & Co, Telford, PA, suit, holster, pistol, mask, and scarf, early 1950s, orig box 500.00
Mary Hartline 45.00
Mr Spock, 1967 . . . . 55.00
Porky Pig, Warner Bros, plastic mask, cloth suit and cap, orig box, 1950s 30.00
Red Skull, Ben Cooper, 1980 . . . . 40.00
Skeleton, black cowl, c1940 . . . . 35.00
Spock, Collegeville, 1967 . . . . 25.00
Tinkerbell, Ben Cooper, Disney, c1958 . . . . 40.00
Tweety Bird 20.00
Wicked Witch, Wizard of Oz, orig box 50.00
Woody Woodpecker, Collegeville, 1950 . . . . 50.00

COUNTRY STORE

There is something special about country stores. My favorite is Bergstresser's in Wassergass, Pennsylvania. There is probably one near you that you feel as strongly about. Perhaps the appeal is that they continue to deny the present. I am always amazed at what a country store owner can dig out of the backroom, basement, or barn.

Country store collectibles focuses heavily on front counter and back counter material from the last quarter of the nineteenth century and first quarter of the twentieth century. The look is tied in closely with Country. It also has a strong small town, real rural emphasis.

Drop in and prop your feet up on the potbelly stove. Don't visit a country store if you are in a hurry.

Cash Register, American, candy store, brass, emb, marble ledge, 24" h, restored $1,100.00
Coin Changer, oak and iron, one cent to one dollar, 12½ x 10¼ x 10½" 25.00
Display Case, Brighton Garter, wood and glass, 8 shelves, stenciling on 3 sides, 18" h 100.00
Display Case, Hohner Harmonica, wood, tri-fold, paper marquee displaying different people of the world playing Hohner Harmonicas, complete with 9 litho tin harmonica boxes and 18 fully illus cardboard harmonica boxes, 5½ x 10½" 800.00
Display Case, Hunt's Pens, wood and glass, countertop, large decal on glass depicting "Round Pointed C. Howard Hunt Pen Co. Tip," pull-out drawer contains 16 compartments that contains variety of pen tips, 12 x 10" 100.00
Display Rack, Beech-Nut/Beechies, metal, 2 shelf 20.00
Receipt Dispenser, cast iron, ornamental filigree in front and back, 19 x 8 x 6½" h 400.00
Scale, butcher's, Toledo, emb fancy filigree on sides, beveled mirror above dial, plaque on back reads "Toledo Honest Weight and Values Guaranteed" 400.00
Showcase, Meyers Drugs, wood frame, etched glass on 3 sides, 28 x 66½ x 19½" 100.00
Sign, Brown Shoes, Baby's First Shoes, 1901 . . . . 375.00
Sign, Dr Bell's Pin Tar Honey Cures Coughs, cardboard, large blue bell, white ground, printed by Globe Co, Akron, OH, 13 x 14" 75.00

COUNTRY WESTERN COLLECTIBLES

You don't have to be a "rhinestone cowboy" to enjoy Country Western music and you don't have to travel to Nashville to find its memorabilia. With a large assortment of items available such as sheet music, signed photographs, and record albums, Country Western collectibles won't bring ya' back home empty handed. So go ahead and enjoy yourselves, and "Ya'll come back now, ya' here?"

Newsletter: *Disc Collector,* P.O. Box 315, Cheswold, DE 19936.

Periodical: *American Cowboy,* P.O. Box 6630, Sheridan, WY 82801.

Autograph, Cash, June Carter, sgd photo **$15.00**
Autograph, Davis, Jimmie, sgd calling card **5.00**
Autograph, Fargo, Donna **6.00**
Autograph, Guthrie, Arlo, sgd photo **10.00**
Autograph, Nelson, Willie, sgd photo **25.00**
Autograph, Pride, Charley **5.00**
Autograph, Tubb, Ernest, sgd 45 rpm record sleeve **3.00**
Bumper Sticker, Davis, Jimmie, "Davis for Governor" **15.00**
Letter, Carter, Wilf, typewritten, sgd, c1975 . . . . . **8.00**
Membership Card, Tex Ritter Fan Club **15.00**
Photograph, Gayle, Crystal, sgd, framed, 8 x 10" **8.00**
Photograph, Parton, Dolly, sgd, 8 x 10" **24.00**
Poster, Kincaid, Bradley, performance **20.00**
Record, Allen Brothers, *It Can't Be Done,* Bluebird, 5533 . . . . . **15.00**
Record, Autry, Gene, *That's How I Got My Start,* Superior, 2681 . . . . . **50.00**
Record, Carter Family, *Broken Hearted Lover,* Vocalion **18.00**
Record, Carter Family, *Keep On The Sunny Side,* Bluebird, 5006 . . . . . **6.00**
TV Guide, Hee Haw feature, sgd by Grandpa Jones **6.50**

COW COLLECTIBLES

Holy cow! This is a moovelous category, as entrenched collectors already know.

Club: *Cow Observers Worldwide,* 240 Wahl Ave., Evans City, PA 16033.

Advertising Trade Card, Carnick's Lacto Preparata & Soluable Food, man holding child on knee milking cow **$45.00**
Advertising Trade Card, Dwight's Saleratus, black, white, and gold, cow image on front, text on back, 1890s, 3¼ x 5¼" **15.00**
Book, *Herd Book,* Holstein Breeder's Assoc, cov with engraved and litho cow and bull illus, 1884, 684 pp. **18.00**
Bowl, china, full color Elsie and family portraits, Universal-Cambridge Pottery, ©1940 Borden, 10¼" d **100.00**
Box, Country Dairy Butter, cows image, dated 1917, 3½" d, 3" h **3.00**
Box, Cow Butter, Pine Grove Dairy, cows in pasture, 1940s, 2½ x 2½ x 5" **3.00**
Cookie Jar Lid, ceramic, Elsie, unmkd, 4 x 5 x 6" **40.00**
Display, standup, Holstein adv, tin, cow shape, black and white, 6" l **75.00**
Figure, Ferdinand, rubber, Seiberling, ©Walt Disney Enterprises, c1930, 3 x 5½ x 4" **75.00**
Figure, Hereford calf, Beswick **75.00**
Mug, Elsie, china **75.00**
Postcard, Evaporated Milk—Pure Cow's Milk, black and white cows, green ground, 1940 . . . . . **8.00**
Sign, American Stock Food, Uncle Sam with farm animals in barnyard **375.00**
Sign, Elsie, "M-M-M Look," diecut cardboard, easel back, countertop, Borden Co, ©1940s, 10½ x 11½" **90.00**
Tray, Carnation Milk adv, oval, cows in pasture, 3½ x 5½" **20.00**

Calendar, Louella Butte, 1936, paper, color litho scene of girl with calf in pasture, American Stores Co, 25" h, 12" w, $44.00. Photo courtesy Collectors Auction Services.

COWAN POTTERY

R. Guy Cowan founded the Cowan Pottery in 1913 in Cleveland, Ohio. It remained in almost continuous operation until financial difficulties forced it to close in 1931. Initially, utilitarian redware was produced. Cowan began experimenting with glazes, resulting in a unique lusterware glaze.

Club: American Art Pottery Assoc., P.O. Box 1226, Westport, MA 02790.

Periodical: *Cowan Pottery Journal* (Cowan Pottery Museum), 1600 Hampton Rd., Rocky River, OH 44116.

Bookends, pr, figural unicorn, 7" h **$425.00**
Candlesticks, pr, figural Marlin, 8½" h **400.00**
Compote, diamond shaped, cream, green int, 2" h **20.00**
Console Bowl, canoe shaped, molded sea horse dec, mottled blue glaze, 16" l **110.00**
Figure, sea nymph, nude, unmkd, 9" h **500.00**
Figure, Spanish dancer, male, 8¾" h, 1928 . . . . . **400.00**
Match Holder, chicken, 5¼" h **45.00**
Table Lamp, relief molded flowers on blue lustre glazed base, dragon handles,14" h **750.00**
Soap Dish, sea horse, blue, 4" d **35.00**
Trivet, bust of young girl framed by flowers, scalloped rim, sgd, 6½" d **275.00**
Vase, fan, apple green, gold specks, 5" h **80.00**
Vase, turquosie glaze, 5" h **150.00**

COWBOY HEROES

The cowboy heroes in this category rode the range in movies and on television. In a way, they were larger than their real life counterparts, shaping the image of how the west was won in the minds of several generations. The contemporary westerns may be historically correct, but they do not measure up in sense of rightness.

The movie and television cowboy heroes were pioneers in merchandise licensing. If you were a child in the 1949 to 1951 period and did not own a Hopalong Cassidy item, you were deprived.

Club: Westerns & Serials Fan Club, Rt. 1, Box 103, Vernon Center, MN 56090.

Newsletter: *The Cowboy Collector Newsletter,* P.O. Box 7486, Long Beach, CA 90807.

Periodical: *Spur,* 4700 Western Heritage Way, Los Angeles, CA 90027.

Note: For information on fan clubs for individual cowboy heroes, refer to *Maloney's Antiques & Collectibles Resource Directory* by David J. Maloney, Jr., published by Antique Trader Books.

Annie Oakley, autograph, Gail Davis, photo, glossy, 1950s, 8 x 10" **$50.00**
Annie Oakley, book, *Danger At Diablo,* Whitman, 1955 . . . . . **15.00**
Annie Oakley, game, Milton Bradley, 1955, reissued 1958 . . . . . **35.00**
Annie Oakley, record, 78 rpm, *Annie Oakley Sings,* Little Golden Record, mid 1950s, 6½ x 7½" sleeve **15.00**
Autry, Gene, coloring book, Gene Autry Coloring Book, Whitman, #116915, ©1952 Gene Autry **40.00**
Autry, Gene, guitar, Emenee, MIB **175.00**
Autry, Gene, magazine, *Movie Thrills,* Sep 1950, full color cov photo, 96 pp, 8½ x 11" **50.00**
Autry, Gene, Pistol Horn, squeeze toy, 6½" metal pistol horn, rubber squeeze handle with image of Gene Autry on 1 side and Champion on reverse, orig box with image of Gene Autry and Champion on 2 different sides, c1950 . . . . . **0.00**
Bat Masterson, hat, black felt, fabric picture, Arlington Hats, c1960, 12 x 13 x 4" h **30.00**
Bonanza, photo, Michael Landon as Little Joe, color, early 1960s, 8 x 10" **25.00**
Bonanza, *TV Magazine,* week of Jun 11, 1961 . . . . . **25.00**
Buffalo Bill, Jr, outfit, child's, 2 pc, flannel, plastic fringe trim with simulated fur, late 1950s **75.00**
Daniel Boone, lunch box, King-Seeley Co, ©1965, American Tradition Co **100.00**
Davy Crockett, iron-on transfer, set of 3, titled images, "Great Hunter," Indian Fighter," and "Wild Frontier" **50.00**
Davy Crockett, mug, plastic, red, tan lid, relief portrait image, mid 1950s, 3" h **75.00**
Davy Crockett, toolbox, tin, Fess Parker **75.00**
Gabby Hayes, comic book, Quaker Oats premium, set of 5, orig envelope, 1951, 2½ x 7" **150.00**
Gunsmoke, lunch box, Aladdin Industries, steel, 1962 . . . . . **125.00**
Hopalong Cassidy, birthday card, diecut, front image of Hoppy crouched down with guns drawn, western wagon in background, right boot is attached diecast white metal, card opens to color art image of Hoppy leaning against fence rails with caption "I'm Shootin' It Straight You Bet Your Boots I Think You're Swell," Buzza Cardozo, c1950s, 4½ x 5¾" **40.00**
Hopalong Cassidy, Butter-Nut Bread wrapper **65.00**
Hopalong Cassidy, camera, metal, black, black and silver circular title plate, Glater Products Co, late 1940s, 2 x 2½ x 5" **75.00**
Hopalong Cassidy, coloring book, William Boyd Star of Hopalong Cassidy, Lowe, #1231-15, ©1950 . . . . . **40.00**
Hopalong Cassidy, pinback button, celluloid, metal hanger, c1950, 1¼" d **30.00**
Hopalong Cassidy, tumbler, glass, color art, "Western Series," cowboy branding irons, c1950, 4¾" h **50.00**
Lone Ranger, belt, leather, dark brown, brass accent metal buckle with relief head and shoulder image of Lone Ranger, name at upper left, crown imprint of maker on reverse size 36, late 1930s, 42" l **100.00**
Lone Ranger, book, *The Lone Ranger and the War Horse,* Whitman, #2411, 28 pp, 1951 . . . . . **20.00**
Lone Ranger, book, *The Lone Ranger On Powderhorn Trail,* #11, ©1949, 207 pp **25.00**
Lone Ranger, map, Lone Ranger Hunt Map, full color illus, orig mailing envelope, Silvercup Bread, c1938, 13 x 17" **200.00**
Lone Ranger, sheet music, *Hi-Yo Silver,* Chappell, ©1938, 6 pp, 9 x 12" **45.00**
Lone Ranger, toothbrush holder, figural, plaster, painted, ©1928 Lone Ranger Inc, 4" h **75.00**
Maverick, canteen, plastic, attached diecut metal badge inserted by paper picture of James Garner, 1950s, 4½" d **35.00**
Roy Rogers, binoculars, Roy and Trigger, 3 power, MIB **125.00**
Roy Rogers, book, *Roy Rogers and Trigger to the Rescue,* Whitman, #203825, full color cov photo of Trigger in western desert scene, 24 pp, 1950 . . . . . **20.00**
Roy Rogers, jewelry set, pr cufflinks and tie bar, gold finished metal, cowboy boot shape cuff links, relief western saddle design tie bar, orig card, mid 1950s **45.00**
Tom Mix, belt buckle, decoder, secret compartment **95.00**
Tom Mix, magnifying glass, Ralston premium, Tom Mix Luminous Compass-Magnifying Glass, plastic, ivory, with orig mailing envelope and instructions, 1946 . . . . . **100.00**
Wayne, John, comic book, Oxydol and Dreft Soaps premium, 1950, 3 x 7" **45.00**

Hopalong Cassidy, hat, black felt, white neck string, leather slider, $150.00.

Lone Ranger Guitar, wood, plastic string holders, Supertone Warranted High Quality Musical Instruments, "2183" stamped inside, wear to paint, warping and cracks, no strings, 35½" h, 13" w, $55.00. Photo courtesy Collectors Auction Services.

Wild Bill Hickock, map, paper, "Wild Bill Hickock Treasure Map," Hickock drawing and jingles in lower left corner, western motif, shows over 300 treasure sites, Rand McNally, 1950s, 24 x 36" **60.00**
Wild Bill Hickock, View-Master reel, 3 color view cards, #T-2, #T-18, and #T-19, ©1956, 4 x 5½" envelope **50.00**
Wyatt Earp, badge, Marshall, metal, orig card. **10.00**
Wyatt Earp, mug, milk glass. **22.00**

CRACKER JACK COLLECTIBLES

You can still buy Cracker Jack with a prize in every box. The only problem is that when you compare today's prizes with those from decades ago, you feel cheated. Modern prizes simply do not measure up. For this reason, collectors tend to focus on prizes put in the box prior to 1960.

Most Cracker Jack prizes were not marked. As a result, many dealers have Cracker Jack prizes without even knowing it. This allows an experienced collector to get some terrific bargains at flea markets. Alex Jaramillo's *Cracker Jack Prizes* (Abbeville Press, 1989) provides a wonderful survey of what prizes were available.

Club: Cracker Jack Collectors Assoc., 5469 S. Dorchester Ave., Chicago, IL 60615

Bank, litho tin, book shape, 1920s, 1 x 1¼ x 1¾". **$150.00**
Booklet, 1933 World's Fair, Cracker Jack adv, 8 pp, 1½ x 2½" **75.00**
Bookmark, litho tin, diecut, brown image resembling Spaniel puppy, 1930s **20.00**
Charm, candlestick, diecast lead, ring **5.00**
Charm, fish, diecast lead, ring **5.00**
Charm, plane, diecast lead, ring **5.00**
Charm, stork and baby, diecast lead, ring. **5.00**
Coin, Mystery Club, emb aluminum, presidential profile, back with "Join Cracker Jack Mystery Club/Save This Coin," 1930s, 1" d. **18.00**
Doll, cloth, stuffed, vinyl head, Vogue Dolls, ©1980, unopened display card **25.00**
Drawing Book, blue and white cov design, nursery rhyme characters on each side, tracing sheets between each page, 4 pp, unused, 1920s, 1¼ x 2½" **30.00**
Figure, Sailor Jack and Bingo, plastic, yellow, on rect base, reverse with back image of both and "C.J. Co. 5," 1960s **20.00**
Game, Cracker Jack Toy Surprise Game, Milton Bradley, orig box, 1976 . . . . **25.00**

Truck, tin, red with black hood, 1⅜", 1⅜" l, $60.00.

Game, Magic Words, #7, paper and cardboard, 1920–30, 1½ x 2½". **50.00**
Game, pinball, Pokey the Turtle **10.00**
Hat, paper, red, white, and blue design, "Me For Cracker Jack," early 1900s **65.00**
Top, litho tin, diecut, red, white, and blue, 1930s, 1⅜" d **55.00**
Toy, Cracker Jack Kerchoo Railroad Engine, plastic, red, 1950s **10.00**

CRACKLE GLASS

If crackle glass catches your fancy, beware! It is still being produced by Blenko Glass Company and in foreign countries such as Taiwan and China. Examine prospective purchases carefully. Cracks are often hard to distinguish from the decorative "crackles."

Club: Collectors of Crackle Glass, P.O. Box 1186, N. Massapequa, NY 11758.

Candleholder, pale sea green, Blenko, 5¼" h **$50.00**
Candy Dish, dark topaz, ribbed, drop-over handle, Hamon, 5½ x 2¼". **75.00**
Creamer and Sugar, gold, Kanawha, 3½" h. **50.00**
Decanter, lemon lime, Pilgrim, 6" h **100.00**
Decanter, topaz, ribbed, crystal drop-over handle, Pilgrim, 6¼" h **100.00**
Dish, green, Kanawha, 5¼ x 3" **35.00**
Glass, cream, drop-over handle, 5½" h **35.00**
Miniature Hat, olive green, Pilgrim, 3" h **35.00**
Pitcher, amethyst, drop-over handle, Pilgrim, 3¼" h **35.00**
Pitcher, dark amber, drop-over handle, Pilgrim, 5" h **25.00**
Pitcher, tangerine, pulled back handle, Pilgrim, 3¾" h **30.00**
Syrup Pitcher, blue, pulled back handle, Kanawha, 6" h **50.00**
Vase, jonquil, ftd, crimped top, Blenko, 7¼" h **100.00**
Vase, olive green, double-neck, Blenko, 7" h **75.00**

CRECHE COLLECTIBLES

Once primarily a religious holiday decoration, creches have increasingly become a year-round collectible, with many collectors keeping their sets on display in the non-holiday months.

The creche's philosophical roots lie in the New Testament passages from Luke and Matthew. In its simplest and most basic form, the Nativity set is comprised of three figures known as the Holy Family: the Virgin Mary, Joseph, and the Infant Jesus lying in a manger or creche. These figures are displayed free standing, or they are placed in settings varying from a stable to a cave to castle ruins symbolizing the downfall of the old Pagan beliefs. Typical accompanying figures include an ox and donkey, Three Wise Men (or Magi), one or two shepherds with lambs, and a heralding angel.

The practice of displaying the Christmas Nativity figures is an ancient one, first popularized, although not originated, by St. Francis of Assisi in thirteenth century Italy. By the eighteenth century, the development of the creche figures in Naples had become a fine art, with the foremost artists of the time commissioned by wealthy families to create stunning displays that featured hundreds of accessory village figures in addition to the basic ones. These Neapolitan collections typically reach the secondary market through offerings in the large auction houses.

Until recently, creches rarely were seen in secondary markets outside the holiday season; however, with the popularization of the creche as a collectible, full sets and individual figures are increasingly available all year.

Creche collectors look for all forms of the Nativity display, from the three-dimensional figures to paper cutouts. Pre–World War II European made figures are especially desirable, although examples of well-known brand names such as Hummel or Anri in excellent condition will command a good price.

Collectors are as apt to purchase individual figures to fill out a home display as they are to buy a full matching set.

Advisor: Rita B. Bocher, 117 Crosshill Rd., Wynnewood, PA 19096-3511, (610) 649-7520, Fax (610) 649-5782, e-mail: crecher@op.net, Internet: www.op.net/~bocassoc/

Newsletter: *Creche Herald,* 117 Crosshill Rd., Wynnewood, PA 19096.

Book, Nativity scene, punch-out, #989, Saalfield Publishing Co, designs by Corinne and Bill Bailey, 1933 . . . . . $75.00
Figure, 3 Magi, composition, hollow, mkd "Germany" on bottom, pre-1940, price for each 5.00
Figure, 3 Magi, plaster, faded paint, 1960s, 4" h, price for each 3.00
Figure, 3 Magi, poured clay, painted, c1920, price for each 24.00
Figure, Blue Angel, Hummel, 1961–72, 2" h 48.00
Figure, Infant Jesus, Hummel, 1951, 2" h 60.00
Figure, Infant Jesus, Lenox, white glazed porcelain, 2" h 35.00
Figure, Joseph, ceramic, mkd, European, c1920 . . . . . 35.00
Figure, Baby Jesus, in manger, plastic, 1950s, 2" h 3.00
Figure, Mary, plastic, 1950s, 3" h 2.00
Figure, Mary, with separate Infant Jesus, Hummel, 10" h 395.00
Figure, Mary, Joseph, or Jesus, Fontanini, orig box, 1980s–90s, price for each 10.00
Figure, Mary, Joseph, or Jesus, Fontanini, without box, 1980s–90s, price for each 8.00
Figure, shepherd, composition, painted, Italy, 1960, 6" h, price for each 5.00
Figure, shepherd, Hummel, 12" 250.00
Figure, stable animals, plaster, Germany, 1950s, price for each 5.00
Figure, stand alone Infant Jesus in manger with stable roof, ceramic, "Reg. U.S. Pat. Off., Norcrest—Japan" pasted label on bottom, 1960s, 5" h 12.00
Figure, villagers, Magi, Fontanini, orig box, 1980s–90s, 5" h, price for each 9.00

Set, 13 composition figures, painted, Italy, 1950–60s, $55.00.

Figure, villagers, Magi, Fontanini, orig box, 1980s–90s, 6½" h, price for each 9.50
Figure, villagers, Magi, Fontanini, without box, 1980s–90s, 5" h, price for each 7.00
Figure, villagers, Magi, Fontanini, without box, 1980s–90s, 6½" h, price for each 7.50
Figure, set of 6, 3 Magi, peasant girl, and 2 lambs 16.00
Figure, set of 9, papier-mâché, painted, 1950s 25.00
Plaque, round, white bisque, boxed with papers, c1970s, 10" d 150.00
Set, 7 pcs, glass figures, separate mirror base, China, figures 4" to 5" h 12.00
Set, 7 pcs, porcelain bisque, orig box labeled "Trippie's," Japan, 1990s, 1" to 2" h 6.00
Set, 10 pcs, Anri 95.00
Set, 15 pcs, plaster, mkd "British Zone Germany," post-1940, 4" to 7" 40.00
Set, 16 pcs, painted bisque porcelain, Germany, 1920-30s 395.00
Set, 20 pcs, ceramic, painted, Infant Jesus separate from crib, 1950s, 5" 45.00
Set, Jesus, Mary, Joseph, 6" composition figures glued on floor of wooden stable, Germany, c1960 . . . . . 5.00
Set, stable with 5 plastic figures, worn paint 30.00
Set, stable with 10 plastic figures, moss dec, painted, tallest figure 5" h, 1960s 45.00
Set, stable with 12 plaster figures glued to floor, back wall with pasted night scene and Three Magi, "Made in Italy" stamped on back, c1980 . . . . . 12.00
Water Color on Wood Panel, painted for church stained glass design, 7½ x 7", 1840s 200.00

CUFF LINKS

Many people consider cuff links to be the ideal collectible. Besides being available, affordable, and easy to display and store, cuff links are educational and offer windows to history. They have been around for centuries and have always reflected the styles, economics, and technologies of their era. Cuff link collecting can be profitable. Rare or unusual finds can be worth substantial dollars. Most serious collectors have had the thrill of buying a pair for "pennies" that turned out to be worth a great deal.

Many cuff link collectors specialize in their collections. Some areas of specialization are size, shape, and closure type. Other collectors specialize by subject. Examples of this are cuff links that show animals, sports, advertising logos, cars, boats, etc.

Club: National Cuff Link Society, P.O. Box 346, Prospect Heights, IL 60070.

Abstract Design, enamel over sterling, blue and yellow pastel, c1955 . . . . . $135.00
Advertising, Bon Ami Cleanser, barbell type closure, enamel over sterling, c1895 . . . . . 160.00
Advertising, Coca-Cola, toggle closure, Australian, box with water stain, 1970 . . . . . 75.00
Art Deco, Jem Snap Link, sq metal base, green celluloid with center mother-of-pearl circle dec, orig card, 1920s 25.00
Chance Cuff Buttons, mother-of-pearl insets, Separable adaptation, 1925 . . . . . 100.00
Character, Mickey Mouse logo, black, yellow, and red, orig box with torn edges, c1940 . . . . . 45.00

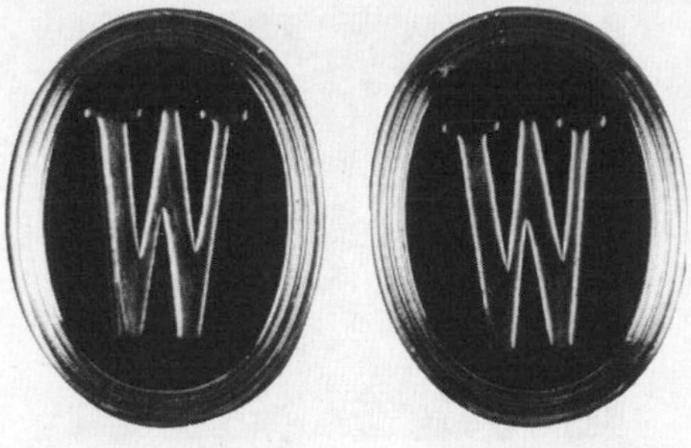

Swank, monogram "W," silver, black ground, matching tie bar, $12.00.

Coin, Mercury dime, pr cuff links and tie tack, 1930s **40.00**
Hickok, knots, gold colored, matching tie bar, 1955 . . . . **15.00**
Kremetz, rect, gray, mother-of-pearl, double faced, gold plating surround, 4 matching studs, orig pouch, 1935, price for set **105.00**
Political, Presidential Seal, Reagan, base metal, orig box with autopen autograph **200.00**
Shields, oval, turquoise stone, silver colored base, back swivel closure, 1975 . . . . **9.00**
Swank, fleur de lis, square shaped, silver and blue, 1960, ¾" w **8.00**
Swank, letter "F," matching tie bar, orig box, 1965 . . . . **6.00**
Swank, rect, paperweight type, reverse painted hunter with raised gun and hunting dog, mother-of-pearl ground, ¾" l **25.00**
Unknown Manufacturer, set, pr cuff links and tie pin, octagonal shape, sivler tone, center ivory celluloid disk set with rhinestones, 1920s **30.00**

CUPIDS

Be suspicious of naked infants bearing bows and arrows. It is not clear if their arrows are tipped with passion or poison.

Club: Cupid Collectors Club, 2116 Lincoln St., Cedar Falls, IA 50613.

Booklet, Diamond dyes, 2 rabbits watching cupid blowing bubbles, 6 x 8", 1901 . . . . **$18.00**
Christmas Ornament, white cupid, gold trim, gold hanger, plastic, 4" h **5.00**
Dresser Scarf, linen, embroidered dec **45.00**

Diamond Dyes Cabinet, litho tin sign, cupids dec, oak case with 52 compartments, rear wood sliding doors, hinged front door with sign, paint chips, fading, 30" h, 21" w, $550.00. Photo courtesy Collectors Auction Services.

Napkin Ring, figural, sitting, legs crossed, SP, combination candleholder and napkin ring **175.00**
Plaque, oval, red paint, gold braid trim, cupid in center, 11 x 7", price for pair **32.00**
Postcard, heart with cupids, shooting hearts and arrows at lovers, green ivy trim, "February 14th," Germany, 1910 . . . . **1.50**
Print, Cupid Awake, Cupid Asleep, Taber Prang, ©1897, unframed, 6 x 8", price for pair **22.00**
Print, woman in gauze dress with cupid on rock, 8 x 10" **30.00**
Valentine, cupid delivering floral garland to girl, "Love Messages," dated 1902 . . . . **3.00**
Valentine, 2 cupids, fold-out, red tissue paper, stand-up, Germany, 6" h **8.00**
Valentine, "Cupid's Temple of Love," honeycomb, c1928 . . . . **15.00**
Wall Hanging, 3 part, cupid on heart, flower, and butterfly **18.00**

CUSPIDORS

After examining the interiors of some of the cuspidors for sale at flea markets, I am glad I have never been in a bar where people "spit." Most collectors are enamored by the brass cuspidor. The form came in many other varieties as well. You could build a marvolous collection focusing on pottery cuspidors.

Within the past year a large number of fake cuspidors have entered the market. I have seen them at flea markets across the United States. Double-check any cuspidor with a railroad marking and totally discount any with a Wells Fargo marking.

Cast Iron, porcelanized, light gray, white int, mkd "Valley RR" **$95.00**
Graniteware, blue **55.00**
Nippon, lady's hand, violets, turquoise beading, green letter "M" in wreath mark **150.00**
Redware, applied tooled floral design, mkd "A.L.S. Manufactured, St. Jobs, Ohio" on base, 2" h **50.00**
Redware, tooled bands, brown and green running glaze with brown dashes, 8 x 4¼" **250.00**
Rockingham, glazed yellow ware, molded shell form, c1850-80, 10" d **80.00**
Salt Glazed, brown highlights, 8½" d **55.00**
Stoneware, emb sponged blue earthworm pattern **120.00**
Tin, smoked white, red stripes and gold stenciled dec, 8¼" d **70.00**
Yellow Ware, green, blue, and tan sponging, 5 x 7½" **60.00**

CUT GLASS

Collectors have placed so much emphasis on American Brilliant Cut Glass (1880 to 1917) that they completely overlook some of the finer cut glass of the post–World War I period. Admittedly, much cut glass in this later period was mass produced and rather ordinary. But, if you look hard enough, you will find some great pieces.

The big news in the cut glass market at the end of the 1980s was the revelation that many of the rare pieces that had been uncovered in the 1980s were of recent origin. Reproductions, copycats, and fakes abound. This is one category where you had better read a great deal and look at hundreds of pieces before you start buying.

Compote, Arbutus pattern, tear drop in stem, Clark, $7^{3}/_{4}$" h, 6" d, $265.00.

Canister Set, pearl luster ground, gold letters, mkd, price for set of 5, $125.00.

Condition is also critical. Do not pay high prices for damaged pieces. Look for chips, dings, fractures, and knife marks. Sometimes these defects can be removed, but consider the cost of the repair when purchasing a damaged piece. Of course signed pieces command a higher dollar value.

Remember, the antiques and collectibles market is governed by "caveat emptor" (let the buyer beware).

Club: American Cut Glass Assoc., P.O. Box 482, Ramona, CA 92065.

Basket, alternating hobstars and pinwheels, rope handle, American Brilliant period, 7" h. **$50.00**
Basket, hat shape, 3 large hobstars and 4 fans, applied rope handle, American Brilliant period, $6^{3}/_{4}$" h **150.00**
Bell, hobstars, fan, and strawberry diamond **275.00**
Bowl, Greek Key design and floral panels, 8-sided, American Brilliant period, 3" h. **50.00**
Bowl, swirled primrose, sgd "Tuthill," $8^{1}/_{4}$" d. **500.00**
Butter Pat, Hobstars. **30.00**
Door Knob, facet cut. **25.00**
Ice Bucket, Harvard pattern, American Brilliant period, $5^{1}/_{2}$" h **150.00**
Mustard, cov, Renaissance pattern, matching underplate. . . . **150.00**
Plate, cut and engraved Colias pattern, clear crystal, Pairpoint, 10" d **115.00**
Plate, Hindoo pattern, Hoare. **115.00**
Punch Cup, hobastars, pedestal, handle **75.00**
Relish, hobstars, 8" l, $3^{1}/_{2}$" w **35.00**
Tray, pinwheels, hobstars and florals, 12" d. **115.00**
Vase, bulbous body, flaring rim, Sillsbee pattern, deep cut leaves and flowers, Pairpoint, $12^{1}/_{2}$" h **300.00**
Wine, hobstars, fans and strawberry diamond. **35.00**

CZECHOSLOVAKIAN

Czechoslovakia was created at the end of World War I out of the area of Bohemia, Moravia, and Austrian Silesia. Although best known for glass products, Czechoslovakia also produced a large number of pottery and porcelain wares for export.

Czechoslovakia objects do not enjoy a great reputation for quality, but I think they deserve a second look. They certainly reflect what was found in the average American's home from the 1920s through the 1950s.

Club: Czechoslovakian Collectors Guild International, P.O. Box 901395, Kansas City, MO 64190.

Bowl, ceramic lustre with flower frog, 6" d. **$7.50**
Card Holder, ornate gold metal frame and base, green ground, glass cameo, $2^{3}/_{4}$" h. **40.00**
Centerpiece, Alien pottery, mkd "Made in Czechoslovakia, $4^{1}/_{2}$" h **50.00**
Chamberstick, Erphila, blue with spatter design, flowers and black handle, $4^{1}/_{2}$" h **30.00**
Cologne Bottle, blue, glossy, bow front, 4" h **12.00**
Decanter, Art Nouveau, 4 part, 11" h. **40.00**
Perfume Bottle, engraved design, amber frosted flowers, stopper, 5" h **25.00**
Plate, Bartered Bride, hp, 9" d, price for pair **50.00**
Rose Bowl, Kralik, glass, ftd, clear with enamel dec, 5" h **50.00**
Salt and Pepper Shakers, pr, figural duck, clear glass bodies, orange porcelain tops, 2" h **42.00**
Vase, glass, goldenrod with brown pulled design, $7^{1}/_{2}$" h. **95.00**
Vase, Loetz, green iridized glass, funnel shaped, Rusticana pattern, $7^{1}/_{4}$" h **160.00**
Vase, opaque, enameled birch trees, house, and barn with red roof, 6" h. **65.00**

DAIRY COLLECTIBLES

For decades, the dairy industry has been doing a good job of encouraging us to drink our milk and eat only real butter. The objects used to get this message across, as well as the packaging for dairy products, have long been favorites with collectors.

Concentrate on the material associated with a single dairy, region, or national firm. If you tried to collect one example of every milk bottle used, you simply would not succeed. The amount of dairy collectibles is staggering.

Clubs: Creamer Separator Assoc., Rt. 3, P.O. Box 189, Arcadia, WI 54612; National Assoc. of Milk Bottle Collectors Inc., 4 Ox Bow Rd., Westport, CT 06800.

Newsletters: *Creamers*, P.O. Box 11, Lake Villa, IL 60046; *The Udder Collectibles,* HC 73 Box 1, Smithville Flats, NY 13841.

Book, *Herd Book,* Holstein Breeder's Association, cov with engraved and litho cow and bull illus, 1884, 684 pp **$18.00**
Box, Borden's Process Cheese Food, wood, red and green logo, 1950s, 4 x 12 x 4". **18.00**
Broom Holder, De Laval Cream Separators, tin, orig envelope, 4 x 4" **115.00**
Calendar, 1943 With Elsie the Borden Cow, color, Elsie cartoon each page, 8 x 14" **50.00**

Ice Cream Cartons, pr, cardboard, Crane's Philadelphia Ice Cream, $3\frac{1}{5}$ x $6\frac{5}{8}$ x $2\frac{3}{4}$"; Furnas Ice Cream, $3\frac{1}{4}$ x $6\frac{3}{8}$ x $2\frac{1}{2}$", unused, with inventor's notes and promotional ad copies, 1920s, price for pair, $632.50. Photo courtesy Wm. Morford.

Cookbook, Carnation Milk, 32 pp, 1915 . . . . **10.00**
Creamer, Rosebud Dairy **9.00**
Doilies, Carver Ice Cream, set of 12, linen-like, emb, Christmas, 1920s **12.00**
Envelope, DeLaval Cream Separator adv, grazing cows, 1932 . . . . **30.00**
Lamp, Elsie and Baby Beauregard, figural Elsie holding Beauregard in her lap, holding opened book beside him, Bordon Co copyright, c1948 . . . . **200.00**
Milk Bottle, Ennes Dairy, H Zupke, Greeley, CO, round, black pyroglaze, 1 qt **35.00**
Milk Bottle, Supreme Dairy, Peru, IL, "Baby's Choice," baby in crib with bottle, tall, round, blue pyroglaze **24.00**
Milk Bottle Cap Opener, Brock Hall Dairy Products, Purity Protected Dacro Sealed Milk on back **5.00**
Playing Cards, Lemke Milk Products, Wausau, WI, white, blue and gold border **3.50**
Postcard, Ebert Ice Cream Co, factory picture **5.00**
Poster, Evaporated Milk—Pure Cow's Milk, black and white cows, green ground, 1940 . . . . **8.00**
Purse, green patent leather, silver metal reinforcement strips with beaded snap fastener balls at top edge, 1 side centered by high relief ivory plastic image of Elmer, missing carrying strap, 1940s, 1 x 6 x 6" **45.00**
Puzzle, jigsaw, cardboard, Borden's milk wagon and milkman, middle piece shaped like milk bottle, 1928, 18 x 11" **100.00**
Puzzle, jigsaw, Green Spring Dairy, Baltimore, MD, dairy processing machinery, missing envelope, $10\frac{3}{4}$ x 9" **30.00**
Puzzle, jigsaw, "Milking Time at a Brookfield Dairy Farm," Swift & Co, dancing cows at center above oval with info about "Brookie" the famous white cow and her pals, figural pcs spell "SWIFT & CO," 12 x 12 box **65.00**

Sign, De Laval, cow and calf, text on reverse of both, diecut litho tin, creases, fading, scuffs, and scratches to both, 3 x 5" cow, 2 x $2\frac{1}{2}$" calf, price for pair, $176.00. Photo courtesy Collectors Auction Services.

DAKIN FIGURES

The term "Dakin" refers to a type of hollow, vinyl figure produced by the R. Dakin Company. These figures are found with a number of variations—molded or cloth costumed, jointed or nonjointed and range in height from 5 to 10".

As with any popular and profitable product, Dakin figures were copied. There are a number of Dakin-like figures found on the market. Produced by Sutton & Son Inc., Knickerbocker Toy Company, and a production company for Hanna-Barbera, these figures are also collectible and are often mistaken for the original Dakin products. Be careful when purchasing.

Bank, Bugs Bunny, standing on yellow basket filled with carrots, gray and white body, yellow gloves, hard plastic and vinyl, movable head and arms, 1971 . . . . **$35.00**
Bank, Speedy Gonzales, standing on cheese wedge, hard plastic and vinyl, movable head, arms, and tail, fabric outfit, 1970, $9\frac{3}{4}$" h **20.00**
Bank, Yosemite Sam, standing on brown trunk, blue hat and pants, yellow shirt, orange hair, black gun belt and boots, hard plastic and vinyl, movable arms, yellow painted hair, orange "cotton" beard, fabric outfit, 1970, 7" h **30.00**
Figure, Autocat, Hanna Barbera Prod, 1969 . . . . **30.00**
Figure, Barney Rubble, orange outfit, brown belt, 1970 . . . . . **50.00**
Figure, Big Boy, holding burger **200.00**
Figure, Bozo the Clown, plastic and vinyl, movable head and arms, orange hair, blue body, white gloves, 1974, $7\frac{1}{2}$" h **12.00**
Figure, Cool Cat, plastic and vinyl, 1968, 9" h **25.00**
Figure, Dino, squeaky head, 1970 . . . . **60.00**
Figure, Dudley Do-Right, Cartoon Theater **20.00**
Figure, Elmer Fudd, white shirt, black coat, yellow pants, red top hat and shoes, 1970 . . . . **35.00**
Figure, Hokey Wolf, vinyl, movable head, arms, feet, and tail, brown body, tan and black markings, 1971, 8" h **20.00**
Figure, Little Liberty Bell, vinyl, orig tag, ©1975, 7" h **55.00**
Figure, Oliver Hardy, plastic and vinyl, 1960s, $7\frac{1}{2}$" h **35.00**
Figure, Pebbles Flintstone, vinyl, 1970, 8" h **28.00**
Figure, Pluto, yellow body, black ears and tail, red tail, Walt Disney Productions **35.00**
Figure, Rocky the Flying Squirrel, in box, Dakin's TV Cartoon Theater, P. A. T. Ward Prod, 1976 . . . . **65.00**
Figure, Smokey the Bear, holding shovel, squeaker, brown body, blue pants, yellow hat, small, 1974 . . . . **20.00**
Figure, Speedy Gonzales, light green shirt, white pants, yellow sombrero, 1968 . . . . **30.00**
Stuffed Toy, bunny, bean bag, glass eyes, 1977 . . . . **25.00**
Stuffed Toy, monkey, astronaut, mohair, glass eyes, velvet uniform, rocket, 1961 . . . . **100.00**

DEARLY DEPARTED

I know this category is a little morbid, but the stuff is collected. Several museums have staged special exhibitions devoted to mourning art and jewelry. Funeral parlors need to advertise for business.

I did not put one in the listing, but do you know what makes a great coffee table? A coffin carrier or coffin stand. Just put a piece of glass over the top. It's the right size, has leg room underneath, and makes one heck of a conversation piece.

Beer Stein, Germany, book as base, pewter lid with insert, base mkd "GOMME, RS BUCH," anchor marking on bottom, 4¾" h, $165.00. Photo courtesy Bill Bertoia Auctions.

Bottle, Frigid Fluid, embalming fluid, paper label, screw top, 1940s, 7½" h. **$10.00**
Catalog, Derma Surgery with Complete Catalog of Embalmer's of Embalmer's Supplies, H S Eckels and Co, Philadelphia, PA, c1927, 324 pp, 9 x 12" **35.00**
Catalog, Oliver Johnson, Inc, Chicago, IL, illus, grave digger tents, decorations, markers, ground thawer, lawn equipment, etc, prices, 1930, 31 pp. **22.50**
Clothing, burial suit, child's, tuxedo, black, white shirt, black pants, 1940s **35.00**
Coffin, child's, white velour ext, white satin int, Bakelite handles, 1940s, 36½ x 12½" **295.00**
Cooling Board, portable, wood, brass hardware, B F Gleason, Rochester, NY, late 19th C **150.00**
Grave Marker, 1898 Cuba War **15.00**
Mortician's Basket, woven, adult size **125.00**
Mourning Jewelry, brooch, celluloid, black, emb, "In Memorian," 1870s, 2 x 2½" **100.00**
Salt and Pepper Shakers, pr, plastic, yellow and white, emb "Wilson Funeral Home," c1960s. **10.00**
Sheet Music, *Funeral March,* Eclipse Publishing Co, c1914 . . . . **12.00**

DEEDS AND DOCUMENTS

A document is any printed paper that shows evidence or proof of something. Subject matter ranges from baptismal certificates to scholastic awards to stocks and bonds. Flea markets are loaded with old documents. Though they generally have minimal value and are usually copies of the original forms, it makes good sense to check before discarding. It may be of value to its original owner or to a paper-ephemera collector.

Many eighteenth and early nineteenth century deeds are on parchment. In most cases, value is minimal, ranging from a few dollars to a high of $10. First, check to see if the deed is the original document. Most deeds on the market are copies; the actual document is often on file in the courthouse. Second, check the signatures. Benjamin Franklin signed a number of Pennsylvania deeds. These are worth a great deal more than $10. Third, check the location of the deed. If it is a city deed, the current property owner may like to acquire it. If it is for a country farm, forget it.

Finally, a number of early deeds have an elaborate wax seal at the bottom. When framed, these make wonderful display pieces in attorneys' offices.

Club: International Bond & Share Society, P.O. Box 814, Richboro, PA 18954.

Stocks & Bonds, Black Canyon Gold Mining Co, 500 shares capital stock, ornated black and white sheet engraving, official seal in green, 1907, 11 x 8¼", $35.00.

Agreement, Ulster Co, NY, saw mill built by 2 men, hand written, 1813, 4 pp **$16.00**
Bill of Sale, Black Raven Coal and Coke Co, ornate, raven logo, 1906 . . . . **6.50**
Bill of Sale, H J Thompason, Inc, Jun 4, 1906 . . . . **10.00**
Check, Sonoma Vineyards, L M Martinia Grape Products, Kingsburg, CA, canceled, 1939 . . . . **8.50**
Confirmation Certificate, Abingdon Press, NY and Cincinnati, #80, 1926, 11½ x 16" **8.00**
Land Grant, Miami River, Cincinnati, OH, sgd by John Quincy Adams, 1827. . . . . **350.00**
Land Indenture, Greenland, NH, Jan 9, 1786 . . . . **150.00**
Pay and Allowance, Civil War officer, 11 x 17" **15.00**
Marriage Certificate, Ernst Kaufmann, NY, #105, 1898, 13 x 17" **15.00**
Receipt, A E Miller, Manufacturers & Jobbers of Contectionery, Brattleboro, VT **10.00**
Receipt, Education for Freedom, Memphis, TN, rent for school house to meet the necessities of the colored people for school rooms, paid amount specified $100, sgd by Capt Walker, Apr 1865 . . . . **40.00**
Receipt, Hygeia Bottling Works, Pensacola, FL, Bottlers of Soda Water & Coca-Cola **10.00**
Reward of Merit, Card of Honor, model scholar, Jackson Daily Citizen, 1874 . . . . **20.00**
Stock Certificate, Bank of Binghamton, 10 shares, $100 each, 1859 . . . . **20.00**
Stock Certificate, Holiday Mining Co, General Land Office, CO, 1884 . . . . **35.00**
Summons, Whitley County, KY, summons for court appearance, 1857, 3½ x 7" **18.00**

DEGENHART GLASS

Degenhart pressed glass novelties are collected by mold, by individual color, or by group of colors. Hundreds of colors, some are nearly identical and were produced between 1947 and 1978. Prior to 1972 most pieces were unmarked. After that date a "D" or "D" in a heart was used.

Do not confuse Kanawha's bird salt and bow slipper or L. G. Wright's mini-slipper, daisy and button salt, and 5" robin-covered dish with Degenhart pieces. They are similar, but there are differences. See Gene Florence's *Degenhart Glass and Paperweights: A Collector's Guide to Colors and Values* (Degenhart Paperweight and Glass Museum: 1982) for a detailed list of Degenhart patterns.

Club: Friends of Degenhart, Degenhart Paperweight and Glass Museum, Inc, 65323 Highland Hills Rd., P.O. Box 186, Cambridge, OH 43725.

Animal Dish, cov, lamb, cobalt blue **$40.00**
Bicentennial Bell, canary. **15.00**
Boot, skate, sapphire dark, mkd 1972 . . . . **30.00**
Candy Dish, cov, Wildflower, crystal **15.00**
Coaster, Shamrock, mkd 1975 . . . . **6.00**
Creamer and Sugar, Daisy & Button, Cambridge pink, mkd 1972 . . . . **75.00**
Cup Plate, Heart & Lyre, mulberry, c1977 . . . . **15.00**
Hand, frosty jade **15.00**
Hat, Daisy and Button, amethyst **8.00**
Jewelry Box, heart, fawn **18.00**
Mug, child's, Stork and Peacock, smokey heather **25.00**
Owl, charcoal. **40.00**
Owl, midnight sun **30.00**
Owl, nile green opal, mkd 1967 . . . . **45.00**
Owl, willow blue **48.00**
Paperweight, star flower, John or Charles Degenhart **70.00**
Priscilla, periwinkle. **75.00**
Salt, Star and Dew Drop, forest green **12.00**
Salt and Pepper Shakers, pr, bird, ruby **50.00**
Shoe, figural, high button, light blue **25.00**
Slipper, bow, caramel **30.00**
Toothpick Holder, Colonial Drape and Heart, ruby **20.00**
Toothpick Holder, Forget-Me-Not, caramel. **8.50**
Wine, Buzz Saw, honey amber **15.00**

DEPRESSION ERA GLASSWARE

Depression Era Glass refers to glassware made between the 1920s and 1940s. It was mass-produced by a number of different companies. It was sold cheaply and often given away as a purchasing premium.

Specialize in one pattern or color. Once again, there is no way that you can own every piece made. Also, because Depression Era Glass was produced in vast quantities, buy only pieces in excellent or better condition.

A number of patterns have been reproduced. See Gene Florence's *The Collector's Encyclopedia of Depression Glass* (Collector Books, revised annually) for a complete list of reproductions.

Clubs: The National Depression Glass Assoc., P.O. Box 8264, Wichita, KS 67209.

Newspaper: *The Daze,* P.O. Box 57, Otisville, MI 48463.

Aunt Polly, U S Glass, ashtray, green **$30.00**
Aunt Polly, U S Glass, berry bowl, 7⅞" d, iridescent **20.00**
Aunt Polly, U S Glass, butter, cov, green. **210.00**
Aunt Polly, U S Glass, candy, ftd, 2 handled, green. **75.00**
Aunt Polly, U S Glass, salt and pepper shakers, pr, blue **225.00**
Aunt Polly, U S Glass, sherbet plate, 6" d, green **6.50**
Aunt Polly, U S Glass, tumbler, 8 oz, 3⅝" h, blue **26.00**
Colonial Knife & Fork, Hocking, berry bowl, 4½" d, green **17.00**
Colonial Knife & Fork, Hocking, bread and butter plate, 6" d, crystal. **4.50**
Colonial Knife & Fork, Hocking, butter, cov, crystal **37.00**

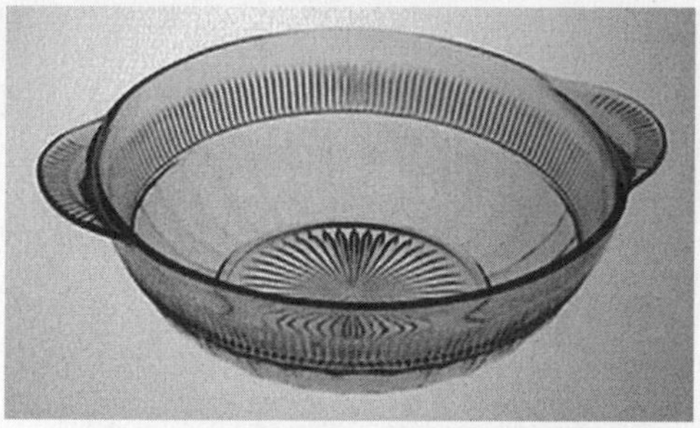

Coronation, "Banded Rib or Saxon," Hocking, berry bowl, 8" d, $3.50.

Colonial Knife & Fork, Hocking, cocktail, 3 oz, 4" h, crystal. **14.00**
Colonial Knife & Fork, Hocking, creamer, crystal **17.00**
Colonial Knife & Fork, Hocking, cup and saucer, green. **18.00**
Colonial Knife & Fork, Hocking, cup and saucer, pink, ... **17.00**
Colonial Knife & Fork, Hocking, dinner plate, 10" d, green **45.00**
Colonial Knife & Fork, Hocking, grill plate, 10" d, pink. **46.00**
Colonial Knife & Fork, Hocking, platter, oval, 12" l, green. . . . **25.00**
Colonial Knife & Fork, Hocking, sherbet, ftd, 3⅜" h, pink **10.00**
Colonial Knife & Fork, Hocking, tumbler, ftd, 5 oz, 4" h, pink **28.00**
Coronation, "Banded Rib or Saxon," Hocking, bowl, 4¼" d, green **45.00**
Coronation, "Banded Rib or Saxon," Hocking, cup, royal ruby **6.50**
Coronation, "Banded Rib or Saxon," Hocking, luncheon plate, 8½" d, pink **4.50**
Coronation, "Banded Rib or Saxon," Hocking, nappy, handled, 6½" d, royal ruby **12.00**
Coronation, "Banded Rib or Saxon," Hocking, sherbet, green **75.00**
Coronation, "Banded Rib or Saxon," Hocking, sherbet plate, 6" d, pink **2.00**
Coronation, "Banded Rib or Saxon," Hocking, tumbler, 10 oz, 5" h, pink. **30.00**
Criss Cross, Hazel Atlas, bowl, no lip, 5" d, crystal **15.00**
Criss Cross, Hazel Atlas, butter, cov, 1 lb, cobalt blue **140.00**
Criss Cross, Hazel Atlas, butter, cov, 1 lb, green **60.00**
Criss Cross, Hazel Atlas, creamer, crystal **16.50**
Criss Cross, Hazel Atlas, pitcher, 54 oz, crystal. **100.00**
Criss Cross, Hazel Atlas, reamer, large, crystal **12.00**
Criss Cross, Hazel Atlas, sugar, cov, pink **225.00**
Criss Cross, Hazel Atlas, refrigerator dish, cov, 4 x 4," cobalt blue **30.00**
Criss Cross, Hazel Atlas, tumbler, 9 oz, crystal **25.00**
Criss Cross, Hazel Atlas, water bottle, 8¾," crystal **19.50**
Cubist, Jeannette, butter, cov, pink **70.00**
Cubist, Jeannette, coaster, pink **7.00**
Cubist, Jeannette, creamer and sugar, cov, large, pink **25.00**
Cubist, Jeannette, cup and saucer, pink **9.00**
Cubist, Jeannette, dessert bowl, 4½" d, green **7.00**
Cubist, Jeannette, dessert bowl, 4½" d, pink. **6.50**
Cubist, Jeannette, pitcher, pink. **245.00**
Cubist, Jeannette, plate, 8" d, green **9.00**
Cubist, Jeannette, powder jar, cov, green **28.00**
Cubist, Jeannette, sherbet, ftd, green **7.00**
Cubist, Jeannette, tumbler, 9 oz, 4" h, green **65.00**

Dogwood, MacBeth-Evans, tumbler, 5" h, pink, $35.00.

Dogwood, MacBeth-Evans, berry bowl, $8^1/_2$" d, pink **50.00**
Dogwood, MacBeth-Evans, cup, monax **36.00**
Dogwood, MacBeth-Evans, cake plate, pink, 13" d **110.00**
Dogwood, MacBeth-Evans, cereal bowl, $5^1/_2$" d, pink **25.00**
Dogwood, MacBeth-Evans, creamer, green **53.00**
Dogwood, MacBeth-Evans, creamer, pink, thin, $3^1/_4$" h **14.00**
Dogwood, MacBeth-Evans, creamer and sugar, pink, thick **35.00**
Dogwood, MacBeth-Evans, cup, monax **36.00**
Dogwood, MacBeth-Evans, cup and saucer, green **45.00**
Dogwood, MacBeth-Evans, cup and saucer, pink, thick **15.00**
Dogwood, MacBeth-Evans, juice, pink **315.00**
Dogwood, MacBeth-Evans, pitcher, decorated **165.00**
Dogwood, MacBeth-Evans, plate, 6" d, pink **8.00**
Dogwood, MacBeth-Evans, plate, 8" d, green **8.00**
Dogwood, MacBeth-Evans, plate, 9" d, pink **38.00**
Dogwood, MacBeth-Evans, saucer, green **10.00**
Dogwood, MacBeth-Evans, saucer, pink **4.50**
Dogwood, MacBeth-Evans, salver, pink **24.00**
Dogwood, MacBeth-Evans, sugar, pink, thick **14.00**
Doric and Pansy, Jeannette, berry bowl, $4^1/_2$" d, ultramarine **15.50**
Doric and Pansy, Jeannette, creamer, green **115.00**
Doric and Pansy, Jeannette, creamer, pink **75.00**
Doric and Pansy, Jeannette, dinner plate, 9" d, green **27.50**
Doric and Pansy, Jeannette, salad plate, 7" d, green **38.00**
Doric and Pansy, Jeannette, salt and pepper shakers, pr, green **400.00**
Doric and Pansy, Jeannette, tray, handled, 10" d, green **30.00**
Doric and Pansy, Jeannette, tumbler, green **70.00**
Iris, Jeannette, berry bowl, beaded, $4^1/_2$," crystal **35.00**
Iris, Jeannette, butter, cov, crystal **45.00**
Iris, Jeannette, creamer and sugar, cov, crystal **25.00**
Iris Jeannette, cup and saucer, crystal **27.00**
Iris, Jeannette, pitcher, crystal **37.50**
Iris, Jeannette, sandwich plate, $11^3/_4$" d, crystal **34.00**
Iris, Jeannette, sherbet, $2^1/_2$," crystal **25.00**
Iris, Jeannette, soup bowl, $7^1/_2$" d, iridescent **60.00**
Iris, Jeannette, tumbler, ftd, 6" h, iridescent **16.00**
Jubilee, Lancaster, candlesticks, pr, pink **185.00**
Jubilee, Lancaster, cheese and cracker set, yellow **250.00**
Jubilee, Lancaster, cocktail, 3 oz, $4^7/_8$" h, yellow **150.00**
Jubilee, Lancaster, cup and saucer, yellow **24.00**
Jubilee, Lancaster, fruit bowl, $11^1/_2$" d, pink **195.00**
Jubilee, Lancaster, juice tumbler, ftd, 6 oz, 5" h, yellow **95.00**
Jubilee, Lancaster, mayonnaise and plate, orig ladle, yellow **250.00**
Jubilee, Lancaster, sandwich tray, center handle, 11" d, pink **195.00**
Madrid, Federal, butter dish, cov, amber **60.00**
Madrid, Federal, cookie jar, cov, amber **45.00**
Madrid, Federal, cream soup, $4^3/_4$" d, amber **14.00**
Madrid, Federal, creamer, ftd, blue **20.00**
Madrid, Federal, creamer and sugar, cov, ftd, amber **57.00**
Madrid, Federal, creamer and sugar, open, ftd, amber **10.50**
Madrid, Federal, cup and saucer, pink **12.50**
Madrid, Federal, grill plate, $10^1/_2$" d, amber **8.50**
Madrid, Federal, juice pitcher, 36 oz, $5^1/_2$" h, amber **50.00**
Madrid, Federal, luncheon plate, $8^7/_8$" d, amber **5.50**
Madrid, Federal, luncheon plate, $8^1/_8$" d, green **9.00**
Madrid, Federal, pitcher, sq, 60 oz, 8" h, pink **35.00**
Madrid, Federal, salad bowl, 8" d, amber **17.00**
Madrid, Federal, salt and pepper shakers, pr, flat, $3^1/_2$" h, amber **36.00**
Madrid, Federal, sauce, 5" d, amber **6.00**
Madrid, Federal, shaker, ftd, $3^1/_2$" h, amber **65.00**
Madrid, Federal, soup bowl, 7" d, blue **30.00**
Madrid, Federal, tumbler, flat, 5 oz, $3^7/_8$" h, amber **11.50**
Madrid, Federal, tumbler, ftd, 10 oz, $5^1/_2$" h, amber **20.00**
Madrid, Federal, vegetable bowl, oval,10" d, amber **18.00**
Manhattan, Hocking, ashtray, round, crystal **9.00**
Manhattan, Hocking, berry bowl, $4^1/_2$" d, crystal **9.00**
Manhattan, Hocking, candlesticks, pr, double, crystal **32.90**
Manhattan, Hocking, candy, ftd, pink **12.00**
Manhattan, Hocking, cereal bowl, $5^3/_4$" d, handled, pink **17.90**
Manhattan, Hocking, coaster, crystal **15.00**
Manhattan, Hocking, creamer and sugar, pink **18.50**
Manhattan, Hocking, fruit bowl, ftd, $9^1/_2$" d, pink **37.00**
Manhattan, Hocking, relish insert, royal ruby **6.00**
Manhattan, Hocking, sherbet, pink **15.00**
Newport, "Hairpin," Hazel Atlas, berry bowl, $4^3/_4$," cobalt **20.00**
Newport, "Hairpin," Hazel Atlas, cream soup, $4^3/_4$," amethyst **18.00**

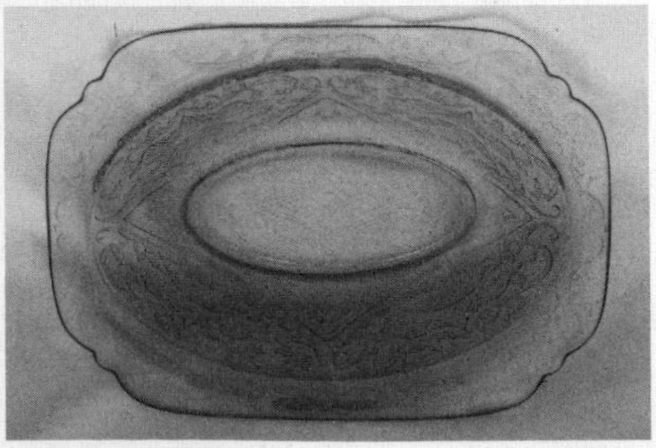

Madrid, Federal, vegetable bowl, oval, 10" l, amber, $15.00.

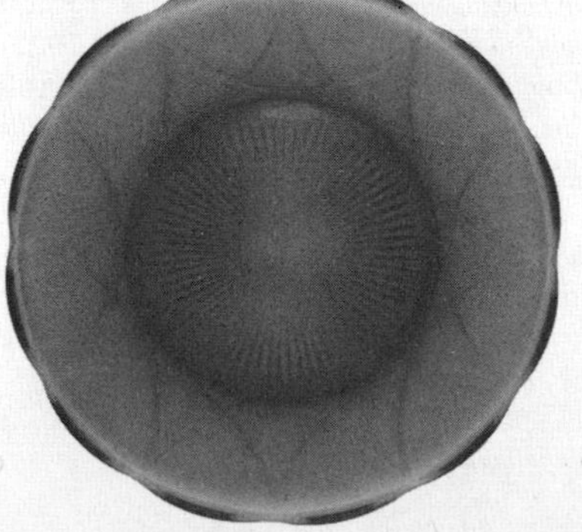

Newport, (Hairpin), Hazel Atlas, sandwich plate, $11^3/_4$" d, $40.00.

Newport, "Hairpin," Hazel Atlas, dinner plate, $8\frac{13}{16}$" d, cobalt 30.00
Newport, "Hairpin," Hazel Atlas, salt and pepper shakers, pr, amethyst 40.00
Newport, "Hairpin," Hazel Atlas, tumbler, 9 oz, $4\frac{1}{2}$" h, cobalt 40.00
Patrician, Federal, berry bowl, individual, 5" d, amber 11.00
Patrician, Federal, berry bowl, master, $8\frac{1}{2}$" d, pink 35.00
Patrician, Federal, bread and butter plate, 6" d, green 7.00
Patrician, Federal, cereal bowl, 6" d, amber 25.00
Patrician, Federal, cream soup, $4\frac{3}{4}$" d, amber 16.00
Patrician, Federal, cup and saucer, amber 17.00
Patrician, Federal, dinner plate, $10\frac{1}{2}$" d, amber 7.00
Patrician, Federal, dinner plate, $10\frac{1}{2}$" d, green 40.00
Patrician, Federal, pitcher, molded handle, clear 100.00
Patrician, Federal, platter, oval, $11\frac{1}{2}$" l, amber 30.00
Patrician, Federal, salt and pepper shakers, pr, green 60.00
Patrician, Federal, sherbet, ftd, green 8.00
Patrician, Federal, sugar, open, green 6.00
Patrician, Federal, tumbler, ftd, 8 oz, $5\frac{1}{4}$" h, green 55.00
Patrician, Federal, tumbler, flat, 14 oz, $5\frac{1}{2}$" h, pink 46.00
Panelled Ring-Ding, Hocking, goblet, 9 oz, $7\frac{1}{4}$" h, red, yellow, black, orange, green painted bands 14.00
Panelled Ring-Ding, Hocking, ice tea tumbler, ftd, $6\frac{1}{2}$" h, red, yellow, black, orange, green painted bands 13.00
Panelled Ring-Ding, Hocking, juice tumbler, 5 oz, $3\frac{1}{2}$" h, red, yellow, black, orange, green painted bands 6.50
Panelled Ring-Ding, Hocking, sherbet, ftd, $4\frac{3}{4}$" h, red, yellow, black, orange, green painted bands 9.00
Panelled Ring-Ding, Hocking, tumbler, 9 oz, $4\frac{1}{4}$" h, red, yellow, black, orange, green painted bands 10.00
Patrick, Lancaster, bowl, 9" d, yellow 50.00
Patrick, Lancaster, cheese and cracker set, pink 140.00
Patrick, Lancaster, cup and saucer, yellow 52.00
Patrick, Lancaster, sherbet, pink 45.00
Patrick, Lancaster, sugar, pink 75.00
Patrick, Lancaster, tray, 2 handles, 11" d, yellow 60.00
Princess, Hocking, bowl, 9" d, green 36.00
Princess, Hocking, cake stand, ftd, 10" d, green 20.00
Princess, Hocking, cereal bowl, 5" d, green 25.00
Princess, Hocking, cereal bowl, 5" d, yellow 26.00
Princess, Hocking, creamer, yellow 17.50
Princess, Hocking, grill plate, handled, $10\frac{1}{2}$" h, green 12.50
Princess, Hocking, salt and pepper shakers, pr, green 50.00
Princess, Hocking, sherbet, ftd, yellow 32.00
Princess, Hocking, tumbler, flat, 9 oz, 4" h, green 28.00
Princess, Hocking, tumbler, flat, 9 oz, 4" h, yellow 17.00
Princess, Hocking, vegetable bowl, oval, 10" l, green 23.00

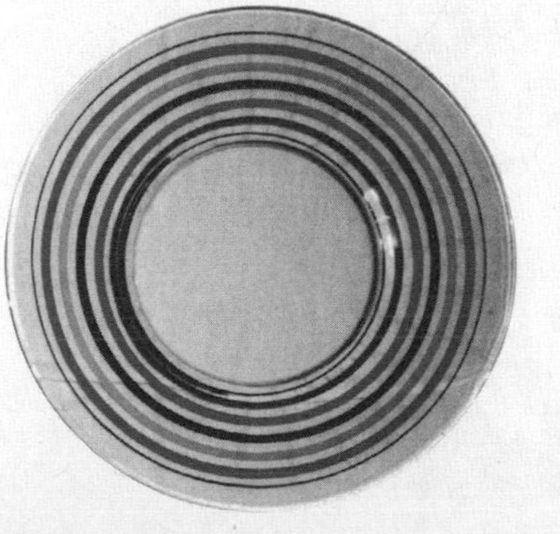

Panelled Ring-Ding, Hocking, plate, crystal, crystal with black, red, yellow, orange, green, and black stripe pattern, 8" d, $4.50.

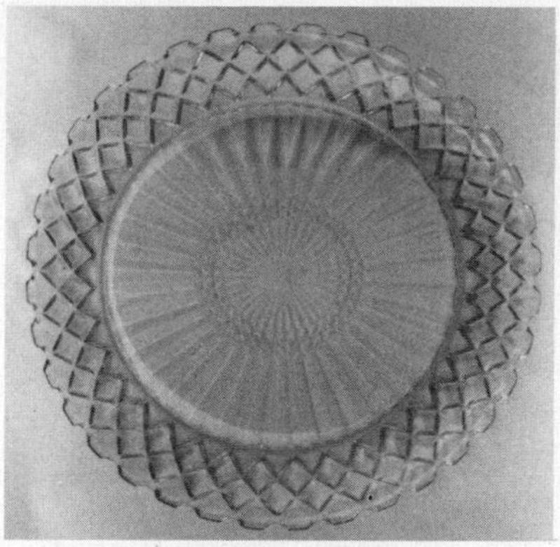

Waterford, "Waffle," Hocking, dinner plate, $9\frac{1}{2}$" d, $11.00.

Starlight, Hazel Atlas, cereal bowl, closed handles, $5\frac{1}{2}$" d, pink 12.00
Starlight, Hazel Atlas, creamer, oval, crystal 5.00
Starlight, Hazel Atlas, dinner plate, 9" d, white 7.50
Starlight, Hazel Atlas, luncheon plate, $8\frac{1}{2}$" d, white 5.00
Starlight, Hazel Atlas, relish, white 15.00
Starlight, Hazel Atlas, sandwich plate, 13" d, pink 18.00
Starlight, Hazel Atlas, sherbet, white 15.00
Strawberry, U S Glass, bowl, $6\frac{1}{2}$" d, green 18.00
Strawberry, U S Glass, compote, iridescent 18.00
Strawberry, U S Glass, plate, $7\frac{1}{2}$" d, pink 13.00
Strawberry, U S Glass, sugar, green 32.00
Strawberry, U S Glass, tumbler, 8 oz, $3\frac{5}{8}$" h, crystal 18.00
Sunflower, Jeannette, cake plate, 3 legs, 10" d, pink 15.00
Sunflower, Jeannette, cup and saucer, pink 20.00
Sunflower, Jeannette, dinner plate, 9" d, green 20.00
Sunflower, Jeannette, tumbler, 9 oz, $4\frac{3}{4}$" h, pink 28.00
Tulip, Dell, bowl, 6" d, blue 20.00
Tulip, Dell, candy, cov, ftd, amethyst 75.00
Tulip, Dell, creamer, blue 20.00
Tulip, Dell, decanter, with stopper, amber 85.00
Tulip, Dell, juice tumbler, blue 25.00
Tulip, Dell, plate, 9" d, amethyst 37.50
Tulip, Dell, sherbet, flat, $3\frac{3}{4}$" d, amber 18.00
Tulip, Dell, whiskey tumbler, amber 20.00
U S Swirl, U S Glass, berry bowl, $4\frac{3}{8}$" d, green 5.50
U S Swirl, U S Glass, butter, cov, green 110.00
U S Swirl, U S Glass, comport, green 20.00
U S Swirl, U S Glass, creamer, pink 16.00
Victory, Diamond Glass-Ware, bon bon, 7", amber 11.00
Victory, Diamond Glass-Ware, bowl, rolled edge, 11" d, black 50.00
Victory, Diamond Glass-Ware, candlesticks, pr, 3" h, amber 30.00
Victory, Diamond Glass-Ware, creamer, pink 15.00
Victory, Diamond Glass-Ware, goblet, 7 oz, 5" h, blue 50.00
Victory, Diamond Glass-Ware, luncheon plate, 8" d, pink 7.00
Victory, Diamond Glass-Ware, platter, 12" d, green 30.00
Victory, Diamond Glass-Ware, sandwich server, center handle, black 75.00
Victory, Diamond Glass-Ware, sherbet, ftd, blue 26.00
Waterford, "Waffle,"Hocking, berry bowl, $4\frac{3}{4}$," pink 13.00
Waterford, "Waffle," Hocking, creamer, oval, crystal 5.00
Waterford, "Waffle," Hocking, cup, crystal 35.00
Waterford, "Waffle," Hocking, pitcher, tilted ice lip, 80 oz, crystal 32.00
Waterford, "Waffle," Hocking, salad plate, $7\frac{1}{8}$" d, pink 8.00
Waterford, "Waffle," Hocking, sherbet plate, 6" d, pink 6.00

Denby Pottery, Gypsy pattern, dinner plate, $10.00.

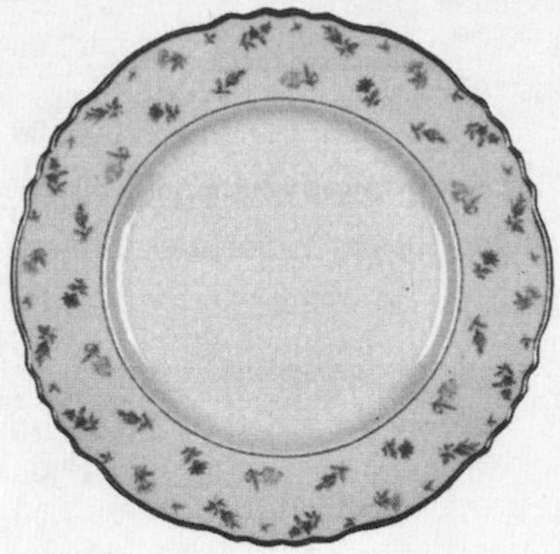

Syracuse China, Suzanne, Federal Shape, dinner plate, 10" d, $22.00.

DINNERWARE

There is a growing appreciation for the thousands of dinnerware patterns that graced the tables of low-, middle-, and some upper-income families during the first three-quarters of the twentieth century. Some of America's leading industrial designers were responsible for forms and decorative motifs.

Collectors fall into three groups: those who collect the wares of a specific factory or factories, often with a strong regional emphasis; individuals who are reassembling the set they grew up with; and those who are fascinated by certain forms and motifs. The bulk of the books on the subject appeared in the early 1980s.

Several of the companies have become established collecting categories in their own right. This is why you will find companies such as Blue Ridge and Hall elsewhere in this book.

Club: International Willow Collectors, P.O. 13382, Arlington, TX 76094; Porcelier Collectors Club, 21 Tamarac Swamp Rd., Wallingford, CT 06492.

Newsletter: *Coors Pottery Newsletter*, 3808 Carr Place N, Seattle, WA 98103.

Periodicals: *The Daze,* P.O. Box 57, Otisville, MI 48463; *The Pottery Collectors Express*, P.O. Box 221, Mayview, MO 64071.

Block China, Poinsettia, Watercolors, bread and butter plate **$2.00**
Block China, Poinsettia, Watercolors, cereal bowl, coupe shape, 5⁷/₈" d **5.00**
Block China, Poinsettia, Watercolors, chop plate, 12" d **12.00**
Block China, Poinsettia, Watercolors, coffeepot, cov **18.00**
Block China, Poinsettia, Watercolors, demitasse cup and saucer **5.00**
Block China, Poinsettia, Watercolors, dinner plate, 10¹/₂" d **5.00**
Block China, Poinsettia, Watercolors, salad plate, 8" d **3.50**
Block China, Poinsettia, Watercolors, sugar, cov **10.00**
Block China, Poinsettia, Watercolors, teapot, cov **15.00**
Block China, Poinsettia, Watercolors, vegetable, 7³/₄" d **12.00**
Coors Pottery, Rosebud, bread and butter plate, 6" d **12.00**
Coors Pottery, Rosebud, casserole, Dutch, 3³/₄ pt **55.00**
Coors Pottery, Rosebud, eggcup, 3" d **28.00**
Coors Pottery, Rosebud, sugar shaker **35.00**
Crooksville China, Quadro, creamer **5.00**
Crooksville China, Quadro, dinner plate, 9¹/₂" d **6.00**
Crooksville China, Quadro, gravy liner **5.00**
Crooksville China, Quadro, saucer **2.00**
Crooksville China, Quadro, vegetable bowl **10.00**
Denby Pottery, Camelot, cereal bowl, coupe shape, light green, 6⁵/₈" d **8.00**
Denby Pottery, Camelot, cup and saucer, flat, light green, 2¹/₂" **6.50**
Denby Pottery, Camelot, dinner plate, light green, 10¹/₈" d **6.00**
Denby Pottery, Camelot, salad plate, light green, 8³/₄" d **5.00**
Denby Pottery, Castile, creamer, blue, shaped rim, 3¹/₈" **12.00**
Denby Pottery, Castile, cup and saucer, ftd, blue, shaped rim, 3³/₈" **5.50**
Denby Pottery, Gypsy, creamer **12.00**
Denby Pottery, Gypsy, cup and saucer, flat, 2¹/₂" **8.00**
Porceleir Mfg Co, Barock-Colonial, sugar shaker **15.00**
Porceleir Mfg Co, Geometric Cattails, creamer **12.00**
Porceleir Mfg Co, Rose and Wheat, coffeepot, 6 cup **25.00**
Syracuse China, Stansbury, dinner plate, Federal shape, 10³/₈" d **12.00**
Syracuse China, Stansbury, fruit bow, Federal shape, 5¹/₈" **8.00**
Syracuse China, Stansbury, salad plate, Federal shape, 8" d **7.50**
Syracuse China, Stansbury, vegetable, Federal shape, round, 9" d **30.00**
Syracuse China, Suzanne, bread and butter plate, Federal shape, 6¹/₂" d **5.00**
Syracuse China, Suzanne, cream soup and saucer, Federal shape **16.00**
Villeroy & Boch, Acapulco, cup and saucer, flat, 2¹/₄" **14.00**
Villeroy & Boch, Acapulco, salt and pepper shakers, pr. **24.00**
Villeroy & Boch, Petite Fleur, luncheon plate, 9⁵/₈" d **9.00**
William Adams & Sons, bread and butter plate, Empress shape, blue design, 6¹/₄" d **5.00**
William Adams & Sons, dinner plate, Lancaster, Hexagon/Chinese shape, floral border, 10³/₈" d **15.00**

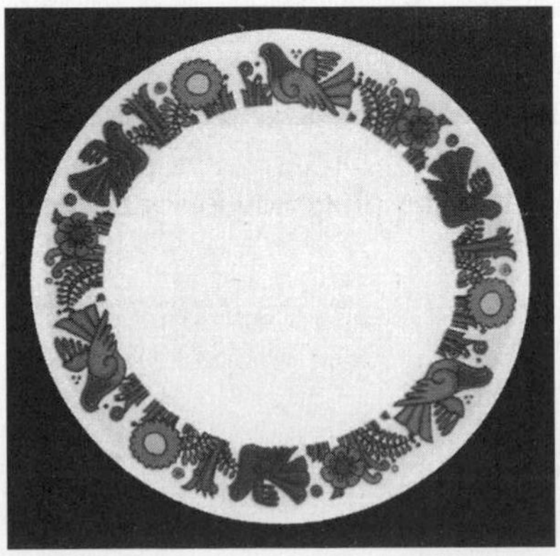

Villeroy & Boch, Acapulco, dinner plate, $12.00.

DIONNE QUINTUPLETS

On May 28, 1934, on a small farm in Callander, Ontario, Canada, five baby girls weighing a total of 10 pounds 1¼ ounces were delivered into this world with the help of Dr. DaFoe and two midwives.

Due to their parents' poor financial circumstances and the public's curiosity, the quintuplets were put on display. For a small fee, the world was invited to come and see the quints at play in their custom-built home or to buy a souvenir to mark their birth.

The field of collectibles for Dionne Quintuplets memorabilia is a very fertile one!

Club: Dionne Quint Collectors, P.O. Box 2527, Woburn, MA 01888.

Book, *Dionne Quintuplets Play Mother Goose,* Dell, 1938 . . . . **$25.00**
Book, *The Dionne Quintuplets Growing Up,* brown and white cov, 1935, 8½ x 11" **40.00**
Calendar, 1938, full color portrait, unused, 8 x 11" **30.00**
Calendar, 1945, Harvesy Day, full pad, 10 x 7" **15.00**
Candy Box, Dionne Pops, Vitamin Candy Co, Providence, RI, 1936, 4 x 10½ x 1" **125.00**
Cereal Bowl, premium, Quaker Oats, chrome plated metal, late 1935, 5⅞" d **25.00**
Doll, Madame Alexander, mohair wig, painted brown eyes, 7½" h **250.00**
Fan, Howard M Davies Funeral Chapel adv on back, cardboard, wooden handle, picture of quint and ducks at stream on front **25.00**
Game, Line Up The Quints **30.00**
Magazine Cover, *Look,* Oct 11, 1938, Dr. Dafoe **5.00**
Paper Dolls, Let's Play House with the Dionne Quints, #4, uncut **50.00**
Photograph, tinted color, first year, 7¼ x 9" photo, 10 x 12" glass frame with cardboard easel **25.00**
Pinball Game, Place The Quintuplets In The Carriage, green tin frame, 3½ x 5" **18.00**
Sheet Music, *Quintuplets' Lullaby,* tinted photo front cov, 6 pp **15.00**

DISNEYANA

"Steamboat Willie" introduced Mickey Mouse to the world in 1928. Walt and Roy Disney, brothers, worked together to create an entertainment empire filled with a myriad of memorable characters ranging from Donald Duck to Zorro.

Early Disney items are getting very expensive. No problem. Disney continues to license material. In thirty years the stuff from the 1960s and 1970s will be scarce and eagerly sought. Now is the time to buy it.

Clubs: National Fantasy Fan Club for Disneyana Collectors & Enthusiasts, P.O. Box 19212, Irvine, CA 92713; The Mouse Club, 2056 Cirone Way, San Jose, CA 95124.

Periodicals: *Storyboard Magazine,* 80 Main St., Nashau, NH 03060; *Tomart's Disneyana Digest,* 3300 Encrete Ln., Dayton, OH 45439.

Bank, Pinocchio **$30.00**
Bank, Snow White, ceramic, Snow White standing next to well, green foliage, pr of birds on front of well, roof of well with raised text and gold "Wishing And Saving Will Make It So," orig trap, orig foil Enesco label, 1960s, 3 x 4½ x 5" **90.00**
Big Little Book, *Mickey Mouse Sails For Treasure Island,* Whitman, #750, ©1933 . . . . **65.00**
Birthday Card, Mickey Mouse, front diecut flap of Mickey holding birthday cake, inside of card is gold and black with illus of stove and diecut slot where cake is placed, int inked name and inscription, Hallmark, 1930s, 4½ x 4½" **40.00**
Book, *Mickey Mouse Crusoe,* Whitman, 72 pp, 1936, 7 x 9½ **90.00**
Booklet, *Guide To Disneyland,* color photos of attractions and areas of park, Walt Disney photo on front cov, ©1959, 8 x 11½" **65.00**
Box, Mickey Mouse Straws, 1960 . . . . **15.00**
Charm Bracelet, enameled metal figures **35.00**
Clock Radio, Mickey Mouse, General Electric, Youth Electronics, 1950s **175.00**
Coloring Book, Mickey & Minnie Mouse Coloring Book, Saalfield, 28 pp, 1933 . . . . **200.00**
Cookie Jar, Dumbo, mouse finial **95.00**
Cookie Jar, Winnie the Pooh, Walt Disney Productions **85.00**
Drinking Glass, set of 8, Alice in Wonderland, "Queen Of Hearts and The White Rabbit," front illus of King of Hearts behind Queen, red text on back with "Alice in Wonderland," c1951, 4⅝" h **40.00**
Figure, Dopey, bisque, 5½" h **65.00**
Figure, Figaro, ceramic, Brayton Laguna, 1940, 2 x 4 x 3¼" **20.00**
Figure, Mickey Mouse, jointed, decal, early 1920s **275.00**
Figure, Three Little Pigs, musicians, bisque **145.00**
Lamp, Bambi, scent, porcelain, Goebel **295.00**

Stuffed Toy, Mickey Mouse, drum major, green jacket, yellow hands, red papier-mâché shoes, orig hat and baton, $95.00.

Rug, Pluto, Flower, and Thumper, brown, gray, black, red, blue, green, and pink, 1950s, 22" h, 40" w, $82.50. Photo courtesy Collectors Auction Services.

Mickey Mouse Club Newsreel with Sound Outfit, plastic camera, cardboard screen, record, film, and pinback button, $55.00.

Lunch Box and Thermos, Sport Goofy, metal, emb, color illus of Goofy in various sports activities, Aladdin Industries, c1983 . . . . **20.00**
Menu, Carnation Ice Cream Parlor, Disneyland, souvenir mailer, paper seal tab on front cov, 1955, 4¾ x 9" **45.00**
Mug, Donald Duck, ceramic, painted, high relief design on front with color portrait of Donald against dark bluish green textured circular ground, "Disneyland" on reverse, letter "D" shaped handle in blue, Disneyland label on underside, c1960s, 3" h **20.00**
Mug, Winnie the Pooh and Piglet, front scene of Pooh and Piglet stuffing themselves on pots of honey, separate smaller image of Pooh with honey pot on reverse, gold trim on rim and handle, "From The Cartoon film Winnie The Pooh And The Honey Tree/Keele St. Pty. Co. Ltd./England," ©1965, 4" h **75.00**
Napkin, linen, Snow White with Dopey, Disney label **25.00**
Napkin Rings, pr, Mickey and Minnie, celluloid, 2¼" attached hollow celluloid figure on front, mkd "Made in England," 1930s **200.00**
Necktie, Snow White and Seven Dwarfs, white fabric, repeated dwarf illus in brown, red, blue, and yellow, repeated music notes, and "Hi-Ho," c1938, 37" l **25.00**
Ornament, Mickey Mouse, celluloid, 3-D Mickey figure holding accordion with his head turned to 1 side, 1930s, 3¼" h **65.00**
Paper Dolls, One Hundred and One Dalmatians, Whitman, 1960, unused **65.00**
Pattern, Cinderella, apron, paper **8.00**

Book, *Walt Disney Annual,* Whitman/WDE–1937, hard cov, dj, 123 color and black/white pp, 10 x 14", $141.00. Photo courtesy New England Auction Gallery.

Pinback Button, Mickey Mouse, celluloid, "Good Teeth," Mickey brushing Big Bad Wolf's teeth, red, black, and white, 1¼" d **150.00**
Playset, Disney World Town Square, diecut cardboard and plastic pcs, vinyl playset mat, colorful cardboard backdrop depicting castle, Sears, 1988, MIB **40.00**
Press Box, Alice in Wonderland, uncut, 1974 . . . . **15.00**
Record Album, *Who's The Leader,* Mickey Mouse Club, 1955 . . . . **55.00**
Salt and Pepper Shakers, pr, Pinocchio, 1940s **45.00**
Sand Pail, Mickey Mouse Happynak, colorful character portraits, England, 1940s **95.00**
Sheet Music, *Snow White,* Walt Disney Enterprises, 1938 . . . . **40.00**
Tablecloth, child's, Alice in Wonderland, color storybook illus, 1950s **65.00**
Toothbrush Holder, Three Little Pigs, bisque, white pigs, painted outfits, green base, 1930s, 1¾ x 4 x 4" **75.00**
Tea Set, child's, Donald Duck, porcelain, 13 pcs, orig box **395.00**
Tea Set, child's, Mickey Mouse, litho tin, Happynak, 7 pcs, orig box **375.00**
Telephone, Mickey Mouse Talking Phone, battery operated, hard plastic, Hasbro, orig box, 1983 . . . . **20.00**
View-Master Set, Zorro, set of 3 reels, orig booklet, ©1958 . . . . **20.00**
Watering Can, Snow White and Seven Dwarfs, Ohio Art, 1938 . . . . **145.00**
Windup, Donald Duck, mechanical wheelbarrow, plastic, Marx, orig box, 1973 . . . . **90.00**
Windup, Nautilus, 20,000 Leagues Under the Sea, tin, orig box, 1930s **295.00**

DOG COLLECTIBLES

The easiest way to curb your collection is to concentrate on the representations of a single breed. Many collectors focus only on three-dimensional figures. Whatever approach you take, buy pieces because you love them. Try to develop some restraint and taste and not buy every piece you see. Easy to say, hard to do!

Club: Canine Collectors Club, 736 N. Western Ave., Ste. 314, Lake Forest, IL 60045; Wee Scots, P.O. Box 1597, Winchester, VA 22604.

Newsletters: *COLLIEctively Speaking!*, 428 Philadelphia Rd., Joppa, MD 21085.

Advertising Trade Card, New Home Sewing Machine, diecut, racng greyhound, girl in Victorian dress riding on back, "Light Running," **$25.00**
Ashtray, scottie, black full figure with tray **20.00**
Book, *Dogs of Today,* Harding Cox, illus, 1931 . . . . **5.00**
Bookend, terrier, porcelain, black and white **150.00**
Calendar, 1949, Morrel Circus, collie, wolfhound, poodle, and terrier performing tricks, 8½ x 11" **15.00**
Calendar Plate, boxer, white, gold trim, 1910, 8⅝" d **45.00**
Catalog, Dog Furnishings, 1920 . . . . **24.00**
Catalog, St Louis Kennel Club, Third Annual Dog Show, 1899, photos, color cov with woman and St Bernard, 110 pp **40.00**
Cigar Label, Two Friends, woman petting St Bernard **6.00**
Doorstop, Boston Terrier, cast iron, 2 pcs **75.00**
Doorstop, wirehaired terrier, orig paint, c1929 . . . . **115.00**

Match Safe, plated metal, unmkd English, 2¹/₈" l, $150.00.

Planter, scottie, chalkware, 5 x 6" 10.00
Stock Certificate, dog vignette, Osborn Mills, Fall River, MA, 1910 . . . . 30.00
Stuffed Toy, cocker spaniel, 4¹/₂" h 30.00
Tie Tack, Mack bulldog, brass, 1950s 12.50
Trading Card, various breeds, full color, 48 cards, 1961, 1³/₈ x 2⁵/₈" 20.00
Windup, Romping Puppy, plush, black, litho tin bone in mouth, T N, Japan, orig box, 1950s 75.00

DOLL HOUSES AND FURNISHINGS

Doll houses and doll house furnishings have undergone a current craze and are highly collectible. Many artists and craftsmen devote hours to making scale furniture and accessories. This type of artist-oriented doll house furnishing affects the market by offering the buyer a choice of an old piece versus a present-day handmade piece.

Petite Princess, Plastic Art Toy Corporation, Tootsietoy, and Renwal are just four of hundreds of major manufacturers of machine-made doll house furniture. Materials range from wood to injection molded plastic. This furniture was meant to be used, and most surviving examples were. The period packaging is its supporting literature can double the value of a set.

Club: Dollhouse & Miniature Collectors, P.O. Box 16, Bellaire, MI 49615.

Periodicals: *Doll Castle News,* P.O. Box 247, Washington, NJ 07882; *Miniature Collector,* 30595 Eight Mile, Livonia, MI 48152;.

DOLL HOUSE

Combination Dollhouse, Stirn & Lyon, stenciled wood building sections decorated with crayons, litho paper illus on cov, patented 1881, 15" h $172.50
Country Cottage, Wolverine, #800, 1980s 40.00
Dolly's Playhouse, McLoughlin Bros, litho paper on board, folding, 2 rooms, folding printed paper furniture, orig box cov, 18¹/₂" h house, late 19th C 375.00
Miniature Dollhouse, Ohio Art, #95, litho tin, complete with 28 pcs of plastic furnishings, 3 x 8¹/₂ x 5¹/₄" 75.00
Ranch House, Child Life Toys, Inc, removable roof, picture windows, 1950s, 24 x 36" 120.00
Ranch House, T Cohn, litho tin, 1950s 75.00
Ranch House, Marx, side porch, litho tin, 1960s 65.00
Spanish Two-Story, T Cohn, patio, litho tin, 1948 . . . . 150.00
Suburban, Marx, litho tin, 1950s 110.00
Three-Story, Fisher-Price, #0250, 5 rooms, spiral stai case, 2 figures, complete with instructions, 1970s 45.00

DOLL HOUSE FURNISHINGS

Accessory Set, Marx, #1427, 20 figures, playground equipment, and swimming pool, 1950s, MIB $160.00
Bathroom Set, Fisher-Price, #253 . . . . 3.00
Bedroom Suite, Ideal, 4 pc set, plastic, c1940, MIB 25.00
Candelabra, Petite Princess, Ideal 20.00
Doll, maid, bobbed hair, short blue dress, lace trimmed apron, 5" h 60.00
Floor Lamp, black, soft metal, gilded frame, with glass beaded shade, 4" h 100.00
Foot Warmer, brass, working drawer, ³/₄" 35.00
Nursery Set, Fisher-Price, #257 . . . . 3.00
Refrigerator, Arcade, cast iron, white lacquer, gray trim, mkd "Leonard," 5³/₄" h 35.00
Settee, Arcade, cast iron 80.00
Side Chair, Petite Princess, Ideal, red satin, MIB 20.00
Suite, Arcade, Curtis, 3 pc set, cast iron, white lacquer finish, 2 high backed benches, matching 4³/₄" l table, openwork legs, 1936 . . . . 50.00
Suite, Tootsietoy, Daisy, 8 pc set, circular pedestal table, 4 chairs, buffet, sideboard, and tea cart, orig box 65.00
Table, Petite Princess, Ideal, MIB 20.00
Table and Chairs, Renwal, price for table and 4 chairs 20.00

DOLLS

People buy dolls primarily on the basis of sentiment and condition. Most begin by buying back the dolls they remember playing with as a child.

Speculating in dolls is risky business. The doll market is subject to crazes. The doll that is in today may be out tomorrow.

Place great emphasis on originality. Make certain that every doll you buy has the complete original costume. Ideally, the box or packaging also should be present. Remember, you are not buying these dolls to play with. You are buying them for display.

Note: The dolls listed date from the 1930s through the present. For information about antique dolls, see Jan Foulke's *13th Blue Book Dolls and Values* (Hobby House Press: 1997) and Dawn Herlocher's, *200 Years of Dolls,* (Antique Trader Books: 1996).

Skookum Indian Doll, papier-mâché face, wood feet, wool clothes, paper label on bottom of foot mkd "Trade Mark Registered, U.S.A., SKOOKUM, Bully Good), INDIAN PATENTED, " 8" h, $75.00.

Horsman, plastic head and hands, molded, painted features, rooted curly hair, bean bag body, pink flannel hat and top, yellow flannel pants, laced trim, mid "Horsman Dolls Inc.," 11" h, $6.00.

Clubs: Chatty Cathy Collectors Club, P.O. Box 140, Readington, NJ 08870; Ideal Toy Co. Collector's Club, P.O. Box 623, Lexington, MA 02173; Madame Alexander Doll Club, PO Box 330, Mundelein, IL 60060; United Federation of Doll Clubs, 10920 N. Ambassador Dr., Kansas City, MO 64153.

Newsletters: *Doll-E-Gram* (Black Dolls), P.O. Box 1212, Bellevue, WA 98009; *Rags* (Raggedy Ann and Andy), P.O. Box 823, Atlanta, GA 30301.

Periodicals: *Doll Reader*, 6405 Flank Dr., Harrisburg, PA 17112; *The Cloth Doll Magazine*, P.O. Box 2167, Lake Oswego, OR 97035.

Advertising, Burger King, Knickerbocker, ©1980 Burger King Corp, orig box, 20" h **$40.00**
Advertising, Campbell Soup, 1963, 10" h **95.00**
Advertising, C & H Sugar, set, cloth stuffed, tanned brown body, boy doll has printed colorful floral briefs, lei, and orchid in hair, girl doll has printed floral sarong with grass skirt, lei, and hair flower, orig stitched "Hawaiian Huggables" tag, c1971–73, 15" h **20.00**
Advertising, Del Monte, Sweet Pea, 12" h **10.00**
Advertising, Jolly Green Giant, soft vinyl, Product People, Inc, orig box, 1970s, 9¼" h **75.00**
Advertising, Marky Maypo, soft vinyl, formed in seated position for placement of cereal bowl between sprawled legs, 1960s, 9¼" h **65.00**
Advertising, Mrs Butterworth's Syrup, 11" h **5.00**
Advertising, Swiss Miss, cloth, 17" h **15.00**
American Character, Betsy McCall, nylon teddy, socks, white shoes, 1958, 8" h, MIB **200.00**
American Character, Tiny Toodles, vinyl, molded and painted hair, 1958, 10½" h **35.00**
Arranbee, Nancy Lee, composition, blonde wig, blue sleep eyes, closed mouth, orig red and white taffeta dress, c1947, 14" h **150.00**
Arranbee, Taffy, plastic, socket head, blue eyes, brunette saran wig, straight walker legs, blue striped satin skirt, white organdy blouse, rufled sleeves, straw hat, 1954, 23" h **175.00**
Cameo, Miss Peeps, vinyl, brown skin, 1973, 19" h **35.00**
Cosmopolitan Doll Co, Ginger, hard plastic, glued on wig, walker, head turns, 1955, 7½" h **35.00**
Cosmopolitan Doll Co, Little Miss Ginger, vinyl head, hard plastic body, rooted ash blonde hair, closed mouth, high heel feet, 1956, 8½" h **20.00**
Deluxe Topper, Dancing Dawn **30.00**
Eegee, Newborn Baby, vinyl head and limbs, cloth body, 1963, 16" h **20.00**
Ideal, Dopey, molded composition head, cloth body and legs, oil cloth arms, cotton shirt and pants, missing hat, mid 1930s, 14" h **86.00**
Ideal, Flatsy Casey, 4½" h **30.00**
Ideal, Saucy Walker, hard plastic head, walker, c1951, 17" h, MIB **150.00**
Ideal, Growing Hair Crissy, vinyl head, plastic body, rooted hair, 17½" h **120.00**
Ideal, Toni, impressed head and body, orig dress, pink jumper with yellow polka dot blouse, 14" h **196.50**
Kenner, Baby Wet and Care, 13" h, MIB **90.00**
Madame Alexander, Amy, Little Women Series, #411, 8" h, complete with period box **22.00**
Madame Alexander, Little Bo-Peep, #483, 8" h, complete with period box **41.00**
Marx, First Love, posable, baby powder scent, 16" h, 1970s **40.00**
Mattel, Cathy Quick Curl, complete with brush and comb, 15" h **55.00**
Mattel, Mrs Beasley, stuffed cloth, yellow yarn hair, 1973, 14" h **65.00**
Nancy Ann Storybook, hard plastic **10.00**
Remco, Littlechap Family, Dr John **20.00**
Skookum Indian, wood face, composition body, orig label, 9½" h **40.25**
Vogue, Brickette, rooted curly strawberry blonde hair, sleep eyes, polka dot dress, straw hat, 18" h, 1979–80 . . . . **65.00**

DOORSTOPS

Cast-iron doorstops have gone through a number of collecting crazes over the past twenty years. The last craze occurred just a few years ago, raising the prices to such a level that doorstops are more likely to be found at antiques shows than at flea markets.

Reproductions abound. A few helpful clues are: check size (many reproductions are slightly smaller than the period piece); check detail (the less detail, the more suspicious you need to be); and check rust (bright orange rust indicates a new piece).

Club: Doorstop Collectors of America, 2413 Madison Ave., Vineland, NJ 08630

Note: Doorstops listed are cast iron unless otherwise noted.

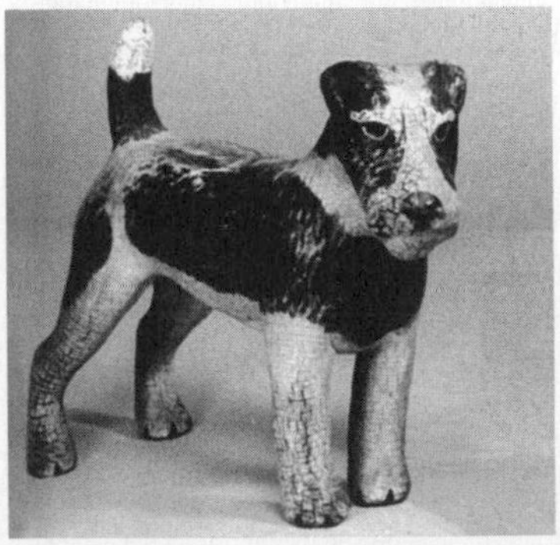

Dog, rubber, 10¾ x 13½", $110.00. Photo courtesy Bill Bertoia Auctions.

Cape Cod, Eastern Specialty Mfg Co, emb "Eastern Specialty Mfg. Co. No. 14," 5½ x 8½" $352.00
Clipper Ship, Kleistone Rubber Specialties, mkd "Old Ironsides," 11 x 8" 165.00
Conestoga Wagon, 8 x 11" 95.00
Corgi, full figure, 8 x 9½" 308.00
Frog, sitting, yellow and green, 3" h 40.00
Fruit Basket, Albany Foundry, 10⅛ x 7½" 275.00
Fruit Bowl, Hubley, mkd "456," 6⅞ x 6⅝ 165.00
High Heel Shoe 75.00
Imp & His Bone, mkd "GHR c. 1921, #142," 5¼ x 8¼" 352.00
Mutt & His Bone, 8¼ x 5½" 220.00
Rabbit by Fence, Albany Foundry, mkd "59," 6⅞ x 8⅛" 440.00
Scottie, Wilton Products, Inc, Wrightsville, PA, 7¾ x 4½" . . . 198.00
Tulip Pot, National Foundry, 8¼ x 7" 242.00
Welsh Corgi, Bradley & Hubbard, 8¼ x 5⅞" 308.00
Whippet, Creation Co, 8 x 8½" 242.00
Windmill, ivory, red roof, green base, 6¾" h. 95.00

DRAG RACING

Drag racing is an acceleration contest between two cars racing in a straight line for a quarter of a mile. The first drag race probably took place shortly after the invention of the wheel. However, drag racing as we know it began in the late 1940s in Southern California. By the early 1950s drag strips were popping up nationwide.

The formation of the national Hot Rod Association in 1951 brought organization to drag racing. The NHRA promoted safety in racing and began to sanction drag strips across the country. The promotion of these races and the ephemera generated as a result of conducting the races provides the source for the drag racing collectibles that are sought today. The drag racing items listed in this section are representative of what is available. The prices are the actual selling prices for the objects listed.

Advisors: Michael and Cheryl Goyda, P.O. Box 192, East Petersburg, PA 17520, (717) 569-7149, fax (717) 569-0909.

Newsletter: *Quarter Milestones,* 53 Milligan Ln., Johnson City, TN 37601.

Jacket, York US 30, cotton, name of strips and class champion $200.00
Jacket, Muncie Dragway, cotton, name of strip with embroidered dragster 300.00
Model Kit, Exterminator, Lindberg, 2 in 1 dragster kit 250.00

Model Kit, Exterminator, Lindberg, 1/8 scale, 1964, $250.00.

Poster, The Weekend Warriors, filmed at NHRA Races by Dempsey Associates, 1963, 27 x 41", $150.00.

Model Kit, MPC, Color Me Gone, 1/25 scale, 1968, MIB . . . 175.00
Pennant, Beech Bend, Bowling Green, KY, pictures from engine dragster and super stock car 50.00
Pennant, Islip Speedway, Islip, NY, pictures front engine dragster 60.00
Poster, Drag Strip, American International Pictures, 1957, 22 x 28" 150.00
Poster, NHRA, heavy stock, multicolored, John Jodauga artwork, features Snake and Mongoose funny cars, 1979, 22 x 28" 100.00
Poster, Indy Nationals, cardboard, features 2 front engine dragsters, 1963, 14 x 22" 175.00
Vehicle, dragster, Processed Plastics, late 1950s, 7" l. 35.00
Vehicle, Mustang funny car, Japan, metal, 1969 . . . . 50.00

Jacket, Peterson Drag-Way, cotton, $150.00.

DRINKING GLASSES, PROMOTIONAL

It is time to start dealing seriously with promotional glasses given away by fast-food restaurants, garages, and other merchants. This category also includes drinking glasses that start out life as product containers.

Most glasses are issued in a series. If you collect one, you better plan on keeping at it until you have the complete series. Also, many of the promotions are regional. A collector in Denver is not likely to find a Philadelphia Eagles glass at his favorite restaurant.

Just a few washings in a dishwasher can cause a major change in the color on promotional drinking glasses. Collectors insist on unused, unwashed glasses whenever possible. Get the glass, and drink your drink out of a paper cup.

Newsletter: *Collector Glass News,* P.O. Box 308, Slippery Rock, PA 16057.

Mobil, NFL, Philadelphia Eagles, single green bands, 1988, $5^{1}/_{2}$" h, $4.00.

Tin, Oakley's Talc, litho tin, $4^{5}/_{8}$ x $2^{1}/_{2}$ x $1^{3}/_{8}$", $176.00. Photo courtesy Wm. Morford.

A & W Root Beer, bear **$2.50**
Arby's, Currier & Ives, 1978. . . . . **3.00**
Arby's, Looney Tunes Adventures, 1988 . . . . . **4.00**
Big Boy, 50th anniversary **3.00**
Big Top Peanut Butter, Old Time Songs, 1950s **2.00**
Burger Chef, Burger Chef and Jeff Go Trail Riding, 1976 . . . . . **8.00**
Burger King, Have It Your Way, 1776–1976, Liberty Bell **4.00**
Burger King, See These Burgers, 1978 . . . . . **11.00**
Chuck E Cheese, Pizza Time Theater **5.00**
Coca-Cola, Hollie Hobby and Robby, Christmas, 1978, American Greetings Corp **3.00**
Country Time Lemonade, Grandpa's Girl, Norman Rockwell, *Saturday Evening Post* scene. **5.00**
Godfather's Pizza, The Goonies, ©Warner Bros, 1985. . . . . **3.00**
Holly Farms, Washington Redskins, 16 oz **3.00**
Jewel Tea Jelly, Old Time Series **2.00**
Kentucky Fried Chicken, bucket and balloon **6.50**
Kentucky Fried Chicken, Wizard of Oz, Kansas Land of Ahs: Tin Man. **45.00**
Pepsi-Cola, Harvey Cartoons Action series, 5" h **8.00**
Pepsi-Cola, James Bond 007, 1985 . . . . . **10.00**
Pepsi-Cola, Ringling Bros & Barnum & Bailey Circus, chariot racing, 1975 . . . . . **5.00**
Pepsi-Cola, Superman the Movie: From Kal-el the Child to Man of Steel, 1978 . . . . . **8.00**
Pizza Hut, ET Collector Series, Be Good, 1982. . . . . **2.50**
Pizza Hut, Green Bay Packers, Willie Davis **5.50**
Popeye's Fried Chicken, Swee' Pea, 1979 . . . . . **10.00**
Seven-Up, Indiana Jones and the Temple of Doom, 1984 . . . . . **6.00**
Sneaky Pete's Hot Dogs, Al Capp series, 1975 . . . . . **40.00**
Subway, Sandwiches and Salads Sponsored by 98 WIYY, We Rock Baltimore, red and black on yellow panel, $5^{5}/_{8}$" h **3.00**
Welch's, Kagran Howdy Doody: Clarabell Gets a Kick Out of Circus Mule! **21.00**
Wendy's, Roger Hargreaves Series, plastic **1.00**
Wendy's, Sesame Street, plastic **1.00**
Wyler's, Family Circus, plastic **1.00**

DRUGSTORE COLLECTIBLES

Corner drugstores, especially those with a soda fountain, were major hangouts in almost every small town in the United States. Almost all of them dispensed much more than medically related products. They were the 7-11's of their era.

This category documents the wide variety of material that you could acquire in a drugstore. It barely scratches the surface. This is a new collecting approach that has real promise.

Newsletter: *The Drug Store Collector,* 3851 Gable Lane Dr. #513, Indianapolis, IN 46208.

Advertising Trade Card, Hibbard's Rheumatic Syrup, Greatest Blood Purifier Known & Testimonials int, litho **$25.00**
Advertising Trade Card, Johnson's Anodyne Liniment. **10.00**
Advertising Trade Card, Lydia E Pinkham's Vegetable Compound, text on back, color, illus, 1890s, 3 x $4^{1}/_{2}$" **10.00**
Book, *Merck's 1907 Index: An Encyclopedia for the Chemist, Pharmacist and Physician,* 472 pp. **12.00**
Booklet, *Alka-Seltzer Song Book,* c1935 . . . . . **2.50**
Bottle, Walgreen Lilac Bouquet Beard Gloss, barber screw cap, blue and green label, 1920, 12 oz, $7^{1}/_{2}$" h **12.00**
Bottle, Walgreen Tar Soap Shampoo, barber screw cap, 12 oz, 1920, $7^{1}/_{2}$" h **15.00**
Bottle, Wallace Laboratories, Brunswick, NJ, Soma Carisoprodol **6.50**
Box, Dr Hobson's Ox Marrow Pomade, lady illus, includes bottle, $3^{1}/_{2}$ x 2 x 2" **15.00**
Box, Smith Brothers Cough Drops, wood, 39 x 18 x 10" **75.00**
Canister, Calonite Powder, Research Labs, cardboard, vertical round, orange and blue, 1920, 3 oz, 4" h **22.00**
Container, Rexall Cold Cream, red, turquoise letters, $4^{1}/_{4}$" d **11.00**
Display, Smart Peppermint Gum, True Blue Gum Co, Grand Rapids, Mich, complete with 20 orig packs, 1 x 6 x $4^{1}/_{4}$" **160.00**
Display Cabinet, Dr Calvin Crane's quaker Remedies, walnut, slat front lift top, adv images on 3 sides, 10 x $14^{3}/_{4}$ x $10^{1}/_{4}$" **725.00**
Fan, Rubifoam Tooth Powder on front, Hoyt's Colognes on back, diecut cardboard, bamboo stick handle, 13 x 7" **350.00**
Fan, Tums, 1920s **18.50**
Pocket Mirror, Star Soap **20.00**
Pocket Mirror, Walgreen's Green Bay store opening, 1938. . . . . **60.00**
Rectal Dialators, set of 4, black hard rubber, #1 and #4, emb with number and "Dr. Young's Rectal dialator," c1920s, price for set **50.00**
Sign, Alt-Lo-Pho-Ros Rheumatism and Neuralgia Remedy, cardboard, 3 pc screen type window display, $18^{3}/_{4}$ x $20^{1}/_{4}$" **275.00**
Sign, Dr Haile's Ole Injun System Tonic, color litho, "Kidneys, Liver & Stomach," Indian wearing headdress, 1950, 13 x 20". **50.00**
Sign, Nature's Remedy, porcelain **265.00**
Thermometer, Ex-Lax, porcelain, 8 x 36" **135.00**

Thermometer, Ramon's Kidney Pills, painted wood, 21 x 9" 425.00
Tin, Dearso Respicoal Ointment 15.00
Tin, Dr White's Cough Drops, litho tin, 75 x 3½ x 2¼" 600.00
Tin, Carmen Condoms, litho tin, colorful pin-up image, ⅝ x 1⅝" 170.00
Tin, Gold-Pak Condom, Crown Rubber Co, Akron, OH, litho tin, 1½ x 5" 400.00
Tin, Milk of Magnesia Tablets, flat, light blue and cream, 1945, ½ x ½ x 3¼" 12.00
Tin, Quick-Strips Bandages, 1940, 1 x 2¼ x 3½" 12.00
Tin, Uth Stocking Treatment, litho tin, different image of girl on both sides, 5⅞ x 2" 210.00
Toiletry Kit, Peau-Doux brand, includes talc, styptic powder, and shaving cream, red box, 1938 . . . . 125.00

EASTER COLLECTIBLES

Now that Christmas and Halloween collectibles have been collected to death, holiday collectors are finally turning their attentions to Easter. The old Easter bonnet still hangs in the Clothing Collectibles closet, but chicken and rabbit collectors now have to contend with Easter enthusiasts for their favorite animal collectible.

Bank, figural rabbit, plastic, red and white check top, orange felt skirt, mkd "Roy Des of Fla," 1968 . . . . $20.00
Basket, reeded, pink, handle, Germany, 6" h 20.00
Book, *Uncle Wiggily Starts Off,* 1940s 12.00
Box, Kauffman's Egg Dye, wood, early 1900s 75.00
Cake Mold, rabbit, Griswold 275.00
Candy Container, duck, yellow composition, ribbon around neck, standing on 3" d round cardboard box, opens at base, Germany, 4" h 35.00
Candy Container, rabbit, potbelly, white, head and ears on wire spring, white glass beaded trim, separates at belt line, mkd "US Zone Germany," 8" h 15.00
Candy Container, rabbit, pressed cardboard, 8" h 75.00
Dinner Bell, ceramic, rabbit on top, mkd "Happy Easter 1979" 15.00
Display, cardboard, Easter bunny holding colored food dyes 25.00
Egg Dye Packet, PAAS, 1930–40 . . . . 10.00
Greeting Card, girl climbing out of egg shell, fringed, German, 19th C 12.00
Greeting Card, "Joyous Easter," angel in oval, daisies and emb dec, c1910 . . . . 2.00

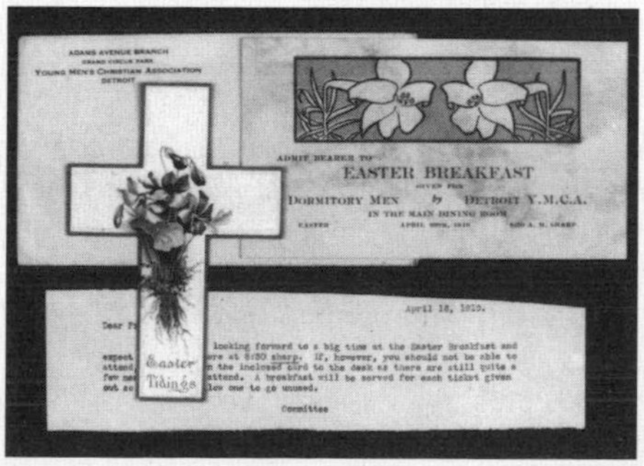

Ticket, YMCA Easter Breakfast, printed color, emb diecut cross, orig envelope, 1919, 6 x 3½", $10.00.

Toy, Windup Bunny Carriage, celluloid and tin, mkd "Made in Japan/O.K.D.," orig box, 6½" h, $77.00. Photo courtesy Collectors Auction Services.

Greeting Card, "Loving Wishes For Easter," cherub on emb ground, crucifix motif, emb flowers on edge, 1890-1900 . . . . 3.00
Greeting Card, mechanical, bunny drinking soda, soda flows through straw, 1920s 8.00
Ice Cream Mold, Easter lily, pewter, early 20th C 50.00
Piñata, rabbit with carrot, standing, Mexican, unused, mid 20th C 35.00
Postcard, "Easter Greetings," children watching 2 rabbits kissing, 1910 . . . . 2.00
Postcard, "To Greet You on Easter Day," bunny discovering girl in basket, Raphael Tuck & Sons 10.00
Pull Toy, rabbit, wood, cardboard cart, 1940s 50.00
Rabbit, hard plastic, mother rabbit dressed in yellow, brown glasses, 5" h 7.00
Windup, egg, plastic, tin chick inside, 1950s 40.00

EGGBEATERS

America has borne a grudge against eggs for decades—evidence the innumerable gadgets invented for beating them. There were well over 1,000 patents issued for eggbeaters since 1856. Any collector should be able to assemble a large collection of eggbeaters without any duplication.

A & J, metal, "Beats Anything in a Cup or Bowl," 7½" h $15.00
A & J, metal, "Lady Bingo #72," 10¾" h 15.00
A & J, metal, Super Speed Spinnit Cream and Egg Whip, 11½" h 30.00
A & J, Whirlpool Whipper, 8" h 55.00
Androck, Beats-All, 11" h 18.00
Androck, Turbine Egg Beater, mfg by Cassady-Fairbank Co, Chicago, 10" h 60.00
Androck, Turbine Beater, 11½" h 18.00
Archimedes Type, F Ashley, pat May 1, 1860, 14" h 500.00
Archimedes Type, George R Flowers, Phila, "The Up To Date Egg Cream Whip," pat Apr 10, 1906, 11½" h 150.00
Archimedes Type, Roberts, with dasher stoppper, 13½" h 65.00
Archimedes Type, Spear, 20th Century Egg & Cream Whipper, mkd "Improvements Allowed Nov 29, 1913," 12½" l 100.00
Archimedes Type, Sterling, 13¾" h 40.00
Aurelius, Ideal Mille Lacs Mfg, 10¾" h 30.00
Aurelius, Master Egg Beater, 11½" h 300.00
Dazey, Churn #20, 2 qt 125.00
Dazey, Mix-er-ator, 10" h 20.00
Dover, beveled wheel, 1870, 10" h 65.00
Dover, cast iron, 12" h 75.00

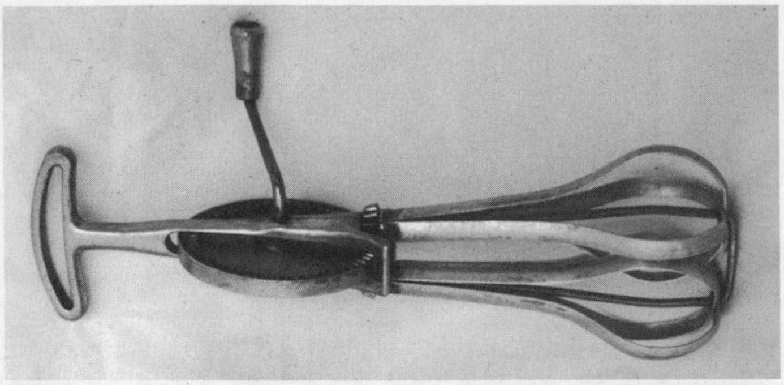

Aluminum, rotary, c1920, 10½" l, $15.00.

Edlund Co, ST blades, red painted wood handle and knob 8.00
EKCO, 9¾" h 5.00
EKCO, Mary Ann, 11¼" h 10.00
EKCO, One Hand Beater, 10" h 7.00
Holt-Lyon, Cream Whip, 1897, 10" h 120.00
Holt-Lyon, Jar Cream Whip and Mayonnaise Mixer, qt jar, 1900, 11½" h 300.00
Ladd, #00, pat Oct 18, 1921 United Royalties Corp, 11" h . . . 12.00
Ladd, Saturn Beater, "B," 10½" h 25.00
Landers, Frary & Clark, Universal Cake Mixer, 9" d 50.00
Landers, Frary & Clark, Universal Churn #25 . . . . . 400.00
Made In Germany, Minit-Mixer, plastic jar, emb on bottom "The Original Minit-Mixer Patented Made in Germany," 9" h 20.00
Taplin, clear plastic cup, 6" h 60.00
Taplin, Light Running, 12½" h 50.00
Taplin, wooden handle, 5½" h 15.00
Turner & Seymour, Merry Whirl, cast iron frame, 11½" h 20.00
Turner & Seymour, Super Whirl, Bakelite handle, 11½" h 20.00
Turner & Seymour, Triumph, 9½" h 200.00
Turner & Seymour, Turner Egg Beater, pat Sep 26, 1876, 10" h 300.00

EGGCUPS

Where modern Americans would be hard-pressed to recognize, let alone know how to use, an eggcup, their European counterparts still utilize the form as an everyday breakfast utensil. Their greatest period of popularity in America was between 1875 and 1950—long before cholesterol became a four-letter word.

A plain white porcelain eggcup works just as well as a fancy decorated one. The fact that so many different and highly decorative eggcups exist shows our unwillingness to accept the mundane at the breakfast table.

Collectors place a premium on character eggcups. You can make a great collection consisting of eggcups from breakfast services of hotels, railroads, steamships, or restaurants. As tourists, many of our ancestors had a bad case of sticky fingers.

Finally, do not forget the various scissor-like devices designed to decapitate the egg. Would you even recognize one if you saw one? I saw one once at a flea market marked as a circumcision device. *Ouch!*

Newsletter: *Eggcup Collectors' Corner,* 67 Stevens Ave., Old Bridge, NJ 08857.

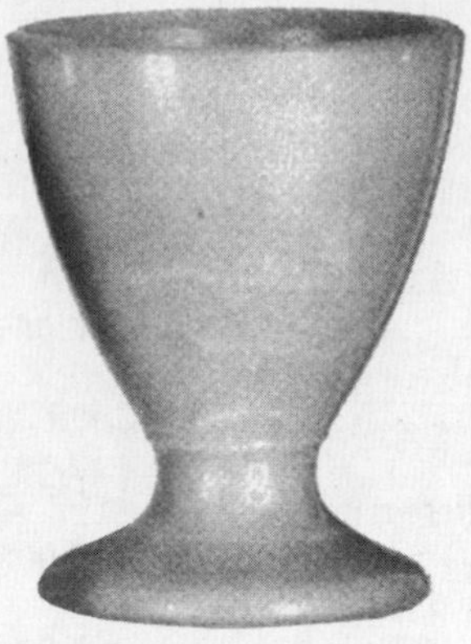

McKee Glass Co, Skokie Green, $15.00.

Advertising, Cadbury Creme Egg, brown glaze, yellow chickens, 1989 . . . . . $10.00
Advertising, Nescafe, red, white lettering and int, Carlton Ware, 1980s 20.00
Character, Charlie McCarthy, orange lusterware, Japan 95.00
Character, Holly Hobbie, with blue bonnet, 1960s 12.00
Character, Humpty Dumpty, sitting on red brick wall, red bow tie, yellow pants, Mansell Print Ltd, 1985 . . . . . 25.00
Character, Supercar, white, raised Supercar, mkd "Keele St Pty Co, Ltd, England," 1962 AP Film Ltd copyright, 2¼" h 80.00
Character, Tom and Jerry, plastic figures holding onto block of cheese, removable cup, MGM Inc, Made in Hong Kong, 1970 . . . . . 25.00
Columbia Glass Co, Hobnail, white milk glass 18.00
Commemorative, Prince William Birth, color portrait with Prince and Princess of Wales, Coronet Pottery, 1982 . . . . . 25.00
Duncan, Beaded Swirl, clear 12.00
Hazel Atlas, double, milkglass, flared base, 1930s 8.00
Homer Laughlin, Yellowstone pattern, Southweatern motif decal 20.00
Lehneware, wood, turned, ftd, orig red, green, black, and yellow strawberry dec, salmon pink ground 525.00
Limoges, France, multicolored florals, 2½" h 12.00
Occupied Japan, dog, white, brown tail, blue cup 18.00
Pressed Glass, opalescent, oval panels of hobnails, c1890 . . . . . 25.00
Susie Cooper, double, beige and yellow flowers 25.00
Taylor, Smith & Taylor, Lu Ray pattern, Sharon Pink 18.00
Universal Pottery, double, Ballerina pattern 15.00
Watcombe Pottery, Torquay pattern, cottage dec, "Straight From The Nest" motto, 1¾" h 12.00

ELEPHANT COLLECTIBLES

Public television's unending series of documentaries on African wildlife has destroyed the fascination with wild animals. By the time parents take their children to the zoo or circus, elephants are old hat, blase. Boo, hiss to public television—those pompous pachyderms. We want the mystery and excitement of wildlife returned to us.

Things were different for the pre-television generations. The elephant held a fascination that is difficult for us to comprehend. When Barnum brought Jumbo from England to America, English children (and a fair number of adults) wept.

Bookends, pr, Blenko, 1980, 6⁵/₈" h, $18.00.

There are a few elephant-related political collectibles listed. It is hard to escape the G.O.P. standard bearer. However, real elephant collectors focus on the magnificent beasts themselves or cartoon representations ranging from Dumbo to Colonel Hathi.

Club: The National Elephant Collector's Society, 380 Medford St., Somerville, MA 02145.

Newsletter: *Jumbo Jargon*, 1002 W. 25th St., Erie, PA 16502.

Advertising Trade Card, The Sacred White Elephant, Light of Asia, Forepaugh's White Elephant of Siam **$25.00**
Book, *Little Orphan Annie and Jumbo, the Circus Elephant*, pop-up, 1935, 8 x 9¹/₄" **125.00**
Book, *Walt Disney's Dumbo of The Circus*, Garden City, 1941, 52 pp, 10 x 11" **50.00**
Chocolate Mold, tin, 3 cavities **75.00**
Diecut, elephant balancing on ball, emb, printed color, 5 x 6¹/₂" **20.00**
Figure, 3 elephants, celluloid **15.00**
Figure, Fantasia Elephant, ceramic, wearing pink dress, American Pottery, 5¹/₂' h **150.00**
Lapel Stud, walking elephant, white metal, "Coolidge," 1" l **12.00**
Perfume Bottle, figural elephant, brown and white **75.00**
Pin, figural elephant, diecut, silvered brass, inscribed "Carlsberg Beer," 1" d **15.00**
Pinback Button, "Dewey In 1948," white, dark blue elephant illus, 2¹/₂" d **25.00**
Pitcher, Dumbo, ceramic, white, pink and blue dec, Leeds China, mkd "Walt Disney Dumbo 2 Qt Jug," 1947 . . . . **85.00**
Poster, "Jumpy? Those Who Keep Their Heads Over Little Things Make The Biggest Headway, Size It Up And Keep Cool!," elephant scared by mouse, orange, purple, brown, Mathes Co, Chicago, 1929, 36 x 44" **225.00**
Toy, squeaker, dumbo, rubber, movable head, Walt Disney Productions copyright, 1950s, 6¹/₂" h **20.00**
Windup, Expander Elephant, plush, blue, litho tin ears and eyes, built-in key, T N Japan, orig box, 1960s **75.00**

ELONGATED COINS

Although the elongation of coinage first begain in 1893 at the Columbian Exposition in Chicago as souvenirs of that event, the revival of producing and collecting elongated coins began in earnest in the early 1960s. Initially available to the hobbyists and souvenir collectors from a few private roller/producers, the elongation of coins advanced by way of commercial enterprises beginning in 1976 during the Bicentennial celebration. Automated vending rolling machines producing souvenirs are all over the United States and abroad, from historical sites to national parks and amusement areas.

Elongated coins are now on the Internet. Most of the coins are trading and since so many are being produced, there is little value in them. The more serious collectors still deal with "Classic" specimens and of the older productions.

For further information on elongated coins, old and modern, contact the advisor listed below.

Advisor: Angelo A. Rosato, 70 Grove St., New Milford, CT 06776, (860) 354-5684.

Club: The Elongated Collectors, 203 S. Gladiolus St., Momence, IL 60954.

ELVIS

Elvis was hot, is hot, and promises to be hot well into the future. Elvis collectibles are bought from the heart, not the head. A great deal of totally tacky material has been forgiven by his devoted fans.

Elvis material breaks down into two groups: (1) items licensed while Elvis was alive and (2) items licensed after his death. The latter are known as "fantasy" items. Fantasy Elvis is collectible but real value lies in the material licensed during his lifetime.

Beware of any limited edition Elvis items. They were manufactured in such large numbers that the long-term prospects for appreciation in value are very poor. If you love an item, fine. If you expect it to pay for your retirement, forget it.

Club: Elvis Forever TCB Fan Club, P.O. Box 1066, Pinellas Park, FL 33281.

Badge, purple pleated fabric border around black and white paper disk with Elvis portrait, red fabric ribbons at bottom, c1957, 6" d **$65.00**
Bangle Bracelet, brass, photo portrait, 1960s **85.00**
Book, *Elvis Portrait Portfolio*, Sean Shaver, Timus Pub, black and white photos, 1st ed, sgd and numbered, 304 pp, #554 of 1956, 1983 . . . . **125.00**
Calendar, pocket size, glossy stiff paper, color photo, 1964, 2¹/₄ x 4" **5.00**
Christmas Card, Elvis wearing Army uniform, 1959 . . . . **15.00**

Limited Edition Plate, "The King," The Bradford Exchange, Remembering Elvis series, Nate Giorgio, 95 days, 1995, 8¹/₈" d, issue price $30.00.

Hat, fabric, black top and brim, wide band with multicolored song titles and portrait illus, Magnet Hat and Cap Corp, ©1956 Elvis Presley Enterprises, orig car board tag, 8½" l **60.00**
Keychain Viewer, plastic, purple and clear, attached chain, color photo of Elvis wearing red shirt, early 1970s, 2" l **12.50**
Letter, Tom Diskin of Col Tom Parker Management, concerning Elvis tour, 1973 . . . . **10.00**
Magazine, *Fans' Star Library,* "Elvis in the Army" cov, 1959 . . . . **15.00**
Movie Poster, *Girls! Girls! Girls!,* Paramount Pictures, 1960 . . . . **20.00**
Newspaper, *Memphis Press-Scimitary,* death of Elvis, front page banner headline and color photo, related articles and photos inside, Aug 17, 1977 . . . . **30.00**
Pennant, felt, blue, printed white "Elvis The King Of Rock And Roll," and picture frame, black and whtie photo of Elvis holding crown attached to front, white trim, 1970s, 9 x 24" **18.00**
Photo, black and white, glossy, Elvis photo with blue facsimile signature, 1955, 5 x 7" **70.00**
Pinback Button, "Best Wishes Elvis Presley," black and white photo, 1956, 2½" d **65.00**
Pinback Button, "Elvis Presley For President/Lou Monte Campaign Manager," white and dark blue, 1½" d **40.00**
Pinback Button, "You're Nothin' But A Houn' Dog," red, white, and blue, Elvis copyright on curl, 1956, ⅞" d **10.00**
Postcard, "Easter Greetings, Elvis Presley," 1967 . . . . **20.00**
Poster, "Welcome Home Elvis," Billy Joe Burnette tribute song, 1979 . . . . **15.00**
Pocketknife, memorial, front grip with color portrait and birth and death dates on pale blue ground, dark red plastic grip on back, 2 blades, unused, late 1970s, 3½" l **15.00**
Record Sleeve, *Jailhouse Rock/Treat Me Nice,* full color, 7 x 7" **40.00**
Record Sleeve, *Wear My Ring Around Your Neck/Doncha' Think It's Time,* full color, 7 x 7" **40.00**
Sheet Music, *You Don't Know Me,* young Elvis photo cov, 1955 . . . . **10.00**

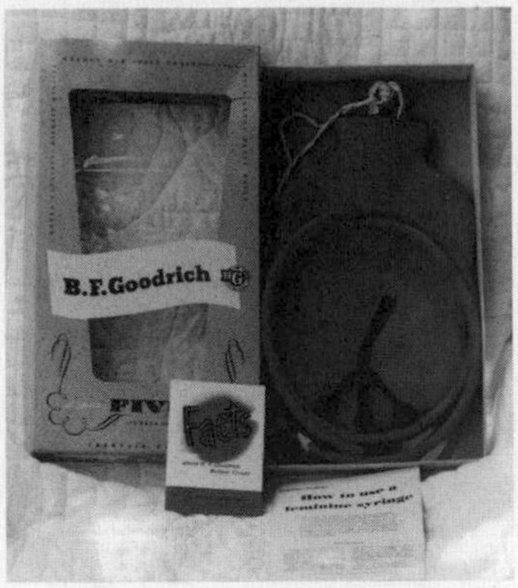

Fountain Syringe, BF Goodrich, red, 2+ quarts, attachments, literature, orig box, $8.00.

ENEMA & FEMININE HYGIENE PRODUCTS

Enemas have been in use for many years. There are pictographs from ancient Egypt which show people receiving enemas. The enema was originally used for medicinal purposes. An excellent treatise on the history of the enema can be found in the book *The Enema as an Erotic Art,* by David Barton-Jay. Now, of course, due to "wise" heads in medicine, the enema is losing favor as a treatment, and those wonderful red, yellow, green, black, and blue bags with black nozzles are being pushed aside in favor of the bane of modern society...disposables.

Feminine hygiene products have a less lengthy history. The emphasis on being "fresh and clean" dates from the 19th century, but shows no signs of abating today, as companies place new products in the market. However, those new products share a common trait with those in the rectal hygiene field: disposable.

The items in both arenas now available and collectible date primarily from the 1920s through the 50s, though it is not uncommon to find irrigators, like the Allen Sanitary Fountain, which was patented in 1899, or the boxed tips of the Tyler syringe, which dates from 1875. Unless a bag has been cared for quite well, whether through continual use or just being left in the box in a dark closet, the rubber in most of the pre-1900 syringes has deteriorated to the point of not being useable. Fortunately, there are collectors in the United States (and probable elsewhere) who have these relics safe and sound in good storage conditions.

Rubber syringes for enema and douche purposes are not a popular collecting item. Most people have bad memories of enemas from childhood. Others just can't imagine collecting something so esoteric. In spite of their primary function of cleansing the body, it just seems so "dirty." There are a few, however, who recognize that, despite the memories, an item that once hung in many bathrooms is something worth saving.

Advisor: Atled Delta, PhD, 2911 NW 122nd St., Ste. 262, Oklahoma City, OK 73120-1900, (405) 751-0859, e-mail: atleddelta3@netscape.net.

Allen Sanitary Fountain, galvanized metal, without attachments or box, 4 qts **$50.00**
Arrow, Seamless Rubber Co, combination water bottle and fountain syringe, with attachments, orig box **6.00**
Bronze, National Package Drugs, combination syringe, red, with attachments, orig box **6.00**
Comfy, Davol Rubber Co, fountain syringe, red, with attachments, orig box **6.00**
Crest, Seamless Rubber Co, combination water bottle and fountain syringe, red, with attachments, orig box **8.00**
Criterion, B F Goodrich, combination water bottle and fountain syringe, red, with attachments, orig box **6.00**
Defender, Rexall, fountain syringe, red, with attachments, orig box **6.00**

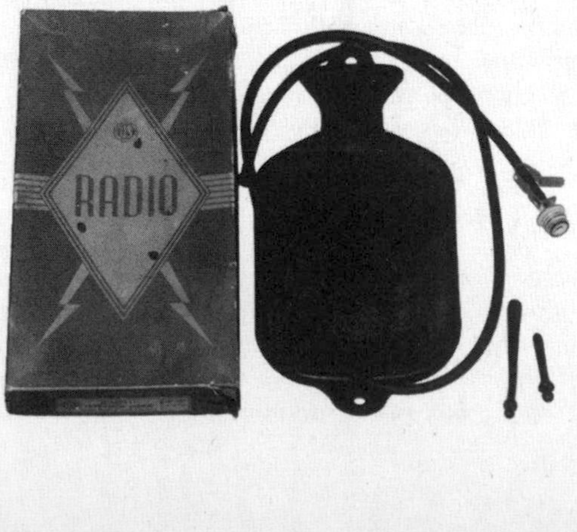

Radio, combination syringe, US Rubber Company, black, complete with all attachments, $8.00.

Near Kid, combination water bottle and fountain syringe, The Seamless Rubber Co., red, 2+ qts, orig box, $6.00.

Dila-Spray, vaginal dilating syringe, orig box 8.00
Disposable Fountain Syringe, unknown manufacturer, 2 qt sheet plastic bag with plastic tube for nozzle, orig box. 3.00
Enema Can, S Maw, English, metal tip, flaking paint 350.00
Fem Aide, Hygienic Vaginal Jelly, with rubber bulb applicator, orig box. 12.00
Hygiox, vaginal douche tablets, orig box 3.00
Iris, Davol Rubber Co, fountain syringe, red, with attachments, orig box 10.00
Irrigator, graduated, with detachable spout, bone white enamel and metal, no hose or tips 10.00
Irrigator, Jones Medical Co, white enamel/metal, without attachments. 5.00
Kantlek, Rexall, combination water bottle and fountain syringe, red, with attachments 8.00
Kloratubes, vaginal powder, plastic case of 18 . . . . 10.00
Petal, Davol, combination water bottle and syringe, red, with attachments, 2 plus qts, orig box. 12.00
Radio, U S Rubber Co, combination syringe, black, with attachments, orig box 8.00
Roxbury, United Drug Co, combination syringe, red, with attachments, orig box. 6.00
Sunburst, B F Goodrich, combination water bottle and syringe, red, with attachments, orig box 6.00
Tyler Rubber Co, nozzle tips, 1 vaginal, 4 rectal, orig wooden box, syringe missing 35.00
Victoria, Rexall, combination water bottle and fountain syringe, red, with attachments, orig box 8.00
Wearever, metal container for traveling fountain syringe, with syringe and attachments. 8.00
Young's Vaginal Dialators, set of 4, hard black rubber or Bakelite, orig box 25.00

ENESCO

Enesco's product line includes more than 12,000 gift, collectible, and home accent items including the Precious Moments and Cherished Teddies collection. It also markets licensed gifts and collectibles such as Lilliput Lane and David Winter Cottages.

In 1983 Enesco became a wholly-owned subsidiary of Westfield, Massachusetts-based Stanhome, Inc., a multinational corporation. In 1997 The Bradford Group entered into a long-term licensing agreement to market the product lines of Stanhome's subsidiary, Enesco Giftware Group. In 1998 Stanhome, Inc., changed its name to Enesco Group, Inc. Today, Enesco products are distributed in more than thirty countries including Japan, Mexico, and Germany.

Figurine, Meeting Special Friends Along The Way, Memories of Yesterday, M Attwell, 1 year, 1997, 5" h, issue price $85.00.

Bank, bear holding set of blocks that spells "Baby," Cherished Teddies, 1996, 7" h $22.50
Candleholder, angel carrying basket of fruit, International Collections' Via Vermont, 1996, 4½" h 15.00
Clock, "Rock-A-Bye-Baby," bears, bottle, pacifier, and baby book at base of moon face, Cherished Teddies, 1996, 6¾" h 55.00
Figurine, Bless You Little One, Memories of Yesterday A Loving Wish For You, M Attwell, 1995. . . . . 25.00
Figurine, bunny, Just In Time For Spring, Cherished Teddies, P Hillman, 1995. . . . . 14.00
Figurine, Friends For Life, Maud Humphrey Bogart, Collectors' Club Members Only, M Humphrey, 1991 . . . . . 65.00
Figurine, Hilary Hugabear, Cherished Teddies Club, P Hillman, 1995. . . . . 20.00
Music Box, "Don't Change a Single Spot," puppy in hat box, Walt Disney's 101 Dalmatians, plays *I Feel Pretty*, 6" h 40.00
Night Light, bear wearing diaper with baby blocks, Cherished Teddies, 4½" h. 12.50
Ornament, Baby in Swing, Miss Martha's Collection, M Holcombe, 1992. . . . . 50.00
Ornament, Beth on Rocking Reindeer, Cherished Teddies, P Hillman, 1992. . . . . 30.00
Ornament, Look Out Below, 1981 . . . . 20.00
Ornament, Special Delivery!, Memories of Yesterday, M Attwell, 1988 . . . . 25.00
Ornament, Straight To Santa, J Davis, 1991. . . . . 14.00
Plate, Barbie, Silver Screen Barbie, FAO Schwarz Exclusive, 1994. . . . . 30.00
Plate, Girl In Green Dress, Cherished Teddies, P Hillman, 1995. . . . . 35.00
Plate, Join Me For A Little Song, Memories of Yesterday, M Attwell, 1995 . . . . 50.00

ERTL BANKS

This is another of those highly speculative areas that are addressed as the need arises. The 1980s and 1990s saw a surge in the number of cast-iron banks produced by several companies, Ertl being the most dominant. These banks were often made to commemorate special events or used as promotions or fundraising efforts for local charities.

Most of the Ertl banks were recently manufactured in Hong Kong. They should only be purchased if in fine condition or better and only if the originally packaging is included. All of the banks are marked and numbered. Avoid any that are not marked. The serial numbers and series numbers are important in cataloging and pricing these items.

Club: Ertl Collectors Club, P.O. Box 500, Dyersville, IA 52040.

ACE Hardware, Runabout, #9019, 1989 . . . . **$75.00**
Agway, Model T Van, #5, #7514, 1990 . . . . **35.00**
Allis-Chalmers, Mack Truck, #1201, 1984 . . . . **40.00**
Amoco, Model T Van, #9150, 1987 . . . . **155.00**
Anthracite Battery, Ford Delivery Van, #9264, 1987 . . . . **45.00**
Baker Oil Tools, Mack Truck, #9210UP, 1990 . . . . **35.00**
Banjo Matthews, Ford Panel, #2784 . . . . **55.00**
Barrett Jackson Car Auction, Chevy Panel, #9361UP, 1990 . . . **40.00**
Bell System, horse and carriage, #9801, 1988 . . . . **30.00**
Boone Co Fair, Ford Delivery Van, #9716, 1988 . . . . **30.00**
Breyer's Ice Cream, Ford Delivery Van, #9617, 1989 . . . . **45.00**
Briggs & Stratton, Runabout, #9986, 1988 . . . . **145.00**
Celotex, Model T Van, #9317, 1987 . . . . **550.00**
Dairy Queen, school bus, #3257 . . . . **28.50**
Dallas Cowboys, Model T Van, #1247, 1984 . . . . **30.00**
Diamond Walnut, hawkeye Box Truck, #9881 . . . . **34.00**
Dr Pepper, Mack Truck, #9235 . . . . **35.00**
Fina, Mack Tanker, #9186, 1987 . . . . **90.00**
Happy Birthday, Hawkeye, #9450 . . . . **16.00**
Humble Oil, Kenworth Tanker, #3 in series, #3839 . . . . **20.00**
Indianapolis 500, Ford Runabout, #9813, 1988 . . . . **45.00**
Jim Beam, Sugar River Beamers, Ford Delivery Van, #2125UO, 1990 . . . . **30.00**
John Deere, Seagraves Fire Engine, #1 in series, #5710 . . . . . . **21.00**
Kraft Dairy Group, Model T Van, #9675, 1989 . . . . **35.00**
Lea & Perrins, Model T, #917OB **32.50**
Leidy's, Ford Tractor Trailer, #9578UO, 1989 . . . . **30.00**
LePage Glue, Model T Van, #2120, 1984 . . . . **35.00**
Lolli Pups, Model T Van, #2146, 1984 . . . . **40.00**
Los Angeles Times, Model T Van, #7667UA, 1990 . . . . **45.00**
Marshall Fields, Model T Van, #1650, 1983 . . . . **65.00**
Matco, Step Van, #9659, 1989 . . . . **65.00**
Minnesota Vikings, Model T Van, #1246, 1984 . . . . **55.00**
NASA, Step Van, #9467, 1989 . . . . **40.00**
Old El Paso, Ford Delivery Van, #7636UO, 1990 . . . . **45.00**
Pepsi-Cola, Ford Runabout, #6936, 1989 . . . . **55.00**
Phillips 66, Mack Tanker, #9787 . . . . **35.00**
Renninger's Antique Market, Adamstown, PA, Ford Delivery Van, #9712, 1988 . . . . **35.00**
Riverview Nursery, Ford Tractor Trailer, #9804, 1988 . . . . **45.00**
Schneider Meats, Ford Panel, #9229, 1985 . . . . **115.00**
Shop Rite, Mack Truck, with crates, #9666, 1989 . . . . **25.00**
Steamtown USA, Mack Tanker, #9167B **75.00**
Sunholidays Travel, Ford Runabout, #9618, 1988 . . . . **35.00**
Sunmaid Raisins, Step Van, #9576, 1990 . . . . **40.00**
Terminix, Ford, #9086 . . . . **20.00**
Texaco, Dodge, #10 in series, #9500 . . . . **18.00**
Texaco, Ford Runabout, #5 in series, #9740 . . . . **90.00**
Texaco, Kenworth, #9 in series, #9385 . . . . **25.00**
Trappey "Bull Brand" Hot Sauce, Ford Delivery Van, #1311, 1990 . . . . **35.00**
Turner Hydraulics, Hawkeye Truck, #2106UP, 1990 . . . . **30.00**
United Airlines, Model T, #9223 . . . . **27.00**
Universiry of Wisconsin, Model T Van, #9655, 1989 . . . . **30.00**
Valley Forge, Mack Truck, #9616, 1989 . . . . **100.00**
Western Auto, Model T Van, #1328, 1981 . . . . **110.00**
Wilson Foods, Runabout, #9897, 1988 . . . . **35.00**
Yoder Popcorn, Step Van, #9627, 1989 . . . . **55.00**
Yuengling Beer, Ford Delivery Van, #9176, 1987 . . . . **135.00**

FANS, ELECTRIC

Collecting old electric fans is becoming increasingly popular. Old fans have become "trendy." In the past year alone demand for older fans has doubled. Fortunately, the supply is vast enough to accommodate the interest, except for the oldest/rarest fans. Many people think they have a gold mine when they come across a brass bladed fan. This is most often not the cast. Plenty of common mass-produced brass bladed fans are still available, hence not all such fans are valuable. With these fans, the condition determines price. If, for example, the paint is very good and the brass is polished/buffed to a luster, the price may jump up to 50% compared to a similar fan in tarnished/rusty condition.

Fans from the late 1930s thru the 40s—mostly steel and aluminum bladed with "bullet-back" motor covers—have stayed constant/unchanged in value. The main factor making these more desirable will be if "new/in box" or near mint.

The high dollar values still belong to the older/rarer models like, Edison, Crocker Curtis and other makes with exposed coils or unique features like light bulbs on top of the motors. Alternate powered fans are also sought after.

Art Deco and unusual mechanisms on fans are in high demand by collectors and interior decorators alike. Watch TV programs and movies carefully and you will see old fans in the background setting the mood. Fan popularity is at an all time high. They look good and are also useful.

Advisor: Mike Roberts, 4416 Foxfire Way, Ft. Worth, TX 76133, (817) 294-2133.

Club: American Fan Collectors Assoc., P.O. Box 5473, Sarasota, FL 34277.

EMERSON

44A, Northwind, 8" blades, gold paint, 4 S-shaped wires on cage **$35.00**
450, Northwind Series, 10" blades, oscillating, heavy cast iron base, 3-speed slide switch **45.00**
6250, Anniversary Fan, copper blades, commemorative of Emerson's 50 years of business, 1940 . . . . **100.00**
16646, tiered/step base, 12" scalloped/Bulwinkle horn shape brass blades, cast iron blade hub, non oscillating **150.00**
19645, 10" blades, yoke/ Y motor support on step base, brass and brass, non oscillating **125.00**
73668, residential fan, 6 brass 16" blades, painted steel guard, heavy cast metal motor and base, late 1920s **100.00**

General Electric, "Star Oscillator," 12" blades, brass blades and guard, four-point handles, motor tag on side, 1917, $100.00.

77646AD, oscillating floor fan, same design as 77646, mounted on floor stand, 1938 . . . . **120.00**
79648, 16" painted steel blades, cast base with sliding switch, bullet back cov, 1941 . . . . **40.00**
99646, non oscillating, 12" blades, tin, chrome plated cage, plastic front name badge on cage, 1950s **15.00**

GENERAL ELECTRIC

Bullet-Backed Tin Fan, round brown Bakelite base, 10" blades, motor supported by C-shape steel neck, 1940s **$35.00**
GE Whiz, 9" brass blades, dark green paint, motor supported in circle housing, 1924 . . . . **50.00**
Non Oscillating Desk Fan, 6" blades, dark green **70.00**
Oscillating Floor/Pedestal Fan, "X" shaped 4 ftd base, 4 fat aluminum blades inside multi-wire cage, medium brown paint **120.00**
"Sidegear," 398950, exposed gear oscillator, rear gear box built sideways, large gear exposed, motor supported in yoke, brass blades and cage **500.00**
Tin Fan, 12" pressed sheet metal blades, tin housing and base, c1940s. **20.00**
Vortelex, 3 tapered tipped 16" blades, multi-wire guard **40.00**

WESTINGHOUSE

12PA2, 12" overlapping blades, bullet back, Duckbill heavy cast iron base, large open ring on center guard, plastic name ring, 1940s **$25.00**
1648641, 6 steel 12" blades, S wire guard with outside/support ring, aluminum name badge, 1923 . . . . **65.00**
31575, 12" fiber blades, blades rotate counter-clockwise, 1920s. **40.00**
"Tank," 12" brass blades and guard, smooth trumpet style base with sliding speed switch, large open ring on center guard, banner name tag, non oscillating, 1912. . . . . **160.00**

OTHER

Guth, ceiling/light fan, 12" circle blade assembly with vented "blades" punched in, disc shaped blade hangs beneath ornate 6 light fixture, 1920s **$250.00**
Kisco, "Hassack," tin/sheet metal housing with tubular supports, 1950s. **45.00**
Mathis, furniture/box fan, 10" aluminum fat overlapping blades, wooden housing, square or rounded front, thin verticle slats front and rear guards, approx 16 x 20" **65.00**
Samson, "Safeflex," 4 thick rubber blades, motor atop gooseneck support. **45.00**
Singer, 3 elasticated cloth blades, brown Bakelite housing and base, 1940s. **100.00**

Colonial, front oscillator, 12" blades, oscillating mechanism between blades and front of motor, large DC brush-caps on rear of motor, $200.00.

FARM COLLECTIBLES

The agrarian myth of the rugged individual pitting his or her mental and physical talents against the elements remains a strong part of the American character in the 1990s. There is something pure about returning to the soil.

The Country look heavily utilizes the objects of rural life, from cast-iron seats to wooden rakes. This is one collectible area in which collectors want an aged, i.e., well-worn, appearance. Although most of the items were factory-made, they have a handcrafted look. The key is to find objects that have character—a look that gives them a sense of individuality.

Clubs: Antique Engine, Tractor & Toy Club, 5731 Paradise Rd., Slatington, PA 18080; Cast Iron Seat Collectors Assoc., P.O. Box 14, Ionia, MO 65335.

Periodical: *Farm Antique News,* 812 N. Third St., Tarkio, MO 64491; *Farm Collector,* 1503 SW 42nd St., Topeka, KS 66609.

Advertising Trade Card, Empire Riders, Reapers & Mowers, Sunrise, 1884 Krebs Litho **$6.00**
Advertising Trade Card, J I Case Steam Tractor **8.00**
Advertising Trade Card, Minneapolis Threshing Machine Co **10.00**
Billhead, pr, Curtis Mfg Co Agricultural Implements, green and red plow vignettes, 1874 . . . . **30.00**
Booklet, *80 Pictures of Farm Experiences,* Celotex Insulation Corp, 1936, 35 pp **5.00**
Calendar, 1910, Empire Cream Separator **350.00**
Calendar, 1914, McCormick Machinery **175.00**
Calendar, 1917, De Laval Cream Separators, girl and collie, full pad, 12 x 23" **325.00**
Calendar, 1929, Minnesota Binders, DeLavel Separators, Oliver Implements, flapper girl illus **28.00**
Catalog, Boggs Mfg Co, Standard Potato Graders, Onion Graders and Warehouse Equipment, 1928, 24 pp **25.00**
Catalog, Case Cultivator, 400 Series Tractors, 1961, 1953 . . . . **10.00**

Booklet, *Better Hay, How to Make and Market it,* John Deere, Moline, IL, black and white photo illus, tinted cov, 36 pp, 1916, 7¾ x 8¾", $15.00.

Sign, Farm Bureau Association, metal, 18" h, 18" w, $126.50. Photo courtesy Collectors Auction Services.

Catalog, Farm Barns, Beatty Bros, Fergus, Ontario, illus, barns, tolls, equipment, c1920, 352 pp **15.00**
Catalog, Kraus Farm Cultivators, 1911, 62 pp **20.00**
Catalog, Louden machinery, illus, hay, dairy, horse, etc, hard cov, 1917, 224 pp **15.00**
Catalog, Oliver Chilled Plow Works, 1924, 18 pp, 4 x 8½" **24.00**
Catalog, Wiard Plow Co, Batavia, NY, 32 pp, 6¾ x 9¾" **27.00**
Certificate, Stockman Protective Assoc, OK, 3 large farm vignettes, 1926 . . . . **6.00**
Corn Sheller, Gray Brothers **350.00**
Hinge, barn, wrought iron, strap, 27" l **60.00**
Magazine, *The Farmer's Wife,* 1929 . . . . **12.00**
Milking Stool, wooden, 3 short legs **50.00**
Photograph, Strangeland & Halverson Farm Implements Co, front view, c1890, 7 x 5" **12.50**
Pinback Button, Frick Company, red, white, gold, and lavender, Eclipse farm tractor **15.00**
Pinback Button, Minneapolis-Moline Co, 1944 union member **25.00**
Pinback Button, P & O Canton Plows, celluloid, multicolored, 1¼" d **70.00**
Pinback Button, Rumley Oil Pull Tractor, multicolored, tractor image **100.00**
Pinback Button, Twin City Tractors, red, white, and blue, 1920s **50.00**
Poster, Granite Iron Ware, woman carrying milking pail, cow, 12½ x 28" **575.00**
Sign, Capewell Horsenail Co, family eating dinner, horse reaching through door being hand fed by mother, "One of the Family," framed, c1910, 19 x 25" **215.00**
Stickpin, Moline Plow, brass **35.00**
Watch Fob, Gardner Denver Jackhammer **25.00**

FARM TOYS

The average age of those who play with farm toys is probably well over thirty. Farm toys are adult toys. Collectors number in the tens of thousands. The annual farm toy show in Dyersville, Ohio, draws a crowd in excess of 15,000.

Beware of recent "limited" and "special edition" farm toys. The number of each toy being produced hardly qualifies them as limited. If you buy them other than for enjoyment, you are speculating. No strong resale market has been established. Collectors who are not careful are going to be plowed under.

Clubs: Ertl Collectors' Club, P.O. Box 500, Dyersville, IA 52040; Farm Toy Collectors Club, P.O. Box 38, Boxholm, IA 50040.

Newsletters: *Spec-Tacular News,* P.O. Box 368, Dyersville, I-A 52040; *Turtle River Toy News & Oliver Collector's News,* RR1, Box 44, Manvel, ND 58256.

Periodicals: *The Toy Tractor Times,* RR3 Box 112-A, Osage, IA 50461; *Toy Farmer,* 7496 106th Ave. SE, LaMoure, ND 58458; *Tractor Classics CTM,* P.O. Box 489, Rocanville, Saskatchewan SOA 3LO Canada.

Animal Farm Set, Buddy L, 6½" l Giraffe Truck, 6¼" l Jr Kitty Kennel, 11¼" l Jr Pony Trailer with Sportster, 1968 . . . . **$185.00**
Climbing Tractor, Marx, with Chain Pull, tin wind-up, 1929, 7½" l **225.00**
Corn Picker, Tru-Scale, pressed steel, 1/16 scale, Carter, 1971 . . . . **70.00**
Covered Wagon, Marx, litho tin, friction, 9" l **30.00**
Dairy Farm Set, Buddy L, #5050, includes blue #5210 Milkman Truck, red and gray #5260 Milk Tanker, and orange #5270 Farm Tractor, boxed set, 1961 . . . . **65.00**
Elevator, John Deere, pressed steel, 1/16 scale, Carter, 1960 . . . . **85.00**
Farm Set, Marx, tin wind-up, 7" l red plastic tractor, 1950 . . . . **125.00**
Farmyard Animals, Dinky, #2, pre-1933 . . . . **35.00**
Harvester, Ertl, Farmall 300, #2513 . . . . **15.00**
Harvester, Marx, International, diesel, driver and set of tools, 1/12 scale, 1954 . . . . **125.00**
Hay Rake, Dinky, #27-K, 1953 . . . . **20.00**
Hen Pulling Cart, tin windup, polychrome paint, chick passenger, squeak box not working, 9¼" l **50.00**
Horse Cart, with removable seat, cast iron, red, white, black, and gold, mkd with patent dates 1880, 1881, 1882, 1883, and 1884, 10½" l, no driver, horse rocks **192.50**
Horse Transporter, Corgi, #1105-B, 1976–80 . . . . **50.00**
Livestock Trailer Truck, Dodge, Corgi, #484-A, 1967–72 . . . . . **50.00**
Manure Spreader, Dinky, #27-C, 1949 . . . . **45.00**
Milk Trailer Set, Tootsietoy, tractor with 3 milk tankers, #0192 . . . . **100.00**
Planter, White **15.00**
Playset, Lazy Day Farm Set, Marx, 100 pcs, 1960 . . . . **165.00**
Plow, Arcade, Oliver, cast iron, red, 1/16 scale, 1940 . . . . . . **115.00**
Thresher, Arcade, McCormick-Deering, various colors, gold striping, red grain pipe, 1936, 9½" l **250.00**
Tractor, Arcade, Allis-Chalmers, cast iron, 1934, 3" l **95.00**
Tractor, Arcade, Avery, cast iron, gray frame with gold stripe, red wheels, 1929, 4½" l **150.00**

Tractor, Hubley, diecast, painted red, emb "Hubley Jr.," large rubber tread tires with yellow hubs, orig box, 7" l, $110.00. Photo courtesy Bill Bertoia Auctions.

End Loader, Structo, #340, pressed steel, 3 decals, Structo black rubber tires, orig box, 13½" l, $110.00. Photo courtesy New England Auction Gallery.

Tractor, Arcade, Ford, cast iron, 1/12 scale, 1941 . . . . **150.00**
Tractor, Arcade, Fordson, cast iron, 1932, 5¾" l **150.00**
Tractor, Arcade, McCormick-Deering M, cast iron, wooden wheels, 1942, 4¼" l **250.00**
Tractor, Buddy L, Husky, yellow body, 1970, 13" l **45.00**
Tractor, Ertl, Deutz-Allis 6620 All Wheel, #2332. . . . . **3.00**
Tractor, Ertl, Fordson Super Major, 1/16 scale, #0307 . . . . **19.00**
Tractor, Hubley, c1950 . . . . **75.00**
Tractor, Marx, American, tin wind-up, with accessories, 1926, 8" l **225.00**
Tractor, McCormick Farmall Super-A, #0250 . . . . **9.00**
Tractor, SCA, Allis Chalmers, D-17, 1/16 scale, #FF-0136 . . . . **35.00**
Tractor, SCA, Allis Chalmers, U, Farm Show, #FT-0456 . . . . . . **60.00**
Tractor, SCA, Ford 976, 4WD, 1/64 scale, #FA-0001 . . . . **8.00**
Tractor, SCA, Oliver 70, 1/16 scale, #FF-0138 . . . . **32.00**
Tractor, Tootsietoy, Caterpillar, #108, miniature. **25.00**
Tractor, Tootsietoy, Caterpillar, #4646, 1931 . . . . **30.00**
Tractor, Tootsietoy, Ford, red, with loader, diecast, 1/32 scale. **40.00**
Tractor, Tootsietoy, International. **15.00**
Tractor, Tootsietoy, with scoop shovel and wagon, red, silver scoop, flatbed trailer, 1946–52 . . . . **185.00**
Tractor, Tootsietoy, with driver, #4654 . . . . **100.00**
Tractor, White 185, 1/16 scale, #FA-004. . . . . **4.00**
Tractor and Trailer, Arcade, Allis-Chalmers, with Earth Mover, cast iron, 1934, 5" l **145.00**
Tractor and Trailer, Marx, litho tin, multicolored, self-reversing, orig box, 1936. . . . . **85.00**
Tractor and Wagon, Auburn, orange tractor, bright red spreader wagon. **115.00**
Wagon, Arcade, John Deere, wooden box, iron running gear, cast iron, 1/16 scale, 1940. . . . . **225.00**
Wagon, Kenton, ox drawn, cast iron, with driver, red, yellow, brown, black and maroon paint, wooden ox yoke added, 16" l **577.50**

FAST-FOOD COLLECTIBLES

If you haunt fast-food restaurants for the food, you are a true fast-food junkie. Most collectors haunt them for the giveaways. If you stop and think about it, fast-food collectibles are the radio and cereal premiums of the second half of the twentieth century. Look at what you have to eat to get them.

Whenever possible, try to preserve the original packaging of the premiums. Also, save those things which are most likely to be thrown out. I see a great many Happy Meals toys and few Happy Meals boxes.

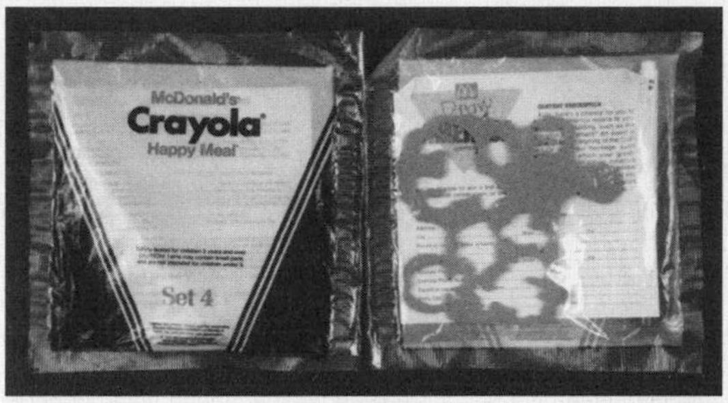

Crayola Stencils, McDonald's Happy Meal, set 3 and set 4, yellow and green, unopened, ©1986, 7" w, 7½" h, $3.00.

Club: McDonald's Collectors Club, 1153 S. Lee St., Ste. 200, Des Plaines, IL 60016.

Newsletter: *Collecting Tips Newsletter*, P.O. Box 633, Joplin, MO 64802.

Activity Book, Long John Silver's, Adventure on Volcano Island Paint and Water Book, 1991. . . . . **$2.50**
Adventure Kit, Burger King, 1991. . . . . **1.50**
Backpack, Hardee's, orange. **2.00**
Ball, Jack In The Box, Bouncing Buddies, 1993. . . . . **2.00**
Ball, Wendy's, Saurus Sports, 1991 . . . . **1.50**
Bank, Chuck E Cheese, figural **10.00**
Bath Mitt, Burger King, sea creatures, 1989 . . . . **4.00**
Beach Ball, Dairy Queen, logo on side **3.00**
Beach Ball, McDonald's, Olympic theme, 1984 . . . . **3.00**
Book, Arby's, *Babar's Read and Get Ready,* 1991 . . . . **2.00**
Book, McDonald's, *An American Tail,* 1986 . . . . **2.00**
Book, Taco Bell, *Little Critter's Bedtime Storybook,* 1987. . . . . **5.00**
Bookmark, Dominos Pizza **8.00**
Bucket, Burger King, Aladdin. **3.00**
Bowl, White Castle, plastic orange. **3.00**
Cards, Denny's, Jetsons Space Cards, 1992. . . . . **2.00**
Cards, Domino's Pizza, Quarterback Challenge, pack of 4, 1991. . . . . **1.00**
Cartoon Viewer, Lee's Famous Recipe Fried Chicken, cartoon characters. **10.00**
Cassette Tape, Burger King, Christmas Sing-A-Long, 1989 . . . . . **3.00**
Clock, McDonald's, prototype, Ronald McDonald below dial, hamburgers replace numerals, electric, 12" w, 28" h **125.00**
Coloring Book, Denny's, Jetsons Space Travel Coloring Book, with 4 crayons, 1992 . . . . **3.00**
Coloring Book, Taco Bell, Zoobilee Zoo series, 1984 . . . . **4.00**
Crayon Holder, Little Caesars. **3.00**
Crown, Burger King, cardboard, jewel-like design, "Have It Your Way" slogan. **7.00**
Cup, Carl's Jr, plastic, shark theme, 1993 . . . . **2.00**
Doll, Burger King, cloth, King, 1972, 16" h **20.00**
Doll, Burger King, cloth, plastic, The Simpsons, 1991 . . . . **3.00**
Doll, International House of Pancakes, cloth, Susie Strawberry, 1992 . . . . **6.00**
Doll, Little Caesars, Meatsa Man, 1990 . . . . **5.00**
Doll, Sonic Drive-In, Treasure Trolls, 1993 . . . . **2.00**
Doll, Wendy's, cloth, 11½" h. **5.00**
Figure, Arby's, Little Miss, 1981 . . . . **3.00**
Figure, Burger King, characters from *Aladdin,* 1992 . . . . **2.00**
Figure, Burger King, characters from *Beetle Juice,* 1990. . . . . . . **2.00**

NBA Fantasy Packs, McDonald's, foil package, 4½" h, 2½" w, $3.00.

Figure, Carl's Jr, Stung Grip Geckos, 1991 . . . . . **2.00**
Figure, Chuck E Cheese, bendie **10.00**
Figure, Dunkin' Donuts, bendie, Munch-Kins, 1989 . . . . . **5.00**
Figure, Kentucky Fried Chicken, Col Sanders, papier-mâché, 1960s, 7" h **50.00**
Figure, Ronald McDonald, 1980, MIP **15.00**
Figure, Roy Rogers, Cup Critters, 1994 . . . . . **2.00**
Figure, Sonic Drive-In, Brown Bag Buddies, 1993 . . . . . **2.50**
Figure, Wendy's, *All Dogs Go to Heaven,* 1989 . . . . . **2.00**
Finger Puppet, Burger King, *Hunchback of Notre Dame,* 1996 . . . . . **2.00**
Finger Puppet, Wendy's, Play-Doh Fingles, 1989 . . . . . **3.00**
Frisbee, Burger King, plastic, emb character, 3¾" d **6.50**
Frisbee, Hardee's, white, yellow imprinting, 4¾" d **1.50**
Glass, Domino's Pizza, frosted design and logo, 4⅛" h **2.00**
Glass, Wendy's, white, black, and pink, "Where's the Beef?," 1984, 5⅞" h **6.00**
Hand Puppet, Dairy Queen, vinyl, Strawberry Bear, 1991 . . . . . **1.00**
Hand Puppet, Pizza Hut, Eureeka's Castle, 1990 . . . . . **3.00**
Kaleidoscope, Long John Silver's, Sea Watchers, 1991 . . . . . **3.00**
Kite, Big Boy, Big Boy image, 1960s **10.00**
License Plate, Arby's, "Babar's World Tour" across top, red "Arby's" at bottom, colored sticker with name of city/country, 1990 . . . . . **2.00**
Little Golden Book, Hardee's, *The Little Red Caboose* **2.00**
Lunch Box, Burger King, plastic, blue, emb logo **2.00**
Magnet, Carl's Jr, food items, 1988 . . . . . **3.00**
Meal Box, Burger Chef, 1977 . . . . . **10.00**
Meal Box, Burger King, Super Powers, 1987 . . . . . **5.00**
Meal Box, Carl's Jr, 50 Happy Star Years, 1991 . . . . . **2.00**
Meal Box, Hardee's, Smurf, 1987 . . . . . **3.00**
Meal Box, Kentucky Fried Chicken, cardboard, "Colonel's Kids," features Foghorn Leghorn, 1987 . . . . . **2.00**
Mug, Arby's, Yogi & Friends, ceramic, full color decal, 1994 . . . . . **2.50**
Mug, McDonald's, ceramic, white, gold arches and red lettering, 4⅞" h **7.00**
Noise Maker, Dairy Queen, plastic cylinder, makes duck-like sound when shaken, logo on side, 1993 . . . . . **2.50**
Ornament, McDonald's, cloth, Fry Guy and Fry Girl, 3½" h **3.00**
Pen, Sonic Drive-In, secret decoder, 1988 . . . . . **4.00**
Pen, White Castle, bendies, 1993 . . . . . **1.50**
Pinback Button, Burger King, metal, "Happy Face," eyes made of Burger King Corp logo, ¾' d **3.50**
Playing Cards, Dairy Queen, 1993 . . . . . **2.50**
Puppet, Pizza Hut, Eureka's Castle, 1991 . . . . . **3.00**
Puzzle, Jack In The Box, Back In Time, cardboard, frame tray, 5 x 8" **2.50**
Ring, Arby's, plastic, Looney Tunes, 1¼" d changeable picture disc on top, 1987 . . . . . **5.00**
Ring, Roy Rogers, eraser ring, 1986 . . . . . **4.00**
Ring, Wendy's, plastic, Fun Flyer, 3½" d **1.00**
Scratch and Smell Stickers, Jack In The Box, 1991 . . . . . **1.00**
Shoelaces, Wendy's **1.00**
Sipper Bottle, Jack In The Box **4.00**
Socks, Burger King, rhinestone accents **2.00**
Stamp Set, Kentucky Fried Chicken, WWF, Canadian issue, 1996 . . . . . **2.00**
Sunglasses, Pizza Hut, *Back to the Future,* Solar Shades, 1989 . . . . . **3.00**
Telescope, Carl's Jr, plastic, Star Gazers, logo on ey piece, 1988 . . . . . **3.00**
Vehicle, Big Boy, race car, 1992 . . . . . **2.50**
Vehicle, Hardee's, Days of Thunder Racers, 1990 . . . . . **3.50**
Wrist Pouch, Carl's Jr, 1989 . . . . . **3.00**

FENTON GLASS

Frank L. Fenton founded the Fenton Art Glass Company as a glass-cutting operation in Martins Ferry, Ohio, in 1905. In 1906 construction began on a plant in Williamstown, West Virginia. Production began in 1907 and has been continuing ever since.

The list of Fenton glass products is endless. Early production included carnival, chocolate, custard, pressed, and opalescent glass. In the 1920s stretch glass, Fenton dolphins, and art glass were added. Hobnail, opalescent, and two-color overlay pieces were popular in the 1940s. In the 1950s Fenton began reproducing Burmese and other early glass types.

Throughout its production period, Fenton has made reproductions and copycats of famous glass types and patterns. Today these reproductions and copycats are collectible in their own right. Check out Dorothy Hammond's *Confusing Collectibles: A Guide to the Identification of Contemporary Objects* (Wallace-Homestead: 1979, revised edition) out-of-print, for clues to spotting the reproductions and copycats of Fenton and other glass manufacturers of the 1950s and 1960s.

Clubs: Fenton Art Glass Collectors of America, Inc, P.O. Box 384, Williamstown, WV 26187; National Fenton Glass Society, P.O. Box 4008, Marietta, OH 45750.

Newsletter: *Butterfly Net,* 302 Pheasant Run, Kaukauna, WI 54130.

Animal Dish, cov, hen, rose pastel, 9" h **$75.00**
Ashtray, Hobnail, blue opalescent, fan **32.50**

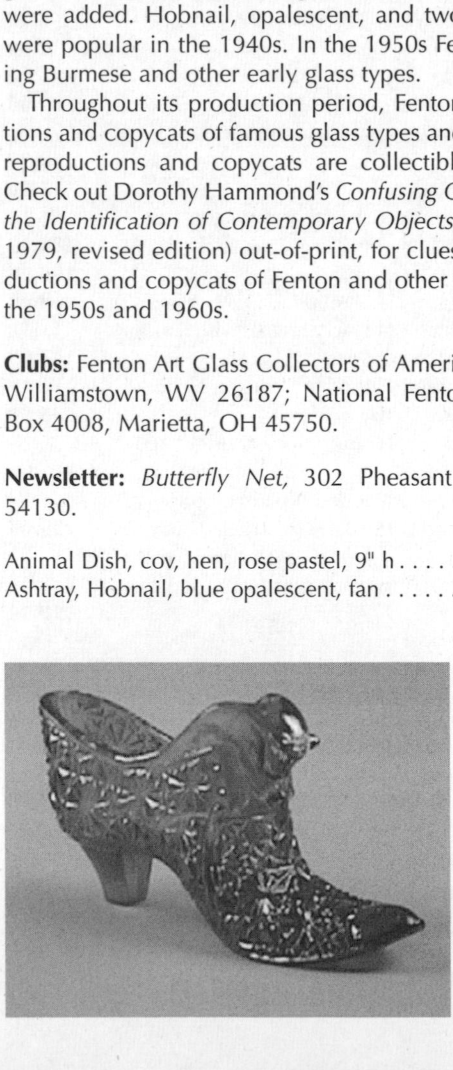

Shoe, #1995, kitten slipper, Daisy & Button, carnival, emb "Fenton" in oval on sole, 1970, 3½" h, 5¾" l, $15.00.

Basket, red carnival, dated 1994, sgd "Tom Fenton," 8½" h 55.00
Bonbon, cov, Stretch, irid, purple, #643 . . . . . 50.00
Bowl, mandarin red, flare, #950, 12" d 85.00
Bowl, stiegel blue, lace edge, 7" d 26.00
Bowl, Thistle, carnival, marigold, ruffled edge, 8" d. 90.00
Candlesticks, pr, Hobnail, blue opalescent, cornucopia, 3½" h 42.00
Champagne, Hobnail, French opalescent 18.00
Champagne, Plymouth, red 12.50
Compote, Apple Blossom Crest, #7329 . . . . . 60.00
Condiment Set, Hobnail, blue opalescent, individual creamer, sugar, and mustard. 37.00
Console Set, Jade, #1600 dolphin bow, pr #318 candlesticks, price for 3 pc set 125.00
Cookie Jar, cov, Big Cookies, black amethyst, wicker handle 95.00
Creamer, Lincoln Inn, pink 15.00
Creamer, Turquoise Crest 50.00
Creamer and Sugar, Hobnail, white opalescent, tall, price for pr 27.50
Juice Tumbler, Hobnail, blue opalescent. 110.00
Juice Tumbler, Plymouth, red 15.00
Mayonnaise and Liner, Hobnail, blue opalescent 75.00
Petal Bowl, Jade, #848 . . . . . 25.00
Pitcher, Button and Braids, green opalescent. 175.00
Plate, Silver Crest, 6" d 6.50
Relish Dish, Silver Crest, heart shaped, handle 25.00
Rose Bowl, Blue Overlay, beaded melon, 3½" h 30.00
Salt and Pepper Shakers, pr, Georgian, amber. 75.00
Salt and Pepper Shakers, pr, Hobnail, blue opalescent 45.00
Shoe, Hobnail, blue opalescent 24.00
Sugar, Silver Crest, ruffled top 45.00
Tidbit Tray, Silver Crest 30.00
Vase, Apple Blossom Crest, dec, 4" h 40.00
Vase, Burmese, hp roses, 4" h 35.00

FIESTA WARE

Fiesta was the Melmac of the mid 1930s. The Homer Laughlin China Company introduced Fiesta dinnerware in January 1936 at the Pottery and Glass Show in Pittsburgh, Pennsylvania. It was a huge success.

The original five colors were red, dark blue, light green (with a trace of blue), brilliant yellow, and ivory. Other colors were added later. Fiesta was redesigned in 1960, discontinued about 1972, and reintroduced in 1986. It appears destined to go on forever.

Values rest in form and color. Forget the rumors about the uranium content of early red-colored Fiesta. No one died of radiation poisoning from using Fiesta. However, rumor has it that they glowed in the dark when they went to bed at night.

Clubs: Fiesta Club of America, P.O. Box 15383, Loves Park, IL 61132; Fiesta Collectors Club, P.O. Box 471, Valley City, OH 44280.

Ashtray, dark green $90.00
Bowl, chartreuse, 4½" d 22.00
Bowl, cobalt blue, 4¾" d. 18.00
Bowl, green, 4¾" d 15.00
Bread and Butter Plate, ivory, 6" d 2.50
Cake Server, Kitchen Kraft, light green 165.00
Candlesticks, pr, tripod, cobalt blue 850.00

Salad Bowl, yellow, 9½" d, $45.00.

Casserole, cov, ivory 125.00
Chop Plate, cobalt blue, 13" d. 65.00
Chop Plate, yellow, 13" d 20.00
Coffeepot, cov, ivory 150.00
Coffeepot Base, after dinner, green. 175.00
Compote, green, 12" d 125.00
Cream Soup, yellow 40.00
Deep Plate, yellow 24.00
Demitasse Cup and Saucer, ivory. 55.00
Dessert Bowl, red, 6" d 40.00
Dinner Plate, red, 10" d. 40.00
Egg Cup, light green 45.00
Fork, Kitchen Kraft, green 115.00
Fruit Bowl, chartreuse, 5½" d, chartreuse 25.00
Grill Plate, turquoise, 15" d 22.00
Luncheon Plate, chartreuse, 9" d 15.00
Mixing Bowl, turquoise, #4 . . . . . 220.00
Mug, yellow 35.00
Platter, cobalt blue 25.00
Relish Center, green 55.00
Salad Plate, ivory, 7" d. 35.00
Sauce Boat, gray 85.00
Sauce Boat, turquoise 40.00
Shaker, red, ... 12.00
Syrup, cobalt blue. 375.00
Syrup, red. 375.00
Syrup, yellow 325.00
Teapot, cov, light green, medium 75.00

FIGURINES

Looking for a "small" with character? Try collecting ceramic figurines. Collecting interest in the colorful figurines produced by firms such as Ceramic Arts Studio, Florence Ceramics, Vernon Kilns, and others has grown considerably during the past ten years. Pieces are starting to become pricey. However, there are still bargains to be found. A surprising number of these figurines are found at garage sales and flea markets at prices below $10.

Clubs: Abingdon Pottery Club, 210 Knox Hwy. 5, Abingdon, IL 61410; Arkansas Pottery Collectors Society, P.O. Box 7617, Little Rock, AR 72217; Ceramic Arts Studio Collectors Assoc., P.O. Box 46, Madison, WI 53701; Florence Collector's Club, P.O. Box 122, Richland, WA 99352.

Newsletter: *Vernon Views*, P.O. Box 945, Scottsdale, AZ 85252.

Abingdon Pottery, nude, kneeling, 7" h. $160.00

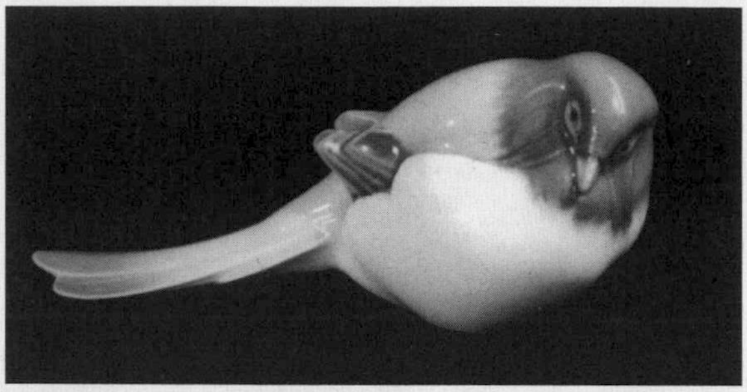

Bing & Grondahl, bird, seated, #1635R, blue, gray, and white, $4\frac{1}{2}$" l, $70.00.

American Glass, boxer dog, clear . . . **50.00**
Baccarat, shark, clear . . . **110.00**
Beswick, foal . . . **85.00**
Brush Pottery, frog, reclining, 10" l . . . **75.00**
Cambridge, frog, crystal satin . . . **20.00**
Ceramic Arts Studio, Colonial man . . . **30.00**
Clay Sketches, cockatoo . . . **25.00**
Fenton, raccoon, ruby iridized . . . **22.00**
Florence Ceramics, choir boys . . . **35.00**
Florence Ceramics, Grace . . . **195.00**
Florence Ceramics, Linda Lou . . . **95.00**
Fostoria, sea horse, clear, 8" h . . . **90.00**
Japan, kitten, white, on brown shoe, 3" l . . . **9.00**
Lladro, swan . . . **160.00**
Midwest Potteries, long neck goose, white, yellow dec, 1940-44, $5\frac{3}{4}$" h . . . **8.00**
New Martinsville, baby bear, sun colored . . . **35.00**
Niloak Pottery, frog . . . **20.00**
Pennsbury Pottery, hen, cream body, brown trim, 11" h . . . **225.00**
Roselane, stylized giraffe, glossy gray . . . **20.00**
Vernon Kilns, unicorn, black, from Disney's *Fantasia* . . . **200.00**
Weller, boy, fishing . . . **215.00**

FINCH, KAY

After over a decade of ceramic studies, Kay Finch, assisted by her husband, Braden, opened her commercial studio in 1939. A whimsical series of pig figurines and hand-decorated banks were the company's first successful products.

An expanded studio and showroom located on the Pacific Coast Highway in Corona de Mar opened on December 7, 1941. The business soon had forty employees as it produced a wide variety of novelty items. A line of dog figurines and themed items were introduced in the 1940s. Christmas plates were made from 1950 until 1962.

When Braden died in 1963, Kay Finch ceased operations. Freeman Mc-Farlin Potteries purchased the molds in mid-1970s and commissioned Finch to model a new series of dog figurines. Production of these continued throught the late 1970s.

Bank, pig, floral dec, 10" h . . . **$75.00**
Cane Vase, #T509A, cane, 8" section, carnelian glaze, 1949 . . . **25.00**
Candleholder, white flower, 14" h . . . **25.00**
Console Set, Oriental, Celadon green, 2 ladies and vase, sgd, price for 3 pcs . . . **145.00**
Figure, Choir Boy, singing . . . **55.00**
Figure, Court Lady, pink pearl matte glaze, #401, $10\frac{1}{2}$" h . . . **185.00**
Figure, Jezebel Cat . . . **125.00**
Figure, Madonna and Child, white . . . **60.00**
Figure, Mr Bird, #453, brown, applied leaves, $4\frac{1}{2}$" h . . . **45.00**
Figure, Peep and Jeep . . . **85.00**
Figure, Scandia Girl . . . **30.00**
Figure, turkey . . . **45.00**
Figure, Yorkie Puppy . . . **125.00**
Mug, Santa, #4950 . . . **50.00**
Shell, #5406, rosy pink, 4" h . . . **15.00**

FIRECRACKER PACKS, LABELS, & RELATED

This hobby includes, but is not limited to, the collection of Chinese artwork as found on the colorful and often artistic labels found on old packages of firecrackers, and sometimes the firecrackers themselves. The artwork is of a great variety of animals, mythical and comic characters, and patriotic and sporting themes. There are perhaps a thousand different brands that were sold in the United States since about the middle of the 19th century. Since firecrackers originally sold for as little as one cent per thousand and still can be purchased for about one cent each, their labels represent true popular art. The labels range in size from that of a postage stamp to those nearly as large as a newspaper page. a large label was usually pasted on a parcel or "brick" of 20 to 250 packages, and each package also had a label. Some brands also had their name or the object named by the brand on a label wrapped around each individual firecracker. Some common brands such as Camel, Zebra, and Black Cat were continuously marketed for decades, whereas others were on the market for only a few seasons. Some old brands of firecrackers are still sold in retail fireworks stands across the country and new brands appear annually. Catalogues, posters, postcards, and advertising depicting firecrackers or fireworks are also collected, as are the cast iron cannon and mortars that used firecrackers for ammunition.

Firecracker collectors should look for labels without "I.C.C.," "D.O.T.," or "U.N.O." markings. These are acronyms for government agencies and began to be used in the 1950s as regulatory agencies became concerned with the transportation and safety aspects of fireworks. Large "Caution" and "Warning" panels detract greatly from the beauty and artistic design of modern firecracker labels. Prices generally rise for larger labels and those with special artistic appeal. However, some collectors prefer to collect packs or labels from the smallest sizes, called "penny packs." A few prefer to collect individual firecrackers.

Greyhound Brandy by Ming Hing, empy box, $100.00; full box $300.00.

Others in the hobby collect fireworks-related items used to celebrate Independence Day, and in the South, Christmas. These items include domestically produced salutes, torpedoes, caps, sparklers, snakes, smokes, whistles, rockets, and many other devices. Yet others collect documents and photographs related to the many fireworks companies that once flourished in the United States. Those mostly interested in capbombs, capcanes, capguns, capstrikes, firecracker mortars, cannon, and pistols and other hardware items usually are considered toy collectors.

Advisor: Hal Kantrud, Rt. 7, Jamestown, ND 58401, (701) 252-5639, e-mail: halk995@daktel.com.

Newsletter: *The Phoenix,* Rt. 7 Box 52, Jamestown, ND 58401.

Periodical: *Pyrofax Magazine,* P.O. Box 2010, Saratoga, CA 95070.

Note: Prices listed are for labels. Full packs usually command prices about 25 to 50% higher.

Ape **$5.00**
Batman **5.00**
Battleship **75.00**
Bazooka **20.00**
Big Chief **20.00**
Big Jake . . . . . **.25**
Black Fury **3.00**
Black Hawk . . . . . **.25**
Black Prince **75.00**
Blue Shark **150.00**
Bob Cat **1.00**
Boomer . . . . . **.25**
Bulldog **10.00**
Cats **10.00**
Celebration Sam . . . . . **.25**
Champ **5.00**
Cock **1.00**
Dragon Lady **1.00**
Father Christmas **500.00**
Golliwog **50.00**
Happy Penguin **200.00**
Jubilant Jeep **300.00**
Jungle **20.00**
Mustang **10.00**
Nightraider . . . . . **.25**
Polar Bear **20.00**
Pyramid **300.00**
Round One **75.00**
Samson **30.00**
Supercharged . . . . . **.25**
Super Maelstrom . . . . . **.25**
Tom Cat **100.00**
Touch-Down **50.00**

FIREHOUSE MEMORABILIA

Who hasn't heard the wail of the fire truck siren and wished they could respond to save the damsel in distress? Well, collecting firehouse memorabilia is the next best thing!

Firehouse collectors are everywhere. They are doctors, lawyers, businessmen, housewives, as well as firefighters, and they live in every city across America.

Helmets, fire alarm equipment, speaking trumpets, and fire truck equipment are only a few categories of many Firehouse collectibles. Many of the items are over 100 years old, and as with other collectibles, condition is of the utmost importance.

Fire helmets were used to protect the firemen from falling debris, and are a very popular item. The foremen of the fire companies used speaking trumpets to shout orders to their men. Trumpets, or bugles as they were sometimes called, are still symbols of authority in the fire department today. Large silver plated trumpets were carried in parades or given as gifts on many occasions.

Alarm boxes were placed on the street so passing citizens could signal the fire department incase of fire. Each fire station had a very ornate wood cased gongs that would ring out the number of the box pulled. Before the time of electricity fire engine oil lanterns were used to light the way and are highly sought after.

Badges are another area of collecting. They are very popular because they are plentiful and relatively inexpensive.

Advisor: Marvin Karsten, Old Tyme Fire Classics, 6217 Crystal Dr., Alta Loma, CA 91701, (909) 987-5084, e-mail: firegoods@aol.com.

Club: Antique Fire Apparatus Club of America, 5420 S. Kedvale Ave., Chicago, IL 60632; Fire Collectors Club, P.O. Box 992, Milwaukee, WI 53201; The Fire Mark Circle of the Americas, 2859 Marlin Dr., Chamblee, GA 30341.

Badge, silver tone, eagle on top, steam fire engine in center, "Cumberland Fire Co. Carlisle, Pa," mkd "C.D. Reese, 57 Warren St, New York" on back **$50.00**
Badge, SS, eagle on top, motorized fire truck in center, "Driver, Dickson City Fire Dept, Pa" **75.00**

Sam Yik Sui Kee of Canton: empty box, $30.00; full box $50.00.

Eclipse Fire Lantern, nickel over brass, blue over clear globe, mkd "The Fire Extinguisher Co," $1,400.00.

Presentation Trumpet, SP, bell, hose carriage engraved on bell, "Presented to John N. Sitterlen by the Officers and Men of Page Hose Co No 5 Dec. 27, 1875," 21" h, 8" bell, $1,250.00.

Fire Alarm Equipment, fire station gong, Gamewell, wood cased, ornate, 3 indicating numbers under glass top, 8½" bell at bottom, fan type dec top . . . **4,000.00**
Fire Alarm Equipment, fire station gong, wood cased, ornate, various styles, 15" bell at bottom . . . **3,000.00**
Fire Alarm Equipment, street box, aluminum, cottage style, Gamewell Fire Alarm Telegraph Co, 16½ x 10½ x 5¼" . . . **125.00**
Fire Alarm Equipment, street box, cast iron, cottage style, Gamewell Fire Alarm Telegraph Co, "Fire Alarm Telegraph" on door with operating instructions . . . **200.00**
Fire Engine Lantern, brass, C T Ham Co . . . **450.00**
Fire Engine Lantern, Dietz King, brass or nickel over brass, mkd "Fire Dept" on fuel tank, patented 1907 . . . **175.00**
Fire Engine Lantern, Dietz King, "Fire Dept," mkd "Seagrave Co." on watershield . . . **450.00**
Fire Engine Lantern, Dietz King, mkd "American LaFrance Fire Engine Co. Elmira, New York" on watershield . . . **265.00**
Fire Engine Lantern, Dietz King, tin with copper tank, "Fire Dept" . . . **125.00**
Fire Engine Lantern, Eclipse, mkd "Fire Extinguisher Co. Chicago, Ill. Patented 1886" on bottom of tank . . . **850.00**
Fire Grenade, "HNS" nutting hand grenade, amber diamond panel, 1 pt . . . **190.00**
Fire Grenade, hand fire extinguisher, turquoise blue, "Harden's" quilted pattern mkd "No. 1, patented Aug. 14, 1883," 1 pt . . . **125.00**
Fire Grenade, "Harden's" star hand grenade, turquoise blue, 1 pt . . . **100.00**
Fire Grenade, Red Comet fire extinguisher, bulb type, metal wall bracket and spring loaded mechanism with fusible firing mechanism . . . **45.00**
Fire Grenade, Red Comet fire extinguisher, bulb type, plastic wall bracket with no firing mechanism . . . **25.00**
Fire Grenade, Sure Stop 6 Pack, metal box hangs on wall, 6 frosted bulb extinguishers . . . **125.00**
Fire Nozzle, brass, for 1½" hose, American LaFrance Co, with shut off, 8" h . . . **60.00**
Fire Nozzle, brass, for 1½" hose, Elkhart, with shut off, 8½" h . . . **50.00**
Fire Nozzle, brass, for 2½" hose, Akron, with shut off and plastic handles, 22" h . . . **100.00**
Fire Nozzle, brass, for 2½" hose, Larkin Mfg Co, with shut off and leather handles, 19" h . . . **125.00**
Helmet, aluminum, flat metal finial, 6" leather frontispiece . . . **125.00**
Helmet, fiberglass composition, Bullard or MSA, 4" leather frontispiece . . . **45.00**
Helmet, leather, brass eagle finial, 8" leather frontispiece . . . **370.00**
Helmet, leather, flat metal finial, 6" leather frontispiece . . . **175.00**
Match Safe, hammered copper, applied silver medallion, "Fireman's Fund Insurance Co—Christmas Greetings 1915" giveaway, depicts fireman rescuing child from flames . . . **350.00**
Match Safe, SS, Home Insurance Co of New York giveaway, depicts 2 firemen with hose and nozzle . . . **450.00**
Match Safe, SS, "Presented by the Home Insurance Co. of New York," depicts a steam fire engine pulled by 2 horses . . . **400.00**
Parade Axe, viking style, large rounded blade, curving spike on back . . . **325.00**
Pocket Watch, coin silver, Elgin, steam fire engine engraved on back . . . **500.00**
Pocket Watch, gold, Howard, inside case engraved "Presented to Captain William McAllister, by officers & members of Engine Co. 8, January 1st, 1925," New York City Fire Department badge engraved on back . . . **900.00**
Pocket Watch, gold, Waltham, inside case engraved "Presented to Engineer Adolph Banzer by the officers & members of Engine Co. No. 16 on completion of twenty years service New York Fire Department. November 25, 1929...1909-1929," gold New York City badge with steamer affixed to back . . . **1,300.00**
Speaking Trumpet, brass or nickel plated brass, 18" h, 6" d across bell, works . . . **425.00**
Speaking Trumpet, silver plated, parade or presentation horn, engraved steam fire engine, inscribed on shaft "Presented to Chief Ralph W. Emerson from Eagle Hose Co. No. 2, July 4, 1886," 21" h, 7½" d across bell . . . **1,100.00**

FIRE-KING

Remember those great coffee mugs you used to find at diners? Those nice big warm cups filled to the brim by a smiling waitress, not the Styrofoam of this decade. Chances are they were Fire-King mugs. Fire-King dinnerware and ovenware was sold in sets from the 1940s through the 1970s. The company guaranteed to replace broken pieces and their colorful wares were quite popular with housewives. While Fire-King has been around for many years, collectors are now discovering quantities at flea markets and many are enjoying this new collecting area.

Club: Fire-King Collectors Club, 1406 E. 14th St., Des Moines, IA 50316.

22 K Gold, creamer . . . **$5.00**
22 K Gold, dinner plate . . . **6.00**
22K Gold, sugar, open . . . **5.00**
Black Dot, salt and pepper shakers, pr . . . **60.00**
Charm Square, cup and saucer, azurite . . . **3.00**
Coupe Shape, cup, white, silver border . . . **3.00**
Fleurette, cup . . . **3.50**
Fruits, casserole, open, 1 qt . . . **9.00**
Fruits, refrigerator jar, cov, hp, white ground, 4⅛" sq . . . **8.50**
Golden Anniversary, dinner plate . . . **7.00**
Golden Anniversary, sugar, open . . . **5.50**
Golden Shell, cup and saucer . . . **3.50**
Golden Shell, sugar, cov . . . **8.00**
Golden Shell Swirl, dinner plate, 9" d . . . **5.00**

Ivory Swirl, dinner plate 4.50
Ivory Swirl, sugar, cov 7.00
Jadeite, egg cup 21.00
Jadeite, refrigerator jar, cov, 5 1/8 x 9 1/8" 40.00
Jane Ray, cereal bowl, jadite 7.00
Jane Ray, vegetable, jadite, 8 1/2" d 15.00
Ovenware, sapphire blue, custard, 5 oz 3.00
Ovenware, sapphire blue, loaf pan, 9 1/8 x 5 1/8" 18.00
Peach Lustre, dinner plate 7.00
Restaurantware, luncheon plate, jadeite, 9" d 14.00
Restaurantware, mug, jadeite, thin 6.00
Soreno, cup and saucer, avocado 3.50
Swirl Azurite, platter 14.00
Swirl Jadeite, vegetable bowl, large 8.50
Tulips, mixing bowl, white, 8 1/2" d 15.00
Turquoise Blue, sugar 5.00
White Swirl, dinner plate, 7 1/2" d 2.50

FISHBOWL ORNAMENTS

Long after the goldfish and guppies have been flushed down the toilet or consumed by some hungry predator, aquarium owners find they still may have the ceramic castle, lighthouse, mermaid, pagoda, shipwreck, or other furniture that once graced the bottom of their tank.

Aquarium furniture manufactured in Germany, Japan, and the United States between 1870 and 1970 is the most collectible. Most examples sold at neighborhood five and dime stores.

Looking for an interesting subcollection? Consider fish food containers.

Castle, ceramic, fluorescent colors, 6" h $5.00
Castle and Tower, ceramic, joined by bridge, multicorored, matte glaze, 4" h. 20.00
Castle, ceramic, blue and brown, glossy glaze, Japan, 6" h 22.00
Castle, ceramic, multicolored, glossy glaze, Japan, 2 3/4" h 20.00
Castle and Windmill, ceramic, multicolored, glossy glaze, Japan, 3 3/4" h 15.00
Diver, plastic, gray 3.00
Dragon, ceramic, 3 parts, Japan 2.00
Pagoda, ceramic, multicolored, glossy glaze, Japan, 3 3/4" h 18.00
Sunken Ship, plastic, bubble stone 3.00
Treasure Chest, ceramic, brown, glossy glaze, 2" h 8.00

FISHER-PRICE TOYS

In 1930 Herman Guy Fisher, Helen Schelle, and Irving R. Price founded the Fisher-Price Toy Company in Birmingham, New York. From that year forward, Fisher-Price toys were built with a five-point creed: intrinsic play value, ingenuity, strong construction, good value for the money, and action. With these principles and manufacturing contributions, the Fisher-Price Toy Company has successfully maintained quality and creativity in the toy market.

The collectibility of Fisher-Price toys is a direct reflection upon their desirability due to their unique characteristics and subject matter.

Club: Fisher-Price Collectors Club, 1442 N. Ogden, Mesa, AZ 85205.

Dapper Donald Duck, #460, diecut figural Donald on wheeled platform, paper litho, wings missing, c1936, $132.00. Photo courtesy New England Auction Gallery.

Note: Listings for toys in good condition.

Allie Gator, #653, 1960 . . . . $40.00
Barky Buddy, #150, 1934 . . . . 400.00
Bouncy Racer, #8, 1960 . . . . 45.00
Cash Register, #972, 1960 . . . . 35.00
Chatter Telephone, wood wheels, #747, 1962 . . . . 25.00
Cowboy Chime, #700, 1951 . . . . 150.00
Dandy Dobbin, #765, 1941 . . . . 150.00
Family Play Barn, 1969 . . . . 15.00
Gabby Goose, #120, 1936 . . . . 35.00
Jack & Jill TV Radio, #148, 1959 . . . . 25.00
Lady Bug, #658, 1961 . . . . 30.00
Lop Ear Looie, #415, 1934 . . . . 150.00
Merry Mousewife, #662, 1962 . . . . 35.00
Merry Mutt, #473, 1949 . . . . 45.00
Molly Moo-Moo, #190, 1956 . . . . 65.00
Musical Sweeper, #225, 1953 . . . . 85.00
Nosey Pup, #445, 1956 . . . . 45.00
Peter Bunny Engine, #715, 1941 . . . . 70.00
Prancing Horses, #766, 1937 . . . . 175.00
Pushy Piggy, #500, 1932 . . . . 350.00
Rainbow Stack, #446, 1960 . . . . 15.00
Shaggy Zilo, #738, 1960 . . . . 40.00
Suzie Seal, with ball, #460, 1961 . . . . 25.00
Tabby Ding Dong, #730, 1939 . . . . 200.00
Tailspin Tabby, #455, 1939 . . . . 125.00
Woodsy-Wee Circus, #201, 1931 . . . . 500.00

FISHING COLLECTIBLES

There has been a lot written recently about the increasing value of fishing tackle of all types. What has not been said is that the high-ticket items are very limited in number. The vast majority of items sell for less than $5.

Fishing collectors emphasize condition. If a rod, reel, lure, or accessory shows heavy use, chances are that its value is minimal. The original box and packaging are also important, often doubling value.

You will make a good catch if you find wooden plugs made before 1920 (most that survive were made long after that date), split bamboo fly rods made by master craftsmen (not much value for commercial rods), and reels constructed of German silver with special details and unique mechanical action. Fishing collectors also like to supplement their collection with advertising and other paper ephemera. Find a pile of this material and you have a lucky strike.

Clubs: American Fishing Decoy Assoc., 624 Merritt St., Fife Lake, MI 49633; National Fishing Lure Collectors Club, 22325 B Drive S, Marshall, MI 49068; Old Reel Collectors Assoc., 849 NE 70th Ave., Portland, OR 97213.

Newsletter: *The Fisherman's Trader*, P.O. Box 203, Gillette, NJ 07933.

Periodical: *Fishing Collectibles Magazine*, 20005 Tree House Ln., Plano, TX 75023.

Calendar, 1906, Oakwood Market, OH, man fishing, 8½ x 5½" **$90.00**
Catalog, Weller Deluxe Tackle, punched for binder, 89 pp, 1963, 8 x 10½" **20.00**
Creel, split willow, classic shape, 6" ruler attached to top, orig leather latch strap and hinges, damage along rear of lid **60.00**
Creel, crushed willow, leather bound, 14 x 9 x 7" **24.00**
Creel, whole willow, Brady, trout size, leather harness and shoulder strap, canvas cov, large front pocket, 2 pouches **150.00**
Decoy, Sletten, cast aluminum, unopened, 1950s **22.00**
License, pinback button, Pennsylvania, resident fishing license, maroon, white ground, black serial number, 1948 . . . . . **15.00**
Lure, Hedon, Frog pattern, crazy crawler, wood **35.00**
Lure, Abbey & Imbrie Glowbody Minnow, glass tube body of luminous material attached to spinning keels, orig flattened picture box, c1920 . . . . . **82.50**
Poster, Canadian Pacific adv, hooked rainbow trout, silkscreen design, Ewart illus, "Canada For Game Fish," c1935, 24 x 35" **325.00**
Reel, fly, "J. B. Moscrops Patent—Manchester," brass, orig black finish, both foot ends filed, 1 foot end shortened, 3⅛" d, 1" w **55.00**
Reel, fly, "Orvis Magnalite Multiplier," multiplying reel with exposed rim and drag switch, 3⅛" d, ⅞" w **55.00**
Reel, salmon, The Ambassador, Farlow, single action, back plate drag adjustment, 4" d, ¾" w **82.50**
Reel, Takapart, #480, A F Meisselback Mfg, patent 1904–09 . . . . . **40.00**
Rod, fresh water, Edwards Quadrate, Special Luxor, medium fresh water action spinning rod, 2 pc, full length, no bag or tube, 7' l **55.00**
Rod, trout, F E Thomas, Bangor, ME, Browntone Special, top of the Line Model, 3 pc, 1 tip, agate stripper, tip top guides, blued hardware, long cork handle with thumb depression, bag and tube, 8½" l **175.00**

Booklet, *Where to Fish in Western Michigan,* published by The Grand Rapids Herald, includes folded "Official Michigan Service Map," numerous black and white maps, soft cov, 64 pp, 1932, 6 x 9", $8.00.

Sheet Music, *American Patrol,* orig ©1885 by Frank W. Meacham, $8.00.

FLAGS AND FLAG COLLECTIBLES

There certainly was a great deal of flag waving as a result of Operations Desert Shield and Desert Storm. Many collectors have salted away "yellow ribbon" flags. Unfortunately, they forgot a basic rule of collecting—the more made, the lower the future value. Ask anyone who owns a 48-star flag.

Flags themselves are difficult to display. Old flags are quite fragile. Hanging them often leads to deterioration. If you own flags, you should be aware of flag etiquette as outlined in Public Law 829, 7th Congress, approved December 22, 1942.

Many collectors do not collect flags themselves but items that display the flag as a decorative motif. A flag-related sheet music collection is one example.

Club: North American Vexillological Assoc., 1977 N. Olden Ave, Ste. 225, Trenton, NJ 08618.

Advertising Trade Card, flag draped woman holding glas of beer, Anheuser Busch Brewing Assoc adv, 1893 . . . . . **$30.00**
Blotter, large flag image, gold highlights, "Victory," Follansbee Brothers Co Roofing Tin adv, Jun 1898 calendar inset **15.00**
Certificate, Betsy Ross Flag Association, serial #38181, Series N, C H Weisgerber painting, 1917, 12 x 16" **40.00**
Flag, 36 stars, parade, mounted on stick, 5-point star design, 6,6,6,6,6,6, star pattern, 21½ x 36" **125.00**
Flag, 37 stars, parade, printed muslin, 1867–1877, 16 x 24" **40.00**
Pinback Button, Cleveland Yacht Club adv, sepia image of *Flagship Priscilla,* blue inscription "Inter lake Yachting Assn./Cleveland Yacht Club," stickpin shaft and small red, white, and blue fabric flag appendages, early 1900s **10.00**
Playing Cards, Delta Air Lines, Washington adv, color illus of American flag, capitol building, and Abraham Lincoln **10.00**
Pocket Mirror, multicolored, transport aircraft in flight against sunset sky under rippling flag **40.00**
Postcard, American flag, banner type sheet music for *Star Spangled Banner,* and stars illus, Int Art Co, NY **5.00**
Poster, "History of Old Glory," lithograph, Babbitt soap giveaway, 14 x 29" **145.00**
Sheet Music, *Our Flag,* Clark, 1859 . . . . . **25.00**
Sheet Music, *Stars and Stripes Forever,* J Philip Sousa, 1897 . . . . . **35.00**
Stickpin, metal, 13 stars, c1925, 2" l, ⅜ x ⅝" **4.00**
Toy, drum, emb flag and portrait of Admiral Dewey, orig drum sticks, c1899, 9" d **300.00**

Thermometer, souvenir, ceramic, pink, Made in Japan, 6" h, $5.00.

FLAMINGOS

The fabulous flamingo offers a wide range of collectibles, from a lovely art glass vase to those ever-present pink plastic yard birds. The most popular flamingos are the graceful ceramic figurines produced en masse in the late 1940s and early 1950s by such artists and companies as Will George, Brad Keeler, Maddux, Lane, and California Pottery. These figurines were sold mostly in pairs with one bird standing upright and the mate standing in a head-down position. Measurements for pairs always refers to the upright flamingo.

The raised wing or in-flight flamingos, TV lamps and planters are more difficult to find. A few white flamingos were produced, but they hold little interest to collectors compared to those birds depicted in dark rose and pink. Also highly prized are both the mirror-framed air-brushed prints produced by Turner and copycats from that period.

Advisor: Lynn Rogers, 1997 Sherman Ave., North Bend, OR 97459, (541) 756-4678.

Console Set, pr flamingos with bowl and candlesticks, Will George, 10" h **$395.00**
Demitasse Cup and Saucer, 2 birds **20.00**
Figure, bone china, raised wing, Kelvin, 2½" h **15.00**
Figure, elegant, Lefton China, 5½" h, price for pr **45.00**
Figure, elegant, Maddux, 9½" h **35.00**
Figure, large body, leaf base, unmkd, 11" h **65.00**
Figure, mother and 2 babies, raised wing, unmkd, 9" h **50.00**
Figure, papier-mâché, 48" h **75.00**
Figure, pot metal, Victorian, 6" h **35.00**
Planter, raised wing, Maddux, 6" h **35.00**
Plate, 2 birds and palms, Harker Brothers, 8¼" h **25.00**
Print, Turner, 2 flamingos, orig frame, 16 x 22" **75.00**
Television Lamp, Lane, 4" h **150.00**
Vase, art glass, huge leaves and flamingos, 15" h **250.00**

FLASHLIGHTS

Old flashlights have become collectible. They are generally not expensive and they can replace your emergency light. Most people take them for granted; however, they can be so much more than simple tools. There are beautiful, unusual, and decorative varieties. The flashlight was invented about 1896. In 1897, Conrad Hubert founded American Electrical Novelty and Manufacturing Company, which went on to become Eveready. The Eveready name appeared in 1899 as "Ever Ready."

Flashlights were so named because they would not give a steady stream of light. The batteries were very weak and bulbs were inefficient, only allowing it to be flashed on for a few moments at a time. The advances and design of the switch over time is often what makes one flashlight worth more than another.

What is there to collect in flashlights? Name brands, early lights, unusual lights, lanterns, military lights, comic character or personality lights, gun-shaped lights, penlights, novelty lights, new innovative lights, etc. Most collections grow in a haphazard way. You buy the ones in your price range. Some of the quality names in flashlights are Bond, Bright Star, Burgess, Eveready, Franco, French Flasher (Ray-O-Vac), Kwik-Lite, Micro-Lite, USA-Lite, and Winchester. Condition counts.

Advisor: Stuart Schneider, P.O. Box 64, Teaneck, NJ 07666, (201) 568-3336.

Club: Flashlight Collectors of America, P.O. Box 4095, Tustin, CA 92681.

Note: Price listed for flashlights in excellent working condition.

Advertising, Miller Beer, plastic, bottle shape **$12.00**
Bond, tubular light, copper, 1930s **22.00**
Burgess, "Snaplight," Art Deco, 1930s **45.00**
Eveready, house light, wood, 1910s **85.00**
Eveready, Masterlight Tablelight, chrome, black, 1936 . . . . **18.00**
Eveready, Tiffany pocket light, SS, 1912 . . . . **250.00**
Eveready, tubular light, nickel plated, 1920s **35.00**
Eveready, tubular light, nickel plated, 1930s **18.00**
Franco, pocket light, nickel plated, 1910s **35.00**
Kwik-Lite, nickle plated, opens in middle tubular light, 1920s **40.00**
Micro-Lite, "Space Satellite," 1956 . . . . **65.00**
Ray-O-Vac, Captain Ray-O-Vac, tubular light **50.00**
Ray-O-Vac, French Flasher, tubular light, 1915 . . . . **75.00**
Ray-O-Vac, Ray-O-Lite, tubular light, 1920 . . . . **40.00**
Stewart R Browne, tubular light, Bakelite, 1940 . . . . **30.00**
USA-Lite, "Red Head," tubular light, 1930s **175.00**
USA-Lite, "Silly Symphonies," 1936 . . . . **350.00**
Winchester, tubular light, copper and brass, 1937 . . . . **65.00**
Winchester, tubular light, patent date 1926 . . . . **65.00**
Winchester-Olin, tubular light, 1940s **35.00**
Winchester-Olin, tubular light, plastic **30.00**

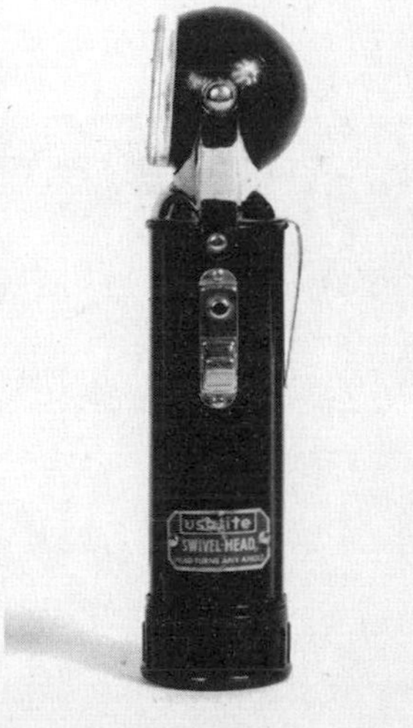

Top: Dacolite, Dynamo Hand Generator, 1940s, $25.00.
Right: USA-Lite, "Swivel Head," 1948, $45.00.

FLATWARE

Flatware refers to forks, knives, serving pieces, and spoons, There are four basic types of flatware: (1) sterling silver, (2) silver plated, (3) stainless, (4) Dirilyte.

Sterling silver flatware has a silver content of 925 parts silver per thousand. Knives have a steel or stainless steel blade. Silver plating refers to the elctroplating of a thin coating of pure silver, 1,000 parts silver per thousand, on a base metal such as brass, copper, or nickel silver. While steel only requires the addition of 13% of chromium to be classified stainless, most stainless steel flatware is made from an 18/8 formula, i.e., 18% chromium for strength and stain resistance and 8% nickel for a high luster and long-lasting finish. Dirilyte is an extremely hard, solid bronze alloy developed in Sweden in the early 1900s. Although gold in color, it has no gold in it.

Most flatware is purchased by individuals seeking to replace a damaged piece or to expand an existing pattern. Prices will vary widely, depending on what the seller had to pay and how he views the importance of the pattern. Prices listed below represent what a modern replacement service quotes a customer.

Abbreviations used in the listings include:

FH	Flat Handle	SS	Sterling Silver
HH	Hollow Handle	ST	Stainless Steel
SP	Silver Plated		

Dirilyte, Regal, baby spoon, $5^{1}/_{8}$" $25.00
Dirilyte, Regal, bonbon spoon, $5^{3}/_{4}$" 25.00
Dirilyte, Regal, butter spreader, FH, $7^{1}/_{4}$" 25.00
Dirilyte, Regal, cocktail fork, 6" 20.00
Dirilyte, Regal, fork, 7" 22.00
Dirilyte, Regal, iced tea spoon, $8^{3}/_{8}$" 22.00
Dirilyte, Regal, serving fork, cold meat, $8^{5}/_{8}$" 50.00
Gorham, Andante, SS, fork, $7^{1}/_{8}$" 55.00
Gorham, Andante, SS, knife, HH, modern blade, 9" 40.00
Gorham, Andante, SS, sugar spoon, $5^{7}/_{8}$" 45.00
Gorham, Colonial Tipt, ST, butter knife, HH, 7" 12.00
Gorham, Colonial Tipt, ST, gravy ladle, 7" 17.00
Gorham, Colonial Tipt, ST, iced tea spoon, $7^{3}/_{4}$" 10.00
Gorham, Melon Bud, ST, fork, 8" 10.00
Gorham, Melon Bud, ST, knife, HH, modern blade, $9^{1}/_{4}$" 15.00
Gorham, Melon Bud, ST, iced tea spoon, $7^{5}/_{8}$" 10.00
International, Joan of Arc, SS, butter serving knife, HH, 7" 32.00

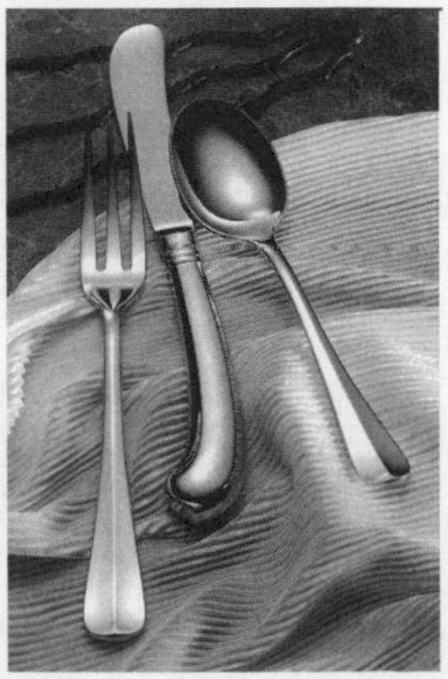

Gorham, Colonial Tipt, ST, Fork, $8^{1}/_{8}$", $10.00; Knife, pistol grip, modern blade, $9^{1}/_{4}$", $15.00; Teaspoon, $6^{1}/_{8}$", $7.00.

Oneida, Alexis, ST, Salad Fork, $6^{3}/_{4}$", $12.00; Fork, $7^{1}/_{4}$", $15.00; Knife, HH, modern blade, 9", $15.00; Tablespoon, $8^{3}/_{8}$", $15.00; Teaspoon, 6", $10.00.

International, Joan of Arc, SS, carving knife, ST blade, $10^{3}/_{4}$" 50.00
International, Joan of Arc, SS, cream soup spoon, round bowl, 6" 40.00
International, Joan of Arc, SS, soup spoon, $7^{1}/_{4}$" 45.00
Oneida, Alexis, ST, cocktail fork, 6" 10.00
Oneida, Alexis, ST, gravy ladle, $7^{3}/_{4}$" 17.00
Oneida, Alexis, ST, iced tea spoon, $7^{5}/_{8}$" 12.00
Oneida, Heiress, SS, butter spreader, FH, $5^{3}/_{4}$" 20.00
Oneida, Heiress, SS, fork, $7^{1}/_{8}$" 40.00
Oneida, Heiress, SS, salad fork, $6^{1}/_{4}$" 30.00
Oneida, Twin Star, ST, butter serving knife, FH, $6^{5}/_{4}$" 12.00
Oneida, Twin Star, ST, infant feeding spoon, $5^{5}/_{8}$" 15.00
Oneida, Twin Star, ST, salad fork, $6^{1}/_{4}$" 10.00
Oneida, Twin Star, ST, tablespoon, pierced, $8^{3}/_{8}$" 15.00
Wallace, Waltz of Spring, SS, butter spreader, HH, padded ST blade, $6^{1}/_{4}$" 32.00
Wallace, Waltz of Spring, SS, gravy ladle, HH, ST bowl, $8^{1}/_{4}$" 50.00
Wallace, Waltz of Spring, SS, steak knife, $9^{3}/_{8}$" 55.00
Wallace, Waltz of Spring, SS, teaspoon 35.00

FLORENCE CERAMICS

Florence Ward of Pasadena, California, began making ceramic objects as a form of therapy in dealing with the loss of a young son. The products she produced and sold from her garage workshop provided pin money during the Second World War.

With the support of Clifford, her husband, and Clifford, Jr., their son, Florence Ward moved her ceramics business to a plant on the east side of Pasadena in 1946. Business boomed after Ward exhibited at several Los Angeles gift shows. In 1949 a state-of-the-art plant was built at 74 South San Garbiel Boulevard, Pasadena.

Florence Ceramics is best known for its figural pieces, often costumed in Colonial and Godey fashions. The company also produced birds, busts, candle holders, lamps, smoking sets, and wall pockets. Betty Davenport Ford joined the company in 1956, designing a line of bisque animal figures. Production ended after two years.

Scripto Corporation bought Florence Ceramics in 1964 following the death of Clifford Ward. Production was shifted to advertising specialty ware. Operations ceased in 1977.

Club: Florence Collector's Club, P.O. Box 122, Richland, WA 99352.

Amelia, brown, $9^{1}/_{4}$" h $150.00
Belle 125.00

Camille, blue, 9" h **225.00**
Douglas, white **230.00**
Elizabeth **325.00**
Gary, green **230.00**
Jeannette **160.00**
Joyce, pink **280.00**
Lady Pompadour **300.00**
Lillian, gray **110.00**
Marie Antionette **430.00**
Marilyn **125.00**
Melanie **125.00**
Rose Marie, rose **290.00**
Shi-Ti and Kui, white, pr **430.00**
Wickum Boy and Girl, pr **240.00**

FOOD MOLDS

Commercial ice cream and chocolate molds appear to be the collectors' favorites. Buying them is now a bit risky because of the large number of reproductions. Beware of all Santa and rabbit molds.

Country collectors have long touted the vast array of kitchen food molds, ranging from butter prints to Turk's head cake molds. Look for molds with signs of use and patina.

Do not forget the Jell-O molds. If you grew up in the 1950s or 1960s, you ate Jell-O and plenty of it. The aluminum Jell-O molds came in a tremendous variety of shapes and sizes. Most sell between 10¢ and $1, cheap by any stretch of the imagination.

Butter, deep carved geometric design, rect cased, cherry, 4½ x 6⅞" **$110.00**
Cake, Santa Shape-A-Cake, orig instructions, MIB **8.50**
Chocolate, bicycle with boy, 2 parts, 8¾" **375.00**
Chocolate, cowboy, tin, clamp style **48.00**
Chocolate, heart, 2 cavities, 6½ x 6" **65.00**
Chocolate, teddy bear, 2 pcs, clamp type, mkd "Reiche" **275.00**
Chocolate, turkey, pewter **35.00**
Cookie, basket with leaves and grape hyacinths, cast iron, oval, c1830, 4 x 6" **165.00**
Cookie, leaf, stamped tin, c1904 . . . . **10.00**
Food, grapes and leaf center design, oval, Wedgwood Creamware, 3 x 5 x 7" **110.00**
Food, turk's head, redware, swirled fluting, brown sponged rim, 9" d **45.00**
Ice Cream, asparagus, pewter, individual, 3⅝" **25.00**
Ice Cream, castle, chess game piece, mkd "S & Co" **60.00**
Ice Cream, pear, mkd "S & Co, #17" **250.00**
Ice Cream, smoking pipe, pewter **65.00**
Maple Candy, fruit and foliage design, wood, 2 part, 5½ x 8" **28.00**
Pudding, pineapple, tin and copper, oval **65.00**

FOOTBALL CARDS

Football cards are hot. It was bound to happen. The price of baseball cards has reached the point where even some of the common cards are outside the price range of the average collector. If you cannot afford baseball, why not try football?

Football card collecting is not as sophisticated as baseball card collecting. However, it will be. Smart collectors who see a similarity between the two collecting areas are beginning to stress Pro-Bowlers and NFL All-Stars. Stay away from the World Football material. The league is a loser among collectors, just as it was in real life.

Periodicals: *Beckett Football Card Magazine,* 15850 Dallas Parkway, Dallas, TX 75248; *Sports Cards,* 700 E. State St., Iola, WI 54990; *Tuff Stuff,* P.O. Box 569, Dubuque, IA 52004.

Note: The prices listed below are for cards in good condition.

Bowman, 1948, complete set (108) **$800.00**
Bowman, 1948, common card (1-108) **2.50**
Bowman, 1948, #80, Bill Dudley **12.50**
Bowman, 1950, complete set (144) **500.00**
Bowman, 1950, common card (1-144) **2.50**
Bowman, 1950, #72, Bill Johnson **2.50**
Bowman, 1951, complete set (144) **425.00**
Bowman, 1951, common card **2.30**
Bowman, 1951, #61, Don Doll **2.50**
Bowman, 1953, complete set (96) **350.00**
Bowman, 1953, common card **3.00**
Bowman, 1953, #43, Frank Gifford SP **40.00**
Bowman, 1955, complete set (160) **200.00**
Bowman, 1955, common card (65-160) **1.00**
Bowman, 1955, #152, Tom Landry **22.00**
Fleer, 1960, complete set (132) **100.00**
Fleer, 1960, common card . . . . **.45**
Fleer, 1960, #4, Bob White . . . . **.50**
Fleer, 1962, complete set (88) **105.00**
Fleer, 1962, common card . . . . **.75**
Fleer, 1962, #39, Goose Gonsoulin **1.00**
Fleer, 1963, complete set (88) **230.00**
Fleer, 1963, common card **1.00**
Fleer, 1963, #87, Chuck Gavin **1.00**
Philadelphia Gum, 1964, complete set (198) **115.00**
Philadelphia Gum, 1964, common card . . . . **.25**
Philadlephia Gum, 1964, #139, Philadelphia Eagles . . . . **.25**
Philadelphia Gum, 1965, complete set (198) **100.00**
Philadelphia Gum, 1965, common card . . . . **.25**
Philadlephia Gum, 1965, #19, Mike Ditka **3.80**
Philadelphia Gum, 1967, complete set (198) **80.00**
Philadelphia Gum, 1967, common card . . . . **.22**
Philadlephia Gum, 1967, #1, Atlanta Falcons . . . . **.22**
Pinnacle, 1992, complete set (13) **11.50**
Pinnacle, 1992, common card . . . . **.50**
Pinnacle, 1992, #6, Michael Irvin/Eric Allen **1.00**
Playoff, 1994, complete set (336) **6.00**
Playoff, 1994, common card . . . . **.02**
Playoff, 1994, #1, Joe Montana . . . . **.50**
Score, 1990, complete set (660) . . . . **.95**
Score, 1990, common card . . . . **.01**
Score, #40, Boomer Esiason . . . . **.02**
Topps, 1957, complete set (154) **275.00**
Topps, 1957, common card (1-88) . . . . **.50**
Topps, 1957, #59, Kyle Rote **1.25**
Topps, 1959, complete set (176) **115.00**
Topps, 1959, common card (1-88) . . . . **.30**
Topps, 1959, #46, Green Bay Packers . . . . **.40**
Topps, 1965, complete set (176) **500.00**
Topps, 1965, common card . . . . **.95**
Topps, 1965, #122, Joe Namath **200.00**
Topps, 1967, complete set (132) **80.00**
Topps, 1967, common card . . . . **.40**
Topps, 1967, #25, Ron McDole . . . . **.40**
Topps, 1968, #65, Joe Namath **38.00**

Topps, 1970, complete set (263) **57.50**
Topps, 1970, common card (1-132) . . . . **.09**
Topps, 1970, #50, Daryle Lamonica . . . . **.40**
Topps, 1975, complete set (528) **38.00**
Topps, 1975, common card . . . . **.04**
Topps, 1975, #33, Bubba Smith . . . . **.25**
Topps, 1975, #163, Tom Dempsey . . . . **.05**

FOOTBALL COLLECTIBLES

At the moment, this category is heavily weighted toward professional football. Do not overlook some great college memorabilia. Local pride dominates most collecting. Taking an item back to its hometown often doubles its value. Because of their limited production and the tendency of most individuals to discard them within a short time, some of the hardest things to find are game promotional giveaways. Also check the breweriana collectors. A surprising number of beer companies sponsor football broadcasts. Go Bud Light!

Periodical: *Sports Collectors Digest,* 700 E. State St., Iola, WI 54990.

Beer Can, 1975 Steelers Commemorative, aluminum, Iron City Beer, 12 oz, 5" h **$15.00**
Book, *American Football,* Walter Camp, NY, 1st ed, 1891 . . . . **660.00**
Booklet, *Gulf Football Manual,* Gulf Oil premium, 1933, 24 pp **5.00**
Cigarette Lighter, Baltimore Colts, musical, MIB **75.00**
Game, All-American Football, Cadaco, 1960 . . . . **30.00**
Magazine, *All-Pro Football,* Johnny Unitas, 1959 . . . . **43.00**
Magazine, *Football Digest,* Chuck Bednarik, 1948 . . . . **70.00**
Magazine, *Sports Today,* Joe Namath, 1971 . . . . **20.00**
Media Guide, Dallas Cowboys, helmet, 1964 . . . . **18.00**
Media Guide, Miami Dolphins, logo and year, 1970 . . . . **12.00**
Media Guide, NY Giants, logl, 1955 . . . . **25.00**
Nodder, Atlanta Falcons, gold round base **25.00**
Nodder, Green Bay Packers, composition, inked "1961 Champions" **50.00**
Patch, Super Bowl V, Baltimore and Dallas, 1970 . . . . **60.00**
Pennant, St Louis Cardinals, felt, red and white, c1967 . . . . . **15.00**
Pinback Button, St Louis Cardinals, black, red, and white, football and cardinal, 1960s **5.00**
Program, Lincoln University vs Howard University, 1949 . . . . **15.00**
Program, National Football Conference Championship, Minnesota vs LA Rams, 1974 . . . . **18.00**
Ticket, AFC Wild Card, Houston vs Miami, 1976 . . . . **10.00**

Magazine Cover, *The Saturday Evening Post,* Nov 15, 1913, J. C. Leyendecker illus, sepia and red, 10¼ x 14", $35.00.

Ticket, Ohio State, seating diagram on back, 1978 . . . . **1.50**
Ticket Stub, 1955 NFL Championship **65.00**
Ticket Stub, 1971 Super Bowl VI **45.00**
Yearbook, Buffalo Bills, 1989 . . . . **6.00**
Yearbook, St Louis Cardinals, 1967 . . . . **30.00**

FOSTORIA GLASS

The Fostoria Glass Company was founded in Fostoria, Ohio, in 1887 and moved to Moundsville, West Virginia, in 1891. In 1983 Lancaster Colony purchased the company but produced glass under the Fostoria trademark.

Fostoria is collected by pattern, with the American pattern the most common and sought after. Other patterns include Baroque, Georgian, Holly, Midnight Rose, Navarre, Rhapsody, and Wister. Hazel Weatherman's *Fostoria, Its First Fifty Years,* published by the author about 1972, helps identify patterns.

Clubs: Fostoria Glass Collectors, P.O. Box 1625, Orange, CA 92856; Fostoria Glass Society of America, P.O. Box 826, Moundsville, WV 26041.

American, basket, reed handle **$95.00**
American, butter, cov, ¼ lb **30.00**
American, cake plate, 3 toed **22.00**
American, hat, 3" h **20.00**
American, juice tumbler, 5 oz **8.00**
Baroque, cake plate, 10" d **12.00**
Bouquet, goblet **28.00**
Century, basket, 10" l **100.00**
Century, bowl, 3 ftd, rolled, 10½" d **55.00**
Century, mayonnaise, orig liner **30.00**
Chintz, comport, 5½" d **40.00**
Coin, bowl, #1372, blue, 8" d **50.00**
Coin, nappy, #1372, green, handle, 5⅜" d **40.00**
Colony, bonbon, #2412, 7" d **14.00**
Colony, bowl, #2412, 12" d **35.00**
Colony, lemon dish, #2412 . . . . **15.00**
Heather, wine, #6037 . . . . **35.00**
Heirloom, pitcher, yellow opalescent, 9" h **85.00**
Jamestown, sherbet, amethyst, 6½ oz **15.00**
Pinecone, bowl, flared, 12" d **45.00**
Pioneer, coaster, green **6.00**
Versailles, goblet, blue **45.00**
Vesper, platter, green, 11" l **100.00**

FRANCISCAN

Charles Gladding, Peter McBean, and George Chambers organized the Gladding, McBean and Company pottery in 1875. Located in California, the firm's early products included sewer pipes and architectural items. In 1934 the company began producing dinnerware under the Franciscan trademark. The earliest forms consisted of plain shapes and bright colors. Later, the company developed molded, underglaze patterns such as Desert Rose, Apple, and Ivy.

Franciscan ware can be found with a great variety of marks—over 80 were used. Many of the marks include the pattern name and patent dates and numbers.

Club: *Franciscan Collectors Club,* 8412 5th Ave. NE, Seattle, WA 98115.

Apple, ashtray **$15.00**
Apple, berry bowl **3.50**
Apple, cigarette box **95.00**
Apple, compote, large **60.00**
Apple, cream soup **8.00**
Apple, cup and saucer, jumbo **50.00**
Apple, gravy boat and underplate **30.00**
Apple, luncheon plate, 9½" d **8.00**
Apple, milk pitcher, 6¼" h **70.00**
Apple, relish, 3 part **75.00**
Apple, salad plate, 10" d **115.00**
Apple, sherbet, ftd **24.00**
Apple, soup bowl, ftd **32.00**
Apple, teapot, cov **95.00**
Coronado, bread and butter plate, yellow, 6½" d **3.50**
Coronado, chocolate set, pot, after dinner cups and saucers, turquoise **90.00**
Coronado, cream soup, with underplate **20.00**
Coronado, demitasse cup and saucer, yellow **14.00**
Desert Rose, butter pat **18.00**
Desert Rose, cereal bow, 6" d **14.00**
Desert Rose, cup and saucer **8.00**
Desert Rose, gravy, with liner **35.00**
Desert Rose, dinner plate, 9½" d **14.00**
Desert Rose, salt and pepper shakers, pr, small, rosebud **20.00**
Desert Rose, soup bowl, ftd, 5½" d **17.50**
Desert Rose, vegetable bowl, divided, 10" d **45.00**
Desert Rose, water pitcher **100.00**
Duet Rose, ashtray, large **35.00**
Duet Rose, cup and saucer **10.00**
Duet Rose, salad plate **8.00**
Duet Rose, vegetable bowl, oval **18.00**
Eldorado, creamer and sugar, gold and gray **18.00**
Eldorado, salt and pepper shakers, pr, gold and gray **8.00**
Ivy, cereal bowl **25.00**
Ivy, cup and saucer **40.00**
Ivy, water tumbler **40.00**
Poppy, dinner plate, 10" d **40.00**
Sycamore, creamer **3.00**
Sycamore, dinner plate **4.00**
Wildflower, salad plate **75.00**

FRANKART

Every time there is an Art Deco revival, Frankart gets rediscovered. Frankart was founded in the mid 1920s by Arthur Von Frankenberg, a sculptor and artist. The key is to remember that his pieces were mass-produced.

Frankart figures are identified through form and style, not specific features. Do I have to tell you that the nudes are the most collectible? Probably not. Nudes are always collectible. Do not overlook other human figures or animals.

Almost every Frankart piece is marked with the company name followed by a patent number or "pat. appl. for." Avoid unmarked pieces that dealers are trying to pass as Frankart. Frankenberg's wares were frequently copied during the late 1920s and early 1930s.

Ashtray, caricatured monkey supporting 3" d glass ash receiver in tail, 7" h **$85.00**
Ashtray, nude figure growing from tobacco plant holding scalloped glass tray overhead, 25" h **625.00**
Bookends, pr, antelopes leaping **275.00**
Bookends, pr, horse heads, flowing manes **45.00**
Centerpiece Bowl, 8½" h nude, 15" d dish, flower frog **275.00**
Figure, elk, bronze patina finish, 6¼" h **120.00**
Lamp, 2 back to back dancing nudes supporting 11" sq glass cylinder satin finish shade **750.00**
Lamp, nude holding globe, #L210 . . . . **500.00**
Smoker's Set, seated nude leaning back, geometric base, arms resting on removable glass box, 3" d removable glass ashtray at feet, 7" h **285.00**

FRANKOMA

This is one of those potteries, such as Gonder and Hull, that runs hot and cold. Last edition, I suggested it was freezing. There has been a mild thaw, especially in the Midwest. Frankoma is great fifties. It's just that collectors and dealers have not yet discovered it as such.

In 1933 John N. Frank, a ceramic art instructor at Oklahoma University, founded Frankoma, Oklahoma's first commercial pottery. Originally located in Norman, it eventually moved to Sapulpa, Oklahoma, in 1938. A series of disastrous fires, the last in 1983, struck the plant. Look for pieces bearing a pacing leopard mark. These pieces are earlier than pieces marked "FRANKOMA."

Club: Frankoma Family Collectors Assoc, P.O. Box 32571, Oklahoma City, OK 73123.

Bookend, mountain girl, #425 . . . . **$94.00**
Bowl, cactus, carved, 10" d **40.00**
Christmas Card, 1969 . . . . **18.50**
Compote, Gracetone, pine cone, #85 . . . . **20.00**
Creamer and Sugar, #42/A **66.00**
Figure, circus horse, #138, Ada **130.00**
Figure, coyote, Willard Stone, #102 . . . . **15.50**
Figure, panther, green, sgd, early, 7½" l **40.00**
Figure, squirrel, Willard Stone, #105 . . . . **15.50**
Flower Holder, duck, #184, prairie green **368.50**
Lazybones, soup cup, #4SC, brown satin, Sapulpa **7.00**
Match Holder, #89A, royal blue, 1942 . . . . **40.00**
Mug, Political, donkey, 1980 . . . . **13.00**
Mug, Political, elephant, 1972 . . . . **20.00**
Pitcher, #835, 24 oz **25.00**
Plainsman, creamer, #5A, flame **5.00**
Plainsman, dinner plate, #5F, desert gold, 10½" d **12.00**
Planter, elephant, #390 . . . . **15.25**
Planter, pig, #391 . . . . **23.00**
Plate, Bicentennial Series, 1976 . . . . **7.00**
Plate, Christmas, 1977 . . . . **8.00**

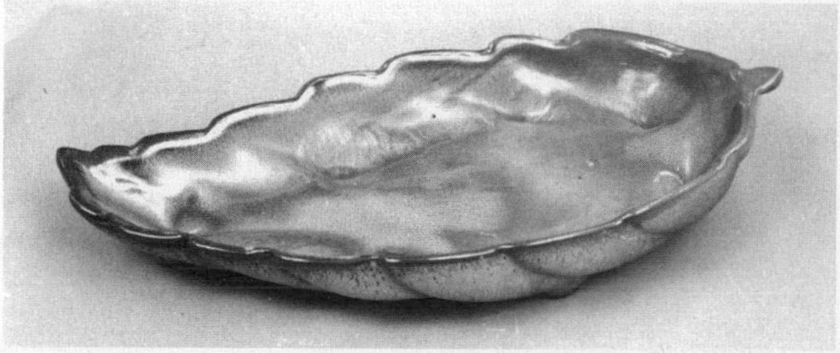

Dish, leaf shaped, Gracetone, green and brown, ftd, imp "Frankoma 226," 12¼" l, 6⅛" w, 1⅞" h, $15.00.

Refrigerator Jug, #86, prairie green **100.00**
Salt and Pepper Shakers, pr, barrel, #97H **37.00**
Salt and Pepper Shakers, pr, wagon wheel, #94H **16.00**
Saucer, #94E, desert gold, Ada **5.00**
Teacup, #5CC, prairie green, 5 oz **8.00**
Trivet, eagle, #2TR **66.00**
Vase, #228, swan, prairie green, Sapulpa **15.00**
Wall Pocket, boot, #133 . . . . **20.00**

FRATERNAL ORDER COLLECTIBLES

In the 1990s few individuals understand the dominant societal role played by fraternal orders and benevolent societies between 1850 and 1950. Because many had membership qualifications that were prejudicial, these "secret" societies often were targets for the social activists of the 1960s.

As the 20th century ends, America as a nation of joiners also seems to be ending. Many fraternal and benevolent organizations have disbanded. A surprising amount of their material has worked its way into the market. Lodge hall material is often given a "folk art" label and correspondingly high price.

The symbolism is fun. Some of the convention souvenir objects are downright funky. Costumes are great for dress-up. Do not pay big money for them. Same goes for ornamental swords.

Benevolent & Protective Order of Elks, bookmark, elk's head, SS **$18.00**
Benevolent & Protective Order of Elks, matchbook cover **2.25**
Benevolent & Protective Order of Elks, plate, elk's head, BPOE & 463, Johnson Bros, England, 10" d **45.00**
Brotherhood of Railroad Trainsmen, shaving mug, "S.T. Shope," base stamped "J.S. Germany," 3³/₄" h **165.00**
Fraternal Order of Eagles and Shriners, shaving mug, "J.E. Henkel," 3⁵/₈" h **110.00**
Fraternal Order of the Eagle No. 293, shaving mug, "Bill Wagner," base stamped "P. Germany" and "P. Eismann 4.11" in gold, 3³/₄" h **209.00**
Fraternal Order of Elks, shaving mug, "Liberty, Truth, Justice, Equality," eagle standing on rock **15.00**
Independent Order of Odd Fellows, ribbon, Michigan, red and black, Sep 1893 . . . . **25.00**
Knights of Columbus, postcard, Knights of Columbus Hut, U S Training Station, Newport, RI, Albertype Co, Brooklyn, NY **3.50**
Knights of Templar, souvenir book, adv, 160 pp, 1895 . . . . **30.00**
Masonic, Bible, leather binding, illus, 22 k gold stamping, 1,200 pp, c1931, 9¹/₂ x 11¹/₂ x 2¹/₂" **65.00**

Plate, 51st Annual Conclave Knights Temple of Penna, No. 75, York, PA, 1904, 9" d, $25.00.

Masonic, book, *Revised Encyclopedia of Freemasonry,* 2 vol, illus, 1,217 pp, 1929 . . . . **55.00**
Masonic, certificate, Maine, membership in Lodge 86, ornate, red printing **15.00**
Masonic, cigar box label, Infinity, Masonic symbols **45.00**
Order of Odd Fellows, booklet, *Odd Fellows Pillar Encampment,* rules, practices, and member information, 50 pp, 1905 . . . . **11.00**
Order of Eastern Star, pencil, mechanical **15.00**
Shrine, letter opener, 32nd emblem, c1920 . . . . **20.00**
Shrine, tie tack, gold, jeweled dec **28.00**

FROG COLLECTIBLES

A frog collector I know keeps her collection in the guest bathroom. All the fixtures are green also. How long do you think it took me to find the toilet? Thank goodness I have good bladder control.

In fairy tales frogs usually received good press. Not true for their cousin, the toad. Television introduced us to Kermit the Frog, thus putting to rest the villainous frog image of Froggy the Gremlin. I am willing to bet Froggy's "magic twanger" would not get past today's TV censors.

Club: The Frog Pond, P.O. Box 193, Beech Grove, IN 46107.

Advertising Trade Card, frogs dressed as sailors, smoking pipe and cigarette, Austin, Nichols & Co, NY **$25.00**
Bank, Leap Frog, cast iron **145.00**
Clicker, Life of Party Products, Kirchhof, Newark, NJ, 3" l **6.00**
Figure, frog with black eyes and clear crown, #7642nr48, Swarovski Crystal, SC or swan logo **90.00**
Figure, frog sitting on leaf, Vienna, 1" h **25.00**
Game, Frantic Frogs, Milton Bradley, 1965 . . . . **20.00**
Game, Frog Who Would A-Wooing Go **60.00**
Planter, frog playing instruments near water lily, 3 x 3" **12.00**
Snowdome, Kermit the Frot, sitting on brown trunk, clear dome, round base, mkd "Koziol" on bottom, 1980s, 3¹/₂ x 3" **20.00**
Stickpin, bronze, figural frog wearing suit, c1900 . . . . **20.00**
Stuffed Animal, felt, orig neck tag, 4" **45.00**
Stuffed Animal, frog smoking pipe, 8" h **45.00**
Wind-up, cloth over tin, glass eyes, Germany **50.00**

FRUIT JARS

Most fruit jars that you find are worth less than $1. Their value rests in reuse for canning rather than in the collectors' market. Do not be fooled by patent dates that appear on the jar. Over 50 different types of jars bear a patent date of 1858 and many were made as long as 50 years later.

However, there are some expensive fruit jars. A good price guide is Douglas M. Leybourne, Jr.'s *The Collector's Guide to Old Fruit Jars: Red Book No. 8*, published privately by the author in 1997.

Clubs: Ball Collectors Club, 22203 Doncaster, Riverview, WI 48192; Federation of Historical Bottle Collectors, Inc., 88 Sweetbriar Branch, Longwood, FL 32750; Midwest Antique Fruit Jar & Bottle Club, P.O. Box 38, Flat Rock, IN 47234.

Newsletter: *Fruit Jar Newsletter*, 364 Gregory Ave., West Orange, NJ 07052.

"Clarke/Fruit Jar Co./Cleveland O.," aqua, 1/2 gal, smooth base, ground lip, orig glass lid and metal closure, $50.00. Photo courtesy Glass-Works Auctions.

Amazon Swift Seal, clear, glass lid, wire bail, qt **$5.00**
Atlas Special, blue, zinc lid, pt **25.00**
Ball Deluxe, clear, glass lid, wire bail, pt **4.00**
Bulach, green, glass lid, wire clip, qt **3.00**
Canton Domestic, clear, glass lid, wire bail, qt **75.00**
Durham, green, glass lid, wire bail, qt **15.00**
Federal, olive, glass lid, wire bail, qt **95.00**
Gem, clear, glass lid, screw band, 1908 . . . . **6.00**
Globe, amber, pt **88.00**
Heroine, The, aqua, glass lid, screw band, qt **30.00**
J P Smith & Son Co, Pittsburgh, aqua, wax seal, qt **35.00**
Kentucky L G Co, green, wax seal, qt **35.00**
Kerr Economy Trade Mark, clear, metal lid, clip, pt **4.00**
Mason's, Improved, light green, qt **15.00**
Mason's, Sealtite Wide Mouth, green, metal screw top, qt **10.00**
Mason's, Shield union, aqua, mismatched zinc lid **240.00**
Pacific S F Glass Works, aqua, glass lid, screw band, qt **30.00**
Swayees Improved Mason, amber, qt **38.00**
Victory, clear, glass lid, top emb "Victory Reg'd 1925," pt **5.00**
Weidman Boy Brand, Cleveland, clear, glass lid, wire bail, pt **6.00**
Woodbury, aqua, glass lid, metal clip, pt **25.00**

FURNITURE

Much of the furniture found at flea markets is of the secondhand variety.

Bar Seat, painted metal, foliate back, hide seat **$75.00**
Bed, mahogany veneer, incised lines, applied decorative medallions, shell shaped crest, 4 turned high posts, 1920, 50" h **200.00**
Bed, maple, 24" w, 73" d, 28" h **250.00**
Bedroom Suite, maple, twin bed, chest of drawers, matching wall mirror, night stand with 1 drawer **125.00**
Blanket Chest, pine, hinged lid, dovetailed case and base molding, brown rainbow shaped vinegar graining, light blue trim, lid replaced, 38 1/2" w, 17" d, 16 1/2" h **170.00**
Blanket Chest, walnut veneer, cedar lined, diamond shaped molding on front, Lane, 1930s **150.00**
Bookcase, mahogany and mahogany veneer, molded top, pr glazed doors with Gothic type mullions, adjustable shelved int, French Restauration scrolling feet **400.00**
Candlestand, cherry stain, tilt top, splayed legs, 25 1/2" w, 16 1/2" d, 27 1/4" h **225.00**
Chair, armchair, tiger's eye maple, brown leather inserts, red lacquered fretwork, 1935 . . . . **500.00**
Chair, caned back, armchair, laminated ash, leather seat cushion, metal tag, Edward Wormley for Dunbar, 32 x 24 1/2 x 23" **225.00**
Chair, ladderback, armchair, maple, acorn finials, 4 slats, woven splint seat, 44" h **75.00**
Chair, ladderback, dining, accentuated flaring tall back with 6 vertical slats, woven reed seat, Italian black lacquered finish, c1950, 46 x 17 x 17", price for 6 . . . . . . **850.00**
Chair, overstuffed, matching overstuffed ottoman, carved mahogany frame, foliage carved apron, carved scrolling legs, animal paw front feet, new cut velvet floral upholstery, 36 1/2" h, price for 2 pcs **50.00**
China Cabinet, oak, bow front, convex glass side panels, 4 shelves, mirrored back, 1920s, 38" w, 60" h **575.00**
Coffee Table, kidney shape, walnut frame, blue glass top . . . **175.00**
Coffee Table, turtle shaped top, 4 pc V-matched striped walnut veneer, center bleached striped walnut veneer, holly inlay border, 4 red dyed flower accents, cabriole legs with carved knees, 34" w, 19" d, 17" h **180.00**
Cradle, walnut, heart cutout on headboard and footboard, scrolled headboard, arched footboard, dovetailed case, shaped runners, c1839 . . . . **650.00**
Desk, child's, oak, roll top, 3 drawers, matching chair **125.00**
Dining Table, extension, walnut veneer, molded apron, 6 legs, U-shaped stretchers, 1925, 60" w **175.00**
Dining Table, Hepplewhite style, mahogany, inlay, D-shaped drop leaf ends, 78" l, 46" w, 29 1/2" h, minor wear and damage **100.00**
Dressing Table, oak, adjustable side mirrors, arched center mirror, 2 small drawers, scalloped apron, long front cabriole legs, straight back legs, 1925 . . . . **250.00**
Jelly Cupboard, poplar, 2 nailed drawers over double raised panel doors, wooden pulls, cutout feet, brown paint, burn grained door panels and drawer fronts, nailed repair on 1 door, 41" w, 14 1/2" d, 54 1/4" h **400.00**
Night Stand, walnut, waterfall veneer, open shelf above single cupboard door, 1935 . . . . **200.00**
Parlor Table, oak, sq top, spiral turned legs, base shelf, claw and ball feet **175.00**
Piano Bench, oak, rect top, sq legs, 40" w **125.00**
Plant Stand, Regency style, mahogany, 3 tiers, 3 legs, brass feet, 10 1/2" d, 47" h, c1930, price for pr **250.00**
Porch Rocker, woven splint back and seat, wide arms **95.00**
Sewing Stand, Priscilla type, painted red, dark trim, floral decal, rod carrying handle, 1930s, 25" h **28.00**

Sidechairs, contemporary, maple, orig green fabric upholstery, orig finish, designed by Paul McCobb for O'Hearn Furniture Co, unmkd, c1950, price for set of 4, $167.50. Photo courtesy David Rago Auctions.

Side Table, walnut, 2 board top, single drawer frieze with turned knob handle, sq tapered legs, old refinishing, 30" w, 28¼" d, 28½" h **525.00**
Telephone Stand, cherry and poplar, gently curved sides and front, single dovetailed drawer, high back, cutout sides, old worn finish, 23" w, 14¾" d, 36" h **250.00**
TV Stand, champagne oak finish, rect top, canted sides, medial shelf, bowed half-round tapered legs, color and maker's mark stamped on underside of shelf, Heywood-Wakefield, 26" w, 24½" d, 26" h, refinished . . . **300.00**
Vanity, walnut, large round mirror, flanked by two 3-drawer sections, dropped center well, 1935. . . . . **250.00**
Work Table, 1 board top, sq legs, base shelf, sq nail construction, worn red paint, loose top, 21" w, 15¼" d, 24" h **150.00**

GAMBLING COLLECTIBLES

Casinos and other types of gambling are spreading across the country, just as they did over a century ago. Gaming devices, gaming accessories, and souvenirs from gambling establishments—from hotels to riverboats—are all collectible.

Gambling collectors compete with Western collectors for the same material. Sometimes the gunfight gets bloody. With the price of old, i.e., late nineteenth- and early twentieth-century, gambling material skyrocketing, many new collectors are focusing on more modern material dating from the speakeasies of the 1920s and the glitz of Las Vegas in the 1950s and 1960s.

You might as well pick up modern examples when you can. Some places last only slightly longer than a throw of the dice. Atlantic City has already seen the Atlantis and Playboy disappear. Is Trump's Taj Mahal next?

Club: Casino Chip & Gaming Token Collectors Club, P.O. Box 63, Brick, NJ 08723.

Ashtray, cigar, glass, brass rim, cigar rests, and match holder int design of hand holding 5 playing cards, c1900, 5½" d **$70.00**
Book, *Confessions of a Poker Player,* by "King Jack," NY, I Washburn, Inc, 209 pp, 1940 . . . . **20.00**
Book, *The Game of Draw Poker,* John Keller, NY, 1887, 84 pp, 4½ x 4¼". **25.00**
Card Box, black lacquer, rect, double deck, 4 etched silver cards on lid, c1880, 5 x 6½ x 1½" **110.00**
Card Press, dovetailed, holds 10 decks, handle, 9½ x 4½ x 3". **140.00**
Cigarette Lighter, emb, poker chips and enameled aces on sides, Sgt Lee, c1945 . . . . **27.50**
Dice, weighted, always total 12, set of 3 . . . . **35.00**

Card and Chip Caddy, Bakelite, butterscotch, with over 150 Bakelite chips, 7¼ x 3¼", $201.25. Photo courtesy Jackson's Auctioneers & Appraisers.

Tavern Horse Race Game, counter top, foreign machine with pay out, colorful dial, 27" h, $302.50. Photo courtesy Collectors Auction Services.

Matchsafe, roulette, enameled roulette wheel, c1900 . . . . . . **550.00**
Poker Chip Box, wood, rect, woodburned dec, horse head framed by horseshoe and cards, above banner inscribed "Good Luck," fitted int, c1920, 7 x 10 x 2" **30.00**
Poker Chips, ivory, scrimshawed, eagle **30.00**
Poker Chips, molded rubber, dollar **4.00**
Poker Dice, leather cup. **35.00**
Roulette Wheel, wood, inlaid dec, F Denzleer, Denver, CO, 31½" d **75.00**
Slot Machine, Keeney, Operator Bell, 25¢, counter top model, oak and metal cabinet, 16 x 25 x 16". **1,450.00**
Slot Machine, Mills, Diamond, 3 reel, 50¢, chrome front, c1950, 15 x 25" **950.00**
Slot Machine, Mills, Skyscraper, 3 reel, 5¢, c1933, 16 x 20" **850.00**
Table Cover, dice, chips, score pad, and poker hands, c1920, 30" sq **130.00**
Wheel of Fortune, wood, 15 numbers, stenciled dec, 20½" d **30.00**

GAMES

Many game collectors make distinctions between classic games—those made between 1840 and 1940—and modern games—those dating after 1940. This is the type of snobbishness that gives collecting a bad name. In time, 1990s games will be one hundred years old. I can just imagine a collector in 2090 asking dealers at a toy show for a copy of the Morton Downey "Loudmouth" game. I am one of the few who have a mint-condition example put aside.

Condition is everything. Games that have been taped or have price tags stuck to their covers should be avoided. Beware of games at flea markets where exposure to sunlight and dirt causes fading, warping, and decay.

Avoid common games, e.g., "Go to the Head of the Class," "Monopoly," and "Rook." They were produced in such vast quantities that they hold little attraction for collectors.

Most boxed board games found are in heavily used condition. Box lids have excessive wear, tears, and are warped. Pieces are missing. In this condition, most games fall in the $2 to $10 range. However, the minute a game is in fine condition or better, value jumps considerably.

Club: American Game Collectors Assoc., P.O. Box 44, Dresher, PA 19025; Gamers Alliance, P.O. Box 197, East Meadow, NY 11554.

Periodicals: *Toy Shop,* 700 E. State St., Iola, WI 54990; *Toy Trader,* P.O. Box 1050, Dubuque, IA 52004.

Family Feud, Milton Bradley, 1977, $12.00.

Say When!!, Parker Brothers, 1961, $20.00.

Air Traffic Controller Game, Schaper, 1974 . . . . **$25.00**
All in the Family, Milton Bradley, 1972 . . . . **15.00**
American History, The Game of, Parker Brothers, c1890 . . . . . **45.00**
Animal Game, Saalfield Publishing co, c1920s **50.00**
Are You Being Served?, Toltoys, 1977 . . . . **20.00**
Art Linkletter's Game of "People Are Funny," Whitman, 1954 . . . . **35.00**
Authors, E. E. Fairchild, #623-3, c1945 . . . . **15.00**
Avilude, or Game of Birds, West & Lee Game Co, 1873 . . . . . **35.00**
Bamm Bamm Color Me Happy Game, Transogram, 1963 . . . . **60.00**
Bantu, Parker Brothers, 1955 . . . . **20.00**
Battles, Game of, or Fun for Boys, McLoughlin Bros, 1889 . . . . **500.00**
Bobbsey Twins on the Farm Game, The, Milton Bradley, 1957 . . . . **30.00**
Cabby, Selchow & Righter, 1938–40s **60.00**
Calling All Cars, Parker Brothers, c1938 . . . . **45.00**
Corn & Beans, E G Selchow & Co, 1875 . . . . **45.00**
Deduction, Ideal, 1976 . . . . **7.00**
Down the Pike with Mrs Wiggs at the St Louis Exposition, Milton Bradley, 1904 . . . . **25.00**
Excursion to Coney Island, Milton Bradley, c1885 . . . . **30.00**
Fame and Fortune, Whitman, 1962 . . . . **18.00**
Gilligan, The New Adventures of, Milton Bradley, 1974 . . . . . **20.00**
Hands up Harry, Transogram, 1964 . . . . **45.00**
Hi-Ho Cherry-Ho, Whitman, 1960 . . . . **5.00**
Hollywood Squares, Ideal, 1974 . . . . **10.00**
I've Got A Secret, Lowell, 1956 . . . . **40.00**
Intrigue, Milton Bradley, 1955 . . . . **35.00**
Jack Straws, Milton Bradley, c1900 . . . . **15.00**
Kate Smith's Own Game America, Toy Creations, 1940s **55.00**
Knockout Andy, Parker Brothers, 1926 . . . . **40.00**
Leaping Lena, Parker Brothers, 1920s **95.00**
Marble Maze, Hasbro, 1966 . . . . **15.00**

Mystic Skull, Ideal, 1964, $40.00.

Mastermind, Invicta, 1972 . . . . **8.00**
Mystery Date Game, Milton Bradley, 1965 . . . . **50.00**
National Velvet Game, Transogram, 1961 . . . . **35.00**
Operation, Milton Bradley, 1965 . . . . **12.00**
Pac-Man Game, Milton Bradley, 1980 . . . . **12.00**
Qwik Quiz Game, Transogram 1958 . . . . **25.00**
Romper Room Magic Teacher, Bar-Zim, 1960s **20.00**
Spedem Auto Race, Alderman-Fairchild, 1922 . . . . **95.00**
Tell Bell, The, Knapp Electric, Inc, 1928 . . . . **30.00**
Tom Sawyer, The Game of, Milton Bradley, c1937 . . . . **75.00**
Underdog, Milton Bradley, 1964 . . . . **25.00**
Voyage Round the World, Game of, Milton Bradley, c1930s **125.00**
Wagon Train Game, Milton Bradley, 1960 . . . . **30.00**
What's My Line?, Lowell, 1954–55 . . . . **40.00**
You Don't Say Game, Milton Bradley, 1964–69 . . . . **10.00**
Yours For A Song, Lowell, 1961 . . . . **25.00**

GAS STATION COLLECTIBLES

Approach this from two perspectives—items associated with gas stations and gasoline company giveaways. Competition for this material is fierce. Advertising collectors want the advertising; automobile collectors want material to supplement their collections.

Beware of reproductions ranging from advertising signs to pump globes. Do not accept too much restoration and repair. There were hundreds of thousands of gasoline stations across America. Not all their back rooms have been exhausted.

Club: International Petroliana Collectors Assoc., P.O. Box 937, Powell, OH 43065.

Periodical: *Mobilia,* P.O. Box 575, Middlebury, VT 05753; *Petroleum Collectibles Monthly*, 411 Forest St., P.O. Box 556, LaGrange, OH 44050.

Attendant's Shirt, Phillips 66, size 14-14$^{1}/_{2}$, slightly soiled **$20.00**
Bank, Sohio, glass, emb lettering, 4$^{3}/_{4}$" h **50.00**
Blotter, Sunoco, cardboard, "A-596-800M-8-37," 3$^{3}/_{4}$" h **5.50**
Bowl, Mobil, china, mkd "Shenango China, U.S.A.," 2$^{1}/_{4}$" h **50.00**
Calendar, 1941, Atlantic Petroleum Products, paper, 28$^{3}/_{4}$" h **45.00**
Chart, Texaco Lubrication, paper, 18$^{1}/_{4}$" **70.00**
Dealer Hat, Sunoco, vinyl and cloth, metal enameled badge, size 7$^{1}/_{4}$, overall vinyl cracking and wear **215.00**

Pump Globe, Power "G," glass body, 1 lens, 13½" d, $165.00. Photo courtesy Collectors Auction Services.

Fan, Phillips 66, Van's Service Station, Downtown Fairbury, IL, shild shape, wood handle, 14 x 8½" **20.00**
Knife, Esso Standard Oil, metal, gas pump shape, 2⅞" h **55.00**
Knife/Scissors, Shell, metal, "Mileage is our Business," 2⅜" l **50.00**
Lamp, Amoco, plastic and metal, electric, 18¼" h **135.00**
Lamp, Texaco, plastic and metal, electric, 18¼" h **280.00**
License Attachment, Tydol Man and Flying Horse **35.00**
Motor Oil Rack, wire, 4 emb glass bottles with metal spouts, 9" w **225.00**
Poster, "Super-Shell," paper, linen backing, 32½" h **198.00**
Pump Globe, Blue Sunoco, blue and yellow glass inserts, metal body, blue lettering on yellow diamond, 16" d **175.00**
Pump Globe, Lion, black and orange glass inserts, milk glass body, lion poised above lettering, 15" d **425.00**
Pump Globe, Mutual Gasoline, glass inserts, plastic body, running rabbit image, blue and red, 15" d **100.00**
Pump Globe, Shamrock, plastic body, 13½" d **300.00**
Pump Globe Lens, Essolene, 15" d, price for pr **190.00**
Radio, Champion Spark Plug, figural spark plug, plastic, Japan, 5" w, 14½" h **100.00**
Salesman Ship Service Book, Esso, hardcover, 73 pp, ©1935, 7¾" h **38.50**
Salt and Pepper Shakers, pr, Texaco, plastic, "Fire Chief" salt, "Sky Chief" pepper, orig box, 2¾" h **65.00**
Sign, Amoco, "Courtesy Cards Honored Here," porcelain, double sided, 15" h **75.00**
Sign, BP, double sided, 31⅝" h **275.00**
Sign, Conoco Gasoline, round, colonial soldier illus, 25" d **850.00**
Sign, Esso Garantie Lube, porcelain, double sided, "Renaud Morez MAI 1932" at bottom, 9½" h **145.00**
Sign, Fisk Tires/Tubes/Service Station, reflective, double sided, 14" h **425.00**
Sign, Hudson Essex, porcelain, double sided, 15⅝" h **330.00**
Sign, Indian Gasoline, porcelain, 1940, 12 x 18" **335.00**
Sign, Mobilgas, porcelain, 12" h **225.00**

Hat, child's, Imperial Esso, promotional giveaway, paper, 4" h, 22¾" l, $22.00. Photo courtesy Collectors Auction Services.

GAUDY ITALIAN

While not all items marked "Made in Italy" are gaudy, the vast majority are. They are collected for their kitsch, not aesthetic value.

The Mediterranean look was a popular decorating style in the late 1950s and early 1960s. Etruscan style-pieces, reproduction and copycats of Etruscan antiquities painted in light yellows and greens, often relief decorated with sea motifs including mythical sea creatures, and featuring a high gloss, majolica-type glaze, were the most popular. Production values were crude.

The Mediterranean look fell out of favor by the mid-1960s. Those gaudy Italian's that did not wind up in the garbage dump were relegated to basements, attics, and other damp and foreboding places. Some wish they stayed there.

Vases are the most commonly found form. The modestly decorated examples sell in the $15 to $25 range. A large elaborate example fetches $40 or more. The gaudiness of the piece affects its value—the more gaudy, the higher the perceived value.

GAY FAD GLASSWARE

In the late 1930s Fran Taylor and her husband, Bruce, founded the Gay Fad Studios, a firm that decorated glass and metal wares for sale in the tabletop market. The business flourished. In 1945 the Taylors transferred their operations from Detroit to Lancaster, Ohio, just across the street from the Anchor Hocking Glass Co.

Gay Fad glassware is found in hundreds of different designs. Many appeared as sets, e.g., the eight glass Gay Ninety Family Portrait series. Gay Fad glassware is usually marked with an interlocking "G" and "F" or "Gay Fad." Not all pieces were marked. Also look for decanters, juice sets, tea and toast sets, and waffle sets.

Gay Fad pieces were imitated. Gay Fad frosted glass is smooth to the touch, like silk. Imitators used a rougher feeling frosting.

Cocktail Glass, Bentware, Beau Brummel **$8.00**
Decanter, frosted, Bartender **8.00**
Glass, Currier & Ives, hp, silk-screened **3.00**
Glass, 48 States **2.00**
Pilsner Glass, Gay Ninety Family Portrait **8.00**
Server, rect, 3 pocket, gold and black leaves dec, sgd, 8 x 22" **20.00**
Snack Tray, abstract pattern **15.00**
Tumbler, "Democrats/Say When," donkeys, 3 oz **3.00**
Tumbler, Gal of Distinction, 12 oz **6.00**
Tumbler, "Merry Christmas from Gay Fad," stylized dove **10.00**
Tumbler, Rich Man, Poor Man **8.00**
Tumbler, stylized cats **4.00**
Tumbler, Zombies **8.00**

GEISHA GIRL

Geisha Girl porcelain is a Japanese export ware whose production began in the last quarter of the nineteenth century and still continues today. Manufacturing came to a standstill during World War II.

Collectors have identified over 150 different patterns from over one hundred manufacturers. When buying a set, check the pattern of the pieces carefully. Dealers will mix and match in an effort to achieve a complete set.

Beware of reproductions that have a very white porcelain, minimal background washes, sparse detail coloring, no gold, or very bright gold enameling. Some of the reproductions came from Czechoslovakia.

Bamboo Tree, bread and butter plate, 6" d $10.00
Bamboo Tree, cup and saucer, mkd "Made in Japan" 8.50
Bamboo Tree, teapot 12.00
Bamboo Trellis, bowl, ftd, 7½" d 35.00
Bamboo Trellis, chocolate set, pot, 6 cups and saucers, cobalt blue, lattic work ground 225.00
Bird Cage, bread and butter plate, 6" d 12.00
Bird Cage, tete-a-tete, pot, 2 cups and saucers, red-orange, gold 8.00
Flat, bowl, red, gold trim, 6½" d 24.00
Ikebana in Rickshaw, bowl, ftd, yellow, 8" d 40.00
Ikebana in Rickshaw, teapot, cobalt blue, gold 35.00
Long-Stemmed Peony, creamer 12.00
Porch, cup and saucer, after dinner, dark green, Made in Japan 10.00
Porch, nut bowl, master, cobalt blue, Torii Nippon 25.00

G.I. JOE

The first G.I. Joe 12" tall posable action figures for boys were produced in 1964 by the Hasbro Manufacturing Company. The original line was made up of one male action figure for each branch of the military. Their outfits were styled after World War II, Korean Conflict, and Vietnam Conflict military uniforms.

In 1965 the first black figure was introduced. The year 1967 saw two additions to the line—a female nurse and Talking G.I. Joe. To stay abreast of the changing times, Joe was given flocked hair and beard in 1970.

The creation of the G.I. Joe Adventure Team made Joe the marveled explorer, hunter, deep-sea diver, and astronaut, rather than just an American serviceman. Due to the Arab oil embargo in 1976, the figure was reduced in height to 8" and was renamed the Super Joe. In 1977 production stopped.

It wasn't until 1982 that G.I. Joe made his comeback, with a few changes to the character line and to the way in which the Joe team was viewed. "The Great American Hero" is now a posable 3¾" tall plastic figure with code names corresponding to the various costumes. The new Joe must deal with both current and futuristic villains and issues.

Clubs: G.I. Joe Collectors Club, 12513 Birchfalls Dr., Raleigh, NC 27614; G.I. Joe: Steel Brigade Club, 8362 Lomay Ave., Westminster, CA 92683.

Periodical: *G.I. Joe Patrol,* P.O. Box 2362, Hot Springs, AR 71914.

ACTION FIGURE, 12" h

Action Pilot, #7800 .... $85.00
Adventurer, Negro, #7404, orig box, MIB 275.00
Annapolis Cadet, Parade Dress, #7624, MIB 375.00
Astronaut, silver space suit 135.00
German Soldier, #8100, MIB 395.00
Man of Action, #7284, MIB 225.00
Sea Adventurer, #7492, MIB 175.00
Sky Dive to Danger, MIB 275.00
Talking Commander 200.00
West Point Cadet, Parade Dress, #7537, MIB 200.00

CLOTHING AND ACCESSORIES

Adventure Team Pith Helmet $25.00
Ammo Belt, green 12.00
Australian Jungle Fighter Hat 15.00
Canteen 2.00
Crutch 4.00
Dress Outfit, Navy, orig tie, complete 75.00
Folding Shovel, with shovel bag 6.00
Jumpsuit, orange 20.00
Sailor Cap 2.00
Scuba Tank 25.00
Shirt and Pants, sailor 15.00

PLAYSETS AND VEHICLES

Air Chariot $45.00
Armadillo 15.00
Battle Wagon 30.00
Cobra, F.A.N.G. 25.00
Crew Fire Truck 35.00
GI Joe Training Center 100.00
Helicopter, orig accessories, 1970s 68.00
Jet Fighter Plane, #5396, Irwin, 1967 .... 350.00
Python Patrol Viper 10.00
Secret Mountain Outpost, #8040 .... 75.00
Special Training Center, sears, MIB 300.00
Weapon Transport 10.00

OTHER

Figure, Airborne, unpackaged, orig file card, 1983 .... $15.00
Figure, Doc, unpackaged, orig file card, 1983, 3¾" h 15.00
Figure, Flash, unpackaged, orig file card, 1982, 3¾" h 20.00
Figure, Recondo, unpackaged, orig file card, 3¾" h 9.00
Game, GI Joe Commando Attack, Milton Bradley, 1985 .... 10.00
Game, GI Joe Marine Paratroop, Hasbro, 1965 .... 40.00
Puzzle, Mural, 221 pcs, scene #2, 1988 .... 5.00

GIRL SCOUTS

Girl Scout collectors started about twenty years behind Boy Scout collectors, but are catching up fast in knowledge and enthusiasm. So far, antique dealers are not in tune with their interests. However, there is a network of specialist Scouting dealers selling through the mail, and they are including Girl Scout items among their Boy Scout offerings. In addition, on-line auctions are selling a lot of Girl Scout collectibles.

Many active Girl Scout collectors are acquiring for their local Girl Scout Council Museums. They focus on different kinds of uniforms with suitable accessories. They need hats, belts, socks, and some badges but they don't need a complete set of all badges. They also like showy things like cameras and dolls.

Other Girl Scout collectors want a complete set of each type of badge and pin, plus all the calendars, and as many different Girl Scout dolls as possible. These are the true collectors.

The supply of Girl Scout collectibles is way below the demand. The problem is partly that people don't realize Girl Scout things have value. Some valuable things get discarded. Since antique dealers don't know the values of the various badges or uniforms, many of them steer clear of Girl Scout things. We need to get more information to those who can bring these items out of hiding and offer them for sale.

Golden Eaglet Pins, left: miniature, 1930–38. 13mm wide, 10k gold, $400.00; center: Second Type, 1934–38, 22mm wide, 10k gold, $500.00; right: First Type, 1919–34, 29 mm wide, gold plated, $500.00.

Pin, left, Community Service, green enamel, 20mm d, 1922–31, $150.00.
Right: War Service, blue enamel, 1918–19, $450.00.

Advisor: Cal Holden, Box 264, Doylestown, OH 44230, (330) 658-2793.

Badge, Senior Interest Badge, Trailblazer, 1955–60, 3" d **$90.00**
Blanket, green, woven Girl Scout logo, c1930s. **150.00**
Book, *Girl Scout Collector's Guide,* Degenhardt & Kirsch, out-of-print, 1987. . . . . **100.00**
Calendar, color illus, 1950, used **15.00**
Diary, Girl Scout, 1936, partially used **30.00**
Doll, Brownie, black, Effanbee, 8" h, MIB **90.00**
Doll, Girl Scout, white, Beehler Arts, 1959–60, 8" h, MIB . . . **125.00**
Equipment Catalog, 1936 . . . . **50.00**
First Aid Kit, Johnson & Johnson, complete with contents and cloth belt pouch, 1930s **35.00**
Handbook, *Girl Scout Handbook,* 1st printing **12.00**
Handbook, *Girl Scout Handbook,* 2nd printing, blue cov. **75.00**
Handbook, *Girl Scout Handbook,* 23rd printing, 1953 . . . . **4.00**
Handbook, *Junior Girl Scout Handbook,* 1st printing, 1963. . . . . **6.00**
Handbook, *Scouting for Girls,* 3rd printing, 1922 . . . . **22.00**
Lunch Box, metal, brown, illus on sides, 1920s, complete with cov insert, 7½ x 5 x 4". **90.00**
Patch, Brownie Bridge-to-Bridge Juniors Patch, with 3 segments **5.00**
Patch, cloth, embroidered, curved bar, 1940–47 . . . . **35.00**
Patch, First Class, bright green with crimped edges, early 1950s **10.00**
Patch, Senior Roundup, 1962. . . . . **25.00**
Patch, Senior Service Scout Leader's, with Civil Defense triangle **95.00**
Pin, Challenge Pin, Community Action, 1963–80 . . . . **8.00**
Pin, curved bar, 1948–63 . . . . **7.00**

Pin, left, First Brownie, brass, brass, pre–1938, $95.00.
Patch, right, Brownie Golden Hand, brown felt, pre–1938, $75.00.

Pin, Golden Eaglet, 1st type, gold plated, 1919–30. . . . . **500.00**
Pin, Mariner, pot metal, safety pin clasp, Lyons Bros **25.00**
Pin, Mariner, sterling, rotary clasp, Robbins **40.00**
Pin, Second Trefoil, no ribbon in eagle's mouth, c1918–23 . . . . **50.00**
Pin, Senior Roundup, oval, orig card, 1965 . . . . **40.00**
Pin, Wing Scout, Robbins, 1948–63 . . . . **125.00**
Ring, Brownie, sterling, rect face, adjustable, 1950s **15.00**
Ring, Girl Scout, sterling, green hexagon with gold trefoil logo, 1945–48. . . . . **80.00**
Uniform, khaki, complete with 10 khaki badges on sleeves, brimmed hat, and web belt, c1915–28. . . . . **250.00**

GOLD

Twenty-four-karat gold is pure gold. Twelve-karat gold is fifty percent gold and fifty percent other elements. Many gold items have more weight value than antique or collectible value. The gold-weight scale is different from our regular English pounds scale. Learn the proper conversion procedure. Review the value of an ounce of gold once a week and practice keeping that figure in your mind.

Pieces with gold wash, gold gilding, and gold bands have no weight value. Value rests in other areas. In many cases the gold is applied on the surface. Washing and handling leads to its removal.

Take time to research and learn the difference between gold and gold plating before starting your collection. This is not an area in which to speculate. How many times have you heard that an old pocket watch has to be worth a lot of money because it has a gold case? Many people cannot tell the difference between gold and gold plating. In most cases, the gold value is much less than you think.

Gold coinage is a whole other story. Every coin suspected of being gold should first be checked by a jeweler and then in coin price guides.

GOLF COLLECTIBLES

Golf was first played in Scotland in the fifteenth century. The game achieved popularity in the late 1840s when the "gutty" ball was introduced. Although golf was played in America before the Revolution, it gained a strong foothold in the recreational area only after 1890.

The problem with most golf collectibles is that they are common while their owners think they are rare. This is an area where homework pays, especially when trying to determine the value of clubs.

Do not limit yourself to items used on the course. Books about golf, decorative accessories with a golf motif, and clubhouse collectibles are eagerly sought by collectors. This is a great sports collectible to tee off on. (No pun intended!)

Clubs: Golf Collectors' Society, P.O. Box 20546, Dayton, OH 45420; Logo Golf Ball Collector's Assoc., 4552 Barclay Fairway, Lake Worth, FL 33467; The Golf Club Collectors Assoc., 640 E. Liberty St, Girard, OH 44420.

Newsletter: *US Golf Classics & Heritage Hickories*, 5407 Pennock Point Rd., Jupiter, FL 33458.

Bag, leather, Tony Lema, 1964 British Open Champion **$50.00**
Ball, D & M Skull, Draper-Maynard Co, Plymouth, NH, mesh pattern, mkd "Skull & Crossbones" between "D" and "M" in black ink on both poles, c1920–30s **75.00**
Ball, Goodyear "B," Goodyear Tire & Rubber Co, Akron, OH, mesh pattern, repainted, c1926 . . . . **125.00**
Ball, U S Royal, United States Rubber Co, Providence, RI & NYC, mesh pattern, mkd "U. S. Royal" in blue ink on both poles, c1930s **95.00**
Ball, Whippet, A J Reach Co, Philadelphia, PA, mesh pattern, stamped "Whippet" in green ink on both poles, 8 green mesh squares around equator, c1920s **65.00**
Book, *Golfing Illustrated,* Beldam, George W, 1st ed, London, Gowans & Gray, notes by John L Low, illus from photographs by Beldam, pictorial wrappers, 1908 . . . . **63.25**
Book, *On Many Greens: A Book of Golf and Golfers,* Bantock, Miles, 1st ed, NY, Grosset & Dunlap, introduction by Findlay S Douglas, illus, 1901 . . . . **373.75**
Book, *Portrait of a Professional Golfer,* Palmer, Arnold, 1st ed, South Norwalk, Golf Digest, illus, pictorial boards, sgd by Palmer on front free endpaper, 1964 . . . . . **110.00**
Book, *The Sorrows of a Golfer's Wife,* Kennard, Mrs Edward, 2nd ed, London, F V White, orig pictorial chromolithograph boards, 1897 . . . . **207.00**
Club, iron, Spalding F-4, wood shaft, c1922 . . . . **10.00**
Club, iron, Tom Stewart lofter, smooth face, wood shaft **45.00**
Club, putter, Mills, "L" model, aluminum head **37.50**
Club, putter, Tommy Armour IMG Ironmaster, steel shaft **85.00**
Cookbook, *Golfer's Cookbook,* 92 pp, 1968 . . . . **4.00**
Doorstop, golfer putting, green cap, red shoes, coat, and knickers, 6½ x 8" **65.00**
Game, The Game of Golf, Clark & Sowdon, #352, c1905 . . . **200.00**
Matchsafe, SS, golfer swinging club motif, 2½ x 1¾ x 6½" h **20.00**

Cap, Arnold Palmer, Doubleday, "Play Great Golf," green, white, and gold, ASI, one size fits all, $5.00.

Jigsaw puzzle mailing envelope for Goofy Golf, Sty Meee in Chinee, Richfield premium, #4, envelope with Alex Morrison's golf lesson on back, 7 x 9", 1933, $25.00.

Pinback Button, "B P O E '93' Country Club Caddy, Hamilton, Ohio," sample 000 serial number, black lettering, dark red ground, 1930s, 1¾" d. **10.00**
Postcard, cartoon golf scene **10.00**
Program, Bob Hope Desert Classic, 1967 . . . . **15.00**
Sign, The Original Canadian Dry, cardboard, golfing scene, 1920s, 13½ x 12" **75.00**
Souvenir Spoon, SS, golfer, Milford, PA **80.00**
Tee, Super Golf Tees, orig package, 1920s **30.00**
Utensils, bar type, Art Deco, silver and chrome **125.00**

GONDER POTTERY

In 1941 Lawton Gonder established Gonder Ceramic Arts, Inc., at Zanesville, Ohio. The company is known for its glazes, such as Chinese crackle, gold crackle, and flambé. Pieces are clearly marked. Gonder manufactured lamp bases at a second plant and marketed them under the trademark "Eglee." Gonder Ceramic Arts, Inc. ceased production in 1957.

Club: Gonder Collectors Club, 917 Hurl Dr., Pittsburgh, PA 15236.

Newsletter: *Gonder Collector Newsletter*, P.O. Box 4263, North Myrtle Beach, SC 29597.

Basket, twisted handle, brown glaze, L-19, 9" h **$45.00**
Candlesticks, pr, turquoise, pink coral int, mkd "E-14 Gonder," 4¾" h **20.00**
Creamer and Sugar, cov, brown speckles and drips on ivory ground, large **12.50**
Ewer, bulbous, mottled maroon, 7½" h **25.00**
Figure, collie, gray, 9" l **15.00**
Figure, elephant, raised trunk, rose and gray **40.00**
Figure, panther, #217, 15" l **115.00**
Figurine, Oriental Coolie, pink and green glaze, 8" h **20.00**
Flower Frog, blue and brown glaze, swirl pattern, 7¾ x 7" . . . **20.00**
Planter, gondola, yellow and pink **25.00**
TV Lamp, seagull, black, flying over yellow waves, 12" h **75.00**
Vase, ewer, brown and yellow glaze, H-33, 9" h **35.00**
Vase, mottled green, twisted, 6" h **12.00**
Vase, rect, yellow, H-74, 8½" h **20.00**

GOOFUS GLASS

Goofus glass is a patterned glass on which the reverse of the principal portion of the pattern is colored in red or green and covered with a metallic gold ground. It was distributed at carnivals between 1890 and 1920. There are no records of it being manufactured after that date. Crescent Glass Company, Imperial Glass Corporation, LaBelle Glass Works, and Northwood Glass Company are some of the companies who made Goofus glass.

Value rests with pieces that have both the main color and ground color still intact. The reverse painting often wore off. It is not uncommon to find the clear pattern glass blank with no painting on it whatsoever.

Goofus glass is also known as Mexican Ware, Hooligan Glass, and Pickle Glass. Says a lot, doesn't it?

Newsletter: *Goofus Glass Gazette*, 9 Lindenwood Ct., Sterling, VA 20165.

Bonbon, red and green strawberry dec, gold ground **$35.00**
Bowl, carnations, 9" d **25.00**
Bowl, water lilies dec, gold ground, 10½" d **50.00**
Candy Dish, red strawberries and green leaves, molded applied ring handle **12.00**
Coaster, red floral dec, gold ground, 3" d **8.00**
Compote, red strawberries and green leaves, gold ground, ruffled, 9½" d **45.00**
Dish, chrysanthemum sprays, red and gold, scalloped rim, 11" d **70.00**
Dresser tray, oval, red and black florals, 6½" l **15.00**
Jar, butterflies, red and gold **20.00**
Pitcher, red rose bud, gold leaves **45.00**
Plate, red and gold roses, scalloped rim, 11" d **25.00**
Plate, red flowers, gold ground, 10¾" d **12.00**
Salt and Pepper Shakers, pr, Poppy, 3" h **35.00**
Vase, red roses, gold ground, 12" h **40.00**

GRANITEWARE

Graniteware, also know as agateware, is the name commonly given to iron or steel kitchenware covered with an enamel coating. American production began in the 1860s and is still going on today.

White and gray are the most common colors. However, wares can be found in shades of blue, brown, cream, green, red, and violet. Mottled pieces, those combining swirls of color, can be especially desirable.

For several years there was a deliberate attempt by some dealers to drive prices upward. This scheme was quite successful until the 1990 recession. Never lose sight of the fact that graniteware was inexpensive utilitarian kitchen and household ware. Modern prices should reflect this humble origin.

Club: National Graniteware Society, P.O. Box 10013, Cedar Rapids, IA 52410.

Bedpan, gray mottled **$60.00**
Bucket, gray, bail handle, miniature **30.00**
Cake Pan, gray, 10 x 14" **10.00**
Chamber Pot, gray, child's, paper label **20.00**
Coffeepot, light blue and white, conical, C-shaped black handle, hinged rounded lid with ball finial, 9⅜" h overall **180.00**
Colander, gray, 11½" d **55.00**
Dipper, red and white **15.00**
Double Boiler, white, red trim **20.00**
Funnel, gray mottled **20.00**
Kettle, cov, gray mottled, 9" h **45.00**
Lunch Pail, light blue and white, cylindrical shape, lid with arched handle, wire bail handle with turned wooden grip painted black, 7" h with lid **110.00**
Milk Pan, blue and white swirl **45.00**
Miner's Lunch Pail, blue and white on solid blue, stacked, consists of iron rack with round handle on top, round dish at bottom with round holes around sides, 3 round individual dishes stacked on top, plain blue graniteware rounded lid, 11⅛" h **45.00**
Muffin Pan, gray mottled, 9 cup **40.00**
Pail, dark blue and white, matching lid, white int, knob finial on lid, wire bail handle, 6¼" h **45.00**
Pan, green and white, flared sides, rounded rim, 3⅜" h **90.00**
Pan, light blue and white, flated sides, rounded rim, white int, black rim, 2" h **5.00**
Percolator, light blue and white, hinged lid, glass dome top, aluminum coffee basket and parts, black handle and rims, flat bottom with rounded base and straight sides, rounded lid, 5⅜" d at base, 8¼" h **45.00**
Pie Pan, gray **20.00**
Pitcher, white, black trim **45.00**
Plate, blue and white swirl **15.00**
Pudding Pan, cobalt blue and white swirl, 8" d **40.00**
Roaster, cream and red, large **30.00**
Soap Dish, blue and white swirl **25.00**
Strainer Insert, brown and white mottled, straight sides, wire bail, 8½" d **55.00**
Tube Pan, gray mottled, octagonal **40.00**
Wash Basin, blue and white marbelized, 13½" d **35.00**

GREETING CARDS

Greeting cards still fall largely under the wing of postcard collectors and dealers. They deserve a collector group of their own.

At the moment, high-ticket greeting cards are character-related. But, someday collectors will discover Hallmark and other greeting cards as social barometers of their era. Meanwhile, enjoy picking them up for 25¢ or less.

Birthday, children illus, 19th C. **$4.00**
Birthday, floral design, blue fringe, c1880 . . . . **20.00**
Christmas, "Best Wishes," cherub holding dove, raised message, ribbon on top, c1900 . . . . **1.50**
Christmas, birds and flowers, blue fringed, c1880 . . . . **35.00**
Christmas, Flash Gordon, 1951, unused **12.00**
Christmas, "My Lips May Give a Message," Kate Greenaway, girl holding letter, c1880 . . . . **50.00**

Birthday, printed color cov with Scottie dog, Greetings, Inc, bi-fold, 1948, 4¾ x 6", $7.50.

Christmas, Nativity scene, fold-out, c1820 . . . . **8.00**
Easter, angels, Whitney, NY, 19th C **5.00**
Easter, floral, religious, Tuck **15.00**
Easter, "Joyous Easter," angel in oval, daisies and emb dec, c1910 . . . . **2.00**
New Year, "Here Comes the New Year with Lots of Good Cheer," child with Christmas tree and toys, c1870. . . . . **15.00**
New Year, "Wishing You a Happy new Year," girl on front, man on back, fringed, tasseled cord, L Prang and Co, c1884 . . . . **25.00**
Thanksgiving, family seated at table, mid 20th C **3.00**
Thanksgiving, turkey, feather tail, 1930s **8.00**
Valentines Day, "Best Valentine Wishes," woman wearing winter clothing reading valentine card, c1920. . . . . **1.50**

GRISWOLD

Normally when one hears Griswold, one thinks cast iron household wares. They also made commercial electrical appliances.

Matthew Griswold purchased the Selden family interest in Selden & Griswold in 1884. Griswold became a cast iron king in the early 20th century under the leadership of Marvin Griswold, Matthew's son. Roger Griswold, son of Matthew, Jr., became president in 1926. The family's involvement ended in 1944. In 1957 the Griswold trade name was sold to Wagner Manufacturing Company, one of its major competitors. The additional sales eventually resulted in the company being part of the General Housewares Corporation.

Beware of reproductions and fantasy pieces. Many are made in India and imported with easily removable, country of origin paper labels.

Club: Griswold & Cast-Iron Cookware Assoc., P.O. Box 243, Perrysburg, NY 14129.

Newsletter: *Kettles 'n' Cookware,* P.O. Box 247, Perrysburg, NY 14129.

Breadstick Pan, #22, Erie **$50.00**
Brownie Golf Pan, #9 . . . . **175.00**
Cake Mold, rabbit **270.00**
Cake Mold, Santa **650.00**
Cake Mold, Turk's Head, #140 . . . . **200.00**
Coffee Trivet, small **300.00**
Corn/Wheat Pan, ftd **200.00**
Cornstick Pan, #262 . . . . **60.00**
Crispy Corn Stick, #283 . . . . **200.00**
Deep Patty Bowl, #72 . . . . **45.00**
Dutch Oven Trivet, #7 . . . . **45.00**
Dutch Oven Trivet, #10 . . . . **60.00**
Egg Separator **450.00**
Egg Skillet, #53, sq **25.00**
Gem Pan, #1 . . . . **150.00**
Gem Pan, #3, variation 1 . . . . **240.00**
Gem Pan, #17, mkd **150.00**
Golfball Pan, #19, full writing **550.00**
Ice Shaver, #1 . . . . **125.00**
Loaf Pan **400.00**
Patty Mold Set, #3, with patty bowl, orig box **125.00**
Popover Pan, #18, satin chrome **55.00**
Puritan Skillet, #8 . . . . **30.00**
Roaster Lid, #7, oval **125.00**
Skillet, #7, Erie **35.00**
Skillet, #9, with heat ring **75.00**
Tite-Top Dutch Oven, #7, smooth lid **180.00**
Tite-Top Dutch Oven Lid, #9 . . . . **40.00**
Waffle Iron, #9, American Waffle **65.00**
Whole Wheat Pan, #28 . . . . **225.00**

HALL CHINA

In 1903 Robert Hall founded the Hall China Company in East Liverpool, Ohio. Upon his death in 1904, Robert T. Hall, his son, succeeded him. Hall produced refrigerator sets and a large selection of kitchenware and dinnerware in a wide variety of patterns. The company was a major supplier of institutional (hotel and restaurant) ware.

Hall also manufactured some patterns on an exclusive basis: Autumn Leaf for Jewel Tea, Blue Bouquet for the Standard Coffee Company of New Orleans, and Red Poppy for the Grand Union Tea Company. Hall teapots are a favorite among teapot collectors.

For the past several years, Hall has been reissuing a number of its solid-color pieces as the "Americana" line. Items featuring a decal or gold decoration have not been reproduced. Because of the difficulty in distinguishing old from new solid-color pieces, prices on many older pieces have dropped.

Club: Hall Collector's Club, P.O. Box 360488, Cleveland, OH 44136.

Note: For additional listings see Autumn Leaf.

Blue Blossom, teapot, cov, Streamline **$395.00**
Crocus, ball jug **195.00**
Crocus, cake plate **30.00**
Crocus, dinner plate, 9" d **12.00**
Crocus, gravy boat **35.00**
Crocus, platter, 13¼" l **35.00**
Drip-O-Lator, Cathedral, orange, gray and blue floral decal, large **16.50**
Drip-O-Lator, Crest, Minuet decal **33.00**
Drip-O-Lator, Drape, floral decal, aluminum insert **25.00**
Drip-O-Lator, Rounded Terrace, floral decal, small **19.25**
Drip-O-Lator, Waverly, daffodils, large **19.25**
Drip-O-Lator, Waverly, yellow rose, small **22.00**
Monticello, cup and saucer **6.00**
Orange Poppy, bread and butter plate, 6" d **6.00**
Orange Poppy, casserole, cov, 8" l **65.00**
Orange Poppy, teapot, Melody shape **240.00**

Teapot, Aladdin, cadet blue, gold trim, mkd "Hall 06695, 6 Cup, Made in USA," in gold, decal on bottom is banner with "Chester W. Va.," flame finial, 10½" l, $45.00.

Peach Blossom, platter, 15" l	**40.00**
Pinecone, E style, cup and saucer	**9.00**
Poppy and Wheat, jug, cov, #5	**125.00**
Red Poppy, cereal bowl, 6" d	**15.00**
Red Poppy, drip jar	**30.00**
Red Poppy, pie baker	**38.00**
Red Poppy, teapot, New York shape	**75.00**
Rose Parade, salad bowl	**22.00**
Silhouette, casserole, Medallion, 6" d	**12.00**
Springtime, dinner plate, 9" d	**9.00**
Taverne, pretzel jar	**85.00**
Tulip, nesting bowls, set of 3	**75.00**
Wildfire, casserole, cov, tab handle	**35.00**
Wildfire, dinner plate, 9" d	**12.00**

HALLMARK ORNAMENTS

Hallmark Cards, Inc., was founded by Joyce C. Hall. Hallmark Keepsakes were first marketed in 1973 and these first-year ornaments are avidly sought by collectors. Handcrafted Keepsakes were added to the line in 1975, followed the next year by Baby's First Christmas and Bicentennial ornaments.

Collecting Hallmark Keepsake Ornaments became a popular hobby in 1987, leading to the creation of The Keepsake Ornament Collector's Club, whose membership roles now exceed 250,000. As with any contemporary collectible, keep in mind that secondary market values can be speculative.

Clubs: Hallmark Collectors Club Connection, P.O. Box 110, Fenton, MI 48430; Hallmark Keepsake Ornament Collectors Club, P.O. Box 412734, Kansas City, MO 64141.

Newsletter: *Hallmarkers,* P.O. Box 97172, Pittsburgh, PA 15229.

Periodical: *The Ornament Collector*, 22341 E. Wells Rd., Canton, IL 61520.

1973, Little Girl, yarn, #125XHD825	**$25.00**
1973, Mrs Santa, yarn, #125XHD752	**20.00**
1973, Snowman, yarn, #150QX1041	**25.00**
1974, Charmers, glass, #250QX1091	**45.00**
1974, Soldier, yarn, #150QX1021	**25.00**
1975, Betsey Clark, satin, set of 2, #350QX1671	**43.00**
1975, Marty Links, glass, #300QX1361	**55.00**
1976, Bicentennial Charmers, glass, #300QX1981	**60.00**
1976, Drummer Boy, yarn, #175QC1231	**25.00**
1977, Desert, glass, #250QX1595	**36.00**
1977, Disney, Mickey Mouse, satin	**65.00**
1978, Christmas Spirit, satin, #350QX1335	**60.00**
1978, Peanuts, satin, #250QX2036	**65.00**
1979, Holiday Wreath, acrylic, #350QX3539	**40.00**
1979, The Light of Christmas, glass, #350QX2567	**29.00**
1980, Angel Music, fabric, #200QX3439	**20.00**
1980, Christmas Cardinals, glass, #400QX2241	**30.00**
1981, First Christmas Together, acrylic, #550QX5055	**23.00**
1986, Child's Third Christmas, fabric, #650QX4136	**20.00**
1986, Son, handcrafted, #575QX4303	**30.00**
1987, Sister, wood, #600QX4747	**12.00**
1988, Candy Cane Elf, handcrafted, #300QXM5701	**15.00**
1988, Happy Santa, glass, #450QXM5614	**15.00**
1989, Strollin' Snowman, porcelain, #450QXM5742	**15.00**
1990, Peace, brass, #300QXM5796	**5.00**
1994, Buster Bunny, handcrafted, #575QXM5163	**10.00**
1995, Catch the Spirit, handcrafted, #795QX5899	**15.00**
1996, Baby Tweety, handcrafted, #575QXM4014	**25.00**
1996, Feliz Navidad, handcrafted, #995QX6304	**15.00**

1976, Santa, Yesteryear Collection, handcrafted, #500QX1821, $100.00.

HALLOWEEN

Halloween collectibles deserve a category of their own. There is such a wealth of material out there that it nearly rivals Christmas as the most-decorated holiday season.

Remember how much fun it was to play dress-up as a kid? Collectors have rediscovered children's Halloween costumes. While you may be staggered by some of the prices listed below, I see costumes traded at these prices all the time.

Newletters: *Boo News*, P.O. Box 143, Brookfield, IL 60513; *Trick or Treat Trader*, P.O. Box 499, Winchester, NH 03470.

Candy Box, 3 Musketeers, cardboard, "Some Pumpkins for "Tricks or Treats," 1940s	**$45.00**
Candy Container, devil, papier-mâché, cone shaped, Germany, 7" h	**28.00**
Chocolate Mold, 3 witches in a row, metal	**125.00**
Costume, Cabbage Patch Kids, Tiny Tot, orig box	**20.00**
Costume, Ghostbusters, Ben Cooper, vinyl, orig box	**25.00**
Costume, wicked witch, Wizard of Oz, orig box	**50.00**
Display, A & H Rootbeer, Happy Halloween from the Munsters, cardboard	**50.00**
Fan, litho, 2 black cats, arched backs, wood handle, mkd "DRGM Germany"	**15.00**
Game, Green Ghost, Transogram, glow-in-the-dark gameboard, 1966	**80.00**
Game, Haunted House, Ideal, 1962	**60.00**

Decoration, diecut cat, mechanical, black with orange outline, color one side, c1940s, $15.00.

Jack-O'-Lantern, pressed paper, orange, black and white eyes, c1950, 4½" h, $40.00.

Jack-O-Lantern, glass globe, tin base, bail handle, battery operated **45.00**
Mask, Batman, rubber **45.00**
Mask, pirate, papier-mâché, string ties, mkd "Germany" **100.00**
Noisemaker, ratchet, wood, small black composition cat on top, 5½" l. **72.00**
Postcard, "Halloween Greetings," woman bobbing for apples, jack-o-lantern border, E C Banks, 1909 . . . . **12.00**
Postcard, "Wishing You a Merry Halloween," black cat driving jack-o'-lantern carriage, pulled by 6 mice, checked border, 1912 . . . . **15.00**
Sign, "Dr Pepper/Drink A Bite To eat at," cardboard, pumpkin head, corn stalks **45.00**
Sucker Mold, metal Lorann, MOC **8.00**
Toy, hard plastic, with and jack-o'-lantern on motorcycle, painted black accents **110.00**
Trick or Treat Bag, litho pumpkin head, "Happy Halloween," 1940 . . . . **18.00**

HANNA-BARBERA

How much is that gorilla in the window? If it's Magilla Gorilla, it could be pricey. Merchandise associated with Hanna-Barbera cartoon characters is becoming increasingly popular as baby boomers rediscover their childhood. Keep in mind that these items were mass-produced. Condition is a key element in determining value.

Atom Ant, game, Transogram, 1966 . . . . **$50.00**
Breezly, squeaker toy, Ideal, soft vinyl, white, orange accent hat and scarf, smiling seated position holding rifle in right hand over shoulder, 1960s, 6" h **60.00**
Cindy Bear, push puppet, Kohner Bros, blue body, yellow hat, 1960s, 3¾" h **40.00**
Flintstones, ashtray, Barney, ceramic, ©1961 Arrow Houseware Products of Chicago. **35.00**
Flintstones, figure, wood, smiling full figure Fred, blonde wood block feet, dark green suded tunic over shoulders, gray rabbit fur hair, black eye accents with wood-burned smile, Arne Basse©Hanna-Barbera, 1963, 5½" h **55.00**
Flintstones, Fuzzy Felt Set, Standard Toycraft, contains felt shapes of Flintstones and friends with illus instruction booklet, 1961, orig 8 x 13" box. . . . . **100.00.**
Flintstones, game, Bamm Bamm Color Me Happy, Transogram, 1963 . . . . **60.00**
Flintstones, game, The Flintstones Present Dino the Dinosaur Game, Transogram, 1961 . . . . **65.00**

Scooby Doo, game, Scooby-Doo Where Are You?, Milton Bradley, 1973, $20.00.

Flintstones, lunch box, Aladdin, metal, relief image of Bedrock Festival on 1 side, reverse with Flintstones Kids at moonlit parkint spot pointing at mad rabbit, with matching vinyl thermos showing Flintstone Kids in prehistoric drag race, 1971, 7 x 8 x 3¾" **85.00**
Flintstones, model kit, Fred Flintstones Rock Crusher, AMT, 3¾ x 5¼ x 7½" box with Fred on top of dinosaur, cutouts on sides of Barney and Mr Slate, 1974. . . . . **40.00**
Flintstones, ornament, Dino, vinyl, purple, black spots, tan muzzle, ©1976, 4' h **25.00**
Flintstones, windup, Marx, Fred riding Dino, litho tin, vinyl head, 1963, 3 x 8 x 5". **175.00**
Huckleberry Hound, coloring book, Whitman, #1117, 1959. . . . . **25.00**
Huckleberry Hound, game, Huckleberry Hound Western Game, Milton Bradley, 1959. . . . . **30.00**
Huckleberry Hound, record, *Howl Along with Huckleberry Hound and Yogi Bear,* A A Records, GLP55, LP, 12¼ x 12¼" color illus sleeve,©1960 Hanna-Barbera Productions **15.00**
Jetsons, candy box, The Jetsons Candy Sprockets, yellow, repeated image of Elroy in outer space rocket sled on both sides, World Candies, Inc, Brooklyn, NY, 1960s, 2 x 3¼ x ¾", full box. **40.00**
Magilla Gorilla, coin purse, Estelle Toy Co, #4911-P, blue vinyl, red and yellow accents, name at bottom, mid 1960s, MOC **15.00**
Magilla Gorilla, figure, Ideal, #4920-5, soft vinyl, poseable, 6" h smiling full figure Magilla wearing green felt suspenders and red felt shorts, light green cather's mitt and white bat, ©1965 Hanna-Barbera Productions, 3 x 7¼ x 2½" box **60.00**

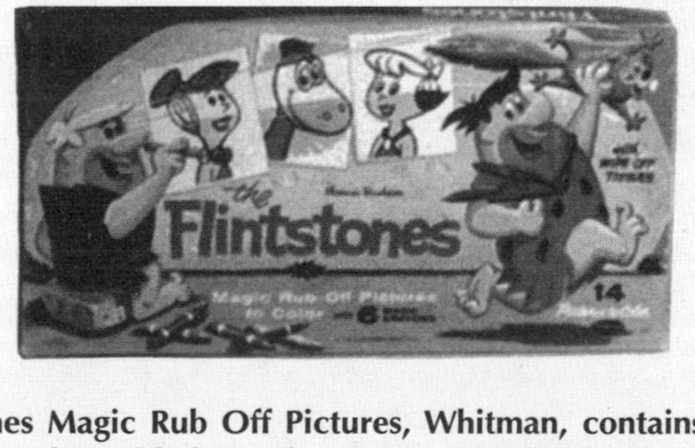

Flintstones Magic Rub Off Pictures, Whitman, contains 14 pictures to color with box of crayons, 1962, orig 9 x 15" box, $88.00. Photo courtesy New England Auction Gallery.

Yogi Bear, stuffed toy, plush, green hat, white collar, yellow tie, $65.00.

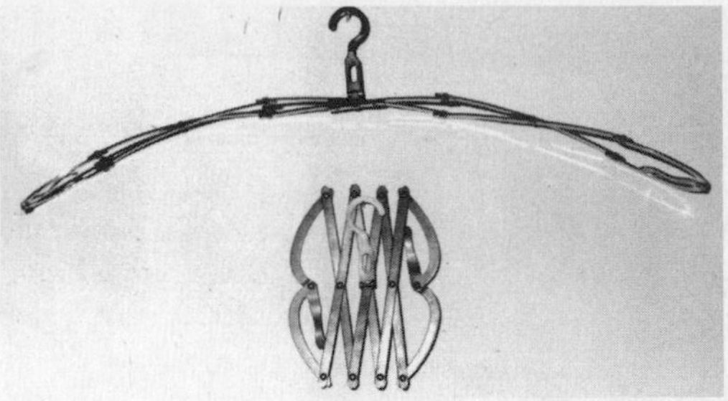

Travel Hanger, (shown extended and folded), stamped "Korrect Form Co. Chicago, Ill, Trade Mark Co–VES–PA U.S. pat. & foreign p' d' g.," $35.00.

Quick Draw McGraw, figure, ceramic, smiling full figure Quick Draw leaning on brown post with initials "HB" atop, green base with name, ©Hanna-Barbera Products, 1960s, 7¼" h 65.00
Quick Draw McGraw, windup, Linemar, litho tin, 1962, 4" h 375.00
Ruff and Reddy, Little Golden Record, *Ruff and Reddy and Their Friends,* 45 rpm, EP 571, color illus sleeve, 1959 . . . . 15.00
Scooby Doo, gumball bank, Hasbro, plastic, smiling face holding white bone, yellow base, 1968, 9" h 15.00
Secret Squirrel, frame tray puzzle, Whitman, #4559, color image of Secret using robot hand on hat to pick pear from tree, Morocco Mole holding basket, 1967, 11½ x 14½" 15.00
Secret Squirrel, push puppet, Kohner, #4995, holding binoculars, yellow base, 1960s, 5½" h 15.00
Wacky Races, Nutty Dragster, Laramie, #9705, purple plastic dragster with decals of Rufus Ruffcut on front and flower on roof, 1971, MOC 15.00
Yogi Bear, Play Fun Coloring Set, Whitman, #4755, 30 x 30" coloring sheet, 6 cardboard punch-out sheets, box of crayons, ©1964 Hanna-Barbera Productions, Inc 65.00
Yogi Bear, mocassins, pr, soft vinyl, simulated white fur around opening, red, yellow, and black smiling Yogi face with name on top, early 1960, 5¼ x 9¼ x 3" box 35.00
Yogi Bear, roly poly toy, Irwin Toys, hard vinyl, white, blue accent face, hat and collar, yellow accent arms, tie and ears, orig paper label, 1970s, 7½" 35.00

HANGERS

Clothing hangers have been manufactured with an imaginative variety of forms depending upon their specific use. Some have been fashioned to hold coats, suits, skirts, pants, belts, ties, a hat and any combination of garments. There are even hangers made for a pair of shoes.

Hangers designed for traveling purposes have employed folding sides, telescoping arms and accordion extensions. Hangers for drying may use a framework with clothes pins or take the contoured shape of a glove, stocking, sweater or pants.

Many hangers have patent dates from the 1890s through the 1920s. The most common type of hanger has a loop of steel wire which fits in each shoulder of the garment. Prices tend to rise as the construction and shape become more elaborate. Though not frequently encountered, antique hangers display fascinating design innovations and are often stunning sculptural works. They are generally inexpensive, easy to store and may still be used for their intended purposes.

Advisors: Cheryl and Roger Brinker, 3140-B W. Tilghman St., #165, Allentown, PA 18104, (610) 432-8393.

Drying Hanger, wire, contoured hand form **$10.00**
Drying Hanger, wire, contoured stocking form **8.00**
Grim's Pres-Gard Hanger, Extenso Hanger Co, NY, horizontal tin extension arm with metal clip at ends **20.00**
Hanger, wire hook and arms with clothes pin at ends **12.00**
Hanger, wire hook with tapering Bakelite shoulder supports **45.00**
Midget, folding travel hanger, patented Jan 7, 1913 . . . . **35.00**
Shoe, holds pr, bent wire, wooden toe supports **30.00**
Trouser Hanger, flat plated metal strips, slide closing latch **10.00**
Wire Hanger, with graduated wire coil extended across shoulders **55.00**

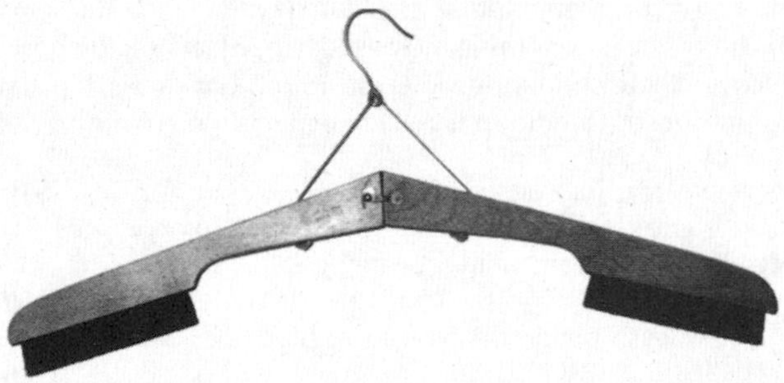

Coat Hanger, wood with brush ends, USA (design) pat no 77134, December 4, 1928, $30.00.

HARDWARE

Ornate hardware on the entry door was, at one time, a sign of pride of the builder and owner. This "jewelry of the building" was available at any hardware store in a tremendous variety. From 1870 to about 1920 manufacturers produced an estimated 5,000 patterns and there was one to complement every building. Decoration was the privilege and almost a necessity of the day. Even the bathtub and the kitchen stove were artistic statements.

Classic Green themes, natural life, and geometric tracery was embossed on nearly everything.

The trend to utilitarianism banished such decoration and by 1920 there was little to admire. The finest hardware ever made went the way of the draft horse, and five millenniums of development of the metalworker's art disappeared. Surely there is a lesson in anthropology here.

Antique hardware has been "discovered" by decorators and builders, much to the delight of everyone. Collectors in all states are preserving this national heritage. The Antique Doorknob Collectors of America (ADCA), PO Box 31, Chatham, NJ, 07928-0031, conducts research and provides identification and fellowship. Join the club!

Advisor: Charles W. Wardell, P.O. Box 195, Trinity, NC 27370.

Club: Hardware Companies Kollectors' Club, 715 W. 204th Ave., Hutchinson, KS 67502; The Antique Doorknob Collectors of America, P.O. Box 126, Eola, IL 60519.

Cherub on eagle's back, Branford Lock Co, 1885 . . . . **$200.00**
Classic Greek Floral Knob, Yale & Towne Co, 1905. . . . . **50.00**
Emblematic Elk's knob and escutcheon, Yale & Towne Co, 1895. . . . . **175.00**
Floral Design Knob, various makers, 1890–1910 . . . . **35.00**
Gothic, various makers, 1880–1920. **20.00**
Hexagon, Corbin Lock Co, 1874 . . . . **200.00**
Hound Dog Knob, Russell & Erwin Co, 1870 . . . . **500.00**
Hummingbird Knob, Russell & Erwin Co, 1880 . . . . **350.00**
Ornate Doorbell, 4" brass gong, Russell & Erwin Co, 1880. . . . . **300.00**
Pierced Flowers Knob, Reading Hardware Co, 1905 . . . . **75.00**
Standing Indian, Mallory-Wheeler Co, 1880. . . . . **450.00**

HARKER POTTERY

In 1840 Benjamin Harker of East Liverpool, Ohio, built a kiln and produced yellowware products. During the Civil War, David Boyce managed the firm. Harker and Boyce played important roles in the management of the firm through much of its history. In 1931 the company moved to Chester, West Virginia. Eventually, Jeannette Glass Company purchased Harker, closing the plant in March 1972.

Much of Harker's wares were utilitarian. The company introduced Cameo ware in 1945 and a Rockingham ware line in 1960. A wide range of backstamps and names were used.

Periodical: *The Daze*, P.O. Box 57, Otisville, MI 48463.

Amy, cake plate, 10½" h **$8.00**
Amy, pie lifter. **15.00**
Amy, sugar scoop **35.00**
Black-Eyed Susan, bread and butter plate. **3.00**
Cameoware, bread and butter plate, Dogwood. **2.00**
Cameoware, creamer, Ivy Wreath **6.00**
Cameoware, cup and saucer, Everglades, Harmony House label **7.00**
Cameoware, dinner plate, Cock O'Morn **6.00**
Cameoware, platter, Provincial Tulip **8.00**
Cameoware, salt and pepper shakers, pr, Rose **8.00**
Cameoware, syrup jug, Daisy **15.00**
Colonial Lady, cup and saucer. **12.00**
Colonial Lady, dinner plate **5.00**
Colonial Lady, spoon. **25.00**
Corinthian, cup and saucer **3.00**
Corinthian, soup bowl. **5.00**
Dresden Duchess, cake set, plate, 4 dessert plates, Royal Gadroon shape, 7½" d. **15.00**
Mallow, berry bowl. **4.00**
Mallow, bread and butter plate **5.00**
Monterey Zephyr, casserole, cov **8.00**
Petit Point Rose, dinner plate, 9" d. **10.00**
Petit Point Rose, pie baker, 9" d **20.00**
Pinecone, tidbit tray, 2 tier. **20.00**
Red Apple, mixing bowl, 10" d **30.00**
Red Apple, pie server **20.00**
Red Apple, utility plate **20.00**
Tulip, cake plate, round, orange. **5.00**
Tulip, cereal bowl **3.00**
Tulip, salt and pepper shakers, orange **4.00**
Water Lily, dinner plate. **5.00**

HARMONICAS AND RELATED ITEMS

Since this section came out in the Fourth Edition, harmonica collecting has surged in popularity. Many people are out beating the flea market bushes and coming up with some very interesting instruments. As with most collectibles, the more unusual models are the most popular and therefore costly; those with bells or large brass horn attachments, or with cover plates made to look like airships, old cats, etc, will command three figure prices.

Collecting harmonicas is appealing for several reasons: the endless variety of models—some quite bizarre; compact size for storage and display; the fact that you can play them as well as look at them; and reasonable coast for conventional models. Since this section was written for the last edition, we have doubled our estimate of the number of different harmonica models made since 1880 to about 40,000. If this is hard to believe, consider that The Harmonika Museum in Trossingen, Germany has about 25,000 models. Several US collectors have about 2,000 models each in their private collections, many of them are not in the German museum. Early catalogs show thousands of models never seen by anyone.

To anyone just getting started, we recommend getting a copy of the latest Hohner price list from Hohner, Inc, P.O. Box 9375, Richmond, VA 23227. Many harmonicas seen for sale as "antiques" or "old" are in Hohner's current line. New models may cost less—sometimes a lot less—than what uniformed dealers may think their used harmonica is worth. For Hohners, at least check

All American, Harmonic Reed Corp, Philadelphia, resembles streamline railroad car, red, white, and blue dec on harmonica and box, $35.00.

for the star in the trademark. It is found on the side opposite the model name and consists of a star in a circle held by two hands. This indicates pre-1940 vintage. Later Hohners have no star. Not all Hohner harmonicas have this trademark, but most do.

The prices listed are for harmonicas or related items in nice collectible condition, with minimal dents, rust spots or other defects, and with original box in fine condition (unless otherwise indicated).

Advisors: Alan G. Bates, 495 Dogwood Dr., Hockessin, DE 19707, (800) 597-7012, e-mail: harmonicas@compuserve.com; Buzzie Nightingale, May/Oct-P.O. Box 447, Madison, NH 03849, (603) 367-4459, Nov/Apr-701 SE 15th St. #2, Pompano Beach, FL 33060, (954) 785-2729.

Club: A new collectors club has just been formed called Harmonica Collectors International. Anyone interested in receiving more information and membership application should write HCI, P.O. Box 6081, St. Louis, MO 63006-6081, or e-mail hcrain@harleysharps.net.

HARMONICAS

Alpina, Koch, double-sided model, 20 double holes per side, large holes on cov plates with metal strips across diameter of each hole, telescoping end on box **$75.00**

Auto-Valve Harp, Hohner, 10 double holes, octave tuned, with star in trademark, ornate box **55.00**

Bravo, Hohner, 14 double holes, conductor leading harmonica band on box cov, no star **35.00**

Babe's Musical Bat, miniature, 5 hole harmonica is mounted in souvenir baseball bat, sometimes found with Babe Ruth's signature, 3³/₄" l, price without signature **100.00**

Brass Band Clarion, Ch Weiss, 10 double holes, octave tuned, with "organ pipes" covering reeds, distinctive label inside box cov showing Weiss and Prussian general playing harmonica, US Pat. 592850, 1897 . . . . **90.00**

Butterfly Harmonica, Nippon Gakki, Japan, 10 holes, butterfly trademark on both sides **25.00**

Camping, Hohner, 20 double holes, anodized gold covers, plastic comb, clamshell case **45.00**

Chordomonica-I, Hohner, Chamber-Huang System, 10 hole model, slide button like chromatic, leather pouch **75.00**

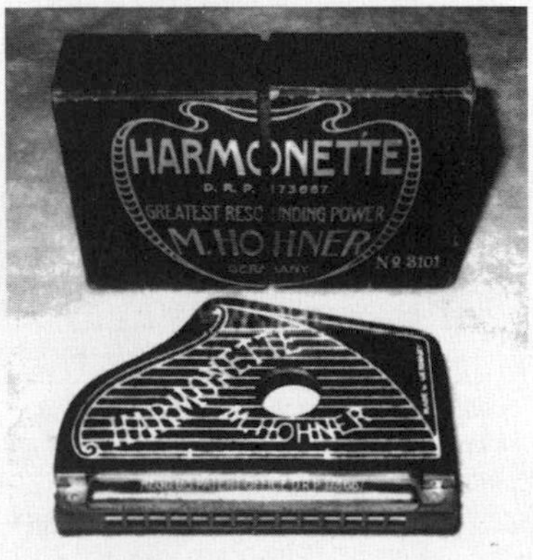

Harmonette, Hohner, harp shaped, wooden resonator chamber with painted dec, 14 double holes, 4⁵/₈" l, with telescoping box, $125.00.

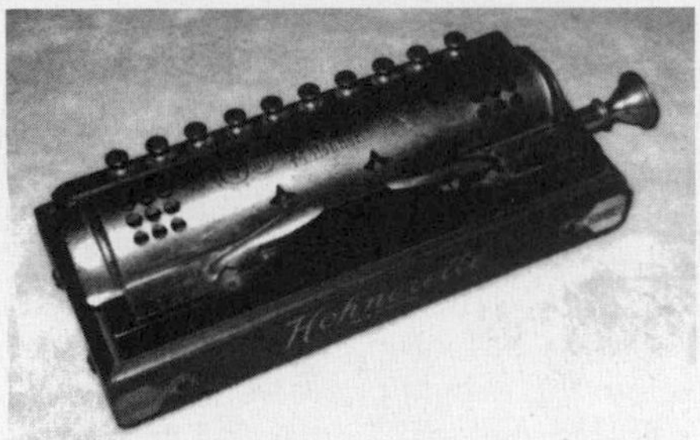

Hohnerette, Hohner, unadorned model, trumpet–like mouthpiece, 10 buttons, chord and bass keys, with wind box, $125.00.

Clover No. I Harmonophone, funnel shaped resonator, cov plates stamped with US patents #483160 (1892), and 605083 (1899), wooden box with sliding top **300.00**

Echo/Bell Metal Reeds, Hohner, double sided, 16 double holes per side, boldly raised cov plate designs with star shaped perforations, sleeves on trademark have zig-zag cut off, star in trademark, "The Echo Star" with Alpine scene on box **85.00**

Echo Elite, Hohner, streamlined design, 24 double holes per side, red enamel, nickel plating and powder blue mouthpiece, red, blue and silver box with rounded ends, 7⁵/₈" l **95.00**

Echo-Luxe, Hohner, 14 double holes, curved front and back, Art Deco design on cov plates with no flaked areas in enamel, "Century of Progess" on box. **125.00**

Echophone, Hohner, bullet shaped brass resonator, 10 holes, 4¹/₂" l, no box **90.00**

Echo Super Vamper, Hohner, 10 holes, with star **45.00**

Harmonetta, Hohner, harmonica type mouthpiece, honeycomb system of 32 buttons, introduced in 1966, discontinued in 1980, 6 x 7" **550.00**

Hohnerette, Hohner, with wind box containing harmonica, trumpet-like mouthpiece, 10 buttons, 5 brass horns, orig box **350.00**

Hohner Band, 12 double holes, curved front and back, with star, young ladies on box **50.00**

Hohner Orchestra I, 4-10" holes, metal clad hole dividers, conductor leading harmonica band scene on box, no star. **45.00**

Little Bandmaster, Seydel Söhne, Germany, mini, 5 holes, flaring horns in high relief on side plates, 1⁵/₈" l. **40.00**

Loudspeaker, Strauss, 10 holes, single horn projecting from back, with instruction folder and box **175.00**

Marine Orchestra-2 Bells, Hohner, 14 double holes, 2 different size bells with ringer springs mounted behind cov plate, no box **275.00**

My Little One, F A Rauner, mini, 5 holes **25.00**

New Echo, Hohner, 14 double holes, basket weave pattern on cov plates, with star **40.00**

Organette, Hohner, cylindrical, with mouthpiece, 10 note keys, chord and bass keys, brass, black, or brown finish **125.00**

Philmonet, Chris Kratt Instrument Co, USA, 10 holes, black plastic body, c1950 . . . . **25.00**

Polyphonia No. 5, Hohner, chromatic, 56 reeds, plays on blow and draw, with star in trademark, telescoping box with cloth cov **150.00**

Presciosa, Hohner, 20 double holes, with star, metallic gold box **60.00**

Roy Rogers Riders, Harmonic Reed Corp, Phila, with pristine bubble wrap store card **95.00**
Sinfonet, Wm Kratt Co, USA, 10 holes, wooden body, c1950 . . . . **35.00**
Sousa's Band Professional Model, made in Germany, 10 holes, rounded ends, John Philip Sousa's signature on harmonica and blue-green box, 4" l **50.00**
Siamese Twins, Hohner, 2 harmonicas attached at 30 degree angle to single outer cov plate which wraps around back, each harmonica has 14 double holes, c1905, no box **100.00**
Siamese Twins, Hohner, 2 harmonicas attached at 30 degree angle to single outer cov plate which wraps around back, each harmonica has 14 double holes, c1905, with box **250.00**
Super Scout, Magnus Harmonica Corp, Newark, NJ, 10 holes, cowboy on harmonica and box, c1948. . . . . **25.00**
Thorens No. 63 Color Harmonica, made in Switzerland, assorted pastel colors, enameled body and cov plates **50.00**
Unsere Lieblinge, Hohner, 14 double holes, curved front and back, star in trademark, 2 young ladies on box cov, 4½" l **45.00**
Vest Pocket Harp, Hohner, 10 holes, no star in trademark, 3⅛" l **20.00**
World Reknown, Hohner, Model 3CND, 10 double holes, octave tuned, Alpine scene on box **60.00**

HARMONICA RELATED

Booklet, *How-to-Play the Harmonica,* Hohner, cov scene of young man playing harmonica, with instructions, music, and pictures of US Marine Band, Navy Band, etc, 1925 . . . . **$15.00**
Revolving Obeslisk Display, Hohner, windup rotary base with display top shaped like Washington Monument, brackets and clips on each 4 faces to mount harmonica boxes, painted on prices and model numbers for each harmonica, complete with all hardware and windup crank **650.00**

HARTLAND PLASTICS, INC

Although the Hartland trade name survives today, Hartland Plastic collectibles focus on plastic television cowboy and sports figures issued in the 1950s. The baseball figures were reissued in 1989. They have a "25" in a circle on their back just below the belt. Do not confuse them with the earlier figures.

Most figures came with accessories. These need to be present in order for the figure to be considered complete. There are two Lone Ranger figures, the second bearing a much closer resemblance to Clayton Moore.

After a period of rapid rise in the early 1990s, especially for sports figures, prices are now stable. In fact, commonly found figures are a hard sell at full book price.

Annie Oakley, 9½" h **$90.00**
Babe Ruth, late 1950s, 7½" h **75.00**
Blessed Virgin Mary, soft blue outer rober over white robe accented by gold collar, brown hair, gold halo, mkd "B150 by Hartland Plastics, Inc" on underside, orig box with repeated design of church steeple and circular window, 6½" h figure, 2¼ x 2½ x 8¾" box **40.00**

Dale Evans & Butttermilk, includes Buttermilk, Dale, hat, saddle, and reins, no guns, orig box, $317.00. Photo New England Auction Gallery.

Brave Eagle, 9½" h **140.00**
Buffalo Bill, complete **175.00**
Cactus Pete, 8" h **75.00**
Clay Hollister, Tombstone Territory, complete with 2 guns, 8" h **75.00**
Dale Evans, olive green outfit, white hat, with horse **175.00**
Hoby Gilman, Trackdown, late 1950s **175.00**
Jim Hardie, Tales of Wells Fargo, brown shirt, dark blue pants, complete with brown hat and gun, 7¾" h **175.00**
Lone Ranger, complete with 2 pistols **75.00**
Lucas McCain, The Rifleman, 1950–60s **175.00**
Matt Dillon, yellow shirt, brown vest, 7" h figure, 8¼" gray horse with black saddle **75.00**
Mickey Mantle, white uniform, blue cap, 1960s, 7" h **100.00**
Nellie Fox, red and black uniform, early 1960s. **200.00**
Paladin, 9½" h **175.00**
Ted Williams, late 1950s, 7½" h. **75.00**
Tom Jeffords, Broken Arrow, complete **175.00**
Tonto, complete with gun, knife, saddle, and replacement feather **75.00**
Yogi Berra, blue and white uniform, early 1960s. **125.00**

HATPIN HOLDERS AND HATPINS

Women used hatpins to keep their hats in place. The ends of the pins were decorated in a wide variety of materials—ranging from gemstones to china—and the pins themselves became a fashion accessory. Since a woman was likely to own many hatpins and they were rather large, special holders were developed for them.

Clubs: American Hatpin Society, 20 Monticello Dr., Rolling Hills Estate, CA 90274; International Club for Collectors of Hatpins and Hatpin Holders, 1013 Medhurst Rd., Columbus, OH 43220.

HOLDERS

Art Nouveau, SS, 4 ring or neck-chain holders, c1905, 6½" h **$150.00**
Belleek, pink and maroon floral dec, green leaves, gold top, mkd "Willets Belleek," dated 1911, 5¼" h **125.00**
China, hp, floral dec, artist sgd, Austria, 4½" h **75.00**
Figural, golf bag, SS, mkd "sterling 950," 3" l **170.00**
Limoges, grapes, pink roses, matte finish, sgd **60.00**
Nippon, relief serpent dec, mottled ground, 5" h **165.00**
Royal Bayreuth, art nouveau lady, 16 pin holes, 4½" h **475.00**
Royal Rudolstadt, lavender and roses dec **25.00**
Schlegelmilch, RS Prussia, floral and scroll dec, gold accents, ftd **170.00**

PINS

Advertising, Economy Stoves and Ranges, 10" l. **$45.00**
Art Deco, plastic, free form design in 2-mold mottled color, c1925, 7" l steel pin **25.00**
Art Nouveau, gilt over brass, 2 polished free-form amethysts on steel pin, c1905, 8" l **80.00**
Art Nouveau, SS, 4-sided, 12" l **85.00**
Art Nouveau, SS, stylized woman, 1905, 8¾" l. **80.00**
Brass, openwork, amber setting **45.00**
Carnival Glass, figural rooster, amber **35.00**
Figural, tennis racket, SP **25.00**
Mercury Glass, elongated cased teardrop **70.00**
Mother-of-Pearl, snake motif, ruby head, gold top, USA **175.00**
Porcelain, hp, gold overlay, Victorian motif, c1890, 1¾" l . . . **150.00**
Porcelain, scenic design, ornate mounting **35.00**
St Louis World's Fair, enamel dec, 1904 . . . . **30.00**

HATS, LADY'S VINTAGE

Stop! Don't think about throwing those old hats away! Hats are a very important part of fashion history. Hats can still be found to purchase at reasonable prices throughout the country and abroad. However, condition is of great importance as well as uniqueness and age. Millinery items such as hat blocks, hat stands, hat boxes, feathers, vintage ornamentation, millinery advertisements and books are in demand by collectors. There are many unique and intriguing hats being designed and constructed today for future collectors of hats from the late 1900s. Happy hat hunting!

Advisors: Danielle Ware and Stephanie Castellini, 1199 S. Main Rd., Vineland, NJ 08360, (609) 794-8300.

Club: The Costume Society of America, 55 Edgewater Dr., P.O. Box 73, Earleville, MD 21919, (800) CSA-9447 or www.costumesocietyamerica.com.

Felt, brown and beige swirled, with pheasant feather, Deauville, 1940s **$55.00**
Felt, cloche, white back and hot pink, Mary McDonnell, 1930s **40.00**
Felt, fric frac, gold, orig paper style tag, early 1940s **45.00**
Felt, wide brimmed, black with black grosgrain ribbon and netting on brim, Merrimac Hat Co, 1930s **25.00**
Felt, yellow, with tapered brim covered with black fishnetting, yellow/white buckles on yellow grosgrain ribbon, Margaret Longfellow, Philadelphia, late 1930s **45.00**
Silk, bonnet, black, with black silk flowers, Altosenberg Fine Millinery, Philadelphia, 1900s. **65.00**
Silk, bonnet, black,with black lace encircling black jet bead ornamentation, early 1900s **125.00**
Silk, bonnet, black, with lavender ostrich feathers, black jet heads and silk violets, long black silk ties, late 1800s **55.00**
Silk, bonnet, black with black silk ribbon ties, 1890s **75.00**
Silk, cloche, silk, beige with brown geometric designs attached with french knots, 1920s **45.00**
Straw, cap, navy blue with white feather and attached rhinestones, blue netting, early 1950s. **35.00**
Straw, cloche, powder blue with silk lining, 1930s **95.00**
Straw, picture hat, crimped wide brim, natural straw color with black grosgrain ribbon around rim, 1950s **65.00**
Straw, wide brim, blue with velvet ribbon and 2 silk magnolias, 1920s **65.00**

Group of Hats, $25–$150.00. Photo courtesy Gene Harris Antique Auction Center, Inc.

HAWAIIANA

Since Missionary times, visitors to Hawaii have been bringing back souvenirs.

This century, photos, postcards, steamship and airline items, menus, dolls, figurines, lamps, jewelry, clothes, ukuleles, artwork, books, perfume bottles and many other souvenirs were brought back to the mainland United States. All are now sought by collectors of Hawaiiana, with an emphasis on pre-1960 items.

Advisor: Anne Moore, P.O. Box 604, Bingen, WA 98605, (509) 493-4463.

Bookends, bronzed cast iron, palm trees and antheriums, c1930s, 7" **$95.00**
Chalkware, hula girl, c1930s, 16", some paint chips **150.00**
Cribbage Board, koa wood, pineapple shape, c1950s, 12" **35.00**
Doll, hula girl, fabric, hp face, c1940s, 10" **45.00**
Doll, hula girl, Suzette, Effanbee, composition, c1930s, 11½". **275.00**
Figurine, hula girl, ceramic, Hedi Schoop, c1940s, 11½". **275.00**
Handkerchief, large print of hula girl and Diamond Head on yellow ground, c1940s, 19" sq **25.00**
Lamp, hula girl, bronzed pot metal, motorize hip movement, c1940s, 19" **575.00**
Lamp, hula girl, chalkware, c1950s, 30". **300.00**
Magazine, *Paradise of the Pacific,* Nov 1946 . . . . **15.00**

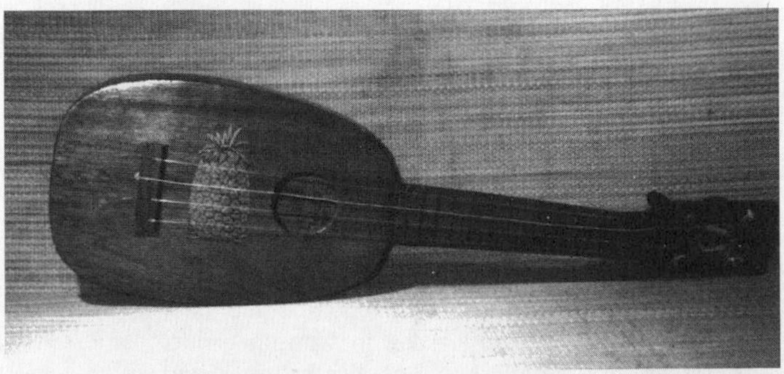

Kamaka Pineapple Ukelele, orig decals, c1920s, 21" l, $375.00.

Doll, "Hanna," composition body, china head, sleep eyes, Schoenau & Hoffmeister, c1920s, 7" h, $225.00.

Poster, "Hawaii by Clipper," Pan American, c1950s, 28 x 42", $225.00.

Menu, Matson, colorful artwork by E Savage, stylized scenes of Hawaiian life printed on front and back, c1940s 60.00
Menu, Outrigger Canoe Club, c1940s 30.00
Paintings, airbrush watercolors of Hawaiian flowers by various artists such as Mundorff, Hale Pua, and Tip Freeman, c1940s, approx 16 x 20", price listed for each 175.00
Pennant, blue felt, "Hawaii" with hula girl and canoe, c1930s, 26½" 35.00
Perfume Bottle, carved monkey pod wood, flower shape, c1940s, 4½" 50.00
Pillow Slip Cover, pink cloth, fringe, colorful graphics of hula girl and surfer, 17" sq 35.00
Plate, "Lei Lani," Vernon Kilns, c1940s, 10½" 45.00
Salt and Pepper Shakers, pr, hp, hula girls, Japan, c1950s, 3½" h 45.00
Sheet Music, *Song of the Islands,* Chas E King, hula girl illus, c1920s 8.00
Sheet Music, *Ukulele Lady,* Gus Kahn, c1930s 12.00
Spoon, sterling, "Hawaii" with Diamond Head in relief, c1940s, 5½" l 25.00
Stationary, Royal Hawaiian Hotel,, single sheet of paper with drawings of the Royal Hawaiian Hotel and Moana Hotels dec, c1920s 8.00
Tie Rack, koa wood, surf board shape, Hawaiian seal decal, 1940s, 12" 65.00
Tray, round, koa wood, center Hawaiian seal decal, 1930s, 7½" d 40.00
Yearbook, Mid-Pacific Institute, 1928 . . . . 20.00

"Shaker" Doll, spring between legs and body, magnet on bottom, Made in Japan, c1950, 7" h, $75.00.

HEISEY GLASS

A. H. Heisey Company of Newark, Ohio, began operations in 1896. Within a short period of time, it was one of the major suppliers of glass to middle America. Its many blown and molded patterns were produced in crystal, colored, milk (opalescent), and Ivorina Verde (custard). Pieces also featured cutting, etching, and silver-deposit decoration. Glass figurines were made between 1933 and 1957.

Not all Heisey glass is marked. Marked pieces have an "H" within a diamond. However, I have seen some non-Heisey pieces with this same marking at several flea markets.

It is important to identify the pattern of Heisey pieces. Neila Bredehoft's *The Collector's Encyclopedia of Heisey Glass, 1925–1938* (Collector Books: 1986) is helpful for early items. The best help for post–World War II patterns is old Heisey catalogs.

Club: Heisey Collectors of America, 169 W. Church St, Newark, OH 43055.

Newsletter: *The Newscaster*, P.O. Box 102, Plymouth, OH 44865.

Basket, Lariat, no loops, 7" $100.00
Bookends, pr, fish 230.00
Bowl, Provincial, crystal, rolled edge, 12" d 35.00
Candlesticks, pr, Crystolite, crystal, sq base 50.00
Candy Jar, cov, Lariat 125.00
Champagne, Colonial, crystal 10.00
Cocktail, Arcadia, crystal 16.00
Cocktail, Duquesne, tangerine bowl, 3 oz 130.00
Cologne, Lariat, enamel dec 50.00
Cruet, Fandango, faceted stopper, 4 oz 50.00
Cruet, Greek Key, stopper, 4 oz 95.00
Custard, Colonial, crystal 5.00
Goblet, Creole, sahara bowl, 11 oz 45.00
Goblet, Duquesne, tangerine bowl, 9 oz 210.00
Pitcher, Beaded Panel & Sunburst, ½ gal, mold marks 75.00
Plate, Greek Key, 5½" d 17.50
Relish, Crystolite, oval, 3 part, 9½" l 15.00
Saucer Champagne, Carcassone, cobalt bowl, 6 oz 45.00
Salt and Pepper Shakers, pr, Empress, Old Colony etch 40.00
Sherbet, Galaxy, flamingo, 6 oz 5.00
Soda, Banded Flute, 14 oz 100.00
Toothpick, Fancy Loop, emerald 120.00
Torte Plate, Crystolite, 13" 65.00
Torte Plate, Spanish, 14" 20.00
Vase, Cathedral, 8" h 70.00
Vase, Warwick, moongleam, 9" h 460.00

HI-FI EQUIPMENT

Remember your "hi-fi" from the 1950s and 60s? The equipment used those glowing little bulbs called vacuum tubes, and music came from black vinyl discs called records, not CD's.

Well, now it's the 1990s, and some of that old hi-fi gear is now collectible. Items that are in demand are U.S. made vacuum tube type amplifiers, pre-amplifiers, AM/FM tuners and receivers. Also desirable are certain brands of speakers and record turntables from the U.S. and Europe. Certain old vacuum tubes if new and in the original boxes are also collectible.

The key to ascertaining an item's value is to know the manufacturer or brand, and the model number. Some of the amplifiers to look for include Audio Research, Conrad Johnson, McIntosh, marantz, Western Electric, Altec, Acrosound, Heathkit, H. H. Scott, and Harmon Kardon. Speakers to look for include Altec, Tannoy, JBL, QUAD, and Lowthar. Record turntable names include Thorens and SME.

WARNING! NEVER plug old hi-fi gear into an AC outlet with the power on! Tube equipment uses high voltage circuits, and old power cords are almost always deteriorated—creating a potential hazard of shock or electrocution!

Advisor: Jeffrey Viola, 784 Eltone Rd., Jackson, NJ 08527, (732) 928-0666.

Acrosound, Model ULII, amplifier, Ultra Linear, mono, 60 watts, EL 34 output tubes **$120.00**
Acrosound, Model Stereo 120, amplifier, Ultra Linear, stereo, 120 watts, EL 34 output tubes **120.00**
Altec, Model 350A, amplifier, mono, 60 watts, 6550 output tubes **100.00**
Altec, Model 605A, speaker, coaxial horn, 16 ohms **50.00**
Audio Research, Model D60, amplifier, stereo, 6650 output tubes **200.00**
Audio Research, Model SP-7, pre-amplifier, tube, stereo **100.00**
Conrad Johnson, Model PV-2, pre-amplifier, tube, stereo **75.00**
Heathkit, Model W5-M, amplifier, mono, 25 watts, KT66 output tubes **75.00**
Marantz, audio consolette, pre-amplifier, tube **100.00**
Marantz, Model 5, amplifier, mono, 30 watts, EL 34 output tubes, meter **200.00**
Marantz, Model 7-C, pre-amplifier, stereo, tubes, wood case, metal knobs **250.00**
Marantz, Model 8-B, amplifier, stereo, 70 watts, EL 34 output tubes **400.00**
McIntosh, Model C-20, pre-amplifier, stereo, tubes, wood case **250.00**
McIntosh, Model MC-75, amplifier, mono, chrome chassis, 75 watts, 6550 tubes **150.00**
Sonex, Model Ultra Linear, amplifier, mono, 25 watts **50.00**
Tannoy, speaker, 12 or 15" dual concentric **50.00**
Western Electric, Model 300-B, vacuum tube, output, triode **25.00**

HIGGINS GLASS

Michael Higgins and Frances Stewart Higgins were actively involved in designing and decorating glass in their Chicago studio by the early 1950s. Between 1958 and 1964, the couple worked in a studio provied for them by Dearborn Glass, an industrial company located outside Chicago. Pieces were mass produced. A gold signature was screened on the front of each piece before the final firing. During the period with Dearborn, the Higgins developed new colors and enamels for their double-layered pieces and experimented with weaving copper wire into glass, fusing glass chips to create crystalline forms, and overlaying colors onto glass panels.

After leaving Dearborn, the Higgins established a studio at Haeger. In 1966 they re-established their own studio. During the late 1960s and early 1970s, the Higgins manufactured large quantities of glass plaques, often framed in wood. In 1972 they purchased the building in Riverside, Illinois, that currently serves as their studio. Pieces made after 1972 have an engraved signature on the back. Unless stated otherwise, all of the listings below have a gold signature. When they retire, the Higgins plan to close their studio rather than allow a successor to continue.

Ashtray, blue fish motif, 10 x 14" **$82.50**
Ashtray, blue waves with sand dollars, 5 x 7" **49.50**
Ashtray, orange and green psychedelic florals, 11½ x 7" **38.50**
Bowl, blue with gold sunbursts, 11½" d **104.50**
Bowl, pink and blue amobae, 5 cornered, 3 ftd, Stickman, etched signature, 8½ x 8" **148.50**
Bowl, turquoise and black dot ray, 5 cornered, ftd, Stickman signature, 8½ x 9" **93.50**
Box, hardwood, orange ray lid, 2 x 4" **66.00**
Charger, green spike, 17" d **137.50**
Charger, purple spike, 12½" d **99.00**
Condiment, orange, green, and red rays, gold swirl dec, 3 part, Stickman and gold signature, 7 x 19" **77.00**
Dish, black and gray dot ray, bowite shaped, etched signature with Stickman, 10" l **93.50**
Dish, daisies, 3 part, ftd, 8½" d **110.00**
Dish, red, orange, and avocado rays, off center, Stickman and gold signature, 9 x 7" **55.00**
Finger Rings, pr, etched signature, approximately 1" sq **110.00**
Pendant, trees and setting sun motif, etched signature, 2 x 3" **82.50**
Plate, blue scroll, 13½" d **82.50**
Plate, chartreuse and white stripes with gold seaweed, 8½" d **55.00**
Plate, red and orange spike, 7½" d **38.50**
Tray, balloons, 9" d **49.50**
Tray, balloons in smoke, off center, 14½ x 12" **159.50**
Tray, chartreuse and white stripe with gold seaweed, 2 part, Stickman and gold signature, orig paper label, 7 x 14" **71.50**

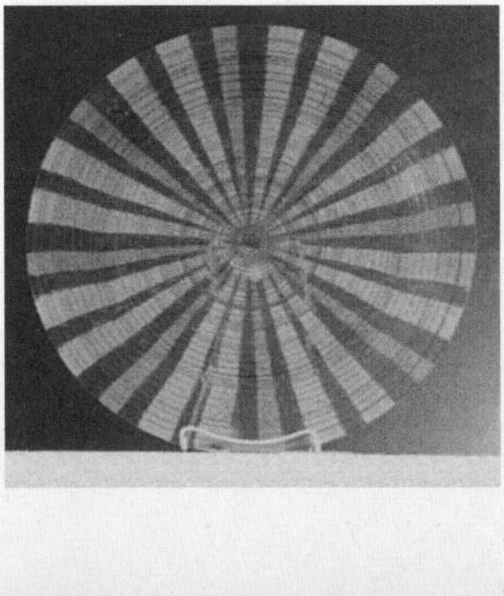

Charger, yellow and chartreuse ray, gold signature, 17" d, $165.00. Photo courtesy Jackson's Auctioneers & Appraisers.

Book, *Do It!*, Jerry Rubin, Simon & Schuster, NY, 1970, $200.00.

HIPPIE MEMORABILIA

The "Hippies" continued the "Beatnik" attitudes and conduct of rebellious, free-thinking nonconformity during the tumultuous 1960s. In 1964, students at the University of California at Berkeley began the first organized student protests, known as "The Free Speech Movement." As the Vietnam War escalated, a number of groups such as the Students for a Democratic Society (SDS), the Youth International Party (Yippies), led by Abbie Hoffman and Jerry Rubin, and the Weather Underground formed to protest the war with varying degrees of fervor.

The Haight-Ashbury area of San Francisco became the center for the emerging "counterculture." New and outrageous styles of clothes, music, art, theatre, attitudes, behavior, and politics emerged. Harvard professor Timothy Leary began controlled experiments with hallucionegic drugs (legal at the time). The watershed event of the counterculture, which took place in August, 1969, was the Woodstock music and Art Fair, which attracted at least 400,000 people. Rock bands proliferated across the country.

The era produced many thousands of highly collectible items. Basic categories include books, records, posters, underground newspapers and comics, magazines, bumper stickers, pinback buttons, etc.

Advisor: Richard M. Synchef, 22 Jefferson Ave., San Rafael, CA 94903, (415) 507-9933.

Note: Prices listed for items in excellent to near mint condition. All books are first editions with dust jackets in near fine or better condition.

Book, *Quotations From Chairman Mao Tse-Tung,* Foreign Language Press, Peking, 1966. . . . . **$250.00**
Book, *Rebellion in Neward,* Hayden, Tom, Random House, New York, 1967. . . . . **75.00**
Book, *Revolution for the Hell of It,* by Free (Abbie Hoffman pseudonym), Dial Press, New York, 1968 . . . . . . **300.00**
Book, *Woodstock Craftman's Manual,* Young, Jean, Prager Publishers, Inc, New York, 1972 . . . . **70.00**
Bumper Sticker, "The People Want McCarthy," orange letters on blue ground, 1968, 15 x 4" **60.00**
Comic Book, underground, El Perfecto Comics, Print Mint, Berkeley, CA, benefit comic for Timothy Leary Defense Fund, 1973 . . . . **125.00**
Handbill, Human Be-In, A Gathering of the Tribes, Stanley Mouse, Alton Kelley and Michael Bowen, artists, The Bindweed Press, San Francisco, Jan 14, 1967, 8½ x 11" **500.00**
Handbill, March Against the War, Los Angeles, Apr 22, 1970, Student Mobilization Committee, San Francisco, 8½ x 11" **125.00**
Handbill, Zenefit—Zen Mountain Center Benefit, Nov 13, 1966 . . . . **225.00**
Jigsaw Puzzle, Life, Peter Max, Schisgall, New York, 500 pcs, 1970, 9 x 11" box. **125.00**
Magazine, *Avant Garde,* Ginsburg, Ralph (ed), New York, issue #2, Marilyn Monroe issue, Bert Stern prints, Mar 1968 . . . . **225.00**
Magazine, *Life,* "Tragedy at Kent State," May 25, 1970 . . . . . . **40.00**
Newspaper, *San Francisco Oracle,* issue #5, The Human Be-In, same image as poster and handbill **250.00**
Paperback Book, *Electric Tibet,* Doukas, James, Dominion, North Hollywood, early study of San Francisco rock bands, 1969 . . . . **80.00**
Paperback Book, *LSD on Campus,* Young, Warren, & Hixon, Joseph, Dell, New York, 1966 . . . . **80.00**
Poster, "Can You Pass the Acid Test?," Ken Kesey and the Merry Pranksters, Norman Hartweg, artist, 1965 . . . . . . **2,600.00**
Poster, "Dick Gregory for President, Mark Lane for VP," Peace & Freedom Party, with photos, 1968 . . . . **500.00**
Poster, Monterey Pop Festival, Jan 16–18, 1967, Monterey County Fairgrounds **2,400.00**
Program, *Woodstock,* Warner Brothers, 48 pp, 1970. . . . . **50.00**
Record, *FSM'S Sounds & Songs of the Demonstration!,* FSM Records, Berkeley, CA, monaural LP, early student protest documentary, 1964 . . . . **250.00**
Record, *Murder at Kent State University,* Pete Hamill, narrated by Rosko, Flying Dutchman Records, monaural LP, 1970 . . . . **150.00**
Record, *Wake Up America,* Abbie Hoffman, Big Toe Records, limited to 1,000 copies, 1969. . . . . **300.00**
Ticket, Woodstock Music and Art Fair, Globe Ticket Co, Aug 1969 . . . . **100.00**

HOLIDAY COLLECTIBLES

Holidays play an important part in American life. Besides providing a break from work, they allow time for patriotism, religious renewal, and fun. Because of America's size and ethnic diversity, there are many holiday events of a regional nature. Attend some of them and pick up their collectibles. I have started a Fastnacht Day collection.

This listing is confined to national holidays. If I included special days, from Secretary's Day to Public Speaker's Day, I would fill this book with holiday collectibles alone. Besides, in fifty years is anyone going to care about Public Speaker's Day? No one does now.

Fourth of July, postcard, emb, red, white, blue, and gold, divided back, International Art Pub Co, 5¼ x 3¼", $4.50.

Club: National Valentine Collectors Assoc., P.O. Box 1404, Santa Ana, CA 92702.

Newsletter: *St. Patrick Notes,* 10802 Greencreek Dr., Houston, TX 77070.

Periodical: *Pyrofaz Magazine,* P.O. Box 2010, Saratoga, CA 95070.

Birthday, hat, Sweet Sixteen, crown type, cardboard, silver covered, glitter dec, 1930. . . . . **$5.00**
Birthday, puzzle, post card type, "Birthday Wishes," dove, heart, florals, and anchor, perforated cardboard pcs, German, c1909 . . . . **8.00**
Father's Day, sign "Father's Day Special," Winchester Arms, 1966 . . . . **12.00**
Fourth of July, bottle carrier, Coca-Cola, July Fourth, 6 box wrapper, c1935 . . . . **70.00**
Fourth of July, pinback button, multicolored Miss Liberty, 1906-07 . . . . **30.00**
Fourth of July, sheet music, *Stars and Stripes Forever*. **10.00**
Memorial Day, postcard, "Memorial Day Greetings," flag, draped red, white, and blue curtain, soldier's hat, crossed swords, gun, and bugle, fort scene bac ground, 1909 . . . . **6.00**
New Year's Day, book, child's, *Miss Flora McFlimsey And The Baby New Year,* Mariana, Lothrop, Lee & Shepard, 1951, dj **22.00**
New Year's Day, hat, cone shape, cardboard, crepe paper dec, cutout silver foil, 1928 . . . . **12.00**
New Year's Day, noisemaker, litho tin, wood handle, Kirchhof **20.00**
New Year's Day, ticket, admission to New Year's Eve Festival, Concord, OH, festival vignette, blue printing, white ground, 1858. . . . . **50.00**
President's Day, diecut, George Washington, 3 different scenes, set of 3, $2\frac{1}{2}$" h. **8.00**
President's Day, postcard, "Three Cheeres for George Washington," children waving flag beneath Washington's portrait, 1909 . . . . **1.75**
St Patrick's Day, diecut, gold harp entwined with shamrocks and green ribbon, mkd "Germany" **1.50**
St Patrick's Day, pin, shamrock shape, emb tin, silver luster, early 1900s **20.00**
St Patrick's Day, postcard, "The Charm of the Morn to You, Here's Wishing You A Bright and Happy St Patrick's Day," girl holding flower bouquet, 1916 . . . . **15.00**
Thanksgiving, napkin, printed, Pilgrims and Indians, cellophane package, 1940s **5.00**

Ground Hog Day, postcard, $20.00.

Thanksgiving, postcard, Grand Dinner Thanksgiving menu, 1913 . . . . **3.00**
Thanksgiving, postcard, "Here's To A Rough And Ready Thanksgiving Greeting" **3.00**
Thanksgiving, postcard, "Wishing You A Happy Thanksgiving," children feeding turkey, Clapsaddle artwork, International Art Publishing Co, 1908 . . . . **4.00**
Valentine's Day, chocolate mold, aluminum, heart shape, emb "Happy Valentine's Day," 1940 . . . . **10.00**
Valentine's Day, cookbook, *Valentine Queen of Hearts,* Jell-O, early 20th C **35.00**

HOLT-HOWARD

A. Grant Holt and brothers John and Robert J. Howard formed the Holt-Howard import company in Stamford, Connecticut, in 1948. The firm is best known for its novelty ceramics, including the Cat and Christmas lines and the popular Pixie Ware line of condiment jars. Designed by Robert J. Howard and produced between 1958 and the early 1960s, these ceramic containers proved to be so successful that knock-offs by Davar, Lefton, Lipper & Mann, M-G, Inc., and Norcrest quickly found their way into the market. Kay Dee Designs purchased Holt-Howard in 1990.

Authentic Pixieware is easily identified by its single-color vertical stripes on a white jar, flat pixie-head stopper (with attached spoon when appropriate), and condiment label with slightly skewed black lettering. An exception is three salad dressing cruets which had round heads. All pieces were marked, either with "HH" or "Holt-Howard,' a copyright symbol followed by the year "1958" or "1959," and "Japan." Some pieces may be found with a black and silver label.

Coq Rouge, candle holders, pr, $4\frac{3}{8}$" h **$30.00**
Coq Rouge, cereal bowl, 6" d **12.00**
Coq Rouge, coffeepot, 6 cup **60.00**
Coq Rouge, dinner plate, $9\frac{1}{2}$" d. **12.00**
Coq Rouge, flour canister **60.00**
Coq Rouge, jam jar **35.00**
Coq Rouge, ketchup jar. **30.00**
Coq Rouge, salt and pepper shakers, pr, large. **20.00**
Coq Rouge, snack dish **15.00**
Cozy Kitchen Kitties, ashtray, $4\frac{1}{2}$" d **55.00**
Cozy Kitchen Kitties, bud vase, Tabby and Tom Charmers, $6\frac{3}{4}$" h, price for pr. **80.00**
Cozy Kitchen Kitties, butter dish, cov, 7" l **95.00**
Cozy Kitchen Kitties, creamer **60.00**
Cozy Kitchen Kitties, Merry Measure, 3 x $3\frac{1}{2}$" **70.00**
Cozy Kitchen Kitties, salt and pepper shakers, pr **15.00**
Cozy Kitchen Kitties, wall caddy, 7" h **70.00**
Daisy 'Dorables, bud vase, $5^1/$" h. **65.00**
Daisy 'Dorables, candle holder, 4" h **30.00**
Jeeves, chip dish, $6\frac{3}{4}$" **75.00**
Jeeves, decanter, $10\frac{1}{2}$" h **150.00**
Pixieware, berry bowl **95.00**
Pixieware, hors d' oeuvre dish, Party Pixies **150.00**
Pixieware, condiment jar, chili sauce **175.00**
Pixieware, honey jar, $5\frac{1}{2}$" h. **300.00**
Pixieware, mustard dish, Mustard Max. **95.00**
Pixieware, salt and pepper shakers, pr, winking duo **175.00**
Winking Santa, candle holder, #6268, sgd, 6" h **30.00**
Winking Santa, egg nog pitcher, 40 oz, $4\frac{1}{2}$" h **45.00**
Winking Santa, punch bowl set, 10 pcs, 3 qt bowl, 8 six oz mugs, candy cane striped ladle **115.00**

Blotter, "That Christmas May Live On! Buy Extra War Bonds," 1940s, 6 x 3", $5.00.

Platter, Nautilus shape, gold trim, 13⅝" l, $12.00.

HOME-FRONT COLLECTIBLES

Home-front collectibles emerged as a separate collecting category approximately three years ago. The fact that it took so long is surprising. However, many home-front collectibles have been sold for years in crossover categories; e.g., post cards and magazines. See the Anti-Axis listing for related items.

Club: Society of Ration Token Collectors, 618 Jay Dr., Gallipolis, OH 45631.

Badge, Civil Defense, "Aux Police Eerie County NY," center "CD" emblem, USA, WWII **$20.00**
Banner, "Relative In Service," red, white field and blue star center, with 11 x 15" black wood post and gold cord, USA, WWII **28.00**
Compact, brass, snap lid, blue enamel top with raised Army brass emblem in center, contains powder puff, powder, and mirror, 3½" **55.00**
Earrings, pr, screw back, AAF emblem on face, ST, USA, WWII **20.00**
Gas Mask, child's, rubber, 1 pc curved lense above respirator valve, attached canister/filter and elastic headband, mkd "Small Child's" **25.00**
Gas Mask, civilian's, green rubber mask with straps, flat aluminum filter, inked Waffenamt stamp on filter, Germany, WWII **20.00**
Glow Button, Air Raid Warden, celluloid, red, white and blue, "Buy War Bonds at Minnesota Federal Savings & Loan Association" on back **35.00**
ID Bracelet, SS, regular links and clasp, curved Combat Infantry Badge ID bar, USA, WWII **33.00**
Pendant, Gold Star Mother, bronze, gold star insert over liner and statue of Liberty and Eiffel Tower, given by the US Lines, numbered on rim, loop for hanging, USA, WWI, 1½" d **26.00**
Pin Cushion, painted bent-over Hitler figure with cushion affixed at rump, base mkd "Stick a Pin in the Axis," and "Mason Co." 6½" h **145.00**
Pin, "Son In Service," gilt and enamel pinback brooch with Great Nation Seal design attached by small chain, orig box, USA, WWII **20.00**
Ring, SS, AAF emblem on crest, WWII **56.00**
Signet Ring, Airborne, SS, red stone in face with airborne images on sides and "Airborne U.S. Army" around stone, miniature jump wings fixed on stone, USA, WWII **46.00**
Sweetheart Ring, copper, Air Cadet Wings on crest and symbols on sides **34.00**

HOMER LAUGHLIN

Homer Laughlin and his brother, Shakespeare, built two pottery kilns in East Liverpool, Ohio, in 1871. Laughlin became one of the first firms in America to produce whiteware.

In 1896, William Wills and a Pittsburgh group led by Marcus Aaron bought the Laughlin firm. New plants were built in Laughlin Station, Ohio, and Newall, West Virginia. Plant advances included continuous tunnel kilns, spray glazing, and mechanical jiggering.

The original trademark used from 1871 to 1890 merely identified the products as "Laughlin Brothers." The next trademark featured the American eagle astride the prostrate British lion. The third mark featured a monogram of "HLC," which has appeared, with slight variations, on all dinnerware produced since about 1900. The 1900 trademark contained a number which identified month, year and plant at which the product was made. Letter codes were used in later periods.

Prices for Homer Laughlin china (with the possible exception of Virginia Rose pieces) are still moderate. Some of the patterns from the 1930 to 1940 period have contemporary designs that are very artistic.

REPRODUCTION ALERT: Harlequin and Fiesta lines were reissued in 1978 and marked accordingly.

Newsletter: *The Laughlin Eagle*, 1270 63rd Ter. South, St. Petersburg, FL 33705.

Note: For additional listings see Fiesta Ware.

Amberstone, creamer **$4.50**
Amberstone, dinner plate **5.00**
Blue Willow, cup and saucer **3.00**
Blue Willow, soup bowl **8.00**
Conchita, cake server, Kitchen Kraft **95.00**
Epicure, creamer, pink **16.00**
Epicure, gravy **20.00**
Epicure, dinner plate, 10½" d **14.00**
Epicure, sugar, pink **16.00**
Harlequin, ashtray, basket, rose **65.00**
Harlequin, ball jug, maroon **55.00**
Harlequin, berry bowl, individual, rose **8.00**
Harlequin, butter base, maroon **50.00**
Harlequin, candlesticks, pr, mauve **495.00**
Harlequin, casserole, maroon, oval **215.00**
Harlequin, creamer, red, novelty **30.00**
Harlequin, cup, rose **8.00**
Harlequin, deep plate, maroon **35.00**

Harlequin, eggcup, double, maroon **22.00**
Harlequin, oatmeal bowl, gray **20.00**
Harlequin, sugar, cov, mauve **15.00**
Harlequin, teacup, dark green **6.00**
Riviera, butter dish, cov, green, 1/4 lb **185.00**
Riviera, casserole, green **165.00**
Riviera, dinner plate, green, 10" d **95.00**
Riviera, juice tumbler, green **85.00**
Virginia Rose, butter, cov **45.00**
Virginia Rose, gravy **6.50**

HORSE COLLECTIBLES

This is one of those collectible categories where you can collect the real thing, riding equipment ranging from bridles to wagons, and/or representational items. It is also a category where the predominant number of collectors are women.

The figurine is the most-favored collectible. However, horse-related items can be found in almost every collectible category from Western movie posters to souvenir spoons. As long as there is a horse on it, it is collectible.

A neglected area among collectors is the rodeo. I am amazed at how much rodeo material I find at East Coast flea markets. I never realized how big the eastern rodeo circuit was.

Club: North American Model Horse Show Assoc., P.O. Box 50508, Denton, TX 76206.

Newsletter: *The Model Horse Trader,* 143 Mercer Way, Upland, CA 91786.

Periodicals: *Hobby Horse News,* 2053 Dryehaven Dr., Tallahassee, FL 32311; *TRR Pony Express,* 71 Aloha Cir., North Little Rock, AR, 72120.

Advertising Trade Card, Galena Axle Grease Co **$5.00**
Advertising Trade Card, Lion Coffee, woman riding horse **12.00**
Bank, cast iron, figural, emb "Beauty" on side, painted black, Arcade, early 1900s, 4" h **80.00**
Book, *Old Bones the Wonder Horse,* 1918 . . . . **10.00**
Booklet, *How To Ride & Train the Saddle Horse* **5.00**
Bridle, braided leather strips, 1930s **45.00**
Calendar, 1907, cardboard, cowgirl on horse, Dousman Milling adv, 10 x 20" **50.00**
Comb, mane and tail, mkd "Oliver Slant Tooth," 1940s **15.00**
Game, Merry-Go-Round, Milton Bradley, #4688, c1910 . . . . . **25.00**

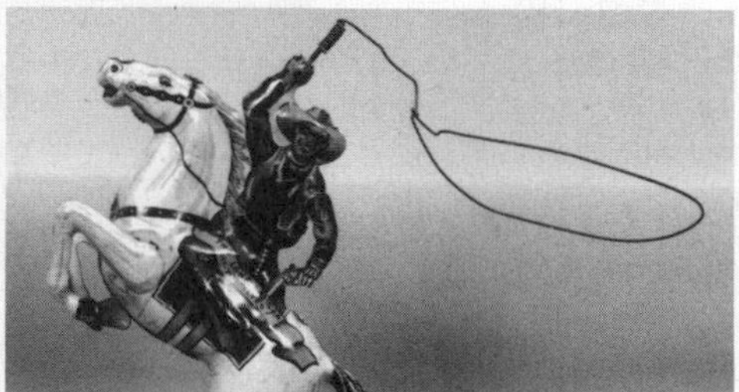

Windup, Lone Ranger, litho tin, Marx, ©1938 The Lone Ranger, Marx logo on right side of horse blanket, $210.00. Photo courtesy Gene Harris Antique Auction Center, Inc.

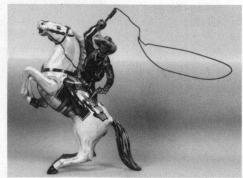

Pin, Mobilgas Pegasus Horse, 1 1/8" w, 7 1/8" h, $166.00. Photo courtesy Collectors Auction Services.

Game, Mister Ed, Parker Brothers, 1962 . . . . **35.00**
Horseshoe, Hopalong Cassidy, "Good Luck," orig insert card, 1950 . . . . **20.00**
Magazine, *Life,* Dec 22, 1952, Midget Horse **5.00**
Magazine Tear Sheet, adv, Cream of Wheat, "Where The Mail Goes—Cream of Wheat Goes," man on horse back delivering mail, framed **25.00**
Pincushion, metal, horseshoe shape **10.00**
Poster, Anheuser Busch, 50th Anniversary, Clydesdales horses, 1933–83 . . . . **8.00**
Pull Toy, horsehair mane and tail, glass eyes, wood base, red wood wheels, late 19th C, 16" h **600.00**
Puzzle, Follow Your Dream, Springbok, A Mini Jigsaw Puzzle, Pegasus illus **5.00**
Souvenir Spoon, Cheyenne, WY, bucking horse, SS **22.00**
Toothpick Holder, wooden, pony with cart **3.00**

HORSE RACING COLLECTIBLES

The history of horse racing dates back to the domestication of the horse itself. Prehistoric cave drawings show horse racing. The Greeks engaged in chariot racing as early as 600 B.C. As civilization spread, so did the racing of horses. Each ethnic group and culture added its own unique slant.

The British developed the thoroughbred breed from a group of horses that were descendants of three great Arabian stallions: Carley Arabian, Byerley Turk, and Goldolphin Arabian. Receiving royal sponsorship, horse racing became the sport of kings.

Horse racing reached America during the colonial period. By the 1800s four-mile match races between regional champions were common. In 1863 Saratoga Race Track was built. The first Belmont Stakes was run at Jerome Park in 1867. As the nineteenth century ended, over 300 race tracks operated a seasonal card. By 1908, society's strong reaction against gambling reduced the number of American race tracks to 25.

Of course, the premier American horse race is the Kentucky Derby. Programs date back to 1924 and glasses, a favorite with collectors, to the late 1930s.

There are so many horse racing collectibles that one needs to specialize from the beginning. Collector focuses include a particular horse-racing type or a specific horse race, a breed or specific horse, or racing prints and images. Each year there are a number of specialized auctions devoted to horse racing, ranging from sporting prints sales at the major New York auction houses to benefit auctions for the Thoroughbred Retirement Foundation.

Plate, Dan Patch, Champion Harness Horse of the World, photo print, tinted, East Liverpool Potteries, $60.00.

Book, *The American Racing Manual,* track diagrams, photos, and record, 1947, 978 pp **$15.00**
Catalog, John Middling, Middling Two Wheelers, harness racing sulkies, 6 different models, prices and descriptions, 1910, 34 pp **50.00**
Cigar Label, La Diana, female jockey, horse race scene. **15.00**
Disk, Prince Albert, celluloid, double sided, black and white, engraving style portrait on front, back with text for 1901 Allentown Fair, $1\frac{3}{4}$" d **30.00**
Game, Giant Wheel Thrills & Spills Horse Race Game, Remco, 1958 . . . . **55.00**
Game, Kentucky Derby Racing Game, 11 x 7" **35.00**
Game, Win, Place & Show, 3M, 1966 . . . . **15.00**
Glass, 1959 Kentucky Derby **32.50**
Glass, 1963 Kentucky Derby **45.00**
Glass, 1973 Kentucky Derby **25.00**
Glass, 1974 Preakness, Pimlico, frosted white panel, black portraits of famous Triple Crown winners, lists winners from 1873 through 1973, $5\frac{1}{4}$" h **15.00**
Hartland Statue, horse and jockey, dark brown horse with wrapped ankles and bobbed tail, jockey wearing red jacket, white cap and trousers, black boots **85.00**
Magazine, *TV Guide,* Jun 10–16, 1950, Thoroughbred Horse Racing cov **40.00**
Pennant, Derby Day, felt, red and white design with pink accents, white lettering, 1939, 18" l **15.00**
Pinback Button, Bergen, jockey, yellow polka dotted shirt, "Celebrated American Jockey," American pepsin Gum text on back, c1900, $\frac{7}{8}$" d **15.00**
Tray, 100th Running Kentucky Derby, litho tin, full color race scene, lists derby winners and times from 1865 through 1973, issued 1974, $21\frac{1}{2}$" l. **25.00**

Model Kit, 1930 Ford Yellow Jacket, Monogram, #PC–76, issued 1962, MIB, $75.00.

HOT RODS

Although the modification of the automobile to increase its performance began shortly after its invention, the term "Hot Rod" did not come into general use until after WWII. The debate as to what constitutes a hot rod has continued ever since. Generally speaking, however, the typical hot rod is a pre-war automobile that has been modified both mechanically and appearance wise.

The critical factor, of course, is the modification of the engine. This is accomplished either by the addition of speed equipment to the existing engine or most frequently by the replacement of the engine with a later and much higher displacement engine, most often a V-8.

The modifications to the appearance include such things as chopping the top, removing the fenders and lowering the entire car. The latter is accomplished by either modifying the suspension or actually channeling the body down over the frame rails.

All of these modifications combine to create a vehicle that is uniquely American. My personal response when asked what a hot rod is, "You'll know it when you see one."

There are numerous hot rod related collectibles. Prices for most items are quite reasonable, but will continue to escalate as more AARP members like myself try to recapture their youth.

Advisors: Cheryl and Michael Goyda, P.O. Box 192, East Petersburg, PA 17520, (717) 569-7149, fax (717) 569-0909.

Periodical: *Mobilia,* P.O. Box 575, Middlebury, VT 05753.

Jacket, Universals, Napierville, IL, cotton, embroidered roadster. **$350.00**
Model Kit, 1932 Deuce Coupe, #232, issued 1960, MIB. **50.00**

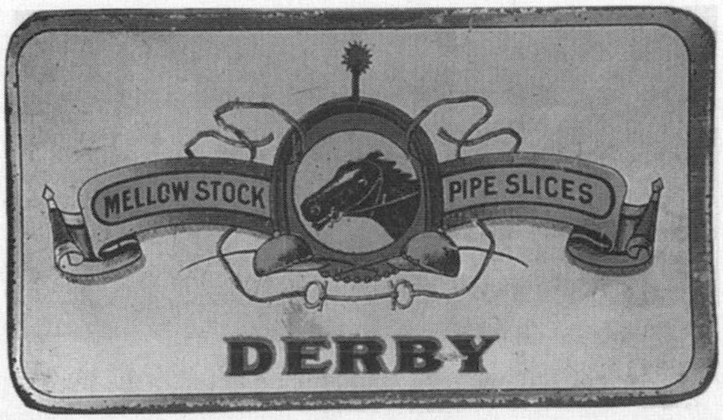

Derby Tobacco Tin, painted tin, red, blue, yellow, black, gold, and white, $22.00. Photo courtesy Collectors Auction Services.

Plaque, "Clock Pushers/Detroit," red, black, and white enamel on aluminum, $150.00.

Jacket, Flywheels, Hanover, corduroy, black with red and yellow embroidered winged flywheel, $200.00.

Model Kit, 1932 Ford Orange Crate, Revell, #H-1289, issued 1963, MIB . . . **60.00**
Plaque, Gents, Venice, CA, name and city, red painted ground . . . **75.00**
Plaque, Grinder's, NJ, features interlocking gears on black ground . . . **120.00**
Plaque, Ridge Runner, Little Rock, features 50's custom on salmon ground . . . **125.00**
Poster, Green Spot Cola Co, cardboard, shows kids drinking soda and working on hot rods, 14 x 22" . . . **175.00**
Poster, Niagara Falls 1st Rod & Custom Show, cardboard, shows the "Orange Crate," 1960, 14 x 20" . . . **150.00**
Record, *Little Deuce Coupe,* Capitol, 1963 . . . **25.00**
Toy, All-American Hot Rod, cast aluminum, can be converted to gas powered, orig condition . . . **250.00**
Toy, Mystery Action Hot Rod, Japan, tin windup, MIB . . . **300.00**
Toy, rubber hot rod with driver, Renwal, 5½" l, M . . . **45.00**

Record, *Hot Rod Rumble,* Liberty, 1957, $100.00.

HOT WHEELS

In 1968 Mattel introduced a line of two-inch long plastic and diecast metal cars. Dubbed "Hot Wheels," there were originally sixteen cars, eight playsets, and two collector sets.

Hot Wheels are identified by the name of the model and its year, which are cast on the bottom of each vehicle. The most desirable Hot Wheels cars have red striping on the tires. These early vehicles are the toughest to find and were produced from 1968 to 1978. In 1979 black tires became standard on all models. The most valuable Hot Wheel vehicles are usually those with production runs limited to a single year or those in a rare color.

Hop in your own set of wheels and race to your nearest flea market to find your own hot collectibles.

Club: Hot Wheels Collector Club, 2263 Graham Dr., Santa Rosa, CA 95404.

Newsletter: *Hot Wheels Newsletter,* 26 Madera Ave., San Carlos, CA 94070

CARS

'31 Doozie, orange . . . **$8.00**
'56 Hai Tail Hauler, orange . . . **10.00**
American Hauler, blue . . . **7.00**
American Victory, light blue . . . **8.00**
Aw Shoot, olive . . . **15.00**
Buick Wildcat, Demolition Man Series . . . **5.00**
Captain America, Scene Machine, white . . . **40.00**
Corvette 4-Rotor, Sizzler . . . **20.00**
Custom Barracuda, purple . . . **55.00**
Custom Camaro, green . . . **28.00**
Custom Corvette . . . **16.00**
Custom Eldorado, gold . . . **30.00**
Double Boiler, Sizzler . . . **10.00**
Fireworks, Sizzler . . . **50.00**
Inferno, yellow . . . **35.00**
Jack Rabbit . . . **7.00**
Jet Threat, light green . . . **10.00**
King Kuda, blue . . . **27.00**
Live Wire, Sizzler . . . **15.00**
Long Count, Sizzler . . . **15.00**
Mantis, light blue . . . **12.00**
Maserati Mistrial brown . . . **32.00**
Mighty Maverick, dark blue . . . **40.00**
Mustang, Vintage II, light blue . . . **5.00**
Silhouette, red . . . **18.00**
Stingray Corvette . . . **12.00**
Torero, green . . . **9.00**

PLAYSETS & MISC.

Automatic Lap Counter . . . **$15.00**
Dash & Crash Speedway . . . **20.00**
Dual Lane Road Runner Set . . . **40.00**
Game, Hot Wheels Wipe-Out Race Game, Mattel, 1968 . . . **25.00**
Hot Curves Race Action Set, 2 cars, 1969 . . . **45.00**
Jump Ramp Accessory Pack . . . **12.00**

HOWARD JOHNSON'S MEMORABILIA

Howard Johnson is one of the best known names ever to appear in the American restaurant business. Howard had the perception that the American public's most important artifact was to be the automobile. In 1925, at the age of 28, he took over a patent medicine store in Wollaston, Massachusetts, that included a newspaper franchise and soda fountain. Howard wanted to expand the business and started making his own ice cream with 18% butterfat and only natural ingredients. With hand-turned freezers in the basement, Howard made the usual flavors of vanilla, chocolate, and strawberry, but also started making ice cream flavors no one had heard of before. Business grew at a steady rate and Howard began selling his ice cream to local restaurants. Within a year, he opened stands on Wollaston Beach selling ice cream, clams, and frankfurters. In 1929, Howard opened his own restaurant in Quincy, Massachusetts, and expanded his line to 28 flavors of ice cream. He understood the importance of a family oriented establishment and was already using Simple Simon & The Pie Man as his restaurant trademark. With the stock market crash, Howard had many challenges to his dream of owning a chain of roadside restaurants. Using the concept of franchising, the restaurants grew to 25 through Massachusetts by 1935. Howard built most all of his businesses on the edge of towns or located halfway between two towns, essentially creating the American highway restaurant.

Howard wanted an easily identifiable building and chose bright orange roof tiles to get the public's attention. He liked the color of aged copper and chose this blue-green to compliment the orange. The glass enclosed, lighted cupolas became synonymous with Howard Johnson's. In 1939, Howard built a $750,000 restaurant near the New York World's Fair that served as many as 6,000 customers a day. By 1940, there were 100 Howard Johnson's from Massachusetts to Florida. Howard's business ideology was to provide quality food products served in clean, homelike settings. The cottage style buildings in bright white featuring dormers, turquoise shutters, and landscaping reminded the traveling public of someone's home. Howard wanted a customer stopping for dinner in Connecticut to expect the same attention to detail and great food as in Georgia. This business savvy proved to be quite successful. By 1946 these restaurants were being seen on American roadways from Maine to Florida and as far west as Ohio. In 1950, there were 230 units using his name.

Howard Johnson's Motor Lodges were established in 1954 with the first in Savannah, Georgia. All motor lodge complexes were to include the familiar orange roof restaurant to provide the public a one-stop convenience. Like the rest of America with the growth of suburbia, Howard Johnson's restaurants now being designed with a ranch house styling with large expanses of plateglass windows, low roof lines, and with a modern cupola of a lighted turquoise pyramid. Howard further expanded his restaurants by opening locations along the New Jersey, Maine, and Pennsylvania turnpikes. During the 1950s Howard was a quiet pioneer in the field of convenience frozen foods. He built commissaries in the Boston and Miami areas that delivered pre-portioned and pre-cooked foods to the Howard Johnson's up and down the east coast. By the late 1950s, Howard was averaging annual sales of more than three million gallons of ice cream and "28 Flavors" remained an advertising slogan. The twenty-eight flavors hardly remained static over the years with new concoctions replacing a poor seller. In 1959, there were 550 Howard Johnson's Restaurants and 75 Motor Lodges, with an annual sales figure of $89 million. The American public continued to love the Pie Man and by 1966 there were 290 Motor Lodges in 35 states. The number of restaurants was now at over 800 locations along the highways of this country.

The 1970s saw most new Howard Johnson's being built as high-rise complexes with hundreds of guest rooms, exercise rooms, saunas, banquet facilities, parking garages, and cocktail lounges. The company had opened a couple dozen Red Coach Grill restaurants through the 1960s. The Ground Round was added to the Howard's Johnson's family in 1969. These two restaurants were open for lunch and dinner only. The high-rise complexes included the orange roof restaurant, as well as one of these other dining establishments for their guests to choose from.

Howard Johnson's have been a familiar site around the United States for over 50 years. The original company was sold and disbanded in 1979. This historical review and listing of items includes only a very small look at this famous restaurant and motor lodge system.

Advisor: Jeffrey C. McCurty, P.O. Box 882, Pleasant Valley, NY, 12569-0882.

Ashtray, clear glass, octagonal, orange "Howard Johnson's," turquoise roof dome trademark, 1968–1979, 4½" **$8.00**

Ashtray, clear glass, square, orange or turquoise, mkd "Howard Johnson's Ice Cream Shops and Restaurants," Pie Man trademark, 4½" sq **15.00**

Bank, restaurant building, cottage style, white plastic, painted orange roof, 2-sided elevation features 1940s restaurant, mkd "Howard Johnson's Restaurants" across top of both sides, 5 x 3½ x 3¼" **10.00**

Bank, restaurant building, ranch style, white plastic, painted orange roof and turquoise roof dome, 2-sided elevation features 1960s restaurant, mkd "Howard Johnson's" across top of both sides, 5¼ x 4 x 3½" **15.00**

Candy Container, cardboard, mkd "Howard Johnson's Personal Selection Package, Assorted Chocolates, Net. Weight 1 Pound. Howard Johnson's Candies, Quincy, Mass.," orange and turquoise, Howard Johnson's road sign with cottage restaurant and cars in background, 7½ x 5 x 1¾" **50.00**

Candy Container, metal can, mkd "Howard Johnson's Assorted Chocolates One pound Net. Quincy, Mass," orange, turquoise, and white, Simple Simon & The Pie Man trademark, 5 x ¼" h **35.00**

Cup and Saucer, Caribe China, Puerto Rico, USA, white, maroon design, scalloped edge, Pie Man trademark, 5½" d saucer **25.00**

Dinner Plate, Caribe China, W C Ayres Co, Inc, white, maroon design, smooth edge, Americana scenes with restaurant and road sign, mkd "Howard Johnson's Ice Cream Shoppes and Restaurants," 9½" d **45.00**

Dinner Plate, Walker China, Bedford, OH, white, maroon design, scalloped edge, Simple Simon & The Pie Man trademark, 9¾" d **35.00**

Drinking Glass, clear, Ho Jo Cola, roof dome/weathervane logo in white, orange, and turquoise, 8 oz **25.00**

Drinking Glass, clear, Simple Simon & The Pie Man, white Pie Man trademark, 8 oz **20.00**

Weather Vane, Lamplighter with Simple Simon, pot metal, painted gold, c1960, 10 lbs, 36 x 42", $1,000.00.

Drinking Glass, clear, turquoise "Howard Johnson's Motor Lodges," shows Lamplighter figure with Simple Simon logo in reverse plate image, 8 oz **5.00**

Map, Rand McNally, features locations of restaurants and motor lodges in Eastern half of US, 1957, 19 x 35" opened size **10.00**

Menu, child's, heavy paper, Simple Simon & The Pie Man trademark on cov, white, turquoise, and orange, lists various meals with nursery rhyme names, back cov has Simple Simon nursery rhyme, 4 x 7". **20.00**

Menu, child's, paper, "Amuse-A-Menu," full color illus, various themes, educational information, puzzles, coloring, crosswords, etc, 8 pp, early 1970s, 7 x $11^1/_2$" **8.00**

Menu, red, white, and blue cov, Howard Johnson's Restaurant and Pie Man logo with WWII scenes, various dinners and specials listed inside, Maine to Florida, 1942, $8^1/_2$ x 11". **25.00**

Menu, white, orange, and turquoise cov, roadsign and cottage restaurant scene, various products listed, early 1950s, 7 x 10" and $8^1/_2$ x 11" **15.00**

Motor Lodge Directory, lists 750 restaurants and 230 motor lodges in 37 states, features full description of each motor lodge and various services available, 64 pp, 1965. $8^1/_2$ x 4". **8.00**

Sandwich Plate, Caribe China, W C Ayres, Philadelphia, oval, white, maroon design, smooth edge, Americana scenes with restaurant and road sign, $9^1/_2$" l **15.00**

Sandwich Stick, plastic, Simple Simon & The Pie Man on top, mkd "Howard Johnson's," and "Snac-Pic," orange or turquoise, 3" l **3.00**

Service Pin, gold plated, features roof dome trademark with "Howard Johnson's," 1968–1979, $^1/_2$ x $^3/_8$" **25.00**

Soda Can, H J Bottling Co, Garfield, NJ, features orange and turquoise roof dome trademark, soda flavor mkd in corresponding color, 1968–79, 12 oz, $4^3/_4$" h **10.00**

Souvenir, Pennsylvania Turnpike Plate, full color illus, various scenes of Turnpike and restaurant, mkd "Vernon Kilns, Made Expressly For Howard Johnson's Turnpike Shops," c1950, $10^1/_2$" d **25.00**

Stirrer, plastic, Simple Simon & The Pie Man on top, mkd "Howard Johnson's," various colors, $5^3/_4$" l **3.00**

Toy, eraser, rubber, cottage restaurant building shape, white, orange painted roof, mkd "Howard Johnson's 1925-1975," $1^3/_4$ x $^3/_4$ x $1^3/_4$" **5.00**

Toy, pocket pins, Plasticworld Inc, Masbeth, NY, round, tin, bend over tab, various colors, features ice cream cone smile face graphic, mkd "Happiness Comes in 28 Flavors," 1" d **3.00**

Toy, soda fountain, Ideal Toy Corp, Hollis, NY, #4108-7, plastic, white, orange, and turquoise, working beverage dispenser, various ice cream dishes, cup holders, and scoop, Simple Simon & The Pie Man logo on dispenser, orig box, 1963, 22 x 8 x 12". **125.00**

Toy, truck, Marx, plastic, white body, black wheels, available in 2 styles, Pie Man trademark on decal with 1950s logos and "Landmark for Hungry Americans," and "Host of The Highways." orig cardboard box shows scenes of ranch style restaurant with people inside and truck parked in front, or 1940s restaurant elevation drawing and "Ice Cream Shoppes and Restaurants" on decals, $10^1/_4$ x $3^3/_4$ x $4^3/_4$" **175.00**

Travel Guide, "From Maine To Florida With Howard Johnson's," features company history, photos, lists various travel sites, ice cream shops and restaurants along east coast, 44 pp, 1939, $5^3/_4$ x $8^1/_4$" **25.00**

Uniform Patch, cloth, oval, white, turquoise, and orange roof dome trademark with "Howard Johnson's," 1968 to 1979, 5 x 3" **15.00**

Winross Truck, Friday Clam Fry Special, white, orange, turquoise, and gold, features clam cartoon figures, mkd "Seconds On The House," roof dome trademark, 1973. . . . . **50.00**

Winross Truck, Ice Cream Cone Model, sides of truck features 6 smile face ice cream cones in various color combinations, mkd "Happiness Comes In 28 Flavors," roof dome trademark. **60.00**

Winross Model Truck, motor lodge reservation promotion, features yellow suitcase with orange and turquoise roof dome trademark, white, brown, yellow, and orange, includes toll free 800 phone number, 1977. . . . . **50.00**

Winross Truck, Roof Dome Trademark Model, mkd "Howard Johnson's Host of The Highways Coast To Coast," white, turquoise, and orange, 1968. . . . . **60.00**

HOWDY DOODY

The Howdy Doody show is the most famous of early television's children's programs. Created by "Buffalo" Bob Smith, the show ran for 2,343 performances between December 27, 1947, and September 30, 1960. Among the puppet characters were Howdy Doody, Mr. Bluster, Flub-A-Dub, and Dilly-Dally. Princess Summerfall-Winterspring and Clarabelle, the clown, were played by humans.

There is a whole generation out there who knows there is only one answer to the question: "What time is it?"

Club: Howdy Doody Memorabilia Collectors Club, 8 Hunt Ct., Flemington, NJ 08822.

Activity Set, Howdy Doody TV Studio Cut-Outs, "Doodyville," Kagran, complete with instruction sheet, partially assembled, 1954. . . . . **$231.00**

Bag, Howdy Doody Fudge Bar, red, white, and blue, waxed paper, premium offer on back, unused, 4 x $5^1/_4$". . . . **18.00**

Catalog, products and illus, 22 pp, reprint, 1955 . . . . **10.00**

Howdy Doody's Clarabell Hug-Me Toy or Laundry Bag, Kagran, lithoed 9 x 11" lid, contents complete, orig box, 1950s, $95.00. Photo courtesy New England Auction Gallery.

Doll, Princess, Beehler/Kagran, plastic, open/close eyes, full outfit, 7" h, orig litho 5 x 9" box, unused, $230.00. Photo courtesy New England Auction Gallery.

Cornucopia Vase, Wildflower, W-10, 1946–47, 8½" h, $130.00. Photo courtesy Gene Harris Antique Auction Center, Inc.

Cookie Jar, ceramic, Puriton Pottery, early 1950s, 9 x 9 x 8½" 350.00
Game, Howdy Doody's Electric Doodler Game, Harett-Gilmar, 1951 . . . . 40.00
Handkerchief, fabric, printed Howdy image beside pony head, yellow ground with white border, ©Bob Smith c1948–51, 8¼ x 8½" 15.00
Handkerchief, linen-like weave cotton, printed Clarabell image holding yellow balloon, 9 x 9" 15.00
Iron-On Transfer, unused 30.00
Little Golden Book, *Howdy Doody and the Princess,* 24 pp, color illus, Simon & Schuster, ©1952 Kagran, 6½ x 8" 10.00
Premium, Blue Bonnet Sue, Doodyville Theater on 4 unpunched sheets, full color, orig envelope, 18½ x 11½" 344.00
Premium, Luden's, Howdy Doody Magic Kit, uncut cutouts, with orig envelope 216.00
Push Puppet, Princess Summerfall Winterspring, Kohner, ©Bob Smith, c1948-51 . . . . 175.00
Shopping Bag, paper, full color Howdy Doody image and "I've Been To The Howdy Doody Show" 456.00
Sign, "Howdy Doody Ice Cream Bar," paper, "Be Sure To Save All Howdy Doody Bags For Swell Prizes," Americana Enterprises Co, ©Kagran, c1951-56, 10½ x 14" 85.00

HULL POTTERY

Hull Pottery traces its beginnings to the 1905 purchase of the Acme Pottery Company of Crooksville, Ohio, by Addis E. Hull. By 1917 a line of art pottery designed specifically for flower and gift shops was added to Hull's standard fare of novelties, kitchenware, and stoneware. A flood and fire destroyed the plant in 1950. When the plant reopened in 1952, the Hull products had a new glossy finish.

Hull is collected by pattern. A favorite with collectors is the Little Red Riding Hood kitchenware line, made between 1943 and 1957. Most Hull pieces are marked. Pre-1950 pieces have a numbering system to identify pattern and height. Post-1950 pieces have "hull" or "Hull" in large script letters.

Club: Hull Pottery Assoc., 4 Hilltop Rd., Council Bluffs, IA 51503.

Newsletters: *Hull Pottery News,* 466 Foreston Place, St. Louis, MO 63119; *Hull Pottery Newsletter,* 11023 Tunnell Hill NE, New Lexington, OH 43764.

Basket, Bow Knot, B-25, blue and green, emb "Hull Art B25," 6½" h $300.00
Candlesticks, pr, Magnolia, 12" h 11.50
Console Bowl, Dogwood, #511, cream and aqua, 11½" d 165.00
Ewer, Magnolia, #5, 7" h 130.00
Flowerpot, Tulip, #116-33, 6" h 75.00
Pitcher, Camelia, #128, 4¾" h 35.00
Planter, Basket Girl, 8" h, price for pr 63.00
Planter, poodle, red and green, 8" h 17.00
Planter, ducks, imp "Hull," 7½" h 17.00
Planter, woman with flowing skirt, 7" h 29.00
Planter with Underplate, water lily, pink, 6" h 57.50
Tea Set, teapot, sug and creamer, magnolia gloss, gold decor 69.00
Vase, Magnolia Gloss, double cornucopia, emb "Hull Art H-15," 12" h 40.00
Vase, Magnolia Matte, 2 handled, pink and blue, imp "Hull Art, U.S.A. 2," 8½" h 115.00
Vase, Magnolia Matte, 2 handled, yellow and dusty rose, emb "Hull Art, U.S.A. 2," 8½" h 80.00
Vase, Mardi Gras, pink and white, imp "U.S.A.47," 9" h 40.00
Vase, Water Lily, 2 handled, pink, 5½" h 46.00
Vase, Wild Flower, pink and blue, paper label, mkd in relief "Hull Art USA, 59," 10½" h 220.00
Vase, Woodland, cornucopia, emb "Hull W2," 5½" h 35.00
Vase, Woodland, rose and chartreuse, emb "Hull W9-8¾" USA" 110.00
Wall Pocket, Little Red Riding Hood, imp design number, 9½" h 345.00

HUMMELS

Hummel items are the original creations of Berta Hummel, a German artist. At the age of 18, she enrolled in the Academy of Fine Arts in Munich. In 1934 Berta Hummel entered the Convent of Siessen and became Sister Maria Innocentia. She continued to draw.

In 1935, W. Goebel Co. of Rodental, Germany, used some of her sketches as the basis for three-dimensional figures. American distribution was handled by the Schmid Brothers of Randolph, Massachusetts. In 1967 a controversy developed between the two companies involving the Hummel family and the convent. The German courts decided The Convent had the rights to Berta Hummel's sketches made between 1934 and her death in 1964. Schmid Bros. could deal directly with the family for reproduction rights to any sketches made before 1934.

All authentic Hummels bear both the M. I. Hummel signature and a Goebel trademark. There were various trademarks used to identify the year of production. The Crown Mark (trademark 1) was used from 1935–1949, Full Bee (trademark 2) 1950–1959, Stylized Bee (trademark 3) 1957–1972, Three Line Mark (trademark 4) 1964–1972, Last Bee Mark (trademark 5) 1972–1980, Missing Bee Mark (trademark 6) 1979–1990, and the Current Mark or New Crown Mark (trademark 7) from 1991 to the present.

Hummel lovers are emotional collectors. They do not like to read or hear anything negative about their treasures. At the moment, they are very unhappy campers. The Hummel market for ordinary pieces is flat, with little signs of recovery in the years ahead.

Hummel material was copied widely. These copycats also are attracting interest among collectors. For more information about them, see Lawrence L. Wonsch's *Hummel Copycats With Values* (Wallace-Homestead: 1987).

Clubs: Hummel Collector's Club, 1261 University Dr., Yardley, PA 19067; M. I. Hummel Club, Goebel Plaza, P.O. Box 11, Pennington, NJ 08534.

A Fair Measure, #345, trademark 5, 5½" h **$137.50**
Apple Tree Boy, #142 3/0, trademark 3, no paper title, 4" h **88.00**
Apple Tree Girl, #141 4/0, trademark 5, no paper title, 4 h **66.00**
Book Worm, #3/1, trademark 5, 5½" h **132.00**
Brother, #95, trademark 3, 5¼" h **99.00**
Busy Student, #367, trademark 4, 4½" h **99.00**
Carnival, #328, trademark 5, 6" h **99.00**
Chicken Licken, #385, trademark 5, 4¾" h **121.00**
Cinderella, #337, trademark 5, 4½" h **90.00**
Goodnight, #214/C, trademark 7, 3½" h **55.00**
Happiness, #86, trademark 3, no paper title, 4¾" h **66.00**
Little Bookkeeper, #306, trademark 5, 4¾" h **99.00**
Little Fiddler, #4, trademark 5, 4¾" h **88.00**
Little Hiker, #16/1, trademark 3, 6" h **121.00**
Little Shopper, #96, trademark 5, 5" h **66.00**
Mischief Maker, #342, trademark 5, 5" h **110.00**
Mother's Darling, #175, trademark 5, 5½" h **121.00**
Stitch In Time, #255, trademark 4, 6¾' h **143.00**
The Builder, #305, trademark 4, 5½" h **110.00**
Wayside Harmony, #111/1, trademark 6, 5" h **110.00**
Worship, #84/0, trademark 3, no paper title, 4" h **121.00**

HUMMEL LOOK-ALIKES, ERICH STAUFFER FIGURINES

"Original Child Life Subjects. Designed by Erich Stauffer. Completely Hand Made & Hand Painted" are the words found on blue, triangular tags that luckily are sometimes found on these child-like figures; they look like Hummels, but are not. Also, on some of these figures, still adhering to its base, is a blue and gold sticker with "Original Arnart Creation, Japan." They were imported to the United States during the late 1950s thru the 1980s as interesting, Hummel-look-alikes, inexpensive to buy and a delight to display.

A Hummel collector, of course, can tell at a glance these are not the "real thing," but the novice qualifies them as very good imposters indeed! However, though they are sometimes referred to as "Hummel-look-alikes," even by their collectors, they really should be known as the "Stauffer" figures. Their mark (in blue script) reads "Designed by Erich Stauffer," and is usually accompanied by either two crossed arrows or a crown motif, but always with a style number.

The most interesting fact about these figures is that not only one figure was made with a particular number, but sometimes up to six or even eight different ones! Therefore, no matter whatever the activity is, all six or eight will carry the same style number! Indeed, this is not only confusing for a potential collector, but for the advanced collector as well!

Occasionally, one will come across on of these figures without the name Stauffer—only crossed arrows and a style number. Identical figures having the same style number and which do have Stauffer's name on them have been found. (It's anybody's guess if the non-Stauffer-marked figures were made before or after the Stauffer-marked ones.) It is interesting to note too that many of these figures often have the letters "S" or "U" on front of its style/series number. At this point in time, it is unknown if there is any definite significance concerning their use.

Besides the Stauffer-marked children, one might come across similar figures that have "Arnart Imports, NY," and "Hand-painted" stamped on the base. At some point in time, some of them were reissued and made up in larger size. In doing so they were each given a different number than the originals. This fact alone makes for inconsistent cataloging, creating a need for a crossover index for both the Stauffer figures and those marked Arnart.

When new, each figure came with a small strip of paper on the front edge of each figure, giving a title to its figure. It is a bonus if some figures still retain them. If a figure is not washed and cleaned carefully, the paper comes off easily.

These figures measure from 4¼ up to 12" high, Most small-to-medium size have rectangular bases; those of medium height will often either have a standing figure or one sitting on a fallen log; those bases are usually round, but not always. It is unusual to find more than one figure on a base, i.e. "Dancing Time" that has three children or sometimes just two girls or a boy and a girl. Another rarity is finding a 12" high figure. Not so rare, but making a figure even more interesting, is one that features a small dog, a rabbit, one or two geese, a chicken, a doll, or a musical instrument.

A guide to pricing today is $3 to $3.50 an inch, heightwise, for 4–5" figures, and $4 to $5 and inch, heightwise, for the 5" h and up, depending upon condition. If the title is still intact or the blue tag is still there, that is a bonus for you.

Advisor: Joan Oates, 685 S. Washington, Constantine, MI 49042.

Erich Stauffer Figures: left, "Sore Thumb," U8536, 7½" h, $30.00; right, #5511059, 4¾" h, $18.00.

Erich Stauffer Figure, "Junior Doctor," 6½" h, $25.00.

ARNART FIGURES

1546N, News Boy, boy with bundle of newspapers under arm, goose at side, 4¼" h **$18.00**
1550 , Sandy Shoes, girl holding orange slipper, 5½" h **18.00**
15/1540, School Days, boy with hand in pocket, school books under arm, 4⅜" h **13.00**
55/1880, Picnic, boy holding bun, 5" h **15.00**

STAUFFER FIGURES

44/173, Little Hikers, boy with pick axe and knapsack on back, 5½" h **$20.00**
55/475, Pray Every Day, girl praying, rooster at side, 5½" h **18.00**
55/512, Big Game Hunter, boy holding bow, 2 geese at side, 5½" h **20.00**
55/1551, Life On The Farm, girl with hands on basket of grapes, blue bird on fence post, 4⅞" h **15.00**
2579, Rainy Days, boy with open umbrella, patch on knee, 4" h **16.00**
8218, Spring Time, girl with closed umbrella, basket over arm, 5½" h **18.00**
S8218, Summer Time, boy holding sprinkling can in both hands, 5½" h **15.00**
8218, Winter Time, boy with shovel in hand, snowball in other, 5" h **20.00**
8263, boy climbing tree, goose beside him, 5" h **18.00**
8268, Farm Chores, girl with bunch of carrots and lettuce, 5" h **15.00**
8316, Spring Time: A Nun!, basket over arm, closed umbrella in other hand, 4⅞" h **25.00**
8336, God's Children, girl, sitting beside shelter with Virgin Mary inside, goose beside girl, 5" h **22.00**
8386, A Planter!, girl, sitting in front of stone wall, holding basket of grapes, base 4¼" l x 1¾" w **25.00**
U8394, Life On The Farm, boy with violin, 2 geese behind, 5⅛" h **20.00**
U8515, Young Folks, boy with rake, sitting on stump, 6¼" h **15.00**
U8536, Little Sprinkler, girl with blue sprinkling can in her lap, 7½"h **20.00**
S8541, Life On The Farm, boy with shovel, orange bird on post, 6¾" h **25.00**
U8561, Sandy Shoes, girl holding orange slipper, 6⅝" h **18.00**
U8588, Junior Doctor, standing boy with doll at feet. **25.00**

Ammunition Box, Winchester Ranger, 12 gauge, 1 pc, full, 4 x 4 x 2½", $66.00. Photo courtesy Past Tyme Pleasures.

HUNTING COLLECTIBLES

The hunt is on and the only foxes are good flea market shoppers. It is time to take back the fields and exhibit those beautiful trophies and hunting displays. I do not care what the animal activists say. I love it. Old ammunition boxes, clothes, signs, stuffed beasts, photographs of the old hunting cabins or trips, and the great array of animal-calling devices. Oh yeah, this is the stuff that adventures and memories are made from.

Care and condition are the prime considerations when collecting hunting-related items. Weapons should always be securely displayed, insect deterrents and padded hangers are best for clothing or accessories, and humidity-controlled areas are suggested for paper ephemera. Good luck and happy hunting!

Club: Call & Whistle Collectors Assoc., 2839 E. 26th Place, Tulsa, OK 74114; Callmakers & Collectors Assoc. of America, 137 Kingswood Dr., Clarksville, TN 37043.

Periodical: *Sporting Collector's Monthly,* P.O. Box 305, Camden, Wyoming, DE 19934.

Ammunition Box, Ace, Gamble's, 12 gauge, 1 pc, yellow, blue, buff, and red with shot shell on both end panels, full **$21.00**
Ammunition Box, Hiawatha-Ace, .410 gauge, 1 pc, brown, yellow, and white, full **35.00**
Ammunition Box, Peters HV, 12 gauge, #2 chilled shot size, 1 pc, empty **17.00**
Book, *Colt Guns,* Marin Rywell, 1953 edition, blue hard cov, 136 pp **136.00**
Bullet Mold, Winchester, .40-82, walnut handle, bright blue **63.00**
Catalog, Smith & Wesson, red, black, and light brown, textured cov, 40 pp, c1934, 9½ x 7½" **55.00**
Crow Call, SR&C "Ranger," walnut barrel, red painted top and bottom band, orig cardboard tube, 5¼" l **95.00**
Decoy, Bluebills, sgd "Harold Dinham Waubaushene," Ontario, Canada, orig paint, glass eyes, 13" l **35.00**
Decoy, Woodduck Drake, sgd and initialed by "Miles Smith," Marine City, Michigan, orig paint with stamped feather design, glass eyes, 16" l **60.50**
Disk, brass, "Shot With A Remington Rifle" 1 side, "Shot With A Kleanbore Remington Cartridge" other side **12.00**
Pinback Button, "1950 Ducks Unlimited," image of flying duck, celluloid, multicolored **49.00**
Pinback Button, Du Pont Smokeless Powder, multicolored quail illus center, black border, white letters **65.00**

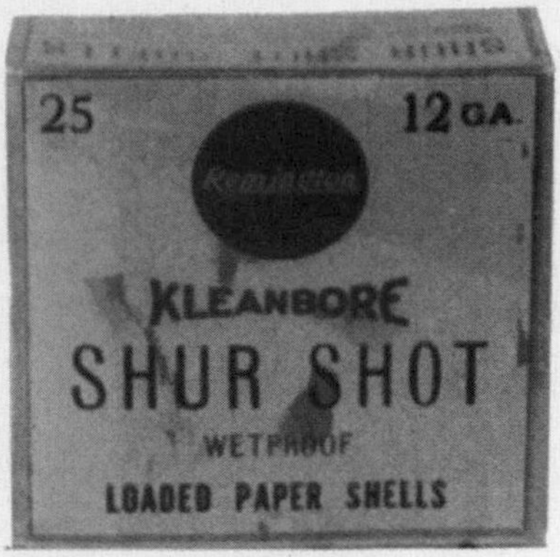

Remington Shur Shot Paper Shells, 2 pc box, full, 4 x 4 x 1¾", $143.00. Photo courtesy Past Tyme Pleasures.

Shotgun, Stevens, double barrel, 16 gauge, 28" l blued barrels, simple engraving on receiver, serial #H23700 . . . . **220.00**
Sign, Remington Arms, paper, hunter with dogs, pump shotgun leaning on fence, orig metal strips top and bottom, 17 x 25" **450.00**
Tin, Du Pont Indian Rifle Gunpowder, red, chromolithograph paper label, Indian with rifle, 1908 . . . . **195.00**

ICE SKATING

I hope that I am not skating on thin ice by adding this category to the book, but the staff has found many skating-related items and they were hard to ignore. Since ice skating has been around for centuries and is something I have never gotten the knack of, I can only hope that this is better than letting all these goodies go unnoticed.

Autograph, Sonja Henie, black and white portrait pose, 7 x 9" **$95.00**
Box, Sonja Henie Knitwear, winter cap, c1940 . . . . **15.00**
Catalog, Bradford & Anthony, Wholesale Price List of Winslow's Skates and Skate Straps, 16 pp, pictorial wrappers, 1869 . . . . **125.00**
Catalog, Spauding, A G & Bros, Fall & Winter Sports, 128 pp, variety of sports equipment, 1907 . . . . **100.00**
Catalog, Winslow's Ice Skates/Roller Skates, Worcester, MA, 2 pp, 1906 . . . . **20.00**
Coloring Book, features Sonja Henie, Merrill Publishing Co, #3418, 1941, uncut **50.00**
Paper Dolls, Sonja Henie, Merrill Publishing Co, #3418, 1941, uncut **50.00**
Pinback Button, Ice Capades, Donna Atwood photo portrait, black lettering on yellow ground, late 1950s **12.00**
Program, Transcontinental Tour, Sonja Henie, Presented by Hollywood Ice Productions, Chicago, 1941–42 . . . . **25.00**
Skates, pr, German, Jackson Haines era, clamp attachment, c1848 . . . . **250.00**
Skates, pr, child's, Union Hardware, Torrington, CT, clamp-on, tighten with key, all metal, metal toe and heel plates, c1900 . . . . **45.00**

IMPERIAL GLASS

The history of Imperial Glass dates back to 1901. Initially the company produced pattern and carnival glass. In 1916 an art glass line, "Free-Hand," was introduced. However, Imperial's reputation rests on a wide variety of household glassware products.

Imperial was responsible for some neat Depression Era Glassware patterns. They were practical, plentiful, and very affordable. Today their bright colors delight collectors.

The company made a practice of acquiring molds from firms that went out of business, e.g., Central, Cambridge, and Heisey. Imperial used a variety of marks over time. Beware of an interlaced "I" and "G" mark on carnival glass. This is an Imperial reproduction.

Club: National Imperial Glass Collectors Society, P.O. Box 534, Bellaire, OH 43906.

Ashtray, purple slag, 6" sq **$25.00**
Berry Bowl, Katy, blue opalescent, flat rim **30.00**
Bowl, Beaded Block, amber, 5½" sq. **7.50**
Bowl, Beaded Block, milk white, 6¾" d **16.00**
Bowl, Pillar Flutes, light blue **22.50**
Cake Plate, Molly, opalescent green **45.00**
Candlesticks, pr, Jewels, blue luster **50.00**
Cereal Bowl, Katy, blue opalescent, flared **60.00**
Compote, Jewels, iridescent teal blue, 7½" d **60.00**
Cream Soup Bowl, Diamond Quilted, green, 4¾" d **8.00**
Decanter, Cape Cod **60.00**
Goblet, Cape Cod, amberina **28.00**
Jelly Compote, Beaded Block, pink, 4½" d **10.00**
Marmalade, Cape Cod **30.00**
Sherbet, Victorian, yellow **10.00**
Vase, Beaded Block, opalescent cobalt blue **75.00**
Whiskey, Cape Cod, crystal **10.00**

INK BOTTLES

In the eighteenth and early nineteenth centuries, individuals mixed their own ink. The individual ink bottle became prevalent after the untippable bottle was developed in the middle of the nineteenth century. Ink bottles are found in a variety of shapes ranging from umbrella style to turtles. When the fountain pen arrived on the scene, ink bottles became increasingly plain.

Periodical: *Antique Bottle and Glass Collector*, P.O. Box 180, East Greenville, PA 18041.

Barrel, "Pat. March-1, 1870," smoky clear, smooth base, rolled lip, c1870-80, 2" h **$71.50**
Carter's Ink, amethyst, mold blown, applied lip **4.00**
Cottage, S I Comp, bluish aqua, smooth base, tooled mouth, c1885-92, 2½" h **187.00**

Clover Leaf Ink, "Carter's" on base, American, medium cobalt blue, 6-sided, smooth base, ABM lip, c1920–30, 2⅞" h, $165.00. Photo courtesy GlassWorks Auctions.

Master, Cathedral, deep cobalt blue, "CA-RT-ER" around base, "Carter's" on smooth base, ABM lip, orig lable, c1920–30, 9³/₄" h 154.00. Photo courtesy Glass-Works Auctions.

Farley's, "Farley's Ink," 8-sided, medium olive green, open pontil, flared lip, c1845–55 . . . . **467.50**
Geometric, blown 3-mold, olive amber, open pontil, applied disc mouth, c1820–35, 1¹/₂" h **231.00**
Harrison's, "Harrison's Columbian Ink," 12-sided, aqua, "Patent" on shoulder, pontil scarred base, applied mouth, c1845–55 . . . . **231.00**
Master, Field's Blue-Black Ink, jug type, stoneware, English, dark brown, applied handle, orig label, "Bourne Denby" on oval stamp near base, 13¹/₈" h **50.00**
S O Dunbar, Taunton, MA, aqua, pontil scarred base, applied sloping collar mouth, 5⁵/₈" h. **88.00**
Turtle, Davids', medium teal, smooth base, tooled lip, c1870–80, 1³/₄" h. **412.00**
Turtle, Dessauer's Jet Black Ink, bluish aqua, smooth base, ground lip, c1870–1880, 2" h **148.50**
Turtle, J & I E M, medium amber, smooth base, ground lip, 1⁵/₈" h **93.50**
Umbrella, 8-sided, light emerald green, pontil scarred base, rolled lip, c1845–55, 2¹/₂" h. **132.00**
Umbrella, 12-sided, light blue green, open pontil, rolled lip, c1845–55, 2¹/₈" h. **77.00**
W E Bonney, aqua, smooth base, applied mouth with pour spout, c1855–65, 5¹/₈" h. **165.00**

INKWELLS

Inkwells enjoyed a "golden age" between 1870 and 1920. They were a sign of wealth and office. The common man dipped his ink directly from the bottle. The arrival of the fountain pen and ball-point pen led to their demise.

Inkwells were made from a wide variety of materials. Collectors seem to have the most fun collecting figural inkwells—but beware, there are some modern reproductions.

Club: The Society of Inkwell Collectors, 5136 Thomas Ave. South, Minneapolis, MN 55410.

Brass, Bradley & Hubbard **$45.00**
Cast Metal, camel, painted **275.00**
Cone, light greenish aqua, open pontil, rolled lip, c1835–55, 2¹/₄" h. **80.00**
Cut Glass, brass collar, glass stopper, 4³/₄" h **95.00**
Cut Glass, canary yellow, polished base, 3 pen shelves, orig brass hinged collar, c1880–1900, 2¹/₂" h **412.50**
Cylindrical, blown 3-mold, dark olive amber, disk mouth, 1³/₈" h **140.00**
Glass, clear, dome shape, 16 point stare on base, round brass hinged lid, 2¹/₂" d **95.00**
Glass, clear, turtle shape, 1⁷/₈ x 3³/₄" **145.00**
Metal, figural, tree stump, whippet, painted white, orig insert **125.00**
Pattern Glass, Daisy and Button, vaseline, matching loose lid, 2" sq **175.00**
Pewter, pen rest with cherub dec, glass insert, floral dec on cov **65.00**
Porcelain, red, green, and blue floral design, 3¹/₈" h **50.00**
Pottery, woman's slipper, light brown and tan glaze, 1¹/₄" h **140.00**

INSULATORS

Insulators were a trendy collectible of the 1960s and prices have been stable since the 1970s.

Insulators are sold by "CD" numbers and color. Check N. R. Woodward's *The Glass Insulator in America* (privately printed, 1973) to determine the correct CD number. Beware of "rare" colors. Unfortunately, some collectors and dealers have altered the color of pieces by using heat and chemicals to increase the rarity value. The National Insulators Association is leading the movement to identify and stop this practice. They are one of the few clubs in the field that take their policing role seriously.

Club: National Insulator Assoc., 1315 Old Mill Path, Broadview Heights, OH 44147.

Periodical: *Crown Jewels of the Wire*, P.O. Box 1003, St. Charles, IL 60174.

CD 102, So Mass Tel Co, aqua. **$65.00**
CD 112, New England Telegraph & Telephone, aqua **35.00**
CD 117, Ampersand, deep aqua **35.00**
CD 121, Brookfield, green. **35.00**
CD 134, Pettingell Andrews, bluish aqua **335.00**
CD 143, Canadian Pacific, royal purple **45.00**
CD 145, Brookfield/New York, aqua **5.00**
CD 154, Dominion 42, dark red amber **55.00**
CD 160, Hemingray 14, clear **6.00**
CD 162, Hemingray, #19, cobalt **310.00**
CD 164, B C Drip. **45.00**
CD 200, Star, blue aqua **110.00**
CD 203, Zicme, grayish green **150.00**
CD 214, Telegraphos/Nacionales, bright orange amber **90.00**
CD 228, Brookfield. **225.00**
CD 241, Hamingray, orange amber **65.00**

CD 123, "E.C.&M.Co. S.F." emb on skirt, yellow green/chartreuse, $40.00.

Rocker Iron, The Erie Fluter, Griswold Mftg Co, Erie, PA, clip-on handle, c1875, 5½" l, $100–$150.00.

Slug Iron, English, #10, all brass construction, lift-up gate, mid 1800s, 7¾" l, $150–$200.00.

IRONS

Country and kitchen collectors have kept non-electric iron collecting alive. The form changed little for centuries. Some types were produced for decades. Age is not as important as appearance—the more unusual or decorative the iron, the more likely its value will be high. There are still bargains to be found, but cast iron and brass irons are becoming expensive. Electric irons are the iron collectible of the future.

Advisor: David Irons, 223 Covered Bridge Rd., Northampton, PA 18067, (610) 262-9335, fax (610) 262-2853.

Clubs: Club of the Friends of Ancient Smoothing Irons, P.O. Box 215 Carlsbad, CA 92008; Midwest Sad Iron Collectors Club, 24 Nobltill Dr., St. Louis, MO 63138.

Newsletter: *Iron Talk,* P.O. Box 68, Waelder, TX 78959.

Note: David Irons is the author and publisher of *Irons By Irons, More Irons By Irons,* and *Pressing Iron Patents.*

Charcoal, double chimney, NE Plus Ultra, 1902 . . . . **$180.00**
Charcoal, Dragon, German, dragon head chimney **550.00**
Charcoal, turned chimney, European, many variations **130.00**
Flat Iron, Asbestos Sad Iron, metal cov over base **35.00**
Flat Iron, Enterprise, cord handle, 2 pc, wood handle **20.00**
Flat Iron, French, Le Caiffa #5, low profile cast iron **65.00**
Flat Iron, Ober #6, ribbed handle, all cast **45.00**
Flat Iron, Weids's, cord handle, handle flips back **180.00**
Fluter, charcoal, with rocker fluter side plate **180.00**
Fluter, Clarks, base holds slug, roller type. **160.00**
Fluter, Crown, machine type, orig paint and striping **150.00**
Fluter, The Best, rocker typc, 2 pcs **80.00**

Goffering Iron, double, European, brass barrels and standard, ornate cast iron base, mid 1800s, 10" h, $300–$500.00.

Goffering, single, round base, Clark, with poker **100.00**
Liquid Fuel Iron, British Boudoir Iron **65.00**
Liquid Fuel Iron, Diamond Iron, gasoline, rear tank **50.00**
Liquid Fuel Iron, GME, natural gas. **65.00**
Liquid Fuel Iron, Jubilee Iron, double ptd iron **130.00**
Liquid Fuel Iron, Vulcan Gas Iron, natural gas with pipes **80.00**
Slug, Magic, sensible, top lifts off. **220.00**
Slug, oxtongue, European, saw grip handle. **100.00**
Small, charcoal, tall chimney, 3½" **190.00**
Small, Enterprise, holes through handle, 2½" **80.00**
Small, oval cap, French, 3½" **50.00**
Small, Swan, all cast, 2" **85.00**
Small, Swan, all cast, orig paint **150.00**
Small, wood grip, star with "10" **80.00**
Special Purpose, egg on a stand, French, tripod base **160.00**
Special Purpose, flower, G Molla, top and bottom brass, wood handle. **100.00**
Special Purpose, hat, electric press and stretcher **100.00**
Special Purpose, long sleeve, oral end with dec, French, 19" **150.00**
Special Purpose, MAB Cooks, polisher, rounded sides. **50.00**
Special Purpose, sleeve, Grand Union Tea Co, detachable handle. **40.00**
Special Purpose, Sweeney Iron, polisher, 1896 . . . . **140.00**

IRONSTONE POTTERY

This was the common household china of the last half of the nineteenth century and first two decades of the twentieth century. This ceramic ware was supposed to wear like iron— hence the name "ironstone." Many different manufacturers used the term ironstone when marking their pieces. However, the vast majority of pieces do not bear the ironstone mark.

Piece that are all white, including the pattern, are known as White Patterned Ironstone. A more decorative appearance was achieved by using the transfer process.

Club: White Ironstone China Assoc., Inc., RD #1 Box 23, Howes Cave, NY 12092.

Butter Dish, cov, Moss Rose, handled, Meakin, no insert, 6½" w. **$12.50**
Compote, Gothic shape, white, pedestal, 10-sided, handled, black "Ironstone China, J. Meir & Son" mark, c1850, 7½" h **95.00**
Creamer, Oriental style shape, transfer, mkd "Mason's Patent Ironstone," 4" h **75.00**
Cup and Saucer, Moss Rose, 3½" h **50.00**

Cup and Saucer, Wheat, black "Robert Cochran & Co. Glasglow, Imperial Ironstone China" mark, 1860s 30.00
Gravy Boat, Wheat and Blackberry, white, Meakin, 1860s, 5" h 40.00
Nappy, Moss Rose, Edwards Bros, 4½" d 12.00
Pitcher, Wheat and Blackberry, white, Taylor and Hanley, 9" h 65.00
Plate, Corn, white, Davenport, 10½" d 20.00
Platter, Lily of the Valley, Meakin, 14½" l 40.00
Salt and Pepper Shakers, pr, Moss Rose, SS tops, Rosenthal, 5" h 50.00
Sauce Dish, Moss Rose, Meakin, 4¾" d, price for pr 80.00
Soup Plate, Wheat and Clover, white, Turner & Tomkinson, 9" d 25.00
Spooner, Moss Rose, Meakin 60.00
Sugar Bowl, white, Fuchsia, Meakin 40.00
Toothbrush Holder, Hyacinth, white, Wedgwood 60.00
Toothbrush Holder, Moss Rose, J W Pankhurst, 5¾" h 100.00
Tray, Moss Rose, handled, gold trim, Wedgwood, 9" l 15.00
Tureen, cov, white, cabbage leaves, bud finial 120.00

ITALIAN GLASS

Italian glass, also known as Venetian glass, is glassware made in Italy from the 1920s into the early 1960s and heavily exported to the United States. Pieces range from vases with multicolored internal thick and thin filigree threads to figural clowns and fish.

The glass was made in Murano, the center of Italy's glass blowing industry. Beginning in the 1920s many firms hired art directors and engaged the services of internationally known artistsand designers. The 1950s was a second golden age following the flury of high-style pieces made from the mid-1920s through the mid-1930s.

Newsletter: *Verti: Italian Glass News,* P.O. Box 191, Fort Lee, NJ 07024.

Ashtray, creamy opaque with cobalt center, Gabberts paper label, 6½" d $33.00
Basket, handled, Murano, translucent blue, Murano circular label, 13" h 137.50
Bottle, Murano, with stopper, paper label, 18" h 137.50
Cup and Saucer, latticinio white with gold leafed base and handle, 4" h 38.50
Dish, boomerang shape, emerald green with whirlpool of copper flecks, unsgd, 14 x 18" 93.50

Bottle and Stopper, attributed to Fratelli Toso, blue and white cane glass, unmkd, 18" h, $110.00. Photo courtesy David Rago Auctions, Inc.

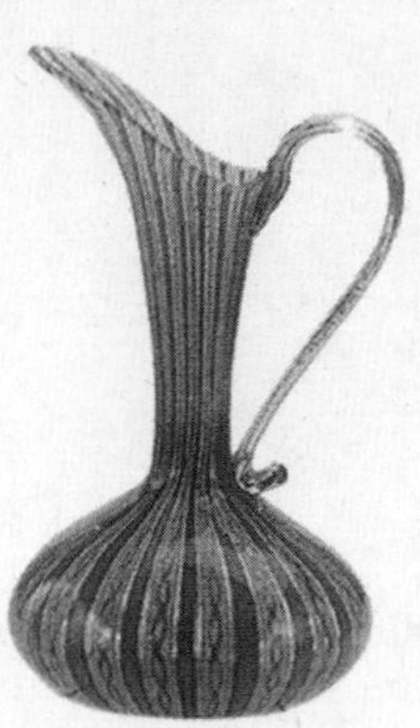

Ewer, attributed to Fratelli Toso, blue and white latticino glass with copper ribbons and gold leaf, unmkd, 11½" h, $165.00. Photo courtesy David Rago Auctions, Inc.

Figure, 2 dancers, turquoise with gold flecks, bell shaped plinths, 12" h 330.00
Figure, longneck bird, amber to blue shading, 21" h 93.50
Figure, sea horse, blue, green, and amber, 13" h 82.50
Paperweight, Vianello, clear with angel fish, paper label, 4" h 170.50
Vase, Balboa Venetian, blue handkerchief with white lattice, 7" d 104.50
Vase, Seguso, stretched iridescent with mottled gold leaf, sgd "Des. L. Seguso," 8½" h 247.50

IVORY

Ivory is a yellowish-white organic material that comes from the teeth and tusks of animals. In many cases, it is protected under the Endangered Species Act of 1973, amended in 1978, which limited the importation and sale of antique ivory and tortoiseshell items. Make certain that any ivory you buy is being sold within the provisions of this law.

Vegetable ivory, bone, stag horn, and plastic are ivory substitutes. Do not be fooled. Most plastic substitutes do not approach the density of ivory nor do they have crosshatched patterns. Once you learn the grain patterns of ivory, tusk, teeth, and bone, a good magnifying glass will quickly tell you if you have the real thing.

Club: International Ivory Society, 11109 Nicholas Dr., Silver Spring, MD 20902.

Button, stylized bird, ¾" sq $8.00
Cigarette Holder, 24k gold ferrule, black hinged case, 2" l 30.00
Crochet Hook, carved 12.50
Drum, ceremonial, oval, carved, cords with stone beads 220.00
Figure, apple, carved scene inside, 3" h 120.00
Figure, seated Buddha, 3" h 95.00
Figure, woman with lute, Chinese, 12¾" h 225.00
Frame, oval, easel style, carved dragon, scroll, and heart, 5¼" h 60.00
Mask, carved, man and woman, jeweled headdresses, Chinese, 5" h, price for pr 100.00
Memo Pad, silver fittings, 1½ x 2¾" 25.00
Napkin Ring, relief carved bird, 2" d 12.00
Pie Crimper, pewter wheel, wood handle, 6¼" l 30.00
Pincushion, red velvet cushion, pedestal base, 2" h 40.00
Snuff bottle, floral and figural carved sides, stone stopper, Chinese, 2¼" h 130.00
Stiletto, turned top, 3" l 32.00
Tape Measure, spinning top shape 50.00

Earrings, AMA, gold with black, red, yellow, and green insignia, $55.00. Photo courtesy Collectors Auction Services.

JEWELRY

All jewelry is collectible. Check the prices on costume jewelry from as late as the 1980s. You will be amazed. In the current market, "antique" jewelry refers to pieces that are one hundred years old or older, although an awful lot of jewelry from the 1920s and 1930s is passed as "antique." "Heirloom/estate" jewelry normally refers to pieces between twenty-five and one hundred years old. "Costume" refers to quality and type, not age. Costume jewelry exists for every historical period.

The first step to determining value is to identify the classification of jewelry. Have stones and settings checked by a jeweler or gemologist. If a piece is unmarked, do not create hope where none deserves to be.

Finally, never buy from an individual that you cannot find six months later. The market is flooded with reproductions, copycats, fakes, and newly made pieces. Get a receipt that clearly spells out what you believe you bought. Do not hesitate to have it checked. If it is not what it is supposed to be, insist that the seller refund your money.

Club: American Society of Jewelry History, 215 East 80th St., New York, NY 10022.

Newsletter: *Old Jewelry News*, P.O. Box 272, Evanston, IL 60204.

Bracelet, composed of 5 oval scrimshaw plaques, 3 depicting nautical scenes, sgd by Howard Weyahok, joined by 14k yellow gold trace link chain **$55.20**
Brooch, 3 flowers. 14k yellow gold, citrine, tourmaline, and amethyst, faceted gemstone leaves, centered by round diamond **230.00**
Brooch, Victorian, hp dec **58.00**
Bracelet, rect pierece links, white gold-topped 14k yellow gold, 7½" l **86.25**
Bracelet, Victorian, 14k yellow gold and enamel, hinged, central black enamel band, engraved accents **175.00**
Cuff Links, shamrock motif, SS. **80.00**
Lapel Pin, SS, Budweiser 3 Million Barrel Team, inset ruby, 1941 . . . . **30.00**
Necklace, Art Deco, enamel dec, SS links, set with lapis color glass. **165.00**
Pendant/Brooch, 18k yellow gold, depicting female in ¾ length pose wearing pink dress, in oval frame with scroll accents and blue enamel sides **230.00**
Pendant, scroll form design, gilt silver, gem-set blister pearls and faceted amethysts, highlighted by polychrome enamel, Austro-Hungarian **287.50**
Pin, Egyptian Revival, centered by cultured pearl flanked by opposed crested bird motifs and falcon wings in black enamel, 18k yellow gold mount **230.00**
Ring, amethyst, in seed pearl frame, pierced bi-color 14k gold mount. **143.75**
Ring, Victorian, 14k yellow gold, hardstone cameo depicting female in profile **55.00**
Stickpin, turtle shape, 14k yellow gold, half pearls, and demantoid garnet, mkd "Riker Brothers," with handkerchief holder **287.50**

JEWELRY, COSTUME

Diamonds might be a girl's best friend, but costume jewelry is what most women own. Costume jewelry is design and form that has gone mad. There is a piece for everyone's taste—good, bad, or indifferent.

Collect it by period or design—highbrow or lowbrow. Remember that it is mass-produced. If you do not like the price the first time you see a piece, shop around. Most sellers put a high price on the pieces that appeal to them and a lower price on those that do not. Since people's tastes differ, so do the prices on identical pieces.

Club: Vintage Fashion/Costume Jewelry Club, P.O. Box 265, Glen Oaks, NY 11004.

Brooch, 2 gilt metal cupped flowers with rhinestone baguette stems, tremblant centers and small pearl springs, 1940s **$92.00**
Brooch, flower, petals set with cinnamon pâte de verre, center with single pearl surrounded by rhinestones, 1960s **80.00**
Earrings, Chanel, 7 asymmetrically shaped gilt metal nuggets in graduated sizes, sgd **80.00**
Earrings, Stanley Hagler, oversized teardrop pearls with gilt metal filigree mount, sgd "Stanley Hagler NYC," c1967. . . . . **34.00**
Necklace, Art Deco, rose quartz beads and green carved glass medallion with marcasite frame, 1930s **143.00**
Necklace, De Lillo, blue and white stones set in gilt metal 8-pointed stars, with large tassel pendant, sgd **57.00**
Necklace, Kenneth Jay Lane, faux turquoise cabochons set in gilt metal rings, 1970s **46.00**
Necklace, Victorian, silver metal strands with elaborate filigree, stone and pearl clasp. **172.00**

Flower Basket Pin, Trifari, painted yellow, with red and blue flowers, rhinestone accents, sgd, 1950s, $201.00. Photo courtesy William Doyle Galleries.

Pin, cross, faux lapis cabochons and gilt metal sprays with rhinestones, sgd "Sandor" 69.00
Pin, lizard, cold cast, painted yellow, mkd "Austria," early 20th C 80.00
Pin, rooster, SS, set with marcasite and pale green stones, mkd "Germany Sterling," 1940s 80.00

JOHNSON BROTHERS DINNERWARE

The Johnson Brothers, Alfred, Frederick, and Henry, acquired the J. W. Pankhurst pottery located in the Staffordshire district of England in 1882 and began manufacturing dinnerware the following year. Another brother, Robert, joined the company in 1896 and took charge of American distribution.

Over the years the company produced hundreds of variations of patterns, shapes, and colors. One of the most popular and readily found patterns is blue and white Coaching Scenes, first introduced in 1963. Although it was also made in green and white, pink and white, and brown multicolored, only blue and white was shipped to the United States. Other popular patterns include Old Britain Castles and Friendly Village.

Coaching Scenes, coffeepot, cov $60.00
Coaching Scenes, cup and saucer, flat, 2¾" 15.00
Coaching Scenes, gravy boat with underplate 40.00
Coaching Scenes, luncheon plate, 8½" d 10.00
Coaching Scenes, sugar, cov 30.00
English Chippendale, cereal bowl, flat, 6¼" d 15.00
English Chippendale, creamer 30.00
English Chippendale, dinner plate, 10" d 16.00
English Chippendale, salad plate, 7½" sq 10.00
English Chippendale, vegetable, oval, 9" l 30.00
Friendly Village, butter dish, cov, ¼ lb 30.00
Friendly Village, dessert plate, 7" d. 3.00
Friendly Village, dinner plate, 9⅞" d 8.00
Friendly Village, relish, 3 part, 13⅞" 40.00
Friendly Village, serving tray, 2 tier 22.00
Hearts & Flowers, creamer 20.00
Hearts & Flowers, dinner plate, 10" d 16.00
Hearts & Flowers, platter, oval, 14" l 45.00
Hearts & Flowers, salad plate 12.00
Old Britain Castles, bread and butter plate, 6¼" d, blue 8.00
Old Britain Castles, chop plate, 12" d, pink 45.00
Old Britain Castles, cup and saucer, flat, 2¼", blue 16.00
Old Britain Castles, dinner plate, 10" d, pink 10.00
Old Britain Castles, fruit bowl, 5⅛", blue 10.00
Sheraton, dinner plate, 10" d 16.00

Coaching Scenes, vegetable bowl, open, 8¼" d, $35.00.

JOSEF FIGURINES

Josef Originals were designed and produced by Muriel Joseph George. She began sculpting ceramics in California during World War II. Around 1946 she and her husband, Tom, began planning their own pottery. In 1959, in order to compete with cheap imitations that were being made in Japan, they formed a partnership with George Good's "George Imports" and went to Japan to have their figurines produced there. The partnership was merged with other George Good lines and became "George-Good Corporation" in 1974. Muriel Joseph retired in 1980–81, but continued designing until 1984–85. George Good sold the company to Applause Co in 1985. While some lines continued to be made, no new designs can be produced under the Josef Original name, Muriel passed away in 1995.

California Josef figurines are marked with a black oval paper label that reads "Josef Original California." In addition, the pieces may have an incised Josef Original marking on the bottom or sometimes merely an incised "X." The Japan pieces usually have two paper labels, an oval black label that reads "Josef Original," and a separate small oval sticker that reads "Japan." Some pieces were also ink stamped, and large pieces almost always have an incised Josef Original signature on the bottom.

Advisors: Sam and Anna Samuelian, P.O. Box 504, Edgmont, PA 19020, (610) 566-7248, fax (610) 566-7285., e-mail info@smsnoveltiques.com.

Newsletter: *Josef Original,* P.O. Box 475, Lynnwood, WA 98046.

Animal, bunny, California, Nip or Tuck, light blue, raised flowers, price for each $30.00
Animal, bunny, Japan, flocked light brown, gel or dark brown, glossy eyes, 1–3" h. 5.00
Animal, bunny, Japan, tan and brown, satin finish, 1–3" h. 10.00
Animal, cat, California, Puff or Fluff, light blue, raised flowers, price for each 30.00
Animal, chihauhua, Japan, satin finish 25.00
Animal, dog, California, Chili or Dilly, black and white, raised flowers, price for each 30.00
Animal, elephant, Japan, baby sprinkling water over back 20.00
Animal, elephant, Japan, flowers on head, satin finish. 30.00
Animal, German Shepard, Japan, satin finish 25.00
Animal, poodle, California, Cherie or Coco, light gray, gold highlights, raised flowers, price for each 30.00
Animal, mouse, Japan, satin finish, 1–2" h 10.00
Animal, penguin, Japan, satin finish, 4¾" h 25.00

Animal, Boxer Dog with Shoe, $25.00.

Birthday Angel Girl #12, $30.00.

Figure, Birthstone Doll, Japan, 4" h 15.00
Figure, California Belle series, 3" h. 35.00
Figure, Denise, California, 5" h 45.00
Figure, The Engagement, Japan, Romance series, girl in blue gown with large diamond ring, 8" h 80.00
Figure, Gail, California, 5" h 45.00
Figure, Graduation Angels, pink, blue or gray 30.00
Figure, Heddy, California, 4" h. 40.00
Figure, Henri, California, 5" h 45.00
Figure, Japan Belle series, $3^1/_2$" h 30.00
Figure, Mama, California, various colors and poses, $7^1/_2$" h . . . 80.00
Figure, Mary Ann, California, various colors and poses, $3^1/_2$" h 35.00
Figure, Tammy, Japan, musical series, girl playing piano 30.00
Figure, Teddy, California, 4" h 40.00
Music Box, *A Pretty Girl Is Like a Melody,* Japan, girl in green gown. 60.00
Music Box, *Anniversary Waltz,* Japan, girl in lavender gown 60.00
Music Box, *Fascination,* Japan, girl playing violin 50.00
Rosary Box, Japan. 35.00
Salt and Pepper Shakers, pr, Mr & Mrs Clause, Japan 10.00
Salt and Pepper Shakers, pr, owls, Japan. 10.00
Salt and Pepper Shakers, pr, Santa heads, Japan 12.00
Salt and Pepper Shakers, p, snowmen, Japan 12.00
Wall Pocket, owl, Japan, 3 owls on log with "Bless Our Nest" 35.00

JUGTOWN

Jugtown is the pottery that refused to die. Founded in 1920 in Moore County, North Carolina, by Jacques and Julianna Busbee, the pottery continued under Julianna and Ben Owens when Jacque died in 1947. It closed in 1958 only to reopen in 1960. It is now run by Country Roads, Inc., a nonprofit organization.

The principal difficulty in identifying Jugtown pottery is that the same type of wares and glazes are used on modern pieces as were used decades ago. Even the mark is the same. Since it takes an expert to distinguish between the new and old, this is certainly one category which novices should avoid until they have done a fair amount of study.

Carolina pottery is developing a dedicated core group of collectors. For more information read Charles G. Zug III's *Turners and Burners: The Folk Potters of North Carolina* (University of North Carolina Press: 1986).

Bowl, Chinese blue glaze, honey brown stain, mkd, $10^5/_8$" h $175.00
Bowl, tea bowl shape, mottled ochre glaze, $5^1/_2$" d 75.00
Cookie Jar, cov, green glaze, 6" h. 95.00
Creamer, cov, yellow, mkd, $4^3/_4$" h 45.00
Creamer, intertwined incised linear design, salt glaze finish with cobalt accents on handle and rim, imp "Jugtown Ware," $3^1/_3$" h 60.00
Mug, applied handle, medium brown glaze, imp "Jugtown Ware," 5" h. 30.00
Pie Plate, orange ground, black concentric circles dec, $9^1/_2$" d 70.00
Plate, orange glaze, 6" d 40.00
Plate, redware body, $10^1/_2$" d 30.00
Pot, burnt orange glaze, 2 handles, $3^1/_2$" h 65.00
Sugar, cov, clear glaze, orange clay body, imp "Jugtown Ware," 5" h. 45.00
Vase, Chinese White flowing glaze 70.00
Vase, ovoid, narrow neck, white crackle drip glaze, bisque body, $6^1/_2$" h 175.00

JUICERS

Finding juicers (or reamers as they're often called) in mint condition is next to impossible. The variety of materials from which they were made is staggering, ranging from wood to sterling silver. As in many other categories, the fun examples are figural. Scholarly collectors might enjoy focusing on mechanical examples, although I am not certain that I would mention on the cocktail circuit or the church social hall that I collect "mechanical reamers."

Reamers are identified by a number system developed by Ken and Linda Ricketts in 1974. This cataloging system was continued by Mary Walker in her two books on reamers. Edna Barnes has reproduced a number of reamers in limited editions. These are marked with a "B" in a circle.

Club: National Reamer Collectors Assoc., 47 Midline Court, Gaithersburg, MD 20878.

Aluminum, Handy Andy, table type, crank, red base, ... $20.00
Aluminum, Lemon-Lime Roto Squeezer, scissor type 5.00
Aluminum, Rival Mfg Co, Kansas City, MO, lever action, c1935 . . . . 40.00
China, Hall, 1 pc, green, flat, large, mkd 155.00
China, happy face, l2 pcs, emon rind textured surface, yellow spots, green leaves and handle, painted face, white ground, Japan, c1950 . . . . 50.00
Glass, Anchor Hocking, fired on, ribbed, tab handle. 12.00
Glass, Federal, green transparent, pointed cone, tab handle 28.00

Sunkist, #330, yellow, $50.00.

Glass, Fenton, baby, 2 pcs, red and white elephant and "Orange" inscription on base 75.00
Glass, Fry, canary vaseline, tab handle 60.00
Glass, Hazel Atlas, cobalt blue, tab handle. 225.00
Glass, Hazel Atlas, Crisscross, green 18.00
Glass, Jeannette, Jennyware, ultra marine 120.00
Glass, Jeannette, light jadite, loop handle, large 20.00
Glass, McKee, Sunkist 70.00
Glass, US Glass, Party Line, 4 cup pitcher and top 175.00
Mechanical, Sealed Sweet, clamps to table, tilt model 40.00
Plastic, chef, combination reamer/lemon slicer, red, c1950 . . . . 5.00
Porcelain, Presto Juicer, metal stand 60.00
Steel and Aluminum, Kwikway Products, Inc, St Louis, MO, hand held, wire reamer, domed lid with crank, hinged handles, patent 1929 . . . . 18.00

KEWPIES

Kewpies are the creation of Rose Cecil O'Neill (1876–1944), artist, novelist, illustrator, poet, and sculptor. The Kewpie first appeared in the December 1909 issue of *Ladies Home Journal*. The first Kewpie doll followed in 1913.

Many early Kewpie items were made in Germany. An attached label enhances value. Kewpie items also were made in the United States and Japan. The generations that grew up with Kewpie dolls are dying off. ONeill's memory and products are being kept alive by a small but dedicated group of collectors.

Club: International Rose O'Neill Club, P.O. Box 688, Branson, MO 65616.

Bank, bisque, "Koin Keeper," pink, 6 white Kewpies illus, 5½ x 5" $175.00
Bell, brass 60.00
Book, *The Kewpies & Dotty Darling,* Rose O'Neill, 88 pp, 1912, 8/2 x 11", dj 275.00
Cake Topper, bride and groom 40.00
Chocolate Mold, pewter, 6" h 70.00
Clock, Jasperware, green 625.00
Display, Royal Society, Christmas, easel back, 1913, 13" h 150.00
Doll, bisque, O'Neill, 5" h. 60.00
Doll, composition, red heart, orig clothes and shoes, 11" h 130.00
Doll, porcelain, movable arms, legs together, incised "O'Neill" on bottom of foot, copyright sticker on back, 6" h 135.00
Feeding Dish, child's, Kewpies and alphabet border, 10" d 150.00
Postcard, Christmas, Gibson, pricted color illus, divided back 20.00
Recipe Book, Jell-O. 30.00
Soap, orig container, 1917. . . . . 95.00
Tin, round, 9 Kewpies, 2 on tightrope, 2 on ground, 5 clinging to rope, c1935, 3½" h 20.00

KEY CHAINS

Talk about an inexpensive collecting category. Most examples sell under $10.00. If you are really cheap, you can pick up plenty of modern examples for free. Why not? They are going to be collectible in thirty years and antiques in a hundred. Who knows, maybe you will live that long!

One of the favorite charity fundraising gimmicks in the 1940s and 1950s was the license plate key chain tag. There is a collectors' club devoted to this single topic.

Club: License Plate Key Chain & Mini License Plate Collectors, 888 Eighth Ave., New York, NY 10019.

Advertising, Atlantic Motor Oil, diecut, plastic figural barrel formed by 2 panels joined by grommet. red and white stripes with front inscription "Atlantic Petrol," and back inscription "Atlantic Refining Company Of Africa Ltd," late 1930s $15.00
Advertising, Chalmers Motor Co, enameled brass, disk with name and initials logo, c1907 . . . . 40.00
Advertising, Esso Gasoline, gold finished metal, raised tiger head symbol, Esso log under slogan, "Put A Tiger In Your Tank," serial number on back for Happy Motoring Club, 1960s, 1⅜" d. 8.00
Advertising, Exxon Travel Club, aluminum tag with logo and club title on front, engraved serial number on reverse, c1970s 5.00
Advetising, Hercules Powder Co, rect, brass, logo and company name, reverse with "Fiftieth Anniversary 1912-1962," 1¼" l. 12.00
Automobile, keychain gauge, plastic cylinder with markings and turning gauge wheel to remember parking times per instruction slip inside, inscription for auto supply dealer, c1940s 8.00
Automobile, Lexington Motors, "The Lexington-Howard Co./Connersville, Ind. USA.," c1914. . . . . 40.00
Automobile, license plate, metal, "1941 New York State," yellow and black replica insert, reverse with postage guarantee if found. 5.00
Automobile, oil change reminder, white plastic, diecut, text on both sides, 1940s. 10.00
Political, Richard Nixon, brass case, 2 pull knife blades, white plastic sides, red and blue lettering reads "President Nixon, Now more than ever' 15.00
Premium, P F Sneakers, ivory plastic, large animal tooth shape, logo and antelope head dec, built-in siren whistle, sun dial, and alphabet code, 1960s, 3" l 25.00

KEYS

There are millions of keys. Focus on a special type of key, e.g., automobile, railroad switch, etc. Few keys are rare. Prices above $10 are unusual.

Collect keys with a strong decorative motif. Examples include keys with advertising logos to cast keys with animal or interlocking scroll decorations. Be suspicious if someone offers you a key to King Tut's Tomb, Newgate Prison, or the Tower of London.

Cabinet, barrel type, brass, decorative bow, 2½". $5.50
Cabinet, bronze, gold plated bow, decorative, 1½". 8.50
Car, Chrysler "Omega" keys, brass Yale, 1933, price for 5 pc set. 15.00
Car, Dodge, nickel-silver, reverse "Caskey-Dupree" 1.50
Car, Ford, Model T, dealers key 3.50
Car, Ford, Model T, nickel-silver, Ford logo. 1.75
Casting Plate, bronze, 6" 29.00
Clock, brass, Ingraham & Co, 2" 22.00

Folding, jackknife, bronze and steel, bit cuts, maker's name, 5" l 18.00
Gate, bronze, bit type, 6" 12.00
Hotel, steel, bit type, bronze tag 3.00
Jail, bronze, lever tumbler cut, Folger-Adams, oval bow with "A," 4½" 18.00
Jail, steel, flat, lever tumbler, cut, Folger-Adams 18.00
Pocket Door, bronze, slide stem, "T" bow, knurled nut 9.00
Presentation, Key to the City, white metal, "Be A Golden Key For Happiness," 2½" 1.50
Railroad, AT&SF Atchison Topeka & Santa Fe 15.00
Railroad, DT RR Detroit Terminal 18.50
Railroad, MC RR Michigan Central 18.00
Ship, bit type, iron/steel, bronze tags, 3–4" 3.00
Souvenir, 1933 Chicago Expo, "Good Luck," silver luster metal key with image of 4 exhibit buildings above "World's Fair 1933," "Keep me For Good Luck" with horseshoe symbol and 4-leaf clover, Master Lock Co, Milwaukee text on reverse 10.00
Watch, Art Nouveau, brass, loop bow 9.00

KITCHEN COLLECTIBLES

Kitchen collectibles are closely linked to Country, where the concentration is on the 1860–1900 period. This approach is far too narrow. There are a lot of great kitchen utensils and gadgets from the 1900 to 1940 period. Do not overlook them.

Kitchen collectibles were used. While collectors appreciate the used look, they also want an item in very good or better condition. It is a difficult balancing act in many cases. The field is broad, so it pays to specialize. Tomato slicers are not for me; I am more of a chopping knife person.

Clubs: International Society for Apple Parer Enthusiasts, 17 E. High, Mount Vernone, OH 43050; Jelly Jammers, 110 White Oak Dr., Butler, PA 16001; Kollectors of Old Kitchen Stuff, 501 Market St., Mifflinburg, PA 17844.

Newsletters: *Kettles 'n Cookware*, P.O. Box 247, Perrysburg, NY 14129.

Biscuit Cutter, nested set of 3, stamped aluminum, Calumet Pastry Cutter, Wearever, 1931 patent #1797859, 1½, 2¼, and 3¼" d $18.00
Bread Skillet, sq 40.00
Butter Churn, table top type, stave construction, handle 110.00
Butter Stamp, swan, wood, long handle, English, 3⅛" h, 2⅝" d 75.00

Can Opener, Can-O-Mal, Rival Mfg. Co., wall mount, apple green metal, plastic crank knob, c1946, 7½" l, $5.00.

Salt and Pepper Shakers, pr, Jeannette Glass Co., blue delphite, square, $150.00.

Can Opener, flat wood handle, bulbous head, brass ferrule, cutting blade mkd "Wynn & Timmins," c 1900, 6½" l 15.00
Chocolate Mold, candy bars, cast metal tray type, Wilbur Candy Co 18.00
Coffee Canister, glass, clear, emb zipper pattern 22.00
Coffee Grinder, lap type, wood 20.00
Coffeepot, copper, slant sided, tin lid, copper ring finial, wire bail with wood grip, mid 1800s 75.00
Colander, perforated tin, ring foot, 3¾" h, 9¾" d 15.00
Cookie Press, tin cylinder, wooden plunger, star shaped opening, 10½" l 30.00
Corn Stick Pan, Griswold 65.00
Flour Sifter, Mystic Sifter, crossbars and wire agitator, Wire Goods Co, Worcester, MA, 1915, 6½" d 15.00
Griddle, wood handle, Wagner, #9, stylized logo 65.00
Jelly Mold, fish, stamped tin, 19th C 25.00
Knife Sharpener, Eversharp, iron, wood handle, early 20th C 20.00
Knife Sharpener, Silver Duplex, screw-clamped cast iron frame, 2 steel sharpening sticks, Silver & Co, Brooklyn, c1910 . . . . . 25.00
Mayonnaise Mixer, Wesson Oil Mayonnaise Mixer, glass tumbler, metal screw-on lid with mixer blade shaft, horizontal convex perforated metal dasher, 11" h 20.00
Mixing Bowl, graniteware, yellow and white marbleized, 9½" d 30.00
Napkin Doll, pink and yellow dress, hp eyes, stamped "Japan," 9¼" h 25.00
Napkin Doll, wood, red skirt, matching hat with silver accents, Servy-Etta, 11¾" h 18.00
Onion Chopper, glass jar, paper label 10.00
Salt and Pepper Shakers, pr, black chef and maid, chalkware, 2½" h 40.00
Spatula, emb metal, Swansdown, Egleheart Brothers, Evansville, IN, 12" l, 1¼" w 15.00

KNOWLES DINNERWARE

In 1900 Edwin M. Knowles established the Edwin M. Knowles China Company in Chester, West Virginia. Company offices were located in East Liverpool, Ohio. The company made semi-porcelain dinnerware, kitchenware, specialties, and toilet wares and was known for its commitment to having the most modern and best equipped plants in the industry.

In 1913 a second plant in Newell, West Virginia, was opened. The company operated its Chester, West Virginia pottery until 1931, at which time the plant was sold to the Harker Pottery

Company. Production continued at the Newell pottery. Edwin M. Knowles China Company ceased operations in 1963.

Knowles dinnerware liens enjoyed modest sales success. No one line dominated. Some of the more popular lines with collectors are Deanna (a solid color line occasionally found with decals—introduced in 1938), Esquire (designed by Russel Wright and manufactured between 1956 and 1962), and Yorktown (a modernistic line introduced in 1936. Yorktown can be found in a variety of decal patterns such as Bar Harbor, Golden Wheat, Penthouse, and Water Lily, in addition to solid colors.

When collecting decal pieces, buy only pieces whose decals are complete and still retain their vivid colors. Edwin M. Knowles China Company also made a Utility Ware line which is gaining favor with collectors.

Do not confuse Edwin M. Knowles China Company with Knowles, Taylor, and Knowles, also a manufacturer of fine dinnerware. They are two separate companies. The only Edwin M. Knowles China Company mark that might be confusing is "Knowles" spelled with a large "K."

In the 1970s the Edwin M. Knowles Company entered into a relationship with the Bradford Exchange to produce limited edition collector plates, with titles such as *Gone With the Wind* and *The Wizard of Oz* in addition to Norman Rockwell subjects.

Alice Ann, casserole . . . **$20.00**
Alice Ann, cup and saucer . . . **7.00**
Alice Ann, sou bowl, 7½" d. . . . **10.00**
Beverly, cream soup cup . . . **12.00**
Beverly, salt and pepper shakers, pr . . . **8.00**
Deanna, cake plate, lug handle, 11" d . . . **10.00**
Deanna, cup and saucer, yellow . . . **10.00**
Deanna, demitasse cup . . . **10.00**
Deanna, dinner plate, 10" d. . . . **10.00**
Deanna, platter, Daisies . . . **8.00**
Fruits, pitcher, cov, Utility Ware . . . **25.00**
Fruits, shaker . . . **12.00**
Marion, dinner plate, 10" d . . . **10.00**
Marion, platter, 13¾" d . . . **12.00**
Tia Juana, bread and butter plate, 6" d . . . **3.00**
Tia Juana, dinner plate, 9½" d . . . **6.00**
Tia Juana, mixing bowl . . . **30.00**
Tia Juana, shaker . . . **12.00**
Tulip, pie plate, Utility Ware . . . **15.00**
Tuliptime, vegetable bowl, octagonal . . . **12.00**
Williamsburg, cake plate, lug handle, 10" d . . . **10.00**
Williamsburg, dish, lug handle, 5¼" d . . . **2.00**
Yorktown, cereal bowl, green, 6" d . . . **6.00**
Yorktown, dinner plate, Picket Fence, 10" d . . . **10.00**
Yorktown, dish, 6" d . . . **4.00**
Yorktown, gravy boat, Penthouse . . . **10.00**
Yorktown, platter, 15" d . . . **20.00**

LABELS

Labels advertising anything from cigars and citrus fruits to soaps and tobacco make great make great decorative accents. Properly framed and displayed, they become attractive works of art.

The first fruit crate art was created by California fruit growers about 1880. The labels became very colorful and covered many subjects. Most depict the type of fruit held in the box. The advent of cardboard boxes in the 1940s marked the end of fruit crate art and the beginning of a new collecting category. When collecting paper labels, condition is extremely important. Damaged, trimmed, or torn labels are significantly less valuable than labels in mint condition.

Can, My Choice Salmon, red and blue, 4⅛ x 9¾", $8.00.

Clubs: Cigar Label Collectors International, P.O. Box 66, Sharon Center, OH 44274; The Citrus Label Society, 131 Miramonte Dr., Fullerton, CA 92365; Florida Citrus Label Collectors Assoc., P.O. Box 547636, Orlando, FL 32854; International Seal, Label & Cigar Band Society, 8915 E. Bellevue St, Tucson, AZ 85715; The Fruit Crate Label Society, Rt. 2, Box 695, Chelan, WA 98816.

Newsletter: *Please Stop Snickering*, 4113 Paint Rock Dr., Austin, TX 78731.

Beverage, Old Style Beer, stagecoach, Indians, teepee, train, airplane, and car . . . **$.50**
Beverage, Palm Springs Soda, silver Art Deco design, black and gold ground, dated 1935 . . . **.50**
Cigar, Castle Hall, castel, soft colors . . . **1.00**
Cigar, La Boda, wedding ceremony . . . **2.00**
Cigar, La Miretta, lady and plantation. . . . **3.00**
Cigar, Uncle Jake's Nickel Seegar, comical man with beard and cat, c1925 . . . **3.00**
Food, Blue Hill White Corn, house and river scene. . . . **3.00**
Food, Elkay Cocoa, emb, cup of cocoa, dark blue, gold, and white . . . **10.00**
Food, Farmer's Pride Catsup. . . . **.25**
Food, Pastore Olive Oil, Indian chief with raised hands, bead work border, 7 x 10" . . . **1.00**
Food, Roseco Evaporated Milk, cow, milking stool, and bucket, red rose . . . **2.00**
Fruit Crate, Better 'N Ever, half sliced grapefruit, blue ground . . . **.50**
Fruit Crate, Don't Worry, little boy holding apple, black ground . . . **1.00**

Baggage, Hotel Royal, Bangkok, black on orange, 1920s, $60.00.

Fruit Crate, Great Valley, scenic, orange orchard, Orange Cove 1.00
Fruit Crate, Pete's Best, laughing boy, red apple, yellow ground 1.00
Health and Beauty, Essence Jam Ginger, floral, blue and white 50
Health and Beauty, Mentholated Cream, emb, gilt, floral and leaf dec 50
Health and Beauty, Talcum Powder, beautiful women on black ground 1.50
Household, Furniture Oil for Oiling Walnut, C Schrock & Son, Philadelphia, black and white 10.00
Household, Skysweep Broom, bi-plane, dated 1931 50
Soda, Orang-O-3, three oranges and leaves 25
Tobacco, Cora, child seated by giant flowers, 7 x 14" 37.50
Tobacco, International, clipper ship, Liberty ladies and topless nude, 7 x 14" 45.00
Tobacco, Sailor's Hope, woman wearing nautical dress on dock, clipper ship, 7 x 14" 27.00
Travel, Barbizon Plaza Hotel, black, white, and silver, 1930s 4.00
Travel, Hotel Mount Everest, Darjecting, Indian, blue and red 15.00
Whiskey, More's Malt Whiskey, 5 x $3\frac{1}{2}$" 1.00
Whiskey, Rocking Chair, MNr Boston and rocking chair, $3\frac{1}{4}$ x 5" 1.50

LACE

While there are collectors of lace, most old lace is still bought for use. Those buying lace for reuse are not willing to pay high prices. A general rule is the larger the amount or piece in a single pattern, the higher the price is likely to be. In this instance, the price is directly related to supply and demand.

On the other hand, items decorated with lace that can be used in their existing forms, e.g., costumes and tablecloths, have value that transcends the lace itself. Value for these pieces rests on the item as a whole, not the lace. Learn to differentiate between handmade and machine-made lace.

Club: International Old Lacers, Inc, P.O. Box 481223, Denver, CO 80248.

Periodical: *The Lace Collector*, P.O. Box 222, Plainwell, MI 49080.

LADY HEAD VASES

Heart shaped lips and dark eyelashes mark the charm of the typical lady head vase. Manufactured in the early 1950s, these semiporcelain glazed or matte finished vases were produced in Japan and the United States. The sizes of lady head vases range from $4\frac{1}{2}$" to 7" high. The decoration is thoughtfully done with a flare for the modeled feminine form. Many of the vases have the character shown from the shoulders up with elaborate jewelry, delicate gloves, and a stylized hair-do or decorated hat. A majority of the head vases are marked on the base with the company and place of manufacture.

Club: Head Vase Society, P.O. Box 83H, Scarsdale, NY 10583.

Inarco, E-1852, Jackie Kennedy, paper label, mkd, $5\frac{7}{8}$" h . . **$275.00**
Inarco, #4611, Eskimo with earrings, paper label, $6\frac{3}{4}$" h. . . . 325.00
Japan, young black lady, downcast eyes, yellow turban, red sarong, large gold hoop earrings, 3-strand pearl necklace, 5" h 30.00
Lefton, #PY641, white hair with gold accents, upswept styled hair, white skin, downcast eyes, gold arched eyebrows and eyelashes, pink flounced hat with yellow rose dec, matching dress, $5\frac{3}{4}$" h 15.00
Napco, #C32872A, fingers on chin, painted earrings, bracelet, mkd, paper label, 1958, 5" h 60.00
Napcoware, #C7494, blond hair, black hat, gray bow and dress, pearl drop earrings, pearl necklace, orig silver foil label 22.50
Norcrest, blond hair, blue bonnet, pink dress, paper label, 6" h 20.00
Norleans, Japan, blond hair, downcast eyes, white bonnet with blue ribbons, white ruffled dress, gold accents, $7\frac{1}{2}$" h 25.00
Parma, AAI, Japan, long blond hair, straight bangs, ponytail on top of head with blue flowers, eyes looking right, raised hand, slender neck, blue dress, $5\frac{1}{4}$" h 12.50
Reliable Glassware and Pottery, #3088, blond hair, blue eyes looking right, open-mouth smile, rosy cheeks, large red hat tied with red bow under chin, holly leaves dec, red and white candy-striped mittens, red coat with white fur cuffs and gold button, 6" h 22.00
Rubens, #495, gloved crossed hands beneath chin, earrings, mkd, $5\frac{5}{8}$" h 50.00
Shawnee Pottery, Island Girl, #896, carrying basket on head, wearing hibiscus in black hair, downcast eyes, green sarong, 6" h 25.00
Stanfordware, Sterling, OH, Spanish Doña, black hair, white skin, blue eyes, tilted head, white and gold dress, tiara, and mantilla, gold necklace, $6\frac{1}{2}$" h 28.00
Unknown Manufacturer, baby, blond hair, open eyes, pink cheeks, open mouth, pink ruffled bonnet tied under chin, pink dress, $5\frac{3}{4}$" h 20.00
Unknown Manufacturer, nurse, short blond hair, downcast eyes, raised right hand, white cap with Red Cross insignia, white uniform with gold accents, painted fingernails, $5\frac{1}{4}$" h 30.00

LAMPS

Collecting lamps can be considered an *illuminating* hobby. Not only is the collection practical, versatile, and decorative, but it keeps you out of the dark. Whether you prefer a particular lamp style, color, or theme, you will find a wonderful and enlightening assortment at any flea market.

Left: Kerosene, 2 pc, Bradford base, frosted pattern font, $93.50. Photo courtesy Gene Harris Antique Auction Center, Inc.
Right: Miniature, milk glass, apple blossom, chip on shade, $100.00.

Note: For addition listings see Aladdin and Motion Lamps.

Advertising, Texaco, platic and metal, electric, 18¼"h, 18½" d **$280.00**
Banquet, miniature, bronze pedestal, brass font, base with 4 ornate feet, milk glass globe, 17" h **220.00**
Betty, tin, saucer base, 7¼" h **192.50**
Boudoir, Art Nouveau, tall tubular octagon shaped pink Depression Era Glass shade with emb nudes on 4 sides, square black metal base **85.00**
Character, Davy Crockett, Davy, tree, and bear ceramic base, Davy Indians, and fort on shade, 1950s, 16" h **180.00**
Character, Fred Flintstone, painted vinyl, black metal base, missing shade, 13¼" h **45.00**
Figural, crowing rooster, ceramic, red, black, and white, circular paper shade with hex sign dec, 1950s **12.00**
Figural, desk-type telephone, plaster, turquoise, black and white speckled, clock face replacing dial, removable receiver with built-in cigarette lighter, matching rectangular venetian blind shade **35.00**
Figural, fish, ceramic, brown, leaping out of waves, brown and ivory circular paper shade. **25.00**
Figural, football player, hollow plater, standing next to football standard, linen over cardboard shade, WK, Japan, Sears, Roebuck, 1978, 14½" h **20.00**
Figural, french poodle, ceramic, pink, circular base, pink paper shade **25.00**
Figural, stylized flowers, 3 flaring wrought iron stems with curlicue leaves, plastic globular shades, circular brass base, 1930s **45.00**
Figural, Tara, Southern belle, glass, fired-on pink, matching glass parasol shade **60.00**
Grease Lamp, stoneware, with saucer base and handle, dark brown Albany slip, 4¼" h **357.50**
Hand Lamp, pewter, burning fluid burner with snuffer caps, 5" h plus burner **165.00**
Lard Lamp, tin, weighted base, flat drum shaped font with 2 wicks, 6⅜" h **165.00**
Miniature Oil Lamp, basket lamp, white milk glass, emb. **90.00**
Miniature Oil Lamp, beauty night lamp, nickel. **55.00**
Miniature Oil Lamp, bull's-eye pattern, clear glass stem **45.00**
Miniature Oil Lamp, finger lamp, green milk glass **65.00**
Miniature Oil Lamp, geometric design, milk glass, emb **45.00**
Miniature Oil Lamp, hobnail, vertical ribs **5.00**
Miniature Oil Lamp, medallion pattern, white milk glass, emb **45.00**
Miniature Oil Lamp, satin glass, white, emb, painted flowers **95.00**

Table, sculptural, by Paul Evans, wide twisted brass ribbon, large white cylindrical shade, unmkd, 54" h, 19¼" d shade, $165.00. Photo courtesy David Rago Auctions, Inc.

Advertising, Amoco, plastic and metal, electric, 18¼" h, 8½" d, $148.50. Photo courtesy Collectors Auction Services.

Novelty, lava, bottle shaped, Lava Simplex Corp, Chicago, IL **50.00**
Peg Lamp, clear, brass collar, burning fluid burner, 5⅞" h **88.00**
Petticoat Hand Lamp, pewter, burning fluid burner with snuffer caps, 3¼" h plus burner **71.50**
Table, astral style, gilded brass and marble, cut prisms, frosted and cut to clear shade, electric, 31" h **375.00**
Table, Tiffany type, gilded white metal framework with emb flowers and leaves, domed shade with caramel slag glass panels, tapered cylindrical form base with caramel slag glass panels, circular base, with double socket lamp with night light in base **325.00**
Whale Oil Lamp, pewter, "R. Dunham" touch, missing 1 spout, 7⅝" h. **137.50**

LAW ENFORCEMENT COLLECTIBLES

Do not sell this category short. Collecting is largely confined to the law enforcement community, but within that group, collecting badges, patches, and other police paraphernalia is big. Most collections are based upon items from a specific locality. As a result, prices are regionalized.

There are some crooks afoot. Reproduction and fake badges, especially railroad police badges, are prevalent. Blow the whistle on them when you see them.

Newsletter: *Police Collectors News*, RR1, Box 14, Baldwin, WI 54002.

Brochure, Plymouth Police Cars, Best On Any Beat, 1957, closeup face of policeman, 1957 . . . . . . **$8.00**
Catalog, Edward K Tryon Co, Philadelphia, PA, 400 pp, 12 pp of police goods, 1924 . . . . . . **100.00**
Game, Calling All Cars, Parker Brothers, c1938 . . . . . . **45.00**
Game, Point of Law, 3M, 1972 . . . . . . **10.00**
Game, The FBI Game, Transogram, 1961 . . . . . . **45.00**
Handcuffs, Fujihira, Japan, swing-thru type, bows controlled by pinwheel, single locking, laminated steel chrome plated. **50.00**
Handcuffs, Hiatt's, modern, swing-thru type, chrome plated or bright metal, 1960, 12½ oz **80.00**
Handcuffs, Takeda, Taiwan, model 660, steel and aluminum **10.00**
Helmet riot type, leather, New York City. **200.00**
Leg Irons, pr, Straus Engineering Co, Crawford, GA, WWII model, parkerized finish. **120.00**
Mirror, San Diego Police Dept, framed with badge and legend, "To Protect & To Serve," wood frame, 16 x 28" **65.00**

Photograph, motorcycle squad, 3 policemen posed on motorcycles in front of station #6, Kansas City, MO. 10.00
Postcard, "The Seat of Trouble," policeman approaching 2 children 3.00

L. E. SMITH

L. E. Smith Glass Company was founded in 1907 in Mount Pleasant, Pennsylvania, by Lewis E. Smith, Although Smith left the company shortly after its establishment, it still bears his name, Early products were cooking articles and utilitarian objects such as glass percolator tops, fruit jars, sanitary sugar bowls, and reamers.

In the 1920s, green, amber, canary, amethyst, and blue colors were introduced along with an extensive line of soda fountain wares. The company also made milk glass, console and dresser sets, and the always popular fish-shaped aquariums. During the 1930s, Smith became the largest producer of black glass. Popular dinner set lines were Homestead, Melba, Do-Si-Do, By Cracky, Romanesque, and Mount Pleasant.

L. E. Smith presently manufactures colored reproduction glass and interesting decorative objects. A factory outlet is available as well as factory tours. Contact the factory for specific times.

Animal, rooster, black, c1930 . . . . **$15.00**
Animal, swan, white opaque, small **15.00**
Aquarium, King-Fish, green, c1920, 10" h, 15" l **250.00**
Bookends, pr, rearing horse, emerald green **100.00**
Bread and Butter Plate, Melba, amethyst, 6" d **5.00**
Candlesticks, pr, Romanesque, pink **10.00**
Cologne Bottle, Colonial, black **30.00**
Compote, cov, Moon 'n Star, amberina **35.00**
Cookie Jar, cov, Amy, black **95.00**
Creamer, Honestead, pink **5.00**
Cruet, Moon 'n Star, ruby **30.00**
Cup and Saucer, Do-Si-Do, pink, gold trim **6.50**
Dinner Plate, Mt Pleasant black, 8" d **20.00**
Fern Dish, Greek Key, 3 ftd, white, opaque, 1930s **8.00**
Salad Tray, Mt Pleasant, 2 handles **50.00**
Sherbet, Romanesque, black **10.00**
Soda Glass, Soda Shop **6.00**
Sugar, cov, Kent **6.50**
Tray, crystal, oval, 15 x 6" **10.00**
Vase, dancing girls, #433, black, 7" h. **18.00**
Water Goblet, Moon 'n Star, amberina **15.00**

L. G. WRIGHT

The time is right for L. G. Wright. Thanks to James Measell and W. C. Roetteis' *The L. G. Wright Glass Company* (Glass Press, 1997) collectors now have the checklist they need to properly collect L. G. Wright Glass.

L. G. Wright's post–World War II carnival glass, pattern, and overlay reproductions have become collectible in their own right.

L. G. Wright was essentially a glass distributor. The company's products were actually made by a host of American glass manufacturers ranging from Dalzell-Viking and Fenton to New Martinsville and Westmoreland.

Bowl, Priscilla, amber **$5.00**
Cake Plate, pink **40.00**
Castor Bottle, cranberry **210.00**
Compote, ruffled top, blue. **32.50**
Compote, scalloped top, blue **32.50**
Covered Dish, Moon and Star, blue opalescent. **45.00**
Cracker Jar, cov, pink overlay satin floral design **400.00**
Creamer and Sugar, amber **7.50**
Cruet, amber, no stopper **45.00**
Cruet, Daisy and Button, amber **45.00**
Dish, low, Daisy and Button, vaseline **15.00**
Dish, rect, crystal **27.50**
Epergne, 2 pc, amber **85.00**
Figure, Murano-style **50.00**
Salt and Pepper Shakers, pr, Daisy and Button, blue **12.50**
Sugar Shaker, cov, vaseline **17.50**
Tumbler, Mary Gregory style, cobalt. **22.50**
Vase, painted floral dec, white ground, 15" h **35.00**

LEFTON CHINA

Lefton China was founded by George Zoltan Lefton in Chicago, Illinois, in 1941. The company markets porcelain giftware from suppliers in Japan, Taiwan, Malaysia, and China, with the bulk imported from Japan.

Club: National Society of Lefton Collectors, 1101 Polk St., Bedford, IA 50833.

Animal, deer, #521, 5⅝" h. **$28.00**
Animal, fish, #1072, 4½" h **25.00**
Animal, french poodles, set of 3, #80550, stone dec. **45.00**
Animal, otter, #132, 5½" h **32.00**
Animal, Persian Cat, #1513, matte, 3½" h **8.00**
Animal, raccoon, #4752, bisque, 5" h **42.00**
Animal, tiger, #8743, black, white, and gold, 8½" h **50.00**
Bank, lion wearing glasses, #13384, 6" h **50.00**
Bank, pig, #1992, floral dec, 5 x 4" **20.00**
Bank, turtle, #3893, glass eyes. **10.00**
Candleholders, pr, #965, 2 angels playing instruments, pastel bisque with pink roses, 7 x 5½" **125.00**
Cup and Saucer, Holly Garland, #1802 . . . . **25.00**
Jam Jar, #2844, figural pear with tray and spoon. **32.00**
Pickle Castor, cranberry opalescent swirl **475.00**
Pickle Castor, Daisy and Fern, cranberry. **400.00**
Rose Bowl, Inverted Thumbprint, green **20.00**
Spoon Rest, Rustic Daisy, #4123, 7½" h. **12.00**
Vase, double, #591, 2 angels playing instruments **250.00**
Vase, lyre, #955, white china, sponge gold and raised roses dec, 5" h **65.00**
Wall Planter, 2 birds, pastel gray-green bisque finish, #940, 6½" h **65.00**

LENOX

Johnathan Cox and Walter Scott Lenox founded the Ceramic Art Company, Trenton, New Jersey, in 1889. In 1906 Lenox established his own company. Much of Lenox's products resemble Belleek, not unexpectedly since Lenox lured several Belleek potters to New Jersey.

Lenox has an upscale reputation. China service sets sell, but within a narrow price range, e.g., $600 to $1,200 for an ordinary service of eight. The key is Lenox gift and accessory items. Prices are still reasonable. The category has not yet been truly "discovered." Lenox produces limited edition items. Potential for long-term value is limited.

Left: Blue Tree, dinner plate, $10^5/_8$" d, $18.00.
Right: Cinderella, dinner plate, $10^7/_8$" d, $40.00.

Note: For additional listings see Limited Edition.

Blue Tree, bread and butter plate, $6^3/_8$" d. **$20.00**
Blue Tree, cream soup bowl. **80.00**
Blue Tree, demitasse cup and saucer **60.00**
Blue Tree, fruit bowl, $5^1/_2$" d. **40.00**
Blue Tree, salad plate, $8^1/_4$" d **25.00**
Cinderella, cup and saucer, ftd, $2^5/_8$" h **50.00**
Cinderella, luncheon plate, $9^1/_4$" d **17.00**
Cinderella, salad plate, $8^3/_8$" d **27.00**
Cinderella, sugar, cov, no lid **65.00**
Cretan, demitasse cup **40.00**
Cretan, dinner plate, $10^7/_8$" d **30.00**
Cretan, luncheon plate, $9^1/_4$" d **28.00**
Cretan, salad plate, $8^1/_2$" d **20.00**
Cretan, sugar, cov, $3^1/_4$" **85.00**
Cretan, vegetable bowl, $9^3/_4$" l **94.00**
Fair Lady, dinner plate. **15.00**
Fair Lady, salad plate. **12.00**
Fancy Free, bread and butter plate, $6^3/_8$" d **6.00**
Fancy Free, cereal bowl, $6^1/_8$" d **18.00**
Fancy Free, coffeepot, cov **65.00**
Fancy Free, cup and saucer, flat, $2^3/_4$" **14.00**
Fancy Free, dinner plate, $10^3/_8$" d **20.00**
Fancy Free, gravy boat. **55.00**
Fancy Free, roaster, $15^1/_4$" l. **50.00**
Fancy Free, salad plate, 8" d **14.00**
Flirtation, bread and butter plate, $6^5/_8$" d. **8.00**
Flirtation, cup and saucer, ftd, 3" **40.00**
Flirtation, dinner plate. **10.00**
Flirtation, salad plate. **6.00**
Flirtation, sugar, cov **25.00**
Flirtation, vegetable bowl, $8^1/_2$" d **37.00**

Left: Glories on Grey, dinner plate, $10^3/_4$" d, $14.00.
Right: Lace Point, dinner plate, $10^5/_8$" d, $34.00.

For the Grey, bread and butter plate, $6^1/_2$" d **12.00**
For the Grey, cup and saucer. **14.00**
For the Grey, platter, $14^3/_8$" l. **65.00**
Glories on Grey, creamer **27.00**
Glories on Grey, cup and saucer, flat, $2^3/_4$" **15.50**
Glories on Grey, flour canister, 7" h **47.00**
Glories on Grey, salad plate, $8^3/_8$" d **8.00**
Holiday, cup and saucer, ftd **15.00**
Holiday, relish tray, pierced **20.00**
Lace Point, bread and butte plate, $6^3/_8$" d **20.00**
Lace Point, cream soup bowl. **80.00**
Lace Point, salad plate, $8^1/_4$" d **27.00**
Lace Point, sugar, cov **100.00**
Memoir, cup and saucer, ftd, 3" h **60.00**
Memoir, dinner plate, $10^3/_4$" d **34.00**
Memoir, salad plate, $8^1/_4$" d **27.00**

LETTER OPENERS

Isn't it amazing what can be done to a basic form? I have seen letter openers that are so large that one does not have a ghost's chance in hell of slipping them under the flap of a No. 10 envelope. As they say in eastern Pennsylvania, these letter openers are "just for nice."

Advertising letter openers are the crowd pleaser in this category. However, you can build an equally great collection based on material (brass, plastic, wood, etc.) or theme (animal shapes, swords, etc.)

Advertising, Arthur Krisher Feed Mill, Bridgewater Center, OH, plastic and metal, "Mfg: Autopoint of Chicago," c1950, $9^1/_2$" l **$10.00**
Advertising, Dunn & Eldridge Co Brass Goods, Philadelphia, PA, ST, $9^3/_4$" l. **10.00**
Advertising, "Fort Wayne Drug Co, Ft Wayne, Ind-25 Years of Service 1898–1923," bronze, $8^1/_4$" l **25.00**
Advertising, Geo Moser Leather Co, New Albany, IN, celluloid, c1910, $9^1/_4$" l **60.00**
Advertising, Industrial Trust & Savings Bank, bronze, $7^1/_4$" l **5.00**
Advertising, Keystone Telephone Co, celluloid, c1906, 6" l. **40.00**
Advertising, Lincoln National Bank & Trust Co, Ft Wayne, IN, bronze, $8^1/_4$" l **5.00**
Advertising, Olympia Beer, pewter, steel blade, $7^1/_4$" l **15.00**
Advertising, Uneeda Bread Co, litho tin, $8^1/_4$" l **45.00**
Advertising, V F W Ladies Auxilary, ST, 7" l. **5.00**
Abraham Lincoln, copper, 11" l **35.00**
Airplane, brass, "Washington DC," $8^1/_4$" l **45.00**
Bird Head, celluloid, 7" l. **10.00**
Chinese Dragon, in relief, plastic, $7^1/_4$" l **20.00**
Fish, Art Nouveau style, chromed metal, "Chicago 1933" on blade, $9^1/_4$" l. **40.00**
Horse and Rider, copper, gilded paint, $8^1/_2$" l **20.00**
Napoleon, brass overlay, 7" l **40.00**
Nude, Art Deco style, bronze, green paint, 6" l. **40.00**
Owl, wide-eyed, brass, 6" l **20.00**
Parrot, brass, $7^1/_2$" l **10.00**
Roses, antique brass finish, "Charles," $5^3/_8$" l. **45.00**
Souvenir, "Butte, Montana," copper, $9^3/_8$" l **25.00**
Souvenir, Chicago Natural History Museum, bronze, nickel finish, $6^1/_2$" l **25.00**
Souvenir, Fort McHenry, Baltimore, MD, copper, $6^1/_4$" l. **15.00**

Souvenir, Gettysburg, PA, figural sword, brass, 8" l 15.00
Souvenir, "San Francisco, California 1915," copper, 8" l 20.00

LIBERTY BLUE

In 1973 the Grand Union Company, a retail supermarket chain based in New Jersey, commissioned Liberty Blue dinnerware to be offered as a premium in grocery stores throughout the eastern United States. Ironically, though intended to celebrate America's Independence, the dinnerware was produced in Staffordshire, England.

Liberty Blue dinnerware, introduced in 1975, portrayed several patriotic scenes in blue on a white background. It also combined several elements of traditional Staffordshire dinnerware while remaining unique. The Wild Rose border was reproduced from a design dating back to 1784. Original engravings depicted historic buildings and events from the American Revolutionary period.

Liberty Blue is easy to identify, Most pieces contain the words "Liberty Blue" on the underside and all are marked "Made in England." The back of each dish also contains information about the scene illustrated on it.

Bread and Butter Plate, 6" d. $4.00
Cereal Bowl 12.00
Coaster. 12.00
Cup and Saucer, flat, 2⅝" 12.00
Creamer 20.00
Dinner Plate, 10" d 9.00
Fruit Bowl, 5" d. 8.00
Gravy Boat and Liner 50.00
Mug 14.00
Pitcher 135.00
Platter, 12" l 45.00
Salad Plate 12.00
Salt and Pepper Shakers, pr 35.00
Saucer 2.00
Sugar, cov. 30.00
Teapot, cov. 150.00
Vegetable, open, oval 35.00

LICENSE PLATES

The popularity of license plate collecting continues to grow. There are now over 3,000 active members in the Automobile License Plate Collectors Association, an international group and the largest organized club for plate hobbyists.

Plates appeal to collectors because they are colorful, diverse, and can be found virtually anywhere usually for minimal cost. Millions are produced each year, and our mobile society scatters them far and wide. Modern silkscreened graphics are now the rule rather than the exception on America's highways. The wildly colorful and fanciful optional and specialty plates issued to raise funds for favorite causes have transformed the lowly "number plate" into a 6 x 12" artist's palette. A passionate taste for these new issues can be expensive: many collectors will often pay ten to twenty times the price of an ordinary issue from the same state. However, prices usually fall drastically after a few years' production.

Quality older issues continue to rise in value, but prices are often arbitrary, regional, and hard for the novice to accurately determine. Condition is primary; badly chipped porcelains or rusty metal plates with only traces of original paint remaining are usually of little value. Repainting is acceptable to some collectors, but in most cases the resulting value is a fraction of what the item would be worth in original condition. Today's advanced collectors seek out those choice specimens that are well preserved, having been kept indoors away from destructive humidity rather than used as decoration on an outbuilding. Plates from the industrialized North and East are most easily found; pre-war southern and western issues are much less common. Part of the appeal of the plate hobby is that rare early issues still turn up on a regular basis, often from the unlikeliest of locations such as construction sites and from behind walls of old buildings. Wartime scrap drives did not get them all—a good old "tag" is still one of the most probable discoveries for the treasure hunter or flea market frequenter, and the reward for a choice find can be substantial.

Advisor: Dave Lincoln, P.O. Box 331, Yorklyn, DE 19736, (610) 444-4144.

Club: Automobile License Plate Collectors Assoc. (ALPCA), P.O. Box 7, Horner, WV 26372.

Newsletter: *The Plate Trader,* 21 Ridge Run SE, Apt D., Marietta, GA 30067.

Periodical: *PL8S: The License Plate Collector's Hobby Magazine,* P.O. Box 222, East Texas, PA 18046.

Alabama, 1955, "Heart of Dixie" $20.00
Alaska, 1976–82, standing bear graphic 25.00
Arizona, 1932–34, solid copper issue. 150.00
Arkansas, 1911, black and white porcelain 1,200.00
California, sun graphic 5.00
Colorado, 1920s and 1930s. 20.00
Connecticut, lighthouse graphic. 75.00
Delaware, 1940s, porcelain, tab slots, lite chips 35.00
District of Columbia, 1953, Inaugural with Eisenhower and Nixon photos 300.00
Florida, special optional issue, manatee, panther, etc 20.00
Georgia, 1941, peach decal intact 90.00
Hawaii, 1930s, some paint remaining 75.00
Idaho, Centennial or scenic graphic. 6.00
Illinois, 1943–1948, fiberboard issue 12.00
Indiana, 1978–1998, various graphics 3.00
Iowa, 1953, "The Corn State" 10.00
Kansas, 1950s, "Wheat State" 5.00
Louisiana, 1984 World's Fair graphics 15.00

Early Porcelain, $250.00.

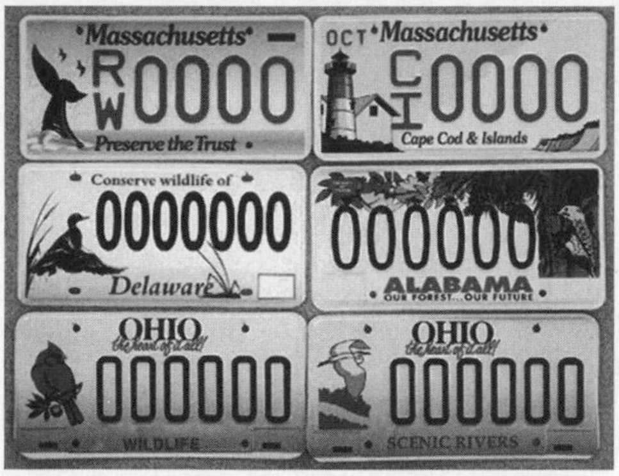

Multicolor Graphics, values range from under $10.00 to over $100.00.

Kosmic Kiddle, "Purple Gurple," 2½" h, $200.00 for complete set.

Massachusetts, 1929, pr of codfish, B prefix **200.00**
Michigan, 1910–1915, porcelain, lite chips **120.00**
Minnesota, 1920–60s **6.00**
Minnesota, 1949 Centennial **15.00**
Mississippi, 1977, magnolia graphic **3.00**
Missouri, 1920–1940s **10.00**
Montana, 1944, fiberboard **35.00**
Nebraska, 1940–1941, state capitol design **30.00**
New Hampshire, 1918 or earlier, porcelain, few chips **60.00**
New Jersey, specialty graphics, woodpecker, lighthouse,etc **50.00**
New Mexico, 1930s and 1940s, with zia symbol **30.00**
New York, 1964 Unisphere World's Fair booster plate, M **50.00**
North Carolina, 1970–1990s **2.00**
Ohio, undated, white and blue porcelain, 5 digits **400.00**
Oklahoma, Native America graphic **3.00**
Pennsylvania, owl and tiger graphic **40.00**
Rhode Island, porcelain, white and black , "Registered in R.I." **1,200.00**
South Carolina, "Keep It Beautiful" with flower **75.00**
South Dakota, 1952–1956, state shape **25.00**
Tennessee, state shape, map, 1935-56 . . . . **25.00**
Texas, 1928–1930, front and rear matched pr **200.00**
Utah, 1942–1948, with slogan **40.00**
Vermont, porcelain, early 1900s **50.00**
Vermont, white and green, with tree **4.00**
Virginia, cardinal graphic **8.00**
Washington, 1940s–50s, motorcycle **125.00**
West Virginia, graphic with state map outline **4.00**
Wisconsin, 1912 and 1913, metal numbers riveted to base **50.00**
Wyoming, 1960–1990s, bronco rider **5.00**

LIDDLE KIDDLES

Between 1965 and 1971, Mattel introduced over 125 different Liddle Kiddle dolls. They ranged in size from less than an inch to four inches in height. Liddle Kiddles came in a wide variety of styles. Some were in soda bottles or ice cream cones. Some represented storybook characters. Others were simply children and were packaged with a small plastic wagon, slide or TV. There were even animal Kiddles (Animiddles) and aliens (Kozmic Kiddles).

The variety of styles available, high quality and extraordinary detail is what made Liddle Kiddles so successful for Mattel and what makes them so coveted by collectors today.

Advisor: Linda Maley, 318 E. Virginia Rd., Fullerton, CA 92831, (714) 446-0736, fax (714) 446-0436.

Club: Liddle Kiddles Klub, 3639 Fourth Ave., La Crescenta, CA 91214.

DOLLS

Alice in Wonderland, blonde hair, blue and white dress and panties, shoes, vinyl rabbit with metal watch, booklet, 3½" h **$150.00**
Animiddles, Lucky Lion, Dainty Deer, Miss Mouse, Tiny Tiger, price for each **25.00**
Annabelle Autodiddle, auburn hair, pink top and shoes, yellow hat and shorts, orange plastic car, plastic type pusher for walking, 4" h **40.00**
Bunson Burnie, red hair, dressed as fireman, red fire engine, white plastic ladders, 3" h **75.00**
Calamity Jiddle, blonde hair, fringed red and white bodysuit and skirt, white boots, black felt hat, spotted plastic rocking horse, 2⅞" h **50.00**
Cinderiddle, blonde hair, blonde hair, gown, shoes, broom, "poor" dress, scarf, booklet, 3½" h **150.00**
Harriet Helididdle, brunette hair, green suit, white shoes, pink plastic goggles, yellow plastic helicopter, plastic pusher for walking, 4" h **50.00**
Heart Pin Kiddle, 1" h beauty queen doll in pink plastic heart with pin on back **25.00**
Heather Hiddlehorse, pink plastic horse, 1969, 4" h **65.00**
Kola Kiddles, 2" doll in 5" plastic soda bottle, 6 different flavors available, price for each **40.00**
Kologne Kiddles, 9 different 2" h floral scented dolls in plastic kologne bottle, price for each **25.00**
Lemon Stiddle, blonde hair, red dress, yellow apron, shoes, lemonade stand, pitcher, and 2 glasses, 3½" h **95.00**
Lenore Limousine, 1969 . . . . **45.00**
Locket Kiddles, plastic locket with chain, doll 2" h **25.00**

Sleeping Biddle, 3½" h, $125.00 for complete set.

Surfy Skiddle, 3" h, $60.00 for complete set.

Yellowish-green rib pattern, sheered ends, American, c1890–1925, 4¾" h, $65.00. Photo courtesy Glass-Works Auctions.

Lola Liddle, blonde hair, red shirt, white pants and shoes, sailor hat, plastic sailboat, 3½" h 50.00
Pretty Priddle, brunette hair, blue dress and panties, white shoes, pink plastic vanity and stool, 3½" h 75.00
Rah-Rah Skediddle, cheerleader, blonde hair, dress and panties, white shoes, crepe paper pom poms, plastic pusher for walking, 4" h. 85.00
Sheila Skediddle, red hair, yellow dress and panties, white shoes, plastic pusher for walking, 4" h. 25.00
Sweet Treat Kiddle Kones, 2" doll in 7" h plastic ice cream cone, 3 different flavors, price for each. 40.00
Tea Party Kiddles, 4 different sets, 3½" h doll in fancy gown, child sized cup and saucer in clear plastic dome with pink plastic base, price for each set. 95.00

OTHER

Case, Kiddles Collector's case, vinyl, pink or green $20.00
Case, Liddle Kiddles Kastle, vinyl, styrene roof, balcony and base, 10" h. 85.00
Case, Liddle Kiddles Kolony, vinyl, styrene roof and base 40.00
Case, Lucky Locket case, vinyl, blue, holds 6 Locket Kiddles 85.00
Coloring Book, Liddle Kiddles Coloring Book, Whitman, Calamity Jiddle on cov 40.00
Kiddle Komedy Theatre, includes 2 puppets, 3 rubber masks, hat, record, and backdrop for theatre, MIB. 75.00
Liddle Kiddles Electric Drawing Set, Lakeside Toys, contains lighted desk with tracing paper and pictures 40.00
Lunchbox, vinyl, light blue, with matching metal thermos 175.00

LIGHTNING ROD BALLS

Lightning rod balls are the ornamental portion of lightning rod systems typically found on the roofs of barns and rural houses from the 1840s to 1930s. The glass balls served only aesthetic purposes and did not contribute to the operation of the lightning rod system.

Glass balls were made in a rainbow of colors ranging from common white or blue milk glass to red and clear. Many clear glass balls turned shades of sun colored amethyst (SCA) through exposure to the sun. Mercury colored balls were created by silvering the interior surface of balls of different colors to produce silver, gold, cobalt, red, and green mercury colors. Lightning rod balls were also colored using flashing and casing techniques.

There are 34 standard shapes or styles of lightning rod balls.

Newsletter: *The Crown Point*, 2615 Echo Ln., Ortonville, MI 48462.

Blue Milk Glass, pumpkin pattern $65.00
Blue Milk Glass, swirl pattern 65.00
Diddie Blitzen, clear, emb "Diddie Blitzen Rods," 4⅛" h. 25.00
Electra, round, cobalt, 51/8" h 50.00
Green Milk Glass, chestnut pattern 60.00
K Ball, gold mercury, emb "K," 5⅛" h 125.00
Plain Round, amber, 4" h. 40.00
Plain Round, amber, 5½" h 20.00
Plain Round, milk glass, rough sheared ends, 4¾" h 56.00
Plain Round, SCA, 3½" h. 85.00
Plastiball, plastic, opaque, snap together halves 3.00
Ruby Red, rough sheared ends, 4¾" h 56.00
Shinn System Round 20.00
White Milk Glass, D&S pattern 10.00
White Milk Glass, quilt pattern, raised 55.00
White Milk Glass, vaseline, 5" h 12.50
Yellow Green, rib pattern, 4¾" h 56.00

LILLIPUT LANE

Collectible cottages, also know as architectural collectibles, are the 1980/90s version of commemorative plates and whiskey bottles. The secondary market is highly speculative; and, there are more than ample signs that the bubble is bursting. Limited Edition and Collector Club models are among the most speculative.

In 1982 David Tate of Skirsgill, near Penrith, Cumbria, England, issued the first series of fourteen Lilliput Lane cottages, inspired by buildings in England's Lake District.

The company has used over a dozen different backstamps on its buildings, making them easy to date. Before buying on the secondary market, always check to see if the building is still in production and what its current suggested retail price is. A cottage needs to have its period box and certificate to be considered complete.

Club: Lilliput Lane Collectors' Club, P.O. Box 498, Itasca, IL 60143.

Anne Hathaway's Cottage, 1989, discontinued 1997, 3¼" h $150.00
Applejack Cottage, 1994, 2½" h 35.00
Banqueting House, 1994, 3" h. 65.00
Bow Cottage, 1992, discontinued 1995, 3½" h. 135.00
Bridge House, 1991, 3" h 20.00
Buttercup Cottage, 1990, discontinued 1992, 2¾" h 75.00
Button Down, 1995, discontinued 1998, 2½" h 30.00
Calendar Cottage, 1996, 3¼" h 55.00
Carrick House, 1989, 2½" h 35.00
Chestnut Cottage, 1989, discontinued 1993, 4½" h. 125.00

Coke Country Five & Dime, cold cast, 3¹/₄" h, $95.00.

Clockmaker's Cottage, 1987, discontinued 1990, 4" h...... **250.00**
Craigievar Castle, 1989, discontinued 1991, 6³/₄" h........ **300.00**
Die Kleine Backerei, 1988, discontinued 1994, 3¹/₂" h **85.00**
Farriers, 1985, discontinued 1990, 2¹/₂" h.............. **100.00**
Greensted Church, 1989, discontinued 1995, 4" h **95.00**
Helmere Cottage, 1989, discontinued 1995, 3¹/₄" h......... **85.00**
Hometown Depot, 1990, discontinued 1993, 3" h **125.00**
John Knox House, 1989, discontinued 1992, 5³/₄" h **150.00**
Kenmore Cottage, 1989, discontinued 1993, 3¹/₂" h **125.00**
Le Petit Montmartre, 1990, discontinued 1997, 5" h **95.00**
Limerick House, 1989, discontinued 1992, 3³/₄" h......... **150.00**
Mrs Pinkerton's Post Office, Oak Cottage, 1989, discontinued 1993, 4¹/₂" h **150.00**
Paradise Lodge, 1991, discontinued 1996, 4¹/₂" h **95.00**
Pat Cohan's Bar, 1989, discontinued 1996, 3¹/₂" h.......... **85.00**
Saddler's Inn, 1987, discontinued 1989, 3" h **95.00**
School Days, 1991, discontinued 1997, 2³/₄" h............ **60.00**
Tudor Merchant, 1991, discontinued 1997, 4¹/₂" h **60.00**
Vine Cottage, 1990, discontinued 1995, 4¹/₂" h........... **125.00**
Wealden House, 1987, discontinued 1990, 4¹/₂" h **175.00**
Wedding Bells, 1992, 3¹/₄" h **50.00**

LIMITED EDITION COLLECTIBLES

Collect limited edition collectibles because you love them, not because you want to invest in them. While a few items sell well above their initial retail price, the vast majority sell between twenty-five and fifty cents on the original retail dollar. The one consistent winner is the first issue in any series.

Whenever possible, buy items with their original box and inserts. The box adds another ten to twenty percent to the value of the item. Also, buy only items in excellent or better condition. Very good is not good enough. So many of each issue survive that market price holds only for the top condition grades.

Clubs: International Plate Collectors Guild, P.O. Box 487, Artesia, CA 90702. In addition, many companies that issue limited edition collectibles have company sponsored clubs. Contact the company for further information.

Periodicals: *Collector Editions,* 170 Fifth Ave., 12th Fl., New York, NY 10010; *Collectors' Bulletin,* 22341 East Wells Rd., Canton, IL 61520; *Collector's Mart Magazine,* 700 E. State St, Iola, WI 54990; *Collectors News,* 506 Second St., P.O. Box 156, Grundy Center, IA 50638; *The Treasure Trunk,* P.O. 13554, Arlington, TX 76094; *White's Guide to Collecting Figures,* 8100 Three Chopt Rd., Ste. 226, Richmond, VA 23229.

Bell, Anri, Christmas, J Ferrandiz, wooden, 1976 .... **$50.00**
Bell, Artists of the World, Festival of Lights, T DeGrazia, 1980... **85.00**
Bell, Belleek, Church, third edition, 1991................ **32.00**
Bell, Belleek, Two Turtle Doves, Twelve Days of Christmas, 1992 .... **30.00**
Bell, Gorham, Currier & Ives, American Homestead, 1977... **25.00**
Bell, Kirk Stieff, Annual Bell 1978, Musical Bells **80.00**
Bell, Lenox China, Deck the Halls, Songs of Christmas, 1992... **50.00**
Bell, Old World Christmas, Santa Bell, first edition, Porcelain Christmas, E M Merck, 1988................ **10.00**
Bell, Reed & Barton, Noel Musical Bell, 1980 .... **50.00**
Bell, River Shore, Flowers for Mother, Rockwell Children Series, N Rockwell, 1977......................... **60.00**
Bell, Roman, Adoration, The Masterpiece Collection, F Lippe, 1979 .... **20.00**
Bell, Schmid, The Guardian Angel, Berta Hummel Christmas Bells, B Hummel, 1974 .... **45.00**
Doll, Annalee Mobilitee Dolls, Baby Witch, A Thorndike, 1987, 3" h........................... **275.00**
Doll, Annalee Mobilitee Dolls, Unicorn, Doll Society, A Thorndike, 10" h, 1986......................... **350.00**
Doll, Anri, Jessica, Sarah Kay Dolls, S Kay, 1991, 7" h...... **300.00**
Doll, Anri, Juanita, J Ferrandiz, 1991, 7" h **300.00**
Doll, Ashton-Drake, Bye-Bye, Baby Talk, Good-Kruger, 1994... **50.00**
Doll, Ashton-Drake, New Year, Calendar Babies, Ashton-Drake, 1995 .... **25.00**
Doll, Ashton-Drake, Rebeccah, Amish Blessings, J Good-Kruger, 1990 .... **100.00**
Doll, Ashton-Drake, Stephanie, Christmas Memories, Y Bello, 1994 .... **60.00**
Doll, Attic Babies, Christmas Baggie Bear, Baggie Collection, M Maschino, 1991...................... **22.00**
Doll, Attic Babies, Rammy Sammy, M Maschino, 1989...... **44.00**
Doll, Dolls by Jerri, Alfalfa, J McCloud, 1986 .... **350.00**
Doll, Dolls by Jerri, Miss Nanny, J McCloud, 1985 .... **275.00**
Doll, Dynasty Doll, Marcella, 1990 .... **90.00**
Doll, Elke's Originals, Kricket, E Hutchens, 1990 .... **400.00**
Doll, Ganz, Sweet Cicely musical doll in basket, Little Cheesers/Cheeserville Picnic Collection, G D A Group, 1992.................................... **85.00**
Doll, Georgetown Collection, Christina Merovina, American Dairy Dolls, L Mason, 1991 .... **130.00**
Doll, Georgetown Collection, Katie, Little Loves, B Deval, 1989.................................. **140.00**

Bell, Bing & Grondahl, Christmas Bell, 1985, 3" h, $45.00.

Doll, Ashton-Drake, Andy, Yesterday's Dreams, M. Oldenburg, 1990, $68.00.

Doll, Goebel of North America, Alexa, Victoria Ashlea Originals, B Ball, 1989 . . . . . 195.00
Doll, Gorham, Friday's Child, Days of the Week, R/L Schrubbe, 1992 . . . . . 98.00
Doll, Gorham, Katrina, Joyful Years, B Gerardi, 1989 . . . . . 375.00
Doll, Gorham, Mother's Helper, Gorham Holly Hobbie Childhood Memories, 1985 . . . . . 175.00
Doll, Hamilton Collection, Amanda, Connie Walser Derek Baby Dolls, C W Derek, 1991 . . . . . 155.00
Doll, Hamilton Collection, Dana, Daddy's Little Girls, M Snyder, 1993 . . . . . 95.00
Doll, Hamilton Collection, First Party, Maud Humphrey Bogart Doll Collection, 1990 . . . . . 150.00
Doll, Hamilton Collection, Ricky, I Love Lucy, porcelain, 1991 . . . . . 350.00
Doll, Ladie and Friends, Bridget Bowman, The Family and Friends of Lizzie High, B K Wisber, 1987 . . . . . 95.00
Doll, Ladie and Friends, Brother Noah Pawtucket, The Pawtuckets of Sweet Briar Lane, B K Wisber, 1986 . . . . . 110.00
Doll, Ladie and Friends, Earth Angel, The Christmas Pageant, B K Wisber, 1985 . . . . . 100.00
Doll, Ladie and Friends, Indian Squaw, The Thanksgiving Play, B K Wisber, 1988 . . . . . 40.00
Doll, Lenox Collections, Hannah, The Little Dutch Maiden, Children of the World, 1989 . . . . . 120.00
Doll, Middleton Doll Co, Christmas Angel, L Middleton, 1988 . . . . . 200.00
Doll, Reco International, Tommy the Clown, Children's Circus Doll Collection, J McClelland, 1991 . . . . . 75.00
Doll, Roman Inc, Chelsea, A Christmas Dream, E Williams, 1990 . . . . . 125.00
Doll, Sarah's Attic, Bobby Doll, Heirlooms from the Attic, 1989 . . . . . 120.00
Doll, Seymour Mann, Baby John, Connossieur Doll Collection, 1989 . . . . . 85.00
Doll, The Collectables, Cassandra, Cherished Memories, P Parkins, 1990 . . . . . 550.00
Doll, The Collectables, Willow, Butterfly Babies, P Parkins, 1990 . . . . . 375.00
Figurine, All God's Children, Amy, M Holcombe, 1987 . . . . . 25.00
Figurine, American Artists, Arab Mare & Foal, Fred Stone Figurines, F Stone, 1986 . . . . . 225.00
Figurine, Anri, All Aboard, Sarah Kay Figurines, S Kay, 1987, 4" h 185.00
Figurine, Anri, Devotion, Ferrandiz Shepherds of the Year, J Ferrandiz, 1984, 3" h 125.00
Figurine, Anri, Golden Sheaves, Ferrandiz Boy and Girl, J Ferrandiz, 1986, 3" h 125.00
Figurine, Anri, Harvest's helper, J Ferrandiz, 1986, 4" h 175.00
Figurine, Anri, Maestro Mickey, Disney Studio, 1988, 4½" h 175.00
Figurine, Armani, Charlie, Clown Series, G Armani, 1995 . . . . . 175.00
Figurine, Armani, Flamingo, Wildlife, G Armani, 1991 . . . . . 420.00
Figurine, Armani, Fresh Fruit, Siena Colleciton, G Armani, 1993 . . . . . 295.00
Figurine, Armstrong's, Clem Kadiddlehopper, The Red Skelton Collection, R Skelton, 1981 . . . . . 150.00
Figurine, Artaffects, Cinderella, The Storybook Collection, G Perillo, 1981 . . . . . 95.00
Figurine, Artaffects, Geronimo, The Chieftains, G Perillo, 1983 . . . . . 135.00
Figurine, Artists of the World, Fesitval Lights, T DeGrazia, 1986 . . . . . 110.00
Figurine, Band Creations, July, Best Friends, Angels of the Month, Richards/Penfield, 1993 . . . . . 10.00
Figurine, Boehm Studios, Elephant, white bisque, 1985 . . . . . 575.00
Figurine, Boyds Collection, Father Chrisbear and Son, The Bearstone Collection, G M Lowenthal, 1993 . . . . . 200.00
Figurine, Byers' Choice Ltd, Singing Cats, J Byers, 1988 . . . . . 15.00
Figurine, Calabar Creations, My Funny Valentine, Dreamsicles, K Haynes, 1992 . . . . . 28.00
Figurine, Classic Collectables by Uniquely Yours, Girl in Sleigh, Dicken's A Christmas Carol, E Tisa, 1988 . . . . . 75.00
Figurine, Creart, Thoroughbred Horse, Horses and Cattle, Perez, 1989 . . . . . 275.00
Figurine, Cybis, Huey, The Harmonious Hare, Animal Kingdom, 1986 . . . . . 275.00
Figurine, Dave Grossman Designs, Graduate, Norman Rockwell Collection, 1983 . . . . . 50.00
Figurine, Department 56, Alpine Shops, 1992 . . . . . 75.00
Figurine, Department 56, Booter and Cobbler, Dickens' Village Series, 1988 . . . . . 110.00
Figurine, Department 56, Nathaniel Bingham Fabrics, New England Village, 1986 . . . . . 155.00
Figurine, Department 56, Little Italy Ristorante, Christmas in the City, 1991 . . . . . 52.00
Figurine, Duncan Royale, The Pixie, History of Santa Claus II, P Apsit, 1986 . . . . . 175.00
Figurine, Eggspressions, Miss Ellie, Whimsical, 1992 . . . . . 45.00
Figurine, Enchantica, Rattajack with Snail, A Bill, 1991 . . . . . 85.00
Figurine, Flambro Imports, Bedtime, Emmett Kelly Jr, 1986 . . . . . 325.00
Figurine, Franklin Mint, Trick or Treat, Joys of Childhood, N Rockwell, 1976 . . . . . 175.00
Figurine, Gartlan USA, Bobby Hull, sgd, L Heyda, 1992 . . . . . 400.00
Figurine, Hamilton Collection, Camelia, D Fryer, 1987 . . . . . 75.00
Figurine, Kaiser, Bear and Cub, white bisque, 1979 . . . . . 375.00

Figurine, Department 56, Going to the Chapel, Snow Village, 1977–95, $20.00.

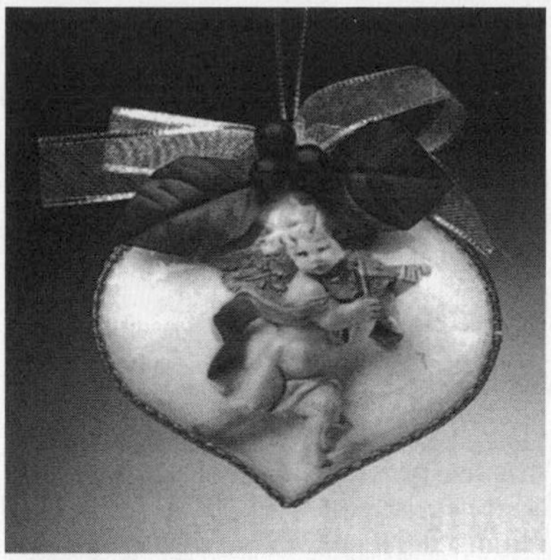

Ornament, Roman, Inc, Fontanini, paper, 4" h, $3.50.

Plate, The Hamilton Collection, Attic Attack, Country Kitties, G Gerardi, 1988, $25.50.

Figurine, Lenox Collections, Governor's Garden Party, American Fashion, 1985 . . . . **95.00**
Figurine, Maruri U S A, Baby Emporer Penguin, Polar Expedition, 1990 . . . . **50.00**
Figurine, Old World Christmas, Teddy Bear, Night Lights, E M Merck, 1986 . . . . **110.00**
Figurine, Pen Delfin, Honey, D Roberts, 1989 . . . . **60.00**
Figurine, Reco, Donkey, Reco Creche Collection, J McClelland, 1988 . . . . **17.00**
Figurine, Roman, Flight into Egypt, Ceramica Excelsis, 1978 . . . . **90.00**
Figurine, R R Creations, Outhouse, Grandpa's Farm Collection Series II, D Ross, 1992 . . . . **5.00**
Figurine, Schmid, Company's Coming, Davis Cat Tales, L Davis, 1982 . . . . **225.00**
Figurine, The Cat's Meow, Jared Coffin House, Nantucket, F Jones, 1987 . . . . **20.00**
Figurine, The Cat's Meow, Limberlost Cabin, Collector Club Gift Houses, F Jones, 1991 . . . . **50.00**
Ornament, Anheuser-Busch, Greatest Triumph, A & Eagle Collector Ornament Series, 1993 . . . . **15.00**
Ornament, Annalee Mobilitee Dolls, Skier, A Thorndike, 1992 . . . . **175.00**
Ornament, Anri, Heavenly Drummer, Ferrandiz Woodcarvings, J Ferrandiz, 1988 . . . . **225.00**
Ornament, Artists of the World, Flower Girl, DeGrazia Annual Ornaments, T DeGrazia, 1988 . . . . **75.00**
Ornament, Bing & Grondhal, Silent Night, Holy Night, E Jensen, 1986 . . . . **30.00**
Ornament, Boyds Collection, Father Christmas, The Folkstone Collection, G M Lowenthal, 1995 . . . . **10.00**
Ornament, Department 56, Shooting Star, bisque light-up, clip-on, 1986 . . . . **6.00**
Ornament, Gorham, sterling snowflake, 1971 . . . . **75.00**
Ornament, Lenox Collections, Lion, 1989 . . . . **20.00**
Ornament, Roman, Kristopher Kolumbus, The Discovery of America, I Spencer, 1991 . . . . **15.00**
Ornament, Roman, Puss in Berries, Catnippers, I Spencer, 1988 . . . . **15.00**
Ornament, Roman, Rarest of Heaven, Sepaphim Collection by Faro, 1994 . . . . **25.00**
Ornament, Schmid, Mailbox, Lowell Davis Country Christmas, L Davis, 1983 . . . . **45.00**
Plate, Allison and Company, Toast To A Mouse, Late to Party, B Allison, 1983 . . . . **35.00**
Plate, American Artists, Cora's Recital, Family Treasures, R Zolan, 1981 . . . . **39.50**
Plate, American Artists, The Eternal Legacy, Fred Stone Classics, F Stone, 1986 . . . . **85.00**
Plate, American Heritage, Down Easter In A Squall, American Sail, E Ries, 1983 . . . . **39.50**
Plate, American Rose Society, Seashell, All-American Roses, 1976 . . . . **135.00**
Plate, Anheuser-Busch, Buddies, Man's Best Friend, M Urdahl, 1990 . . . . **50.00**
Plate, Anna-Perenna, Helping Hands, Annual Christmas, P Buckley Moss, 1985 . . . . **175.00**
Plate, Anna-Perenna, Carnation, Flowers of Count Bernadotte, Count Lennart Bernadotte, 1983 . . . . **95.00**
Plate, Anri, Santa Claus In Tyrol, Christmas, 1981 . . . . **185.00**
Plate, Anri, Alpine Mother And Children, Mother's Day, 1973 . . . . **55.00**
Plate, Artaffects, Nez Perce Nation, America's Indian Heritage, G Perillo, 1988 . . . . **50.00**
Plate, Artaffects, Comanche, Tribal Ponies, G Perillo, 1984 . . . . **100.00**
Plate, Bing & Grondahl, The Magical Tea Party, Children's Day, C Roller, 1985 . . . . **24.50**
Plate, Bing & Grondahl, Danish Farm, Christmas, O Larsen, 1942 . . . . **115.00**
Plate, Blue Delft, Francesco Lana's Airship, Father's Day, 1971 . . . . **30.00**
Plate, Boehm Studios, Edward Marshall, Monarch And Daisy, Butterflies of the World, 1978 . . . . **62.00**
Plate, Bradford Exchange, Rusty's Retreat, Hideaway Lake, 1993 . . . . **35.00**
Plate, Crown Delft, Two Sleigh Riders, Christmas, 1970 . . . . . **20.00**
Plate, Danbury Mint, Molly Pitcher, Bicentennial Silver, 1978 . . . . **125.00**
Plate, Delphi, A Hard Day's Night, Beatles Collection, N Giorgio, 1991 . . . . **50.00**
Plate, Department 56, The Cratchit's Christmas Pudding, A Christmas Carol, R Innocenti, 1991 . . . . **60.00**
Plate, Dresden, Village Scene, Christmas, 1974 . . . . **30.00**
Plate, Fairmont China, Flower Boy, Children of the World, T DeGrazia, 1978 . . . . **45.00**
Plate, Franklin Mint, Washington Crosses The Delaware, American Revolution, A Farnham, 1976–77 . . . . **75.00**
Plate, Gartlan USA, Hockey's Golden Boys, Brett and Bobby Hull, M Taylor, 1991, 8½" d **45.00**
Plate, W S George, Yosemite Falls, American the Beautiful, H Johnson, 1988 . . . . **34.50**
Plate, The Hamilton Collection, Clowns, Greatest Show On Earth, F Moody, 1981 . . . . **70.00**
Plate, The Hamilton Collection, Crayon Creations, Delights of Childhood, J Lamb, 1989 . . . . **29.50**
Plate, The Hamilton Collection, First Day Of Spring, Country Season of Horses, J M Vass, 1990 . . . . **29.50**

Plate, Edwin M Knowles, Office Hours, Friends I Remember, J Down, 1984, $17.50.

Plate, The Hamilton Collection, June's Creation, Gardens of the Orient, S Suetomi, 1983 . . . . **19.50**
Plate, Edna Hibel Studios, Angels' Message, Christmas Annual, E Hibel, 1985 . . . . **45.00**
Plate, Edna Hibel Studios, Peony, Flower Girl Annual, E Hibel, 1989 . . . . **125.00**
Plate, House Of Global Art, Dolly Dingle Visits Germany, Dolly Dingle World Traveler, G Drayton, 1982 . . . . **30.00**
Plate, Hutschenreuther, Spring Morning, Bouquets of the Seasons, 1987 . . . . **24.50**
Plate, Bicentennial Coin, Coin Plates, 1976 . . . . **20.00**
Plate, Imperial, Drummers, Christmas, carnival glass, 1978 . . . . **30.00**
Plate, Incolay She Walks In Beauty, Romantic Poets, G Bright Appleby, 1977 . . . . **80.00**
Plate, Georg Jensen, Christmas Story, 1974 . . . . **25.00**
Plate, Kaiser, Tender Moment, Anniversary, K Bauer, 1975 . . . . **25.00**
Plate, Kaiser, The Rooster, On The Farm, A Lohmann, 1982 . . . . **75.00**
Plate, Kera, Little Peter, Christmas, 1971 . . . . **15.00**
Plate, Kera, The Arabian, Great Achievements in Art, H Young, 1980 . . . . **170.00**
Plate, Edwin M Knowles, All Wrapped Up: Himalayans, Cat Tales, A Brackenbury, 1988 . . . . **45.00**
Plate, Edwin M Knowles, Bathsheba And Solomon, Biblical Mothers, E Licea, 1983 . . . . **39.50**
Plate, Edwin M Knowles, The Singing Lesson, Backyard Harmony, J Thornbrugh, 1991 . . . . **35.00**
Plate, Edwin M Knowles, Christmas Vigil, Sundblom Santas, H Sundblom, 1990. . . . . **50.00**
Plate, Lenox, Colonial Virginia, Colonial Christmas Wreath, 1981 . . . . **90.00**
Plate, Lynell, Olde Country Inn, Betsy Bates Annual, 1979. . . . . **45.00**
Plate, Lynell, Cradle of Love, Norman Rockwell Mother's Day, N Rockwell, 1980 . . . . **40.00**
Plate, Modern Concepts Ltd, Sugar And Spice, Nursery Rhyme Favorites, 1984. . . . . **38.50**
Plate, Pemberton And Oakes, Forests And Fairy Tales, Adventures of Childhood, D Zolan, 1991 . . . . **30.00**
Plate, Pemberton And Oakes, Sharing Secrets, Childhood Friendship, D Zolan, 1988 . . . . **45.00**
Plate, Pickard, Cleopatra, Let's Pretend, I Spencer, 1984 . . . . . **80.00**
Plate, Reco International, Black-Capped Chickadee, Grafburg Christmas, 1975 . . . . **60.00**
Plate, Reco International, Pretty As A Picture, Barefoot Children, S Kuck, 1988 . . . . **30.00**
Plate, River Shore, Founder's Day Harvest, Little House On The Prairie, E christopherson, 1985 . . . . **40.00**
Plate, River Shore, Trial By Jury, We the Children, D Crook, 1988 . . . . **25.00**
Plate, Rockwell Society, Scotty Gets His Tree, Christmas, N Rockwell, 1974 . . . . **100.00**
Plate, Roman, Breezy Day, A Child's Play, F Hook, 1982. . . . . **35.00**
Plate, Roman, Ice Princess, Pretty Girls of the Ice Capades, G B Petty, 1983 . . . . **25.00**
Plate, Rosenthal, Christmas In Wurzburg, 1974. . . . . **100.00**
Plate, Royal Bayreuth, Down Memory Lane, Antique American Art, 1978 . . . . **65.00**
Plate, Royal Copenhagen, Christmas In The Forest, K Lange, 1952. . . . . **175.00**
Plate, Royal Copenhagen, Virgin Islands, Special Issues, 1967. . . . . **25.00**
Plate, Royal Delft, Christmas Star, 1924 . . . . **290.00**
Plate, Royal Doulton, Village Children, All God's Children, L DeWinne, 1980. . . . . **65.00**
Plate, Royal Worcester, Christmas Eve, English Christmas, 1979 . . . . **60.00**
Plate, Schmid, Starlight Angel, Berta Hummel Christmas, B Hummel, 1979. . . . . **38.00**
Plate, Signature Collection, Ring The Bell, Carnival, T Newsom, 1983. . . . . **40.00**
Plate, Villeroy And Boch, Mary With Child, Christmas, 1979. . . . . **198.00**

LITTLE GOLDEN BOOKS

Read me a story! For millions of children that story came from a Little Golden Book. Colorful, inexpensive, and readily available, these wonderful books are a hot collectible. You see them everywhere.

Be careful, you may be subject to a nostalgia attack because sooner or later you are going to spot your favorite. Relive your childhood. Buy the book. You won't be sorry.

Club: Golden Book Club, 19626 Ricardo Ave., Hayward, CA 94541.

Newsletter: *The Gold Mine Review,* P.O. Box 209, Hershey, PA 17033.

Animal Babies, #39, 1947, 42 pp **$14.00**
Baby's House, #80, 1950, 28 pp **15.00**
Bugs Bunny and the Indians, #120, ©Warner Bros Cartoon, Inc, 1951, 28 pp **14.00**

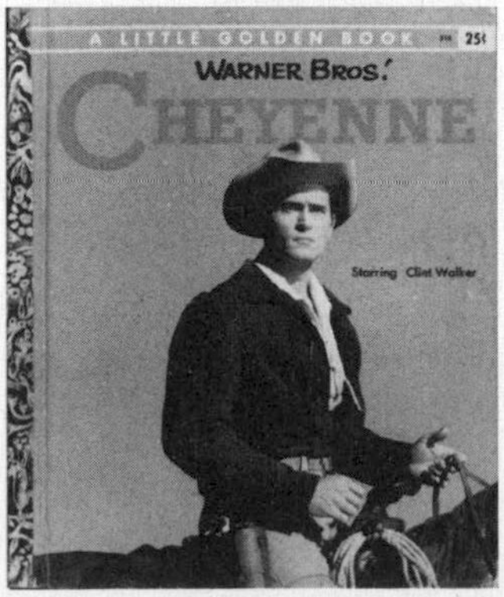

***Cheyenne,* #318, Charles Spain Verral, Al Schmidt illus, Simon & Schuster, NY, 1958, 24 pp, $20.00.**

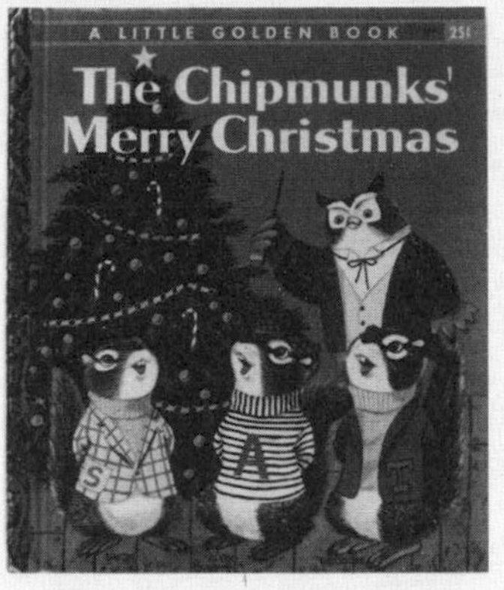

***The Chipmunks' Merry Christmas,* #375, David Corwin, Richard Scarry illus, Golden Press, NY, 1959, 24 pp, $9.00.**

Busy Timmy, #50, 1948, 28 pp **30.00**
Come Play House, #44, 1948, 42 pp **27.00**
Day at the Playground, A, #119, 1951, 28 pp. **25.00**
Doctor Squash The Doll Doctor, #157, 1952, 28 pp **16.00**
Gaston and Josephine, #65, 1949, 42 pp **2.00**
Good Morning, Good Night, #61, 1948, 42 pp. **30.00**
Happy Man and His Dump Truck, The, #77, 1950, 42 pp. . . . **20.00**
This Little Piggy Counting Rhymes, #12, 1942, 42 pp **50.00**
Little Golden Book of Hymns, The, #34, 1947, 42 pp **14.00**
Little Golden Funny Book, The, #74, 1950, 42 pp. **14.00**
Little Red Hen, The, #6, 1942, 28 pp **20.00**
Lively Little Rabbit, The, #15, 1943, 42 pp **25.00**
Magic Next Door, The, #106, 1971, 24 pp **6.00**
Musicians of Bremen, The, #189, 1954, 28 pp **8.00**
My Little Golden Dictionary, #90, 1949, 56 pp. **14.00**
New Baby, The, #41, 1948, 42 pp **30.00**
Pets For Peter, #82, 1950, 28 pp **14.00**
Poky Little Puppy, The, #8, 1942, 42 pp **40.00**
Rabbit and His Friends, #169, 1953, 28 pp **12.00**
Rainy Day Play Book, The, #133, 1951, 28 pp **11.00**
Road To Oz, The, #144, 1951, 28 pp. **25.00**
Scuffy The Tugboat, #30, 1946, 42 pp **25.00**
Toys, #22, 1945, 42 pp **25.00**
Train To Timbuctoo, The, #118, 1951, 28 pp **20.00**
Up in the Attic, #53, 1948, 42 pp **16.00**
We Like Kindergarten, #552, 1965, 24 pp **6.00**
Year on the Farm, A, #37, 1948, 42 pp. **20.00**

LITTLE ORPHAN ANNIE

Little Orphan Annie is one of those characters that pops up everywhere—radio, newspapers, movies, etc. In the early 1930s "Radio Orphan Annie" was syndicated regionally. It went network in 1933. The show's only sponsor was Ovaltine. Many Little Orphan Annie collectibles were Ovaltine premiums.

Actually, Little Orphan Annie resulted from a sex-change operation. Harold Gray, an assistant on the "Gumps" strip, changed the sex of the leading character and submitted the same basic strip concept as a proposal to the *New York News*. The 1924 operation was a success.

Annie's early companions were Sandy, her dog, and Emily Marie, her doll. "Daddy" Warbucks replaced the doll, and the strip went big time. Gray died in 1968. The strip was farmed out to a succession of artists and writers. The result was disastrous.

Radio and cartoon strip Little Orphan Annie material is becoming expensive. Try the more recent movie-and stage-related items if you are looking for something a bit more affordable.

Newsletter: *Annie People,* 517 N. Fenwick St., Allentown, PA 18103.

Apron, fabric, printed color image of Annie and Sandy, trimmed in piping strip contour, single large pocket, Harold Gray copyright, 1930s, 4½ x 8½" folded size. . . . **$100.00**
Bank, ceramic, figural Annie and Sandy, coin slot in top of head, rubber disk trap, Applause of Knickerbocker Toy Co sticker on underside with ©1982 Columbia Pictures and Tribune Syndicate. **20.00**
Bank, dime register, lito tin, missing key, 1936 . . . . **195.00**
Better Little Book, *Little Orphan Annie and the Ancient Treasure of AM,* Whitman, #1468, 1939 . . . . **50.00**
Big Little Book, *Little Orphan Annie in the Movies* **40.00**
Book, *Little Orphan Annie and Jumbo the Circus Elephant,* pop-up, Blue Ribbon Press, Pleasure Books Inc, ©1935, 8 x 9¼" **200.00**
Comic Book, Little Orphan Annie, Dell, #152, ©1947 News Syndicate Co, 48 full color pp **45.00**
Comic Strip Book, *Little Orphanie Annie/A Willing Helper,* Cupples & Leon Co, hard cov, black and white comic strip reprints, 86 pp, ©1931 Chicago Tribune, 7 x 8½". **75.00**
Display Card, cardboard, 7 block announcements of various Annie stage production show awards received in 1977 and 1978, bottom inscription band imprinted for 7 week coming performances at 5th Avenue Theater, 14 x 22". **20.00**
Doll, cloth, stuffed, painted composition head and arms, cloth body, movable arms, fabric dress, woven fabric knee stockings in red oilcloth boots with thin car board soles, 2" d cloth tag pinned to dress, 15" h **200.00**
Doll, cloth, stuffed, yellow soft frizzy hair, red fabric outfit with white felt collar and belt, printed black sandal shoes, orig window display box, made in Taiwan for Well-Made Toy Mfg Corp, ©1973 New York News, 1½ x 3½ x 7" **20.00**
Doll, oilcloth, stuffed, reverse image of cap, jacket, and figure, 1930s, 12½" h **100.00**
Game, Little Orphan Annie Game, Milton Bradley **130.00**
Greeting Card, Christmas, "Merry Christmas And A Great '68," cover art of Annie and Sandy, inner right panel imprinted in red lettering form greeting from Annie and Sandy plus Winifred and Harold Gray followed by their summer and winter addresses, unused, 1967, 5 x 6¾". **75.00**
Lunch Box, vinyl, red with white polka dots, 6½" h plastic bottle with full color front images of Annie on delivery bike and skipping rope, 7 x 9 x 3½" **65.00**

Box, empty, Little Orphan Annie Sweater, Lampl Knitwear Co, litho paper lid, 8 x 11", $280.00. Photo courtesy New England Auction Gallery.

Mug, Ovaltine "50th Golden Annie-Versary," ceramic, white, gold and black inscriptions, black, white, red, and orange image image of Annie and Sandy, 1981–82, 3½" h **20.00**
Nodder, painted bisque, "Orphan Annie" stamped on back, 1930s, 3½" h **150.00**
Ovaltine Premium, bandana, Radio Orphan Annie, "Flying W," red and white printed fabric with brown accents, border horshoe motifs and circular background portraits of Radio Orphan Annie, Sandy, Joe Corntassel, and Ginger, 1934, 17 x 18½" **65.00**
Ovaltine Premium, Orphan Annie Goofy Ciurcus Kit, with envelope, 1939, 10½ x 15" **100.00**
Ovaltine Premium, Orphan Annie's Cold Ovaltine Shake-Up Mug, green Beetleware plastic, red lid, full color decal, 1940, 5" h **75.00**
Ovaltine Premium, Radio Orphan Annie's 1936 Secret Society Manual, full color, 12 pp, illus of 1936 decoder pin and silver star ring premiums, with 4 x 6" order coupon for ring, 6 x 8¾" **65.00**
Ovaltine Premium, Radio Orphan Annie's Welcome to Simmons Corners Map, folded 6 x 9½" sheet opens to 19 x 24" full color aerial view of village in Tucker County, "Where Radio's Little Orphan Annie Has Had So many Thrilling Adventures," 1936 . . . . **65.00**
Pastry Set, child's, baking utensils, Transogram "Gold Medal" Toy, 1930s. **75.00**
Photo, Shirley Bell, black and white, glossy, sgd "To My Friend/Radio's Little Orphan Annie/Shirley Bell," 1932, 8 x 10" **40.00**
Pinback Button, "Little Orphan Annie/Some Swell Sweater," color portrait, white, black print, 1¼" d **50.00**
Salt and Pepper Shakers, pr, plater, Annie and Sandy, 1940s, 3" h **25.00**
Ring, brass, portrait on top, orig luster, 1934 . . . . **75.00**
Sign, "Orphan Annie Secret Guard," diecut cardboard, folding, lower center area for holding tablet of Secret Guard membership application coupons, poster design and back of application picture premiums of official handbook, Slidomatic Radio Decoder, and Mysto-Snapper membership badge clicker, small area for entering local radio station and broadcast times, c1941, 11½ x 23½". **650.00**
Snowdome, plastic, Annie and Sandy, 1970s, ... **10.00**
Whistle, tin, 3 tones **30.00**

LITTLE RED RIDING HOOD

On June 29, 1943, the United States Patent Office issued design patent #135,889 to Louise Elizabeth Bauer, Zanesville, Ohio, assignor to the A. E. Hull Pottery Company, Incorporated, Crooksville, Ohio, for a "Design for a Cookie Jar." Thus was born Hull's Little Red Riding Hood line. It was produced and distributed between 1943 and 1957.

Early cookie jars and the dresser jars with a large bow in the front can be identified by their creamy off-white color. The majority of the later pieces have very white pottery, a body attributed to The Royal China and Novelty Company, a division of Regal China. Given the similarity in form to items in Royal China and Novelty Company's "Old McDonald's Farm" line, Hull possibly contracted with Royal China and Novelty for production as well as decoration.

Great hand painted and decal variation is encountered in pieces, e.g., the wolf jar is found with bases in black, brown, red, or yellow. Prices for many pieces are in the hundreds of dollars. Prices for the advertising plaque and baby dish are in the thousands.

Attempts at determining production levels have been unsuccessful. This category has the potential for an eventual market flooding, especially for the most commonly found pieces. New collectors are advised to proceed with caution.

Undecorated blanks are commonly found. Value them between 25 and 50 percent less than decorated examples.

Club: Red Riding Hood!, P.O. Box 105, Amherst, NH 03031.

REPRODUCTION ALERT: Be alert for a Mexican produced cookie jar that closely resembles Hull's Little Red Riding Hood piece. The Mexican example is slightly shorter. Hull's examples measure 13" high.

Basket, open, large floral decal **$275.00**
Batter Pitcher **400.00**
Butter Dish, cov **375.00**
Coffee Canister **400.00**
Cookie Jar, red hood, floral decal on skirt. **275.00**
Cracker Jar **690.00**
Creamer, side pour **115.00**
Dresser Jar **625.00**
Grease Jar, yellow wolf. **1,000.00**
Match Holder **475.00**
Milk Pitcher, front pour **325.00**
Milk Pitcher, standing, 8" h **275.00**
Mug, hot chocolate **2,000.00**
Mustard, cov, orig spoon, 5½" h **375.00**
Salt and Pepper Shakers, pr, small **90.00**
Salt Canister **850.00**
Spice Jar, allspice, cinnamon, cloves, nutmeg, or pepper, price for each **700.00**
String Holder **2,500.00**
Sugar Canister. **590.00**
Teapot, cov. **325.00**
Toothbrush Holder **75.00**

LITTLE TIKES

Thanks to Beanie Babies, collector interest in infant and juvenile toys is growing. Rubbermaid's Little Tikes' toys and playtime equipment are one of the beneficiaries.

Little Tikes sturdy products are made of heavy-gauge plastic. They have proven virtually indestructible, one of the reasons they frequently appear in the garage sale, recyclable market. In fact, most are bought to be reused rather than collected.

The ideal way to purchase these items is to check the cost of a new example and plan on paying twenty to thirty cents on the dollar. Doll high chairs, lawn and garden carts, and toddler tractors sell between $5 and $8. Expect to pay $20 or more for the Junior Activity Gym or Twin Slide Tunnel Climber.

While you should not expect to find an example factory new, do not buy pieces that have deep scratches, the edges of which are often rather sharp or can catch on clothing. Also make certain that the item you buy is complete, e.g., the Junior Activity Gym has an attached slide.

LLADRO PORCELAINS

Lladro porcelains are Spain's contribution to the world of collectible figures. Some figures are released on a limited edition basis; others remain in production for an extended period of time. Learn what kinds of production numbers are involved.

Lladro porcelains are sold through jewelry and "upscale" gift shops. However, they are the type of item you either love or hate. As a result, Lladro porcelains from estates or from individuals tired of dusting that thing that Aunt Millie gave for Christmas in 1985 do show up at flea markets.

Club: Lladro Collectors Society, 43 W. 57th St., New York, NY 10019.

Bell, Christmas, 1987 . . . . . **$50.00**
Figurine, A New Friend, L-1506-G, 1986 . . . . . **250.00**
Figurine, Baby Jesus, L-1388-G, 1981 . . . . . **190.00**
Figurine, Beagle Puppy, L-1071-G, 1969 . . . . . **225.00**
Figurine, Bear, white, L-1208-G, 1972 . . . . . **75.00**
Figurine, Bearly Love, L-1443-G, 1983 . . . . . **120.00**
Figurine, Best Friend, S-7620, 1993 . . . . . **250.00**
Figurine, Bird, L-1053-G, 1969 . . . . . **100.00**
Figurine, Can I Play?, S-7610, 1990 . . . . . **300.00**
Figurine, Dog and Snail, L-1139-G, 1971 . . . . . **270.00**
Figurine, Eskimo, L-1195-G, 1972 . . . . . **135.00**
Figurine, Flower Song, S-7607, 1988 . . . . . **500.00**
Figurine, Flying Duck, L-1263-G, 1974 . . . . . **90.00**
Figurine, Garden Classic, L-7617-G, 1991 . . . . . **400.00**
Figurine, Girl with Brush, L-1081-G, 1969 . . . . . **300.00**
Figurine, Girl with Geese, L-1035-M, 1969 . . . . . **165.00**
Figurine, Henry VIII, LL-1384 . . . . . **850.00**
Figurine, Kissing Doves, L-1169-G, 1971 . . . . . **150.00**
Figurine, Little Pals, S-7600, 1985 . . . . . **2,000.00**
Figurine, Little Traveler, S-7602, 1986 . . . . . **1,000.00**
Figurine, My Baby, LL-1331, 1976 . . . . . **900.00**
Figurine, Phyllis, L-1356-G, 1978 . . . . . **225.00**
Figurine, Sancho Panza, L-1031-G, 1969 . . . . . **550.00**
Figurine, Star Gazing, L-1477-G, 1985 . . . . . **375.00**
Figurine, Valencian Boy, L-1400-G, 1982 . . . . . **400.00**
Figurine, Waiting Backstage, L-4559-G, 1969 . . . . . **440.00**
Figurine, Young Sailor, L-4810-G, 1972 . . . . . **175.00**
Ornament, Christmas Ball, 1988 . . . . . **60.00**
Ornament, Holy Family, miniature, set of 3, 1989 . . . . . **100.00**
Ornament, Playing Cherub, 1995 . . . . . **120.00**
Ornament, Flying Dove, 1995 . . . . . **45.00**
Ornament, Santa, 1992 . . . . . **55.00**
Tree Topper, Angel, blue or pink, 1990-91 . . . . . **120.00**

Figurine, left: Next at Bat, L–5828, 9" h; right: I've Got It!, L–5827, 5" h, $170.00 each.

Texaco, set of 4, brass, with keys, 2½–5" l, $412.50. Photo courtesy Collectors Auction Services.

LOCKS AND PADLOCKS

Padlocks are the most desirable lock collectible. While examples date back to the 1600s, the mass production of identifiable padlocks was pioneered in America in the mid-1800s.

Padlocks are categorized primarily according to tradition or use: Combination, Pin Tumbler, Scandinavian, etc. Cast, brass, and iron are among the more sought-after types.

Reproductions, copycats, and fakes are a big problem. Among the trouble spots are screw key, trick, iron lever, and brass lever locks from the Middle East, railroad switch locks from Taiwan, and switch lock keys from the U.S. Midwest. All components of an old lock must have exactly the same color and finish. Authentic railroad, express, and logo locks will have only one user name or set of initials.

Clubs: American Lock Collectors Assoc., 36076 Grennada, Livonia, MI 48154.

Combination, Corbin Sesamee, brass case, 2¾" h **$1.50**
Combination, Dialoc, steel, 2¼" h **5.00**
Combination, L & Co Ltd, zinc alloy case, 2½" h **15.00**
Combination, Slaymaker, steel case, zinc alloy dial, 2⅞" h **1.50**
Eight Lever, steel, Reese **12.00**
Gate Lock, iron and brass, manufacturer's name, 10" h **70.00**
Lever, brass, Corbin, 2" h **18.00**
Lever, brass, Sphinx, 2¾" h **15.00**
Lever, iron, Master, #41, 2" h **15.00**
Lever, iron, Yale Junior, 3¾" h **5.00**
Pin Tumbler, brass, Reese US, 1¾" h **5.00**
Pin Tumbler, iron, push key, brass hasp, Yale, 2" h **10.00**
Pin Tumbler, steel, Eagle Lock Co, Pat. June 28, 1896, 2¼" h **8.00**
Pin Tumbler, iron, push key, brass hasp, Yale, 2" h **10.00**
Railroad, C & E I, Yale & Town Mfg Co, iron lever, 3" h **15.00**
Railroad, CSTPM & O, iron, Fraim, 2¼" h **20.00**
Railroad, D L & W RR, 3¼" h **60.00**
Railroad, Illinois Central System, Best, pin tumbler, 2⅛ x 1½" **15.00**
Railroad, Missouri Pacific Railway, 3¾" h **100.00**
Railroad, Pennsylvania RR, switch, steel, Slaymaker, 2¼" h **25.00**
Scandinavian, Corbin, brass, 2½" h **50.00**
Scandinavian, J H W Climax Co, 4" h **25.00**
Scandinavian, Romer & Co, rect keyhole, 1¾" h **20.00**
Six Lever, brass, Yale, 2" h **15.00**
Six Lever, steel, N S H Co **5.00**

LONGABERGER BASKETS

Collectors of antique and vintage baskets will tell you that Longaberger baskets are vastly overrated. While not something a Longaberger basket collector wants to hear, they may regret not paying attention when the current speculative bubble bursts.

Dave Longaberger founded The Longaberger Company, based in Newark, Ohio, in 1973. While the company stresses a hand-made, craft ancestry for its baskets, the fact is they are mass produced. The company sold 7.7 million baskets in 1997, an indication that scarcity is a word that will not be used to describe a Longaberger basket, even fifty years from now.

Internet sales, especially on eBay, are fueling Longaberger basket speculative prices. The key is the price realized for the fifth example offered, not the first, assuming it is lucky enough to receive an opening bid or meet reserve.

BASKETS

Bee Basket, Bee Tie-On, 1998 . . . . . **$10.00**
Booking Basket, Chives Garde, Splendor Lid **10.00**
Christmas, Bayberry Combo, 1993 . . . . . **80.00**
Christmas, Christmas Tie-On, 1996 . . . . . **14.00**
Christmas, Jingle Bell **70.00**
Christmas, Mistletoe Basket, red, 1989 . . . . . **110.00**
Classics Collection, small laundry basket with protector, 1998 . . . . . **175.00**
Collectors Club, Serving Tray Combo, with box, 1996 . . . . . **250.00**
Collectors Club Signatures, Summer/Fall 1997, vol 2, #3 . . . . . **5.00**
Easter, cookie mold, Angel of Hope, 1994 . . . . . **14.00**
Father's Day, Finder's Keepers Divided Protector, 1998 . . . . . **8.00**
Sweetheart Basket, Bee Mine Combo **64.00**
Traditions Collection, Fellowship Lid, 1997 . . . . . **25.00**
Wrought Iron, plant hanger, MIB **35.00**

LINERS

All American Stars & Stripes, Picnic, large **$38.00**
Cherry Red Plaid, Picnic Pal **14.00**
Classic Blue, Horizon of Hope **11.00**
Collectors Club, Thyme **15.00**
Emerald Vine, Thyme **12.00**
Fall Foliage, Harvest, 1993 . . . . . **15.00**
Fall Gingham, Harvest, 1993 . . . . . **15.00**
Father's Day Paisley, Oregano **12.00**
Mother's Day Floral, Button **16.00**
Rose Trellis, Horizon of Hope **12.00**
Traditional Holly, Table Overlay **40.00**
Traditional Plaid, Hospitality **28.00**

LUGGAGE

Until recently luggage collectors focused primarily on old steamship and railroad trunks. Unrestored, they sell in the $50 to $150 range. Dealers have the exterior refinished and the interior relined with new paper and then promptly sell them to decorators who charge up to $400. A restored trunk works well in both a Country or Victorian bedroom. This is why decorators love them so much.

Within the past three years, there is a growing collector interest in old leather luggage. It is not uncommon to find early twentieth century leather overnight bags priced at $150 to $300 in good condition. Leather suitcases sell in the $75 to $150 range.

LUNCH BOXES

Lunch kits, consisting of a lunch box and matching thermos, were the most price-manipulated collectibles category of the 1980s. Prices in excess of $2,500 were achieved for some of the early Disney examples. What everyone seemed to forget is that lunch boxes were mass-produced.

The lunch kit bubble has burst. Prices dropped for commonly found examples. A few dealers and collectors attempted to prop up the market, but their efforts failed. If you are buying, it will pay to shop around for the best price.

Buy lunch kits. Resist the temptation to buy the lunch box and thermos separately. I know this is a flea market price guide, but lunch kits can get pricy by the time they arrive at a flea market. The best buys remain at garage sales where the kits first hit the market and sellers are glad to get rid of them at any price.

Club: Step Into The Ring, 829 Jackson St. Ext., Sandusky, OH 44870.

Periodical: *Paileontologist's* Retort, P.O. Box 3255, Burbank, CA 91508.

A-Team, King-Seeley, steel, plastic thermos, 1985 . . . . . **$25.00**
Barbie and Midge, King-Seeley, vinyl, 1970 . . . . . **65.00**
Beatles, Air-Flite, vinyl, 1965 . . . . . **125.00**
Boating, American Thermos, metal, speedboats, sailboats, and canoes illus, c1958, $6^{1}/_{2}$ x $8^{3}/_{4}$ x 4" **175.00**
Bobby Soxer, Aladdin, vinyl, c1959, 7 x $8^{1}/_{2}$ x 4" **400.00**
Boy on Rocket, Ardee, vinyl, 1960s, 7 x $8^{1}/_{2}$ x $3^{1}/_{2}$" **175.00**
Bullwinkle, King-Seeley, vinyl, 1963 . . . . . **60.00**
Captain Kangaroo, King-Seely, vinyl, thermos, 1964–66 . . . . . **95.00**
Charlie's Angels, Aladdin, steel, 1978 . . . . . **35.00**
Circus Wagon, American Thermos, metal, dome shape **225.00**
Denim, King-Seeley, vinyl, blue denim design, red, white, blue, and yellow patches, red plastic thermos with denim pocket decal, c1970s, 7 x 9 x 4" **65.00**
Disco, Aladdin, steel, plastic thermos, 1979–80 . . . . . **30.00**
Dutch Cottage, American Thermos, metal, dome, c1958, 7 x 9 x $4^{1}/_{2}$" **175.00**
Family Affair, King-Seeley, metal, color illus, ©1969, 7 x 8 x 4" **75.00**
Football, Decoware, litho tin, football shape, removable int silver tray, "Varsity," simulated laces on lid, 1950s **175.00**
Fritos Corn Chips, King-Seeley, metal, c1975, 7 x $8^{3}/_{4}$ x 4" **65.00**
Gene Autry, Melody Ranch, Universal, 1954–55, $6^{1}/_{2}$ x 9 x $3^{1}/_{2}$" **175.00**

Hopalong Cassidy, Aladdin Industries, metal, litho scene, 1954, $150.00.

Roy Rogers & Dale Evans, metal, no thermos, 7¼ x 8¾ x 3¾", $72.00. Photo courtesy Collectors Auction Services.

Hogan's Heroes, Aladdin, dome, 1966 . . . . 75.00
Holly Hobbie, Aladdin, steel, 1973–74 . . . . 16.00
Hot Wheels Sizzlers, Thermos, ©Mattel, vinyl, missing thermos 225.00
I Love A Parade, Bayville, vinyl, red, full color scene on front under clear cov, illus of girl bandleader followed by poodle wearing band uniform as 2 cats watch, orig blue styrofoam thermos with plastic bottle insert, c1970, 7 x 8 x 4" 75.00
James Bond 007, Aladdin, 1966 . . . . 75.00
Jetsons, Aladdin, dome, 1965 . . . . 75.00
Laugh-In, Aladdin, steel, plastic thermos, 1970 . . . . 70.00
Lidsville, Aladdin, emb metal, ©Sid & Marty Krofft Television Products, 1971 . . . . 55.00
Little Red Riding Hood, Ohio Art, metal, illus, c1982, 7 x 9 x 4" 45.00
Man From U.N.C.L.E., King-Seeley, 1966 . . . . 60.00
Mary Poppins, Aladdin, vinyl, white, color illus, c1973, 7 x 9 x 4" 125.00
Munsters, King-Seeley, 1966 . . . . 45.00
Orbit, American Thermos, metal, c1963, 7 x 9 x 4" 125.00
Osmonds, Aladdin, emb metal, 1973 . . . . 50.00
Pebbles & Bamm-Bamm, Aladdin, 1972 . . . . 26.00
Play Ball, King-Seeley, steel, 1969, 7 x 8¾ x 4" 65.00
Popples, Aladdin, 1986 . . . . 25.00
Road Tote, unmkd, vinyl, red, traffic signs illus, 1970s, 6½ x 9 x 4½" 200.00
Roy Rogers and Dale Evans, American Thermos, c1950s 120.00
School Bus, Rel Plastics Corp, plastic, 1951, 4 x 9 x 5¾" 85.00
See America, Ohio Art, color illus on front and back panels, band has road map design in green, black, and red, 1972, 7 x 9 x 4" 40.00
Skateboarder, Aladdin, emb metal, color illus, c1977, 7 x 8 x 4" 15.00
Sleeping Beauty, Aladdin, vinyl, 1970 . . . . 75.00
Snow White, Aladdin, vinyl, 1975 . . . . 55.00
Strawberry Shortcake, Aladdin, vinyl, ©American Greetings Corp, 1980 . . . . 25.00
Street Hawk, Aladdin, emb metal, color illus, thermos, ©1984, 7 x 8 x 4" 200.00
Tarzan, Aladdin, emb metal, 1966, 7 x 8 x 4" 555.00
The Life And Times Of Grizzly Adams, Aladdin, metal, dome shape, color illus, ©1977, 7 x 9 x 4" 75.00
Underdog, Okayt Industries, 1974 . . . . 250.00
Wagon Train, King-Seeley, steel, thermos, 1964 . . . . 40.00
Waltons, Aladdi, metal, 1973 . . . . 60.00
Washington Redskins, Okay Industries, metal, helmet design on front and back, c1970, 7 x 9 x 3½" 175.00
Wild Wild West, Aladdin, 1969 . . . . 50.00

MAD COLLECTIBLES

What kid from the 1960s on doesn't remember Alfred E. Neuman and his zany, somewhat irreverant humor? Alfred is getting older, as are many of his fans, but items adorned with his unforgettable face are very collectible.

Arcade Card, black and white, featuring pre-MAD Alfred E Neuman, 1920s **$20.00**
Decal, full color, Alfred E Neuman illus, "What—Me Worry" on striped and yellow ground, Inprint Art Products, 1960s, 3 x 4¼" **25.00**
Disguise Kit, Alfred E Neuman, contains 2 Alfred ears, red skin and hair color, black tooth, and freckle pencil, Imagineering, 1987, MIB **30.00**
Figure, Alfred E Neuman bust, china bisque, green felt on bottom, no label, 1960, 3¾" h **280.00**
Hand Puppet, Alfred E Neuman, plastic head, cloth body, white shirt, black bottom, red ribbon tie, "What...Me Worry?" on neck, Crestline, 1960, 10" h **362.00**
Mask, full head Alfred E Neuman, latex, with hair, Cesar, 1981 . . . . **55.00**
Matchbook, full color Alfred E Neuman character on back, Bob Adamcik, 1950s, 3½ x 4¼" **61.00**
Paperback Book, *Burning MAD,* Signet **4.00**
Patch, Alfred E Neuman, pink, peel-off sticky back, unlicensed, 1960s, 3" d **20.00**
Poster, *Up The Academy,* 1980, 41 x 26½" **25.00**
Poster, "Who Needs You?," full color, 1991, 22 x 36" **53.00**
Record, *MAD Twists Rock N Roll,* Big Top, LP, 1962 . . . . **100.00**
Record, *Musically MAD,* RCA, LP, mono, 1959 . . . . **20.00**
Stickers, MAD Trouble Stickers, complete set of 64, Fleer, 1983 . . . . **25.00**
TV Guide, Oct 26, 1968, 5 pp article "MAD About Television" **15.00**
Watch, MAD 30th Anniversary, chrome finish, leather band, orig display box, Concepts Plus, 1987 . . . . **93.00**

MAGAZINES

A vast majority of magazines, especially if they are less than thirty years old, are worth between 10 cents and 25 cents. A fair number of pre-1960 magazines fall within this price range as well. There are three ways in which a magazine can have value: the cover artist, the cover personality, and framable interior advertising. In three instances, value rests not with the magazine collector, but with the speciality collectors.

***Collier's,* Oct 28, 1922, Fred Turner cov illus, sgd orange and black color wash, 30 pp, 10½ x 14", $6.00.**

At almost any flea market, you will find a seller of matted magazine advertisements. Remember that the value being asked almost always rests in the matting and not the individual magazine page.

Newsletter: *The Illustrator Collector's News,* P.O. Box 1958, Sequim, WA 98382.

Periodicals: *Paper Collectors' Marketplace* (PCM), P.O. Box 128, Scandinavia, WI 54977; *Pulp & Paperback Market Newsletter,* 5813 York Ave., Edina, MN 55410.

Adirondack Life, 1970s $3.00
Air Trails, 1951 annual 20.00
Airbrush Action, 1980s–90s 5.00
Amazing Stories Quarterly, 1930–50 . . . . 5.00
American Artist, Feb 1975, Wyeth cov 15.00
American Detective, 1930s 8.00
American Economic Review, 1940s 1.00
American Lady, 1930s 10.00
American Rodding, Sep 1964, Vol 1 . . . . 8.00
Auto & Motor Sport, 1960s 4.00
Auto Racing Journal, 1940s 11.00
Baseball Digest, Jan 1949 . . . . 10.00
Basketball All Pro, 1970s Annual 12.00
Better Homes & Gardens, Sep 1935 . . . . 23.00
Blue Book, Jul 1913 . . . . 35.00
Botanical Gazette, 1870–1920s 7.00
Boys Life, Apr 1966, Willie Mays 20.00
Brewers Digest, 1920s 3.00
Buchanan's Journal of Man, Jan 1849, Vol #1 . . . . 25.00
Cadillac Connoisseur, 1980s 3.00
Car & Motor, 1960s 4.00
Classic Photography, Fall 1956, Marilyn Monroe 24.00
Daring Detective, May 1943 . . . . 8.00
Dental Digest, 1920s 2.00
Discovery 1920s 11.00
Dynamic Detective, Sep 1940 . . . . 8.00
Family Circle, Oct 16, 1942, Judy Garland cov 15.00
Farmers Cabinet, 1830 . . . . 12.00
Fortune, Sep 1930 . . . . 40.00
Friends Miscellany, 1830s 10.00
Gentry, Winter 1951 . . . . 35.00
Gleason's Pictorial, May 2, 1851 . . . . 60.00
Good Ole Days, 1966 . . . . 5.00
Grin, Aug 1940 . . . . 15.00
Harper's Monthly, Jan 1920 . . . . 12.00
Harper's Weekly, Aug 1907 . . . . 10.00
Heavy Metal, 1970–80s 3.00

The Mentor, **Jun 1929, features Henry Ford collector, black and white illus, 71 pp, 8½ x 11½", $15.00.**

The Saturday Evening Post, **Nov 27, 1909, Harrison Fisher cov illus, sepia and black wash cover sgd, 44 pp, 11¼ x 14¼", $45.00.**

Hit Parader, 1940s 6.00
Honk!, 1950s 10.00
Horse Shoe Journal, early 1900s 9.00
Hot Rod Cartoons, 1960s 7.00
House & Home, Mar 1954 . . . . 10.00
Ice Capades, 1945, G Petty cov 36.00
Independent Woman, 1930 . . . . 4.00
Inside Story, Jan 1955 . . . . 20.00
Intimate Romances, 1950–70s 5.00
Journal of Living, 1940s 50
Judge's Library, 1890s 20.00
Ladies Circle, 1960s 3.50
Ladies Companion, 1830s 15.00
Ladies Home Journal, May 1893, Palmer Cox Brownies 18.00
Ladies Home Journal, Jan 1960, Pat Boone 5.00
Life, Jun 3, 1941, Statue of Liberty 9.00
Life, Nov 17, 1947, Howard Hughes 15.00
Life, May 1979, Three Mile Island 2.00
Look, Jan 12, 1943, J Stewart cov 15.00
Look, Feb 12, 1963, Grace Kelly cov 25.00
Magazine of Business, 1930s 1.00
McCalls, 1940s 8.00
Mechanics Illustrated, Apr 1959 . . . . 3.00
Modern Bride, 1960–65 . . . . 2.00
Modern Handgun, 1960s 2.00
Muscle Power, Oct 1953, Mr America 3.00
My Story, 1960s 2.00
National Geographic, Dec 1939, Cathedrals 5.00
National Geographic, Aug 1976, Venezuela 1.00
New Thought, early 1900s 4.00
Newsweek, Mar 27, 1939, Supreme Court 5.00
Newsweek, Nov 21, 1955, railroads 3.00
Now, 1950s 2.00
Outdoor Life, Jan 1978 . . . . 1.00
Personality, 1920s 3.00
Playbill, 1950s 3.00
Pleasure Magazine, winter 1937 . . . . 12.00
Popular Horsemen, 1950s 1.50
Popular Photography, Aug 1937, swimsuit cov 22.00
Popular Song Hits, May 1947, Betty Grable cov 10.00
Prisoner's Friend, mid 1800s 4.00
Punch, Nov 10, 1954 . . . . 6.00
Racecar, 1970–80s 3.00
Radio News, 1920–30s 10.00
Railroad Magazine, 1940s 7.00
Real Confessions, 1960s 3.50
Reader's Digest, Spring 1968 25
Rolling Stone, 1969, #37, Elvis 20.00
Saturday Evening Post, Mar 15, 1930, Fangel Milk adv 15.00

Saturday Evening Post, Sep 28, 1963, Vietnam **4.00**
Saturday Evening Post, May 1976, Chris Evert. **1.00**
Scholastic Weekly, 1930–40s . . . . **.25**
Scientific American, Mar 23, 1895 . . . . **10.00**
Sixteen, 1960s. **6.00**
Sports Illustrated, Jun 22, 1964, Tom O'Hara **9.00**
Sports Illustrated, Mar 22, 1976, Tracy Austin **9.00**
Spur, 1930-40s **7.50**
Supercycle, 1970s. **3.00**
Theatre Arts, Aug 1942, Black actors **14.00**
Time, Apr 15, 1935, Dizzy Dean **65.00**
True Confessions, Sep 1945 . . . . **6.00**
True Story, Nov 1947 . . . . **6.00**
TV Guide, May 6, 1950, Hopalong Cassidy **150.00**
TV Guide, Sep 18, 1953, Fall Preview **150.00**
TV Guide, May 21, 1954, Wally Cox cov **12.00**
TV Guide, Nov 27, 1965, Hogan's Heroes cov, Liza Minelli article **10.00**
TV Guide, Sep 23, 1967, Monkees cov, General Custer article. **25.00**
U S Camera, Oct 1952, Ann Blyth **6.00**
Vanity Fair, Nov 1929 . . . . **38.00**
Vette Power, 1970–80s **3.00**
Walt Disneys Magazine, Feb 1958, Annette Funicello cov. **15.00**
Woman's Farm Journal, 1920s **2.00**
World Report, 1940s. **2.00**
Your Physique, Apr 1952 . . . . **5.00**

MAGIC COLLECTIBLES

Presto, chango—the world of magic has fascinated collectors for centuries. The category is broad; it pays to specialize. Possible approaches include children's magic sets, posters about magicians, or sleight-of-hand tricks. When buying a trick, make certain to get instructions—if possible, the original. Without them, you need to be a mystic, rather than a magician to figure out how the trick works.

Magic catalogs are treasure chests of information. Look for company names such as Abbott's, Brema, Douglas Magicland, Felsman, U. F. Grant, Magic Inc., Martinka, National Magic, Nelson Enterprises, Owen Magic Supreme, Petrie-Lewis, D. Robbins, Tannen, Thayer, and Willmann. Petrie-Lewis is a favorite among collectors. Look for the interwoven "P & L" on magic props.

Magicians of note include Alexander, Blackstone, Carter The Great, Germain The Wizard, Houdini, Kar-I, Kellar, Stock, and Thornston. Anything associated with these magicians has potentially strong market value.

Club: Magic Collectors Assoc, P.O. Box 511, Glenwood, IL 60425.

Newsletter: *Magic Set Collector's Newsletter,* P.O. Box 561, Novato, CA 94949.

Big Little Book, *Houdini's Big Little Book of Magic,* Am Oil Co premium **$25.00**
Book, *Life of Robert Houdini, King of the Conjurers,* translated from French, Rochester Pub, 1859 . . . . **60.00**
Book, *Magicians Handy Book of Cigarette Trucks,* 36 pp, 1933. . . . . **15.00**
Booklet, *Easy Magic For Everyone,* c1920, pub by Arthur Felsman, Chicago, 16 pp, photos and drawings. **15.00**
Booklet, *Magic Made Easy,* ©1930, 28 pp **20.00**
Booklet, Mysteries of Magic By Blackstone, over 32 pp, c1940s, 4½ x 6¼". **15.00**
Broadside, De La Mano, magic acts vignettes, c1880, 5 x 24". **85.00**
Bubble Gum Cards, Magic Trick Bubble Gum, Philadelphia Chewing Gum Co, Harry Blackstone magic tricks, bifold, folders explain various magic tricks, 24 cards, 1953, 2 7/16 x 3½". **90.00**
Catalog, Illustrated and Descriptive Catalogue of New and Superior Conjuring Wonders, Martinka and Co, NY, 1898, 144 pp **55.00**
Catalog, Learn to Entertain with Super Magic Tricks & Puzzles. **20.00**
Cigar Label, Wizard, 10 x 6½". **30.00**
Flyer, Ferrante—The Prince of Magic, adv, black and white, photo illus, c1890, 3¼ x 7½" **8.00**
Handbill, 2-sided, "Parlour Magic Without Apparatus, Souvenir U.S. Centennial, 1876, Invented and Manufactured by Robert Nickle" **35.00**
Magazine, *Linking Ring, Magicians of the World,* 1939 . . . . . . **15.00**
Magic Kit, Conjuring Magic, Berwick, England, litho box contains full set of tricks, unused, 13 x 16". **45.00**
Magic Kit, Dr Doolittle Magic Set, features "Oriental Card Trick, Magic Flower Pots, Whispering Colors," Remco, ©1067 20th Century Fox Film Corp, orig 8 x 12 x 3" box. **15.00**
Magic Kit, John Calvert/Master of Mystery Magic Set, Magic City Toy Co, Birmingham, AL, contains illus instruction booklet for 12 magic tricks, and accessories, "No Sleight Of Hand" on both end panels of lid, c1930–40s, 1 x 10 x 15" **85.00**
Magic Kit, Magic Kit of Tricks and Puzzles, Transogram, 1959. . . . . **25.00**
Magic Kit, Scarecrow Magic Kit, Ralston Purina Co premium, 1960s. **25.00**
Magic Kit, Scooby Doo's Box of Magic Tricks, Rand McNally, #09031, lid shows color image of Scooby Doo as magician doing juggling tricks against bright yellow background, Rand McNally, ©Hanna-Barbera Productions, 1977 . . . . **15.00**
Magic Kit, The Young Magician (Easy Conjuring Tricks), colorful box opens to reveal compartments filled with tricks and equipment, c1910, 17 x 13". **80.00**
Manual, Hermann's Wizards Manual, 1915, 66 pp **10.50**
Paperback Book, *Hermann's Art of Magic,* Professor Hermann, early 1900s, 95 pp, 5 x 7" **20.00**

Magic Kit, Merit, lithoed box contains 25 tricks and instruction booklet for "38 super tricks," 1963, 11 x 15", $45.00. Photo courtesy New England Auction Gallery.

Pinback Button, Houdini Convention Club of Wisconsin, blue and white, 1930s **8.00**
Poster, George—The Supreme Master of Magic, Otis Litho, magician floating cards over approving Buddha, 1929, 20 x 27" **150.00**
Poster, Ken Griffic Magic Show, cardboard, "America's Great Touring Illusionist and Master Magician," c1955, 14 x 22" **15.00**
Program, Blackstone/World's Master magician, 20 blue-tone photos from performances, 4 illus pages of magic tricks, biography, announcement of new comic book, late 1940s, 9 x 12" **15.00**

MAGNIFYING GLASSES

The vast majority of magnifying glasses that are offered for sale at flea markets are made-up examples. Their handles come from old umbrellas, dresser sets, and even knives. They look old and are highly decorative—a deadly combination for someone who thinks they are getting a one-hundred-year-old plus example. There are few collectors of magnifying glasses. Therefore, prices are low, often a few dollars or less, even for unusual examples. The most collectible magnifying glasses are the Sherlock Holmes type and examples from upscale desk accessory sets. These often exceed $25.

MAILBOXES

Mailboxes have long been a fixture on the porch or sidewall and are a necessity in some areas. Residential boxes about 6 x 12" will hold all the mail for the average home. Still being made in many sizes and shapes, one may be found that harmonizes with any building. The antiques were heavily ornamented with animals, flowers, gargoyles, and pictures reminiscent of medieval architecture. The more ornate ones are collectible and must be bought at an antique mall or flea market. A demolition site is an excellent place to find them. A "piece of Americana" often is the gleanings from a trip into an old part of the city. The antique boxes, in some cases, are masterpieces of the metalworker's art.

Advisor: Charles W. Wardell, P.O. Box 195, Trinity, NC 27370.

Arts & Crafts, hammered copper, c1920 . . . . **$150.00**
Folk Art, iron strapping, c1915 . . . . **75.00**
Gargoyle, Henry C Hart Co, c1910 . . . . **200.00**
Ornate, cast iron, S C Tatum Co, Cincinnati, c1910, 6 x 12" **250.00**

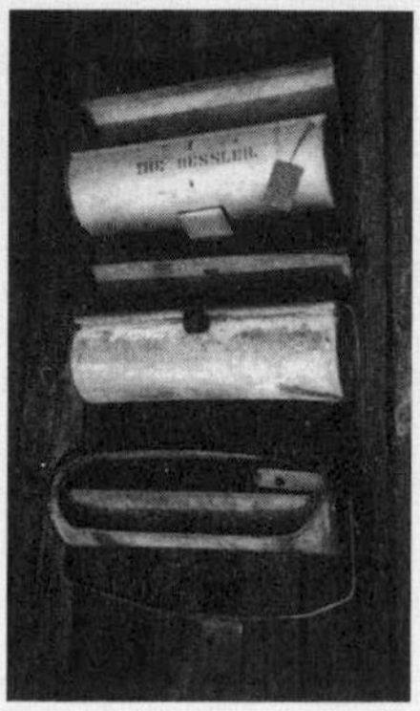

Tubular Mailboxes, sheet iron, early 1900s, 19 x 7", $100.00 each.

Plain Box, Griswold Mfg Co **50.00**
Tubular, sheet iron, Century Mailbox Co, 1910, 19 x 7" **100.00**
Tubular, sheet iron, Deshler Mailbox Co, 1910, 19 x 7" **100.00**
Tubular, sheet iron, H E Hessler Co, 1912, 19 x 7" **100.00**

MARBLES

Marbles divide into handmade glass marbles and machine-made glass, clay, and mineral marbles. Marble identification is serious business. Read and re-read these books before buying your first marble: Paul Baumann, *Collecting Antique Marbles, Second Edition* (Wallace-Homestead, 1991); and Mark E. Randall and Dennis Webb, *Greenberg's Guide to Marbles* (Greenberg Publishing, 1988).

Children played with marbles. A large number are found in a damaged state. Avoid these. There are plenty of examples in excellent condition. Beware of reproductions and modern copycats and fakes. Comic marbles are just one of the types that is currently being reproduced.

Clubs: Marble Collectors' Unlimited, P.O. Box 206, Northborough, MA 01532; Marble Collectors' Society of America, P.O. Box 222, Trumbull, CT 06611; National Marble Club of America, 440 Eaton Rd., Drexel Hill, PA 19026.

HAND MADE

Benningtons **$1.00**
End of Day, Onionskin, 3/4" **35.00**
End of Day, Onionskin, 1 3/4" **275.00**
Lutz, Banded, 5/8" **100.00**
Lutz, Banded, 1" **250.00**
Lutz, Banded, 1 3/4" **450.00**
Lutz, End of Day Onionskin, 3/4" **300.00**
Lutz, Ribbon, 5/8" **300.00**
Mica, 5/8" **10.00**
Mica, 1" **100.00**
Sulphide, 1 1/4" **125.00**
Sulphide, 2" **125.00**
Swirl, Banded, 3/4" **15.00**
Swirl, divided Core, 3/4" **18.00**
Swirl, Indian, 3/4" **75.00**
Swirl, Latticinio core, 1 3/4" **125.00**
Swirl, Peppermint, 5/8" **65.00**
Swirl, ribbon Core, 1 1/2" **100.00**
Swirl, solid core, 2 . . . . **300.00**
Unglazed Painted China **5.00**

MACHINE MADE

Akro Agate, Carnelian agate **$8.00**
Akro Agate, corkscrew, 2 color **1.00**
Akro Agate, Helmet Patch **2.50**
Akro Agate, Limeade corkscrew **18.00**
Akro Agate, metallic stripe **12.00**
Akro Agate, Moonstone **8.00**
Akro Agate, Popeye corkscrew, blue/yellow **25.00**
Akro Agate, Popeye corkscrew, red/blue **60.00**
Akro Agate, slag **1.00**
Akro Agate, opaque corkscrew, white matrix **2.00**
Christensen Agate, cobra/cyclone **750.00**
Christensen Agate, Flame swirl, 2 color **50.00**
Christensen Agate, slag **20.00**

Christensen, M F & Son, Oxblood slag **60.00**
Christensen, M F & Son, slag **5.00**
Marble King, Cub Scout, yellow/blue **5.00**
Marble King, Spiderman, blue/red **150.00**
Marble King, white matrix . . . . **.25**
Master Marble, Sunburst, opaque **3.00**
Peltier Glass, Peerless Patch **2.00**
Peltier Glass, 2 color Rainbo, old type **12.00**

MARILYN MONROE

In the 1940s a blonde bombshell exploded across the American movie screen. Born Norma Jean Mortonson in 1926, she made her debut in several magazines in the mid 1940s and appeared in the Twentieth Century Fox movie *Scudda Hoo! Scudda Hey!* in 1948.

Now known as Marilyn Monroe, she captured the public eye with her flamboyant nature and hourglass figure. Her roles in such films as *The Dangerous Years* in 1948, *Bus Stop* in 1956, *Some Like It Hot* in 1959, and *The Misfits* in 1961 brought much attention to this glamour queen.

Her marriages to baseball hero Joe DiMaggio and famous playright Arthur Miller, not to mention her assorted illicit affairs with other famous gentlemen, served to keep Marilyn's personal life on the front burner. It is commonly believed that the pressures of her personal life contributed to her untimely death on August 5, 1962.

Club: All About Marilyn, P.O. Box 291176, Los Angeles, CA 90029.

Bank, battery operated, insert coin and dress blows up, 7" h **$55.00**
Book, *My Story by Marilyn Monroe*, Stein & Day, 1974, dj, 141 pp **25.00**
Book, *Norman Jean, The Life of Marilyn Monroe*, dj, 1969 . . . . **25.00**
Calendar, 1954, "Golden Dreams," nuded on red ground portrait, glossy, full pad, 11 x 24" **175.00**
Lamp, figural, orig Vandor label **80.00**
Lobby Card, *The Seven Year Itch*, #8, 1955, 11 x 14" **35.00**
Magazine, *Focus*, Nov 1955, full color front cov **7.50**
Magazine, *Marilyn Monroe Pin-Ups*, black and white and color photos, 32 pp, 1953, 8½ x 11" **70.00**
Magazine, *Movie Life*, Dec 1956, black and white Monroe pictorial **12.00**
Magazine, *Rave*, Aug 1956, full color front cov, 28 pp article and photos, 64 pp, 8 x 10¼" **50.00**
Magazine, *TV Guide*, Jan 23-29, 1953, Vol 6, #4 . . . . **35.00**

Pocketknife, color photo under clear plastic handle, Colonial Jack, $50.00.

***Show Book,* Mar 1953 issue, $25.00. Photo courtesy Frank's Antiques.**

Movie Poster, *Let's Make It Legal*, 20th Century Fox, 1951 . . . **150.00**
Movie Poster, *Some Like It Hot*, United Artists, 1959 . . . . **300.00**
Photo, color glossy, wearing yellow 2 pc outfit, A Sheer copyright, late 1950s, 8 x 10" **25.00**
Postcard, *Bus Stop*, French version, sexy Monroe photo **15.00**
Poster, *Bus Stop*, 20th Century Fox, 1956 . . . . **300.00**
Record, *Some Like It Hot*, Ascot, 1964 . . . . **75.00**
Script, *Bus Stop*, Monroe cov, 1956 . . . . **25.00**

MARX TOY COLLECTIBLES

My favorite days as a child were filled with the adventures of cowboys and Indians in their constant struggle for control of Fort Apache. I have only Louis Marx to thank for those hours of imagination and adventure for I was a proud owner of a Marx playset.

The Marx Toy Company was founded after World War I when Louis and David Marx purchased a series of dies and molds from the bankrupt Strauss Toy Company. In the following years the Marx Toy Company produced a huge assortment of tin and plastic toys, including 60 to 80 playsets with hundreds of variations. These playsets, some with lithographed tin structures, are very collectible if complete. Marx also manufactured a number of windup and action toys like Rock-em Sock-em Robots and the very popular Big Wheel tricycle.

The company was bought and sold a number of times before finally filing for bankruptcy in 1980. The Quaker Oats Company owned Marx from the late 1950s until 1978, at which time it was sold to its final owner, the British toy company, Dunbee-Combex.

Action Figure, Mike Hazard Double Agent, posable, brown hair, blue outfit, complete with accessories, 1965, 11½" h **$85.00**

Dan Dipsy Car, second version, litho tin, 1950s, 5¾ x 6", $300.00. Photo courtesy Gene Harris Antique Auction Center, Inc.

Pinocchio The Acrobat, litho tin, jointed composition cardboard legs, 1939, 16" h, 11" w, good condition, $80.00; excellent condition, $250.00. Photo courtesy Gene Harris Antique Auction Center, Inc.

Fix-All Tractor, with tools and accessories, complete in orig box, $105.00. Photo courtesy New England Auction Gallery.

Army Truck, plastic, steel frame, rubbber tires, tailgate opens, olive drab, c1950, 12" l 75.00
Banana Figure on Tricycle, #2173, litho tin, windup 65.00
Bengal Tiger on Wheels, hard plastic, movable mouth. . . . 35.00
Blue and Gray Civil War Miniature Cavalry Set, pr of plastic and metal cap guns with brown plastic holster on orig 6¾ x 9" blister card, 1960 . . . . 15.00
Bravo the Armored Horse, 13½" hard plastic horse, and accessories, for use with Noble Knight series, 1968, orig 13½ x 15 x 4" box 65.00
Brewster Rooster 100.00
Cadillac Coupe, litho tin, windup, orange body, black trim, trunk rack, 1931, 11" l 375.00
Chris Craft Cruiser, plastic, windup, white, brown deck, red keel, 1950s, 18" l 85.00
City Delivery Van, steel, yellow, red fenders, tin grille, 11" l 200.00
Convertible, steel, blue top, red body, white tires, 1930s, 11" l 325.00
Corn Figure on Tricycle, litho tin, windup, green and yellow corn figure with hollow soft plastic body and celluloid feet, bell on back of tricycle with illus of banana, corn, and watermelon characters, 1967, 2½ x 3¾ x 4¼" h 40.00
Dick Tracy Squad Car, litho tin, windup, siren, flashing red spotlight, 2 rubber and 2 wooden wheels, 1949, 11¼" l. . . . 300.00
Drumming Major, litho tin, windup 175.00
Dump Truck, #1013, plastic, c1950, 18" l 150.00
Eagle Air Scout, litho tin, windup, silver body, blue trim, revolving propeller, 1929, 26" l, 26½" wingspan 350.00
Exploding Souvenir Grenade, soft plastic and metal "Sick Hand Grenade" from the "Combat-Line," on 6 x 9" cardboard display card, 1960s, 7½" l, MIP 40.00
Greyhound Bus Terminal, litho tin, 2 pumps, 2 sign boards, 2 garage entrances, drugstore, waiting room, c1938, 16" l, 11" w 300.00
Honeymoon Special, litho tin, windup, train with engine and 3 cars, 1927, 6" d 150.00
International Agent Car, litho tin, friction, mkd "UEA, United Espionage Agency, ©1966, 4" l 85.00
Lone Ranger Adventure Set, Hidden Silvermine Adventure, 1973, MIB 15.00
Midget Tractor, litho tin, red, green, yellow, and black, curved radiator, 1940, 5¼" l 65.00
Mighty Viking Horse, 13½" h hard plastic horse, tan, cream colored accents, plastic wheels under hooves, movable nodding head, black rubber bridle and saddle, "From The Knight And Viking Series, " 1970 . . . . 65.00
Mystic Motorcycle, litho tin, windup, blue, yellow, and white, 1936, 4¼" l. . . . 175.00
Native on Hippopotamus, hard plastic, ramp walker, Black native wearing yellow loincloth on brown/gray hippo, 1950s, 3¼" l, MIP. . . . 40.00
Nutty Mad Car, litho tin, friction, red, soft molded vinyl head, 1960s 60.00
Playset, Army Playset. . . . 30.00
Playset, Desert Storm Air Wars LTD 55.00
Playset, Freight Station, tin, complete 275.00
Playset, Lazy Day Farms 95.00
Playset, Prehistoric Times, #3398, orig booklet, acce sories, 1961 . . . . 135.00
Presidents of the United States, contains complete set of 36 hard plastic 2½" h figures, 20 pp illus booklet, orig 17 x 17 x 1½" box 85.00
Press Lever Top Set, plunger and 2 litho tin globes, 1 with world map, other with faces, pump plunger to spin globes, orig box 175.00
Pro Shot Golf Game, golf bag shaped box with plastic carrying handle, complete, 1960s 40.00
Racer, windup. . . . 35.00
Roadside Rest Service Station, battery operated, 1935, 13½" l, 10" w 500.00
Rosey the Robot, litho tin, windup, ©Hanna-Barbera Productions, 1963, 2¼ x 4¼ x 2¼" h 175.00
Smoky Sam, plastic hat, body, and car, litho tin head and wheels, windup, crazy car, 1950, 6½" l 200.00
Sports Car, #2, plastic, friction, visible Straight Eight engine, black rubber tires, sparking action, needs new flint, orig box, 1950s, 7½" l 175.00
The Enforcer Tommy Gun, brown plastic, cap shooting, 9 x 15" display cards shows Dick Tracy type man capturing gangsters, 1950s, 12½" l, ... 25.00
Trans-Atlantic Zeppelin, litho tin, windup, striped rudder, c1930, 10" l 400.00
Tumbling Monkey, litho tin, windup, 1942, 4½" h 110.00
Walk-Away Baby, hard plastic, ramp walker, orange hair with pair of red bows, blue bib-overalls, red shoes, 1960s, 6" h, orig 4¾ x 6¼ x 2" box 40.00

MARY GREGORY GLASS

Who was Mary Gregory anyway? Her stuff certainly is expensive. Beware of objects that seem like too much of a bargain. They may have been painted by Mary Gregory's great-great granddaughter in the 1950s rather than in the 1880s. Also, watch the eyes. The original Mary Gregory did not paint children with slanted eyes.

Vase, black glass, white enamel design, 10" h, $65.00.

Feature, 20 Strike, Olympic Club, "San Francisco" on saddle, aerial view of clubhouse and "The Olympic Club at Lakeside" on back, line drawing of club int on inside, Lion Match, $12.00. Photo courtesy Ray Morykan Auctions.

Barber Bottle, cobalt blue ground, white enameled boy and girl playing badminton, 7½" h **$120.00**
Beverage Set, pitcher and 6 tumbler, clear ground, white enameled girl in garden setting **275.00**
Box, cov, round, cranberry ground, white enameled girl and floral sprays, hinged lid, 2¾" h **265.00**
Bud Vase, sapphire blue ground, white enameled boy, pedestal foot, 7" h **125.00**
Creamer, green ground, white enameled girl, Inverted Thumbprint pattern, applied green handle, 3¾" h **145.00**
Ewer, cranberry ground, white enameled girl in garden setting, applied clear handle, 10" h **220.00**
Mug, cranberry ground, white enameled girl, applied clear handle, 3" h **75.00**
Plate, cobalt blue, white enamel girl with butterfly net, 6¼" h **125.00**
Salt Shaker, blue ground, white enameled girl in garden, paneled body, brass top, 5" d **180.00**
Toothpick Holder, cranberry ground, white enameled girl and floral sprays **55.00**
Tumbler, sapphire blue ground, white enameled boy, ribbed body, 4½" h **65.00**
Vase, robin's-egg blue ground, girl running through flower field dec, 5" h **125.00**

MATCHBOOKS

Don't play with matches. Save their covers instead. A great collection can be built for a relatively small sum of money. Matchcover collectors gain a fair amount of their new material through swapping. A few collectors specialize in covers that include figural shaped or decorated matches. If you get into this, make certain you keep them stored in a covered tin container and in a cool location. If you don't, your collection may catch fire and go up in smoke.

Clubs: Casino Matchcover Collectors Club, 5001 Albridge Way, Mount Laurel, NJ 08054; Rathkamp Matchcover Society, 1359 Surrey Rd., Vandalia, OH 45377; The American Matchcover Collecting Club, PO Box 18481, Asheville, NC 28814. Note: There are over thirty regional clubs throughout the United States and Canada.

Comic, "Fruity Acres Sanitarium, Screwball Rd., Fruitville, N.Y." on front, "Your Daze Go By Faster at Fruity Acres..." on back, "Phone PSycho 341 Q" on saddle, Metalart Co, 1958 . . . . **$3.00**
Display, Beachcomber and island on front and back, "Home of the Zombie" and zombie on front, dancing zombie and drink on display, nude Hawaiian dancer, shipwrecked sailor, and monkey in palm tree across sticks **$15.00**
Display, "Dick Raymond Finance Company, Phone 8-8573" on front and back, "Bakersfield, California," photo of man with Dick Raymond, address and services **6.00**
Display, "Jack Dempsey's on Broadway" on front, oval bar on back, Dempsey photo display, "J.D." on each match, alternating light blue on dark blue and dark blue on light blue, Feature Matchbook, Lion Match **15.00**
Display, "Oasis Restaurant, Roanoke, Virginia" on front and back, "dial ROanoke 6-3771," palm tree with name and location **5.00**
Feature, 20 Strike, "Andy Won's Chinese Sky Room..., San Francisco" on front, front doors with "Thru These Portals..." on back, 3 Chinese dancers across sticks with "The Wongettes," Lion Match **12.00**
Feature, 20 Strike, "Club 116 Reneo" with champagne glass on front, "Reno's Famous Club 116 Dining Room" on back, name on each stick, Lion Match **8.00**
Feature, 20 Strike, "Colonel Restaurant and Bar" with bearded man on front, "famous for Food and Liquors, 125 N Clark St., Dearborn 1528, Chicago" on back, bar scene with "Colonel Bar" across sticks, Lion Match **10.00**
Feature, 20 Strike, Eleanor Shop, Portsmouth, VA, garment and word "Blouses, Slips, robes, Skirts," or "Sweaters" on each stick, pink, purples, blue, and white, Lion Match **10.00**

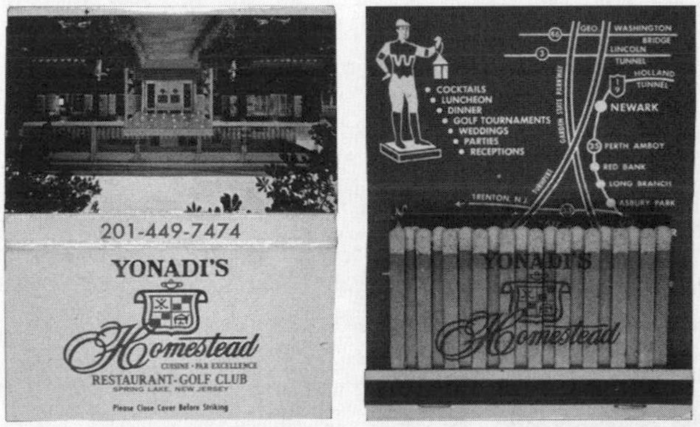

Printed Sticks, Yonadi's Homestead Restaurant Golf Club, full color photo of building front on back, printed sticks with red "Yonadi's Homestead" and coat of arms, Universal Match, $8.00. Photo courtesy Ray Morykan Auctions.

21 Feature, 30 Stick, "The Sands, Las Vegas, Nevada" on front, hotel on back, penguin on each stick, "Why be formal?...Come as you Are!" across sticks, Lion Match, $12.00. Photo courtesy Ray Morykan Auctions.

Feature, 20 Strike, "Indian Rocks" with Indian logo on front, picture of fruit and "Fancy Citrus Fruits..." on saddle, name with colorful logo across sticks **15.00**
Feature, 20 Strike, Longchamps Restaurant, New York City, chef on each stick with "Longchamps" across all sticks, orange and white, Lion Match **12.00**
Girlie, Faiman's Cafe adv on front, girlie and "Station WOW" on back, "We Never Sleep" on saddle **6.00**
Hotel, "Holiday Inn Golden Gateway, San Francisco" and world map on back. **3.00**
Hotel, "Souvenir of Water Gate Inn" with cherry blossoms on back **8.00**
Luckey Sticks, Flemington Glass Company, Inc, Flemington, "New Jersey" on front, "Factory Showrooms" and wine glass on back, white on magenta ground, play instruction inside, 21 sticks each with card symbols for different poker hand on each stick, Lion Match. **10.00**
Midget, "Bamboo Garden Restaurant, 648 Bergenline Ave, West New York, N.J." on front, "Luncheon 40¢, Dinner 75¢" on back, Lion Match **5.00**
Midget, "Blue Mirror Cocktail Lounge, 929 N. Charles St.," and champagne glass on front, same on back with addition of "Balto., MD.," "Air Conditioned" on saddle, Lion Match **5.00**
Midget-Type, Hotel El Tejon, "Say 'Tay-Hone' Bakersfield California, George Bowser, Mgr." on front, "Good Food" on saddle, building, name, and location on back, "200 Delightfully Air-Condition Rooms, Banquet Facilities, Sample Rooms, In the Heart of Bakersfield" inside, black and white, Diamond Match. **6.00**
Military, Air Force, "officers' Club, Victorville, Calif" around winged star on front, blank saddle, bomber action scene on back, blank inside, silver on dark blue, Lion Match. **5.00**
Military, Army, "U.S. Army Combat Developments Command, Ft. Belvoir, Virginia" with insignia on front, blank saddle, "Go Army, Re-Enlist By Choice—Not By Chance" on back **6.00**
Patriotic, "Give to the Greater New York Fund, Keep the Home Front Strong," full length, large soldier with arms spread to encompass crowd of civilians, "Give!" superimposed over "V" and "1942 to the Greater New York Fund" inside, National Match. **8.00**
Patriotic, "Reese Drugs" on front, "Defend Yourself Save with Safety" on saddle, "Remember Pearl Harbor, Buy War Stamps Here" on back **15.00**
Patriotic, "V for Victory" on front and back, blank saddle **5.00**
Patriotic, "Vote Bob Dole For President 1988" **3.00**
Political, "McGovern for President '72" on front, "A Leader of Courage and Integrity!" on saddle, "Vote for the man who will keep faith with you!" on back with silhouette **8.00**
Radio Station, "Faiman's Café" on front, "Station WOW" and girlie picture on back, "We Never Sleep" on saddle **6.00**
Transportation, Railroad, "Broadway Limited" on front, "Pennsylvania Railroad" on bottom flap at the usual striker location, "Safety-Speed-Comfort" on saddle, 4-color photo of streamlined locomotive on back, striker located on flat bottom edge, blank inside, Diamond Match **8.00**
21-Feature, "Alex Novack & Sons, Scrap Iron" and crane on front, US map and outline on back, colorful working crane across sticks **10.00**
21-Feature, "Jimbo's Restaurant...San Bernadino, Calif" on front, restaurant on back, restaurant with name across sticks **10.00**
21-Feature, "Red Lion Inn, Hackensack, New Jersey" on front, red lion logo on back, red lion logo across center 3 sticks, Lion Match **12.00**

MATCHBOX TOYS

Leslie Smith and Rodney Smith founded Lesney Products, an English company, in 1947. They produced the first Matchbox toys. In 1953 the trade name "Matchbox" was registered and the first diecast cars were made on a 1:75 scale. In 1979 Lesney produced over 5.5 million cars per week. In 1982 Universal International bought Lesney.

Clubs: American-International Matchbox Collectors & Exchange Club, 532 Chestnut Street, Lynn, MA 01904; Matchbox Collectors Club, P.O. Box 977, Newfield, NJ 08344; The Matchbox International Collectors Assoc., P.O. Box 28072, Waterloo, 6JB Canada; Matchbox U.S.A., 62 Saw Mill Rd, Durham, CT 06422.

CARS

Airport Coach, #65-E, 1977, 3" l **$10.00**
Atlantic Trailer, #16-A, tan body, 1956, $3^{1}/_{8}$" l **25.00**
Atlas Extractor, #32-G, red and orange body, 1981, 3" l **4.00**
Austin A-50, #36-A, silver grille, no windows, 1957, $2^{1}/_{8}$" l **20.00**
Austin Taxi Cab, #17-B, maroon, 1960, $2^{1}/_{4}$" l **50.00**
Beach Buggy, #30-E, pink, 1970, $2^{1}/_{2}$" l **4.00**

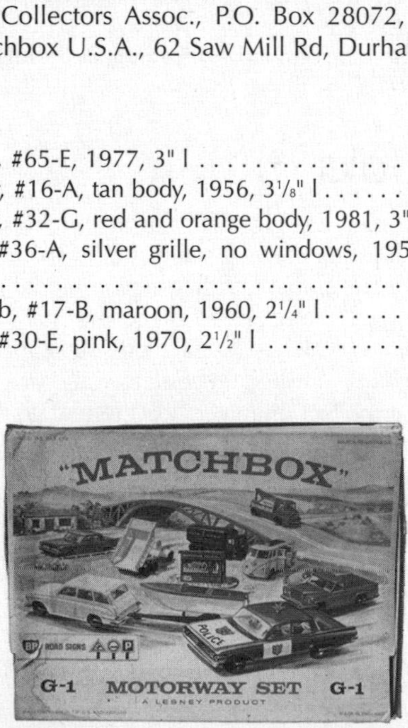

Motorway Set, G–1, assorted behicles from the 1-75 series, cardboard roadway, road signs, $300.00.

Big Banger, #26-E, red body, blue windows, 1972, 3" l ... 6.00
Boat and Trailer, #9-D, white hull, blue deck, 1970, $3\frac{1}{4}$" l ... 5.00
BRM Racing Car, #52-B, 1965, $2\frac{5}{8}$" l ... 20.00
Cadillac Sedan, #27-C, 1960, $2\frac{3}{4}$" l ... 30.00
Caterpillar Tractor, #8-B, 1959, $1\frac{5}{8}$" l ... 35.00
Cement Mixer, #3-A, blue body, orange metal wheels, 1953, $1\frac{5}{8}$" l ... 35.00
Chevy Pro Stocker, #34-G, 1981, 3" l ... 3.00
Combine Harvester, #51-F, red, 1978, $2\frac{3}{4}$" l ... 5.00
Daimler Double-Deck Bus, #74-B, 1966, 3"l ... 15.00
Dodge Challenger, #1-H, red, 1976, 3" l ... 5.00
Dumper Truck, #48-D, yellow body, blue cab, green windows, 1970, 3" l ... 7.00
Fandango, #35-D, white, red int, 1975, 3" l ... 5.00
Flying Bug, #11-F, metallic red, 1972, 3" l ... 7.00
Ford Capri, #54-D, 1971, 3" l ... 4.00
Ford Fairlane Station Wagon, #31-B, 1960, $2\frac{3}{4}$" l ... 30.00
Ford GT, #41, whtie ... 30.00
Ford Mustang, #8-F, 1970, $2\frac{7}{8}$" l ... 25.00
Galaxie Police Car, #55, white, orig box ... 25.00
GMC Refrigerator Truck, #44-D, turquoise, gray plastic opening rear door, red ribbed roof cab, green windows, 1967 ... 10.00
Greyhound Bus, #66-D, silver, 1970, 3" l ... 10.00
Honda Motorcycle and Trailer, #38-C, metallic blue/green, wire wheels, black tires, orange trailer, 1967, $2\frac{7}{8}$" l ... 15.00
Hot Rod Draguar, #36-E, metallic red, clear canopy, spoke wheels, 1970, $2\frac{13}{16}$" l ... 6.00
Ice Cream Truck, #37, Lyons Maid, blue ... 45.00
Jaguar XKE, #32-B, metallic red, ivory int, 1962, $2\frac{5}{8}$" l ... 20.00
Jeep Hot Rod, #2-F, 1971, $2\frac{5}{16}$" l ... 10.00
Lamborghini Marzel, #20-D, 1969, $2\frac{3}{4}$" l ... 20.00
Land Rover Fire Truck, #57-C, red, blue tinted windows, white plastic ladder, 1966, $2\frac{1}{2}$" l ... 15.00
Lincoln Continental, #31, light green, orig box ... 20.00
Mack Dump Truck, #28-E, green, 1970, $2\frac{5}{8}$" l ... 5.00
Mercedes-Benz 230SL, #27-D, 1966 , 3" l ... 25.00
Mercury Cougar, #62-D, 1970, 3" l ... 5.00
MG Midget, #19-A, white, red seats, tan driver, 1956, 2" l ... 60.00
Peterbilt Cement Truck, #19-H, green, orange barrel, decal on hood, 1982 ... 3.00
Police Patrol, #20-E, white, orange side stripe with "Police," orange int, 1975, $2\frac{7}{8}$" l ... 8.00
Porsche 928, #59-G, metallic brown, 1978, 3" l ... 5.00
Rallye Royal, #14-G, metallic gray, 1973, $2\frac{7}{8}$" l ... 4.00
Road Tanker, #11-B, red, black plastic wheels, 1958, $2\frac{1}{2}$" l ... 55.00
Safari Land Rover, #12-D, 1965, $2\frac{1}{3}$" l ... 10.00
Siva Spider, #41-E, metallic red, 1972, 3" l ... 7.00
Sun Burner, #37-H, black, red and yellow flames on hood and sides, 1972, 3" l ... 3.00
Tanzara, #53-E, orange, 1972, 3" l ... 4.00
U S Mail Jeep, #5-G, blue, white base, bumpers, and canopy, black plastic seat, 1978, $2\frac{3}{8}$" l ... 10.00
Volkswagen 1500 Saloon, #15-D, off-white, "137" on doors, 1968, $2\frac{7}{8}$" l ... 20.00

OTHER

Devil's Leap Speed Set, 1973 ... $20.00
Double Super Loop Race Set, 1970 ... 40.00
Fire Station, white building, brick face, red roof, 1963 ... 75.00
Highway Express Truck Stop, 1982 ... 20.00
Lap Counter, 1970 ... 10.00
Laser Wheels Speed of Light Stunt Set, 1988 ... 12.00
Matchbox City Case Playset, 1972, MIB ... 35.00
Motorcity 500 Superset, 1991 ... 25.00
Motorcity Fold-N-Go Garage, 1991 ... 20.00
Service Station, 1979 ... 35.00
Super Spin Car Wash, reissued 1983 ... 15.00
Stunt Loop, 1973 ... 10.00
Two-Story Garage, white building, green base, 1961 ... 70.00
Yesteryear Carry Case, blue vinyl, 1969 ... 20.00

MCCOY POTTERY

Like Abingdon Pottery, this pottery is attractive and is sought by those who no longer are able to afford Roseville and Weller pottery. Commemorative cookie jars and planters seem to be rapidly increasing in price, like the Apollo Spaceship cookie jar at $45.00. These speciality items bring more from secondary collectors than from McCoy collectors who realize the vast quantity of material available in the market.

Beware of reproductions. The Nelson McCoy Pottery Company is making modern copies of their period pieces. New collectors are often confused by them.

Newsletters: *The NM Express,* 3081 Rock Creek Dr., Broomfield, CO 80020.

Periodical: *The Pottery Collectors Express,* P.O. Box 221, Mayview, MO 64071.

Ashtray, fish, honey brown glaze, 4" l ... $5.00
Basket, basketweave design, green and white ext, white int, 1957 ... 25.00
Bookends, pr, white horse, gold trim, 8" h ... 100.00
Bookends, pr, swallow, 6 x $5\frac{1}{2}$" ... 125.00
Bud Vase, matte green, 8" h ... 5.00
Cookie Jar, Fireplace ... 95.00
Cookie Jar, Raggedy Ann ... 95.00
Cookie Jar, W C Fields ... 150.00
Corn Dish, brown drip, 1966, 9 x $3\frac{1}{4}$" ... 10.00
Dog Feeding Dish, "Man's Best Friend, His Dog" around sides, 1930s, $7\frac{1}{2}$" d ... 50.00
Jardiniere, brown, 9" h ... 50.00
Paperweight, figural baseball boy, blue hat and glove, 1978, 6" h ... 40.00
Planter, basket, basketweave design, 1957, 9 x $5\frac{1}{4}$" ... 35.00
Planter, frog, green ... 8.50

Strawberry Pot, mottled brown glaze, #3021, 7" h, 10" w, $35.00.

Planter, scotties, green and ivory, brown spray, 1949, 8" l 30.00
Planter, snowman, 6 x 4" 50.00
Planter, stork, "NM" mark, 1940s, 7" h 250.00
Planter, trolley car, 1954, 7 x 3$^{3}/_{4}$" 35.00
Platter, emb rooster, 1974, 16 x 11" 40.00
Reamer, 1949, 8" l 45.00
Salt and Pepper Shakers, pr, cabbage, 4$^{1}/_{2}$" h 50.00
Spittoon, frog dec 125.00
Teapot, Pine Cone 75.00
Vase, Blossomtime, yellow, applied pink flower, orig paper label, 1946, 8" h 60.00
Vase, donkey, unmkd, 1940s, 7" h 50.00
Vase, double tulip, white, yellow dec, 1948 . . . . 50.00
Vase, parrot, "NM" mark, 7$^{1}/_{2}$" h 35.00
Vase, Uncle Sam, white, yellow, and green, 1940s, 7$^{1}/_{2}$" h 40.00
Wall Pocket, butterfly, "NM" mark, 7 x 6" 200.00
Wall Pocket, cornucopia, yellow, brown bisque glaze, mkd, 8 x 6$^{1}/_{2}$" 65.00

MEDICAL ITEMS

Anything medical is collectible. Doctors often discard instruments, never realizing that the minute an object becomes obsolete, it also becomes collectible. Many a flea market treasure begins life in a garbage can behind the doctor's office. Stress condition and completeness. Specialize in one area. Remember some instruments do not display well. My wife will not let me keep my rectal examiners in the living room.

Club: Medical Collectors Assoc., Montefiore Medical Park, 1695A Eastchester Rd., Bronx, NY 10461.

Newsletter: *Scientific, Medical & Mechanical Antiques*, P.O. Box 412, Taneytown, MD 21787.

Amputation Bow Saw, metal, fenestrated handle, finger ring, mkd "Tiemann & Co," with blade, c1885 . . . . $80.00
Apothecary Bottle, Sunnybrook Medicinal Whiskey, apothecary, sealed, orig box with prescription storage window, color graphics 85.00
Artificial Eye, glass, lifelike iris and pupil 32.00
Book, *People's Medical Lighthouse,* Dr Harmon Knox 20.00
Book, *Science and Health With Key to the Scriptures,* 700 pp, Boston, 1906 . . . . 20.00
Book, *Surgical Emergencies In Children,* 1936 . . . . 25.00
Book, *The Evolution of Modern Medicine,"* 1943 . . . . 75.00

Alcohol Burner, sterilizer, brass, 2$^{1}/_{2}$" h, $36.00.

Flange Sign, Red Cross, 2-sided porcelain, 11" h, 14" h, $170.00. Photo courtesy Collectors Auction Services.

Bottle, Chlorate Potassique, clear, pontil, painted brown, 6$^{1}/_{2}$" h 20.00
Bottle, Ether, clear glass, cork, emb "Boardman & Norton, Portsmouth, N. H.," c1930 . . . . 18.00
Catalog, Codman & Shurtleff General Operating Instruments, illus, 400 pp, Boston, MA, 1965 . . . . 45.00
Chloraform Mask, Yankauer, metal, gauze between mesh dome, spring loop for chloraform drops, c1910 . . . . 50.00
Cupping Glass, set of 3, clear, dome shaped, c1890, 2 x 1$^{1}/_{2}$" 35.00
Ear Syringe, glass, tow-wrapped plunger, curved tip becomes bulbous with narrowed injection tip, c1890 . . . . 36.00
Formaldehyde Fumigator, blue glazed metal, 2 candles in base, orig box with instructions, "Pat. Sept. 12, 1911" 22.00
Glass Eye, human size 20.00
Handbill, Barnes' Family Pills, sgd by Finlay Barnes, c1870, 9 x 4" 10.00
Jar, Confection of Senna, white ceramic, black printing, green senna lant illus, Boots Chemists, c1880 . . . . 38.00
Leg Splint, hardwood, stamped "Gus V. Olson Successor to George Fowler, Manufacturers of Surgical Splints, Amesbury, Mass," c1880 . . . . 40.00
Medicine Case, black leather, locking, hinged int with 2 sides, 16 purple velvet compartments holding 6 metal-capped square medicine bottles, c1900, 9$^{1}/_{2}$ x 3$^{1}/_{2}$ x 3" 80.00
Medicine Glass, with minim measure, leatherette cylindrical container, nested green and red int, c1880 . . . . 75.00
Pill Box, wooden, "Dr Jacobs' Nerve Harmonizong, Blood Purifying And Invigorating Vegetable Pills," on violet and black label 28.00
Poster, Hygienic Water Cure Sanitorium, "Our Home on the Hillside," Dansville, NY, building and horse-drawn carriages illus, Sage, Sons & Co litho, 36 x 24" 100.00
Quack Gadget, massager, with disc applicator on black wooden handle, c1940s 9.00
Sign, Henry, Johnson & Lord, tin, various products listed and illus, 14 x 20" 500.00
Thermometer, white enameled metal, red and black lettering, wall mount screws, adv for Mass pharmacist, orig box 12.00
Tin, Jim Dandy Veterinary Product, colorful animal illus 70.00
Tonsil Snare, Beck-Schneck, snare tube, "Aloe Germany," c1890 . . . . 28.00
Uterine Dilator, gutta-percha handles, c1870 . . . . 75.00
Vaginal Speculum, DeVilbiss, screw-handle closure, c1918 . . . . 55.00

MELMAC

Durable Melmac dinnerware was all the rage in the late 1960s and early 1970s. Children could finally be assigned the chore of washing the dishes without fear of loss and breakage. Despite its claims of being indestructable, continued dishwasher washing will takes its toll. If you plan to collect Melmac and use, it you'll have to revert to hand washing.

Club: Melmac Collectors Club, 6802 Glenkirk Rd., Baltimore, MD 21239.

Brookpark, cup and saucer	**$3.00**
Brookpark, salad plate	**4.00**
Brookpark, serving bowl	**4.00**
Brookpark, soup bowl	**5.00**
Brookpark, sugar, cov	**6.00**
Debonaire, creamer	**1.50**
Debonaire, dinner plate	**2.00**
Debonaire, sugar, cov	**3.00**
Fostoria, butter, cov	**15.00**
Fostoria, serving bowl, divided	**15.00**
Fostoria, sugar, cov	**12.00**
Harmony House, creamer	**5.00**
Harmony House, dinner plate	**4.00**
Holiday, platter	**8.00**
Holiday, serving bowl, divided	**8.00**
Imperial Ware, dinner plate	**2.00**
Imperial Ware, sugar, cov	**3.00**
Lucent, cereal bowl	**7.00**
Lucent, dinner plate, Sun Petal pattern	**6.00**
Lucent, serving bowl, divided	**15.00**
Mallo-Ware, gravy boat	**5.00**
Mallo-Ware, cup and saucer	**2.50**
Mar-Crest, fruit bowl	**1.50**
Mar-Crest, soup bowl	**3.00**
Monte Carlo, bowl	**2.00**
Monte Carlo, cup and saucer	**2.50**
Prolon, dinner plate, Beverly pattern	**4.00**
Prolon, salad bowl, ftd	**4.50**
Prolon, serving bowl, divided	**8.00**
Restraware, bread plate	**1.00**
Restraware, creamer	**1.00**
Restraware, salt and pepper shakers, pr	**4.00**
Royalon, dinner plate	**2.50**
Royalon, salad plate, Jubilee pattern	**2.50**
Royalon, sugar, cov	**3.50**
Spaulding, cup and saucer	**2.00**
Spaulding, dinner plate	**2.00**
Spaulding, sugar, cov	**3.00**
Stetson, butter, cov	**5.00**
Stetson, serving bowl, divided	**4.00**
Texas Ware, dinner plate, flag design	**3.00**
Texas Ware, salad plate, San Jacinto design	**3.00**
Watertown, cup and saucer	**3.00**
Watertown, water pitcher, cov	**20.00**
Westinghouse, dessert bowl	**2.00**
Westinghouse, serving bowl	**4.00**

METLOX

In 1921 T. C. Prouty and Willis, his son, founded Proutyline Products, a company designed to develop Prouty's various inventions. Metlox (a contraction of metallic oxide) was established in 1927. The company began producing a line of solid color dinnerware similar to that produced by Bauer. In 1934 the line was fully developed and sold under the Poppytrail trademark. Other dinnerware lines produced in the 1930s include Mission Bell, Pintoria, and Yorkshire. In the late 1930s Metlox introduced a line called Modern Masterpieces featuring bookends, busts, figural vases, figures, and wall pockets.

The California Ivy pattern was introduced in 1946, California Provincial and Homestead Provincial in 1950, Red Rooster in 1955, California Strawberry in 1961, Sculptured Grape in 1963, and Della Robbia in 1965. A number of new shapes and lines came out in the 1950s, among which are Aztec, California Contempora, California Free Form, California Mobile, and Navajo.

When Vernon Kilns ceased operation in 1958, Metlox bought the trade name and select dinnerware molds, establishing a separate Vernon Ware branch. This line rivaled the Poppytrail patterns.

Between 1946 and 1956 Metlox made a series of ceramic cartoon characters under license from Walt Disney. A line of planters and Poppets were marketed in the 1960s and 1970s. Recent production includes novelty cookie jars and Colorstax, a revival solid color dinnerware pattern. The company ceased operations in 1989.

Periodical: *The Pottery Collectors Express*, P.O. Box 221, Mayview, MO 64071.

Antique Grape, compote	**$80.00**
Antique Grape, flour canister	**95.00**
Antique Grape, salt and pepper shakers, pr	**30.00**
Brown-Eyed Susan, chop plate, $12^{3}/_{8}$" d	**20.00**
Brown-Eyed Susan, cup and saucer	**10.00**
Brown-Eyed Susan, dinner plate, $9^{3}/_{4}$" d	**10.00**
California Confetti, fruit bowl	**12.00**
California Ivy, casserole, cov	**42.00**
California Ivy, creamer and sugar, cov	**15.00**
California Ivy, dinner plate, $10^{1}/_{4}$" d	**10.00**
California Ivy, serving bowl, round	**40.00**
California Ivy, vegetable, 9" d	**20.00**
California Provincial, berry bowl	**8.00**
California Provincial, marmalade jug	**45.00**
California Strawberry, canister, small	**15.00**
California Strawberry, dinner plate	**6.00**
California Strawberry, pitcher, $4^{1}/_{2}$" h	**30.00**
California Strawberry, vegetable, 8" d	**30.00**
Della Robbia, cup and saucer	**15.00**
Della Robbia, luncheon plate, 9" d	**22.00**
Della Robbia, sugar, cov	**35.00**

Left: California Ivy, dinner plate, $10^{3}/_{8}$" d, $8.00.
Right: Della Robbia, dinner plate, $15.00.

Green Rooster, flour canister 125.00
Green Rooster, creamer and sugar 20.00
Green Rooster, salt and pepper shakers, pr, handled 27.00
Green Rooster, tumbler, 5" h 20.00
Homestead Provincial, creamer 7.00
Homestead Provincial, cup and saucer 6.50
Provincial Blue, coffeepot 95.00
Provincial Blue, salad plate, 7" d 10.00
Red Rooster, mug, small 22.00
Red Rooster, salad bowl, large 95.00

MEXICAN COLLECTIBLES

When you live on the East Coast and do not roam west of Chicago, you are not going to see South of the Border collectibles except for the tourist souvenirs brought home by visitors to Central and South America. However, the growing Hispanic population is looking back to its roots and starting to proudly display family and other items acquired south of the border.

Within the past year there has been a growing interest in Mexican jewelry. In fact, several new books have been published about the subject. Mexican pottery and textiles are also attracting collector attention. At the moment, buy only high-quality, handmade products. Because of their brilliant colors, Mexican collectibles accent almost any room setting. This is an area to watch.

MICROSCOPES

Microscopes are the best collectible to epitomize the history of science. High quality, signed, all-brass instruments are hard to find, but easy to sell. Signatures are important, although turn-of-the-century microscopes signed "Bausch & Lomb" or "Spencer" are quite common. American-made microscopes are generally more valuable than imported instruments.

Do not polish instruments you plan to resell. Collectors hate this! Be wary of missing or replaced parts, especially the mirror. Having a large antique microscope's original case can increase its value by $50 to $100. Most serious microscope and toy collectors are uninterested in toy microscopes, although exceptions do exist.

Advisor: Randy D. Watson, MD, 545 SE Oak, Ste. D, Hillsboro, OR 97123.

Clubs: Historical Microscope Society of Canada, RR #2, Priceville, Ontario, Canada NOC 1KO; Microscope Historical Society, 14 Tall Acres Dr., Pittsford, NY 14534.

Bausch & Lomb, American, $350.00–$500.00.

Bausch & Lomb, binocular microscope, black, brass trim . . $150.00
Bausch & Lomb, black, nickle plated knobs and lenses, c1930, full size 75.00
Bausch & Lomb, Harvard Model, brass, with case, c1890 . . . . 350.00
Bausch & Lomb, Model BB, brass, black horseshoe base, full size 150.00
Bausch & Lomb, Model R, plastic body with nickle body tube, walnut case 50.00
Bausch & Lomb, monocular, black, brass knobs and lenses, jug handle, full size 125.00
Bausch & Lomb, Little Gem, student, brass, green stand, velvet lined cardboard case, small 75.00
Bausch & Lomb, New Gem, student, nickle plated tube, black base, small 55.00
Bioscope, projection microscope, for classroom use 75.00
Blister, student set, c1950 . . . . 15.00
Gilbert, toy, with metal case, c1960 . . . . 15.00
Gilbert, toy set, cardboard case, c1950 . . . . 15.00
Gilbert, toy set, green or yellow wood case, c1940 . . . . 25.00
Gundlach, case mounted, c1905 . . . . 275.00
Hensold, Met-Tami, German, portable 100.00
Hensold, Pro-Tami, German, portable 175.00
Hensold, Tami, German, portable 75.00
Junior, field microscope, tripod legs, Germany 65.99
Leitz, black, brass knobs and lenses, full size 150.00
Meccano, toy set, cardboard box 15.00
Meccano, toy set, green wood case 35.00
Meccano, toy set, large metal case 50.00
Microset, toy set, Model 2M, cardboard box 15.00
Microset, toy set, Model 3M, cardboard box 20.00
Microset, toy set, Model 3X, cardboard box 25.00
Microtome, slide-making machine 75.00

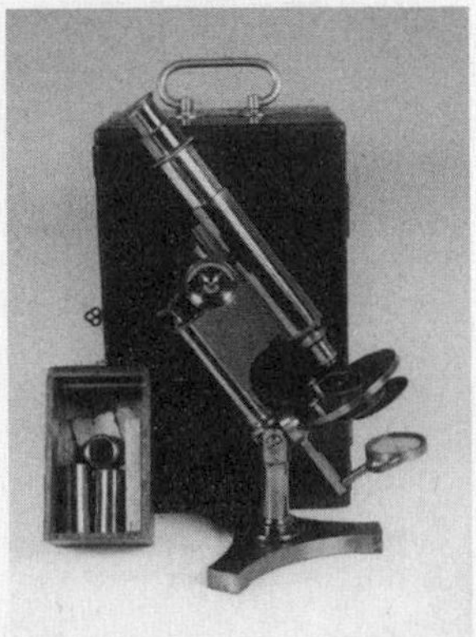

Bausch & Lomb, Investigator, c1885, $350.00–$500.00.

Queen & Co, American, $400.00–$600.00.

Tolles, American, $800.00–$1,000.00.

Porter, Microscraft, toy set, blue wood box 15.00
Porter, Microscraft, toy set, #309, cardboard box 30.00
Porter, Microcraft, toy set, metal case 15.00
R&J Beck, binocular, c1870 . . . . 850.00
Ring, toy set, black cardboard box 20.00
Ring, toy set, red and blue wood case 25.00
Ring, toy set, red and yellow cardboard box 20.00
Skillcraft, toy set, metal case 15.00
Spencer, dissecting microscope 85.00
Spencer, dissecting microscope, single eyepiece 50.00
Spencer Lens Co, monocular, black body, brass knobs and lenses, full size 75.00
Student, drum microscope, brass, round base, with case, 6" h 50.00
Tasco, Japan, toy set, cardboard box 5.00
Tasco, Japan, toy set, 600X, mahogany wood case 15.00
Tasco, Japan, toy set, 750X, mahogany wood case 15.00
Tasco, Japan, toy set, 900X, mahogany wood case 20.00
Tasco, Japan, toy set, 1200X, mahogany wood case 20.00
Wollensak, student, 250X, round base 35.00
Wollensak, student, 450X, horseshoe base, walnut case 350.00
Zeiuss, research microscope, black and brass 300.00
Zent Meyer, Histologic, brass, walnut case, c1870–1880 . . . . 350.00

MILITARIA

Soldiers have returned home with the spoils of war as long as there have been soldiers and wars. Look at the Desert Storm material that is starting to arrive on the market. Many collectors tend to collect material relating to wars taking place in their young adulthood or related to re-enactment groups to which they belong.

It pays to specialize. The two obvious choices are a specific war or piece of equipment. Never underestimate the enemy. Nazi material remains the strongest segment of the market.

Reproductions abound. Be especially careful of any Civil War and Nazi material.

Clubs: American Society of Military Insignia Collectors, 526 Lafayette Ave., Palmerton, PA 18071; Assoc. of American Military Uniform Collectors, P.O. Box 1876, Elyria, OH 44036; Company of Military Historians, North Main St., Westbrook, CT 06498; Imperial German Military Collectors Assoc., 82 Atlantic St, Keyport, NJ 07735;

Periodicals: *Militaria International,* Box 43400, Minneapolis, MN 55443; *Military Trader,* P.O. Box 1050, Dubuque, IA 52004; *North South Trader's Civil War,* PO Drawer 631, Orange, VA 22960.

CIVIL WAR

Ammunition Pouch, unofficial badge for division of the Union 6th Corps, curved brass plate with cross device attached to face, mounted by loop and lug $75.00
Binoculars, USA, Army, France, brass construction, leatherette covered barrels, string cord neckstrap, French made hallmark on eyepiece 23.00
Book, *Pictorial History of Civil War of Union,* Stevens 90.00
Canteen, USA, Army, pewter spout with chain and stopper, 7½" d 110.00
Compass, USA, Army, pocket, 8-point azimuthal ring with floating pointer and locking lever, glass cov with brass case, octagonal box with blue velour lining and blue satin int padded top 164.00
Drumstick, USA, Army, oak, leather padded tipm mkd "US/1861" near grip 87.00
Field Glasses, brass, Lemaire Fabt, Paris, 7½" l 125.00
Knapsack, USA, Army, black treated cloth, black leather straps 132.00
Letter, USA, Army, from soldier in 12th Regiment, Massachusetts Volunteers, to his wife, discusses ongoing fighting, includes envelope addressed to wife in Natick, MA, posted in 3¢ stamp, 5 x 7" lined paper 115.00
Medical Instruments, USA, Army, set of glass drawing cups and wood gripped veining knife 80.00
Mess Kit, USA, Army, 8" d steel bowl and dish with rolled edges, fork and spoon with "US" stmaped on handles 91.00
Photograph, USA, Army, sepia color print depicting young Union soldier standing, wearing frock coat and cap, 12 x 17" 93.00
Shell Jacket, Union Cavalry, buttons, lining, and inspector's marks 425.00

KOREAN WAR

Boots, USA, Army, Arctic, felt, thick white felt bodies, thick composition soles, lace insteps, white canvas/leather 2-buckle uppers, with thick white wool felt liners, size large $21.00
Cap, field, pile, Model Quartermaster 1, dark olive drab cotton with alpaca-lined fold-down earflaps and 1950 quick release tag, chevron on front of stitched bill, all labels intact, size 7 . . . . 19.00
Cartridge Belt, USA, Army, dark olive drab web with brass fittings, includes 2 dark olive drab web Carlisle bandage pouches, dated 1952 and 1945 . . . . 20.00

Souvenir Program, U S Government War Exposition, Lake Front, Chicago, Sep 2–5, 1917, "How the Mighty Have Fallen," black and white photos, 32 pp, 6 x 9", $15.00.

Magazine Tear Sheet, Asbestos adv, 1940s, 10¼ x 13", $15.00.

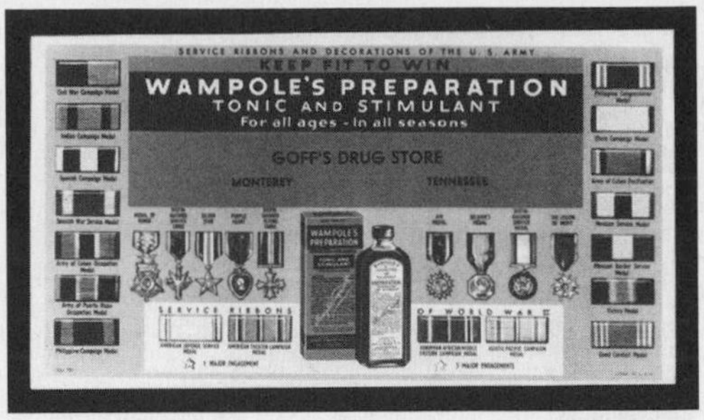

Blotter, Wampole's Preparation Tonic and Stimulant adv, printed color, WWII service ribbons illus, 1940s, 6⅜ x 3½", $8.00.

Helmet, USA, Navy, flight, pilot wing decal and gothic initials on front, ridged gold finish top pattern, boom mike on right side, adjustable straps on outside, padded leather headband, web restraints and shock pad liners, Gentexite label, handwritten names and 1954 date on ear covers 86.00

Lighter, USA, Air Force, brushed silver finish flip-top case, 1 side brass with enameled 5th Air Force patch design insignia and engraved "Officers Open Mess," other side engraved "K. 55" with likeness of Korea and locations 41.00

Pillow Case, red cotton body, large color machine embroidered 8th Army patch design in center, yellow machine embroidered "11th Evac Hospital Pusan Korea," 17 x 17" 30.00

Plaque, USA, Air Force, oak, hp center emblem with"5th Air Force" above and "Korea" below 53.00

VIETNAM WAR

Baseball Hat, USA, Army, officer, olive drab, vented, elasticized sweatband and embroidered white eagle on frong, Saigon tailors mark on sweatband $125.00

Beret, flash, USA, Army, for 75th Ranger Battalion, applied cotton panel and hand embroidered color design on olive drab ripstop base, Vietnam made, 2 x 2¼" 55.00

Book, *82nd Airborne Division, Vietnam History,* USA, Army, 3rd Brigade, illus, hardback, orig mailing sleeve 30.00

Grenade, USA, Army, green smoke, light green painted top, pin in fuse, bottom drilled out 20.00

Helmet, combat, Viet Cong, woven bamboo with string chin ties, 11" d 75.00

Helmet, tropical, USA, Army, tan cotton cov fiber shell, green lining, adjustable sweatband, web chinstrap, metal grommet vents 13.00

Knife, combat, USA, Army, parkerized blade, knuckle bow welded to guard and mated to pommel, 3 wide ribs on underside, checkered black grips, "US M8A 1" on scabbard, Milpar hallmark on guard, developed from M6 baylonet 145.00

WORLD WAR I

Belt, dress, USA, USMC, for dress blue uniform, white buff leather, no fittings or buckle, 40" l $20.00

Blanket, USA, Army, wool, light olive drab, brown stripe at ends 35.00

Boots, field, USA, Army, brown leather, rawhide lace fronts, cap toes, leather and rubber soles, 14" h 76.00

Compass, USA, Army, alloy case in pocketwatch form, Wittnaur hallmark on face, black leather pouch 37.00

Dog Tag, USA, Navy, oval, man's name, dated 1917 and mkd "USN" on front with thumbprint on reverse side 28.00

First Aid Pouch, USA, Army, tan canvase pouch, snap flap, web strap and belt clip, mkd "US" on front, dated "10-18" inside, complete contents 40.00

Helmet, combat, USA, Army, semi-smooth olive drab finish steel shell, "145" above large crossed cannons, no chinstrap 75.00

Poster, USA, "Hun or Home? Buy More Liberty Bonds, " color illus of German soldier with spike helmet in pursuit of woman and child, 20 x 30" 66.00

Trench Art, USA, model, from scrap brass, bullet and coins, fuselage is safed rifle round and wings and tail are from scrap, coins make wheels moveable pr peller, upper wing missing 26.00

Watch Fob, USA, Army, 44th Division, brass, mkd "Co/A/114 INF/ 44dth Div" in raised letters, cowhide strap 28.00

WORLD WAR II

Ammunition Pouch, Italy, Army, 2 pockets, field gray leather with flap tabs, tab posts and rear belt loops $20.00

Banner, "Relative In Service," USA, red and white, blue star center, black wood post and gold cord, 11 x 15" 28.00

Belt, officer's, USA, Army, web trouser, olive drab web, gilt tip, Gemsco, orig box mkd "U.S. Officers Web Belt" with lift-off lid, 36" l 38.00

Book, *Rear Area Security in Russia,* USA, Army, Russian WW II historical reference work, historical study covering Soviet second front behind Germany lines, Department of the Army publication, 1951 . . . . 20.00

Buckle, German, Army, enlisted man, stamped gray pebble body with 4 tab roundel, silver painted finish 35.00

Bugle, USA, Army, brass, nickel plated mouthpiece, mkd "US Regulation" on throat of horn 50.00

Canteen Cup, USA, Army, dark blue porcelain over metal, metal hinged handle 75.00

Dog Tag, with chain, USA, Army, name, address and 1941 date 20.00

Flashlight, USA, Army, olive drab green plastic case, Model MX944/U, uses 3 D-size batteries 29.00

Gas Mask, Germany, civilian, green rubber, with straps, flat aluminum filter, inked Waffenamt stamp on filter. 20.00

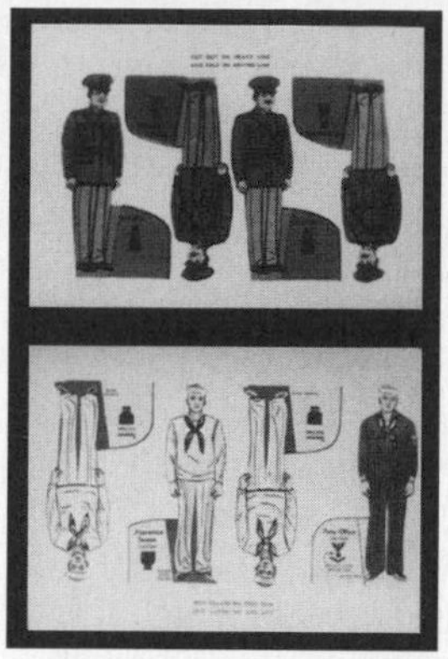

Paper Soldiers, cardboard, printed color, four 3½" h figures with insignia, 6¾ x 5", 1940s, price for each card, $9.00.

Grenade, USA, Army, MK-11 A1, complete with pin, arm, and fuse case, some rust **20.00**
I D Bracelet, USMC, SS, oval, worn emblem with name and home town, chain with clasp, 2" l **36.00**
Map Case, Germany, Army, dark brown leather body, full flap, aluminum closure adjustment and empty tool fittings, dated 1936 with maker stamped, 3 inked owner's names **40.00**
Metal, Distinguished Flying Cross, USA, Army, on slot brooch-mounted ribbon, leatherette presentation case **30.00**
Periodical, *The Forward Observer*, USA, Army, publication of the 492nd Armored Field Artillery Battalion at Camp Cooke, CA, dated Aug 5, 1944 . . . . **6.00**
Postcard, Hitler, Germany, black and white drawing of chest-up profile with overcoat and peaked hat, unused, 1938 . . . . **28.00**
Poster, USA, "Confidence" over picture of Franklin D Roosevelt, 18 x 24" **9.00**
Ring, Germany, black enamel swastika on silver disc, chipped red borders, size 8½ **145.00**
Sweetheart Pin, USA, hp eagle with "In Service" on chest, sweetheart banner in talons **20.00**
Sweetheart Ring, USA, copper, Air Force Cadet Wings on crest and other symbols on sides **34.00**
Telescope, USA, Army, olive drab finished metal tube, optics and scale on 1 lens, brackets for mounting clamps, Model 76 carrying case **23.00**
Trench Art, USA, salt and pepper shakers, pr, from turned aluminum, with threaded tops, engraved names **55.00**

MILK BOTTLES

There is an entire generation of young adults to whom the concept of milk in a bottle is a foreign idea. In another fifteen years a book like this will have to contain a chapter on plastic milk cartons. I hope you are saving some.

When buying a bottle, make certain the glass is clear of defects from manufacture and wear and the label and/or wording in fine or better condition. Buy odd sized bottles and bottles with special features. Don't forget the caps. They are collectible too.

Club: National Assoc. of Milk Bottle Collectors, Inc., 4 Ox Bow Rd., Westport, CT 06880.

Newsletter: *The Udder Collectibles*, HC 73 Box 1, Smithville Flats, NY 13841.

Adderholdt Bros Creamery, Gainesville, GA, round, red pyro, reverse with Uncle Sam holding glas of milk, outline of USA, and "A Healthy Nation is a Strong Nation/Milk the Nation Builder," qt **$60.00**
Alaska Dairy Products Corp, Anchorage, AK, sq, green pyro front, red pyro back, qt. **175.00**
Alameda County Milk Dealers Assoc, Oakland, round, orange pyro, "Milk Builds Great Champions" with baseball and football player on back, ½ gal **45.00**
Anchorage Dairy, Anchorage, AK, orange pyro, qt. **165.00**
Athens Cooperative Creamery, round, green pyro, reverse with "War Bonds For Victory/Milk For Strength," Uncle Sam holding glass of milk, qt **55.00**
Augusta Dairies, Inc, Staunton, VA, round, black pyro, 3 children playing with "Milk for Health," qt **32.00**
Ausable Dairy Corp, NY, round, emb, pt **5.00**
Bangor Dairy, Bangor, MI, round, black pyro, farm scene on back, qt **23.00**
Batchelder's Dairy, Hampton Falls, NH, round, orange pyro, qt. **22.00**
Ben Jansing Farm Dairy, Licking Pike, Newport, NY, red pyro, reverse with picture of man and "Yes Sir!," qt. **45.00**
Blairs Dairy Farm, Blairs, VA, emb pt **30.00**
Blake's Creamery, Manchester, NH, red pyro, qt **28.00**
Borden, sq, red pyro, Elsie head, yellow plastic bale, gal. **55.00**
Brookfield Dairy, Hellertown, PA, round, emb baby face, ½ pt **100.00**
Bryson's Farm Fresh Grade A, Augusta, GA, sq, red pyro, "Jack is Nimble and Jack Is Quick, Bryson's Milk Explains the Trick," qt **25.00**
Calhoun County Creamery, AL, emb, qt **12.00**
C Decracker, Williamson, NY, emb, qt **20.00**
Chas A Hoak's Modern Sanitary Dairy, round, emb, qt **40.00**
Clearview Farm, Swedesboro, NJU, round, orange pyro, qt **35.00**
Clover-Dale Farms, Binghamton, NY, emb, qt. **32.00**
Cop the Cream, Rochester, NY, round, emb, qt. **175.00**
Cream Separator, Ashenhurst Dairy, Viola, IL, round, emb **125.00**
Crystal Creamery Co, squat, black pyro, qt. **30.00**
Dairylee Milk, sq, double baby face, red and yellow pyro, qt. **50.00**
Dartmouth Dairy, orange pyro, qt **24.00**
Edgewood Farms, Troy, PA, emb, pt **25.00**
El-Fre Nubian Goat Farm, Ebenezer, NY, sq, blue pyro, "All Our Goats are Registered and T.V. Inspected," qt **40.00**
Essex Dairy, Irvington, NJ, round, maroon pyro, reverse with minute man and "United Nation is a Strong Nation," ½ pt **34.00**

Baby Face, "Cop the Cream/Glenside Dairy/Deep Water, N.J.—It Whips!," clear, smooth base, ABM lip with cap seat, 20th C, pt, $93.50. Photo courtesy Glass-Works Auctions.

"A.G.S./& Co./Patent/App'd For," clear, metal handle, lightning type closure, tin lid emb "A.G. Smalley & Co.," smooth base, tooled lip, c1885–95, pt, $100.00. Photo courtesy Glass-Works Auctions.

Farmers Fairfield Dairy Co, Reading, PA, squat, red pyro, qt **60.00**
Frederick's Farm Dairy, Conyngham, PA, brown pyro, qt **35.00**
George Signor, Keeseville, NY, round, emb, pt **4.00**
HiAcre Milk Farms, squat, orange pyro, qt **30.00**
Hidden Acres Farms, Washington, NJ, sq, clear, baby face, 4-leaf clover, qt **30.00**
H L Green, Grade A Raw, Golden Guernsey Products, Chester, NY, round, orange pyro, reverse with story carrying baby, qt **30.00**
Katahoin Creamery, Patton, ME, sq, green pyro **23.00**
Jersey Farm Dairy, Fresno, CA, emb, qt **40.00**
Landgren's Dairy, Kenosha, WI, maroon pyro, qt. **35.00**
Lawnton Dairy, Camden, NJ, emb, pt. **30.00**
Lycoming Dairy Farms, emb, ½ pt **25.00**
Maola Milk & Ice Cream Co, New Bern, NC, round, orange pyro, front with picture of baby holding bottle, reverse with "Food Fights Too/Plan Your Meals For Victory," qt **45.00**
Maplewood Dairy, Fair Haven, VT, red pyro, qt. **22.00**
Margrove Inc Cream Craft Products, NY, sq, red pyro, qt. **5.00**
Meadowview Dairy, Johnsonville, CA, red pyro, ½ pt **15.00**
Melrose Dairy, Ormand, FL, blue pyro, reverse with milk bottle jumping, qt **35.00**
Phelp's Dairy, round, orange pyro, qt **25.00**
Pine Grove Dairy, Skaneateles, NY, green and orange pyro, qt. **28.00**
Purelac Dairy, Waterville, ME, sq, red pyro. **23.00**
Queen City Dairy, Inc, Cumberland, MD, round, "Cream Top Pat. Mar. 3, 25," qt **52.50**
Roper Dairy Farm, Trussville, AL, emb, pt. **22.00**
Rosedale Dairy, round, green pyro, qt **12.00**
Ruff's Dairy, St Clair, MI, squat, orange pyro, qt **30.00**
Slosek's Farm, orange pyro, qt **15.00**
Smith Dairy, Boardman, OH, red pyro, qt. **20.00**
Smith's Dairy, Verda, KY, black pyro, reverse with cow and calf and "Pure Bred Herds," qt. **50.00**
Snyder's Dairy, Hazelton, PA, round, red pyro, pt **12.00**
Statham's Dairy, Cordele, GA, round, black pyro, qt **60.00**
Sunrise Dairy, Lewiston, ME, red pyro, qt **20.00**
Sunny Dale Dairy, IN, round, pyro, qt **10.00**
Toothache Cream Top, Peninsula Dairy, VA, sq, emb, qt **125.00**
Westmoreland, sq, orange and red pyro, cow head with crown, "Queen of Quality," orange plastic bale, orig plastic overcap, gal **45.00**
White Oak Dairy, Covington, VA, emb qt. **22.00**
Wood's, Petersburg-Hopewell, VA, sq, orange pyro, double baby face, qt **135.00**
Yurko Farm Dairy, Sweet Valley, PA, sq, green pyro, ½ pt . . . **100.00**

MILK GLASS

Milk glass is an opaque white glass that became popular during the Victorian era. A scientist will tell you that it is made by adding oxide of tin to a batch of clear glass. Most collect it because it's pretty.

Companies like Atterbury, McKee, and Westmoreland have all produced fine examples in novelties, often of the souvenir variety, as well as household items. Old timers focus heavily on milk glass made before 1920. However, there are some great pieces from the post-1920 period that you would be wise not to overlook.

Milk glass has remained in continuous production since it was first invented. Many firms reproduce old patterns. Be careful. Old timers will tell you that if a piece has straw marks, it is probably correct. Some modern manufacturers who want to fool you might have also added them in the mold. Watch out for a "K" in a diamond. This is the mark on milk glass reproductions from the 1960s made by the Kemple Glass Company.

Club: National Milk Glass Collectors Society, 46 Almond Dr., Hershey, PA 17033.

Animal Dish, cov, cat on drum, Portieux, blue, 4¾" d. **$75.00**
Animal Dish, cov, cow, relief design, oblong, orig paint, Vallerystahl, 7" l, 4¼" w. **125.00**
Animal Dish, cov, fish, Vallerystahl, blue **425.00**
Animal Dish, cov, hen, red glass eyes, 6⅞" l. **50.00**
Animal Dish, cov, jack rabbit, 6" l **350.00**
Animal Dish, cov, lion, picket base, Atterbury. **150.00**
Animal Dish, cov, squirrel, acorn base **125.00**
Animal Dish, cov, turkey, nest base **85.00**
Ashtray, Beaded Grape, Westmoreland, 6½" sq. **15.00**
Bowl, Ball and Chain pattern, openwork rim, 8" d **45.00**
Bowl, Old Quilt pattern, ftd, Westmoreland, 9" d **40.00**
Butter Dish, cov, Paneled Grape, Westmoreland, 9" d. **50.00**
Candlestick, pr, Beaded Grape, Westmoreland, 4" h **20.00**
Candy Container, suitcase, tin closure, white **65.00**
Compote, Jenny Lind, blue **85.00**
Compote, open hand **35.00**
Covered Dish, cabbage, Portieux, blue. **40.00**
Covered Dish, Santa on Sleigh. **55.00**
Covered Dish, trunk with strap, 5½" l. **90.00**
Creamer, owl, orig eyes. **25.00**
Creamer, Paneled Wheat pattern **30.00**
Eggcup, kingfisher. **10.00**
Jar, cov, scottie, pink **45.00**
Lady's Shoe, floral, blue, gold paint dec **15.00**
Lamp, Columbus, bearded, miniature **1,250.00**

Covered Dish, strawberry with snail, some orig paint, Vallerysthal, $247.50. Photo courtesy Gene Harris Antique Auction Center, Inc.

Shaker, Johnny Bull, $44.00. Photo courtesy Gene Harris Antique Auction Center, Inc.

Lamp, Goddess of Liberty, clear frosted font, 11" h . . . **360.00**
Mantel Dogs, pr, Atterbury, 5" h, 7" l . . . **1,700.00**
Match Holder, Indian head, wall type, 5" l . . . **65.00**
Match Safe, Bible, blue . . . **25.00**
Match Safe, elf, hanging . . . **210.00**
Mug, child's, duck and swan . . . **20.00**
Mustard, owl, glass insert, orig threaded top, Atterbury, 5" h . . . **150.00**
Pickle Dish, sheaf of wheat . . . **12.50**
Pitcher, Dart and Bar pattern, rect handle, ftd, blue . . . **95.00**
Plate, Blackberries pattern, beaded rim, Westmoreland, 7½" d . . . **12.00**
Plate, Cherries pattern, beaded rim, white, Westmoreland, 7½" d . . . **12.50**
Plate, Eagle pattern, star rim, Fenton, 8" d . . . **40.00**
Plate, Easter Bunny and Egg, orig gold border . . . **50.00**
Salt, master, swan, head down, 3¼" h, 5½" l . . . **25.00**
Salt and Pepper Shakers, pr, Paneled Grape pattern, Westmoreland . . . **24.00**
Sugar, cov, Sunflower pattern . . . **50.00**
Toothpick, monkey with hat . . . **130.00**
Tray, Moses in the Bulrushes . . . **50.00**

MODEL KITS

A plastic model kit is a world of fun and fantasy for people of all ages. Model kit manufacturers such as Revell/Monogram, Aurora, and Horizon, create and produce detailed kits that let the builders imagination run wild. Creative kits give movie monsters a creepy stare, F16 fighter planes a sense of movement, and hot rod roadsters that race on a dragstrip across a tabletop.

Most model kits were packed in a decorated cardboard box with an image of the model on the surface. It contained the requisite pieces and a set of assembly instructions. Model kits are snapped together or glued together. Painting and decoration is up to the assembler. Model kits are produced from plastic, resin, or vinyl, often requiring a bit of dexterity and patience to assemble.

Buying model kits at flea markets should be done with a degree of caution. An open box spells trouble. Look for missing pieces or lost instructions. Sealed boxes are your best bet, but even these should be questioned because of the availablity of home shrink wrap kits. Don't be afraid—inquire about a model's completeness before purchasing it.

Clubs: Kit Collectors International, P.O. Box 38, Stanton, CA 90680; Society for the Preservation and Encouragement of Scale Model Kit Collecting, 3213 Hardy Dr., Edmond, OK 73013.

Periodical: *International Figure Kit Club,* P.O. Box 201, Sharon Center, OH 44274.

1930 Ford Woody, Monogram, 1/24 scale . . . **$35.00**
1951 Chevy Fleetline, AMT . . . **43.00**
1957 Flip Nose Vette, MPC, 1/25 scale . . . **30.00**
1957 Chevy Nomad, AMT, 1/16 scale . . . **43.00**
1962 Chrysler 300 Hardtop, Jo-Han . . . **45.00**
1965 Mustang Fastback, AMT, 1/32 scale . . . **43.00**
1966 T-Bird, AMT . . . **40.00**
1969 Buick Riviera, AMT . . . **40.00**
1977 Camaro Type LT, MPC . . . **30.00**
1978 Corvette, MPC, 1/20 scale . . . **30.00**
A-Team Van, AMT, 1983 . . . **20.00**
Alien Exoskeleton ID4, Lindberg . . . **20.00**
American Wilderness Bald Eagle, Lifelike . . . **30.00**
B-17G Flying Fortress, Monogram, 1975 . . . **30.00**
B-26 Invader Four Star, Monogram, 1955 . . . **40.00**
Badman 55 Chevy Street Funnycar, Monogram, 1973 . . . **50.00**
Baja Beast Street 'N Beach Set, Monogram . . . **40.00**
Banana Splits Banana Buggy, Aurora, 1969 . . . **325.00**
Bearcat F8F, Monogram, 1967 . . . **25.00**
Beer Wagon, Monogram, 1967 . . . **40.00**
Big Rod Show Car, MPC, 1/25 scale . . . **50.00**
Blackbird Trans Am, MPC . . . **30.00**
Black Knight of Milan, Aurora, 1961 . . . **125.00**
Blank Vulcan Pirate Ship, Aurora, 1950s . . . **25.00**
Blue Nose Schooner, Aurora, 1957 . . . **40.00**
Boeing 707 Astrop Jet, Aurora . . . **55.00**
British SE-5 Scout, Aurora, 1963 . . . **35.00**
Bushwacker Offroad Jeep, MPC, 1977 . . . **30.00**
Camaro T-Top, AMT, #2213 . . . **20.00**
Captain Kidd Bloodthirsty Pirate, Aurora . . . **200.00**
Cherokee Sports Roadster, Hawk, 1964 . . . **25.00**
Cherry Bomb Turbine Powered Sho-Rod Chopper and Trailer, Monogram, 1973 . . . **48.00**
Classic Lincoln Continental, Monogram, 1/24 scale, 1967 . . . **45.00**
Classic Rolls Royce Phantom II, Monogram, 1966 . . . **25.00**
Cobra Tee Way-Out Rod, Pyro, 1/16 scale . . . **90.00**
Coors Courier Revell, 1978 . . . **30.00**
Corsair F40-1, Revell, 1/32 scale, 1970 . . . **30.00**
Curls Girl Surfer Figure Kit, MPC . . . **130.00**
Deep Sea Lobster, Educational Products, 1962 . . . **70.00**
Dick Tracy Sports Coupe, Aurora . . . **235.00**
Disney's Haunted Mansion, Vampire Madness, MPC . . . **165.00**
Don the Snake Prudhomme, Revell, 1/25 scale rear engine dragster, 1974 . . . **90.00**
Dornier Flying Pencil WWII Bomber, Monogram . . . **25.00**

Robotch, Revell, 2-in-1 Kit, 1964, $200.00 MIB.

Dragula, Blueprinters series, AMT/Ertl, 1991 . . . . **20.00**
Dr Crazy, Marx, 1960s **350.00**
Ecklers Corvette Hatchback, AMT, #3102 . . . . **30.00**
Evil Knievel's Sky Cycle X2, Addar, 1974 . . . . **25.00**
F-16 Airforce Fighter, Monogram, 1976 . . . . **20.00**
Folgers Monte Carlo Stock Car, Monogram, 1986 . . . . **20.00**
Ford "T" Pick-Up, Monogram, 1975 . . . . **35.00**
Frantic Cats, Hawk **140.00**
Frantics, Steel Plunkers, Hawk, 1965 . . . . **45.00**
French Galley La Reale Ship, Lindberg **23.00**
Galaxy Runner, Message from Space, Entex, 1978 . . . . **20.00**
Gemini Astronaut, Revell, 1967 . . . . **90.00**
George Washington, Aurora, 1965 . . . . **125.00**
German WWI Albatross, Aurora, 1956 . . . . **45.00**
Giant Killer VW Bug, MPC **20.00**
Glow Hunchback of Notre Dame, Aurora, 1969 . . . . **160.00**
Hardy Boys Van, Revell, 1978 . . . . **35.00**
High Roller Ramcharger, Monogram **30.00**
Human Brain, Lindberg, 1972 . . . . **20.00**
Jaguar XK120 Roadster, Aurora, 1961 . . . . **35.00**
Ice Cream Truck Show rod, MPC **48.00**
Illya Kuryakin, Aurora **250.00**
Indian Warrior, Pyro, 1960 . . . . **60.00**
Indy Special Fuel Injection, Aurora, with instructions, 1953 . . . . **25.00**
Jerry West Great Moments in Sports, Aurora **200.00**
King Kong The Last Stand, Mego, 1976 . . . . **75.00**
Leonardo DaVinci Moveable Crane, AMT **35.00**
L'il Van Custom Rod, Monogram, Tom Daniels design, 1973 . . . . **55.00**
Lotus Checker Flag Series, AMT, 1/25 scale **55.00**
Madame Tussaud's Chamber of Horrors Guillotine, Aurora **650.00**
Mercedes Roadster, Lindberg, motorized, 1/32 scale **25.00**
North American P-51D Mustang, Lindberg **23.00**
Northern White Rhino, Revell, 1974 . . . . **16.00**
Nova, MPC **35.00**
Nutty Nose Nipper, Aurora, 1965 . . . . **165.00**
P-38 Lightning War Plane, Monogram, 1973 . . . . **30.00**
Pilgrim Observer Space Station, MPC **55.00**
Planet of the Apes, Addar **40.00**
Ratfink's Mother's Worry, Revell, 1963 . . . . **115.00**
Redstone Mercury Rocket, Revell, 1961 . . . . **100.00**
Road Hog, Lindy Loonys, Lindberg, 1964 . . . . **145.00**
Roadster, Mannix, MPC, 1968 . . . . **75.00**
Sand Worm, Dune, Revell, 1985 . . . . **20.00**
Shogun Warrior Mazinga, Monogram **65.00**
Street Fever Vette, MPC, 1978 . . . . **30.00**
Stroker McGurk and His Surf/Rod, MPC, 1964 . . . . **125.00**
Superman, Monogram, 1974 . . . . **18.00**
Tarzan, Aurora, 1972, MIB **45.00**
U S Army Guided Missile, Hawk, 1969 . . . . **45.00**
U S S Fletcher Destroyer, Revell, 1964 . . . . **40.00**
Viper Vette, MPC, 1/20 scale **38.00**
Volkswagen Beetle, Pyro **30.00**
Wacky Back Wacker Machine, Aurora, 1965 . . . . **350.00**
Warlord Trans Am, MPC **35.00**
W A S P Aircraft Carrier, Lindberg, 1950s **45.00**
Welcome Back Kotter, Sweathogs car, MPC, 1976 . . . . **40.00**
Xtasy Chevy Custom Van, AMT, #T-401 . . . . **40.00**
Zero, Revell, 1967 . . . . **40.00**

MONSTERS

Collecting monster related material began in the late 1980s as a generation looked back nostalgically on the monster television shows of the 1960s, e.g., *Addams Family, Dark Shadows,* and *The Munsters*, and the spectacular monster and horror movies of the 1960s and 1970s. Fueling the fire was a group of Japanese collectors who were raiding the American market for material relating to Japanese monster epics featuring reptile monsters such as Godzilla, Rodan, and Mothra. It did not take long for collectors to seek the historic roots for their post–World War II monsters. A collecting revival started for Frankenstein, King Kong, and Mummy material. Contemporary items featuring these characters also appeared.

This is a category rampant with speculative fever. Prices rise and fall rapidly depending on the momentary popularity of a figure or family group. Study the market and its prices carefully before becoming a participant. Stress condition and completeness. Do not buy any item in less than fine condition. Check carefully to make certain that all parts or elements are present for whatever you buy. Since the material in this category is of recent origin, no one is certain how much has survived. Hoards are not uncommon. It is possible to find examples at garage sales. It pays to shop around before paying a high price.

While an excellent collection of two-dimensional material, e.g., comic books, magazines, posters, etc., can be assembled, stress three-dimensional material. Several other crazes, e.g., model kit collecting, cross over into monster collecting, thus adding to price confusion.

Clubs: Count Dracula Fan Club, 29 Washington Sq. West, New York, NY 10011; Dark Shadows Fan Club, P.O. Box 69A04, West Hollywood, CA 90069; Munsters & The Addams Family Fan Club, P.O. Box 69A04, West Hollywood, CA 90069.

Star Trek USS Enterprise, illuminated, Desilu, 1996, $11.00. Photo courtesy Gene Harris Antique Auction Center, Inc.

Godzilla, toy, plastic Godzilla on wheels flashes out tongue, with pretend flame action and push button for firing claw, orig box, Mattel, 1977, 19½" h, $265.00. Photo courtesy New England Auction Gallery.

Addams Family, game, The Addams Family Family Reunion Game, Pressman, 1991, $12.00.

Wolfman, soaky bottle, blue pants, Colgate-Palmolive, 1963, $80.00.

Addams Family, game, Addams Family Card Game, 1965 . . . **$48.00**
Addams Family, puzzle, Addams Family Mystery, Milton Bradley, orig box, ©1965, 14 x 24" . . . **75.00**
Creature From the Black Lagoon, costume, Collegeville, ©1980 Universal City Studios, Inc, orig 8½ x 11 x 3" box . . . **40.00**
Creature From the Black Lagoon, display, Creature From the Black Lagoon 3-D Pinball, diecut plastic, countertop, issued for Bally pinball machine, ©1982 Universal City Studios, Inc, early 1990s, 8½ x 8½" . . . **40.00**
Creature From the Black Lagoon, pinback button, litho metal, color illus, Elwar Ltd, 1963, 3½" d . . . **35.00**
Creature From the Black Lagoon, snowdome, MIB . . . **15.00**
Dark Shadows, magazine, *Barnabas Collins Famous Monsters of Filmland,* #59 . . . **35.00**
Dracula, action figure, Remco, ©1980 Universal City Studios, Inc, 8½" h . . . **40.00**
Dracula, doll, Count Dracula, coffin box and death certificate, Travelers, 1985 . . . **75.00**
Dracula, flicker ring, silver base, 1960s . . . **50.00**
Dracula, game, Dracula Mystery Game, Hasbro, orig box, ©1963 Universal Pictures Corp. . . . **125.00**
Dracula, souvenir program, *Bela Lugosi In Dracula,* issued at theater performances of Dracula presented by Harry H Oshrin, 12 pp, c1943, 8½ x 11" . . . **15.00**
Dr Jekyll and Mr Hyde, model kit, Aurora Glow Monster Kit, 1972 . . . **225.00**
Elvira, display, Coors Beer, life size standup . . . **45.00**
Frankenstein, action figure, Remco . . . **40.00**
Frankenstein, *Castle of Frankenstein 1967 Monster Annual,* Warren Publishing, 66 pp, c1974, 8½ x 11" . . . **15.00**
Frankenstein, doll, cloth body, vinyl head and hands, rooted hair, removable clothjing, Universal Studios, 18" h . . . **175.00**
Frankenstein, figure, Bend-em, 1990, MOC . . . **20.00**
Frankenstein, lobby card, *Jesse James Meets Frankenstein's Daughter,* South American, oversized, paper, inset black and white photo depicting western fish fight with color graphics of Jesse James, Frankenstein and Frankenstein's daughter, 1966, 12 x 16" . . . **15.00**
Frankenstein, magazine, *Castle of Frankenstein,* Vol 1, #1, Jan 1962, Gothic Castle Publishing Co, black and white photos, articles on Boris Karloff, 8¼ x 11" . . . **40.00**
Frankenstein, magazine, *Life,* Vol 64, #11, Mar 15, 1968, 10 pp article on Frankenstein . . . **15.00**
Frankenstein, photo, *Ghose of Frankenstein,* black and white glossy, 1970s, 8½ x 11" . . . **18.00**
Frankenstein, puzzle, 81 pcs, APC, 1977 . . . **12.00**
Frankenstein, waste can, with lid, litho tin, wrap-around design depicting Frankenstein's body, molded plastic lid designed as top of his head with textured hair design, Chein, 1970s, 16" h . . . **90.00**
Godzilla, coloring book, The Cool Ghoul Monster Coloring Book, Wanamaker, 32 pp, 1964, 15 x 9", unused . . . **20.00**
Hunchback of Notre Dame, figure, glow-in-the-dark, Uncle Milton, 1990, MOC . . . **10.00**
Karloff, Boris, comic book, Die Monster Die Movie Classic . . . **35.00**
Karloff, Boris, lobby card, *The Haunted Strangler,* Mexican, oversized, inset black and white photo of Karloff as Strangler with woman in blue dress by graveyard, 1958, 12½ x 16" . . . **15.00**
King Kong, bank, hard vinyl, Relic Art Ltd, ©1977 RKO General Inc, missing trap, 12½" h . . . **50.00**
King Kong, belt, leather, glossy finish, repeated designs of 3 different scenes, Pyramid Belt Co, ©1976 Paramount Pictures Corp . . . **15.00**
King Kong, comic book, Giant Classic King Kong, Whitman, 64 pp, 1969, 10¼ x 13¼" . . . **10.00**
King Kong, doll, cloth, 1970s, 20" h . . . **38.00**
King Kong, doll, vinyl head, hands, and feet, holding Fay Raye figure, 15" h . . . **35.00**
King Kong, game, Ideal, 1978 . . . **40.00**
King Kong, colorforms, King Kong Panorama Playset, ©1976 Dino de Laurentiss Corp, 12¾ c 16 x 1" . . . **15.00**
Mummy, puzzle, mummy carrying screaming victim, Jaymar, orig box, 1963 . . . **100.00**
Mummy, wallet, vinyl, illus of Mummy on 1 side and Dracula on other, inside snap closure compartment, small magic slate with wood stylus, and pockets for picture, with set of 4 monster club cards, ID card with skull and snake, ©1963 Universal Pictures Co, Inc, 3½ x 4½" . . . **175.00**
Munsters, book, *The Munsters and the Great Camera Caper,* Whitman, hard cov, 212 pp, 1965, 5½ x 8" . . . **15.00**
Munsters, costume, Lily Munster, orig box . . . **75.00**
Munsters, puppet, Herman Munster, talking mechanism . . . **150.00**
Nightmare on Elm Street, figure, Talking Freddy, Matchbox, 18" h . . . **90.00**
Nightmare on Elm Street, Freddy Fright Squirter, LJN, 1989, MIB . . . **30.00**
Nightmare on Elm Street, game, A Nightmare On Elm Street/The Freddy Game, Cardinal, ©1989 New Line-Huron Venture, 15 x 16x 3½" . . . **15.00**
Phantom of the Opera, iron-on transfer, Kaumagraph Toy Division, ©1964, 9 x 12", price for pair . . . **50.00**

Tales From the Crypt, movie poster, Australian, 1972, 13 x 30" 40.00
Vampirella, model kit, Aurora Monster Scenes Kit 115.00
Wolfman, jigsaw puzzle, 5½ x 4" cardboard canister, 11¼ x 17¼" assembled size, ©1974 APC 15.00
Wolfman, Mix 'N Mold Figure Maker Set 50.00
Wolfman, soaky bottle, soft plastic, hard plastic head, 1960s, 10" h 75.00

MORTON POTTERIES

Morton is an example of a regional pottery that has a national collecting base. Actually, there were several potteries in Morton, Illinois: Morton Pottery Works and Morton Earthenware Company, 1897–1917; Cliftwood Art Potteries, 1920–1940; Midwest Potteries, 1940–1944; and, Morton Pottery Company, 1922–1976.

Prior to 1940 local clay was used and fired to a golden ecru. After 1940 clay was imported and fired white. Few pieces are marked. The key to identifying Morton pieces is through the company's catalogs and Doris and Burdell Hall's books, *Morton's Potteries: 99 Years,* (published by the authors, 1982), and *Morton Potteries Vol. 2,* (L-W Book Sales, 1995).

American Art Potteries, console set, stylized petal design, 10" d bowl, 1¾" h candleholders $25.00
American Art Potteries, creamer, bird, curved tail handle 10.00
American Art Potteries, creamer and sugar, stylized flowers, blue, peach spray glaze, 3" h 18.00
American Art Potteries, figural lamp, gnarled tree trunk, 12" h 20.00
American Art Potteries, figural lamp, poodle, 15" h 25.00
American Art Potteries, figure, pig, white, gray spots, 5" h 40.00
American Art Potteries, figure, squirrel, 5½" h 15.00
American Art Potteries, figure, wild horse, brown spray glaze, 11½" h 35.00
American Art Potteries, planter, cowboy boot, blue, pink spray glaze, 6" h 12.00
American Art Potteries, planter, reclining deer and log, 6½" l 18.00
American Art Potteries, planter, wheel barrow, parrot shape, 6½" h 12.00
Cliftwood Art Potteries, candlesticks, pr, sq base, choc late drip glaze, 11" h 50.00
Cliftwood Art Potteries, creamer, barrel shape 35.00
Cliftwood Art Potteries, figure, bald eagle, natural colors, 8½" h 95.00
Cliftwood Art Potteries, lamp, owl on log, yellow, 7½" h 35.00

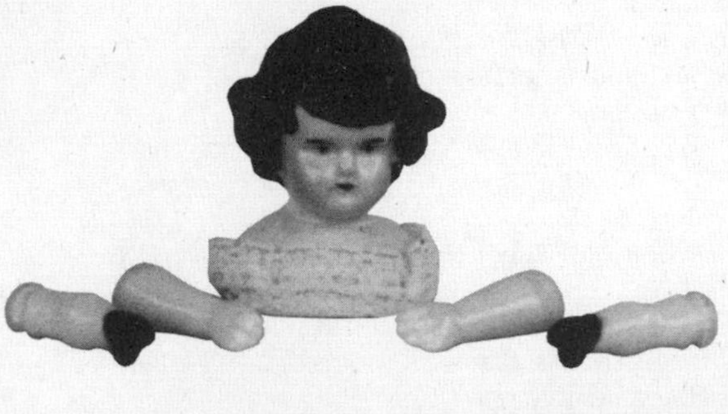

American Art Potteries, doll parts, 3" h head and appendages, $55.00.

Midwest Potteries, figure, crane, 11" h, $30.00.

Cliftwood Art Potteries, match box holder, wall mount, turquoise and pink over white 50.00
Cliftwood Art Potteries, sweetmeat bowl, cov, sq, green and yellow drip glaze 45.00
Cliftwood Art Potteries, water pitcher, brown drip glaze, 7¾" h 50.00
Midwest Potteries, figure, afghan hound, white, gold dec, 7" h 35.00
Midwest Potteries, cowboy, riding bucking bronco, black glaze, 7½" h 25.00
Midwest Potteries, figure, heron, blue air brush, 14k gold dec, 11" h 25.00
Midwest Potteries, figure, pony, yellow, gold dec, 3½" h 18.00
Midwest Potteries, figure, rearing stallion, 10¾" h 25.00
Midwest Potteries, figure, squirrel, brown, white drip, 9" h . . . 35.00
Midwest Potteries, figure, stylized female dancer, white, gold dec, 8½" h 25.00
Midwest Potteries, miniature, goose, white, gold dec, 2" h 6.00
Midwest Potteries, planter, dog, wearing bow tie, 5¼" h 15.00
Midwest Potteries, planter, lioness, 3 x 6½" 12.00
Morton Pottery Co, bank, log cabin school, brown 25.00
Morton Pottery Co, bank, pig, wall hanger, blue 25.00
Morton Pottery Co, bookends, pr, eagles, natural colors 40.00
Morton Pottery Co, deviled egg tray, hp underglaze, spray glazing, center rooster 30.00
Morton Pottery Co, figure, cat, pouncing, cold painted bow at neck, small 8.00
Morton Pottery Co, figure, colt, wood pump and barrel 40.00
Morton Pottery Co, rabbit, creeping, light brown, 7½" l, 4½" h 15.00
Morton Pottery Co, grass grower, Jake, #777, 5" h 20.00
Morton Pottery Co, grass grower, Jolly Jim 20.00
Morton Pottery Co, grass grower, soldier 25.00
Morton Pottery Co, lamp, teddy bear 25.00
Morton Pottery Co, pie bird, white, multicolored wings and back, 5" h 22.00
Morton Pottery Co, planter, cowboy and cactus, natural colors, 7" h 12.00
Morton Pottery Co, planter, Scottie dog 8.00
Morton Pottery Works and Modern Earthenware Co, coffeepot, brown Rockingham glaze, ornate emb dec, 5 pt 90.00
Morton Pottery Works and Modern Earthenware Co, crock, Rockingham glaze, 1 gal 50.00
Morton Pottery Works and Modern Earthenware Co, miniature, chamber pot, Yellow Ware 25.00
Morton Pottery Works and Modern Earthenware Co, miniature, pitcher, bulbous body, green glaze, 1¼" h 25.00

Magazine Tear Sheet, Whitman's Chocolates and Confections adv, Pioneer Woman statue illus, $8.00.

MOTHER'S DAY COLLECTIBLES

It's not fair. The amount of Mother's Day memorabilia is about ten times that of Father's Day memorabilia. It has something to do with apple pie. A great deal of the Mother's Day memorabilia seen at flea markets is "limited edition." The fact that you see so much is an indication that few of these issues were truly limited. Insist on excellent or better condition and the original box when buying.

Since so many collectors are focusing on limited edition material, why not direct your efforts in another direction, for example, greeting cards or pinback buttons. Your costs will be lower, and your collection will be out of the ordinary, just like your mother.

Bell, Mother's Love, porcelain, Avon, 1988, 3" h. **$10.00**
Candle, front decal "A Mother's Gift is Love 1986," Avon, 4" h. **3.00**
Compact, goldtone, heart, rhinestone script "Mother" and U S N emblem, framed mirror, 3 x 2¾ x ½". **75.00**
Figurine, Little Things, Avon, porcelain boy, hp, 3¾" h **18.00**
Figurine, Motherhood, musical, Artaffects, 1987. . . . . **65.00**
Figurine, Cherished Moments, girl, hp porcelain, 1983-84, 4" h **18.00**
Ornament, "Mom 1991," handcrafted, Hallmark **17.00**
Ornament, "Mother," ceramic/bisque, Hallmark, 1990 . . . . . . **20.00**
Pin, mother-of-pearl, "Mother" written in gold wire on leaf. **10.00**
Pinback Button, "Anna Jarvis Founder Philadelphia, Mother's Day," carnation, multicolored, ¾" d **3.00**
Pinback Button, "Gimbels Mother's Day Reminder," black and white, pink carnations, green stems, 1940-50, 1¾" d. **12.00**
Pinback Button, white carnation, red ground, white lettering, 1920s, ⅞" d **18.00**

Plate, Birds and Chicks, Bing & Grondahl, Mother's Day 1970, Henry Thelander, $10.00.

Plate, Alpine Mother and Children, Mother's Day series, Anri, 1972 . . . . **50.00**
Plate, Mother's Day Special Memories, porcelain, Avon, 1985, 5" d. **10.00**
Print, "Greetings To Mother," Donald Art Co, Inc, N Y, framed **1.00**
Trinket Box, cedar, printed verse and photo on lid, c1920s **5.00**

MOTION CLOCKS

Novelty clocks with some type of motion or animation go back hundreds of years and were used in windup or spring powered clocks. Today these clocks are quite desirable and therefore are very expensive. Much more affordable and ever growing in popularity are electric clocks with animation, or motion clocks.

First appearing in the late thirties, they reached their peak production period in the fifties. They declined somewhat in the sixties, and by the seventies were rather uncommon. With the advent of battery operated quartz movements, manufacturers again created many novelty clocks. Some even had multiple motions and sound effects. These clocks are being made today, and while too new to be classified as collectibles, look for them to be popular with collectors in the near future as most are made only for short periods of time and in limited quantities.

Our coverage will focus on electric clocks with animation that were made from the fifties to the seventies. Of these, four companies (Mastercrafters, United, Haddon, and Spartus) led the field by producing clocks that are not only very collectible today, but are also fun to own and operate. Enough were produced to allow for the availability of many different models, and finding them should not be too difficult since many were made for years and years. One word of caution: most parts are not longer available for these clocks, so try to find them in good running order. Parts can be gotten from junk or donor clocks, but this will add to your coast and will also require a degree of repair skill.

Note that many motion clocks feature lighted scenes with a switch to turn off the light, which is usually a long-lasting seven watt night light type bulb.

Advisors: Sam and Anna Samuelian, P.O. Box 504, Edgmont, PA 19028, (610) 566-7248, fax (610) 566-7285, e-mail: info@smsnoveltiques.com.

Note: Prices listed are for complete clocks in very good condition. Missing parts will devalue quite a bit. Fully restored clocks will be worth $50 to $75 more. Names have been assigned when original names were unknown.

Haddon, Home Sweet Home, grandmother rocks in chair while fire flickers in fireplace in lighted room setting. **$125.00**
Haddon, kitten, eyes move from side to side along with tail **200.00**
Haddon, Rancho, cowboy rides bucking horse in lighted outdoor western setting **225.00**
Haddon, Ship Ahoy, celluloid ship moves up and down in waves in lighted marine setting. **250.00**
Haddon, Teeter Totter, boy and girl ride moving see-saw in lighted outdoor country scene **190.00**
Mastercrafters, antique auto, 2 headlights flicker on automobile **75.00**

Mastercrafters, waterfall, $100.00.

Mastercrafters, blacksmith, man strikes anvil with hammer while fire flickers in hearth **125.00**
Mastercrafters, carousel, carousel with 5 figures turns around, snap on front piece often missing. **250.00**
Mastercrafters, church, man pulls rope while bell in tower above moves back and forth **100.00**
Mastercrafters, fireplace, realistic fire appears to burn behind andirons and logs, fireplace grate is often missing **85.00**
Mastercrafters, golfer, man swings golf club from side to side **225.00**
Mastercrafters, Perky, coffeepot percolates by means of flickering light **65.00**
Mastercrafters, swinging bird, yellow bird swing on perch, cage front piece often missing **175.00**
Mastercrafters, swinging girl, girl swings back and forth in country cottage setting **140.00**
Spartus, cat, eyes move up and down while tails swings left and right **50.00**
Spartus, panda bear, eyes move from side to side **40.00**
Spartus, waterfall and Wheel, wheel moves by lighted waterfall in old mill setting **75.00**
United, ballerina, girl dances while music plays, wood case with metal accents **125.00**
United, bobbing chicks, 2 yellow chicks bob in and out of nest **75.00**
United, cowboy, man twirls lasso **150.00**
United, dancers, 4 ballroom dancers move while turntable they are on turns around **175.00**
United, fireplace, realistic fire burns in fireplace set to right of clock **90.00**
United, hula girl, topless girl moves her hips while drummer boy beats drum **250.00**

United, lighthouse, $225.00.

United, majorette, girl twirls baton **125.00**
United, owl, eyes move from side to side **125.00**
United, windmill, windmill turns in lighted scene **150.00**
Unknown Manufacturer, chef, eyes move from side to side **150.00**
Unknown Manufacturer, God Bless America, litho tin, flag waves above Statue of Liberty **100.00**
Unknown Manufacturer, Klocker Spaniel, dogs eyes and tail move from side to side **90.00**

MOTION LAMPS

Motion lamps feature a scene that lights and gives the illusion of motion. They first appeared in the 1920s and are still produced today, but their popularity peaked in the 1950s. Early lamps were constructed of metal and glass, while later lamps were primarily plastic. All feature some type of rotating cylinder that spins from the power of the heat produced by the bulb.

Most lamps need clear 25–40 watt bulbs to work properly. Using frosted bulbs will result in muddy or poor animation. Be careful not to use high wattage bulbs as damage will likely occur. Today's motion lamps use simple colorful cylinders whose moving images project onto the surface of an outer shade, but the earlier lamps used a more complex system, of animation sleeves that produce much more sophisticated motions like water running, wheels turning, fire blazing, etc.

Motion lamps are novelty items that were produced in limited quantities, making them somewhat hard to find in good condition today. However, many different models were made by a number of noteworthy manufacturers, leaving hundreds of various lamps for collectors to search out. Besides scenic lamps, psychedelic, advertising, and figural lamps are among others that are collectible.

The value of motion lamps has risen steadily since the publication of the 1991 pioneer book *Animated Motion Lamps* by Bill and Linda Montgomery, (L-W Books, out-of-print.) The 1998 book *Collector's Guide to Motion Lamps* by Sam and Anna Samuelian features over 550 lamps with 750 color photos and a price and rarity guide. It is available from the authors.

Advisors: Sam and Anna Samuelian, P.O. Box 504, Edgmont, PA 19028, (610) 566-7248, fax (610) 566-7285, e-mail: info@smsnoveltiques.com.

Note: Values listed below are for complete lamps in very good condition that are free of cracks, dents, and scratches, and have good color. Perfect or restored examples will be more valuable. Names have been assigned when original names were unknown.

Econolite, Antique Auto, Stutz Bearcat on 1 side, Model T Ford on reverse, wheels turn, ground underneath moves, trees and houses in background **$200.00**
Econolite, butterflies, various types of butterflies fly by **175.00**
Econolite, ducks, ducks moving wings while water moves below **225.00**
Econolite, forest fire, fire rages while water in stream flows **125.00**
Econolite, Hopalong Cassidy, 2 styles produced, Hoppy chasing stagecoach scene, or Hoppy before moving waterfall and burning campfire **400.00**
Econolite, Miss Liberty, NY harbor scene of boats with stacks smoking and rippling water, Statue of Liberty with lit torch **300.00**

L A Goodman, firefighters, $300.00.

Econolite, Mother Goose, nursery rhyme characters spin around carousel style framework 175.00
Econolite, Niagara Falls, water flows, churns, and moves downstream 100.00
Econolite, Old Mill, water flows downstream over mill wheel, waterfalls in background 140.00
Econolite, picture frame lamps, various scenes, glass cov, wood frame 175.00
Econolite, snow scene, snow gently falls on country scene with cottages and church 175.00
Econolite, steamboats, Robert E Lee and Natchez steamboats with water moving under vessels, smoke and fire pour from stacks, small flags wave in the wind 225.00
Econolite, trains, The General and John Bull steam locomotives on opposite sides, 6 different motions 225.00
Econolite, tropical fish, colorful swimming fish 200.00
Econolite, waterski, waterskiers with water spraying underneath them and the boat, moving palm tree scene background 375.00
L A Goodman, bowl shape, pleated framework, various scenes 175.00
L A Goodman, firefighters, antique fire engine flames and smokes while horses stir up dust, reverse shows water pulsing through hoses as ground moves underneath firemen and nearby building blazes 300.00
L A Goodman, flying geese, clouds move above and water moves below flying geese 175.00
L A Goodman, Fountain of Youth, country boy urinating into lake as animals watch 150.00
L A Goodman, Ocean Creatures, octopus and other sea life swim by sunken ship 250.00
L A Goodman, Oriental Fantasy, volcano erupts intermittently as water ripples before Oriental people 225.00
L A Goodman, sailboats, colorful sailboats pass by wooded setting 250.00
L A Goodman, Santa and reindeer, Santa in sleigh with reindeer flying over black silhouette roof tops, pedestal base 400.00
L A Goodman, waterfall-campfire, waterfall on 1 side, reverse with campfire burning near western campers 140.00
Revolite, pagoda shape frame 200.00
Scene-In-Action, Colonial Fountain, fountain sprays up and down at top, then flows in to water below and ripples 225.00
Scene-In-Action, forest fire, fire blazes in trees and nearby cabins 150.00
Scene-In-Action, Japanese Twilight, water ripples in lake before Mt Fuji 200.00
Scene-In-Action, marine, lighthouse beacon flashes and waves crash into shore on 1 side, reverse with water moving under sailing ship 250.00
Scene-In-Action, Niagara Falls, water flows and moves downstream 175.00
Scene-In-Action, Serenader, water ripples in lake setting, heart shaped glass set into metal gondola frame 325.00
Unknown Manufacturer, advertising, various beer makers 100.00
Unknown Manufacturer, chalkware, various figural lamps 175.00
Unknown Manufacturer, metal, features fire burning, with various figures set before fireplace, 1930s 150.00
Unknown Manufacturer, patterns change shape, 1970s 75.00

MOTORCYCLE COLLECTIBLES

Some of these beauties are getting as expensive as classic and antique cars.

Motorcycles are generational. My father would identify with an Indian, my son with the Japanese imports, and I with a BMW or Harley Davidson. I suspect that most users of this book are not likely to buy an older motorcycle. However, just in case you see a 1916 Indian Power Plus with sidecar for a thousand or less, pick it up. It books at around $15,000.00.

Do not overlook motorcycle related items.

Club: American Motorcyclist Assoc., 33 Collegeview Rd., Westerville, OH 43081; Antique Motorcycle Club of America, P.O. Box 300, Sweetser, IN 46987.

Periodicals: *Motorcycle Shopper Magazine*, 1353 Herndon Ave., Deltona, FL 32725; *Old Bike Journal*, 6 Prowitt St., Norwalk, CT 06855.

Book, *The Big Five Motorcycle Boys at the Front,* hard cov, cover shows motorcyclists on twin cylinder bikes delivering dispatches in WWI Belgium, c1915, 283 pp $90.00
Buckle, AMA Gypsy Tour, gold with AMA enameled logo, 1955 . . . . 90.00
Carbide Lamp, "Old Sol," Hawthorne Mfg, Bridgeport, CT, nickel-plated, 3 jeweled reflectors, mounting clamp, c1913, 10" h, 4½" d lens 210.00
Catalog, 1948 Indian Accessories, sepia, red and white highlights, featuring clothing, jackets, goggles, kidney belts, hats, saddlebags, jewelry, parts, and accessories, oil can adv, 8½ x 11" 275.00

Decal, Oilzum Motorcycle Oil, racer on cycle, orange, white, and blue, 1950s, 4 x 4", unused, $50.00. Photo courtesy Dunbar's Gallery.

Badge, Indian, red with gold-colored emb Silver Chief logo and "Indian," 1950s, 1½" d, $135.00.

Game, Hollywood Movie Bingo, Whitman Publishing Co, #3046, "The Game of the Movie Stars," 1937, $40.00.

Figure, bisque, Santa on motorcycle, c1920s, 2" l **165.00**
Harley-Davidson, 1979 XLCR 1000, unrestored **6,000.00**
Honda, 1973 SL 125 Trail, single cylinder 122cc 4-stroke engine with overhead camshaft, 5 speed **3,500.00**
Magazine, *Motor Cycling,* Nov 30, 1914, 64 pp **70.00**
Manual, 1951 Indian Riders Instruction Book, fold-out lube chart with motorcycles, 42 pp, 7" h, 5" w **140.00**
Patch, cloth, solemn Indian with winged Indian logo, red, white, and black, 7 x 2½", unused **60.00**
Pin, 1958 AMA Gypsy Tour Award, gold with green, red, and yellow enamel, on card, 2¾" h, 2¼" w, unused **60.00**
Postcard, 3 motorcycles with 2 riders, left bike is Indian Twin, 3" h, 5½" w **40.00**
Sheet Music, *Black Denim Trousers & Motorcycle Boots,* The Cheers & Les Baxter, bike with rider on cov, ©1955 Capitol **15.00**
Toy, Cop Cycle Whistle, plastic, blue, 3¾" l **150.00**
Triumph, 1969 TR5 Trophy, 650cc, single carburettor, restored **3,750.00**
Visor, Harley Davidson, leather, unused **30.00**
Wrench, steel, Indian adv, incised, 6" l **160.00**

MOVIE MEMORABILIA

The stars of the silent screen have fascinated audiences for over three-quarters of a century. In many cases, this fascination had as much to do with their private lives as their on-screen performances.

This is a category where individuals focus on their favorites. There are superstars in the collectibles area. Two examples are Charlie Chaplin and Marilyn Monroe.

Posters are expensive. However, there are plenty of other categories where a major collection can be built for under $25 per object. Also, do not overlook present day material. If it's cheap, pick it up. Movie material will always be collectible.

Club: The Manuscript Society, 350 N. Niagara St., Burbank, CA 91505.

Periodicals: *Big Reel,* P.O. Box 1050, Dubuque, IA 52004; *Collecting Hollywood Magazine,* 2512 Broad St., Chattanooga, TN 37409; *Movie Advertising Collector,* P.O. Box 28587, Philadelphia, PA 19149; *Movie Collector's World,* Box 309, Fraser, MI 48026.

Almanac, 1947-48 Motion Picture, hard cov, over 1,000 pp, 6½ x 9" **$55.00**
Blotter, *Hunchback of Notre Dame,* Lon Chaney, pictorial scene **40.00**
Book, *Harold Lloyd "The Freshman,"* Pathe Pictures, Grosset & Dunlap, hard cov, 6 pp of stills, dj with color portrait of Lloyd in title role, ©1925, 345 pp, 5¼ x 7½" **15.00**
Booklet, *Famous Recipes of the Movie Stars,* Tower Books, sepia, 48 pp, ©1931, 7 x 10" **15.00**
Cookbook, *Gone With the Wind,* paperback, Pebeco Toothpaste premium, 48 pp, c1940, 5½ x 7½" **45.00**
Game, Director's Choice, Direct Broadcast Programs, Inc, "Watch the movie, Play The Game, The Ultimate Game for Movie Lovers," includes video tape, 1984 . . . . . . **10.00**
Game, *Goodbye, Mr Chips,* Parker Brothers, 1969 . . . . **28.00**
Game, Hollywood Stars, The Game of, Whitman, 1955 . . . . . **10.00**
Game, Popular Actors, The Game of, Parker Brothers, ©1893 . . . . **75.00**
Lobby Card, *Gang Busters,* color photo, Visual Drama, Inc, 1950s **25.00**
Lobby Card, *Gun Brothers,* color photo, United Artists, 1956 . . . . **15.00**
Lobby Card, *Singing In The Rain,* full color photo of Gene Kelly, Donald O'Connor, and Debbie Reynolds **75.00**
Lobby Card, *The Crimson Skull,* starring Bill Pickett, 1921, 11 x 14", price for pair **132.00**
Lobby Card, *The Kidnappers,* black and white, manson, 1964 . . . . **20.00**
Magazine, *Life,* "Portrait of Hollywood," May 3, 1937, black and white cov photo of Jean Harlow, 10½ x 14" **15.00**
Magazine, *Modern Screen,* Jun 1935, full color Mae West cov, 124 pp, 8½" x 11½" **35.00**
Magazine, *Motion Picture,* Dec 1927, full color art, 120 pp, 8½ x 11½" **25.00**
Magazine, *Screen Album For 1936,* Dell Publishing Co, sepia, 52 pp, Claudette Colbert cov, 8¼ x 11¼" **20.00**
Magazine, *Sheilah Graham's Hollywood Romances,* Vol #1, Feb 1954, black and white photos, 100 pp, front cov shows color photo of Elizabeth Taylor, 8½ x 10½" **20.00**
Mask, Charlie Chaplin, *The Gold Rush,* movie promotion, diecut paper, fleshtone tint face, 8½ x 10½", unused **65.00**
Movie Poster, *Black Gold,* 14 x 22" **185.00**
Movie Poster, *Bomba And The Jungle Girl,* Monogram Picture, 6 sheet, 1952, 12 x 15" folded **200.00**
Movie Poster, *Panther Girl of the Kongo,* Republic Pictures, full color, starring Phyllis Coates, 10½ x 11½" folded **65.00**
Movie Poster, *Sea of Sand,* British, The Rank Organization, 1958, 12 x 14" folded **100.00**
Movie Poster, *The Real Glory,* United Artists, Gary Cooper, 1939, 27 x 41", linen **230.00**

Poster, *The Sea of Grass,* Spencer Tracy, Katharine Hepburn, paper, ©1947 Loew's Pic, $27\frac{1}{2}$ x 22", $44.00. Photo courtesy Collectors Auction Services.

Movie Poster, *Untamed Women,* United Artists, 1962, 12 x 14" folded **175.00**
Movie Poster, *War and Peace,* Paramount, Audrey Hepburn, Henry Fonda, 1956, 27 x 41", linen **200.00**
Paperback Book, *Cool Hand Luke,* Fawcett, Paul Newman cov, 1965 . . . . **8.00**
Paperback Book, *The Desperate Hours,* Perma Books, Humphrey Bogart and Fredric March cov, 1955 . . . . **10.00**
Photo, sgd, James Caan, black and white **12.00**
Photo, sgd, Joan Crawford, black and white, 5 x 7" **65.00**
Photo, sgd, Maureen O'Hara, black and white, glossy, blue ink "To Rosa From Maureen O'Hara," c1940s, 5 x 7" **50.00**
Program, *Gone With the Wind,* souvenir from first theater performance, full color portraits, cast and production facts, c1939-40, 9 x 12" **65.00**
Sheet Music, *"April Showers,"* from 1949 movie *The Jolson Story,* cartoon illus on border, blue and red **6.00**
Sheet Music, *"Let The Rest of the World Go By,"* from 1947 movie *Irish Eyes Are Smiling,* cov with Dick Haynes and June Haver dancing **10.00**
Sheet Music, *"Moon Song,"* from 1932 movie *Hello Everybody,* Kate Smith cov **10.00**
Sheet Music, *"The Rose In Her Hair,"* from 1935 movie *Broadway Gondolier,* Dick Powell cov **8.00**
Sheet Music, *"You Do,"* from 1945 movie *Mother Wore Tights,* Betty Grable cov **12.00**
Sign, cardboard, Lever Bros "Golden Jubilee" 50th anniversary, black and white photo of Dorothy Lamour in bathrobe holding bar of Lux soap, name and *Road To Utopia* in black, 11 x 14" **65.00**
Tablet, Rock Hudson, color photo, 1950s, 8 x 10" **15.00**
Tin, litho tin, full color portrait of Rudolph Valentino as *The Sheik,* facsimile signature with "Paramount Star," c1921, $7\frac{1}{2}$" d **65.00**
Watch, Jerry Lewis caricature profile portrait center dial face, red leather straps, silvered metal buckle, c1960s **90.00**
Window Card, *To The Shores of Tripoli,* cardboard, red lettering, local showing information printed in black for benefit performance related to WWII war effort, 1942, 14 x 22" **40.00**

MUGS

The problem with every general price guide is that it does not cover the broad sweeping form categories, e.g., wash pitchers and bowls, any longer. A surprising number of individuals still collect this way.

If you stay away from beer mugs, you can find a lot of examples in this category for under $10.00. Look for the unusual, either in form or labeling. Don't forget to fill one now and then and toast your cleverness in collecting these treasures.

Club: Advertising Cup and Mug Collectors of America, P.O. Box 680, Solon, IA 52333.

A & W Root Beer, clear, circular logo **$5.00**
Arby's, A Boy and His Dog series, Norman Rockwell artwork, ©1956 Brown & Bigelow and ©1984 the Norman Rockwell Museum, Inc, mid-1980s **4.00**
Arby's, glass, clear, etched Christmas motif **3.00**
Batman, white milk glass, black Batman illus **6.00**
Big Boy Restaurant, glass, clear **3.00**
Dunkin Donuts, white milk glass **3.00**
Frosty Root Beer, glass, clear, price for 6 . . . . **30.00**
Care Bears, days of week, American Greetings Corp **2.00**
Coca-Cola, pewter, dura-cast, "Enjoy Coke" **30.00**
Davy Crockett, red milk glass, "Davy Crockett, Indian Fighter," Hazel Atlas **6.00**
Fisher Dry Roasted Peanuts, "Mug of Nuts," glass, clear, NFL and college team logos **4.00**
Gulliver's Travels, china, gold accent, Hammerly & Co, England, c1939, $3\frac{1}{4}$" h **125.00**
Hopalong Cassidy, white milk glass, facsimile signature **10.00**
Jiggs, ceramic, yellow cane handle, mkd "Jiggs" and "Puck" on back, 1960s, 5" h **125.00**
Lefty Lemon, plastic, yellow, black, white, and red accents, baseball bat handle, orig mailing box, ©1969 The Pillsbury Co, $3\frac{1}{2}$" h **22.00**
McDonald's, ceramic, celebrating opening 100th store in Japan, 1976 . . . . **70.00**
McDonald's, glass, clear, 1984 Olympics **3.00**
McDonald's, glass, clear, Garfield illus, 1978 . . . . **3.00**
McDonald's, glass, smoke colored, emb Hamburgler playing hockey, 1977, $5\frac{5}{8}$ x $6\frac{1}{4}$" **6.00**
Mickey Mouse, china, color image of Mickey and dog, orange rim and handle, mkd "Made In Japan," 1930, $3\frac{1}{4}$" h **100.00**
Nestle's Quik, plastic, figural bunny head, ear handles, back with raised "Quik," mkd "The Nestle Co Inc," 1970s, 4" h **20.00**
Ranger Joe, white milk glass **6.00**
Ringling Bros Circus, glass, 1976 . . . . **10.00**
Snoopy, white milk glass, Snoopy and Woodstock dancing, "At Times Life is Pure Joy!," **4.00**

Hilliard Oil & Gas, glass, etched lettering and oil derrick scene, scratches, $5\frac{1}{2}$" h, $55.00. Phot courtesy Collectors Auction Services.

MUSICAL INSTRUMENTS & RELATED

Didn't you just love music lessons? Still play your clarinet or trumpet? Probably not! Yet, I bet you still have the instrument. Why is it that you can never seem to throw it out?

The number of antique and classic musical instrument collectors is small, but growing. Actually, most instruments are sold for reuse. As a result, the key is playability. Check out the cost of renting an instrument or purchasing one new. Now you know why prices on "used" instruments are so high. Fifty dollars for a playable instrument of any quality is a bargain price. Of course, it's a bargain only if someone needs and wants to play it. Otherwise, it is fifty dollars ill-spent. Do not overlook music related items.

Clubs: American Musical Instrument Society, Rd. 3 Box 205-B, Franklin, PA 16323; Automatic Musical Instrument Collectors Assoc., 919 Lantern Glow Trail, Dayton, OH 45431; Miniature Piano Enthusiast Club, 633 Pennsylvania Ave., Hagerstown, MD 21740.

Periodicals: *20th Century Guitar,* 135 Oser Ave., Hauppauge, NY 11788; *Concertina & Squeezebox,* P.O. Box 6706, Ithaca, NY 14851; *Vintage Guitar Classics,* P.O. Box 7301, Bismarck, ND 58507.

Banjo, Bacon Banjo Co, style C, 17 fret neck, hardshell case **$175.00**
Banjo, Regina, 18 hooks, 17 fret, peghead and fingerboard inlaid with mother-of-pearl crescent moons, double thick wood and metal rim, tone ring, metal resonator, 1920 patent date **125.00**
Banjo, Wondertone, S S Steward, walnut, marquetry inlay, 1920s **185.00**
Banjo Bag, cloth, green, button closure **10.00**
Book, *History of English Music,* Davey, London, 1895 . . . . **12.00**
Bugle, officer's, c1900 . . . . **100.00**
Catalog, Needham Organ & Piano Co, 1900, 16 pp, 7 x 9¼" **30.00**
Catalog, Rudolph Wurlitzer Co, 1920, 176 pp, 8 x 10¼" **95.00**
Catalog, Thomas A Edison, Inc, 1919, 12 pp, 5 x 8" **20.00**
Clarinet, Laube, 13 keys, 2 rings, Grenadilla wood, C, low pitch **350.00**
Drum, bass, Acme Professional, c1900, 24" d **175.00**
Drum, snare, Acme Professional, c1900, 14" d **175.00**
Guitar, Cambridge, rosewood back adn sides, spruce top, ebony fingerboard, nickel-plated head, early 1900s **145.00**
Guitar Case, canvas, brown, leather bound edges, strap, buckle, and handle, 1890–1900 . . . . **15.00**
Mandolin, Ballinger, mahogany and maple, black wood strips, rosewood cap, faux tortoiseshell guard plate, early 1900s **50.00**
Piano Stool, wood, circular seat, plain design, adjustable height, 1880–1915 . . . . **75.00**
Piccolo, Atlas, cast metal, c1900 . . . . **45.00**
Poster, Woody Herman, "America's New Sensation!," Herman with clarinet illus, c1951, 14 x 22" **185.00**
Saxophone, Dupont, baritone, B-flat, polished brass **350.00**
Sheet Music, *Bugle Call Rag,* The Benny Goodman Story, drawing of Goodman, inset of Steve Allen and Donna Reed, 1951 . . . . **8.00**
Sheet Music, *June in January, Here Is My Heart,* Bing Crosby, Kitty Carlisle, 1934 . . . . **3.00**

Guitar, child's, 6-string, 25½" h, $10.00.

Tambourine, Mexican, c1900 . . . . **80.00**
Toy, Accordion, "Golden Piano Accordian," unknown manufacturer, plastic body, 18 keys, 52 tuned reeds, complete with cardboard case, song book, and harness strap, 1957 . . . . **35.00**
Toy, Golden Symphonette Toy Music Set, Spec-Toys, set of 5 hard plastic musical instruments, 12 x 7" box shows jazz musician laughing with 2 children, c1950s **30.00**
Toy, guitar, Partridge Family, Carnival, plastic, David Cassidy decal on body, 19" l, 1970s **65.00**
Toy, Michael Jackson Cordless Electronic Microphone, orig box, MJJ Productions, Inc, ©1984 . . . . **25.00**
Tuning Hammer, zither, ivory handle, early 1900s **8.00**
Violin, Otto Hoyer, round stick with ivory face, silver and ebony frog, plain sides, silver-sheathed adjuster **300.00**

NAPKIN RINGS

If you really get lucky, you may find a great Victorian silver plated figural napkin ring at a flea market. Chances are that you are going to find napkin rings used by the common man. But do not look down your nose at them. Some are pretty spectacular. If you do not specialize from the beginning, you are going to find yourself going around in circles. Animal shaped rings are a favorite.

Advertising, Worcester Salt, salt sack illus **$15.00**
Bird, wings spread over nest of eggs **145.00**
Boy, holding drumstick, sitting on bench **180.00**
Bulldog, SP, Dirigo Boy **125.00**
Cat, bisque, Japan **20.00**
Cherries, stems, leaf base, ball feet **70.00**
Deer, standing next to fence **175.00**
Dog, glass eyes, 1 paw raised, hammered finish **200.00**

Swans, swimming, individual oval bases, $175.00.

Fawn, standing next to ring, floral garland around neck, emb angel on ruffled edged holder, leaf design base, Reed & Barton **200.00**
Flowers and Butterfly, Noritake **15.00**
Fox, creeping around bush, ring on back, Derby Silver Co **200.00**
Frog, leaping, holder on back, overlapping leaves base, Southington Cutlery **200.00**
Girl, with flowing hair, SS, Art Nouveau, 11½" d **25.00**
Goat, alongside round holder, dec design on top **175.00**
Grapes, celluloid, emb **12.00**
Hen, SS, sgd "Meriden" **195.00**
Hobstars and Diamonds, cut glass **85.00**
Horse, rearing, standing on top of ring, sq arrangement of leaves on base with acorn shaped feet **200.00**
Horse, standing next to ornate ring **175.00**
Iron, James W Tufts **175.00**
Peacock, standing, SS . . . .
Sailboat, bisque, yellow, 2" d **60.00**
Scottie Dog, SS **35.00**
Sheep, reclining, scroll edged base, applied dec center band, Meriden **200.00**
Top Hat and Hand, on sq base. Meriden **200.00**
Turtle, SP **30.00**

NAUTICAL

There is magic in the sea, whether one is reading the novels of Melville, watching Popeye cartoons, or standing on a beach staring at the vast expanse of ocean. Anyone who loves water has something nautical around the house. This is one case where the weathered look is a plus. No one wants a piece of nautical material that appears to have never left the dock.

Club: Nautical Research Guild, 62 Marlboro St., Newburyport, MA 01950.

Periodicals: *Nautical Collector*, One Whole Whale Rd., New London, CT 06320.

Book, *Masting, Mast-making and Rigging of Ships,* Robert Kipping, 1877, orig cov **$90.00**
Business Card, The Island Tool Store, Ship Builders, 171 Lewis St, New York City, green card, black printing, c1875 . . . . **40.00**
Catalog, Marine Hardware, P & F Corbin, New Britain, CT, 278 pp, looseleaf format, illus, brass and bronze hardware, c1920 . . . . **35.00**
Catalog, Steamship and Yacht Ranges, Bramhall, Deane Company, New York, NY, 16 pp, illus, nautical supplies, includes list of boats outfitted by Bramhall, Deane Company **40.00**
Cigar Label, Cutter cigars, sailing yacht flying U S flag, 1887, 5" sq **32.00**
Document, Bill of Sale, "U.S. of America Bill of Sale of Enrolled Vessel," parchment, sailing ship vignette, ... **15.00**
Harpoon Head, whale ivory, incised designs, 3⅛" l **100.00**
Label, Defender Tomatoes, 2 sailing ships along coastline, 9 x 3½" **2.00**
Sea Chart, Chart of the North and Baltic Seas, J Thompson, outline colored, 1816, 23 x 19" **35.00**
Stock Certificate, Pioneer Steamship Co, steamship vignette, ornate border, 1914 . . . . **20.00**

Barrel, souvenir, "From The Timber Of *H.M.S. Cornwall,* Launched Bombay, 1815," 3" h, $50.00.

NEWSBOY COLLECTIBLES

For those of us who heaved newspaper from bike baskets in the rain and snow, then spent hours collecting from subscribers who always seemed to be away, collecting items related to newsboys is a labor of love.

Newsboys and newspaper carriers were given a variety of items to make their jobs easier to retain subscribers. Collectibles range from metal and celluloid newsboy badges, authorizing the sale and delivery of newspapers, to aprons and bags emblazoned with the name of the paper, to awards received for a job well done.

Newsboy collectibles also include the freebies distributed to faithful customers, such as ornate carrier greetings and calendars (most pre-dating World War I), rulers, pocket mirrors, pinback buttons and related memorabilia, all carrying the name of the newspaper or magazine it represented.

Advisor: Tony Lee, P.O. Box 134, Monmouth Junction, NJ, 08852, (973) 429-1531.

Club: Newspaper Memorabilia Collectors Network, P.O. Box 797, Watertown, NY 13601.

Apron, *The Springfield Daily News,* Largest Evening Circulation, shows newsboy, red and white on blue **$45.00**
Badge, celluloid, "I Bring Your Press Earlier Now," blue letters on white clockface, 3" d **15.00**
Badge, celluloid, "I Sell the Fort Worth Telegram," oval, blue letters, white ground **25.00**
Badge, metal, Boston Newsboy, Licensed 1911, octagon shield with leather strap **45.00**
Badge, metal, Newsboy, Woburn, oval, black letters **25.00**

Badge, celluloid, "Evening American League of Junior Salesmen, 578," red and black lettering on yellow ground, 2¼" d, $20.00.

Sign, porcelain, red letters on white ground, 8 x 6", $75.00.

LA PORTE ARGUS-BULLETIN

***La Porte Argus-Bulletin,* Apr 17, 1912, "Night of Horror...," Titantic sinking headline, 16 pp, 16 x 24¹/₂", $200.00.**

Badge, metal, Official Bridgeport Times Carrier, 5-pointed star shield **50.00**
Badge, metal, Oklahoma City Newsboy, small shield **60.00**
Badge, metal, Richmond News Leader vendor, oval, gold **30.00**
Belt Buckle, The Spokesman-Review Merit Award, gold, 2³/₄ x 1³/₄" **30.00**
Blotter, celluloid, Carrier's Greeting 1911, *Daily Sun,* Waukegan, IL **50.00**
Calendar, Aug 1911, *Syracuse Herald,* 2 x 6" **4.00**
Calling Card, brass, Cleveland Press Carrier of the Month, red, white, and blue, 3¹/₂ x 2" **75.00**
Crew List, whale ship *Montpelier,* Sep 6, 1853, names, positions, numbe of shares in voyages to be received **125.00**
Fog Horn, brass, 19th C, 30" l **85.00**
Key Chain, plastic, "I Deliver the Home News," gold on white **2.00**
Patch, Union-Bulletin Star Carrier, round, star in center, gold on green, 5" d **12.00**
Photograph, newsboy on bike wearing *The Record* delivery bag, 2 x 4" **18.00**
Pin, cardboard, Newspaperboys for Radio Free Europe, red, white, and blue, 3¹/₂ x 2" **75.00**
Ribbon, Newsboy's Dinner, Belmont Mansion, July 5, 1880, gold letters on red ground, 11 x 1³/₄" **30.00**
Whistle, plastic, train shape, *Milwaukee Journal/Sentinel,* Spring Sales Campaign, black letters on yellow ground, 1967, 5" l **6.00**

NEWSPAPERS

"Read All About It" is the cry of corner newspaper vendors across the country. Maybe these vendors should be collected. They appear to be a vanishing breed. Some newspapers are collected for their headlines, others because they represent a special day, birthday, or anniversary. Everybody saved the newspaper announcing that JFK was shot. Did you save a paper from the day war was declared against Iraq? I did.

Club: Newspaper Collectors Society of America, 6031 Winterset, Lansing, MI 48911.

Periodical: *Paper Collectors' Marketplace (PCM),* P.O. Box 128, Scandinavia, WI 54977.

1685, *The Observator,* exhorts readers to stop criticisms and begin Reformation at home . . . . **$30.00.**
1783, Nov 6, *Salem Gazette,* U S Congress passed resolution, half pay pension for Revolutionary War officers **55.00**
1799, Feb 15, *Massachusetts Mercury,* front page adv for Mass Mutual Fire Ins, Co, inside notice of meeting to choose committee for honoring George Washington's birthday **35.00**
1813, Sept 1, *Columbian Centinel,* War of 1812 issue, front page report on Naval Affairs on Lake Ontario, British account of capture and destruction of 4 schooners **16.00**
1832, Oct 18, *Boston Atlas Extra,* electoral votes, race againt General Jackson, 8 pp **20.00**
1837, *Sunday Morning News,* political and commercial matters, 4 pp **9.00**
1841, Aug 21, *Philadlephia Saturday Courier,* fire on steamboat *Erie* kills 170, 4 pp **12.00**
1847, Oct, 22, *Lynn News,* articles on discoveries in Egypt, protection of King Louis Phillippe **10.00**
1864, Nov 11, *The Liberator,* Abraham Lincoln re-elected **75.00**
1871, Oct 28, *Leslie's Illustrated,* Great Chicago Fire **150.00**
1873, *Ogden Junction,* joining of 2 railroad track lines at Promontory Point, 4 pp **28.00**
1876, Jul 15, *Chicago Times,* Bull's Braves, Sitting Bull interview **30.00**
1881, Sep 20, *Boston Daily Globe,* Garfield Dies headline, 4 pp **35.00**
1882, Apr 5, *Chicago Tribune,* Jesse James Killed **500.00**
1906, Apr 18, *Chicago Daily News,* San Francisco earthquake **110.00**
1915, May 7, *Boston American,* sinking of *Lusitania,* photos, 20 pp **75.00**
1921, Aug 3, *Nashville Tennessean,* Black Sox acquitted by jury **25.00**
1927, *Galveston Daily News,* Baby Ruth's 60th Homerun **82.00**
1929, *Nashville Tennessean,* Ruth's wife dies in fire **11.00**
1936, Jul 16, *The Sporting News,* Jimmy Fox, Lefty Grove, and Joe Cronin, 12 pp **25.00**
1941, Dec 8, *San Francisco Chronicle,* Pearl Harbor attack **55.00**
1945, May 7, *New York Sun,* German Surrenders headline **14.00**
1963, Jan 13, *The Observer,* 36 pp **16.00**
1977, *Los Angeles Times,* Elvis Presley dies **27.00**

NILOAK POTTERY

When you mention Niloak, most people immediately think of swirled brown, red, and tan pottery, formally known as Mission Ware. However, Niloak also made items in a host of other designs through 1946. These included utilitarian wares and ceramics used by florists that can be bought for a reasonable price. If Niloak prices follow the trend established by Roseville prices, now is the time to stash some of these later pieces away.

Club: Arkansas Pottery Collectors Society, P.O. Box 7617, Little Rock, AR 72217.

Ashtray, figural hat, blue **$7.50**
Bowl, Mission Ware, brown, tan, and turquoise swirl, 8 x 3" **60.00**
Bowl, Mission Ware, white and blue swirl, 7½ x 3½" **250.00**
Bowl, red, cream, blue, and green, 5" d **35.00**
Bud Vase, Ozark Dawn II, Hywood Line, 8" h **25.00**
Candlesticks, pr, Mission Ware, blue, brown, and cream marbleized swirls, 8½" h **125.00**
Chamber Pot, Mission Ware, 6¼ x 2½" **250.00**
Creamer and Sugar, rose, Hywood Line **24.00**
Drinking Glass, Mission Ware, 3½" h **80.00**
Ewer, dark brown, Hywood Line, orig sticker, 6¾" h **15.00**
Figurine, bathtub, green, "Hot Springs, Arkansas," 1½" h **35.00**
Figurine, canoe, white matte, 7½" l **30.00**
Figurine, frog, seated on lily pad, 4" h **35.00**
Figurine, parrot, white, orange accents, 5" h **12.00**
Figurine, Scottie dog, Hywood Line, 3¾" h **45.00**
Figurine, squirrel **20.00**
Match Holder, duck, brown and white swirls **15.00**
Paperweight, rabbit, orig paper label **30.00**
Pitcher, dark green, 7" h **15.00**
Pitcher, eagle, 10" h **30.00**
Pitcher, peacock blue, Art Deco style, incised Hywood, 7½" h **40.00**
Planter, camel, 3" h **22.00**
Planter, clown, blue, incised Niloak, 7½" h **40.00**
Planter, duck, rose, 4½" h **20.00**
Planter, frog, rose glaze, Hywood Line **27.50**
Planter, log, white, 7" l **15.00**
Planter, swallow, green, 2" h **8.50**
Planter, wishing well, dusty rose, 7¼" h **12.00**
Salt and Pepper Shakers, pr, green, 2¼" h **25.00**
Shot Glass, Mission Ware, 2¼" h **75.00**
Vase, green, wing handles, 6" h **25.00**
Vase, aqua, Hywood Line, orig paper label, 8" h **18.00**
Vase, Mission Ware, marbleized swirls, corset top, bulbous bottom, 8" h **125.00**
Vase, Mission Ware, scroddled brown, rust, white, and blue bisque-fired clay, imp "Niloak," 10 x 4¾" **450.00**
Vase, Ozark Dawn II, emb pinecones, Hywood Line, 7½" h **35.00**
Wall Pocket, Mission Ware, conical, 6" h **225.00**

Niloak Pottery Group, Mission Ware, $100.00–$150.00. Photo courtesy Gene Harris Antique Auction Center, Inc.

NIPPON

Nippon is hand painted Japanese porcelain made between 1891 and 1921. The McKinley tariff of 1891 required goods imported into the United States to be marked with their country of origin. Until 1921, goods from Japan were marked "Made in Nippon."

Over two hundred different manufacturer's marks have been discovered for Nippon. The three most popular are the wreath, maple leaf, and rising sun. While marks are important, the key is the theme and quality of the decoration.

Nippon has become quite expensive. Rumors in the field indicate that Japanese buyers are now actively competing with American buyers.

Club: International Nippon Collectors Club, 1417 Steepe St., Fort Meyers, FL 33901.

Ashtray, hand of cards in full house scene, attached rest, green "M" in Wreath mark, 4" d **$35.00**
Basket, handled, hp sailboats scene, enameled beading, blue Rising Sun mark, 5½" h **58.00**
Biscuit Jar, large purple iris on stippled ground, acanthus leaf brackets molded in relief, blue Maple Leaf mark, 7½" h **515.00**
Biscuit Jar, moriage pine cones decor, 2 handles, no lid, unmkd, 5½" h **45.00**
Bowl, floral dec in moriage, blue Maple Leaf mark, 9" l **172.00**
Candlesticks, pr, gold floral bands, magenta "M" in Wreath mark, 6" h **62.00**
Candlesticks, pr, house in meadow scene, Green Kinso Nippon mark, 5½" h **80.00**
Chocolate Pot, moriage dec, unmkd, 9" h **200.00**
Chocolate Set, 6 pc, house in meadow behind black silhouette of trees with gold highlights, green "M" in wreath mark **170.00**
Cuspidor, pr, 1 with windmill scene, other with poppies, mkd "Studio Hand Painted Nippon," 3½" h **115.00**
Demitasse Set, 10 pc, pot, creamer and sugar, 6 cups and saucers, tray, yellow panels between black striping, blue Rising Sun mark **125.00**
Dresser Set, 4 pc, tray, hat pin holder, powder box, and hair receiver, sailboat scene, pink border with gold scrolls and blue jewels, blue TEOH mark **200.00**
Egg Warmer, cartoon style scene, blue Rising Sun mark, 7" d **92.00**
Hatpin Holder, red and pink roses, blue Maple Leaf mark, 4½" h **25.00**

Pitcher, melon rib form, hp rose below gold scrollwork and cartouches, blue Maple Leaf mark, 8½" h, $143.75. Photo courtesy Jackson's Auctioneers and Appraisers.

Hatpin Holder, scenic, jeweled lattice, blue Maple Leaf mark, 4½" h **25.00**
Mug, gamblers motif, smoky ground, green "M" in wreath mark, 5" h **145.00**
Mug, tree lined shore with cherry blossoms scene, green "M" in Wreath mark, 5" h **58.00**
Nappy, sq, handled, mountain cottage scene, orange, green, and black, green "M" wreath mark, 5" sq **35.00**
Nut Dish, chestnuts molded in relief, geen "M" in Wreath mark, 9½" h **58.00**
Nut Dish, leaf shape, acorns molded in relief, green "M" in Wreath mark, 8" l **70.00**
Pitcher, man stealing geese scene, enameled jewels on rim, green Wreath Studio Handpainted mark, 5¼" h **115.00**
Pitcher, melon rib form, hp rose below gold scrollwork and cartouches, blue Maple Leaf mark, 8½" h. **140.00**
Plaque, 3 men on camels scene, beaded rim, green "M" in Wreath mark, 9" d **150.00**
Plaque, girl with horn chasing geese scene, enameled rim, 7½" d **80.00**
Plaque, windmill scene, green "M" in Wreath mark, 7¾" d **35.00**
Plaque, hp white moriage bird, resting on cherry branch, blue Maple Leaf mark, 7¾" d **85.00**
Sauce Dish, cov, with underplate, band of flowers dec, blue Rising Sun mark, 4" d. **35.00**
Soap Dish, cov, with insert, windmill scne, enameled and jeweled borde, blue Maple Leaf mark, 5" l **172.00**
Table Setting, 5 pc, mustard, toothpick, salt and pepper, tray, gold scrolling and cobalt band dec, RC Nippon mark. **160.00**
Tea Set, service for 6, polychrome ivory band of flowers on white ground, green "M" in Wreath mark **25.00**
Toothpick Holder, cottage and apple tree scene, 2 handles, green "M" in Wreath mark, 2¼" h **70.00**
Tray, house in meadow scene, pierced handle of Indian's profile molded in relief, 8¼" l, price for pair. **100.00**
Vase, apple blossoms on blue shaded ground, enameled handles, Blue Sendai mark, 5¼" h. **58.00**
Vase, floral scene accented in moriage, white and brown Wedgwood style shoulder and handles, blue Maple Leaf mark, 8½" h. **200.00**
Vase, flying geese with moriage accents, green "M" in Wreath mark, 6" h. **150.00**
Vase, lake shore at sunset scene, pretzel handles with enamel beading, green "M" in wreath mark, 6" h **62.00**
Vase, large yellow and pink roses over gold ringwork, blue "M" in Wreath mark, 12" h. **115.00**
Vase, scrolled moriage design throughtout, central rooster motif on burgundy ground, hp florals, 11½" h. **345.00**
Vase, tri-corner form, large painted roses bheind scrolled gold acanthus leaves resting on protruding spade shaped feet, 13½" h, price for pair **690.00**

NORITAKE AZALEA

Noritake china in the azalea pattern was first produced in the early 1900s. Several backstamps were used. They will help date your piece.

Azalea pattern wares were distributed as a premium by the Larkin Company of Buffalo and sold by Sears, Roebuck and Company. As a result, it is the most commonly found pattern of Noritake china. Each piece is hand painted, adding individuality to the piece. Hard-to-find examples include children's tea sets and salesmen's samples. Do not ignore the hand painted glassware in the azalea pattern that was manufactured to accompany the china service.

Cranberry Bowl, 5¼" d **$48.00**
Dinner Plate, 10" d **30.00**
Fruit Bowl, 5¼" d **8.00**
Butter Tub. **80.00**
Cake Plate, handled, 9¾" d **38.00**
Celery Dish, 12½" d **45.00**
Compote, 2¾" d **80.00**
Condiment Tray. **30.00**
Creamer, gold finial. **45.00**
Cup and Saucer, flat, 2¼" h **16.00**
Dinner Plate **20.00**
Fruit Bowl. **50.00**
Grill Plate, 10½" d **145.00**
Lemon Dish **20.00**
Luncheon Plte, 8½" d **20.00**
Mustard Jar, cov, no lid, no spoon **30.00**
Olive Dish, 7⅛" d. **52.00**
Platter, oval, 11¾" l. **50.00**
Platter, oval, 16¼" l. **425.00**
Relish, oval, 8¼" l. **25.00**
Snack Set, plate and cup **30.00**
Syrup, cov, with underplate **125.00**
Teapot, cov. **100.00**
Toothpick Holder **100.00**
Tray, glass, hp, 10" l **50.00**
Whipped Cream, with underplate and ladle. **35.00**

NORITAKE CHINA

Noritake is quality Japanese china imported to the United States by the Noritake China company. The company, founded by the Morimura Brothers in Nagoya in 1904, is best known for its dinnerware lines. Over one hundred different marks were used, which are helpful in dating pieces. The Larkin Company of Buffalo, New York, issued several patterns as premiums, including the Azalea, Briarcliff, Linden, Savory, Sheridan, and Tree in the Meadow patterns, which are readily found.

Be careful. Not all Noritake china is what it seems. The company also sold blanks to home decorators. Check the artwork before deciding that a piece is genuine.

Club: Noritake Collectors' Society, 145 Andover Pl., West Hempstead, NY 11552.

Plate, mkd "Noritake, Hand Painted, Made in Japan, ""M" in green, 7¼" d, $35.00.

Asian Song, dinner plate, $20.00.

Blue Moon, dinner plate, $10\frac{3}{8}$" d, $16.00

Asian Song, bread and butter plate, $6\frac{3}{8}$" d	**$6.50**
Asian Song, cup and saucer, ftd, 3" h	**20.00**
Asian Song, fruit bowl, $5\frac{5}{8}$" d	**15.00**
Asian Song, gravy boat, attached underplate	**55.00**
Asian Song, platter, oval, $11\frac{5}{8}$" l	**55.00**
Asian Song, salad plate, $8\frac{3}{8}$" d	**12.00**
Asian Song, sugar bowl, cov	**30.00**
Asian Song, vegetable bowl, oval, $10\frac{1}{8}$" l	**40.00**
Belmont, bread and butter plate, $6\frac{1}{4}$" d	**3.00**
Belmont, cream soup and saucer	**8.00**
Belmont, creamer	**15.00**
Belmont, cup and saucer, flat	**15.00**
Belmont, demitasse saucer	**2.50**
Belmont, fruit bowl, $5\frac{3}{4}$" d	**8.00**
Belmont, platter, oval, $12\frac{1}{8}$" l	**35.00**
Belmont, salad plate, $8\frac{1}{4}$" d	**8.00**
Belmont, vegetable bowl, cov, $10\frac{1}{2}$" d	**30.00**
Blue Haven, bread and butter plate, $3\frac{5}{8}$" d	**6.00**
Blue Haven, butter dish, cov, $\frac{1}{4}$ lb	**30.00**
Blue Haven, cup and saucer, flat	**12.00**
Blue Haven, gravy boat	**40.00**
Blue Haven, salad plate, $8\frac{1}{4}$" d	**12.00**
Blue Haven, salt and pepper shakers, pr	**20.00**
Blue Haven, sugar, cov	**20.00**
Canton, cup and saucer	**15.00**
Canton, demitasse cup	**2.50**
Canton, gravy boat, attached underplate	**30.00**
Canton, salad plate, $7\frac{7}{8}$" d	**8.00**
Canton, soup bowl, coupe shape	**8.00**
Crestmont, bread and butter plate, $6\frac{1}{4}$" d	**2.50**
Crestmont, cereal bowl, lug, $6\frac{3}{4}$" d	**10.00**
Crestmont, demitasse cup and saucer	**16.00**
Crestmont, gravy boat, attached underplate	**35.00**
Crestmont, sugar, cov	**20.00**
Holly, butter pat	**10.00**
Holly, coffeepot, cov	**110.00**
Holly, cup and saucer, ftd	**25.00**
Holly, dinner plate	**15.00**
Holly, mug, $3\frac{5}{8}$" h	**28.00**
Holly, napkin ring	**12.00**
Holly, salad plate, $8\frac{3}{8}$" d	**16.00**
Kilkee Keltcraft, bread and butter plate	**8.00**
Kilkee Keltcraft, casserole, cov, $6\frac{1}{8}$" d	**70.00**
Kilkee Keltcraft, dinner plate, $10\frac{1}{2}$" d	**15.00**
Kilkee Keltcraft, gravy boat	**30.00**
Kilkee Keltcraft, salad plate, $7\frac{5}{8}$" d	**10.00**
Kilkee Keltcraft, salt and pepper shakers, pr	**20.00**
Marseille, bread and butter plate, $6\frac{3}{8}$" d	**6.00**
Marseille, creamer	**20.00**
Marseille, fruit bowl, $5\frac{5}{8}$" d	**8.00**
Marseille, salt and pepper shakers, pr	**30.00**
Marseille, sugar, cov	**12.00**
Marseille, vegetable, cov, 10" l	**40.00**
Mirano, coffeepot, cov, no lid	**60.00**
Mirano, cream soup and saucer	**25.00**
Mirano, cup and saucer, flat	**8.00**
Mirano, dinner plate	**18.00**
Mirano, platter, 12" l	**40.00**
Mirano, sugar, cov	**30.00**
Mirano, vegetable, cov, round	**85.00**
Norma, bread and butter plate, $6\frac{1}{2}$" d	**6.00**
Norma, cup and saucer, ftd	**18.00**
Norma, dinner plate	**20.00**
Norma, sugar, cov	**30.00**

NORITAKE TREE IN THE MEADOW

If you ever want to see variation in a dinnerware pattern, collect Tree in the Meadow. You will go nuts trying to match pieces. In the end you will do what everyone else does. Learn to live with the differences. Is there a lesson here?

Tree in the Meadow was distributed by the Larkin Company of Buffalo, New York. Importation began in the 1920s, almost twenty years after the arrival of azalea pattern wares. Check the backstamp to identify the date of the piece.

Bread and Butter Plate, 6" d	**$10.00**
Butter Tub	**58.00**
Cake Plate, sq, $7\frac{1}{2}$"	**25.00**
Celery Tray	**40.00**
Centerpiece Bowl, wreath with M mark, $7\frac{1}{2}$" d	**105.00**
Coffeepot, cov	**185.00**
Condiment Set, 5 pc, mustard pot, ladle, salt and pepper shakers, and tray	**40.00**
Cruet, oil and vinegar, price for pair	**140.00**
Demitasse Coffeepot	**375.00**
Demitasse Cup and Saucer	**35.00**
Dinner Plate, $8\frac{1}{2}$" d	**15.00**
Fruit Bowl, shell shape, $7\frac{3}{4}$" l	**275.00**
Gravy Boat	**50.00**
Humidor, cov	**375.00**
Lemon Dish, center ring handle, $5\frac{1}{2}$" d	**15.00**
Mug	**100.00**
Nappy	**15.00**
Salt and Pepper Shakers, pr	**30.00**
Snack Set, tray and cup	**25.00**
Tile, chamfered corners, green mark, 5" w	**25.00**

Toothpick Holder, fan shape, 7" 75.00
Vegetable Dish, oval, Noritake mark, 9¾" l 30.00

NUTCRACKERS

Tracking down nutcrackers for a collection can become a real treasure hunt, and a fun one indeed. While no formal invention date has ever been assigned to the nutcracker, we do know that in an early inventory of the contents of the Louvre in Paris (1420) a gilded silver nutcracker is listed. Furthermore, King Henry VIII gave Anne Bolyn a gift of a nutcracker.

The first nutcrackers were probably nothing more than two large stones. The nut was placed on the bottom stone and was hit with a heavier rock. This type is very easy to find. You may have several right in your backyard. Nutcrackers, in fact, are as versatile as people themselves. They come in all shapes, colors, sizes, and weights. There are three basic types of nutcrackers, The first is the screw type. A nut is placed in a hollowed-out interior, and a wooden screw is turned into it. The pressure of the end of the screw against the nut will break or crack the nut open. The second type has a handle that serves as a lever and pivots at one end. Some have even been reinforced with metal and are not uncommon. Last, there is sort which works on indirect pincer action. Two levers are pivoted off center with the short end jaws closing as a result of pressure on the long ends of the levers. Many of this kind are animal that crack the nuts in their mouth. There are many nutcrackers that employ both direct and indirect methods.

Nutcrackers can be as small as two inches and and tall as a six-foot man. Some of the most beautiful nutcrackers are made of wood and are one of a kind specimens. Nutcrackers are made of wood, metal, porcelain or even glass. Some are even made of ivory. Painted nutcrackers in the form of people often have folklore elements. They feature the costumes of a region and are brightly colored. Most of these are from Germany. The most popular makers are Christian Steinbach and Christian Ulbricht. Each year there are new editions and new series. These are true collectibles, and some of them become quite valuable. Have fun collecting, or should I say, "GO NUTS."

Advisor: Claudia J. Davis, E. 4400 English Point Rd., Hayden Lake, ID 83835, (208) 772-6801.

Club: Nutcracker Collectors' Club, 12204 Fox Run Dr., Chesterland, OH 44026.

Aluminum, Miller, Patent No. 3966810, 7" h **$20.00**
Aluminum, nut shape, made in Taiwan 10.00
Brass, kissing couple, East India 75.00
Brass, squirrel, mkd "made in Taiwan," reproduction 10.00
Cast Iron, dog, cracked nut in mouth 45.00
Cast Iron, elephant, painted, 9" l 325.00
Cast Iron, parrot, 10" l 75.00
Cast Iron, squirrel, black, base patent dated May 28, 1878, Patent No. 204,255 . . . . . . 700.00
Nickel Plated Cast Iron, wolf or dog head 75.00
Wooden, barrel shape, screw type, 4 x 2" 5.00
Wooden, bird, screw type, 7" l 100.00
Wooden, Filipino female 25.00
Wooden, fish, 8" l 50.00
Wooden, peasant woman, painted scarf on head 125.00
Wooden, peasant woman, scarf on head, carved spectacles 95.00
Wooden, soldier, brightly painted, made in China 5.00
Wooden soldier, hp vivid colors, no teeth, Milford, USA 150.00

OCCUPIED JAPAN

America occupied Japan from 1945 to 1952. Not all objects made during this period are marked "Occupied Japan." Some were simply marked "Japan" or "Made in Japan." Occupied Japan collectors ignore these two groups. They want to see their favorite words.

Beware of falsely labeled pieces. Rubber-stamp marked pieces have appeared on the market. Apply a little fingernail polish remover. Fake marks will disappear. True marks are under glaze. Of course, if the piece is unglazed to begin with, ignore this test.

Club: The Occupied Japan Club, 29 Freeborn St., Newport, RI 02840.

Ashtray, ceramic, "Georgia" with map illus, mkd "H.L Moore Co., West Yarmouth, Mass," 6⅜" **$25.00**
Ashtray, chrome plated, pierced floral rim, 6¾" d 10.00
Bookends, pr, sailing ships, emb wood 75.00
Cigarrette Set, plated metal, cov box, with Scottie dog, matching lighter 20.00
Cornucopia, china, white, pink roses, gold trim 35.00
Creamer, cottage, 2⅝" h 15.00
Creamer, honeycomb design, blue, 2⅝" h 12.50
Demitasse Cup and Saucer, dragonmotif 20.00
Doll House Furniture, china, refrigerator, white, Philco, 2½" h 18.00
Figure, bird, pink body, gray wings, yellow beak 20.00
Figure, donkey, china 8.00
Figure, Oriental girl, blue and green outfit, gold trim 28.00
Figure, Santa, china, 6½" h 65.00

Wood, nut cracks in back, $100–$175.00.

Trapeze Toy, windup, celluloid figure, wire frame, mkd "My Friend" in globe on acrobat's back, inspection sticker on leg, 1930s, 8¼" h, $60.00.

Figure, swan, wings spread, 3¾" h **18.00**
Lamp Base, colonial couple, bisque, gold trim, 7¼" h. **45.00**
Nodder, donkey, celluloid **40.00**
Perfume Bottle, glass, blue, 4" h. **15.00**
Planter, baby booties, blue trim **8.00**
Planter, dog, brown spots, sticking tongue out, front paws on top hat, 3⅝" h **10.00**
Planter, donkey, pulling wagon, 4¾" l **10.00**
Planter, duckling, with basket **8.00**
Planter, girl, with book, hp **10.00**
Planter, zebra, with basket. **8.00**
Salt and Pepper Shakers, pr, cat **18.00**
Salt and Pepper Shakers, pr, cottage **20.00**
Salt and Pepper Shakers, pr, mug **15.00**
Salt and Pepper Shakers, pr, pigs, large ears **12.00**
Salt and Pepper Shakers, pr, squirrel. **15.00**
Stein, man and woman with dog, 8½" h. **40.00**
Sugar, cov, figural tomato **18.00**
Teapot, cov, blue stoneware, bamboo handle **30.00**
Teapot, cov, floral dec, brown ground, 6½" h **22.00**
Toy, windup, dancer, litho tin and celluloid, man standing by black and white tin street sign "Hollywood" and "Vine," 3½ x 4½ x 8½". **165.00**

OCEAN LINER COLLECTIBLES

Although the age of the clipper ships technically fits into this category, the period that you are most likely to uncover at at flea markets is that of the ocean liner. Don't focus solely on American ships. England, Germany, France, and many other countries had transoceanic liners that competed with and bested American vessels. Today is the age of the cruise ship. This aspect of the category is being largely ignored. Climb aboard and sail into the sunset.

Clubs: Steamship Historical Society of America, Ind., 300 Ray Drive, Ste. #4, Providence, RI 02906; Titanic Historical Society, 208 Main St., Indian Orchard, MA 01151; Titanic International, Inc, P.O. Box 7007, Freehold, NJ 07728.

Ashtray, funnel shape, *SS France,* ceramic, blue, white, red, and black, molded "France" on bottom, 7" l. **$100.00**
Banner, for gangway of *SS United States,* canvas, rect, blue lettering "United States Lines," white ground, red border. **748.00**
Book, *Wreck of the Titanic,* Everett, 320 pp **30.00**
Brooch, *SS France,* figural memaid cradling ocean liner, metal gold colored base, mkd "AB," "Transatlantique," and "Ile de France," 1¾" h. **550.00**
Cabinet Card, 1890s steamboat **36.00**
Champagne Bucket, *Holland America Line,* logo on front, stamped "K. Sola 90 V.A. Waneburg" on bottom, 14" h **200.00**
Compact, *Empress of Canada,* Canadian Pacific Line, Stratton, line flag logo, ship's name in enameled front medallion **40.00**
Creamer, *Cunard White Star,* white, tan and light gray striping, logo on bottom, 1930s, 3" h **50.00**
Cruise Book, *Scythia,* 1929 . . . . **30.00**
Deck Plan, *SS Manhattan,* 10 pp, 1936, unfolds to 28 x 9". **50.00**
Goblet, *Queen Elizabeth II,* Cunard Line, souvenir, etched image and name, Stuart Crystal, #1305 . . . . **225.00**
Menu, *Liberte,* Dec 10, 1956, 4 pp, 9 x 11½". **75.00**
Menu, *SS Oakwood,* American Export Lines, Christmas 1939. . . . . **5.00**
Passenger List, *Transylvania II,* Anchor Line, Jun 22, 1938 . . . . **18.00**
Poster, *SS United States,* full color scene, T C Skinner, 1952, 28 x 17" **200.00**
Sheet Music, "Wreck of the Titanic," A Stauffer Publishing, 1912 . . . . **125.00**
Sign, *Kaiserin Victoria,* tin, steamship sailing from New York harbor image, statue of Liberty background, Fred Pansing illus, 32 x 29½". **800.00**
Thermos, plated, incised *"United States Lines"* around eagle, complete with stopper, 10½" h. **110.00**

Postcard, "T.S.S. Titanic," poster design for White Star Liner, published by Tuck, England, after the sinking, $200.00. Photo courtesy Postcards International.

OLYMPIC COLLECTIBLES

Why has the collecting of Olympic memorabilia lagged behind other sports collectibles?

There are several reasons: the frequency of the Olympics; the international flavor of the event; the "baggage" of social, political and economic factors: and the failure, with few exceptions, to develop and market the super athletes that have participated.

Since the 1984 Los Angeles Olympics, pin collecting has been the driving force bringing the Olympics to public attention. In most cases the initial expense is small and the pin collectors trade frequently, putting the emphasis on pin collecting as a hobby, rather than an investment.

In addition to the above, there is a group of "elite" collectors who collect those items which are directly connected to the athletes and the official Olympic games material.

Olympic items can be found at garage sales, flea markets, auctions, and antique shows. For the beginning collector it would be best to focus on a certain type of collecting category.

1952, Oslo, 6th Winter Olympic Games, dish, ceramic, hp by Br. V., Norway, 6½" d, $287.50. Photo courtesy Ingrid O'Neil Sports and Olympic Memorabilia.

Advisor: Ray Smith, P.O. Box 254, Elizabeth, NJ 07207-0254, (908) 354-5224, Fax (908) 352-1576.

Club: Olympic Pin Collector's Club, 1386 5th St., Schenectady, NY 12303.

1912, Stockholm, 5th Olympic Games, postcard, color illus, Olympic stadium scene, unused **$75.00**
1912, Stockholm, 5th Olympic Games, tin cup, sides illus of Stadium over Olympic Games Stockholm legend, crowned and draped Swedish royal coat of arms and marathon runners crossing finish line **220.00**
1924, Paris, 8th Olympic Games, patch, wool, red, white, and blue American shield with "American Olympic Boxing Team, Paris, 1924," 5½ x 6½" **330.00**
1924, Paris, 8th Olympic Games, pin, silvered, with orange ribbon **175.00**
1924, Paris, 8th Olympic Games, postcard, souvenir, May-Jun 1924, Colombes Stadium, features rugby, pole vault, and running, writing on back **100.00**
1928, Amsterdam, 9th Olympic Games, program, #22, opening ceremony, Jul 28, 24 pp, 2 opening addresses in 4 different languages **120.00**
1928, Amsterdam, 9th Olympic Games, tickets, Jun 16, 1928, LA Coliseum, used **62.00**
1928, Amsterdam, 9th Olympic Games, vase, commemorative, hp, Olympic rings and Amsterdam coat of arms on side, by Koninklyk Goedewaagen, Gouda, Holland **260.00**
1932, Los Angeles, 10th Olympic Games, charm, silver, discus thrower, rings, and Los Angeles Olympic legend **160.00**
1936, Berlin, 11th Olympic Games, coaster, pearl, handmade, color rings over "Berlin," 1 pearl missing, 7½ x 7" **200.00**
1936, Berlin, 11th Olympic Games, pin, silvered, Olympic bell on black Bakelite **200.00**
1936, Garmisch-Partenkirchen, 4th Olympic Games, postcard, Czechoslovakian ice hockey team, autographs on back, used **190.00**
1940, Helsinki, 12th Olympic Games, medal, silvered, Dutch Olympia Cyling Championship, red and black Amsterdam shield, reverse with "20 K.M./1st NWL/A Snijders/'40," with loop and ring **100.00**
1952, Helsinki, 15th Olympic Games, plate, ceramic, light blue, high relief gilt Olympic legend and color rings over Olympic stadium, 9" d **275.00**
1952, Oslo, 6th Olympic Winter Games, pin, silvered, British Olympic Ski Team Supporter **160.00**
1960, Squaw Valley, 8th Olympic Winter Games, flag, silk, British Olympic Games, blue and gold, framed, 6 x 4½" **160.00**
1964, Tokyo, 18th Olympic Games, brochure, Regulations Governing Identity Cards for the Games of the XVIII Olympiad, Tokyo, 31 pp, English and French, 4 x 6" **90.00**
1964, Tokyo, 18th Olympic Games, program, Tokorozawa Clay Pigeon Shooting Range, Oct 15–17, 32 pp, 6 x 8" **90.00**
1968, Grenoble, 10th Olympic Games, ticket, closing ceremony, Feb 18, 1968, Stade de Glace **165.00**
1972, Muenchen, 20th Olympic Games, plate, porcelain, stadium and tower, Munich in background, Kaiser Porcelain Mfg, 7½" d **150.00**
1988, Seoul, 24th Olympic Games, medal, bronze, Steffi Graf facsimile autograph, biographical data on back **95.00**

1956, Melbourne, 16th Summer Olympic Games, souvenir scarf, hand rolled, "Olympic Games/ Melbourne/22 Nov–8 Dec 1956," Made in Japan, $123.00. Photo courtesy GVL Enterprises.

OWL COLLECTIBLES

Most people do not give a hoot about this category, but those who do are serious birds. Like all animal collectors, the only thing owl collectors care about is that their bird is represented.

Bank, tin, owl on side, 2 x 2½" **$50.00**
Bell, brass, emb feathers and features, 4" h **45.00**
Book, *Owls In The Family,* Mowat, Farley, Little, Brown & Co, 1961 . . . . . **.35**
Calendar Plate, 1912, owl on open book, Berlin, NE **25.00**
Candy Container, glass, screw cap closure, 4⅜" h **125.00**
Cheese Dish, cov, glass, Owl and Pusssy Cat, clear **195.00**
Clock, wood, hand carved, 6½" h **110.00**
Creamer, Sugar, and Shaker Set, gold, green trim **20.00**
Decoy, papier-mâché, double faced, glass eyes, brown, small white area on chest **65.00**
Fairy Lamp, double faced figure, pyramid size, frosted cranberry glass, lavender enameled eyes, Clarke base, 4⅛" h **200.00**
Figure, carnival glass, Mosser, 4" h **20.00**
Inkwell, brass, glass inset, hinged lid, pen tray, 2" owl figure, 8 x 4" **75.00**
Match Holder, metal, hanging type, 8" h **18.00**
Medal, Natural History Society of Montreal, bronze, cast, owl with branch in beak, 1¾" **20.00**
Napkin Ring, SP, owl standing **145.00**
Pin, diecut, white celluloid, blue accents, tiny mounted thermometer, early 1900s, 1½" h **30.00**

Fruit Crate Label, Snow Owl Apples, red and yellow, 8½ x 10½", $25.00.

Sugar Shaker, cobalt blue, $925.00.

PADEN CITY

The Paden City Glass Manufacturing Company, Paden City, West Virginia, was founded in 1916. The plant closed in 1951, two years after acquiring the American Glass Company. Paden City glass was handmade in molds. There are no known free-blown examples. Most pieces were unmarked. The key is color. Among the most popular are opal (opaque white), dark green (forest), and red. The company did not produce opalescent glass.

Berry Bowl, Crows Foot, amber, 5¼" sq **$7.00**
Cake Plate, silver overlay, crystal ground, 3 toed, 12" d. **15.00**
Candy Dish, Mrs B, 3 sections, red, gold trim **50.00**
Cocktail Shaker, Utopia, 3 pc, crystal **165.00**
Compote, Gothic Garden, yellow, 7" d. **35.00**
Compote, Peacock Rose, green, ruffled edge **55.00**
Creamer and Sugar, Luli, ruby **40.00**
Cup and Saucer, Crows Foot, amber, sq **7.00**
Figure, rooster **70.00**
Goblet, Cupid **15.00**
Goblet, Penny Line, ruby, 6" h **20.00**
Gravy Boat, with underplate, pink, gold encrusted rim **40.00**
Ice Bucket, Black Forest, pink **75.00**
Ice Bucket, Party Line, amber **25.00**
Ice Cream Soda, Party Line, ftd, pink, 7" h **25.00**
Pitcher, cov, Party, green **60.00**
Plate, Chavalier Line 90, ruby, 8" d **15.00**
Plate, Crows Foot, amber, 9" d. **10.00**
Plate, Largo, blue, ftd **18.00**
Plate, Wotta Line, ruby, 8" d **7.00**
Salt and Pepper Shakers, pr, Party Line, orig tops **45.00**
Server, Black Forest, green, center handle **35.00**
Serving Plate, Gazebo Etch, 11¼" d **38.00**
Tumbler, Penny Line, red, 6" h **12.00**
Vase, Black Forest, black, 10" h **110.00**
Vase, Utopia, green, 10½" h **125.00**

PAINT-BY-NUMBER SETS

Paint-By-Number Sets are most frequently collected according to subject matter. Crossover collectors are the biggest customers. To date there is little interest in the category by itself. Perhaps someday a generic animal picture painted on black velvet will be collectible in its own right.

Batman Sparkle Paint Set, Kenner, 6 pre-numbered sketches of Batman, 1966 . . . . . **$45.00**
Buck Rogers, Craft Master, 1980s **10.00**
Bullwinkle and Rocky Presto Sparkle Painting Set, 6 pictures, 2 comic strip panels, Kenner, 1962 . . . . . **35.00**
Combat Oil Paint By Number Set, Hasbro, 1963 . . . . . **100.00**
Flipper "Stardust" Paint Set, Hasbro, two 7 x 11" pictures, 6 paint vials, application, and instruciton sheet, 1966 . . . . . **20.00**
Flying Nun Paint By Number Set, Hasbro, 1967 . . . . . **50.00**
Green Hornet Paint By Number Set, Hasbro, 1966 . . . . . **90.00**
Herman & Katnip Deep View Paint Set, Pressman, box contains 3-D picture with painted background, 6 paints, water bowl, and brush, 1961 . . . . . **55.00**
Howdy Doody Paint Set, Milton Bradley, 1950s **50.00**
Hulk Comics Paint By Number Set, Hasbro, No. 1, 1982 . . . . . **15.00**
Jonny Quest Paint By Number Set, Transogram, 1965 . . . . . **130.00**
Maverick Oil Painting By Numbers Set, Hasbro, ©Warner Bros, 1958 . . . . . **200.00**
Pebbles and Bamm Bamm Paint By Numbering Coloring Set, Transogram, 8 inlaid paint tablets, plastic paint tray, 8 pre-numbered sketches, and brush, 1965 . . . . . **55.00**
Popeye Paint By Number Set, Hasbro, 1981 . . . . . **10.00**
Sleeping Beauty Magic Paint Set, Whitman **50.00**
Snoopy Paint By Number Set, Craft House, 1980s **20.00**
Space Traveler Paint-By-Number Set, Standard Toykraft, 1950s **100.00**
Star Trek Paint By Number Set, Hasbro, 1972 . . . . . **30.00**
Superman Paint By Number Watercolor Set, Transogram, 1954 . . . . . **200.00**
Wyatt Earp Paint By Number Set, Transogram, 1958 . . . . . **60.00**

PAINT CANS

Furniture, automobile and interior design can be viewed on the labels of early paint cans. Paint companies took great pride in the way their labels looked, and thus the labels themselves are works of art. The fine, lavish colors and art ability of the designs on these cans can never be duplicated by computer.

Paint cans were opened, used and thrown away, thus making the hunt for mint cans more of a challenge. Gallon cans are much harder to find in good condition, as paint was spilled over the edges and stored in damp outbuildings and the cans were then thrown away. The small cans, on the other hand, were purchased and then stored in a cabinet for future use.

Paint can collectors should look for unusual shapes and sizes. Colorful paper or tin labels with complex designs are the most desirable, but will also cost more. Full paint cans are also more desirable. There are still lots of wonderful 1930s cans available to collectors at a collector's price.

Chicago Paints, Inc, Seminole Truck & Tractor Enamel, paper label with Indian Chief, gal, $75.00, qt, $35.00.

Ohio Varnish Co, Everwhite Enamel, cone-style can, metal label, gal, $325.00, qt, $175.00.

The Steel Company of Canada Limited, Tiger White Lead, metal label, gal, $125.00.

Advisor: Irene Davis, 27036 Withams Rd., Oak Hall, VA 23416, (757) 824-5524.

August Miller & Son, Oriole Ready Mix, paper label with Baltimore Oriole, gal **$55.00**
Baer Bros, Bruin Paint, paper label, 2 bears painting wall, gal **95.00**
Baer Bros, Bruin Wire Screen Enamel, 2 bears painting screen, pt **65.00**
Boston Varnish Co, Dinah black, paper label with black mammies, half pint **95.00**
Colonial Works, Lus-Tro-Lac, paper label with car, woman, and boat, qt **33.00**
Colonial Works, Wagon and Implement Paint, paper label with wagon and plow, 1/8 gal **45.00**
Cook Paint and Varnish Co, Rapidry Enamel metal label with boy painting, pt **45.00**
Dutch Boy, pail, black with yellow print, various sizes **25.00**
Dutch Boy, white lead, metal label, yellow and black with boy, half pt **12.00**
Hirshberg Paint Co, Stag Wood Stain, paper label with stag, qt **22.00**
John Lucas Co, wagon paint, paper label with wagon, qt **40.00**
Larkin Automobile, paper label with colonial home, qt **23.00**
Martin Seymour, Glo-Tone, paper label with furniture, 1930s, pt **15.00**
McCloskey Varnish Co, paper label of race horse, qt **33.00**
Nu-Enamel Paint Co, Nu-Enamel Automobile Finish, tin label, 1930s automobile, pt **18.00**
Ohio Varnish Co, Everwhite Enamel, cone style can, metal label, qt **175.00**
Pittsburg Plate Glass Co, Wallhide, paper label with sun logo, gal **15.00**

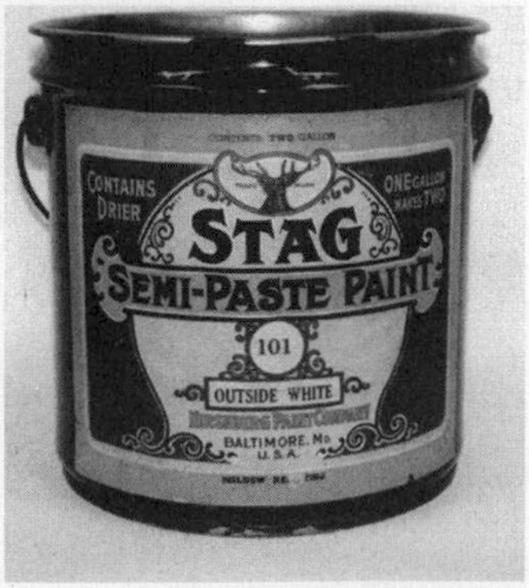

Hirshberg Paint Co, Stag Semi-Paste Paint, paper label, gal, $125.00.

Pittsburg Plate Glass Co, Waterspan Enamel, paper label with sun logo, pt **25.00**
Platt and Lambert. Effecto Automotive, paper label with 1930s automobile, pt **34.00**
Sapolin Paint, Mel-Lux Enamel, paper label with paint brush, qt **15.00**
Sapolin Paint, Varnish Stain, paper label, "free sample" **25.00**
Sherwin-Williams, Enameloid, paper label with blue and yellow, qt **10.00**
Sherwin-Williams, Enameloid, paper label with "Cover the Earth," pt **15.00**
Sherwin-Williams, House Paint, paper label with blue ground, qt **15.00**
Sherwin-Williams, Soda Bottle, 4½" h paper label, "Hat Brite" **30.00**
Technical Color and Chemical, high gloss polyurethane enamel, metal label with full devil, 1900s **15.00**
Technical Color and Chemical, Red Devil, paper label with devil face, qt **20.00**
Tredennick Paint Mfg Co, Little Trojan, paper label with house, half pt **20.00**
Yarnall Paint Co, LiqUidEne, enamel, orange paper label with woman, pt **15.00**
Yarnall Paint Co, LiqUidEne, enamel, orange paper label with woman and dresser, pt **15.00**
Yarnall Paint Co, LiqUidEne, varnish stain, orange paper label with woman, pt **15.00**

PAPERBACK BOOKS

This is a category with millions of titles and billions of copies. Keep this in mind before paying a high price for anything.

A great deal of the value of paperbacks rests in the cover art. A risqué lady can raise prices as well as blood pressure. Great art can make up for a lousy story by an insignificant author. However, nothing can make up for a book's being in poor condition, a fate which has befallen a large number of paperbacks.

For a detailed listing, I recommend consulting Kevin Hancer's *Hancer's Price Guide to Paperback Books, Third Edition* (Wallace-Homestead, 1990, out-of-print) and Jon Warren's *The Official Price Guide to Paperbacks* (House of Collectibles, 1991). Both are organized by company first and then issue number. Hence, when trying to locate a book, publisher and code number are more important than author and title.

The vast majority of paperbacks sell in the 50¢ to $2.50 range.

Periodical: *Paperback Parade*, P.O. Box 209, Brooklyn, NY 11228.

PAPER DOLLS

Paper dolls have already been through one craze cycle and appear to be in the midst of another. The publication of Mary Young's *A Collector's Guide To Magazine Paper Dolls: An Identification & Value Guide* (Collector Books, 1990) is one indication of the craze. It also introduces a slightly different approach to the subject than the traditional paper doll book.

The best way to collect paper dolls is in uncut books, sheets, and boxed sets. Dolls that have been cut out, but still have all their clothing and accessories, sell for fifty percent or less of their uncut value.

Paper doll collectors have no desire to play with their dolls. They just want to admire them and enjoy the satisfaction of owning them.

Club: The Original Paper Doll Artists Guild, P.O. Box 14, Kingfield, ME 04947.

Newsletters: *Paper Doll News*, P.O. Box 807, Vivian, LA 71082; *Yesterday's Paper Dolls*, 808 Lee Ave, Tifton, GA 31794.

Periodical: *Paperdoll Review*, P.O. Box 485, Princeton, IN 47670.

Ann Sheridan, Whitman, #986, 1944 . . . . **$125.00**
Barbie and Ken, Whitman, 1970 . . . . **8.00**
Betsy McCall, Artcraft, ©1965 McCall **15.00**
Betty Grable, Whitman, 1943 . . . . **90.00**
Bridal Party, Whitman, 1964 . . . . **15.00**
Chatty Baby, Whitman, 1963 . . . . **25.00**
Chitty Chitty Bang Bang, Whitman, 1968 . . . . **15.00**
Dinah Shore, Whitman, 1958, folder **80.00**
Dolly Dingle, uncut sheet **30.00**
Grace Kelly, Whitman, 1956 . . . . **90.00**
Jane Russell, Saalfield, 1955 . . . . **65.00**
Janet Leigh Cutouts & Coloring, Merrill Publishing **45.00**
Julie Andrews, Saalfield, 1957 . . . . **40.00**
Let's Play Paper Dolls, McLoughlin, 1938 . . . . **20.00**
Kewpie-Kin Paper Doll Book, Saalfield, 1967 . . . . **20.00**
Lana Turner, Whitman, 1947 . . . . **65.00**
Lennon Sisters, Whitman, ©1962 Teleklew Productions **40.00**
Malibu Francie, Lowe, 1973 . . . . **10.00**
Miss America Magic Doll, Parker Bros, 1953 . . . . **18.00**
Mod Fashions Paper Doll Book Featuring Jane Fonda, Saalfield, 1966 . . . . **40.00**
Natalie Wood, Whitman, 1958 . . . . **75.00**
Shirley Temple, Saalfield, Christmas, uncut **60.00**
Sleeping Beauty, Whitman, 1970 . . . . **60.00**

National Velvet Cut-Outs, Whitman, #1948, ©1962, $35.00.

Storybook Kiddles Sweethearts, Whitman, ©1969 Mattel **40.00**
Swing Your Partners, Abbott, 1940s **40.00**
The Models, Saalfield, 1973 . . . . **20.00**
The Waltons, Whitman, 1974 . . . . **8.00**
Tricia Nixon Paper Doll & Game Book, Saalfield, 1970 . . . . . . **15.00**
Wishnik Paperdoll Book, Whitman, ©1966 Uneeda Doll **20.00**

PAPER MONEY

People hid money in the strangest places. Occasionally it turns up at flea markets. Likewise early paper money came in a variety of forms and sizes quite different from modern paper currency. Essentially, paper money breaks down into three groups—money issued by the federal government, by individual states, and by private banks, businesses, or individuals. Money from the last group is designated as obsolete bank notes.

As with coins, condition is everything. Paper money that has been heavily circulated is worth only a fraction of the value of a bill in excellent condition. Proper grading rests in the hands of coin dealers. Krause Publications (700 East State Street, Iola, WI 54990) is a leading publisher in the area of coinage and currency. *Bank Note Reporter*, a Krause newspaper, keeps collectors up-to-date on current developments in the currency field. There is a wealth of information available to identify and price any bill that you find. Before you sell or turn in that old bill for face value, do your homework. It may be worth more than a Continental, which by the way, continues to be a real "dog" in the paper money field.

PAPERWEIGHTS

This is a tough category. Learning to tell the difference between modern and antique paperweights takes years. Your best approach at a flea market is to treat each weight as modern. If you get lucky and pay modern paperweight prices for an antique weight, you are ahead. If you pay antique prices for a modern paperweight, you lose and lose big.

Paperweights divide into antique (prior to 1945) and modern. Modern breaks down into early modern (1945 to 1980) and contemporary (1980 and later). There is a great deal of speculation going on in the area of contemporary paperweights. It is not a place for amateurs or those with money they can ill afford to lose. If you are not certain, do not buy.

Clubs: International Paperweight Society, 761 Chestnut St., Santa Cruz, CA 95060; Paperweight Collectors Assoc., Inc., P.O. Box 1059, Easthampton, MA 01027.

Advertising, Best Pig Forceps, compliments J Reimers, Davenport, IA, glass, pig shape, 6" d **$100.00**
Advertising, Chisholm Steel Shovel works, Cleveland, OH, glass **65.00**
Advertising, Crane Bros, dark luster white metal, figural crane, feeding on small frog, inscription "Crane Bro's/Westfield, Mass/Gold Medal Linen Ledger & Record Papers," underside inscription "Use Crane Bro's Gold medal Linen Ledger Paper In All Your Blank Books," c1930s, 3" d **85.00**
Advertising, Donnelly Machine Co, Brockton, MA, rect, scalloped edge, vintage factory, 3 x 4½" **58.00**
Advertising, Dutch Boy Paints, figural Dutch Boy painter with inscription on base front, 4" h **90.00**

Apple with Worm, modern, orange, etched design, Zimmerman, $50.00.

Advertising, Henry Hooker & Co, rect, horse drawn carriage, 2 1/2 x 4" 115.00
Advertising, Heywood Shoe, rect, vintage shoe and "Heywood Is In It," 2 1/2 x 4" 46.00
Advertising, Laco Drawn Wire Quality, ceramic, whtie ground, black letters, half-lightbulb shape, backstamped "Rosenthal" 60.00
Advertising, New England Mutual Accident Assoc, rect, multicolored, vintage railroad 1 side, paddle stea boat other side, 2 1/2 x 4". . . . 144.00
Advertising, Northern Wood Fuel Co, metal, figural sawn tree tunk log on base with company name inscribed on both sides, and "1902-Chicago-1923," orig green felt skid pad on underside, 2 x 2 x 5" 75.00
Advertising, Oscar R Boehne & Co, rect, gold scale, 2 1/2 x 4" 70.00
Advertising, Pike Sharpening Stones, glass, whetstone block, fused glass cov on oil-stone bae, multicolored paper label pictures pike and sharpening tools, c1900s, 1/2 x 2 x 3" 65.00
Advertising, Star Line Goods, cast iron, brass colroed, figural turtle, 1" oval celluloid shell, inscription in center of shell, 1904 copyright, 1 3/4 x 2 1/4 x 1/2" 80.00
Character, Snoopy and Woodstock, glass, color image of Snoopy hugging Woodstock, red and blue ground, applied green felt base on underside, ©1965 United Features Syndicate, Inc, c1980, 2 3/4" d 15.00
Commemorative, astronauts, sulphide, 4 astronauts cameo, translucent turquoise ground, D'Albret, limited edition of 1,000, 1971, 3 7/8"d 143.00
Commemorative, Chesapeake & Ohio Railways, glass, inner paper full color portrait on yellow ground, with "Peake—Chessie's Old Man," late 1940s–early 1950s, 3/4 x 2 3/4 x 4 1/4" 65.00
Commemorative, Churchill Downs, Louisville, KY, metal, horseshoe image, center shield, brass finish, early 1900s, 2 1/4 x 2 1/2". . . . 25.00
Commemorative, Eleanor Roosevelt, double overlay sulphide, amethyst over white double overlay with cameo insdie, ftd, 3" d. . . . 275.00
Commemorative, Gen George G Meade, glass, sepia portrait image, inscribed "Gettysburgh 1863," 1920s, 2 3/4 x 4 1/4 x 3/4". . . . 40.00
Commemorative, Mahatma Gandhi, sulphide, cameo on star cut ground, circular top facet with fluted sides, 2 7/8" d 220.00
Commemorative, Prince Charles and Lady Diana Spencer, etched portraits, purple ground, Caithness, 3" d 175.00
Commemorative, Titanic, glass, mirror underside, paper ship image with 3 hand-drawn flags, hand-lettered "RMS Titanic" in black, c1912, 7/8 x 2 3/4 x 4 1/4" 175.00
Political, McKinley, glass, rect, sepia photo, inscribed "Pres McKinley, Wife and Home, Canton, O," mkd "Cent Glass & Nov Co" on reverse, 1900s, 1 x 2 1/2 x 4". . . . 50.00
Souvenir, 1939 New York World's Fair, copper luster white metal, detailed replica of Theme Center with inscription on perimeter of base "New York World's Fair" 40.00

PARKING METERS

I have seen them for sale. I have even been tempted to buy one. The meter was a lamp base, complete with new lamp wiring and an attractive shade. To make the light work, you put a coin in the meter. I'm not sure why, but they are rather pricey, usually in the $50 to $100 range. Maybe it has something to do with the fine that you will pay if you obtain one illegally. Might be a good idea to stash a few coin-operated meters away. Have you experienced one of the new electronic meters? Isn't progress wonderful?

PATRIOTIC COLLECTIBLES

Americans love symbols. We express our patriotism through eagles, flags and shields, the Liberty Bell, Statue of Liberty, and Uncle Sam. We even throw in a few patriots, such as Benjamin Franklin.

Club: Statue of Liberty Collectors' Club, 26601 Bernwood Rd., Cleveland, OH 44122.

Note: For addition listings see Flags and Flag Collectibles.

Benjamin Franklin, bookends, pr, cast white metal, bronzed $35.00
Benjamin Franklin, pinback button, "Franklin Life Insurance Co," sepia, bust portrait, red rim, white lettering, c1910, 1/4" d 12.00
Eagle, cookie cutter, tin, 6 1/2" l 85.00
Eagle, pin, diecut silvered metal eagle with shield symbol on chest, holding miniature replica brass alarm clock, c1890. . . . 30.00
Eagle, pinback button, All American Shoe, red, white, and blue, brown eagle against cloudy sky, red inscription, orig back paper ad. . . . 18.00
Flag, clock, mantel, God Bless America, American flag second hand waves back and forth, Howard Miller 125.00

Statue of Liberty, jar, American, clear glass, smooth base, ground rim, orig green and gold paint, c1886–90, 12 1/2" h, $70.00. Photo courtesy Glass-Works Auctions.

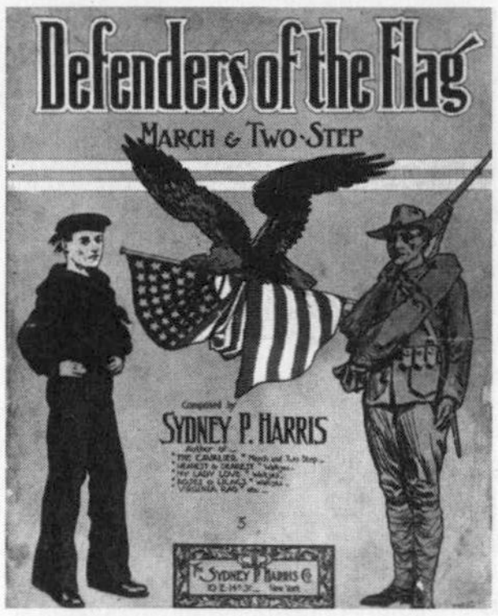

Flag, sheet music, "Defenders of the Flag," march, 2-step, music by Sydney P. Harris, cov by Starmer, published by Sydney P. Harris & Co., NY, ©1909, incomplete, $3.00.

Flag, matchbook cover, "I am proud to be an American," outline illus of person saluting, red, white, and blue, Match Corp of America, Chicago, empty **5.00**
Flag, sheet music, "Your Flag And My Flag," H Woods **10.00**
Flag and Shield, pinback button, litho tin, Humphrey/Muskie Jugate, black adn white photos, white ground, red, white, and blue shield, 1¾" d **10.00**
George Washington, tray, porcelain, George and Martha Washington portraits, Mt Vernon, VA, "Washington's Home, Mt Vernon, VA" in center, multicolored, enhanced enameling, sq corners, gold trim, mkd "Germany," 7½ x 11" **75.00**
Liberty Bell, bank, pot metal and wood, brown, mkd "USA, 1947," 4½" h **32.00**
Liberty Bell, bookmark, diecut, celluloid, shield shape, red, white, and blue, bronze colored Liberty Bell, bank name on back, c1920 . . . . **40.00**
Liberty Bell, bread plate, glass, clear, Liberty Bell, Constitution signers' names, emb 1776–1876 . . . . **80.00**
Liberty Bell, paperweight, cast iron, figural, 6" h **50.00**
Liberty Bell, pinback button, General Accident Insurance, Philadelphia, center Liberty Bell, blue and white, c1901, ¾" d **10.00**
Liberty Bell, sheet music, "Liberty Bell Time To Ring Again," 1918 . . . . **3.50**
Shield, stickpin, silvered brass, engraved "McK" for McKinley below 3 tiny glass stone acents in red, white, and blue, c1896, 1¾" h **20.00**
Stars and Stripes, drinking glass, Willkie, red and blue stars, white stripes, white Willkie face illus, for nomination event Aug 17, 1940, 4½" h **20.00**
Statue of Liberty, hat, heavy paper, "Liberty," red, white, and blue, picture of Statue of Liberty, c1918 . . . . **20.00**
Statue of Liberty, milk bottle, Augusta Dairies, Augusta, GA, clear glass, emb, orange lettering, Statue of Liberty flanked by company name, "God Bless America," and "The Land of The Free," qt, 9½" h **85.00**
Statue of Liberty, night light, white metal, dark copper finish, Statue of Liberty, battery operated, c1920, 5½" h **35.00**
Uncle Sam, advertising trade card, Frank Millers Blacking adv, Uncle Sam type shaving with straight razor, using polished boot as mirror, eagle looking at reflection in other boot, 3½ x 5¼" **18.00**
Uncle Sam, figure, Uncle Sam holding defense gun and binoculars, white pants, red stripe, blue belt, c1917, 10" h **35.00**
Uncle Sam, ornament, Uncle Sam Keepsake Ornament, pressed tin, Hallmark, 1984 . . . . **25.00**
Uncle Sam, pinback button, East End Imporvement Society, multicolored, Uncle Sam in center surrounded by firecrackers, July 4th 1920 celebration, black letteirng, 1¾" d **75.00**
Uncle Sam, pinback button, "National IB of EW Defense," civilian worker shaking hands with Uncle Sam, industrial background **15.00**
Uncle Sam, pinback button, Uncle Sam, multicolored, back paper for "Play Button Gum" series, c1920 . . . . **15.00**
Uncle Sam, pinback button, "Uncle Sam Citizenship Training Corps," multicolored, lieutenant rank, c1920, ⅞" d **18.00**
Uncle Sam, salt and pepper shakers, pr, painted plaster, figural, glossy white, black, and red accents, red, white, and blue top hat, 1½ x 2½ x 2" **45.00**
Uncle Sam, sign, "Use Jaxon Soap," Uncle Sam leaning on fence, jack knife in hand, whittling on stick, easel back, 4½ x 8" **25.00**

PEANUTS

Peanuts is a newspaper cartoon strip written and illustrated by Charles M. Schulz. The strip started about 1950 and starred a boy named Charlie Brown and his dog, Snoopy. Its popularity grew slowly. In 1955, merchandising was begun with the hope of expanding the strip's popularity. By the 1970s Charlie Brown and the gang were more than just cartoon strip characters. They greeted every holiday with TV specials; their images adorned lunch boxes, pencils, pins, T-shirts, and stuffed toys. Macy's Thanksgiving Day Parade wouldn't be complete without a huge Snoopy floating down Seventh Avenue.

Club: Peanuts Collector Club, Inc., 539 Sudden Valley, Bellingham, WA 98226.

Activity Book, Peanuts Trace and Color, Saalfield, 1960s **$25.00**
After Shave Bottle, milk glass, figural Snoopy, wearing baseball cap, Avon, 1970s **10.00**
Bank, Peppermint Patty, baseball series, papier-mâché, Determined, 1973 . . . . **45.00**
Bank, Woodstock, standing, papier-mâché, #1503, Determined, 1970s **12.00**
Bell, Snoopy and the Beaglescouts, Schmid, orig box, 1984 . . . . **25.00**
Book, *Happiness Is a Warm Puppy,* Charles M Schulz, Determined, hard cov, Lucy hugging Snoopy cov illus, 1962 . . . . **3.00**
Brush and Comb Set, plastic, figural Snoopy brush, Avon, 1970 . . . . **15.00**
Colorforms, Snoopy & Belle, 1970–80s **15.00**
Comic Book, Peanuts, Dell, #878, Charlie Brown and Snoopy watching TV cov illus, 1958 . . . . **20.00**
Cookie Cutter, plastic, orange, Snoopy lying on pumpkin, Hallmark, 1972, 5½ x 6½", MIP **150.00**
Doll, Lucy, plastic, jointed, red dress, shoes, Determined, #378, orig box, 1970s **35.00**
Doll, Snoopy Tub-Time, rubber, Knickerbocker, 1980s **25.00**
Drinking Glass, set of 8, Snoopy and Woodstock, rainbow background, Anchor Hocking, 1980s **20.00**
Figure, Woodstock on skateboard, Aviva, 1970s **15.00**
Frame, desk top **20.00**
Game, Peanuts, Selchow & Righter, 1959 . . . . **45.00**
Game, Snoopy Come Home, Milton Bradley, 1973 . . . . **15.00**

Limited Edition Plate, Schmid, Peanuts Christmas, "Snoopy Guides The Sleigh," Charles Schulz, ©1972 United Features Syndicate, Inc.," $10.00.

Ice Bucket, vinyl, white, dancing Snoopy and Woodstock on rainbow illus, Shelton Ware, #9002, 1979 . . . . . . **50.00**
Jam Jar, cov, ceramic, Snoopy on lid, 1970s, 4¼" h. **30.00**
Magnets, set of 2, ceramic, Snoopy on top of dog house, 1994 . . . . . . **6.00**
Marionette, Snoopy, Pelham Puppets, England, 1979, 8" h **50.00**
Mirror, Snoopy in hot-air balloon surrounded by flying Woodstocks illus, Determined, 1970s, 8 x 10½" **20.00**
Napkin, paper, Snoopy as Red Baron, "A Distinguished Combat Hero!/Snoopy For President," Hallmark, 1970s, 5 x 5", orig pkg **10.00**
Pillow, cotton, stuffed, Snoopy, 1970s **8.00**
Planter, ceramic, Snoopy, standing, hand on hip, "Merry Christmas," 1970s **65.00**
Sheet, cotton, Snoopy and Woodstock on top of dog house scene, "Love Is A Friend," 1970s **15.00**
Soap Dish, Snoopy, lying on back, stomach is soap holder, Avon, 1968 . . . . . . **15.00**
Soap Dispenser, Snoopy Soaper, plastic, Kenner, 1975 . . . . . . **35.00**
Spoon, baby's, ST, figural Snoopy on end, Determined, 1980s **3.00**
Toy, guitar, plastic, Snoopy and Charlie Brown playing baseball scene on front, windup handle on side, Mattel, 1960s **25.00**
Toy, pull type, plastic, Snoopy holding Woodstock, Snoopy's ears twirl, Romper Room/Hasbro, 1980s **15.00**

PENCIL CLIPS AND PAPER CLIPS

Paper clips clip pieces of paper together. Pencil clips hold pencils in one's pocket. Both were popular; both were used to advertise products. Neither form is used much today. After seeing several hundred examples, I think they should be missed.

The listings below are for paper clips with celluloid buttons and metal spring clips, all dating from the early 1900s. Pencil clips have celluloid buttons with metal pencil holders.

PAPER CLIPS

Art Deco, ornate design, SS, mkd "B.K. & Co." **$80.00**
Art Deco, red and black scarab on brass, 3" l **65.00**
Boston Varnish Co, multicolored, gold inscription, 1¼" l **30.00**
Figural, elephant's head, brass, 6" l **15.00**
Figural, hand, brass, English, 5" h **30.00**
Figural, heart, SS, dragons, cherubs, and gargoyle face at base, English, 5" l **125.00**
Figural, pineapple, brass, 3½" l **10.00**
Figural, whale, brass, tail forms clip **8.00**
Lane Mfg Co, Montpelier, VT, black and white sawmill illus, 2½" l **25.00**
Peacock Condoms, litho metal, yellow, green, and red design, c1940, 2 x 2" **35.00**

PENCIL CLIPS

Allentown Dairy Co, Inc, "Drink More Milk," green and white **$24.00**
Allis Chalmers, "AC, Suggestions $ Pay $," black and orange ground **22.00**
Amsterdam Broom Co, Amsterdam, NY, black on white ground **25.00**
Braender Tires, image of dog and tire, red, white, and blue **40.00**
Chevrolet, "We Are Out to Beat Last Year's Record," white on blue ground **17.00**
Clark Certified Concrete, blue on white ground, clip foxed **20.00**
Dreikorn's Bread, "Reach For Dreikorn's," bread loaf, multicolor **34.00**
Gerber, image of Gerber baby, blue on white ground **30.00**
Habbersett's Quality Pork Products, red and blue on cream ground **36.00**
HAS Novelties Ltd, "We Make Buttons," green on yellow ground **14.00**
Home Kraft Fresh Bread, red and blue on white ground **30.00**
Keen Kutter, "The Reflection of Quality," red, black, and white **25.00**
Merchant's Hotel, W S Bachman, Reading, red and blue on white ground **33.00**
Missouri Pacific Lines, gray, red, and white **18.00**
Peter G Teneyck for Congress, image of Teneyck, black and white **42.00**
Shapleigh Hardware Co, "Diamond Edge...," black, red, and white **40.00**

PENNANTS, FELT

Pennants were produced in large enough quantities for collectors to be picky. Buy pennants only if they are in good condition. Images and lettering should be crisp and the pennant should show no signs of moth or insect damage.

When storing pennants, keep them flat or roll them on a cylinder. Do not fold! Creases left from years of folding can be very difficult to remove.

Indianapolis Speedway, 8¾ x 26", $137.50. Photo courtesy Collectors Auction Services.

1934 Chicago Expo, blue, matching streamers, white inscription, white felt trim strip, image of "Hall of Science" in yelow, green, and blue, 5½ x 18" $20.00
1939 Detroit Tigers, black, dark orange inscription, orange trim, image of tiger head, 11½ x 29" 65.00
1939 New York World's Fair, "Aviation Building," green, white lettering, 8 x 25" 40.00
1940 New York World's Fair, yellow, blue inscription for visitor on closing day Oct 27, 1940, 4 x 9" 40.00
1962 Seattle World's Fair, black, white inscription, inked "Century 21 Exposition" in blue, yellow, lavender, and orange, 9 x 27" 20.00
Al Simmons/Tigers, purple, gold inscription, 2¼ x 4¼" 15.00
Ali-Frazier, white, red and black inscription, black and white screened photos of Muhammad Ali and Joe Frazier, each on yellow square ground, c1970s, 8 x 21" 25.00
Captain Marvel, printed image and name, ©Fawcett Publications, Inc, 8½ x 14½" 90.00
Caravan Of Stars, dark brown, white inscription, green accent, musical and dancer images, 3 x 3" Hopalong Cassidy image in white on brown, 9½ x 27" 90.00
Franklin Roosevelt, red and yellow, white image of Roosevelt, Capitol dome and "I Was At The 1st Third Term Inauguration January 20, 1941," yellow streamers, 4½ x 12" 65.00
I Like Ike, white, yellow, and blue, from Gettysburg, PA, 5 x 6" image of Ike in white, gray accents and tie, 8½ x 26½" 15.00
Indianapolis Speedway, May 30, 1939, annual Memorial Day event, 11½ x 26½" 65.00
Paul Derringer/Reds, gold, turquoise blue inscription, c1936, 2¼ x 4¼" 15.00
Paul Waner/Pirates, maroon, white inscription, c1936, 2¼ x 4¼" 15.00
Remember Pearl Harbor, blue, white inscription, image of Uncle Sam rolling up his sleeve flanked by civilian workers on left and military personnel on right, 7 x 23" 50.00
Sunset Carson Republic Pictures, dark blue, yellow streamers, colorful image of Carson, white lettering, "Sunset Carson Souvenir Of Republic Pictures, Hollywood, Calif," 1940s, 8½ x 26" 40.00
World War I, 27th Division 24.00
Zeke Bonura/White Sox, navy blue, white inscription, 2¼ x 4¼" 15.00

PENNSBURY POTTERY

Henry and Lee Below established Pennsbury Pottery, named for its close proximity to William Penn's estate "Pennsbury," three miles west of Morrisville, Pennsylvania, in 1950. Henry, a ceramic engineer and mold maker, and Lee, a designer and modeler, had previously worked for Stangl Pottery in Trenton, New Jersey. Henry Below died on December 21, 1959, leaving the pottery in trust for his wife and three children with instructions that it be sold upon the death of his wife. Lee Below died on December 12, 1968. In October 1970 the Pennsbury Pottery filed for bankruptcy. The contents of the company were auctioned off on December 18, 1970. On May 18, 1971, a fire destroyed the pottery and support building. Many of Pennsbury's forms, motifs, and manufacturing techniques have Stangl roots. A line of birds similar to those produced by Stangl were among the earliest Pennsbury products. While the carved design technique originated at Stangl, high bas-relief molds did not.

Pennsbury products are easily identified by their brown wash background. The company also made pieces featuring other background colors. Do not make the mistake of assuming that a piece is not Pennsbury because it does not have a brown wash. Pennsbury motifs are heavily nostalgic, farm, and Pennsylvania German oriented. The pottery made a large number of commemorative, novelty, and special-order pieces. Marks differ from piece to piece depending on the person who signed the piece or the artist who sculpted the mold.

Concentrate on one pattern or type. Since the pieces were hand carved, aesthetic quality differs from piece to piece. Look for pieces with a strong design sense and a high quality of execution. Buy only clearly marked pieces. Look for decorator and designer initials that can be easily identified.

Many of the company's commemorative and novelty pieces relate to businesses and events in the Middle Atlantic States, thus commanding their highest price within that region.

Look-Alike Alert: The Lewis Brothers Pottery, Trenton, New Jersey, purchased fifty of the lesser Pennsbury molds. Although they were supposed to remove the Pennsbury name from the molds, some molds were overlooked. Further, two Pennsbury employees moved to Lewis Brothers when Pennsbury closed. Many pieces similar in feel and design to Pennsbury were produced. Many of Pennsbury's major lines, including the Harvest and Rooster patterns, plaques, birds, and highly unusual molds, were not reproduced.

Amish, beer mug, 5" h. $38.50
Amish, creamer and sugar, 4" h 27.50
Amish, pitcher, 5" h. 27.50
Amish, plaque, 4½" h 22.00
Amish Woman, pitcher, 5" h 27.50
Black Rooster, butter dish 49.50
Black Rooster, cake stand 82.50
Black Rooster, plate, 10" d. 33.00
Black Rooster, salt and pepper shakers, pr, black tops 27.50
Boy and Girl, plate, 11" d 176.00
Commemorative, tray, "Fidelity Mutual Life". 13.75
Commemorative, tray, "Iron Horse Ramble, Reading Railroad, 1960". 49.50
Eagle, pitcher, 5¼" h 38.50
Eagle, plate, 8" d. 82.50
Figurine, gold finch, #102, sgd "K" 247.50
Figurine, wren, #109, sgd "K" 126.50
Gay Ninety, beer mug, 5" h 33.00
Harvest, plate, 8" d 82.50

Gay Ninety, pretzel bowl, $45.00.

Hex, coffeepot, 2 cup, 5½" h **55.00**
Hex, creamer and sugar, 2¾" h **30.00**
Hex, gravy boat, 4" h **22.00**
Hex, powder jar, 6½" d **55.00**
Hex, pretzel bowl **60.50**
Hex, teapot **50.00**
Holly, serving tray **55.00**
Red Barn, pitcher, 6¼" h **44.00**
Red Rooster, bowl, 11" d **132.00**
Red Rooster, butter dish **33.00**
Red Rooster, coffeepot, 2 cup, 5½" h **55.00**
Red Rooster, pitcher, 5" h **27.50**
Red Rooster, plate, 8" d **15.00**
Red Rooster, plate, 13½" d **93.50**
Red Rooster, tray, 7½ x 5½" **33.00**
Tulip, tray, 7½ x 5½" **22.00**
Two Birds Over Heart, desk basket, 5" **49.50**

PENS AND PENCILS

Forget the ordinary and look for the unusual. The more unique the object or set is, the more likely it is that it will have a high value. Defects of any kind drop value dramatically. When buying a set, try to get the original box along with any instruction sheets and guarantee cards (you will be amazed at how many people actually save them).

Clubs: American Pencil Collectors Society, R.R. North, Wilmore, KS 67155; Pen Collectors of America, P.O. Box 821449, Houston, TX 77282; Pen Fancier's Club, 1169 Overcash Dr., Dunedin, FL 34698.

Newsletter: *Float About,* 1676 Millsboro Rd., Mansfield, OH 44906; *Pens*, P.O. Box 64, Teaneck, NJ 07666.

Periodical: *Pen World Magazine,* P.O. Box 6007, Kingwood, TX 77325.

PENS

A&W/Nightmare Before Christmas, plastic, clear body, paper insert, repeated portraits of Jack and pumpkin, ©1994 Cadbury Beverages, Inc, 6¾" l **$15.00**
Bell Telephone, Waterbury, ballpoint, MIB **25.00**
Conklin, Model 20, #2, point-nib, black crescent filler #20, gold clip, narrow gold band on cap, patent date May 28, 1918 stamped on clip, 5 5/16" l **85.00**
Conklin, Model 30, black hard rubber, 1903 . . . . **80.00**

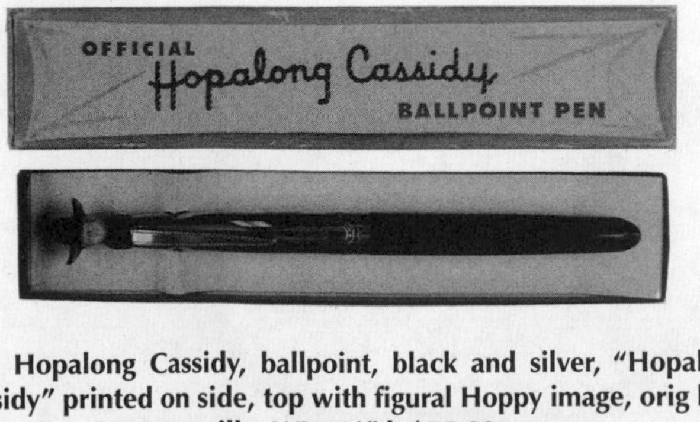

Pen, Hopalong Cassidy, ballpoint, black and silver, "Hopalong Cassidy" printed on side, top with figural Hoppy image, orig box, Parker Pen Co, Janesville, WI, 5¾" l, $75.00.

Eversharp, Doric, desk type, gold seal, green marble cov, lever fill, large adjustable nib, 1935 . . . . **200.00**
Floaty Pen, King Kong, floating up and down outside New York City's Empire State Building, Eskesen **4.00**
Floaty Pen, mama bear and cub walking through winter landscape of Great Smoky Mountains **4.00**
Floaty Pen, souvenir, Hawaii, school fo sunfish swimming **4.00**
Floaty Pen, tugboat and barge sailing by London's Houses of Parliament **4.00**
Floaty Pen, Walt Disney World, Tinkerbell floats up and down in front of Magic Kingdom, Eskesen **4.00**
Jefferson, fountain, red and orange marbleized Catalin, brass clip, 5¼" l **20.00**
Moore, rose color, fancy band around cap, warranted nib, side lever filler **100.00**
Parker, Lucky Curve, push button filler, 1917 . . . . **195.00**
Parker, Model 48, ring top, gold filled barrel and cap, button filled, 1915 . . . . **275.00**
Regal, fountain, olive green, tan, and black marbleized Catalin, 5¼" l **25.00**
Sheaffer, Lifetime, black, brown stripe **50.00**
Sheaffer, White Dot, green jade, gold plated trim, lever filled, 1923 . . . . **140.00**
Tom Mix, marbleized, rope script, 14K, gold plated, Southern Pen Co, c1920, 4¾" l **75.00**
Wahl, Tempoint, #305-A, gold filled metal mounted, eyedropper, 1919 . . . . **180.00**
Waterman, Ideal, #452, SS, 1925 . . . . **150.00**

PENCILS

Coca-Cola, wood, bat shape, gold luster metal tip, red inscription "Enjoy Coca-Cola" on bat, 1950s, 5¾" l **$20.00**
Lone Ranger, Liquid Viewer Pen and Pencil Set, plastic and metal ballpoint pen and mechanical pencil, transparent clear plastic in upper barrel holds 1" h miniature painted Lone Ranger figure in clear liquid, Progressive Products, Inc, ©Lone Ranger, Inc, with orig warranty insert paper, orig box, c1950s **90.00**
Missouri Pacific Lines, mechanical, yellow marbleized plastic and metal, "Sunshine Special, The Scenic Limited, Air Conditioned, A Service Institution," 5½" l **30.00**
Mobilgas, mechanical, celluloid, silvered brass tip and pencil clip, clear cylinder holding miniature diecut

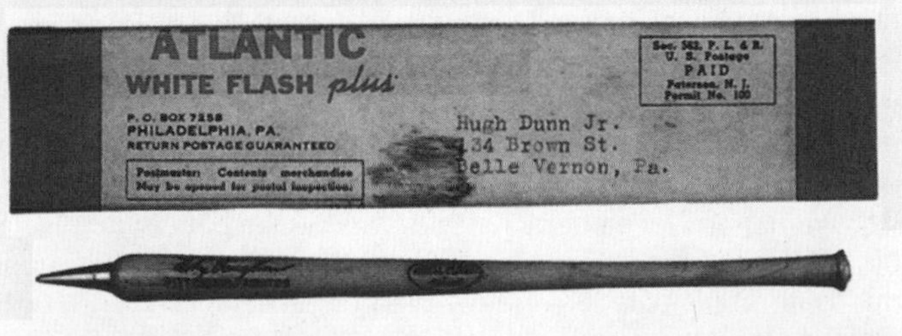

Top: pencil, Lion Head Motor Oil, plastic and metal, with sample of oil sealed in top, 5½" l, $66.00.
Bottom: Atlantic White Flash, metal and wood, wooden baseball bat sgd "Arky Vaughan, new old stock in orig box, 6½" l, $44.00. Photos courtesy Collectors Auction Services.

fish, ivory celluloid barrel with red and blue logo and inscription for Socony-Vacuum Co, barrel has names of local agent in Marlin, TX, 1930s, 6" l **40.00**
Mr Peanut, mechanical, brass tip, 1¹/₄" h plastic Mr Peanut figure at upper end, name repeated around barrel, "Planter's" on brass pencil clip, late 1940s-50s, 5¹/₂" l **20.00**
New York Mets, wood, lead, soft vinyl smiling baseball head mounted at top, light green barrel with batter, pitcher, and catcher, symbol figures "Mr Met" and "Lady Met" with Shea Stadium and team emblem, late 1960s, 10³/₄" l **15.00**
Parker, Duofold, marbleized green **170.00**
Popeye, mechanical, metal, silver-gray, black and dark red illus and text, Eagle Pencil Co, 1930–40, 10¹/₂" l **25.00**
Wahl-Eversharp, gold filled metal mounted, 1919. . . . . **60.00**

PEPSI-COLA

Caleb D. Bradham, a pharmacist and drugstore owner in New Bern, North Carolina, developed "Brad's Drink," a soda mix, in the mid-1890s. By 1898, Brad's Drink had become Pepsi-Cola. By 1902 Bradham was promoting Pepsi-Cola on a full-time basis. Two years later he sold his first franchise.

By the end of the twentieth century's first decade, Bradham had organized a network of over 250 bottlers in 24 states. The company's fortunes sank shortly after World War I when it suffered large losses in the sugar market. Bankruptcy and reorganization followed. Roy Megargel, a Wall Street financier, rescued and guided the company out of its difficulties. Pepsi-Cola survived a second bankruptcy in 1931.

Pepsi-Cola's fortunes soared in 1933 when the company doubled its bottle size and held its price to a nickel. Under the direction of Walter Mack from 1938–1951, Pepsi challenged Coca-Cola for the number one spot in the soda market. One of the most popular advertising jingles of the 1950s was "Pepsi-Cola Hits The Spot, Twelve Full Ounces That's A Lot."

Pepsi-Cola, a division of Beatrice, enjoys a worldwide reputation, outselling Coca-Cola in a number of foreign countries.

Beware of a wide range of Pepsi-Cola reproductions, copycats, fantasy items, and fakes. A Pepsi and Pete pillow issued in the 1970s, a Pepsi glass-front clock, and a 12" high ceramic statue of a woman holding a glass of Pepsi are a few examples.

Club: Pepsi-Cola Collectors Club, P.O. Box 1275, Covina, CA 91722.

Bookmark, paper, figural leaf with bottlecap on bottom, 1940s, 3 x 12". **$35.00**
Bottle, glass, applied color label, 1960s, 32 oz. **50.00**
Bottle, plastic, throwaway, 1960s, 16 oz. **10.00**
Bottle Carrier, cardboard, striped sides, "Hostess Size," holds 2 bottles, 1960s **50.00**
Bottle Carrier, cloth bag, "For Pepsi-Cola Bottles Save Paper—Use This Bag" on side, 1940s, 8 x 6". **60.00**
Bottle Carrier, wood, holds 24 bottles, 1940s **65.00**
Bottle Opener, plastic handle, 1950s, 6" l. **25.00**
Calendar, 1952, Bottling Company of ADA, "Season's Greetings," 6 x 10¹/₂" **250.00**
Cash Register Topper, cardboard, information on how to spot counterfeit currency on back, 1930–40s **550.00**
Certificate, Rogers Silverware sponsor, 1917. . . . . **12.00**

Flange Sign, masonite, metal connector, 1940s, 12 x 13", $242.00. Photo courtesy Gary Metz's Mudding River Trading Co.

Clock, double dot light-up, orig standing easel attached to back, Telechron, 1940s **300.00**
Coaster, cardboard, 1950s, 4" d. **20.00**
Dispenser, countertop, "Drink Pepsi-Cola Ice Cold" on side, 1950s **525.00**
Display, cardboard, refilled and recapped Pepsi bottle on front, 1930–40s, 6¹/₂ x 13". **650.00**
Door Handle, "Enjoy Pepsi-Cola/Bigger Better," 1940s **145.00**
Door Push, tin, raised edge, 1930s, 3¹/₂ x 13¹/₂" **950.00**
Door Push, wrought iron, 1960s **95.00**
Mileage Chart, tin, framed. **45.00**
Pinback Button, tin, "I Drank A Pepsi, Did You?," 1970s, 2" d **10.00**
Ruler, tin, "Be Sociable Have a Pepsi," 1950s, 12" l **20.00**
Serving Tray, round, bottle cap illus and "Have a Pepsi," 1950s, 13" d **75.00**
Sign, celluloid over tin, orig hanging pack, string, cardboard and instruction on back, "Pepsi-Cola 5¢/12 Ounces," 1930s, 5¹/₄ x 121/2" **1,100.00**
Sign, glass, orig wooden base, bottle cap with "Pepsi-Cola," "20¢," "10¢," 1950–60s, 17 x 12" **210.00**
Sign, porcelain, red, white, and blue banner, double dotted logo, "American's Biggest Nickel's Worth," 18 x 6" . . . **300.00**
Sign, tin, polar bear and iceberg scene, 1950s, 23" sq. **220.00**
Straws, box of 50, unopened **650.00**
Thermometer, litho tin, "Bigger/Better," 1930–40s, 6¹/₂ x 16". **400.00**
Ticket, Russel Bros Circus, Pepsi adv, 1930s **50.00**
Toy, truck, metal, Tonka, 1978, 7¹/₂" l **65.00**
Tray, round, bottle cap shape, 1940 . . . . **325.00**
Walkie-Talkie, bottle shape **25.00**

PERFUME BOTTLES

Perfume bottles come in all shapes and sizes. In addition to perfume bottles, there are atomizers (a bottle with a spray mechanism), colognes (large bottles whose stoppers often have an application device), scents (small bottles used to hold a scent or smelling salts), and vinaigrettes (an ornamental box or bottle with a perforated top). The stopper of a perfume is used for application and is very elongated.

Perfume bottles were one of the hottest collectibles of the 1980s. As a result of market manipulation and speculative buying, prices soared. The wind started to blow in the wrong direction. The field began to stink. Many prices collapsed. The wind is changing again as new collectors follow the scent. Today's collectors are also interested in commercial bottles. They enjoy their pretty shapes and colors as well as those sexy names.

Clubs: International Perfume Bottle Assoc., P.O. Box 529, Vienna, VA 22183; Miniature Perfume Bottle Collectors, 28227 Paseo El Siena, Laguna Niguel, CA 92677.

Blown Three Mold, glass, light sapphire blue, pontil scarred base, flared lip, c1815–30, $5^{1}/_{4}$" h **$120.00**
Blown Three Mold, glass, pale aqua, Gothic Arch, cork stopper, c1825 . . . . **110.00**
Blown Three Mold, glass, violet cobalt blue, pontil scarred base, rolled and flared lip, c1815–30, $5^{1}/_{4}$" h **650.00**
Cologne, American, glass, aqua, emb basket of flowers design, pontil scarred base, rolled lip, c1845–55, $4^{3}/_{8}$" h **70.00**
Cologne, American, clear glass, violin pattern and shape, pontil scarred base, rolled lip, c1845–55, $5^{1}/_{2}$" h **70.00**
Cologne, European, glass, clear, gold flake splotch pattern, smooth base, c1870–1900, 4" h **50.00**
Cologne, European, cobalt blue, pontil scarred base, sheared and rolled lip, c1870–1900, 4" h **50.00**
Cologne, Sandwich type, American, polygonal form, deep cobalt blue, smooth base, rolled lip, c1865–80, $4^{3}/_{4}$" h **425.00**
Commercial, Black Satin **8.00**
Commercial, Fragonard, miniature bottles, set of 3 . . . . **48.00**
Commercial, Harrison's Columbian Perfumery, glass, clear, smooth base, flared lip, 1855–65, $5^{1}/_{8}$" h **35.00**
Figural, crystal palace, clear, smooth base, tooled mouth, orig ground glass stopper with sphere, $13^{3}/_{8}$" h **60.00**
Figural, fish, bluish aqua, smooth base, sheared lip, c1890–1910, 11" h **60.00**
Figural, lady and parrot, china, blue, white, black, yellow, green and orange, metal and cork stopper, $3^{3}/_{8}$" h **70.00**
Figural, shoe, black amethyst, smooth base, ground lip, orig metal screw cap and painted toe, c1890–1910, $3^{5}/_{8}$" h **110.00**
Lucien Long, 3 pc set **95.00**
Schiaparelli Shocking, orig leather case, 3" h **245.00**
Czechoslovakian, glass, opaque black, clear stopper, $3^{5}/_{8}$" h **85.00**
Figural, heart shape, glass, cut flowers on front and back, clear cut faceted stopper, $5^{1}/_{2}$" h **75.00**
Perfume, Givenchy, orig red silk box **45.00**
Scent, Prince of Wales Feathers Scent, deep blue, raised feather pattern, open pontil, $2^{1}/_{4}$" h **110.00**
Scent, Sandwich, milk glass, fiery opalescent, smooth base, ground lip, missing cap, 1865–75, 3" h **20.00**
Scent, shield shape, purple amethyst, pontil scarred base, smooth lip, c1800s, 3" h **450.00**

Cologne Bottle, American, bluish aqua, open pontil, round lip, c1845–55, $5^{3}/_{4}$" h, $66.00. Photo courtesy Glass–Works Auctions.

Poster, World's Fair, Knoxville, 1982, $75.00.

PETER MAX COLLECTIBLES

Peter Max has been creating collectibles since 1967. He's the quintessential pop icon whose works symbolized the colorful 1960s hippie era. Interest in Peter Max collectibles has escalated since the first Psychedelic Show in New York City in 1995.

Collectors should note that items dated pre-1973 are most in demand. Unsigned Peter max look-alike items should be avoided. Find the Peter Max signature on the item before purchase. Since Peter Max owns the copyrights to all his designs, he has not authorized any reproductions or reprints to his works. Prices continue to rise in this area, as well as the entire psychedelic era field.

Advisor: Lee Hay, P.O. Box 14898, Cincinnati, OH 45250-0898, (513) 621-6034, e-mail: heywood@sprintmail.com.

Bag, Borden Yogurt, vinyl, with zipper, c1969. . . . . **$325.00**
Bead Craft Set, Walco, 1972 . . . . **150.00**
Belt, cloth, metal buckle, c1970 . . . . **50.00**
Book Set, *Land of Red, Land of Yellow, Land of Blue,* 1970. . . . . **125.00**
Book, *Needlepoint,* 1972 . . . . **35.00**
Book, *Paper Airplane,* 1971 . . . . **25.00**
Book, *Poster,* 1970 . . . . **75.00**
Book, *Superposter,* 1971 . . . . **75.00**
Book, *Teen Cuisine,* 1969 . . . . **35.00**
Book Cover, paper, c1969, 21 x 14 . . . . **15.00**
Canister Set, 3 pc, enamel, c1973 . . . . **450.00**
Chess Game, Kontrell, 1971 . . . . **350.00**
Clock, alarm, GE, 3 designs, c1968 . . . . **225.00**
Clock, wall, GE, 6 designs, 1968 . . . . **150.00**
Coffeepot, enamel, c1973, $8^{1}/_{2}$" h. **275.00**
Cup, Jello Pudding, plastic, 1972. . . . . **15.00**

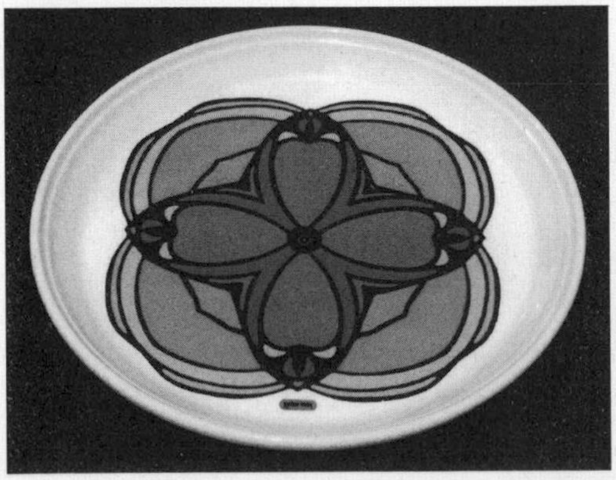

Plate, Love, Iroquois, c1968, 10" d, $75.00.

Necklace, ceramic, c1968 . . . . . **50.00**
Perfume Bottle, Sunshine, Frangipani flavored, Iskcon, 1973 . . . . . **125.00**
Pillow, inflatable, vinyl, 8 designs, c1969 . . . . . **35.00**
Poster, Contemporary Arts Center, Cincinnati, OH, c1970, 51 x 73" **500.00**
Puzzle, *Life Magazine,* butterfly, 1970 . . . . . **35.00**
Scarf, zodiac, c1969, 21 x 21" **45.00**
Serving Tray, Happy, c1970 . . . . . **75.00**
Skillet, enamel, c1973 . . . . . **250.00**
Sunglasses, with case, c1969 . . . . . **150.00**
Tennis Shoes, c1968 . . . . . **500.00**
Tie **45.00**
Towel, stars, c1970, 25 x 42" **60.00**

PEZ DISPENSERS

The Pez dispenser originated in Germany and was invented by Edvard Haas in 1927. The name "Pez" is an abbreviation of the German word for peppermint—*pfefferminz*. The peppermint candy was touted as an alternative to smoking.

The first Pez container was shaped like a disposable cigarette lighter and is referred to by collectors as the non-headed or regular dispenser.

By 1952 Pez arrived in the United States. New fruit flavored candy and novelty dispensers were introduced. Early containers were designed to commemorate holidays or favorite children's characters including Bozo the Clown, Mickey Mouse, and other popular Disney, Warner Brothers, and Universal personalities.

Collecting Pez containers at flea markets must be done with care. Inspect each dispenser to guarantee it is intact and free from cracks and chips. Also, familiarize yourself with proper color and marking characteristics.

Newsletter: *PEZ Collector's News,* P.O. Box 124, Sea Cliff, NY 11579.

Bambi, black nose **$65.00**
Barney Bear **35.00**
Batman, with cape **100.00**
Bubbleman **15.00**
Captain Hook **95.00**
Charlie Brown, eyes closed, German, MOC **110.00**
Clown Totem **35.00**
Cockatoo, blue, yellow beak **65.00**
Cow, orange **120.00**
Cowboy, black hat **350.00**
Dalmation Pup **60.00**
Daniel Boone **240.00**
Droopy Dog, short ears **6.00**
Dumbo, blue **40.00**
Elephant, orange, blue flat hat **125.00**
Football Player **175.00**
Goofy, red cap **25.00**
Henry Hawk **80.00**
Icee Bear, purple stem **6.00**
Icee Bear, white stem, MOC **15.00**
Indian Chief, blue headress **250.00**
Indian Squaw **225.00**
King Louie **15.00**
Petunia Pig **35.00**
Pilgrim, yellow band **225.00**
Policeman **60.00**
Pony, orange head **100.00**
Rooster, white **45.00**
Smurf, red, blue stem **7.00**
Smurfette, blue, yellow stem **7.00**
Uncle Sam **275.00**
Wylie Coyote **55.00**
Yappy Dog, orange **75.00**

Jiminy Cricket, orig cello with 2 candles and pamphlet, $230.00. Photo courtesy New England Auction Gallery.

PFALTZGRAFF

The name Pfaltzgraff is derived from a famous Rhine River castle, still standing today, in the Pfalz region of Germany. In 1811 George Pfaltzgraff, a German immigrant potter, began producing salt-glazed stoneware in York, Pennsylvania.

The Pfaltzgraff Pottery Company initially produced stoneware storage crocks and jugs. When the demand for stoneware diminished, the company shifted its production to animal and poultry feeders and red clay flowerpots. The production focus changed again in the late 1940s and early 1950s as the company produced more and more household products, including its first dinnerware line, and giftwares.

In 1964 the company became The Pfaltzgraff Company. Over the next fifteen years, Pfaltzgraff expanded via construction of a new manufacturing plant and distribution center at Thomasville, North Carolina, the purchase of the Stangl Pottery of Trenton, New Jersey, and the acquisition of facotries in Dover, Aspers, and Bendersville, Pennsylvania. Retail stores were opened in York County, Pennsylvania; Flemington, New Jersey; and Fairfax, Virginia.

America, custard cup, 2¾" h **$8.00**
America, mixing bowl, 7" d **30.00**

Heirloom, dinner plate, $8.00.

America, pie plate, $9\frac{5}{8}$" d . . . **40.00**
America, sherbet, 3" d . . . **10.00**
America, soup bowl, flat, $8\frac{3}{4}$" d . . . **14.00**
America, spice shaker, $6\frac{1}{2}$" h . . . **20.00**
Christmas Heirloom, cup, flat, $3\frac{1}{4}$" h . . . **16.00**
Christmas Heirloom, mug, $4\frac{7}{8}$" h . . . **14.00**
Gourmet, cereal bowl, coupe, $5\frac{5}{8}$" d . . . **6.00**
Gourmet, chip and dip . . . **30.00**
Gourmet, gravy boat . . . **30.00**
Gourmet, pitcher, $7\frac{1}{2}$' h . . . **12.00**
Heirloom, batter bowl, $5\frac{3}{4}$" . . . **38.00**
Heirloom, coffee canister, $6\frac{1}{2}$" h . . . **20.00**
Heirloom, coffeepot, cov . . . **30.00**
Heirloom, creamer . . . **20.00**
Heritage, sugar canister, 7" h . . . **14.00**
Village, cup and saucer . . . **8.00**
Village, salad plate, 7" d . . . **4.00**
Windsong, cereal bowl, flat, $6\frac{1}{8}$" d . . . **10.00**
Windsong, coffeepot, cov . . . **50.00**
Windsong, salad plate, 7" d . . . **6.00**
Yorktowne, baker, individual, $6\frac{5}{8}$" . . . **12.00**
Yorktowne, cup and saucer . . . **10.00**
Yorktowne, custard cup, $2\frac{3}{4}$" h . . . **2.00**
Yorktowne, salt shaker . . . **6.00**

PICTURE FRAMES

We have reached the point where the frame is often worth more than the picture in it. Decorators have fallen in love with old frames. If you find one with character and pizzazz at a flea market for a few dollars, pick it up. It will not be hard to resell. Who said picture frames have to be used for pictures? They make great frames for mirrors. Use your imagination.

Club: International Institute for Frame Study, P.O. Box 50130, Washington, DC 20091.

Art Deco, beveled glass, etched floral and leaf design, c1940, $14\frac{1}{2}$ x 17" . . . **$85.00**
Art Deco, brass, half circle projection on 2 sides, easel back, 6 x 8" . . . **80.00**
Art Deco, glass, light blue tine, tin-plated, corner mounts . . . **22.00**
Art Deco, wood and glass, black and white diagonal stripe design . . . **75.00**
Art Nouveau, brass, 2 oval openings, easel back, 7 x 12" . . . **125.00**
Art Nouveau, cast iron, oval, gilded, folding stand, ope work scrolls and leaves, $10\frac{1}{2}$ x 8" . . . **50.00**
Curly Maple, refinished, $16\frac{3}{4}$ x $20\frac{1}{2}$" . . . **90.00**
Folk Art, assorted soft woods, 14 x 17" . . . **125.00**
Folk Art, mahogany, laminated, pyramid dec, old varnish finish, 9 x $12\frac{3}{4}$" . . . **45.00**
Tramp Art, rect, chip carved, diamond shape projections on each corner, 1915, $17\frac{1}{4}$ x $19\frac{1}{2}$" . . . **45.00**

Art Deco, silver colored metal, silver and black cardboard mat, easel back, 7 x 9", $1.00.

PIE BIRDS

Pie birds and pie funnels continue to be a 1990s hot collectible and functional kitchen novelty. Because of the frantic search for pie birds, everything and anything with a hole(s) is being labeled "pie bird." The basic criteria for pie birds are: ceramic pottery (e.g. stoneware, porcelain), glazed inside and outside, 3 to 5 inches tall, arches (cutouts) at the base to allow steam to enter and exit through a top vent hole. There are Pyrex and aluminum (non-US) pie funnels.

Examples of non-pie birds are: dated brass bird (toy whistle), birds with stems (plant waterers), multi-holed chickens (hors d'oeuvre holders), bird on base with many holes (flower frogs), elephant with clover (ring holder).

From the 1980s to the present, many novelty pie vents have been added to the market for variety and the enjoyment of both the baker and the collector. These are made by commercial (including Far East importers), and local enterprises in Australia, Canada, England and the United States. A new category for the 1990s includes an array of holiday-related pie vents. Beware of figural pie vents from England that are stained with brown gook that allude to age and usage. Note: age crazing is a process that can be applied to new pie vents.

Advisor: Lillian Cole, 14 Harmony School Rd., Flemington, NJ 08822, (908) 782-3198.

Club: Pie Bird Collectors Club, 158 Bagsby Hill Ln., Dover, TN 37058.

Newsletter: *Piebirds Unlimited Newsletter* (Lillian Cole, editor), 14 Harmony School Rd., Flemington, NJ 08822.

Blackbird, English, mkd "Midwinter" or "Newport Pottery," mass produced . . . **$25.00**
Blackbird, porcelain, poorly painted yellow or white beak, new, Taiwan . . . **4.00**
Chef, black-faced, imported, blue, yellow, or green, 1940-60s . . . **100.00**
Chef, black-faced, round spoon, multicolored, new import . . . **10.00**

Speckled Blue Bird, U S, mid 1940–60s, $4\frac{1}{2}$" h, $40.00.

Cook, black faced lady, round spoon, multicolored, new import 10.00
Figural, variety, mkd "SB, England" 30.00
Funnel, emb "Tala 1899," England, new 1996–present 15.00
Funnel, "T.G. Green" motif, England, new 1990s 25.00
Funnel, "Squab Vit-Porcelain," Australia 50.00
Josef Originals, man chef or lady baker, Japan, 1970s 25.00
Josef Originals, yellow chick, US and Japan, mass produced, 1970–80s 25.00
Long-Neck Duckling, blue, yellow, or pink, US, mass produced, 1950–60s 35.00
Pie Boy, sombreros on pants, hands cupped to mouth, 1950s 85.00
Pie Funnels, plain white, various sizes, no markings, English 15.00
Rooster, mkd "Cleminson" or "Cb," mass produced 1940–60s 25.00
Shawnee Pottery Pie Chic, pink or blue base, US, 1950–60s 25.00
Songbird, blue, pink, or light brown, mass produced, 1940–60s 35.00
Songbird, blue with speckles, US, 1950–60s 50.00
Songbird, gold trim beak, feet, and feathering, US, 1950–60s 50.00
White Bird, porcelain, imported, Taiwan, new 4.00

PIERCE, HOWARD

Howard Pierce established his pottery studio in LaVerne, California, in 1941. Initially he produced small pewter animal figurines. A lack of metal supplies during World War II forced him to close. He reopened in 1945 and produced a line of contemporary ceramic figurines.

Pierce's work was sold in high-end gift shops and department stores. A satin-matte brown on white combination glaze was his favorite. In 1956 he introduced a line of Jasperware products.

Pierce entered semi-retirement in 1968 when he moved to Joshua Tree, a desert community near Palm Springs. He still produces a small range of limited production pieces that are sold through select outlets.

Bank, pig, porcelain, brownish gray gloss glaze, black ink stamp "Howard Pierce," 4 x 7" $150.00
Box, cov, mint green, Art Deco gazelles on side, imp "Howard Pierce Claremont Calif.," 4 x 5" 1125.00
Dish, triangular, gray glaze, unmkd, 16 x 12" 85.00
Figure, bird, gold, unmkd, 2½ x 5½" 35.00
Figure, bison, white, black ink stamp "Pierce," 2½ x 3⅓" 50.00
Figure, cat, black, 10¼" h, black ink stamp 60.00
Figure, gazelle, brown high gloss glaze, imp "Howard Pierce" and "100P," 11¼ x 4" 100.00
Figure, girl, beside 2 jugs, holding open container, "Howard Pierce" black ink stamp, 9 x 3½" 85.00
Figure, madonna and child, 13 x 2½" 85.00
Figure, monkey, matte gray flecked glaze, black hig lights, "Howard Pierce" black ink stamp, 6¼ x 3" 75.00
Magnet, figural rabbit, porcelain, unmkd, 3¼" h 50.00
Planter, mint green matte glaze, leaf motif, imp "Howard Pierce Claremont Calif.," 4¼ x 6½" 50.00
Teapot, cov, light blue, shepherd and sheep on front, 6" h 150.00
Vase, green gloss glaze, white fish insert, imp "Howard Pierce Claremont Calif.," 8 x 7" 100.00

PIG COLLECTIBLES

This is one animal that does better as a collectible than in real life. Pig collectibles have never been oinkers.

Established pig collectors focus on the bisque and porcelain pigs of the late 19th and early 20th centuries. This is a limited view. Try banks in the shape of a pig as a specialized collecting area. If not appealing, look at the use of pigs in advertising. If neither please you, there is always Porky. "That's All, Folks!"

Club: The Happy Pig Collectors Club, P.O. Box 17, Oneida, IL 61467.

Ashtray, 1 pig bowling, other watching, pink with green, 5" $95.00
Bank, china, Royal Copley 65.00
Bank, Porky Pig, plastic 25.00
Cookie Jar, Harley-Davidson Hog, McCoy, ©1984HD 300.00
Figure, 2 pigs riding in car 55.00
Figure, caboose, 2 pigs 80.00
Gravy Boat, porcelain, 2 pink pigs swinging 45.00
Matchsafe, bisque, pink pig, "Scratch My Back" and "Me Too," 5" h 100.00
Paperweight, figural, glass, Best Pig Forceps, compliments J Reimers, Davenport, IA 100.00
Pin Dish, 3 little pigs around water trough, 2½" h 50.00
Pinback Button, The Yankee Pig, pig dancing on island of Cuba, multicolored, Spanish-American War era, c1898 . . . . 85.00
Salt and Pepper Shakers, pr, figural, 1 playing accordion, other playing saxophone, glazed and painted, mkd "Japan," c1930, 4" h 45.00
Souvenir, bank, "Souvenir of Danville, IL," front pink pig sticking out of bank, back end sticking out other end, gold pig, yellow pouch 50.00
Souvenir, toothpick holder, "Watertown, NY, stamped "Made in Germany," 3" d 55.00
Toothpick Holder, 2 pigs in front of egg, 2¾" h 50.00
Vase, red devil's arm around pink pig, sitting on log 110.00

PINBACK BUTTONS

Around 1893 the Whitehead & Hoag Company filed the first patents for celluloid pinback buttons. By the turn of the century, the celluloid pinback button was used as a promotional tool covering a wide spectrum, ranging from presidential candidates to amusement parks, not that there is much difference between the two.

Chevrolet, "New Chevrolet Six," litho tin, Ceraghty & Co, ⅞" d, $5.00.

This category covers advertising pinback buttons. To discover the full range of non-political pinbacks consult Ted Hake and Russ King's *Price Guide To Collectible Pin-back Buttons 1896–1986* (Hake's Americana & Collectibles Press: 1986).

Ball Brand Trade Mark All Knit, red, black, and white **$10.00**
Brecht's Candy, monkey dressed as bellhop, multicolored, 1930s, $1\frac{1}{4}$" d **65.00**
Buck Brand Coffee, multicolored, "One Pound Free For Every Ten Wrappers Returned," c1900s **22.00**
Bunny Bread, rabbit illus, "Reach For Bunny Bread," 1950s **15.00**
Canada Dry Ginger Ale, "Now Canada Dry Ginger Ale 5¢," green and white, red lettering, 1930–40s **20.00**
Cascarets, "Don't Kick! Take Cascarets Candy Cathartic, blue and white **14.00**
Delco Battery, "Save A Battery, Service Twice A Month," orange, black, and white **5.00**
Freihoffer's Bread, color illus of boy in striped shirt eating slice of jelly bread, 1950s, $2\frac{1}{2}$" d **20.00**
Gerber, baby illus, "I Have Visited The Gerber Baby," 1930s **10.00**
Heinz, multicolored, pickle illus, white ground, c1896, $\frac{7}{8}$" d **10.00**
Hobo Bread, red and yellow, man playing banjo, dog watching, "Order A Loaf Now! Hobo Light Bread," 1930s, $2\frac{1}{2}$" d **20.00**
Hudson, "Ride The Green Lane Of Safety In A New 1939 Hudson," green, blue, black, and white **15.00**
International Harvester, Whetstone Bark River Culvert & Equipment, Co, "Our 50th Year," red and gold **12.00**
Koveralls, "Look For The Label," red, black, and white **8.00**
Majestic Ranges, multicolored **24.00**
Nabisco, multicolored, cookie jar holding Nabisco products illus, "America's Cookie Jar," white ground, red lettering, 1970s **5.00**
Overland, multicolored, car image **15.00**
Planter's Peanuts, Mr Peanut center, blue and white, red rim, 1940s **20.00**
Pulver's Gum, "Get a Collection of Buttons," red and white, early 1900s **20.00**
Syracuse Herald, dog with black spot on eye, red ground "I Am The Syracuse Herald Snuggle Pup" around sides, $1\frac{1}{8}$" d **10.00**
Wesley's Bread, "Eat Wesley's Bread/Delivered Direct To Your Door," multicolored, stuffed calico bear toy illus, white ground, blue lettering, 1930s **20.00**

PIN-UP ART

The stuff looks so innocent, one has to wonder what all the fuss was about when it first arrived upon the scene. Personally, I like it when a little is left to the imagination.

George Petty and Alberto Vargas (the "s" was dropped at *Esquire's* request) have received far more attention than they deserve. You would be smart to focus on artwork by Gillete Elvgren, Billy DeVorss, Joyce Ballantyne, and Earl Moran. While Charles Dana Gibson's girls are also pinups, they are far too respectable to be considered here.

Newsletters: *Glamour Girls: Then and Now*, P.O. Box 34501, Washington, DC 20043; *The Illustrator Collector's News*, P.O. Box 1958, Sequim, WA 98382.

Playing Cards, 53 Vargas Girls, plastic coated, $75.00.

Booklet, World's Smallest Pin-Up Book, 16 fold-out photos of nude nymphs, vinyl bound, 1955-60 . . . . . . **$5.00**
Box, candy, DeVorss, color image, 1930s, 11 x 16" **150.00**
Calendar, 1939, Earl Moran, litho, 15 x 33" **175.00**
Calendar, 1940, Petty, Old Gold Cigarette adv, Petty girl for each month, 18 x 10" **55.00**
Calendar, 1941, Elvgren, paper, "Help Wanted!," full color art, 2 x 18" cardboard tube mailer **65.00**
Calendar, 1946, DeVorss, Jeanne, full pad, 16 x 33" **95.00**
Calendar, 1946, Moran, full color, "Sitting Pretty," $5\frac{1}{2}$" x $7\frac{1}{2}$" **20.00**
Calendar, 1946, Varga, pocket folder, Vargas and *Esquire* copyrights, 3 x $4\frac{1}{2}$" closed size, opens to $4\frac{1}{2}$ x $21\frac{1}{2}$" strip **60.00**
Calendar, 1949, Moore, "Esquire Girl," spiral bound, orig 9 x $12\frac{1}{2}$" envelope **40.00**
Calendar, 1951, McPherson, "Cutouts For Grown-Ups," spiral bound, orig 10 x 13" envelope **65.00**
Calendar, 1954, Golden Dreams, nude Marilyn Monroe, full color, 9 x 15" **75.00**
Calendar, 1956, Thompson, "Studio Sketches," spiral bound, orig envelope, $8\frac{1}{2}$ x 11" **65.00**
Calendar Pad, 1947, Sept, Rolf Armstrong, "See You Soon," salesman's sample, 11 x 23" **45.00**
Calendar Pad, 1955, Dec, Elvgren, "Stepping Out," 16 x 33" **85.00**
Cigarette Lighter, chrome, Petty, 1950s **45.00**
Folder, Sally of Hollywood & Vine, cardboard, sliding insert changes dress to underwear to nude **22.00**
Magazine, *Carnival of Beauty,* Vol 1, #1, Oct–Nov 1950, 68 pp **20.00**

The MacPherson Sketchbook for 1950 Calendar, paper in orig wrapper, "Rahway Valley Railroad Co. Kenilworth, N.J.," various poses of nudes, $12\frac{1}{2}$" h, $9\frac{1}{2}$" w, $82.50. Photo courtesy Collectors Auction Services.

Magazine, *Hollywood Tales,* Vol 1, #36, full color art, 1930s, 24 pp. **30.00**
Playing Cards, MacPherson, "Win, Lose or Draw," 2 complete decks, cardboard hinged box, 1940s **65.00**
Playing Cards, Petty Pippins, cowgirl leaning against fence, c1940, orig box. **15.00**
Poster, Otto, full color, woman in shorts walking dog, c1951, 17 x 33" **50.00**
Print, Armstrong, brunette in bibbed shorts, yellow blouse, matted and framed, 11 x 14" **30.00**
Print, Moran, "Sheer Delight," #5464, calendar sample, ©A Scheer, 12 x 13¾" **20.00**
Print, Vargas, *Esquire,* Phil Stack verse, WWII, matted and framed, 11 x 14" **65.00**
Program, New York City Dutch Treat Club, diecut, octagonal, 1936, 96 pp, 8 x 8" **40.00**

PLANTERS

No, I am not talking about Planter's Peanuts. I am chronicling those strange and decorative containers that people seem intent to force vegetation to grow from. If I had a "You Have To Be Nuts To Own It" category in this book, I might have been tempted to include planters in it. Don't you find it just a bit strange to see English ivy growing out of the top of a ceramic pig's head?

A planter is any container suitable for growing vegetation. It may be constructed of any number of materials ranging from wooden fruit crates and painted tires found on suburban front lawns to ceramic panthers stalking 1950s television sets. If you thought all those planters you got from the florist were junk, read on. Too bad you threw them out or sold them for a dime each at your last garage sale. This category deals with the figural ceramic variety found in abundance at all flea markets.

Angel, with halfmoon, "Your Lucky Star Guardian Angel," Napco, 4¼" h **$8.00**
Baby Ballerina, haeger, 5½" h **8.00**
Baby Scale, Japan, 6½" h. **9.00**
Baseball Glove, 6" h **18.00**
Basket, black and white, mkd "McCoy USA" **12.00**
Bird, sitting on fence, 3¾" h **6.00**
Butterfly on Log, brown and white, glossy, mkd "Shawnee 502" **30.00**
Cherub, made in Japan, 5" h **8.00**
Clock, Metlox, California Provincial. **95.00**
Clown, riding pig, McCoy **30.00**
Coal Scuttle, 6½" l **7.00**
Cradle, blue, semi gloss, emb basketweave design with flowers and swags dec, mkd "McCoy" **8.00**
Dancer, stylized, #234, unmkd, 8¼" h **15.00**
Dutch Couple, beside wishing well, Shawnee, 8½" l. **25.00**
Elf, sitting on large elf shoe, multicolored, glossy, mkd "Shawnee 765" **6.00**
Elf, with wheelbarrow, Shawnee, 3¾" h **12.00**
Girl, leaning on barrel, Royal Copley, 6¼" h. **15.00**
Globe, blue and green globe on yellow stand, glossy, mkd "Shawnee USA" **12.00**
Godiva on Horse, stamped "Japan," 7" l **18.00**
Golf Bag, 7" h. **9.00**
Guitar, black, semi gloss, mkd "Red Wing USA #M-1484" **15.00**
Hand, McCoy, 8⅝" h **8.00**
Hat and Pipe, Lefton, #H5959, 3¾ x 7½" **15.00**
Log, applied squirrel figure, gray spray glaze, American Art Potteries, 7" h **15.00**
Mortar and Pestle, gold trim, 6½" h **7.00**
Oaken Bucket, with pump, Inarco, 5¼ x 5¼" **9.00**
Oriental Girl, with fan, 9" h. **10.00**
Pelican, turquoise, matte, McCoy, mkd "NM USA" **10.00**
Phonograph, green, 7¼" h **12.00**
Rolling Pin, hp flowers, Clinchfield Artware Pottery, 14" l **10.00**
Steeplechaser, 12" l **25.00**
Watering Can, basketweave design, Shawnee, 5½" h **15.00**

PLANTER'S PEANUTS

Amedeo Obici and Mario Peruzzi organized the Planter's Nut and Chocolate Company in Wilkes-Barre, Pennsylvania, in 1906. The monocled Mr. Peanut resulted from a trademark contest in 1916. Standard Brands bought Planters only to be bought themselves by Nabisco. Planter's developed a wide range of premiums and promotional items. Beware of reproductions.

Club: Peanut Pals, P.O. Box 4465, Huntsville, AL 35815.

Bank, figural Mr Peanut, cast iron, 5 x 11½ x 3½" **$25.00**
Blotter, Planters Peanut Butter, diecut cardboard, image of soft yellowish-tan peanut shell with full color jar illus, 1930a, 3½ x 7" **65.00**
Book, *Soup to Nuts,* 1970 . . . . . **5.00**
Canister, figural peanut, plastic, reissue, 11 x 5 x 5" **5.00**
Cookie Jar, Mr Peanut, ceramic, MIB **25.00**
Display Box, Planters Salted Peanuts, waxy cardboard, 2-pc with lift-off top, holds 5¢ bags, marquee image of smiling girl holding bag of peanuts, 8¾ x 9 x 3⅛" **632.50**
Earrings, pr, plastic, figural Mr Peanut, clip-on type, 1¼ x ⅞" **70.00**
Jar, barrel shaped, emb running peanut on sides, peanut finial, 13" h, 8" d **150.00**
Jar, hexagonal, Mr Peanut painted on 3 panels, "Planters" painted on alternating 3 panels, glass lid with large knob finial, 10" h to top of finial. **200.00**
Jar, sq, emb "Planters" on sides, glass lid with peanut finial, 9½" h to top of finial **150.00**
Jars, pr, Planters Peanut Butter, clear glass, paper label with Mr Peanut image on front and premium mail-in offers on back, 5½ x 3½" **110.00**
Letter Opener, brass, Mr Peanut **150.00**
Mask, Mr Peanut face, cardboard, no rubber band, 7¾ x 8¼" **357.50**

Jar, countertop, clear glass, highly emb Mr Peanut running and Mr Peanut standing on 2 sides, glass lid with peanut finial, emb Mr Peanut characters painted silver, 12" h to top of finial, $200.00.

Paperweight, metal, Mr Peanut figure, "Mr Peanut" and "Compliments Planter's Nut & Chocolate Company" emb on base, 7" h 575.00
Punchboard, Planters Cocktail Peanuts, "2¢ each," winning number receives free ½ lb tin of salted peanuts, early 1940s, 7¾" h 65.00
Thermometer, diecut tin, Mr Peanut, 16" h 55.00
Toy, Mr Peanut Vendor, plastic 575.00
Toy, Tractor Trailer, 2 pc, red cab, yellow and blue trailer with "Planters Peanuts" and Mr Peanut image, Pyro Toy Co, 1950s, 1¾ x 5½" 230.00

Mug, pedestal base, tan, Femlin in black, "Playboy Club Hall China" stamped "Hall China" on bottom, 1960s, $12.00.

PLAYBOY COLLECTIBLES

Playboy memorabilia, from magazines to calendars to Playboy Club items is a popular collecting category, especially now since all the clubs have closed. Hugh M. Hefner began his empire in 1953 with the debut of the first issue of *Playboy Magazine*. Marilyn Monroe graced its cover and centerfold. Many Playboy collectibles can be found at yard sales, swap meets, flea markets, collectible shows, and antique malls. Value on items listed are in good condition, but will be higher if they are in excellent condition and/or unopened or unused such as sealed puzzles and playing cards.

Advisor: Ronnie Keshishian, P.O. Box 2654, Glendale, AZ 85311, (602) 435-2665, e-mail: ronniek@goodnet.com.

Club: Playboy Collectors Assoc., P.O. Box 653, Phillipsburg, MO 65722.

Beer Pitcher, yellow lettering, black rabbit heads, 1970s **$25.00**
Bottle, Playmate Perfume, ½ oz, 1960s **15.00**
Calendar, 1958–59, wall size, orig envelope **50.00**
Calendar, 1960–63, wall size, orig envelope **40.00**
Calendar, 1964–67, wall size, orig envelope **30.00**
Calendar, 1968–72, wall size, orig envelope **20.00**
Calendar, 1973–80, wall size, orig envelope **10.00**
Calendar, 1981–98, wall size, orig envelope **3.00**
Candle, multicolored vase style, wood base, 1960s **35.00**
Casino Tokens, Atlantic City Club, price for each **5.00**
Cocktail Napkins, Jack Cole design, 36 per box, 1956 . . . . . **20.00**
Cuff Links, pr, orig box, 1960s **25.00**
Doll, cheerleader rabbit, with Playboy flag, 1960–70s **40.00**
Golf Putter, pink, ladies, 1960s **60.00**
Key Card, pink playmate, with pouch and box, 1960s **50.00**
Key Chain, square, rabbit head, 1960s **10.00**
Lighter, jumbo size, 1960s **75.00**
Lighter, lucite, Playboy Club key inside, 1960s **75.00**
Magazine, Dec 1953, Vol 1, No 1, Marilyn Monroe cov **600.00**
Magazine, Jan 1954, Vol 1, No 2 . . . . . **500.00**
Magazine, Jan 1955, Vol 2, No 2, Bettie Page centerfold **75.00**
Magazine, Feb 1954–May 1954 . . . . . **75.00**
Magazine, Jun 1954–Dec 1954 . . . . . **50.00**
Magazine, Feb 1955–Dec 1955 . . . . . **20.00**
Magazine, 1956–59 . . . . . **15.00**
Magazine, 1960–64 . . . . . **10.00**
Magazine, 1965–1998 . . . . . **3.00**
Mug, beer, black and white, Femlin kicking up her legs, 1960s, 22 oz **15.00**
Mug, clear, specific club name and address, 1970s, 5½" h . . . **10.00**
Mug, coffee, black and white, Femlin kicking up her legs, 1960s, 10 oz **12.00**
Paperweight, crystal, 2 different designs, 1970s **25.00**
Puzzle, coffee can size, 24 different **10.00**
Puzzle, life size, 4 different, 1971, 150 pcs **25.00**
Rabbit Head, electric, plug it in and ears move back and forth, used in clothing shops on mannequin dressed in tuxedo, 1969 . . . . . **100.00**
Statue, Femlin, 4 different poses, 1961 . . . . . **150.00**
Towel, king size, colorful, 1964, 66 x 36" **25.00**

Cappuccino Cup and Saucer, tan, Femlin in black, "Playboy Club Hall China" stamped on bottom, 1960s, $25.00.

PLAYING CARDS

The key is not the deck, but the design on the deck surface. Souvenir decks are especially desirable. Look for special decks such as Tarot and other fortune-telling items.

Always buy complete decks. There are individuals who just collect Jokers and have a bad habit of removing them from a deck and then reselling it. Also, if you are buying a playing card game, make certain that the instruction card is included. Prices listed are for complete decks.

Clubs: Chicago Playing Card Collectors, Inc., 1826 Mallard Lake Dr., Marietta, GA 30068; 52 Plus Joker, 8127 Mesa Dr., #B391, Austin, TX 78759; International Playing Card Society, 3570 Delaware Common, Indianapolis, IN 46220.

A-1 Tire Company, "Buy War Bonds" **$7.50**
American Presidential Lines **10.00**
Avis, "Avis Features GM Cars" **5.00**
Budweiser, "King of Beers" **10.00**
C & O Railroad, Peake Chessie's Old Man **5.00**
Caesars Palace, Las Vegas, NV, gold logos, dark blue ground **5.00**
Carling Black Label Beer, can shape, red, white, and black **17.50**

Century of Progress, Chicago 1934, view of Belgian village, gilt edges, 3¾ x 2½", $25.00.

Central Banknote Company, Chicago/New York, eagle illus . . . 10.00
Continental Motors, flag with "Army/Navy," center circle "Continental Motors/America's Standard/Powerful as a Nation," red white, and blue . . . 7.50
Delta Air Lines, San Francisco . . . 10.00
Dorney Park, Allentown, PA, Alfundo the clown illus . . . 5.00
Hotel Fremont and Casino, Las Vegas, NV, red and white, diamond design . . . 5.00
Ideal Electric . . . 5.00
Keebler Zesta Saltine Crackers . . . 10.00
Kennedy Space Center, FL, Space Shuttle, lift off photo . . . 6.50
Life Savers, roll of Life Savers Candy illus . . . 5.00
New York, New Haven & Hartford, orig wrapper and box . . . 40.00
Pacific Western Airlines, "We're with you all the way" . . . 6.00
Prince of Wales National Relief Fund, England, WWI, De La Rue, 1914, MIB . . . 30.00
Santa Clausland, Santa Claus, IN, Santa photo . . . 7.50
Sears Tower, Chicago, skyline . . . 7.50
Sinclair Oil, red oil well logo, white ground, gold and red borders . . . 5.00
Tee-Up, golf cartoon on each card, orig box, c1950 . . . 10.00
Winston Cigarettes, "Rodeo Awards," cowboy on bucking horse illus, red, white, and black . . . 17.50
World's Fair, 1984, New Orleans, "Ozark Flies Your Way" . . . 10.00

POLITICAL ITEMS

Collect the winners. For whatever reason, time has not treated the losers well, with the exception of the famous Cox-Roosevelt pinback button. This is a good category to apply my Thirty Year Rule—"For the first thirty years of anything's life, all its value is speculative." Do not pay much for items less than thirty years old. But, do remember that time flies. The Nixon-JFK election was over thirty years ago.

Also concentrate on the non-traditional categories. Everyone collects pinbacks and posters. Try something unusual. How about political ties, mugs, or license plates?

Clubs: American Political Items Collectors, P.O. Box 340339, San Antonio, TX 78234; Third Party & Hopefuls, 503 Kings Canyon Blvd, Galesburg, IL 61401.

Newsletter: *The Political Bandwagon*, P.O. Box 348, Leola, PA 17540.

Periodical: *The Political Collector*, P.O. Box 5171, York, PA 17405.

Bush, George, pinback button, "George Bush For President," black and white, red lettering, 1980 . . . **$10.00**
Carter, James E, keychain, figural peanut, metal, brass luster, c1976 . . . 10.00
Carter/Mondale, door hanger, diecut, stiff paper, double sided, "Elect Carter/Mondale," blue-tone photo, red, white, and blue, attached string, AFL-CIO, 1976 . . . 10.00
Cox, James, pinback button, black and white photo, "For President" and "Peace-Progress-Prosperity," ¾" d . . . 175.00
Democrat, badge, National Convention, Philadelphia, brass hanger with Betsy Ross house, fob with City Hall and Wm Penn statue, blue enameled "Press" bar, white fabric ribbons, 1948, 1½ x 5½" . . . 18.00
Eisenhower, Dwight D, bandanna, red, white, and blue, blue-tone photo of Eisenhower, 26" sq . . . 85.00
Goldwater, Barry, bracelet, brass, charm in shape of United States, ©J Freides . . . 15.00
Goldwater, Barry, lighter, gold finish, black outlined elephant wearing glasses, caption "Au H20," mkd "Park Lighter," 2¼" h . . . 45.00
Harding, Warren G, pinback button, center portrait, white, dark brown . . . 10.00
Hoover, Herbert, pinback button, blue-tone photo, blue lettering, white ground, reverse with St Louis Button Co back paper, 1¼" d . . . 40.00
Kennedy, John F, cigarette lighter, black and bronze finish, front with full name, portrait, and dates of birth and death, reverse shows close-up of Statue of Liberty . . . 20.00
Kennedy, John F, sponge, tan and red, "John F. Kennedy For President, center Kennedy image with United States outline, 1960, 2½ x 4" . . . 40.00
Kennedy, Ted, pinback button, black lettering, yellow ground, "Edw. Kennedy/President-John Conyers Vice President" . . . 10.00
Lincon, Abraham, pinback button, celluloid, 1809–1909 . . . 30.00
McGovern, George, ring, metal, silver luster, imp image of donkey on top, expandable band, 1972 . . . 10.00
McKinley, William, spoon, SS, raised image at end of handle, inscribed "Wm McKinley," c1900, 5½" l . . . 10.00
Nixon, Richard M, bobbing head, composition, figural elephant, white tusks, blue eyes, red hat, red and white striped pants, black shoes, mkd "Japan" on bottom base, 1960, 5½" h . . . 100.00
Nixon, Richard M, hat, soft cloth, red, white, and blue, "Nixon Now," 1968, 6" h, 12" w brim . . . 10.00
Nixon, Richard M, patch, cloth, dark blue ground, elephant design and Nixon's name in gold metallic thread, reverse mkd "Made in India," 1¾" d . . . 10.00

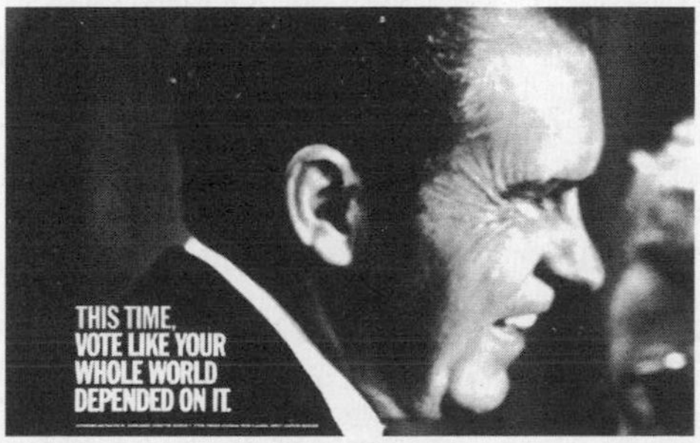

Nixon, Richard M, campaign poster, Nixon/Spiro Agnew, 1968, 21 x 13½", $20.00.

Roosevelt, Franklin D, pamphlet, "Promise and Performance," anti FDR, red and blue on white, 16 pp, 1936, 4 x 8$^{3}/_{4}$", $15.00.

Reagan, Ronald, matchbook holder, brass, hinged, inscribed "50th American Presidential Inaugural," 1984, 1$^{1}/_{2}$ x 2$^{3}/_{4}$" 20.00
Republican, pennant, GOP Replublican National Convention, Chicago, elephant head and building, 1952 . . . . 25.00
Roosevelt, Franklin D, sheet music, "Anchors Aweigh," FDR portrait on cov, 1935 . . . . 20.00
Stevenson, Adlai E, record, *Stevenson Speaks ,* black and white photo overlaid with thin plastic 78 rpm record, issued by AFL-CIO, Philadelphia address on back, 7" sq 25.00
Taft, William, watch fob, black and white celluloid, black leather fob, orig strap, "Taft For President," 2" d 65.00
Wallace, George, bumper stickers, "Wallace For President" 5.00
Wallace, George, license plate, tin, emb, center bluetone dot pattern photo of Wallace, red, white, and blue, Dixie Seal Atlanta, c1968, 6 x 12" 20.00

POODLE COLLECTIBLES

People who collect dog and cat memorabilia are a breed apart. While most cat collectors collect items with any cat image (except Siamese collectors), dog collectors tend to specialize. Poodle collectors are more fortunate than most because the poodle was a popular decorating motif during the 1950s and 60s. Poodles were featured on everything from clothing to lamps.

Ashtray, pink poodle design, Lefton $12.00
Book, *Playtime Poodles,* Helen Wing 6.00
Dish Towel, linen, poodle standing under Fifth Avenue canopy 8.00
Doll, Peteena, Hasbro, 1966, MIB 50.00
Dress, shift, sleeveless, poodle appliqué in gingham and terry cloth, Miss Jane, Miami label, 1960s 35.00
Figure, ceramic, recling poodle on couch wearing crown, looking in mirror 50.00
Greeting Card, poodle sitting under hair dryer reading newspaper, Hallmark, 1950s 2.00
Luggage, child's, 3 pc set, vinyl, Miss Traveler, Ponytail 100.00
Magazine Tear Sheet, *Seventeen,* Play-Tano adv, high-wire walking poodle, 1947 . . . . 1.00
Pattern, poodle skirt, child's, Simplicity, 1950s 3.00
Perfume and Powder Set, French Bouquet 50.00
Planter, Hull 95.00
Purse, figural, wicker, leash handle, Maybelle Marie Birch California 50.00
Puzzle, frame tray, mother poodle pushing stroller full of puppies, Built-Rite, 1960s 6.00
Puzzle, jigsaw, little girl in convertible with poodle and teddy bear, Whitman, 1958 . . . . 10.00
Shirt, felt, 2 poodles and other dogs appliqué, Beacon Hill Co 40.00
Skirt, black felt, "Cafe de Paris" and 2 poodles, 1 sitting on chair by table, other holding umbrella, 1950s 70.0
Stuffed Animal, Mimi the Parisian Poodle, C&M Srery Co 10.00
Thermometer, wall hanger, chalk, poodle taking bubble bath, 1950s 10.00
Waste Can, tin, hp, rhinestone trim, Ransburg of Indianapolis 15.00

POSTCARDS

This is a category where the average golden age card has gone from 50¢ to several dollars in the last decade. Postcards' golden age is between 1898 and 1918. As the cards have become expensive, new collectors are discovering the white border cards of the 1920s and 30s, the linens of the 1940s, and the early glossy photograph cards of the 1950s and 1960s.

It pays to specialize. This is the only way that you can build a meaningful collection. The literature is extensive and can be very helpful.

Club: Deltiologists of America, P.O. Box 8, Norwood, PA 19074.

Periodicals: *Barr's Post Card News,* 70 S. 6th St., Lansing, IA 52151; *Postcard Collector,* P.O. Box 1050, Dubuque, IA 52004. Note: *Barr's* and *Postcard Collector* list over fifty regional clubs scattered across the United States.

Advertising, Coca-Cola, "Ice Cold," woman standing beside horse $40.00
Advertising, Falstaff Beer, real photo, Lemp Brewery, St Louis 85.00
Advertising, Glidden's Racket Store, Tampa, FL, stork delivering new baby 75.00
Advertising, Iron Horse Machine Silk, adv text on back, Belgium 45.00
Advertising, Lily White Flour, "Yes Ma'am Lily White is The Flour the Best Cooks use," Valley City Milling Co, Grand Rapids, MI, c1910 . . . . 50.00
Advertising, Marie Louise Perfume, Paris 50.00
Advertising, Pontiac, "Pontiac for 1948" 8.00
Advertising, Trump Sandals, German 65.00

Advertising, The Famous North Carolina Gospel Singers, Mt Carmel Baptist Church, Philadelphia, PA, 7th Anniversary Show, black and white photograph on cardboard, 1920s, 6 x 7$^{1}/_{2}$", $30.00.

Teddy Bears, emb, printed color, International Art Publishing Co, Series 791, Germany, divided back, 3½ x 5½", $30.00.

Art Nouveau, Milic of Kromeriz, published by Neubert, from The Slav Epic set of 6, brown and white, 1928 . . . . . . **50.00**
Art Nouveau, woman with clowns, published by Koch & Bitriol, Dresden, Germany **50.00**
Art Nouveau, woman with umbrella, semi-nude, black and white with hand applied orange and yellow coloring **60.00**
Automobile, Hupmobile, "4-Passenger Touring Car, On the Way Around the World," Hupp Motor Car, Detroit, 1911 . . . . **100.00**
Aviation, real photo, Pan American, "Pan Am welcomes George R Wright Company" **45.00**
Aviation, Wright Brothers, commemorative, J B Miller & Sons, Dayton, OH, 1909 . . . . **35.00**
Black , Cuddle Toys, linen, prices for toys listed on back. **75.00**
Black, real photo, "Mr. Eugene Stratton," Rapid Photo Co, London, c1910 . . . . **45.00**
Boy Scout, real photo, carrying first aid kit, with cane and gear, pencil notations on back "Nelson A. Butler, Age 17 yr., 1914" **40.00**
Circus, Ringling Bros, Barnum & Bailey Circus, Sarasota, FL, real photo, elephants standing on hind legs. **65.00**
Holiday, Christmas, real photo, girl sitting in front of tree with dolls, 1909 . . . . **85.00**
Holiday, Christmas, real photo, Santa beside child on donkey **40.00**
Holiday, Halloween, with and her brew, emb, c1910 . . . . **40.00**
Military, anti-axis, "Look Who's Listening," Seagram Distillers, sgd "Goff" **30.00**
Military, "Tank Destroyer Forces," Camp Hood, TX **40.00**
Military, "USA Fleet, Welcome To America," 1908 . . . . **65.00**
Motorcycle, Harley-Davidson, with side car, "Legless one-arm driver, now on 50,000 mile tour of the United States," 1918 . . . . **75.00**
Motorcycle, 3 passengers on René Gillet motorcycle, real photo, German **45.00**
Motorcycle, "Boone Races, Aug 12, 1914, The Start of the First Event, Stock Twins," real photo **75.00**
Nautical, Nautical School, issued for third day of technology by the Alfredo Cappellini Institute of Nautical Technology, Italy **35.00**
Ocean Liner, Cunard to Canada, "A Welcome Awaits You" **100.00**
Political, "President Harding Playing Golf," real photo, portrait of Harding with his club, published by "Groganized," IL, black and white **150.00**
Railroad, Northern Pacific Railroad, "A Delicious Northern Pacific Breakfast," A W Thompson, Superintendent Dining Cars, St Paul, MN **35.00**
Sports, wrestlers, real photo, portrait of wrestlers from different countries, each person numbered in pen with corresponding list of names and countries on back, includes black wrestler V Thomson from US, black and white, dated 1930 . . . . **100.00**
Zoo, Philadelphia Zoo, real photo, "Josephine, African Elephant" **60.00**

POSTERS

Want a great way to decorate? Use posters. Buy ones you like. This can get a bit expensive if your tastes run to old movie or advertising posters. Prices in the hundreds of dollars are not uncommon. When you get to the great lithography posters of the late 19th and early 20th century, prices in the thousands are possible.

Concentrate on one subject, manufacturer, illustrator, or period. Remember that print runs of two million copies and more are not unheard of. Many collectors have struck deals with their local video store and movie theater to get their posters when they are ready to throw them out. Not a bad idea. But why not carry it a step further? Talk with your local merchants about their advertising posters. These are going to be far harder to find in the future than movie posters.

Because so many people save modern posters, never pay more than a few dollars for any copy below fine condition. A modern poster in very good condition is unlikely to have long-term value. Its condition will simply not be acceptable to the serious collector of the future.

Periodical: *Collecting Hollywood Magazine,* P.O. Box 2512, Chattanooga, TN 37409.

Advertising, Atlantic Car Conditioning Service, full color clown, "Suggested Posting date May 1, 1956 Litho in U.S.A.," 28 x 44" **$40.00**
Advertising, L&M Cigarettes, cardboard, Gunsmoke characters photo, facsimile James Arness signature, 21 x 22" **90.00**
Advertising, Mack Trucks, bulldog illus, framed, 26 x 21¼" **55.00**
Advertising, Shell, "Let Us Check Your Oil," 32 x 48" **50.00**
Advertising, Nash Airflite, "Stick out your chest, like you owned a Nash Airflite/Let Us Give You A Demonstration," 33 x 18" **75.00**
Advertising, Sinclair H-C Gasoline, blue, red, green, and black **55.00**
Advertising, Weed Chains, "Put On Here," 39½ x 22" **40.00**

Carson and Barnes Wild Animal Circus, paper, 33½ x 42", $44.00. Photo courtesy Collectors Auction Services.

Advertising, Quaker State, paper, multicolor, "Keep 'Em Rolling...," $66.00. Photo courtesy Collectors Auction Services.

Auto Racing, Rhinebeck Speedway, "250 Lap, Sat Aug 10," red, white, and blue, 22½ x 28½" **125.00**
Circus, King Brothers Combined 3 Ring Circus, crouching tiger, woodcut style, 1950s, 28 x 40" **50.00**
Circus, Seils Sterling Circus, The Maniton Troupe, World's Youngest Acrobats, blue and orange on white paper, 1930s, 21 x 28" **72.00**
Concert, David Cassidy, cardboard, Curtis Hixon Hall-Tampa, Sun, Sep 26, 1971, "David Cassidy Of The Partridge Family," 15 x 22½" **40.00**
Concert, Donovan, Cow Palace, Fri Sep 22, 1967, Bill Graham, 14 x 21¼" **40.00**
Concert, Family Dog, Avalon Ballroom, May 3, 1968, 13½ x 20" **75.00**
Concert, Santana, Long Beach Arena, Jan 30, 1977, sgd, 23 x 29" **90.00**
Concert, The Jefferson Airplane, Fillmore Auditorium, Feb 4–6, 1966, 14¼ x 20" **40.00**
Movie, *Brother Rat,* Warner Bos, Ronald Reagan, Jane Wyman, 1938, 27 x 41" **200.00**
Movie, *Four Boys and A Gun,* United Artists, red, white, sepia photos, scattered tack holes, 1956, 27 x 41" **45.00**
Movie, *Honky Tonk,* MGM, Clark Gable, Lana Turner, linen, 1941, 27 x 41" **258.00**
Movie, *The Glory Stompers,* American International Picture, black, white, and red, 1967, 27 x 41" **50.00**
Movie, *The Man Who Knew Too Much,* Paramount, James Stewart, line, 1956, 41 x 81" **230.00**
Movie, *The Real Glory,* United Artists, Gary Cooper, line, 1939, 27 x 41" **230.00**
Political, Ford/Dole, full color glossy, statesmen-like image, 15 x 24" **35.00**
Political, "LBJ For The USA," clear plastic, black and white image, 20 x 30" **20.00**
Political, Mondale/Ferraro, cardboard, red, white, and blue, 13½ x 12" **15.00**
Political, "Nixon's The One," red lettering, white ground, Nixon photo, 14 x 22" **20.00**
Political, "Reagan, He'll Provide The Strong New Leadership America Needs," black and white photo, blue border, 17 x 21" **10.00**
Psychadelic, "Hippie Love, Groovie, Flower Power," stylistic text, Snoopy in balloon, characters on bottom half, Sparta Poster #2, Dave Schiller ©1967, 17 x 22" **100.00**
Railroad, 20th Century Limited, black and white, dated Oct 16, 1926, 20 x 28" **75.00**
Rock and Roll, Elton John, color caricature illus of John and band, c1970, 22 x 35" **25.00**
Social Cause, "NRA/We Do Our Part," red, white, and blue, orig folds, 21 x 27" **90.00**
Theater, Hoyt's A Trip To Chinatown, "The Strobridge Lith. Co. Cin. NJ. & Lon.," 30 x 40½" **120.00**
World War I, "Letter Home," letter writer and text of letter, unidentified artist, black, white, and green **30.00**
World War I, "The Watch On The Rhine," unidentified artist, black, white, 2 shades of orange **30.00**
World War I, "War Savings Stamps," 20 x 30" **40.00**
World War II, "Buy That Invasion Bond!," full color, 20 x 28" **90.00**
World War II, "Volunteer For Victory," Red Cross, 22 x 28" **65.00**

PRAYER LADIES

Prayer Ladies are highly prized figurines manufactured by Enesco in the mid 1960s. Originally they were sold under the name of Mother-in-the-Kitchen. Helen Gallagher sold the figurines as Prayer Ladies in her mail order catalog. Many other gift companies such as Calaco, Adriane and Gift Creations purchased this line from Enesco and distributed it across the country.

The figurines are made of highly glazed porcelain. Her reddish brown hair is swept up into a bun, her head is bowed, eyes closed, and her hands are folded or holding a household object. The dress is high necked with long sleeves and a prayer is on her white apron. The prayers range from "We give you thanks for all your gifts" to a prayer of thirteen lines!

Pink is the dress color that is most commonly found. Blue is much harder to find, and white with blue trim is the hardest to find of all colors. The most common pieces t o find are the napkin holder, toothpick holder, and the salt and pepper shakers. The rarest pieces to locate are the sprinkler bottle and the canister set.

Advisor: April M. Tvorak, P.O. Box 94, Warren Center, PA 18851, (717) 395-3775, e-mail: april@epix.net.

BLUE

Bell **$95.00**
Cookie Jar **495.00**
Flat Spoon Rest **45.00**
Instant Coffee **145.00**
Mug **145.00**
Napkin Holder **35.00**
Salt and Pepper Shaker, pr **20.00**
Soap Dish **45.00**
Spoon Holder **55.00**

Pink, Sprinkler Bottle, 6½" h, $300.00.

Pink, string holder, 6½" h, $150.00.

Teapot, creamer and sugar. **400.00**
Toothpick Holder **28.00**

PINK

Air Freshener **$150.00**
Bank. **145.00**
Bell **85.00**
Bud Vase **125.00**
Candle Holders, pr **145.00**
Canister Set, price for each **300.00**
Cookie Jar. **295.00**
Crumb Sweeper Set, brush and tray **145.00**
Egg Timer **135.00**
Flat Spoon Rest. **35.00**
Instant Coffee **125.00**
Mug **135.00**
Napkin Holder **25.00**
Photo Holder **135.00**
Planter **125.00**
Ring Holder **48.00**
Salt and Pepper Shaker, pr. **16.00**
Soap Dish. **38.00**
Spoon Holder. **45.00**
Teapot, creamer and sugar. **250.00**
Toothpick Holder **20.00**
Wall Plaque **100.00**

WHITE, BLUE TRIM

Cookie Jar. **$425.00**
Flat Spoon Rest. **50.00**
Instant Coffee **160.00**
Napkin Holder **40.00**
Salt and Pepper Shaker, pr. **22.00**
Toothpick Holder **32.00**

PUNCHBOARDS

Punchboards that are unpunched are collectible. A punched board has little value unless it is an extremely rare design. Like most advertising items, price is determined by graphics and subject matter.

The majority of punchboards sell in the $8 to $3 range. The high end of the range is represented by boards, such as Golden Gate Bridge at $85 and Baseball Classic at $100.

Punchboards are self-contained games of chance made of pressed paper containing holes with coded tickets inside each hole. For an agreed amount the player uses a "punch" to extract the ticket of his or her choice. Prizes are awarded to the winning ticket. Punch prizes can be 1¢, 2¢, 3¢, 5¢, 10¢, 20¢, 50¢, $1.00 or more.

Not all tickets were numbered. Fruit symbols were used extensively as well as animals. Some punchboards had no printing at all, just colored tickets. Other ticket themes included dice, cards, dominoes, words, etc. One early board had Mack Sennett bathing beauties.

Punchboards come in an endless variety of styles. Names reflected the themes of the boards. Barrel of Winners, Break the Bank, Baseball, More Smokes, Lucky Lulu, and Take It Off were just a few.

At first punchboards were used to award cash. As legal attempts to outlaw gambling arose, prizes were switched to candy, cigars, cigarettes, jewelry, radios, clocks, cameras, sporting goods, toys, beer, chocolate, etc.

The golden age of punchboards was the 1920s to the 1950s. Attention was focused on the keyed punchboard in the film *The Flim Flam Man*. This negative publicity hurt the punchboard industry.

Advisor: Clark Phelps, 127 N. Main, Midvale, UT 84047, (801) 255-4731.

200 Hole Push Card, 10 x 10". **$3.00**
Ace High, 13 x 17". **90.00**
Barrel of Cigarettes, 10 x 14½" **50.00**
Bars & Bells, 13 x 18⅛". **135.00**
Baseball Push Card, 7 x 10". **10.00**
Beat the Seven, 10 x 10" **35.00**
Best Hand, 6½ x 11". **40.00**
Big Game, 8 x 10½" **30.00**
Bowling Club, 10 x 13". **4.00**
Candy Special, 4½ x 7½" **24.00**
Cash In, 8½ x 9". **18.00**
Double or Nothing, 9 x 10". **36.00**
Extra Bonus, 13 x 12" **40.00**
Fin Baby, 19 x 6". **32.00**
Five On One, 11 x 11" **18.00**
Five Tens, 10 x 13" **18.00**
Girlie Board, 9 x 13". **32.00**
Glades Chocolates, factory wrapped, 7 x 9" **25.00**
Good Punching, 9½ x 10". **36.00**
Home Run Derby, 10 x 12" **75.00**
Jackpot Bingo, 10 x 8". **10.00**
Joe's Special, 11 x 14". **20.00**

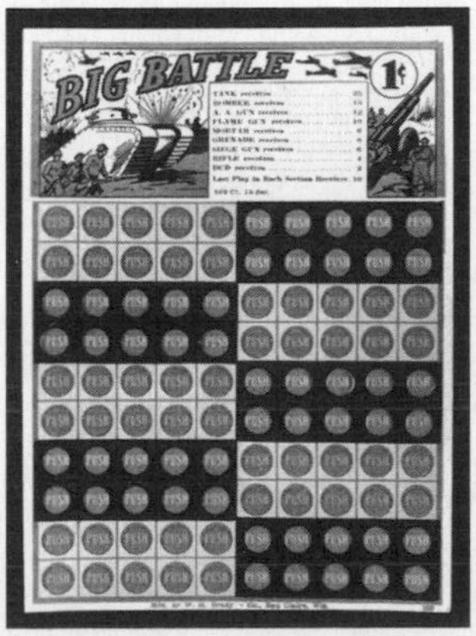

Big Battle, "W.H. Brady & Co., Eau Claire, Wis.," $25.00.

Lu Lu Board, 10 x 11" 28.00
More Smokes, red, white and blue tickets, 10½ x 10½" 24.00
Musical Money, 12 x 14" 43.00
Nestle's Chocolate, 2¢ board, 9 x 8½" 45.00
Nickel Charlie, 10 x 9" 18.00
No Losers Push Card, 7 x 9½" 5.00
Odd Pennies, Small Change 2¢ and 3¢ Board, 6¾ x 11" 45.00
Palm Chart, orig envelope, 1936, 20 x 11½" 8.00
Perry's Prizes, 9½ x 13" 60.00
Pocket Boards, cartoon graphics, 5 different 35.00
Positive Prizes, 12 x 17" 25.00
Pots A Plenty, 11 x 17½" 26.00
Professor Charlie, ©1946, 10 x 12" 16.00
Section Play, 8½ x 10" 18.00
So Sweet, 13½ x 13" 40.00
Speedy Tens, 10 x 13" 18.00
Stars & Stripes, 9 x 14" 26.00
Take It Or Leave It, 12 x 14" 85.00
Tavern Maid, 9½ x 13½" 55.00
Three Sure Hits, 10 x 14" 24.00
Tu Pots, 12 x 18" 44.00
Valuable Prizes, 10 x 12" 20.00
Win A Buck, 4½ x 7½" 12.00

PUPPETS

No, somebody is not pulling your strings, there really is a category on puppets. This category covers marionettes and related jointed play toys, as well as finger and paper puppets. There are bound to be a few of your favorite character collectibles hanging around this new category.

Finger, Fred Flintstone, Knickerbocker, 1972 . . . . **$15.00**
Finger, Monkees, Davy Jones, vinyl, sticker with 1970 Columbia Pictures, Inc copyright, 5" h 25.00
Finger, Peanuts, Peanuts Showtime Finger Puppets, Ideal, 1977 . . . . 35.00
Finger, Prince Charming, Mego, 1977 . . . . 30.00
Finger, Spiderman, Ideal, 1965 . . . . 85.00
Hand, Bamm Bamm, Ideal, 1964, 10" h 20.00
Hand, Barney Google 50.00
Hand, Batman, plastic body, vinyl head, Ideal, 1966 . . . . 70.00
Hand, Beetle Bailey, Gund 65.00
Hand, Bozo the Clown, Capital, 1962 . . . . 25.00
Hand, Court Jester 20.00
Hand, Droop-A-Long, Ideal 45.00
Hand, Green Hornet, Ideal, 1966 . . . . 185.00

Hand Puppet, Gumby's Pal Pokey, orange cloth body, vinyl head, Lakeside, 1965, $35.00.

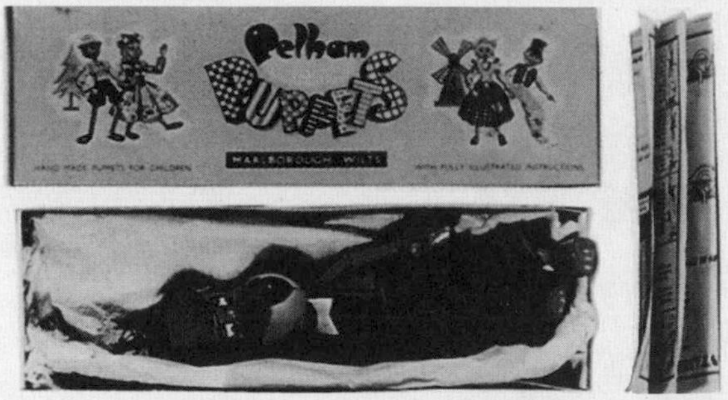

Marionette, Huckleberry Hound, composition body, hp details, fabric hat and jump suit, with handles and instructions, Pelham Puppets/Screen Gems, 1960s, 9½" h, $477.00. Photo courtesy New England Auction Gallery.

Hand, Gumby, Lakeside, 1965 . . . . 30.00
Hand, Huckleberry Hound, Knickerbocker, 1959 . . . . 22.00
Hand, Jerry Lewis 90.00
Hand, Lone Ranger, Ideal, 1966 . . . . 50.00
Hand, Mad Hatter, cloth body, 1960s 20.00
Hand, Magilla Gorilla, Ideal, 1960s, 19" h 140.00
Hand, Mr Magoo, cloth body, vinyl head, 1960s 55.00
Hand, Nightmare Before Christmas, Santa, Hasbro, MIB 30.00
Marionette, Alice In Wonderland, Peter Puppet Playthings, 1950s 60.00
Marionette, Donald Duck, Peter Puppet Playthings, 1950s, 6½" h 55.00
Marionette, Donny and Marie Osmond, dressed in matching blue glitter polyester outfits, performing on stage powered by electric motor, orig box, Madison Ltd, 1979 . . . . 180.00
Marionette, Snoopy, Pelham/Tiderider, 1979, 27" h 42.00
Push Button, Batman, plastic, Kohner, 1966, 3" h 45.00
Push Button, Charlie Brown, Ideal, 1977 . . . . 45.00
Push Button, Davy Crockett, wood, plastic, Kohner, 1956 . . . . 65.00
Push Button, Joe Cool, Ideal, 1977 . . . . 35.00
Push Button, Mr Jinx, plastic, Kohner, 3" h 20.00
Push Button, Ricochet Rabbit 45.00
Push Button, Rocky Squirrel, 1965 . . . . 40.00
Push Button, Snoopy, sheriff, Ideal 14.00
Push Button, Wally Gator, Kohner, 1964 . . . . 25.00

PURINTON POTTERY

Bernard Purinton founded Purinton Pottery in 1936 in Wellsville, Ohio. In 1941 the pottery relocated to Shippenville, Pennsylvania. Dorothy Purinton and William H. Blair, her brother, were the chief designers for the company. Maywood, Plaid, and several Pennsylvania German designs were among the patterns attributed to Dorothy Purinton. William Blair designed the Apple and Intaglio patterns.

Purinton did not use decals, as did many of its competitors. Greenware was hand painted and then dipped into glaze. A complete dinnerware line and many accessory pieces were produced for each pattern.

The plant ceased operations in 1958, reopened briefly, and then closed for good in 1959.

Newsletter: *Purinton Pastimes*, P.O. Box 9394, Arlington, VA 22219.

Apple, beer mug $115.00
Apple, breakfast plate 14.00
Apple, coffee canister 60.00
Apple, cookie jar, wide oval 55.00
Apple, cruets, pr, oil and vinegar, sq 55.00
Apple, cup and saucer 10.00
Apple, juice mug 12.00
Apple, relish, 3-part 22.50
Apple, tumbler 10.00
Brown Intaglio, candy dish, ring handle 60.00
Brown Intaglio, coffee mug 25.00
Brown Intaglio, coffeepot, 8 cup 45.00
Brown Intaglio, honey jug 110.00
Chartreuse, candy dish, ring handle 90.00
Chartreuse, chop plate 55.00
Chartreuse, creamer and sugar 47.50
Chartreuse, dutch jug, 5 pt 70.00
Fruit, canister, half oval, red trim 15.00
Fruit, creamer and sugar, mini 25.00
Fruit, Dutch jug, 5 pt 25.00
Heather Plaid, chop plate 60.00
Heather Plaid, creamer, mini 37.50
Heather Plaid, salt and pepper shakers, mini jug 25.00
Mountain Rose, cruet, round, right handled 60.00
Mountain Rose, rum jug 55.00
Normandy Plaid, bean cup, individual 30.00
Normandy Plaid, chop plate 26.00
Normandy Plaid, coffeepot, 8 cup 50.00
Normandy Plaid, Dutch jug, 1 pt 32.50
Normandy Plaid, pitcher 45.00
Normandy Plaid, tea and toast set 12.00
Normandy Plaid, tumbler 9.00
Palm Tree, honey jug 120.00
Petals, creal bowl 15.00
Petals, dessert bowl 20.00
Petals, salad plate 37.50
Red Ivy, creamer and sugar, mini 35.00
Red Ivy, salt and pepper shakers, range size 15.00

PURSES

It is amazing what people will carry draped over their shoulders! Remember those alligator purses, complete with head and tail? Or how about those little metal mesh bags that held a lady's hankie and a book of matches, at most? As impractical as they were, these are are some of the most collectible purses on the market. Where value is concerned—think unusual.

Club: California Purse Collector's Club, P.O. Box 572, Campbell, CA 95009.

Alligator, beige, adjustable strap, self cov drawstring threaded through gilt-metal ringed holes, sgd "Morabito 1 Place Vendome Paris," 1970s $460.00
Alligator, brown, elegant trapezoidal form, fold-over flap closure with gold metal clasp, sgd "Lucille de Paris," 1950s 110.00
Beaded, fancy floral design, string closure 65.00
Beaded, Jaqueline Mode 17.50
Beaded, jet black, string closure 30.00
Beaded, red, white, and blue, string closure 45.00
Beaded, silver, brown, and white, possibly Czechoslovakian 100.00

Enamel Mesh, floral design, white-silver metal frame, chain link fringe, $75.00.

Chatelaine, crocheted, steel beads, ornate German silver frame, hook, early 1900s 125.00
Enamel Mesh, allover diamond pattern, multicolor, zigzag bottom edge, Whiting and Davis 83.00
Enamel Mesh, Art Deco allover swirl design, blue, pink, yellow, and brown, zigzag bottom edge, Whiting and Davis 105.00
Enamel Mesh, Art Deco design, multicolor, zigzag bottom edge, Whiting and Davis 165.00
Enamel Mesh, Art Nouveau design, black, yellow, and pale green, zigzag bottom edge, Whiting and Davis 94.00
Enamel Mesh, central floral medallion, black, white, and yellow, zigzag bottom edge, sgd "El-Sah" 72.00
Enamel Mesh, diamond grid pattern, cream and browns, zigzag bottom edge, Whiting and Davis 83.00
Enamel Mesh, repeating geometric design, pink, brown, and greens, zigzag bottom edge, Whiting and Davis 100.00
Enamel Mesh, snakeskin pattern, green and yellow, straight bottom edge with band of cresed waves, Whiting and Davis, replaced chain 66.00
Fabric, blue peacock design, Pavan, 9" h, 15" w 40.00
Lizard, envelope bag, black, gilt-metal handle and double G monogram, sgd "Germaine Guérin, orig box, 1960s 70.00
Mesh, silver, jeweled frame, Whiting and Davis 150.00
Papier-mâché, rect, leaves and flowers dec 50.00
Plastic, box bag, mottle tan, padded, outlined with brass studs, sgd "Judith Leiber," 1960s 172.00
Plastic, lucite, pearlized, round lid, twisted handle, seashell dec 18.00
Suede, evening bag, black suede with mint green enamel, silver ornament, and clasp, sgd "S & F 935 Austria Sterling" 460.00

Hermés, black calf with gilt-metal oval catch, sgd, 1960s, $172.00. Photo courtesy William Doyle Galleries.

Suede, pouch, dark brown, silk cord drawstring through gilt-metal rings, sgd "Cartier," 1970s **143.00**
Velvet, evening bag, blush pink, embroidered with gold bouillon and rhinestones, sgd "Nettie Rosenstein," 1950s **172.00**
Wood, flip-top, color vintage car dec, glass stones dec, double handled, 5½" h, 11½" w, 4¼" d **50.00**
Wood, "Roadrunner," gold jewels dec, 7" h, 8½" w, 3" d **45.00**
Wood, "Sophistikit," hp cat, blue jeweled eyes, gold and clear colored jewel dec, dated 1964, 11 x 9 x 3" **75.00**

PUZZLES

The keys to jigsaw puzzle value in order of importance are: (1) completeness (once three or more pieces are missing, forget value); (2) picture (no one is turned on by old mills and mountain scenery); (3) surface condition (missing tabs or paper or silver fish damage causes value to drop dramatically); (4) age (1940 is a major cutting off point); (5) number of pieces (the more the better for wood); and (6) original box and label (especially important for wooden puzzles). Because of the limitless number of themes, jigsaw puzzle collectors find themselves competing with collectors from virtually every other category.

Jigsaw puzzle collectors want an assurance of completeness, either a photograph or a statement by the seller that they actually put the puzzle together. "I bought it as complete" carries no weight whatsoever. Unassembled cardboard puzzles with no guarantees sell for $1 or less, wooden puzzles for $3 or less. One missing piece lowers price by 20 percent, two missing pieces by 35 percent, and three missing pieces by 50 percent or more. Missing packaging (a box or envelope) deducts 25 percent from the price.

Clubs: American Game Collectors Assoc., P.O. Box 44, Dresher, PA 19025; National Puzzler's League, P.O. Box 82289, Portland, OR 97282.

Note: The following retail prices are for puzzles that are complete, in very good condition, with their original box.

Jigsaw, adult, diecut, American News Company and Branches, Miss America Puzzle Series, #4, In Blossom Time, over 300 pcs, 1933, 13¼ x 10" **$25.00**
Jigsaw, adult, diecut, Automatic Products Co, Transportation building, Indianapolis, IN, Tip-Top Jigsaw Puzzle, "Paradise Valley," garden terrace with mountains in background, 391 pcs, 11⅝ x 15¾", orig box **20.00**
Jigsaw, adult, diecut, Brundage, J R, Empire Jig Picture Puzzle, A Canadian Landscape, over 400 pcs, box eatures sketch of Empire State Building **8.00**
Jigsaw, adult, diecut, Built-Rite, Interlocking Picture Puzzle, Hospitality, over 350 pcs, 19⅝ x 15⅝", guide picture on box **5.00**
Jigsaw, adult, diecut, Consolidated Paper Box Co, Big 10, Grandma's Birthday, over 275 pcs, approx 15½ x 10¼" **8.00**
Jigsaw, adult, diecut, Einson-Freeman, Long Island City, NY, #27, The Cradle Maker, mother with baby looks over shoulder of young boy making cradle from carton scraps, Walter Beach Humphrey illus, 165 pcs, 10½ x 14¼" **18.00**
Jigsaw, adult, diecut, Milton Bradley, Buckingham Jig Picture Puzzle, Hector, the Protector, over 240 pcs, guide picture on box **12.00**
Jigsaw, adult, hand cut, A-1 Puzzle Club, untitled Impressionist landscape by August Renoir, wood, woman strolling along shady road, c1910, 24 x 20", box missing **10.00**
Jigsaw, adult, hand cut, Bliss, R W, Wallaston, MA, The Flower Market, Van Vreeland print of Dutch flower market by canal, interlocking cut, 200 pcs, c1930, 9 x 12", period box **25.00**
Jigsaw, adult, hand cut, Cotton, Robert, Soldier Boy, soldier surrounded by ammunition, 76 pcs, cut Jan 22, 1943, back of puzzle is cigar box lid, boxed **25.00**
Jigsaw, adult, hand cut, Full o'Cheer Picture Puzzles, Boston, MA, Contentment Cottage, T Noel Smith country scene of cottage and garden by stream, color line cutting, 132 pcs, 9 figurals, c1930s, 12 x 9", period box missing **25.00**
Jigsaw, adult, hand cut, Houser, Glad, The Rug Merchant, Near Eastern woman showing a rug to elderly gentleman buyer, Balesio Roman Tivol artist, 100 pcs, c1920, 8 x 6", orig box **15.00**
Jigsaw, adult, hand cut, Milton Bradley, Tyrolean Waters, alpine scene with castle, lake, and mountains, 300 pcs, 1937, 15 x 11", orig box **40.00**
Jigsaw, advertising, Birds Eye, "Birds Eye Puts It All Together Jigsaw Puzzle," diecut cardboard, lid shows "Clarence Birdseye...the man who started an industry" standing in front of Birds Eye Frosted Foods freeder in old-fashioned country store, unopened, 9 x 6 x 2" box **10.00**
Jigsaw, advertising, Burger Chef, Dragon Wagon, part of Timetraveler Funmeal Fest, frame tray, 16 pcs, 1980, 9½ x 6⅝" **10.00**

Jigsaw, adult, diecut, Einson-Freeman, Every Week Jig-Saw Puzzle, #30, In Conference, Ray Morgan illus, photo by Seaf, 14¼ x 10¼", $25.00.

Jigsaw, adult, hand cut, Parker Brothers, Visiting the Invalid Dog, over 150 pcs, 11⅝ x 10", $35.00.

Jigsaw, children's, diecut cardboard, E. E. Fairchild Corp, #1652, Freddy Flameout: The Way Out Jet Jockey, 100 pcs, 1963, 15 x 10½", $30.00.

Skill, dexterity puzzle, Nabisco Shredded Wheat Juniors, fighting Blue Devils, 101st Cavalry, tin and plastic, 1¼" d, $35.00.

Jigsaw, advertising, Cocomalt, R B Davis Co, The Windmill Jig-Saw Puzzle, windmill and harbor at low tide, 65 pcs, 10 x 6½", paper envelope **10.00**
Jigsaw, advertising, New Jersey Bell, "The Answer To Your Communication Puzzle: BELL," 9 pcs, 8 x 8", period packaging missing **8.00**
Jigsaw, advertising, Our Gang Gum, #8, 1 of series of 25, aerialist dangling from wire using mouth grip, c1933, 3⁹⁄₁₆ x 5⅛" **8.00**
Jigsaw, advertising, Springmaid, frame tray, Abdullah Bulbul Amir defending his sheet, battle scene on front between Abdullah Bulbul Amir and Ivan Skavinsky Skivar, poem on back, c1951, 14 x 11" **15.00**
Jigsaw, advertising, Taco Bell, premium, frame tray, Parasaurolophus, 1 of series, 15 pcs, 1993, 5 x 8" **4.00**
Jigsaw, children's, Horsman, E J, Prize Mother Goose Pictures Dissected **75.00**
Jigsaw, children's, McLoughlin Brothers, Composition Board Puzzles A New Dissected Map of the United States, c1887, 12 x 8", wood box **60.00**
Jigsaw, children's, Parker Brothers, Little People's Picture Puzzle, 2 puzzle set, multicolored litho, sgd by Alice Hirschberg, c1915 . . . . **75.00**
Jigsaw, children's, Samuel Gabriel Sons & Co, Our Defenders Puzzles, set of 3, 1940s, 12 x 16" box **50.00**
Jigsaw, children's, Louis Marx & Co, Cottage of Dreams/Moon Mullins, wood, double sided, double set, 145 pcs, 9½ x 6¾",m cardboard box mkd "150 pcs" **85.00**
Jigsaw, children's, Milton Bradley, Captain Kangaroo Puzzles, #4501-5, diecut cardboard 4 puzzle set, each puzzle approx 6¼ x 10", 20 pcs each puzzle, cardboard box with 2 partial guide pictures **25.00**
Jigsaw, children's, Milton Bradley, Dissected Outline Map of the United States of America, wood, reversible, U S Map and scenes, c1880, 8 x 9¾", wood box **125.00**
Jigsaw, children's, Saalfield Publishing Co, Kitty-Cat Picture Puzzle Box, #567, 6 puzzle set, Fern Biesel Peat illus, each puzzle approx 7⅞ x 9⅞" **50.00**
Jigsaw, children's, Whitman Publishing Co, Tarzan Big Little Book Picture Puzzles, 1938, 11 x 8" box **150.00**
Jigsaw, children's, Wilkie Picture Puzzle Co, Everybody, #24, A Winter Day, G Fleissner illus, 310 pcs, mid 1930s, orig box, 15¾ x 11⅞" **10.00**
Jigsaw, game, Cadco-Ellis, Jingo: The Jigsaw Bingo Game, 1941, 13¼ x 10 x 1" box **35.00**
Jigsaw, photograph, American Studios, LaCrosse, WI, personalized, individual's home, 1965, boxed **15.00**
Jigsaw, postcard, Statue of Joseph Warren, Picture Puzzle Post Card, U S 616, Roxbury, MA, perforated, 18 pcs, 3½ x 5½", mailing envelope **15.00**
Skill, Head and Tail Puzzle, Calumet Baking Powder, match colors and 4 sides of baking powder cans **25.00**
Skill, Letter Dissection, Royal Typewriter Co, NY, The "R" Puzzle, Royal logo on front, 7 pcs, 4½ x 3" paper envelope **20.00**
Skill, Sequential Movement, Puzzle-Peg, Lubbers & Bell Mfg Co, Clinton, IA, c1920s **15.00**

PYREX

I'll bet everyone has at least one piece of Pyrex glassware in his/her house. This heat resistant glass can be found in many forms, including casserole dishes, mixing bowls, sauce pans, and measuring cups. Pyrex was manufactured by Corning Glass Works.

Bowl, Gooseberry Cinderella, #442 . . . . **$7.00**
Bowl, Gooseberry Cinderella, #444 . . . . **10.00**
Cake Dish, red, 8¼" d **8.00**
Casserole, cov, Butterprint, white on turquoise, 1 qt **10.00**
Casserole, cov, clear, round, 2 qt **12.00**
Casserole, cov, Colonial Brown, ½ qt **12.00**
Casserole, cov, Daisy, 2½ qt **20.00**
Casserole, cov, Golden Pine, 2 qt **15.00**
Casserole, cov, Holiday, 2 qt **15.00**
Casserole, cov, Hospitality, 2 qt **15.00**
Casserole, cov, individual, 8 oz **4.00**
Casserole, cov, Zodiac, 2½ qt **18.00**
Chip and Dip Set, gold on white, 1961 . . . . **22.00**
Dish, cov, Town and Country, 1½ qt **15.00**
Divided Dish, cov, yellow, 1½ qt **15.00**
Loaf Pan, clear, 1½ qt **8.00**
Nesting Bowl, Early American **5.00**
Nesting Bowl, Orange Dot **6.00**
Nesting Bowl, Terra, set of 3 . . . . **20.00**
Nesting Bowl, yellow **8.00**
Percolator, Flameware, Deluxe, 4 cup **8.00**
Pie Plate, clear, 10" d **8.00**
Ramekin, red, 7 oz **4.00**
Refrigerator Dish, cov, blue opal, 1½ cup **5.00**
Saucepan, Flameware, 1 qt **8.00**
Saucepan, Flameware, detachable band, 1½ qt **10.00**
Serving Bowl, Bluebelle, 1½ qt **15.00**
Serving Bowl, with candle warmer, 2½ qt, 1959 . . . . **20.00**
Teapot, Flameware, thin handle **22.00**
Utility Dish, oblong, yellow, 2 qt **10.00**

RADIO CHARACTERS AND PERSONALITIES

Radio dominated American life between the 1920s and the early 1950s. Radio characters and personalities enjoyed the same star status as their movie counterparts. Phrases such as "The Shadow Knows" or "Welcome Breakfast Clubbers" quickly date an individual.

Many collectors focus on radio premiums, objects offered during the course of a radio show and usually receive by sending in proof of purchase of the sponsor's product. Make certain an object is a premium before paying extra for it as part of this classification.

Many radio characters also found their way into movies and television. Trying to separate the products related to each medium is time consuming. Why bother? If you enjoyed the character or personality, collect everything that is related to him or her.

Clubs: Friends of Vic & Sade, 7232 N. Keystone Ave., Lincolnwood, IL 60646; National Lum 'n' Abner Society, #81, Sharon Blvd., Dora, AL 35062; North American Radio Archives, 134 Vincewood Dr., Nicholasville, KY 40356; Oldtime Radio-Show Collectors Assoc., Rt. 1, Box 197, Belpre, OH 45714; Pow-Wow (Straight Arrow), P.O. Box 24751, Minneapolis, MN 55424; Radio Collectors of America, 8 Ardsley Cir., Brockton, MA 02402.

Newsletter: *Hello Again,* P.O. Box 4321, Hamden, CT 06514;

Periodicals: *Old Time Radio Digest,* 10280 Gunpowder Rd., Florence, KY 41042.

Allen, Jimmie, model airplane, Thunderbolt, 19" l, 24" wingspan, orig box, 1930s **$100.00**

Amos 'n Andy, game, Card Party, M Davis Co, 2 score pads, 8 tallies, orig obx, 1938 . . . . **70.00**

Amos 'n Andy, map, Pepsodent Co premium, 1935 copyright, 1937, 5 x 8" **85.00**

Amos 'n Andy, paperback book, *Amos & Andy,* vertical format, 16 pp, dusty, heavily soiled covers, extensive wear, c1930s, 4 x 6" **150.00**

Amos 'n Andy, sheet music, "The Perfect Song/Musical Theme Of The Pepsodent Hour," ©1937, 8 pp, 9 x 12" **25.00**

Amos 'n Andy, sticker, "Check 'N Double Check! That's Amos And Andy. We Don't Want Any Double Checks. Just A Single Check For $...Will Satisfy Us. How About It?," Hartford Insurance Co adv, black and white, red border, unused, 1930s, $2\frac{1}{4}$ x $3\frac{1}{2}$" **40.00**

Archie, pinback button, "Meet 'Archie' Thursday Night, white lettering, dark red ground, c1940, $2\frac{3}{4}$" **45.00**

Sophie Tucker, cigar bag, Chevrolet adv on reverse, 4 x $6\frac{1}{2}$". $10.00.

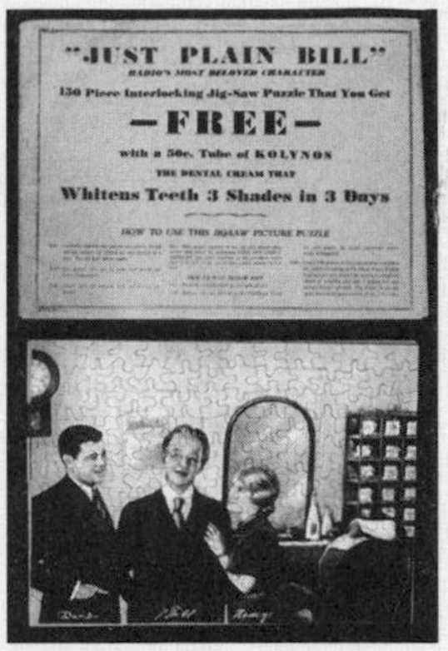

Just Plain Bill, puzzle, Kolynos Dental Cream giveaway, 150 pcs, orig envelope, 12 x 9", $30.00.

Benny, Jack, program, Jack Benny Show, black and white photos, Phil Harris signature, 12 pp, late 1930s **24.00**

Cantor, Eddie, transcription disk, mkd in pen on each side, "NBC Symphony Pines of Rome, 3/11/52," and "NBC Cantor Show Biz, 12/15/51," orig plain green sleeve, 16" d disk **40.00**

Captain Midnight, photo, Chuck Ramsey, black and white, matte, white facsimile signature, Skelly Oil, c1939, 6 x $7\frac{1}{2}$" **65.00**

Fibber McGee and Molly, fan card, glossy black and white photo neatly mounted on cardboard, 1930s, 8 x 12" **50.00**

Fibber McGee & Molly, menu, stiff paper, Brown Derby Restaurant, autographed, $9\frac{1}{2}$ x $12\frac{1}{4}$" **100.00**

Green Hornet, fan card, color photos, back with brown and white facsimile signature, $3\frac{1}{2}$ x $5\frac{1}{2}$". **60.00**

Green, Mitzi, pinback button, photo and "I'm on the Air, Mitzi Green, in Happy Landings" in center, "Ward's Soft Bun Bread, WKAN, Tues & Thurs, 6 pm" in white lettering on rim, 1930s, $1\frac{1}{4}$" d **5.00**

Lone Ranger, ring, brass bands, 6-gun, sparking, 1947 . . . . . **75.00**

Lum and Abner, family almanac, orig mailing envelope, Horlick's Malted Milk, 1936, 34 pp, 6 x 9" **40.00**

McCarthy, Charlie, book, *A Day With Charlie McCarthy,* soft cov, color photo cov, 32 pp, K K Publications, Inc, ©1938 McCarthy, Inc, $9\frac{1}{4}$ x 10" **20.00**

McCarthy, Charlie, perfume bottle, clear glass, removable black plastic hat, late 1930s, $3\frac{1}{2}$" h. **40.00**

Paul, Les, song folio, 1951 . . . . **3.00**

Penner, Joe, valentine, mechanical, diecut, Penner holding duck on shoulder, eyeballs and mouth move back and forth, "I'll Gladly Buy A Duck," 1930–40, $4\frac{1}{2}$ x 7" **20.00**

Purvis, Melvin, ring, brass, adjustable, eagle and shield design, 1936 . . . . **30.00**

Sgt Preston, coloring book, Whitman, 32 pp, unused **20.00**

Skelton, Red, postcard, radio show cast photo, matte finish, postmarked 1948, $3\frac{1}{2}$ x $5\frac{1}{2}$" **20.00**

Sky King, newspaper adv, Name-A-Plane Contest, 1950s, $11\frac{1}{2}$ x $15\frac{1}{2}$" **25.00**

Superman, ring, Superman Crusader, silvered brass **160.00**

The Shadow, blotter, Blue Coal, red, white, blue, and yellow, 1940s, unused pr, 4 x 9" **75.00**

The Shadow, matchbook cover, silhouette image of Shadow on front with skull, reverse depicts skeleton holding bloody knife with "The Shadow Radio's Thrilling Mystery Drama/Brought To You," printed name and address, inside 15 matched mkd "Listen To The Shadow Every Sunday Mutual Network" **100.00**

Uncle Don, membership card, Don Winslow Squadron of peace, stiff paper, issued by Kellogg's Wheat Krispies, includes individual registration number and facsimile signature, orig recipient's name in black ink, 1939, 2½ x 4" 20.00
Uncle Don, book, *U S N Secret Code Book,* Whitman, ©1935, 16 pp 90.00
Uncle Don, pinback button, "Uncle Don Good Humor-GHHC," Uncle Don in uniform, blue letters, 1¼" d 25.00

RADIOS

If a radio does not work, do not buy it unless you need it for parts. If you do, do not pay more than $10. A radio that does not work and is expensive to repair is a useless radio.

The radio market went through a number of collecting crazes in the 1980s and 1990s. It began with Bakelite radios, moved on to figural and novelty radios, and now is centered on early transistors and 1940s plastic case radios. These crazes are often created by manipulative dealers. Be suspicious of the prices in any specialized price guide focusing on these limited topics. There are several general guides that do a good job of keeping prices in perspective.

Clubs: Antique Radio Club of America, 81 Steeple Chase Rd., Devon, PA 19333; Antique Wireless Assoc., 59 Main St., Bloomfield, NY 14469.

Periodicals: *Antique Radio Classified*, P.O. Box 802, Carlisle, MA 01741; *Radio Age,* P.O. Box 1362, Washington Grove, MD 20880; *The Horn Speaker,* P.O. Box 1193, Mabank, TX 75147.

Addison, Model 2-A, ridges around body and left grill wrap over top in contrasting color, green or maroon body, small, 1939 . . . . $700.00
Admiral, Model 4V18, portable, semicircular dial and oversized pointer at top, gray, maroon or green with gold trim, 1952 . . . . 35.00
Admiral, Model 6T01, table, rect, Bakelite, molded grill louvers across front, white or brown, 1946 . . . . 25.00
Admiral, Model 7T10E-N, table, plastic, right front sq dial, left horizontal louvers, 2 knobs, broadcast, AC/DC, 1947 . . . . 35.00
Advertising, Miracle Whip 30.00
Advertising, Nabisco, Oreo shaped, plastic 25.00
Advertising, Lipton Cup-of-Soup, box shaped 30.00
Advertising, Pepsi, dispenser shaped 25.00

Emerson, Bakelite, dial mkd, "Emerson Radio and Phono. Corp. N.Y. U.S.A.," front mkd "Emerson Radio & Television," 5" h, 9" w, 4½" l, $27.50. Photo courtesy Collectors Auction Services.

Telefunken Operette #6, glass, cloth, plastic, orig papers and parts, Superheterodyne, Serial #468561, Western Germany, 14½" h, 21½" w, 8¼" d, $176.00. Photo courtesy Collectors Auction Services.

Airline, Model 14BR-514B, table, plastic, ivory painted, Art Deco style, right slide rule dial, push button, left horizontal louvers, 2 knobs, 1946 . . . . 100.00
Arvin, Model 253T, table, black Bakelite, 1948 . . . . 35.00
Belmont, Model 5D128, table, Bakelite, Art Deco, rounded left side, small dial at left with push buttons, tuning knob on right side, 1940 . . . . 65.00
Bendix, Model 55P2, table, plastic, imitation walnut, slide rule dial, vertical grill bars, rear handle, 2 knobs, broadcast, AC/DC, 1949 . . . . 40.00
Capehart, Model 504PR, console, wooden, sq, AM/FM, phono, space for TV, 1949 . . . . 45.00
Character, He-Man/Skeletor, hard plastic, 2 dimensional image of He-Man on 1 side, Skeletor on back, blue, yellow, and flesh-tone, red raised names, ©1985 Mattel, 2½ x 4 x 5" 20.00
Character, Mickey Mouse, Emerson, wooden, painted black, metal Mickey cutout over grill, Disney characters on metal corners 1,500.00
Crosley, Model 9-113, table, plastic, brown, elongated dial under oversized speaker cloth, 1949 . . . . 15.00
Crosley, Model 11-1204, white 135.00
Emerson, Model 77, console, Art Deco, 7-tube set with veneer inlays, simple dial, 3 knobs on front, mid 1930s 75.00
Emerson, Model 511, marbleized plastic 150.00
Emerson, Model 825B, clock radio, rect, sq clock face center, knobs on right side, 1955 . . . . 15.00
Emerson, Model 883, series B, table, blue, sleep timer 35.00
Firestone, Model 4-A-78, table, plastic, oblong panel, right semi-circular dial, left grill, 2 knobs, broadcast, AC/DC, 1950 . . . . 45.00
General Electric, Model 422, plastic, elongated dial between 2 knobs on bottom, brown or white, AM, 1951 . . . . 15.00
General Electric, Model A-65, console, Art Deco, vertical wooden grill, 2-band dial, 4 knobs, 1935 . . . . 100.00
Motorola, Model 52H, table, rect, large station numbers on clear plastic front, gray, green, white or brown, 1952 . . . . 25.00
Motorola, Model L14E, portable, transistor, plastic, right dial knob, lower horizontal bars, left knob, handle, AM, battery, 1960 . . . . 25.00
Philco, Model 42-KR5, refrigerator, wood, rounded sides, right dial, left clock, curved base to fit top of refrigerator, 1942 . . . . 60.00
Philco, Model 50-1727, radio/phono, double doors over speaker cloth, AM/FM, 1959 . . . . 25.00
RCA, Model 1X51, Blaine, table, semicircular dial, 1952 . . . . 15.00

RCA, Model 54B5, Solitarire, portable, Catalin panel behind dial, gold plating on trim, 1947 . . . . 75.00
RCA, Model 56X, plastic, brown, Art Deco dial 45.00
Silvertone, Model KT, Cameo, table, Bakelite, rect, brown or white 15.00
Sparton, Model 100, table, Bakelite, elongated dial a top edge, black or white, 1947. . . . . 25.00
Stewart Warner, Model 9170, Gadabout, portable, folding handle on top near dial and controls. 35.00
Stromberg-Carlson, Model 515-M, console, Art Deco, long dial and push buttons below long dial, c1940 . . . . 55.00
Sylvania, Model 548, clock radio, plastic, sq clock face at left, radio dial on right side, tan, black, red or green, 1957. . . . . 15.00
Westinghouse, Model H-107, console, left door pulls out phono, right door opens to expose radio and controls, 1946 . . . . 15.00
Zenith, Model 6D015, table, Bakelite, grill and dial form large semicircle, brown or white, 1946. . . . . 45.00

RADIOS, TRANSISTOR

In the early 1960s transistor radios were the rage. Music was now both portable and convenient. Today, the transistor has gone the way of the early hand held calculator—both are clumsy and obsolete.

Newsletter: *Transistor Network,* 32 W. Main St., Bradford, NH 03221.

Admiral, Model 581, coat-pocket set, recessed volume control above larger tuner at right front, no handle or earphone jack, 1959 . . . . $50.00
Admiral, Model 739, Palomar, gray leatherette covering, volume at left, tuner at right, 1959 . . . . 20.00
Arvin, Model 61R13, plastic, pink, shirt pocket, grill below offset V-shaped metal area with large tuner, 1961 . . . . 20.00
Bulova, Model 670, Bantam, shirt pocket, metal front with small glass jewel above perforatged grill and logo, 1961 . . . . 45.00
Continental, Model TR-208, 2-tone, shirt pocket, strip with tuner across front, 2 jacks at top edge, 1959 . . . . 35.00
Emerson, Model 842, leather cov, tuner at top front center, 1956 . . . . 50.00
General Electric, Model P745, coat pocket, grill slots at left, large tuner and recessed volume control at right, black with gold trim, 1958. . . . . 25.00
General Electric, Model P760, plastic, 2-tone, knobs on sides, plastic handle on top, 1958 . . . . 20.00
Hitachi, Model TH-621, plastic, shirt pocket, tuner above slot grill, recessed volume knob on right, white or black, 1958. . . . . 75.00
Magnavox, Model CR-729, coat pocket, large metal grill, "all-transistor" above "Magnavox," 1957. . . . . 200.00
Novelty, alligator, General Electric, plastic, green 30.00
Novelty, binoculars, Japanese, Bakelite, controls on top 60.00
Novelty, champagne bottle, oversized 45.00
Novelty, gasoline pump, "Sunoco" on front 10.00
Novelty, Panda Bear, platic, white and black 20.00
Novelty, Polaroid Film, plastic, blue, paper label 15.00
Novelty, skate, plastic 20.00
Novelty, Snoopy, black details, white body. 25.00

Standard Amoco, 4¼" h, 2½" w, 1½" d, $33.00. Photo courtesy Collectors Auction Services.

Olympic, Model 781, shirt pocket, metal grill at bottom, circular window, black or tan. 35.00
Philco, Model T-4J, coat pocket, large tuner dial at right front, earphone jack, black 75.00
RCA, Model 1BT-3, leatherette cov, metal grill on front, 1958. . . . . 45.00
Silvertone, Model 220, Transistor 600, oversized leatherette case, controls at sides, 1960 . . . . 15.00
Sony, Model TFM-825, coat pocket, long dial on left edge, AM/FM, 1965. . . . . 10.00
Sony, Model TR-650, coat pocket, oversized circular grill, 1965 . . . . 20.00
Westinghouse, Model H-655, coat pocket, grill over large tuner, metal handle, white and gray, 1959 . . . . 30.00

RAILROADIANA

Most individuals collect by railroad, either one near where they live or grew up or one for which they worked. Collectors are split fairly evenly between steam and diesel. Everyone is saddened by the current state of America's railroads. There are Amtrak collectors, but their numbers are small.

Railroad collectors have been conducting their own specialized shows and swap meets for decades. Railroad material that does show up at flea markets is quickly bought and sent into that market. Collectors use flea markets primarily to make dealer contacts, not for purchasing.

Railroad paper from timetables to menus is gaining in popularity as railroad china, silver plated flat and hollow wares, and lanterns rise to higher and higher price levels. The key to paper ephemera is that it bear the company logo and have a nice displayable presence.

THE PULLMAN COMPANY—Passenger's Check. To identify accommodations purchased.
LOUISVILLE to NASHVILLE, Tenn.
TRAIN M SEAT 3 CAR 77
Property taken into car will be entirely at owner's risk.
OFFICE 14-1 FORM 17 $0.80
1313

Ticket, The Pullman Co, Louisville to Nashville, TN, $6.00.

Clubs: Key, Lock and Lantern, Inc., 31 Sandle Dr., Fairport, NY 14450; Railroadiana Collectors Assoc., Inc., P.O. Box 4894, Diamond Bar, CA 91765; Railway & Locomotive Historical Society, P.O. Box 1418, Westford, MA 01886;

Periodical: *The Main Line Journal,* P.O. Box 121, Streamwood, IL 60107.

Ashtray, C & O Railroad, white, 4 rests, blue outer band, inner yellow pinstripe, center black Chessie kitten, 4" d **$85.00**

Badge, American Electric Railway Association Convention, 1926 . . . . **18.00**

Badge, Delaware & Hudson Railroad, silvered brass rim frame, clear cello over black and white identification paper, c1930s **10.00**

Baggage Check, Northern Pacific Yellowstone Park Line logo, strap, 2¼ x 2½" **45.00**

Berry Bowl, Baltimore & Ohio Railroad **50.00**

Book, *Commodore Vanderbilt, An Epic of the Steam Age,* Wheaton J Lane, Alfred H Knoff, NY, hard cov, 1942, 357 pp, 6 x 8¾" **15.00**

Bottle Opener, Missouri Pacific Lines, metal head pearlized handle, "Air Conditioned", 2½" l **15.00**

Butter Pat, Baltimore & Ohio Railroad **55.00**

Broadside, Central Vermont Railroad, Rand Avery & Company **250.00**

Calendar, Missouri Pacifc Lines, tin, green, color litho of steam passenger locomotive at top, complete set of orig removable green date cards below, 13 x 19" **165.00**

Calendar, Union Pacific Railroad, 1958 . . . . **10.00**

Candy Container, glass, signal lantern shaped, green, tin screw top lid, wire handle, mkd "Avor 1 oz. USA," 3½" h **15.00**

Celery Tray, Chicago & Northwestern Railroad **20.00**

Cereal Bowl, Baltimore & Ohio Railroad, 6½" d **60.00**

Chocolate Mold, tin, early 6-wheel locomotive, hinged, 4½ x 6" **65.00**

Conductor's Cap, Amtrak, letters and logo on sq shaped gold badge affixed to standard royal blue cloth uniform cap **35.00**

Cork Screw, Soo Line, metal, folding, "For Hunting, For Fishing, Take The Soo Line" on handle, 3 x 3" opened size **35.00**

Cream Soup, Baltimore & Ohio Railroad **75.00**

Creamer, PRR, International Silver Co, soldered, seamless, "PRR" on bottom **100.0**

Dinner Plate, Missouri Pacific, states and wildflowers illus, Syracuse China, 10½" d **55.00**

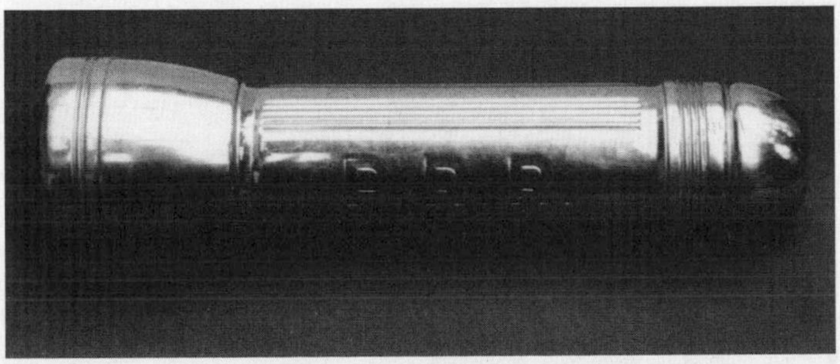

Flashlight, Pennsylvania Railroad, P. R. R., Bright Star, domed glass, 7½" l, $50.00.

Menu, Pennsylvania Railroad, National Railway Historical Society, Phila Chapter, Apr 6, 1957, dinner, red, black, and gold, 6 x 9", $8.00.

Dinner Plate, child's, Union Pacific, clown illus **175.00**

Handkerchief, C & O Railroad, cotton, white, Chessie, Peake, and kittens in corners and center, multicolored, 14 x 14½" **35.00**

Head Rest, Illinois Central, cloth, brown on tan, script at buttonholes, 15 x 15½" **10.00**

Lantern, Adlake Non Sweating Lamp, Chicago, yellow, red, blue, and clear lights, 17½" h **150.00**

Lantern, Missouri Pacific Railroad, hand, 4" clear globe **75.00**

Letter Opener, Northern Pacific, plastic, red, "Main Street of the Northwest, 8½" l **6.00**

Menu, Great Northern Railway, Club Breakfast Service, front cov shows couple seated in lobby of Prince of Wales Hotel, logo at bottom, 1928, 7 x 10¼" **15.00**

Milk Bottle, Missouri Pacific Lines, emb, buzz saw logo, 9¾" h, qt. **65.00**

Napkin, cloth, Union Pacific, cotton, white, winged streamliner motif printed in corner, yellow border, 11 x 16" **10.00**

Photograph, Soo Line Railroad, passenger train arriving at Eden Valley depot, people waiting on platform, matted and framed, c1890, 6 x 8½" **60.00**

Pinback Button, New York Central, "20th Century," litho full color frontal view of engine froms treamlined train service, 1930s, 11/16" **10.00**

Pinback Button, "PA Railroad Co Baggage Room Employee," red and white, center black and white serial number, 1930–40 . . . . **10.00**

Pinback Button, Railroad Union Campaign, multicolored, "Brotherhood of Locomotive Firemen & Engineers" and "100,000," early 1900s **40.00**

Pinback Button, "Santa Fe Railroad Safety Monitor," yellow and black, 1950s **10.00**

Plate, New York Central Railroad, veterans, diesel engine dec, 1951 . . . . **30.00**

Playing Cards, Denver & Rio Grande Railways, complete deck **35.00**

Pocket Mirror, Burlington Northern, green plastic rect case, 2½ x 3" **5.00**

Poster, Great Northern & Northern Pacific Railroad, paper, black and white, pioneers crossing prairie, "The Path of Empire," 38¼ x 27" **95.00**

Poster, Ohio Valley Scenic Railroad, "Take The Yellow Car, To Niagara Falls, Round Trip 50¢, conductor pointing to yellow trolley car, 21 x 28" **275.00**

Sign, Atlantic Coast Line, metal, round, stenciled black lettering, reflective gold ground, 29½" d **85.00**

Thermometer, metal, "G.N.RY," indented black numerals on brass ground, 2½ x 10" **50.00**

Timetable, Great Northern Railway, 1948 . . . . **8.00**
Timetable, Lehigh Valley Railroad, Jan 4, 1945 . . . . **5.00**

RAMP WALKERS

These comical toys have waddled their way into many toy collections. While you may find some ramp walkers made from metal, wood, or celluloid, the majority of those available are plastic. Subjects vary from advertising figures to generic animals to popular television cartoon characters.

Astro and George Jetson, Marx **$90.00**
Baby Walking Baby, plastic, moving eyes, cloth dress, Marx **40.00**
Baseball Player, plastic, with bat and ball **40.00**
Bison with Native, plastic, Marx **25.00**
Bull, plastic, cream colored, brown and black accents, Marx, 4" l **40.00**
Bunnies, carrying carrot **40.00**
Bunny, pushing cart, Marx **40.00**
Camel, plastic, tan muzzle and underbelly, red, silver, and yellow saddle, with movable head, Made in Hong Kong, 1960s, 3" h **40.00**
Chilly Willy, being pulled on sled, Marx **25.00**
Chipmunks Marching Band, plastic, 2 brown chipmunks, yellow feet, wearing red and yellow band uniforms, 1 playing drum, other with trumpet, Marx, 1950s, 3¼" l **30.00**
Circus Horse, Marx **15.00**
Clown on Dinosaur, Marx, 4" l, MIP **65.00**
Cow, plastic, metal legs, Marx **15.00**
Davy Crockett, holding rifle over shoulder, brown and yellow outfit, with brown dog, Marx, 3" l **40.00**
Dutch Boy and Girl, Marx **30.00**
Flash Turtle, Long John Silver premium, with coin weight **15.00**
Funny Face, set of 4, Pillsbury premium, orig shipping box, 1971 . . . . **200.00**
Horse, plastic, rubber ears, string tail, Marx **30.00**
Kangaroo, with baby in pouch, Marx, 3" h **25.00**
Little Red Riding Hood, Wilson **40.00**
Mickey Mouse, pushing lawn mower, Marx, 3¼" l **50.00**
Nora the Nursemaid, plastic Nora figure with baby carriage, 1¼" h soft rubber Bonnie Braids figure, includes litho tin ramp with Dick Tracy, Tess Trueheart, Bonnie Braids, and BO Plenty illus, hp facial features, Marx, ©1951 FA Syndicate, orig 5 x 12 x 1½" box **100.00**
Olive Oyl, Wilson **175.00**
Pinocchio, Wilson **175.00**
Quinn Penguin, Long John Silver premium **15.00**
Reindeer, Marx **35.00**
Santa and Mrs Claus, faces on both sides **40.00**
Sydney Dinosaur, Long John Silver premium, 1989 . . . . **15.00**

RECORDS

Most records are worth between 25¢ and $1. A good rule to follow is the more popular the record, the less likely it is to have value. Who does not have a copy of Bing Crosby singing "White Christmas?" Until the mid-1980s the principal emphasis was on 78 rpm records. As the decade ended 45 rpm records became increasingly collectible. By 1990 33⅓ rpm albums, especially Broadway show related, were gaining in favor.

To find out what records do have value, check Jerry Osborne's *Rockin Records,* 17th Ed., Antique Trader Books, 1995. By the way, maybe you had better buy a few old record players. You could still play the 78s and 45s on a 33⅓ machine. You cannot play any of them on a compact disc player.

Club: Assoc. of Independent Record Collectors, P.O. Box 222, Northford, CT 06472; International Assoc. of Jazz Collectors, 15745 W. Birchwood Ln., Libertyville, IL 60048.

Periodicals: *DISCoveries*, P.O. Box 1050, Dubuque, IA 52004; *Goldmine*, 700 E. State St., Iola, WI 54990.

AC/DC, *Problem Child/Let There Be Rock,* 45 rpm, Atco, 1977 . . . . **$1.00**
Archies, The, *Sugar Sugar/Melody Hill,* 45 rpm, Calendar, 1968 . . . . **1.50**
Baez, Joan, *We Shall Overcome/What Have They Done To The Rain?,* 45 rpm, Vanguard, 1963 . . . . **2.00**
Beach Boys, *Surfin' U S A/Shut Down,* 45 rpm, Capitol, orange and yellow swirl label, 1963 . . . . **3.50**
Banana Splits, The, *The Tra La La Song/Toy Piano Melody,* 45 rpm, Decca, 1970, 32429 . . . . **2.00**
Bugs Bunny in Storyland, 78 rpm, 2 records, Capitol, ©1949 . . . . **35.00**
Carpenters, The, *We've Only Just Begun/All My Life,* 45 rpm, A&M Records, 1970 . . . . **1.50**
Donald Duck Golden Record, 45 rpm, colorful paper sleeve, 7 x 8" **25.00**
Fink Along With Mad, 33⅓ rpm, Big Top, 1961 . . . . **40.00**
Jackson 5, The, *Mama's Pearl/Darling Dear,* 45 rpm, Motown, picture sleeve, 1971 . . . . **2.50**
Jerry Lee Lewis, *Great Balls of Fire,* Sun, 281 . . . . **20.00**
Josie & The Pussycats, *Voodoo/If That Isn't Love,* Capitol, picture sleeve, 1972 . . . . **5.00**
Kiss, *Rock And Roll All Nite/Rock And Roll All Nite,* 45 rpm, Casablanca, 1975 . . . . **1.00**
Laugh In '69 Cast Album, 33⅓ rpm, Reprise, 1969, 12⅓ x 12⅓ cardboard cov **10.00**
Lone Ranger, Little Golden Record, 45 rpm, ©1958, 7 x 8" cardboard dust cov **40.00**
Monty Python Examines the Life of Brian, 33⅓ rpm, Warner Bros, 1979 . . . . **12.00**
Sinatra, Frank, *Come Swing With Me!,* 33⅓ rpm, Capitol, 1961 . . . . **8.00**
Songs Girl Scouts Sing Album, two 78 rpm records, 12 scouting songs, c1940, 10¼ x 10¼" cov **15.00**
Soupy Sales, *Spy With a Pie,* 33⅓ rpm, Reprise, 1962 . . . . **10.00**
Soundtrack, *Pollyanna,* 45 rpm, Disneyland, 1960 . . . . **20.00**

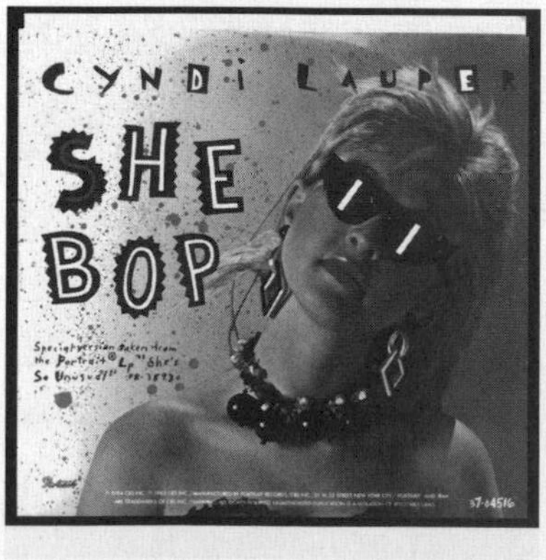

Lauper, Cyndi, *She Bop,* 45 rpm, Epic, ©1984, $1.00.

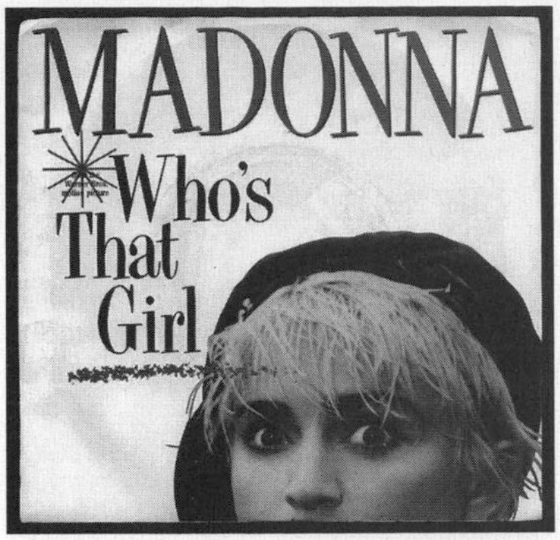

Madonna, *Who's That Girl,* 45 rpm, Sire, 28341–7, 1987, $1.00.

Soundtrack, *The Stooge,* Dean Martin, 33$^1/_3$ rpm, Capitol, 1953 . . . . 35.00
Soundtrack, *To Kill A Mockingbird,* 45 rpm, Ava, 1962 . . . . . . 30.00
Statler Brothers, *Flowers on the Wall,* 33$^1/_3$ rpm, Columbia, 1966 . . . . 10.00
The Untouchables, 33$^1/_3$ rpm, Capitol, early 1960s, 12$^1/_4$ x 12$^1/_4$" cardboard cov 15.00
Van Dyke, Dick, *Songs I Like,* 331/3 rpm, Command, 1963. . . . . 8.00
Walt Disney's So Dear To My Heart, 4 records, Capitol label, ©1949, 10$^1/_2$ x 12" thick cardboard cov. 85.00

RED WING

Red Wing, Minnesota, was home to several potteries. Among them were Red Wing Stoneware Company, Minnesota Stoneware Company, and The North Star Stoneware Company. All are equally collectible. Red Wing has a strong regional base. The best buys are generally found at flea markets far removed from Minnesota. Look for pieces with advertising. Red Wing pottery was a popular giveaway product.

Club: Red Wing Collectors Society, Inc, P.O. Box 184, Galesburg, IL 61402; The Rumrill Society, P.O. Box 2161, Hudson, OH 44236.

Art Pottery, candleholders, pr, #B1409, white/green, tear drop shaped, 5" h $20.00
Art Pottery, compote, #690, fluted sides, white, 9" h 35.00
Art Pottery, vase, #892, fan shaped, white/green, 7$^1/_2$" h 35.00
Art Pottery, vase, #1170, white/green, sawtooth design, 6$^3/_4$" h 40.00
Art Pottery, vase, #1360, green/white, emb flowers, 7$^1/_2$" h 30.00
Art Pottery, water glass, walnut green, Greek motif, 4$^3/_4$" h 25.00
Blossom Time, berry bowl 3.00
Blossom Time, dinner plate, 10$^1/_2$" d. 5.00
Bob White, butter dish, cov 30.00
Bob White, centerpiece, figural quail on tray 95.00
Bob White, cocktail tray 40.00
Bob White, cup and saucer 8.00
Bob White, nappy 15.00
Bob White, water cooler, orig spigot and base 525.00
Bob White, water jug, 60 oz 40.00
Brittany, creamer and sugar, cov 30.00
Brittany, dinner plate, 10" d 15.00
Brittany, gravy boat 45.00
Cookie Jar, Dutch girl, tan 110.00
English Garden, cnadleholder, #1190, ivory/brown wipe, 6" h 25.00
Magnolia, bowl, #1223, ivory/brown wipe, 12$^1/_2$" d 50.00
Magnolia, candleholders, pr, #1029, 7$^1/_2$" h 40.00
Magnolia, vase, #1213, ivory/brown wipe, tapered, 9" h. 45.00
Morning Glory, egg plate, cov 75.00
Morning Glory, creamer 8.00
Morning Glory, cream soup bowl, cov 12.00
Normandy, bread and butter plate, 6" d 8.00
Normandy, chop plate, 12" d. 45.00
Normandy, salt and pepper shakers, pr. 20.00
Random Harvest, fruit dish 15.00
Random Harvest, platter, 13" l 25.00
Random Harvest, salt and pepper shakers, pr 25.00
Random Harvest, sugar, cov 20.00
Renaissance, centerpiece bowl, #526, ivory/brown wipe, 12" l 50.00
Round Up, casserole, large 70.00
Round Up, cup and saucer 40.00
Round Up, platter, 13" l. 135.00
Round Up, salad bowl, 5$^1/_2$" d 40.00
RumRill, bowl, #672, Neo-Classic Group, 3 x 10" 60.00
RumRill, horn of plenty vase, #K8, white, 12" l. 40.00
RumRill, planter, #259, swan, white, 6" h. 45.00
RumRill, planter, #493, trumpet flower, white and green blend, 5$^1/_2$" h 60.00
RumRill, vase, #183, lilac, green over lavender, 8$^1/_4$" h 45.00
RumRill, vase, #576, nude seated on turtle, suntan, green int, Athenian Group, 10$^1/_2$" h. 300.00
RumRill, vase, #664, Neo-Clasic Group, 9$^1/_8$" h 85.00
Turtle Dove, after dinner cup and saucer 10.00
Turtle Dove, bread and butter plate, 6" d 6.00
Turtle Dove, cereal bowl 12.00
Turtle Dove, teapot, cov 50.00
Village Brown, chop plate, 14" l 25.00
Village Brown, coffee mug. 10.00
Village Brown, syrup jug 15.00
Village Brown, vegetable dish, divided. 18.00
Village Green, bread and butter plate, 6" d. 6.00
Village Green, casserole, cov. 24.00
Village Green, cup and saucer. 10.00
Vintage, casserole, cov 50.00
Vintage, celery dish. 20.00
Vintage, vegetable dish, divided. 30.00
Zinnia, cereal bowl. 15.00
Zinnia, chop plate. 35.00
Zinnia, salt and pepper shakers, pr. 25.00

Jardiniere, brushware with emb lilies and cattails, unmkd, 15" h, $275.00. Photo courtesy Jackson's Auctioneers & Appraisers.

ROAD MAPS

The collecting of road maps as we know them is a relatively new category of collectibles and has risen with popularity of all gas station memorabilia. There are many reasons one collects road maps. 1) a specific brand of gasoline, 2) a certain year of issue, 3) a certain state or area, 4) to track highway development, 5) colorful graphics, 6) an almost endless supply, and 7) they are inexpensive.

The majority of collectible maps were issued after 1910 since there were not too many roads prior to that period. Previously, maps were issued by railroads, and from the turn of the century to 1920 guide books were issued for bicycle routes and brave early automobile owners.

In the mid-1920s a uniform national highway marking system was adopted, roads got better and America became mobile. Maps were published and given free to motorists by oil companies and state governments. Other private interests published atlases and special maps. However, the oil companies and state issues have the largest following among collectors. Maps derive their value from the graphic appeal as well as scarcity due to the fact an obscure or small regional oil company may have been the publisher.

After the second World War the maps published by major oil companies became very plentiful and their value has remained modest.

As in all collectibles, especially paper items, condition is all important. Prices listed are for road maps in excellent condition.

Advisor: Peter Sidlow, 5895 Duneville St., Las Vegas, NV 89118, (702) 873-1818, fax (702) 248-4288.

Club: Road Map Collector of America, 2214 Princeton Blvd., Lawerence, KS, 66049.

AAA Issued, 1931–40 . . . . . **$50.00**
AAA Issued, 1941–50 . . . . . **3.00**
AAA Issued, 1951–present. **1.00**
AAA Issued, pre–1930. . . . . **6.00**
Amoco, 1929 . . . . . **100.00**
Associated, 1953 . . . . . **12.00**
Barnesdale, 1937 . . . . . **28.00**
Chevron, 1938 . . . . . **15.00**
Cities Service **20.00**
Conoco, 1931. . . . . **45.00**
Esso, 1952 . . . . . **12.00**
Gulf, 1953 . . . . . **15.00**
Hi Speed, 1940. . . . . **10.00**
Kendall, 1940. . . . . **12.00**
Marathone, 1936 . . . . . **20.00**
Mobil Gas, 1950. . . . . **6.00**
Pan Am, 1948. . . . . **20.00**
Phillips, 1941 . . . . . **15.00**
Pure, 1932 . . . . . **24.00**
Richfield, 1947. . . . . **18.00**
Shell, 1933. . . . . **30.00**
Sinclair, 1939 . . . . . **18.00**
Skelly, 1940 . . . . . **10.00**
Standard Oil of Indiana, 1936 . . . . . **10.00**
Standard Oil of Kentucky, 1930 . . . . . **30.00**
Standard Oil of New York, 1931 . . . . . **20.00**
State Issue, Arizona, 1940 . . . . . **18.00**
State Issue, Michigan, 1955 . . . . . **10.00**
State Issue, Montana, 1941 . . . . . **20.00**
State Issue, Nevada, 1946 . . . . . **15.00**
State Issue, New Mexico, 1942 . . . . . **18.00**
State Issue, Wyoming, 1940. . . . . **10.00**
Sunoco, 1964. . . . . **8.00**
Texaco, 1933 . . . . . **22.00**
Tydol, 1937 . . . . . **18.00**
Union, 1934. . . . . **25.00**

Sinclair, Kansas, 5 panel, 2-sided paper, 1934, 19½" l, $88.00. Photo courtesy Collectors Auction Services.

ROBOTS

This category covers the friction, windup, and battery operated robots made after World War II. The robot concept is much older, but generated few collectibles. The grandfather of all modern robot toys is Atomic Robot Man, made in Japan between 1948 and 1949.

Robots became battery operated by the 1950s. Movies of that era fueled interest in robots. R2D2 and C3PO from *Star Wars* are the modern contemporaries of Roby and his cousins.

Robots are collected internationally. You will be competing with the Japanese for examples.

When buying at a flea market, take time to make certain the robot is complete, operates (carry at least two batteries of different sizes with you for testing), and has the original box. The box is critical.

Action Planet Robot, Yonezawa, Japan, Robbie style, black, red plastic hands, walks, sparks through face, red feet, clockwork mechanism, orig box, 1965–70, 8⅜" h **$488.00**
Astro Captain Robot, Daiya, light tin face behind domed helmet, white plastic arms with claw hands, sparking torso, clockwork mechanism, 1965–70, 6¾" h **285.00**

Cragstan Astronaut, Yonezawa, Japan, litho tin, windup crank handle, advances with moving arms, 10" h, $561.75. Photo courtesy New England Auction Gallery.

Golden Gear Robot, SH, Japan, battery operated, advances with moving legs and arms, flashing light on head, plastic eyes, orig box, 9" h, $603.75. Photo courtesy New England Auction Gallery.

Atlas, built-in key, litho tin, plastic feet, soft plastic rocket attached to back, orig box, mkd "Industria Argentina" in English and Spanish on toy and box, 1960s, 2 x 6 x 3¾" 325.00
Blazer Superhero Robot, Bullmark, tin, red, yellow, black, and blue, plastic arms, windup, orig box 170.00
Captain Robo, Yonezawa, light blue and fluorescent pink tank style robot, friction driven, matching cream plastic trailer with pink bubble over drivers, orig box, 1970s, 13" l 140.00
Dalek, Marx, plastic, battery operated, red body, black base, orig box, 6½" h. 185.00
Ding-A-Lings, Claw, Topper, plastic, red, blue, yellow, and green, 1970s, 3 x 3 x 5½" h 40.00
Extractor, Japan, plastic, blue, litho tin chest plate, silver accents, mkd "Made in Japan," c1970, 9½" h 50.00
Fighting Robot, Japan, plastic, brown, double firing machine guns in torso, battery operated, orig box, 1970s, 9½" h. 200.00
Forbidden Robot Robby Robot, Modern Toys, plastic, windup, metallic gray, clear plastic dome on head, silver face plate, antenna, box mkd "MGM/UA Entertainment Co," 1984, 4¼" h. 50.00
Godaikin Voltes V Super Robot, Bandai, diecast metal, plastic, complete with accessories, transforms into 5 different military machines or giant tank, 1980s, 16" h . . . 100.00
Great Garloo, The, Marx, battery operated, fabric leopard skin skirt, plastic "Garloo" medallion around neck, metal link chain bracelet on wrist, orig box, 1960s, 18" h 550.00
Lost In Space, Remoc, plastic, red, metallic blue arms and legs, clear dome head, claw hands, ©1966 Space Productions, 12" h. 400.00
Mechanical Space Man, Yoshia, light blue litho, 4 blade propeller on orange helmet, astronaut face, fixed arms, clockwork mechanism, 1960s, 6" h. 230.00
Mighty Robot, Japan, metallic green litho, sparking chamber, clockwork mechanism, 1960s, 5½" h. 140.00
Piston Robot, S J M, Taiwan, battey operated, litho tin, plastic, black plegs and arms, red feet, clear platic head with litho tin inserts, silver colored eyes and ears, 1970s, 11" h 100.00
R-35, Marx, tin, remote control, battery operated, plastic battery box, 1950s, 8" h 185.00
Radar Hunter Robot, Busy Bee, Hong Kong, hard plastic, windup, built-in key, walks forward as antenna spins, colorful box with display window, 1970s, 2½ x 4 x 6½" 65.00
Robert the Robot, Ideal, battery operated, eyes light up, orig box, 1950s, 14" h 200.00
Robot 2500, Durham Industries, Inc, battery operated, silver colored, red light on torso, orig box, 10" h. 80.00
Roto Robot, Horikawa, battery operated, gray, hinged plastic arms, 3 guns on chest, walks, rotates while firing lit guns, 1965-70, 8¾" h. 172.00
Star Strider, Japan, battery operated, gray, astronaut walks forward, body rotates as guns fire from chest, 1970s, 12½" h. 170.00
Video Robot, S H, Japan, battery operated, plastic, litho tin, metallic blue, gold and silver accents, 1970s, 9" h . . . 100.00

ROCK 'N' ROLL COLLECTIBLES

Most collectors focus on individual singers and groups. The two largest sources of collectibles are items associated with Elvis and the Beatles. As revivals occur, e.g., the Doors, new interest is drawn to older collectibles. The market has gotten so big that Sotheby's and Christie's hold Rock 'n' Roll sales annually.

Club: *Kissaholics Magazine,* P.O. Box 22334, Nashville, TN 37202.

Beatles, mug, white ceramic, black and white portrait photos with facsimile signitures, mkd "England," c1964, 4" h $85.00
Berry, Chuck, record, *My Ding-A-Ling/Johnny B Goode,* 45 rpm, Chess, 1972 . . . . 2.00
Byrds, The, song books, *The Byrds Bag,* and *Younger Than Yesterday,* words and music with black and white photos, color cov, Tickson Music Co, ©1967 Ludlow Music, Inc, 9 x 12", price for set 40.00
Cass, Mama, doll, Hasbro, 1967, 4½" h. 90.00
Chapin, Harry, poster, cardboard, concert # 7 in the Chapin/PAF Benefit Series, Sun, Jun 5, 1977, Huntington High School, autographed, 17 x 22". 175.00
Checker, Chubby, autograph, black and white photo . . . .
Checker, Chubby, record, *Limbo Rock/Popeye (The Hitch-Hiker),* 45 rpm, Parkway, 1962 . . . . 5.00
Cher, doll, Growing Hair Cher, Mego, ©1976, 12¼" h, orig window display box, MIB 65.00
Chiffons, The, record, *My Boyfriend's Back/I Got Plenty Of Nuttin',* 45 rpm, Laurie, 1966 . . . . 2.00
Clapton, Eric, ticket stub, 1975 Tampa, FL concert, black and white, blue-tone photos, 2¼ x 3". 15.00
Clark, Dick, doll, plush stuffed body, molded vinyl head and hands, mkd "Juro" on back of neck, c1950, 25" h. . . . 150.00

Jefferson Starship, record, *Spitfire,* ©1976 Grunt Records, mfg by RCA Records, NY, $3.00.

Clark, Dick, magazine, *Dick Clark Official American Bandstand Yearbook,* 40 pp, color and black and white photos, c1950, 9 x 12" **25.00**

Doors, The, poster, full color, green bottom border, white Doors logo, ©1968 Doors Production Corp, 24 x 36" **20.00**

Dylan, Bob, magazine, *Sing Out! The Folk Song Magazine,* Vol 12, #4, Oct–Nov 1962, 68 pp, $5\frac{1}{2}$ x $8\frac{1}{2}$" **20.00**

Edgar Winter Group, The, pinback button, "They Only Come Out At Night," litho tin, full color photo, $2\frac{1}{4}$" d **5.00**

Fats Domino, autograph, full color photo, sgd "God Bless And Rock Around The Clock," 8 x 10" **20.00**

Freddie and the Dreamers, program, 20 pp, late 1960s, 10 x 13" **25.00**

Garcia, Jerry, pinback button, "Jerry Garcia For President 1980," black and white photo, yellow lettering, $2\frac{1}{8}$" sq **10.00**

Gibb, Robin, lunch box, metal, color photo of Gibb and Bee Gees, King-Seeley, ©1978 Bee Gees **20.00**

Jefferson Starship, record, *Find Your Way Back,* 45 rpm **1.00**

John, Elton, pinback button, "Elton John/Central Park 1980 Keep It Green," 3" d **20.00**

Jones, Davy, costume, girl's, 1 pc rayon mini dress with Monkees logo, molded thin plastic mask, Bland Charnas Co, Inc, ©1967 Rayburt Productions, Inc, orig box **60.00**

Jones, Davy, pinback button, "I Rave For Dave," celluloid, black and white, bright orange, reverse with Screengems and Raybert copyrights, 1966, $\frac{13}{16}$" d **20.00**

Kiss, comic book, *Kiss Marvel Comics Super Special,* Vol 1, #1, 1977, $8\frac{1}{4}$ x 11" **40.00**

Monkees, The, flicker ring, Kellogg's premium **20.00**

Osmond, Donny and Marie, game, Donny & Marie Osmond TV Show Game, Mattel, ©1976 Osbro Productions, Inc, $9\frac{1}{2}$ x $18\frac{3}{4}$ x $1\frac{1}{2}$" **35.00**

Presley, Elvis, belt buckle, brass, diecut name, late 1970s, $1\frac{3}{4}$ x 3" **20.00**

Santana, ticket, Carlos Santana/Mahavishnu John McLaughlin, stiff paper, Fri, Aug 31, 1973, Chrysler Arena, MI, purple and light blue, photos of Santana and McLaughlin, $4\frac{1}{4}$ x $5\frac{1}{2}$" **40.00**

Woodstock, book, *Woodstock 69,* Joseph J Sia, Scholastic Book Services, ©1970, 124 pp **25.00**

Woodstock, jigsaw puzzle, cardboard and tin canister, American Publishing Corp, ©1970, $3\frac{1}{2}$ x $5\frac{1}{2}$" **20.00**

ZZ Top, pinback button, "WMMR Welcomes ZZ Top Afterburner Tour," black on gold, event at Philadelphia Spectrum, 1986, $1\frac{3}{4}$" d **5.00**

ROCKWELL, NORMAN

The prices in this listing are retail prices from a dealer specializing in Rockwell and/or limited edition collectibles. Rockwell items are one of those categories for which it really pays to shop around at a flea market. Finding an example in a general booth at ten cents on the dollar is not impossible or uncommon.

When buying any Rockwell item, keep asking yourself how many examples were manufactured. In many cases, the answer is tens to hundreds of thousands. Because of this, never settle for any item in less than fine condition.

Club: Rockwell Society of America, P.O. Box 705, Ardsley, NY 10502.

Postcard, Fish Tires adv, "Time to Re-tire. Get A Fish," sgd, red, black, and white, 1924, $150.00. Photo courtesy Postcards International.

Book, *My Adventures As An Illustrator,* Rockwell, 1960 . . . . . **$20.00**

Book, *The Secret Play,* Barbour, 1916 . . . . **100.00**

Calendar, 1920, Painting the Kite, De Laval adv **325.00**

Calendar, 1948, Boy Scouts, Men of Tomorrow **75.00**

Catalog, Montgomery Ward, 1925 . . . . **35.00**

Catalog, Top Value Stamp Catalog, 1967 . . . . **30.00**

Limited Edition, figurine, Grandpa's Guardian, River Shore, 1982 . . . . **195.00**

Limited Edition, figurine, High Hopes, Christmas, Museum Collections, 1983 . . . . **165.00**

Limited Edition, figurine, Little Mother, Rockwell Museum, 1981 . . . . **50.00**

Limited Edition, figurine, Spirit of America, Commemorative, Museum Collecitons, 1982 . . . . **175.00**

Limited Edition, figurine, The Graduate, Dave Grossman, 1983 . . . . **30.00**

Limited Edition, plate, America's Favorite Cowboy, Gene Autry Collection, Rockwell Museum, 1984 . . . . **45.00**

Limited Edition, plate, Cats, Rockwell Cats, River Shore, 1982 . . . . **40.00**

Limited Edition, plate, First Prom, American Family I, Rockwell Museum, 1979 . . . . **35.00**

Limited Edition, plate, Memories, Mother's Day, Lynell Studios, 1982 . . . . **30.00**

Limited Edition, plate, Toy Maker, Heirtage, Rockwell Society, 1977 . . . . **80.00**

Limited Edition, stein, Braving The Storm, Rockwell Museum **60.00**

Lithograph, Weighing In, #14/100, sgd, $23\frac{1}{2}$ x 13" **700.00**

Magazine Cover, *Life,* Nov 22, 1917 . . . . **40.00**

Magazine Cover, *Saturday Evening Post,* 1940 . . . . **20.00**

Poster, Maxwell House Coffee, 1931-32 . . . . **325.00**

Sheet Music, "Little French Mother, Goodbye," 1919 . . . . . . **45.00**

Limited Edition, plate, Grandpa's Guardian, Rockwell Single Issue, River Shore, $80.00.

ROSEMEADE

If you live in the Dakotas, you probably know about Rosemeade. If you live in California, Georgia, or Maine, I am not so sure. Rosemeade is one of the many regional pottery manufacturers that American collectors rediscovered in the past decade.

Rosemeade is actually a trade name for ceramic pieces made by the Wahpeton Pottery Company between 1940 and 1953 and Rosemeade Potteries between 1953 and 1961. Laura Taylor and Vera Gethman were the company's two principal designers. The company produced a wide range of objects from commemorative and souvenir pieces to household and kitchen wares.

Rosemeade prices are stronger in the Midwest and Plains states than elsewhere across the country. Figurines and figural pieces command top dollar.

Club: North Dakota Pottery Collectors Society, P.O. Box 14, Beach, ND 58621.

Cranberry Dish, cov, turkey, 4½" h **$15.00**
Creamer, turkey, 3¾" h **135.00**
Dispenser, cotton, rabbit, white, hp ear int and eyes, 5" h **125.00**
Figurine, elephant, gray, 1¾" h **60.00**
Figurine, pony, brown and black, 4" h **125.00**
Figurine, skunk, ½ and ¾" h, price for set **20.00**
Pin, prairie rose, 2 x 2" **375.00**
Planter, deer on log **50.00**
Planter, swan, white **50.00**
Salt and Pepper Shakers, pr, cats **60.00**
Salt and Pepper Shakers, pr, chickens, 2¾" h **65.00**
Salt and Pepper Shakers, pr, Chinese ring-necked pheasant, 7 x 11½" **250.00**
Salt and Pepper Shakers, pr, dolphins, green, 2¼" h **50.00**
Salt and Pepper Shakers, pr, fish, pink 2¾" h **50.00**
Salt and Pepper Shakers, pr, flamingos, 3¾" h **65.00**
Salt and Pepper Shakers, pr, leaping deer **60.00**
Salt and Pepper Shakers, pr, quail, feather top knot **75.00**
Spoon Rest, pansy, 3¾" h **50.00**
Vase, yellow and brown swirl, 4" h **125.00**
Wall Pocket, 4-H Club, 4¼" h **85.00**

ROSEVILLE POTTERY

Roseville rose from the ashes of the J. B. Owen Company when a group of investors bought Owen's pottery in the late 1880s. In 1892 George F. Young became the first of four succeeding generations of Youngs to manage the plant.

Roseville grew through acquisitions of another Roseville firm and two in Zanesville. By 1898 the company's offices were located in Zanesville. Roseville art pottery was first produced in 1900. The trade name Rozane was applied to many lines. During the 1930s Roseville looked for new product lines. Utilizing several high gloss glazes in the 1940s, Roseville revived its art pottery line. Success was limited. In 1954 the Mosaic Tile Company bought Roseville.

Pieces are identified as early, middle (Depression era), and late. Because of limited production, middle period pieces are the hardest to find. They also were marked with paper labels that have been lost over time. Some key patterns to watch for are Blackberry, Cherry Blossom, Faline, Ferella, Futura, Jonquil, Morning Glory, Sunflower, and Windsor.

Clubs: American Art Pottery Assoc., P.O. Box 1226, Westport, MA 02790; Roseville's of the Past Pottery Club, P.O. Box 656, Clarcona, FL 32710.

Periodical: *Pottery Collectors Express,* P.O. Box 221, Mayview, MO 64071.

Basket, Columbine, 12¼ x 10¼" **$450.00**
Basket, Freesia, #391-8, green **140.00**
Basket, Iris, #30-4, blue **68.00**
Basket, Peony, yellow, 10" d **65.00**
Basket, Zephyr Lily, #395-10, green **120.00**
Bowl, Clematis, blue **50.00**
Bowl, Laurel, oval, gold, 9" l **60.00**
Bowl, Wincraft, #228-12, blue **85.00**
Bud Vase, Pinecone, brown, 7½ x 5" **375.00**
Candleholder, pr, Cherry Blossom, 4¼ x 4¾" **450.00**
Candleholder, pr, Magnolia, green **35.00**
Candleholder, pr, Rosecraft, orange dec, brown ground, "Rv" mark, 8½ x 5" **550.00**
Candleholder, pr, White Rose, 2¼" h **30.00**
Centerpiece Bowl, Topeo, silver label, 4 x 13" **100.00**
Compote, Florentine **40.00**
Dish, cov, Volpatto, ftd, satin white, silver label, 4¾ x 5¼" **275.00**
Ewer, Dawn, #834-15, pink **450.00**
Ewer, Fuschia, handled, green leaves and brown flowers, brown and green ground, foil label, imp mark, 10½ x 5" **275.00**
Flower Frog, Ixia, pink **60.00**
Flower Frog, Poppy, #35, brown **105.00**
Hanging Basket, Mostique, yellow and green spade shaped flowers, pebbled gray ground, 6½ x 6½" **350.00**
Jardiniere, Donatello, ivory, 5" h **70.00**
Jardiniere, Foxglove, #659-5, blue **60.00**
Jardiniere, Poppy, green, 3" h **25.00**
Jug, Wisteria, #629-4, brown, 4" h **225.00**
Planter, Vista, #249-6, yellow, green, and pink flowers, green and lavender ground, 3½ x 7" **150.00**
Sugar, Snowberry, pink **20.00**
Vase, Baneda, pink, 6¼" h **225.00**
Vase, Blackberry, ovoid, 2 handles **550.00**
Vase, Carnelian II, red, 5" h **100.00**
Vase, Columbine, brown, 8" h **120.00**
Vase, Donatello, 4" h **45.00**
Vase, Earlham, bulbous, 2 handles, 7 x 8" **375.00**
Vase, Ferrella, 2 handled, bulbous, stylized red and green flowers, burgundy ground, reticulated rim, 5½ x 6½" **550.00**

Basket, Water Lily, #380, handled, mkd "Waterlilly 380 12," 12" h, $99.00. Photo courtesy Collectors Auction Services.

Vase, Fuschia, #895, blue, 7" h **120.00**
Vase, Jonquil, stovepipe neck, bulbous base, 2 handles, white and amber blossoms, orange-brown ground, 9½" h **450.00**
Wall Pocket, Dahrose, triangular, angular handles, white blossoms, orange ground, 10" h **325.00**
Window Box, Dahrose, rect, yellow flowers and green leaves, brown ground, orig liner, 6¼ x 16". **450.00**

ROYAL CHINA

The Royal China Company, located in Sebring, Ohio, utilized remodeled facilities that originally housed the Oliver China Company and later the E. H. Sebring Company. Royal China began operations in 1934. The company produced an enormous number of dinnerware patterns. The backs of pieces usually contain the names of the shape, line, and decoration. In addition to many variations of company backstamps, Royal China also produced objects with private backstamps. All records of these markings were lost in a fire in 1970.

In 1964 Royal China purchased the French-Saxon China Company, Sebring, Ohio, which it operated as a wholly owned subsidiary. On December 31, 1969, Royal China was acquired by the Jeannette Corporation. When fire struck the Royal China Sebring plant in 1970, Royal moved its operations to the French-Saxon plant. The company changed hands several times, until operations ceased in August 1986.

Collectors tend to concentrate on specific patterns. Among the most favored are Bluebell (1940s), Currier and Ives (designed by Gordon Parker and introduced 1949–50), ColonialHomestead (1951–52), Old Curiosity Shop (early 1950s), Regal (1937) Royalty (1936), and blue and pink Willow Ware (1940s). Because of easy accessibility, only purchase pieces in fine to excellent condition.

Club: The Currier & Ives Dinnerware Collectors Club, 29470 Saxon Rd., Toulon, IL 61483.

Colonial Homestead, bowl, 5½" d **$6.00**
Colonial Homestead, bread and butter plate, 6½" d **2.00**
Colonial Homestead, cake plate, lug handle, 10" d. **10.00**
Colonial Homestead, cereal bowl, 6¼" d **5.00**
Colonial Homestead, cup and saucer. **4.00**
Colonial Homestead, gravy boat **12.00**
Colonial Homestead, sugar **8.00**
Currier & Ives, casserole, 7¾" **50.00**
Currier & Ives, chop plate, 12" d **20.00**
Currier & Ives, gravy boat, 6" l. **12.00**

Currier & Ives, dinner plate, 10" d, $8.50.

Currier & Ives, cup and saucer, blue, $4.00.

Currier & Ives, gravy liner, boy at well **6.00**
Currier & Ives, sandwich server, center handle, 13¼" d. **55.00**
Currier & Ives, sugar, steamboat. **2.00**
Currier & Ives, tidbit, 3-tier **40.00**
Currier & Ives, tumbler, barn in trees, blue on white, frosted, 8 oz, 5½" h. **10.00**
Currier & Ives, tumbler, steamboat, white on blue, 3½" h **6.00**
Memory Lane,
Regal, bowl, oval, 9" l **10.00**
Regal, creamer **5.00**
Regal, cup and saucer. **6.00**
Regal, gravy boat **12.00**
Regal, teapot, cov **20.00**
Royalty, casserole **20.00**
Royalty, dinner plate, 9¼" **8.00**
Royalty, gravy boat **12.00**
Royaly, teapot, 6 cup. **20.00**
Windsor, bread and butter plate, 6¼" d **2.00**
Windsor, casserole **20.00**
Windsor, creamer and sugar **15.00**
Windsor, dinner plate, 9¼" d. **8.00**

ROYAL COPLEY

Royal Copley ceramics were produced by the Spaulding China Company located in Sebring, Ohio. These attractive giftware items were most often marked with a paper label only, making identification a challenge. For hints on identifying unmarked Royal Copley, refer to Leslie C. and Marjorie A. Wolfe's *Royal Copley (plus Royal Windsor and Spaulding)* published by Collector Books, 1992.

Newsletter: *The Copley Courier,* 1639 N. Catalina St., Burbank, CA 91505.

Ashtray, bow and ribbon, "Watch those ashes Friend," 5" . . . **$15.00**
Ashtray, leaf and bird **7.00**
Bank, rooster, coin slot at top of tail, paper label, "Chicken Feed" on front of base, 7½" h **38.00**
Bank, teddy bear, paper label, 7¼" h **42.00**
Bowl, bird perched on side, green stamp, 4" d **8.00**
Bud Vase, parrot, 5" h **10.00**
Figurine, angel, blue, 6¼" h. **16.00**
Figurine, cockatoo, 7¼" h **24.00**
Figurine, cocker spaniel, paper label, 6¼" h. **18.00**
Figurine, kitten and ball of yarn, paper label, 6¼" h **22.00**
Figurine, sparrow, 5" h **12.00**
Pitcher, floral decal, gold stamp on bottom, 6" h. **10.00**

Planter, coach, 3¼ x 6" 15.00
Planter, cocker spaniel, sgd with raised letters on back 10.00
Planter, elephant and ball, paper label, 7¼" h 22.00
Planter, Indian boy and drum, paper label, 6¼" h 12.00
Planter, jumping salmon, paper label, 11¼" l, 6¼" h 35.00
Planter, kitten and ball of yarn, paper label, 8¼" h 20.00
Planter, kitten and bird house, paper label, 7¼" h 38.00
Planter, kitten and boot, paper label, 7¼" h 28.00
Planter, Oriental dragon motif, ftd, paper label, 5¼" h 10.00
Planter, Oriental girl with wheelbarrow, paper label 25.00
Planter, poodle, resting, paper label, 8¼" l, 6¼" h 30.00
Planter, salt box, 5¼" h 18.00
Planter, Siamese cats, paper label, 9" h 55.00
Planter, woodpecker, 6¼" h 12.00
Vase, Ivy, ftd, paper label, 7" h 10.00
Vase, stylized leaf dec, paper label, 5¼" h 8.00
Window Box, Ivy, paper label, 4 x 7" 10.00

ROYAL DOULTON

Chances of finding Royal Doulton at flea markets are better than you think. It often is given as a gift. Since the recipients did not pay for it, they often have no idea of its initial value. The same holds true when children have to break up their parents' household. As a result, it is sold for a fraction of its value at garage sales and to dealers.

Check out any piece of Royal Doulton that you find. There are specialized price guides for character jugs, figures, and toby jugs. A great introduction to Royal Doulton is the two-volume videocassette entitled *The Magic of a Name*, produced by Quill Productions, Birmingham, England.

Clubs: Royal Doulton International Collectors Club, 700 Cottontail Ln., Somerset, NJ 08873; Royal Doulton International Collectors Club (Canadian Branch), 850 Progress Ave, Scarborough, Ontario M1H 3C4 Canada.

Periodicals: *Collecting Doulton*, B.B.R. Publishing, P.O. Box 310, Richmond Surrey TW91FS, U.K.; *Doulton Divvy*, P.O. Box 2434, Joilet, IL 60434.

Ashtray, Welsh Ladies, sgd "Noke," 3⅝" d $35.00
Biscuit Jar, mountains, castles, and lakes with boats in blue on white ground, SP handle, rim, and lid, 8⅝" h 155.00
Bowl, Rosalind, 9¼" d 70.00
Character Jug, Bacchus, D6499, large 55.00
Character Jug, Blacksmith, D6578, small 60.00
Character Jug, Cardinal, D6129, miniature 45.00

Figurine, Genevieve, HN 1962, 1941–75, 7" h, $425.00. Photo courtesy Gene Harris Antique Auction Center, Inc.

Character Jug, Fortune Teller, D6497, large 425.00
Character Jug, Gladiator, D6556, miniature 375.00
Character Jug, Paddy, 1¼" h 100.00
Character Jug, Sancho Panza, miniature 60.00
Character Jug, Santa Claus, reindeer handle 100.00
Figurine, Artful Dodger, HN546 . . . . 55.00
Figurine, Balloon Man, HN1954 . . . . 110.00
Figurine, Bedtime, HN1978 . . . . 80.00
Figurine, Biddy, HN1445 . . . . 145.00
Figurine, Boy From Williamsburg, HN2183 . . . . 75.00
Figurine, Buttercup, HN2309 . . . . 155.00
Figurine, Cocker Spaniel, HN1078, black and white 65.00
Figurine, Song of the Sea, HN2729 . . . . 160.00
Figurine, Tuppence a Bag, HN2320 . . . . 120.00
Mug, Old Salt 60.00
Pitcher, The Castle Inn at Marlborough 95.00
Plate, Sam Weller, Dickens Ware, 8½" d 60.00
Plate, Shakespeare Plays, 10" d 45.00
Sauce Dish, Fat Boy, Dickens Ware 45.00
Teapot, Gold Lace, H4989, 9½" h 95.00
Toby Jug, Happy John, D6070, c1939, 5½" h 45.00
Toby Jug, Mr Pickwick, D6261 . . . . 180.00
Toby Jug, Sairy Gamp, D6263 . . . . 175.00
Tray, Cecil Aldin's Dogs, 11" l 135.00

ROYAL HAEGER

David H. Haeger founded Haeger Potteries in Dundee, Illinois, in 1871. The company produced its first art pottery in 1914. The Royal Haeger line was introduced in 1938 upon the arrival of Royal Arden Hickman. In 1939 Haeger Potteries purchased a building in Macomb, Illinois, to produce pottery for the florist trade and organized the Royal Haeger Lamp Company.

Many Haeger pieces can be identified by molded model numbers. The first Royal Haeger mold was assigned the number "R-1," with subsequent numbers assigned in chronological order. Giftware in the Studio Haeger line, designed by Helen Conover, have an "S" number. Royal Garden Flower wares, produced between 1954 and 1963, have an "RG" number.

The initial collecting craze that established Royal Haeger as an independent collecting category is over. Prices have stabilized for commonly found pieces. Speculative price prevails for high-end pieces.

Club: Haeger Pottery Collectors Club of America, 5021 Toyon Way, Antioch, CA 94509.

Ashtray, #2145, green, leaf and acorn design, 1976 . . . . $15.00
Ashtray, #2609, White Earth Graphic Wrap, center reservoir, c1970, mkd "Royal Haeger, 2069 ©, U.S.A." 15.00
Ashtray, brown, "1934 Century of Progress," 3¼" w 50.00
Ashtray, R-1817, boomerang shaped, orange, 13½" l 15.00
Bookends, pr, R-475, Calla Lily, amber, 6⅛" h 60.00
Centerpiece Bowl, R-1824, palm leaf shaped, 26" l 35.00
Cigarette Lighter, table, #889, mandarin orange, ribbed, foil label, 5" h, 3" d 15.00
Compote, #3003, cotton white ext, turquoise int, 4½" h 20.00
Figure, R-784, elephant, chartreuse and honey, 6" h 15.00
Lamp Base, #5398, figural mermaid, gray, green agate base 200.00
Lamp, wall, #5240, horse head, ebony, c1947, foil label, 9¼" l, 5¼" base 200.00
Pitcher, H-608, Persian blue, rooster handle, 9" h 40.00

Planter, fan tail pouter pigeon, peach agate glaze, c1934, 8" h 75.00
Vase, R-186, Bird of Paradise 25.00
Vase, R-452, morning glory, mauve agate, 16½" h 90.00
Wall Pocket, R-16275, figural fish, antique white, 13¼" l 100.00

ROYAL WINTON

Royal Winton is more than chintz, a fact appreciated by collectors familiar with Eileen Busby's Royal Winton Porcelain: Ceramics Fit For A King (Glass Press, 1998). Royal Winton production includes commemorative and patriotic ware, handpainted ware, an assortment of luster wares, mottled ware, mugs and jugs, pastel ware, souvenir ware, and transfer ware.

In 1885 Sidney and Leonard Grimwade founded the Grimwade Brothers Pottery in Stoke-on-Trent. The firm became Grimwades, Ltd., when it acquired the Winton Pottery Company and Stoke Pottery in 1900. Atlas China, Rubin Art Pottery, Heron Cross Pottery, and Upper Hanley Pottery was added in 1906–07. The "Royal" attribution grew out of the company's promotion of a visit to the plant in April 1913 by King George V and Queen Mary.

Royal Winton's first chintz patterns were introduced in the late 1920s and flourished in the 1930s. In 1997 the company began making limited reproductions of some of its most popular 1930s chintz pieces.

Club: Royal Winton International Collectors Club, 600 Columbia St., Pasadena, CA 91105.

Basin, mkd "Wisteria" and "Rd No 484760," c1900, 16½" d **$160.00**
Bed Pan, slipper shaped 90.00
Biscuit Barrel, Cottage Ware, beehive shaped, raffia handle, mkd "Beehive" 390.00
Bowl, Byzanta, blue lustre, white lustre on underside, branch with fruit and green leaves int, 6" d 90.00
Bowl, Nursery Ware, Charles Dickens scene on int, mkd "Dickens Souvenir," 6¼" d 130.00
Box, cov, Pastel Ware, cream, gilded edge 90.00
Cake Plate, Transfer Ware, coral center with Egyptian motif on yellow band, chrome handle, 1930 mark, 8½" d 60.00
Chamber Pot, mkd "Flaxman," pre-1900 backstamp, 9¼" d 160.00
Character Mug, King George VI, cream, 2¾" h 200.00
Cheese Dish, cov, Cottage Ware, Ye Olde Mill 350.00
Commemorative, teacup and saucer, "Queen Elizabeth II Crowned June 2, 1953" 50.00
Cup, Byzanta, bluish-gray tree and city scene with silhouetted dancers on yellow ground, bottom mkd "Watteau" 80.00
Demitasse Cup and Saucer, Mottled Ware, rouge, gilded edge and handle 65.00
Jug, hp Art Deco floral design, gilded edge and sun rays with orange accents on white ground, 6½" h 140.00
Mug, horse and buggy village scene, plays "I Love to Go a 'Wandering" 220.00
Plate, Cottage Ware, Anne Hathaway's Cottage, mkd "Olde England Hand Painted," 8¼" d 170.00
Relish Dish, divided, Cottage Ware, mkd "Lakeland" 220.00
Teacup and Saucer, commemorative, Franklin D Roosevelt and Winston Churchill on both, c1940s 140.00
Vase, Byzanta, top and bottom black bands on orange ground, black silhouette classical musical scene center, 7½" h 130.00

RUGS

You have to cover your floors with something. Until we have antique linoleum, the name of the game is rugs. If you have to own a rug, own one with some age and character. Do not buy any rug without unrolling it. Hold it up in the air in such a way that there is a strong light behind it. This will allow you to spot any holes or areas of heavy wear.

Periodical: *Rug Hooking,* 500 Vaughn St., Harrisburg, PA 17110.

Braided, black bands and variegated bands of red, blue, and brown, circular, Mennonite or Amish, 39" d **$165.00**
Chain Stitch, floral design, blue, green, and red, 48 x 62" 27.50
Embroidered, floral design, dark pink and ivory, 95 x 115" 225.00
Embroidered, floral design, pastel colors on light green ground, 20th C, 48 x 72" 125.00
Hooked, abstract, cross in center, colorful, 29 x 41" 17.50
Hooked, cottage and bridge in winter landscape with full moon, shades on blue, green, and gray with black, red, and white, oblong, wear and stains, repairs, 23 x 42" 82.50
Hooked, eagle, red, white, and blue 100.00
Hooked, floral, browns, gray, and faded pink, unfinished, orig frame, 26½ x 33" 55.00
Hooked, floral center in red, green, black, and yellow on bluish gray ground, stylized border in beige, multicolored stripes, and black, rect, wear, edges rebound, 25 x 43" 55.00
Hooked, Little Bo Peep, 3 sheep, 18½ x 37" 220.00
Hooked, morning glories, pastel shades, ivory ground, deep purple border, slight color bleeding, 26 x 38" 27.50
Hooked, oval pond with white and black swans floating at either end amid red and green flowers, magenta border, rect, 25½ x 38" 55.00
Hooked, stylized landscape, dog, 2 fawns, birds, and trees, multicolored, 19 x 40½" 175.00
Hooked, swan, cattails, water lilies, blues, greens, brown, black, and white, braided border, modern, mounted on frame, 20 x 36" 70.00
Hooked, white cocker spaniels with black spots in landscape with picket fence, rect, worn and faded colors, 25 x 45" 88.00

Indian, 55" l, 28" w, Photo courtesy Collectors Auction Services.

Oriental, Heriz pattern, red ground, 39 x 66" 195.00
Oriental, Kurd Rug, Northwest Persia, 2 colums of "Memling" guls in navy and sky blue, red, gold, and ivory on dark brown field, ivory border, late 19th C, 84 x 42" 545.00
Oriental, Luri Kelim, Southeast Persia, 3 colums of 6 serrated squares in midnight and navy blue, red, orange, aubergine, and blue-green on ivory field, multicolored border, 93 x 56". 575.00
Rag, bluish gray and white, blue warp, 36 x 180" 90.00

RUSSEL WRIGHT

Russel Wright was an American industrial engineer with a design passion for domestic efficiency through simple lines. Wright and his wife, Mary Small Einstein, wrote *A Guide To Easier Living* to explain the concepts.

Some of his earliest designs were executed in polished spun aluminum. These pieces, designed in the mid 1930s, included trays, vases, and teapots.

Russel Wright worked for many different companies in addition to creating material under his own label, American Way. Wright's contracts with firms often called for the redesign of pieces which did not produce or sell well. As a result, several lines have the same item in more than one shape. Among the companies for which Wright did design work are Chase Brass and Copper, General Electric, Imperial Glass, National Silver Company, and the Shenango and Steubenville Pottery Companies.

Though most collectors focus on Wright's dinnerware, he also designed glassware, plastic items, textiles, furniture, and metal objects. His early work in spun aluminum often is overlooked as is his later work in plastic for the Northern Industrial Chemical Company.

ALUMINUM

Gravy Boat $100.00
Bowl 50.00
Ice Bucket 60.00
Tidbit Tray, 2 tier 125.00
Vase, round 100.00

CHINA

American Modern, baker, seafoam, 10¾" l $10.00
American Modern, coaster, seafoam. 15.00
American Modern, casserole, stick handle 32.00
American Modern, coffeepot, after dinner, white 130.00
American Modern, creamer, granite 12.00
American Modern, dinner plate, chartreuse, 10" d 12.00
American Modern, pickle dish, with liner, chartreuse 8.00
American Modern, pitcher, coral 40.00
American Modern, salt and pepper shakers, pr, granite 20.00
Highlight, bowl, white, 7" d. 15.00
Highlight, charger, blueberry, 15" d 55.00
Highlight, creamer, blueberry 18.00
Highlight, dinner plate, white 10.00
Iroquois Casual, casserole, ocv, oyster, 2 qt 20.00
Iroquois Casual, cereal bowl, cov, avocado, 5" d 12.00
Iroquois Casual, cup and saucer, white 10.00
Iroquois Casual, fruit bowl, ice blue, 5½" d 4.00

GLASS

American Modern, cordial, smoke, 2 oz, 2" h. $30.00
American Modern, iced tea, coral, 15 oz, 5¼" h 25.00
American Modern, sherbet, seafoam, 5 oz, 2¾" h. 25.0
American, water goblet, seafoam, 11 oz, 4½" d 35.00
Flair, juice tumbler, crystal, 6 oz 40.00
Flair, water goblet, crystal, 11 oz 45.00
Twist, juice tumbler, crystal 25.00

PLASTIC DINNERWARE

Flair, Ming Lace, dinner plate $8.00
Flair, Ming Lace, sugar, cov 10.00
Meladur, cereal bowl 6.00
Meladur, dinner plate, 9" d 6.00
Residential, dinner palte 7.00
Residential, tumbler 10.00

SALT AND PEPPER SHAKERS

Hang on to your hats. Those great figural salt and pepper shaker sets from the 1920s through the 1960s have been discovered by the New York art and decorator crowd. Prices have started to jump. What does this say about taste in America?

When buying a set, make certain it is a set. Check motif, base, and quality of workmanship. China shakers should have no cracks or signs of cracking. Original paint and decoration should be present on china and metal figures. Make certain each shaker has the right closure.

Salt and pepper shaker collectors must compete with specialized collectors from other fields, e.g., advertising and black memorabilia. I have been searching for a pair shaped like jigsaw puzzle pieces. So far I have neither seen a pair nor found a dealer who has seen one but I will not give up.

Aluminum, punch set, punch bowl, undertray, ladle, and 12 cups with wooden handles, imp marks, $550.00.

Winnie and Smiley Pig, pink, Shawnee, $121.00. Photo courtesy Gene Harris Antique Auction Center, Inc.

Club: Novelty Salt & Pepper Shakers Club, P.O. Box 3617, Lantana, FL 33465.

Advertising, Ball Canning Jar, glass, orig box, 2¾" h **$40.00**
Advertising, Florida Oranges **4.00**
Advertising, Kool Cigarettes, Willie and Millie Penguin, 1940s, 3½" h **65.00**
Advertising, Mobilgas, shield shaped **25.00**
Advertising, Seagram's Seven, plastic **8.00**
Advertising, Texaco, gas pumps, plastic, decal dec **18.00**
Babies in Basket **75.00**
Bananas, ceramic, yellow and tan **6.50**
Black Chef and Maid, chalkware, 2½" h. **40.00**
Bookcase, wooden **10.00**
Cactus, Rosemead. **15.00**
Cake and Cut Slice, miniature **15.00**
Cat, winking, Enesco. **15.00**
Character, Campbell Kids, plastic, 1950s, 4½" h. **35.00**
Character, Chilly Willy and Charlie Chicken, china, ©1958 Walter Lantz, 4" h **80.00**
Character, Col Sanders, white plastic, 4¼" h. **40.00**
Character, Dick Tracy and Junior **35.00**
Character, Donald Duck, china, white glaze, blue, black, red, and yellow, Leeds, ©1942, 3" h. **25.00**
Character, Fred Flintstone and Barney Rubble. **55.00**
Character, Garfield **18.00**
Character, Little Orphan Annie and Sandy, plaster, 2¾" h **65.00**
Character, Robin Hood and Marion, Twin Winton. **125.00**
Character, Woody Woodpecker, and girlfriend **45.00**
Dutch Boy and Girl, Shawnee, large **40.00**
Flying Saucer, ceramic, Coventry Ceramics, 2½ x 3 x 1". **65.00**
Hammer and Nail, ceramic, gray nail, brown and black hammer **12.00**
Huggems, bears, china, tan or yellow. **20.00**
Huggems, rabbits, white or yellow **20.00**
Lobster, red, claws held above head, attached to green base by springs, Japan **24.00**
Maid and Butler, Kessler **10.00**
Mice and Cheese, plastic. **12.00**
Owls, Lefton. **30.00**
Philmont Scout Ranch, white china, 3½" h. **20.00**
Pixies, ceramic, blue outfit, yellow hair **10.00**
Rotisserie, plastic **200.00**
Souvenir, Florida, pink flamingos, hp, 3" h **6.50**
Souvenir, New York, Empire State Building, Statue of Liberty, silvered cast metal. **8.00**
Souvenir, Washington DC, Washington Monument and White house, silvered cast metal **5.00**
Spanish Dancers, Ceramic Art Studio, 7½" h **100.00**
Thimble and Spool, miniature **15.00**
Windmills. **18.00**
WWII Victory Bombs, plaster, hp, "V" inscription, orig box, 2½" h **65.00**

SAND PAILS

The illustrations found on litho tin sand pails are truly works of art. Innumerable child's themes from animals to cartoon characters have graced the sides of these seashore toys. Despite the fact that sand and salt water are natural enemies of tin toys, concentrate on pails in very good condition with little surface damage. Pails were mass-produced in large quantities, making condition an important part of value.

Ohio Art, Donald Duck, mkd "Walt Disney Productions," and "Ohio Art Co., Bryan, Ohio, Made in U.S.A." around base, $250.00.

Advertising, Jello Instant Pudding, yellow plastic, 2 red mini shovels **$10.00**
J Chein, cat family, 3½" h **125.00**
J Chein, Mother Goose, "15 cents" rubber stamped on bottom, 4" h **100.00**
J Chein, The Story of Peter Rabbit, 8" h. **100.00**
French, Ch Jovienot Boites & Capsules, Paris-Montrouse, straight sided, with lid, continuous scene of children and sailboats, 4¾" h **200.00**
Heidelberger Confectionary Co, Philadelphia, PA, candy container, "A Kiddie Sand Pail," green and white, children and dog illus, 3" h **150.00**
Kirchof, children and dogs on beach, red, yellow, and black, 4" h **125.00**
Ohio Art, children playing at sea shore scene, early 1900s, 4¼" h. **225.00**
Sandy Andy At The Seashore, comical figure dancing, airplane, and ocean liner on blue ground, mkd "Made in Pittsburgh, PA, U.S.A.," early 1900s, 5"h. **300.00**
U S Metal Toy Mfg Co, children playing in garden with animals, 7½" h **125.00**
U S Metal Toy Mfg Co, children water skiing, metallic blue and silver, yellow, 6½" h **50.00**
U S Metal Toy Mfg Co, circus scene, red and yellow, 5¼" h **150.00**
Western Germany, children in train and boat around sides, 5¼" h **75.00**

SCHOOL MEMORABILIA

"School Days, School Days, good old golden rule days." I've been singing this refrain ever since I moved into the former Vera Cruz elementary school in Pennsylvania.

Stapler, King Features Syndicate Characters, metal stapler with raised enamel images, complete with insert, staples, and instructions, orig box, Idealine, 1962, $214.20. Photo courtesy New England Auction Gallery.

The World Book Encyclopedia, ©1963, full set plus yearbooks 1966 through 1973, $10.00.

Bell, teacher's desk, cast brass, 3½" d base **$20.00**
Blackboard Liner, hardwood handle, 5 wire chalkboard holders, 5¼ x 8" **12.00**
Book, *School Memories,* unused, 1920s **18.00**
Catalog, J B Clow & Sons, *Modern Plumbing for Schools,* 1916, 88 slick pps, photos and names of schools as nationwide clients, 9½ x 12" **45.00**
Certificate, Teacher's Elementary School Certificate, Perry Country, OH, sunrise over mountain vignette, 1905, 9¼ x 13" **15.00**
Chalk Holder, wood, for single chalk stick,31/8" l. **10.00**
Desk, student's, formica, metal legs, rect top, c1950 . . . . **10.00**
Game, Pinky Lee's Alphabet Game, 1950s **7.00**
Game, Romper Room Magic Teacher, 1960s **20.00**
Game, The World Educator and Game, W S Reed Toy Co, 1919 . . . . **45.00**
Game, Top Scholar, Cadaco-Ellis, 1957 . . . . **12.00**
Magazine, *Collier's,* School Days cov, Maxfield Parrish, 1908 . . . . **85.00**
Pencil Box, tin, 3 int compartments, tin pencilholder on underside of lid **30.00**
Pencil Case, vinyl, zipper closure, Pony Tail **25.00**
Pencil Sharpener, metal, crank style, Automatio Pencil Sharpener Co, Chicago, 1907 . . . . **80.00**
Pencil Sharpener, plastic, alligator, blue and red, wheels under feet, head bobs up and down, 1960s **15.00**
Pencil Sharpener, plastic, yellow smiley face, crank handle, 1970s **15.00**
Pinback Button, Gaston Grammar School, multicolored, c1915, 1" d **2.00**
Reward of Merit, Card of Merit, Model Scholar, attached cut girl scrap, 1889 . . . . **10.00**
Reward of Merit, Certificate of Honor, 60 Merits, printed, red and white, 1877 . . . . **20.00**
Reward of Merit, Promotion Notice, cardboard, 1908, 2½ x 4⅜" **5.00**
Reward of Merit, Testimonial of Approbation, black and white, 1872, 8½ x 10¼" **12.00**
Sheet Music, "School Day Sweethearts," Glen Edwards, 1923 . . . . **5.00**
Sheet Music, "The Schoolhouse Blues," Irving Berlin, 1921 . . . **10.00**
Water Color Set, orig contents, "Prang—Water Colors Box No. 16" in gold and black on lid, unused **25.00**

SECONDHAND ROSES

This is a catchall category—designed specifically for those items which are bought solely for their utilitarian use. Anyone who regularly attends country auctions, flea markets, or garage sales has undoubtedly seen his fair share of "recycled" household goods. Ranging from wringer washers to electronic video games, these products and appliances are neither decorative nor financially lucrative. They are strictly secondhand merchandise.

There is not much reason to focus on brand names, with two exceptions—Maytag and Craftsman. First, Maytag, widely regarded as the Cadillac of washers and dryers, consistently realizes higher prices than any other brand. Second, Craftsman hand tools, distributed by Sears, generally bring higher prices due to the company's generous replacement policy.

As a result of advances in technology and space constraints in modern homes, several larger sized appliances have little or no value on today's market. For example, console stereos and large chest freezers can often be had free for the hauling.

All items listed below are in good, clean condition. All parts are intact and appliances are in working order. The prices are designed to get you in the ballpark. Good luck in getting a hit.

Air Conditioner, purchased in Fall or Winter **$50.00**
Air Mattress, double **8.00**
Attaché Case, leather, fitted int, locking **10.00**
Answering Machine **15.00**
Bedroom Suite, French Provincial, painted white, gold trim, single bed, night stand, chest of drawers, and dresser with mirror **150.00**
Bicycle, 16", coaster brakes **15.00**
Big Wheel, plastic, 3 wheels **3.00**
Bird Bath, concrete, bowl and pedestal **10.00**
Booster Seat **5.00**
Car Seat **10.00**
Coffee Table, wood, modern **20.00**
Dehumidifier, 15 pt **25.00**
Diaper Bag **2.00**
Dishwasher, portable, over 5 years old **50.00**
Dutch Oven **5.00**
Exercise Bicycle, stationary **25.00**
Fan, exhaust, battery operated, hand-held **1.00**
Fan, window, purchased in Summer **20.00**
Filing Cabinet, metal, 4 drawers **45.00**
Freezer, upright, full size, over 5 years old **100.00**
Garden Tools, hoe, rake, and shovel **5.00**
Grill Cover **3.50**
Grill Mitts, pr **1.00**
Hair Dryer, hand held, full size, multiple settings **3.00**
Highchair, metal, plastic, and vinyl **15.00**
Kerosene Heater **50.00**
Ladder, wooden **30.00**

Battery Charger, General Electric, Charge 8, c1985, $5.00.

Cooler, Coleman, plastic, locking, drain plug, blue and white, $7.00.

Lawn Mower, electric 25.00
Linens, new condition 10.00
Microwave Oven, large, 1–5 years old 85.00
Mixer, counter top, 2 bowls 12.00
Movie Projector, 8mm or Super 8 . . . . 20.00
Nintendo Game Boy 25.00
Nintendo Video Game System, full size 30.00
Playpen, wood slats 5.00
Pots and Pans, 8 pc set, SS 50.00
Radar Detector 15.00
Refrigerator, bar size 50.00
Rug Shampooer 20.00
Sega Game Gear 50.00
Sewing Machine, portable, modern, electric 30.00
Space Heater 15.00
Stemware, 3 sizes, 24 pcs 45.00
Stereo, turntable, 2 speakers, name brand 25.00
Stroller 15.00
Television, color, over 5 years old 75.00
Television Stand, casters 10.00
Trailer Hitch 12.00
Traveling Liquor Cabinet, complete 20.00
Tupperware, salad set, 6 qt bowl, 6 individual bowls, and 2 servers 2.00
Typewriter, electric 20.00
Vacuum Cleaner, canister or upright 35.00
Umbrella, child's, plastic 1.00
VCR, VHS, over 5 years old 85.00
Video Games, any size, any brand 15.00
Wallet, women's, leather, checkbook style, with change purse 2.00
Wardrobe, metal 20.00
Weight Lifting Bench 15.00
Whirligig, wood 20.00

SEWING ITEMS

This is a wide open area. While many favor sterling silver items, only fools overlook objects made of celluloid, ivory, other metals, plastic, and wood. An ideal specialty collection would be sewing items that contain advertising.

Collecting sewing items received a big boost as a result of the Victorian craze. During the Victorian era a vast assortment of practical and whimsical sewing devices were marketed. Look for items such as tape measures, pincushions, stilettos for punchwork, crochet hooks, and sewing birds (beware of reproductions).

Modern sewing collectors are focusing on needle threaders, needle holders, and sewing kits from hotels and motels. The general term for this material is "20-Pocket" because pieces fit neatly into 20 pocket plastic notebook sleeves.

Clubs: International Sewing Machine Collectors Society, 1000E. Charleston Blvd., Las Vegas, NV 89104; National Button Society, 2733 Juno Pl., Apt. 4, Akron, OH 44313; Thimble Collectors International, 8289 Northgate Dr., Rome, NY 13440; The Thimble Guild, P.O. Box 381807, Duncanville, TX 75138; Toy Stitchers, 623 Santa Florita Ave., Millbrae, CA 94030.

Newletter: *Thimbletter,* 93 Walnut Hill Rd., Newton Highlands, MA 02161.

Advertising Trade Card, Gray & Grace's Sewing Machines, 1858 . . . . **$45.00**
Advertising Trade Card, Household Sewing Machine Co, spirit of '76 scene, dated 1885 . . . . 6.00
Advertising Trade Card, Wheeler and Wilson, family watching sewing machine delivery 4.00
Book, *Florence Home Needlework,* Nontuck Silk Co, 1887, 96 pp 15.00
Book, *The Singer Drawing Book For Young Artists,* 1930s, 3¼ x 5½" 10.00
Booklet, *Shakespear Boiled Down,* New Home Sewing Machine, 1890s, 30 pp 20.00
Bookmark, Merrick Spool Cotton 10.00
Button, celluloid, black, metal center strip, 1¼ x 2" 35
Button, wood, brass rim, 1¼" d 50
Catalog, C B Barker & Co, Price List of Genuine Sewing Machine Parts, New York, NY, c1870 144 pp, replacements parts for sewing machines 75.00
Catalog, Victor Sewing Machine Co, Middletown, CT and Philadelphia, accordion style, 8 panels, c1880 . . . . 20.00
Darner, slipper shape, maple wood base, 5½" l 8.00
Manual, Singer, #221 . . . . 35.00
Mending Kit, Bakelite, purple, German 14.00
Needle Book, Red Owl Food Stores adv, diecut, logo shape 5.00
Needle Case, bone, turned, awl tip 60.00
Pincushion, Lustreware, c1930 . . . . 25.00
Pincushion, open flower, linen 15.00
Print, San Diego Sewing Machine adv, little girl, red and pink roses, Compliments of the New Home Sewing Machine Co, early 1900s, 10 x 41" 50.00
Sewing Machine, Singer, 221 Featherweight, black 200.00
Sewing Scissors, Oriental silk case 20.00
Tape Measure, Colman's Mustard adv, celluloid, white, yellow illus, black lettering 25.00
Thimble, SS, kitten with ball 45.00

Pattern, Simplicity #6208, doll clothes, ©Ideal Toy Co., 1965, 5½ x 8¼" envelope, $18.00.

Toy Sewing Machine, Holly Hobbie, No. 5825, plastic, foot pedal, manual or battery operated, light, Durham Industries, 7" h **40.00**
Toy Sewing Machine, Sew Big, die cast, blue, hand operated, two foot high convertible ivory plastic table, 13" h round blue plastic storage hassock, Marx, 1960s, 5 x 8½" **55.00**

SHAWNEE POTTERY

The Shawnee Pottery company was founded in Zanesville, Ohio, in 1937. The plant, formerly home to the American Encaustic Tiling Company, produced approximately 100,000 pieces of pottery per working day. Shawnee produced a large selection of kitchenware, dinnerware, and decorative art pottery. The company ceased operations in 1961.

Club: Shawnee Pottery Collectors Club, P.O. Box 713, New Smyrna Beach, FL 32170.

Periodical: *Pottery Collectors Express,* P.O. Box 221, Mayview, MO 64071.

Butter Dish, cov, Queen Corn, #72 . . . . . **$29.00**
Casserole, cov, King Corn, #74 . . . . . **85.00**
Casserole Lid, Queen Corn, individual **25.00**
Cereal Bowl, King Corn, #94 . . . . . **55.00**
Cookie Jar, cov, Drum Major **475.00**
Cookie Jar, cov, Jack, yellow pants **75.00**
Cookie Jar, cov, Jill, blue and white **300.00**
Cookie Jar, cov, Jo Jo **185.00**
Cookie Jar, cov, Muggsy **425.00**
Cookie Jar, cov, Muggsy, gold trim **850.00**
Cookie Jar, cov, owl, gold trim **240.00**
Cookie Jar, cov, Queen Corn, #66 . . . . . **143.00**
Cookie Jar, cov, Smiley, blue bib, cold paint **100.00**
Cookie Jar, cov, Smiley, red bib, cold paint **80.00**
Cookie Jar, cov, Smiley, shamrock **250.00**
Cookie Jar, cov, Winnie, blue collar **250.00**
Creamer, King Corn, #70 . . . . . **30.00**
Dinner Plate, Queen Corn, #68, 10½" d **9.00**
Fruit Bowl, Queen Corn, #92, 6" d **11.00**
Mixing Bowl, King Corn, #5 . . . . . **40.00**
Pitcher, hot coffee, Queen Corn, #7, 1 qt **48.00**
Plate, Queen Corn, 7¼" d **3.00**
Relish Tray, King Corn, #79 . . . . . **40.00**
Salt and Pepper Shakers, pr, Chanticleers, large **55.00**
Salt and Pepper Shakers, pr, Chef, small **20.00**
Salt and Pepper Shakers, pr, Milk Cans, small **20.00**
Salt and Pepper Shakers, pr, Queen Corn, small **20.00**
Teapot, cov, Queen Corn, #75 . . . . . **125.00**
Vegetable Bowl, Queen Corn, #95, 9" l **27.00**

Salt and Pepper Shakers, pr, King Corn, $35.00.

SHEET MUSIC

Just like postcards, this is a category whose ten cent and quarter days are a thing of the past. Decorators and dealers have discovered the cover value of sheet music. The high ticket sheets are sold to specialized collectors, not sheet music collectors.

You can put a sheet music collection together covering almost any topic imaginable. Be careful about stacking your sheets on top of one another. The ink on the covers tends to bleed. If you can afford the expense, put a sheet of acid-free paper between each sheet. Do not, repeat do not, repair any tears with Scotch or similar brand tape. It discolors over time. When removed, it often leaves a gummy residue behind.

Advisor: Wayland Bunnell, 199 Tarrytown Rd., Manchester, NH 03103.

Clubs: City of Roses Sheet Music Collectors Club, 4312 S.E. Flavel St., Portland, OR 95206; National Sheet Music Society, 1597 Fair Park Ave., Los Angeles, CA 90041; New York Sheet Music Society, P.O. Box 1214, Great Neck, NY 11023; Remember That Song, 5623 N. 64th Ave., Glendale, AZ 85301.

Newsletter: *The Rag Times,* 15222 Ricky Ct., Grass Valley, CA 95949.

Periodical: *Sheet Music Magazine,* P.O. Box 8629, Boulder, CO 80321.

"A Royal Thorobred," Verge, arranged by Mayberry, dedicated to Prince of Wales, Fisher drawing large door, American and British flags behind, sgd by composer at top, 1926 . . . . . **$10.00**
"Darkies Mardi Gras," Wenzlik, 2/4 rag/march, black people at Mardi Gras, 1906 . . . . . **40.00**
"Do You Believe In Dreams," Britt/J R Robinson/Little, Barbelle man and woman embracing in full moon, inset blackface Ubert Carlton, 1926 . . . . . **5.00**
"Hail to the Spirit of Liberty," John Philip Sousa, black and white photo of Sousa in center, wreaths, flags, and shields, 1900 . . . . . **12.00**
"Heart and Soul," H Carmichael, Loesser, Four Aces photo in large red heart, 1938 . . . . . **5.00**

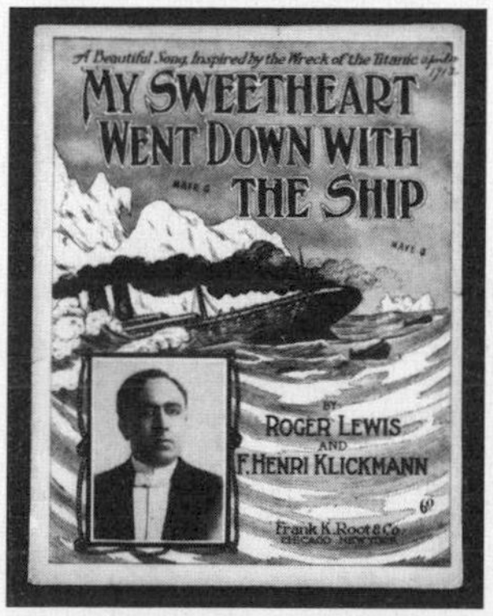

"My Sweetheart Went Down With the Ship," Roger Lewis and F. Henri Klickman, McKinley Music Co., Chicago, IL, greentone cov illus, 1912, 10¼ x 10½", $55.00.

"Hearts of Stone," Jackson, Ray, large music staff and notes, overlapping frames, large inset of Red Foley, 1954 . . . . 4.00
"I See Two Lovers," Wruble, Dixon, *"Sweet Music,"* large photo of Rudy Vallee, horizontal baton, tuxedo, 1934 . . . . 12.00
"I Think I'm Beginning To Fall In Love," Stephens, *"The Bliss of Mrs Blossom,"* Shirley Macline, Attenborough, and Booth scenes, 1948 . . . . 7.00
"I Won't Dance," Kern, Hammerstein/Harbach, Fred Astaire and Ginger Rogers, Irene Dunne, 1935 . . . . 10.00
"Keep That Twinkle In Your Eye," *"Paddy O'Day,"* head photo of Jane Withers, 1936 . . . . 8.00
"Let's Call A Heart A Heart," *"Pennies From Heaven,"* Burke, Johnston, Bing Crosby, 1936 . . . . 7.00
"Maids On Parade," *"Captain of the Guard,"* Roemheld, Dugan, John Boles and Laura LaPlante, battle scene below, 1930 . . . . 12.00
"Man Without Love," large photo of Engelbert Humperdinck, 1968 . . . . 3.00
"Mona Lisa," Livingston/Evans, Alan Ladd, Wanda Hendrix, teal blue and gray, 1949 . . . . 4.00
"Okay Toots," *"Kid Millions,"* Eddie Cantor caricature 8.00
"One Tin Soldier," *"Billy Jack,"* Lambert/Potter, Tom Laughlin and Delores Taylor, 1969 . . . . 6.00
"Satin Sheets," Volinkaty, full page photo of Jeanne Pruett, 1973 . . . . 5.00
"She'll Be Comin Round The Mountain," brown and white mountain scene, 1930 . . . . 4.00
"Strangers In The Night," *"A Man Could Get Killed,"* black and white word cov, Kaempfert, Snyder, Singleton, 1966 . . . . 3.00
"Swastika Spirit," Minchew, Peace, red and gray stylized flowers, flags with swastikas, dedicated to Swastika Canoe Club, 1911 . . . . 8.00
"Thank Heaven For You," *"International House,"* Rainger, Robin, large head photo of Rudy Vallee, 1933 . . . . 12.00

SHOE-RELATED COLLECTIBLES

This is a category with sole. Nothing more needs to be said.

Club: Miniature Shoe Collectors Club, P.O. Box 2390, Apple Valley, CA 92308.

Advertising Trade Card, Bixby & Co Shoe Polish, Lady Liberty holding shoe polish **$8.00**
Bag, paper, Red Goose Shoes, Gilbert **50.00**
Bank, Poll-Parrot Treasure Boot, plastic **20.00**

Sign, Red Goose, cardboard hanger, emb, 4 x 9", $98.00. Photo courtesy Frank's Antiques.

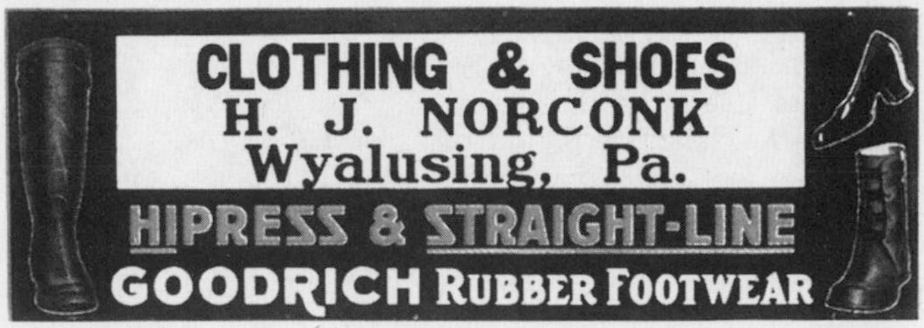

Sign, Goodrich Rubber Footwear, emb tin, 13¾" h, 39½" w, $38.00. Photo courtesy Collectors Auction Services.

Booklet, *Happy Days of Tess and Ted,* Star Brand Shoes **5.00**
Bookmark, Peters Weatherbird Shoes, 4" l **15.00**
Bookmark, Poll Parrot Shoes, 5¾" l **15.00**
Charm, miner's knee boots, made from compressed anthracite coal, pr attached to orig card, c1930 . . . . **50.00**
Clicker, Peters Weatherbird Shoes **28.00**
Clicker, Sundial Bonnie Laddie **5.00**
Comic Book, premium, PF Magic Shoe Adventure Book, *Rocket Kids Moon Story,* BF Goodrich, 1962 . . . . **22.00**
Display, Peters Shoes, metal holder, 7½ x 9½" l **95.00**
Display, U S Rubber Boot, large buckled rubber boot made from Froyal tempered rubber, working brass buckles, 28" h **150.00**
Jump Rope, Peters Weatherbird Shoes **20.00**
Key Tag, Armour Leather Company, shoe sole shape, brown leather, inscribed "Leather—Key To Foot Health," c1930 . . . . **15.00**
Pencil, mechanical, Peters Shoe Co, celluloid **20.00**
Pencil, mechanical, Poll-Parrot Shoes **15.00**
Pencil Box, Peters Weatherbird Shoes, 10" l **30.00**
Pocket Mirror, Cherry Blossom Boot Polish adv, product tin illus, 1920s **60.00**
Pinback Button, Buster Brown Shoes, "Member Brown Bilt Club," Buster and Tige illus **15.00**
Pinback Button, Friedman Bros Shoe Co, St Louis, "Our Little Samson" **33.00**
Pinback Button, Hanover Shoe, red and black high button shoe and inscription, white ground, dated 1905 . . . . **25.00**
Pinback Button, Poll Parrot Shoes, "I Wear Pre-Tested Poll-Parrot Shoes For Boys and Girls," parrot illus **10.00**
Pinback Button, Star Brand Shoes, "Star Branc Are Better Shoes," red star in center on blue ground **2.00**
Pinback Button, Tess and Ted School Shoes, multicolored, well dressed boy and girl illus, white ground **30.00**
Pocketknife, Star Brand Shoes, 1 blade, metal, "Society Shoe" **75.00**
Ring, plastic, Poll-Parrot Shoes adv, Howdy Doody image **65.00**
Ruler, Peters Weatherbird Shoes adv, wooden, 6" l **18.00**
Shoehorn, Queen Quality, celluloid, curled handle, color portrait of lady, c1900, 2 x 6" **35.00**
Shoehorn, Red Goose Shoes **10.00**
Shoehorn, Star Brand Shoes **4.00**
Shoe Shine Kit, child's, Shinola, 1953, MIB **20.00**
Spinner, Poll-Parrot Shoes **35.00**
Spinner, Weatherbird Shoes **15.00**
String Holder, Red Goose Shoes, handing, diecut tin goose above holder, 27" h **825.00**
Whistle, Peters Weatherbird Shoes, green **25.00**
Whistle, Poll Parrot Shoes, 2" l **25.00**
Whistle, Weather Bird Shoes **20.00**

Reverse Paint on Glass, Daniel Webster, printed paper room scene, period gilt frame, 8¹/₄ x 5¹/₂", $402.50. Photo courtesy Butterfield, Butterfield & Dunning.

SILHOUETTE PICTURES

Eighteenth and nineteenth silhouettes (shades) are profiles produced by hollow cutting or mechanical tracing. Additional detail was often added by painted highlights.

Etienne de Silhouette, a French Minister of Finance, introduced the process. Silhouettes were popular in colonial America. Examples by the Peale family, who marked their work with an impressed "PEALE" or "PEALE MUSEUM" stamp are highly desirable.

Hollow cut and mechanical traced silhouettes lost their appeal in the mid-nineteenth century due to advent of the photograph. A brief revival occurred between the 1930s and the mid-1950s. Silhouette stands were common attraction on seaside boardwalks and other tourist stops.

Marlys Sellers' *Encyclopedia of Silhouette Collectibles on Glass* (Shadow Enterprises, 1992) introduced collectors to colored pictures in a silhouette style that were painted on the back of a piece of flat or convex glass that were popular from the 1920s through the early 1950s. They are usually found with a paper scenic or tinted background or a background of textured foil. A popular promotional giveaway, examples are found with an imprinted advertising message. Forms range from a simple two-dimensional picture to a jewelry box.

Cut, hollow, gentleman, white ink detail on black cloth, 5¹/₂ x 4¹/₂" frame size, early 19th century **$200.00**

Cut, hollow, woman, white ink hair and dress detail, sgd. "D. Hubbard," oval brass frame, 4 ³/₄ x 5 ³/₄" frame size, early 19th century **400.00**

Cut, mechanical, pasted, lady, faded gilt detail, black frame, 6 x 4³/₄" frame size, early 19th century **140.00**

Painted, convex glass, picture, untitled, Benton Glass Company, two kittens at pond's edge watching duckling enter water, plain white background, simple metal frame, 1930s–40s **15.00**

Painted, flat glass, picture, The Dance, Buckbee-Brehem Company, features couple in colonial dress doing minuet in garden setting, cellist and flutist in background, plain tan ground, simple black painted wood frame, 1930s **18.00**

Painted, flat glass, picture, untitled, Fisher Hand Painted Silhouettes, couple in colonial dress kissing on arched bridge in marsh setting, background of dried flowers, simple black painted wood frame, 1930s **22.00**

Painted, jewelry box, flat glass picture lid, Art Deco style woman walking greyhound, gold painted accents, gold painted elaborately molded wood frame **45.00**

Mustard Pot, red insert, 4" h, $55.00.

SILVER PLATED

G. R. and H. Ekington of England are credited with inventing the electrolytic method of plating silver in 1838. In late nineteenth-century pieces, the base metal was often Britannia, an alloy of tin, copper, and antimony. Copper and brass also were used as bases. Today the base is usually nickel silver.

Rogers Bros., Hartford, Connecticut, introduced the silver-plating process to the United States in 1847. By 1855 a large number of silver-plating firms were established.

Extensive polishing will eventually remove silver plating. However, today's replating process is so well developed that you can have a piece replated in such a manner that the full detail of the original is preserved.

Identifying companies and company marks is difficult. Fortunately there is Dorothy Rainwater's *Encyclopedia of American Silver Manufacturers, 3rd Edition* (Schiffer Publishing, 1986).

Bread Tray, Daffodil **$95.00**

Cigarette Lighter, Ronson, oval, Art Nouveau design, ftd **18.00**

Clock, Birmingham, Art Deco, circular shape, guilloche-enameled black and white with applied marcasite dec, 1930s **100.00**

Cocktail Fork, Remembrance pattern, International Silver, 5¹/₂" l **10.00**

Compact, La Mode, heart shaped. **60.00**

Creamer and Sugar, mkd "Meriden" **100.00**

Cruet Set, Victorian, cut glass bottles, minor nicks, mid 19th C, 10³/₄" h **350.00**

Flatware Service, luncheon set, 12 knives and forks, 2 crumbers, serving knife and fork, engraved blades, ivory handles. **125.00**

Grapefruit Spoon, Grenoble pattern, Oneida, 6⁷/₈" l **8.00**

Ice Bucket, Baroque pattern, thermos lined, Wallace. **225.00**

Infant Spoon, Coronation pattern, Oneida, 5⁵/₈" l **8.00**

Pie Server, Daffodil pattern, International Silver, 10³/₄" d **50.00**

Knife Rest, dolphin, Pairpoint. **35.00**

Matchsafe, textured pattern **40.00**

Napkin Ring, Victorian, floral bouquets **15.00**

Salad Fork, First Love pattern, International Silver, 6³/₄" l **17.00**

Salad Set, 2 pcs, Flair pattern, International Silver. **50.00**

Sugar Tongs, Danish Princess pattern, International Silver, 4¹/₈" l **30.00**

Syrup, geometric and floral strap work body, figural finial, Meriden, 1865, replated. **85.00**

Tea Tray, 2 handles with folitate dec, 28" l, price for 4. . . . . . **750.00**

Toothpick Holder, Colonial lady. **65.00**

Watch Holder, figural child and dog. **275.00**

Top: Roller Derby, #10, red, metal wheels, $12.00.
Bottom: Super Surfer, wood deck, clay wheels, $14.00.

SKATEBOARDS

Skateboards have been around since a very inventive person with only one rollerskate broke it in half and nailed it to a 2 x 4" board.

The progression of the sport was slow until the sixties. Surfers who were bored with no ocean swells and flat seas, saw a resemblance in skating to surfing. The same stance and movement to initiate a turn, made surfers out of land-locked people all over the world.

In the late 1970s, major design changes put production, quality, and prices on a meteoric rise. Professionals would endorse certain models during this time frame, stimulating a lot of sales for the company.

Advisor: Thomas J. VanderHorst, 9011 West End Dr., Kalamazoo, MI 49002, (616) 327-6248.

Brewer, Dick Brewer "Snowboards" **$40.00**
Dog Town Skates, Jim Mulc, Bob Biniar, Wes Hampton or Shogo Kubo 35.00
Flying Banana 130.00
Gordon Smith, Fiberflex, 67" 100.00
Hobie, fiberglass, Mike Weed 50.00
Huffy, Thunder Road 5.00
Keebler, Elf, in box 75.00
Magazine, *Quarterly Skateboarder,* Vol 1, #1 . . . . 25.00
Magazine, *Thrasher,* Vol 1, #1 . . . . 15.00
Magazine, *Transworld Skateboarding,* Vol 1, #1 . . . . 8.00
Makaha, XL10, aluminum 120.00
Makaha, Zipees 80.00
Nash, Duke Kahanamoku 120.00
Nash, Sidewalk Surfer Shark 60.00
Nash, Spiker Dozer 5.00
Santa Cruz, Bevel 30.00
Schmitt Stik, Chris Miller 65.00
Sidewalk Surfer, maple deck, clay wheels 14.00
Sims, Lester Kasi, Lonnie Toft or Super Ply 35.00
Sims, Pure Juice 65.00
Tony Alva 30.00
Thrusher, Flite Surf Co 60.00
Tracker, Rocket Deck 65.00

SLOT CARS

Aurora, the premier name in slot car racing, marketed its first electric slot car play set in the fall of 1960. Since then, slot cars have successfully competed with electric trains for their share of the model hobbyist's dollars.

Club: H.O. Slot Car Collecting & Racing Club, P.O. Box 255, Monroe, CT 06468.

Newsletter: *Lots of Slots,* 503 Boal St., Cincinnati, OH 45210; *Slot Car Trader,* P.O. Box 1868, Elyria, OH 44036.

Accessory, Aurora, modular bridge posts, 1/32 scale **$15.00**
Accessory, Aurora, Spin-Out shoulder ends, 1/32 scale 15.00
Accessory, Aurora Thunderjet, country bridge and roadway 20.00
Accessory, Aurora Thunderjet, guard rails and rail posts set 15.00
Accessory, Aurora Thunderjet, speed control unit 15.00
Accessory, Gilbert, Railway-Highway, crossing, MIB 22.00
Accessory, Monogram, 6 curved track, 21" radius 25.00
Accessory, Revell, 6" model car race track, 12 pk spin-out apron transitions 15.00
Accessory, Strombecker, lap counter 22.00
Car, Aurora, Blazin' Brakes, Corvette GT, white, red, yellow, and orange 15.00
Car, Aurora, Cats Eye, GMC Blazer, white, red, orange, and yellow 20.00
Car, Aurora, Magna-Sonic, Baja Bug, red and white 20.00
Car, Aurora, Scre-E-Echers, Rapid Rescue, yellow and red 5.00
Car, Aurora, Speed Steer, Thunderbird Stock Car, blue, green, white, and yellow 20.00
Car, Aurora, Vibrator, #1542, Mercedes, yellow 55.00
Genuine Duncan Yo-Yo Tournament Top 77, wood, solid color lacquer finish with contrasting airbrushed stripe, yellow decal with black and red print, 1946-49 . . . . 60.00
Car, Aurora Thunderjet, Bushwacker, blue and white 40.00
Car, Aurora Thunderjet, Ferrari, white, red stripes 30.00
Car, Aurora Thunderjet, Hot Rod Coupe, tan 35.00
Car, Aurora Thunderjet, Mako Shark, red 45.00
Car, Aurora Vibrator, Hot Rod Roadster, tan 45.00
Car, Aurora Vibrator, Mercedes Benz, black 70.00
Car, Cox, Ferrari, red, 1/24 scale 70.00
Car, Eldon, Thunderbird Coupe, 1/32 scale 25.00
Car, Lionel, Porsche Power passer, white 20.00
Car, Marklin, #1317, Porsche Carrera Sportswagon, red, 1/32 scale 120.00
Car, Marx, Jaguar XKE, 1/32 scale 50.00
Car, Revell, Ford Cobra Racer, burgundy, 1/24 scale 95.00
Car, Strombecker, Barracuda, 1/32 scale 150.00
Car, Tyco, Z-28 Camaro, #7, red, white, and blue 8.00
Race Set, Aurora, 12 Hours at Sebring 65.00
Race Set, Aurora, Jackie Stewart Oval 8, HO scale, orig box 80.00
Race Set, Aurora, #2703, Mario Andretti GP International Challenge, HO scale, orig box 50.00
Race Set, Elden, Power Pack 8, 1/32 scale, orig box 45.00
Race Set, Marx, Grand Prix Race Set, 1/32 scale, orig box 65.00
Race Set, Strombecker, Indianapolis 5/1 Race Set, 1/32 scale, orig box 120.00
Race Set, Strombecker, International Road Racing Set, includes 4" l Porsche RS61, Lotus MKXIX, track, safety fence, figures, decal sheet, safety cones, control units, and 32 pp manual, missing electric power box, 1960s 65.00
Race Set, Topper, Johnny Lightning Indy 500 Set, 500 Unit, dual lane lap counter, two 180 degree turns, 2 crossovers, 3 straights, 8 bases, uprights, and couplers, 2 cars, 26 x 18 x 8" red and white illus box 25.00

Soaky, Lander, $25.00.

SMOKEY BEAR

It is hard to believe that Smokey Bear has been around for more than fifty years. The popularity of Smokey started during the Second World War, as part of a national awareness campaign for the prevention of forest fires. The National Forest Service ran slogans like "Keep 'Em Green; Forests are Vital to National Defense" in an attempt to keep the public's attentions on the war effort.

From then to now Smokey has been more the just a crusader for fire awareness and prevention; he has been a collectible character and a source of enjoyment to many admirers. There was a wide variety of Smokey collectibles produced: watches, radios, toys, posters, and many games and books. Most had short production runs and were used as Forest Service giveaways or were sold by a select number of department store chains.

Good luck in your collecting and remember only you can prevent forest fires.

Alarm Clock, metal, Bradley, 1970s, 6½" h. **$200.00**
Ashtray, figural, log shape, ceramic, raised Smokey head on end, other end with "Prevent Forest Fires," 1950s, 3½ x 4½ x 6" **50.00**
Bobbing Head, composition, 1960. . . . . **50.00**
Booklet, *Smokey Bear's Story of the Forest,* Oregon State Board of Forestry, 1964 . . . . **15.00**
Bookmark, U S Department of Agriculture, 1954, 6¼" l **15.00**
Coloring Book, Whitman, 1960s, 8 x 10½" **12.00**
Doll, rust color plush body and limbs, vinyl painted head, hands and feet, cotton stuffed, glassene eyes, complete with levi's, belt with buckle, badge, and shovel, Ideal, 1953, 14" h **125.00**
Forest Ranger Kit, Smokey the Bear Jr, complete contents, orig envelope, 1960s **100.00**
Game, Smokey Bear Game, Milton Bradley, 1973 . . . . **30.00**
Game, Smokey the Forest Fire Preventin' Game, Ideal, 1961. . . . . **40.00**
Handbook, *Junior Forest Ranger,* 24 pp, 1974. . . . . **15.00**
Lunch Box, black vinyl, King-Seely Thermos Co, c1965, 7 x 9½ x 4". **85.00**
Mug, ceramic, 1960s, 3¼" h **45.00**
Pamphlet, "Suppose You Went Camping" **10.00**
Patch, embroidered, "Please be Careful," 1970s, 3 x 4". **15.00**
Pinback Button, "I Prevent Forest Fires," ¾" d. **15.00**
Ruler, wooden, ""A Rule To Prevent Forest Fires..." **10.00**
Salt and Pepper Shakers, pr, ceramic, 1950s, 4" h. **60.00**
Sign, cardboard, "Prevent Woods Fires," 1960s, 11½ x 14" **60.00**
Song Book, *Forest Fire Prevention Song Book* **20.00**

SNACK SETS

The earliest snack sets (originally called tea and toast sets) were porcelain and earthenware examples manufactured overseas. Glass sets produced in the United States were a popular hostess accessory during the boom years following World War II. American dinnerware manufacturers of the time, such as Purinton and Stangl, also produced sets to match their most popular dinnerware patterns.

Newsletter: *Snack Set Searchers' Newsletter*, P.O. Box 908, Hallock, MN 56738.

Note: The following snack sets are for two piece sets unless noted otherwise.

Anchor Hocking, Fleurette, 8 pc set **$32.00**
Anchor Hocking, turquoise blue **6.00**
Anchor Hocking, Wheat, milk glass, 8 pc set **28.00**
Anniversary Rose **13.00**
Colonial Lady, crystal cup **7.00**
Colonial Lady, red cup **11.00**
England, floral, Queen Anne **36.00**
Federal, Homestead, crystal, 8 pc set **15.00**
Federal, Patio, milk glass, 8 pc set **14.00**
Federal, Rosecrest, milk glass, 8 pc set **32.00**
Fleurette **8.00**
Gay Fad, Magnolia **15.00**
Harker, Antique Cars, 8 pc set **30.00**
Hazel Atlas, Daisy **5.00**
Hazel Atlas, Dogwood, milk glass, 8 pc set **12.00**
Hazel Atlas, Seashell, capri blue, 8 pc set **58.00**
Holt Howard, Tomato **25.00**
Indiana Glass, Harvest, lime green carnival **18.00**
Indiana Glass, Harvest, milk glass, 8 pc set **25.00**
Jeannette, Dewdrop **4.00**
Lefton, Blue Paisley **32.00**
Lefton, Heirloom Rose. **38.00**
Lefton, Lilac Chintz. **36.00**
Lefton, Rose Chintz. **34.00**
Lefton, Rose Heirloom. **32.00**
Lefton, Spring Time **22.00**
Lefton, Summertime **18.00**
Made In Japan, bite shape, floral **5.00**
Made In Japan, shell shape, floral **5.00**
Noritake, Azalea **45.00**
Primrose. **10.00**
Salem, Antique Cars, 8 pc set **30.00**
Salem, Game Birds, 8 pc set **30.00**

Hazel Atlas, Pebbletone, crystal, $6.00.

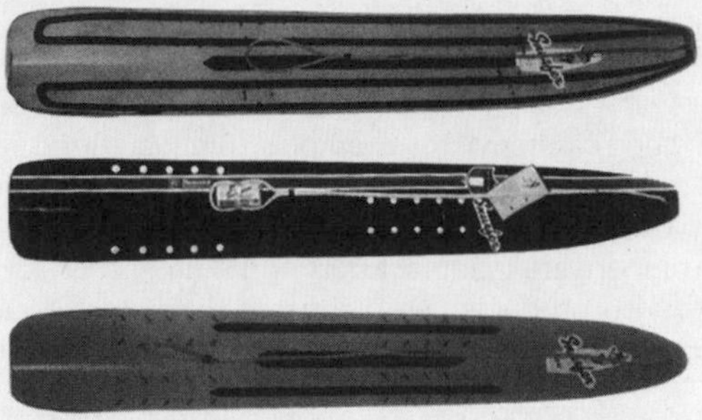

Snurfers, Brunswick, top: yellow, $30.00, middle: Super Racing, $25.00, bottom: Gem, $20.00.

SNOWBOARDS

Snowboarding, as an organized sport, has only been around since the early 1980s. Sliding down a hill on one plank probably dates back to the first viking who broke a ski and had to make it down to town, surf style.

People went skiing and sledding for outdoor winter recreation until a wise man, named Sherman Poppen, invented a stand up "water ski" with staples for traction and a rope for handle. That was in 1964. With a combination of surf and snow the "snurfer" was born. That little yellow sled evolved into the multimillion dollar sport that is snowboarding today.

Advisor: Thomas J. VanderHorst, 9011 West End Dr., Kalamazoo, MI 49002, (616) 327-6248.

Brunswick, Snurfer, red	**$40.00**
Burton, Backhill	**70.00**
Burton, Burton Board	**120.00**
Burton, Elite	**60.00**
Marina, Snow Skimmer	**20.00**
Nash, Skifer	**20.00**
Sims, Lonnie Toft	**120.00**
Star Surfing Co	**25.00**
Swing-Bo	**29.00**
Winterstick, split swallow or V-tail	**65.00**

SNOW GLOBES

The majority of plastic and glass snow globes found at flea markets are imported from the Orient. A few are produced in France, Germany, and Italy. There are no American manufacturers, but rather dozens of large gift companies who design and import an array of styles, shapes, and themes. Enesco Corporation of Elk Grove Village, Illinois, is one of the largest.

Club: Snowdome Collectors Club, P.O. Box 53262, Washington, DC 20009.

Newsletter: *Roadside Attractions,* 7553 Norton Ave., Apt. 4, Los Angeles, CA 90046.

Advertising, American Express, double sided	**$15.00**
Advertising, Coca-Cola, woman holding bottle of Coke	**12.00**
Advertising, Flamingo Productions	**15.00**
Advertising, Knorr, double sided	**12.00**
Advertising, Newsweek	**60.00**
Advertising, New York Times, 1987	**100.00**
Advertising, Skelly Tire Co, "Your Surety of Service"	**35.00**
Advertising, White Star Trucking, gold crown, black base	**65.00**
Ashtray, Florida, flamingos, glass and plastic, pink	**35.00**
Character, Betty Boop, Bully, Germany, 1986	**15.00**
Character, Felix the Cat, Determined, 1987	**12.00**
Character, Flintstones, "Bedrock City," 1975	**25.00**
Character, Hansel and Gretel, German	**10.00**
Character, Lone Ranger, glass globe	**75.00**
Character, Marilyn Monroe	**35.00**
Character, Snoopy, lying on dog house, Willits, 1966	**18.00**
Character, Teenage Mutant Ninja Turtles, 1990	**12.00**
Commemorative, 1958 Brussels World's Fair	**35.00**
Commemorative, 1992 Winter Olympics, Albertville, France	**12.00**
Commemorative, Seattle World's Fair	**15.00**
Commemorative, moon landing	**20.00**
Figural, apple, "#1 Teacher"	**8.00**
Figural, baby bottle	**6.00**
Figural, bell, Christmas scene	**8.00**
Figural, Bugs Bunny	**85.00**
Figural, coffeepot	**15.00**
Figural, frog, souvenir	**12.00**
Figural, heart shape, red, New York	**12.00**
Figural, lantern	**15.00**
Figural, Santa Claus, deer over shoulders	**15.00**
Figural, witch, holding crow, "Best Witches"	**15.00**
Music Box, Snow White, glass globe, plays "Some Day My Prince Will Come," Walt Disney	**40.00**
Pencil Topper, Simpsons characters	**6.00**
Pencil Sharpener, Niagara Falls, Canada	**10.00**
Salt and Pepper Shakers, pr, Christmas scene	**12.00**
Salt and Pepper Shakers, pr, Florida, flamingos	**15.00**
Salt and Pepper Shakers, pr, Grauman's Chinese Theater, Los Angeles, TV shape	**25.00**
Salt and Pepper Shakers, pr, Seattle Space Needle	**20.00**
Souvenir, Europe, flags	**12.00**
Souvenir, Las Vegas, calendar base	**15.00**
Souvenir, London, bottle shaped	**15.00**
Souvenir, Louisiana, oval, state map, lobster, pelican, and boat	**10.00**
Souvenir, Memphis, skyline and river boat scene	**6.00**
Souvenir, New York, Statue of Liberty	**10.00**
Souvenir, Paris, Eiffel Tower	**18.00**
Souvenir, Switzerland, panda bear	**15.00**
Souvenir, Texas, yellow map, cowboy with lasso	**10.00**
Souvenir, Urie's, Wildwood, NJ	**8.00**
Sports, New York Yankees	**6.00**
Sports, University of Alabama, Crimson Tide, "We're #1" on base	**6.00**

Man and Dog, Atlas Crystal Works, 4 1/2" h, $40.00.

Race Car, Tidy Toys, Colgate-Palmolive, 1960s, $25.00.

SOAKIES

Soaky bottles are plastic bubble bath containers molded in the shape of popular children's characters. The first Soakies were marketed by the Colgate-Palmolive Co., in the 1960s and were an innovative marketing tool designed to convince kids (especially boys) that "Bathtime Is Funtime."

As with any profitable idea, copycats soon appeared. One successful line produced by the Purex Company was called the Bubble Club. These containers were fashioned after Hanna-Barbera characters. The bottles included in this category are all plastic figural containers and range in size from 6" to 11" high.

Advisor: Greg Moore, P.O. Box 1621, Castle Rock, WA, 98611, (360) 274-7424.

Atom Ant, Purex, 1965 .... **$60.00**
Bullwinkle, Colgate-Palmolive, 1966 .... **45.00**
Casper, Colgate-Palmolive, 1960s **30.00**
El Cabong, Purex, 1964 .... **70.00**
Explosives Truck, Colgate-Palmolive, 1960s **25.00**
Frankenstein, Colgate-Palmolive, 1965 .... **75.00**
Gravel Truck, Colgate-Palmolive, 1960s **25.00**
Little Orphan Annie, Lander, 1977 .... **25.00**
Magilla Gorilla, Purex, 1960s **70.00**
Morocco Mole, Purex, 1966 .... **75.00**
Mr Magoo, Colgate-Palmolive, 1960s **30.00**
Mush Mouse, Purex, 1960s **45.00**
Paul McCartney, Colgate-Palmolive, 1965 .... **100.00**
Punkin' Puss, Purex, 1966 .... **45.00**
Quick Draw McGray, Purex, 1960s **25.00**
Ricochet Rabbit, Purex, 1964 .... **45.00**
Rocky, Colgate-Palmolive, 1962 .... **25.00**

Huckleberry Hound, Purex, 1960s, $25.00.

Secret Squirrel, Purex, 1966 .... **75.00**
Smokey the Bear, Lander, date unknown **25.00**
Snow White, Colgate-Palmolive, movable arms, 1960s **20.00**
Speedy Gonzales, Colgate-Palmolive, 1960s **30.00**
Superman, Colgate-Palmolive, 1965 .... **50.00**
Tennessee Tuxedo, Colgate-Palmolive, 1965 .... **30.00**
Wolfman, Colgate-Palmolive, blue pants, 1963 .... **80.00**
Woodsy Owl, Lander, date unknown **60.00**
Woody Woodpecker, Colgate, 1977 .... **40.00**
Yogi Bear, Purex, 1960s **20.00**

SOAP COLLECTIBLES

At first you would not think that a lot of soap collectibles would survive. However, once you start to look around, you'll see no end to the survivors. Many Americans are not as clean as we think.

There is no hotel soap listed. Most survivors sell for 50¢ to $2.00 per bar. Think of all the hotels and motels that you have stayed at that have gone out of business. Don't you wish you would have saved one of the soap packets? You don't? What are you—normal or something?

Advertising Trade Card, Doty's Washer, folder type, red, black, and buff, 1873 price list **$15.00**
Advertising Trade Card, Dreydroppel's Soap, "True Story of the White Elephant," blue and white **25.00**
Advertising Trade Card, Higgins Soap, afternoon in Central Park, horse and carriage, color **6.00**
Advertising Trade Card, Scourine, "Arrest All Dirt" **8.00**
Advertising Trade Card, Williams Yankee Soap, red, white, and blue flag, beige ground **100.00**
Advertising Trade Card, Wool Soap, "My Mama Used Wool Soap," diecut **14.00**
Bookmark, Dingman's Soap, baby illus **9.00**
Box, Argo Starch, 1930s, unopened **10.00**
Box, Bear Cleaner, polar bear illus, 1930s, 2 x 4 x 6" **3.00**
Box, Honor Bright Soap, cardboard **5.00**
Box, Larkin Sweet Home Soap, wood **45.00**
Calendar, Suchan's Carbolic Soap, 1891, full pad **25.00**
Display, Ivory Soap, inflatable **25.00**
Playing Cards, Best Grand Laundry, "We wash ever thing with Ivory Soap" **5.00**
Pocket Mirror, Lava Chemical Resolvant Soap, celluloid, c1910, 2½" d **35.00**
Poster, Lifebuoy, cardboard, "Laugh with Bob Burns," 10 x 14" **10.00**
Poster, Lux, cardboard, Ann Sheridan with "My Beauty Care," 14 x 11" **30.00**
Poster, Lux, paper, "Holiday Special, a useful gift!," 2-sided, 13 x 18" **35.00**
Poster, Oxydol, cardboard, box shaped, 5½ x 7¾" **92.00**
Poster, Rinso, cardboard, "Values for Thrifty Shoppers," 11 x 14" **5.00**
Poster, Rinso, paper, Amos N' Andy, "Shop Early," 1944, 11 x 14" **110.00**
Sign, Ivory Soap, cardboard, little girl washing doll's clothing, Maud Humphrey illus, 17 x 24½" **450.00**
Sign, Lava Soap, cardboard, full color, c1910, 8 x 8" **20.00**
Sign, Proctor & Gamble Soap, "Purity," Victorian woman wearing bonnet and lacy scarf, 17½ x 22" **130.00**
Soap, Betty Boop Toilet Soap, 3 bars with different top decal depicting Betty in different poses, orig 3 x 6" lithoed box, Pictorial Products/Fleischer, 1931 .... **340.00**

Sign, Lenox Soap, porcelain, 6" h, 10" w, $110.00. Photo courtesy Collectors Auction Services.

Postcard, "Votes For Women/Let's Pull Together!," sgd "Emily Hall Chamberlain," published by the National Woman Suffrage Pub. Co., NY, 1915, $100.00. Photo courtesy Postcards International.

Soap, Hanna-Barbera Bath Soap, Roclar, Yogi Bear, Yakky Doodle, and Chopper on wrapper, 1976, 3 x 2 x 1" bar **8.00**
Soap, Snow White Perfumed Soaps, 7 bars with character's image and name on each, orig box, Kerk Guild/WDE, 1938 . . . . **520.00**
Soap Dish, porcelain, Blue Onion, drain **58.00**
Thermometer, Lincoln Laundry, wood, early 1900s, 12 x 3" **25.00**

SOCIAL CAUSE COLLECTIBLES

Social cause collectibles are just now coming into their own as a collecting category. Perhaps this is because the social activists of the 1960s have mortgages, children, and money in their pockets to buy back the representations of their youths. In doing so, they are looking back past their own protest movements to all forms of social protest that took place in the twentieth century.

Great collections can be built around a single cause, e.g., women's suffrage or the right to vote. Much of the surviving material tends to be two-dimensional. Stress three-dimensional items the moment you begin to collect. As years pass, these are the objects most likely to rise in value.

Club: American Political Items Collectors, Labor History Chapter, P.O. Box 407, Dallas, NC 28034.

Book, *Prisoners of Poverty: Women Wage Workers, Their Trades and Their Lives,* Helen Campbell, Little, Brown, and Co, Boston, 1900, 257 pp, red cloth cov **$40.00**
Calendar, American Red Cross, 1919, 28 x 10½" **35.00**
Journal, *The Official Organ of the White Ribbon Army,* WCTU, 1887 . . . . **12.00**
Leaflet, "Let the People Speak," anti-war demonstration, Aug 28, 1968, 7½ x 10½" **42.00**
Matchbook Cover, Air Line Pilot's Association vs National Airlines, boy carrying sign "Bobby Brown...World's Youngest Picket—A Strikebreaker Is Flying His Daddy's Airplane," 1948 . . . . **10.00**
Medal, Peace, emb brass, Angel of Peace waving palm branch, text on back with dates of beginning and ending of World War I, 1¾" d **15.00**
Pinback Button, "Defend the Park!," "People for Parks Parks for People," Berkeley People's Park, 1½" d **48.00**
Pinback Button, "Free Speech for H.S. Students," 1½" d **15.00**
Pinback Button, "Gay Love, It's the Real Thing," 2¼" d **25.00**
Pinback Button, "Stop the War on Viet Nam—SPU," Student Peace Union, 1¼" d **18.00**
Pinback Button, "Today's Pig—Tomorrow's Bacon," Black Panthers, black lettering on green ground, 1½" d **23.00**
Pinback Button, "Vietnam March for Peace, Nov. 27," 1" d **10.00**
Postcard, "Equal Suffrage—Woman's Birthright," unused **30.00**
Postcard, "I Want To Be A Suffragette," red and green litho of woman trying on pants, 1914 postmark **20.00**
Poster, Peace flag on stars ground, red, white, and blue, 1970, 21 x 33" **138.00**
Poster, "The End of the War, 1973," paper, red and black on blue ground, "Straight Theatre, Nov 5, 8 PM," 15¾ x 23" **125.00**
Ribbon, United Labor Party, Hamilton Co, Cincinnati, OH, 1880s, 1¾ x 3¾" **184.00**
Watch Fob, Transport Workers Union **10.00**

SODA FOUNTAIN AND ICE CREAM COLLECTIBLES

The local soda fountain and/or ice cream parlor was the social center of small town America between the late 1880s and the 1960s. Ice cream items appeared as early as the 1870s.

This is a category filled with nostalgia—banana splits and dates with friends. Some concentrate on the advertising, some on the implements. It is all terrific.

Clubs: National Assoc of Soda Jerks, P.O. Box 115, Omaha, NE 68101; The Ice Screamer, P.O. Box 465, Warrington, PA 18976.

ICE CREAM

Change Tray, Velvet Ice Cream, young woman eating ice cream **$275.00**
Cone Dispenser, glass jar, nickel plated insert holds stacked cones upright, metal lid, 14" h, 6½" d **300.00**
Display, figural ice cream cone, papier-mâché, 18" h **100.00**
Fudge Warmer, Howell's Hot Fudge **48.00**
Light Fixtures, pr, figural ice cream cones, painted metal, 15" h, 10' d **110.00**
Scoop, cone shaped bowl, Clipper Cone Dish, thumb lever, Geer Mfg Co, Troy, NY **300.00**
Scoop, cone shaped bowl, tin and steel, Ice Cream Measure and Mold, V Clad Co, Philadelphia, PA, 1878 . . . . **40.00**
Scoop, round bowl, aluminum, Erie Specialty Co **100.00**
Scoop, round bowl, Indestructo, Benedict Mfg Co **75.00**
Serving Tray, Collins Ice Cream, rect, mother serving small children **675.00**

Sign, Johnston Hot Fudge Sundaes, plastic and masonite, light-up, emb sundae, c1950s, 9" d, $176.00. Photo courtesy Gary Metz's Muddy River Trading Co.

Serving Tray, Moore's Ice Cream, tin, children's birthday party scene, 13½" d. **75.00**
Sign, Empress Ice Cream, tin, 28 x 44". **65.00**
Sign, "It's Hood's Ice Cream," emb tin, 28 x 20" **425.00**
Sign, Peter Pan Ice Cream, tin, character illus **115.00**
Sign, Rich Valley Ice Cream, yellow and red, 1940s, 9" d **40.00**
Thermometer, Puritas Ice Cream, cardboard, c1923, 12½" h **35.00**

SODA FOUNTAIN

Brochure, White Mountain Ice Cream, woman making ice cream illus. **$125.00**
Catalog, Dean Foster Co, soda counter goods, 1908 . . . . **48.00**
Cup Holder, SP, lily shaped, set of 6. . . . . **30.00**
Fan, Lee's Drug Store, Natrona Heights, PA, diecut car board, sundae, candy, fruit, and milkshake illus **75.00**
Glass, Modox, emb Indian Chief image, 5" h. 3" d **50.00**
Menu, Hook's Dependable Drug Store Fountain Menu, 1920-30 . . . . **35.00**
Poster, chocolate shakes and shakers, repeated designs of shakes and aluminum shaker canisters, Anon, c1950, 25 x 11" **30.00**
Poster, "Trip O' Shakes," 3 images of hand gripping frothy chocolate shakes, Anon, 1947, 29 x 22" **25.00**
Sign, Orange Crush, tin with blackboard **65.00**
Straw Holder, glass, green, pressed design, 4-sided, no lid, 9½" h **100.00**
Syrup Dispenser, Ward's Lemon Crush, lemon shaped. **450.00**

SOFT DRINK COLLECTIBLES

National brands such as Coca-Cola, Canada Dry, Dr Pepper, and Pepsi-Cola dominate the field. However, there were thousands of regional and local soda bottling plants. Their advertising, bottles, and giveaways are every bit as exciting as those of the national companies. Do not ignore them.

Clubs: Crown Collectors Society International, 4300 San Juan Dr., Fairfax, VA 22030; Dr Pepper 10-2-4 Collector's Club, 3508 Mockingbird, Dallas, TX 75205; Grapette Collectors Club, 2240 Hwy. 27N, Nashville, AR 71852; National Pop Can Collectors, P.O. Box 7862, Rockford, IL 61125; New England Moxie Congress, 445 Wyoming Ave., Millburn, NJ 07041; Painted Soda Bottle Collectors Assoc., 9418 Hilmer Dr., La Mesa, CA 91942.

Newsletter: *Painted-Label Soda Bottles,* 192 Ridgecrest Dr., Goodlettsville, TN 37072.

Periodical: *Club Soda,* P.O. Box 489, Troy, ID 83871.

Note: For addition listings see Coca-Cola and Pepsi-Cola.

Baseball Glove, child's, emb "drink Coca-Cola in bottles" in back of glove, 1930s **$575.00**
Belt Buckle, Dr Pepper, enamel, 1930s. **200.00**
Bottle Cap, Dad's, emb, "you'll love Dad's...taste's like Root Beer should!," late 1940s–50s, 30" d **275.00**
Bottle Topper, Hire's Root Beer, metal and rubber **12.00**
Bottle Topper, Whistle, diecut cardboard, pretty girl and "Thirsty? Just-Whistle," 1920s, 8 x 12" **253.00**
Change Tray, Moxie, woman holding glass, 6" d **110.00**
Checkerboard, Hire's Root Beer, adv back flaps with pointing boy and "Exhilarating and Appetizing," 12 x 12" open size **350.00**
Cigarette Lighter, Royal Crown Cola, bottle shaped. **45.00**
Clock, Kist Beverages, round, light-up **215.00**
Cooler, 7-Up, aluminum **50.00**
Disc, B-1 Lemon Lime Soda, round, mounted on heavy wood frame, 3" d. **75.00**
Disc, Bubble Up, oval, 1940s-50s, 8 x 12". **325.00**
Disc, Old Colony Lemonade, round, colonial man holding glass of lemonade, 1940s–50s, 9" d **161.00**
Disc, Orange Crush, round, "Enjoy Orange Crush," 1940s–50s, 9" d. **110.00**
Dispenser Stand, Mission Orange, 16" h. **130.00**
Door Push, White Rock Sparkling Water. **100.00**
Drinking Glass, Moonshine Soda, flared, syrup line **45.00**
Fan Pull, Orange Crush, cardboard, double sided, c1930, 7 x 8" **126.00**
Ice Cream Scoop, Hires, plastic **10.00**
Menu Board, Hire's Root Beer, tin, "Hires R-J Root Beer With Real Root Juices Ice Cold 5¢ Bottles" above chalkboard, 1950s, 15 x 29" **130.00**
Menu Board, Nesbitt's, tin, "Drink Nesbitt's California Orange" and bottle image above chalkboard, late 1930s, 14 x 22". **103.00**
Menu Board, Squirt, tin, "Enjoy Squirt, Never and After-Thirst" and green bottle at top, 1959 . . . . **115.00**
Mirror, Kist, round, bottle graphic and "Get Kist Today!" **28.00**
Puzzle, Hood's Sarsaparilla, cardboard, double horse drawn buggy carrying doctor away from laboratory and factory building, 15 x 10" **95.00**
Sidewalk Marker, 7-Up, brass, emb "Drink 7Up, Safety First". **110.00**
Sign, Brownie Chocolate, tin, emb, "Drink Brownie Chocolate it's delicious," 1950s, 20 x 28". **275.00**
Sign, Grape Ola, tin, "Drink Grape Ola It's Real Grape," emb, early 1920s, 20 x 28" **475.00**

Cigarette Lighter, Dr Pepper, complete with orig instructions and box, c1940s, $176.00. Photo courtesy Gary Metz's Muddy River Trading Co.

Catalog, Nehi Bottling Co. premium, red and black on white, 6 pp, 1920s, 5³/₈ x 8¹/₄", $25.00.

Sign, Grapette, cardboard, easel back, reverse glass, "Drink Grapette Soda Thirst's Best Bet," c1930s, 9 x 13" **200.00**
Sign, Grapette, plastic, counter top, bottle and "Thirsty or Not Remember Buy Grapette," 1940s–50s, 8¹/₂ x 6¹/₂" **325.00**
Sign, Hires Root Beer, tin, diecut bottle, c1940s–50s, 16 x 57" **425.00**
Sign, Squeeze, tin, "Squeeze That Distinctive Orange Drink," c1930s, 20 x 28" **625.00**
Sign, Squirt, tin, emb, "Enjoy Squirt Never An After Thirst," 1959 . . . . . **100.00**
Sign, Vernor's Ginger Ale, man with barrel and "Drink Vernor's Ginger Ale," 1940s, 18 x 54" **550.00**
Stand-Up, Pal Orange, diecut cardboard, boy standing between 2 oversized soda botles, 12 x 20" **35.00**
Syrup Dispenser, Texberry, barrel shaped, c1920, 11¹/₂" h . . . **150.00**
Thermometer, Dr Pepper, tin, round, "Hot or Cold Drink Dr Pepper," 12" d **300.00**
Thermometer, Hires Root Beer, tin, round, "Hires" and mug, 12" d **325.00**
Thermometer, Mason's Root Beer, tin, bottle and "Drink Mason's Root Beer," 26" h **150.00**
Thermometer, Nesbitt's Orange, tin, bottle and "Drink Nesbitt's California Orange," 27" h **130.00**
Thermometer, Squirt, tin, round, bottle and "Drink Squirt," c1940–50s, 9" d **500.00**
Tray, Frank's Dry Ginger Ale, color litho of bottle, 1930s **50.00**

SOUVENIRS

This category demonstrates that, given time, even the tacky can become collectible. Many tourist souvenirs offer a challenge to one's aesthetics. But they are bought anyway.

Tourist china plates and glass novelties from the 1900 to 1940 period are one of the true remaining bargains left. Most of the items sell for under $25. If you really want to have some fun, pick one form and see how many different places you can find from which it was sold.

Clubs: Statue of Liberty Collectors' Club, 26601 Bernwood Rd., Cleveland, OH 44122.

Newsletter: *Antique Souvenir Collectors' News*, P.O. Box 562, Great Barrington, MA 01230.

Apron, cloth, Ghost Town/Knott's Berry Farm, CA, 1950s **$7.00**
Bank, ceramic, Hawaii, figural hula girl, 4" h **10.00**
Bank, plaster, Franklin Institute, Philadlephia, PA, buffalo nickel shaped, 1970s, 12" h **15.00**
Brochure, *Chicago Today,* Art Deco cov photo of family watching television, orig envelope, 64 pp, 1939, 6¹/₄ x 9¹/₂" **18.00**
Brochure, *Illustrated Souvenir of New York,* full color Art Deco cov with Indians in foreground and sailing ship in bay, story of New York with view guide, photos, 48 pp, 1946 . . . . . **15.00**
Brochure, *New York the Wonder City,* revised edition, full color cov, black and white photos, 48 pp, 1945, 6¹/₂ x 9¹/₄" **15.00**
Brochure, *Our Nation's Capital, Washington, D C,* full color cov photo of Capitol building and patriotic shields, black and white photos, 64 pp, 1942, 6¹/₂ x 9³/₄" **15.00**
Bud Vase, Mt Rundle, ceramic, multicolored scene, Japan, 3¹/₂" h **8.00**
Compact, Hawaii, Elgin **30.00**
Cup and Saucer, Casino Santa Cruz, CA, multicolored scene, blue luster glaze, Japan **4.00**
Drinking Glass, Canada, "1966 Newfoundland Come Home Year," Confederation Building, Star of Logy Bay song on back, blue and white, 5³/₄" h **3.00**
Drinking Glass, Laurel Caverns, Uniontown, PA, 5¹/₂" h **8.00**
Drinking Glass, "Provencial Flowers of Canada," mult colored flowers on frosted panel, 4³/₄" h **8.00**
Drinking Glass, Texas, "1836–1986," Alamo, oil rigs, cowboys, and spaceman, 3⁷/₈" h **3.00**
Flicker, Mt Rushmore, full color image changes from "before" view of rocky mountain cliff to "after" view of completed Mt Rushmore, Japan, 1960s **20.00**
Handkerchief, Harrisburg, PA, orig "H H Hermann Handkerchief/Hand Rolled Hem" paper label, 13" sq **8.00**
Handkerchief, Minnesota, state name and printed state motif, scalloped hem, Franshaw, 13" sq **8.00**
Map, San Francisco and the San Francisco Bay Metropolitan Area, United Nation's Conference Center, published by San Francisco Chamber of Commerce **7.50**
Map, travel map and guide to Chicago's attractions, "Ride the L" above congested traffic, black and white, 1930s **6.00**
Measuring Spoon Holder, ceramic, owl and tree stump, "Spooning for you in Tennessee," tree stump is spoon holder, 5" h **10.00**
Menu, The Brown Derby Restaurant, Dec 1, 1947 . . . . . **8.00**
Pencil, Hershey Park, Hershey, PA, scented **1.00**

View Book, Panama Canal, I. L. Madaro's Souvenir Store, Panama, color litho cov, black and white photo illus, c1910, 32 pp, 10 x 8", $30.00.

Pennant, felt, Ringling Bros Barnu, & Bailey Circus, white lettering on brown ground, circus scenes, yellow trim and streamers, c1940 . . . . **25.00**
Pennant, felt, Indianapolis Speedway, 8¾ x 26" **125.00**
Pinback Button, Concord State Fair, multicolored, portrait of blonde woman in ornate dark red gown and matching hat, white lettering, red rim, 1901 . . . . **20.00**
Pinback Button, Niagara Falls night scene, multicolored, 1920–30s **40.00**
Pinback Button, Panama-Pacific Expo, white text on green ground, gold rim, 1915 . . . . **10.00**
Pinback Button, Yazoo Valley, multicolored, yellow ear of cornin green husk on white ground, black lettering, early 1900s **20.00**
Plate, Dayton Beach, FL, Rosland & Marsellus **44.00**
Plate, Historical Boston, Rowland & Marsellus **33.00**
Pocketknife, Disneyland, dark brown plastic grips with black and silver aluminum plaque with Disneyland name and copyright, 3 blades, 2 openers, miniature scissors, corkscrew, and small file, late 1950s, 2" l plus brass loop **50.00**
Salt and Pepper Shakers, pr, Mt Rushmore, plastic **25.00**
Salt and Pepper Shakers, pr, Texas, ceramic, figural cowboy hat **20.00**
Snow Dome, Memphis, TN, bottle shaped, Graceland, memphis River front skyline, paddlewheel boat against bue sky scene, 1960s **65.00**
Toothpick Holder, Florida, pink flamingo standing in green grass, Japan, 3" h **2.00**

SOUVENIR BUILDINGS

Miniature cities boasting United States skyscrapers, French churches, German castles, suburban banks, and Chicago water towers delight collectors of souvenir buildings. These three-dimensional replicas of mostly famous buildings and monuments were originally made as souvenirs for travelers or to commemorate a particular occasion, building, or person. Many are still being made today for the same reasons. Collectors prefer metal, especially pot metal with a high lead content, which produces buildings with fine detail. Age is not as important as rarity, condition, detail, and architectural interest. Most souvenir buildings measure between 1" and 7" high.

Advisor: Dixie Trainer, P.O. Box 70, Nellysford, VA 22958-0070, (804) 361-1739, e-mail: souvenirbu@aol.com.

Club: Souvenir Building Collectors Society, P.O. Box 70, Nellysford, VA 22958-0070.

Newsletter: *Souvenir Building Collector,* P.O. Box 70, Nellysford, VA 22958-0070.

Note: Prices listed are for metal buildings unless noted.

Adler Planetarium, Chicago **$115.00**
Arc de Triompe, Paris, copper finish **5.00**
Atomium, 1958 Brussels World Fair **80.00**
Banker's Life Tower, New York City **135.00**
Castle, Nuremburg, Germany **50.00**
Castle, Wartburg, Germany **140.00**
Cathedral, Aachen, Germany **35.00**
Cathedral, Strasbourg, France **35.00**

First Federal Savings & Loan Association, Greenville, S. C. $75.00.

Cathedral of the Immaculate Conception, Washington, DC, large **45.00**
Cathedral of the Immaculate Conception, Washington, DC, small **20.00**
Cologne, Koln, Germany Cathedral, large **60.00**
Cologne, Koln, Germany Cathedral, small **10.00**
Colosseum, Rome, large **45.00**
Colosseum, Rome, small **10.00**
Eiffel Tower, Paris, large **25.00**
Eiffel Tower, Paris, small **10.00**
Empire State Building, New York City, large **125.00**
Empire State Building, New York City, small **5.00**
First Nation Bank of Riverside **575.00**
Ft Wayne, IN, Citizens Federal Bank **80.00**
General Motors Building, Detroit **385.00**
George Washington Masonic National Memorial, Washington DC **35.00**
Houston Astrodome **70.00**
Jefferson Memorial, Washington DC **15.00**
Kraft Headquarters, Chicago **120.00**
Kremlin Tower, Moscow **85.00**
Leaning Tower of Pisa, composition, 3" h **12.00**
Leaning Tower of Pisa, copper, 3" h **35.00**
Lighthouse, Bar Harbor, Maine, with thermometer **16.00**
Mormon Temple and Tabernacle, Salt Lake City, Utah, salt and pepper set **25.00**
New York City Cityscape **45.00**
Oil Well Rig, Texas **10.00**
Paris, double inkwell with Sacre Coeur **50.00**
Parthenon, Athens, composition, metalized in silver **20.00**
People's Bank of St Louis, MO **750.00**
Pilgrim Memorial Monument, painted metal, with thermometer **35.00**

Bologna Monument, Italy, $40.00.

Sacre Coeur, Paris, large 25.00
Sacre Coeur, Paris, small 10.00
Sears Tower, Chicago, small. 8.00
Sears Tower, Chicago, large 95.00
Seattle Space Needle, large 35.00
Seattle Space Needle, small. 5.00
Singing Tower, Lake Wales, Florida, large 25.00
Singing Tower, Lake Wales, Florida, small. 5.00
St Paul's Cathedral, London, pencil sharpener. 90.00
Stadium, Ohio State University, ashtray 35.00
TransAmerica Building, San Francisco 50.00
Unisphere, 1964 New York City World's Fair 15.00
Washington Monument, Washington DC, large 20.00
Washington Monument, Washington DC, small 4.00

SOUVENIR SPOONS

Collecting commemorative spoons was extremely popular from the last decade of the 19th century through 1940. Actually, it has never gone completely out of fashion. You can still buy commemorative spoons at many historical and city tourist sites. The first thing to check for is metal content. Sterling silver has always been the most popular medium. Fine enamel work adds to value.

Clubs: American Spoon Collectors, 7408 Englewood Ln., Kansas City, MO 54133; The Scoop Club, 84 Oak Ave., Shelton, CT 06484.

Absecon Lighthouse, Atlantic City, NJ, lighthouse handle, pear shaped bowl $40.00
Albany, NY, Shepard Mfg. 30.00
Albert Memorial, London 20.00
Atlantic City, NJ, SS, skyline, ocean scenes. 45.00
Bangor, ME, SS 15.00
Bloomington, IL, SS. 35.00
Brooklyn Bridge, SS, "New York" on handle 38.00
Calgary, Alberta, Canada, SS, Robert Hendery mark 15.00
Capitol Building, Washington, D C, SS, Capitol on bowl, Watson Co, 1879–1905. . . . . 400.00
Checolah, OK, SS, 3 figures on handle. 20.00
Chicago, skyline handle, "Public Library". 50.00
Church of Guadalupe 20.00
Colorado, SS. 10.00
Costa Rica, 25 centavos coin bowl. 20.00
Disney Characters. 8.00
George Washington. 100.00
Glace Bay, Nova Scotia, SS 25.00
Gulfport, MI, SS 100.00
Havana, Cuba, "Souvenir/Havana" on handle. 15.00
Lima, Peru 15.00
Little Miss Tuffet 50.00
Melbourne, Australia. 20.00
Missouri, SS, woman and "Show Me I'm From Missouri, Watson Co 225.00
Nassau, nickel silver 10.00
New Year's, SS 35.00
New York City, skyline handle, "Public Library" 40.00
Postage Stamp. 40.00
St Augusine, FL, Coat of Arms, WmB Durgin Co 75.00
San Antonio, TX, The Alamo, SS. 40.00
Taunton, MA, SS, "1639–1939," Reed & Barton 25.00
Walla Walla, Washington, SS, figural Indian handle, Mayer & Bros 75.00

Buck Rogers, Atomic Pistol, $220.00. Photo courtesy Gene Harris Antique Auction Center, Inc.

SPACE COLLECTIBLES

This category deals only with fictional space heroes toys. My father followed Buck Rogers in the Sunday funnies. I saw Buster Crabbe as Flash Gordon in the movies and cut my teeth on early television with Captain Video. My son belongs to the Star Trek generation. Whichever generation you choose, there is plenty to collect.

Club: Galaxy Patrol, 22 Colton St., Worcester, MA 01610.

Buck Rogers, Buck Rogers Electronic Communications Outfit, complete with 2 plastic phones, secret decoder, electric wire, and box insert featuring buck inside TV-like screen, Buck Rogers featured on box, Remco/Dille $95.00
Buck Rogers, Dixie Lid, sepia photo of star Matthew Crowley, "Star Of Cream Of Wheat Radio Program," 1935. . . . . 45.00
Buck Rogers, handkerchief, Wilma, Cream of Wheat premium, 1933–35. . . . . 300.00
Buck Rogers, pencil box, American Pencil Co, 1934–38 . . . . 150.00
Buck Rogers, rubber stamp, set of 11, yellow, wood back, Wilma, Buddy, Alura, and 2 different Buck Rogers, c1930. . . . . 90.00
Buck Rogers, Sonic Ray Flashlight Gun, plastic, black, green, and yellow, code signal screw, Norton-Honer, 1950s, 7 1/4" l 120.00
Buck Rogers, Super Foto Camera, Norton-Honer, 1955 . . . . . 70.00
Buck Rogers, Telescope, Popsicle premium, 1939 . . . . 90.00
Buck Rogers, wristwatch, G L J Toys, 1978 . . . . 15.00
Captain Video, game, Captain Video Space Game, Milton Bradley, early 1952. . . . . 150.00
Captain Video, goggles 50.00
Captain Video, Troop Transport Ship, Lido, MIB 150.00

Tom Corbett, Space Cadet, puzzle, orig box contains set of 3 puzzles, Saalfield/Rockhill, 1952 $144.90. Photo courtesy New England Auction Gallery.

Captain Video, Video Rangers Rocket Launcher, plastic, includes rocket launcher and parts with missiles, box reverse has 2 unpunched Video ranger figures **238.00**
Defenders of the Earth, Phantom Skull Copter, Galoob, 1985 . . . . **10.00**
Dr Who, Dalek Shooting Game, Marx, 1965 . . . . **330.00**
Dr Who, Talking K-9 Doll, battery operated, plastic, Palitoy, 1978, 3½ x 6 x 8½", MIB **160.00**
Flash Gordon, action figure, Beastman, Mattel, 1979, 3¾" h **30.00**
Flash Gordon, Better Little Book, *Flash Gordon in the Forest Kingdom of Mongo,"* #1492, ©1938 King Features Syndicate **75.00**
Flash Gordon, lobby card, *Flash Gordon Conquers the Universe,* Universal Pictures, 11 x 14" **50.00**
Flash Gordon, pocket watch, Ingersoll, c1939 . . . . **350.00**
Flash Gordon, ray gun, hard plastic, Nasta, 1976, on 6 x 8" blister card **20.00**
Flash Gordon, wallet, faux leather, zipper closure, ©1949 KFS **75.00**
Rocky Jones, record, *Adventures In Outer Space,* 45 rpm, Columbia, 1950s **20.00**
Space: 1999, coloring book, #C1881, cov shows space ship orbiting around moon, Saalfield **15.00**
Space: 1999, Eagle Transport, #360, diecast, Dinky, 1975 . . . . **35.00**
Space: 1999, Moon Car, plastic, yellow, 3 tires on each side with silver wheel cov, 2 astronaut figures in orange outfits in vehicle seat, "Space: 1999" paper sticker, Ahi, 1976 . . . . **65.00**
Space Patrol, Rocket Lite Flashlight, Rayovac, MIB **325.00**
Space Patrol, Space-O-Phone, Ralston Purina mailer, pr of 3" l yellow and blue plastic space phones, attached string, instruction sheet with order blank, 1950s **100.00**
Thunderbirds, gun, plastic, red, blue front sight, fires spring loaded darts, Lone Star, 1965, 8½" l **60.00**
Tom Corbett, Space Cadet, book, *Wonder Book of Space,* Rockhill Radio Recording, hard cov, 24 pp, color illus, 1953, 5½ x 8" **12.00**
Tom Corbett, Space Cadet, costume, girl's, cloth, gray top and skirt with polka dots around neck and cuff, yellow felt section around chest and back area with red and blue logo **85.00**

SPACE EXPLORATION COLLECTIBLES

There can be no greater thrill than collecting an artifact of man's greatest adventure. Space exploration collecting covers a wide range of items from rocket models to autographs of men who walked on the moon! Autographs from astronauts can be had for free by writing to NASA and making a request. Autographs from former astronauts can be had by making a request to the astronaut or from an autograph dealer.

Mission patches from the earliest days of space exploration are also highly collectible. Mission patches are small works of art depicting the goals and members of a particular mission. Mission patches can be found at flight museums or through mail order or home retailers.

One of the most exciting areas of space collecting is that of items actually used to help send Man to the moon. These items include hardware, manuals, and almost anything used in the quest for space. While these items can be hard to find, they can still be had from many of the people who were involved with, but have retired from, the space program. Other space items include presentation and manufacture models, art, books, space collector cards, postal covers, medallions, coin sets, and collector pins.

Limited Edition, plate, Apollo Moon Landing, Reco, Royale, $80.00.

Advisor: Dennis Kelly, P.O. Box 9942, Spokane, WA 99209 (509) 456-8488.

Newsletter: *Space Autograph News,* 862 Thomas Ave., San Diego, CA 92109.

Flag, U S, flown abord Gemini V, 6 x 4" **$400.00**
Food Packet, flown in space **300.00**
Hard-Hat, Gordon, Richard, Gemini **250.00**
Mission Patch, Schirra, Walter, sgd, Beta Crew, 5 x 7" **200.00**
Pen, Cooper, Gordon, flown aboard Mercury 9 . . . . **110.00**
Photograph, Aldrin, Buzz, sgd, 8 x 10" **125.00**
Photograph, Armstrong, Neil, sgd, 8 x 10" **275.00**
Photograph, Bean, Alan, sgd, 8 x 10" **75.00**
Photograph, Borman, Frank, sgd, 8 x 10" **80.00**
Photograph, Collins, Michael, sgd, 8 x 10" **200.00**
Photograph, Conrad, Charles, sgd, 8 x 10" **80.00**
Photograph, Cooper, Gordon, sgd, 8 x 10" **110.00**
Photograph, Lovell, James, sgd, 8 x 10" **125.00**
Photograph, Schirra, Walter, sgd, 8 x 10" **100.00**
Photograph, Stafford, Thomas, sgd, 8 x 10" **65.00**
Photograph, White, Edward, sgd, 8 x 10" **425.00**
Space Collector Card **2.00**

SPARK PLUGS

Over 4,000 different plug names have been identified by collectors, the most common of which are Champion, AC, and Autolite. Spark plugs are classified into six types: name plugs, gadget plugs, primer plugs, visible plugs, coil plugs, and quick detachable (QD) plugs.

There is no right or wrong way to collect spark plugs. Some people collect a certain style of plug, while others grab any plug they can find.

Use care when examining old spark plugs. Many have fragile labels which can be destroyed through improper handling.

Club: Spark Plug Collectors of America, 14018 NE 85th St., Elk River, MN 55330.

Aim Long Henry **$45.00**
Anderson, glass insulator, 18mm **45.00**
Apollo, brass **100.00**
Asko, brass **75.00**

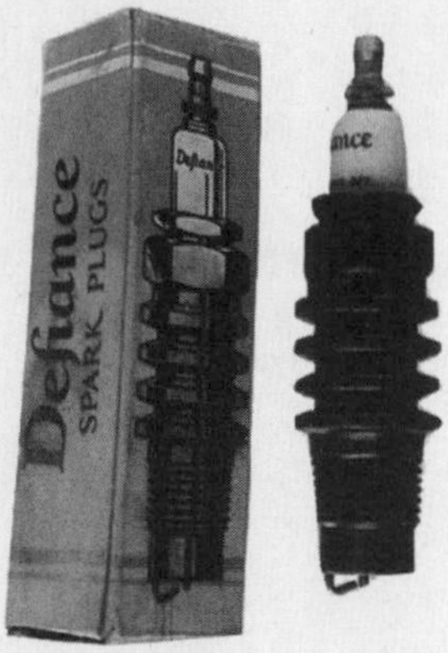

Defiance, 4½" l, $33.00. Photo courtesy Collectors Auction Services.

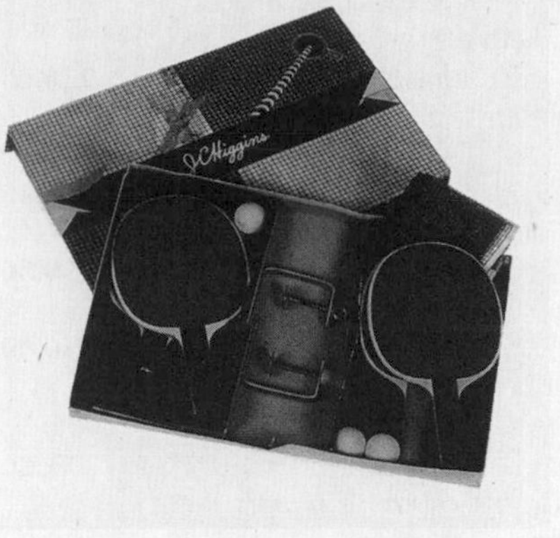

Table Tennis Equipment, J. C. Higgins #2700, 4 paddles and balls, 2 holders, and net, "Sears Roebuck & Co.," $15.00. Photo courtesy Collectors Auction Services.

Auto Lite, T-7 . . . . **4.00**
Beacon Lite, glass insulator **45.00**
Blue Crown Husky **4.00**
Bodin, marblelite, white porcelain, blue letters **65.00**
Bowers **4.00**
Cities Service **5.00**
DeFiance **5.00**
Firestone, M-2 . . . . **4.00**
Fisk **3.00**
Helfi **45.00**
Jewel, Pittsfield Coil Co, brass/mica **50.00**
Joly **55.00**
Kant Break **70.00**
King Bee **65.00**
Kopper King, metal can **85.00**
Lissen, mica, steel,a nd brass **65.00**
Parkin **50.00**
Prosper C **10.00**
Renault, brass/mica **75.00**
Rentz, Buick **10.00**
Sphinx **45.00**
Shurhit **15.00**
Titan, #2, 14mm **3.00**

SPORTS AND RECREATION COLLECTIBLES

There has been so much written about sport cards that equipment and other sport-related material has become lost in the shuffle. A number of recent crazes, such as a passion for old baseball gloves, indicates that this is about to change. Decorators have discovered that hanging old sporting equipment on walls makes a great decorative motif. This certainly helps call attention to the collectibility of the material.

Since little has been written outside of baseball and golf collectibles, it is hard to determine what exactly are the best pieces. A good philosophy is to keep expenditures at a minimum until this and other questions are sorted out by collectors and dealers.

Club: Boxiana & Pugilistica Collectors International, P.O. Box 83135, Portland, OR 97203;

Periodical: *Boxing Collectors News,* 3316 Luallen Dr., Carrollton, TX 75007.

Badge, "1 Mile Run 1st Prize," reverse "St Patrick's Field Day May 30, 1910," copper plated white metal, engraved **$15.00**
Bank, plastic, figural jointed-arm bowler and bowling alley, battery operated, orig box, M B Daniel & Co, Japan, 1950s, 4¼" h **40.00**
Baseball, Mickey Mantle and Willie Mays Zipee Baseball, white plastic, whiffle style, 3 x 4" black and white card of Mays and Mantle reads "The Champion's Choice," Transogram, 1960s, unused **75.00**
Book, *The Spectacle of Sports from Sports Illustrated,* 1957, 320 pp, dj **25.00**
Booklet, *Keds Handbook of Sports,* 1926 . . . . **20.00**
Figure, female swimmer in swimsuit and cap in crouched starting position pose, white plastic, Rugby Sportwear premium, Marx, c1956, 2¼" h **20.00**
Figure, soccer player Pat Bonner, Kenner Starting Lineup, 1989 . . . . **35.00**
Figural Lamp, cast metal, woman bowler, alley, and pins, wood stand, painted fiber shade, 16" w, 9½" h base **25.00**
Handbook, *Handbook of Light Gymnastics,* Lucy B Hunt, 92 pp, 1887, hard cov **50.00**
Ice Skates, pr, Dutch, child's, plain blade, wooden foo plate, leather straps, 1950s **40.00**
Lunch Box, Boston Bruins, steel, Okay Industries, 1973 . . . . . **90.00**
Magazine, *Sport,* Mar 1969, sgd by Jerry West **20.00**
Magazine Cover, *Life,* close-up photo of child wearing turned cap while biting tongue and sighting his white shooter marble toward others, 84 pp, May 10, 1937 . . . . . . **40.00**
Nodder, San Diego Gulls, Sports Specialities **150.00**
Pinback Button, "National Association of Amateur Oarsmen," 1890s **20.00**
Pinback Button, "World Pillow Fighting Championships," maroon on ivory white, blue inscriptions, 1970s, 3" d **20.00**
Popcorn Popper, endorsed by Joe Namath, orig paper and box, Hamilton Beach, 1970s **40.00**
Postcard, hockey match, "At Madison Square Garden between the Atlantic city Sea Gulls and the Crescent-Hamilton Athletic Club of Brooklyn," real photo by "Jack Frank of the New York Herald-Tribune, made with Kalart Photoflash Synchronizer...," advertising text on back for Synchronizer camera equipment, by Kalart Com New York City, black and white, 1935 . . . . **320.00**
Postcard, wrestlers, real photo of wrestlers from different countries, each person numbered in pen with corresponding list of names and countries on back, includes black wrestler V Thomson from U S, black and white, dated 1930 . . . . **100.00**
Poster, Larry Csonka, *Sports Illustrated,* 1968–71 . . . . **20.00**

Program, AAU National Amateur Boxing Championships in Toledo, OH, Apr 7–9, 1960, red, white, and blue "A.A.U" and "U.S.A." emblem on cov, Cassius Clay illus inside 288.00

Salt and Pepper Shakers, pr, china, white, 5¼" h salt topped by image of bowling pin, 4¼" h pepper topped by image of gold bowling ball, souvenir of Women's International Bowling Congress event, "Syracuse, N.Y." on reverse base, cork stopper 20.00

Tennis Racquet, Prince Classic, aluminum, green throat piece, 1960s 8.00

Toy, Golf Caddy, metal shaft golf clubs, golf balls, and tees, red and black plaid, 1950s, Fairway, Suburban Toy Co, PA, orig 5 x 7¼ x 31" box, MIB 75.00

Toy, Zorro Target & Dart Shooting Rifle Set, 21" l plastic rifle, black plastic darts, and target, T Cohn, 1960s 125.00

STAMPS, MISCELLANEOUS

Trading stamps were offered by retail stores to attract customers and increase sales. The more money spent, the more stamps you could earn. The stamps could be redeemed for merchandise, either from the store that issued the stamps or from redemption centers that offered catalog merchandise. The first independent trading stamp company was set up in 1896. The use of trading stamps has declined, but some companies still give them out to stimulate sales. So far, a secondary market has not been established.

Other nonpostage stamps of interest to collectors include revenue stamps (often collected by philatelists), savings bond stamps, and war ration stamps.

Clubs: American Revenue Assoc., 701 S. First Ave., Arcadia, CA 91006; State Revenue Society, 22 Denmark St., Dedham, MA 02026.

STAMPS, POSTAGE

When I was a boy, everybody and his brother had a stamp collection. In today's high tech world that is not often the case. Most stamps found at flea markets will be cancelled and their value is negligible. They can usually be bought in batches for a few dollars. However, there are rare exceptions. Who knows? If you look long and hard enough you may find an "Inverted Jenny."

Club: American Philatelic Society, P.O. Box 8000, State College, PA 16803.

Periodicals: *Linn's Stamp News,* P.O. Box 29, Sidney, OH 45365; *Scott's Stamp Monthly,* P.O. Box 828, Sidney, OH 45365; *Stamp Collector*, 700 E. State St., Iola, WI 54990; *Stamps,* 85 Canisteo St., Hornell, NY 14843.

Air Mail, 1957, 50th Anniversary of Air Force, 6¢ . . . . $.15
Air Mail, 1959, Pan American Games, Chicago, 10¢ 25
Air Mail, 1963, Amelia Earhart, 8¢ 15
Postage, 1953, 50th Anniversary of the Trucking Industry, 3¢ 15
Postage, 1956, Wildlife Conservation, 3¢ 15
Postage, 1959, Oregon Statehood, 4¢ .15
Postage, 1960, Boy Scouts of America, 4¢ 15
Postage, 1960, Water Conservation, 4¢ 15
Postage, 1964, Register To Vote, 5¢ 15
Postage, 1987, American Wildlife, set of 50, used 10.00
Postage, 1976, Bicentennial State Flags, set of 50, used 10.00
Postage, 1982, Birds and Flowers, set of 50, used 12.50
Postage, 1982, Wildflowers, set of 50, used 12.00

STANGL POTTERY

Stangl manufactured dinnerware between 1930 and 1978 in Trenton, New Jersey. The dinnerware featured bold floral and fruit designs on a brilliant white or off-white ground.

The company also produced a series of three-dimensional bird figurines that are eagerly sought by collectors. The bird figurines were cast in Trenton and finished at a second company plant in Flemington. During World War II the demand for the birds was so great that over 60 decorators were employed to paint them. Some of the birds were reissued between 1972 and 1977. They are dated on the bottom.

Club: Stangl/Fulper Collectors Club, P.O. Box 538, Flemington, NJ 08822.

Bird, bluebirds, #3276D, 1978, 8¼" h $200.00
Bird, bluejay, with peanut, #3715, antique gold, repaired beak, 10¼" h 95.00
Bird, Brewer's blackbird, #3591, 3½" h 95.00
Bird, broadtail hummingbird, #3626, blue flower, 6" h 100.00
Bird, canary, #3747, blue flower, 6¼" h 175.00
Bird, cardinal, #3444, 6¾" h 130.00
Bird, chickadees, #3581, black and white, orig price tag 350.00
Bird, cliff swallow, #3852, 3¾" h 110.00
Bird, duck, running, #3431, 5" h 350.00
Bird, European finch, #3722, 4½" h 125.00
Bird, hen pheasant, #3491, 6¼ x 11" 175.00
Bird, painted bunting, #3452, 5" h 90.00
Bird, passenger pigeon, #3450, 9¼ x 19¼" 1,100.00
Bird, turkey, #3275, 3⅜" h 375.00
Bird, vermillion flycatcher, #3923, 5¾" h 500.00
Bird, white-crowned pigeons, #3518D, 7⅞ x 12½" 600.00
Children's Dish Set, Ginger Girl, 3 pcs, 1957 . . . . 450.00
Children's Dish Set, Playful Pups, 2 pcs 190.00
Country Garden, cake stand 30.00
Country Garden, coffeepot, 4 cup 50.00
Country Garden, cup and saucer 15.00
Country Garden, dinner plate, 11" d 35.00
Country Garden, shaker 10.00
Daisy, creamer and sugar, green 18.00
Daisy, dinner plate, yellow, 10" d 20.00
Daisy, vegetable bowl, blue, 10" l 25.00
Harvest, cup and saucer 20.00

Terra Rose, basket, #3624, twisted vine handle, paper label, 9½" h, 7½" w, $25.00.

Harvest, teapot, cov **70.00**
Orchard Song, bread and butter plate **5.00**
Orchard Song, creamer **8.00**
Orchard Song, eggcup. **10.00**
Orchard Song, saucer **3.00**
Prelude, bread and butter plate **6.00**
Prelude, dinner plate. **10.00**
Terra Rose, butter, cov. **20.00**
Terra Rose, cereal bowl, 5½" d **10.00**
Terra Rose, gravy, with liner. **18.00**
Terra Rose, salt and pepper shakers, pr. **12.50**
Thistle, coffeepot, cov **25.00**
Thistle, dinner plate, 10" d. **10.00**
Thistle, salad plate **7.50**
Wild Rose, cup and saucer **10.00**

STANLEY TOOLS

Mention the name Stanley to a carpenter and the first tool that comes to mind is a plane. While Stanley planes are the best documented and most widely collected planes on the market, Stanley also produced many other tools, many of which are becoming desirable to tool collectors.

Periodical: *Stanley Tool Collector News*, 208 Front St., P.O. Box 227, Marietta, OH 45750.

Carpenter's Bell Faced Claw Hammer, Stanley Rule & Level, sweetheart trademark, c1920s, 13" l **$45.00**
Bench Plane, RB10 . . . . **15.00**
Blade Honing Guide, #200 . . . . **15.00**
Butt Gauge **14.00**
Cabinetmakers' Scraping Plane, #81 . . . . **20.00**
Chamfer Shave, #65 . . . . **15.00**
Combination Plane, type "55," complete with all cutters, instruction booklet, orig box **150.00**
Dowelling Jig **15.00**
Fore Plane, #6, type "20," blue finish, 1962–67 . . . . **45.00**
Fore Plane, #6C, type "9," blade spent, cleaned with Japanning enhanced, 1902–07. . . . . **60.00**
Hand Reeder, #66. . . . . **15.00**
Heavy Jack Plane, #51/2H, type "9," S & W Hart iron spent, cleaned with Japanning enhanced, 1902–07. . . . . . **650.00**
Jack Plane, #5, type "6," cleaned and refurbished, 1888–92 . . . . **20.00**
Open Throat Router Plane, #71P, Stanley Rule & Level, orig box, 8" l. **85.00**
Plow Blade, #41, type "4," Millers patent adjustable, fillister bed and extra fence, with 9 of 10 cutters **950.00**
Plumb Bob, #1, Stanley Rule & Level, brass, retractable reel, patented Apr 28, 1874 . . . . **225.00**
Router Plane, #7C, 3 irons, fence, and throat closing attachment **55.00**
Rule, #32, 4-fold, brass bound, 12" l **35.00**
Smooth Plane, #2, type "BB" mark on iron, cleaned and lightly repainted, 1936. . . . . **175.00**
Smooth Plane, #3, type "15," cleaned and refurbished, 1931–32 . . . . **45.00**
Smooth Plane, #4, type "18," cleaned and refurbished, 1946–47 . . . . **15.00**
Spirit Level, #30, fruitwood **25.00**
Victor Smooth Plane, #1004, gray frame, red frog, stained red handle and knob, orig box, 1936–41 . . . . **100.00**

STAR TREK COLLECTIBLES

In 1966, a new science fiction television show aired that introduced America to a galaxy of strange new worlds filled with new life forms. The voyages of author Gene Roddenberry's starship *Enterprise* enabled the viewing audience to boldly go where no man had gone before. These adventures created a new generation of collectors: "Trekkies." From posters, costumes, and props to pins, comic books, and model kits, there is no limit to the number of Star Trek collectibles that can be found.

With the release of Paramount's *Star Trek: The Motion Picture* in 1979, the Star Trek cult grew. The Enterprise's new devotees inspired the inevitable new sequels: *Star Trek II: The Wrath of Khan, Star Trek III: The Search for Spock, Star Trek IV: The Voyage Home, Star Trek V: The Final Frontier, Star Trek VI: The Undiscovered Country, Star Trek: Generations, and Star Trek: First Contact.*

In 1988, Trekkies demanded the return of the *Enterprise* to television and were rewarded with *Star Trek: The Next Generation*. A new starship, manned by a new crew, retained the same desire to reach out into the unknown. More recent spinoffs include *Star Trek: Deep Space 9 and Star Trek: Voyager.* Whether you are an old Trekkie or a Next Generation Trekkie, keep seeking out those collectibles. May your collection live long and prosper.

Clubs: International Federation of Trekkers, P.O. Box 84, Groveport, OH 43125; Starfleet, 200 Hiawatha Blvd., Oakland, NJ 07436; Star Trek: The Official Fan Club, P.O. Box 111000, Aurora, CO 80042.

Action Figure, Dr McCoy, Mego, ©1974 Paramount Pictures Corp, 8" h, MOC **$65.00**
Action Figure, Ferengi, *The Next Generation,* Galoob, 1988. . . . . **9.00**
Action Figure, Klingon, brown adn dark maroon outfit, belt, phaser and communicator, Mego **40.00**
Action Figure, Lt Uhura, red dress, tricorder, Mego. **65.00**
Action Figure, Mr Spock, blue and black outfit, belt, light blue phaster, communicator and tricorder, Mego **45.00**
Activity Book, Punch Out and Play Album, Saalfield, 1975. . . . . **45.00**
Belt Buckle, bust of Kirk and Spock, coppe, 3-D, 1979 . . . . . . **20.00**
Book, *I Am Not Spock,* Leonard Nimoy, 1975 . . . . **12.00**
Book, *Star Fleet Technical Manual,* Ballantine, 1968 . . . . **3.00**

Snow Globe, *U.S.S. Enterprise* suspended on lucite rod, glass ball, plastic bse and rotating hood, green glitter, Made in China, base mkd "Hallmark Authorized User/Willitts Designs, Item No. 47051, NCC 1701 Lighted Star Globe," 1972, 7" h, $50.00.

Action Figure, Scotty, Where No Man Has Gone Before, Playmates Toys, mid-1990s, MOC, $8.00.

Book, *Star Trek 1978 Annual,* World Distributors, ©Paramount Pictures Corp, full color comic book style stories, puzzles, color photos, 64 pp, used **15.00**
Book, *The Trouble With Tribbles,* Ballantine, 1973 . . . . **2.00**
Comic Book, *Star Trek V Movie Special, The Final Frontier,* DC Comics, 1989 . . . . **3.00**
Costume, Mr Spock, molded plastic mask, 1 pc rayon and vinyl outfit, orig box, Ben Cooper, 1978. . . . . **40.00**
Decanter, ceramic, figural Dr Spock, Grenadier, ©1979 Paramount Pictures Corp, orig box **15.00**
Drinking Glass, *Enterprise,* Dr Pepper, 1978. . . . . **40.00**
Figure, *U S S Enterprise,* diecast metal and plastic, 4 x 10 x 7 3/4" window box with photo of Spock and Kirk on front and illus of *Enterprise* and Klingon battle cruiser on back, complete with unopened plastic bag containing 8 white plastic disks and small orange space vessel, Dinky, ©1977 Paramount Pictures Corp **90.00**
First Aid Kit, *The Motion Picture,* 1979. . . . . **10.00**
Flashlight, Star Trek Phaser Ray Gun/Space Flashlight, battery operated, hard plastic, black, silver accents, raised logo on side, click action noise, Azrak-Hamway, ©1976 Paramount Pictures Corp, 3 1/2" l **45.00**
Frisbee, Star Trek Flying *U S S Enterprise,* plastic, applied label with portrait of Spock and "Throw It...It Flys Like A Real Spaceship," Remco, ©1967 Desilu Productions, Inc, 8 1/2" d **85.00**
Kite, vinyl, images of *Enterprise* and Klingon Cruiser, Hi-Flyer Mfg Co, 1975, 36" l, MIP **20.00**
Lunch Box, *Star Trek the Next Generation,* blue plastic box with full color cast photo on reflective silver background, blue and white plastic thermos with red, whtie, and silver *Enterprise* decal, Thermos, ©1988 Paramount Pictures Corp **20.00**
Model Kit, *U S S Enterprise,* AMT, ©Paramount Pictures, 8 1/2 x 10 x 3" box **20.00**
Model Kit, *U S S Enterprise Command Bridge,* AMT, ©1975 Paramount Pictures Corp, includes figures of Kirk, Spock, and Sulu, 8 1/2 x 10 1/2 x 3" box **45.00**
Napkins, paper, Party Creations/Tuttle Press, unopened, 1976. . . . . **3.50**
Ornament, Galileo, Hallmark **20.00**
Paint Set, canvas portrait, orig box, Hasbro, 1974, 12 x 16" **50.00**
Pinback Button, *The Wrath of Khan,* crew image, Image Products, 1980s **2.00**
Playset, Command Bridge, *The Motion Picture,* 1979 . . . . **30.00**
Playset, Star Trek *Enterprise* Action Playset, vinyl, complete with accessories, Mego, 32" open width. **65.00**
Premium, ring, issued by McDonald's, plastic, secret compartment, emb designs on top of characters, Enterprise, and logo, 1979 . . . . **20.00**
Premium, Star Trek Action Fleet, issued by M&M/Mars, ©1979 Paramount Pictures corp, includes 11 x 25" paper poster with photos and blueprints, set of 6 cardboard punch-out spaceships and instruction sheet, orig mailing envelope **65.00**
Record, *Leonard Nimoy Presents Mr Spock's Music From Outer Space,* 33 1/3 rpm, Dot Records **20.00**
Toy, Authentic Hand Phaster Water Pistol, hard plastic, silver, Aviva Enterprises, Inc, ©1979 Paramount Pictures Corp, 7" l, on 7 1/2 x 8 1/4" l blister card **20.00**
Trading Cards, *The Search for Spock,* laminated ship cards, set of 20, FTCC **8.00**
Vehicle, Shuttlecraft Galileo, *The Next Generation,* Galoob **15.00**
View-Master Set, 3 reels and storybook, 1968 . . . . **40.00**

STAR WARS

It was in a galaxy not so long ago that author/director George Lucas put into motion events that would change the way we think of space. In 1977 a movie was produced that told the story of an evil Empire's tyrannical rule over the galaxy and of the attempts of a young man from a distant world to end this tyranny. Luke Skywalker's adventures became the *Star Wars* saga and spanned six years and three separate movies: *Star Wars, The Empire Strikes Back, and Return of the Jedi.*

The enormous success of the *Star Wars* movies inspired the release of a wide range of movie-related products including toys, games, costumes, records, and comic books. As you travel through the flea market aisles in search of *Star Wars* treasure, "May the Force Be With You."

Club: Official Star Wars Fan Club, P.O. Box 111000, Aurora, CO 80042.

Newsletter: *The Star Wars Collector,* 20982 Homecrest Ct., Ashburn, VA 22011.

Action Figure, Ben Kenobi, Kenner, 12" h. **$180.00**
Action Figure, Boba Fett, complete with accessories, Kenner, 1979, 13 1/2" h **85.00**
Action Figure, Hans Solo, Kenner, 1979, 12" h. **85.00**

Model Kit, AT ST (All Terrain Scout Transport), commemorative edition, *The Empire Strikes Back/Return of the Jedi,* ©1984, 1992 LucasFilm Ltd., 10 x 7" box, $25.00.

Dixie Cups, box of 100 five oz cups with 40 different scenes, $15.00.

Bank, Darth Vader, ceramic, Roman Ceramics 28.00
Coloring Book, *The Empire Strikes Back,* Chewbacca, Han, Leia, and Lando on cov, Kenner 4.00
Cookie Jar, C-3PO, ceramic, Roman Ceramics 75.00
Costume, Klaatu, *"Revenge of the Jedi"* on chestplate, Ben Cooper 25.00
Display Sign, Star Wars Action Figures, diecut cardboard, double sided, photos of "Original 12" and "#9 New" action figures, "Collect All 21," Kenner, ©1979 20th Century Fox Film Corp, 18¼ x 20¼" 90.00
Doll, Chewbacca, stuffed, brown, plastic eyes and nose, brown vinyl cartridge belt, gray plastic cartridges, orig tag, Kenner, 1977, 18" h 40.00
Doll, R2-D2, stuffed cloth, shiny silver fabric top, movable legs, squeaking noise made when squeezed, orig tag, Kenner, 1978, 8½" h 40.00
Drinking Glass, Chewbacca, Burger King, Coca-Cola 8.00
Game, Star Wars Adventures of R2-D2 Game, Kenner, 1978 . . . . 20.00
Game, Star Wars Battle at Sarlacc's Pit Game, Parker Brothers, 1983 . . . . 12.00
Game, Star Wars Wicket the Ewok, Parker Brothers, 1983 . . . . 10.00
Model Kit, Darth Vader, battery operated, rasping breathing sound and illuminated eyes, orig box, MPC, ©20th Century Fox Film Corp, 10¾" h 40.00
Model Kit, Millennium Falcon, lights, Modern Plastics Co, 1977 . . . . 55.00
Mug, figural Chewie, ceramic, brown, black accents, blue eyes, California Originals, 6½" h 65.00
Paint Set, figurine, C-3PO, Craft Master 8.00
Paint Set, glow-in-the-dark, Darth Vader 12.00
Patch, *Revenge of the Jedi* 20.00
Playset, Ice Planet Hoth 80.00
Playset, Star Wars Creature Cantina Action Playset, Kenner 1979 . . . . 65.00
Puppet, hand, Yoda, vinyl, white life-like hair, molded outfit, brown wood cane, orig box, Kenner, 1980, 8" h 45.00
Puzzle, frame tray, Leia and Wicket, Craft Master 3.00
Race Set, Star Wars Duel At Death Star Racing Set, Lionel, Fundimensions, A Division of the General Mills Fun Group, Inc, ©1978 20th Century Fox Film Corp 90.00
Robot, R2-D2, remote control unit, plastic, blue and silver accents, moves foreard and backward, head turns, eye lights up, "beep" sounds, orig box, Kenner, 1978 . . . . . 85.00
Toothbrush, Jedi Masters, Oral-B 3.00
Toy, Hans Solo Laser Pistol, *Empire Strikes Back,* Kenner 20.00
Trading Cards, *Star Wars,* Topps, 1st series, blue, set of 66. . . . 18.00
Vehicle, Land Speeder, re-issue, Kenner, 1983 . . . . 20.00
Vehicle, Millennium Falcon, Kenner, 1981 . . . . 185.00
Vehicle, Rebel Armored Snowspeeder 25.00
Vehicle, Speeder Bike 15.00
Vehicle, Tie Fighter, diecast metal and plastic, black and white, removable solar panels and Darth Vader figure attached to removable seat, 3¼" h, Kenner, 1978, orig 7 x 10" blister card 20.00
Wall Clock, *The Empire Strikes Back,* Bradley, 1980 . . . . 20.00
Wallet, vinyl, *Return of the Jedi,* color Yoda illus, orig blister card, Adam Joseph Industries 25.00

STEIFF

Margarete Steiff was born in Giengen, Germany in 1847. At the age of two she contracted polio, which left her paralyzed and confined to a wheelchair. Despite her handicap, she became a wonderful seamstress. While working as a dressmaker in 1880, Margarete used scraps of felt to make several elephant pin cushions which she gave as gifts to family and friends. The first Steiff toy was born. Soon she was making donkeys, horses, camels and even a pig. By 1897, her five nephews had joined her company and the now famous identification "Button in Ear" was created. Her nephew Richard Steiff designed and exhibited the first teddy bear at the Leipzig trade fair in 1903. The bear was a great success. During the 1950s, known as "the Golden Age of Steiff," the company experienced their most productive years. Exportation of the button in ear brand quality play things was at its highest. As a result, many examples of these detailed fine toys can be readily found today. These are avidly sought by collectors. The Margarete Steiff Company still remains in existence, a tribute to its founder.

Advisor: Beth B. Savino, The Toy Store, P.O. Box 798, Holland, OH 43528, (419) 473-9801, (800) 862-8697, fax (419) 473-3947.

Clubs: Steiff Club USA (company sponsored), 225 Fifth Ave., Ste. 1033, New York, NY, 10010; Steiff Collectors Club, P.O. Box 798, Holland, OH 43528.

Puppet, Bunny Rabbit, #317, light brown mohair, white ears tipped with black, 1950–78 . . . . $50.00
Puppet, Foxy Fox Terrier, #317, 1951–78 . . . . 30.00
Puppet, Lion, #517, gold brown mohair, 1949–61 . . . . 50.00
Puppet, Tiger, #317, gold, white, and black striped mohair, 1952–78 . . . . 30.00
Puppet, Wittie Owl, #317, green and yellow eyes, brown spotted body, 1955–78 . . . . 30.00

Leo Lion, #2322.1 in ear tag, chest tag, button in ear with yellow stock tag, 1956–58, 9" l, $100.00.

Jocko Chimpanzee, brown mohair plush, fully jointed, 6" h sitting,1949–58, $75.00.

Baccarat, Montaigne, water goblet, 7" h, $35.00.

Stuffed Toy, Cockie Cocker Spaniel, with chest tag and button in ear, leather collar, 1957–58, 5" h **75.00**
Stuffed Toy, Nelly Snail, #2410,03, velveteen and plastic body, brown or greenish blue, 1961–63 . . . . **150.00**

STEMWARE

There are two basic types of stemware: (1) soda-based glass and (2) lead or flint based glass, often referred to as crystal. Today crystal is also a term synonymous with fine glassware and used to describe glass that is clear. Lead crystal, which must contain a minimum of 24% lead oxide, has a brilliant clarity, durability, and a bell-like tone that emanates when the glass is struck.

Free blown, mold blown, and pressed are the three basic methods used to make. Decorating techniques range from cutting to etching. Color also is used to create variety.

There are thousands of different stemware patterns. If you do not know your pattern, consider sending a drawing of the stem and rubbing of its decoration to Replacements, Ltd. (P.O. Box 26029, Greensboro, NC 27420). Replacements has an excellent research staff. Also check *Harry L. Rinker's Stemware of the 20th Century: The Top 200 Patterns* (House of Collectibles, 1997) and/or Bob Page and Dale Frederiksen's *Crystal Stemware Identification Guide* (Collector Books, 1998). If you do not find your specific pattern, you will find ample comparables.

Stemware usually was sold in sets of four, six, or eight. Previously, a value premium was added if the set was complete. Today's buyers expect a discount when buying in quantity.

The following is a simple approach to determining a quick price per stem for your stemware: (1) soda glass stem, plain, $2 to $4; (2) soda glass stem, pressed, $5 to $8; (3) soda glass stem, elaborately decorated, $12 to $15; (4) lead glass stem, plain, $15 to $18; (5) lead glass stem, simple decoration, $20 to $25; (6) lead glass stem, elaborate decoration, $25 to $30; and (7) lead glass stem, streamline modern or post-war modern design style, $15 to $20. Add a 20% premium for patterns from companies such as Baccarat, Gorham, Lenox, Waterford, and Wedgwood.

Baccarat, Montaigne, champagne, 4⅞" h **$35.00**
Baccarat, Montaigne, champagne, fluted, 6⅞" h **35.00**
Baccarat, Montaigne, claret, 5¾" h **30.00**
Baccarat, Montaigne, iced tea **35.00**
Baccarat, Montaigne, wine, 4⅞" h **35.00**
Cambridge, Rose Point, champagne, 6½" h **14.00**
Cambridge, Rose Point, cocktail **30.00**
Cambridge, Rose Point, cordial **36.00**
Cambridge, Rose Point, iced tea, ftd. **18.00**
Cambridge, Rose Point, oyster cocktail **25.00**
Cambridge, Rose Point, wine **28.00**
Duncan & Miller, Sandwich, champagne, 5" h **14.00**
Duncan & Miller, Sandwich, cocktail, 4¼" h **10.00**
Duncan & Miller, Sandwich, tumbler, ftd, 3¾" h **8.00**
Duncan & Miller, Willow, highball, 5⅝" h **20.00**
Duncan & Miller, Willow, old fashioned, 3¼" h **20.00**
Durand International, Longchamp, brandy, 5¼" h **10.00**
Durand International, Longchamp, champagne, 5⅝" h **4.00**
Durand International, Longchamp, cordial, 45/8" h **4.00**
Durand International, Longchamp, tumbler, flat, 5" h **4.00**
Durand International, Versailles, highball **10.00**
Durand International, Versailles, wine, 4⅞" h **10.00**
Fostoria, Buttercup, champagne, 5⅝" h **20.00**
Fostoria, Buttercup, cocktail, 5¼" h **16.00**
Fostoria, Buttercup, cordial, 3⅞" h **35.00**
Fostoria, Carousel, champagne, 4¾" h **20.00**
Fostoria, Carousel, claret, 6 oz, 5¾" h **28.00**
Fostoria, Carousel, cocktail, 4⅜" h **20.00**
Fostoria, Carousel, water goblet, 6¾" h **25.00**
Gorham, First Lady, champagne, 4⅝" h **18.00**
Gorham, First Lady, cocktail, 4⅛" h **18.00**
Gorham, First Lady, juice, 6½" h **18.00**
Gorham, First Lady, water goblet, 6⅝" h **20.00**
Gorham La Scala, champagne, 5" h **35.00**
Princess House, Heritage, beer glass, 5½" h **4.00**
Princess House, Heritage, brandy, 4½" h **2.00**
Princess House, Heritage, champagne, 4⅞" h **2.50**
Princess House, Heritage, cocktail, 5" h **2.50**
Princess House, Heritage, iced tea **3.00**
Princess House, Heritage, juice, flat, 3½" h **2.00**
Sasaki, Wings, cocktail, 4⅛" h **25.00**
Sasaki, Wings, iced tea, 6⅜" h **25.00**
Sasaki, Wings, juice, 3⅞" h **20.00**

STRADIVARIUS VIOLINS

In the late 19th century inexpensive violins were made for sale to students, amateur musicians, and others who could not afford an older, quality instrument. Numerous models, many named after famous makers, were sold by department stores, music shops, and by mail. Sears, Roebuck sold "Stradivarius" models. Other famous violin makers whose names appear on paper labels inside these instruments include Amati, Caspar DaSolo, Guarnerius, Maggini, and Stainer. Lowendall of Germany made a Paganini model.

All these violins were sold through advertisements that claimed that the owner could have a violin nearly equal to that of an antique instrument for a modest cost; one "Stradivarius" sold for

$2.45. The most expensive model cost less that $15. The violins were handmade, but by a factory assembly line process.

If well cared for, these pseudo antique violins often develop a nice tone. The average price for an instrument in playable condition is between $100 and $200.

STRING HOLDERS

I have fond memories of the plaster face of a Dutch girl with a piece of string coming out of her mouth that hung in my mother's kitchen. I also remember saving string, attaching accumulated pieces and wrapping them into a ball.

Few save string any longer. It is a lost art. Fortunately, plenty of collectors are saving the countertop and wall hanging string holders that were found in virtually every kitchen from the 1920s through the 1950s.

Beware of fake stringholders made by hollowing out the back of a figural head wall plaque and drilling a hole in the mouth, e.g., a Chinese or Siamese man or woman, or altering a figural wall lamp, e.g., a pineapple or apple face.

Apple, bird after worm, chalkware **$110.00**
Apple, stem to left, chalkware **25.00**
Bird, scissors through head, Royal Copley **50.00**
Black Cat, red ball of string, chalkware **25.00**
Boy, gold hat and pipe, chalkware **35.00**
Bride, groom, and bridesmaid, ceramic **70.00**
Bridesmaid, blue dress, ceramic **85.00**
Dutch Girl, green hat, chalkware **45.00**
Girl, maroon bonnet, chalkware **75.00**
Girl, yellow bonnet, chalkware **45.00**
Mammy, with flowers, ceramic **350.00**
Pear, chalkware **35.00**
Sailor, with pipe, chalkware **50.00**
Sailor Boy, chalkware **100.00**
Señor, chalkware **50.00**
Strawberry Face, chalkware **50.00**
Tiger Cat, red ball of string, chalkware **45.00**

STUFFED TOYS

Stuffed toys is a generic term for plush toys, a technical toy marketing term that has become well known thanks to the recent Beanie Baby craze. I grew up calling them stuffed toys, and stuffed toys they will remain in my price guides.

Normally one thinks first of the teddy bear when considering stuffed toys. Yet, virtually every animal and a fair number of characters and personalities have appeared as stuffed toys. Margarette Steiff's first stuffed toy was not a bear but an elephant.

The stuffed toy was a toy/department store fixture by the early 1920s. Many companies, e.g., Gund, Ideal, and Knickerbocker, competed with Steiff for market share. Collectors pay a premium for examples from these companies. The 1970s stuffed toys of R. Dakin Company, San Francisco, are a modern favorite.

Following World War II, stuffed toys became a favorite prize of carnival games of chance. Most are inexpensive Asian imports and hold only modest interest for collectors. Do not pay more than a few dollars for these poorly quality examples.

Periodical: *Soft Dolls & Animals,* 30595 Eight Mile, Livonia, MI 48152.

Rabbit, plush, purple and white, Prettique, c1990, $2.00.

Alf, plush, brown, padded, furry composition, attached label, Allen Productions, 1986, 17" h **$20.00**
Annie, cloth, orange yarn hair, red dress, Sandy dog in pocket, Knickerbocker, 16" h **30.00**
Beany, cloth, molded plastic vinyl head, hands and shoes, plastic propeller on cap, pull-string talker, Mattel, 1962, 18" h **150.00**
Bugs Bunny, plush, gray and white, molded vinyl face and hands, pull-string talker, Mattel, 1962, 27" h **100.00**
Care Bear, Funshine Bear, plush, yellow and white, embroidered depiction of smiling sun on tummy, Kenner, 1983, 13½" h **20.00**
Dog, glass eyes, black embroidered nose, mouth, and claws, Steiff, 1913, 5½" h **172.00**
Dog, cloth, attached paper tag, Herman Pecker & Co, Made in Japan, 9" l **30.00**
Dog, corduroy, "Made in Japan" tag, 3¾ x 4¾ x 2¼" **25.00**
Felix the Cat, cloth, glass eyes and nose, Chad Valley, 9" h **90.00**
Flip Wilson/Geraldine, cloth, Geraldine character front, Flip Wilson on back, pull-string talker, orig box, Shindana Toys, 1970, 16" h **80.00**
Gingerbread Man, plush, tan, Knickerbocker, 12" h **65.00**
Gremlins Gizmo, plush, squeaking sound, Hasbro, 9" h **25.00**
Huckleberry Hound, plush, vinyl face, 17" h **20.00**
Magilla Gorilla, "Twistables," cloth, vinyl face, posable, Ideal, 1964, 8" h, window display box 10 x 5 x 4" **50.00**
Mickey Mouse, plush, California Stuffed Toys, 15" h **20.00**
Monkey, mohair, red, metal face, felt ears, hands, and feet, Schuco, 1930s, 2½" h **150.00**
Pink Panther, plush, orig tag, Warner Bros Mighty Star, 13" h **25.00**
Popeye, cloth sailor suit, molded vinyl head and arms, Gund, 1958, 20" h **100.00**

Teddy Bear, red velvet heart, red bow, Dakin, 1983, 7" h, $20.00.

Reddy, plush, hard plastic face, emb "Reddy" on red collar, Knickerbocker, 1960, 15" h **100.00**
Scooby Doo, light orange and brown, dark brown accents, J S Sutton and Sons, 1970, 14" h **50.00**
Snoopy, plush, black and white, wearing red and white Santa cap, 1968, 10½" h **20.00**
Spaniel Puppy, mohair, golden brown, glass eyes, felt nose and tongue, cloth chest tag, jointed head, Knickerbocker, 1930–40s, 10¾" h **86.00**
Teddy Bear, plush, light brown, yellow ribbon around neck, musical, keywind, plays "Rock A Bye Baby," Knickerbocker, 14" h **55.00**
Yes/No Monkey, brown fur, metal face and eyes, felt hands and feet, Schuco, 1930s, 5" h **100.00**

SUGAR PACKETS

Do not judge sugar packets of the 1940s and 1950s by those you encounter today. There is no comparison. Early sugar packets were colorful and often contained full color scenic views. Many of the packets were issued as sets, with a variety of scenic views. They were gathered as souvenirs during vacation travels.

There is a large number of closet sugar packet collectors. They do not write much about their hobby because they are afraid that the minute they draw attention to it, prices will rise. Most sugar packets sell for less than $1. It's time to let the sugar out of the bag. Get them cheap while you can.

Club: Sugar Packet Clubs International, 15601 Burkhart Rd., Orrville, OH 44667.

SUNBEAM

In 1932 Sunbeam first produced a standing mixer that had no handle and was operated with a switch on the base. This unit also included a large green bowl with no lip, small green bowl, green juice bowl, extractor, spout, and screen basket. Shortly after producing this mixer Sunbeam came out with a standing mixer which had a handle, but could be used as a hand mixer.

Bottom control mixers are difficult to find and command the highest prices, providing they are complete. Original attachments include mixer blades and green mixing bowls. They should be in working order and retain their egg-yellow paint finish and Sunbeam insignia and stickers. If cared for properly, vintage mixers will last a lifetime. Sunbeam also produced a myriad of small kitchen appliances, gadgets and related material.

Advisor: Norman Hagey, 19672 Stevens Creek Blvd., #424, Cupertino, CA 95014, (408) 973-8129.

Clock, Externating Kitchen Notifier, Model E-83, green, jet black benzel, 5½" h **$24.00**
Coffeemaster Buffet Set, Model C-22 . . . . **20.00**
Dough Hook, for Model #225 and #235 . . . . **3.00**
Egg Cooker **7.00**
Heater Fan **18.00**
Heating Pad, Model H-581 . . . . **7.00**
Iron, automatic, Model C-890, 660 watt. **6.00**
Mixer, JMC Hand Mixer, yellow, pink, white, turquoise and white **10.00**
Mixer, Junior Mixer, Model J, creamy yellow and white. **12.00**
Mixer, Model K, complete with bowls and book. **75.00**
Mixer, Model M-4C, complete with bowls and book. **120.00**
Mixer, Model M-4F, complete with bowls and book **100.00**
Mixer, Model M-4H, complete with bowls and book **80.00**
Mixer, Model #1, complete with bowls and book. **50.00**
Mixer, Model #3, complete with bowls and book. **40.00**
Mixer, Model #3-A, complete with bowls and book **40.00**
Mixer, Model #3-B, complete with bowls and book **40.00**
Mixer, Model #5, complete with bowls and book. **25.00**
Mixer, Model #5-B, complete with bowls and book **25.00**
Mixer, Model #5-1, complete with bowls and book **25.00**
Mixer, Model #7, complete with bowls and book. **25.00**
Mixer, Model #7-B, complete with bowls and book **25.00**
Mixer, Model #7-1, complete with bowls and book **25.00**
Mixer, Model #12, yellow, turquoise, pink, and white. **70.00**
Mixer Beaters, Vista, large and small, with bowl, 1962 . . . . . . **18.00**
Mixer Cover **4.00**
Mixing Bowl, cov, meal, heavy plated, highly polished, 3 qt **8.00**
Waffle Iron, Model F-3 . . . . **25.00**

SUPER HERO COLLECTIBLES

Super heroes and comic books go hand in hand. Superman first appeared in *Action Comics* in 1939. He was followed by Batman, Captain Marvel, Captain Midnight, The Green Hornet, The Green Lantern, The Shadow, Wonder Woman, and a host of others.

The traditional Super Hero was transformed with the appearance of The Fantastic Four—Mr. Fantastic, The Human Torch, The Invisible Girl, and The Thing.

It pays to focus on one hero or a related family of heroes. Go after the three-dimensional material. This is the hardest to find.

Clubs: Air Heroes Fan Club (Captain Midnight), 19205 Seneca Ridge Ct., Gaithersburg, MD 20879.

Newsletter: *The Adventures Continue (Superman),* 935 Fruitville Pike #105, Lancaster, PA 17601.

Captain America, coloring book, Whitman, 1966 . . . . **$30.00**
Captain America, kite, plastic, color, Pressman, 1966 . . . . **60.00**
Captain Marvel, book, *Captain Marvel's Fun Book,* games, tricks, riddles, and puzzles, 96 pp, Samuel Lowe Co, ©1944 Fawcett Publications, Inc, 6¾ x 9½" **75.00**
Captain Marvel, iron-transfer, Captain Marvel with hands on hips, cape flying, saying "Shazam!," full color, 1972–73, 8 x 10" sheet, unused **12.00**
Captain Marvel, postcard, Captain Marvel's Secret Message, blue, dip in water to reveal message, 1940s. **75.00**

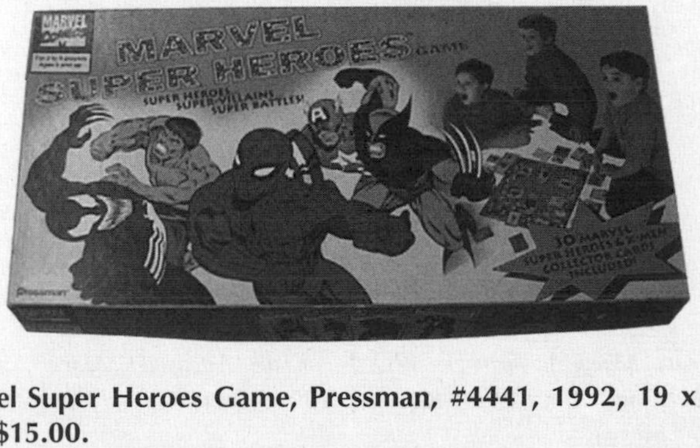

Marvel Super Heroes Game, Pressman, #4441, 1992, 19 x 9½" box, $15.00.

Spider-Man, jigsaw puzzle, The Amazing Spider-Man, The Rainbow Works, NY, 63 pcs, 11½ x 15", $8.00.

Captain Midnight, mug, Ovaltine premium, red plastic, complete decal, 1953, 3" h 45.00
Green Hornet, coloring book, Watkins-Strathmore, ©1966, 8 x 11", unused. 30.00
Green Hornet, drinking glass, illus of Green Hornet, hornet insect, and Black Beauty car, ©1966 Greenway Productions, Inc, 4¾" h 200.00
Green Hornet, model Kit, Black Beauty car, 1966 Chrysler Imperial, plastic, 1/32 scale, Aurora, 1966, MIB 700.00
Green Hornet, photograph, sgd, glossy, full color Green Hornet and kato, sgd "Van Williams "The Green Hornet" in blue felt tip pen, 8 x 10" 40.00
Green Hornet, poster, Black Beauty car, from orig Aurora model kit box artwork, limited edition, 1990, 14 x 22" 15.00
Incredible Hulk, book, paperback, black and white reprints of early Hulk comics, illus, 1966, 5 x 7" 18.00
Incredible Hulk, record, 4 stories, Neal Adams artwork, Peter Pan, 1978 . . . . 8.00
Spider-Man, doll, plush, red, whtie, and black outfit, orig tag, ©Marvel Comics Group, 1978, 20" h 20.00
Spider-Man, figure, The Amazing Energized Spiderman," battery operated, complete with plastic spider web, spider beam flashlight, spider clamp, and energy belt, Remco, 1978, 12" h, MIB 75.00
Spider-Man, radio, figural Spiderman bust, red, black and white eyes, Amoco, 5" h, MIB 45.00
Spider-Man, water gun, plastic, Ahi, ©1979 Marvel Comics Group, 5" l, MOC 20.00
Superman, activity book, punch-out, "Three Exciting Scenes To Assemble And Hang," Whitman, ©1966 National Peirodical Publications, Inc, 8½ x 11¾" 100.00

Captain Marvel Picture Puzzle: One Against Many, Fawcett Publications, Inc., Minneapolis, MN c1941, 10 x 7" paper envelope, $60.00.

Superman, greeting card, Superman & Friends, set of 48, 1978 . . . . 50.00
Superman, lunch box, metal, Universal, 1954 . . . . 200.00
Superman, membership kit, includes letter with Superman illus, unfolded stiff paper code folder with blue printing, certificate, and pinback button, complete in orig mailing envelope, 1955 . . . . 375.00
Superman, movie viewer, plastic viewer, 2 boxes film, Acme, 1965, MOC 30.00
Superman, pennant, felt, red, white logo, white, pink, and yellow Superman illus, ©National Periodical Publications, Inc, 1966, 11 x 29" 60.00
Superman, *TV Guide,* Sep 25, 1953, Vol 1, #26, New York edition, 3 pp article about TV series starring George Reeves, color and black and white photos 175.00
Superman, Underoos, boy's, extra large, 1978, MIP 20.00
Wonder Woman, action figure, Mego, 1973, 8" h, MIB. 175.00
Wonder Woman, cake pan set, silver metal pan, hard plastic color face attachment, instruction booklet, Wilton, 1978. . . . . 15.00
Wonder Woman, doll, Steve Trevor, wearing pilot uniform . . . 70.00
Wonder Woman, drinking glass, illus on front, logo and name on back, Pepsi issue, ©D C Comics, 1978, 6¼" h 18.00
Wonder Woman, lunch box, vinyl, Aladdin, 1977 . . . . 65.00

SWANKYSWIGS

Swankyswigs are decorated glass containers that were filled with Kraft Cheese Spreads. They date from the early 1930s. See D. M. Fountain's *Swankyswig Price Guide* (published by author in 1979) to identify pieces by pattern.

Most Swankyswigs still sell for under $5. If a glass still has its original label, add $5.

Club: Swankyswigs Unlimited, 201 Alvena, Wichita, KS 67203.

Antique, green $4.00
Antique, red 4.00
Bands, black and red. 3.00
Bands, blue and white. 4.00
Bicentennial, yellow, Coin Dot 10.00
Bustling Betsy, brown, 1953 . . . . 4.00
Bustling Betsy, orange, 1953 . . . . 4.00
Checkerboard, white and blue. 18.00
Circles, green 3.00
Circle and Dot, blue, 4¾" h. 10.00
Coin, clear, 3¾" h. 2.00
Cornflower, dark blue, #2, 3½" h. 3.00
Cornflower, light blue, #2, 3½" h. 3.00
Dots and Diamonds, red, 3½" h 8.00
Forget-Me-Not, red, 3½" h. 3.00
Jonquil 3.00
Kiddie Kup, pig and bear, blue. 2.00
Lattice and Vine, white and blue, 3½" h. 8.00
Red Fox, Sportsmen Series, black. 5.00
Sailboat, crystal, white dec, 4¾" h 6.50
Stars, black. 5.00
Stars, red 4.00
Tavern, silver, 4¾" h 15.00
Texas Centennial, 1936. . . . . 8.00
Tulips, Bachelor's Button 2.50
Tulips, green. 3.00

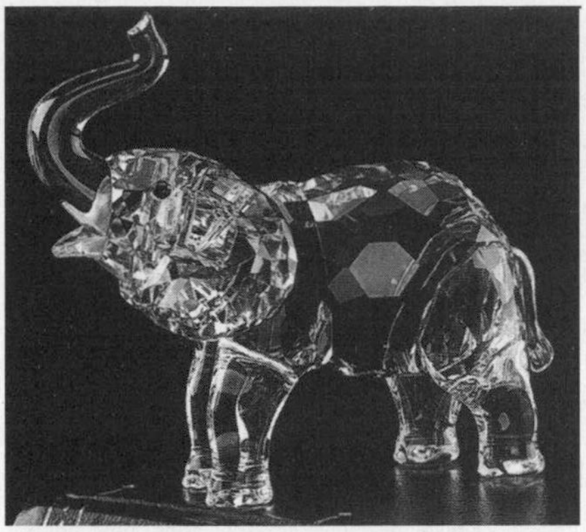

Baby Elephant, 1¼" h, $155.00.

SWAROVSKI CRYSTAL

One of today's popular contemporary collectibles comes from a family business that goes back over 100 years. After decades of glass production and technological innovation, Swarovski introduced charming crystal decorative accessories in the 1970s and immediately found a warm response in the marketplace. A very high lead content, stringent quality control and remarkable design sophistication are hallmarks of Swarovski crystal pieces which set them apart from crystal bibelots produced by other manufacturers.

For many years, the family-owned Swarovski company produced cut crystals for the costume jewelry industry. Precision cutting techniques perfected for this purpose have been expanded to other product lines which include Swarovski jewelry and Swarogem, Swarovski Optik, Daniel Swarovski fashion accessories and others, including Swarovski Silver Crystal. It is the Silver Crystal line upon which most collectors focus, although collectors have become increasingly interested in other lines produced by the company, such as Trimlite, Giftware Suite, Crystal Memories, and private label editions.

The Swarovski Collectors Society (SCS) was formed in 1987, and with this development came a series of figurines only available to members. As the number of members has grown, retired figurines have seen significant increase in value. In addition to each annual figurine, a few special designs have been released only to SCS members. Renewal gifts, anniversary designs, dealer display pieces and numbered limited editions are also of interest to collectors.

The Swarovski logo, in one of its several variations, should appear on all pieces, but legitimate unmarked items have appeared in the marketplace. So far, there is no significance attached to this phenomenon in terms of value. The early mark was a block style SC, and was changed to a stylized swan in 1990. Club pieces are augmented with the letters SCS. The mark is generally applied to the bottom as a small, acid etched symbol. If the copyright symbol © appears next to the Swarovski mark, the item has been prepared for retail sale in the USA. Many advanced collectors are interested in variations among items sold in the USA and similar items sold in Europe or Asia as well as the pursuit of items available only in certain regional markets.

Occasionally you will find a piece bearing the artist's signature in script. The autograph was added during a personal meeting, and some collectors are willing to pay an additional 10% for this feature, but it is subjective and somewhat controversial among Swarovski enthusiasts. Collectors of Swarovski crystal are very keen on obtaining complete original packaging, without which prices are compromised 10–25%. Only the annual and numbered limited editions came with certificates of authenticity,

Advisor: Maret Webb, 4118 East Vernon Ave., Phoenix, AZ 85008-2333.

Club: Daniel Swarovski Corporation AG, General Wille-Strasse 88, CH-8706, Feldmeilen, Switzerland, www.swarovski.com; Swarovski Collectors Society; Swan Seekers Network, 9740 Campo Road, Ste. 134, Spring Valley, CA 91977, www.swanseekers.com; Swarovski Collectors Society, 2 Slateer Rd., Cranston, RI 02920.

Birthday Cake, #003-0169678	**$200.00**
Cactus, 1988 renewal gift	**150.00**
Cat, standing, #7634nr70	**140.00**
Crystal Rhapsody Barbie	**450.00**
Dolphins, #do1x901	**1,000.00**
Dragon, #do1x971	**500.00**
Dumbo, blue eyes, 1993	**475.00**
Ebeling & Reuss Animal Bust	**300.00**
Elephant, #do1x931	**1,500.00**
Giftware Suite 1988 Christmas Ornament	**100.00**
Hedgehog, small, #7630nr30	**500.00**
Hummingbird on Flower, gold trim, #7553nr100	**1,750.00**
Mouse, large, #7631nr50	**750.00**
Paperweight, blue swan	**150.00**
Peacock, #7607nr000002	**6,000.00**
Perfume Bottle, Lancome Tresor, 1995	**350.00**
Rhinoceros, large, #7622nr70	**150.00**
Trimlite Candy Cane Bear from Zales	**100.00**
Turtledoves, #do1x891	**1,000.00**
Woodpeckers, #doqx881	**1,750.00**

SWIZZLE STICKS

They just do not make swizzle sticks like they used to. There is no end of the ways to collect them—color, motif, region, time period, and so on.

You can usually find them for less than $1. In fact, you can often buy a box or glass full of them for just a few dollars. Sets bring more, but they must be unusual.

Club: International Swizzle Stick Collectors Assoc., P.O. Box 1117, Bellingham, WA 98227.

1939 World's Fair and 1939 New York Expo, set of 12	**$140.00**
Candy Cane Shape, glitter filled, whistle on end	**.50**
Christmas Motif, set of 6	**20.00**
Cowgirl, "Afiliado al Diners Club"	**3.00**
Fruit, glass, set of 12, includes stand	**55.00**

"Spike-Stirs," plastic, nail-shaped, set of 8, Dorcy Mfg. Co., $15.00.

Golf Clubs, plastic, red golf bag holder with corkscrew **6.00**
Jack Dempsey Restaurant, green and orange. **18.00**
Mallet, wooden **2.00**
Mermaid, plastic, Kempro **1.00**
Paint Brush and Palette, plastic . . . . **.50**
Piccadilly Circus Bar. **2.00**
Playing Cards, glass and plastic, set of 8. . . . . **18.00**
Sterling Silver, monogrammed, set **5.00**
Stick, glass, rolled piece of paper inside. **1.00**
Tuxedoed Men, glass, set of 6 . . . . **15.00**
Wood, painted bar name. **12.00**
Zulu, 1950s, MOC **16.00**

TAYLOR, SMITH & TAYLOR

W. L. Smith, John N. Taylor, W. L. Taylor, Homer J. Taylor, and Joseph G. Lee founded Taylor, Smith, and Taylor in Chester, West Virginia. In 1903 the firm reorganized and the Taylors bought Lee's interest. In 1906 Smith bought out the Taylors. The firm remained in the Smith family's control until it was purchased by Anchor Hocking in 1973. The tableware division closed in 1981.

One of Taylor, Smith, and Taylor's most popular lines was Lu-Ray, produced from the 1930s through the early 1950s. Designed to compete with Russel Wright's American Modern, it was produced in Windsor Blue, Persian Cream, Sharon Pink, Surf Green, and Chatham Gray. Coordinating colors encouraged collectors to mix and match sets. Taylor, Smith, and Taylor used several different backstamps and marks. Many contain the company name as well as the pattern and shape names.

A dating system was used on some dinnerware lines. The three number code included month, year, and crew number. This system was discontinued in the 1950s.

Autumn Harvest, cup and saucer **$4.00**
Autumn Harvest, dinner plate, 10" d **3.00**
Autumn Harvest, sugar **5.00**
Beverly, cup and saucer **5.00**
Beverly, sugar, cov **8.00**
Boutonniere, bread and butter plate, 6¾" d **2.00**
Boutonniere, creamer and sugar **10.00**
Boutonniere, cup and saucer. **4.00**
Boutonniere, dinner plate **3.00**
Boutonniere, platter, round **12.00**
Empire, dinner plate, 8¼" d. **4.00**
Empire, platter, oval, 11½" l. **10.00**
Fairway, casserole **20.00**
Fairway, eggcup **10.00**
Laurel, creamer and sugar **12.00**
Laurel, cream soup cup. **12.00**
Lu-Ray, bowl, tab handle, blue **12.00**
Lu-Ray, cream soup, blue **75.00**
Lu-Ray, cup and saucer, pink. **7.50**
Lu-Ray, dinner plate, blue **13.00**
Lu-Ray, grill plate, yellow **25.00**
Lu-Ray, lug soup **21.00**
Lu-Ray, mixing bowl, pink, 5½" d **40.00**
Lu-Ray, platter, green, 13½" d **18.00**
Lu-Ray, relish, 4 part, blue. **135.00**
Lu-Ray, salad plate, pink, 7" d **4.00**
Lu-Ray, salt and pepper shakers, pr, blue **20.00**
Lu-Ray, sugar, cov **12.00**
Lu-Ray, vegetable, round, gray, 8" d **28.00**
Lu-Ray, water pitcher, pink **48.00**
Marvel, cup and saucer. **5.00**
Marvel, gravy boat **12.00**
Plymouth, creamer **6.00**
Plymouth, saucer **2.00**
Taverne, berry bowl, 5¼" d **8.00**
Taverne, bread and butter plate, 6" d **5.00**
Taverne, creamer and sugar, cov **30.00**
Taverne, dinner plate, 9" d. **12.00**
Versatile, wheat pattern, cup and saucer **6.00**
Versatile, wheat pattern, luncheon plate. **5.00**
Versatile, wheat pattern, platter, 13" l **8.00**
Vistosa, eggcup, yellow **10.00**
Vistosa, dinner plate, cobalt blue, 9" d. **8.00**

TEDDY BEARS

Teddy bear collectors are fanatics. Never tell them their market is going soft. They will club you to death with their bears. Do not tell anyone that you heard it here, but the Teddy Bear craze of the 1980s has ended. The market is flooded with old and contemporary bears.

The name "Teddy" Bear originated with Theodore Roosevelt. The accepted date of their birth is 1902–1903. Early bears had humped backs, elongated muzzles, and jointed limbs. The fabric was usually mohair; the eyes were either glass with pin backs or black shoe buttons.

The contemporary Teddy Bear market is as big or bigger than the market for antique and collectible bears. Many of these bears are quite expensive. Collectors speculating in them will find that getting their money out of them in ten to fifteen years will be a bearish proposition.

Clubs: Good Bears of the World, P.O. Box 13097, Toledo, OH 43613; Teddy Bear Boosters Club, 19750 SW Peavine Mtn. Rd., McMinnville, OR 97128.

Periodicals: *National Doll & Teddy Bear Collector*, P.O. Box 4032, Portland, OR 97208; *Teddy Bear & Friends*, 11 Commerce Blvd., P.O. Box 420235, Palm Coast, FL 32142; *Teddy Bear Review,* 170 Fifth Ave. 12th Flr., New York, NY 10010.

BEAR

Character Novelty Co, synthetic plush, cinnamon, plastic eyes, label sewn in ear, c1960, 15" h. **$60.00**
Ideal, ginger mohair, fully jointed, excelsior stuffing, black shoe-button eyes, black embroidered nose, mouth, and claws, felt pads, fur loss, c1919, 20" h **460.00**

Unknown Maker, saffron mohair, fully jointed, excelsior stuffing, embroidered nose and mouth, beige felt pads, glass eyes, 14" h, $130.00. Photo courtesy Skinner, Inc., Boston, MA.

Unknown Maker, dark brown, movable arms and legs, glass eyes, 21" h, much hair loss, $55.00. Photo courtesy James D. Julia, Inc.

Ideal, light blonde mohair, fully jointed, excelsior stuffing, shoe-button eyes, black embroidered nose, mouth, and claws, beige felt pads, fur loss, felt damage, c1905, 14¾" h **431.00**
Ideal, Musical Clown Bear, cinnamon synthetic plush, white pants with brown and yellow spots, paw pads, and ear linings, yellow felt hat, molded soft vinyl face, plastic eyes, label on shoulder seam, c1950, 15" h **135.00**
Knickerbocker, brown mohair, jointed, flat face, 20" h **100.00**
Schuco, gold mohair over metal form, wire jointed, black metal eyes, black thread nose and mouth, 2½" h **300.00**
Schuco, Yes/No Bear, beige mohair, fully jointed, excelsior stuffing, black and brown glass eyes, black embroidered nose, mouth, and claws, felt pads, some fur loss, 1950s, 13" h **345.00**
Steiff, ginger mohair, fully jointed, black steel eyes, black embroidered features and claws, pads replaces, needs stuffing, some fur loss, fabric damage on muzzle, c1905, 12" h **288.00**
Unknown Maker, Cricket, gold mohair, dark brown backing, fully jointed, straw stuffed, black shoe-button eyes, black floss nose, no claws, c1915, 16½" h **400.00**
Unknown Maker, probably American-made Stuffed Toy Co, NY, Electric-Eye Teddy Bear, red, white, and blue mohair, jointed arms, fur and fabric loss, mechanism missing, 19" h **115.00**
Unknown Maker, probably Schuco, blonde and brown mohair, straw stuffed, glass eyes, black floss nose and claws, hard innersoles under mohair pads, c1930, 10" h **230.00**
Unknown Maker, rust mohair, shoe-button eyes, sliced-in ears, c1915, 15" h **350.00**

BEAR RELATED

Book, *Mother Goose's Teddy Bears,* Frederick L Cavally, color illus, worn edges. **$365.00**
Book, *The Teddy Bears,* Bray illus, Judge, set of 8, 1907 . . . . **160.00**
Fan, cardboard, Smokey the Bear by campfire, 1950s, 7 x 8" **18.00**
Figurine, bear dressed as monkey, Enesco, L Rigg artist, 1990. . . . . **15.00**
Figurine, Boo Boo Bear, Russ Berrie and Co, Teddytown Village Collection, 1995 . . . . **2.50**
Paper Doll, Teddy Bear and His Friends, Platt & Munk Co, 3 book set, boxed **45.00**
Paper Doll, The Three Bears' Home, Patten Beard, illus by Violet Moore Higgins, MdLoughlin Bros, 1933 . . . . **35.00**
Postcard, Molly and her Teddy Bear, sgd "M Greiner" **8.00**

TELEPHONE CARDS

One of the newest collecting crazes is telephone cards, commonly known as telecards. They have been big in Europe for years. Look for an explosion in the United States during the last half of the 1990s. Telecards are credit cards issued by major telephone companies and many private companies. You purchase a card and then use up the credit each time you place a call. Once the credit value of the card is exhausted, you have an instant collectible.

Some telecards are produced as part of a series, some are limited editions. Most stand alone. The cards are issued in quantities that start in the hundreds and continue into the tens of thousands. Collector value rests in a card's graphics, issuing telphone company, and the number issued. Prices are highly speculative. Only time will tell how this new collectible will "reach out and touch" collectors.

Prices listed here are from current sales lists issued by several individuals selling directly to collectors. The market has yet to determine if a premium is to be paid for cards unexpended credit balances.

Periodicals: *Premier Telecard Magazine*, P.O. Box 4614, San Luis Obispo, CA 93403.

Access Telecom Inc (ACT), Heinken Beer & Ornament, 10 units **$14.00**
ACMI (ACI), Endangered-Cheetah, $3 value **11.00**
ACMI (ACI), Fed EX. **75.00**
ACMI (ACI), Marilyn Monroe, $6 value **10.00**
ACMI (ACI), Ryder Truck Rentals **90.00**
American Express Telecom (AMX), AIDS Memorial Quilt, $5 value **8.00**
American Express Telecom (AMX), Daisies, $20 value. **20.00**
American National Phone Card (ANPC), Betty Boop/New York Jumbo, 20 units. **125.00**
American National Phone Card (ANPC), Guardian Angel Xmas, 10 units **8.00**
Ameritech (AMT), Claude Monet-Water Lilies, 20 units. **13.00**
Ameritech (AMT), Michigan Bell Cash Card, $2 value. **100.00**
AT&T (ATT), Apollo Lunar Module, 10 units **65.00**
AT&T (ATT), Art Deco District, Miami Beach, 25 units **70.00**
AT&T (ATT), Flintstones & Rubbles, 25 units. **24.00**
AT&T (ATT), Holiday Treats, 10 units **20.00**
AT&T (ATT), Nabisco-Oreo Cookie, 10 units **8.00**
AT&T (ATT), New York Skyline, 10 units. **46.00**
ATS, 1957 Chevy Corvette Convertible, 10 minutes **9.00**
ATS, Hammermill Paper, 20 minutes **12.00**
ATS, Memorial Park Funeral Home, 20 units. **12.00**

Watch F–R–I–E–N–D–S on NBC, 15 minutes, $15.00.

ATS, Olan Mills Photo Studios, 20 minutes **15.00**
Bell Atlantic (BAT), James Earl Jones, green, $5 value **10.00**
Bell South Telecom (BST), Mobility: Sea Life, $60 value **60.00**
Continental Plastics (CNP), Windy City-Am TelExpo '97, 5 minutes **16.00**
Frontier Communications (FRO), X Files, $10 value **8.00**
GTI, Dr No, $5 value **5.00**
GTI, Ralston Purina/Golden Retriever, 10 minutes **3.00**
GTE Hawaii (GTH), Diamond Head-Sunrise, 3 units **35.00**
GTE Hawaii (GTH), Lanai, 30 minutes **30.00**
Nynex (NYN), New York State Fair, $5 value. **8.00**
Nynex (NYN), Summer in the City, $5.25 value **10.00**
Pacific Bell, Santa & Phone, $5 value **39.00**
Sprint (SPR), Animal Series/Exotic Birds, 100 units **30.00**
Wachovia Corporation (WAC), Journal Constitution-Atlanta, $10 value **15.00**

TELEPHONES AND TELEPHONE RELATED

If you ask people when they think the telephone was invented, most will give you a date in the early 20th century. The accepted answer is 1876, when Alexander Graham Bell filed his patent. However, crude telegraph and sound-operated devices existed prior to that date.

Beware of reproduction phones or phones made from married parts. Buy only telephones that have the proper period parts, a minimum of restoration, and are in working order. No mass-produced telephone in the United States made prior to 1950 was manufactured with a shiny brass finish.

Concentrating on telephones is only half the story. Telephone companies generated a wealth of secondary material from books to giveaway premiums. Dig around for examples from local companies that eventually were merged into the Bell system.

Clubs: Antique Telephone Collectors Association, P.O. Box 94, Abilene, KS 67410; Mini-Phone Exchange, 5412 Tailden Rd., Bladensburg, MD 20710; Telephone Collectors International, Inc., 19 N. Cherry Dr., Oswego, IL 60543.

Blotter, AT&T, Bell logo, "Don't Write—Talk, Local and Long Distance Telephone," red, white, and blue, c1916, 8 x 4" **$20.00**
Booth, wood, no doors **125.00**
Catalog, Western Electric Co, NY, Inter-Phones and Accessories, 60 pp, wholesale and retail price lists, illus, 1916. . . . . **50.00**
Fan, Bell System logo, blue and white **12.00**
Pencil, lead, Bell Telephone, Auto Point **25.00**
Pinback Button, Chicago Telephones, white lettering on red ground, 2¼" d **25.00**
Playing Cards, The Telephone, One Hundred Years of Service, 1876–1976, light blue and white. **5.00**
Pocket Mirror, Missouri and Kansas Telephone Co, Bell System, American Telephone & Telegraph, celluloid, blue and white, early 1900s, 2½" l **65.00**
Sign, porcelain enamel on steel, "Public Telephone," 8½ x 11" **75.00**
Telephone, candlestick, straight pipe, dial. **185.00**
Telephone, desk, Leich, Bakelite finish, 5¾ x 9" **50.00**
Telephone, desk, Grab-A-Phone, Federal Tel & Tel Co, NY, c1915–25, 8 x 10" **200.00**
Telephone, desk, US Army, mkd "Connecticut". **40.00**

Pay Telephone, reconditioned and rewired with plug, 23" h to top of marquee, $400.00. Photo courtesy James D. Julia, Inc.

Telephone, desk, Western Electric, model #202, metal, gold, c1930s **150.00**
Telephone, novelty, American Flag, candlestick, American Telecommunicatopns Corp, c1970s, 12½ x 7 x 5¼". **50.00**
Telephone, novelty, Batmobile, black and yellow, bat logo on top, DC Comics, made in China, 1989, 2½ x 4 x 10" **65.00**
Telephone, novelty, Garfield Climbing Wall Telephone, Model #1209, Tyco, May Yung Enterprises Co, made in Taiwan, c1980s, 12 x 9½ x 6" **75.00**
Telephone, novelty, Heinz 57 Tomato Catsup Bottle, HJ Heinz, Pittsburgh, PA, made in Taiwan, c19080s, 8½ x 2½" **45.00**
Telephone, Pay Phone, GTE Automatic Electric, Model #120-A, 21 x 6". **130.00**
Telephone, single box, wood, plain front, 1915–20. . . . . . . **200.00**
Telephone, wall, American Electric, rotary **27.50**
Toy, Smurf, plastic, H G Toys, NY, 1982, 9" h **20.00**

TELEVISION CHARACTERS AND PERSONALITIES

The golden age of television varies depending on the period in which you grew up. Each generation thinks the television of its childhood is the best there ever was. TV collectibles are one category in which new products quickly establish themselves as collectible. The minute a show is cancelled, something that happens rather rapidly today, anything associated with it is viewed as collectible.

The golden age of TV star endorsements was the 1950s through the 1960s. For whatever reason, toy, game, and other manufacturers of today are not convinced that TV stars sell products. As a result, many shows have no licensed products associated with them. Because of the absence of three-dimensional material, collectors must content themselves with paper, such as *TV* Guide and magazines.

Periodicals: *Big Reel,* P.O. Box 1050, Dubuque, IA 52004; *Television Chronicles,* 10061 Riverside Dr., #171, North Hollywood, CA 91602; *The TV Collector,* P.O. Box 1088, Easton, MA 02334.

Note: Consult *Maloney's Antiques & Collectibles Resource Directory, 4th Edition* by David J. Maloney, Jr. for additional information about fan clubs for individual television shows.

Ben Casey MD, game, contains cardboard Casey figures, plastic stands, 66 cards, dice, and instruction sheet, Transogram, 1961, $30.00.

Soupy Sales, book, *Soupy Sales,* Barbara Gellman and Robert Shorin, illus by Tony Tallarico, Wonder Books, #7904, Grosset & Dunlap, NY, 1965, soft cov, 48 pp, 8 x 11", $8.00.

All In the Family, doll, Joey Stivic, MIB **$75.00**
Andy Griffith Show, coloring book, "Ron Howard of the Andy Griffith Show Pictures to Color," #5344, 224 pp, Saalfield ©1962 Mayberry Enterprises, Inc, 8 x 10¾" **65.00**
Arthur Godfrey Show, book, *Godfrey The Great,* Jack O'Brian, photos, 64 pp, 1951 . . . . . **30.00**
Ben Casey MD, comic book, Dell, #3, 1962 . . . . . **5.00**
Ben Casey MD, overnight case, vinyl, Casey photo portrait on lid, ©1962 Bing Crosby Productions, 12" d **45.00**
Beverly Hillbillies, magazine cov, *Saturday Evening Post,* Feb 2, 1963 . . . . . **10.00**
Bewitched, writing tablet, cast photo on cov, 1964, 8 x 10" **15.00**
Candid Camera, game, The Allen Funt Candid Camera Game, Lowell, 1963 . . . . . **20.00**
Captain Kangaroo, coloring book, dot-to-dot, 150 pp, Whitman, 1959, 8 x 11", partially colored **10.00**
Car 54, Where Are You?, record, *Toody and Muldoon on Patrol,* 33⅓ rpm, Allison, 1961 . . . . . **20.00**
Charlie's Angels, gum card wrapper, Topps, 1977 . . . . . **8.00**
Dennis the Menace, record, *The Misadventures of Dennis the Menace,"* 33⅓ rpm, Colpix, 1960s **30.00**
Donna Reed Show, TV Guide, Jun 29, 1963 . . . . . **20.00**
Dr Kildare, bobbing head, composition, name decal on base, Metro-Goldwyn-Mayer Productions sticker, 1960s, 6¼" h **90.00**
Dragnet, coloring book, "Jack Webb's Safety Squad," 64 pp, Lowe, 1956 . . . . . **25.00**
Ed Sullivan Show, bobbing head, Topo Gigio, ceramic, metal eyes, hard plastic whisker hairs, 1950s, 5½" h **45.00**
Family Affair, sticker book, Mrs Beasley Sticker Book, 12 pp, Whitman, 1972, 10¼ x 12" **20.00**
Flipper, stuffed toy, plush, gray and pink, plastic jiggle-eye disks, cloth sailor's vest and cap, Knickerbocker, 1976, 13" l **20.00**
Get Smart, lunch box, metal, King-Seeley ©1966 Talent Associates, 7 x 9 x 4" **65.00**
Gilligan's Island, writing tablet, Alan Hale and Bob Denver full color cov photo, c1960s **20.00**
Gleason, Jackie, coloring book, 16 pp, Abbott ©1956 VIP Corp, 11 x 12¼" **20.00**
Happy Days, bubble gum box, Topps, 1976 . . . . . **15.00**
Hawaii Five-0, book, *Hawaii Five-0/The Octopus Caper,* 212 pp, Whitman, 1971 . . . . . **15.00**
H R Pufnstuf, coloring book, 128 pp, Whitman, 1970 . . . . . **20.00**
I Love Lucy, comic book, #535, Dell, 1954 . . . . . **90.00**
I Love Lucy, magazine cov, *Newsweek,* Jan 19, 1953 . . . . . **20.00**
Kojak, Corgi Junior Kojak New York Police Set, ©1971 Universal City Studios, 5¼ x 8", MOC **20.00**
Kukla, Fran and Ollie, postcards, set of 2, "Kukla, Fran and Ollie Sing the Musical Alphabet," Curtiss Candy premium, each designed as 78 rpm record with color photo and songs "Sleep Baby Sleep" and "The Musical Alphabet," candy bar add and illus on reverse,1957, 3½ x 5¼" **60.00**
Land of the Giants, publicity photo, black and white, glossy, cast member's in giant's hand, attached "ABC Press Information" paper, 1968, 7¼ x 9" **20.00**
Linkletter, Art, pinback button, "Art Linkletter and I Sell RC," salesman's, bluetone photo of Art, white lettering on red ground, 1950s, 4" d **45.00**
Little House on the Prairie, colorforms playset, complete with color cast photo, Colorforms ©Ed Friendly Productions, Inc, 12½ x 16 x 1", MIB **20.00**
Man From UNCLE, Secret Print putty, Colorforms, MOC **25.00**
Mod Squad, figure, Pete Cochran, plastic, Aurora, 1969, 3" h **20.00**
Mork & Mindy, doll, Mork, talking backpack, MIB **75.00**
Nancy Drew Mysteries, lunch box, metal, with plastic thermos, King-Seeley, 1977 . . . . . **45.00**
Police Woman, doll, 8" h, MIB **50.00**
Sea Hunt, divers' watch and sunglasses, Ja-Ru, MOC **10.00**
Simpsons, bendie figure, set of 5, Jesco, MOC **60.00**
Six Million Dollar Man, activity book, Steve Austin punch-out plaque and "Race In Space" game with playing pcs, 24 pp, Rand McNally, 1974, 10 x 12½" **10.00**
Soupy Sales, pinback button, "Soupy Sales Society," red lettering on white ground, 1960s, 3½" d **10.00**
That Girl, coloring book, 64 pp, Saalfield, 1967 . . . . . **20.00**
Time Tunnel, coloring book, Artcraft, 1966 . . . . . **75.00**
Untouchables, The, Eliot Ness and the Untouchables Sawed Off Shotgun, complete with 2 red and 2 green plastic shotgun shells and bullets, Transogram ©Desilu, 9 x 24" box with Robert Stack illus **200.00**
Voyage to the Bottom of the Sea, cast photo, full color, facsimile signatures on reverse, 3½ x 5½" **12.00**
Waltons, The, game, Milton Bradley, 1974 . . . . . **10.00**

TELEVISION LAMPS

What 1950's living room would be complete without a black ceramic gondola slowly drifting across the top of the television set? Long before the arrival of VCRs, Home Box, and Nintendo systems, figural lamps dominated the tops of televisions. The lamps were made of colorful high gloss ceramics and the subject matter ranged from the relatively mundane dog statue to the more exotic (tasteless?) hula dancer.

Gazelle, chalkware, red, brown, and gold, c1950s, $60.00.

A collection of ten or more of these beauties will certainly lighten up the conversation at your next party. On second thought, it does not take ten. The pink poodle lamp on my television is more than enough to do the job.

Buffalo, brown, standing on rocks **$32.00**
Cat, brown, black highlights, green eyes. **20.00**
Crown, 12" h **40.00**
Dachshund, fiberglass shade, 10" h **70.00**
Deer, glass insert, 14" h. **50.00**
Fish, white, round metal base **18.00**
Fish and Sea Shell. **40.00**
Flamingos, pink and black, Lane **50.00**
Hearth, green, yellow and orange screen **28.00**
Horse, reclining, rust colored, black mane, 9" h **30.00**
Lighthouse and Cottage, multicolored **32.00**
Mallard, airbrushed, green and brown, wings spread, planter base **35.00**
Medusa, aluminum tubing, chrome, 52" h **300.00**
Panther, black, stalking pose, white screen background, green oval base **25.00**
Poodles, pr, pink and black, black oval planter base **30.00**
Ram, green, 14" h **45.00**
Scottie Dog, pouncing pose, gold **18.00**

TELEVISIONS

Old television sets are becoming highly collectible. It is not unusual to see a dozen or more at a flea market. Do not believe a tag that says "I Work." Insist that the seller find a place to plug it in and show you. A good general rule is the smaller the picture tube, the earlier the set. Pre-1946 televisions usually have a maximum of five stations, 1 through 5. Channels 7 through 13 were added in 1947. In 1949 Channel 1 was dropped. UHF appeared in 1953.

In order to determine the value of a television, you need to identify the brand and model number. See *Harry L. Rinker The Official Price Guide to Collectibles* (House of Collectibles: 1999) for a more detailed list.

Club: Antique Wireless Assoc., 59 Main St., Bloomfield, NY 14469.

Periodical: *Antique Radio Classified,* P.O. Box 2, Carlisle, MA 01741.

Admiral, F2817, console, double door, 27" tube, 1954 . . . . . **$20.00**
Admiral, 14R12, tabletop, Bakelite, 2 large knobs below screen, 1951, 14" **25.00**
Air King, A-1001, console, wooden cabinet, 1949, 10" **100.00**
Air King, A-2000, tabletop, wooden, 1949, 10" **75.00**
Apex, 70, console, 4 legs, speaker below radio **75.00**
Arvin, 4080T, tabletop, metal, painted mahogany cabinet, 1950, 8" **100.00**
Bendix, 6001, console, double doors, 16" **20.00**
Crosley, 348-CP, Deluxe Spectator, Swing-a-View picture tube, tilt-out controls and radio, pull-out phono, 1948, 10" **175.00**
Emerson, 600, portable, leatherette cov, side handle, 1949, 7" **125.00**
Emerson, 614, tabletop, Bakelite, 1950, 10" **75.00**
Fada, 930, tabletop, wooden, 1949, 12". **85.00**
General Electric, 16K1, AM/FM radio and phono behind left door, screen behind right door, 1950, 16" **20.00**
Hallicrafters, 514, portable, with handle, 1948, 7" **200.00**
Motorola, 14K1, console, gold bezel around sq screen, 1950, 14" **50.00**
Motorola, VT-71, tabletop, wooden, 1948, 7" **75.00**
Muntz, 17PS, portable, painted metal, handle and tuner on top, 1959 . . . . **25.00**
Philco, 51-T1604, tabletop, wooden, 4 knobs below screen, 1951, 16" **15.00**
RCA, GG846, console, color, 1959 . . . . **10.00**

TENNIS BALL CANS

Tennis balls originally came in bags and cardboard boxes. In 1926, Wilson introduced the first metal tennis ball can. It opened with a small key like a can of ham and had a flat lid that would not stay on the can after it was opened. After 1942, the lid was improved so that it could be put back on the can after opening to hold the balls securely. This lid was slightly dome-shaped instead of flat. Dome lid cans were also of the key wind opening type. Most English key wind cans had flat lids, regardless of when they were made and should not be confused with the rare United States flat-lid cans. However, the older English cans had a small solder spot either on the lid or the bottom of the can, and four sets of ridges in groups of two to four horizontally around the can. The newer English cans had no solder spot and only one ridge near the top.

Around 1972, the easy opening pull-ring cans were introduced. The best cans are the big 12-ball cans, four-ball cans, and flat-lid cans made in the United States, and cans with a famous player on them. The newer pull-ring cans are still very common and are only worth 50 cents to $10. Some balls are still sold in boxes. Pre-1960 boxes are hard to find and are worth $50 to $200. Boxes that predate cans are extremely rare and can cost $100 or more.

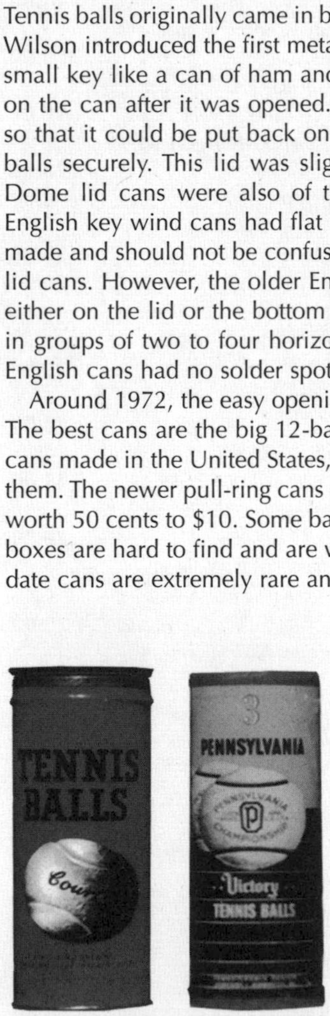

Left: Court, black, white, and red, English, $80.00.
Right: Victory, yellow, black, and white, cardboard canister, c1940, $300.00.

Advisor: Larry W. Whitaker, 2920 Jessie Ct., San Jose, CA 95124, (408) 377-8120, e-mail: LWhita@aol.com.

Club: The Tennis Collectors Society, Gerald Gurney, Guildhall, Great Bromley, Colchester, U.K., C077TU.

Aeroplane, gray and blue, made in China **$80.00**
Bancroft, "Winner," black, gold, and white **25.00**
Caprico, Wimbledon Cup, blue, black, and white, Czechoslovakia **145.00**
Chemold, Tony Roche on red can with Australian flag **30.00**
D & M, blue and red, flat lid **45.00**
Davega, yellow and black, cardboard can **175.00**
Dunhill, green and red, English **80.00**
Dunlop, Warwick, light green paper label, Old English **175.00**
Earls Court, brown paper label, Old English **150.00**
Imperial, green with racket and ball, English **75.00**
MacGregor, black, red and white plaid **25.00**
Oxford, purple, 12-ball can **125.00**
Pennsylvania, Centre Court, black and white, USA, dome lid **20.00**
Pennsylvania, yellow, black and white paper label, 12 ball cans, c1940 . . . . **400.00**
Rawlings, sea green, black, red, USA, dome lid **125.00**
Spalding, white with red and blue on front, USA, dome lid **20.00**
Volt, green and white, dome lid **25.00**
Wards, green top and bottom, white middle, USA, flat lid **300.00**
Wilson, dark blue, red, white, USA, flat lid **250.00**
Wilson, Jack Kramer, red and white, English **75.00**
Wilson, yellow top, red bottom, white spot, USA, dome lid **20.00**
Wisden, olive green with white ball, English, disc lid **150.00**
Wright & Ditson, True-Flite, blue and white, USA, dome lid **50.00**

TENNIS COLLECTIBLES

One of the latest sports collectibles to receive attention is tennis memorabilia. The recent publication of *Tennis Antiques and Collectibles* by Jeanne Cherry (Amaryllis Press, 1995) has given collectors a much needed and well researched reference source. A Tennis Collectors Society has been in existence for several years and the membership continues to grow, particularly in the United States. Collectors are seeking racquets, trophies, tournament programs, ball cans, prints, jewelry, and anything else with a tennis or racquet motif. The earlier the better.

The single most popular symbol of the sport is the racquet, the most sought after models being those with unusual head shapes, i.e., lob or tilt-tops or flat-top frames. The earliest racquets usually had the maker's name incised or stamped into the wood. Decals usually indicate a post-1900 racquet. Handles of early racquets are wooden. Leather bound models first appeared in the late 1930s. Boxed sets for tennis included racquets, net, net posts, rules book, balls, and a sturdy wooden box with a lawn tennis lithograph on the inside lid. Collectors dream of finding a complete matched set.

Trophies won by famous players at well-known tournaments or clubs command the highest prices. Trophies with tennis images are also desirable. Finally, the most sought after collectible in the tennis field is original period art; oils and stained glass being two examples.

Racquet, Spalding Smash Bash, aluminum, zippered vinyl case, c1994, $12.00.

Advisor: Ken Benner, 217 Hewett Rd., Wyncote, PA 19095, (215) 885-5876.

Club: The Tennis Collectors Society, Guildhall Orchard, Great Bromley, Colchester, C07 7TU U.K.

Annual, *Wright & Ditson,* results of tournaments, rules, adv, etc, soft cov, 1908 . . . . **$12.00**
Autograph, Tilden, William T, tennis book **50.00**
Book, *Match Play and the Spin of the Ball,* Tilden, William T, first ed, hardbound, 1923 . . . . **45.00**
Box, wood, tennis lithograph on inside lid, held complete tennis set **100.00**
Cigarette Cards, set of 50, each with famous tennis player from 1930s, green **25.00**
Fan, cardboard, wood stick handle, lady holding tennis racquet image, adv on reverse **15.00**
Game, Set Point SV Productions, 1971 . . . . **30.00**
Magazine, *American Lawn Tennis,* 1920s **5.00**
Magazine, *Harper's Weekly,* full pp print of ladies playing tennis in Prospect Park, New York City, 1880s **12.50**
Napkin Ring, silver, racquet and ball, c1890s **90.00**
Net, with turned wood posts **50.00**
Photograph, tennis players holding racquets, court in background, 1880s **20.00**
Program, USLTA, Forest Hills, 1936 . . . . **15.00**
Program, Wimbledon, All England Lawn Tennis Club, player image on cov, 1950s **4.00**
Racquet, Dayton, wood handle, steel head, wire strings, no string breaks, diamond-shaped trademark decal on handle, 1930s **15.00**
Racquet, Harrry C Lee, Dreadnought Driver, big handle, c1903 . . . . **25.00**
Racquet, Hazell's Streamline, 3-shaft construction, made in England, c1930s **90.00**
Racquet, Horsman, flat top, wood handle, model name and "Horsman" stamped into wood, thick orig gut strings, c1890s **70.00**
Racquet, Prince Classic, aluminum, green throat pc, 1960s **7.50**
Racquet, Spalding, The Hub, decals, wood handle, c1905 . . . . **20.00**
Racquet, Wilson, Famous Player Series, Don Budge, 1940s **10.00**
Racquet, Winchester, wood handle, trademark decal, 1930s **40.00**
Trophy, silver, 1905 Seabright Lawn Tennis and Cricket Club, 10" h **90.00**

THERMOMETERS

The thermometer was a popular advertising giveaway and promotional item. Buy only thermometers in very good or better condition that have a minimum of wear on the visible surface. Remember, thermometers had large production runs. If the first example you see does not please you, shop around.

Club: Thermometer Collectors Club of America, 6130 Rampart Dr., Carmichael, CA 95608.

AC Spark Plug, metal body and face, glass front, "T.W. O'Connell & Co. Chicago 7, ILL. U.S.A.," 12" d **$225.00**
Boston Shoe Co, wooden, shoe shape, diecut, 6 x 21" **250.00**
Carter White Lead Paint, porcelain, "The All Weather Paint," 7 x 27" **170.00**
Cat, figural, bisque, Bradly label, Japan, 7½" h **22.00**
Champion Spark Plugs **20.00**
Clark Bar, wooden, 1920–30s, 5½ x 19" **275.00**
Doan's Pills, wooden. **175.00**
Dr Pierce's Chemical Co, Bakelite, 1931 . . . . **18.00**
Goodyear Tires, wooden, 11½" h **50.00**
Hills Bros Coffee, tombstone shape, man in nightgown drinking coffee, red ground, white rim, c1920s, 21" h **275.00**
Ken-L Mill Dog Food, "For Best Results Feed Your Dog Ken-L Meal," 1950s, 7 x 27" **190.00**
Lake Contrary Park, St Joseph, MO, "Big Free Show Every Night" **375.00**
Lincoln Laundry, wooden, early 1900s, 12 x 3" **25.00**
Mack Trucks, tin face, glass front **200.00**
Mail Pouch Tobacco, porcelain, "Chew Mail Pouch Tobacco/Treat Yourself To The Best," 15 x 62" **225.00**
Mission Orange, vertical panel, soda bottle, white ground, 1950s, 17" h **150.00**
O-Pee-Chee Chewing Gum, wood, 6 x 24" **130.00**
Prestone, porcelain, 36" h **185.00**
Rochester American Insurance Co, NY, porcelain **27.00**
Sohio, metal, "You Start Or We Pay," 6½" h **80.00**
Sun Crest, vertical oval shape, bottle floating in lake, "Drink Sun Crest, Whether It's Hot Or Not You'll Enjoy It!," 1940s, 16" h **120.00**
Tracto Weather Station, tin, orig box **75.00**
Tru Ade, vertical oval, soda bottle above yellow band with red button, dark blue ground, white rim, "Drink Tru Ade, A Better Beverage, Not Carbonated," 1940s. **175.00**
Trutype Seeds, porcelain, yellow, 7 x 27" **150.00**
White House Coffee, man holding cup of coffee, 4 x 15" . . . **150.00**
World's Fair, 1964 New York World's Fair, metal and plastic, diamond shape, full color illus, 6 x 6". **25.00**

Dri-Power, curved glass over metal, 12" d, $187.00. Photo courtesy Wm. Morford.

TICKET STUBS

Next time you attend a paying event, don't throw away that ticket stub! It may be worth something in twenty years.

Baseball, 1945 World Series, Chicago Cubs and Detroit Tigers, Wrigley Field **$15.00**
Berlin Olympics, 1936, German text **50.00**
Bowling, 32nd International Tournament, Detroit, MI, 1932, 5 x 3" **6.00**
Boxing, Frazier/Ali, Mar 8, 1971 . . . . **75.00**
Bus, Wasworth Transfer Co, 1 bus fare **3.00**
Concert, The Beatles, paper, yellow, black text, Aug 18, 1966, Suffolk Downs, East Boston, MA, complete with letter of authenticity, 1½ x 4", unused. **75.00**
Grand Negro Jubilee Concert, Southland Nightingales-Company of Negro Jubilee Singers, c1890 . . . . **28.00**
International Aviation Meet, Long Island, 1911, unused **22.00**
Kansas State Lottery, multicolored, 1894 . . . . **8.00**
King Bros Circus, 1930s, unused **17.00**
Parking, Freedomland Amusement Park, Bronx, NY, 50¢, 1940s **20.00**
Railroad, R L & N F Railroad, 1860s **50.00**
Railroad, Wisconsin Central, 1910. . . . . **3.50**
Roosevelt/Garner Inaugural Parade, orange, black type **40.00**
Truman and Barkley Inauguration, red, white, blue, and gold, black and white inset photo, reverse with seating information **20.00**
World's Fair, Centennial Exposition, Philadelphia, 1876, admission **20.00**
World's Fair, New York, 1940, black and white, 50¢ admission, serial number printed in red, reverse with circular image of Trylon and Perisphere on stylized engraved ground **10.00**

TINS

The advertising tin has always been at the forefront of advertising collectibles. Look for examples that show no deterioration to the decorated surfaces and that have little or no signs of rust on the insides or bottoms.

The theme sells the tin. Other collectors, especially individuals from the transportation fields, have long had their eyes on the tin market. Tins also play a major part in the Country Store decorating look. Prices for pre-1940 tins are still escalating. Before you pay a high price for a tin, do your homework and make certain it is difficult to find.

Club: Tin Container Collectors Assoc., P.O. Box 440101, Aurora, CO 80044.

Baking Powder, Grand Union Tea Co, paper label, multicolored litho image of 2 children, 1 lb, 5¼" h. **$231.00**
Baking Powder, Nabob Brand, kelly, Douglas Co, Vancouver, B C, American Can, colorful picture of strawberry cake, red lettering, 5 lb, 7½" h. **60.00**
Cigar, New Bachelor, multicolored image of man smoking cigar and playing solitaire, 4¼ x 2¼ x 5⅜" h **132.00**
Cigar, Postmaster Smokers, image of postmaster smoking cigar, black and white, red ground, 5¼" h. **137.00**
Cigar, Rose-O-Cuba, multicolored litho of senorita and roses both sides, 5½" h **88.00**
Cocoa, Hershey's Chocolate Cocoa, 5 x 12¼" **25.00**

Carrel Paisley's Lavender Scented Talcum Powder, litho tin, 3 oz, 1940, $4\frac{3}{4}$" h, $30.00.

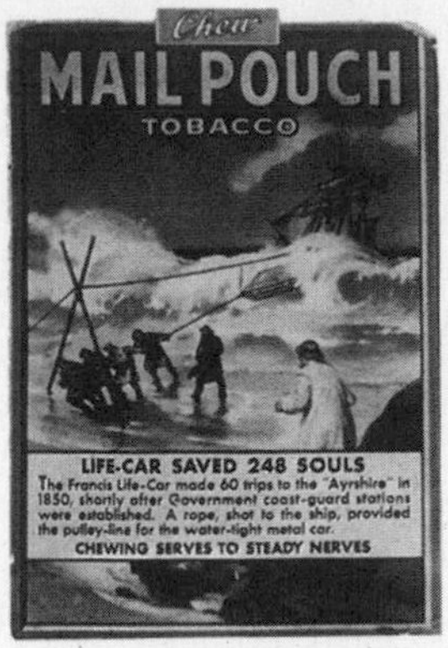

Sign, Mail Pouch Tobacco, standup, cardboard, 1 sided, $20\frac{1}{4}$" h, $13\frac{3}{4}$" w, $170.50. Photo courtesy Collectors Auction Services.

Cocoa, Millar's Magnet, multicolored cocoa harvesting scene each side, 6" h **105.00**
Coffee, Campbell Brand, bale handle, detailed camels and desert scene, 4 lb, 8" h **100.00**
Coffee, Columbia, picture of world map surrounded by leaf and berries on sides, $2\frac{3}{4}$ x $2\frac{1}{4}$" **55.00**
Coffee, Deep-Rich, keywind, red, black, and white, 1 lb, 4" h **72.00**
Cosmetics, Golden Brown Hair Dressing, sq, $\frac{1}{2}$ x $1\frac{1}{8}$ x $1\frac{1}{8}$" **18.00**
Cosmetics, Jarnac Skin Cleansing Cream, round, sample, $\frac{1}{4}$ x $1\frac{3}{8}$" **12.00**
Dental, John & Johnson Dentotape Dental Floss, $1\frac{1}{8}$ x $1\frac{1}{2}$" **6.00**
Gun Powder, Dead shot, American Powder Mills, picture of just-shot flying duck, red ground, 1 lb, 4 x $1\frac{1}{4}$ x $5\frac{3}{4}$" h **176.00**
Lighter Fluid, Old Faithful, red, black, and white, with picture of geyser, 2 x 1 x 4" h. **55.00**
Medicine, Anacin Aspirin, $\frac{1}{4}$ x $1\frac{1}{4}$ x $1\frac{3}{4}$" **5.00**
Medicine, Herbaline Mountain Rose, Springsteen Medicine Co, Cleveland, multicolored, screw cap, 3 x 3" h **55.00**
Medicine, Scott's Sure-eez Corn Remedy, round, $\frac{1}{2}$ x $1\frac{1}{4}$" **5.00**
Needles, Better Needle Phonograph Needles, $\frac{1}{4}$ x $1\frac{1}{8}$ x $2\frac{3}{8}$" **15.00**
Needles, Zenith Extra Loud, $\frac{1}{4}$ x $1\frac{1}{4}$ x $1\frac{3}{4}$" **18.00**
Pipe Polish, Middleton John, round, $\frac{3}{4}$ x $1\frac{5}{8}$" **8.00**
Shoe Polish, Uncle Sam, image of Uncle Sam on red ground, white lettering on black border, $1\frac{1}{2}$" h **132.00**
Stove Polish, Easybright, No 5, round, 1 x $3\frac{3}{4}$" **25.00**
Tobacco, California Nugget Chop Cut, flat pocket tin, yellow, red, and green, $4\frac{1}{2}$ x $2\frac{3}{4}$ x $\frac{3}{4}$" h **66.00**
Tobacco, Forest & Stream Tobacco, pocket size **75.00**

TOBACCO RELATED COLLECTIBLES

The tobacco industry is under siege in the 1990s. Fortunately, they have new frontiers to conquer in Russia, Eastern Europe, Asia, and Africa. The relics of America's smoking past, from ashtrays to humidors, are extremely collectible. Many individuals are not able to identify a smoking stand or a pocket cigar cutter. Today, tobacco growing and manufacturing have virtually disappeared. Is it possible that there will be a time when smoking disappears as well?

Clubs: Cigar Label Collectors International, P.O. Box 66, Sharon Center, OH 44274; International Seal, Label, and Cigar Band Society, 8915 E. Bellevue St, Tucson, AZ 85715; Society of Tobacco Jar Collectors, 3011 Falstaff Rd. #307, Baltimore, MD 21209; Tobacco Tin Tag Collectors Club, Rt. 2 Box 55, Pittsburg, TX 75686.

Newsletter: *The Cigar Label Gazette,* P.O. Box 3, Lake Forest, CA 92630.

Booklet, *Honest Scrap Tobacco,* color illus, "An Everyday Scrap," 12 pp **$30.00**
Box, Marksman Cigars, cardboard, 2 men shooting guns, 5¢, 3 x 5 x 1" **25.00**
Calendar, 1918, Chiquez Le Tebec Stag, "Invincible," sailor, framed, 22 x 39" **150.00**
Catalog, United Cigar Stores, 1916, 48 pp **12.00**
Cigar Band, Mark Twain **40.00**
Cigar Band, Seneca Chief **24.00**
Cigar Box Label, Adieu **45.00**
Cigar Box Label, Clover Queen **45.00**
Cigar Box Label, Saturn **170.00**
Cigar Cutter, Blackstone, marquee emb "Waitt & Bond's Blckstone, leads the World," professionally restored with copper tiger striping, $4\frac{3}{4}$" h **345.00**
Cigarette Paper, B & W, red **8.00**
Cigarette Paper, Country Gentleman **11.00**
Cigarette Paper, Duke's Cameo **24.00**
Cigarette Paper, Prince Albert, 15 leaves **2.00**
Cigarette Paper, Target, Long Cut **12.00**
Display, Blue Ribbon Cigars, cardboard, standup, logo on green and white ground **35.00**
Package, Cincy Chewing and Smoking Tobacco, red, white, and blue, unused **30.00**
Playing Cards, Royal Lancer Cigars, pinochle deck, adv text on aces, orig box **25.00**
Poster, General Cigar Co, National Brands, factory vignettes, $23\frac{1}{2}$ x $34\frac{1}{2}$" **300.00**
Sign, Crusader Tobacco, c1900, 13 x 7" **25.00**
Sign, Time Plug Tobacco, cardboard, 12" sq **25.00**
Tin, Eagle Brand Snuff, $1\frac{1}{4}$ x $2\frac{1}{8}$ x $1\frac{1}{2}$" **30.00**
Tin, Half & Half **5.00**
Tin, Larkin & Morrill Snuff Scotch, $1\frac{1}{2}$ x $2\frac{1}{4}$" **35.00**
Tobacco Tag, Battle Ax, diecut ax, white on red ground **1.50**
Tobacco Tag, Spur, diecut spur, emb **7.00**

TOKENS

Token collecting is an extremely diverse field. The listing below barely scratches the surface with respect to the types of tokens one might find.

The wonderful thing about tokens is that, on the whole, they are very inexpensive. You can build an impressive collection on a small budget. Like match cover and sugar packet collectors, token collectors have kept their objects outside the main collecting stream. This has resulted in stable, low prices over a long period of time in spite of an extensive literature base. There is no indication that this is going to change in the near future.

Clubs: American Numismatic Assoc, 818 N. Cascade Ave., Colorado Springs, CO 80903; Token and Medal Society, Inc.,9230 SW 59th St., Miami, FL 33173.

American Legion Post 91, Mt Carmel, PA, brass **$11.00**
Baltimore Oriole Celebration, white metal, "Sep 12, 13, 14, 1882" **5.00**
Bank of Upper Canada **15.50**
Chain O' Lakes, Antrim County, MI **6.00**
Community Cigar Store, Mahanoy City, PA, aluminum **15.50**
Conrad's, Boston, MA, gold-plated **25.00**
Fada Radio **15.00**
Gimble Bros, New York City, white metal, oval **18.00**
Globe Fire Insurance Co, NY, copper, eagle holding Liberty Bell and "Centennial 1776 1876" on front, reverse with world globe and company name and address **4.00**
Halifax Steamboat Co, Canada, ferry token **25.00**
King's Daughters Hospital, Middlesborough, KY, brass **22.00**
Lion Buggy Co, Cincinnati, OH, brass **5.00**
Northern Transit Co, Atwood, ND, "One Fare" **8.00**
Northwestern Consolidated Milling Co, Minneapolis, MN, aluminum **15.50**
Palmer House Barber Shop, copper-nickel alloy **15.00**
Paul's Place, Lake Benton, MN, brass **1.00**
Petty Jewelry Co, Jewelers & Optometrists, Mt Pleasant, TN, aluminum, "Good For 50¢ On A Pair Of Spectacles Or Eyeglasses. Good For $1.00 On A Cash Purchase Of $20.00 Or Over" **13.00**
Presbyterian Orphans Home, aluminum **25.00**
Rainbow Club, Strandquist, MN, brass, "Good For One Drink" **4.00**
Remington, brass, "Shot With A Kleanbore Remington Cartridge" on front, reverse with "Shot With A Remington Rifle," 1¼" d **8.00**

TOOLS

Every flea market has at least a half a dozen tables loaded with tools. The majority are modern tools sold primarily for reuse. However, you may find some early tools thrown in with the bunch. Dig through tool boxes and the boxes under the tables. Decorators like primitive tools for hanging on walls in old homes. Other desirable tools include those that are handwrought or heavily trimmed with brass. Names to look for include Stanley, Keen Kutter, and Winchester. Refer to the Stanley and Winchester listings for further information on these brand names.

Club: The Early American Industries Assoc., 167 Bakersville Rd., South Dartmouth, MA 02748.

Newsletter: *Tool Ads,* P.O. Box 33, Hamilton, MT 59840.

Periodical: *The Fine Tool Journal,* 27 Fickett Rd., Pownal, ME 04069.

Socket Set, ¼" and ⅜" drive, complete, $20.00.

Blueberry Rake, 11½" w with 2¾" teeth, wooden handle . . . **$85.00**
Buggy Wrench, Joys, "Patent Feb 1'98," nickel-plated, 10" l **75.00**
Calipers, ladies legs, heavy gauge steel, 8¼" l **85.00**
Chisel, Ohio Tool Co, socket handled, V-shape **25.00**
Clapboard Slick, D-handled, smith-made, mkd "HMC," 24" l, 3½" w **55.00**
Cooper's Adze, French, flat blade, 8" handle with 2 small rosette touchmarks, 4¼" w **55.00**
Corner Brace, Millers Falls, probably McClillan patent 6-29-1897 . . . . **250.00**
Expanding Bit, "J. Anderson Pat. Seacomb, Eng," for early type brace, 5/16" **30.00**
Gutter Plane, lignum vitae, beech handle, replaced wedge, unmkd, 11¼" l **55.00**
Hacksaw, nickel-plated, "Millers Falls," #300, red plastic handle **30.00**
Hammer, Vigeant, J, Marlboro, MA, #1, double-headed shoe hammer, pat Jan 7, 1868, 12" l **75.00**
Leather Draw Gauge, early, rosewood and steel, mkd "C.S. Osborne" with assembly #63 on frame and fence **35.00**
Leather Punch, brass base, hollow pins, 9" l **15.00**
Plumb Bob, brass, turnip shape, steel point, 2½ lb, 4½" l . . . **115.00**
Rule, circular, solid box wood, 36" l **75.00**
Saw, child's, Cresson, W, Philadelphia, imp "W. Cresson," c1860, 10" l **185.00**
Soldering Iron, shepherd's crook shape, pitted, 12" l **35.00**

TOOTHBRUSH HOLDERS

Forget your standard bathroom cup or mounted wall toothbrush holders. They have no pizzazz. No one collects them.

Collectors want wonderful ceramic figural toothbrush holders from the 1930s through the 1960s. Images are generation driven, from a bisque boy holding an umbrella seated on a fence from the 1920s to a high-glazed seated elephant from the 1950s. Licensed characters from comic strips, children's literature, and cartoons, especially Disney, are plentiful. Prices for pre-1940 examples begin around $60.00 and extend into the hundreds.

If you find these vintage toothbrush holders pricey, consider modern plastic examples, many of which are found in the shaped of licensed characters from children's television shows and comics. Do not overlook figural electrical toothbrush sets. I already have several in my collection.

Club: Toothbrush Holder Collectors Club, P.O. Box 371, Barnesville, MD 20838.

Skeezix, "Pro-phy-lac-tic Listerine," tin, diecut, 3³/₄ x 6", $154.00. Photo courtesy Past Tyme Pleasures.

Pattern Glass, Pretty Maid, clear, $55.00. Photo courtesy Gene Harris Antique Auction Center, Inc.

Annie Oakley, 2 holes, Japan, 5³/₄" h **$95.00**
Bear, chalkware, 1 hole, 6¹/₈" h **50.00**
Bear, 1 hole, Goldcastle/Japan, 6" h **90.00**
Bell Hop, holding flowers, 1 hole, Japan, 5¹/₄" h **70.00**
Boy, holding umbrella, 2 holes, Japan, 4³/₄" h **70.00**
Bulldog, red tongue, 1 hole, 3¹/₂" h **55.00**
Cat, black, arched back, 1 hole, 4" h **135.00**
Cat, 2 holes, Goldcastle/Japan, 5³/₄" h **75.00**
Doc, from Snow White, "Doc says Brush Your Teeth, "Snow White," 1 hole, 4¹/₄" h **90.00**
Dog, begging, Lustre, 2 holes, 3³/₄" h **90.00**
Dog, holding basket in mouth, 1 hole, Japan, 5³/₄" h **85.00**
Donald Duck, 2 holes, bisque, 5¹/₄" h **250.00**
Donkey, 1 hole, Goldcastle/Japan, 5³/₄" h **90.00**
Duckling, chalkware, 2 holes, 4³/₄" h **40.00**
Elephant, trunk in air, 3 holes, Japan, 5¹/₂" h **80.00**
Flapper Girl, holding purse, 2 holes, 4¹/₄" h **115.00**
Frog, playing mandolin, 1 hole, Goldcastle/Japan, 6" h **90.00**
Girl, holding basket, 2 holes, Japan, 4¹/₂" h **60.00**
Lion, black accents, 2 holes, Japan, 6" h **80.00**
Mexican Boy, 2 holes, Japan, 5¹/₂" h **80.00**
Old Mother Hubbard, shaker top, Germany, 6¹/₄" h **350.00**
Penguin, 3 holes, Japan, 5¹/₂" h **90.00**
Rabbit, sitting up, 1 hole, Norwood/Germany, 5¹/₂" h **80.00**
Soldier, red pants and hat, 1 hole, Japan, 6³/₄" h **75.00**
The Three Bears, 2 holes, Japan, 5" h **80.00**

TOOTHPICK HOLDERS

During the Victorian era, the toothpick holder was an important table accessory. It is found in a wide range of materials and was manufactured by American and European firms. Toothpick holders also were popular souvenirs in the 1880 to 1920 period.

Do not confuse toothpick holders with match holders, shot glasses, miniature spoon holders in a child's dish set, mustard pots without lids, rose or violet bowls, individual open salts, or vases. A toothpick holder allows ample room for the toothpick and enough of an extension of the toothpick to allow easy access.

Club: National Toothpick Holder Collectors Society, P.O. Box 417, Safety Harbor, FL 34695.

Aluminum, souvenir, "Niagara Falls" **$40.00**
Aluminum, souvenir, "World's Fair St Louis 1904" **40.00**
Art Glass, amber bottom half, ruby ruffled top half, etched Bohemian type design **200.00**
Art Glass, Mother-of-Pearl, Diamond Quilt, crimp top, SP frame, probably Thomas Webb & Sons **300.00**
Bisque, figural boy, 4¹/₂" h **45.00**
Bisque, figural dwarf, 4¹/₂" h **25.00**
China, hp, Nippon, 2¹/₂" h **40.00**
China, portrait of Queen Louise, unmkd **50.00**
China, souvenir, "Wapakoneta, Ohio" **30.00**
Copper, bail handle, leaf dec **50.00**
Custard Glass, souvenir, Belvedere, IL **35.00**
Cut Glass, Gravic Carnation, cut star under base, notched rim, gray cut carnations on body, mkd "T.G. Hawkes & Co.," 3¹/₄" h **200.00**
Cut Glass, Star Feather, cut star under base, flashed stars and feather on body, mkd "Libbey Glass Co.," 2⁵/₈" h **110.00**
Glass, Beaded Grape, U S Glass Co **60.00**
Glass, Beaded Panel & Sunburst, crystal, Heisey **100.00**
Glass, Daisy & Button, Fenton **30.00**
Glass, hat, Hobnail, topaz opalescent, Fenton **25.00**
Glass, opaline, Baccarat **50.00**
Milk Glass, figural barrel, white, metal hoops **25.00**
Milk Glass, Keystone, McKee **45.00**
Pattern Glass, Feather, clear **65.00**
Pattern Glass, Hobnail, vaseline **20.00**
Pattern Glass, King's Crown, ruby stained **38.00**
Pattern Glass, Three Dolphins, amber **45.00**
Porcelain, Jasperware, mkd "Wedgwood, England" **125.00**
Pressed Glass, clear, Lacy Floral, Westmoreland **35.00**
Pressed Glass, clear, nude woman on front, flower on back, wrap-around brass trim, 23/4" h **30.00**
Pressed Glass, clear, silver overlay of grapes on center panels, flowers on other panels **50.00**
Ruby Stained, Button Arches, "Mother 1947" **20.00**
Silver Plate, figural cat and bucket, Babcock **50.00**
Silver Plate, figural chick and egg, Wilcox Silver Plate Co, Meriden, CT **100.00**
Silver Plate, figural rooster, engraved "Picks," 2" h **48.00**
Sterling Silver, cup, 2 handles, mkd Black, Star And Frost," stamped "Dinner Of The First Panel, Sheriff's Jury, Jan. 14, 1897" **100.00**
Wood, figural beaver, painted features, broad tail, hollowed out trunk **5.00**

TORTOISE SHELL ITEMS

It is possible to find tortoise shell items in a variety of forms ranging from boxes to trinkets. Tortoise shell items experienced several crazes in the 19th and early 20th centuries, the last occurring in the 1920s when tortoise shell jewelry was especially popular. Anyone selling tortoise shell objects is subject to the Endangered Species Act and its amendments. Tortoise shell objects can be imported and sold, but only after adhering to a number of strict requirements.

Bracelet, bangle, silver inlay, 3" d **$35.00**
Brooch, figure-eight ribbon inlaid with scalloped ovals and X's, $1^{1}/_{2}$" w **295.00**
Coin Purse, silver inlaid dec, 3 x 2" **150.00**
Comb, ornate design, Spanish, $5^{1}/_{2}$" l **45.00**
Hairpin, carved poppy blossoms **140.00**
Letter Opener, silver fox head handle, 12" l **225.00**
Model, rickshaw, hinged hood, spoked wheels, metal poles, 8" l **110.00**
Neckchain, tortoise shell chain links with yellow gold star piqué on fronts and backs, horseshoe shaped closure, 21" l **750.00**
Pill Box, small ivory feet, $2^{1}/_{2}$" l **80.00**
Shaving Brush, inlaid mother-of-pearl dec handle **40.00**
Stickpin, carved fly perched on coral branch, gold filled pin **75.00**
Stickpin, Piqué, yellow gold, domed disk, inlaid circles, c1880 . . . . **200.00**

TOYS

The difference between men and boys is the price of their toys. At thirty one's childhood is affordable, at forty expensive, and at fifty out of reach. Check the following list for toys that you may have played with. You will see what I mean.

Clubs: Diecast Toy Collectors Assoc., P.O. Box 1824, Bend, OR 97701; The Antique Toy Collectors of America,Inc., Two Wall St., New York, NY 10005; Toy Car Collectors Club, 33290 W. 14 Mile Rd. #454, West Bloomfield, MI 48322.

Periodicals: *Antique Toy World,* P.O. Box 34509, Chicago, IL 60634; *Toy Car & Vehicles,* 700 E. State St., Iola, IWI 54990; *Toy Trader,* P.O. Box 1050, Dubuque, IA 52004.

Amsco, Doll-E-Dish Time, complete with small box of Brillo pads, DuPont sponge, Rymplecloth polishing fabric, bottle brush, and brittle plastic sink strainer, 1955 . . . . **$10.00**
Auburn, Telephone Truck, 7" l **16.50**
Bandai, Chevy Convertible, friction, $9^{1}/_{2}$' l, orig box **475.00**
Bandai, Plymouth Ambulance, friction, white, red cross on doors, 1960s, 12" l **45.00**
Big Bang Cannons, The Conestoga Company # 5T, Motor Tank, cast iron hull, rubber wheels, $9^{1}/_{2}$" l **350.00**
Britains, Toy Soldier, Set #229, U S West Point Cadets, 8 pcs, orig box **126.00**
Buddy-L, Anti-Aircraft Unit, 15" **60.50**
Buddy-L, Ladder Fire Truck, 31" **82.50**
Buddy-L, Texaco Tanker, 23" **187.00**
Chein, Fish, tin windup, $11^{1}/_{2}$" l **40.00**
Corgi, Deluxe Lincoln Continental Limousine Car, diecast metal, 2-tone gold and black, opening doors, hood, and trunk, simulated jewel headlights, 1960s, 6" l **30.00**
Daiya, Japan, Boeing 707, tin, friction, orig box, 10" l. **110.00**
Dinky, Hawker Hurricane, #62H, 1939–41 . . . . **75.00**
Doepke, Barber Greene Bucket Loader, 19" **176.00**
Doepke, Unit Crane and Shovel, 23" **170.50**
Ideal, Motorific Boat The Sea Wolf, battery operated, plastic, complete with blue plastic display stand, 1960s, 6" l **40.00**
Japan, Buick Roadmaster Sedan, friction, 1951, $11^{1}/_{2}$" l **35.00**
Kenner, Easy Bake Oven, 1960s **35.00**
Kuzan, Kuzan's Astro Zapper, futuristic plastic gun with ammo **84.00**
Linemar, Donald Duck Car, tin, windup, $6^{1}/_{2}$" l **258.00**
Lupor, Taxi, litho tin, yellow and red, orig box, 7" l. **128.00**
Marx, Army Mobile Search Light, 12" **55.00**
Marx, Exploding Souvenir Grenade, soft plastic and metal, 1960s, MIP **40.00**
Mattel, Creeple People Thingmaker Set, complete, 1965 . . . . . **80.00**
Metal Craft, C W Coffee Truck, 11" **385.00**
Mignot, Toy Soldiers, British Grenadiers of the 33rd Regiment, 1776, 12 pcs, orig box **316.00**
Modern Toys, X-07 Space Surveillant, battery operated, bump-and-go action, flashing lights, animated tin astronaut under canopy, orig box, 9" l **258.00**
Newell, Atomic "5" Pistol, #149, red plastic pistol with spring firing action useds table tennis balls, 1950s, $9^{1}/_{2}$" l **168.00**
Nylint, Caterpillar GMC Semi, 22", MIB **44.00**
S Japan, Betty Boop Tambourine, litho tin, 6" d. **198.00**
Structo, Dump Truck, 20" **50.00**
Structo, Macinery Hauler, 13" **55.00**
Thomas Toys, Battle Stations—Sea & Air Combat Action Set, plastic, includes exploding battleship, 7 x 9" l atom bomber with bombs, and 10" l submarine with torpedoes, orig box **235.00**
TN Japan, Hot Rod, tin, battery operated, classic hot rod styling with tin collegiate driver, floating superpower motor with animated fan blade, bump-and-go action, orig box, 1950s, 10" l **184.00**

Cragstan, Mystery Action Satellite, includes styro-saucer, 3 actions, 1960s, 9" l, $80.00. Photo courtesy Gene Harris Antique Auction Center, Inc.

Schuco, Micro-Racer, metal windup with rubber tires, "Made in U.S. Zone Germany," orig box, $214.50. Photo courtesy Collectors Auction Services.

Tonka, Car Carrier, 43" **28.00**
Tonka, Ladder Fire Truck, 36". **50.00**
Tonka, Rovin' Wrecker, #2202, 14", MIB **22.00**
Tootsie Toy, Mobile Gas Truck, 9". **22.00**
Topper, Suzy Homemaker, washer and dryer, battery operated **95.00**
Unique Art, G I Joe and his Jouncing Jeep, tin windup, with figure, 8" l **200.00**
Wolverine, Drum Major, tin windup, 14" h. **144.00**
Wyandotte, Hook & Ladder Fire Truck, 25". **82.00**

TRAINS, TOY

Toy train collectors and dealers exist in a world unto themselves. They have their own shows, trade publications, and price guides. The name you need to know is Greenberg Books, now a division of Kalmbach publishing, 21027 Crossroads Circle, Waukesha, WI 53187. If you decide to get involved with toy trains, write for a catalog. The two most recognized names are American Flyer and Lionel, and the two most popular gauges are S and O. Do not overlook other manufacturers and gauges.

The toy train market has gone through a number of crazes—first Lionel, then American Flyer. The current craze is boxed sets. Fortunately, the market is so broad that there will never be an end to subcategories to collect.

Clubs: American Flyer Collectors Club, P.O. Box 13269, Pittsburgh, PA 15243; Lionel Collector's Club of America, P.O. Box 479, La Salle, IL 61301; National Model Railroad Assoc., Inc., 4121 Cromwell Rd., Chattanooga, TN 37421; Train Collectors Assoc., P.O. Box 248, Strasburg, PA 17579.

Periodical: *Classic Toy Trains,* 21027 Crossroads Circle, P.O. Box 1612, Waukesha, WI 53187.

American Flyer, American Flag and Post, diecast, painted blue with gold shield emb "Old Glory," tall wooden flag pole, mfg's plate on bottom. **$660.00**
American Flyer, car, 23787, remote control Log Loader, missing man **99.00**
Amercian Flyer, coal loader, 23785, 3 button controller **363.00**
American Flyer, engine, 405, Silver Streak, Alco Pa, 1952. . . . . **80.00**
American Flyer, engine, 212374, Chesapeake and Ohio, GP-7, 1961–62 . . . . **110.00**
American Flyer, hopper, Lehigh New England, gray, white lettering, S gauge, 1946–53 . . . . **2.00**
American Flyer, passenger car, Columbus, 1957–58 . . . . **45.00**

American Flyer, set, green litho tin, includes locomotive 0-4-0 and 2 coaches mkd "Pleasant View" and "America," $418.00. Photo courtesy Bill Bertoia Auctions.

American Flyer, set, 0-4-0, 4653 locomotive, 2 Bunker Hill passenger coaches, Yorktown observation car, orange **715.00**
American Flyer, set, 4643, litho tin Pleasant Valley, America, and United States Mail coaches, green **462.00**
American Flyer, tank car, Baker's Chocolate, 1961–72 . . . . . . **25.00**
Buddy L, flat car, 1006, black **675.00**
Buddy L, gondola, 54, red **105.00**
Dorfan, caboose, #600, narrow gauge **25.00**
Ives, bridge, stonework ramps, double viaduct center, lattice type girders, 0 gauge, 31" l **70.00**
Ives, caboose, 70, O gauge **4.00**
Ives, drawing room car, #129, "The Ives Railway Lines," green steel litho, gray roof, 1928–24 . . . . **85.00**
Ives, parlor car, "The Ives Railway Lines" above windows, 0 gauge, 1914–15 . . . . **150.00**
Ives, tank car, orange and black, 66 Standard Oil, 0 gauge **30.00**
Lionel, box car, State of Maine, 1956-58 . . . . **55.00**
Lionel, box car, Timken, #6464-500, yellow and white, tab-end trucks, orig box **220.00**
Lionel, caboose, #217, orange and maroon, standard gauge **231.00**
Lionel, fire car, #52, orig box. **302.50**
Lionel, girl's train hopper, 6436-500. . . . . **385.00**
Lionel, lamp post, double light, dark green, 1929. . . . . **55.00**
Lionel, locomotive and tender, #255 and #263W, gunmetal **770.00**
Lionel, lumber loader, red or green roof, 1946–50 . . . . **175.00**
Lionel, searchlight car, #520, green and nickel, standard gauge **231.00**
Lionel, transformer, 90 watt, 1948 . . . . **45.00**
Lionel, signal bridge, #440, 440C panel board in red **357.50**
Lionel, tank car, Lionel Lines, 1958–59 . . . . **5.00**
Lionel, trestle bridge, gray **52.00**
Lionel, whistle controller, #167, 1950–66 . . . . **15.00**
Marx, caboose, plastic, brown and white **10.00**
Marx, crossing gate, plastic, 81/4" l. . . . . **.15**
Marx, dump car, "New York Central," tender for steam locomotive, 4 wheel, blue, 1934–41 and 1950–55 . . . . **20.00**
Marx, locomotive, "The Chief," plastic. **45.00**
Marx, refrigerator car, tin, "C & S," sliding doors. **15.00**
Marx, set, Old Time Western, plastic, battery operated, black locomotive and tender, yellow gondola, and red caboose **80.00**
Marx, tank car, "Allstate," plastic, turquoise **5.00**
Unique, circus car, tin, "Unique U Circus," 7 1/2" l **90.00**
Unique, passenger car, tin, "Garden City," blue and silver body, white and black lettering. **75.00**

TRAPS

Animal traps have been collected for many years; however, condition means everything. Many thought the more rust on the trap the better, but this is not the case for the "dyed in the wool" collectors. Usually there is "stamped in lettering" located on the pan (the round or sometimes oval item that the animal places its foot onto.) This lettering should be readable, which helps identify the trap. Many trap collectors also collect mouse traps, glass fly traps, minnow traps, and of course, the large bear traps.

Advisor: Tom Parr, P.O. Box 94, Galloway, OH 43119, (614) 878-6011.

Mouse, Electrocuter, 1940s, $35.00.

Tritzels Pretzels, Perfect Food, Inc., Lansdale, PA, 10" d, $30.00.

Club: North American Trap Collectors Association, P.O. Box 94, Galloway, OH 43119.

Bear, Herter's #41AX, 1960s **$500.00**
Bear, Mackenzie Dist Fur Co **175.00**
Bear, Newhouse ATC #6, with teeth **1,000.00**
Bear, Newhouse #15, Oneida Community **350.00**
Beaver, handforged, symmetrical shape, strong springs, complete **75.00**
Bigelow Humane Killer Trap, round, flat steel, made in Ohio **20.00**
Fly Trap, glass **35.00**
Minnow, Camp Glass, cone shaped holes **95.00**
Mouse, wood, 4-hole choker with stamped in printing **20.00**
Muskrat, Diamond Trap #51, Walloper **45.00**
Muskrat, wooden stretcher board, handmade **5.00**
Otter, Newhouse #3½, complete with chain **125.00**
Rabbit, Victor #10, made in USA for Australia **75.00**
Rat, Gibbs Gladiator, wood base with metal tray **50.00**
Scent Bottle, with label and wood or cardboard shipping container **20.00**
Spring Trap, Blake & Lamb #1 . . . . **5.00**
Tree Trap, Oneida Community, 4 sizes **30.00**
Woods & Water Fur Trap, wire, early 1980s **5.00**

TRAYS

Tin lithographed advertising trays date back to the last quarter of the 19th century. They were popular at any location where beverages, alcoholic and nonalcoholic, were served.

Because they were heavily used, it is not unusual to find dents and scratches. Check carefully for rust. Once the lithographed surface was broken, rust developed easily.

Smaller trays are generally tip trays. Novice collectors often confuse them with advertising coasters. Tip trays are rather expensive. Ordinary examples sell in the $50 to $75 range.

Coca-Cola,1976 Cotton Bowl Champs, tin **$25.00**
Commemorative, center with flag and Francis Scott Key medallion below "1814-1914," flag shield border, compliments C D Kenny Co. **50.00**
Cottolene Shortening, multicolored illus on black ground, NK Fairbanks Co, 4½" d **40.00**
Fairy Soap, tip, tin **38.00**
Firestone, Carriage Convention, souvenir, brass, 1914, 6½" d **20.00**
Genessee Twelve Horse Ale, horse team illus **75.00**
Hyroller Whiskey, change **25.00**
Incandescent Light and Stove Co, tip **75.00**
Kentucky Derby, 100th Running, 13¼ x 21½" **55.00**
Parsely Salmon, change **40.00**
Peerless Beer, oval **125.00**
Red Raven, serving, woman hugging red raven, 12" d **95.00**
Straus, Gunst & Co, Full Dress Maryland Rye, tip, 1907, 12" d **100.00**
Taft and Sherman, tip, litho tin, jugate portraits, "Grand Old Party/1856 To 1908" on rim, black and gold border, 4½" d **125.00**
Taka Cola, tip **75.00**
Tom Moore Cigars, change **20.00**
Valley Forge, souvenir, "Washington's Headquarters" **40.00**
Velvet Ice Cream, change, woman eating ice cream, oval **275.00**
Yellowstone Park, souvenir, copper, silver wash, 4" l **12.00**
World's Fair, 1933 Chicago, Century of Progress, brass, emb, raised detailed exhibit buildings, 4¾" d **25.00**

TROLLS

The modern troll craze was originally born in the 1960s. A second wave of popularity swept the nation in the 1990s, and trolls became popular with both boys and girls. Although trolls have been made in all shapes and sizes, their unique facial features and hair easily distinguish them from other dolls.

Newsletters: *Troll Monthly,* 216 Washington St., Canto, MA 02021; *Troll'n,* P.O. Box 601292, Sacramento, CA 95860.

Activity Book, Hobnobbins Paint with Water Book, Golden **$1.50**
Bank, Dam, Santa Claus, 7" h **50.00**
Bank, Dam, white hair, dark red-amber eyes, green and red outfit, 7" h **40.00**
Doll, Bijoy Toy, Neanderthal Man, blonde hair, painted brown eyes, 7½" h **35.00**
Doll, Dam, Caveman, yellow hair, green eyes, 12" h **115.00**
Doll, Dam, Cowboy, felt costume, blue hair, 7" h **45.00**
Doll, Dam, Elephant, yellow hair, 1960s, 6" h **150.00**
Doll, Dam, Giraffe, yellow hair, amber eyes, 12" h **85.00**
Doll, Dam, Girl, wearing raincoat, 7" h **40.00**
Doll, Dam, Hula Girl, 6" h **15.00**
Doll, Dam, Indian Girl **45.00**
Doll, Dam, Lion, Limited Edition, 5" h **65.00**
Doll, Dam, Pirate, 7" h **45.00**
Doll, Dam, Playboy Bunny, 5½" h **45.00**
Doll, Norfin, Grandpa Claus, 14" h **90.00**

Doll, Russ, Bridesmaid, pink hair, brown eyes, 4" h **4.00**
Doll, Russ, gray hair, shirt with "Life Begins at 60", 4" h **7.50**
Doll, Russ, Little Red Riding Hood, 4½" h **9.00**
Doll, Uneeda Wishnik, Cowhand, blue hair, blue and white neckerchief, blue pants, red hat, 3½" h **15.00**
Doll, Uneeda Wishnik, doll faced, red hair and eyes, red and white petal shaped dress, 7" h **20.00**
Doll, Uneeda Wishnik, Graduate, 8" h **10.00**
Doll, Uneeda Wishnik, Hula-Nik, orange hair, purple skirt, 5" h **30.00**
Doll, Uneeda Wishnik, Hunt-Nik, bright red hair, amber eyes, red and black checkered flannel shirt, red pants, blue cap, orig container, 3" h **20.00**
Doll, Uneeda Wishnik, salt and pepper hair, blush pink cheeks, inset light amber eyes, 3" h **12.00**
Ornament, Norfin Santa, painted body, red and white outfit, 2½" h **3.00**
Pin, Dam, Astronaut, orange hair, 1½" h **20.00**
Premium, Burger King, Jaws, glow-in-dark, 3" h **5.00**
Stocking, red, white, and green plush, green hair, brown eyes, wearing Santa hat, 7" h **3.00**

TROPHIES

There are trophies for virtually everything. Ever wonder what happens to them when the receiver grows up or dies? Most wind up in landfills. It is time to do something about this injustice. If you plan on collecting them, focus on shape and unusual nature of the award. Set a $5 limit—not much of a handicap when it comes to trophy collecting. Always check the metal content of trophies. A number of turn-of-the-century trophies are sterling silver. These obviously have weight as well as historic value. Also suspect sterling silver when the trophy is a plate.

TURTLE COLLECTIBLES

Turtle collectors are a slow and steady group who are patient about expanding their collection of objects relating to these funny little reptiles. Don't you believe it! My son is one of those collectors, and he's not at all slow when it come to expanding his collection. Turtle collectibles are everywhere. Like all animal collectibles, they come in all shapes and sizes. Candles, toys, storybooks, jewelry, and ornaments featuring turtles can be found at almost any flea market. Watch out for tortoise shell items. This material is subject to the provisions of the Federal Endangered Species Act.

Baseball Glove, Teenage Mutant Ninja Turtles, green, yellow, red mask, purple trim, orig paper tag, #18535, Endorsed by Raphael, Major League model, Remco, 9" h **$20.00**
Brooch, figural, painted dec **8.00**
Cookie Jar, Timmy Turtle, McCoy **40.00**
Dish, figural, amber glass, removable shell lid **95.00**
Doorstop, full figure, Wilton **700.00**
Figure, ceramic, brown and green, unmkd, 10" l. **15.00**
Figure, Weller, Coppertone, 5½" h **85.00**
Game, Touché Turtle, Transogram, 1962 . . . . **60.00**
Pin, wooden, carved clear lucite shell **50.00**
Planter, figural, white matte glaze, McCoy **5.00**
Pincushion, figural, cast iron body, stuffed velvet shell cushion. **25.00**
Salt and Pepper Shakers, pr, figural, ceramic, walking upright, dark green shells, brown bodies **6.00**
Telephone, figural, green, shell handset **40.00**
Toothpick Holder, figural, SP, child holding umbrella seated on turtle, Pairpoint **175.00**
Toy, Teenage Mutant Ninja Turtles, Pizza Thrower, 1989 . . . . . **35.00**
Toy, Tuggy Turtle, Fisher-Price, #139. . . . . **80.00**

TYPEWRITERS

The first commercially produced typewriter in America was the 1874 Shoels and Gliden machine produced by E. Remington & Sons. The last quarter of the 19th century was spent largely in experimentation and attempting to make the typewriter an integral part of every office environment, something that was achieved by 1910. Although there were early examples, the arrival of a universally acceptable electric typewriter dates from the 1950s.

The number of typewriter collectors is small, but growing. Machines made after 1915 have little value, largely because they do not interest collectors. Do not use the patent date on a machine to date its manufacture. Many models were produced for decades. Do not overlook typewriter ephemera. Early catalogs are helpful in identifying and dating machines.

Clubs: Internationales Forum Historishe Burowelt, Postfach 500 11 68, D-5000 Koln-50, Germany; Early Typewriter Collectors Assoc., 2591 Military Ave., Los Angeles, CA 90064.

Newsletters: *Ribbon Type News,* 28 The Green, Watertown, CT 06795; *The Typewriter Exchange,* 2125 Mt. Vernon St, Philadelphia, PA 19130.

Booklet, Smith Premier Typewriter Co, diecut typewriter shape, 6 pp **$30.00**
Booklet, *The Typewriter: A Short History,* Zellers, 1873–1948 . . . . **7.00**
Brochure, Oliver Typewriter Co, Chicago, New Model 9 Typewriter, 1922, 8½ x 10½" opened size **8.00**
Catalog, Oliver Typewriter Co, Chicago, c1902, 24 pp **75.00**
Ribbon Tin, American Brand, 2½" d **10.00**
Ribbon Tin, Amneco, 2½ x 2½". **8.00**
Ribbon Tin, Battleship Brand, 2⅛ x 2⅛" **15.00**
Ribbon Tin, Bundy, 2½" d **12.00**
Ribbon Tin, Columbia classic, 2¼ x 2¼" **12.00**
Ribbon Tin, Deluxe, 2½ x 2½". **6.00**
Ribbon Tin, Flint Brand, 2¼ x 2¼" **5.00**
Ribbon Tin, 2½ x 2½" **5.00**
Ribbon Tin, Hercules, 2½ x 2½" **7.00**

Ribbon Tin, Chieftain, 2⅝ x ¾", $357.50. Photo courtesy Wm. Morford.

Ribbon Tin, Kleenertype, 2½ x 2½" **6.00**
Typewriter, Bar-Lock, copper fancy front. **350.00**
Typewriter, Bennett Junior **100.00**
Typewriter, Century 10 . . . . **50.00**
Typewriter, Corona, folding, with tripold stand **100.00**
Typewriter, Corona, 4-row, animal keyboard **100.00**
Typewriter, Emerson, 3 row, pivot frontstrike. **150.00**
Typewriter, Hammond, curved keyboard **150.00**
Typewriter, Hammond, Multiplex, straight keyboard **60.00**
Typewriter, Keaton Music Typewriter **300.00**
Typewriter, Pittsburgh Visible, #11 . . . . **50.00**
Typewriter, Remington, #5, upstrike **150.00**
Typewriter, Remington, Rem-Blick, Baby-Rem **85.00**

UMBRELLAS

Umbrellas suffer a sorry fate. They are generally forgotten and discarded. Their handles are removed and collected as separate entities or attached to magnifying glasses. Given the protection they have provided, they deserve better.

Look for umbrellas that have advertising on the fabric. Political candidates often gave away umbrellas to win votes. Today baseball teams have umbrella days to win fans.

Seek out unusual umbrellas in terms of action or shape. A collection of folding umbrellas, especially those from the 1950s, is worth considering.

Advertising, Coca-Cola **$25.00**
Beach, multicolored **5.00**
Character, Davy Crockett, vinyl **85.00**
Child's, New York World's Fair, multicolored, 1939, 28" d **40.00**
Folding Type **3.00**
Man's, black cloth, figural golf club handle **45.00**
Plastic, child's, pink, plastic handle **2.00**
Plastic, dome shape, clear, 1960–70s **20.00**
Silk, plastic handle **5.00**
Silk, wooden handle, striped **8.00**

UNITED STATES MARINE CORPS

A recent survey indicated that there are currently over 2,000,000 former United States Marines. Not many of these former (never "ex") Marines can—or will—allow the U.S.M.C. insignia, commonly referred to as the "Eagle, Globe and Anchor," go unnoticed when they see it today. It may be on the cover of a book or magazine, the side of a toy truck or train, on a recruiting or movie poster, printed or embroidered on many types of wall hangings or tapestries or many other formats than can be mentioned here. A great many of these former Marines and countless other militaria collectors are constantly in search of almost any items that relate to or were used at some point by U.S. Marines. Toy soldiers, Guidebooks for Marines, toys of all types, U.S.M.C. or the Eagle, Globe and Anchor are all in demand to these collectors. Some of these items have little monetary value, but whether it be monetary or sentimental worth, collectors of United States Marine memorabilia and collectibles are out in great numbers. If you have any of the above mentioned items or others not listed and would like to dispose of them, please let me know. Semper Fidelis!

Advisor: Stan Clark, 915 Fairview Ave., Gettysburg, PA 17325, (717) 337-1728, Fax ((717) 337-0581, e-mail: usmc@mail.wideopen.net.

Emblem, wood, carved, 15 x 19", $75.00.

Book, *Guidebook for US Marines,* 1967 . . . . **$30.00**
Book, *Heroes, U. S. Marine Corp* **100.00**
Carte de Visite, Civil War Marine **250.00**
Collar Discs, pr, WWI **75.00**
Decanter, Jim Beam, "Devil Dog" **25.00**
Decanter, Jim Beam, "Once A Marine, Always A Marine" **25.00**
Doll, Stars and Stripes Barbie and Ken, in blue dress USMC uniforms. **40.00**
Doll, Vintage GI Joe Action Marine, complete, orig box **150.00**
Figure, bulldog, chalkware **40.00**
Helmet, WWI 4th Marine Brigade, painted insignia **150.00**
Jet, litho tin, made in Japan **75.00**
Letter, handwritten, General John A Lejeune **250.00**
Lobby Card Set, *Call Out the Marines* **75.00**
Medal, Good Conduct, USMC, engraved owner's name and dates, WWI **30.00**
Movie Poster, *Devil Dogs of the Air* **300.00**
Movie Poster, *Fighting Devil Dogs,* 27 x 41" **200.00**
Movie Poster, *Sands of Iwo Jima,* 27 x 41" **200.00**
Pillowcase, USMC, WWI/WWII, colorful, mother, sister, sweetheart **25.00**
Pillowcase Cover, Camp Lejeune, WWII. **15.00**
Playset, Marine Beachhead, Marx, complete with box. **250.00**
Playset, Sands of Iwo Jima, Marx, complete with box **75.00**
Postcard, real photo, WWI Marine **12.50**
Record, *The Making of a Marine,* 1960s **10.00**
Recruiting Poster, paper, "Be A U.S. Marine," James Montgomery Flagg. **300.00**
Recruiting Poster, "Enlist Now—U. S. Marines," Iwo Jima, Guadalcanal, Saipan, Arawa, Bouganville, WWII **150.00**
Statue, Iwo Jima, pewter, Danbury Mint, 5½ x 7½". **40.00**
Sweetheart Doll, dress blues **35.00**
Sweetheart Necklace, USMC emblem, WWII **25.00**
Sword, Mamelule Marine Officer's, German **200.00**
Sword, Marine NCO, with scabbard, German. **150.00**
Train Set, Land, Air and Sea, Lionel **400.00**
Uniform, USMC, WWI **150.00**
Vehicle, USMC Amphibious, metal, 22" l **65.00**

UNIVERSAL POTTERY

Universal Potteries of Cambridge, Ohio, was organized in 1934 by The Oxford Pottery Company. It purchased the Atlas-Globe plant properties. The Atlas-Globe operation was a merger of the Atlas China Company (formerly Crescent China Company in 1921, Tritt in 1912, and Bradshaw in 1902) and the Globe China Company.

Even after the purchase, Universal retained the Oxford ware, made in Oxford, Ohio, as part of its dinnerware line. Another Oxford plant was used to manufacture tiles. The plant at Niles, Ohio, was dismantled.

Three of Universal's most popular lines were Ballerina, Calico Fruit, and Cattail. Both Calico Fruit and Cattail had many accessory pieces. The 1940 and 1941 Sears catalogs listed an oval wastebasket, breakfast set, kitchen scale, linens, and bread box in the Cattail pattern. Unfortunately, the Calico Fruit decal has not held up well over time. Collectors may have to settle for less than perfect pieces.

Not all Universal pottery carried the Universal name as part of the backstamp. Wares marked "Harmony House," "Sweet William/Sears Roebuck and Co.," and "Wheelock Peoria" are part of the Universal production line. Wheelock was a department store in Peoria, Illinois, that controlled the Cattail pattern on the Old Holland shape.

Ballerina, bowl, 36s **$8.00**
Ballerina, creamer. **5.00**
Ballerina, eggcup **10.00**
Ballerina, mug **12.00**
Ballerina, pie baker, 10" d **10.00**
Ballerina, platter, 13" d **10.00**
Ballerina, teapot, 6 cup **25.00**
Ballerina, tidbit tray, 2 tier **10.00**
Bittersweet, creamer **6.00**
Bittersweet, cup **6.00**
Bittersweet, dish, lug handle **5.00**
Bittersweet, mixing bowl, 2 qt **12.00**
Bittersweet, plate, 7⅞" d **5.00**
Bittersweet, platter, 13½" l **15.00**
Bittersweet, stack set, round, 4 pc **45.00**
Calico Fruit, jug, cov. **40.00**
Calico Fruit, refrigerator set, 3 round jars, 4", 5", and 6" **45.00**
Calico Fruit, soup bowl, tab handle **6.00**
Camwood, casserole, emb lug handle, 9½" d **20.00**
Camwood, cup and saucer **6.00**
Camwood, gravy boat **12.00**
Camwood, grill plate, 9¾" d **12.00**
Cattail, casserole, cov, 8¼" d **15.00**
Cattail, gravy boat **20.00**
Cattail, platter, oval **20.00**
Mount Vernon, creamer **10.00**
Mount Vernon, cup and saucer **5.00**
Mount Vernon, teapot **30.00**
Netherlands, cup and saucer **5.00**

Ballerina, sugar, cov, burgundy, $12.00.

URINALS

When you gotta go, you gotta go—any port in a storm. You have been in enough bathrooms to know that all plumbing fixtures are not equal.

The human mind has just begun to explore the recycling potential of hospital bedpans. Among the uses noted are flower planters, food serving utensils, and dispersal units at the bottom of down spouts. How have you used them? Send your ideas and pictures of them in action to the Bedpan Recycling Project, 5093 Vera Cruz Road, Emmaus, PA 18049.

VALENTINES

There is far too much emphasis placed on adult valentines from the 19th century through the 1930s. It's true they are lacy and loaded with romantic sentiment. But, are they fun? No!

Fun can be found in children's valentines, a much neglected segment of the valentine market. If you decide to collect them, focus on the 1920 through 1960 period penny valentines. The artwork is bold, vibrant, exciting, and a tad corny. This is what makes them fun.

There is another good reason to collect 20th century children's valentines. They are affordable. Most sell for less than $2, with many good examples in the 50¢ range. They often show up at flea markets as a hoard. When you find them, make an offer for the whole lot. You won't regret it.

Club: National Valentine Collectors Assoc., P.O. Box 1404, Santa Ana, CA 92702.

Greeting Card, Art Nouveau, heart shape **$5.00**
Greeting Card, "Best Valentine Wishes," woman wearing winter clothes reading card, c1920 . . . . **1.50**
Greeting Card, Dainty Dimples Series **5.00**
Greeting Card, diecut, "Valentine's Greetings," Germany **7.00**
Greeting Card, fold-out, "To My Sweetheart," cupid holding package, red tissue paper, 8" h. **7.50**
Greeting Card, "Hearts Are Ripe," children picking heart shaped apples **5.00**
Greeting Card, honeycomb, "Cupid's Temple of Love," c1928 . . . . **15.00**
Greeting Card, "Lady Killer," A J Fisher, NY, c1850 . . . . **30.00**
Greeting Card, mechanical, "Such Is Married Life," c1950 . . . . **45.00**
Greeting Card, "Remember Me, Yours Forever," printed poem, paper lace, c1900 . . . . **2.00**
Greeting Card, standup, Little Lulu and Tubby **15.00**

Greeting Card, Bang Gum wrapper, adv, Frank Fleer Corp, Philadelphia, PA, USA, 1930s, 5¼ x 5", $77.00. Photo courtesy Past Tyme Pleasures.

Greeting Card, "To My Sweetheart, boy in striped shirt playing rugby, c1920 . . . . . **1.50**
Greeting Card, "Valentine's Forever," flower dec **2.00**
Postcard, "A Valentine Reminder," verse on bottom, red hearts, woman with valentine, John Winsch **18.00**
Postcard, "February 14th," heart with cupids, green ivy trim, Germany, 1910 . . . . . **1.50**
Postcard, "My Valentine Think Of Me" **3.00**
Postcard, "St Valentine's Greetings," Clapsaddle, sgd **5.00**
Postcard, "To My Sweet Valentine," sepia tones **1.50**
Postcard, "To My Valentine," Gibson girl on swing, on gilded ground **2.00**
Postcard, "To My Valentine," cupids holding garland of hearts, London, 1910 . . . . . **1.50**
Postcard, "To My Valentine," top verse with pumpkin head man and woman seated on bench **5.00**

VENTRILOQUIST DUMMIES

Ventriloquist dummies have been very popular throughout the last sixty years. Even though ventriloquism itself dates back to ancient times, it really wasn't until the popularity of Edgar Bergen and Charlie McCarthy that ventriloquism became as popular as it did. Ironically they became popular on the radio, which is very strange since Edgar was a ventriloquist and Charlie was his wisecracking sidekick piece of wood. Charlie's popularity was so great that they licensed many items, including tin toys by Marx, puppets, dummies, glasses, spoons, books, soap, records, pins, paddle balls, game, and just about any other popular toy you could think of. Since many of these items were made around 1937 in the height of their popularity, they are very old and now very collectible, especially the composition dummies and puppets. Edgar also had two other very popular follow-up characters to Charlie. They were Mortimer Snerd and Effie Klinker. They too had many licensed products based on their popularity.

After Bergen and McCarthy came Paul Winchell and Jerry Mahoney with their TV series called *Winchell/Mahoney Time* during the 1950s. Jerry also became extremely popular and soon after, Paul added another sidekick named Knucklehead Smiff. They had dummies, puppets, hand puppets, toys, keychains, and many more items. Another very popular ventriloquist was Jimmy Nelson with his sidekick Danny O'Day. He became popular on the *Milton Berle Texaco Star Theatre Show*. He also had dummies, toys, and many other licensed products. He then followed up the success of his Danny O'Day with another memorable character named Farfel, who was the Nestle's chocolate dog on the commercials for years.

You can still find many amazing and interesting items on ventriloquism and ventriloquists, including photos, playbills, and professional or mass produced toy dummies. I have the best luck at flea markets, antique shows, and when I travel I find a lot of interesting items.

Advisor: Andy Gross, P.O. Box 6134, Beverly Hills, CA 90212-1134, (310) 820-3308, e-mail: pop@LAmagictoy.com.

Note: Listings are for items MIB.

Charlie McCarthy, dummy, Effanbee, 1937 . . . . . **$950.00**
Charlie McCarthy, dummy, Juro, c1960 to present **50.00**
Charlie McCarthy, hand puppet, Ideal, composition, c1937 . . . . . **300.00**

Mickey Mouse, Horsman, hollow body, head stick with trigger for mouth, red jacket, black tux with tails, 1970s, $350.00.

Charlie McCarthy, Jim Beam Whiskey decanter, c1970s **200.00**
Charlie McCarthy, puppet, cardboard, movable mouth and eyes, c1937 . . . . . **450.00**
Charlie McCarthy, tin windup, Marx, c1937 . . . . . **900.00**
Danny O'Day, dummy, Jimmy Nelson's Danny O'Day, Texaco outfit, c1950s **750.00**
Danny O'Day, dummy, Juro, plastic, headstick **350.00**
Danny O'Day, dummy, Juro, string behind neck **65.00**
Dummy Dan, dummy, composition, c1920s **450.00**
Humphrey Higsby, dummy, Jimmy Nelson's, half glasses . . **1,000.00**
Humphrey Higsby, hand puppet, Jimmy Nelson Enterprise, soft vinyl, ©JNE Inc, c1952 . . . . . **250.00**
Jerry Mahoney, dummy, Juro, composition, green suit with tag, c1950s, 24" h **600.00**
Jerry Mahoney, dummy, Paul Winchell, c1966, 24" h **600.00**
Knucklehead Smiff, dummy, Juro, with tag, 1950s 825.00
Knucklehead Smiff, hand puppet, Paul Winchell, vinyl, 1966 . . . . . **150.00**
Jerry Mahoney, hand puppet, beanie cap, moving mouth, c1950s **170.00**
Jerry Mahoney, hand puppet, Juro, green suit **185.00**
Jerry Mahoney, hand puppet, Paul Winchell, vinyl, 1966 . . . . **125.00**
Moe, The Three Stooges, dummy, Horsman, hollow body, headstick with trigger for mouth, c1970s **425.00**
Mortimer Snerd, dummy, c1960 to present **50.00**
Mortimer Snerd, figural Jim Beam Whiskey decanter, 1970s **185.00**
Mortimer Snerd, hand puppet, Ideal, composition, c1937 . . . . . **350.00**
Mortimer Snerd, puppet, cardboard, movable mouth and eyes, c1937 . . . . . **475.00**
Mortimer Snerd, tin windup, Tricky Car, Marx, c1937 . . . . **1,200.00**
Simon Sez, dummy, Horsman, hollow body, headstick with trigger, c1970s **425.00**

VERNON KILNS

Founded in Vernon, California, in 1912, Poxon China was one of the many small potteries flourishing in southern California. By 1931 it was sold to Faye G. Bennison and renamed Vernon Kilns, but it was also known as Vernon Potteries Ltd. Under Bennison's direction, the company became a leader in the pottery industry.

The high quality and versatility of its product made Vernon ware very popular. Besides a varied dinnerware line, Vernon Kilns also produced Walt Disney figurines and advertising, political, and fraternal items. One popular line was historical and commemorative plates, which included several plate series featuring scenes from England, California missions, and the West.

Surviving the Depression, fires, earthquakes, and wars, Vernon Kilns could not compete with the influx of imports. In January, 1958, the factory was closed. Metlox Potteries of Manhattan Beach, California, bought the tradename and molds along with the remaining stock.

Newsletter: *Vernon Views,* P.O. Box 945, Scottsdale, AZ 85252.

Periodical: *The Pottery Collectors Express,* P.O. Box 221, Mayview, MO 54071.

Brown-Eyed Susan, casserole, individual . . . **$35.00**
Brown-Eyed Susan, chop plate, 12" d . . . **25.00**
Brown-Eyed Susan, cup and saucer . . . **12.00**
Brown-Eyed Susan, gravy boat . . . **20.00**
Brown-Eyed Susan, soup bowl . . . **18.00**
Chatelaine, bread and butter plate . . . **12.00**
Chatelaine, cup and saucer . . . **20.00**
Chatelaine, salad bowl, 12" d . . . **50.00**
Coronado, bread and butter plate . . . **4.00**
Coronado, creamer . . . **10.00**
Coronado, dessert dish, 5½" d . . . **5.50**
Coronado, soup bowl . . . **12.00**
Coronado, tumbler . . . **5.00**
Homespun, pitcher, 2 qt . . . **45.00**
Melinda, casserole, 8" d . . . **40.00**
Melinda, chop plate, 12" d . . . **20.00**
Melinda, eggcup . . . **15.00**
Melinda, salad bowl, 12½" d . . . **50.00**
Moby Dick, bread and butter plate, blue, 6" d . . . **18.00**
Moby Dick, dinner plate, blue, 9" d . . . **60.00**
Modern California, creamer, azure . . . **18.00**
Modern California, luncheon plate, pistachio, 9½" d . . . **15.00**
Organdie, chop plate, 14" d . . . **55.00**
Organdie, tumbler, 14 oz . . . 28.00
Tickled Pink, butter, ¼ lb . . . **25.00**
Tickled Pink, chop plate, 13" d . . . **20.00**
Tickled Pink, fruit dish . . . **5.00**
Tickled Pink, gravy boat . . . **15.00**
Tickled Pink, jug, 1 qt . . . **20.00**
Tickled Pink, tidbit tray, 2 tier . . . **15.00**
Tradewinds, dinner plate, 10" d . . . **15.00**

VIDEO GAMES

At the moment, most video games sold at a flea market are being purchased for reuse. There are a few collectors, but their numbers are small.

It might be interesting to speculate at this point on the long-term collecting potential of electronic children's games, especially since the Atari system has come and gone. The key to any toy is playability. A video game cartridge has little collecting value unless it can be put into a machine and played. As a result, the long-term value of video games will rest on collectors' ability to keep the machines that use them in running order. Given today's tendency to scrap rather than repair a malfunctioning machine, one wonders if there will be any individuals in 2041 that will understand how video game machines work and, if so, be able to get the parts required to play them.

Next to playability, displayability is important to any collector. How do you display video games? Is the answer to leave the TV screen on twenty-four hours a day?

Video games are a fad waiting to be replaced by the next fad. There will always be a small cadre of players who will keep video games alive, just as there is a devoted group of adventure game players. But given the number of video game cartridges sold, they should be able to fill their collecting urges relatively easily.

What this means is that if you are going to buy video game cartridges at a flea market, buy them for reuse and do not pay more than a few dollars. The more recent the game, the more you will pay. Wait. Once a few years have passed, the sellers will just be glad to get rid of them.

VIEW-MASTER

William Gruber invented and Sawyer's Inc., of Portland, Oregon, manufactured and marketed the first View-Master viewers and reels in 1939. The company survived the shortages of World War II by supplying training materials in the View-Master format to the army and navy.

Immediately following World War II a 1,000-dealer network taxed the capacity of the Sawyer plant. In 1946 the Model C, the most common of the viewers, was introduced. Sawyer was purchased by General Aniline & Film Corporation in 1966. After passing through other hands, View-Master wound up as part of Ideal Toys.

Do not settle for any viewer or reel in less than near-mint condition. Original packaging, especially reel envelopes, is very important. The category is still in the process of defining which reels are valuable and which are not. Most older, pre-1975, reels sell in the 50¢ to $1 range.

Club: National Stereoscopic Assoc., P.O. Box 14801, Columbus, OH 43214.

Camera, Personal 3-D, custom film cutter . . . **$175.00**
Projector, Sawyer's, plastic, single lens . . . **10.00**
Projector, Stereomatic 500, 3-D, 2 lens, carrying case . . . **250.00**
Reel, #26, Grand Canyon . . . **2.00**
Reel, #62, Hawaiian Hula Dancers . . . **3.00**
Reel, #92, Oregon Caves National Monument . . . **2.00**
Reel, #101, Rocky Mountain National Park . . . **2.00**
Reel, #137, Washington DC . . . **3.00**
Reel, #151, Columbia River Highway, OR . . . **1.00**
Reel, #196, Grand Coulee Dam, Washington, 1949 . . . **2.00**
Reel, #253, Carlsbad Caverns National Park . . . **4.00**
Reel, #338, Lookout Mountain, Chattanooga, TN . . . **1.00**
Reel, #501, Mexico City and Vicinity . . . **3.00**
Reel, #510, Lake Pitzcuaro and Paricutin Volcano . . . **6.00**

Reel, #955, Hopalong Cassidy, $5.00.

Reel, #623, Ruins of Pachacamac 20.00
Reel, #942, Life with the Cowboys. 2.00
Reel, #3308, People of the Nile Valley, Egypt 3.00
Reel, #9055, Prehistoric Cliff Dwellers of Mesa Verde. 5.00
Reel, #SAM-1, Adventures of Tom Sawyer 4.00
Reel, #SP-9039, San Diego, CA, 1949 . . . . 1.00
Reel Set, #A-102, Eskimos of Alaska 8.00
Reel Set, #A-81, Los Angeles, CA, Edition B 6.00
Reel Set, #A-360, Arizona, State Tour Series 6.00
Reel Set, #A-635, Historic Philadelphia, Edition A 12.00
Reel Set, #B-146, Castles of Europe 10.00
Reel Set, #B-215, Grand Tour of Asia 15.00
Reel Set, #B-343, Mark Twain's Huckleberry Finn 30.00
Reel Set, #B-503, Dark Shadows, Edition A, 1968. . . . . 20.00
Reel Set, #B-610, Butterflies of North America 6.00
Reel Set, #BB-432, Treasure Island 6.00
Reel Set, #CH-6A, B, and C, Birth of Jesus 3.00
Reel Set, #EA-1, 2, and 3, Easter Story 4.00
Reel Set, #FT-31A, B, and C, Christmas Carol 3.00
Viewer, Model F, lighted, dark brown plastic, pressure bar on top 18.00
Viewer, Model H, GAF, lighted, round bottom, front logo, 1967-81 . . . . 15.00

VOGUE PICTURE RECORDS

Vogue picture records are attracting the interest of a growing number of collectors. They were invented by Tom Saffady and manufactured by his company Sav-Way Industries in Detroit, Michigan in 1946–1947. These innovative high quality 78 rpm records were constructed with a central aluminum core for durability. A colorful paper illustration covering the entire record was applied to the core and then sealed in clear vinyl.

The beautiful multicolored pictures are often romantic, at times whimsical, and frequently represent the song title. A small black-and-white photo of the artist appears as an insert at the margin of the illustration. The regular production Vogues were issued with a number in the range R707 to R788.

A wide variety of music can be found on Vogue picture records, including big band swing, jazz, country, Latin, fairy tales for children, and even dance illustrations. Seven albums each containing two records are known to have been released. Unfortunately, the record division of Sav-Way Industries was forced into bankruptcy after only fifteen months of production, somewhat limiting the availability of these attractive and highly collectible records.

Advisor: John Coates, 324 Woodland Dr., Stevens Point, WI 54481, (715) 341-6113.

Note: Prices listed for records in good average used condition.

R708, *S'posin'/I Surrender Dear,* The King's Jesters and Louise. $95.00
R720, *Grandpa's Gettin' Younger Ev'ry Day/Time Will Tell,* Lulu Belle & Scotty 75.00
R722, *Tear It Down/Put That Ring on My Finger,* Clyde McCoy & His Orchestra. 60.00
R726, *Rhapsody in Blue—Part II/Blue Skies,* The Hour of Charm All Girl Orchestra 55.00
R730, *All Through The Day/Piper's Junction,* Art Mooney & His Orchestra 65.00
R732, *I Don't Know Why/In the Moonmist,* Art Mooney & His Orchestra 75.00

R733, *Blue Skies/ Seville,* The Hour of Charm All Girls Orchestra and Choir, $25.00.

R738, *Rhumba Lesson No 2/Give Me All Of Your Heart,* Paul Shahin/Dick La Salle & His Society Orchestra 65.00
R744, *Don't Tetch It/Flat River, Missouri,* Nancy Lee & The Hilltoppers/Judy & Jen 65.00
R746, *The Trial Of "Bumble" The Bee Part II/The Boy Who Cried Wolf Part II,* The Jewell Playhouse, directed by James Jewel. 85.00
R752, *Baby, What You Do To Me/(Ah Yes) There's Good Blues Tonight,* Clyde McCoy & His Orchestra 75.00
R755, *Serenade To A Pair Of Nylons/Broadjump,* The Charlie Shavers Quintet 75.00
R761, *Go West, Young Man, Go West/More Than You Know,* Joan Edwards 75.00
R764, *Whatta Ya Gonna Do!/I Guess I'll Get The Papers,* Shep Fields & His Orchestra. 85.00
R767, *This Is Always/Love Means The Same Old Thing,* Joan Edwards 65.00
R772, *Sniffle Song/All By Myself,* Frankie Masters & His Orchestra 75.00
R775, *Clementine/I Love You In The Daytime Too,* Sonny Dunham & His Orchestra 75.00
R776, *Majercita/Vem Vem,* Enric Madriguera & His Orchestra 75.00
R777, *La Rumbita Tropical/Tiqui Tiqui Tan,* Enric Madriguera & His Orchestra 75.00
R781, *Sooner Or Later/I Love You (For Sentimental Reasons),* Art Kassel & His Orchestra 55.00
R785, *The Echo Said No/My Adobe Hacienda,* Art Kassel & His Orchestra 65.00

WADE CERAMICS

Red Rose Tea issued several series of small Wade animals. Like many of my other collections, I will not be happy until I have multiple sets. "Drink more tea" is the order of the day at my office. How much simpler it would be just to make a list of the missing Wades and pick them up at flea markets where they sell in the 50¢ to $1 range.

Club: Wade Watch, 8199 Pierson Ct., Arvada, CO 80005.

Ashtray, tortoise center $30.00
Bank, Thomas the Tank Engine, blue. 60.00
Basket, Gothic 95.00
Butter Dish, cov, Basket Ware 38.00
Candle Holder, Disney Light series, panda, 1960s 50.00
Commemorative, vase, Charles and Diana 55.00
Creamer and Sugar, Copper Luster. 32.00

Dish, "Remember? Broadway" **10.00**
Frame, heart shaped, emb flower and leaves **60.00**
Pipe Rest, German Shepherd **25.00**
Pitcher, rabbit and trees, emb, green, Heath **80.00**
Red Rose Tea Premium, Corgi **9.00**
Red Rose Tea Premium, lion **6.00**
Red Rose Tea Premium, Little Jack Horner **6.00**
Red Rose Tea Premium, otter **7.00**
Red Rose Tea Premium, Queen of Hearts **15.00**
Red Rose Tea Premium, rabbit **8.00**
Red Rose Tea Premium, squirrel **5.00**
Red Rose Tea Premium, wild boar **2.00**
Salt and Pepper Shakers, pr, Mr and Mrs Penguin **360.00**
Souvenir, turtle, mkd "Devil's Hole, Bermuda" **20.00**
St Bruno Tobacco Premium, St Bernard **20.00**
Tankard, barrel **15.00**
Teapot, Bramble Ware **90.00**

WALL POCKETS

The wall pocket—what can be said? What is a wall pocket? My mother used them for plants. A "rooter" she called them. Now they are used as match holders and places for accumulating small junk.

Most of the common wall pockets were produced between the 1930s and 1960s; though there are some that date to the Victorian era. Wallpockets can be made of wood, tin, glass or ceramic. Ceramic examples have been produced both domestically and abroad. Wall pockets come in all shapes and sizes, but all have a small hole on the back side for the insertion of the wall hook.

Dirt build-up and staining is very common, albeit most collectors prefer them to be neat and clean. Carefully check any wall pocket prior to purchase; dirt can hide cracked or broken areas as well as common household repairs.

Club: Wall Pocket Collectors Club, 1356 Taniti, St. Louis, MO 63128.

California Pottery, dust pan, inverted **$12.00**
Camark, cat, climbing wall **35.00**
Czechoslovakia, bird at well, mkd "Made in Czechoslovakia 5676 A" **48.00**
Frankoma, acorn, light brown, mkd "Frankoma 190" **20.00**
Frankoma, cowboy boot, blue and white speckled **24.00**
Hull, flying goose, 8" h **45.00**
Hull, whisk broom, Sunglow, 5½" h **50.00**
Japan, baby and diaper, mkd "4921, Japan" **12.00**
Japan, parrot and pink flowers, hp, Japanese lusterware **40.00**
L & F Ceramics, broom, inverted, mkd "L & F Ceramics ©Hollywood, Hand Made" **20.00**
Made In Japan, geese, basketweave and palm tree background **25.00**
McCoy, apple, 7" h **25.00**
Morton Potteries, cockateel, #578 . . . . **18.00**
Morton Potteries, peacock, 6½" h **20.00**
Red Wing, cornucopia, pink, mkd "Red Wing 441" **30.00**
Roseville, apple blossom, blue, 8½" h **150.00**
Roseville, magnolia, 8½" h **120.00**
Royal Copley, angel, 6" h **20.00**
Royal Copley, cocker spaniel **15.00**
Royal Copley, walking rooster, 5½" h **25.00**
Shawnee, teapot, pink apple dec **25.00**
Treasure Craft, elf on bucket **12.00**
West Coast Pottery, peacock **45.00**

WALLACE NUTTING

Wallace Nutting (1861–1941) was America's most famous photographer of the early twentieth century. A retired minister, Nutting took more than 50,000 pictures, keeping 10,000 of his best and destroying the rest. His most popular and best-selling scenes included exterior scenes (apple blossoms, calm streams, and rural American countrysides), interior scenes (usually featuring a colonial woman working near a hearth), and foreign scenes (typically thatch-roofed cottages). His poorest selling pictures, which have become today's rarest and most highly collectible pictures, are classified as miscellaneous unusual scenes and include categories not included above: animals, architecturals, children, florals, men, seascapes, and snow scenes. Process prints are 1930s machine-produced reprints of twelve of Nutting's most popular pictures. These have minimal value and can be detected by using a magnifying glass. Nutting sold millions of his hand-colored platinotype pictures between 1900 and his death in 1941.

While attempting to seek out the finest and best early American furniture as props for his colonial interior scenes, Nutting became an expert in early American antiques. He published nearly twenty books in his lifetime, including his ten-volume State Beautiful series, and various other books on furniture, photography, clocks, and his personal biography. He also became widely known for his reproduction furniture. His furniture shop reproduced hundreds of different furniture forms, all clearly marked with a distinctive paper label glued directly to the piece or his block or script signature brand.

The overall synergy of the Wallace Nutting name—pictures, books, and furniture—has made anything Wallace Nutting quite collectible.

Club: Wallace Nutting Collectors Club, 2944 Ivanhoe Glen, Madison, WI 53711.

Birthday Card, narrow stream and tall trees scene over 4-line verse **$260.00**
Book, *England Beautiful,* 1st ed, green cov **55.00**
Book, *Furniture Treasury,* 1928–9, Vol 1–3 . . . . **350.00**
Book, *Pennsylvania Beautiful,* 1st ed, dj, 1924 . . . . **35.00**
Furniture, ladderback side chair, #392 . . . . **200.00**
Furniture, Windsor side chair, bowback, #305 . . . . **725.00**
Furniture, Windsor stool, oval, paper label **225.00**
Furniture, Windsor tripod candlestand, #17, block branded signature **475.00**

Print, The Meeting Place, $2,255.00. Photo courtesy Michael Ivankovich Antiques, Inc.

Print, A Fleck of Sunshine, 14 x 17" 250.00
Print, A Friendly Reception, 11 x 14" 130.00
Print, Affectionately Yours, 18 x 22" 180.00
Print, An Elm Birch Arch, 14 x 20" 95.00
Print, An Old Drawing Room, 12 x 16" 45.00
Print, Birch Brook, 13 x 16" 85.00
Print, Cathedral Brook, 9 x 11" 50.00
Print, Farm Borders, 10 x 16" 70.00
Print, Flush Banks, 10 x 12" 55.00
Print, Hollyhock Cottage, 13 x 16" 135.00
Print, LaJolla, 13 x 16" 70.00
Print, Larkspur, 11 x 14" 75.00
Print, Provincetown Hollyhocks, 13 x 16" 150.00
Print, The Coming Out of Rosa, 14 x 17" 130.00
Print, The Italian Spring, 10 x 13" 65.00
Print, The Lane to Uncle Jonathan's, 10 x 16" 115.00
Print, The Maple Sugar Cupboard, 16 x 20" 150.00
Print, The Way of the Blessed, 18 x 22" 115.00
Print, Towards the Mountains, 13 x 16" 65.00

WASH DAY COLLECTIBLES

I keep telling my wife that women's liberation has taken all the fun out of washing and ironing. She quickly informs me that it was never fun to begin with. The large piles of unironed clothes around the house are ample proof.

Wash day material is a favorite of advertising collectors. Decorators have a habit of using it in bathroom decor. Is there a message here?

Activity Book, Gold Dust Twins At Work and Play, color cov, 20 pp, 1904 . . . . $50.00
Advertising Trade Card, Adams Steam Carpet Cleaning 15.00
Advertising Trade Card, Gold Dust Washing Powder, diecut, 1890s, 3 x 3½" 35.00
Carpet Beater, wire, braided loop, wood handle 25.00
Catalog, National Washboard Co, 36 pp, c1925 . . . . 100.00
Catalog, Savage Arms Corp, Freedom from All Washday Bondage, 16 pp, c1930 . . . . 35.00
Clothes Dasher, Ward Vacuum Washer 35.00
Clothespin, carved, late 19th C 10.00
Clothespin Bag, cotton, wire handle 10.00
Dustpan, tin, tubular handle, 8" w 40.00
Fan, Gold Dust & Fairy Soap, Gold Dust Twins overlooking 1904 World's Fair 70.00
Iron, Ober, #12, open handle holes, emb 15.00
Label, broom, Winner, woman holding torch 50
Laundry Basket, woven splint, rim handles, oval 35.00

Box, Gold Dust Washing Powder, "Lever Brothers Company, New York, N.Y., U.S.A.," cardboard, with contents, $50.00. Price for pair. Photo courtesy Collectors Auction Services.

Magazine Tear Sheet, Preston's Braided Wire Carpet Whip, *House Furniture Review,* Dec 1910 . . . . 8.00
Scrub Board, wooden, handmade, orig paint 110.00
Sign, Borax Dry Soap, metal, red and white 45.00
Sign, Gold Dust Washing Powder, 1900, 8 x 11" 75.00
Sign, Kitchen Kleanzer, cardboard 45.00
Sign, Rising Sun Stove Polish, "A Thing of Beauty Is A Joy Forever," 1880s, 13 x 29" 650.00
Sticker, New York Housewares, Atlantic City, Art Deco design, emb, blue and white 5.00
Wash Stick, 36" l 12.00

WASHING MACHINES

For collection purposes clothes washing machines fall into two distinct categories; automatic and wringer. This category pertains to the collection of vintage automatic washers. Automatic washers fill themselves with water, wash and rinse the clothes, extract the water from both the clothes and the machine and turn themselves off without any help from the operator, whereas laundry operations with wringer machines are performed manually.

Bendix sold the very first automatic washer in 1938. It was a front loading washer, called the Model S. It had to be bolted to the floor to keep it from jumping into the air during the spin cycle. Blackstone and Westinghouse were about to market their very first automatic washers in 1941 when World War II forced a halt in domestic appliance production as factories converted to supply materials for the war effort. In 1947 automatic washers from Frigidaire, Thor, Blackstone, GE, Westinghouse, Launderall, AMC, Kenmore and the 1900 Corporation (soon to become Whirlpool) appeared for the very first time, but they were extremely expensive, hard to get and long waiting lists formed to purchase one the these new machines. The automatic washer became quite popular by the early 1950s, even though its cleaning ability was below that of a wringer washer. The conveniences of having an automatic washer well outweighed its limitations. Bendix pioneered another first in 1953, the combination washer/dryer, which was a front loading machine. It did both washing and drying in one machine. In the 1950s the styling of automatics was similar to cars, with heavy usage of chrome, lighted dials, audible signals, windows in the lids, and cabinet colors such as pink, turquoise, pastel yellow, and sea foam green (the yellow and green colors of the 1950s were very different than the harvest gold and avocado colors of the 1970s). Famous industrial designers were brought in to stylize their machines such as Raymond Lowey, who was hired by Frigidaire in the 1940s and 50s.

Vintage 1940s and 50s automatic washers are now extremely rare. They were complicated machines of a new technology and they tended to break down more than any other home appliance. Modern restoration of the automatics is quite time consuming and expensive as national searches for original factory parts must be performed. Most of these vintage parts haven't been available for over thirty years. To keep up the value of a machine, restoration of either the mechanics or aesthetics must be done by an expert in this field; anything else greatly reduced its value. Having the matching dryer to go with the washer will certainly add to its value, but vintage dryers were less complicated and they are still easy to find.

Advisor: Robert Seger, 3629 15th Ave. South, Minneapolis, MN 55407, (612) 729-7561, e-mail: Robert.seger@AEXP.com.

Frigidaire, Model WL-60, 1949, $300.00.

Club: Maytag Collectors Club, 960 Reynolds Dr., Ripon, CA 95366.

Note: Prices listed for machines in complete, unrestored condition. They are in good shape aesthetically and mechanically.

ABC-O-Matic, window lid models, 1950–1958 . . . . **300.00**
ABC-O-Matic, windowless lid models, 1950–1958 . . . . **200.00**
AMC and AMC Coronado, orig model with round glass lid, 1947 . . . . **200.00**
AMC and AMC Coronado, 1950–1959 . . . . **50.00**
AMC and AMC Coronado, 1948–1949 . . . . **100.00**
Apex Wash-A-Matic & Universal, 3000 Series, 1949 . . . . **300.00**
Apex Wash-A-Matic & Universal, windowless lid models, 1950–1956 . . . . **200.00**
Bendix & Philco Bendix, agitator automatics, 1956–1958 . . . . **100.00**
Bendix & Philco Bendix, Duomatic, 27" cabinet, 1959–1967 . . . . **50.00**
Bendix & Philco Bendix, Duomatic, controls mounted on front of cabinet, 1956 . . . . **200.00**
Bendix & Philco Bendix, Duomatic, front loading washer/dryer combination, 1953–1955 . . . . **200.00**
Bendix & Philco Bendix, Economatic, agitator automatics with rubber squeeze tub, 1951–1954 . . . . **200.00**
Bendix & Philco Bendix, Energy Disk Top Loading Washer, with formica top, 1953–1956 . . . . **300.00**
Bendix & Philco Bendix, post-war Model S and Deluxe Model washer, bolt down type, 1946–1950 . . . . **100.00**
Bendix & Philco Bendix, wobbling agitator automatics, perforated baskets, 1960s **100.00**
Bendix & Philco Bendix, wobbling agitator automatics, solid basket, 1959 . . . . **200.00**
Easy, Velapower Direct Drive Transmission models, 1958–1964 . . . . **50.00**
Easy, combination washer/dryer, 1956–1963 . . . . **100.00**
Frigidaire, Multimatic Models, 1959–1964 . . . . **50.00**
Frigidaire, Control Tower Unimatic Model WI-57, pink or charcoal gray, with matching dryer Model DI-57, 1957 . . . . **600.00**
Frigidaire, Control Tower Unimatic Models WI-57, white WDU-57, 1957 . . . . **200.00**
Frigidaire, Custom Imperial Model WCI-58, white WI-58 . . . . **100.00**
Frigidaire, Imperial Unimatic Models WV-65, white WI-56 . . . . **150.00**
Frigidaire, Imperial Unimatic Models WV-65, green, yellow, and pink Model WI-56 . . . . **200.00**
Frigidaire, Model WJ-60, orig white perforated tub and harmonizer, 1947 . . . . **700.00**
Frigidaire, Model WK-60, orig white perforated tub and harmonizer, 1948 . . . . **500.00**
Frigidaire, Model WL-60, orig rimless black speckled solid tub and harmonizer, 1949 . . . . **300.00**
Frigidaire, Models WO-65 and WO-65-2, 1950–1954 . . . . . . **200.00**
Frigidaire, Pulsamatic Models WV-35, WS-56, WD-56, WS-57, WD-57, WS-58, WD-58 . . . . **100.00**
General Electric, combination washer/dryer, 1954–1957 . . . . **200.00**
General Electric, combination washer/dryer, 1958–1963 . . . . . **75.00**
General Electric, combination washer/dryer, 1964 . . . . **50.00**
General Electric, early V12 perforated basket models, 1961–1964 . . . . **25.00**
Hotpoint, coaxial transmission models, 1953–1959 . . . . **50.00**
Kelvinator, window lid models, 1959–1966 . . . . **50.00**
Kelvinator, windowless lids models, 1959–1966 . . . . **25.00**
Kelvinator, window lid models, 1950–1958 . . . . **300.00**
Kelvinator, windowless lid models, 1950–1958 . . . . **200.00**
Kenmore, bolt down models, 1947–1953 . . . . **200.00**
Kenmore, combination washer/dryer, 29" w **50.00**
Kenmore, combination washer/dryer, 33" w **100.00**
Kenmore, Lady Kenmore, 1957–1962 . . . . **100.00**
Kenmore, Lady Kenmore, pink, turquoise, 1962–1964 . . . . . . **50.00**
Kenmore, top of the line models, 1950–1956 . . . . **100.00**
Launderall, 1947–1951 . . . . **150.00**
Maytag, combination washer/dryer, Models 340W, 440C, 1958–1965 . . . . **250.00**
Maytag, Helical Drive Models 142, 160, 1958–1960 . . . . **25.00**
Maytag, Model AMP, 1948-1952 . . . . **100.00**
Maytag, Models AM2P, AM3P, AM4P, 101, 102, 130, 140, 1943–1957 . . . . **50.00**
Montgomery Ward/Wardomatic, fluid drive AMC design models, 1952–1956 . . . . **100.00**
Montgomery Ward/Wardomatic, front loading washers, (Westinghouse designed), 1957–1964 . . . . **150.00**
Norge/Hamilton, combination washer/dryer, 1958–1964 . . . . **200.00**
Norge/Hamilton, Dispensomat, 1959–1960 . . . . **100.00**
Norge/Hamilton, front loading, Model AW204, 1950 . . . . . . **250.00**
Thor, 1953–1955 . . . . **200.00**
Thor, semi-automatic clothes washer/dishwasher combination with both clothes and dish washer tubs, 1947–1952 . . . . **400.00**
Westinghouse, Models B-1-3, B3, C-1-3, C3, front loading, 1950–1953 . . . . **250.00**
Westinghouse, Models L4, L5, LB6, L8, L9, front loading, 1950–1956 . . . . **150.00**
Whirlpool, combination washer/dryer, 1957–1960, 33" w **100.00**

General Electric, AW5 Line, 1951, $200.00.

Litho Tin, Super Mario Bros., ©1988 Nintendo of America, Inc.," 13" h, $10.00.

Good Year Tires, cloisonné porcelain, inlaid, $187.00. Photo courtesy Wm. Morford.

WASTEBASKETS

Wastebaskets are not just for garbage. Many collectors are just beginning to appreciate the great lithographed artwork found on many character cans.

Litho Tin, painted poodle with umbrella scene **$10.00**
Litho Tin, *Star Wars, Return of the Jedi* **18.00**
Litho Tin, Teenage Mutant Ninja Turtles **10.00**
Metal, Charlie Brown, "Good Grief!," Charlie Brown looking at report card, Chein Co, 1970s, 13" h **20.00**
Metal, Snoopy kissing Peppermint Patty, Chein Co, 1970s, 13" h **20.00**
Plastic, blue finish, gold stars on sides **5.00**
Sheet Metal, stamped and slit, copper plated, green paint, Dandee, Erie Art Metal Co, pat 1909, 16" h. **50.00**
Steel, corrugated sides, raised bottom, green enamel finish, 11¾" h **5.00**
Steel, white finish, expanded, solid steel inside collar, 12" h **30.00**
Tin, painted dec, 11½" h **15.00**
Tin, white finish, perforated sides, Central Stamping Co, 1920, 11⅝" h **40.00**
Wicker, painted white, plastic insert. **15.00**
Wire, openwork basketweave, sheet iron bottom, 22" h **25.00**

WATCH FOBS

A watch fob is a useful and decorative item attached to a man's pocket watch by a strap. It assists him in removing the watch from his pocket. Fobs became popular during the last quarter of the 19th century. Companies such as The Greenduck Company in Chicago, Schwabb in Milwaukee, and Metal Arts in Rochester produced fobs for companies who wished to advertise their products or to commemorate an event, individual, or group.

Most fobs are made of metal and are struck from a steel die. Enameled fobs are scarce and sought after by collectors. If a fob was popular, a company would order restrikes. As a result, some fobs were issued for a period of twenty-five years or more. Watch fobs still are used today in promoting heavy industrial equipment.

The most popular fobs are those relating to old machinery, either farm, construction, or industrial. Advertising fobs rank second in popularity.

The back of a fob is helpful in identifying a genuine fob from a reproduction or restrike. Genuine fobs frequently have advertising or a union trademark on the back. Some genuine fobs do have blank backs but a blank back should be a warning to be cautious.

Club: International Watch Fob Assoc., Inc., P.O. Box 1051, Palmetto, GA 30268.

Avery Tractor Co **$85.00**
Bronco Brand Overalls **125.00**
Bryan-Kern, nickel-plated, red and blue enameled details, eagles and flags center, strap **30.00**
Bull Durham. **75.00**
Case Plow **60.00**
Caterpillar, strap **24.00**
Diamond Edge **32.00**
Fordson Tractor **40.00**
Gold Dust Twins **225.00**
Heinz 57 . . . . **55.00**
International Harvester **65.00**
Kansas Livestock Co **45.00**
Knights of Pythias, bronze, 1906 . . . . **10.00**
Labor Day, 1913 . . . . **55.00**
Mack Bulldog **35.00**
Mayflower, calf skin, German **12.50**
Miller Bros, 1010 Ranch, ornate **190.00**
Oshkosh Beer, porcelain **150.00**
Red Man Tobacco **30.00**
Roosevelt-Fairbanks, brass, figural elephant **30.00**
Souvenir, Atlantic City, city seal, 1854 . . . . **20.00**
Souvenir, Texas, arrowhead, saddle **35.00**
Souvenir, Toronto, Peace Bridge, 1930 . . . . **2.00**
Studebaker, enameled, tire design **38.00**
Wards Tip Top Bread **50.00**
Woodrow Wilson, brass, emb, black ribbon **55.00**

WATT POTTERY

Watt Pottery, located in Crooksville, Ohio, was founded in 1922. The company began producing kitchenware in 1935. Most Watt pottery is easily recognized by its simple underglaze decoration on a light tan base. The most commonly found pattern is the Red Apple pattern, introduced in 1950. Other patterns include Cherry, Pennsylvania Dutch Tulip, Rooster, and Star Flower.

Clubs: Watt Collectors Assoc., P.O. Box 1995, Iowa City, IA 52244; Watt Pottery Collectors USA, Box 26067, Fairview Park, OH 44126.

Apple, baker, 1½ qt. **$50.00**
Apple, casserole, 8½" d. **175.00**
Apple, casserole, tab handles, 5" d. **175.00**
Apple, cereal bowl, 5½" d. **35.00**

Apple, pitcher, #17, ice lip, $225.00. Photo courtesy Gene Harris Antique Auction Center, Inc.

Apple, creamer, 4¼" h. 90.00
Apple, nappy, cov 300.00
Apple, pie plate 175.00
Apple, pitcher. 60.00
Apple, refrigerator pitcher, 3 leaf, ice lip. 140.00
Apple, salad bowl, 9½" d 75.00
Apple, spaghetti bowl, 11½" d. 100.00
Autumn Foliage, carafe, open, ribbon handle 150.00
Autumn Foliage, mug 200.00
Autumn Foliage, pie baker, 9" d. 135.00
Autumn Foliage, salad bowl. 80.00
Cherry, casserole, 9" d. 135.00
Cherry, pitcher 85.00
Cherry, platter, 15" d 120.00
Cherry, salt shaker. 90.00
Dutch Tulip, casserole, French handle, 8" d 250.00
Eagle, cereal bowl, 5½" d 100.00
Eagle, mixing bowl, ribbed, 6" d 135.00
Morning Glory, creamer 350.00
Morning Glory, mixing bowl, 6" d 90.00
Nassau, salad set, salad bowl, vinegar and oil, salt and pepper shakers 275.00
Rio Rose, chop plate. 55.00
Rio Rose, cookie jar 150.00
Rio Rose, cup and saucer 90.00
Rio Rose, pitcher. 150.00
Rooster, baker, 5" d. 100.00
Rooster, ice bucket, cov. 295.00
Rooster, jug, 2 pt. 80.00
Rooster, mug. 80.00
Rooster, platter, 15" d 150.00
Starflower, casserole, cov, 8½" d 40.00
Starflower, drip bowl. 95.00
Starflower, grease jar. 250.00
Starflower, platter, silhouette, 15" l. 90.00
Starflower, salad bowl, 9½" d 90.00
Starflower, salt and pepper shakers, pr, #117 and #118, 4 petal, raised letter. 215.00
Tear Drop, bean pot, #76 . . . . . 125.00
Tear Drop, canister, #72 . . . . . 430.00
Tulip, mixing bowl, ribbed, #7. . . . . 45.00
Tulip, nappy, cov, #05 . . . . . 300.00
Tulip, berry bowl. 30.00
Tulip, cereal bowl 30.00
Tulip, creamer. 225.00
Tulip, cookie jar, 8¼" h 375.00
Tulip, mixing bowl, #65 . . . . . 135.00
Tulip, pitcher, #16. . . . . 175.00

Basalt, teapot, black, flower and scroll, 11¼ oz, 6¾" h, $150.00.

WEDGWOOD

It is highly unlikely that you are going to find 18th, 19th, and even early 20th century Wedgwood at a flea market. However, you will find plenty of Wedgwood pieces made between 1920 and the present. The wonderful and confusing aspect is that many Wedgwood pieces are made the same way today as they were hundreds of years ago.

Unfortunately, Wedgwood never developed a series of backstamps to help identify a piece's age. As a result, the only safe assumption by which to buy is that the piece is relatively new. The next time you are shopping in a mall or jewelry store, check out modern Wedgwood prices. Pay 50 percent or less for a similar piece at a flea market.

Clubs: The Wedgwood Society, The Roman Villa, Rockbourne, Fordingbridge, Hants, SP6 3PG, U.K.; Wedgwood Society of New York, 5 Dogwood Ct, Glen Head, NY 11545.

Basalt, candlestick, classical figures, scroll designs, 7¾" h $100.00
Basalt, figure, bulldog, 2⅞" h. 250.00
Basalt, figure, seated raven, oval base, tail repaired, 4½" h 165.00
Basalt, jar, cov, classical figures, 3" h 80.00
Basalt, pitcher, classical figures, putti, imp "Wedgwood," 7⅜" h 160.00
Basalt, teapot, squat, "Capri" enamel floral dec, 7¾" d 128.00
Basalt, vase, geometric and rams head design, flared lip, imp "Wedgwood," 7½" h. 130.00
Basalt, vase, putti and garlands, 7½" h 130.00
General, baking dish, yellow ware, applied vintage and vegetables, 11½" l. 215.00
General, chop plate, Kutani pattern, 12½" d. 75.00
General, creamer and sugar, Old Vine pattern 20.00
General, cup and saucer, encaustic, rust enamel trim, spiral handle 175.00
General, honey pot, attached underplate, beehive shape, white stoneware, 4" h 130.00
General, pitcher, copper grapes, cream ground, 6½" h 42.00
General, teapot, white classical cameos, olive green ground 50.00
Jasperware, box, cov, yellow, sprigged with white prunus, imp "Wedgwood," late 19th C, 3¾" d 92.00
Jasperware, jam pot, tri-color, yellow body, black grapevine festoons ending in lion heads, white borders, silver plate cov, imp "Wedgwood," late 19th C, 3¼" h 172.50

Jasperware, pitcher, black, tapered cylindrical form, "Maternal Affection" beneath border of fruiting vine, rope handle, imp "Wedgwood, Etruria, England, 1948, 3¾" h 230.00
Luster, bowl, Butterfly, Z4830, 3½" d 65.00
Luster, pitcher, bulbous, blue ext, red int lip, 2" h 260.00
Stoneware, honey pot, beehive shape, attached underplate, 4" h 130.00
Vase, Greora 90.00
Vase, Lavonia, 10" h 130.00
Vase, Louwelsa, bulbous, roses, stamped, 8½" h 150.00
Vase, Louwelsa, cornflowers, squat 150.00
Vase, Panella, green, 10½" h 60.00
Vase, Sicard, tapered, fig shaped, sgd, 4" h 400.00
Vase, Silvertone, 11½" h 160.00
Wall Pocket, Hobart Girl 350.00

WELLER POTTERY

Weller's origins date back to 1872 when Samuel Weller opened a factory in Fultonham, near Zanesville, Ohio. Eventually, he built a new pottery in Zanesville along the tracks of the Cincinnati and Muskingum Railway. Louwelsa, Weller's art pottery line, was introduced in 1894. Among the famous art pottery designers employed by Weller are Charles Babcock Upjohn, Jacques Sicard, Frederick Rhead, and Gazo Fudji.

Weller survived on production of utilitarian wares, but always managed to produce some art pottery production until cheap Japanese imports captured the market immediately following World War II. Operations at Weller ceased in 1948.

Club: American Art Pottery Assoc., P.O. Box 834, Westport, MA 02790.

Periodical: *Pottery Collectors Express*, P.O. Box 221, Mayview, MO 64071.

Basket, Wild Rose, 6" h $60.00
Bowl, Flemish, ftd, daisies, 8½" d 165.00
Bowl, Scandia, 6½" d 75.00
Bud Vase, Roma, double 65.00
Bud Vase, Woodcraft, 6½" h 35.00
Cigarette Holder, Coppertone, figural frog 200.00
Comport, Creamware, ftd, 2 handles 85.00
Ewer, Etna, 9" h 150.00
Ewer, Knifewood, green, 9" h 450.00
Hanging Basket, Woodcraft, 6" h 125.00
Jardiniere, Rosemont, 8" d 160.00
Mug, Souevo, #30 . . . . 145.00
Pitcher, Ivoris, 6" h 40.00
Planter, Klyro, die stamped, 4" sq 60.00
Plate, Zona dinnerware, 10" d 20.00
Vase, Baldin, blue, emb apples, 10¼" h 500.00
Vase, Chase, 9" h 345.00
Vase, Eocean, bulbous, mauve, gray leaves, 6½" h 375.00
Vase, Etna, corseted, red poppy, gray ground, 10" h 150.00

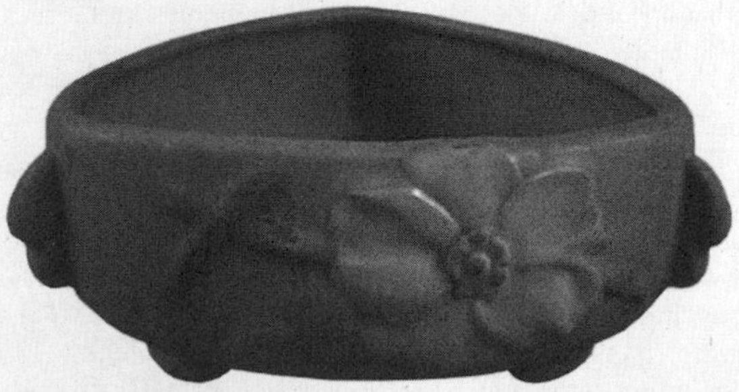

Bowl, Wild Rose pattern, triangular, handled, dogwood blossom on front, peach ground, mkd "Weller," 2⅞" h, 7¼" w, $35.00.

WESTERN COLLECTIBLES

Yippy Kiyay partner, let's get a move on and lasso up some of those western goodies.

The western collectible is a style or motif as it relates to the object. The western theme presents itself in the decorative imagery of the item. The use of western materials for construction of the item also defines it as a possible western collectible; i.e. cattlehide carpets and wall hangings, or items constructed from bull horns. The western motif may also be defined as any item that relates to the western frontier culture. Native American Indian and Mexican cultures are also part of the western collectible theme. It is these cultures that contribute so much of the color to the western heritage.

Club: 101 Ranch Collectors, 10701 Timbergrove Ln., Corpus Christi, TX 78410; National Bit, Spur & Saddle Collectors Assoc., P.O. Box 3035, Colorado Springs, CO 80934.

Newsletter: Cowboy Guide, P.O. Box 6459, Santa Fe, NM 87502.

Periodicals: *American Cowboy*, P.O. Box 6630, Sheridan, WY 82801.

Badge, Tuscon Police Department $165.00
Bag, Indian Territory, gold 145.00
Belt Buckle, brass, emb, Stetson 18.00
Book, *2-Gun Montana,* Better Little Book, 1939 . . . . 10.00
Book, *The Pioneers, A Tale of the Western Wilderness,* R M Ballantyne, 1872 . . . . 80.00
Book, *Wild Life On The Plains, Horrors of Indian Warfare,* W L Holloway, illus, leather bound, 1891 . . . . 95.00
Brand Certificate, Montana, 1917 . . . . 12.00
Catalog, Ottawa Log and Tree Saws, Ottawa, KS, 16 pp, orig mailing envelope, 9 x 12" 30.00
Catalog, Visalia Saddle Company, 128 pp, 1935 . . . . 75.00
Cookie Jar, cowboy boots, American Bisque . . . .
Document, land certificate, Creek nation, 1899 . . . . 65.00
Letterhead, Montana, longhorn steer, 1911 . . . . 15.00

Bookends, pr, Will Rogers, emb leather, green and gold dec on white ground, mkd "Durand, Chicago," $75.00.

Map, Nevada Pony Express Map, chromolithograph, published by Nevada Pony Express Centennial Committed, 23 x 17", framed 250.00
Photograph, cowboys roing and branding cattle on prairie, c1920, 6 x 4". 22.50
Pin, Texas Cousins Farm and Ranch 30.00
Pouch, 101 Ranch & Wild West Show, canvas 250.00
Print, thoroughbred horse, framed, set of 4. . . . . 100.00
Program, World Championship Rodeo, Roy Rogers photos, 1944 . . . . 15.00
Ribbon, 1938 Texas Cowboy Reunion, Stamford, attached fob 75.00
Rope, horsehair. 40.00
Salt and Pepper Shakers, pr, figural cactus, tray with figural cowboy, California 25.00
Scarf Holder, SS, figural saddle 15.00
Ticket, Wild West Show, 1905 . . . . 300.00
Wall Decoration, water buffalo horns, mounted 100.00
Watch Fob, Kansas Livestock Co 45.00

WESTMORELAND GLASS

Westmoreland Glass Company made a large assortment of glass. Some early pieces were actually reproductions of earlier patterns and are now collectible in their own right. Other patterns have been produced for decades.

Expect to pay modest prices. Flea market prices are generally much lower than contemporary department store prices.

Clubs: National Westmoreland Glass Collectors Club, P.O. Box 625, Irwin, PA 15642; Westmoreland Glass Society, P.O. Box 2883, Iowa City, IA 52240.

Newsletter: *The Original Westmoreland Collectors Newsletter*, P.O. Box 143, North Liberty, IA 52317.

Beaded Grape, bowl, cov, #1884, flared, ftd, 5" sq **$25.00**
Beaded Grape, candlesticks, pr, #1884. . . . . 22.50
Beaded Grape, candy box, cov 28.00
Beaded Grape, honey pot, cov, #1884, gold grapes, 5" 50.00
Beaded Grape, salt and pepper shakers, pr, ftd 22.00
Della Robbia, candlesticks, pr, 4" h 120.00
Della Robbia, candy dish, cov, scalloped edge 75.00
Della Robbia, cocktail. 20.00
Della Robbia, cup and saucer 20.00
Della Robbia, salt and pepper shakers, pr. 50.00
Della Robbia, sherbet 16.00
English Hobnail, ashtray, amber, 4½" sq 7.50

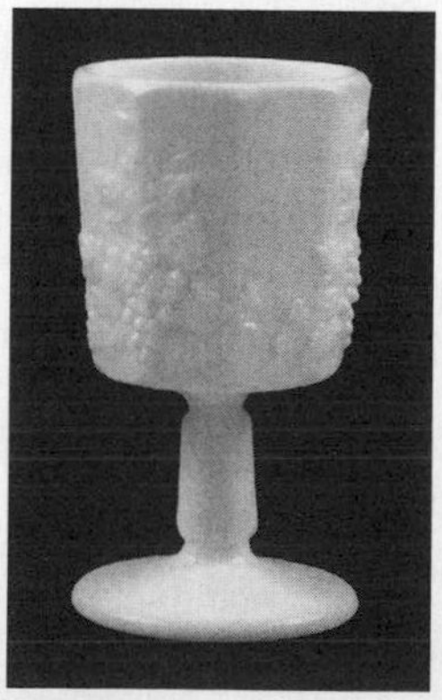

Paneled Grape, water goblet, milk glass, 6" h, $15.00.

English Hobnail, basket, 5" h 15.00
English Hobnail, celery, 9" l. 15.00
English Hobnail, cocktail. 8.00
English Hobnail, puff box, cov, amber, 6" d 18.00
Old Quilt, butter dish, cov, white milk glass, ¼ lb 35.00
Old Quilt, cheese dish, cov, white milk glass 52.00
Old Quilt, creamer, small 10.00
Old Quilt, fruit bowl, #43, crimped, ftd, 9" 45.00
Old Quilt, sugar, small 10.00
Old Quilt, water set, pitcher and 6 ftd tumblers, white milk glass 90.00
Paneled Grape, bud vase, 9" h 18.00
Paneled Grape, cake salver, white milk glass 65.00
Paneled Grape, cake stand, #1881, skirted, 11" h 70.00
Paneled Grape, cruet. 20.00
Paneled Grape, jardiniere, 6½" h 35.00
Paneled Grape, nappy 15.00
Paneled Grape, parfait. 15.00
Paneled Grape, planter, 8½" h 20.00
Paneled Grape, relish, 4-part 30.00
Paneled Grape, salt and pepper shakers, pr, 3½" h 15.00

WHAT'S IN THE CASE?

After years of wandering around the country visiting flea markets of every shape and size, there is one phrase I hear over and over again, "What's in the case?"

"What's in the case?" deals with items found in glass-covered tabletop showcases. Their numbers are infinite. Their variety limitless. They are in the case because they are the smallest of the small, too delicate, or expensive. Showcases have also helped to discourage the unfortunate, but all-too-common disappearing act performed by many pocket-size collectibles.

Items under glass are generally valuable and to handle them without a dealer's permission is practically a sacrilege. Arrangement in the case may be haphazard or organized, depending on the dealer's selling methods. Don't be surprised if you find a number of cases packed to overflowing.

WHEATON

The Wheaton Glass Company, Millville, New Jersey, manufactured commemorative bottles, decanters, and flasks between 1967 and 1974. Series included Christmas, Great Americans, Movie Stars, Political Campaigns, and Space.

The Wheaton Historical Association continued production of the Christmas and Presidential series from 1975 to 1982. The Millville Art Glass Co. obtained a licensing agreement from the Wheaton Historical Association and added some additional bottles to the series.

The Wheaton Glass Company also manufactured copycat (stylistic copies) of 19th century bottles and flasks between 1971 and 1974. Most were marked "Nuline," "W," or "Wheaton, NJ" on the base. Amber, amethyst, blue, green, milk, and ruby were the colors used.

Club: Classic Wheaton Club, P.O. Box 59, Downingtown, PA 19335.

Apollo I, burnt amber **$25.00**
Christmas, 1971, frosted 10.00
Christmas, 1973, red. 5.00

John F. Kennedy, Presidential Series, 1st edition, blue, 1967, $10.00.

Famous First Ed. No. 5, Yacht 1851, America 1970 R.M.E., $35.00

Christmas, 1975, blue **5.00**
Christmas, 1980, blue **5.00**
Clark Gable, Burley **6.00**
Democratic Donkey, green, 1968 . . . . . **5.00**
Franklin Pierce, green **10.00**
George Washington, frosted flint **5.00**
Great American Series, 17 bottles, price for each **5.00**
Jean Harlow, topaz, 1972 . . . . . **20.00**
Jimmy Carter, blue **5.00**
John Quincy Adams, dark amber **6.00**
John Wayne **6.00**
Republican Elephant, amethyst, 1972 . . . . . **5.00**
Richard Nixon, green, miniature **5.00**
Ronald Reagan, cobalt blue **5.00**
Skylab I, frosted **15.00**

WHISKEY BOTTLES, COLLECTORS' EDITIONS

The Jim Beam Distillery issued its first novelty bottle for the 1953 Christmas market. By the 1960s the limited edition whiskey bottle craze was full blown. It was dying by the mid 1970s and was buried sometime around 1982 or 1983. Oversaturation by manufacturers and speculation by non-collectors killed the market.

Limited edition whiskey bottle collecting now rests in the hands of serious collectors. Their bible is H. F. Montague's *Montague's Modern Bottle Identification and Price Guide* (published by author, 1980). The book used to be revised frequently. Now five years or more pass between editions. The market is so stable that few prices change from one year to the next.

Before you buy or sell a full limited edition whiskey bottle, check state laws. Most states require a license to sell liquor and impose substantial penalties if you sell without one.

Club: Jim Beam Bottle & Specialties Club, 2015 Burlington Ave., Kewanee, IL 61443; National Ski Country Bottle Club, 1224 Washington Ave., Golden, CO 80401.

Ballantine, Silver Knight **$15.00**
Cyrus Noble, assayer, Mine Series **175.00**
Cyrus Noble, bear and cubs, 1st ed, 1978 . . . . . **115.00**
Cyrus Noble, dancers, South of the Border, 1978 . . . . . **35.00**
Cyrus Noble, harp seal, 1979 . . . . . **50.00**
Cyrus Noble, moose and calf, 1st ed **100.00**
Double Springs, Mercedes Benz, 1975 . . . . . **25.00**
Double Springs, New York, Bicentennial Series **12.00**
Ezra Brooks, Betsy Ross, 1975 . . . . . **12.00**
Ezra Brooks, goose, 1974 . . . . . **15.00**
Ezra Brooks, Iowa Farmer, 1977 . . . . . **65.00**
Ezra Brooks, panda, 1972 . . . . . **15.00**
Ezra Brooks, penguin, 1973 . . . . . **10.00**
Ezra Brooks, stagecoach, Overland Express, 1969 . . . . . **10.00**
Ezra Brooks, totem pole, 1973 . . . . . **10.00**
Ezra Brooks, Winston Churchill, 1969 . . . . . **10.00**
Garnier, pheasant, 1969 . . . . . **30.00**
Grenadier, Bicentennial Series, 1976 . . . . . **12.00**
Grenadier, General Robert E Lee, Civil War Series, 1976, ½ gal **120.00**
Grenadier, Moose Lodge, 1970 . . . . . **14.00**
Grenadier, soldier, miniature, 1975 . . . . . **15.00**
Hoffman, accordion player, 1987 . . . . . **12.00**
Hoffman, blue jays, 1979, price for pr **35.00**
Jim Beam, Blue Hen Club, 1982 . . . . . **25.00**
Jim Beam, Bob Hope Desert Classic, 1974 . . . . . **10.00**
Jim Beam, cable car, 1983 . . . . . **55.00**
Jim Beam, Colorado Centennial, Pike's Peak, 1976 . . . . . **10.00**
Jim Beam, Denver Club, 1970 . . . . . **12.00**
Jim Beam, Five Seasons Club, 1980 . . . . . **10.00**
Jim Beam, Fox Uncle Sam, 1971 . . . . . **12.00**
Jim Beam, Golden Nuggets, 1969, 12½" h **35.00**
Jim Beam, Kentucky Derby, 1971 . . . . . **7.00**
Jim Beam, Model T Ford, black, 1913 . . . . . **35.00**
Jim Beam, Mortimer Snerd, 1976 . . . . . **30.00**
Jim Beam, Nevada, 1963 . . . . . **35.00**
Jim Beam, Stutz Bearcat, yellow, 1977 . . . . . **35.00**
Jim Beam, Texas Rose, 1978 . . . . . **15.00**
J W Dant, American Legion, 1969 . . . . . **6.00**
J W Dant, Ft Sill, 1969 . . . . . **10.00**
J W Dant, Wrong-Way Charlie **18.00**
Lionstone, Betsy Ross, Bicentennial Series **25.00**
Lionstone, Sons of Freedom, Bicentennial Series **30.00**
Lionstone, Sad Sam, Clown Series **40.00**
Lionstone, snake charmer, Circus Series **15.00**
McCormick, Drake Bulldogs, 1974 . . . . . **20.00**
Old Mr Boston, clown head, 1973 . . . . . **20.00**
Ski Country, dancer, ceremonial buffalo, 1975 . . . . . **120.00**
Ski Country, Mill River Country Club, 1977 . . . . . **40.00**
Ski Country, polar bear, miniature **25.00**
Wild Turkey, Lore Series, 1979 . . . . . **40.00**

WHISKEY-RELATED

Whiskey and whiskey-related items are centuries old. Normally, the words conjure up images of the Western saloon and dance hall. Since the taste of similar whiskeys varies little, manufacturers relied on advertising and promotions to create customer loyalty.

Sign, Nutwood Kentucky Whiskey, Max Selliger & Co. Distillers, Louisville, KY, reverse glass, $7\frac{1}{4}$ x 10", $165.00. Photo courtesy Wm. Morford.

Clubs: The Shot Glass Club of America, 5071 Watson Dr., Flint, MI 48506; Whiskey Pitcher Collectors Assoc. of America, 19341 W. Tahoe Dr., Mundelein, IL 60060.

Advertising Trade Card, Capital Fine Whiskey, Washington Capital view **$75.00**
Book, *Melrose: Honey of Roses,* Stirling Graham, 3rd printing, 95 pp, 1944 . . . . . **8.00**
Fan, Four Roses Whiskey **15.00**
Flask, gold, front with "I Love Jim Beam," back with outline map of Washington, Regal China, 1976, 14 oz, $6\frac{1}{2}$" h **40.00**
Football Guide, Kessler Whiskey premium, 1972 . . . . . **4.00**
Glass, Duncan Miller, Tear Drop pattern, crystal, 2 oz. **15.00**
Glass, Fostoria, American pattern, crystal, $2\frac{1}{2}$" h. **10.00**
Label, Old Crow, distillery scene, sepia **1.00**
Matchbook, Carstairs White Seal Blended Whiskey, blue, gold, and red, seal balancing ball on cov and matches, 1940s, oversized **10.00**
Oil Lamp, Seagrams Whiskey **20.00**
Pinback Button, Gallagher & Burton, Philadelphia Distillery, logo trademark, early 1900s **10.00**
Pinback Button, Old Crow Whiskey, "Vote For The Whiskey of Famous Men," 1930s **5.00**
Pitcher, Canadian Windsor, figural guard **25.00**
Pitcher, Michter's Bourbon, PA Dutch symbol **10.00**
Pitcher, Old Grandad, medallion, sq **12.00**
Shot Glass, Bottoms Up, cobalt **8.50**
Sign, Sam Clay Whiskey, tin, black, white, and gold, monogrammed center, $18\frac{1}{2}$ x $26\frac{1}{2}$" **200.00**
Swizzle Stick, blue and crystal, clear spoon **2.50**

WHISTLES

Webster defines a whistle as an instrument for making a clear, shrill sound. No wonder children love them. Collectors can whistle a happy tune at virtually every flea market. The most desirable whistles are those associated with well-known characters and personalities. They can command prices that are hardly child's play.

Club: Call & Whistle Collectors Assoc., 2839 E. 26th Place, Tulsa, OK 74114.

Butter Nut Bread, 1920s **$20.00**
Cowboy, tin, $3\frac{1}{2}$" l **10.00**
Dairy Queen, figural ice cream cone, plastic **5.00**
Figural, wristwatch, litho tin, rect yellow face, red, white, and blue bands, Japan **15.00**

Agfa Film, red and blue on black ground, $20.00.

Jack & Jill, Gelatin, litho tin **30.00**
Jack Armstrong, ring, brass, Egyptian symbols on sides, built-in siren top, 1938 . . . . . **70.00**
NewYork Evening Telegraph, brass, chain **40.00**
Oscar Meyer Weinermobile, plastic, 2" l **8.00**
Peters Weatherbird **44.00**
Planters Peanuts, plastic **15.00**
Poll Parrot Shoes, 2" l **16.00**
Poll Parrot Solid Leather Shoes **22.00**
Red Goose Shoes **16.00**
Royal Luncheon, litho tin, Germany **12.00**
Weather Bird Shoes **15.00**
Wenner Beverages, wood **14.00**
Whistle Soda, 2" l **16.00**

WHITE-KNOB WINDUPS

White Knob Windups are small, plastic mechanical toys. They arrived on the market in the mid-1970s. Their name is derived from the small white ridged knob found at the end of the metal rod that extends from the body and winds the motor.

Club: White Knob Wind-Up Collectors Club, 61 Garrow St., Auburn, NY 13021.

Blinky Ghost, Tomy, red **$15.00**
Box Pops, Tomy, 1981 . . . . . **15.00**
Bumbling Boxing Game, Tomy, 1982 . . . . . **10.00**
Cabbage Patch Kids, Tomy, boy with basketball, 1985 . . . . . **10.00**
Cabbage Patch Kids, Tomy, Rocking Babies **15.00**
Flip Floppers, Tomy, 1983 . . . . . **3.00**
Great Gonzo, Tomy, pop-over, 1983 . . . . . **12.00**
Hamburger, Russ, hopper **10.00**
Hilarious Hats Walkers, police, Tomy, 1983 . . . . . **8.00**
Home Run Homer Game, Tomy, 1982 . . . . . **12.00**
Inch-A-Longs, Bandai America, 1981 . . . . . **6.00**
Inky Ghost, Pac Man, Tomy, blue, 1982 . . . . . **12.00**
Kermit the Frog, Tomy, swimmer, 1983 . . . . . **10.00**
Li'l Big Toppers, Tomy, 1983 . . . . . **15.00**
Mad Ball Rollers, Spearhead, 1986 . . . . . **3.00**
Major League Baseball, Russ, hoppers, team logo, 1989 . . . . . **6.00**
Mickey Mouse, Durham Industries **30.00**
Mini Appliances, Galoob, 1979 . . . . . **5.00**
Mini Tools, jigsaw, Galoob, 1980 . . . . . **5.00**
Miss Piggy Swinetrek, Flip-Flopper, Tomy, 1983 . . . . . **12.00**
Mity Machines, bulldozer, Galoob, 1984 . . . . . **7.00**
Pocket Pets Hoppers, Tomy, 1983 . . . . . **2.00**
Prancing Ponys, Tomy, 1983 . . . . . **12.00**
Rascal Robots, Tomy, 1977 . . . . . **6.00**
Santa Hopper, Russ **6.00**

Cradle, 2 pc, stick and ball, $137.50. Photo courtesy Gene Harris Antique Auction Center, Inc.

WICKER

Wicker and rattan furniture enjoyed its first American craze during the late Victorian era. It was found on porches and summer cottages across America. It realized a second period of popularity in the 1920s and 30s and a third period in the 1950s. In truth, wicker has been available continuously since the 1870s.

Early wicker has a lighter, airier feel than its later counterparts. Look for unusual forms, e.g., corner chairs or sewing stands. Most wicker was sold unpainted. However, it was common practice to paint it in order to preserve it, especially if it was going to be kept outside. Too many layers of paint decreases the value of a piece.

Chair, funeral parlor, woven triangle design in upper back, openwork on lower half, painted white, 42" h **$150.00**
Chaise Lounge, double row of X's on back, lidded magazine pocket arms, serpentine footrest, ball feet, painted white, 54" l. **750.00**
Cradle, rocking frame, painted white, 50" h **150.00**
Creel Basket, center lid hole, early 1900s. **55.00**
Fainting Couch, sleigh back, straight skirt, upholstered, painted white **150.00**
Footstool, rect upholstered top, woven sides, wrapped legs, painted white, 16" w **150.00**
High Chair, barrel shaped, wooden seat and footrest, painted white, 32½" h **225.00**
High Chair, shell design back, machine woven cane seat, wooden footrest, turned wooden legs, natural finish, c1880 .... **275.00**
Parlor Table, circular top with basketweave pattern, curlicue trim, circular base shelf with cane insert, white, 30¼" h, 27½" d. **125.00**
Sewing Stand, spiderweb caned top basket, hinged circular cov, lower shelf open basket, 3 legs, natural finish, c1870 .... **300.00**
Side Chair, shaped woven crest, vase shaped ornate splat, pressed seat, 39" h, 17½" w **175.00**
Smoking Stand, brass tray, 28" h **60.00**
Sofa, scrolled back, diamond design, upholstered seat, 65" l, 37" h **275.00**
Top Hat, 6" h **45.00**
Towel Bar, hanging, oval beveled mirror, 24" l **80.00**

WILLOW WARE

The traditional Willow pattern, developed by Josiah Spode in 1810, is the most universally recognized china pattern. A typical piece contains the following elements in its motif: willow tree, "apple" tree, two pagodas, fence, two birds, and three figures crossing a bridge.

Willow pattern china was made in almost every country that produces ceramics. In the 1830s over 200 English companies offered Willow pattern china. Buffalo China was one of the first American companies to offer the pattern. Japanese production started about 1902, around the same time Buffalo made its first pieces.

Since the Willow pattern has been in continuous production, the term reproduction has little meaning. However, the Scio Pottery, Scio, Ohio, is currently producing an unmarked set that is being sold in variety stores. Because it lacks marks, some collectors have purchased it under the mistaken belief that it was made much earlier.

Club: International Willow Collectors, P.O. Box 13382, Arlington, TX 76094.

Adderly, biscuit jar, cov, Two Temples II, cane handle, 4½" h **$130.00**
Buffalo, cream soup **10.00**
Copeland, child's cup and saucer, pink **55.00**
Copeland, teacup and saucer, Auld Lang Syne, verse printed on int rim, rust-orange **50.00**
England, eggcup, pink. **22.00**
England, salt and pepper shakers, pr, blue **60.00**
Gibson & Sons, candleholder, chamberstick type, scalloped edge, gold trim, blue, 5" d **150.00**
Homer Laughlin, platter, blue **20.00**
Ideal Toys, child's tea set, plastic, orig box **65.00**
Imperial Royal Nimy, Belgium, dish, c1920, 9" d **45.00**
Japan, ashtray, figural fish, open mouth, attached wire handle, 5" l **25.00**
Japan, grill plate, blue, 10¼" d **15.00**
Japan, kerosene lamp, wall mount, reflector, blue, 8" h. **85.00**
Japan, pie plate, unglazed base, 10" d **50.00**
Japan, pitcher, blue, 6½" h **35.00**
Japan, spoon rest, 9" l **35.00**
Johnson Brothers, bowl, blue, 6" d. **5.00**
Maastricht, grill plate, blue, 11" d **10.00**
Meakin, vegetable bowl, blue, 8½" l **35.00**
Occupied Japan, child's plate, 3¾" d **12.00**
Occupied Japan, child's plate, 4¼" d **60.00**
Occupied Japan, child's platter, blue, oval **47.00**
Occupied Japan, child's saucer, blue, 3¼" d. **8.00**
Occupied Japan, child's teapot, blue, 4" h **50.00**
Occupied Japan, demitasse set, coffeepot, creamer, 6 cups and saucers **100.00**

England, bowl, mkd "Allertons/Made in/England, 3¼" h, 6⅛" d, $35.00.

Shenango China, grill plate, mkd "Shenango China New Castle, PA," $10\frac{1}{4}$" d, $15.00.

Ridgway, creamer, blue, $3\frac{1}{2}$" h. **12.00**
Ridgway, gravy boat, blue **35.00**
Ridgway, sugar bowl, cov, blue, 5" h **45.00**
Shenango China, soup plate, blue, 9" d **20.00**
Stevenson & Sons, plate, blue, $5\frac{3}{4}$" d. **30.00**

WINCHESTER

Mention Winchester and the first thing that comes to mind is the Wild Wild West and the firearms used to tame it. Today, the Winchester name is collectible whether it is found on tools and cutlery or advertising and sporting goods.

Club: The Winchester Arms Collectors Assoc., Inc., P.O. Box 6754, Great Falls, MT 59406.

Ammunition Box, Ranger, 20 gauge, "Super Target Load" . . . **$70.00**
Ammunition Box, Repeater, 12 gauge, multicolored **26.00**
Bank, wood and plastic, cylindrical, "Time Payment Plan," red, white, and black, $8\frac{1}{2}$" h **154.00**
Book, *Winchester For Over a Century,* Bill West, 1st ed, over 300 pp, 1966. . . . . **67.00**
Bullet Mold, 40-65 caliber, walnut handles, lightly freckled. **70.00**
Calendar, 1914, hunter and dogs in cornfield, 30 x 15". **100.00**
Camp Ax, replaced oak handle, brown patina, $5\frac{1}{4}$ x 4" head. **50.00**
Carving Set, 3 pc, carving knife, meat fork, and sharpening steel, French ivory handles, German silver bolsters **80.00**
Catalog, Winchester Repeating Arms Co, #81, New Haven, CT, revision slip pasted in front, illus, 216 pp **100.00**
Catalog, color illus, 48 pp, 1965 . . . . **16.00**

Poster, heavy paper, Winchester Cartridge Shop, "Reveille for Workers/Taps for Japs," 22 x 14", $209.00. Photo courtesy Wm. Morford.

Dispay, cardboard, standup, jacketed bullets, lead bullets, cartridges, wads, prime shells, and primers illus, color, 21 x 27" **22.50**
Envelope, rifles and cartridges, 2 hunters, c1920, $6\frac{1}{2}$ x $3\frac{1}{2}$" **40.00**
Handbook, salesman's, color illus, 1856, 84 pp **80.00**
Handbook, sgd by George Madis, 1st ed, 287 pp, 1981 . . . . . **40.00**
Pinback Button, "Always Shoot Winchester Cartridges," "W" in center bull's-eye, white, black, and red **133.00**
Pinback Button, "Winchester Claybird Tournament" **15.00**
Postcard, Winchester Repeating Arms Co, Boston, MA, gun dealer adv, rifle adv, 1881 . . . . **15.00**
Screwdriver, flat head, hickory handle, brass bolster, 8" blade, $13\frac{1}{2}$" l overall **33.00**
Window Card, Leader Paper Shot Shells, box shape, color, c1910, 8" sq **100.00**

WOOD

There is something great about the grain, patina, and aging qualities of wood. The objects are utilitarian, yet classic for their type.

Barber Pole, painted black, red, and white, iron brackets, 31" l **$350.00**
Ballot Box, poplar, old cherry finish, lock and key, $9\frac{1}{2}$" l. **80.00**
Bible Box, pine, chip carved design on facade, rose head wrought iron nail construction, old dark patina, age cracks, replaced hinges, $17\frac{1}{4}$" l **120.00**
Bowl, oblong, burl, end handles, 20" l **175.00**
Bucket, stave constructed, laced wooden bands, swivel bentwood handle, 11" h **150.00**
Candle Box, birch, dovetailed, finger grips on beveled sliding lid, stained red, 9" l **175.00**
Candle Box, pine, sliding lid, old green paint, "G.M.D. 1858" in white, $11\frac{1}{2}$" l **150.00**
Churn, keg shaped, small round top door, metal bands, wrought iron fittings, hand crank, dasher, sawbuck base, 39" h, $29\frac{1}{2}$" l **60.00**
Clothes Tree, hickory, 6 peg hooks, tripod base, arched legs, Old Hickory Furniture Co, IN, c1935, 68" h **125.00**
Decoy, Canada Goose, old worn and weathered paint, 25" l **200.00**
Drying Rack, pine, 3-part, folding, 5 bars, leather hinges, old patina, each section measures $37\frac{1}{4}$"w, $71\frac{1}{2}$" h **30.00**
Grain Measure, nesting set of 4, sizes graduated from $8\frac{3}{4}$" to 15" d, painted gray **150.00**
Knife Box, bentwood, cutout handle, sq nail construction, 15" l **50.00**

Crate, Father Johns' Medicine, dovetail edges, 11" h, 10" w, 11" d, $22.00. Photo courtesy Collectors Auction Services.

Mortar and Pestle, turned, age cracks, 7" h 35.00
Planter, ftd, log, cedar, bark cov, upright pickets surrounding sq box, 24" l 35.00
Salt Box, hanging, chip carved dec, wire nail construction, 10" h 150.00
Spoon, rope twist handle, turned ivory finial, $8^1/_4$" l. 45.00

WORLD'S FAIRS COLLECTIBLES

It says a lot about the status of world's fairs when Americans cannot stage a fair in 1993–1994 that is even half as good as the 1893 Columbian Exposition in Chicago. Was the last great world's fair held in New York in 1964? Judging from recent fairs, the answer is an unqualified yes. Although it is important to stress three-dimensional objects for display purposes, do not overlook the wealth of paper that was given away to promote fairs and their participants.

Club: 1904 World's Fair Society, 529 Barcia Dr., St. Louis, MO 63119; World's Fair Collectors' Society, P.O. Box 20806, Sarasota, FL 34276.

Periodical: *World's Fair Inc.,* P.O. Box 339, Corte Madera, CA 94976.

1876 Centennial, label, Burton Ale, oval $15.00
1876 Centennial, pocket album 25.00
1876 Centennial, ticket, exhibitor pass, punched 100.00
1893 Columbian, bell, glass, etched, frosted handle 65.00
1893 Columbian, calendar, World's Fair Mfg and Liberal Arts Building, chromolithograph, adv for R H Jones Liquors, Reading, PA, full pad 60.00
1893 Columbian, medal, white metal, bust portrait and inscription, 2" d 20.00
1893 Columbian, paperweight. 75.00
1893 Columbian, puzzle, egg shape, silvered brass, Christopher Columbus portrait 50.00
1893 Columbian, spoon, set of 6, orig box. 125.00
1895 Atlanta, sheet music, *King Cotton March,* John Phillip Sousa, black and white 30.00
1901 Pan-American, bond, Pan-American Exposition Co First Mortgage Bond, $500, brown and white, gold seal, 4 coupons at bottom, 17 x 11" 100.00
1901 Pan-American, change purse 15.00
1901 Pan-American, stickpin, figural frying pan, emb buffalo head 36.00
1901 Pan-American, view book, photo and artwork illus, glossy paper, captions, 80 pp, $6^1/_2$ x 9" 25.00

1939 New York World's Fair, postcard, $5.00.

1933 Century of Progress, Chicago, paperweight, glass globe with flattened base, Tailors' Building in center, "John A. Griffith & Co., Incorporated, 1893–1921, Tailors' Trimmins," 3" d, $40.00.

1904 Louisiana Purchase, egg tin 65.00
1904 Louisiana Purchase, inkwell, porcelain 45.00
1904 Louisiana Purchase, postcard, eggshell paper. 10.00
1909 Hudson-Fulton Celebration, brochure, State of New York Education Dept, 64 pp 30.00
1926 Philadelphia Sesquicentennial, postcard, "Greetings to you from Philadelphia, The Sesqui Centennial," Liberty Bell, garland, and shields, blue Sesqui Centennial seal on divided back, unused 18.00
1929 Philadelphia Sesquicentennial, bank, Liberty Bell replica, cast iron, $3^1/_2$" h. 25.00
1933–34 Century of Progress, bookmark, etched metal, set of 10 . . . . 150.00
1933–34 Century of Progress, coasters, set of 4 . . . . 20.00
1933–34 Century of Progress, compact, chrome 12.00
1933–34 Century of Progress, handkerchief, Japanese silk, set of 3 . . . . 50.00
1933–34 Century of Progress, nesting cup set, set of 6, plastic, slate blue, decal for Travel and Transport Building above "A Century of Progress/Chicago-1933," standing jester figure on lid 50.00
1933–34 Century of Progress, pamphlet, Durkee Famous Foods, 16 pp 5.00
1933–34 Century of Progress, pinback button, "A Century of Progress," black and silver. 28.00
1933–34, Century of Progress, salt and pepper shakers, pr, silver luster over white metal, "Travel and Transport Building/Chicago World's Fair, 1933-34" in raised relief, sides with relief image of Federal Building, Hall of Science, and Illinois Host House, made in Japan, $3^1/_4$" h 50.00
1933–34 Century of Progess, thermometer, Havoline Tower replica, cast iron, inscribed "Havoline Thermometer Tower, Chicago World's Fair, 1933–1934," $4^1/_2$" h 75.00
1934 New York, ticket 25.00
1935 California, booklet, *National Parks of the West,* Standard Oil premium, 16 pp, orig envelope, 5 x 8" 4.00
1936 Texas Centennial, ribbon badge, celluloid, attached fabric ribbon, inscribed "Member of Longhorns at Your Service," $4^1/_2$" l. 15.00
1939 New York, bud vase, china, hp, "New York World's Fair" inscription, underside stamped "Japan," $4^3/_4$" h 75.00
1939 New York, dresser scarf, felt, multicolored inked artwork, purple ground, $8^1/_2$ x $11^1/_2$" 50.00
1939 New York, drinking glass, Libbey. 15.00
1939 New York, guide book, exhibits listing, illus, foldout aerial view grounds map, 256 pp, 5 x 8" 20.00
1939 New York, map, 20 x 28" 25.00

1939 New York, pencil, oversized, wooden, lead, ruber eraser in silvered metal holder, orange barrel with blue and silver picture of Electric Power and Light Building, Solar Fountain, Unisphere, Swiss Sky Ride, and General Motors Building, 10½" l **20.00**
1939 New York, pennant, felt, green, white lettering, "Aviation Building," blue felt streamers, 25" l **50.00**
1939 New York, playing cards, Perisphere and Trylon, red border **22.00**
1962 Century 21, program *King and His Court,* 12 pp, 7 x 10" **24.00**

WRESTLING MEMORABILIA

Collecting wrestling memorabilia can be a very frustrating activity. There are no price guides, and most sellers I have encountered profess to having little or no knowledge of any aspect of professional wrestling. In recent years, wrestling has continued to lose the respect it had decades ago. From the 1800s to the 1950s, the results of important wrestling matches could be found in your local newspaper on page one of the sports section. Not anymore. Today, many fans and collectors do not like to admit to following the sport or collecting memorabilia pertaining to this wonderful slice of Americana.

Prices for wrestling memorabilia can vary tremendously. Sellers usually have no idea what to charge when they come across odd wrestling pieces. Pay only what the item is worth to you.

Advisor: John Pantozzi, 1000 Polk Ave., Franklin Square, NY 11010, (516) 488-7728.

Alarm Clock, talking, WWF, Hulk Hogan **$12.00**
Baking Pan, Wilton, WWF **15.00**
Baseball Glove, WCW, Hulk Hogan **25.00**
Baseball Glove, WWF, Hulk Hogan **25.00**
Can Cooler, puppet, WWF, Hulk Hogan **10.00**
Car, Racing Champions Wrestler Car **5.00**
Comic Book, Ultimate Warrior, #1 . . . . **5.00**
Cup, plastic, set of 6, NWA Great American Bash **25.00**
Falk Cabinet Card, William Muldoon, 1800s **40.00**
Flip Flops, WCW **5.00**
Game, Falls, 1950s **50.00**
Kite, WCW, Hulk Hogan **5.00**
Magazine, *TV Wrestlers,* Buddy Rogers cov, 1961 . . . . **30.00**
Photograph, Bill Goldberg, color, sgd, 8 x 10" **20.00**
Photograph, Hulk Hogan, color, sgd, 8 x 10" **20.00**
Picture Disc, Jesse the Body Ventura **10.00**
Poster, Ali vs Inoki closed circuit, 1975 . . . . **25.00**

Ringside Card, 1950s, $10.00.

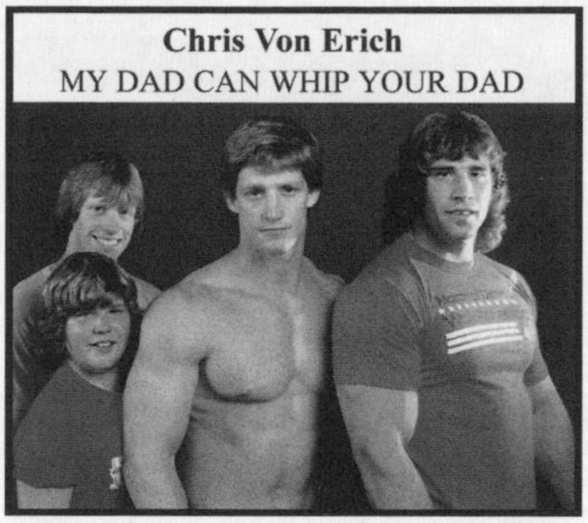

Chris Von Erich
MY DAD CAN WHIP YOUR DAD

Record, *My Dad Can Whip Your Dad,* Chris Von Erich, 45 rpm, $5.00.

Record, Gentrys with Jimmy Hart, 45 rpm **5.00**
Record, *Wrestling Album, The* **10.00**
Trading Card, Spalding, 1926 . . . . **100.00**
Trading Card, WWF, Coca-Cola, set of 20, 1987 . . . . **10.00**
VCR Game, Remco, AWA All Star Wrestling **25.00**

WRISTWATCHES

The pocket watch generations have been replaced by the wristwatch generations. This category became hot in the late 1980s and still is going strong. There is a great deal of speculation occurring, especially in the area of character and personality watches.

Since the category is relatively new as a collectible, no one is certain exactly how many watches have survived. I have almost a dozen that were handed down from my parents. If I am typical, the potential market supply is far greater than anyone realizes.

Club: National Assoc. of Watch & Clock Collectors, Inc., 514 Poplar St., Columbia, PA 17512.

Newsletter: *The Premium Watch Watch,* 24 San Rafael Dr., Rochester, NY 14618; *The Swatch Collectors Club,* P.O. Box 7400, Melville, NY 11747.

Periodical: *Comic Watch Times,* 106 Woodgate Terrace, Rochester, NY 14625; *International Wrist Watch,* P.O. Box 110204 Stamford, CT 06911.

Advertising, Big Boy, Windert **$85.00**
Advertising, Fruit Stripe Gum **50.00**
Advertising, Hawaiian Punch, 1970s **60.00**
Advertising, McDonald's, digital, MOC **10.00**
Advertising, Nabisco Ritz Crackers **60.00**
Character, Barbie, Bradley, ©1971 Mattel **100.00**
Character, Chipmunks, Bradley, not working **25.00**
Character, Flipper, ITF, chromed metal expansion band, 1960s **75.00**
Character, Holly Hobbie, Bradley, 1972, not working **40.00**
Character, Lucy Van Pelt, Peanuts, United Features Syndicate, Inc, full figure Lucy wearing yellow dress, white straps, 1952 copyright on face, c1970 . . . . **40.00**
Character, Mickey Mouse, Ingersoll, no picture **90.00**
Character, Nightmare Before Christmas, Timex, black and white plastic and vinyl, 3-D dial with digital display, ©1993 Touchstone Pictures, MIP **25.00**
Character, Ren & Stimpy, Nickelodeon Bigtime Enterprises, orig warranty and case, 1992 . . . . **50.00**
Character, Shirt Tales, Timex, 1981 . . . . **40.00**

Character, Hopalong Cassidy, United States Time Corp., $70.00.

Character, Uncle Scrooge, Lorus, black vinyl strap, c1990 . . . . 75.00
Character, Wonder Woman, DC Comics, 1975 . . . . 150.00
Lady's, Accutron, Bulova, leather bands, 14K case 125.00
Lady's, Antionette, Girod, 14K yg case 150.00
Lady's, Hamilton, Haddon, 17j, 1953 . . . . 90.00
Lady's, Longines, 14K yg case, orig box 250.00
Lady's, Rolex, 17j, gold filled, c1945 . . . . 60.00
Man's, Bulova, Sky Chief, 17j, steel, c1940 . . . . 225.00
Man's, Elgin, Sportsman, 17j 25.00
Man's, Illinois, Aviator, 17j, gold filled 175.00
Man's, Swiss, mesh golf ball shape 110.00
Swatch, Beach Graffiti/Bikini, GJ 105 . . . . 80.00
Swatch, Calypso Beach/Rotor, GS 400 . . . . 230.00
Swatch, D J Ten-Strikes/Rave, GK 134 . . . . 40.00
Swatch, Granita Di Fruta, Banana 110.00
Swatch, Leonardos/Engineer, GB 139 . . . . 90.00
Swatch, Medieval/Tristan, LK 120 . . . . 40.00
Swatch, Morgans/Mezza Luna, GB 107 . . . . 120.00
Swatch, Mosaiques/Ravenna, GR 107 . . . . 90.00

YARD-LONG PRINTS

Yard-long prints cover a wide variety of subject matter. Desirability rests not so much with subject as with illustrator. The more recognized the name, the higher the price.

Calendar, 1907, diecut, little girl wearing red hat and boots holding puppy, ©1906 Grand Union Tea Co, Brooklyn, NY, 10 x 30" $200.00
Calendar, 1910, Priscilla, Schlitz Malt Extract adv, Jos Schlitz Brewing Co, Milwaukee, adv on back for medicine with pictures of Priscilla, John Alden, and Miles Standish, 7¼ x 36" 350.00
Calendar, 1911, Fancies Groceries, Hay and Grain, woman wearing yellow coat and matching bonnet, R W Harkin's Co adv, 12 x 32" 250.00
Calendar, 1911, Pompeian Beauty, logo at bottom, full calendar on back, 8½ x 29" 200.00
Calendar, 1914, A Walk-Over Girl, sgd C Everett Johnson 300.00
Calendar, 1917, woman holding basket of flowers, Selz Good Shoes adv, The Snyder Mercantile Co, Washtucna, WA, 12 x 40" 350.00
Calendar, 1922, Harvest Moon, John Clay & Company Live Stock Commissiion adv on front and back, sgd Frank H. Desch, 12 x 35" 300.00
Calendar, 1924, woman wearing black gown and red wrap with black fur trim, Selz Good Shoes, sgd Gene Pressler, Geo Peterman's Shoe Store, Belle Plaine, Iowa adv 300.00
Calendar, 1927, woman wearing tassel-hemmed dress and gold robe with blue lining, Selz Good Shoes, by McClelland Barclay, Peterman's Shoe Store, Belle Plaine, Iowa adv 250.00

Print, 1909, Walk-Over Shoe Co., sgd E. Vernon, $200.00. Photo courtesy Gene Harris Antique Auction Center, Inc.

Calendar, 1929, woman wearing sleeveless red gown and fringed shawl, Selz Good Shoes, sgd Earl Chambers, Hughes Clothing Co, Sabetha, Kansas adv 275.00
Photograph, family reunion 30.00
Photograph, military graduation 35.00
Photograph, school graduation class 20.00
Photograph, tourist group 30.00
Print, Bride, R J Taylor, National Stockman and Farmer magazine, 1911 . . . . 300.00
Print, ducklings in water, W M Carey 150.00
Print, Easter Greetings, sgd Paul DeLongpre, litho, Knapp Co, 1894, 6½ x 24" 300.00
Print, Greetings from the Peoria Evening Star Carrier Boy, 1914 calendar on back 250.00
Print, Honeymooning in the Alps, sgd Gene Pressler, Pompeian Beauty adv, 1923 . . . . 150.00
Print, Our Feathered Pets, 12 birds sitting on lattice-work fence, sgd Paul DeLongpre 200.00
Print, Our White House Queen For 1911, White House Shoes adv, sgd Cordially Yours, Maxine Elliott 350.00
Print, kittens climbing tree, sgd Helena Maguire 175.00
Print, woman wearing sailor outfit, Clay, Robinson & Co Live Stock Commission, sgd R Ford Harper, c1914, 9½ x 24" 250.00

YO-YOs

Yo-yos are the only collecting category I know of where the collector is sometimes accused of being what he collects! In recent years, however yo-yos have become increasingly recognized as one of the hottest new collectibles. Some makes and models of vintage yo-yos from the 1920s through the 1960s are now worth hundreds of times their original retail price, depending on their condition and rarity.

The most desirable yo-yos are often the old wooden tournament and metal models by companies such as Flores, Bandalor, Duncan, Royal, Chico, Cheerio, Hi-Ker, Goody, Alox, Jewel, Fli-Back, Sock-It, Kayson, Festival, Lumar, Medalist, Ka-Yo, and HYLO. Wooden "Demonstrator-carved" tournament models are particularly desirable. These were embellished by professional yo-yo demonstrators with carvings of tropical ocean scenes featuring palm trees, sailboats, sunsets, flowers, seagulls, and birds of paradise. Other carved models may depict animals, children's names, and contest award certification. Wooden "Jeweled" tournament models inset with glass rhinestones of clear and various colors are also highly desirable and equally rare. Some early plastic models from the late 1940s to mid-1960s by companies such as Whirl-E-

Gig, Duncan, Royal, Festival, Dell's, and Kusan are also quite valuable. Yo-yos encased in lavishly embossed sterling silver shells by companies such as Gorham, L. S. M., Towle, and Alvin are a delight to any collector.

In order for a yo-yo to be a valuable collectible, its general condition must range from good to mint and it must have a good legible identification seal, which usually gives the manufacturer's name and the model. If the seal is missing, too severely damaged, or the paint is too badly chipped, the yo-yo lacks any real collectible value. Other yo-yo related collectibles of value include 5" diameter award yo-yos, contest award patches, sweaters, trophies, string packs, posters, boxes, trick books, and sheet music featuring yo-yo songs.

Although no organized club of yo-yo collectors presently exists in the United States, an excellent museum which contains much of the Duncan Family Yo-Yo Collection and many other vintage yo-yos is located in Northern California. A collector's fair is presently being planned in conjunction with their annual Nation Yo-Yo Contest, held in October.

National Yo-Yo Museum, c/o Bob Malowney, Director, 320 Broadway, Chico, CA 95928, (530) 893-0545. Open 7 days a week. Free admission. e-mail: www.nationalyoyo.org.

Advisor: Bill Caswell, 1512 Cherokee Pl., Bartlesville, OK, 74003, (918) 336-5130, e-mail: rosicas@juno.com.

Club: American Yo-Yo Assoc., 627 163rd St. South, Spanaway, WA 98387.

Newsletter: *Yo-Yo Times,* P.O. Box 1519, Herndon, VA 22070.

Note: Prices listed for yo-yos in mint condition.

Cheerio 25 Tournament Practice Return Top, wood, lacquer finish, airbrushed contrasting stripe, with gold foil sticker with black and red ink, mid 1940s–mid 1950s **$75.00**

Cheerio 55 Beginners, wood, solid color lacquer paint, die-stamp, 1954–57 . . . . **75.00**

Cheerio 55 Beginners Return Top, wood, 2-tone lacquer finish, silver foil sticker with black ink print, mid 1940s–mid 1950s **75.00**

Cheerio Glitter Spin, wood, solid color lacquer finish, gold foil sticker with black and red ink lettering **175.00**

Cheerio Official Pro 99 Tournament, wood, natural finish, gold foil sticker with blue and red ink print, maple leaf logo design, mid-1940s–mid-1950s **75.00**

Chico Superb Junior Top, wood, gold die stamp, 5-star design, 2-tone paint **35.00**

Duncan Bo-Yo Sportsline-Amflite Bowling Ball, black ball shaped plastic, with hot stamped logo on front, 1965 . . . . **30.00**

Duncan Butterfly Yo-Yo, wood, butterfly model, solid color glitter paint, gold die-stamp butterfly logo, mid-1950s **40.00**

Duncan Disney's Wonderful World of Color Yo-Yo Return Top, plastic with silver or colored embedded stars, clear plastic side lenses with gold hot stamp logo, 1962 . . . . **35.00**

Duncan Imperial Yo-Yo, plastic with gold hot stamped Fleur-de-lis logo and Imperial in lower case letters, transparent, translucent, opaque, or swirled plastic, early-mid-1960s **35.00**

Duncan Imperial Yo-Yo Tops, plastic with gold hot stamped logo, transparent, translucent, opaque, or swirled plastic, Chevron "V" logo with "Tenite" below, script Imperial logo, 1954–early 1960s **35.00**

Duncan Litening Yo-Yo Return Top, wood, crackled enamel finish resembling lightning bolts, gold and white foil sticker with lightning bolt across, late 1950s . . . **100.00**

Duncan O-Boy Yo-Yo Pat Pend, wood, red and black tumbled lacquer finish, silver die-stamp, 1932 . . . . **60.00**

Duncan O-Boy Whistling Yo-Yo, litho tin color design, four 1/4" whistle holes on each side, black in logo, 1930s **125.00**

Duncan Pony Boy Yo-Yo Top Model 22, plastic rims with clear or colored side lenses, hidden bb's placed inside cause rattle effect, 1955 . . . . **60.00**

Duncan Seattlite Space Needle Yo-Yo Return Top, wood, each side resembles top of Seattle Space Needle, souvenir of 1962 Seattle Century 21 Exposition World's Fair **100.00**

Duncan Shrieking Sonic Satellite Yo-Yo, wood, flying saucer shape with air "portholes" around each rim and metal whistles inserted in each side, solid color or 2-tone glitter paint on each side, gold die-stamp logo, 1962 . . . . **60.00**

Duncan Super Yo-Yo Tournament Tops, Model 77, wood, solid color lacquer finish with contrasting airbrushed stripe, gold die-stamp, trademark ® under hyphen in "Yo-Yo," "Super" in logo, early–late 1950s **50.00**

Duncan Yo-Yo Return Top M-1 Satellite, wood, flying saucer shape, 1960 . . . . **40.00**

Festival Big Zapper Yo-Yo, wood, solid lacquer colors with gold contrasting stripe, gold die-stamp logo **20.00**

Festival Screamer Yo-Yo, tin, whistling, checkerboard or zebra stripe designs, paper sticker label, 1972 . . . . **25.00**

Flores Yo-Yo Pat Pend, wood, solid color lacquer finish with black paint seal, late 1920s–early 1930s **225.00**

Genuine Duncan Jeweled Yo-Yo, wood, solid color lacquer finish, 4 clear rhinestones on each side in straight line, gold die-stamp logo, 1930s–early 1960s **65.00**

Genuine Duncan Tournament Yo-Yo Tops Reg US Pat Off, wood, color lacquer finish, airbrush stripe, gold decal with black print, "Genuine" in logo, 1930s **60.00**

Genuine Duncan Whistling Yo-Yo, litho tin color designs, four 1/4" whistle holes on each side, "Genuine" in logo, 1930s **100.00**

Genuine Duncan Yo-Yo Tournament Top 77, wood, solid color lacquer finish with contrasting airbrushed stripe, yellow decal with black and red print, 1946–49 . . . . **60.00**

Duncan, Butterfly, #3058NP, green, mail-in offer and instructions on back, $12.00.

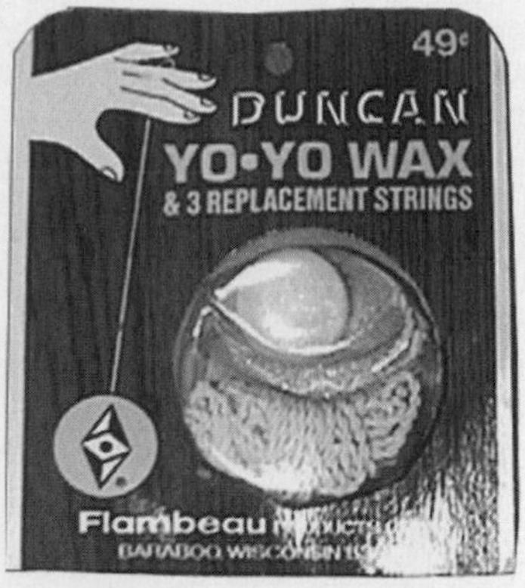

Duncan Yo-Yo Wax and 3 Replacement Strings, Flambeau Products Corp., 4 x 4½", $5.00.

Snow Globe, Turtle Back Zoo, 3 injection-molded panels, mkd "Made in Hong Kong," 1970s, 2¼" h, 6½" w, $8.00.

Genuine Goody Master Filipino Twirler, wood, solid color lacquer with airbrushed contrasting stripe, silkscreened paint seal, 1 jewel in center of logo side, 1940s–50s **75.00**
Genuine Goody Comet Filipino Twirler, wood, solid color lacquer with airbrushed contrasting stripe, silkscreened paint seal, 2 jewels on logo side, 1940s–50s **100.00**
Genuine Goody Champion Filipino Twirler, good, solid color lacquer with airbrushed contrasting stripe, silkscreened paint seal, 3 jewels on logo side, 1940s–50s **100.00**
Genuine Goody Trophy Filipino Twirler, wood, solid color gold or silver lacquer with silkscreened paint seal, 4 or 5 jewels on logo side, 1940–50s **150.00**
Goody Rainbow Filipino Twirler, solid black lacquer color with or without gold airbrushed contrasting stripe, silkscreened paint seal, 7 jewels of various colors on logo side, 1940s–50s **200.00**
Genuine Goody Atomic Filipino Twirler, wood, lacquer paint, silkscreened paint seal, 1940–50s **100.00**
Genuine Goody Filipino Twirler, wood, 2-tone lacquer, silkscreened paint seal, 1940s–50s **50.00**
Hallmark, Peanuts, plastic **15.00**
Hasbro Glow-Action Yo-Yo **25.00**
Hi-Ker Original Flat Top, butterfly model, wood, solid color lacquer, airbrushed contrasting stripe, gold die-stamp with aircraft carrier logo, mid–late 1950s **50.00**
Hi-Ker Professional Top Tournament Model, wood, solid color lacquer, airbrushed contrasting stripe, gold die-stamp, mid–late 1950s **50.00**
Hi-Ker Sparkle Master, wood, solid color lacquer pearl luster paint, 4 rhinestone jewels in box pattern on each side, gold die-stamp, 1955 . . . . **175.00**
Hi-Ker Spin Master, wood, solid color glitter or pearl luster lacquer with gold die-stamp, mid–late 1950s **125.00**
Kayson Streamline Top, wood, 2-tone lacquer paint with decal, 1930s **80.00**
Musical Ka-Yo, litho tin multicolor design and logo, two ¼" whistle holes on each side, 1930s **150.00**
Royal Official Tournament Yo-Yo Tops, wood, color lacquer finish with decal crown logo, jeweled with 4 rhinestones inserted on each side in straight line, 1959 . . . . **75.00**
Royal Thunderbird, wood, butterfly model, solid lacquer colors, Thunderbird decal logo, 1962 . . . . **50.00**
Whistling Ka-Yo, tin, wood grain sheet plastic overlay finish, black and white, or pink paper sticker, four ¼" whistle holes on each side, 1940s **150.00**

ZOO COLLECTIBLES

I have been trying for years to find "Z" categories to end antiques and collectibles price guides. Finally, a book in which zoo collectibles are not out of place!

Ashtray, glass, Denver Zoo, center decal **$5.00**
Book, *Albert's Stencil Zoo,* Little Golden Book, 1951 . . . . **25.00**
Game, Fun at the Zoo, 1902 . . . . **200.00**
Game, Marlin Perkins Zoo Parade, Cadaco, 1955 . . . . **90.00**
Game, Zoo Hoo, 1924 . . . . **55.00**
Medal, Philadelphia Zoo, silver finish, c1960 . . . . **10.00**
Pennant, felt, green, Philadelphia Zoo, white lettering and animal illus, 25" l **10.00**
Pennant, felt, San Francisco Zoo **5.00**
Pinback Button, Audubon Society, multicolored, red cardinal perched on dogwood branch, light green ground, c1920–30 . . . . **12.50**
Pinback Button, San Diego Zoo, multicolored, elephants and tigers **5.00**
Plate, Limited Edition, Zoological Gardens, Kern, Elephants, M Carroll, 1983 . . . . **55.00**
Playing Cards, Wild Animal Park, San Diego, color **30.00**
Sign, door hanger type, "City Zoo," white and yellow, "Do Not Disturb" on back **1.50**
Stein, Endangered Species Series, cougar, 1995 . . . . **35.00**
View-Master Reel, #295, St Louis Zoological Park **3.00**

Part Three

REFERENCE SOURCES

FLEA MARKETEER'S ANNOTATED REFERENCE LIBRARY

A typical flea market contains hundreds of thousands of objects. You cannot be expected to identify and know the correct price for everything off the top of your head. **You need a good, basic reference library.**

As a flea marketeer, there are two questions about every object that you want to know: "What is it?" and "How much is it worth?" A book that answers only the first question has little use in the field. Titles in the "Books About Objects" list contain both types of information.

This basic reference library consists of fifty titles. I admit the number is arbitrary. However, some limit was necessary. Acquiring all the titles on the list will not be cheap. Expect to pay somewhere between $1,250 and $1,500. You can occasionally find some of these books at clearance prices—25% to 75% off—from the publishers or at discount book sellers.

The list contains a few books that are out-of-print. You will have to pursue their purchase through various used-book sources.

Many antiques and collectibles book dealers conduct book searches and maintain "wants" lists. It is common to find one or more of these specialized dealers set up at a flea market. Most advertise in the trade papers, especially ***The Antique Trader Weekly*** (PO Box 1050, Dubuque, Iowa 52002) and "Books For Sale" in the classified section of ***AntiqueWeek*** (PO Box 90, Knightstown, IN 46148). One dealer that I have found particularly helpful in locating out-of-print books is Joslin Hall Rare Books, PO Box 516, Concord, MA 01742.

Many reference books are revised every year or every other year. The editions listed are those as of Spring 1999. When you buy them, make certain that you get the most recent edition.

One final factor that I used in preparing this list was a desire to introduce you to the major publishers and imprints in the antiques and collectibles field. It is important that you become familiar with Antique Publications (Glass Press), Antique Trader Books, Avon, The Charlton Press, Collector Books, House of Collectibles, Krause Publications and its various imprints, L-W Book Sales, Schiffer Publishing, and Tomart Publications.

GENERAL PRICE GUIDES

Rinker, Harry L., ***Harry L. Rinker The Official Price Guide to Collectibles, 3rd ed.*** (New York: House of Collectibles: 1999). This listing is totally self-serving. I firmly believe I author the best price guide to post-1920 collectibles and that you should own it. This guide is truly comprehensive, containing dozens of collecting categories not found in other "collectibles" price guides.

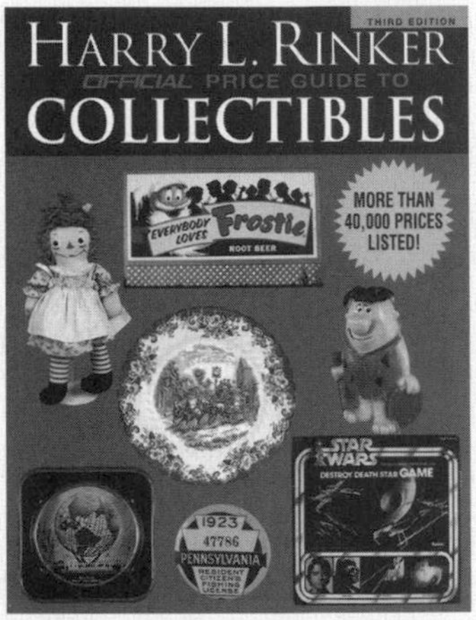

The introduction to each category contains a brief history, list of reference books, names and addresses of periodicals and collectors' clubs, and information about reproductions. It is the perfect companion to ***The Official Price Guide to Flea Market Treasures.***

Does a flea marketeer need a general antiques and collectibles price guide? The realistic answer is no. As each year passes, antiques play a smaller and smaller role in the flea market environment. General antiques and collectibles price guides tend to be heavily weighted toward the antiques portion of the market. Most flea marketeers, whether buyers or sellers, deal primarily in 20th century collectibles.

Yet, I believe every flea marketeer should maintain a multiple year run of one general antiques and collectibles price guide for the purposes of tracking market trends and researching and pricing objects that fall outside their knowledge level. The worst mistake a flea marketeer can make is to buy a different general antiques and collectibles price guide from one year to the next. Find the guide that best serves your need and stick to it.

The following three price guides are listed in the order of frequency that I see them being used in the field. The order is not by my personal preference. However, I am putting aside personal feelings and reporting facts.

Huxford, Sharon and Bob, ed., ***Schroeder's Antiques Price Guide, 17th ed.*** (Paducah, KY: Collector Books: 1999).

Kovel, Ralph and Terry, ed., ***Kovels' Antiques & Collectibles Price List for the 1999 Market, 31st ed.*** (New York: Three Rivers Press: 1999).

Husfloen, Kyle, ed., ***Antique Trader Books Antiques and Collectibles Price Guide, 15th ed.*** (Dubuque, IA: Antique Trader Books: 1998).

Starting with the **Seventeenth Edition**, Rinker Enterprises assumed the editorship of the ***Official Price Guide To Antiques and Collectibles*** (New York: House of Collectibles, 1999). Our goal is to make it one of the top three general antiques and collectibles price guides by 2002. Those titles that appear above are forewarned.

IDENTIFICATION OF REPRODUCTIONS AND FAKES

Hammond, Dorothy, ***Confusing Collectibles: A Guide to the Identification of Contemporary Objects.*** This book provides information about reproductions, copycats, fantasy Items, fakes, and contemporary crafts from the late 1950s through the 1960s. Much of this material appears regularly in today's flea markets. Some is collectible in its own right. The best defense against being taken is to know what was produced.

Hammond, Dorothy, ***More Confusing Collectibles, Vol. II.*** (Wichita, KS: C. B. P. Publishing Company: 1973). Out-of-print. ***Confusing Collectibles*** took a broad approach to the market. ***More Confusing Collectibles*** focuses primarily on glass. It contains all new information, so you really do need both volumes.

Lee, Ruth Webb, ***Antiques Fakes and Reproductions*** (published by author: 1938, 1950). Out-of-print. Note: This book went through eight editions. The later editions contain more information. A good rule is to buy only the fourth through eighth editions. Dorothy Hammond followed in Ruth Webb Lee's footsteps. Lee's book chronicles the reproductions, copycats, fantasy items, and fakes manufactured between 1920 and 1950. While heavily oriented toward glass, it contains an excellent chapter on metals, discussing and picturing in detail the products of Virginia Metalcrafters.

Antique & Collectors Reproduction News. This is not a book, yet it belongs on this list. This monthly publication tracks the latest reproductions, copycats, fantasy items, and fakes. An annual subscription costs $32, an amount you are certain to save several times over during the course of a year. Consider acquiring a full set of back issues. Write *Antique & Collectors Reproduction News,* PO Box 12130, Des Moines, IA 50312.

BOOKS ABOUT OBJECTS

Austin, Richard J., ***The Official Price Guide To Military Collectibles, 6th ed.*** (New York: House of Collectibles: 1998). This book covers military collectibles from medieval to modern times. The book is organized topically, e.g., uniforms and footwear, helmets and headgear, etc. It also includes chapters on military images, military paper, military art, and homefront collectibles. It provides one-volume coverage of the material found in Ron Manion's three-volume set ***American Military Collectibles Price*** (1995), ***Japanese & Other Foreign Military Collectibles*** (1996), and ***German Military Collectibles*** (1995), all published by Antique Trader Books.

Baker, Mark, ***Auto Racing Memorabilia and Price Guide*** (Iola, WI: Krause Publications: 1997). Auto racing collectibles replaced baseball collectibles as the hot sport collecting category of the 1990s. Collecting auto racing memorabilia, from dirt track to Indy cars, has shed its regional cloak and become national in scope. Baker's book is the first off the starting line. James Beckett and Eddie Kelly's ***Beckett Racing Price Guide and Alphabetical Checklist*** only covers trading cards and diecast cars. A checkered flag for Baker because he includes these and much, much more.

Barlow, Ronald S., ***The Antique Tool Collector's Guide to Value*** (Gas City, IN: L-W Book Sales: 1991, 1999 value update). This is the book for tools. Barlow has compiled auction and market prices from across the United States. Since this book is organized by tool type, you need to identify the type of tool that you have before you can look it up. There are plenty of illustrations to help. Treat the pricing with some caution.

Bagdade, Susan and Al, ***Warman's American Pottery and Porcelain*** (Radnor, PA: Wallace-Homestead: 1994, available from Krause Publications). Recommended because of its wide range of coverage. The category introductions provide a wealth of good information, including a large number of drawings of marks. Pricing that is auction based is clearly indicated. Use to cross-check information in Duke's ***The Official Price Guide to Pottery and Porcelain.***

The Bagdades also authored ***Warman's English & Continental Pottery & Porcelain, 3rd ed.*** While most ceramics found at American flea markets are American in origin, European pieces do slip into the mix. If you encounter English and Continental ceramics on a regular basis, consider adding this second Bagdade book to your library.

Bunis, Marty and Sue, ***Collector's Guide to Antique Radios, 4th ed.*** (Paducah, KY: Collector Books: 1997). There is a wealth of radio books in the market. This one is tuned in to a wide band of radios. Organization is by manufacturer and model number. Although heavily illustrated, the book does not picture the majority of the models listed. The book also covers radio parts and accessories.

Collectors' Information Bureau's Collectibles Market Guide & Price Index, 16th ed. (Barrington, IL: Collectors' Information Bureau: 1998). The best thing about this book is that it covers a wide range of limited edition types, from bells to steins. It serves as a collector's checklist.The worst thing is that it is industry-driven. Important negatives and warnings about the limited edition market are minimized. When the issue value and secondary value are identical or within a few dollars assume the real secondary market value is between 20% and 40% of the issue price.

Cornwell, Sue, and Mike Kott, ***House of Collectibles Price Guide to Star Trek Collectibles, 4th ed.*** (New York: House of Collectibles: 1996). There is no question that *Star Trek* collectibles will "live long and prosper." This price guide covers over 5,000 items licensed for the initial *Star Trek* television program, the movies, and television spin-off series, *Star Trek: The Next Generation, Star Trek: Voyager,* and *Deep Space 9*. Includes some foreign licensed materials. Unfortunately, a chapter on convention souvenirs is nowhere to be found.

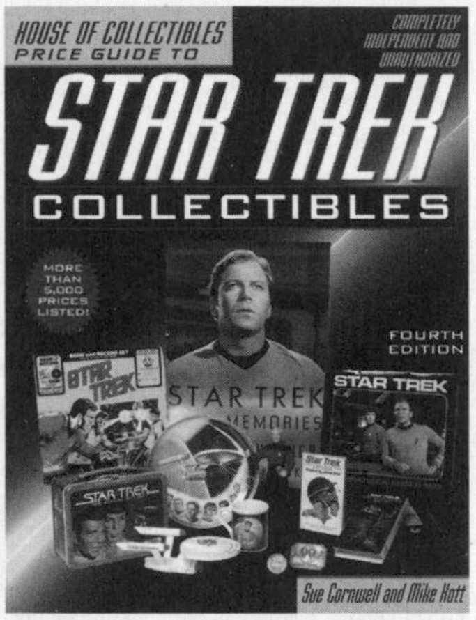

Cornwell, Sue and Mike Kott, ***House of Collectibles Price Guide To Star Wars Collectibles, 4th ed.*** (New York: House of Collectibles: 1997). *Star Wars* won the galactic battle over *Star Trek* for universal dominance in the field of space collectibles with Lucas' 1997 re-release of the *Star Wars* trilogy. When the first of the prequels premiers in May 1999, the world will go *Star Wars* mad. Many, myself among them, are predicting a major pricing jump in older *Star Wars* material. This book documents values prior to their jump to light speed.

Cunningham, Jo, ***The Collector's Encyclopedia of American Dinnerware*** (Paducah, KY: Collector Books: 1982, 1998 price update). This is a profusely illustrated guide to identifying 20th century American dinnerware. In spite of the fact that many new companies and patterns have been discovered since Cunningham prepared her book, it remains a valuable identification tool, especially since its pricing is updated periodically.

Dale, Jean. ***The Charlton Standard Catalogue of Royal Doulton Beswick Figures, 6th ed.*** (Toronto: The Charlton Press: 1998). This is one in a series of four books edited by Dale covering the products of Royal Doulton Beswick. The others are: ***The Charlton Standard Catalogue of Royal Doulton Animals, 2nd Ed.*** (1998); ***The Charlton Standard Catalogue of Royal Doulton Beswick Jugs,* 4th ed.** (1995); and ***The Charlton Standard Catalogue of Royal Doulton Beswick Storybook Figurines, 4th ed.*** (1998). A feature of each of these books is that pricing information is provided in English pounds, Canadian dollars, and American dollars. Americans should pay more attention to books published by The Charlton Press. The title list includes books on chintz and hockey trading cards.

Duke, Harvey, ***The Official Identification and Price Guide to Pottery and Porcelain, 8th ed.*** (New York: House of Collectibles: 1995). This book is dinnerware, kitchenware, and accessory oriented. As such it is the perfect companion to Cunningham. Duke covers many of the companies and lines of which Cunningham was unaware when she first published her book in the early 1980s. Illustrations are minimal, making it necessary to know the name of your pattern before looking anything up. The book is well-balanced regionally. Many West Coast pottery manufacturers finally receive their due. Its major drawback is the lack of an index, hopefully something that will be corrected in the next edition, due out in 2000.

Florence, Gene, ***The Collector's Encyclopedia of Depression Glass, 13th ed.*** (Paducah, KY: Collector Books: 1998). This is the Depression glass collector's bible. Among its important features are a full listing of pieces found in each pattern and an extensive section on reproductions, copycats, and fakes. One difficulty is that there are hundreds of glass patterns manufactured between 1920 and 1940 that are not found in this book because they do not have the Depression Glass label. Supplement the book with Gene Florence's ***Kitchen Glassware of the Depression Years,*** also published by Collector Books, and Ellen Schroy's ***Warman's Depression Glass: A Value & Identification Guide*** (Krause Publications, 1997).

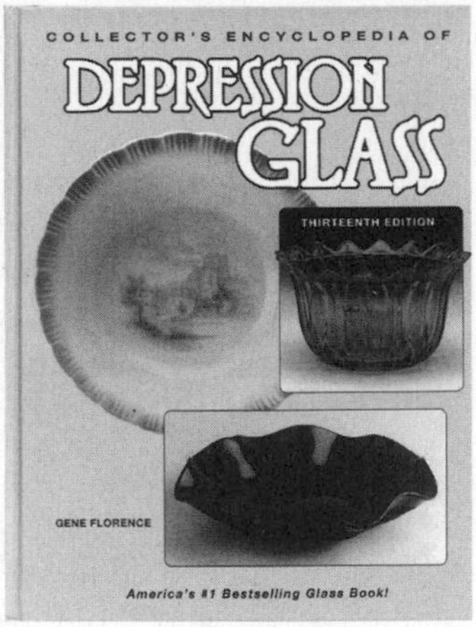

Foulke, Jan, ***13th Blue Book Dolls and Values*** (Grantsville, MD: Hobby House Press: 1997). Foulke is the first place doll collectors turn for information. The book is high-end, turning its back on many of the post–World War II and contemporary dolls. Within the doll field, it sets prices more than it reports them. Cross-check Foulke's prices in Dawn Herlocher's ***200 Years of Dolls: Identification and Price Guide*** (Antique Trader Books).

Franklin, Linda Campbell, ***300 Years of Housekeeping Collectibles*** (Books Americana, now an imprint of Krause Publications, Iola, WI: 1993). Books Americana split the second edition of ***300 Years of Kitchen Collectibles*** into two separate volumes, albeit retaining the edition number for one of the spin-offs. Now, instead of paying $10.95 for a handy-to-use single source, you have to pay $47.90 for two volumes. Hopefully a publisher will see an opportunity and once again put this information in a single volume. Until such time, it makes sense to buy the two Franklin volumes.

Franklin, Linda Campbell, ***300 Years of Kitchen Collectibles, 4th ed.*** (Iola, WI: Krause Publications: 1997). The fourth edition's format is a considerable improvement over that of the third edition. The book is much easier to use. The wealth of secondary material may be great for researchers and specialized collectors, but it is a pain to wade through when you just want to look up something quickly. This focus is primarily in 19th and early 20th century material. It is not the source to use if your kitchen item dates from the post-1945 era.

Gibbs, P. J., ***Black Collectibles Sold in America*** (Paducah, KY: Collector Books: 1987, 1996 value update). Black collectibles have gone through a number of collecting cycles in the past fifteen years. Popular among both white and black collectors, Black memorabilia is likely to cycle several more times in the years ahead. Because of this, prices in any Black collectibles book have to be taken with a grain of salt.

Hagan, Tere, ***Silverplated Flatware, revised 4th ed.*** (Paducah, KY: Collector Books: 1990, 1998 value update). You do not see a great deal of sterling silver at flea markets because most dealers sell it for weight. Silver-plated items are in abundance. This book concentrates only on flatware, the most commonly found form. While you can research silver-plated hollowware in Jeri Schwartz's ***The Official Identification and Price Guide to Silver and Silverplate, 6th ed.*** (House of Collectibles, 1989), disregard the prices. The market has changed significantly.

Hake, Ted, ***Hake's Guide to ...*** series (Radnor, PA: Wallace-Homestead). In the first half of the 1990s, Ted Hake authored a five-book priced picture-book series focusing on material sold in Hake's Americana & Collectibles Mail Auction. Each collecting category is introduced with a brief history, often containing information not readily available to the collector. The series consists of: ***Hake's Guide to Advertising Collectibles: 100 Years of Advertising From 100 Famous Companies*** (1992); ***Hake's Guide to Comic Character Collectibles: An Illustrated Price Guide to 100 Years of Comic Strip Characters*** (1993); ***Hake's Guide to Cowboy Character Collectibles: An Illustrated Price Guide Covering 50 Years of Movie and TV Cowboy Heroes*** (1994); ***Hake's Guide to Presidential Campaign Collectibles: An Illustrated Price Guide to Artifacts from 1789–1988*** (1992); and, ***Hake's Guide to TV Collectibles: An Illustrated Price Guide*** (1990). Several titles are out-of-print. Some are still available from Krause Publications. Allowing this series to die was one in a long list of mistakes made by Chilton Books in the company's final years as publisher of Wallace-Homestead and Warman titles.

Hake, Ted, ***Overstreet Presents: Hake's Price Guide to Character Toys Including Premiums, Comic, Cereal, TV, Movies, Radio & Related Store Bought Items, 2nd ed.*** (Timonium, MD: Gemstone Publications, 1997; distributed by Avon Books as part of its The Confident Collector Series). Hake is the king of collectibles. If anyone knows, he does. This title covers 350 categories and 200 different types of items. Its 7,000 listings range from common to one-of-a-kind premiums. The category introductions provide historical data not available elsewhere. Also be sure to read the front matter. It provides insights into the latest market trends.

Herlocher, Dawn, ***200 Years of Dolls: Identification and Price Guide*** (Dubuque, IA: Antique Trader Books: 1997). Doll identification and pricing information presented in a fresh, new, and extremely usable format. Covering 125 doll manufacturers, the book features a mix of antique and collectibles dolls. Use to cross-check the information and pricing in Foulke's ***Blue Book of Doll Values.***

Huxford, Bob, ***Huxfords Old Book Value Guide, 10th ed.*** (Paducah, KY: Collector Books: 1998). There are always piles of old books at any flea market. Most are valued at less than 50 cents. However, there are almost always sleepers in every pile. This book is a beginning. If you think that you have a really expensive tome, check it out in the most recent edition of ***American Book Prices Current,*** published by Bancroft-Parkman.

Martinus, Norman E., and Harry L. Rinker, ***Warman's Paper*** (Radnor, PA: Wallace-Homestead: 1994).The paper market is hot and getting hotter. Paper is available and affordable. The market already has dozens of specialized shows. ***Warman's Paper,*** is organized into seventy-five collecting topics and over two hundred subject topics. Of all the books with which I have been involved, this title ranks number three on my "most proud" list, right behind ***Harry L. Rinker The Official Price Guide to Collectibles*** and ***Warman's Furniture.***

Melillo, Marcie, ***The Ultimate Barbie Doll Book*** (Iola, WI: Krause Publications: 1997). Barbie—the vinyl goddess, the billion dollar baby—has become so important she deserves a separate listing. There are dozens of Barbie price guides available. This is my favorite full coverage guide. When I want information on contemporary Barbies, my choice is the new edition of Jane Sarasohn-Kahn's ***Contemporary Barbie: Barbie Dolls 1980 and Beyond*** (Antique Trader Books, 1998). Also consider adding a Barbie price guide that includes information on costumes and accessories, two hot Barbie subcollecting categories in the late 1990s.

Morykan, Dana G., ***The Official Price Guide to Country Antiques and Collectibles, 4th ed.***, (New York: House of Collectibles: 1999). This is the bible for Country collectibles. Published previously as part of the Warman series, it has found a new home in New York. For those who still feel the need for a picture-oriented guide, check out Don and Carol Raycraft's ***Wallace-Homestead Price Guide to American Country Antiques, 15th ed.,*** (Krause Publications, 1997).

Morykan, Dana G., and Harry L. Rinker, ***Garage Sale Manual & Price Guide*** (Dubuque, IA: Antique Trader Publications: 1995). The only price guide that covers recyclables, objects whose value rests primarily with their reuse and not collectibility. Includes over 100 categories, from adding machines and artificial flowers to umbrellas and video game systems and cartridges. Are garage sale objects sold at flea markets? You bet they are and in large quantities. Just the coverage you need for low–end material. If you can make a buck, why not sell it?

Osborne, Jerry, ***The Official Price Guide to Records, 12th ed.*** (New York: House of Collectibles: 1997). This is the book to which everyone refers. It lists every charted hit single and album from 1950s through 1990. Alas, it provides minimal coverage for pre–1940 records. Today, record collecting is highly specialized. There are dozens of specialized price guides to records, many published by Krause Publications.

O'Brien, Richard, ***Collecting Toys: Identification and Value Guide, 8th ed.*** (Iola, WI: Krause Publications, 1997). The reason that there are no specialized toy or game books on this list is that you have no need for them if you own a copy of O'Brien. The book dominates the field. It is not without its weaknesses, especially in the area of post–World War II toys. However, each edition brings improvement. O'Brien has enlisted the help of specialists to price many of the sections, an approach that greatly strengthens the presentation.

Overstreet, Robert M., ***The Overstreet Comic Book Price Guide, 28th ed.*** (Timonium, MD: Gemstone Publishing: 1998). Distributed by Avon Books. Long live the king. Although focused too heavily on the Golden and Silver Age of American comics and not heavily enough on contemporary American comics, foreign issues, and underground comics, Overstreet is clearly the price guide of choice among adult collectors. This book sets the market more than it reports it.

Petretti, Allan, ***Petretti's Soda Pop Collectibles Price Guide: The Encyclopedia of Soda-Pop Collectibles*** (Dubuque, IA: Antique Trader Books: 1997). This is the latest offering from the king of Coca–Cola collectibles. This priced picture guide is organized first by object type and then alphabetically by soda company. Do not overlook Allan Petretti's ***Petretti's Coca-Cola Collectibles Price Guide, 10th ed.*** (Antique Trader Books, 1997). It introduces the Petretti numbering system, an easy method to describe Coca-Cola collectibles.

Rinker, Harry L., ***Dinnerware of the Twentieth Century: Top 500 Patterns*** (New York: House of Collectibles: 1997). This book provides detailed information on the 500 most popular dinnerware patterns sought by replacement buyers. Each pattern has an illustration of the plate from the set and a comprehensive checklist of the forms available. There are two other titles in this series: ***Stemware of the Twentieth Century: Top 200 Patterns*** covers the 200 most popular stemware patterns and ***Silverware of the Twentieth Century: Top 250 Patterns*** includes the 250 most popular sterling, silver plated, and stainless flatware patterns. Buy all three.

Romero, Christie, ***Warman's Jewelry, 2nd ed.*** (Iola, WI: Krause Publications: 1998). The best general price guide to jewelry available. It utilizes a time period approach, is well illustrated, and features highly detailed listing descriptions. The book is loaded with historical information, hallmarks, manufacturer's marks, reference source referrals, and a time line chronicling the history of jewelry. Appendices include a listing of American costume jewelry manufacturers (with dates of operation) and a glossary.

Schroy, Ellen, ***Warman's Glass, 3rd ed.*** (Iola, WI: Krause Publications: 1999). A comprehensive guide to the traditional glass market. While heavily American focused, it does include information on major English and European glass collecting categories. It has a balanced approach, covering everything from the finest art glass to household utilitarian glass. Check out Mark Pickvett's ***The Official Price Guide to Glassware, 2nd ed.*** (New York: House of Collectibles, 1998), a challenger to ***Warman's Glass*** that gets better and better with each new edition.

Shugart, Cooksey, Tom Engle and Richard E. Gilbert, ***Complete Price Guide to Watches, No. 18*** (Cleveland, TN: Cooksey Shugart Publications: 1998). Although this book has been distributed by four different publishers during the past ten years, it has never failed to maintain its high quality. It is the best book available on pocket and wrist watches.

Sports Collectors Digest, ***Baseball Card Price Guide, 12th ed.*** (Iola, WI: Krause Publications: 1998). This book has become a superstar. It is more comprehensive and accurate than its competition. Supplement it with the ***Sports Collectors Digest 1999 Standard Catalog of Baseball Cards, 8th Edition*** (Krause Publications, 1998). The one-two hitting combination of these two books relegate James Beckett's ***Baseball Card Price Guide,*** to benchwarmer status.

Swedberg, Robert W. and Harriett, ***Collector's Encyclopedia of American Furniture:*** three volumes: ***Volume 1—The Dark Woods of the Nineteenth Century: Cherry, Mahogany, Rosewood, and Walnut*** (1991, 1998 value update); ***Volume 2—Furniture of the Twentieth Century*** (1992, 1999 value update); and ***Volume 3—Country Furniture of the Eighteenth and Nineteenth Centuries*** (1998 value update). (Paducah, KY: Collector Books). The Swedbergs write about furniture. While their most recent work is done for Collector Books, Krause Publications still keeps their Wallace-Homestead series on oak furniture in print. It is worth a referral from time to time. Also do not ignore the ***Swedbergs' Furniture of the Depression Era: Furniture & Accessories of the 1920's, 1930's & 1940's*** (Collector Books, 1987, 1999 value update). All books utilize a priced-picture approach. Text information, including descriptions for individual pieces, is minimal. Sources are heavily Midwest. The plus factor is that the books feature pieces for sale in the field, not museum examples.

Wells, Stuart W., III, ***The Official Price Guide to Action Figures*** (New York: House of Collectibles, 1997). Finally, we have a price guide to action figures, and it is excellent. It provides background information and detailed listings for twenty-four major action figure groups such as the A-Team, Masters of the Universe, Marvel Superheroes, Spawn, Teenage Mutant Ninja Turtles, and X-Men. It even includes *Star Trek* and *Star Wars* figures. Its index is top of the line.

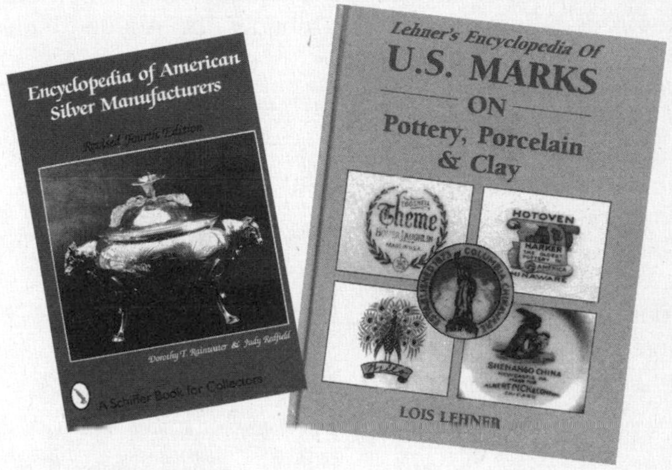

MARK BOOKS

Lehner, Lois, ***Lehner's Encyclopedia of U.S. Marks on Pottery, Porcelain, and Clay*** (Paducah, KY: Collector Books: 1988). This is the best reference book for identifying the marks of United States pottery and porcelain manufacturers. It contains detailed company histories and all known marks and trade names used. Whenever possible, marks and trade names are dated.

Rainwater, Dorothy T., ***Encyclopedia of American Silver Manufacturers, Fourth ed.*** (Atglen, PA: Schiffer Publishing: 1998). This book focuses on hand-crafted and mass-produced factory–manufactured silver and silver plate from the mid-nineteenth century to the present. It is organized alphabetically by company. Each detailed company history is accompanied by carefully drawn and dated marks. A glossary of trademarks is another welcome feature.

BUSINESS REFERENCES

Hyman, Dr. Tony, ***Trash or Treasure: How to Find The Best Buyers of Antiques, Collectibles and Other Undiscovered Treasures*** (Pismo Beach, CA: Treasure Hunt Publications, 1997). Tony Hyman is one of the most magnetic radio personalities that I have ever heard. He writes and compiles. Most importantly, he hustles what he has done. This is a list of people who buy things. One good contact pays for the cost of the book. It is also a great place to get your collecting interests listed.

Johnson, Don, and Elizabeth Borland, ***Selling Antiques & Collectibles: 50 Ways To Improve Your Business*** (Radnor, PA: Wallace-Homestead: 1993). Out-of-print. In a flea market era when there is a proliferation of dealers and fierce competition for customers, this book gives you the competitive edge. It shows you how to stand out from the crowd, increase clientele, and keep customers coming back. The advice is practical and budget conscious.

Maloney, David, Jr. ***Maloney's Antiques and Collectibles Resource Directory, 4th ed.*** (Dubuque, IA: Antique Trader Books: 1997). This is the one reference book to buy if you are only going to buy one. It is a comprehensive directory to the antiques and collectibles market containing approximately 15,000 entries (names, addresses, telephone numbers, and a wealth of other information) in approximately 2,900 categories. It is fully cross-referenced. It covers buyers, sellers, appraisers, restorers, collectors' clubs, periodicals, museums and galleries, show promoters, shops and malls, and many other specialists.

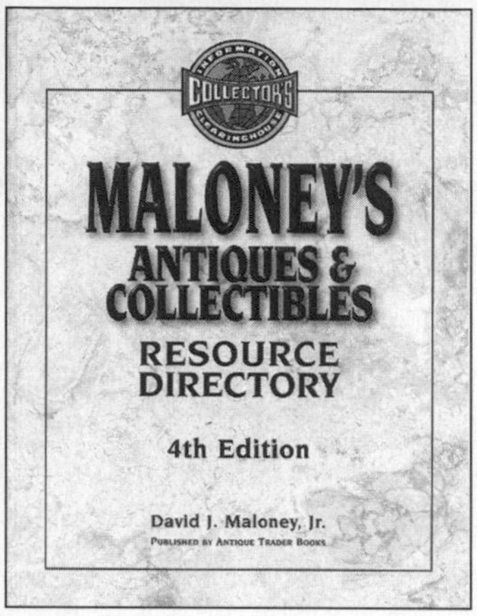

Vesely, Milan, ***Money From Antiques*** (Iola, WI: Krause Publications: 1997). This is one of a number of books that explains how to establish a small business selling antiques and collectibles. In previous editions, I recommended Robert G. Miner's ***The Flea Market Handbook*** (Wallace-Homestead, 1990). Although the information in this book remains the best there is relative to establishing a flea market business, it is out-of-print and difficult to find. Jacquelyn Peake's ***How to Open and Operate A Home-Based Antiques Business: An Unabridged Guide*** (The Globe Pequot Press, 1995) and Lisa Rogak's ***The Upstart Guide To Owning and Managing An Antiques Business*** (Upstart Publishing Co, 1995) offer more traditional business approach than Vesely.

Wanted to Buy, 6th ed. (Paducah, KY: Collector Books: 1997). This is another book listing individuals who want to buy things. If you are a serious collector, write to Collector Books and see if your name and interests can be included in subsequent editions. The book differs from ***Trash or Treasure*** because it contains several dozen listings and prices for most categories.

GENERAL REFERENCES

Kovel, Ralph and Terry, ***Kovels' Antiques & Collectibles Fix-It Source Book*** (New York: Crown Publishers: 1990). Many flea market treasures have not withstood the test of time well. While they should probably be passed by, they all too often wind up in the hands of a collector. This book provides advice on how to fix up these objects.

Rinker, Harry L., ***Rinker on Collectibles*** (Radnor, PA: Wallace–Homestead: 1988). Out-of-print. This book is a compilation of the first sixty test columns from my column, "Rinker on Collectibles." Many are now classics. The book allows you to delve into the mind-set of the collector. It deserves textbook status. I bought the remaining warehouse stock. If you would like a copy, send $10 to: Harry L. Rinker, 5093 Vera Cruz Road, Emmaus, PA 18049. I will even autograph it for you.

Werner, Kitty, ed., ***The Official Directory to U.S. Flea Markets, 6th ed.*** (New York: House of Collectibles: 1998). My opinion of this book is clearly stated in Chapter 2. Nothing has changed since I wrote that section.

JUST FOR THE FUN OF IT

Gash, Jonathan, ***The Sleepers of Erin*** (New York: Viking Penguin: 1983). If you are unfamiliar with Lovejoy the antiques dealer, it is time you make his acquaintance. You will not regret it. I had a hard time picking a favorite. I could have just as easily chosen ***The Judas Pair, Gold by Gemini, The Grail Tree, Spend Game, The Vatican Rip, and The Gondola Scam,*** all in paperback from Viking Penguin. I do not like the more recent Lovejoy novels, e.g., ***The Tartan Sell, Moonspender, and Pearlhanger***. They do not read well.

Rinker, Harry L. ***The Joy of Collecting with Craven Moore*** (Radnor, PA: Wallace-Homestead: 1985). Out-of-print. Try never to become so serious about your collecting or dealing that you forget to laugh and have fun. Find out if you are Craven Moore, Anita Moore, Howie Bys or Constance Lee Bys. Trust me, you are in ***The Joy of Collecting with Craven Moore.*** I guarantee it. Although out-of-print, I still have a few copies around. I will sell you one for $6.00. Send a check or money order to: Harry L. Rinker, 5093 Vera Cruz Road, Emmaus, PA 18049.

ANTIQUES & COLLECTIBLES TRADE NEWSPAPERS

Rinker Enterprises receives the following general and regional periodicals. Periodicals covering a specific collecting category are listed in the introductory material for that category.

NATIONAL MAGAZINES

Antique Trader's Collector Magazine & Price Guide
P.O. Box 1050
Dubuque, IA 52004-1050
(800) 334-7165
web: traderpr@mwci.net

Antiques & Collecting Magazine
1006 S. Michigan Avenue
Chicago, IL 60605
(800) 762-7576
Fax: (312) 939-0053
e mail: LightnerPb@aol.com

Collectors' Eye
6 Woodside Ave., Ste. 300
Northport, NY 11768
(516) 261-4100
Fax: (516) 261-9684
web: www.collectorseye.com

Collectors' Showcase
7134 S. Yale Ave., Ste. 300
Tulsa, OK 74136
(888) 622-3446
web: centralcirculation@webzone.com

Collectibles, Flea Market Finds
Goodman Media Group
1700 Broadway
New York, NY 10019
(800) 955-3870

NATIONAL NEWSPAPERS

The Antique Trader Weekly
P.O. Box 1050
Dubuque, IA 52004-1050
(800) 334-7165
Fax: (800) 531-0880
web: http://www.csmonline.com
e mail: traderpubs@aol.com

Antique Week (Central and Eastern Editions)
27 N. Jefferson St.
P.O. Box 90
Knightstown, IN 46148
(800) 876-5133
Fax: (800) 695-8153
web: http://www.antiqueweek.com
e mail: antiquewk@aol.com

Antiques and the Arts Weekly
The Bee Publishing Co.
P.O. Box 5503
Newtown, CT 06470-5503
(203) 426-8036
Fax: (203) 426-1394
web: http://www.thebee.com
e mail: editor@thebee.com

Collectors News
506 Second Street
P.O. Box 156
Grundy Center, IA 50638
(800) 352-8039
Fax: (319) 824-3414
web: http://collectors-news.com
e mail: collectors@collectors-news.com

Maine Antique Digest
911 Main Street
P.O. Box 1429
Waldoboro, ME 04572
(207) 832-4888 or
(207) 832-7534
Fax: (207) 832-7341
web: www.maineantiquedigest.com
e mail: mad@maine.com

Warman's Today's Collector
700 E. State St.
Iola, WI 54990
(800) 258-0929
Fax: (715) 445-4087
web: www.krause.com
e mail: todays_collector@krause.com

REGIONAL NEWSPAPERS

New England

The Fine Arts Trader
P.O. Box 1273
Randolph, MA 02368
(800) 332-5055
Fax: (781) 961-9044
web: www.fineartstrader.com

MassBay Antiques
152 Sylvan St.
Box 293
Danvers, MA 01923
(800) 982-4023
e mail: mbantiques@cnc.com

New England Antiques Journal
4 Church Street
P.O. Box 120
Ware, MA 01082
(800) 432-3505
Fax: (413) 967-6009
e mail: visit@antiquesjournal.com

New Hampshire Antiques Monthly
P.O. Box 546
Farmington, NH 03835-0546
(603) 755-4568
Fax: (603) 755-3990

Treasure Chest
P.O. Box 245
North Scituate, RI 02857-0245
(800) 557-9662
Fax: (401) 647-0051

Unravel the Gavel
9 Hurricane Rd., #1
Belmont, NH 03220
(603) 524-4281
Fax: (603) 528-3565
web: /www.the-forum.com/gavel
e mail: gavel96@aol.com

Middle Atlantic States

Antiques & Auction News
Rt. 230 West, P.O. Box 500
Mount Joy, PA 17552
(717) 653-4300
Fax: (717) 653-6165

Antiques Tattler (Adamstown)
P.O. Box 457
Adamstown, PA 19501

New York City's Antique News
P.O. Box 2054
New York, NY 10159-2054
(212) 725-0344
Fax: (212) 532-7294

New York–Pennsylvania Collector
P.O. Box C
Fishers, NY 14453
(716) 924-4040 or
(800) 836-1868
e mail: wolfepub@frontiernet.net

Northeast Journal of Antiques & Art
364 Warren St.
P.O. Box 635
Hudson, NY 12534
(518) 828-1616 or
(800) 836-4069
Fax: (518) 828-9437

Renninger's Antique Guide
P.O. Box 495
Lafayette Hill, PA 19444
(610) 828-4614
Fax: (610) 834-1599
web: www.renningers.com

South

Antique Finder Magazine
P.O. Box 16433
Panama City, FL 32406-6433
(850) 236-0543
Fax: (850) 914-9007

Antique Gazette
6949 Charlotte Pike
Ste. #106
Nashville, TN 37209
(800) 660-6143
Fax: (615) 352-0941

The Antique Shoppe
P.O. Box 2175
Keystone Heights, FL 32656
(352) 475-1679
Fax: (352) 475-5326
web: www.antiquenet.com/antiqueshoppe
e mail: EDSOPER@aol.com

The Antique Shoppe of the Carolinas
P.O. Box 640
Lancaster, SC 29721
(800) 210-7253 or
(803) 210-7253
Fax: (803) 283-8969

Carolina Antique News
P.O. Box 241114
Charlotte, NC 28224
(704) 553-2865
Fax: (704) 643-3960

Cotton & Quail Antique Trail
205 East Washington Street
P.O. Box 326
Monticello, FL 32345
(800) 757-7755
Fax: (850) 997-3090

MidAtlantic Antiques Magazine
Henderson Newspapers, Inc.
304 South Chestnut Street
P.O.Box 908
Henderson, NC 27536
(252) 492-4001
Fax: (252) 430-0125

The Old News Is Good News Antiques Gazette
41429 W. I-55 Service Rd.
P.O. Box 305
Hammond, LA 70404
(504) 429-0575
Fax: (504) 429-0576
e mail: gazette@i–55.com

Second Hand Dealer News
18609 Shady Hills Rd.
Spring Hill, FL 34610
(813) 856-9477

Southern Antiques
P.O. Drawer 1107
Decatur, GA 30031
(888) 800-4997
Fax: (404) 286-9727

Southern Antiquing and Collecting Magazine
P.O. Box 510
Acworth, GA 30101-0510
(770) 974-6495 or
(888) 388-7827
e mail: antiquing@go-star.com

20th-Century Folk Art News
5967 Blackberry Ln.
Buford, GA 30518
(770) 932-1000
Fax: (770) 932-0506

The Vintage Times
P.O. Box 7567
Macon, GA 31209
(888) 757-4755
web: www.mylink.met\~antiques
e mail: antiques@mylink.net

Midwest

The American Antiquities Journal
126 East High St.
Springfield, OH 45502
(937) 322-6281
Fax: (937) 322-0294
web: www.americanantiquites.com
e mail: MAIL@americanantiquities.com

The Antique Collector and Auction Guide
Weekly Section of *Farm and Dairy*
185-205 E. State St.
Salem, OH 44460
(330) 337-3419
Fax: (330) 337-9550

Antique Review
12 E. Stafford St.
P.O. Box 538
Worthington, OH 43085
(614) 885-9757
Fax: (614) 885-9762

Auction Action News
1404½ E. Green Bay St.
Shawano, WI 54166
(715) 524-3076
Fax: (800) 580-4568

Auction World
101 12th Street South
Box 227
Benson, MN 56215
(800) 750-0166
Fax: (320) 843-3246
web: ww.finfolink.morris.mn.us/~jfield
e mail: mfield@infolink.morris.mn.us

The Collector
204 S. Walnut St.
P.O. Box 148
Heyworth, IL 61745-0148
(309) 473-2466
Fax: (309) 473-3610

Collectors Journal
1800 West D St.
P.O. Box 601
Vinton, IA 52349-0601
(800) 472-4006
Fax: (816) 472-3117
e mail: antiquescj@aol.com

Discover Mid-America
400 Grand, Ste. B
Kansas City, MO 64106
(800) 899-9730
Fax: (816) 474-1427
web: discoverypub.com/kc
e mail: discoverypub@aol.com

Great Lakes Trader
132 S. Putnam St.
Williamstown, MI 48895
(800) 785-6367
Fax: (517) 655-5380
web: gltrader@aol.com

Indiana Antique Buyer's News, Inc.
P.O. Box 213
Silver Lake, IN 46982
(219) 893-4200 or
(888) 834-2263
Fax: (219) 893-4251
e mail: iabn@hoosierlink.net

Ohio Collectors' Magazine
P.O. Box 1522
Piqua, OH 45356
(937) 773-6063

The Old Times
63 Birch Ave. South
P.O. Box 340
Maple Lake, MN 55358
(800) 539-1810
Fax: (320) 963-6499
web: www.theoldtimes.com
e mail: oldtimes@lkdllink.net

Yesteryear
P.O. Box 2
Princeton, WI 54968
(920) 787-4808
Fax: (920) 787-7381

Southwest

The Antique Traveler
P.O. Box 656
109 E. Broad St.
Mineola, TX 75773
(903) 569-2487
Fax: (903) 569-9080

Antiques & Collectibles Travelers' Guide
P.O. Box 8851
Apache Junction, AZ 85278
Phone/Fax: (602) 596-2935

Arizona Antique News
P.O. Box 26536
Phoenix, AZ 85068
(602) 943-9137

Auction Weekly
P.O. Box 61104
Phoenix, AZ 85082
(602) 994-4512
Fax: (800) 525-1407
web: www.auctionadvisory.com

The Country Register, Inc.
P.O. Box 84345
Phoenix, AZ 85071
(602) 942-8950
Fax: (602) 866-3136
web: www.countryregister.com

West Coast

Antique & Collectables
500 Fensler, Ste. 205
P.O. Box 12589
El Cajon, CA 92022
(619) 593-2930
Fax: (619) 447-7187

Antique Journal
2329 Santa Clara Ave., Ste. 207
Alameda, CA 94501
(800) 791-8592 or
(510) 749-6840
Fax: (510) 523-5262

Antiques Plus
P.O. Box 5467
Salem, OR 97304
(503) 391-7618

Antiques Today
977 Lehigh Cir.
Carson City, NV 89705
(800) 267-4602
Fax: (702) 267-4600

Collector
436 W. 4th St., Ste. 222
Pomona, CA 91766
(909) 620-9014
Fax: (909) 622-8152
e mail: Icollect@aol.com

Old Stuff
VBM Printers, Inc.
336 N. Davis
P.O. Box 1084
McMinnville, OR 97128
(503) 434-5386
Fax: (503) 435-0990
e mail: bnm@pnn.com
web: www.vbmpublishing.com

The Oregon Vintage Times
856 Lincoln #2
Eugene, OR 97401
(541) 484-0049
web: www.efn.org/~venus/antique/antique.html
e mail: venus@efn.org

West Coast Peddler
P.O. Box 5134
Whittier, CA 90607
(562) 698-1718
Fax: (562) 698-1500
web: westcoastpeddler.com
e mail: antiques@westcoastpeddler.com

INTERNATIONAL NEWSPAPERS

Australia

Carter's Homes, Antiques & Collectables
Carter's Promotions Pty. Ltd.
Locked Bag 3
Terrey Hills, NSW 2084
Australia
(02) 9450 0011
Fax: (02) 945-2532
web: carters.com.au
e mail: carters@magna.com.au

Canada

Antique Showcase
Trojan Publishing Corp.
103 Lakeshore Road, Ste. 202
St. Catherine, Ontario
Canada L2N 2T6
(905) 646-0995
web: http://www.vaxxine.com/trojan/
e mail: bret@trojan.com

Antiques & Collectibles Trader
P.O. Box #38095
550 Eglinton Avenue West
Toronto, Ontario
Canada M5N 3A8
(416) 410-7620
Fax: (416) 784-9796

The Upper Canadian
P.O. Box 653
Smiths Falls, Ontario
Canada K7A
(613) 283-1168
Fax: (613) 283-1345
e mail: uppercanadian@recorder.ca

England

Antique Trade Gazette
17 Whitcomb Street
London WC2H 7PL
England

AUCTION HOUSES & PHOTO CREDITS

The following auctioneers and auction companies generously supply Rinker Enterprises, Inc., with copies of their auction lists, press releases, catalogs and illustrations, and prices realized. Those heading the list also supplied numerous photographs for this edition of *The Official Price Guide to Flea Market Treasures.*

Bill Bertoia Auctions
1881 Spring Rd.
Vineland, NJ 08361
(609) 692-1881
Fax: (609) 692-8697
e mail: bba@ccnj.net
web: www.bba.ccnj.net.com

Butterfield, Butterfield & Dunning's
755 Church Rd.
Elgin, IL 60123
(847) 741-3483
Fax: (847) 741-3589
web: www.butterfields.com

Collectors Auction Services
RR 2, Box 431 Oakwood Rd.
Oil City, PA 16301
(814) 677-6070
Fax: (814) 677-6166

William Doyle Galleries, Inc.
175 East 87th St.
New York, NY 10128
(212) 427-2730
Fax: (212) 369-0892
web: www.doylegalleries.com

Dunbars Gallery
76 Haven St.
Milford, MA 01757
(508) 634-8697
Fax: (508) 634-8698
e mail: dunbar2bid@aol.com

Fink's Off the Wall Auction
108 East 7th St.
Lansdale, PA 19446
(215) 855-9732
Fax: (215) 855-6325
web: http://www/finksauctions.com
e mail: lansbeer@finksauction.com

Frank's Antiques
Box 516
Hilliard, FL 32046
(904) 845-2870
Fax: (904) 845-4000

Garth's Auction, Inc.
2690 Stratford Rd.
P.O. Box 369
Delaware, OH 43015
(614) 362-4771
Fax: (614) 363-1064

Glass-Works Auctions
P.O. Box 180
East Greenville, PA 18041
(215) 679-5849
Fax: (215) 679-3068
web: www.glswrk-auction.com

Gene Harris Antique Auction Center, Inc.
203 S. 18th Ave.
Marshalltown, IA 50158
(515) 752-0600
Fax: (515) 753-0226
e mail: ghaac@marshallnet.com

GVL Enterprises
21764 Congress Hall Ln.
Saratoga, CA 95070
(408) 741-5588
Fax: (408) 741-5431
e-mail: jllally@kpcb.com

Michael Ivankovich Antiques, Inc.
P.O. Box 2458
Doylestown, PA 18901
(215) 345-6094
Fax: (215) 345-6692
e mail: wnutting@comcat.com

Jackson's Auctioneers & Appraisers
2229 Lincoln St.
Cedar Falls, IA 50613
(319) 277-2256
Fax: (319) 277-1252
web: jacksonauction.com

James D. Julia, Inc.
P.O. Box 830
Fairfield, ME 04937
(207) 453-7125
Fax: (207) 453-2502

Lang's Sporting Collectables, Inc.
31R Turtle Cove
Raymond, ME 04071
(207) 655-4265

Gary Metz's Muddy River Trading Co.
263 Key Lakewood Dr.
Moneta, VA 24121
(540) 721-2091
Fax: (540) 721-1782

Wm Morford
RD 2
Cazenovia, NY 13035
(315) 662-7625
Fax: (315) 662-3570
e mail: morf2bid@aol.com

Ray Morykan Auctions
1368 Spring Valley Rd.
Bethlehem, PA 18015
(610) 838-6634
e mail: dmorykan@enter.net

New England Auction Gallery
Box 2273
West Peabody, MA 01960
(508) 535-3140
Fax: (508) 535-7522
web: http://www.oldtoys.com

Norton Auctioneers of Michigan, Inc.
Pearl at Monroe
Colwater, MI 49036-1967
(517) 279-9063
Fax: (517) 279-9191
e mail: nortonsold@juno.com

Ingrid O'Neil Sports and Olympic Memorabilia
P.O. Box 60310
Colorado Springs, CO 80960
(719) 473-1538
Fax: (719) 477-0768
e mail: memorabilia@ioneil.com

Past Tyme Pleasures
101 First Street, Ste. 404
Los Altos, CA 94022
(510) 484-4488
Fax: (510) 484-2551

Postcards International
P.O. Box 5398
Hamden, CT 06518
(203) 248-6621
Fax: (203) 248-6628
web: csmonline.com/postcardsint/
e mail: postcrdint@aol.com

Poster Mail Auction Co.
P.O. Box 133
Waterford, VA 20197
(703) 684-3656
Fax: (540) 882-4765

David Rago Auctions, Inc.
333 N. Main St.
Lambertville, NJ 08530
(609) 397-9374
Fax: (609) 397-9377

Skinner, Inc.
Bolton Gallery
357 Main St.
Bolton, MA 01740
(978) 779-6241
Fax: (978) 350-5429
e mail: www.skinnerinc.com

AUCTION HOUSES

Aston Macek
154 Market St.
Pittston, PA 18640
(717) 654-3090

Auction Team Köln, Breker – Die Spezialisten
Postfach 50 11 19
D-50971 Köln, Germany
Tel: 0221/38 70 49
Fax: 0221/37 48 78
Jane Herz, International Rep US
(941) 925-0385
Fax: (941) 925-0487

Action Toys
P.O. Box 102
Holtsville, NY 11742
(516) 563-9113
Fax: (516) 563-9182

Sanford Alderfer Auction Co., Inc.
501 Fairgrounds Rd.
P.O. Box 640
Hatfield, PA 19440
(215) 393-3000
e mail: auction@alderfercompany.com
web: www.alderfercompany.com

American Social History and Social Movements
4025 Saline St.
Pittsburgh, PA 15217
(412) 421-5230
Fax: (412) 421-0903

Arthur Auctioneering
RD 2, Box 155
Hughesville, PA 17737
(800) ARTHUR 3

Butterfield & Butterfield
220 San Bruno Ave.
San Francisco, CA 94103
(415) 861-7500
Fax: (415) 861-8951
web: www.butterfields.com

Butterfield & Butterfield
7601 Sunset Blvd.
Los Angeles, CA 90046
(213) 850-7500
Fax: (213) 850-5843
web: www.butterfields.com

Cards From Grandma's Trunk
The Millards
P.O. Box 404
Northport, IN 49670
(616) 386-5351

Christie's
502 Park Avenue at 59th St.
New York, NY 10022
(212) 546-1000
Fax: (212) 980-8163
web: www.christies.com

Christie's East
219 East 67th St.
New York, NY 10021
(212) 606-0400
Fax: (212) 737-6076
web: www.christies.com

Christmas Morning
1806 Royal Ln.
Dallas, TX 75229-3126
(972) 506-8362
Fax: (972) 506-7821

Cobb's Doll Auctions
1909 Harrison Rd.
Johnstown, OH 43031-9539
(740) 964-0444
Fax: (740) 927-7701

Collector's Sales and Service
P.O. Box 4037
Middletown, RI 02842
(401) 849-5012
Fax: (401) 846-6156
web: www.antiquechina.com
e mail: collectors@antiquechina.com

Copake Auction
Box H, 226 Rt. 7A
Copake, NY 12516
(518) 329-1142
Fax: (518) 329-3369

Dawson's
128 American Rd.
Morris Plains, NJ 07950
(973) 984-6900
Fax: (973) 984-6956
web: idt.net/-dawson1
e mail: dawson1@idt.net

Dixie Sporting Collectibles
1206 Rama Rd.
Charlotte, NC 28211
(704) 364-2900
Fax: (704) 364-2322
web: www.sportauction.com
e mail: gun1898@aol.com

Early Auction Co.
Roger and Steve Early
123 Main St.
Milford, OH 45150
(513) 831-4833
Fax: (513) 831-1441

Etude Tajan
37, Rue de Mathurins
75008 Paris, France
Tel: 1-53-30-30-30
Fax: 1-53-30-30-31
web: www.tajan.com
e mail: tajan@worldnet.fr

Ken Farmer Auctions & Estates, LLC
105A Harrison St.
Radford, VA 24141
(540) 639-0939
Fax: (540) 639-1759
web: kenfarmer.com

Flomaton Antique Auction
277 Old Hwy. 31
Flomaton, AL 36441

Frasher's Doll Auctions, Inc.
Rt. 1, Box 142
Oak Grove, MO 64075
(816) 625-3786
Fax: (816) 625-6079

Greenberg Auctions
7566 Main St.
Sykesville, MD 21784
(401) 795-7447

Marc Grobman
94 Paterson Rd.
Fanwood, NJ 07023-1056
(908) 322-4176
web: mgrobman@worldnet.att.net

Gypsyfoot Enterprises, Inc.
P.O. Box 5833
Helena, MT 59604
(406) 449-8076
Fax: (406) 443-8514
e mail: gypsyfoot@aol.com

Hakes' Americana and Collectibles
P.O. Box 1444
York, PA 17405
(717) 848-1333
Fax: (717) 852-0344

Norman C. Heckler & Co.
Bradford Corner Rd.
Woodstock Valley, CT 06282
(860) 974-1634
Fax: (860) 974-2003

The Holidays Auction
4027 Brooks Hill Rd.
Brooks, KY 40109
(502) 955-9238
Fax: (502) 957-5027

Horst Auction Center
50 Durlach Rd.
Ephrata, PA 17522
(717) 859-1331

Gary Kirsner Auctions
P.O. Box 8807
Coral Springs, FL 33075
(954) 344-9856
Fax: (954) 344-4421

Charles E. Kirtley
P.O. Box 2273
Elizabeth City, NC 27906
(919) 335-1262
Fax: (919) 335-4441
e mail: ckirtley@erols.com

Kruse International
P.O. Box 190
Auburn, IN 46706
(800) 968-4444
Fax: (219) 925-5467

Henry Kurtz, Ltd.
163 Amsterdam Ave., Ste. 136
New York, NY 10023
(212) 642-5904
Fax: (212) 874-6018

Los Angeles Modern Auctions
P.O. Box 462006
Los Angeles, CA 90046
(213) 845-9456
Fax: (213) 845-9601
web: www.lamodern.com
e mail: peter@lamodern.com

Howard Lowery
3812 West Magnolia Blvd.
Burbank, CA 91505
(818) 972-9080
Fax: (818) 972-3910

Mad Mike
Michael Lerner
32862 Springside Ln.
Solon, OH 44139
(216) 349-3776

Majolica Auctions
Michael G. Strawser
200 North Main
P.O. Box 332
Wolcottville, IN 46795
(219) 854-2859
Fax: (219) 854-3979

Manion's International Auction House, Inc.
P.O. Box 12214
Kansas City, KS 66112
(913) 299-6692
Fax: (913) 299-6792
web: www.manions.com
e mail: collecting@manions.com

Ted Maurer, Auctioneer
1003 Brookwood Dr.
Pottstown, PA 19464
(610) 323-1573
web: www.maurerail.com

New England Absentee Auctions
16 Sixth St.
Stamford, CT 06905
(203) 975-9055
Fax: (203) 323-6407
e mail: neaauction@aol.com

Nostalgia Publications, Inc.
21 South Lake Dr.
Hackensack, NJ 07601
(201) 488-4536

Richard Opfer Auctioneers, Inc.
1919 Greenspring Dr.
Timonium, MD 21093
(410) 252-5035
Fax: (410) 252-5863

Ron Oser Enterprises
P.O. Box 101
Huntingdon Valley, PA 19006
(215) 947-6575
Fax: (215) 938-7348
web: members.aol.com/ronoserent

Pacific Book Auction Galleries
139 Townsend St., 4th Fl.
San Francisco, CA 94108
(415) 989-2665
Fax: (415) 989-1664
web: www.nbn.com/pba
e mail: pba@slip.net

Pettigrew Auction Co.
1645 S. Tejon St.
Colorado Springs, CO 80906
(719) 633-7963
Fax: (719) 633-5035

Phillips Ltd.
406 East 79th St.
New York, NY 10021
(800) 825-2781
Fax: (212) 570-2207

Provenance
P.O. Box 3487
Wallington, NJ 07057
(201) 779-8785
Fax: (212) 741-8756

Lloyd Ralston Gallery
109 Glover Ave.
Norwalk, CT 06850
(203) 845-0033
Fax: (203) 845-0366

Red Baron's
6450 Roswell Rd.
Atlanta, GA 30328
(404) 252-3770
Fax: (404) 257-0268
e mail: rbarons@onramp.net

Remmey Galleries
30 Maple St.
Summit, NJ 07901
(908) 273-5055
Fax: (908) 273-0171
e mail: remmeyauctiongalleries@world-net.att.net

L. H. Selman Ltd.
761 Chestnut St.
Santa Cruz, CA 95060
(800) 538-0766
Fax: (408) 427-0111
web: paperweight.com
e mail: selman@paperweight.com

Slater's Americana
1535 N. Tacoma Ave., Ste. 24
Indianapolis, IN 46220
(317) 257-0863
Fax: (317) 254-9167

R. M. Smythe & Co., Inc.
26 Broadway, Ste. 271
New York, NY 10004-1701
(800) 622-1880
Fax: (212) 908-4047

Steffen's Historical Militaria
P.O. Box 280
Newport, KY 41072
(606) 431-4499

Susanin's
Gallery 228 Merchandise Mart
Chicago, IL 60654
(312) 832-9800
Fax: (312) 832-9311
web: www.theauction.com

Theriault's
P.O. Box 151
Annapolis, MD 21404
Fax: (410) 224-2515

Tiques Auction
RRI Box 49B
Old Bridge, J 08857
(732) 721-0221
Fax: (732) 721-0127
web: www.tiques.com
e mail: tiquesauc@aol.com

Tool Shop Auctions
Tony Murland
78 High St.
Needham Market, Suffolk
1P6 8AW England
Tel: 01449 722992
Fax: 01449 722683
web: www/toolshop.demon.co.uk
e mail: tony@toolshop.demon.co.uk

Toy Scouts
137 Casterton Ave.
Akron, OH 44303
(330) 836-0668
Fax: (330) 869-8668

James A. Vanek
7031 NE Irving St.
Portland, OR 97213
(503) 257-8009

Victorian Images
P.O. Box 284
Marlton, NJ 08053
(609) 953-7711
Fax: (609) 953-7768

Tom Witte's Antiques
P.O. Box 399, Front Street West
Mattawan, MI 49071
(616) 668-4161
Fax: (616) 668-5363

York Town Auction, Inc.
1625 Haviland Rd.
York, PA 17404
(717) 751-0211
Fax: (717) 767-7729

If you are an auctioneer or auction company and would like your name and address to appear on this list in subsequent editions, you can achieve this by sending copies of your auction lists, press releases, catalogs and illustrations, and prices realized to: **Rinker Enterprises, Inc., 5093 Vera Cruz Road, Emmaus, PA 18049.**

INDEX

–T–

–U–

–V–

–W–

–Y–

–Z–

CRITICAL THINKING
Consider the Verdict

Fifth Edition

Bruce N. Waller
Youngstown State University

PEARSON
Prentice Hall

Upper Saddle River, New Jersey 07458

Library of Congress Cataloging-in-Publication Data

Waller, Bruce N.
Critical thinking : consider the verdict / Bruce N. Waller.— 5th ed.
p. cm.
Includes bibliographical references and index.
ISBN 0-13-189666-0
1. Critical thinking. 2. Verdicts. 3. Logic. I. Title.

BC177.W3 2004
160'.2'434—dc22

2004006253

Editorial Director: Charlyce Jones-Owen
Senior Acquisitions Editor: Ross Miller
Assistant Editor: Wendy B. Yurash
Editorial Assistant: Carla Worner
Production Liaison: Joanne Hakim
Production Editor: Karen Berry, Pine Tree Composition
Marketing Manager: Kara Kindstrom
Marketing Assistant: Jennifer Lang
Manufacturing Buyer: Christina Helder
Cover Art Director: Jayne Conte
Cover Illustration/Photo: Julie Delton/ Getty Images, Inc.
Director, Image Resource Center: Melinda Reo
Manager, Rights and Permissions: Zina Arabia
Manager, Cover Visual Research & Permissions: Karen Sanatar
Image Permissions Coordinator: Nancy Seise
Composition: Interactive Composition Corporation
Printer/Binder: Hamilton Printing Company
Cover Printer: Coral Graphics

Credits and acknowledgments borrowed from other sources and reproduced, with permission, in this textbook appear on appropriate page within text.

Pearson Education LTD., London
Pearson Education Singapore, Pte. Ltd
Pearson Education, Canada, Ltd
Pearson Education—Japan
Pearson Education Australia PTY, Limited
Pearson Education North Asia Ltd
Pearson Educación de Mexico, S.A. de C.V.
Pearson Education Malaysia, Pte. Ltd
Pearson Education, Upper Saddle River, New Jersey

PEARSON
Prentice Hall

10 9 8 7

ISBN 0-13-189666-0